Encyclopedia of
THE ROMAN EMPIRE

REVISED EDITION

Encyclopedia of
THE ROMAN EMPIRE

REVISED EDITION

Matthew Bunson

Facts On File, Inc.

Encyclopedia of the Roman Empire, *Revised Edition*

Copyright © 2002, 1994 by Matthew Bunson

Facts On File, Inc.
132 West 31st Street
New York NY 10001

Library of Congress Cataloging-in-Publication Data

Bunson, Matthew.
Encyclopedia of the Roman empire / Matthew Bunson.—rev. ed.
p. cm.
Includes bibliographical references and index.
ISBN 0-8160-4562-3
1. Rome—History—Empire, 30 B.C.E.–476 C.E.—Encyclopedias. I. Title.

DG270.B86 2002
937'.06—dc21   2001053253

Text design by Joan Toro
Cover design by Cathy Rincon
Maps and genealogies by Dale Williams, Patricia Meschino,
© Facts On File

Printed in the United States of America

VB FOF 10 9 8 7 6 5 4 3 2

This book is printed on acid-free paper.

In memory of my father,
Lt. Col. S. M. Bunson (1924–1984)

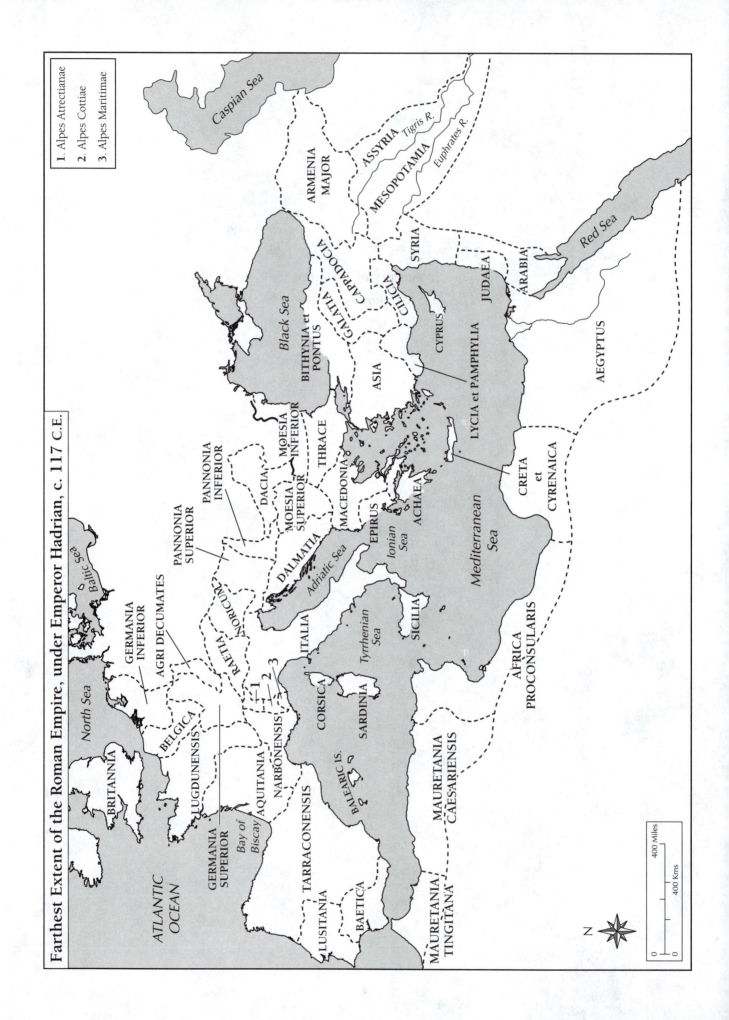

Farthest Extent of the Roman Empire, under Emperor Hadrian, c. 117 C.E.

1. Alpes Atrectianae
2. Alpes Cottiae
3. Alpes Maritimae

Caspian Sea

ASSYRIA

Tigris R.

MESOPOTAMIA

Euphrates R.

ARMENIA MAJOR

Red Sea

SYRIA

CILICIA

CAPPADOCIA

GALATIA

JUDAEA

Black Sea

BITHYNIA et PONTUS

CYPRUS

ASIA

LYCIA et PAMPHYLIA

AEGYPTUS

MOESIA INFERIOR

THRACE

ARABIA

PANNONIA INFERIOR

DACIA

MOESIA SUPERIOR

MACEDONIA

CRETA et CYRENAICA

PANNONIA SUPERIOR

EPIRUS

ACHAEA

Mediterranean Sea

AGRI DECUMATES

NORICUM

DALMATIA

Adriatic Sea

Ionian Sea

Baltic Sea

GERMANIA INFERIOR

RAETIA

ITALIA

Tyrrhenian Sea

SICILIA

AFRICA PROCONSULARIS

North Sea

BELGICA

LUGDUNENSIS

1
2
3

CORSICA

SARDINIA

BRITANNIA

GERMANIA SUPERIOR

Bay of Biscay

AQUITANIA

NARBONENSIS

BALEARIC IS.

MAURETANIA CAESARIENSIS

ATLANTIC OCEAN

TARRACONENSIS

LUSITANIA

BAETICA

MAURETANIA TINGITANA

N

400 Miles

400 Kms

CONTENTS

List of Illustrations and Maps
viii

Introduction
xi

A Note on Names
xiv

Chronology of Major Events
xv

Entries A to Z
1

Appendix I: Emperors of the Roman Empire
27 B.C.E.–476 C.E.
601

Appendix II: Genealogies
603

Glossary
607

Suggested Readings
609

Index
613

List of Illustrations and Maps

Photographs and Illustrations

Bronze *sestertius* of Agrippina the Elder	11
Remains of the sphinxes of ancient Alexandria	14
Coin from the reign of Emperor Antoninus Pius	24
Pont du Gard	29
Arch of Constantine	33
Example of Pompeian-style art	43
Exposed floor of Flavian Amphitheater, or Colosseum	44
Inscription on the Arch of Severus	45
Asclepius, the god of medicine	49
Attila the Hun	55
Silver denarius of Augustus	58
Basilica Aemilia	68
Roman baths in Bath, England	71
Emperor Caracalla	95
Fresco of St. Paul, from the Catacomb of San Gennaro, Naples	101
Mosaic of Christ, from the Cathedral of Il Salvatore, Cefalú, Sicily	110
Coins from the Christian era of the empire	111
Circus Maximus	120
Silver tetradrachm of Claudius	124
Relief of Queen Cleopatra	127
Early imperial coins	131
Middle imperial coins	132
Late imperial coins	133
Flavian Amphitheater (Colosseum)	136
Trajan's Column	138
Coin from the reign of Commodus	140
Gold medallion of Constantine I	143

Christian Constantinople	145
Emperor Constantius I Chlorus	148
Round Temple of Cybele	161
Engraving of the Dacian Wars	166
Samples of the denarius	172
Silver denarius, Domitian	181
Domus in Herculaneum, the House of the Surgeons	184
Library of Ephesus	197
Oven in a house in Herculaneum	216
Warehouse and store in Herculaneum	216
Remains of the Forum Romanum	218
Interior of a house in Herculaneum	222
Mosaic floor in Herculaneum	223
Coin from the reign of Hadrian	250
Remains of Herculaneum	255
Olive press	274
Jerusalem and the Temple of Solomon	283
Destruction of Jerusalem, commemorated on the Arch of Titus	288
Bronze *majorina* of Julian the Apostate	292
Roman legions, from Trajan's Column	307
Armor and weapons of Roman legions	308
Bronze *dupondius* of Livia	327
Hippodrome of Domitian, site of races during the *ludi*	333
Relief of Emperor Marcus Aurelius	350
Temple of Mars Ultor	353
Shrine to Mithras, from Ostia	371
Maison-Carrée, in Nemausus (Nîmes), France	384
Ovid	404
Interior of the Pantheon	411
Coins from the Parthian Empire	414
House from Pompeii	440
Reconstruction of Rome in the early second century C.E.	474
Coins from the Sassanid Persian Empire	489
Temple of Saturn	491
Samples of sesterces	499
Gold aureus of Septimius Severus	500
Mosaic of a warship and a trading vessel	504
Reconstruction of Split, the residence of Emperor Diocletian	513
Temple of Castor	525
Emperor Theodosius I	534
Bridge across the Tiber	538
Silver denarius of Tiberius	540
Commerce in action, from Trajan's Column	548
Gold aureus of Trajan and Plotina	550

Mosaic of trading ships, from Ostia   552

Statue in honor of Vercingetorix   572

Emperor Vespasian   574

Temple of Vesta   575

Vestal Virgin   576

Appian Way   578

Villa in Herculaneum   583

Wall of Hadrian   592

Maps

Farthest Extent of the Roman Empire, under
    Emperor Hadrian, c. 117 C.E.   vi

Roman Empire under Emperor Augustus, c. 14 C.E.   59

Roman Conquest of Britannia, 54 B.C.E.–100 C.E.   80

Spread of Christianity   113

Constantinople in the Fifth Century   147

Provinces under the Reforms of Emperor Diocletian   177

Regions of Italy and Rome under Augustus   278

Languages of the Roman Empire   302

Praetorian Prefectures under the Tetrarchy, c. 300 C.E.   451

Imperial Rome   476

End of the Roman Empire in the West, 476 C.E.   478

Roman Empire under Emperor Septimius Severus, c. 211 C.E.   501

Trade Routes of the First Century C.E.   549

Major Roman Roads   579

INTRODUCTION

The poet Martial once observed, *Eheu fugaces anni* (Alas, for the fleeting years). His words are quite meaningful when applied to the *Encyclopedia of the Roman Empire.* The first edition of this book was published nearly eight years ago. Surprisingly, it remains the only comprehensive A-to-Z reference to the more than 500-year period of Roman imperial civilization. This new edition seeks to build on the original encyclopedia and is marked by considerable revision, improvement, and updating. The extent of the changes will become evident to anyone familiar with the older edition, but the essential task of this work remains unchanged. The encyclopedia covers the most important personalities, terms, and sites that played a part in Roman evolution from the period of Julius Caesar and the Gallic Wars (59–51 B.C.E.) to the fall of the empire in the West (476 C.E.).

As was noted in the last edition, the subject of Roman history, even a seemingly limited aspect such as the imperial epoch, is a complex one. It involves a host of subjects, figures, ideas, and interrelated themes. Even the answering of simple questions proves extremely difficult, due to the amount and variety of information scattered in hundreds of volumes. This reference work thus seeks to provide easy-to-use and readable entries that might be able to shed a little light on a great many topics of interest to readers all over the world.

Among the many changes that are introduced in this edition are new maps and illustrations, the inclusion of suggested reading lists for a large number of individual entries, and an expanded reading list at the end of the book. The volumes selected for these lists are intended for the general reader and are deliberately editions that appeared in the English language. Nevertheless, the volumes chosen represent some of the most up-to-date works available for the specific topics, and all of them are recommended to anyone interested in expanding studies on specific aspects of Roman civilization.

Readers will also note that there has been a change of dating style throughout the text. In keeping with the preferred method of dating for modern historical works, the system of dates according to B.C. (before Christ) and A.D. (*anno Domini*, "in the year of the Lord") has been changed to B.C.E. (before the common era) and C.E. (of the common era). The intention is to make this book consistent with other works on the subject and for purposes of consistent dating in the Facts On File database. The editorial revision of the dating system is undertaken despite the personal preferences of the author.

In terms of individual entries, there are many new topics included in this book, such as China, food and drink, clothing, law, women in Roman society, and transportation; equally, other entries have been expanded for greater depth of coverage and to make them more reflective of contemporary scholarship. Among the broadened topics are philosophy, legions, Christianity, industry, and the calendar.

Clearly, the size and the sheer number of the entries may prove a daunting challenge to readers unfamiliar with the subject. With this in mind, several steps have been taken to make this book as user-friendly as possible. Following this introduction, readers will find a time line covering the major events that are treated in the text. It is recommended that these charts be studied first, to make the general history of Rome clearer and to place it in a proper historical context. The time line serves as the first bridge to the entries that receive more detailed treatment in the A-to-Z section. A brief glossary of terms and words frequently used in the encyclopedia appears in the back of the book and can be used to introduce the reader to a few concepts and the many titles that are so much a part of imperial Roman history. Familiar with these, the reader can better understand the material offered in each entry.

In the encyclopedia itself, the reader may find it useful first to refer to a number of broad, highly explanatory entries that will provide a firm basis on which to investigate subjects of a more complex or specific nature. The following chart should aid in this discovery of the various aspects of Roman life:

Topic	Entries to Be Consulted
Government	census; civil service; coinage; colonies; concilia; consilium; *constitutiones*; consul; finance; freedmen; *princeps*; provinces; senate; taxation
Society	social classes; astrology; astronomy; Christianity; death; divination; Education; Equites; farming; festivals; freedmen; gluttony; marriage and divorce; paganism; Patricians; Plebeians; religion; Senate; tribune; women in Roman society
Daily Life	clothing; death; food and drink; furnishings; Latin language; medicine; marriage and divorce; clothing; personal appearance; villa; writing instruments
Literature and Art	art and architecture; Latin language; literature; philosophy; poetry; satire; theater
Law	law; Lex; civil service; *constitutiones*; Senate; taxation
Trade and Commerce	China, coinage; economy; engineering; India; industry; farming; trade and commerce; provinces; roads; transportation; weights and measures
Warfare	legions; civil war, First Triumvirate & Second Triumvirate, 69 C.E.; Gallic Wars; navy; Praetorian Guard; roads
Religion	Christianity; Imperial Cult; Paganism; philosophy; religion
Other Entries	baths; Colosseum; gladiators; Parthia; Rome; Sassanid dynasty; viae

Included in the back matter are a chronological listing of the emperors and genealogies of the major imperial dynasties and families. After exploring the general entries noted above, the reader might turn to the entries concerning the emperors or other individuals, such as Julius Caesar and Pompey the Great, who were not emperors but had a decisive influence on the late Republic. These biographies will take the reader through every era of Roman history, reflecting the times they influenced and the times that, in turn, shaped them. Several emperors were among the greatest statesmen or generals in history (Augustus, Marcus Aurelius, Diocletian, and Constantine), while others were excellent examples of political aberration (Gaius Caligula, Nero, and Elagabalus). These entries will also be helpful in introducing other topics and areas of interest.

There is an abundance of Roman writings to draw upon for information about the Roman Empire, sources that are useful in painting a clear, accurate, and interesting picture of the imperial epoch. While many ancient writings have been lost to the modern world, a vast number have survived. During the period that historians once termed the "Dark Ages" (fifth–10th centuries), a name

given to this era by Petrarch, knowledge of the classical world was preserved by the monks and the Byzantine Empire. Of equal importance was the work of Arab scholars, who translated the classical manuscripts; thus, when the European scholars turned once again to the classical period, a vast body of material awaited them. Through the monks, the Greek scholars of the Eastern Empire, and the association of Latin and Arab writers and translators in Spain and Italy and in Palestine during the Crusades, what had seemingly been lost forever returned to take part in the intellectual rebirth that characterized the Renaissance. Today it would be impossible to conduct research into the Roman world without utilizing the body of classical writings available.

Most of the sources of historical note are covered in the encyclopedia, not only because they were written by interesting literary figures, but also because many of these figures, such as Tacitus, Ammianus Marcellinus and Dexippus, led very active lives. The study of these authors is also valuable in understanding the political and private circumstances under which they wrote and functioned, and in achieving an awareness of historical events and personalities. Equally, many of these writers composed their works from a particular perspective or with political aims in mind.

Such was the case with the first-century-C.E. historian Velleius Paterculus (who flattered Emperor Tiberius) and with many of the books in the Augustan histories (the *Scriptores Historiae Augustae*). The reader should be warned that many of these sources were biased, exaggerated, or inaccurate. Where possible, they have been described as such, either in the entry on the writer himself or in the entry where the source was used. The inclusion of such material, however, when used with caution, can be of great value in providing an additional source on a topic or a different point of view. Authors naturally vary in their usefulness. Suetonius, while including excellent details about the early emperors and Julius Caesar, has been criticized by classicists as a gossipmonger. Tacitus was a moralist who, in his *Annals,* bemoaned the moral decline of Rome; but his brilliance as a historian made him one of the foremost figures in Roman literature. A few other notable historical writers were Dio, Ammianus Marcellinus, and Josephus. Readers are encouraged to consider the sources as a starting point from which to launch long-term additional study of the writers themselves, beginning with the works used in this encyclopedia. Excellent translations of the classical authors are available today, both the Latin and the Greek.

Aside from the authors noted above, mention must be made of the extensive sources provided scholars through coinage, inscriptions, archaeological work and architectural and artistic remains. Most of these are quite useful for research: two of the best tomes are the *Corpus Inscriptionum Latinarum* (CIL) and the *Prosopography of the Later Roman Empire* (in Latin) two volumes (PLRE I or II), compiled by scholars, archaeologists, and classicists. Excellent, detailed studies such as these serve as vital repositories of information, preserving inscriptions and references to ancient writings. They are less accessible to the average reader but are nevertheless essential to research. There are, finally, periodicals and magazines of immense value, such as the *Journal of Roman Studies* (JRS) and *Archaeology* (Arch.). These are readily available to the public and are recommended enthusiastically.

It is also necessary to discuss one of the pervasive elements of this encyclopedia: Readers will find frequent mention of Hellenism and Hellenic traditions adopted by the Romans. The Romans found in much of Greek culture the qualities and skills that they themselves could emulate. Rome adopted and Latinized elements of Hellenic civilization (which flourished in the fifth–fourth centuries B.C.E.), including its pantheon of gods and key facets of literature, art, and science. The acceptance of Hellenism came gradually, despite the legendary founding of Rome by Aeneas of Troy. During the era of the Republic (founded in 509 B.C.E.), Romans accepted more and more the abundance of Greek tradition and, to their credit, were the first to realize the excellence and timeless nature of Greek works. Through them the Hellenic heritage was preserved, made available not only to the Romans but also to the entire world. Because of this factor, the cultural history of the West was to be enriched during the Renaissance, with the rediscovery of classical knowledge.

It is important to acknowledge the Romans' debt to the Greeks. Cicero and Caesar studied in Greece; Lucretius acknowledged Greek superiority; and Hadrian was more of a Greek in many ways than he was a Roman. Marcus Aurelius wrote his correspondence in Greek, not in Latin. The increasing Hellenization of the Roman Empire was visible in the late third century, with the decline of Rome and the division of the empire by Diocletian. As Rome proved strategically indefensible to the threats on its frontiers, the heart of the empire gravitated eastward, culminating in the decision of Constantine the Great to build his capital at Byzantium, the city renamed Constantinople. The Eastern Empire, based in Constantine's metropolis, began along Latin lines but within centuries was fully imbued with the Hellenic flavor of the region and its history. The dynamism of the Latin that had forged the empire deteriorated in the West, to be amalgamated with the even more vital Germanic peoples who were overrunning it. In the East, the fading Latin culture received a major strengthening by grounding itself in Hellenism, which it earlier had admired grudgingly and adopted gradually. Greek life and traditions allowed the Eastern Empire to reject outright the Germanic influences so dominant in the West during the later imperial era, thereby granting a stay of execution to the Roman Empire itself. While the Western Empire ended in broad terms in 476, the Eastern or Byzantine would endure until 1453, a testament to how much was owed to Hellenism and how important it was to the civilization that had conquered Greece and the known world.

Mention also must be made, of course, of the Latin culture that was spread from the borders of Britain to the waters of the Nile to the shores of the Black Sea. Much as Rome inherited many Hellenistic characteristics from Greece, so did it impart upon much of the occupied Roman world its own Latin traditions. Roman law and justice formed the basis of much of Western legal thinking. Roman architecture served as an inspiration to the medieval builders, who cultivated deliberately the earlier imperial style in the appropriately named Romanesque era of art and architecture. Latin, the language of the empire, allowed imperial citizens to be understood by their fellow subjects or contemporaries, even from distant lands they had never seen or about which they knew nothing. Such was the universality of the Roman Empire. While the empire in the West fell out of Roman hands in 476 C.E., its culture and institutions lived on in the barbarian peoples who had seemingly conquered it.

Finally, there are several individuals to whom a special debt of gratitude is owed for their very kind and generous assistance in the completion of this book. Among them are Fr. Felix Just, S.J.; Warren Esty; John Lavender of Historical Coins, Inc.; Rosa di Salvo of the Hulton Archive; Jane Cavolina; Tyler Ottinger; and Deirdre Mullane, the editor of the first edition and the person who first helped to bring this book to life. Additional thanks are given to my perpetually patient agent, Martha Casselman, and her talented assistant, Judith.

Above all, I would like to give heartfelt thanks to Claudia Schaab, editor at Facts On File, who first suggested that it was time for a revised edition of the encyclopedia to be undertaken. While there were moments when she no doubt pondered whether this project would ever be completed, she made the entire experience an enjoyable one, and I remain honored to have been granted a small role in preserving the history and the legacy of so magnificent and so dreadful a civilization.

A NOTE ON NAMES

In the encyclopedia, individuals are listed according to how they were best known by contemporaneous historians, or, more simply, as tradition dictates. For example, Marcus Tullius Cicero can be found under CICERO, while Lucius Domitius Ahenobarbus is listed by his more familiar adoptive name, Nero. In the latter case, and in analogous cases where the historically familiar name differs from the birth name, the latter follows the entry name in parentheses, in italics. The essential elements of any person's name always appear first, and some names are inverted to illustrate both the primary name(s)—the name by which the individual is known—and the formal order of the "official" name; for example, Cremutius Cordus, Aulus. People with the same name are differentiated by an Arabic numeral in parentheses following the name, e.g., JULIA (1). Cross-references are indicated by SMALL CAPITAL LETTERS.

Abbreviations of names frequently mentioned in imperial Roman history include the following:

A. = Aulus	L. = Lucius
C. = Gaius	M. = Marcus
Cn. = Gnaeus	P. = Publius
D. = Decimus	Q. = Quintus
F. = Fulvius	S. = Sextus
J. = Junius	T. = Titus

Place-names listed by their Latin name have their modern equivalent given parenthetically, where applicable.

CHRONOLOGY OF MAJOR EVENTS

Date	Roman Affairs	Cultural Developments
The Decline of the Republic		
70 B.C.E.	Consulate of Crassus and Pompey	Birth of Virgil
66–63 B.C.E.	Pompey reorganizes the East	
65 B.C.E.		Birth of Horace
63 B.C.E.	Consulate of Cicero	
	Catilinarian Conspiracy	
	Caesar elected pontifex maximus	
60 B.C.E.	First Triumvirate formed among Pompey, Crassus, and Caesar	
59 B.C.E.	Consulate of Caesar	
	Pompey marries Julia, Caesar's daughter	
58 B.C.E.	Caesar begins the Gallic Wars	Caesar writes *Gallic Wars* (58–52 B.C.E.)
55 B.C.E.	Caesar invades Britain	Theater of Pompey completed
53 B.C.E.	Crassus is killed at Carrhae by the Parthians	
51 B.C.E.		Cicero writes *de Republica*
49 B.C.E.	Caesar crosses Rubicon and Pompey flees as civil war begins	
48 B.C.E.	Caesar defeats Pompey at battle of Pharsalus	
47–45 B.C.E.	Caesar campaigns against Pompeians in Africa, Spain, and the East	
	Caesar is dictator until 44 B.C.E.	
46 B.C.E.		Caesar's Forum begun in Rome
45 B.C.E.	Caesar returns to Rome from Spain	Cicero's major philosophical works published (45–44 B.C.E.)
44 B.C.E.	Caesar is assassinated	Cicero attacks Antony in his *Philippics*
43 B.C.E.	Second Triumvirate formed among Antony, Lepidus, and Octavian	
	Cicero murdered	
42 B.C.E.	Liberators defeated at battle at Philippi	
	Brutus and Cassius commit suicide	
41–32 B.C.E.	Antony campaigns in the East	
40 B.C.E.	Antony marries Octavia	
	Treaty of Brundisium signed	
37 B.C.E.	Triumvirate renewed	Horace writes *Satires* (37–30 B.C.E.)

CHRONOLOGY OF MAJOR EVENTS *(continued)*

Date	Roman Affairs	Cultural Developments
36–35 B.C.E.	Campaigns against Sextus Pompey, son of Pompey	
31 B.C.E.	Octavian defeats Antony at battle of Actium	
30 B.C.E.	Antony and Cleopatra commit suicide Egypt annexed by Rome	Horace publishes *Epodes*
29 B.C.E.		Virgil completes *Georgics*

The Empire

Date	Roman Affairs	Cultural Developments
27 B.C.E.	Octavian assumes title of Augustus and becomes first emperor Gaul is organized into a province	Pantheon is completed
25 B.C.E.		Ovid begins *Amores*
24–23 B.C.E.		Publication of Horace's *Odes 1–3*
20 B.C.E.	Peace made with Parthians, who return Roman standards captured at Carrhae	Building of Temple of Mars
19 B.C.E.		Virgil and Tibullus die
18 B.C.E.	Augustan social and marriage reforms begun	
12 B.C.E.	Death of Agrippa Augustus becomes pontifex maximus on death of Lepidus Tiberius's campaign in Pannonia (to 9 B.C.E.)	
8 B.C.E.		Death of Maecenas and Horace
6 B.C.E.–2 C.E.	Tiberius retires to Rhodes Tiberius given tribunician power and adopts nephew Germanicus	Ovid writes *Fasti*
8		Ovid banished to Black Sea
9	Pannonian Revolt (from 6 C.E.)	
19	Death of Germanicus	
20	Death of Drusus, son of the emperor	
27	Tiberius retires to Capri	
31	Sejanus, the Praetorian prefect, is executed	
43	Invasion of Britain under Plautius	
59	Murder of Agrippina by Nero's men	
61	Revolt of Iceni in Britain, led by Boudicca	
64	Fire sweeps Rome, Christians persecuted	Nero's Golden House begun
65	Pisonian Conspiracy	Seneca and Lucan commit suicide
66	Jewish Revolt begins	
69	Year of the Four Emperors: Galba, Otho, Vitellius, and Vespasian	
70	Destruction of the Temple of Jerusalem	
79	Eruption of Vesuvius, with Pompeii and Herculaneum destroyed	Death of Pliny the Elder at Pompeii
80	Fire in Rome, Capitoline Temple destroyed	Colosseum opened
85	Agricola's campaigns end in Britain	Domitian's palace built on Palatine
86	Domitian campaigns against Dacians	Statius, Martial, Quintilian, and Silius Italicus active
98	Trajan becomes emperor	

Date	Roman Affairs	Cultural Developments
101–106	Trajan conquers Dacia	Dio Chrysostom, Epictetus, and Plutarch active
	Arabia becomes a province	
110–111		Tacitus writes *Histories* and *Annals*
112–113		Trajan's Forum and Column dedicated
114–117	Trajan campaigns in Parthia, Armenia, and Mesopotamia, annexing them	Arch of Trajan at Beneventum
115–117	Jewish Revolt	
	The Roman Empire reaches its greatest extent	
117	Hadrian becomes emperor	Hellenism is revived in the empire
132–135	Bar Cochba's revolt; final Diaspora of the Jews	Hadrian's Villa built at Tivoli
		Hadrian's Wall built in Britain
138	Antoninus Pius becomes emperor	
142		Wall of Antoninus Pius built
161	Marcus Aurelius becomes emperor	
162–166	Parthian Wars of Verus	
165–167	Rome suffers from severe plague	Apuleius and Galen
168–175	Marcus campaigns in German Wars	Justin martyred
174–180		Marcus Aurelius writes *Meditations*
193	Septimius Severus becomes emperor	Column of Marcus Aurelius completed
208–211	Severus campaigns in Britain	Philostratus, Clement of Alexandria, Tertullian, Herodian, and Sextus Empiricus active
		Arch of Septimius Severus erected
212	*Constitutio Antoniniana* provides citizenship to all in Empire	
216		Baths of Caracalla completed
223		Ulpian, the prefect and jurist, is killed
226	Ardashir crowned in Iran; launches war against Rome	
235	Beginning of military emperors	
249–51	Decius persecutes Christians	
258		Cyprian martyred
267	Goths invade Greece	
270		Death of Plotinus
271		Aurelian Walls erected in Rome

The Tetrarchies

Date	Roman Affairs	Cultural Developments
284	Diocletian begins reforms; establishes the tetrarchy	
303–305	Persecution of Christians	
306–337	Reign of Constantine the Great	Constantinople is founded as chief city of the empire during Constantine's reign
312	Battle of Milvian Bridge	
	Christianity becomes a sanctioned religion	
313–322		Christian basilica erected in Rome
360–363	Julian the Apostate emperor	
378–395	Theodosius emperor	
395	Rome divided among Theodosius's sons	

CHRONOLOGY OF MAJOR EVENTS (*continued*)

Date	Roman Affairs	Cultural Developments
410	Rome sacked by Alaric the Visigoth	
430		St. Augustine dies
439	Vandals conquer Carthage and Africa	
455	Vandals sack Rome	

The Decline of the empire

Date	Roman Affairs	
476	Fall of Roman Empire in West	
527–565	Justinian labors to restore the Roman Empire	
633–635	Arabs conquer Syria, Egypt, and the Sassanid Persian Empire	
1453	Ottomans conquer Constantinople and end Roman Empire in the East	

ENTRIES A TO Z

Abdagaeses (fl. first century C.E.) *Court official in the kingdom of Parthia*

Abdagaeses aided TIRIDATES in his ascent to the throne. In 35–36, King ARTABANUS III was forced from the throne of PARTHIA, and the Roman-backed Tiridates, a grandson of the old Parthian king PHRAATES III, was established as ruler. The historian Tacitus writes that Abdagaeses exerted control over Tiridates, preventing him from visiting the diverse and ever distrustful Parthian tribes, a policy that kept these clans from uniting behind Tiridates and resulted in civil war. In the face of the rebellion, Abdagaeses advised a retreat into Mesopotamia, claiming advantages were offered by the great rivers there. The Parthians viewed this as cowardice, and Tiridates was ousted from the monarchy. Nothing is recorded about the ultimate end of Abdagaeses.

Ablabius, Flavius (fl. fourth century C.E.) *Prefect of the Praetorian Guard under Constantine the Great, from 329 to 337*

Ablabius governed the Eastern Empire as the personal representative of the emperor, with considerable powers at his disposal. His authority earned him the enmity of members of the imperial court, and his conversion to Christianity was considered a diplomatic move. For some years Ablabius dueled politically with the philosopher SOPATER, eventually winning the intellectual power struggle. His victory was short-lived; when CONSTANTIUS II came to the throne in 337, Ablabius was executed.

Abyssinia *See* AFRICA.

Acacius of Constantinople (d. after 327 C.E.) *Bishop of Constantinople from 327 until his death*

Acacius served as the ranking Christian prelate throughout the final years of the reign of CONSTANTINE the Great (d. 337). He thus enjoyed the emperor's favor at a time when the imperial court exercised considerable influence upon the external affairs of the Christian Church. Acacius was also granted the honorific rank of COMES, with the official title *comes Macedoniae*. Few other details of his life are extant.

Academy Heavily influenced by its Greek predecessor, the Romans adopted this institution of learning as they adopted other Greek intellectual traditions. Roman philosophy was, in fact, based on Hellenic ideas and standards, and during the era of the Republic the philosopher was a respected member of Roman society.

The Academy in Greece was founded in the late fourth century B.C.E. by Plato, as a refuge for intellectual and political idealism, as well as training in mathematics, astronomy, and especially philosophy. Arcesilaus and Carneades were taught for generations in the Roman Academy and thus influenced subsequent Roman philosophical evolution. Gradually, however, the Academy lost much of its status, especially in the second and first centuries B.C.E., as a result of its quarrels with the STOICS and other Roman philosophical groups.

ANTIOCHUS OF ASCALON assumed the chief position in the Academy, succeeding PHILO, sometime around 79 B.C.E. Antiochus revived the institution by terminating its sole reliance upon the philosophical stance of skepticism, a pose adopted by leaders of the past. STOICISM, PLATON-

ISM, the Platonization of other philosophers, and even eclecticism were introduced into the Academy. Under Antiochus's guidance, the so-called New Academy was furthered intellectually by the arrival of Cicero, although the philosophies of the two eventually diverged. Antiochus opted for a more Stoic outlook in the Academy's approach, while Cicero upheld Philo's perspective of skepticism. Under the empire, the Academics were highly regarded, and some of the finest intellects in the Roman world, such as SENECA, were associated with the institution. Emperor JUSTINIAN dissolved the Academy in 529 C.E.

See also PHILOSOPHY.

Accius, Lucius (fl. first century B.C.E.) *A writer and translator*
Accius lived in the first and second centuries B.C.E. and was most noted for his contributions to Roman versification and prose. Accius was famed for his adaptations of 45 Greek tragedies.

acclamatio   Public acclaim that was given by the Romans both out of pleasure and displeasure; heard most commonly at funerals, marriages, in the theater, or at triumphs. The names for the various types of *acclamatio* were: *io triumphe,* for triumphs; *io hymen,* for marriages; the *plaudite,* for spectators at the end of a play; and the *conclamare,* at the time of the death of a loved one. The *acclamatio* was also given to the emperor and his family, with the custom of saluting the ruler developing into a display of flattery. Nero, for example, established the Augustiani, a body of young noblemen who were trained to cheer the emperor enthusiastically. Later emperors also received the *acclamationes* from the Senate, as recorded in the *Scriptores Historiae Augustae.*

See also CLAQUEURS.

Achaea   Roman province; conquered in 146 B.C.E. and eventually composed of a very large part of Greece, including Aetolia, Acarnania, Euboea, the Cyclades, and part of Epirus. Achaea, which had been attached to the wider territory of Macedonia, was secured after a revolt against Roman dominance; Augustus later made Achaea a senatorial province. Achaea benefited from the enlightened attitude of the Roman emperors, who treated pacified provinces in a better manner than their Republican predecessors. The emperors, seeking to maintain a political equilibrium between Rome and its outlying territories, offered such provinces advantages for their status.

The rule of Achaea was in the hands of the SENATE, and a proconsul of Praetorian rank acted as its governor, overseeing the administration of the region from the city of Corinth. This rule remained firmly in place until the reign of DIOCLETIAN, in the late third century.

During the years of the frontier troubles, 15 C.E. to 44 C.E., the province of Achaea was combined with MACEDONIA as part of an imperial province under the governor of Moesia, along the Danube. The Achaeans appear to have relished imperial designation of their lands, as TACITUS recorded that they petitioned for that status. In 67 C.E., as a result of the proclamation of Emperor NERO giving Greece its freedom, the Achaeans ruled themselves. Emperor VESPASIAN, however, in either 70 or 74, reformed the imperial system and reclaimed the province, putting it once again into the hands of the Senate. Aside from the old Achaean League, which was restored, several other religio-sociopolitical unions were tolerated by Rome and allowed to exist freely. A Panhellenic League was encouraged by the Philhellenic emperor HADRIAN. An IMPERIAL CULT, whose head, the *helladarch,* was appointed by league members, also came into being at this time. A facade of independence was consequently maintained by the Achaeans, especially in such cities as ATHENS, CORINTH, SPARTA, and Elis. No garrison was posted to Achaea, and a vast amount of self-determination was tolerated. The *correctores* (first attested for Italy in 216 C.E.) were also present in Achaea, special agents of the emperor who wielded the power to regulate trade or to observe finances. Achaea remained a province until the fall of the Roman Empire.

Achillas (fl. mid-first century B.C.E.) *Skilled soldier in the service of the Egyptian king Ptolemy XIII*
Achillas's notable act was to serve as an accomplice in the murder of POMPEY THE GREAT on September 28, 48 B.C.E. He was subsequently involved in the siege of Alexandria during Caesar's occupation of that Egyptian city, and he also aided in plots against the Roman forces. One of Achillas's intrigues involved Cleopatra's sister Princess ARSINOE, who offered him the post of general of her army. A veteran campaigner, but inept at court politics, Achillas managed to gain Arsinoe's ill will, and he was executed at her command.

Achilleus (d. c. 297 C.E.) *Leader of a nationalistic Egyptian rebellion against Roman domination in 296 or 297*
The years of the tetrarchy under DIOCLETIAN were ones of questionable Roman supremacy in the various regions of the empire, and Achilleus launched an Egyptian campaign for freedom. The revolt was doomed to failure because of internal rivalries and a lack of resources. Achilleus's own leadership was in dispute because many of his coconspirators favored DOMITIUS DOMITIANUS. Diocletian personally put down the revolution by capturing the city of ALEXANDRIA after a siege of six months. Achilleus and his band of rebels were slain.

Acron, Helenius (fl. second century C.E.) *Roman author, whose main works included commentaries on Horace and Persius*
Acron's scholarship concerning other works, such as Terence's *Adelphi* and *Porphyrion*, is now doubted. Little is known of his life.

acta   The laws and decrees enacted by the emperors of Rome. Under the Republic, elected officials swore to uphold the laws of the land. During the empire, this oath was extended to include as well the decrees, or *acta*, of the emperors. Each new emperor took an oath to uphold the *acta*. In many eras, however, these decrees or *acta* were limited only to those promulgated by AUGUSTUS in his time (the decrees of more recent emperors, especially in chaotic periods of the empire, were considered suspect or not worthy of notice). It was the decision of each new emperor whether to swear to uphold the decrees of his immediate predecessor or not. The SENATE possessed the right to rescind decrees of a deceased emperor or to ratify the *acta* of emperors still living (as they did with Augustus in 29 B.C.E.).

Acta were considered important because of the ramifications involved in precedents and posterity. TIBERIUS, for example, refused to allow the Senate to vote oaths to him when he came to the throne, as his monstrous deeds would then be enshrined in the perpetual machinery of the *acta*. CLAUDIUS, meanwhile, made everyone swear to uphold the *acta* of Augustus but, like Tiberius, did not insist upon their taking oaths to him and his personal decrees.

acta diurna   A journal instituted by Julius CAESAR that recounted the great events of Rome, much like a modern newspaper, displayed on a whitened board (*album*) daily. This history was widely read and was used by Roman historians attempting to recreate the events of earlier eras. Tacitus mentions the *acta diurna* in his *Annals*.

acta Senatus   The official records of the proceedings and deeds of the Roman Senate. The records were of interest to various historians, including TACITUS, who used them to put together many of his own books, along with the information available in the ACTA DIURNA.

The record was useful not only in making an account of events and speeches in the Senate, but it also singled out the friends and enemies of an emperor and his lieutenants. Men such as SEJANUS used the *acta Senatus* to keep a close watch on the Senate and its deliberations, courtesy of its own account of itself.

Acte, Claudia (d. after 69 C.E.) *Freedwoman from Asia Minor who became the mistress of Emperor Nero*
Serving as a freedwoman in the imperial household, Acte came to NERO's attention in 55. SENECA, the imperial tutor and adviser, sensed that this infatuation could wean Nero away from his dominant mother, AGRIPPINA THE YOUNGER, and fostered the relationship. The couple, attempting to be discreet, were shielded by various court followers. As was inevitable, Nero lost interest in Acte and took up another mistress. Acte remained devoted, however, appearing after Nero's death to claim his body, which she placed in the family tomb of the Domitii in the Pincian Hills. Acte seems to have amassed considerable wealth during her period of imperial favor.

Actium   An engagement was fought on the Ionian Sea on September 2, 31 B.C.E., just off the coast of this site, near the Ambracian Gulf, between the fleet of Octavian (AUGUSTUS) and the armada of Marc ANTONY and CLEOPATRA. This naval battle, in which Octavian proved victorious, decided the fate of the Roman world.

By 33 B.C.E., most political factions striving for power in the Republic had faded, leaving only the Triumvirs Octavian and Antony as rivals. In May 32, they became dire enemies when Antony divorced Octavian's sister, Octavia (1), and married Cleopatra. Claiming that Cleopatra aspired to become the queen of Rome, and that in his will Antony distributed the Eastern provinces among his illegitimate children by Cleopatra, Octavian roused the Senate and the Roman mob. They called for war against Antony, stripping him of his offices.

Both sides gathered large fleets and assembled legions, but Octavian, with his normal prudence, took his time. Finally, in 31 he set out with hundreds of ships and 40,000 men, landing in Greece and marching south to Mikalitzi, north of Nicopolis on the Bay of Comarus. Antony, possessing a like number of land forces, also had at his command a combined Roman-Egyptian fleet of 480 ships. The advantage rested with Antony because his naval vessels were large and heavy. Octavian, however, possessed two elements that were to prove pivotal to the outcome: his admiral AGRIPPA and his lighter Liburnian ships, which were equipped with the HARPAX, a ram that pinned the opposing vessel and allowed for boarding and capture. Antony, encamped just south of Actium, nevertheless stood a good chance of victory.

The battle was really two encounters in a single day, the fierce naval conflict in the morning and a half-hearted rout on land that afternoon. The naval engagement began with the division of Octavian's fleet into three sections—a center and two wings. Agrippa commanded the northern wing and was admiral in chief. ARRUNTIUS led the center, and Octavian was in charge of the southern wing. On the Egyptian side, Antony took command of the northern squadrons, opposite Agrippa. Marcus Octavius was opposed to Arruntius, and Savius sailed against Octavian's ships. Cleopatra headed a reserve squadron of 60 ships behind the center of the Egyptian fleet.

The tactical advantage fell to the commander who penetrated the other's flanks, and here the battle was won by Agrippa. Antony fought valiantly, but the unreliable and disloyal ships of his center and south wing broke ranks. Cleopatra sailed to safety, probably signaled by Antony to do so, although the historian DIO CASSIUS dismissed her flight as the act of a woman and an Egyptian. Antony, with his own ship pinned by a *harpax*, transferred to another vessel and also fled toward Egypt. Victory at sea was total for Octavian, and Antony's general, CANDIDUS CRASSUS, faced a mutiny in his own ranks and surrendered.

An invasion of Egypt followed in July of 30, but Actium had already established Octavian as the undisputed master of Rome and its far-flung world. By August, Antony and Cleopatra were dead by their own hands. Octavian returned to Rome to become the first Roman emperor, Augustus. PLUTARCH and Dio Cassius wrote extensive versions of the battle.

See also CIVIL WARS (SECOND TRIUMVIRATE) and NAVY.

Acts of the Pagan Martyrs   Literature that dates to the first century C.E., detailing the hardships and trials of Egyptian nationalists in ALEXANDRIA. Written in a dramatic and bitterly anti-Roman style, the work, mainly fragmentary, includes accounts from the period of AUGUSTUS to the era following the reign of MARCUS AURELIUS.

adaeratio   The name given to the imperial process, normally initiated by government decree, in which goods or services could be commuted into issues or into similar monetary transactions.

adlectio   The process by which an individual was chosen to be a Roman senator. Generally, it was accomplished by being enrolled on the lists of the SENATE. This was an arbitrary process at times, and Caesar used it to increase Senate numbers. The tradition was carried on by the emperors with some prudence and hesitation at first, as in the case of Augustus and Claudius, but Domitian, Macrinus, and others used it with enthusiasm.

adoptio   Or *adoptatio,* the name used for adoption, one of two principal areas of domestic relations in Rome with regard to parent and child, the other being lawful marriage. There were actually two variations of the process: *adoptio* and *adrogatio.* Adoption of a person not in the power of a parent (*sui iuris*) was called *adrogatio.* It was originally possible only in Rome and with the vote of the populace (*populi auctoritate*) in the Comitia Centuriata. By the first century B.C.E., the *comitia* was effectively replaced in this matter by 30 lictors who were asked their approval. Those citizens living in the provinces were not eligible for this approbation and were thus required to ask the permission of the emperor, beginning the process that came to be known as the *adrogatio per rescriptum principis.* From the time of Diocletian, this act was mandatory. *Adoptio* involved a complex series of *mancipationes* (emancipations) within the framework of a law in the XII Tables.

By the terms of adoption, a Roman citizen passed from one family to another, a change of family that meant that the *adrogatus* brought with him all persons under his *potestas* into the household of the *adrogator,* while acknowledging the *patria potestas* of the family's head. It served a useful purpose both socially and politically, as a childless individual could adopt and ensure the continuation of the *sacra* of the family, bequeathing not just property to the *heres* (heir), but the family as well, for the new member accepted the name and rank of the adoptive father. Politically, adoption could be used to great advantage as a means of improving one's prospects by becoming adopted into a higher class family—moving from the Plebeian to the Patrician class. The opposite movement had advantages of its own; Pulcher Clodius was adrogated into a Plebeian family by a *lex curiata* in order to be eligible for election as *tribunus plebis* and so continue his struggles with Cicero.

Females could not be taken into a family through adrogation as the transaction involved the *patria potestas.* Adoption became very popular in the early empire as a result of the *lex Julia et Papia Poppaea* (9 C.E.), which granted definite privileges to those citizens with children, such as the eligibility to become praetors. Adoptions were hastily arranged, the office secured and then the *adrogatus* given complete emancipation from the adoptive family. By a *senatus consultum* during the reign of Nero (54–68 C.E.), this practice was curtailed. Antoninus Pius also moved to prevent premature (and potentially disastrous emancipations, the releasing of an adopted heir) by promulgating a law that ensured the rights of succession to the adopted. Under the *adoptiominus plena* by Justinian (ruled 527–565), the adopted maintained a right of succession to the property and name of the former family, and was not subject to the *patria potestas* of the adoptive father; this law had its origins in the custom of the adopted retaining some association with his original *gens,* seen in the new name or *gens,* only the suffix *ianus* was added. An example of this was Emperor Augustus who, as Octavius, was adopted by the testament of his uncle Julius Caesar in 44 B.C.E., taking the full name Gaius Julius Caesar Octavianus. Adoption by testament, of course, was the naming of an heir through a will. However, the adopted was not the heir in the sense of regular *adoptio* or *adrogatio,* receiving only the name and property of the deceased without all of the other benefits or social considerations. Octavius therefore had Caesar's adoption of him by testament made official by the *curiae.*

Adrianople   Site in southern Greece of a battle fought on July 3, 324 C.E., between CONSTANTINE THE GREAT and coemperor LICINIUS. In 312 Constantine had won the battle of MILVIAN BRIDGE, gaining absolute control over the Western Empire. In the East, Licinius vied with MAXIMINUS DAIA for domination, and in 313 marched against this rival. Licinius triumphed; two men now controlled the world in an unstable alliance. In 316 the Danube and Balkan provinces became their battleground. Two collisions (at Cibalae and Mardia) resulted only in stalemate and eventually in a treaty. By 323, Constantine marched once more, against the GOTHS. After routing the barbarians along the Danube, he pursued them into Licinius's territory and one year later forced a showdown.

The two rulers gathered their legions, each army totaling around 130,000 men. On July 3, 324, they engaged at Adrianople. Constantine set a large portion of his army on Licinius's flank, while he led the main assault on the enemy's naturally weakened center. The feint on the flank worked perfectly, and Constantine smashed Licinius's middle. His army routed, Licinius fled, leaving behind some 40,000 men. Constantine pursued him to Byzantium.

Another battle was fought at sea on the Hellespont later in the month, and on September 18, 324, the last confrontation took place at Chrysopolis, where Constantine was again the victor. Licinius was executed in the following year, and Constantine was the sole ruler of the Roman world.

A second battle was fought at Adrianople on August 9, 378, between Emperor VALENS and the Goths. In 376, Valens, the Eastern emperor, received word that the Visigoths were being pushed in great numbers beyond the natural frontier of the Danube. The HUNS had invaded their lands, and the Visigoths, led by FRITIGERN and Alavius, were asking permission to migrate and to settle across the Lower Danube, near Thrace. Valens allowed them to enter the empire with the demand that they surrender their arms and submit all male children as hostages. The hostages were handed over, the arms were not. The arrival of equally alarmed Ostrogothic remnants threw all of Thrace into confusion, and a war broke out. Rome faced Visigoth and Ostrogoth elements, as a general rebellion threatened the entire Danube front. In Thrace, Fritigern (Alavius having been killed in an ambush) joined the Ostrogoth kings, Alatheus and Saphrax (or Safrax), to duel with Valens's Greek legate, Sebastian. The Goths were defeated several times by inferior forces.

GRATIAN, emperor of the West, took steps to pacify the Danube. Sensing that an opportunity was within his reach, not only to crush the barbarian hordes but also to lay claim to greatness for the act, Valens precipitately marched from Constantinople to attack the Goths. The emperor possessed nearly 60,000 men, mostly infantry, while Fritigern and his allies numbered over 100,000 evenly divided between horse and foot. On August 9, 378, Valens, unwilling to wait for Gratian, pressed his legions into battle.

His assault was well-timed, being launched while the mainly Ostrogoth cavalry was away. The Visigoths, facing an organized army with their own limited cavalry on their flanks, were driven back into the large wagon camp that had been erected. Valens pushed on, but suddenly the Ostrogoths turned and made a charge that was to revitalize military tactics for the next thousand years. Crushed, routed and finally annihilated, the immobilized Roman legions were ridden down by the horsemen. Few escaped from the catastrophe. Valens died with 40,000 other Roman soldiers.

The battle of Adrianople was felt more deeply and politically than the number of casualties warranted. St. Ambrose called it "the end of all humanity, the end of the world," a statement that was dramatic and prophetic. Rome was no longer invincible, and the barbarians were pressing on the frontiers.

Adriaticum Mare (Adriatic Sea) The Adriatic sea between Italy and the Balkans that served for many centuries as a conduit of trade and over which Grecian civilization spread throughout Italy. Although always plagued by pirates and natural hazards, the Adriatic played a role in the shaping of Roman economic power. Safe transport of vessels was made possible after the rise to power of Emperor AUGUSTUS (63 B.C.E.–14 C.E.), with the stationing of fleets as monitors of the sea lanes. The home port of these fleets was AQUILEIA, at the head of the Adriatic, the largest trading city in the area.

See also PIRACY.

Aduatuca Also called Atuatuca in some records; an engagement between AMBIORIX and the Romans took place at this site in what is now Belgium in the winter of 54–53 B.C.E. Ambiorix, the tall chieftain of the Eburones, began an uprising against the widely scattered, winter-quartered Roman legions. The attack came as a surprise to Caesar's lieutenant in northern Gaul, Q. Titurius SABINUS. Sabinus's command was spread over the countryside and was vulnerable to assault. Ambiorix was aware of the military risks in a frontal assault against the Roman positions, and offered safe passage to Sabinus and his troops. The Gallic chieftain did not keep his word. Sabinus and his men were slaughtered. Buoyed by his success, Ambiorix attacked Caesar's other commander, Quintus Tullius Cicero, and suffered defeat. The entire region controlled by Ambiorix and his people was eventually overrun by Caesar during the GALLIC WARS, and the rebellion ended.

Adventus, Marcus Oclatinus (160–after 218 C.E.)
Roman general and official
Born in 160, Adventus began a military career and entered the FRUMENTARII, the spy service of the empire, eventually becoming its chief. He later received a procu-

ratorship and served Emperor CARACALLA as one of his two prefects. The other prefect, MACRINUS, murdered Caracalla, thus handing the army the task of choosing an imperial successor. According to the historian Herodian, Adventus was the army's first choice but declined because of his advanced age; Macrinus was elected in his place.

As emperor, Macrinus appears to have felt indebted to Adventus and appointed him a senator, a fellow consul and then prefect of the city. These appointments, made in 218, angered the Senate and the Roman populace, who considered Adventus an assassin. Macrinus tried to make amends by replacing Adventus as prefect with Marius Maximus, which did nothing to appease the Senate. Macrinus died at the hands of Caracalla's family, having no powerful protectors or friends. Adventus, the cause of so many of Macrinus's problems, retired from public life.

advocatus The legal presenter of a case in the Roman judicial system, requiring skill in law, precedence, history, and oratory. The *advocatus* was a gifted speaker who could elevate his defense to an intellectual, philosophical, and rhetorical level that increased the chances of winning. The *advocatus* was distinct from the JURIST in the Roman court system, but in the late empire a decline of jurists caused the roles to overlap and become blurred. Fees were originally banned for the *advocati*, but this tradition was abandoned. One of the greatest *advocati* in Roman history was CICERO.

See also LAW.

Aedesius (c. 280/90–355 C.E.) *Neoplatonic philosopher of the late fourth century*
Aedesius studied in Syria under IAMBLICHUS. Aedesius's students included the future Emperor JULIAN and the historian EUSEBIUS, bishop of Caesarea. Aedesius could be a staunch defender of his beliefs. When another Neoplatonist, Hierocles, placed a virgin into a brothel in Egypt, Aedesius beat him severely with a stick for this act.

See also NEOPLATONISM.

aedile An administrator of Rome, taken from the Latin *aedes*, which meant "temple"; their usefulness and political position increased over the centuries. During the Republic, the aediles supervised the streets, temples, and quarters of Rome and, more important, the CURA ANNONAE, the distribution of the vital corn supply. Augustus, like Caesar before him, made adjustments to their power, in order to create a more professional imperial administration. The historian Tacitus painted a rather clear picture of the role of the aediles during the early empire. They were to tend public buildings, keep the streets clean, police the city (although the URBAN COHORTS also fulfilled this task), and superintend the markets and the games. Also, the aediles helped supervise the cleaning up of the city, an activity that they did not

perform particularly well. Aediles were also charged with the task of destroying any and all books condemned by the Senate and enforced all sumptuary laws.

Aedui A tribe centered in Gallic Burgundy, whose dealings with Rome were both successful and unfortunate. The Aedui became clients of the Republic in the late second century B.C.E., freeing themselves from the yoke of the AVERNI and the ALLOBROGES, for which they showed themselves grateful enough to earn the title of *fratres,* or "brothers." The alliance with Rome allowed them to become the largest of the Gallic tribes. Their capital was founded at AUGUSTODONUM, after Bibracte, their former capital, was abandoned in Caesar's time.

The Aedui were always resentful of Roman domination, and on at least two occasions launched major rebellions against their conquerors. The first was in 21 C.E., when SACROVIR, their king, led 40,000 Aedui and their allies against the legate Gaius SILIUS (1). The battle was quickly decided by Roman might, and Sacrovir killed himself. VINDEX, a Romanized Gaul, and the governor of the pacified region of Gallia Lugdunensis, rose up in 68 C.E., declaring that GALBA should be declared the *princeps;* the Aedui joined him. L. VERGINIUS RUFUS, the master of the legions of Germania Superior, smashed Vindex's hopes in battle. The Aedui were not punished, because Rome's attention was drawn to its own civil war of 69 C.E.

The relationship between the Aedui and the Romans was remarkably cordial and solid over the decades, a unique circumstance among the proud Gallic tribes. The Aedui aided Julius Caesar in his campaigns. Eventually, as clients of Rome, they were able to send representatives to serve in the Senate. As a result of their alliance with Rome, in the third and fourth centuries, the Aedui lands were destroyed by the constant wars of the empire, while the onslaught of barbarians from the east broke Aedui power.

Aegidius (d. 464 C.E.) *A magister militum in Gaul in 458*
Serving Emperor Majorian, he was one of Rome's leading figures in a chaotic era of the Late Empire. Aegidius upheld Roman power at Arles, working with numerous tribes of the region, including the FRANKS and the VANDALS. He was personally responsible for defeating the powerful Theodoric II, king of the VISIGOTHS, who invaded Gaul. By 461, Aegidius was the principal opponent of Rome's true master, RICIMER, the German *magister militum,* who deposed Majorian and replaced him with LIBIUS SEVERUS. Only the continuing wars with Theodoric's Visigoths kept Aegidius from advancing on Rome to take the throne himself. According to Gregory of Tours, the Franks offered him their own throne. Aegidius died in 464, perhaps by poison. He was a devout Christian and a Roman of strict ideals.

Aelian (Claudius Aelianus) (c. 170–235 C.E.) *Writer and rhetorician*

Heavily influenced by STOICISM, Aelian was the author of two books of lasting interest, *Natura Animalium* and the *Varia Historia,* and is considered by some to be the author of the *Peasant Letters* as well.

Aelianus, Casperius (d. 98 A.D.) *Prefect of the Praetorian Guard*

Appointed by DOMITIAN Aelianus was soon replaced in the aftermath of a financial scandal. When Nerva came to the throne in 96, Aelianus regained his position with the Guard. As prefect of the powerful Praetorians, Aelianus drove his troops into a rage over the assassination of Emperor Domitian. The Praetorians raced to the palace and cornered the new emperor, demanding justice and the death of Domitian's slayers (two of Nerva's allies). Nerva was dismissed by the Praetorians. The guilty were soon removed and executed, and Emperor Nerva collapsed and died soon after. Trajan, the new emperor of Rome, summoned Aelianus and all of the other Praetorians involved. They arrived at Trajan's base at Cologne and were promptly slain for their treachery.

Aelius Caesar, Lucius (Lucius Ceionius Commodus) (d. 138 C.E.) *Adopted heir of Emperor Hadrian*

The son of a powerful senatorial family, Aelius came to the attention of Emperor HADRIAN in 136. At the time, Hadrian was searching for an heir. Young, well educated and popular, Aelius was made consul in 136 and 137 and was officially adopted as Hadrian's heir in 136, assuming the name Lucius Aelius Caesar. The emperor ordered the deaths of his own brother-in-law, Julius Servianus, and his grandson, because they could be considered rivals to the throne. Aelius's daughter Fabia was then married to the future emperor, Marcus Aurelius. Aelius subsequently served on the Danube and returned to Rome during the winter of 137. In January 138, he suddenly became ill and died. His son was Lucius Verus.

Aemilian (Marcus Aemilius Aemilianus (d. 253 C.E.) *Roman emperor*

Like others in the long line of third-century political figures, Aemilian rose up to seize the throne and then was slain by a stronger general. He began his career as the governor of Moesia Inferior, assuming command there in 252 in the reign of Trebonianus Gallus. In the spring of 253, when Kniva, the chief of the Goths, demanded that the Roman tributes be increased, Aemilian launched a campaign against the Gothic tribes along the Danube. Elated by Aemilian's victory and aware of the fact that the emperors offered more bounties than governors, his troops declared him emperor. Aemilian then marched to Italy, easily overcame Trebonianus Gallus (who was promptly murdered by his own soldiers), and was proclaimed emperor of Rome by the Senate. VALERIAN, the general of the Rhine legions, marched into Italy almost immediately. Aemilian fell victim to his own men, who, fearing defeat at Valerian's hands murdered their own usurper.

aerarium   Also called the *aerarium Saturni,* the public or state treasury of Rome derived from *aes,* "bronze." Under the Republic, the control of the *aerarium* was one of the bulwarks of the SENATE. During the empire, however, the *aerarium* came to represent both the extent and state of imperial finances and the degree to which the Roman bureaucracy was able to function.

Sources of income for the state treasury were varied. The *tribunii aerarii* collected and deposited payments made by the tribes, allowing few exceptions. There was even a 5% tax on emancipations, and all surplus funds of a region were handed over to the central bureau. This allowed each emperor to inform the people of the provinces that all monies spent on their defense had come originally from the provinces themselves. Equally, the *aerarium* served as a general resource for the empire as a whole; money could be drawn from it and used anywhere in the Roman world, wherever it was needed. The *aerarium,* while substantial, was never enough to cover the mammoth expense of maintaining an empire, and Augustus was forced to use his own sizable sums to finance many projects.

Control over the money under the Republic fell to the *quaestors,* but Caesar, who seized the *aerarium* for himself in 49 B.C.E., placed two AEDILES (administrators) in charge. Augustus at first handed the *aerarium* over to two *praefecti,* but in 23 B.C.E. decided that two praetors were better; each was drawn by lot. The danger of incompetence in the face of a growing bureaucratic system was alleviated by Nero, who appointed two *praefecti aerarii* in 56 C.E., titles that remained into the fourth century. The *aerarium,* along with the *tabularium,* was also the place where state documents of every nature were maintained.

See also FINANCE and FISCUS.

aerarium militare   The military treasury, which was established by Augustus in 6 C.E. and intended to provide bounties for soldiers, both active and retired. The general fund from which it was drawn originated with a donation of 170 million sesterces by Augustus. Three *praefecti aerarii militaris* managed the finances.

Aetius, Flavius (d. 454 C.E.) *Patrician and magister militum in the Western Empire during the reign of Valentinian III (425–55)*

Born at Durostorum, in modern Bulgaria, Aetius was the son of a general by the name of Gaudentius. Aetius succeeded in acquiring a power base around 430 with the help of the Huns (among whom he had been a hostage in his youth), and with them fought against the Visigoths and Burgundians throughout Gaul (432–39).

As a servant of Emperor VALENTINIAN III, Aetius had to contend not only with the Franks, Goths, and Burgundians but also with the emperor's mother, Galla Placidia, the Augusta of the Western Empire. The two were bitter political enemies, and Aetius was forced to defend his position in Gaul when Galla Placidia sent her own champion, Boniface, chief of the African legions, against him. The Huns proved valuable allies during the campaign. While Boniface succeeded in winning several engagements, the commander of the African legions fell in battle, leaving Aetius victorious and de facto ruler of the Western Empire.

Events turned against Aetius in 451, when ATTILA, King of the Huns, swept through Belgica and into Gaul. Aetius summoned the Franks and Goths to aid in the defense of the West. Attila was halted at the bloody battle of the Catalaunian Plain, but the survival of the Hun host permitted Attila to turn south and ravage Italy. Aetius could do little to resist the Hun advance into Italy. He subsequently acquired the enmity of the usurper and future emperor, Petronius Maximus. In 454, Aetius was assassinated. His death hastened the decline and instability of the Western Empire. The following year, Rome was sacked by the Vandals.

Afer, Gnaeus Domitius (d. 59 A.D.) *One of the finest orators of the early Empire*
Afer served as an *advocatus,* both in accusation and in defense, and Emperor Tiberius used him often in the condemnation of his opponents, especially Claudia PULCHRA and Furnius. He was generally unpopular as an individual, and in his later years, when his powers failed him, he could not keep silent. Afer died in 59. He was supposedly from Gallia Narbonensis.

Afranius, Lucius (d. 46 C.E.) *Legate, consul, and an official of Pompey the Great*
Afranius distinguished himself in the CIVIL WAR of the First Triumvirate, more by his persistence than his tactical skills in the field. In 60 C.E., he was appointed consul but could not compete with the far more effective METELLUS CELER; he later acquired the governorship of GALLIA CISALPINA. The Civil Wars gave him further opportunities to advance his career, and in 55, with PETRENIS, he set out for Hispania Citerior (Spain) to serve as Pompey's legate, with three legions under his command. Spain attracted Caesar's attention immediately, and at ILERDA in 49, Afranius was defeated and captured. He was spared by Caesar after vowing not to take up arms again. Undaunted by his oath, Afranius went to Pompey at DYRRHACHIUM and fought at PHARSALUS, escaping after the defeat. He fled to Africa, where Caesar's legate, P. Silius, hunted him down after the battle at THAPSUS in 46; Caesar had him executed.

Africa (province)   Africa's responsibility for the supply of Roman grain made it essential to Rome's survival as an empire. Africa's value as a territory began with the destruction of Carthage in 146 C.E., when the Republic laid claim to all of Carthage's holdings. Most of Africa in the Tunisian region was given back to the original kingdoms from which it had been carved, but the fertile, northeast area of Tunis was converted into the province of Africa Vetus, with a frontier called the *fossa regia.* After the battle of THAPSUS in 46 C.E., Caesar created Africa Nova, sliced out of NUMIDIA.

The empire changed the African borders again. Augustus combined Africa Vetus and Nova into Africa Proconsularis, which stretched from the Cyrenaican frontier westward to the Numidian Kingdom. This arrangement did not last because during Augustus's reign the Roman colonization of the region began in earnest. From then on there was a growing and eventually rich Roman presence in Africa, which the writers APULEIUS, FRONTO, and Tertullian describe. Thirteen colonies were founded in MAURETANIA. The provincial capital was moved from Utica to the larger, reconstructed CARTHAGE. The proconsul there ruled principally through a bureaucracy, for there was never any organized resistance to Roman domination. Only one legion, the III Augusta, was ever stationed there. Gaius Caligula ended the tradition by which the governor controlled the legion and placed the unit under the sole authority of his legate. Further, the troops were subsequently stationed on the frontier near Numidia, which became a separate province by decree of Septimius Severus. Finally, Claudius added two more colonies in Mauretania.

The legion in Africa faced only a few wars and was consequently used almost exclusively in the vital work of construction and engineering. Through centuriation—the organization of the territories into segmented, regular plots and estates—the province came to possess nearly 500 villages or communities, of which 200 were cities. The result of these efforts was total pacification and intense Romanization.

Agriculture was preeminent, with corn serving for centuries as the staple crop. Carthage alone exported annually over half a million tons to Rome. In Tunisia, Numidia, and Mauretania, olives grew readily, and farmers were encouraged to diversify. By the second century, the olive harvest was nearly equal to that of corn, and soon both were joined by cereal, fruits, and textiles.

Africa became one of the leading centers for intellectuals, including Cornelius Fronto, Apuleius, and others, who found the environment rich. A number of senators came from Africa and eventually an emperor (Septimius SEVERUS). Christianity spread quickly through the province, overcoming the Graeco-Roman gods, who themselves had defeated the Punic deities of old.

Africa was, however, swept into the troubles of the empire after the third century. When Emperor GORDIAN I was proclaimed by the landowners of the province and placed on the throne while in Carthage, the legions revolted, in 238 C.E., and ousted the briefly reigning emperor, who probably killed himself rather than die at their hands. As a result, GORDIAN III disbanded the legion. In 308, Domitius ALEXANDER, the prefect of Africa, led a revolt from Carthage and threatened the vital corn supply. The prefect of the Guard, Rufius Volusianus, was sent to Africa and crushed the uprising, destroying much of Carthage in the process.

Emperor Constantine rebuilt the city in the early fourth century and placed the province back into the system adopted by Diocletian, in which Numidia, Tripolitania, Mauretania, and Byzacena were all under the diocese of Africa. Such widening made the province susceptible to even more troubles, as the invasion of the Vandals in 429 demonstrated. Defenses were never strong, as the Moors and other tribes had been easily quelled. The mountainous and desert-like regions made fortifications and permanent *limes* construction difficult, resulting in a province of great wealth that was unable to defend itself.

Africa Nova   The Roman province in AFRICA created in 46 B.C.E. by Julius Caesar, following the battle of THAPSUS. The province was carved out of the kingdom of NUMIDIA. During the reign of Augustus, it was added to Africa Vetus to form the larger province of Africa Proconsularis.

Africa Proconsularis   The combination of the two provinces of Africa Nova and Africa Vetus during the reign of Augustus (27 B.C.E.–14 C.E.).

See also AFRICA.

Africa Vetus   A Roman province in northern Tunisia, governed by a praetor from its capital at Utica. After Carthage fell to the war engines of Scipio Africanus (146 B.C.E.), the Roman Republic seized all of the city's holdings and created the new province.

See also AFRICA.

Agricola, Gnaeus Julius (40–93 C.E.) *General and governor of Britain (78–85)*
Agricola was one of the most successful military men of his era, responsible for imprinting Britain thoroughly with Roman culture. He was the son of Julius Graecinus and Julia Procilla. Graecinus was killed by Emperor Gaius Caligula, and the Lady Julia was murdered by Emperor Otho's troops. But the deaths of his parents had little effect on Agricola's career, which was swift. Agricola served as a tribune in Britain, as quaestor in Asia in 64, as legate in Britain from 71 to 73, as legate of Aquitania from 74 to 77, and as consul in 77.

This last posting was made by the Emperor Vespasian, who favored the able officer and in 78 named him the governor of Britain.

Agricola's campaigns were brilliantly executed, and he Romanized much of the province and extended Roman influence well into Scotland. He conquered North Wales, the Tay, Newstead, Forth, and Clyde, penetrating deep into the Grampian Mountains and into Caledonia. Finally, Agricola's fleet sailed around Britain, a remarkable feat. In 85 C.E., having served there for seven years, Agricola was recalled by Domitian. Agricola married Domitia Decidiana, and his daughter married the historian Tacitus, who provided detailed information about the man and his campaigns in *Agricola*.

See also BRITANNIA (1).

agriculture   *See* ECONOMY and FARMING.

Agrippa I, Marcus Julius (Herod) (d. 44 C.E.) *The grandson of King Herod the Great*
Through political and social connections and assassinations, Agrippa became the ruler of the tetrarchy of Philip Archelaus and hence the king of Judaea from 37 to 44 C.E. Agrippa grew up in Rome and was an intimate companion of CLAUDIUS and the Lady Antonia. His Roman education ended, however, in 23 C.E., with the death of Drusus, and he returned to PALESTINE, where he acquired a reputation for contentiousness, which Josephus the historian made known, and was suspected of treason.

In 36, with borrowed funds, Agrippa returned to Rome and was rescued from prison by Gaius Caligula, who gave him the throne of Philip, Agrippa's uncle, in 37, and then the throne of Herod Antipas as well. Agrippa kept the Great Temple of Jerusalem safe from desecration by Caligula when he persuaded him that it was not necessary to place a statue of himself within the walls. Claudius trusted Agrippa greatly, giving him Judaea as well, but he soon came to regret the gift as Agrippa harbored ambitions of his own. He died before he could make any of his political dreams a reality.

Agrippa II, Marcus Julius (Herod) (fl. mid-first century C.E.) *The son of Agrippa I*
Like his father, Agrippa II spent most of his youth in the Roman Imperial Household. Claudius granted him the kingdom of Chalcis in 50 and then the tetrarchy of Philip, with Abilene and Acene. Agrippa II clearly placated the Jewish element in his territories, but the Jewish revolt of 66 put him in an awkward position. He tried at first to stem the rebellion, but he was wise enough to see the end result and allied himself with the Romans. Josephus reported in *The Jewish War* and in *The Jewish Antiquities* that Agrippa was on hand when the Romans conquered Jerusalem.

See also JUDAEA and PALAESTINA.

Agrippa, Marcus Vipsanius (d. 12 B.C.E.) *Friend, lieutenant, and supporter of Augustus*
Although of common birth (which prevented him from ever wearing the purple robes of an emperor), Agrippa

was Octavian's lifelong companion. Accompanying Octavian in 45 B.C.E. to Apollonia, where Caesar's nephew learned the ways of soldiering, Agrippa was present in 44 B.C.E. when the news of Julius Caesar's assassination arrived. Octavian inherited Caesar's wealth and much of his power, and Agrippa emerged as his representative in all matters. He was even instrumental in raising an army to ensure that Octavian would be part of the newly formed triumvirate, which emerged out of the political chaos after Caesar's murder.

The wars, which were inevitable, allowed Agrippa's multifaceted abilities to shine. He fought against Marc ANTONY's brother, Lucius, in 40 B.C.E., and then helped eradicate the Republican forces at Perusia. Octavian then sent him to Gaul, where he was the only successful agent of the triumvirate. Agrippa defeated a revolt by the Aquitanii, created a Roman site at the Ubii (near Cologne) and made a punitive raid over the Rhine. In 37 B.C.E., he returned to Rome in triumph and was made a consul. At that point Agrippa gave up his general's rank in the army and became an admiral. From 37 to 31 B.C.E., he was a tireless sailor, first creating a powerful fleet and then setting sail for war against the pirate, Sextus Pompey, the son of Pompey the Great. At Mylae and Naulochus, Sextus was defeated.

Octavian, meanwhile, was preparing for the final confrontation between his forces and those of Marc Antony. They met at ACTIUM in 31 B.C.E., and Agrippa commanded the successful left wing in battle. That war ended the rivalries for the throne of Rome. Upon Octavian's return and his assumption of the title of Augustus, Agrippa was instrumental in conducting the census (29–28 B.C.E.) and the reorganization of the Roman institutions so crucial to the subsequent imperial regimes.

After crushing rebellions in Gaul, Agrippa administered the East with the powers given to him by Augustus, which by 13 B.C.E. included those of *censoria potestas* (*see* CENSOR). Agrippa's Eastern tenure, however, prompted a feud with Claudius MARCELLUS, Augustus's nephew, who was being advanced as the emperor's heir. A mission away from Rome to the Black Sea area, Jerusalem and Pannonia, eased the situation.

When Agrippa returned to Rome, he became involved in civic improvements. He built the Pantheon, constructed two aqueducts, built baths, and cleaned the Roman water supply system. He also supervised the building of roads in Lugdunum (Lyons), founded colonies at Berytus and Baalbek, and planned other towns.

Agrippa had three wives: the daughter of Pomponius Atticus, Caecilia; the beautiful and considerably wealthy Marcella, Augustus's niece; and finally, in 21 B.C.E., Julia, Augustus's daughter, who bore him three sons, Gaius, Lucius, and Agrippa, and a daughter, AGRIPPINA.

Agrippa also wrote and drafted a modern map of the empire. He died in 12 B.C.E., still faithful to his friend Augustus, but having outlived his usefulness to the imperial family. He was long honored by the Roman military as the inventor of the HARPAX, the formidable weapon that Octavian used at the battle of Actium.

Agrippa Postumus, Marcus Vipsanius (12 B.C.E.–14 C.E.) *The son of Agrippa and Julia (daughter of Augustus)*

The youngest of three grandsons of AUGUSTUS, Postumus was born after his father's death and grew up in the imperial household. Tacitus considered him "uncultured, with only brute strength to recommend him," and he fell afoul of Empress LIVIA, who had him banished to the island of Planasia (near Elba). In 14 C.E., when his only protector, Augustus, died and Tiberius became emperor, Agrippa was killed. There is some question as to who issued the execution order. Tacitus reported that Tiberius claimed the instructions had been left by Augustus, to be carried out at his death. The historian wrote that Tiberius and Livia were most responsible, Tiberius out of fear and Livia out of spite.

Agrippina (Vipsania Agrippina) (d. 20 C.E.) *A daughter of Marcus Agrippa and for many years the wife of Tiberius*

Desperately loved by Tiberius, according to the historian Suetonius, Agrippina bore him DRUSUS (2) the Younger and was carrying another child in 12 B.C.E., when Tiberius was compelled by Augustus to divorce her to wed JULIA (3), Augustus's own daughter. Later, upon once seeing Vipsania in the marketplace, Tiberius began to weep. The divorce had a profound effect upon the future emperor's psychological stability, and he persecuted Vipsania's second husband, ASINIUS GALLUS, mercilessly. Vipsania died of natural causes.

Agrippina the Elder (fl. early first century C.E.) *The daughter of Julia and Marcus Agrippa and the most bitter opponent of Emperor Tiberius and Livia*

The feud that Agrippina conducted with Tiberius and Livia cost her most of her family, her friends, and eventually her life. Her mother was sent into exile on Pandateria after instigating one of the most sordid sex scandals in Roman history.

Married to the brilliant GERMANICUS, son of Tiberius's brother, Drusus, their union was a happy one and she bore him nine children. Germanicus and Agrippina both cherished republican ideals, a fact that did not endear them to Emperor Tiberius or to his mother Livia. Equally, Agrippina could be harsh, outspoken, and easily angered. Her support of Germanicus was unflagging as he grew in stature in the empire and as Tiberius and Livia began to cast suspicious eyes on them both.

Her devotion was often demonstrated, as during the mutiny of the German legions in 14 C.E. Agrippina stayed at Germanicus's side until the situation became so critical that it was necessary for her to retire to safety, but her

A bronze *sestertius* of Agrippina the Elder, struck under her son, Gaius Caligula, 37–41 C.E. at Rome *(Courtesy, Historical Coins, Inc.)*

departure so shamed the mutineers that the revolt quickly lost momentum. It was during this campaign that the future Emperor GAIUS "CALIGULA" was born to her, and he quickly became a favorite of the soldiers on the frontier. In another campaign against the Chatti and the Germanic tribes under Arminius, Agrippina worked to keep panic from spreading through the great Roman camp on the Rhine by personally distributing food and clothing to the inhabitants. Lucius Aelius SEJANUS, Tiberius's henchman, warned the emperor about this activity and the ensuing popularity of Agrippina and Germanicus among the people of Rome and the empire.

In 17 C.E., Tiberius ordered Germanicus to the East, and once again Agrippina followed him. In Rome, meanwhile, supporters of Germanicus were beginning to clash openly with supporters of Tiberius and with those of Tiberius's son, Drusus. Gnaeus Piso, Tiberius's governor of Syria, was drawn into the affair on behalf of the emperor. As a result, Germanicus died under mysterious circumstances on September 26, 19 C.E., an event that turned Agrippina into an avenging fury. She had always been distant from Tiberius and Livia, but now she regarded them with open hostility. She marched in the Roman funeral of her husband and announced that Tiberius and Livia had slain their own rival. The Romans responded to her grief and to her accusations, but their support could not protect her from Tiberius's revenge.

Sejanus plotted her destruction with his usual deliberate pace, working all the time on Tiberius's animosity for her. Agrippina did not help her cause either. She begged Tiberius to give his consent for her to remarry and then scolded him for the persecution of her friends and allies. When dining with him she refused to eat some apples offered to her by the emperor, thus antagonizing Tiberius; Sejanus had warned Agrippina against accepting

the apples from Tiberius's hands, knowing it would offend the emperor.

In 29, Agrippina was condemned and exiled to the island of Pandateria, where her mother Julia had perished. Tiberius personally flogged her before sending her away, putting out one of her eyes in the assault. At Pandateria she suffered at the hands of her tormentors as well and was fearful that her sons could die at Tiberius's command. Agrippina starved herself to death.

Agrippina the Younger (Julia Agrippina) (15–59 C.E.) *The mother of Emperor Nero and, in her time, one of the most powerful women in the empire*

Agrippina schemed for years to gain the throne for her son, only to succeed and then witness the fading of her power.

Daughter of AGRIPPINA THE ELDER and GERMANICUS, she was married to Gnaeus Domitius Ahenobarbus in 28, giving birth in December of 37 to Lucius Domitius, later called Nero. When her husband died in 39, she and Nero were exiled by GAIUS CALIGULA, so that he could seize their inheritance. The accession of her uncle CLAUDIUS to the throne in 41 brought them back to Rome. By 49, the aging emperor was convinced by the Freedman Pallas to marry his niece, and Agrippina supplied her own considerable charms to make his decision easier. The marriage took place and Agrippina assumed near total control of the state, running the bureaucracy and managing the distribution of gold.

For her son she provided everything possible to ensure his succession to the throne, even to the point of assuming the powerful title of *Augusta* in 50. SENECA was recalled to tutor Nero (an act that she was later to regret). She also developed allies among the Praetorian Guard, especially the prefect, Afranius Burrus, whom she appointed to the office. Nero was adopted by Claudius in 50, marrying the emperor's daughter OCTAVIA in 53. Finally, in 54, having outlived his usefulness, Claudius was poisoned by Agrippina so that her lifelong wish could be fulfilled.

Her power was supreme in the early days of Nero's rule. With the title *Augusta* she ran most of the empire, as Nero was only 17. Nero grew resentful and tired of his mother, however, and ways were found to break her hold on him. Seneca and Burrus were Nero's allies in this effort. Nero and his advisers took every opportunity to reduce Agrippina's role in imperial affairs. The young ruler's relationships with the freedwoman ACTE and POPPAEA, the wife of Otho, were also used to curb her power. When Agrippina dared to suggest that Claudius's young son, Britannicus, might gain support, the lad was poisoned. In 55, she moved out of the palace altogether.

The ruin of Nero, a process in which Agrippina had played a major role, led to her eventual murder. By 59, driven by his realization of unlimited power and by his lust for Poppaea, Nero began to plot Agrippina's death. In one of the most bizarre assassination attempts recorded, Nero placed his mother on a boat designed to collapse off the coast of Baiae. Miraculously she survived, although her close friend, Acerronia, was beaten to death by the oarsmen. Swimming to shore unaided, she made her way to her estates with only a slight injury.

Perplexed by the incident, Agrippina composed a letter to Nero, to the effect that she was saved and would visit him in time. Nero sent the Freedman Anicetus to complete the assassination. Seeing the assembled soldiers around her bed, Agrippina thrust out her abdomen, screaming: "Strike me here!"—the place where she had carried her son. Anicetus obliged her, and Agrippina, *Augusta* of Rome and the mother of the emperor, was hacked to pieces, a victim of the son she had raised to the throne.

Suggested Readings: Barrett, Anthony. *Agrippina: Mother of Nero.* London: Batsford, 1996; ———. *Agrippina: Sex, Power, and Politics in the Early Empire.* New Haven, Conn.: Yale University Press, 1996; Tacitus, Cornelius. *The Annals of Imperial Rome.* Translated with an introduction by Michael Grant. New York: Penguin, 1964; ———. *The Histories.* Translated by Clifford H. Moore. Cambridge, Mass.: Harvard University Press, 1951–56; ———. *The Annals.* Translated by John Jackson. Cambridge, Mass.: Harvard University Press, 1925–1937; ———. *Annales.* Edited by Henry Furneaux. Oxford, U.K.: Clarendon Press, 1965.

Alamanni (or Alemanni)   A group of Germanic tribes who migrated to western Europe as a result of the expansion of the eastern tribes. The Alamanni arrived at the frontier and pushed their way to the Main, Neckar, and Danube regions. In 213 C.E., Emperor Caracalla inflicted a serious defeat upon the Alamanni, but their sheer numbers and the strength of their forces allowed them to expand again. Severus Alexander planned to launch a campaign against the Alamanni in 235 but was slain by his own mutineering troops before he could do so. His successor, Maximinus, crushed them near Baden. The Alamanni had a vengeance of sorts in 258, when they pierced the Alps and threatened Rome itself. This time Emperor Gallienus routed them near Milan (*see* MEDIOLANUM). In 357, Julian defeated them at Strasbourg, but most of Gaul came under their sway and remained so until the Franks overwhelmed the Germans in the fourth century.

Alans (or Alani)   An Asian conglomeration of tribes of Sarmatian extraction, who were pushed out of their homelands in the region of Russia by the movement of the Goths, sometime in the early centuries C.E. Their subsequent migrations from the lands of the Bosporus brought them into confrontation with Parthia and the Roman-controlled province of Cappadocia. The Alans established a considerable empire along the Black Sea and traded with Greece. Continued migrations of tribes, the Huns in particular, drove them deeper into Europe, and hence into conflict with Rome. They were eventually overrun by the Vandals, sometime in the fifth century.

See also SARMATIANS.

Alaric (c. 395–410 C.E.) *King of the Visigoths*
Ruler of the tribe that occupied Lower Moesia after the dramatic battle of Adrianople, Alaric was an ally of Rome, under Theodosius I, who came to accept the Visigoths and to use their presence as a weapon.

Alaric, aware of the potential power in such as arrangement, decided to take advantage of the Western Empire, an effort doomed to failure. In 397, Alaric reached an accord with Constantinople and began to march west. Greece was devastated as a result, and Stilicho, the MAGISTER MILITUM and ruler of the West for Emperor HONORIUS, pursued the Visigoths but failed to destroy the foe because of his own Germanic background. He won a victory against the Visigoths at Pollentia in 402 but did not finish the war by slaying the enemy. As a result, Alaric invaded Italy and chose Rome as the target of his army.

Rome was besieged for two years (408–410), and on the third attempt to breach the city's defenses, the Visigoths were successful. Stilicho, having plotted against the East for so long, stood by as Alaric invaded Rome, and the Alamanni, Burgundians, Vandals, Suebi, and Alans swept across the Rhine. He was executed for his treachery in 408, two years before Alaric's entrance into Rome.

When Rome had been ravaged, Alaric looked for a homeland for his people, not wanting to live in the metropolises they had destroyed. He thought of Africa for a time but managed to get only to southern Italy before he died. The new king of the Visigoths, Athaulf, was unable to establish a territory, and the Visigoths were forced to accept a reduced status in Spain.

Alavius   *See* FRITIGERN.

Alesia   Site in east-central Gaul of the battle and siege between Julius CAESAR and the noted Gallic chieftain VERCINGETORIX. In January 52 B.C.E., Caesar hurried from Rome to the rebelling province of Gaul, where Vercingetorix commanded the Averni and others in the most serious uprising that Rome had ever faced in a nearby province. Caesar immediately seized the initiative, sending his lieutenant, Labienus, orders to do what he could in the northern territories. Caesar tried to extinguish the revolt, but the generally unsuccessful attempts at Avaricum and Gergovia convinced him to recall Labienus and to face Vercingetorix with all of his troops on hand.

His lieutenant joined him at Agendicum, and Caesar set out to find his foe in late June or early July. A brief battle ensued, but the Gauls were driven under Vercingetorix into the city of Alesia (modern Alise), forcing out the women and children to make room for his considerable army of about 60,000 men. Caesar pursued the enemy, built massive siege works and began the battle of Alesia.

With siege battlements of approximately 14 miles in circumference, Caesar and his 45,000 men (mostly in legions but including cavalry of Germanic mercenaries and auxiliaries) prepared to withstand Vercingetorix's attempt to break out of the city. The entrapped Gauls, however, were soon joined by a huge relief army numbering from 100,000 to 250,000 men (sources vary as to the actual number). Caesar decided to rely upon his formidable position, the strength of his siege walls, and upon the iron will of his legions. In three desperate Gallic attacks all of these assets were tested.

The first assault was an onslaught against Caesar's position that was bloodily repulsed. While his outside forces reorganized, Vercingetorix tried to break out himself but failed. Finally, a third assault was attempted but the Romans broke the impetus of the Gauls and forced them to retreat in disorder.

Vercingetorix was too shrewd to believe falsely that he or his people could win. Alesia surrendered, and the Gallic chieftain was taken to Rome and later executed in 46 B.C.E. Caesar then faced a demoralized enemy in the province and was able to pacify the region.

Alexander, Domitius (d. 311 C.E.) *Prefect of Africa in 308*

Alexander was involved in the revolt against the ruler of Italy, the usurper MAXENTIUS. This emperor, outlawed by the tetrarchy, controlled Italy and Africa, but Maxentius's deteriorating political position gave hope to the provinces outside of his immediate reach. Domitius Alexander rose up and declared himself the ruler of Africa. His corn supply cut off and famine breaking out in Rome, in 311 Maxentius dispatched Rufus Volusianus, the prefect of the Guard, to Africa with several cohorts of Praetorians. Alexander was strangled, Carthage was once more destroyed and the revolt was ruthlessly suppressed.

Alexander of Cotiaeon (fl. second century C.E.) *One of the great scholastic minds of his age*

A Homeric expert, grammarian and well-known teacher whose guidance of students was free of vanity and pedantry, Alexander tutored MARCUS AURELIUS, influencing both his thinking and his style. The emperor wrote in his *Meditations* that he learned "From Alexander, the grammarian, to refrain from fault-finding, and not in a reproachful way to chide those who uttered any barbarous or solecistic or strange-sounding expression . . ." Among Alexander's many students, the most noteworthy was ARISTIDES, the rhetorician. The faithful student sent a long, laudatory letter to the people of Cotiaeon upon the occasion of Alexander's death, talking of his goodness, generosity and patronage.

Alexander of Seleucia (fl. second century C.E.) *Sophist and platonic expert*

The head of Marcus Aurelius's Greek secretariat during the last part of his reign, Alexander was born in Seleucia and became one of the empire's leading Platonists, for which he received the name *Peloplato*, the "clay Plato." His gift for words brought him to the attention of Emperor Antoninus Pius. Admiring him also, Marcus Aurelius summoned Alexander during the MARCOMANNIC WARS (166–175, 177–180 C.E.) and sent him to the Danube frontier, where he was given the post of secretary. His time was well rewarded by Herodes Atticus, the tutor and powerful adviser to the emperor. Alexander died at his post but was mentioned in the works of the writer Philostratus and by the emperor in his *Meditations*.

Alexandria

The city in Egypt founded by Alexander the Great in 331 B.C.E.; by the second century B.C.E., Alexandria was a rival of Rome in prosperity and in trade connections, resting as it did on a centrally convenient location that served as a meeting place between the Eastern and Western worlds. Further, the city emerged culturally under the Ptolemies as a center for intellectual achievement. The Great Library of Egypt was located in Alexandria, and the metropolis was inhabited by Greeks, Egyptians, Romans, Syrians, Africans, and large groups of Jews.

Ptolemy X, king of Egypt, came to the realization in 80 B.C.E. that any prolonged resistance to Rome would be futile and requested incorporation into the provincial system. Troubles seemed to haunt the city ever after. King Ptolemy XIII, desiring the sole kingship, feuded with his sister, CLEOPATRA; and Pompey the Great, fleeing to Alexandria in 48 B.C.E., drew Julius Caesar into the struggle. Caesar audaciously tried to hold the city against an Egyptian army led by Achillas and Ptolemy and joined by irate Alexandrians.

Augustus subjected the city to Roman control when he become emperor in 27 B.C.E.; unlike most provinces, strict laws were maintained. A prefect was placed over the territory, with his central administrative office in Alexandria. A large contingent of Roman troops were stationed in the city, because of the continued unrest in the streets. No city council existed, although the magistrates were appointed from the local population, and certain ethnic groups, such as the Jews, maintained private societies.

Social disorder remained a constant factor, but in 200 C.E. Emperor Septimius Severus decreed the creation of city councils. For the rest of the Roman period Alexandria progressed toward full municipalization to match the rest of the province and the empire. But the prefect never lost control, and Roman garrisons were always alert to trouble.

The remains of the sphinxes of ancient Alexandria *(Hulton/Getty Archive)*

That governing Alexandria was difficult was apparent to Julius Caesar: When the local citizens were not fighting Romans they were feuding among themselves. The Jewish population was a special victim of violent attacks; in 41, during a visit by King Herod Agrippa, riots broke out in protest against the Jews. In 66, Tiberius Julius Alexander, the prefect, committed two entire legions to quelling street turmoil; over 50,000 people died in the ensuing confrontations. More riots were recorded in 116, 154, and 172, and Emperor Caracalla slaughtered thousands in 215. Another rebellion broke out during the reign of Aurelian, probably in 272.

Unrest and seething hatred were a result of racial strife, but the intellectual environment of the city also encouraged philosophical and religious upheaval. Christianity spread quickly here, aided by writers and mystics of the time. By the second century C.E., and in the early third century, according to Eusebius in his *Ecclesiastical History,* the Christian community was well founded. In time, persecution in the city, and many writers, such as Origen and Dionysius of Alexandria, were directly touched by the imperial attempt to liquidate an increasingly troublesome sect. Under the late empire, the Alexandrian Church was powerful and existed on a par with those of Antioch, Constantinople and even Rome. The bishops appointed and consecrated their assistants in Alexandria, which brought about the jealousy of Constantinople. Christianity survived, and the religion prospered until the coming of Islam.

The envy of Constantinople was understandable. Alexandria was the jewel of Egypt, and when Diocletian reorganized the empire c. 295, the city was the seat of the *comes Aegypti,* the *praefectus annonae* and most of the other magistrates and officials. The trade that centered in and passed through Alexandria was maintained and remained constant until the Muslims reoriented its economic focus.

Alexandria was planned by the architect Deinocrates and then by Cleomenes of Naucratis. Situated on the extreme western end of the Nile Delta, the city contained a huge harbor and was flanked by the sea and by Lake Mareotis. A bridge called the *heptastadium* connected the mainland with the island of Pharos, with its mighty lighthouse. This construction created two harbors, the smaller Eunostos and the Great Harbor, corresponding to the city sections of Rhacotis and Bruchion.

Although little evidence remains of the actual city plan, some ancient locations can be found. These include the palace, with its own royal harbor, and, most importantly, the museum and library, which reportedly contained all available knowledge of the ancient world, and which was destroyed by Julius Caesar. The Jewish Quarter was in the far eastern part of the city, just within the walls. A little southeast of the Jewish section were the stadium, theater, and the Dicasterium, or Hall of Justice. The west possessed only two notable edifices, the Temple of Serapis and the Canopic Gate.

See also ALEXANDRIA, BATTLE OF.

Alexandria, battle of   The military confrontation in the Egyptian capital between the forces of Ptolemy XIII and the Romans under the command of Julius Caesar. Following the battle of PHARSALUS in Thessaly on August 9, 48 B.C.E., the defeated Pompey the Great fled to Egypt, where he was treacherously murdered. Julius Caesar, in hot pursuit, arrived in Alexandria with only 4,000 men. There he became embroiled in the dynastic dispute between Cleopatra and her brother, King Ptolemy XIII. Caesar sided with Cleopatra and subsequently found himself besieged by an army of over 20,000 Egyptians under the command of the Egyptian general Achillas.

With his troops, Caesar faced one of the most desperate battles of his career. From late August of 48 B.C.E. to February of 47, the Romans fought a series of engagements but proved victorious because of luck and the arrival of reinforcements from across the Republic. The Roman defenses extended only to the section of Alexandria that contained the royal palace. Various attempts were made to break the perimeters, and a large Egyptian fleet of 72 ships menaced Caesar from the sea. He set fire to these vessels, which inadvertently resulted in the burning of the Great Library. His position remained precarious.

With a small fleet Caesar tried to extend his influence, but the presence of another Alexandrian fleet prevented this. After two more bitter battles, Caesar took the offensive and captured the island of Pharos. (Achillas, no longer in command of the Egyptian troops, had deserted to Cleopatra's sister, Arsinoe, who poisoned him.) Caesar then assaulted the *heptastadium,* connecting Pharos and the mainland, but was beaten back with severe losses, having to swim for his life at one point.

By January victory seemed improbable, but news arrived that a large force of approximately 20,000 men had come from the northeastern provinces, under the command of the mercenary, Mithridates of Pergamum. Caesar joined the new forces, leaving a detachment in Alexandria. In February 47 B.C.E., the battle of the Nile was won by the Romans and the mercenaries, and Caesar returned to the city in triumph, thus ending the siege. He had a free hand in Egypt from that point onward.

Alexandria, Library of   The most famous library of the ancient world, created by the command of the first Ptolemaic rulers of Egypt to preserve the light of Hellenic civilization and the sum of ancient Egyptian knowledge. The library was established most likely under Ptolemy I Soter (d. 284) in 290 B.C.E. and was completed under his successor, Ptolemy Philadelphos. The idea for the library is generally credited to the Athenian exile Demetrius of Phaleron, who enjoyed the patronage of Ptolemy I Soter. The first surviving historical reference to the library is in *The Letter of Aristeas* (c. 180–145 B.C.E.). Written by a Jewish scholar working at the library, the letter chronicles the translation of the Septuagint (the Hebrew Old Testament) into Greek by the famed 72 rabbis.

Once opened to scholars, the library acquired a reputation as one of the key centers for learning in the ancient world. It offered vast collections on astronomy, medicine, geography, biology, mathematics, architecture, philosophy, and literature. Virtually every famous or arcane volume was stored on its shelves, available for reading and research. The exact numbers of scrolls, parchments, rolls, and volumes has been reported variously by different ancient writers. Callimachus estimated that there were 490,000 rolls; Seneca estimated that 40,000 rolls were burned in the great fire of 48 B.C.E., although it is thought that he meant 400,000; Demetrius Phalereus put the number of 200,000; Orosius counted 400,000; and Aulus Gellius gave the highest estimate at 700,000. The structure of the library was apparently situated in the Brucchium (northeast) sector of the city, perhaps next to the palace grounds. The library was also adjacent to gardens, columns, laboratories, surgeries, zoological gardens, and study areas that assisted the work of scholars. According to the Greek geographer and historian Strabo, the heart of the library was a Great Hall and a circular domed dining hall with an observatory in its upper terrace. The hall was surrounded by classrooms.

The Ptolemies exercised an aggressive policy of acquiring new books and items for the library. This was partly under the influence of the chief librarians, but it was also a reflection of the rivalry between Alexandria and Pergamum, located in what is today Twhey. The competition was so fierce that for a time the exportation of papyrus to Pergamum was prohibited. The Ptolemies also reputedly had all ships arriving in the harbor of Alexandria searched for any desirable scrolls, keeping all originals and returning hastily inscribed copies to the owner.

The first of the librarians was Zenodotus of Ephesus, who was appointed by Ptolemy I and remained in his post until 245 B.C.E. His successor was Callimachus of Cyrene (c. 305–240 B.C.E.). He was responsible for organizing the first subject catalog, called the *Pinakes,* or Tables, of the more than 120,000 scrolls of the library's holdings. Callimachus was succeeded in 234 B.C.E. by Eratosthenes (234–195 B.C.E.). Notable subsequent librarians were Aristophanes of Byzantium (195–181 B.C.E.) and Aristarchos of Samothrace (181–171 B.C.E.). The library began to decline in importance after the time of Aristarchos. Nevertheless, it was still one of the brightest beacons of knowledge in the Mediterranean when JULIUS CAESAR arrived at Alexandria in late 48 B.C.E. in pursuit of POMPEY THE GREAT.

While waging a bitter fight in the harbor area against the Egyptians, Caesar's troops, in a defensive measure, set fire to ships. The fire spread quickly to the docks and the naval arsenals and then to the library itself, which was situated overlooking the harbor. The conflagration resulted in the destruction of perhaps as many as 400,000 rolls, although there is some question as to whether they were burned in the library or elsewhere. It is considered possible that the contents of the library had been removed and were stored in anticipation of transport to Rome and then burned outside of the library itself. This is supported by the statement made in the *Bellum Alexandrinum* that the harbor had been designed in such a way to prevent serious fires. The loss of the library was still a tragic blow, and Marc Antony subsequently tried to make recompense by granting in 41 B.C.E. 200,000 rolls to Cleopatra, probably taken from the library of Pergamum.

The remnants of the library suffered a series of disastrous losses over the next centuries. In 272 C.E., Queen ZENOBIA of Nabataea launched a war against Emperor AURELIAN and struck into Egypt. The harbor of Alexandria was badly damaged, and it is likely that most of what remained of the library burned in that calamity. The fragments surviving the declining period of the empire were further reduced by the occasional burnings of pagan literature during the Christian ascendancy in Alexandria. What remained at the last perished in fires set by the Arab conquerors of Egypt around 642.

In the 1990s, the Egyptian government, in close cooperation with the United Nations Educational, Scientific and Cultural Organization launched an international effort to rebuild the Library under the form of the Bibliotheca Alexandrina. The new library was built alongside the University of Alexandria Faculty of Arts campus, in Shatby, overlooking the Mediterranean Sea. The total cost of the project has been estimated at $172 million, not including the cost of the land, a conference center, and other expenses reaching $182 million. The official inauguration of the Bibliotheca Alexandrina took place in spring 2001.

See also WRITING INSTRUMENTS AND MATERIALS.

Alexandria Troas   City on the northwest coast of ASIA MINOR, west of MYSIA in the mountainous region of the Troad; named thus because of the legend that the entire region was once ruled by Troy. After the death of Alexander the Great, his General Antigonus became king of Asia, founding the metropolis of Antigoneia, later called Alexandria Troas or Alexandria of the Troad. While it never attained the status or wealth of the fabled Troy, Alexandria Troas was prosperous. After suffering in the CIVIL WAR of the SECOND TRIUMVIRATE, it enjoyed many centuries of peace in the imperial age. The city was considered as the site of the new Constantinople but lost out to Byzantium (about 160 miles away).

Allectus   (fl. late third century C.E.) *A rationalis or minister of finance to the usurper Carausius*
In 293, his ambitions led Allectus to assassinate his master and seize power for himself in Britain and in some provinces of Gaul. He was apparently a gifted soldier and sailor, and his rule lasted for three turbulent years. Sometime around 295–296, Constantius I (Chlorus) resolved to end the usurpation of power and set sail with two fleets to Britain, commanding one fleet and entrusting the other to Praetorian Prefect Asclepiodotus. After losing his enemy in a fog, Allectus disembarked his fleet and prepared for battle. Near Hampshire, Asclepiodotus fought and routed Allectus, and shortly thereafter Allectus was killed. Constantius entered London and thus found a power base for himself and his son, CONSTANTINE THE GREAT.

See also BRITANNIA (1); GALLIA.

Allobroges   A tribe in the province of GALLIA NARBONENSIS (now southern France). This region was annexed early by the Romans. The inhabitants resisted the overtures of the Gallic chieftain VERCINGETORIX when he led a Gallic revolt and were rewarded for their loyalty to Rome. Their capital was Vienne, and Gallia Narbonensis became the birthplace of such great Roman figures as the orator Domitius Afer, the consul Valerius Asiaticus and Emperor Antoninus Pius.

Alps   The principal mountain range surrounding Italy that were important to the empire both as a symbol of strength and protection and a practical barrier for the defense of Rome. The strategic need to defend the frontiers of Italy prompted the acquisition of the Maritime Alps around 14 C.E. and the designation of the territory as a province under the care of a procurator. NERO (r. 54–68 C.E.) later annexed the COTTIAEN ALPS, which helped to maintain a line of communications with Gaul.

Traditionally, the crossing of the Alps by a foe or political enemy (as in the case of usurpers from the provinces) was considered a strategic disaster, and a failure to deal immediately with such an event most often led to defeat. In 69, Otho allowed Vitellius to cross the Alps and was crushed at the battle of BEDRIACUM. In 166, Marcus Aurelius campaigned vigorously to prevent a Germanic invasion of Italy.

Amandus and Aelianus   Imperial aspirants from the Bagaudae tribe. In 286 A.D., these two led a revolt against Rome, citing the barbarian invasions of their lands and the crushing Roman tax system. Diocletian, the newly crowned emperor, sent his trusted aide Maximian to crush the rebellion. The Bagaudae were easily subdued, and Amandus and Aelianus faded from history.

Amaseia   (or Amasia)   A town in GALATIA (later CAPPADOCIA) that served for centuries as the capital of the kings of Pontus. Pompey reorganized the city and used it as an administrative center that survived until the time of Augustus, whose new provincial system made it a part of Galatia. As the east became accessible, Amaseia grew in economic importance. The city was also known for its deliberate and wanton cruelty to Christians during the periods of persecution.

Amathus   City beyond the Jordan River, near Gadara. In 100 B.C.E., Amathus was captured by Jannaeus, also called Alexander, who was aspiring to the throne of Palestine. Pompey the Great reconquered all of the area c. 63 B.C.E., and in 57 B.C.E. Proconsul Galienus broke up Palestine. Amathus, like Jericho and Jerusalem, was a capital for one of five newly created districts.

Ambiorix (d. after 54 B.C.E.) *King of the Eburones*
An opponent of Rome, Ambiorix attacked Julius Caesar's army in 54 B.C.E. The Romans were spread out in a series of winter camps in Gaul (*see* GALLIA) when the Eburones rose in revolt. Ambiorix, their king, was a dubious military strategist but a convincing liar. He lured the Roman legate, Titurius Sabinus, to his destruction at Aduatuca but lost the opportunity to exploit that victory by failing to crush Q. Cicero and his Roman command. Caesar recovered and routed the combined enemy near the Sabis. Ambiorix escaped but was soon overshadowed by another Gallic leader, VERCINGETORIX. Caesar mentioned Ambiorix in the *Gallic Wars*.

Ambrose (339–397 C.E.) *Christian bishop and theologian, and the first Christian prelate to have been born in the faith*
Ambrose was the son of a Praetorian prefect of Gaul and received a thorough education in Roman law. He served as the governor of Liguria and in 374 was called to become the bishop of Milan. Baptized formally, Ambrose set about enforcing orthodoxy within the church. Virginity and the Virgin Mary were important teachings to him, and he wrote a number of treatises on the subject, including: *On Virginity, To Sister Marcellina on Virginity,* and *On Widows.* Most important to Ambrose, however, was the war within the church against heresy, in particular, against ARIANISM. In 381, at the Council of Aquileia, he had the Arian bishops removed. He then wrote his two major works, *On Faith* and *On the Holy Spirit,* both of which attacked Arianism by defending the creed and the orthodox notions established in the Nicene system.

Temporally, Ambrose was a figure of tremendous power, epitomizing the decree to which the church had come to hold sway over the empire. In Milan, which many emperors used as a court, the bishop served officially as the imperial chaplain but unofficially as adviser. Because of his following, he influenced Valentinian I, Gratian, Valentinian II, and Theodosius. He put to use the legal and bureaucratic system of the empire, not for himself but for the church and its policies. Through his influence paganism was sternly opposed. A synagogue in Callinicum was burned to the ground, and when the Empress Justina proposed that a church be given to the Arians, Ambrose and his followers took possession of it, refusing to yield until the empress retreated.

His greatest achievement came in 382, when he convinced Gratian to remove from the Senate the Altar of Victory and then opposed the attempts of the influential Senator Symmachus to have it returned. In 390, when the Emperor Theodosius, angered by unrest in Thessalonica, massacred 7,000 people, Ambrose, as the bishop of Milan, railed against him. The emperor was forced to beg for forgiveness. Ambrose is ranked with Augustine, his greatest student, Gregory and Jerome as one of the most important fathers of the Christian Church.

See also CHRISTIANITY.

amici principis   The Roman concept of the "friends of the ruler," which was one of the foundations for the growth in power of the PREFECT OF THE PRAETORIAN GUARD into the third century. In choosing the prefect (the commander of the bodyguard and, ostensibly, the most direct threat to his person), the emperor invariably chose someone he could trust and on whom he could rely. Very often the person given the post was a reflection of the *princeps.* Great emperors such as Hadrian and Constantine were served by able officials, such as Marcius Turbo and Asclepiodotus, respectively. Emperors like Nero or the aged Tiberius allowed venal officers to rise to power, men such as Tigellinus (Nero's choice) and Sejanus (serving Tiberius).

The concept extended the power of the Praetorian prefecture in ways that went beyond mere affiliation with the emperor. For example, it was a common practice for a ruler to hand to his most trusted servant any tasks that were too vast, too time consuming, or too illegal for personal completion. In this way the prefects, by the third century, were controllers of the imperial finances, administration, and taxation, all under the guise of being the emperor's "friend."

Ammianus Marcellinus (c. 330–395 C.E.) *One of the foremost historians of Rome*
Ammianus was a thorough and prolific writer who detailed the active years of the empire from about 100 C.E. to about 378, in his massive *History.* Of a military background, he served in the army of the Eastern general, Ursicinus, eventually moving to Gaul, where he encountered the future emperor, Julian, whose life was to form a large part of his extant histories. In 363, he accompanied Emperor Julian against Persia, after which he left the army.

After traveling through Greece, Syria, Egypt, and Palestine, Ammianus came to Rome, between 378 and 383. It was here that he began to write the great history that was described by Edward Gibbon in *The Decline and Fall of the Roman Empire* as being "mixed with the narrative of public events a lively representation of the scenes with which he was familiarly conversant." The historian obviously intended to pick up where Tacitus left off, but unfortunately much of his work was lost. Only those writings detailing the times of Constantine II (partly), Julian, Jovian, Valentinian I, and Valens have been preserved, roughly from 350 to 378.

A pagan like his idol Emperor Julian, he admired Christianity and accepted its growing place in Roman society and in the wider context of history.

Suggested Readings: Elliot, Thomas G. *Ammianus Marcellinus and Fourth Century History.* Sarasota, Fla.: S. Stevens, 1983; Jonge, Pieter de. *Philological and Historical Commentary on Ammianus Marcellinus XIX.* Translated by P. de Waard-Dekking. Groningen, Neth.: Bouma's Boekhuis, 1982; Matthews, John. *The Roman Empire of Ammianus.* London: Duckworth, 1989; Rike, R. L. *Apex Omnium: Religion in the* Res Gestae *of Ammianus.* Berkeley: University of California Press, 1987.

Ammonius Saccas (175–242 C.E.) *Neoplatonist philosopher*
Ammonius Saccas had a profound influence on subsequent thinkers, such as PLOTINUS, his student of 11 years, and the Christian theologian Origen. Ammonius Saccas remains a rather enigmatic figure in history because he wrote nothing, delivering his lessons exclusively in the oral tradition. PORPHYRY, in his various writings, was the principal recorder of Sacca's life.

See also NEOPLATONISM.

Ampelius, Lucius (fl. third century C.E.) *Writer and intellectual*
Ampelius's *Liber memorialis* (Book of Knowledge), was a considerable work, encompassing history, mythology, and geography. It is possible to discern the influence of Marcus Terentius VARRO and Nigiduus FIGULUS in his writing.

amphora   A clay pot used throughout the Mediterranean world to hold liquids, such as wine, oil, and even garum (fish sauce), as well as assorted dry products. Termed originally by the Greeks as *amphiphoreus,* meaning a jar that could be carried on both sides, its name was shortened to *amphoreus.* The Romans called it by the even shorter version: *amphora* (pl. *amphorae*).

Amphorae were found in many forms, although the general design was nearly universal. The pottery was shaped with a narrow neck and mouth, the latter with two opposed handles near it; the shape then became wider, with the actual width varying depending upon the specific needs of the maker. The most common size was about three feet three inches (one meter). Some *amphorae* had a flat base to permit free standing, but most had a knobbed or pointed base that served as another handle for pouring. Instead of standing, such amphorae were

stacked. The mouth was narrow enough to allow a cork or seal to be inserted. Seals for the mouth were made of cork or fired clay (*operculum*). Over these was poured a cement seal that could be stamped with any kind of official cipher, such as the name of the merchant who was distributing the goods inside.

Owing to their composition from clay, the amphora was not always entirely sealed and was permeable. To avoid leakage, it was common for a seal to be added to the interior. Types of sealants included varieties of bitumen, resin, rosin, and pitch, although there seems to have been little differentiation in terms for sealants. Those surviving amphorae that did not have an internal seal are of great interest to historians and archaeologists, as the contents might have seeped into the clay. By examining the residue in the clay, it is possible to discern the original contents and thereby increase knowledge of ancient trade and eating habits.

Because of their wide use across the whole of the Roman Empire, amphorae have been found in a host of shapes and sizes. One of the most common areas of preservation is in shipwrecks, as they were a reliable means of transporting liquids and even such solids as olives, nuts, oysters, and figs. Among the best sites for preserved amphorae was the shipwreck of *Albenga,* dated to around the mid-first century. The ship had five layers of amphorae, numbering some 11,000 to 13,500 separate pots of different types.

As there was little change in styles of manufacturing and design, the dating of amphorae can be problematic. Further, there is little information about kilns. Surviving kilns are found in North Africa, Gaul, and Spain. Part of the problems rests in the fact that many kilns were attached to villas and latifundia, supplying the needs of the estate and possibly of the surrounding area. There seems to have been little in the way of an organized amphora industry; instead, the pottery was created at the sites of the producers of wine, oil, fish sauce, etc., to fill the specific needs of the merchants. In trying to systematize knowledge of *amphorae,* the 19th-century scholar Heinrich Dressel classified more than 40 types. Other classifications were added in later years.

Ampius, T. Balbus (fl. first century B.C.E.) *Roman tribune involved in the political struggles of the First Triumvirate*
Of Spanish descent, Ampius gained the rank of citizen through the assistance of the consul of Pompey. He was a remarkable politician, gliding through the chaotic environment of civil-war-torn, Republican Rome. He served Pompey in Spain and then Caesar in Rome, becoming his agent during the GALLIC WARS. Put on trial for various offenses, he was saved by Pompey, Crassus, and Cicero. The officer placed his hopes on Caesar's campaigns and fought for his cause with his associate, C. Oppius.

Andalusia Part of southern Spain that became a vital center of Roman trade and was traversed heavily by marauding barbarian hordes entering Africa via Gibraltar. By 19 B.C.E., the entire area had been Romanized to the extent that the majority of its inhabitants spoke Latin and lived in the Roman style. Andalusia was influenced heavily by trade, and Italian merchants were common. Because of its fertility, the area produced large quantities of agricultural goods for Rome. The Roman name for the region was Baetica.

See also HISPANIA.

Anicetus (fl. first century C.E.) *A freedman and admiral during the reign of Nero*
Anicetus was the prime mover in the murder of AGRIPPINA THE YOUNGER. He was typical of the FREEDMEN of the early empire. Ambitious, thoroughly unprincipled, and dangerous, he came to Nero's attention by volunteering to complete the assassination of Nero's mother, Agrippina, after a previous attempt had failed.

In 55 C.E., Nero sought an end to Agrippina's power and influence. While at the theater, Nero and his tutor Seneca saw a ship split apart as part of a circus act. Nero resolved to build an exact duplicate, so that his mother would drown while sailing on it. Anicetus was probably the supervisor of the ship's construction. When the bizarre contraption failed to achieve its purpose, due to Agrippina's luck and will to survive, Nero searched for an assassin to finish the task. Anicetus is recorded by Tacitus as volunteering to accomplish the deed. He did so, murdering the imperial mother in 59 C.E. with a sword thrust to her womb.

Anicetus was given command of the fleet at Misenum as a reward but performed one last chore for Nero. In 62, while trying to rid himself of his wife OCTAVIA, Nero asked Anicetus to plead guilty to having had an affair with her. Anicetus accepted the role, providing testimony that went far beyond what was required. The freedman was found guilty, exiled to Sardinia, and provided with every possible comfort. He died there of old age. Octavia was exiled to Pandateria, where she died after terrible suffering.

Annalists The earliest Roman historians, who recorded events in a prose style that influenced those who followed in this literary field. Records of magistrates, wars and events of religious importance began to appear after the fourth century B.C.E., and in a variety of forms. Most were written by antiquarians who were anxious to piece together the lives or works of their predecessors. For example, DIONYSIUS OF HALICARNASSUS, historian of the late first century B.C.E., analyzed Fabius Pictor, who lived a century before. These early writers were heavily influenced by their Hellenic counterparts, and adaptation of the Greek style is apparent.

Early works of the Annalists centered on legends and speculative antiquarian history and were often feeble when compared to the prodigious research of later writers, such as the historian Coelius Antipater, who chronicled the Second Punic War. But the later Annalists could consult actual records, and their works, from the Sullan archivists to LIVY in the first century B.C.E., were rich in evidence. SALLUST, for example, took the Annalist Sisennus's work on the civil wars of 91 to 82 B.C.E. and incorporated large portions of it into his own *Histories* in the late first century B.C.E.

It is debatable as to how thoroughly researched many of these works were. Each must be examined individually. Aelius Tubero is reliable, as is Licinius Macer. Gradually the influences became standardized, and Livy helped to formalize a style that was identifiable in the work of later historians, especially TACITUS.

Anna Perena A goddess who was the focus of a great festival on the 15th of March each year. She was the deity of the new year, to whom the Romans prayed and offered sacrifices, especially at the shrines dedicated to her on the Via Flamina. The Romans asked that the year would progress safely and abundantly.

See also GODS AND GODDESSES OF ROME.

Annius Verus, Marcus (fl. early second century C.E.) *Grandfather of Emperor Marcus Aurelius*
A highly successful political figure of the late first and early second centuries C.E., Marcus Annius Verus held a consulship under Domitian but was honored twice more with the post, in 121 and 126. He enrolled in the Patrician class with the sponsorship of Vespasian and Titus and was later prefect of the city. His son of the same name embarked upon a similar career but died while still a praetor. Thus Verus's grandson Marcus passed into his care and received the education that led to his remarkable character and intellect.

annona The Roman supply of corn, a resource that received administrative priority in all eras of the state. The capacity to feed the population of Rome was a source of constant anxiety to the emperors, who recognized that a famine, even of short duration, could cause severe unrest and military intervention.

Augustus, acknowledging the need to maintain control over the distribution of the *annona*, named a *praefectus annonae,* who eventually became an influential figure. In previous eras the *annona* was tended by the AEDILE. Augustus created a *cura annonae* in 22 B.C.E., after a famine. Tiberius, according to Tacitus, paid careful attention to its maintenance, but Claudius, although giving incentives to suppliers, allowed the famine stock to be reduced to a mere 15 days. Trajan, accepting the need to extend the bureaucracy that ran it, placed the *annona* into the hands of a *fiscus frumentarius*.

Egypt and Africa were the principal sources of the corn supply, and every measure was taken to protect them. In 69 C.E., Vespasian withheld the boats needed to feed Rome, as leverage while occupying Egypt; and in 310 C.E., Maxentius sent the Guard itself to Africa to ensure that the grain would flow freely.

Anthemius (1) (fl. early fifth century C.E.) *Prefect of the Praetorian Guard during the reign of Theodosius II (408–450)*

Anthemius was a loyal servant of the previous emperor of the East, Arcadius. On the death of the old ruler in 408, the seven-year-old Theodosius became emperor. Fearing chaos, Anthemius stepped in to serve as regent for the next seven years, becoming a judicious master of CONSTANTINOPLE. His service helped to preserve the power of the East at a time when the West was sinking fast into turmoil. Anthemius repelled the Huns under King Uldine, repaired relations with the West, fortified the cities of Illyricum to act as a bulwark against invasion, and ordered a fleet of 250 ships built as a protective force on the Danube. Most importantly, Anthemius rebuilt, strengthened, and improved the walls of Constantinople. Stretching for miles, from the Golden Gate to the promontory of the city, the Wall of Theodosius was a defensive perimeter of considerable strength, and Anthemius was singularly responsible for this achievement.

As was typical of the increasing intrigue at the Byzantine court, Anthemius found himself the victim of plots. Aelia PULCHERIA, Theodosius's older sister (by two years), was named regent in 414, and Anthemius was replaced by another prefect, Aurelianus.

Anthemius (2) (fl. mid-fifth century C.E.) *Emperor of the West from 467 to 472*

In 467, it was widely accepted that only strict cooperation between the Eastern and Western empires could preserve Roman civilization. After emperor Libius Severus died, the capital at Ravenna went for months without an emperor. Pope Leo I, taking matters into his own hands, chose Anthemius. At first this seemed to be a very good decision. He came from a noble family, had served in the region of Thrace as its *comes*, was a *magister militum* from 454 to 467 and was consul in 455. Further, RICIMER, the power in the West, who watched emperors rise and fall with regularity, became his son-in-law, when he married Anthemius's daughter, Alypia.

With a strong military background (he had defeated both the Huns and the Ostrogoths in 459–467), it was believed that Anthemius was a ruler who could stave off the rapid decline of the West. Hopes were dashed almost immediately as the supposed heir of the great Theodosian line attempted an African expedition of overly grandiose proportions against the powerful king of the Vandals, GEISERIC. A large fleet was organized and launched in 468 under combined leadership. The effort was a debacle, and Anthemius received the first of numerous defeats.

King EURIC of the Visigoths in Gaul next came to Anthemius's attention, and Ricimer allowed this campaign to be conducted mainly by the emperor's son, Anthemiolus. Euric easily crushed him near the Rhone, and Anthemius held Ricimer accountable. In 472, the *magister militum* besieged Anthemius and his Visigoth ally, Bilimes, in Rome. Ricimer intended to play kingmaker again, and with his help Olybrius became emperor, a ruler desired by the Vandals as well. The defense of the city was courageous, but after Bilimes was killed, the city fell. Legend has it that Anthemius tried to flee dressed as a beggar but was recognized and beheaded.

Antinopolis   A city in Egypt, founded on October 30, 130 C.E., by a decree of Emperor HADRIAN. The tremendous scope and vision of Hadrian's mind had been influenced by Eastern thought, and Antinopolis was a living example of this. It was decreed into existence when Antinous, Hadrian's favorite court official, was drowned in the Nile while taking part in an imperial tour. Antinopolis was the official's memorial. Its laws were derived from Greek traditions, and many of the first settlers were Greek. Lying across the Nile from Hermopolis, the city in time became racially mixed, as Egyptians from the Faiyum region settled in its districts.

Antinous (d. 130 C.E.) *Lover and confidant of Emperor Hadrian*

In 130, while traveling through Egypt with the emperor, Antinous, a young, handsome courtier, drowned in the Nile River. He was so mourned by the emperor that Hadrian commanded a series of cultic ceremonies throughout the East. Antinous became Pan, Hermes, and the Greek ideal for beauty and virility in these rituals. The city of ANTINOPOLIS, across the river from Hermopolis, was erected in his honor. Antinous was a Bithynian, originally from the city of Claudiopolis.

Antioch (1)   Resting on the left bank of the Orontes, about 20 miles upriver from the Mediterranean Sea, Antioch served as the capital of the Seleucid Empire (*see* SELEUCIA) in Syria for over 200 years, and then became a major metropolis under Rome's rule. The city was bitterly disputed for centuries. Sometime around 300 B.C.E., Seleucus Nicator chose a fertile valley wherein to build his great city, an economic center named after his father, Antiochus. With a geographical situation similar to Alexandria, and its position on the great trade routes, Antioch became a powerful commercial center and a tempting target for Rome.

In 64 B.C.E., POMPEY THE GREAT seized the city, which was weakened as a result of the broader Seleucid decline. The new province of SYRIA was created, and Antioch made its capital. Around 47 B.C.E., Julius Caesar gave Antioch its own municipal standing. Subsequently, the city was a base of operations for the Roman campaigns against Parthia. In 37 B.C.E., Antony prepared for his abortive Parthian campaign there, and the city was marked by an increasing administrative and martial presence because of the threat posed by the eastern empires.

Augustus stationed at least one legion in the city, which kept the peace and acted as a reserve for the troops on patrol in the north of the province. Emperor Tiberius furthered the Roman presence by instituting a considerable building program of theaters and temples. By 19 C.E. the general Germanicus was centering his expeditions of the East in the city, and eventually died there.

As colonization and trade with the East increased, Antioch grew in both economic vitality and strategic importance. The Syrians responded wholeheartedly, while life in the Syrian provinces was held by the legions to be the easiest and most pleasant tour of duty in the empire. The quality of life in Antioch demonstrated imperial favor and confidence in the city's future, to the point that an imperial mint was established there.

Economic wealth, much like that experienced in Alexandria, encouraged migration and education. People from all over the East came to its gates, causing strife and intellectual achievement to emerge simultaneously. Greeks, Syrians, Italians, Persians, and Jews lived in Antioch, and bitter feuds erupted as a result. When troubles began in Egypt between the Jews and Greeks c. 40 C.E., similar problems appeared in Antioch as well. Antioch was unmatched in the Eastern Empire for the quality and quantity of its schools, philosophers, and writers. Various philosophies not only flourished there but also gave birth to leaders and innovators, including the JURISTS Ulpian and Papinian; Antiochus of Ascalon; the historian Posidonius of Apamea; St. John Chrysostom; the orator and rhetorician Libanius; and the writer and orator Fronto of Emesa.

Religiously, Antioch, like Syria, was a mix of ancient Chaldean, Greek, Roman, and Semitic creeds. But within a short time Christianity seriously impacted upon it; possibly prompted by the appearance of St. Paul, use of the word "Christian" was reported in the city in the first century C.E.'s *Acts of the Apostles*. By the fourth century, Antioch was ranked with Rome, Constantinople, and Alexandria as a seat of one of the four patriarchs of the Christian Church.

A city so seemingly blessed was also beset with troubles. In 115 C.E., Antioch was virtually destroyed in one of the worst earthquakes recorded in the ancient world. Emperor Trajan was visiting at the time but miraculously escaped injury. The historian Dio noted that while many cities suffered, Antioch was the most damaged.

In 194 C.E., after Emperor Septimius Severus defeated the Antioch-supported Emperor Pescennius Niger at the battle of Issus, the city was reduced in status, but was eventually reinstated. Emperor Caracalla based his Parthian campaign of 215 there, and Elagabalus defeated the briefly reigning Macrinus outside of the city walls.

Sometime around 256, the weakness of Rome in Syria was demonstrated by the capture of Antioch by Shapur I, the king of Persia. The historian Ammianus Marcellinus and orator Libanius were both from Antioch and wrote of the capture, stating that it came so quickly that the people were not even aware of it. An actor in a theater stopped his performance and announced to the audience that unless he was dreaming the Persians were present. Such invasions, however, did not prevent the continued flowering of the city. Because of its trade connections and its linen industry, Antioch remained a vital center until late in the history of the empire and the Byzantine Empire.

Antioch, like Syria in general, is remarkably well-preserved archaeologically, and much information is extant as to its design, structure, and pattern of architectural development. Like Alexandria, the city was both a port and a target for land-based caravans. The port of Seleucia on the Mediterranean Sea, near the mouth of the Orontes, handled the sea trade, while the city itself accommodated trade from the desert areas. Antioch fronted the wide stretches of the Syrian landscape leading eastward to the Euphrates River and thence into Parthia. To the south lay the trading centers of Damascus, Tyre, Berytus, and Judaea, while to the north were Cilicia and the provinces of Asia Minor.

Antioch was advanced for its time. Sewers with organized pipe systems were accompanied by aqueducts. Architecturally, the rest of Syria looked to Antioch to establish the styles for their own regions, and Greek, Oriental, and Roman designs all flourished. Originally, Antioch had been erected by the Seleucids to serve as a great city and numerous temples and palaces were built, most of which were eventually supplanted by Greek and Roman structures. However, Oriental designs continued to prevail, as the Eastern Church, influenced by its Greek foundations and the tastes of Constantinople, reigned supreme in the construction of temples and churches.

Antioch (2) A Roman colony built by Augustus circa 19 B.C.E. In 25 B.C.E., Amyntas, the ruler of Galacia who had been granted his kingdom by Marc Antony, died. The region, troubled by hillmen from Homanades and Pisidia, was immediately taken by Augustus, who wanted to stabilize the area and make it more responsive to his broadened Asian policies. To the south, near Pisidia, a community called Antioch had been founded earlier, probably by colonists from Magnesia. To populate the colony, which was given the name Caesarea Antiochus, veterans of two legions, the V and VII Gallica, were brought in. Hardy and militarily capable, these veterans helped pacify the tribes and gave the colony a solid foundation. Slowly Antioch connected itself by roads to such important cities as Iconium, Pergamum, and Antioch of Syria.

See also ASIA; BITHYNIA; CAPPADOCIA.

Antiochus I (fl. late first century B.C.E.) *The ruler of the small kingdom of Commagene, situated on the Upper Euphrates River*

One of the last dynastic kings of the Seleucid line, Anthiochus I was one of the last potentates descended from the time of Alexander and his nation-founding generals. Around 63 B.C.E., the kingdom of Commagene was officially sanctioned by Pompey, who wanted to establish a buffer zone of client states along the Euphrates. Antiochus I, not a strong ruler, was placed at its head.

During Marc Antony's Parthian Campaign (36 B.C.E.), Antiochus was at best indifferent to the Roman cause and at worst pro-Parthian. When retreating Parthians sought sanctuary in Antiochus's city of Samosata, Antony's lieutenant, Bassus Ventidius, pursued them there. Antiochus promptly bribed Ventidius to adopt a sluggish attitude toward his task. As a result, Antony had to take up the pursuit himself. He retaliated by deposing Antiochus in favor of the king's brother, Mithridates II. Apparently Antiochus murdered an envoy sent to Augustus by Mithridates; he was brought to Rome, possibly with the full consent of his brother, and was executed in 29 B.C.E.

Antiochus III (d. 17 C.E.) *Ruler of Commagene*

The reign of Antiochus III was more notable for its conclusion than its duration. When Antiochus III died in 17 C.E. (along with Philopater, the king of Cilicia), the nation was torn apart by internal struggles between those forces desiring independence and those hoping for a Roman occupation. Tiberius placed the area under the control of praetors. Prompted by the troubles in Commagene and Cilicia, Tiberius sent Germanicus to the East.

Antiochus IV (fl. mid-first century C.E.) *King of Commagene*

Antiochus IV was granted his right to rule from GAIUS CALIGULA. For 20 years Commagene had been a part of the provincial system, but in 37 C.E. Gaius allowed Antiochus to assume the throne. Son of Antiochus III, the new king was given a share of other lands, Cilicia and Lycaonia, and also received 100 million sesterces in revenue. Gaius liked Antiochus, whom Dio called equal in tyranny to Emperor Caligula, and probably Herod Agrippa. Gaius, however, deposed Antiochus in 40 C.E., probably because the destitute emperor needed his

money. Claudius reinstated Antiochus, and the grateful king aided the Romans in the Parthian war of 57 C.E.

Antiochus of Ascalon (d. 68 B.C.E.) *A philosopher, intellectual and organizer of the New Academy in the first century B.C.E.*

Antiochus found the ACADEMY, the great philosophical school founded by Plato, in a state of disrepute, undone by feuds and academic rivalries. Taking over the administration of the institution for the Skeptic Philo (c. 78 B.C.E.), he began to energize the sagging Academy by steering it away from the traditional skeptical philosophy by which it had been founded. This intellectual broadening allowed the institution to flourish, and other great intellectuals were drawn to it. CICERO and his contemporaries came to the Academy and brought with them a spirit of healthy debate and rivalry that stimulated the various schools and provided a rich heritage of knowledge and thought. Cicero adhered to the skeptical viewpoint and supported Philo, while Antiochus stuck to his own convictions.

Antipater of Idumaea (fl. mid-first century B.C.E.) *Minister, politician, and power broker in Palestine and Judaea during the period of Aristobulus, Hyrcanus, and Pompey the Great*

The father of Herod the Great, the future King of Judaea, Antipater was the son of Antipas, the governor of Idumaea. Antipater acquired influence at the court, serving in his father's position and then becoming an adviser to Queen Alexandra Salome.

In 67 B.C.E., Alexandra died, leaving the kingdom to her two sons, the elder Hyrcanus and Aristobulus. Aristobulus was strong-willed and difficult while Hyrcanus was weak. Sensing a great opportunity, Antipater became the prime influence on Hyrcanus, and when the two heirs began their violent feuding, Antipater sided with Hyrcanus, although Aristobulus was the proven military commander. Antipater turned to King Aretas III of Arabia, and in 65 B.C.E. an Arabian army marched on Jerusalem to besiege Aristobulus. Roman legions soon arrived on the scene, under the command of Pompey's lieutenant, M. Scaurus.

Rome was the chief power with whom Antipater had to deal. Following Aretas's retreat, he prodded Hyrcanus into making an appeal for kingship directly to Pompey in Damascus. Aristobulus followed suit, but he refused to submit, and Pompey seized him in the Great Temple of Jerusalem in 63 B.C.E. Hyrcanus was given a reduced Judaea to rule, not as king but as a prince or ethnarch. He remained high priest, and Antipater retained his position as the chief minister of state.

For the rest of his life Antipater was thus involved in the affairs of Rome. In 57 B.C.E., when the governor of Syria, Aulus Gabinius, broke Judaea apart, Idumaea was given to Antipater, and he later joined the governor on an expedition to restore Ptolemy XII of Egypt to his throne. The Roman Civil Wars soon followed, and Hyrcanus, through Antipater, supported Pompey. The exiled Aristobulus was rescued in Rome by Julius Caesar and sent with two legions to begin a revolt in Judaea. Fortunately for Antipater, Aristobulus was poisoned before he could achieve anything.

Julius Caesar then won the battle of Pharsalus in 48 B.C.E., and Antipater found a means by which he could placate the victor. He marched to Caesar's aid when the Roman was in serious trouble in Alexandria, and Caesar was grateful enough to reward Antipater with the rank of chief minister of Judaea. This provided him with Roman citizenship, with the right to collect taxes for Rome, accompanied by exemption from personal taxes and the opportunity of keeping large amounts of the Roman monies due. Antipater also placed his sons in major positions in the kingdom. One was Phasael, who governed Jerusalem, and the other was HEROD THE GREAT, then governor of Galilee.

In 44 B.C.E., Caesar was assassinated, and Cassius, one of the murderers, arrived in Syria demanding assistance. Antipater and Hyrcanus were compelled to assist him, and special taxes were collected, especially by Herod, to provide him with funds for his war against Antony. The Jews, however, were no longer tolerant of Antipater's pro-Roman policies, and a group of anti-Romans, led by one Malichus, staged several fiery demonstrations, which climaxed with the poisoning of Antipater himself in 43 B.C.E.

Antonia (1) (36 B.C.E.–37 C.E.) *The daughter of Marc Antony and Octavia and mother of Claudius*
Antonia grew up in the care of Octavia and both loved and married DRUSUS THE ELDER, the brother of Tiberius. He died in 9 B.C.E., after several children were born to the couple, including CLAUDIUS and GERMANICUS and a daughter Livilla. The *lex de maritandis ordinibus* of the period demanded that all widows remarry, but Augustus freed her of the requirement (*see* MARRIAGE AND DIVORCE) and she never remarried.

Her time was spent either in Rome or at her estate in Bauli. She was the closest friend of LIVIA, the mother of Drusus and Tiberius, was amiable to Tiberius and generally tried to help keep order in the divided and resentful environment in which Augustus ruled. When Tiberius inherited the throne, however, the conflicts between Antonia's son Germanicus (and his wife AGRIPPINA THE ELDER) and Tiberius forced her to perform the role of mediator. In 19 C.E., Germanicus died, and Antonia was conspicuously absent during most of the mourning rites. Subsequently she sided with Tiberius and Livia against Agrippina, and Antonia watched impassively as the party of Germanicus was expunged. She did view with growing alarm the increasing power of Tiberius's main execu-

tioner, Lucius Aelius SEJANUS, the prefect of the Praetorian Guard, who earned Antonia's enmity by scheming for the throne. In the process of trying to fulfill his ambitions, he murdered Drusus the Younger (*see* DRUSUS [3]), Tiberius's son and the husband of Livilla.

By 31 C.E., Sejanus had few overt opponents. Antonia, however, sent Tiberius a letter of warning, delivered by her most trusted freedman, PALLAS. Tiberius believed the warning and began the intrigue necessary to bring Sejanus into custody. The prefect died as a result of his crimes, but the episode uncovered yet another schemer within the royal family. Apicata, the former wife of Sejanus, implicated Livilla, who had been Sejanus's mistress, in the murder of Drusus the Younger. Tiberius did not move against Livilla, partly out of respect for Antonia. Dio reported that Antonia imprisoned Livilla, who either starved to death or killed herself because she knew there was no escape from that formidable jailer.

Late in Antonia's life, after Livia's death, her orphaned grandchildren GAIUS CALIGULA and DRUSILLA were in her custody. She entertained several eastern client princes, including Herod AGRIPPA I. Gaius did not forget Antonia's kindness. When elevated to the throne, he gave her the title *Augusta*. Antonia, however, is believed to have committed suicide.

Antonia (2) (fl. early first century C.E.) *Elder sister of Antonia (1), a daughter of Marc Antony and Octavia*
Although overshadowed by her sister, the elder Antonia possessed the same sense of duty and devotion, the lasting gift of their mother. She was, in her own way, responsible for placing a descendant on the throne of Rome. Her marriage to L. Domitius Ahenobarbus resulted in the birth of C. Domitius Ahenobarbus, the father of NERO.

Antonia (3) (fl. mid-first century C.E.) *Imperial family member*
Antonia was the daughter of Claudius and his second wife, Aelia Paetina.

Antonines The dynasty that began with the reign of ANTONINUS PIUS (138 C.E.) and ended with the death of COMMODUS in 192; during this time Rome achieved the greatest heights of power, glory, material accomplishments, and stability that it would ever know. Emperor HADRIAN (117–138 C.E.) actually founded the line by ensuring the adoption of Antoninus Pius and the subsequent adoption of Marcus Aurelius. The emperors involved were: Antoninus Pius (138–161); Marcus Aurelius (161–180), coruled with Lucius Verus (161–169); and Commodus (177–192). The dynasty ended with the assassination of Commodus. The subsequent chaos established a pattern of deterioration from which Rome never fully recovered.

See individual entries for the emperors and PRAE-TORIAN GUARD; DIDIUS JULIANUS; PERTINAX; SEVERUS SEPTIMIUS.

Antonine Wall   *See* WALL OF ANTONINUS.

Antoninianus   A coin issued during the reign of Caracalla (211–217 C.E.) and which, after 256, became the chief silver coin of issue. In weight the Antoninianus was about one-and-one-half times that of its predecessor, the denarius, but its value was double. The coin became representative of the royal overvaluation of the older imperial coinage, for with its distribution the silver content of the coins declined by 75 percent and continued declining throughout subsequent years of minting.

See also COINAGE; DENARIUS.

Antoninus, Arrius (b. 31 C.E.) *The grandfather of Antoninus Pius*
Much praised by Pliny the Younger, Arrius served as consul in the terrible civil war year of 69 C.E. and then aided the victorious VESPASIAN by serving him in Asia. By 96, Antoninus was back in Rome, where he was counted as one of the aged but wise advisers to the short-lived NERVA.

Antoninus Pius (86–161 C.E.) *Emperor of Rome from 138 to 161 C.E. and founder of the dynasty of the Antonines*
Titus Aurelius Fulvus Boionius Antoninus, called Antoninus Pius, came from a good family in Nîmes, in GALIA NARBONENSIS, now southern France. His family's consular history allowed him to serve as a quaestor and as a praetor before receiving the post of *IV vir consularis,* a judicial office in Umbria and Etruria. Around 133–136 he served in Asia as proconsul and there earned the respect of Emperor Hadrian, who appointed him to his *consilium principis,* the royal council. Antoninus Pius served faithfully and distinguished himself so that, upon the death of

his heir L. Aelius Caesar, Hadrian officially adopted him—on February 25, 138—as successor to the throne. On July 10, upon Hadrian's death, and after administering the imperial offices for a time, Antoninus became emperor.

His first act came as a surprise to the Roman Senate. He refused to order the executions of a list of men proposed for such punishment. He declared to the Senate: "I must not begin my reign with such actions." He gained the name Pius as a result, and was later also called the father of the country. Plodding, patient, and administratively inclined, Antoninus ruled the empire with a firm and steady hand. He did not allow an extravagant style at court, and he did not exhibit any great desire to conquer other lands, thus rendering his period of rule uneventful but prosperous.

Antoninus Pius restored the status of the Senate, without losing any of his imperial powers, improved and strengthened the great bureaucratic machinery of the empire, and was a great builder, especially in Italy. Rome and its surrounding provinces were Antoninus's principal areas of concern. The Senate was given back administrative control of many areas, while Antoninus assisted towns and took on the responsibility for construction. He probably never left Italy, preferring his own estate at Lanuvium.

In matters of foreign policy, Antoninus Pius watched the frontiers and outlying Roman holdings with a cautious eye, ensuring the defense of these possessions first by peaceful means, then by administrative and finally military tactics. In Britain the Wall of Antoninus was constructed after 141. In Partian areas of influence Roman control was tightened by the creation of an Armenian kingdom. A similar situation was created along the Danube in 159, with several procuratorships being established. However, by the end of his reign, serious crises were developing in Gaul, Parthia, Dacia, and Africa.

Fortunately, the far-seeing Hadrian had included a clause in his succession document that ensured strength beyond the reign of his immediate heir. Antoninus adopted the young MARCUS AURELIUS as his son. Marcus was elevated over Antoninus's two sons and given all powers to become the next emperor. Antoninus died on March 7, 161.

Antonius, Gaius (d. c. 44 B.C.E.) *Brother of Marc Antony*
A devoted follower of Julius CAESAR, Gaius Antonius unsuccessfully defended Curicta, an island in the Adriatic Sea, in 49 B.C.E., and in 44 was besieged by Brutus in Apollonia and captured by the enemy. Brutus had him executed after he tried to cause a revolt in the army on the site.

Antonius, Iullus (fl. late first century B.C.E.) *The son of Marc Antony by Fulvia*

A coin from the reign of Emperor Antoninus Pius; on the side is a testament to Britannia *(Hulton/Getty Archive)*

Iullus Antonius's career was considerable, as he served as a praetor in 13 B.C.E. and as consul in 9 B.C.E. He married the imperial niece, Marcella, who had been divorced in 21 B.C.E. by Agrippa, who was planning to marry JULIA (3). Antonius's connection to the royal household proved his undoing. In 2 B.C.E., he became involved with the adulterous Julia. When her indiscretions became public, he was executed by imperial decree, possibly for plotting against the throne.

Antonius, Lucius (fl. mid-first century B.C.E.) *A brother of Marc Antony*

Lucius Antonius was a supporter of his campaigns against Octavian (AUGUSTUS) in the civil war. For many years Lucius, as other of his family, had aided Julius Caesar. He served as a quaestor in Asia until 49 B.C.E., when he took over as pro quaestor in charge of the entire province. After Caesar's assassination in 44 B.C.E., Lucius Antony joined Marc in the war against the LIBERATORS (Caesar's killers), eventually becoming consul in 41. After this period his main enemy was Octavian, against whom he organized unhappy farmers and landowners who had been dispossessed by the SECOND TRIUMVIRATE's land grants to veterans. Octavian, seeking to stabilize the Roman political environment, pardoned Lucius in 40 and dispatched him to Spain. He served as consul, with Publius Servilus; but, in actuality, FULVIA (Marc Antony's wife) was his true ally. He received the nickname *Pietas* (devoted or loyal) as a result.

See also PERUSINE WAR.

Antonius Musa (d. after 23 C.E.) *Physician and writer*

The author of several works, Antonius Musa holds the distinction of having been the personal physician of AUGUSTUS. In 23 B.C.E., Augustus fell seriously ill, and it was widely believed that he would not survive. Antonius healed him and acquired a considerable reputation as a result. Using his influence at the imperial court, he encouraged improvements in the water supply of Rome. He later published two widely read books: *De tuenda valetudine ad Macenetum* and *De herba botanica*.

Antony ("St. Antony") (c. 251–356 C.E.) *Hermit, ascetic and influential mystic of the early church*

Beginning circa 269, Antony swore himself to an ascetic's life and by 285 was living in the Egyptian desert, where demons tormented him. Holiness of this type, during the age of persecution, attracted followers, and at the start of the fourth century Antony organized a slightly modified version of a religious order. His close friend was the bishop of Alexandria, Athanasius, with whom he fought against ARIANISM in the Christian Church. The main source of information about Antony is Athanasius's *Vita Antonii*, the *Life of Antony*.

See also CHRISTIANITY.

Antony, Marc (Marcus Antonius) (c. 83–30 B.C.E.) *Triumvir, consul, and imperial aspirant, one of the most important figures from the dying days of the Republic*

Marc Antony was the son of Antonius Creticus, an unsuccessful admiral, and Julia. His father died early in his childhood, and P. Cornelius Lentulus raised him after marrying Julia. In 63 B.C.E. his adoptive father was strangled on Cicero's order for involvement in the famed Catiline Affair, an act Antony did not forget. Subsequent years proved the young Antony an insatiable womanizer and a dissipater.

In 58 or 57, he traveled to Syria, joining the army of Gabinius, where as a cavalry commander he served in Egypt and Palestine with distinction. He was in Gaul in 54 as a staff member for Julius CAESAR. This connection proved useful, for in 52, Marc Antony became a quaestor and the most vocal and dedicated of Caesar's retinue. In 49, while serving as Caesar's tribune in Rome, Antony vetoed the Senate decree stripping Caesar of his command and then joined him in Gaul. Returning to Rome, he watched over Caesar's interests during the general's Spanish campaign and then commanded the left wing of Caesar's forces at the battle of Pharsalus (48), where POMPEY THE GREAT met defeat. For his loyalty Antony was made Caesar's coconsul in 44.

Whatever plans Caesar had for Antony died with his assassination at the hands of the LIBERATORS on March 15 of that year. Antony seized the dead general's papers, read his will, gave the funeral oration, and occupied Caesar's property, representing himself to the people as Caesar's heir.

Antony gained control of Cisalpine Gaul and faced the forces of BRUTUS and Caesar's assassins, who were joined by Cicero and the Roman Senate and Octavian, Caesar's heir. He was defeated in April 43, suffering setbacks at Forum Gallorum and especially at Mutina. He retreated into Gallia Narbonensis, joined by the provincial governors of the West, Plancus, Asinius Pollio, and Lepidus.

The SECOND TRIUMVIRATE was established in November of 43, comprising of Antony, Octavian, and Lepidus. These men and their forces faced the Republicans at Philippi in 42, where the last of the Liberators fell in battle. Antony took control of the East, with plans to carry out Caesar's Parthian expeditions. He was delayed by a meeting with Cleopatra of Egypt, in Tarsus in 41. The growing rift between Antony and Octavian was furthered in the PERUSINE WAR when Fulvia, Antony's wife, and Lucius, his brother, also opposed Octavian in the conflict.

Fulvia's death ended the dispute, and peace was made between Octavian and Antony in 40 B.C.E., at Brundisium; Octavian gave his sister Octavia to Antony in marriage, receiving in return Cisalpine Gaul.

The Parthian Campaign of 36 was less than successful. Antony repulsed King Phraates IV of Parthia around Phraaspa but was forced to retreat because of the heat and the cunning horsemanship of the enemy. He may have carried out the campaigns of Caesar, but he had not proven himself the equal of the murdered general—despite a victory in Armenia in 34. At the same time, Lepidus fell from the triumvirate, leaving mastery of the Roman world to only two combatants.

The East tempted Antony with dreams of unlimited power, and he succumbed completely. Cleopatra and the wealth of Egypt became his principal ally, and Antony drifted further from Rome. A split with Octavian came in 33, followed by a divorce from Octavia. Sensing that universal support would be crucial, Octavian swayed public opinion in Rome by publishing Antony's will, which left large gifts to his illegitimate children by Cleopatra. Antony was stripped of his authority by the senate, and war was declared upon Cleopatra.

The war climaxed at ACTIUM, off the west coast of Greece, on September 2, 31 B.C.E. It proved a disaster for Antony. His personal courage and determination were not enough to overcome the precision of Octavian's fleet or the half-hearted support of the Romans who served Antony's cause. Following the battle he joined Cleopatra in Alexandria, and when Octavian's legions approached the city in August of 30, the two killed themselves.

Suggested Readings: Huzar, Eleanor Goltz. *Mark Antony: A Biography.* London: Croom Helm, 1986; Julius Caesar. *The Civil War.* New York: Penguin, 1967; Julius Caesar. *The Conquest of Gaul.* New York: Penguin, 1982; Plutarch. *Life of Antony.* New York: Cambridge University Press, 1988; Suetonius. *The Twelve Caesars.* Translated and with an introduction by Michael Grant. New York: Penguin, 1979.

Antyllus (d. 30 B.C.E.) *Son of Marc Antony and Fulvia; also called Marc Antony the Younger*
To unite more closely the family of Octavian with that of Antony, Antyllus was betrothed in 37 B.C.E. to Octavian's daughter JULIA (3) (according to Suetonius), but neither side had any intention of allowing this marriage to happen. Designated as his father's heir, Antyllus had coins minted with both their likenesses at the height of Antony's power. He was used as a messenger after the battle of ACTIUM but was unsuccessful in halting Octavian's invasion of Egypt or the continuance of the war to its ultimate end. After Marc Antony and Cleopatra killed themselves, Antyllus and Caesarion, Cleopatra's son by Caesar, were executed.

Anullinus, Publius Cornelius (fl. late second century C.E.) *Proconsul of Africa*
In 193, Anullinus allied himself with SEVERUS, the commander of the Pannonian Legions who marched on Rome and declared himself emperor. In 194, when PESCENNIUS NIGER opposed Severus in Africa and Asia, Anullinus took command of the emperor's legions and inflicted a crushing defeat on Niger at Issus. He later served in the PARTHIAN WAR for Severus and was made urban prefect in 196.

Apamea Cibotus City in Asia Minor, not officially part of the Roman senatorial province of Asia. Apamea Cibotus (also Apamea and Maeandrum) was built by Seleucid ruler Antiochus I Soter on the Meander River in the region of Phrygia, sometime in the third century B.C.E., and later fell under Roman dominance. Located in east-middle Asia Minor, Apamea became one of the leading economic cities of the region and possessed a considerable amount of self-rule and a large population of Roman colonists.

See also CONVENTUS.

Apamea Orontem City built by Nicator on the site of ancient Pella. Located on the Orontes River in a strong defensive position, Apamea fell under the provincial control of Rome and became a leading city of the area. It was connected to Antioch, Seleucia and Emesa, along the route of the Orontes. In the early empire, the city's population probably numbered 170,000. During the reign of Claudius, in 53 C.E., the entire city was devastated by an earthquake and was granted a five-year exemption from the tribute paid to Rome.

Apelles (d. c. 37 C.E.) *Actor*
A first-century actor who was generally held to be the finest tragedian of his era, Apelles endured the time of TIBERIUS (14–37 C.E.), who had exiled actors from Rome. When GAIUS CALIGULA came to the throne in 37, he brought back all performers to Rome and became an obsessive supporter of the arts. Apelles was one of the leading recipients of the emperor's indulgence. Caligula kept Apelles at his side and forced praetors and consuls to fund performances, not just by Apelles, but of all actors.

Aper, Arrius (d. 284 C.E.) *One of the more corrupt of the prefects of the Praetorian Guard*
Aper served the Emperor Carus (282–283) and accompanied him on his initial Pannonian campaign and in 283, on his Persian campaign, when Carus died. Some said that he was struck by lightning, but Aper probably poisoned him, so that NUMERIAN, Carus's son and Aper's son-in-law, could assume the throne. Numerian decided to finish his father's war, but shortly thereafter fell ill. Aper hid him in a litter and in his tent. Finally, the stench arising from the imperial tent confirmed what everyone suspected. The young emperor was dead. Aper showed surprise and ascribed his death to natural causes. The troops put a stop to his ambitions by proclaiming as emperor the commander of the *protectores domestici*, a young and brilliant officer, DIOCLETIAN. A soothsayer had predicted that Diocletian would achieve greatness, but

first had to face an *Aper* (a boar). Aper was dragged before him and declared guilty of murder. Diocletian ran him through with a sword on the spot.

Apicata (d. 31 C.E.) *Wife of Sejanus, the prefect of the Praetorian Guard in the region of Tiberius*
Apicata had borne her husband three children when he divorced her as part of his scheme to gain the throne. She apparently knew much of the plot, for she later revealed considerable details about it. In 31 C.E. her ex-husband fell from power. According to the historian Dio, she was not condemned. Upon hearing of the deaths of her children, however, she retired to her own rooms, composed a letter incriminating LIVILLA in the plot and in the murder of Tiberius's son Drusus, and then killed herself.

Apicius The name bestowed upon gluttons, based upon Marcus Gavius Apicius, author of a lost cookbook in the early first century C.E. The only extant cookbook, *De Re Coquinaria,* is the work of Apicius Caelius (third century C.E.).
See also GLUTTONY; VITELLIUS.

Apis The sacred bull of Egypt, worshiped with the bulls Mnevis of Heliopolis and Buchis of Hermonthis. Apis, whose cult was centered in Memphis, possessed oracular powers and had been honored for centuries on the Nile, remaining a source of interest in the Roman period. It was said that Germanicus, the adopted son of Tiberius, visited Egypt in 19 C.E. The Bull of Apis refused to eat from his hand, an omen that his death was imminent, which was in fact the case. Many characteristics of the Apis rituals were used in the Roman cult of Mithras.
See also RELIGION.

Apollinaris of Laodicea (fl. fourth century C.E.) *Christian scriptural writer*
In 361 C.E., Emperor Julian ordered all Christian teachers to cease teaching pagan doctrines and to center their instruction on the gospels of Matthew and Luke and other Christian writers. Apollinaris and his father, also named Apollinaris, one a grammarian and the other a master of rhetoric, rewrote the Christian scriptures into a classical style. The Old Testament was converted into a 24-book epic in the Homeric style by the father. Apollinaris the Younger rewrote the New Testament in Platonic-style dialogues and became bishop of Laodicea, in Syria.
See also CHRISTIANITY.

Apollo Greek god who was in time accepted by the Romans. When the Greeks were establishing their colonies in Italy, they dedicated their first settlement, at Cumae, to Apollo. The Italians believed in Apollo as a god of healing and medicine, but he was not given admis-

sion into the city of Rome itself because he was a foreign deity. Apollo was, however, a dominant figure in many periods. Although his name was never Latinized, his title of God of the Sun was forgotten. As the god of medicine he could be honored, a custom preserved by the Romans.

AUGUSTUS was responsible for establishing the god officially in the Eternal City. As the young Octavian, he had placed his house and his career into the care of Apollo, and the battle of ACTIUM, in which he seized power from Antony, was supposedly won because of the god's intervention. In honor of this patronage, a small temple was erected to the god in the imperial palace near the Palatine. Later, on private property so as not to violate Roman custom, Augustus constructed the Forum Augustum, housing three important temples: one for Julius Caesar the Divine, one to Mars and one for Apollo. The Sibylline Books were moved from the Temple of Jupiter to Apollo's private shrine. Finally, in 17 C.E. at the *ludi Saeculares* (Secular Games, see *LUDI*) an ancient festival, prayers were offered to the gods, and Augustus added prayers to Apollo, concretizing the deity's role in the religio-political affairs of the empire. In 67 C.E., as a result of a personal vexation over some divinational insult, Emperor NERO abolished the oracles of Apollo.
See also ASTROLOGY; AUGURS AND AUGURY; GODS AND GODDESSES OF ROME.

Apollodorus (fl. early second century C.E.) *Noted imperial architect*
Apollodorus was responsible for the construction of many of Emperor TRAJAN's great works, including the FORUM, the ODEUM and the gymnasium. Upon the accession of Hadrian in 117, his fate would change. The architect had offended Hadrian in the past. According to Dio, when Trajan and Apollodorus were once in consultation on a matter, Hadrian interrupted and was rudely cut short by Apollodorus. Later Hadrian sent him the plans of the Temple of Venus and Roma, after that shrine was completed, demonstrating the fact that such great structures could be erected without Apollodorus's aid. In response, Apollodorus criticized the location of the temple, the height of its statues and the organizational style. Outraged, Hadrian had him murdered in 129.

Apollonius of Tyana (fl. first century C.E.) *One of the leading mystical Pythagoreans of his time*
Among Apollonius's many attested miracles, which included healings and resurrections, was the famous vision in 95 C.E. of the assassination of DOMITIAN. While in Ephesus, he called together all of the townspeople and claimed that Stephanus, one of Domitian's assassins, had done a great deed in smiting the tyrant. This vision supposedly took place at the exact moment that the murder was taking place in Rome. Emperor CARACALLA

admired Apollonius for his magical skills and erected a shrine to him. St. Augustine went to great lengths during the fifth century to refute the claim that Apollonius was similar to Christ. Philostratus wrote his biography circa 220.

Appendix Vergiliana   A group of Latin poems ascribed by ancient authorities to VIRGIL (70–19 B.C.E.). The collection is of widely varying quality, and the attribution to Virgil is considered by scholars to be a most dubious one. Most of the poems in the collection are thought to date from around the time of Augustus, probably in the early first century C.E. or later in the century. The specific works include:

Catalepton: Fourteen poems on assorted subjects, with at least some of them most likely by the hand of Virgil.

Ciris: A work influenced by CATALLUS and the Alexandrian school that tells the tale of Scylla, daughter of Nisus. While there are similarities to the work of Virgil, the poor quality of the poetry makes it almost certainly an imitation.

Copa: A series of phrases derived from Virgil and Sertus PROPERTIUS. They are clearly influenced by Epicurean sensibilities.

Culex: A poem that was considered by Martial, Lucan, and Statius to have been authored by Virgil, although this is unlikely. The poem presents the tale of a gnat and a shepherd. A shepherd is befriended by a gnat, but the insect is soon killed by his friend. The ghost of the gnat then returns to tell of his adventures in the underworld.

Dirae: A poem of a farmer who loses his farm and curses his misfortune. It was often preserved in manuscripts with Lydia.

Eleg. In Maec.: Two elegies on the death of Gaius Maecenas in 8 B.C.E.

Lydia: A poem of lament in which the author expresses his sadness at being separated from his love Lydia.

Moretum: A poem of a farmer preparing his breakfast. The details it presents of country life, and its judgments and attitudes would seem to make it a candidate for potential authorship by Virgil, especially given its similarities to the *Georgics*.

Priapea: Three poems on the god Priapus.

Appian Way   *See* VIAE.

apparitores   The civil servants who attended the magistrates of the Roman government. The *apparitores* were generally drawn from among the freedmen or were sons of freedmen and served as scribes, lictors, and assistants. They were organized into several classes, including *scribae, lictores, viatores, accensi,* and *praecones.* Each received a specific salary from the state, and each held a post for one year on a renewable basis. Over time, it became customary for the *apparitores* to be permitted to hold office for a time well beyond the one-year time period. Civil servants were also organized into formally recognized corporations, with their own panels to oversee their internal organization and bylaws.

Apronius, Lucius   (fl. early first century C.E.) *Roman proconsul and imperial legate*
In 20 C.E., while serving as proconsul in Africa, Apronius attacked and bested the rebel TACFARINAS, avenging the defeat of the general Furius Camillus the previous summer. He took harsh measures to maintain discipline, including the use of lots to single out every tenth man for death, in disgraced units of the army. In the war with Tacfarinas, Apronius used his own son, Caesianus, to finish off the Numidians (*see* NUMIDIA). In 28, the proconsul served as propraetor of Lower Germany (Germania Inferior). He succeeded in driving off a Frisii invasion only after a terrible loss. The embarrassment, normally enough to finish any career, went virtually unnoticed by the Senate, which was preoccupied with the machinations of SEJANUS.

Apuleius   (b. c. 125 C.E.) *Prolific novelist, whose works were widely read in his own era*
Apuleius grew up in the African city of Madura and was educated at Carthage before studying Platonic philosophy at Athens. He traveled extensively, visiting Rome, Asia, and Greece, finally returning to Africa. There, at the urging of his friend Sicinius Pontianus, Apuleius married Pontianus's widowed mother, Pudentilla, a woman of considerable wealth. After domestic troubles in which he was accused of witchcraft, Apuleius moved to Carthage, and there his writings and status as a philosopher, poet, and novelist were celebrated.

He wrote many notable books, the most famous of which was the *Golden Ass* (also known as *Metamorphoses*). The tale concerns Lucius, who is transformed into an ass after dabbling in the world of magic. Isis restores him, but only after he endures a variety of adventures. His other works include the *Florida*, a collection of his orations; the *Apologia*, which defends both magic and himself; and the *De Deo Socratis*, which examines Platonism. Many other works authored by Apuleius have been lost, and others, like *De Dogmate Platonis*, are of dubious originality.

aquae   The Roman term for health-improving spas and baths. The Romans valued such sites and the *aquae* of any given region had much to do with its selection as a place of colonization and development. Some of the major sites included:

Aquae Cutiliae mineral spring in Samnium, near the towns of Cutilia and Reate. This was considered to be the center of Italy, and both VESPASIAN and TITUS died there.

Aquae Patavinae also called Aponi Fons; the warm springs near Patavium. The sick and the dying often visited this site.

Aquae Sextiae site of a Roman colony founded in 122 B.C.E. by Calvinus in GALLIA NARBONENSIS. In 102 B.C.E., Marius routed the Teutons at this spring. During AUGUSTUS's time the colony was renamed Colonia Julia Augusta Aquis Sextus, and in 381 C.E. the site was redesignated as the capital of Gallia Narbonensis. The waters of the site were especially famous in the Roman world.

Aquae Statiellae warm springs in Liguria, near the town of the Statielli.

Aquae Sulis now Bath, England; the most famous of the spas after Aquae Sextiae. In the 19th century C.E., its fame increased and gave impetus to archaeological research, which resulted in great discoveries.

aqueducts Artificial channels by which the Romans conducted water to specific regions. The Romans, like the Greeks before them, were concerned about the acquisition and the supply of water. The Greeks originated the use of tunnels, a scientific and architectural feat improved on by the Romans. Roman engineers, including the famed Marcus Agrippa, experimented with improved forms. The first Roman aqueducts (the Aqua Appia and the Anio Vetus) were, like the Greek models, cut out of tunnels, but added mighty arches to aid in water conveyance. The aqueducts became one of Rome's greatest architectural achievements. The systems at Nîmes (Nemausus) and Segovia survive.

There were three general styles: bridges, arches, and siphons. Bridges were used in the aqueducts of Nîmes and Segovia, while arches were seen in the Aqua Marcia and Anio Novus. Lyons was provided with siphons, replete with pipes laid in concrete.

Nîmes, however, was the most beautiful and the most enduring. Built by Marcus Agrippa from 20 to 16 B.C.E., the system at Nîmes brought water to the settlement from springs 31 miles away. Over the Gardon River, a bridge was built, now the "Pont du Gard," measuring some 323 feet in length and standing 53 feet high, with support arches and tiers. Slightly bent against the course of the water, the stone edifice was magnificent architecturally while serving an absolutely practical purpose.

See also ART AND ARCHITECTURE and ENGINEERING.

The Pont du Gard, one of the greatest of the Roman aqueducts *(Hulton/Getty Archive)*

Aquileia City near the Adriatic Sea, with a large population, and with the province of Illyricum positioned behind it; described by the historian Herodian. The Romans began the city circa 181 B.C.E., to act as a port of entry for Italy and as a defense zone. The road systems of Panonia, Noricum, and Illyricum began there, and the Adriatic fleets of the empire were stationed at its docks. A large population, composed of natives (of Gallic origin) and foreigners (mostly merchants), relied upon the military for protection but also felt secure behind the walls that surrounded Aquileia. The military presence had two general effects on the populace. First, the cult of the Eastern deity Mithras became popular, and second, peace was maintained for so long during the imperial era that the defenses of the city were allowed to deteriorate.

In May of 238 C.E., Aquileia, loyal to Rome and supportive of the joint emperors proclaimed by the Senate, BALBINUS and PUPIENUS, closed its gates to MAXIMINUS I. Resolved to invade Italy to regain his throne, Maximinus placed Aquileia under siege by his entire army. The city responded by building hasty defenses and by repairing its wall; food was abundant. Maximinus failed to take Aquileia, and his losses, coupled with the sinking morale of his troops, brought about a mutiny. On May 10, 238, he was murdered with his son. Herodian described the siege and the city's preparations in some detail.

With a population of nearly half a million, Aquileia remained an economic force on the Adriatic, but in 452, Attila the Hun burned the city to the ground, and malaria struck down the survivors. The city was rebuilt and rose once again to its original prominence, but it was recorded that, during the Hun terror, many residents fled to the Venetian lagoons—the site of modern Venice.

Aquitania The original home of a Gallic people known as the Aquitani. Composed of many tribes, loosely confederated, Aquitania stretched from Garumna, or Garonne, along the Bay of Biscay, down to the Pyrenees. The Aquitani were more similar to the Iberians than to their Celtic neighbors, but they were extremely fierce in war.

See also GALLIA.

Arabia The peninsula situated between the Red Sea and the Indian Ocean; an axe-shaped region divided into three sections in early eras: Arabia Deserta, a vast ocean of sand and stifling heat; Arabia Felix, comprising deserts but also including a fertile strip of land along its western seacoast; and Arabia Petraea, which became a Roman province of the same name.

The NABATAEANS possessed a considerable territory in the north, centered on Petra. Their kingdom became integral to the trade conducted between the Egypt-Palestine area and the Far Eastern kingdoms. Caravans carried spices, gums, and gems back and forth to India, and fabulous wealth was mistakenly believed to reside in Arabia, especially in Arabia Felix. Sailing vessels from Egypt, trading with India via the Red Sea, broke the Arabian trade monopoly, but the chieftains of the main Arabia Felix tribes, the Sabaeans, did what they could to preserve trade routes by land and by sea and give credence to the stories of riches.

Economic advantage was the prime motivation in all Roman efforts in Arabia. After Rome established friendly relations with the Nabataeans, Augustus decided on a campaign to acquire Arabia Felix. In 25 B.C.E., Aelius Gallus, the prefect of Egypt, led 10,000 men in an attempt that was doomed from the start. Gallus was forced to cross a desert of enormous proportions, and then, with his numbers dwindling, retreat across another stretch of sand. The disaster ended with a retreat to Egypt, having accomplished little, except to open relations with the Sabaeans.

Augustus (reigned 27 B.C.E.–14 C.E.) allowed the Nabataeans of Arabia Petraea to retain independence but kept stringent safeguards in effect. King Herod instigated a revolt in 9 B.C.E., and the Nabataean vizier, Syllaeus, protested but was executed. Gaius Caesar, Augustus's grandson, was sent to the east, generally to maintain order, but he was also to impress upon the Petra-based kingdom that it was dangerous to put its vulnerability to the test.

In 105 C.E., Trajan decided that a combination of frontier defense and economic expediency made annexation desirable. Cornelius Palma, with the VI Legion, attacked and conquered the proud Arabians. Outlying tribesmen, according to Ammianus Marcellinus, did fight, but prolonged resistance was impossible. A new province was thus created, and a large road was built from Damascus to the cities of Petra and Bostra, and then to the Red Sea port of Aqaba.

Petra was designated as the capital of the territory, and, as of March 22, 106 C.E., a Praetorian legate commanded the province, with the added weight of the III Legion "Cyrenaica." Massive archaeological remains show a diverse lifestyle in both the city and the province. The city of Bostra was a powerful economic unit along the trade routes and, under Diocletian's reorganization, the capital of a new province simply called Arabia.

Arabia (both Arabia Petraea and Arabia Felix, with Arabia Deserta to a lesser extent) accepted Christianity, but the new religion could not dislodge Sabaean star worship, Judaic admixtures, local religious customs, or the Roman cults, such as that of Dionysus. Such was the situation until the birth of Islam in 610 C.E.

Ara Pacis The Altar of Peace, erected in Rome between 13 and 9 B.C.E. to commemorate the safe return of AUGUSTUS from the provinces to celebrate the Pax Romana throughout the entire empire. Inaugurated on July 4, 13 B.C.E., the altar was more than a piece of art. It served as an important historical document, showing every element of Augustus's vision for Rome's politics, religion, and society, as well as for his own rule. Designed around panels of carved friezes, the Ara Pacis depicted the grand procession to the Campus Martius to celebrate Augustus's triumphant journey home. Using the finest Republican style of art, the panels accomplished two very different purposes: first, the grandeur of the Roman Empire was visible in the superb carving, the excellent interplay of light and shadow in the faces and folds of the garments; second, despite the stiffness of form there was, in the relationship of the figures—men, women, and children—a humanity of the kind that found its finest expression in the reign of Augustus.

The early panels centered on Augustus and Tiberius, the Guards, and then the religious representatives of the Roman state religion, the Vestals and the priesthoods. Behind them were the families of the most powerful men in Rome, including Julia, Augustus's daughter; Antonia; Octavia; and others. Farther behind were the senators, ever present in the Augustan principate but always subservient to the will of Augustus. Most of the Ara Pacis has survived and is displayed in various museums.

See also ART AND ARCHITECTURE.

Arar, battle of   Confrontation between Julius CAESAR and the Helvetians. In June 58 B.C.E., the Helvetians attempted to migrate illegally into Roman territories. Julius Caesar decided to attack at an opportune moment, while the tribal people were crossing the Arar River. With 34,000 men, Caesar drove into the Helvetians, slaughtering over 30,000 of them. The Helvetians fled to the Liger (Loire), with Caesar in pursuit.

See GALLIC WARS.

Arausio (Orange)   One of the leading cities of GALLIA NARBONENSIS; northeast of NEMAUSUS (Nîmes) and just north of Avignon. Arausio was established as a colony in 36 or 35 B.C.E., as part of the extensive program of Romanization in the province. It enjoyed the attention of both Augustus and Tiberius so that by the middle of the first century C.E. it ranked as one of the more prosperous communities in southern Gaul. Following the decline of NARBO in the second century C.E., Arausio was one of the cities that filled the economic vacuum. Arausio possessed temples, baths, an arena, and other Roman buildings. A huge triple arch, the Arch of Tiberius, was built sometime during his reign (c. 26 C.E.) and was unique in being the first such creation to sport three arches, an architectural feat reproduced in the later years of the empire. The theater, also dated to the first century C.E., held more than 7,000 guests and once boasted three tiers of columns and statues. Many other edifices in Arausio were destroyed by Prince Maurice of Nassau during the defense of the city in 1622.

Arbitio, Flavius   (fourth century C.E.) *A magister equitum under Constantius II, Julian and Valens*
One of the first *magistri* of the empire to rise to prominence as the traditional legionary commanders faded in the Roman system, Arbitio helped Constantius II against the usurper Magnentius, at the battle of MURSA Major in 351, earning for himself considerable power. He was made a senator and a consul in 355. Julian used his skills, naming him to preside over the Commission of Chalcedon in 361. He retired but still wielded enough authority to help defeat Valens's rival for the throne, Procopius, in 366 at Nacolea.

Arbogast   (d. 394 C.E.) *A powerful* magister peditum *(master of soldiers) of Frankish descent*
A pagan, Arbogast had served under the *magister militum* BAUTO as an able lieutenant in the reign of Gratian (367–383), traveling with his master to aid Theodosius at Gratian's request.

The wars in the east launched Arbogast's career. Between 385 and 388 Bauto died, and the army called upon Arbogast to take command. Theodosius put his new soldier to use against the usurper Maximus, with his son Flavius Victor. In 388, pleased with this performance, Theodosius gave the new Western emperor, VALENTINIAN II, into Arbogast's care. Valentinian deteriorated from ward to abject prisoner. Arbogast kept him shut in at Vienne in Gaul and ruled the entire Western Empire in his name, placing colleagues and servants in charge of the various imperial departments. Valentinian pleaded with Theodosius for help, but the distant emperor refused to interfere in the affair. Desperate, Valentinian tried to dismiss the general but was impotent in his own court. An assassination attempt was tried but failed, and on May 15, 392, the emperor was found hanged by the neck, probably a suicide.

Arbogast became an imperial power broker, placing Flavius Eugenius, a Christian, on the throne. Civil war was imminent. Despite his pagan preferences, Arbogast had attempted to keep a Christian facade on the empire, refusing the Senate when it wished to restore the Altar of Victory in 384 and promoting a spirit of toleration for all religious beliefs. In 394, Theodosius marched west to finish the struggle. The battle that ensued, that of FRIGIDUS, took place on the fifth and sixth of September and was the end of paganism in the empire. Theodosius was triumphant, and Arbogast was forced to kill himself.

Arcadius, Flavius   (d. 408 C.E.) *Emperor and eldest son of Theodosius I, ruling in the East from 395 to 408 and an important figure in the division of the empire into a definite East and West*
Because Honorius ruled the West independently, Arcadius can be called the first ruler of the "new" Eastern Empire.

His first taste of rule came in 394, when his father marched against the MAGISTER MILITUM Arbogast. Within a year Theodosius was dead, and Arcadius was on the throne. He faced intrigues in his own court from the onset, especially from Stilicho, the *magister militum* of Honorius, who was only 10 years old. Others included Eutropius, the eunuch and court chamberlain, and Flavius Rufinus, the Praetorian prefect of the East.

Like so many other rulers, Arcadius was perpetually hard put to challenge any of his ministers. Events took place without his consent throughout his entire reign, and the power struggles whirling about him were uncontrolled and bloody. The first major confrontations came in 395, when Flavius Rufinus and Stilicho fought for supremacy, using the prefecture of Illyricum as a battleground. Stilicho earned the eternal enmity of Arcadius by having Flavius Rufinus killed in Constantinople, on November 27, 395.

Arcadius next came under the sway of the eunuch Eutropius, who administrated his affairs and kept tight rein on the new Praetorian prefect. Eutropius, however, fell from power circa 399 and was banished, defeated by a new power on the scene, Aelia Eudoxia, the daughter of the *magister militum* Bauto. Eudoxia married Arcadius and then ruled him with an iron hand.

Anyone foolish enough to oppose Eudoxia found himself stripped of rank and exiled. St. John Chrysostom was one such victim of her wrath, facing his punishment in 401. Aelia Eudoxia died in 404, and Arcadius handed over the imperial powers to his Praetorian prefect, Anthemius. This was his wisest act, because Anthemius was genuinely concerned for the empire. When Arcadius died in 408, Anthemius ensured a smooth transition of rule to Theodosius II, the seven-year-old son of Arcadius. Arcadius lived little more than 31 years.

Archelaus (fl. early first century C.E.) *Son of Herod the Great*
Archelaus was sent as a prince of Judaea to be educated in Rome; like his brothers, kings Herod Antipas and Philip, he received control of his own kingdom circa 4 B.C.E. This included Judaea, Samaria and Idumaea, but appears to have been reduced in part by Augustus, who saw the need for breaking up the too centralized kingdom of Herod. As ruler of Judaea, Archelaus from the start was beset with troubles. Public works were halted, and the Roman presence upon which the king relied caused seething hatred on the part of the large Jewish population, especially in the Roman headquarters of Jerusalem.

Further, Archelaus had married the ex-wife of his brother Alexander, who had borne her husband children, a marriage thus considered invalid by Jewish law. Finally, in 6 C.E., Jewish and Samaritan groups demanded that Rome remove him, and Augustus, agreeably accepting a province at the request of its inhabitants, deposed Archelaus. He was sent into exile in Gaul (Gallia Narbonensis), and Judaea became an imperial province under the command of a procurator.

Archelaus of Cappadocia (d. 17 C.E.) *Grandson of the king of same name, who had briefly ruled Egypt, and a king in his own right*
In 40 B.C.E., Marc ANTONY, who controlled the East, was forced to execute the ruler of CAPPADOCIA, Ariarathes, and in his place installed Archelaus. Subsequently, Archelaus became one of the pillars of Antony's support in the East, even though he was powerless to stop Octavian from winning at Actium in 31 B.C. When peace was restored, Archelaus was allowed to keep his kingdom, as part of the broader Roman policy toward Parthia and as a buffer state to Rome. Archelaus ruled for many years but earned the enmity of Tiberius, whom he had snubbed while the future emperor was in self-imposed exile on Rhodes.

Sometime around 17 C.E., Achelaus was summoned to Rome by Tiberius and was put on trial for abuse of funds. He died of natural causes before the end of the trial. Strabo is a major source of information on his kingdom, and Appian refers to him in his chronicles of the Civil War. Tacitus mentions Archelaus, pointing out that upon his death Cappadocia was converted into a province of the empire, although his son did rule, causing a revolt in 36 C.E. among the hill people called the Clitae over taxation.

arches   Architectural form that the Romans brought to near perfection in monuments and other structures. The Romans were gifted in the construction of arches, and many have survived the centuries as remarkable artistic creations of the imperial era.

Early examples of arch-making date to the fourth century B.C.E., but it was another two centuries before the honorific arch, the fornix, (pl., fornices) was created. As the art became more uniform and efficient, more ambitious constructions were attempted, leading to the mighty triumphal arches that are known today.

No precise pattern was ever used in arch construction. Some had more than one vaulted passageway, some had three. Decorations of all varieties were all possible on the *attic*, the top part of the arch, as was true in most support columns. Since an arch was generally built in honor of some personage or event, the decorative emphasis thus contained images of soldiers, prisoners and portraits of the great figures themselves. As one of the leading dedicatory styles in use during the empire, a wide variety and number of arches have survived.

In the provinces, the Arch of Trajan at Beneventum was built around 114 C.E. and seems constructed of a design heavily influenced by the Arch of Titus, with many

The Arch of Constantine, built to commemorate Constantine's victory over Maxentius in 312 *(Hulton/Getty Archive)*

sculpted panels and decorations. In Ancona, a smaller version was constructed to the same emperor's memory. Another Arch of Trajan was erected at a crossroads in the African city of Lepcis Magna.

In Arausio in Gaul, Tiberius, in 26 C.E., ordered the construction of an arch in honor of the defeat of the chieftain Sacrovir in his rebellion of 21. The Arch of Tiberius was notable for its triple-arch construction, while the Arch of Marcus Aurelius, in the African city of Aea, built circa 163, was of marble, pointing to the Romanization of the province and the increasing artistic capacities of its architects and artisans.

The Africans erected a triumphal arch in honor of Emperor Septimius Severus, a native of Lepcis who visited the province in 203. This arch was decorated with reliefs and Corinthian columns. Its depiction of battles, sacrifices and triumphs made a remarkable archaeological find and differed greatly from the arch built in his honor in Rome. Also in Africa (Numidia) was the Arch of Caracalla, built in 219 in honor of that emperor, a gift from the people of Cuicul.

The city of Rome is the best location for the preservation of commemorative arches, with excellent specimens still in existence. These include the arches of Titus, Septimius Severus, and Constantine. Under Augustus great strides were made in the creation of arches, continuing until the time of the Flavians. Two arches were erected by Augustus, the first in 29 B.C.E. to honor his many victories (especially at Actium), and the second was erected in 19 B.C.E., a year after peace was made with the Parthians. This one stood in the Forum. Other early arches includes ones constructed in 19 C.E. to honor the generals Germanicus and Drusus; each stood on a side of the Temple of Mars Ultor. Claudius eventually ordered the Arch of Tiberius, which was placed near the Theater of Pompey.

Later emperors helped develop the form. Titus's Arch was constructed by Domitian. It stood by the Colosseum on the Sacred Way and contained a vaulted arch with columns, strong supporting walls, and various friezes, displaying the conquest of the Jews in 70 C.E. Septimius Severus's Arch was built in 203 and stood in the Forum.

It was innovative in its use of wide carving and depictions of battles, instead of the normal classical style.

In 315, Constantine ordered the carving of a triumphal arch, with the Senate in agreement. The result was a grand artistic creation that in some respects ended the great archbuilding of the empire. Panels were formed, depicting the battle of Milvian Bridge and the victory of Constantine over Maxentius. The presentation of his victory was grandiose, as the emperor himself was carved in superhuman dimensions.

The honorific arch was a genuine Roman art form and one that preserved the glory of its rulers. Emperors were depicted but so too were non-imperial people, as in the arch built in 204 C.E. commemorating the silversmiths of Rome.

See also ART AND ARCHITECTURE, ENGINEERING.

architecture   *See* ART AND ARCHITECTURE.

Ardashir I (d. 241 C.E.) *Founder of the Sassanid Dynasty of Persia in 224 C.E.; ended the Arsacid Dynasty and proclaimed himself "King of Kings"*
Ardashir was one of the great figures of Persian history, a general, prince, and monarch whose cunning and force of will changed Near Eastern history, creating the most potent threat that Rome would face in the East. Under the Arsacid system, local kings were given a free hand in the administration of their territories. Such was the case with Persis, a province of kings whose domains stretched along the Persian Gulf and to the coast of the Arabian Sea. The Persis lands were ostensibly overseen by a larger clan, the Basrangi. One of the local rulers, Papak, broke the power of the Basrangi and came to dominate all of Persia. As there had been no immediate opposition from the Arsacids, Papak understood that their authority was vulnerable.

In time Papak died, leaving his eldest son, Shapur, to rule. Shapur's more talented brother, Ardashir, was a leading general in Persia. In 208 he revolted against Shapur, becoming king almost immediately upon the mysterious death of his brother. A massive war was launched on the adjoining provinces, and victories mounted quickly as Ardashir and his horsemen swept across the Persian plains. Finally, in either 224 or 226, Artabanus, the king of the Arsacids, faced Ardashir in battle and died.

Ardashir entered the city of Ctesiphon, which had been the winter capital of the Arsacids, and declared himself King of Kings. His own dynastic ambitions were satisfied, as he had a son, Shapur, to succeed him. Steps were taken to organize the new Sassanid Empire. Ardashir maintained the general bureaucratic system, but the entire Persian world was now answerable only to him and his successors. No new rival would be allowed to grow in secret. Stricter controls were upheld in the provinces,

especially in the west, in Parthia. This policy brought Ardashir into direct conflict with Rome.

Media fell under attack, and soon after Armenia, but there Ardashir met with failure, as Artabanus's sons, the most important of whom was Artavasdes, were allied with King Chosroes I of Armenia. Ardashir retired temporarily and in 230 invaded Mesopotamia, attacking all of the camps and garrisons of the Romans. Emperor Severus Alexander mustered troops and marched into Syria, launching from Antioch an ill-advised and three-pronged attack on Persia. The first column was to pass into Media, the second to march toward Ctesiphon by way of the Euphrates, and the third, under the personal command of Severus Alexander, to move through Mesopotamia. Ardashir struck first in Media but without result, being called away to the Euphrates to protect his capital. There he met the Romans and defeated them, but not significantly; heavy Persian losses made a stalemate. From 232 until 237, while his western holdings regrouped, Ardashir was centered in the east, where vast areas were available.

In 238, the King of Kings returned to the west and attacked Mesopotamia with his son, Shapur, capturing the fortress of Hatra and the cities of Nisibis and Carrhae. Ardashir died in 241, and Shapur was crowned the ruler of the Sassanids, eager to carry on his father's ambitions. Ardashir was also known as Artaxerxes.

Aretas III (fl. first century B.C.E.) *King of Nabataean Arabia*
In 65 B.C.E. Aretas III invaded Judaea and laid siege to Jerusalem but was driven back to Arabia. Antipater of Idumaea convinced the Nabataean king that it would be in Arabia's best interest to side with Hyrcanus in his feud with his brother, Aristobulus II, over the rule of Judaea. Ambitious, Aretas attacked Aristobulus, satisfying Antipater's ambitions to see him removed. Victory for Aretas was impossible, because Pompey dispatched two servants, A. Gabinius and Aemilius Scaurus, from Syria with orders to pacify the region. Aretas withdrew, but Pompey soon attacked him in Arabia in 63 B.C.E. He could not get to Petra, the capital, before Aristobulus and Hyrcanus attacked one another. Thus the Roman advance was aborted. Scaurus was sent against Petra in turn, but Antipater mediated the situation and brought an end to the confrontation.

Aretas IV (late first century B.C.E.) *King of Nabataean Arabia and ruler of Arabia Petra*
As viceroy of Arabia, Aretas IV faced serious Roman invasions during the reign of Augustus and was very nearly executed by the emperor in 9 B.C.E. He assumed the position of viceroy for the Nabataean king, Obodas, sometime before 24 B.C.E. During this period the country was unsuccessfully invaded by Aelius Gallus, but forever after the Romans possessed considerable influence at Petra, the capital. In 9 B.C.E., Obodas died and Aretas took his

place on the throne without first seeking permission from Augustus. He was finally allowed to rule, but only on the condition that Rome henceforth be consulted in all such matters of state in the land.

Argentoratum   Site of a major battle fought in 357 C.E. between Emperor Julian the Apostate and the Alamanni, near the confluence of the Rhine and Ill rivers and the modern city of Strasbourg. While Julian was campaigning along the Rhine frontier, the large tribe of the Alamanni launched an attack across the Rhine to Gaul. Julian, though pressed to find enough troops to counter the invasion, marched immediately. He and his 13,000 men collided with the Alamanni and a bitter struggle ensued. Using their vast superior numbers, the barbarians tried to overwhelm the Romans, but with their usual discipline the legionaries slowly gained the upper hand and then victory. With thousands of dead littering the field, the Alamanni retreated back to Germany's wild lands. For Julian the triumph was important, both as a military and as a political achievement.

argentus   A Roman silver coin. As part of the reform of the COINAGE, Diocletian in 296 C.E. issued a new silver coin, designed to restore the status of the denarius. This new currency resembled the denarius but came to be known as the *argentus*. Its popularity was such that it replaced the *antonianus* and was minted well into the reign of Julian II.

Arianism   A major heresy that confronted the Christian Church in the fourth century; it posited that Christ is not truly divine but created by God. Arianism took its name from ARIUS (260–336), the heretical priest of Alexandria who formulated its principles and doctrines. A major influence upon the heresy of Arianism was the prevailing pantheistic views of the Hellenic culture.

The doctrinal origins of Arianism can be traced in part to the theories of the theologian Lucian of Alexandria. The doctrine itself set forth a view of the nature of Christ rooted in the Aristotelian concept of unity, negating division and its excessive application to the conception of God. In its understanding of the divine being, Arianism denied the possibility of an active unity in more than one person. As advanced by Arius, then, the unoriginatedness and the unchangeability of the Father made the Logos (Son) necessarily a creation by the will of the Father. In breaking with the subordinationist tradition of the preceding centuries, Arius asserted that the Logos did not participate in creation and was created out of nothing; one of the most controversial tenets of the heresy was that "there was a time when the Son was not."

A conspicuous student of Lucian of Alexandria, the Alexandrian presbyter Arius began around 318 to preach this doctrine that was alarming to his ecclesiastical superiors. As Arius enunciated himself more clearly, he was commanded to silence by his superior, Bishop Alexander of Alexandria. When Arius refused, he was condemned and excommunicated by a synod at Alexandria. Despite his condemnation, however, the heresy continued to spread, ultimately becoming a crisis of such proportions that Emperor CONSTANTINE THE GREAT felt compelled to intervene and attempt to find a resolution. The emperor convened the Council of Nicaea (325) where the anti-Arian party, under the guidance of Athanasius, then a deacon of Alexandria, secured an orthodox definition of the faith and the use of the term *homoousios* (of one substance with) in describing Christ's relationship with God. The Nicene Creed became a powerful refutation of Arian doctrine and began establishing the specifics of crafting a specific language for Christology. The council also exiled a number of Arian prelates, most notably Eusebius of Nicomedia.

While clearly successful in stressing orthodox Christian teaching, Nicaea did not resolve the controversy. Though he was not an Arian, Constantine gradually relaxed his anti-Arian position under the influence of his sister, Constantia, who had certain Arian sympathies, so that Eusebius and others were allowed to return to favor. Eusebius earned the trust of the emperor, and Arian prelates began working for the defeat of the Nicene cause. At the behest of Eusebius of Nicomedia, Constantine attempted to bring Arius back to Constantinople (334–335) and restore him to orthodox favor, but he died while en route in 336. Meanwhile, the Arian party was slowly gaining the upper hand, turning its ire toward their dedicated enemy, Athanasius, now bishop of Alexandria, and Eustathius of Antioch. Athanasius soon faced his first expulsion at Arian hands from his see. The saint, bishop, and theologian subsequently endured severe hardships and is honored by the church not only for his forbearance but his heroic opposition to the heresy even in the face of daunting odds and genuine dangers to his life.

Emperor Constantine died in 337, and the Arians found a dedicated adherent in his successor in the East, Constantius II (r. 337–361). In the West, meanwhile, thanks to the labors of the bishops of Rome and the vast majority of orthodox bishops, Arianism never found a firm foothold.

Starting in 341, however, the Arian adherents gained ascendancy in the Eastern Empire, using a series of councils to establish themselves and to refute Nicaea and the doctrines of *homoousios,* among others. Opposition was so staunch in the West that both Constantius II and his colleague in the Western Empire, Constans (r. 340–350), convened the Council of Sardica in 343. Constans died in 350 and Constantius became sole emperor, an event that heralded a new outbreak of Arianism in the empire and severe persecutions of Catholics who refused to embrace the heterodox doctrine. In 359, the Arians convened the councils of Seleucia and Ariminum and there secured their greatest doctrinal triumph. In perceiving the extent of the danger to the church, St. Jerome wrote that it made the "world groan and wonder to find itself Arian."

At the height of its influence, the Arian party was unable to maintain its unity. Several groups emerged within the Arian cause: the Anomoeans, the most radical, who had favored a sharp difference between the Father and the Son; Homoians, the moderate party; and the Semi-Arians, the Homoiousians, who preferred the theological term *homoiousios* (of similar substance) and stressed the similarities and differences between the Son and Father.

Even as the Arians began to lose their cohesion, theologians in the church became a bulwark against them. The papacy proved a major force in this opposition, but equally important were the great Cappadocians: Gregory Nazianzus, Basil of Caesarea, and Gregory of Nyssa. These renowned theologians gave a firm refutation to Arianism and assisted greatly the doctrinal defeat of the Arian cause. Constantius died in 361, depriving Arianism of its foremost patron. Under Emperor VALENTINIAN (r. 364–375), orthodox Christianity was reestablished in the West and in the East, creating the atmosphere for the final defeat of the Arians.

The inevitable demise of the Arian cause can be dated in practical terms from the death of Emperor VALENS at the disastrous battle of ADRIANOPLE in 378. An ardent Arian, Valens was succeeded on the imperial throne in the East by THEODOSIUS I, a devout orthodox Christian. Theodosius and his co-emperor, Gratian, began moving the empire toward a permanent reinstatement of the faith. Their labors were completed at the Council of Constantinople in 381 that repudiated Arianism, reinstated the Nicene Creed, and reunified the divided Antiochene Church. Through the promulgation of the Nicene-Constantinople Creed, the council achieved the final defeat of Arianism in both the Eastern and Western parts of the church.

The later history of the heresy was centered in the Germanic peoples. The tribes who eventually helped to destabilize and finally overthrow the Roman Empire in the West were most receptive to the cultural influence of the Roman Empire and were also easily enticed by the seemingly straightforward and simple creed of Arianism. Of the Arian figures who had contact with the Germans, the most famous was St. Ulfilas, who preached among the Goths. The Arian Vandal tribes established for themselves a kingdom in North Africa and often persecuted Catholics both there and in Spain. The Vandal Kingdom, the last Arian stronghold in the West, was brought to an end in 534 C.E. by the armies of Emperor JUSTINIAN under the famous general Belisarius.

Ariarathes X of Cappadocia (d. 36 B.C.E.) *A king who ruled from 42 B.C.E. and was one of the last of the Priestly-Kings of Cappadocia*

Antony found Ariarathes an unreliable client in the East. In 36 B.C.E., during the Parthian War, Ariarathes sided with Parthia, aided by Antiochus I of Commagene. For this refusal to aid Rome, Ariarathes was driven from the throne and replaced by the more accommodating Archelaus. The deposed king was taken away and executed.

Ariobarzanes III (d. 42 B.C.E.) *King of Cappadocia and ally of Julius Caesar in his civil war with Pompey the Great*
After the battle of PHARSALUS in 48 B.C.E., Caesar gave Ariobarzanes a slice of Armenia, thus removing the territory from the control of King Deoitarus of Galatia. Later that year the Cappadocian king joined Caesar's lieutenant, Calvinus, in his attempt to defeat the rebellious ruler of Cimmerian Bosporus, Pharnaces. Loyalty was not enough to prevent defeat at Nicopolis in October. Ariobarzanes was present at the battle of Zela (in May 47), when Caesar defeated Pharnaces, and received another portion of Armenia for his efforts. Still loyal to Caesar, in 42 Ariobarzanes refused to settle with Cassius and Brutus in their civil war, and was subsequently arrested and killed by Cassius. He was succeeded by ARIARATHES X.

Ariobarzanes of Media (d. c. 4 C.E.) *Ruler of Media Atropatene*
Ariobarzanes was given Armenia in 4 C.E. by Augustus, at the request of that nation's people and following the murder of the tyrannical Artaxes II by his courtiers. Augustus found in Ariobarzanes a loyal client-king and used the Mede as a key element in his Asian policy. In 1 or 2 C.E., King Tigranes of Armenia was killed in battle, probably with his own people. His queen Erato abdicated, and Gaius Caesar, the son of Augustus, proposed to hand Armenia to Ariobarzanes as well. The Armenians, fiery and proud, refused to have a foreigner rule them, especially a Mede, and they revolted under the leadership of a man named Addon. Gaius reduced the city of Artagira, and Ariobarzanes was made king of Armenia. According to Tacitus, the Armenians eventually came to respect the Mede because of his noble person and spirit. Unfortunately, Ariobarzanes died after a short time and his son Artavasdes was quickly killed.

Ariogaesus (d. after 173 C.E.) *King of the Quadi*
Ariogaesus faced Emperor MARCUS AURELIUS on the Danube. In 172–173, the tribes of the Iazyges and Quadi assisted one another in rebelling against Rome. The Quadi broke all treaties with Rome and in 173 ousted their king, Furtius, replacing him with the chieftain Ariogaesus. Marcus Aurelius refused to recognize Ariogaesus or to negotiate any new treaties, despite the assurances of the Quadi. A reward of 1,000 gold pieces was offered by Rome for Ariogaesus's capture, and 500 gold pieces for his head. Within a short time the king of the Quadi was in the hands of the Romans, but Marcus Aurelius did not

execute him. In keeping with his philosophical policies, the emperor exiled Ariogaesus to Alexandria, where he spent the rest of his days.

Ariovistus (fl. 71–58 B.C.E.) *King of the Suebi and one of the most successful leaders in the era of Julius Caesar*
The Suebi invaded Gaul in 71 B.C.E., crossing the Rhine and defeating the Aedui. These actions and the subsequent victory of Ariovistus, commanding the German forces at Magetobriga (where he defeated a combined Gallic army) in 61 B.C.E., were followed by his request to Rome for official recognition as a rightful king.

The Senate, influenced by the proconsul of Transalpine Gaul, Metellus Celer, and by Julius Caesar (according to the GALLIC WARS), declared Ariovistus a "friend of Rome." Clearly, Ariovistus was considered a counterbalance to the dangerous Gallic tribes; however, when he began to demonstrate further ambitions in the west, Caesar was forced to reconsider this policy. The petitions of the Aedui, sent in 58, convinced the Senate that these Germans occupying the lush Alsace region were too great a threat.

In the summer of 58, Caesar launched his campaign, with about 50,000 men. Ariovistus had an army of almost 75,000. The two generals parried with one another for a time, but Caesar crushed the Germans on September 10, somewhere in Alsace. Ariovistus apparently died sometime later; Dio stated that he escaped over the Rhine.

Aristides, Aelius (Publius Aelius Aristides Theodorus) (117–181 C.E.) *Writer, rhetorician, and adherent of Asclepius, who was a gifted speaker and author*
His career in politics could have been remarkable, but Aristides suffered a series of terrible illnesses, thought by some to have been psychosomatic.

He was born in Adriani in Mysia and studied the classics under Alexander of Cotiaeon, the tutor of Marcus Aurelius, and also studied rhetoric with Herodes Atticus. Rhetoric became his chosen profession, and he traveled to Athens, Egypt, and Rome to continue his studies. While in Rome he wrote and delivered a powerful panegyric to the city, the wonder of the world.

Finding a receptive audience, Aristides could have achieved the greatness of such contemporaries as Herodes Atticus, Cornelius Fronto, and the earlier sophist, Palaemon. Instead, Aristides succumbed to the first of many illnesses, the exact cause and nature of which were never fully clarified. His public career was lost, and he retired to Asia Minor, settling in Smyrna, where he began to write. He was prolific, composing essays, addresses, histories, and religious teachings. He attacked Plato's views on rhetoric and devoted great effort to espousing the creed of Asclepius.

Contemporary medicine offered him little relief from his attacks, but at Pergamum, the Asclepieum gave Aris-

tides desperately needed help, and there a series of visions also confirmed his faith. His *Sacred Teachings,* which examined the beneficence of his cure, was written in six books and is the main source of interest concerning his visionary compositions, also providing a view of the medical practices of his own era.

See also MEDICINE; RHETORIC; SOPHISTRY.

Aristobulus (late third century C.E.) *Praetorian prefect in the reign of Emperor Carinus*
Aristobulus was maintained in his position by Diocletian in 284, despite his having served as co-prefect of the Guard with the infamous Arrius Aper. His tenure as commander of the Praetorians was brief, however, lasting only 13 months. Diocletian moved him to Africa, sometime around 290, where he served as proconsul before assuming duties as prefect of the city (*praefecti urbi*) of Rome in 295.

Aristobulus II (d. 48 B.C.E.) *King of Judaea and one of the two sons of Queen Salome Alexandra of Judaea*
Aristobulus II became high priest and king of Judaea in 67 B.C.E. He was born into the intrigue-filled world of the Palestinian royal houses and grew up during the spiteful reign of Salome, the widow of Jannaeus Alexander, the first priest-king of the Jewish lands. In 67, Salome died, and Aristobulus drove his brother Hyrcanus from the throne. As a result, Antipater of Idumaea, an ally of Hyrcanus, convinced Aretas III, the king of Nabataeans, to invest Jerusalem. Aristobulus took refuge in the Great Temple, watching his siege defenses deteriorate. He was saved by the arrival of Pompey the great and his Roman legions. The combatants on both sides, recognizing Roman superiority, made every effort to gain Pompey's favor.

Hyrcanus was easily swayed, but Aristobulus, fiery to the end, refused to submit so calmly. The Great Temple was put under siege, and finally, in 63, Aristobulus was sent to Rome in chains. His followers were undaunted, however, and civil war raged for several years.

Antipater, deciding which side to aid in the Roman civil war that erupted between Caesar and Pompey, chose Pompey. Aristobulus, aware of the situation in Rome, put himself at Caesar's command. Sometime in 48, he marched into Judaea to cause trouble but was killed before he could be of any worth to Caesar. His son, Mattathiah Antigonus, would try to gain the throne in 40 B.C.E., with the same dire results; his other son, Alexander, married his daughter to Herod the Great.

Aristobulus and Alexander (d. 7 B.C.E.) *Two sons of Herod the Great by his second wife, Mariamne, the daughter of Alexander and granddaughter of Aristobulus II*
As young men, Aristobulus and Alexander were designated as heirs and in 23 B.C.E. were sent to Rome to be educated. They returned in 17 for political marriages but

soon became trapped in the ever perilous domestic squabbles of the House of Herod.

The chief rival facing Alexander and Aristobulus was Antipater, the son of Herod by his first wife, Doris. Rumors and warnings of plots filled Herod's ears, all prompted by Antipater and his allies, and Herod soon demanded that his two designated heirs be tried for treason. Augustus tolerated their trial in 12 but achieved a reconciliation among the family members before any verdict could be reached. In 7 B.C.E. Herod demanded another trial, and this time Augustus agreed. The result of the trial was the death of Aristobulus and Alexander, prompting Augustus to remark that it was safer to be one of Herod's pigs than one of his sons.

Aristophanes (fl. mid-fourth century C.E.) *Government official whose career was saved from disgrace by his friend, the orator Libianus*
Aristophanes was the son of Menander, a leading citizen of Corinth. He learned oratory and philosophy in Athens before returning home. A relative, Flavius Eugenius, laid claim to his inheritance; unable to use legal means to recover his losses, Aristophanes moved to Syria. There, before 357 and through the good graces of the pagan philosopher, Fortunatianus, he became an *agens-in-rebus*, working for the government. In 357, Aristophanes was transferred to Egypt, but in 358 his fortunes changed considerably when Parnasius was named prefect of the province. In 359, both Parnasius and Aristophanes were brought before Modestus at Scythopolis on charges of treason and witchcraft. Aristophanes was fined and exiled for three years until, in 362, Libianus begged Emperor Julian to reinstate him. Convinced by the pleas and impressed by the fact that Aristophanes was a pagan (something that Julian found pleasing) he gave Aristophanes the post of governor, most likely in Macedonia.

See REBUS, AGENTES IN.

Arius (260–336 C.E.) *Heretical theologian, a priest of Alexandria and the founder of the most important heretical doctrine faced by the early Christian Church, Arianism*
Arius was born most likely in Libya. His education ranged from the study of the theologian Origen (who had a tremendous influence on his thinking) to a direct tutelage under Lucian of Antioch, then a leading presbyter of the Eastern Church. Arius became a priest in Alexandria and in 319 began to voice his views on the nature of Christ. Furor and outrage quickly gripped the church as a result, and the tremendous Arian controversy began. Emperor CONSTANTINE called together the Council of Nicaea, where Arius was condemned and exiled to Illyricum. The popularity of his doctrines, however, infected the Eastern episcopacy, and many of the bishops protected him, both physically and politically.

That Arianism gained a firm foothold in the minds of fourth-century religious and political leaders was demonstrated by Constantine's attempts to bring Arius back to Constantinople in 334–335, through the good graces of Eusebius, the bishop of Nicomedia. Fortunately for the principal opponents of the doctrine (Athanasius, Alexander of Alexandria and most of the Western Church), Arius died while en route. Few of his works are extant, and these are mainly fragments of his doctrinal presentations and some letters.

See also CHRISTIANITY.

Arles Called the "Mother of all Gauls"; the city in Gallia Narbonensis that was one of the permanent metropolises of the province and the empire. Founded by Julius Caesar in 46 B.C.E., Arles, like much of southern Gaul, was quickly Romanized, both through construction and architecture and in the placement of *coloniae* (Roman colonists). During the age of Augustus (27 B.C.E.–14 C.E.) extensive building programs were initiated in Arles, most of which are still extant. Water mills were created at Barbegal, just outside of the city, and Arles boasted a number of architectural masterpieces within its limits.

There was a hippodrome and a theater, constructed later in the first century B.C.E. The architect REBURRUS designed the amphitheater in a fashion similar to his amphitheater at Nîmes. Situated on the Rhone River, some 45 miles from the Mediterranean, Arles developed into a major economic center. It was a gateway for merchants traveling by land from Italy to Spain, and was accessible to sea traffic by a canal. By the second century C.E., Arles had replaced Massilia as the leading port of trade along the Gallic coast, and maintained this importance well into the late period of the empire.

With barbarian invasions commonplace in the fifth century C.E., the city was of administrative value because it was close to the direct lines of communications with Italy and was far enough south to remain a key element in defensive operational plans. The prefect of Gaul maintained his watch from there, and eventually a mint was established in the city. Mirroring its power base, the church in Arles was powerful and ambitious, aspiring to acquire other sees (or dioceses) in Gallia Narbonensis. In 417, Pope Zosimus gave the bishop of Arles permission to consecrate the bishops of neighboring episcopacies. Pope Boniface and Pope Celestine revoked this authority, which had made Arles supreme, and Pope Leo reduced the powers that had been held normally. Two councils of the church were held there, one in 314 and the other circa 450.

See also GALLIA.

Armenia and Armenia Minor Territory located to the east of ASIA MINOR, between the Caspian Sea and Black Sea; the focal point of struggles between the Roman

Empire and the empires of the Persians and Parthians. The country was divided geographically by the Euphrates River, and the Armenians were distributed in two regions: Armenia Minor and Armenia Major. Armenia Minor was between Pontus and Cappadocia, while across the great river, Armenia Major extended along part of the wide Parthian frontier. This area was of vital importance to Rome; Armenia Major was the more familiar territory.

For centuries the Caucasian-descended Armenians governed themselves, but the Greek Seleucid dynasty came to rule the country as heir to the Persian Empire. In 189 B.C.E., the Seleucid hold was broken, and an Armenian king controlled Armenia Major. This lasted until the time of King TIGRANES I, who allied himself with his father-in-law, Mithridates VI, the great king of Pontus who had fashioned his domain into one of the greatest kingdoms in Asia and who fought the third Mithridatic War (75–65 B.C.E.).

Following the victory of General Lucullus at Cabira in 72 B.C.E., Mithridates lost Pontus and fled into Armenia. Tigranes refused to yield to the Romans and was himself invaded and broken at Tigranocerta in 69 B.C.E. Lucullus was forced by the hardships of the campaign to withdraw, but Pompey soon arrived and all of Armenia was subdued. Armenia Major was henceforth to be a protectorate, a client state answerable to Rome, while Armenia Minor was attached to Cappadocia.

The next year brought the Armenians into the middle of wider global politics as Rome and the Arsacids fought for control of Asia. Marc ANTONY invaded the Parthian Empire through Armenia in 36 B.C.E. but was repulsed in 34. Artavasdes I of Armenia revolted against his former ally, and Antony crushed the entire country, making it a Roman province. Parthian ambitions were powerful, however; around 30 B.C.E., PHRAATES IV of Parthia reconquered the territory and placed Artaxes on the throne.

Augustus recognized the need for a strong frontier defense and, in or around 20 B.C.E. and as part of his broad peace pact with the Arsacids (see ARSACID DYNASTY), he sent Tiberius into Armenia with legions. Following the murder of Artaxes by his own people, Tigranes was crowned king of Armenia.

The Roman emperors maintained a policy of client kingdoms that were dependent upon Rome but not directly under Roman rule, thus acting as buffers to the enemy. Emperor GAIUS CALIGULA summoned MITHRIDATES I of Armenia to Rome circa 41 C.E., and for no reason threw him into prison and then forced him into exile. Parthia, taking advantage of the situation, moved quickly against Armenia. Emperor Claudius, in 42 or 43, sent Mithridates back to his homeland, where, with Roman assistance, he regained the throne. Nero tried to place a number of doomed pretenders on the throne of Armenia, men such as Tigranes V in 60 C.E., who was quickly deposed by the Parthians. Finally, in 66, Nero officially gave the kingdom to an Arsacid supposedly loyal to Rome: Tiridates. This king played the role of manipulator, paying slight loyalty to Rome while maintaining good relations with his Parthian associates and his brother Vologases I, the king of Parthia.

Tiridates accentuated the general unreliability of Rome's clients, a problem that had only one ultimate solution, adopted by Trajan during his Eastern Campaign of 113–117. Armenia was overrun, Chosroes of Parthia lost Mesopotamia and his capital, Ctesiphon. Armenia was proclaimed a province, garrisoned with Roman troops and ruled by a king who was closely watched. Control was easier with possession of Mesopotamia, but in the third century Rome began to lose its dominance in the East. This weakening led to changes.

The Sassanid destroyers of the Arsacids in Persia immediately initiated ambitious policies. Shapur I, the son of the dynasty's founder, Ardashir, was defeated by Timesitheus, the Praetorian prefect of Gordian III, but the next emperor, Philip the Arab, concluded a peace, reestablishing the old borders at the Euphrates.

Armenia was to be independent, meaning under Roman domination. In 296, Diocletian signed a treaty with Narses, the Sassanid king, giving all Armenia to Rome as a protectorate.

Armenia adopted Christianity very quickly, although the Sassanids did not tolerate its presence during their eras of influence. Christianization was inevitable, given the trade routes that went through Armenia. The kingdom remained under Roman control until 387, when, by agreement, the Sassanids took half, thus allowing a strategic balance. So it remained for nearly three centuries.

Armenia Minor was never so hotly contested. Adhering to the policy of client state buffers, Roman political figures from Pompey to Gaius Caligula, placed various non-Roman claimants on the throne.

RULERS OF ARMENIA MINOR

Deiotorus of Galatia   given throne by Pompey.

Pharnaces   usurped the throne.

Ariobarzanes of Cappadocia   given throne by Julius Caesar in 47 B.C.E.

Polemo of Pontus   given throne by Marc Antony circa 37 B.C.E.

Artavasdes of Media   given throne by Augustus circa 30 B.C.E.

Archelaus of Cappadocia   replaced Artavasdes in 20 B.C.E.

Cotys, grandson of Polemo   given throne by Gaius Caligula in 38 C.E.

Aristobulus, son of Herod of Chalcis   given throne by Nero in 54 C.E.

In 72 C.E., as part of his general reorganization of the empire, Vespasian seized Armenia Minor and placed it under direct Roman supervision. Henceforth Armenians living west of the Euphrates were part of the province of Cappadocia. Dio and Tacitus, along with Strabo, commented on the Armenians themselves. They were a proud people, caught up in the struggles of rival empires. Thus they were wavering in their allegiance and unreliable. Christianity, however, imbedded the concept of nationalism among the people, a factor that no occupying power could suppress with lasting success.

See also ARTAXATA and other individual rulers and imperial and senatorial provinces.

Arminius (Hermann) (d. 19 C.E.) *Prince of the Cherusci and one of Germanic folklore's greatest heroes*

Responsible in 9 C.E. for one of the worst defeats ever inflicted on the Roman legions, Arminius served as an auxiliary of the Roman army but remained loyal to his own tribe. In 7 C.E., VARUS was placed in command of the three legions posted to Germany, with the intention of Romanizing the entire area. These plans were proceeding successfully when, in 9 C.E., Varus advanced to the Weser River, heading to a Roman fort at Aliso.

Arminius, who had previously voiced no opposition to Rome, suddenly led his people and nearly all of the Germanic tribes in revolt. Varus marched his three legions through the rough, impenetrable terrain of the Teutoburg Forest of Lower Saxony, and there he encountered the determined enemy. Nearly 20,000 men were killed in one disastrous episode. Even in the Punic Wars, Rome had never witnessed such a debacle. Imperial policy over the Rhine territory would never recover, and Germany was lost as a province forever. Six years later the gifted Roman general, GERMANICUS, mounted an expedition against the CHATTI, while Arminius was beset with troubles of his own. The Cherusci were divided into two uneven camps because of a quarrel between Arminius and his father-in-law, Segestes. (Arminius had stolen his daughter, although she was betrothed to another man.) Segestes was subsequently besieged by Arminius, and Germanicus, seizing the opportunity offered to him, marched to Segestes's rescue. The Roman pursued Arminius, dispatching his deputy, Aulus Severus Caecina, with 40 cohorts, ahead of him.

Arminius turned to fight, and a general battle followed, with victory to the Romans. The German leader escaped, but four years later, in an attempt to regain his power, he was killed by treachery. Arminius was intensely popular during his days of victory but was hated in his later years, despite his pivotal role in the liberation of Germania.

armor   See LEGIONS.

army   See LEGIONS.

Arria the Elder (d. 43 C.E.) *Wife of the consul Caecina Paetus, who killed herself when her husband was condemned to death by Claudius*

In 42, Furius Camillus Scribonianus, the governor of Dalmatia, attempted to stir a revolt in the legions of the province. He failed, and the hunt started immediately for his fellow conspirators. Caecina Paetus, consul in 37, was one of the plotters. Paetus was captured and brought in chains to Rome. Arria, refused permission to travel at his side, found a way to follow him. When her husband's death was certain, Arria took a dagger, plunged it into her chest, took it out and handed it to Paetus with the famous words: "It does not hurt, Paetus." Pliny wrote of her in one of his *Letters.*

Arria the Younger (d. after 69 C.E.) *Roman widow and exile*

Daughter of Arria, wife of Caecina Paetus, the younger Arria was married to Thrasea Paetus, a senator and an eventual victim of Nero's abuses in 66 C.E. Forced to commit suicide, Thrasea used every argument possible to convince his wife not to join him, as her mother had joined her husband in death. Eventually surrendering to his wishes, Arria watched her husband die and then endured years in exile. In 69, she had the satisfaction of seeing Nero fall, at which time she was returned from exile.

Arrian (Flavius Arrianus) (fl. second century C.E.) *Historian, governor, consul, and Stoic*

Arrian's most vital work was the *Anabasis,* a history of Alexander that is, arguably, the most detailed extant history of the Macedonian kings. Born in Bithynia around 90 C.E., Arrian received an education and showed a talent for Stoicism. He learned philosophy from the famous Epictetus and preserved his teacher's words and lessons in his *Discourses.*

A political career soon followed. Arrian served as consul in 129 and was sent by Hadrian in 134 to serve as governor of Cappadocia. During his term the Alans invaded the region but were repulsed through his efforts. The rest of his achievements were in the literary field. Arrian wrote in Greek, admiring and imitating the style of Xenophon. He penned a now-lost *History of Parthia,* a chronicle of Alexander's successors, *Indike,* a compilation of details from Nearchus and Megasthenes, and possibly a military treatise. None of these, however, could compare with his *Anabasis.* Relying upon the sources of Ptolemy I and Aristobulus, Arrian created a detailed account of Alexander's campaigns. He died during the reign of Marcus Aurelius.

Arsacid dynasty

The rulers of Parthia who dominated the Near East from Syria to India, from 250 B.C.E. to 226 C.E. For nearly 500 years the Arsacids were the second greatest power in the Mediterranean world, vying with Rome for supremacy and influence in the East. They were broken finally by the Sassanids, a new and more vital dynasty led by ARDASHIR I, but only after 37 rulers had sat upon the Arsacid throne.

Around 250 B.C.E., Arsaces, a lord of Parthia, led a revolt against Antiochus II of Syria, destroying his enemy and declaring himself the king of Parthia. From then on the dynasty acquired territories to the east and the west. Arsaces handed the throne to his brother, Tiridates, around 248 B.C.E., upon his death. In his honor Tiridates assumed the title of *Arsaces*.

Despite attacks from Antiochus the Great of Syria, by 210 B.C.E. the Arsacids were a legitimate power. Ambitious, the Parthians involved themselves as far as India itself. In the West, the Arsacid rivalry with Rome was long and bitter. Although in 92 B.C.E. Mithridates II sent an ambassador to Sulla in Rome, wars were commonplace. The Arsacids had their share of victories.

Crassus was annihilated by the Parthian general Surenas at Carrhae in 53 B.C.E., trumpeting a see-saw struggle that raged over Syria, Mesopotamia and Armenia for the next 33 years. Arsacid attempts to seize Syria met with failure. Marc Antony's invasion in 36–34 B.C.E. was repulsed, but civil wars weakened the Parthian position, making a common peace desirable.

Augustus (ruled 27 B.C.E.–14 C.E.) was responsible for the treaty of peace, but the leverage he used on Phraates was the fact that Tiridates, a usurper, had fled the country and had gone to Rome with Phraates's younger son. Here was one of the great handicaps of the Arsacid system: intrigues and dynastic usurpation, which weakened both the succession and the dynasty's hold over far-flung territories. Rome was able to influence the placement of Parthian rulers. The Median King Artabanus, who came to the throne in 16 C.E., was a foreigner, fathering a line of kings that once more fought with Rome.

The later wars were disasters for Parthia. Domitius Corbulo, the commander of the East, in 63 C.E. defeated Vologases I and his brother Tiridates, in Armenia. In 113 C.E., another Roman invasion, under the command of Trajan, routed the forces of Oroses. The capital of Ctesiphon was captured, and Mesopotamia and Assyria were reduced.

Hadrian, in 177 C.E., returned most of the captured territories as part of his policy of establishing stable frontiers. The last great expansionist attempt took place in 162–165 C.E., when Vologases III was defeated by the co-Emperor Lucius Verus (realistically, by his general, Avidius Cassius). Ctesiphon was captured, and a ransom was paid to buy back the kingdom, although much of Mesopotamia was lost.

Subsequently, the Arsacids allowed considerable autonomy on the part of their client kings. In 224 C.E., Ardashir, king of Persia, rose up and conquered the neighboring client states, and Artabanus V rode to quell the rebellion. Ardashir routed Artabanus in a terrible battle, slaying the Arsacid king. As a result, Ardashir founded the Sassanids, and the dynasty of the Arsacids ended.

As the descendants of the Achaemenids, and thus Medes, the Arsacids maintained the Persian influenced system of government and lifestyle in their domain. They possessed satrapies, which the Persians had adopted as their mode of territorial administration, and ruled from Ecbatana and Ctesiphon. Ultimately, however, the lack of a clear, defined dynastic character prompted the stagnation that made the rise of a more truly Persian rule possible.

THE ARSACID KINGS

Arsaces	c. 250–248 B.C.E.
Tiridates	c. 248–227 B.C.E.
Artabanus	c. 211 (208)–191 B.C.E.
Priapitius	c. 191–176 B.C.E.
Phraates	c. 176–171 B.C.E.
Mithridates	c. 171–138 B.C.E.
Phraates II	c. 138–128 or 129 B.C.E.
Artabanus	c. 128 or 129 B.C.E.–124 B.C.E.
Himerus	c. 128–123 B.C.E.
Mithridates II	c. 124–87 B.C.E.
Gotarzes I	c. 90–87 B.C.E.
Unknown	c. 86–85 B.C.E.
Orodes I	c. 80–77 B.C.E.
Sinatrukes	c. 76–69 B.C.E.
Phraates III	c. 70–57 B.C.E.
Orodes II	c. 57–56 B.C.E.
Mithridates III	c. 56–55 B.C.E.
Orodes II	c. 55–38 B.C.E.
Phraates IV	c. 38–2 B.C.E.
Tiridates II	c. 30–25 B.C.E.
Phraataces	c. 2 B.C.E.–4 C.E.
Orodes III	c. 4–7 C.E.
Vonones	c. 7–12 C.E.
Artabanus III	c. 12–38 C.E.
Gotarzes II	c. 38 C.E.
Vardanes	c. 38–47 C.E.
Gotarzes II	c. 47–51 C.E.
Vonones II	c. 51 C.E.
Vologases	c. 51–80 C.E.
Artabanus IV	c. 80–81 C.E.
Pacorus	c. 79–114 C.E.
Osroes	c. 114–122 C.E.
Vologases II	c. 105–147 C.E.
Mithridates IV	c. 128–147 C.E.
Vologases III	c. 149–192 C.E.
Vologases IV	c. 192–207 C.E.
Vologases V	c. 207–224 C.E. (?)
Artabanus V	c. 224–226 C.E.
Artavasdes	c. 226 C.E.

Arsinoe (1) (d. 41 B.C.E.) *A daughter of King Ptolemy XII Auletes and sister of Queen Cleopatra VII and King Ptolemy XIII*

Arsinoe, one in a long line of "Arsinoes" in the Ptolemic dynasty, was involved in the palace intrigues gripping the royal house when Julius Caesar arrived in Alexandria in 48 B.C.E. In the subsequent siege and intense political maneuverings that took place, Arsinoe at first found herself overmatched by her far more skilled sister, Cleopatra; she became a prisoner in the palace.

Arsinoe did manage to escape, however, and then moved to better her position politically. She allied herself with the general of the Egyptian forces, Achillas, but when his loyalty became suspect, she had him killed. Her gamble failed, for Caesar overcame the siege, won the battle of the Nile over Ptolemy III and returned to Alexandria in triumph. Broken, Arsinoe was sent to Italy, where she was part of Caesar's triumph in Rome in 46 B.C.E.

Subsequently returned to Alexandria, Arsinoe lived a dangerous existence. Cleopatra vowed her death but had to wait until Marc Antony acquiesced.

Arsinoe (2) Name given to several Egyptian towns after the royal women named Arsinoe in Egyptian-Ptolemaic history. Two were considered preeminent.

Arsinoe (Heroöpolites) was built (date uncertain) along the Suez Gulf in Lower Egypt, specifically along the Sinus Heropolites or western branch of the Red Sea. It was noted in the early empire for its manufacturing of popular garments.

Arsinoe (Kiman Fares), called Shedyet by the Egyptians, was a substantial city in the Faiyum region of Middle Egypt. For many years Shedyet was the seat of the cult of the crocodile and was called Crocodilopolis. In 215 C.E., the Romans introduced the worship of Jupiter Capitolinus. There are a number of ruins to be found there, including a New Kingdom temple of Ramesses II and Ptolemic temple.

See also RELIGIONS.

art and architecture

ART

The Augustan Age (27 B.C.E.–14 C.E.)
With the dawn of the empire, Roman art revealed a strong Latin influence and embodied AUGUSTUS's vision of imperial grandeur. The greatest example of contemporary sculpture was the Ara Pacis (Altar of Peace), with its relief sculpture glorifying the success of the empire and pictorially augmenting the written record of Augustus's triumphs, RES GESTAE DIVI AUGUSTUS. Built around 10 B.C.E., the altar precinct was part of the CAMPUS MARTIUS complex. Its carvings depict the imperial pageants of the Praetorians, the Vestals and members of the citizenry. The entire design celebrates Augustus, but he is not represented as superhuman; he is part of the procession, not its focal point.

Under Augustus, considerable effort was put into decorating and beautifying altars. A kind of artistic practice emerged in the painting of these altars, best typified by the work preserved in the volcanic ash of Mount Vesuvius at POMPEII, which was buried in the eruption of 79 C.E. The surviving artistic record at Pompeii has allowed historians to discern four general styles of painting, Styles I–IV. These styles are often applied broadly to Roman art. Style III was the most common school of art from the reigns of Augustus and TIBERIUS, continuing through the eras of CALIGULA and even NERO. It is marked by a disdain for realistic perspective, and an emphasis on scale.

Nero to Hadrian (54–117 C.E.)
With the reign of Nero another style of Roman painting, identified generally as Style IV, came into vogue. Style IV relies upon brilliant colors and profuse ornamentation, and is a combination of the previous two styles, synthesizing the abstract qualities of Style III with the more realistic architectural details of Style II. It was during this period that several painters flourished, of whom PRISCUS ATTIUS and Cornelius PINUS were most notable. VESPASIAN used them to decorate the Temple of Honos and Virtus.

The FLAVIANS were the great patrons of Style IV, which, because of its links to Republicanism (Style II), was well received given the more practical attitudes of the later period. The height of painting came just a few years before the Flavians, however, in the works of FORMULUS, who was commissioned by Nero to paint the entire GOLDEN HOUSE, the opulent and excessive imperial palace.

In the provinces, Roman styles were copied by all local artists. An obvious attempt at imitation was demonstrated in the decorative motifs in AQUILEIA. In Gaul, at VIENNE, a number of similar efforts survive but a general scarcity of actual works from the period make a true analysis difficult, even in Italy.

Hadrian (117–138 C.E.)
For some centuries the Hellenic world had been eclipsed by Rome. Artistically, the Greeks heavily influenced Rome, but the styles prevalent in the capital were predominantly Latin. Hadrian's philhellenic tastes changed all that, and he actively patronized Greece. Once more Greek culture was honored, and in art the Latin and Greek styles were incorporated, even as imperial favor ran to the purely Hellenic.

There were several causes for this return to classicism. The empire had expanded to its greatest extent under TRAJAN (97–117 C.E.), and Hadrian inherited a world that embraced many cultures and traditions. A new, outward vision gripped imperial policy, and a rebirth of Greek classicism was part of that intellectual horizon. Under Trajan, Style IV Art, which had begun in the Neronian and Flavian reigns, reached its inevitable conclusion. The reliefs of Trajan's time were beautiful and expressive, particularly the Arch at Beneventum (*see* ARCHES) and, of course, the Column of Trajan (*see* COLUMNS), with their splendid portrayals of the emperor's achievements and his victory over the Dacians. Still, a weakening of the style was inescapable. The revitalizing elements were found in Hadrian's vigor and in his love of the classic style.

Henceforth and until the late empire, Roman art was transformed. The austerity of early sculpture was embellished with classical features. Thus Hadrian's busts and statues displayed a beard and hair more analogous to the age of Pericles than to that of Augustus. This style remained prominent throughout the time of the ANTONINES. Greek artistry was also evident in other forms. For example, a change in burial rites created the sarcophagus as a popular eternal abode for the Romans. Of Egyptian origin, sarcophagi were a testament to the loss of traditional Italian religious notions. The sarcophagi of this era were heavily decorated with reliefs.

Pictorial decoration of a Greek nature spread in Rome and then to the provinces. Examples could be found in Germany and Gaul. But the actual emerging trend exhibited subtle differences. Mosaic artwork used for floors and specific decorations of the second and third centuries belonged entirely to the Roman artisans.

Hadrian's personal life also provided fodder for a specific art movement. The death of his lover ANTINOUS in 130 C.E. caused Hadrian tremendous grief, and he ordered the carving of a series of statues in his honor (as well as a religious cult and a city, which was founded in his name on the Nile). The statues of Antinous came to epitomize the fading glory of the Western Empire. With their idealized proportions, the statues appeared to represent all of the virtues that the empire would need in order to survive.

The Late Empire

From the time of Septimius SEVERUS (193–211) to CONSTANTINE THE GREAT (306–337), official art patronage was concentrated in Rome. These years were ones of much military activity, with a slowly deteriorating social system. Martial scenes dominated painting and relief sculpture. The affairs of the empire influenced the style. When Roman strength waxed, as in the reign of GALLIENUS (c. 253 C.E., who restored Roman military supremacy), art forms reflected Latin characteristics.

Late empire art was still a combination of East and West, but certain trends were evident. Roman sentiment became more nationalistic and decidedly anticlassical. This was a response to the deterioration of the frontiers and the rise of foreign peoples within and outside of the borders. The Greek influence in art fell out of favor. Painting was still popular, and carvings were used on the still popular sarcophagi. Christianity, of course, would

An example of Pompeian-style art. From Herculaneum. *(Courtesy Fr. Felix Just, S.J.)*

lead the empire even further away from its classical heritage.

Beginning with the simple catacomb paintings, Christianity eventually overwhelmed and dominated Western art after the reign of Constantine the Great. The pattern of Roman art, perpetually history-minded and commemorative in nature, functioned alongside remnants of Greek and other provincial elements, but could not maintain its independence. It would reappear in the Middle Ages, and classicism would erupt as a marvelous art form in the Renaissance, but in the late empire it was in decline.

ARCHITECTURE

The Augustan Age

The architecture of the Augustan Age was among the finest in the history of the empire. Rome itself was almost completely rebuilt in this period. Whereas a definite Latin element and remnants of Style II and Republicanism were evident in its painting and sculpture, Rome possessed no such architectural tradition, and building had not been fully organized or of a high quality. SUETONIUS commented that the city was unworthy of its position as capital of the empire. It was, therefore, the privilege of Augustus to determine the style and extent of Rome's reconstruction.

Augustus chose, not surprisingly, the Greeks as a model. Using classicism, the emperor, with the support of Marcus AGRIPPA, built the CURIA (in 29 B.C.E.), the TEMPLE OF DIVUS JULIUS (also in 29 B.C.E.), the TEMPLE OF MARS ULTOR and the TEMPLE OF APOLLO (in 20 B.C.E.), the PANTHEON, new aqueducts (the Aqua Julia and Aqua Virgo) and the Baths of Agrippa. These constructions were only

The exposed floor of Flavian Amphitheater, or Colosseum, one of Rome's greatest architectural achievements *(Courtesy Fr. Felix Just, S.J.)*

a part of the wider Augustan plan for the capital. Eighty-two temples were built or rebuilt, including the great FORUM ROMANUM and FORUM AUGUSTUM.

The Forum Romanum had been greatly expanded by Julius Caesar in 54 B.C.E., but his death put an end to further renovations. Augustus finished the project but increased the prestige of the Forum by installing the greatest buildings of the city and the empire within its confines. Julius Caesar's creation of a basilica was finished by his heir, Augustus, who constructed the BASILICA JULIA (c. 12 B.C.E.), a testament to his grandsons, Gaius and Lucius. It was a prominent part of the Forum, resting opposite the great BASILICA AEMILIA—according to ancient sources, one of the most beautiful structures in Rome.

Rostra (speakers' podiums or lecterns) were built in front of the Temple of Divus Julius and across from it the length of the Forum. Near the first rostra was the excellently carved Arch of Augustus, which was built originally in 29 B.C.E. to commemorate the battle of ACTIUM but was enlarged and made into a triple arch in 19 B.C.E. Augustus's arch stood next to the entrance of the TEMPLE OF CASTOR AND POLLUX (c. 6 C.E.). The last great building

in the Forum Romanum was the TEMPLE OF CONCORD (c. 10 C.E.), located on the Capitoline Hill.

The other great forum was Augustus's own. The Forum Augustum was a long, rectangular-shaped series of structures that was first contemplated in 42 B.C.E. The design was originally to be symmetrical and enclosed, thus realizing the concept of an entire series of buildings as a temple, isolated from the rest of the city. Columns of marble were installed along with statues of prominent Roman figures, from Aeneas, the hero of the Trojan War, to Julius Caesar. The column and statues imbued the Temple of Mars Ultor with color. Mars's temple was in the Corinthian style, and his statue, sword in hand, dominated the building. On either side were statues of Venus and the deified Julius Caesar.

Marble first came into extensive use in the Augustan Age, and the Corinthian style was the dominant architectural form during the empire.

TIBERIUS aided his adoptive father in the continued beautification of Rome, following the death of Marcus Agrippa in 12 B.C.E. In 14 C.E., however, with his accession to the throne, the massive building programs came to an end, although Tiberius did begin the TEMPLE OF DIVUS AUGUSTUS, on the Capitoline Hill. More importantly, two structures were built that displayed the growing centralization of the principate. A palace on the Capitoline replace the old one of Augustus's era, with no expense spared. Then, in 21–22 C.E., at the request of SEJANUS, the prefect of the Praetorian Guard, a permanent barracks for the Guard was placed in the city.

GAIUS CALIGULA followed Tiberius's pattern. He dedicated the Temple of Divus Augustus in 37 C.E. and made grand plans for the palace and a canal through the Isthmus of Corinth. He was killed, and CLAUDIUS, his successor, was far too practical for such projects. Claudius's reign centered architecturally on public building and civil engineering. Aqueducts were built, with fine examples of arches and design, but nothing approached the grandeur or scale of Augustan art. The laudable achievements of Augustus, noted by the famed architect VITRUVIUS and with their emphasis on classicism, were no longer dominant.

Nero to Hadrian

Nero's reign marked a significant change in Roman architecture. Marble faded as the principal construction material, and the use of concrete returned. The DOMUS TRANSITORIA (c. 64 C.E.) was built to connect the various palaces, but was soon destroyed by the great fire of 64. As a result of the conflagration, space was made for the creation of a new palace, the GOLDEN HOUSE. This massive, sprawling complex of suites, parks, and villas was Nero's lasting monument to the architecture of the era and to his own excess.

Such unabashed opulence, among other excesses, helped to bring about Nero's downfall. The Flavians gave the Romans a renewed commitment to sensible rule, and Vespasian went to considerable lengths to placate the citizens of the city and the provinces. Two major architectural undertakings marked that effort: the TEMPLE OF PEACE and the COLOSSEUM. The Temple of Peace was started in 71 C.E. and completed in 75. Designed to commemorate Rome's victory over the Jews, the temple was also a symbolic manifestation that authority and sobriety were once more in effect. The Colosseum was the greatest of the Flavian monumental structures and represented new heights of architectural design and construction.

Later Flavians added to the architectural splendor of the city. TITUS (reigned 79–81 C.E.) built baths, but his less popular brother DOMITIAN (ruled 81–96 C.E. was the one who initiated major works. Domitian was responsible for the Arch of Titus, the Temple of Vespasian on the Capitoline Hill, and a stadium in the Campus Martius. His most notable achievement was on the Palatine Hill, where the architect RABIRIUS designed and built the new imperial palace, the Domus Flavia. With its impressive use of concrete, and of pillars and columns made out of marble, it surpassed Nero's Golden House and became the palace of choice for later emperors. The Domus Flavia

was the culmination of the architectural innovations begun under Nero.

Trajan (ruled 98–117 C.E.) continued them and attempted to pour much of his wealth into construction programs in the city. The great architect of the age was APOLLODORUS of Damascus, and he was responsible for the two major projects of Trajan, the Baths and the Forum. Trajan's Baths, begun in Rome in 104 C.E. and finished in 109, were larger than those of Agrippa, with cross-vaulting and free columns. They were situated on part of the original grounds of Nero's Golden House. Trajan's Forum was an architectural masterpiece. Near the Campus Martius, much of the Quirinal was flattened to accommodate the buildings. The Forum was composed of the huge BASILICA ULPIA (185 feet long), Greek and Latin libraries, and eventually a temple devoted to the divine emperor himself. Also, a column commemorating Trajan's accomplishments was added.

Hadrian
Whereas the greatest architectural works prior to the reign of Hadrian were Roman, in his era they were distributed throughout the empire. Hadrian attempted to build in every province. The importance of Rome faded

The inscription on the Arch of Severus *(Courtesy Fr. Felix Just, S.J.)*

in comparison. Nonetheless, the PANTHEON, though not innovative in style, was one of the most stunning achievements of any age, and Hadrian's palace at TIVOLI was beautiful, large and splendidly suited to the artistic and gifted emperor. It was built between 118 and 134 C.E., and contained courtyards, villas, a Serapeum, baths, a piazza and a library. The influence of Hadrian's world-wide travels was evident in the varied styles upon which the palace was based.

From approximately the time of Trajan, and especially in the reign of Hadrian, Africa was Romanized architecturally. LEPCIS MAGNA, for example, received baths, and building programs in the provinces increased during the late empire. Rome was deemphasized as an artistic or architectural center in direct proportion to imperial aspirations and attention to the rest of the Roman world. Further, the ostentatious styles and imitations of classicism faded in the reawakening of the straightforward Roman or Republican designs. Roman imperial architecture lost vigor in this era, but it was revived in the period following the rule of the Antonines, in the late second century.

The Late Empire

The architecture of the late empire underwent periods of vitality and stagnation, mirroring the political climate of Rome and the empire. Septimius Severus, taking the throne in 193 C.E., ruled Rome with certainty and thus initiated a program of construction both in the city and in his home province of Africa. Rome had been devastated by the fire of 191, and the emperor rebuilt the city, adding to the Palatine palace and creating a new structure, a many-columned building called the Septizonium. Severus's other notable edifice was the Arch, which was traditional in design.

CARACALLA, ruling on his own after 211 C.E., was remembered for one architectural achievement: the Baths of Caracalla. Built from 212 to 216, they were exceptional, with huge decorated rooms: the Calidarium, Natatio, and Frigidarium. Little remains of later reigns, except for the partially rebuilt temples of SEVERUS ALEXANDER's reign. Between the reigns of Caracalla and DIOCLETIAN, from 211 to 284 C.E., few examples of construction are evident. It is known, however, that in 271 the Emperor AURELIAN built sturdy but commonplace walls around the city.

With Diocletian and the Age of the TETRARCHY, Rome was totally eclipsed. The empire was divided into four great areas, and each tetrarch (either an "augustus" or a "caesar") controlled vast territories. Each wished to live in grandeur and built accordingly. The designs used in this period were traditional Roman. Other palaces at TRIER, THESSALONICA, MILAN, and NICOMEDIA displayed architectural splendors. Diocletian's palace at SPLIT, on the Yugoslavian coast, was the most beautiful of these royal residences. The palace at Split was created from 300 to 306 C.E. and was designed much like a great military camp. The walled complex reflected the military activity of the period.

In Rome, during the period from Diocletian to the end of the empire, three lasting achievements became part of the city's heritage. Diocletian constructed Baths (298–306 C.E.) that were more compact and united in theme and design. Constantine, in 315, ordered the carving of a giant Arch, thus marking a return to classicism; and the BASILICA MAXENTIUS was the culmination of the traditional style of architecture in the Western Empire. The new age that would stretch into the Middle Ages began in the East, and its birth was seen in the building of CONSTANTINOPLE.

See also ENGINEERING.

Suggested Readings: Dunbabin, Katherine. *Mosaics of the Greek and Roman World.* Cambridge, U.K.: Cambridge University Press, 2000; Elsner, J. R. *Imperial Rome and Christian Triumph: The Art of the Roman Empire AD 100–450.* Oxford, U.K.: Oxford, 1998; ———. *Art and the Roman Viewer: The Transformation of Art from the Pagan World to Christianity.* Cambridge, U.K.: Cambridge University Press, 1997; Grant, Michael, and Ken Dowden. *Art in the Roman Empire.* New York: Routledge, 1996; Ling, Roger. *Roman Painting.* Cambridge, U.K.: Cambridge University Press, 1991; MacCormack, Sabine. *Art and Ceremony in Late Antiquity.* Berkeley: University of California Press, c. 1981; McDonald, William. *The Architecture of the Roman Empire: An Introductory Study.* New Haven, Conn.: Yale University Press, 1982; McDonald, William. *Architecture of the Roman Empire: An Urban Appraisal.* New Haven, Conn.: Yale University Press, 1988; McKay, Alexander. *Houses, Villas, and Palaces in the Roman World.* Baltimore: Johns Hopkins University Press, 1998; Mortimer Wheeler, Sir Robert. *Roman Art and Architecture.* London: Thames & Hudson, 1985; Myers, Bernard S., and Trewin Copplestone. *The History of Art: Architecture—Painting—Sculpture.* New York: Dorset, 1985; Pischel, Gina. *A World History of Art.* Introduced by Luisa Becherucci. New York: Golden Press, 1996; Ramage, Nancy, and Andrew Ramage. *Roman Art.* New York: Prentice Hall, 2000; Richter, Gisela, and Martin Henig, eds. *A Handbook of Roman Art: A Survey of the Visual Art of the Roman World.* New York: Phaidon Press, 1995; Strong, Donald. *Roman Art.* New York: Viking-Penguin, 1988; Ward-Perkins, John. *Roman Imperial Architecture.* New Haven: Yale University Press, 1992; Wheeler, Mortimer. *Roman Art and Architecture.* Washington, D.C.: Frederic Praeger, 1964.

Artabanus III (d. 38 C.E.) *King of Parthia from 12 to 38 C.E. ousted from his throne on several occasions*
Like so many of the Arsacid princes, Artabanus came to the kingship after a struggle, in his case, with the despised Vonones I. Originating from an Arsacid line, but having served in Media, the prince was chosen by the Parthians to

lead the country, and Vonones was driven into Armenia, and then into Syria and Cilicia, where he died in 19 C.E.

Artabanus possessed only a temporary hold on his throne and was always aware of the dangerous factions involved in court politics. Such concerns prevented him from questioning Germanicus's placement in 18 of the Pontic descendant of Polemo I, Zeno, on Armenia's throne. Instead, he waited and sent a letter of friendship to Rome. The next years were spent solidifying his territorial holdings with a series of successful campaigns. By 34, he felt prepared to carry out his ambitions.

In 34, Zeno (also called Artaxias) died. Artabanus immediately set his own son Arsaces on the throne of Armenia. According to Tacitus, he then sent to Rome threatening letters. Such actions stirred the pro-Roman faction into sending a delegation to Rome, to ask Tiberius for assistance. The emperor dispatched Phraates, the son of Phraates IV of Parthia, to the scene, but he died in Syria and did not reach his destination. Tiberius then sent Tiridates, who was also an Arsacid. Tiridates overcame Artabanus and ruled, albeit briefly (*see* ABDAGAESES).

Artabanus returned to the throne soon after, but in 35, at the instigation of the Romans, Mithridates of the Asian Kingdom of Iberia invaded Parthia. After his generals were defeated, and in the face of invasion by the commander of the legions, Lucius Vitellius, Artabanus accepted Roman supremacy in Armenia. Shortly afterward, another palace intrigue forced him from the throne, but he regained it and died in 38, probably from exhaustion. He was succeeded by his son, Gotarzes.

Artabanus V (d. c. 226 C.E.) *King of Parthia and the last effective ruler of the Arsacid Dynasty*
Artabanus V was destroyed by ARDASHIR I in 226 C.E., losing his troops and his life. The brother of the ruler Vologases V, Artabanus overthrew him and ascended the throne sometime before 224. The perpetual dynastic feuds, however, made the Arsacid line politically unstable. When Ardashir of Persia revolted against the Arsacids in 208, capturing numerous satrapies within the Parthian Empire, Artabanus felt unable to meet the threat immediately. He waited until 224 to confront Ardashir, and by that time it was too late. Ardashir defeated the Parthians and proclaimed himself King of Kings, the traditional Persian title of supremacy. Artabanus was later killed.

Artagira A city in Armenia near Artaxata, in the province of Ararat; a strongly garrisoned site. In 2 C.E., the throne of Armenia was vacant, and Gaius Caesar, with the permission of Augustus, placed Ariobarzanes of Media in the position of king. The Parthians, who had a vested interest in Armenia, stirred up a revolt among their own supporters in the nation. A large force of rebels took refuge in the fortress city of Artagira. Gaius Caesar

arrived there in late August of 3, and on September 9, Addon, the captain of the walls, asked to speak with him. Gaius was wounded in the confrontation and was carried away by his outraged lieutenants. The Romans promptly laid siege to the city and captured the fort after bitter fighting. Gaius died in February of the next year from the wounds received.

Artavasdes (1) (fl. first century B.C.E.) *King of Media Atropatene*
First an ally of PARTHIA against Rome (c. 53 B.C.E.) but later closely connected with Emperor Augustus, Artavasdes turned in 34 B.C.E., from the Parthians and offered his help to Antony. In 30 B.C.E., however, when the Arsacid King Phraates IV conquered both Media and Armenia, Artavasdes was forced to flee to Syria. Seeking a reliable ally on the Euphrates frontier, Octavian (AUGUSTUS) gave Artavasdes the kingdom of Armenia Minor in 30 B.C.E.

Artavasdes (2) (d. 34 B.C.E.) *King of Armenia from 56 to 34 B.C.E.*
An unreliable ally to Marc Antony during his wars against Parthia. Succeeding his father, Tigranes, he participated in the invasion of Parthia in 54 B.C.E. by M. Licinius Crassus. Artavasdes was a half-hearted ally who gave the Roman no aid at all, and when the Parthians invaded Armenia, he changed sides entirely, becoming a vassal of Orodes II. Artavasdes surrendered to Marc Antony in 37 B.C.E. and promised his help. Surprisingly, Antony trusted him, and Artavasdes was given escort duty over Antony's food wagons. The Armenian king betrayed the Romans and allowed them to face a slaughter, forcing Antony to retreat. Antony sought vengeance and in 34 B.C.E. captured the king and two of his sons, Artavasdes and Tigranes; Artaxes, another son, had escaped. The king was taken to Alexandria, where Cleopatra VII had him executed. Plutarch described him as a well educated man, who had a great fondness for all things Greek.

Artaxata Capital of Armenia; located in Ararat Province on the Araxes River. It was built by Artaxes I during the Punic Wars (third–second centuries B.C.E.). Strabo claimed that Hannibal aided in the construction of the city. Its possession subsequently became a symbol of domination between rival powers. The Romans, however, caused the greatest amount of damage and suffering.

In 58 C.E., Gnaeus Domitius Corbulo invaded and reclaimed Armenia for Nero, besieging and then capturing the capital from the east; the city was surrounded on all the other sides by the Araxes River. According to Tacitus, the king of Armenia, Tiridates, watched helplessly as Artaxata was burned to the ground.

In 66, Tiridates gained the favor of Nero, returning home with 200,000 sesterces and with artisans, craftsmen, and gifts, as well as the emperor's permission to rebuild the capital. Artaxata was to be named Neronia, a title that lasted only until Nero's fall in 69.

In 164, Statius Priscus took Armenia and erected a new city to take the old capital's place. Artaxata, however, remained of some importance, for Ammianus Marcellinus mentioned that in 363 the Persians retook Armenia, gaining a sizable portion of the country, including Artaxata.

See also TIGRANOCERTA.

Artaxerxes

The name used for Ardashir I of Persia by the historians Herodian and Dio.

See ARDASHIR I.

Artaxes II (d. 20 B.C.E.) *King of Armenia from 33 to 20 B.C.E.*

The son of Artavasdes I of Armenia, Artaxes regained the throne lost by his father. In 34 B.C.E., Marc Antony captured Artavasdes and brought him to Alexandria. Artaxes had escaped, eventually fleeing to King Phraates IV of Parthia. The Arsacid ruler invaded Armenia in 33 B.C.E. and placed Artaxes on the throne. Spiteful and vengeful, the young king ordered the slaughter of all Roman traders in Armenia, an act that went unavenged. Artaxes was not a popular leader, and a cabal within the palace succeeded in murdering him.

Artemidorus Daldianus (d. after 138 C.E.) *Writer*

Writing during the reigns of ANTONINUS PIUS (86–161) and MARCUS AURELIUS (138–180), Artemidorus was best known for his work *The Interpretation of Dreams*. He was originally from Ephesus but was called Daldianus after Daldis in Lydia, the birthplace of his mother. He lived in Rome for most of his life and there composed his book on the various methods that could be employed to interpret dreams. The subject of dreams was an important one to both the Greeks and especially the Romans. Five sections of the work are extant.

Artemis　*See* DIANA.

Arulenus Rusticus, Q. Junius (d. c. 93 C.E.) *Tribune of the Plebeians in 66 C.E., praetor in 69 and consul suffectus in 92*

An ardent Stoic philosopher, Rusticus was willing to confront the imperial government from the start of his career, defending the political figure Thrasea Paetus in 66. He was a friend of Pliny the Younger, Paetus and Helvidius Priscus, writing a panegyric (c. 93) in honor of the latter two. This affront to the Flavians (both were opponents of Vespasian) was widened by Domitian into a capital crime. Philosophers were banished from Italy, and Rusticus was put to death.

Arval Brethren　The name given to an order of priests in Rome who presided over festivals and important religious holidays. Originally, the Arval was a powerful brotherhood that prayed to Mars, to protect crops from plague, and to the Dea Dia, for crop fertility. By the late Republic, their powers were reduced and membership was declining.

The Arval Brethren was revived by new Emperor AUGUSTUS sometime around 21 B.C.E., with new priests totaling 170. When the group was introduced to Rome, membership was considered an honor. Even members of the Imperial Family opted to join, and the prayers were shifted in emphasis to accommodate the new status of the group.

Henceforth, the Arvals were to pray for crops and growth as part of the tradition, but the imperial institution was the primary beneficiary of their intercessions. No festival was planned without their active participation and presence. The Arval Brethren supervised the following ceremonies: January 1 and 3—the *Ara Pacis Augustae,* where vows were taken for the safety of the state by consuls newly elected and then by imperial or provincial officials; January 7—an Augustan anniversary; and January 16—the reception of the title Augustus.

The Arval also offered prayers throughout the year to Jupiter, Minerva, Dea Dia, and to Divus Augustus, following the emperor's death in 14 C.E. Each emperor then added days to the calendar that he considered important, a process that became impractical after a time. By the late second century, the brotherhood had once more slipped from its elevated status, although a number of dedications, litanies, and prayers used by them are extant through inscriptions.

Arvandus (fl. fifth century C.E.) *Prefect of the Praetorian Guard during the reign of Anthemius (467–472)*

Arvandus was a good friend of the poet and statesman SIDONIUS APOLLINARIS and, in the emperor's name, administered Gaul. His attempts at dealing with the barbaric hordes pouring into the West caused his eventual downfall. Arvandus attempted to bargain with King Euric of the Visigoths, with the aim of placating the entire barbarian enemy. He possessed enemies in Rome, however, and he was brought to the city to answer charges of treason and embezzlement. Arvandus laughed at the attack, but the Senate condemned him. Despite the appeals of Sidonius Apollinaris and a half-hearted ally, the *magister militum* RICIMER, Arvandus was executed.

See also PREFECT OF THE PRAETORIAN GUARD.

as　The principal coin issued by the Republic (pl. asses); came to represent artistically the growing strength of Rome, as made evident by the use of a ship and a god, Janus, on the reverse and obverse sides. First issued in the third century B.C.E., its values as a coin was replaced by the sestertius. By the time Augustus ruled, asses were reduced to a unit of measurement in COINAGE weight.

Asclepiodotus (fl. third century C.E.) *Prefect of the Praetorian Guard from 290 to 296 C.E.*

With a purely military background, a rarity for his era, Asclepiodotus spent much of his career in the service of Probus on the frontiers, fighting there from 276 to 282. Named a prefect of the Guard, he was used on a variety of missions but was noted for his British campaign in 296, against the usurper ALLECTUS. Serving one of the tetrarchs, Constantius I, the prefect commanded an invasion fleet, sailing with his master to Britain. As the admiral of the flotilla, Asclepiodotus achieved not only a successful landing but also the distinction of being the only prefect of the Guard ever to hold a naval position. In Hampshire, later that year, the ex-admiral, now a general, met and defeated Allectus; Constantius then entered London. Asclepiodotus was made consul in 292.

Asclepius (also Aesculapius) Greek god of MEDICINE who was imported into the Roman Empire, attaining immense popularity in the second century C.E. A great physician in Homer's works, he was elevated to divine status and his cult was centered in the Greek city of Epidaurus. Cures were supposedly made there, and in 293 B.C.E., during a tragic plague, the Sibylline Books ordered that a sanctuary be found in Italy to acquire the aid of the god. An island in the Tiber River was chosen as the site of the deity's temple.

There were other places throughout the empire where Asclepius was worshiped. Crete housed the god, and in Cyrenaica he was ranked with Apollo and Venus. But the main center of the cult was at Pergamum during the period of the empire. Thousands traveled to the city on the Aegean Sea coast of Asia Minor in the hope of finding a cure for their illnesses and ailments. One of the pilgrims in the second century C.E. was the writer and rhetorician P. Aelius ARISTIDES.

Asconius Pedianus, Quintus (2 B.C.E.–83 C.E.?) *Also known simply as Asconius, a noted grammarian*

Pedianus probably came from Padua (Patavium) and went blind sometime around 65 C.E. Of his vast writings, only his commentaries on five speeches of CICERO have survived. Among the fragments of these orations were Cicero's *pro Cornelio de maiestate* and *pro Milone,* as well as *in toga candide, in Pisonem* and *pro Scauro.* The commentary of Pedianus was careful, scholarly, and historically valuable. He also wrote a defense of Virgil's poetry, a biography of Salust, (d. 43 B.C.E.) and a Platonic-style "symposium."

Asia A senatorially controlled territory that was, economically and administratively, one of the most impor-

Asclepius, the god of medicine. *(Courtesy Fr. Felix Just, S.J.)*

tant in the empire. Formed along the western coast of ASIA MINOR, Asia composed the territories of MYSIA, LYDIA, PISIDIA and PHRYGIA; RHODES was added later. It was the most desirable posting in the empire because of its regional stability, economic prosperity, and heavy concentration of both Roman and Hellenic influences.

In 130 B.C.E., King Attalus III bequeathed to Rome his kingdom, and Asia became a province under the supervision of a senatorial commission. The borders of the region remained substantially unchanged (with the exception of Vespasian's inclusion of Rhodes) until the time of Diocletian (late third century). In 27 B.C.E., Augustus placed Asia under the authority of the Senate, and it was administered by a proconsul, who was aided by three legates and a quaestor. Procurators served as well, mainly as the upholders of the interests of the emperor. Administration varied from area to area. Many cities that were fairly autonomous under the rule of the Attalid kings retained independence but were still included in the province. Cities directly under the rule of the Romans were allowed city councils, with the usual Roman bureaucratic intrusions. Magistrates, tax collectors, and the *correctores* maintained an imperial presence. Justice was dispensed by nine territorial departments, the *conventus.*

The proconsul administered the province from either Ephesus or Pergamum. There is uncertainty as to which city held sway politically. Pergamum was important, located near the coast, but Ephesus held the public records. Further, when the governor arrived to take control of the province, he was required, historically, to begin in Ephesus.

Asia was enormously prosperous. A variety of crops were grown successfully, including olives and corn. Clothes were dyed as well there. But true economic power came from the province's position directly on the east-west trade routes. Asian harbors at Miletus, Rhodes, Smyrna, and Alexandria Troas contained foreign vessels trading for the wealth of the Mediterranean Sea and beyond.

The cities, in turn, reinvested their capital, most often in themselves, and became some of the most beautiful in the empire. Attractive to Eastern religions, metropolises such as Pergamum emerged as the centers of such deities as Asclepius. A few of these cities received the official Roman status of "metropolis," which brought them even more benefits and privileges. Schools of philosophy, general education, and medicine were opened in Smyrna, Ephesus, and Pergamum.

The wealth of the province made it attractive to colonists. Italians and Romans were lured by the richness and beauty and by the imperial policy concerning rougher regions, which assisted such colonization. Veterans were given parcels of land around Pisidian cities, such as Apamea, or were instructed to found new ones, such as at Antioch. The Greek notions of self-determination were evidenced by the cities, which also displayed a lingering sense of the *polis,* the concept of the city-state with its self-concern and desire to effect policies beneficial to the common workers and their families.

Greek civilization was visible as the people accepted the older Eastern cults, tolerated newer ones,s and then embraced the most important of all, Christianity. It was in the province of Asia that the early church prospered. The Eastern Church, in time, became the bulwark of the Christian creed.

Asia Minor   Name given to Anatolia, the extensive peninsula between the Black Sea and the Mediterranean Sea, fronting the Aegean. Throughout the period of the Roman Empire, Asia Minor contained the provinces of ASIA, LYDIA, CAPPADOCIA, BITHYNIA, and PONTUS, as well as GALATIA and PAMPHYLIA. Connected to the East by Commagene, Armenia, and Parthia, the entire region was one of the most prosperous and well traveled (commercially) areas in the Roman Empire.

Asinius Gallus (d. 33 C.E.) *Senator and consul in 8 B.C.E.*
The son of the famous orator C. Asinius Pollio, Asinius Gallus followed his father's style of blunt speaking. He was singled out for destruction by Tiberius, in one of the most vindictive episodes of that emperor's reign. In 14

C.E. Gallus proposed that Augustus's body be carried to the funeral through the Triumphal Gate and then enraged Tiberius by asking how much of the Roman world the new emperor wished to rule. Tiberius waited for his chance to destroy Gallus for this and for another, greater act. Tiberius divorced his beloved wife VIPSANIA to marry the adulterous Julia, Augustus's daughter. In a moment of astounding political shortsightedness, Gallus wed Vipsania, going so far as to have children and to call Drusus, Tiberius's son, his own.

By 30 C.E., the aged emperor was prepared to seek vengeance. Gallus had added to his sins by constant speechmaking in the Senate. He had an overly ambitious friendship with the soon to be doomed Prefect SEJANUS and an association with Tiberius's enemy, AGRIPPINA. Tiberius summoned Gallus to Capri, entertained him hospitably and then put him in chains. He was condemned and kept under the closest supervision for the next three years. Life was made as horrible as possible for him, as he was never given enough food. The emperor refused to yield, and Gallus died of starvation. Tacitus mentioned Gallus frequently in his *Annals,* usually in a critical fashion. Augustus said that he was a man harboring ambitions for the throne, but lacking the intelligence necessary to achieve such a lofty position. Of his five sons, three became consuls of Rome.

Aspar, Flavius Ardaburius (consul in 434 C.E.) *A Magister Peditum who was one of the most important military and political figures in the Eastern Empire*
Aspar was a member of the Alan people but represented the position of, and received the support of, the Germans. His wife was probably an Ostrogoth, for Theodoric, the powerful Ostrogoth king, was her nephew.

In 425, the magister peditum assisted Empress Galla Placidia and her son Valentinian in their attempts to dislodge John the Usurper from Ravenna. After campaigning in Africa, Aspar received the consulship in 434. He then increased his power through the influence of the Goths, eventually playing kingmaker for the emperors Marcian (Eastern Empire, 450–457) and Leo the Great (Eastern Empire, 457–474).

Leo, however, cultivated new alliances in the East. Despite elevating Aspar's son Patricius to the rank of Caesar in 469–470, he began to view Aspar suspiciously. Aspar's other son, Ardaburius, attempted to bribe Leo's soldiers, the Isaurians, with no success. As a result, Ardaburius and Aspar were slain in the palace by eunuchs.

assassinations   The assassinations of the emperors of Rome were emblematic of the commonplace political instability that characterized much of Roman imperial history. The motives for assassinations varied from personal vendettas (such as that of CASSIUS CHAEREA against Gaius CALIGULA) to political ambition (a common reason to

Emperor	Assassins
Tiberius (14–37 c.e.)	Probably Gaius Caligula
Caligula (37–41)	Praetorian Guards; Cassius Chaerea; Prefect Arrecinus Clemens; and others
Claudius (41–51)	Agrippina the Younger, the empress
Galba (69)	Praetorian Guards
Vitellius (69)	Vespasian's soldiers
Domitian (81–96)	Stephanus; with Petronius Secundus; Norbanus (a chamberlain); and Domitia Longina, the empress
Commodus (180–192)	Narcissus, an athlete; Prefect Quintus Laetus; Marcia (Commodus's mistress); Eclectus (chamberlain); and Pertinax, the urban prefect
Pertinax (193)	Praetorian Guards
Didius Julianus (193)	Soldiers on senatorial orders
Geta (211)	His brother
Caracalla (211–217)	Julius Martialis; with aid of Prefect of the Guard Macrinus
Elagabalus (218–222)	Praetorian Guard in the Castra Praetoria
Severus Alexander (222–235)	Mutinous troops in the Danube Wars
Maximinus I (235–238)	Disaffected troops
Balbinus and Pupienus (238)	Praetorian Guard
Gordian III (238–244)	Soldiers prodded by Praetorian Prefect Philip
Trebonianus Gallus (251–253)	Soldiers
Aemilian (253)	Soldiers
Gallienus (253–268)	Prefect Heraclianus; aided by generals Marcianus, Claudius Gothicus and Aurelian
Postumus (260–268)	Soldiers refused permission to sack city of Moguntiacum
Aurelian (270–275)	Thracian Praetorian officer, Mucapor; and other officers
Florian (276)	Soldiers
Probus (276–282)	Soldiers
Carus (282–283)	Probably the Praetorian Prefect, Arrius Aper, although lightning was listed as the official cause
Carinus (283–285)	One of his imperial officers
Numerian (283–284)	Arrius Aper
Constans I (337–350)	Assassin sent by Magnentius
Gratian (367–383)	Officer named Andragathius
Valentinian II (375–392)	*Magister militum* Arbogast (or possibly by suicide)
Libius Severus (461–465)	Probably by his own men
Julius Nepos (474–475)	Two retainers, Ovida and Viator, with complicity of Glycerius

commit murder) to pure greed. Some of the most frequent participants in the assassinations of emperors were members of the PRAETORIAN GUARD. The guard murdered several emperors, including GALBA, over issues of pay or out of spite that their customary *donativum* was, in their eyes, insufficient. In the later empire, emperors, usurpers, and imperial claimants were slain by their own soldiers following military or political setbacks or when it became clear that they could no longer pay for the loyalty of the troops. A list of the emperors who were assassinated is above.

See also FRUMENTARII and SPECULATORES.

astrology The science given birth in Babylonian Chaldaea and passed on to the Hellenic world. For the Romans, who would adopt virtually anything cultic or of a religious nature, astrology became tremendously popular. During the empire astrology was favored and practiced by all classes of Romans. Its appeal stretched from intellectuals, the Stoics, and the nobility, to the provinces, and even to the common workers and peasants.

The Eastern campaigns of Alexander the Great and the subsequent creation of the Seleucid and Ptolemaic kingdoms ensured enough Asian influences that the art of astrology was scientifically explored. The traditions of stellar influences were accepted by the Ptolemies, and Alexandria, in Egypt, was a center of astrological divination.

Varro (116–27 B.C.E.) was among the first of the Romans to express publicly an interest, but the city itself was at first reluctant to open its gates to such a foreign practice. In 139 B.C.E., the praetor of Rome expelled all astrologers. By the era of Nigidius Figulus (mid-first century B.C.E.), the Pythagorean philosopher and writer (the era of Pompey as well), the astrology movement found support among Posidonius and the Stoicists.

The Stoics gave to astrology precisely the intellectual basis that appealed to the Roman people. A divine linking of the earth with the stars, and a cosmological movement connecting all living things, bore similarities that forged a natural bond between them. The astrologers identified themselves with the Stoics, and the Stoics applied astrological practices.

Romans traditionally had a great interest in the supernatural and the magical; even Tacitus in his *Annals* placed great faith in astrological prophecy. They were curious, generally open-minded, but also highly susceptible to fraud and manipulation, both personal and political. The possibilities for abuse convinced powerful men that astrology would be far too dangerous, and so a series of expulsions took place.

Tiberius, as he did with actors, executed all foreign astrologers in 16 C.E. and exiled all Italian practitioners, this despite his great faith in his own seer, THRASYLLUS. In 52 C.E., Claudius banished astrologers, and Vitellius ordered them out of Rome again in 69. In response, the astrologers issued a notice predicting accurately the day of his demise.

Vespasian had his own seers and granted privileges to BALBILLUS and his city of Ephesus because of his proficiency in the art. In 70, however, finding predictions about his reign a nuisance, he banished everyone connected to astrology.

The most intriguing political use of astrology came circa 95 C.E., when Domitian consulted the diviners about the charts of the men in the empire who might aspire to the throne. He then systematically exterminated them, overlooking Nerva because of his age. In time, Nerva became emperor.

While rulers of the early and middle Empire banned or executed astrologers, no pogrom was launched and no laws were passed to outlaw the practice of the art. The closest law was that of Augustus, in 11 C.E., which forbade the prediction of anyone's death and also prohibited forecasting in private. Astrology, however, was never illegal in Rome, and its popularity made it difficult to erase.

The Eastern cults, which flooded Rome as its empire grew, very often contained many traditional astrological elements; Mithras was intensely popular and largely based on astrology. Influenced by the Mesopotamians and hence Babylonian notions, Mithraism was followed by many legionaries and commoners, placing astrology into the very lowest, hence most populous elements of the empire's citizenry.

Like paganism, astrology could not openly survive orthodox Christianity, which was at odds with all such practices and traditions. Through political pressure, Constantius II in 357 proclaimed divination a crime punishable by death. Astrology was only one of a wider number of divinatory practices in the empire. There were auspices, omens, and the state-administered college of *augura* (*see* AUGURS AND AUGURY). But for capturing the public interest and imagination, all paled alongside astrology.

astronomy A field of interest that was heavily influenced by the East and then developed into an actual science under the Greeks. The Romans had their choice of numerous astronomical theories, but astronomy suffered intellectually during the empire because of the perpetual confusion made between it and astrology.

Nevertheless, astronomy was one of the leading fields of study, and extant works of mathematicians and scientific writers display a variety of ideas. Geocentricism was the accepted theory in Rome, and the heliocentric ideas of Aristarchus of Samos (310–230 B.C.E.) were ignored.

Cicero (d. 43 B.C.E.) an avid follower of Archimedes, studied certain astronomical theories, and the Academy placed the science in its course of study. M. Terrentius Varro (first century B.C.E.) wrote of *astrologia* is his treatise on liberal arts, one among the 488 lost books of which he was author. General acceptance of astronomy was evidenced by the work of Sosigenes, a Greek astronomer who redesigned the Republican calendar.

Other studies were made, especially at Alexandria, the active home of astronomy in many eras. Two names in particular are known: Theon of Smyrna and Claudius Ptolemy (fl. 127–141 C.E.). Theon examined mathematics from an astronomical perspective, while Ptolemy authored the *Great Collection,* which was a vast treatise on the subject, covering the planets and the works of previous Greek astronomers. The *Great Collection,* compiled in the mid-second century C.E., was consulted by the Arabs, who called it *Al-majisti,* and by Europeans until the 16th century.

Sailors of the period knew the stars and, because of astrology, the constellations and the planets of Jupiter, Saturn, Mars, Venus, and Mercury. Unfortunately, the astronomy of the Roman Empire was not particularly original, save for the compilations and extensive calculations of Ptolemy.

Athanasius (St. Athanasius) (c. 295–373 C.E.) *Bishop of Alexandria and a fourth-century theologian who was one of the most active leaders against Arianism in the church*
Receiving a suitable education before becoming a member of the Christian clergy in his home city of Alexandria, Athanasius served under Alexander of Alexandria and accompanied him to the Council of Nicaea in 325, where Arianism was officially condemned. Three years later he was chosen by Alexander to be the bishop of Alexandria.

Constantine I twice listened to the Arians and Melitians, and Athanasius was forced to defend himself in 331 and 335. The second time resulted in his exile to Gaul, after the Council of Tyre expelled him. In 337, Athanasius was reinstated by Constantine II, but was deposed by the Arians, who then refused to accept a synod of bishops that had exonerated him.

Constantius allowed Athanasius to return to Alexandria in 346, but he was condemned again at the Council of Arles (353) and at the Council of Milan (355). Athanasius was then forced to seek shelter in the Libyan desert.

Julian the Apostate became emperor and in February of 362, Athanasius returned to Alexandria. Arianism was strongly condemned by a synod, but a strong attempt at reconciliation was made with the Homoiousians (who believed in the separateness of Christ from the Father), and many so called Semi-Arians were brought back into the church. Julian, however, feared Athanasius's success and exiled him in October of 362. Jovian brought him back, but in 364, Valens (coemperor with Valentinian) sent him away once more.

In less than five months he was back in Alexandria, where he spent his last years. His main works were attacks on Arianism, the most famous being *Discourses Against the Arians, Two Books Against the Pagans* and *On the Incarnation*. Athanasius was a close friend of St. Antony.

Athaulf (d. 415 C.E.) *King of the Visigoths from 410 to 415*
At the end of 410, ALARIC, sacker of Rome and ruler of the Goths, died in southern Italy. His brother Athaulf came to the throne. The most qualified to lead his people, in 412 Athaulf took them over the Alps into Gaul. With GALLA PLACIDA, the sister of Emperor Honorius, and the deposed Emperor Attalus under his control, he bargained with both Honorius and the usurper in Gaul, Jovinus, eventually siding with Honorius. No longer content to ravage the empire, Athaulf in 414 married Galla Placidia and made moves to reconcile himself with Rome. Honorius refused to treat with him, and war broke out in the West. The MAGISTER MILITUM Constantius blockaded the coast of Gaul and much of the southern portion of the country was laid waste. Attalus, who had been temporarily elevated to the throne as a usurper, was captured by Constantius. Whatever plans Athaulf had were cut short by his assassination by followers of a murdered chieftain.

Athena *See* MINERVA.

Athenadorus (fl. late first century C.E.) *Stoic and tutor of Augustus*
Athenadorus, also known as Athenodorus, came from Tarsus and was a correspondent and friend of Cicero. He tutored Augustus and was sent by him to Tarsus, to remove the writer Boethius, the city's leader, who had been appointed by Marc Antony. Athenadorus was considered a good and honorable man by his contemporaries, and Dio related that once he ordered for his use a litter used by the women who were brought into the presence of Augustus. Athenadorus jumped out of the vehicle, sword in hand, demanding to know if Augustus was not concerned that someone could kill him by entering his presence in that fashion. Augustus was grateful for the demonstration.

Athenaeum Institute of learning created by Hadrian in 133 C.E. The Athenaeum specialized in science and literary fields. In 193 C.E., the building was used by the Senate for its deliberations on the fate of Emperor Didius Julianus.

Athens For centuries the city of Athens was the cultural and intellectual center of the Western World. Under the Roman Empire, the city was reduced to a unit of the province of ACHAEA, but remained the seat of intellectualism. In 86 B.C.E., the general Sulla captured Athens after it had rebelled against Roman rule and punished its citizens harshly for trying to break away from Rome.

The first century B.C.E. CIVIL WARS of Rome also proved costly to Athens, as the combatants—Pompey, Caesar, Antony, Brutus, and the Liberators, Octavian—demanded contributions from the inhabitants. Because Antony found great favor with the Athenians, after the battle of ACTIUM (31 B.C.E.), Augustus in revenge terminated the city's right to grant citizenship and to mint its own coinage. When the province of Achaea was officially established, the proconsul administered the territory from Corinth instead of Athens, another display of imperial displeasure. These penalties, however, did not diminish the Athenian spirit of independence.

Supremacy over Greece, let alone the rest of the world, was now out of the question, and Athens found it difficult to compete with the rest of the province economically. Agriculture was helpful, but the city's survival depended upon the assistance and kindness of benefactors, both Greek and Roman. Few figures of provincial Athenian history matched the munificence of HERODES ATTICUS, who used large portions of his personal wealth to build extensively, including such projects as the Odeion. This assistance was small in comparison to what the emperors of Rome could provide, so Athens looked to imperial favor for its survival.

Claudius gave Athens his blessing, and Domitian provided relief. His main contribution came in the confiscation of the wealth of Hipparchus of Athens, whose reduced but still extensive fortune passed to the control of Herodes Atticus. It was HADRIAN (ruled 117–138 C.E.), lover of all things Greek, who became Athens's greatest patron.

According to the historian Dio, Hadrian finished the Olympienum, which housed his statues. He granted to Athens large amounts of money and handed out grain. Equally, Hadrian adopted or imitated the Greek lifestyle, and Athens thus became the focal point of his devotion. Games were given in honor of panhellenism, and the emperor assumed the role of Archon, or Athenian leader. Lastly, he gave Athens the revenue of Cephallenia, which alleviated its economic problems. Marcus Aurelius, taught by many Greek philosophers, in 177–178 ordered the creation of the first great university by endowing chairs at each of the major philosophical schools situated in Athens. Henceforth, despite being sacked by the Goths in 267, Athens's reputation was exclusively educational.

Athens was divided into two major sections, the Acropolis and the Lower City. The Acropolis was the artistic and religious seat, with temples and great statues. The Parthenon dominated the site. Hadrian completed the temple of Olympian Zeus in 124–125 C.E., built his Arch and then constructed a library there. Other construction during the Roman era was limited, the most notable structures being the Agora and the Odeion. Julius Caesar, around 50 B.C.E., made the Agora possible. The Odeion of Agrippa (not the one built by Herodes Atticus) was erected by Marcus Agrippa in 15 B.C.E. but became unusable in the second century C.E.; a new one was constructed by Atticus.

Attalus, Priscus (early fifth century C.E.) *Senator, usurper, and a pawn of the Visigoths*

Attalus was a pagan of Greek origin and was sent in 409 as part of an embassy to the king of the Visigoths, Alaric. The embassy was unsuccessful, and the Goths sacked Rome and attempted to bring Emperor Honorius to his knees at Ravenna, using Attalus as a puppet. Alaric proclaimed Attalus the emperor, because he was serving at the time as urban prefect.

Attalus, however, proved too willful. Alaric made overtures to Honorius and in 410 removed Attalus from the throne. The ex-emperor remained under Alaric's control and was given to Athaulf, who succeeded Alaric, in 412. Two years later, while feuding with Honorius, Athaulf placed Attalus once again on the throne. In 415, however, after losing much of southern Gaul to a blockade, the Goths abandoned Attalus, and he was captured by Honorius's men. Maimed, he was exiled to the island of Lipara.

Attianus, Publius Acilius (fl. early second century C.E.) *A Praetorian prefect under emperors Trajan and Hadrian*

When Hadrian was orphaned as a child, Trajan had ensured that an education in Rome and every possibility for advancement be provided for him. Acilius Attianus, an Equestrian and compatriot of Trajan, was given the task of adopting and raising Hadrian. His influence was considerable, and through Attianus a marriage was arranged between Hadrian and Trajan's relative Vibia Sabina. Hadrian went to various successful commands, while Attianus served as prefect of the Praetorian Guard. Trajan died suddenly in August of 117 in Selinus, a small town beyond Syria. The legions of the East, with Attianus and the Praetorians behind them, proclaimed Hadrian emperor. Because Trajan had not officially adopted Hadrian, the presence of Attianus and Empress PLOTINA ensured the succession.

Attianus immediately took up his post as adviser to the new emperor, still serving as prefect. When a conspiracy of generals who feared Hadrian's nonimperialistic policies was discovered in Rome, Attianus sent agents of the *speculatores* to the rebels. Four generals were executed as a result. Public outrage reached the ears of the emperor, who understood the danger of alienating public sympathy. Attianus, his past services and patronage notwithstanding, was removed from his command but given consular honors and a senatorial rank.

Attila (d. 453 C.E.) *King of the Huns from 434 to 453; he earned the name of the "Scourge of God," a Christian appellation because of his rapacious cruelty*

Attila was the son of the Hun King Mandiuch, succeeding him in 434 along with his brother Bleda, whom he murdered in 444, from which time he ruled alone.

By the fifth century, the Huns occupied an area of considerable size throughout DACIA, PANNONIA, and along the DANUBE. Attila used the first years of his rule (434–443) to solidify his position as king, to extend his holdings in the East and to prepare for an invasion of the Roman Empire. In 443, Attila defeated a Roman army and then demanded tribute and more land. He gained total control over the Huns at the same time, by removing Bleda, and the next years of life were spent earning his fabled, if hideous, reputation. The attacks along the Danube were matched in 447 by the capture of Marcianopolis, thus threatening Constantinople. That great city of the East was a formidable target, even for the Huns, and a treaty was arranged, granting even more of the Danube to Attila to keep him pacified.

The Eastern Empire was well organized, but the West was weak. The last five years of Attila's life (448–453) were centered in the West. He invaded Gaul through Belgica and there encountered, at Orleans, the MAGISTER MILITUM Aetius and his Gothic allies. The Huns were in a difficult position strategically (*see* CATALAUNIAN PLAIN), but in the imperial politics of the time, Aetius could not allow Attila to be annihilated as the balance of power among the Germans would be disrupted.

Defeated, Attila invaded Italy, claiming that he was betrothed to Augusta Honoria, the sister of Emperor Valentinian III. In 452, the city of AQUILEIA was destroyed, but in a famous episode, the bishop of Rome, Pope Leo, convinced Attila that Rome should be left unmolested. The Huns departed, and one year later Attila was dead. He burst an artery on the night of his wedding to the maid Ildico. Attila was described as quintessentially Hunnish, with a broad, squat frame and the harsh features of his people. He was remarkably cunning and dealt adroitly with the political demands of the imperial courts and his own tribes. So central a part did he play as king of the Huns that with his death the Hun empire collapsed.

Attila the Hun, as Flagellum Dei, the "Scourge of God" (*Hulton/Getty Archive*)

Suggested Readings: Bäuml, Franz H., and Marianna D. Birnbaum, ed. *Attila: the Man and His Image*. Budapest: Corvina, 1993; Gordon, Colin D. *The Age of Attila: Fifth-Century Byzantium and the Barbarians*. Ann Arbor: University of Michigan Press, 1966; Howarth, Patrick. *Attila, King of the Huns: Man and Myth*. London: Constable, 1994.

auctoritas   The power, unofficial but unquestionably real, that was possessed by the rulers of the early empire with regard to matters of state or politics. The concept of *auctoritas* was grounded in the belief that the holder of extensive or superior power possessed as well a natural, but not necessarily legal, capacity to exert influence that was greater than that wielded by those around them.

Senatorial resolutions, before becoming legal through the process of *consultum*, carried a very real political weight by virtue of *auctoritas*. Should such a resolution fail to become law, it was still recorded in the ACTA SENATUS and was considered worthy of esteem. Augustus (ruled 27 B.C.E.–14 C.E.) was granted supremacy in virtually all of the Republican institutions, especially in the title of PRINCEPS, and *auctoritas* was added as well. The other emperors maintained the same sort of power until the reign of Vespasian (69–79 C.E.), who assumed the power to do whatever he believed necessary for the good of the state. His *auctoritas* thus came not from divine or inherited authority but from the needs of the time and the inevitable emergence of imperial absolutism.

See also IMPERIUM PROCONSULARES and TRIBUNICIA POTESTAS.

Aufidius Bassus   *See* BASSUS, AUFIDIUS.

Aufidius Victorinus, Gaius (d. c. 186 C.E.) *Considered the most virtuous counselor and friend of Marcus Aurelius; an old schoolmate of the emperor*
Of the senatorial class, Victorinus served as a legate in Germania, proconsul in Africa and later as prefect of the city. Twice consul, the second time in 183, he was sent against the Chatti; he ordered home two underlings, one in Germany and the other in Africa, for displaying greed or corruption. Hated by Emperor Commodus, Victorinus would have been executed except for his reputation. He died shortly after the fall of the Praetorian Prefect Perennis.

Augurium Canarium   The Roman practice conducted in late summer that attempted to determine the favorability of the coming harvests. The rite was held during the time when Sirius, the Dogstar, was in ascendancy.
See also AUGURS AND AUGURY.

augurs and augury   The diviners of Rome did not predict the future but rather determined, as part of their official capacity, whether a given action was proper and accepted by the divinities. The augurs belonged to four classes of priests, along with the PONTIFICES, the SEPTEMVIRI and the QUINDECIMVIRI. They formed their own college, originally with three members, but increased membership to five and then 15 by Sulla's era (c. 80 B.C.E.). In 47 B.C.E., under Julius Caesar, the number was 16.

Augury was a respected practice and the office, especially during the period of the empire, was politically powerful. An augur, wearing his toga of office and his wand, conducted ceremonies designed to determine whether the gods approved of a decision. Two methods were used: *auspicia oblativa* and *auspicia impetrativa*.

Oblativa meant that a sign or portent was unlooked for or unrequested. Most often this pointed to something horrendous. Portents of doom were never wanted, although the Roman histories were full of them, especially those concerning the impending deaths of emperors. In 217 C.E., Caracalla's assassination, according to the historian Dio, was foreshadowed by numerous prophecies and strange happenings. The signs had all been there, for any trained observer to see with clarity.

Auspicia impetrativa was the more formal and routine process of augury. The Roman legions traveled with augurs and birds; before battle it was determined whether the ensuing engagement was blessed. Food was given to usually starved chickens, and, depending upon their appetite, the propitiousness of action was seen. The use of birds was important, and the etymological root of "augury" may be found in the Latin *avis*, or bird, although entrails, especially livers, were also observed, a process known as *haruspicium*.

Divination and the examination of auspices, along with the strict control of all divinatory practices (*see* ASTROLOGY), were maintained by the Roman state, which early on saw the potential for abuse. In 29 B.C.E., Augustus was warned by Marcus Agrippa not to trust diviners and augurs, for they could, at times, lead people to chaos by lies. Traditionally, a magistrate or the *pontifex maximus* held auspices, and the interpretation of an augur could be discounted if they so desired. In practice, however, the diviners wielded considerable influence.

Augusta The title given first to Empress LIVIA in 14 C.E., in honor of her unique position during the reign of AUGUSTUS; later used to designate the role of the wife of the emperor, or that of any woman of power in imperial affairs. The name was also given to a number of Roman colonies and townships (see below).

With the death of Augustus in 14 C.E., the grateful Senate and the people of Rome heaped every honor on the late ruler. Livia, his widow, received the same in honor of her service, and was adopted into the Julian house and given the title Augusta. With this unprecedented act, the Senate made Livia a virtual colleague of the new emperor, her own son TIBERIUS. Augustus's name had been based on the title given to him when he was still Octavian, making him emperor in spirit. Tiberius recognized the reality of the title extended to Livia, and, having no love for his domineering mother, he severely restricted the execution of the powers that complemented the name.

AGRIPPINA THE YOUNGER was next to receive the title, in 50 C.E. She was given her status while Claudius, her emperor husband, was still alive. Unlike Livia, who was limited by Tiberius, Agrippina had Claudius's permission to exercise her powers. They continued in 54 C.E., when her son Nero was named emperor. She shared his office, sitting on an equal station with him, and appeared on imperial coinage with her countenance prominently displayed. In 59, Agrippina was murdered by Nero. Four years later, POPPAEA, Nero's new wife, was granted the title of Augusta, as was her new daughter. Their position, however, was politically impotent, and consequently began the trend that reduced the status of the rank to that of a title given the wife or nearest female relative of the emperor.

Domitian named his wife, DOMITIA LONGINA, to be Augusta as his empress only, with no real powers. Her influence in the palace was such, however, that the assassination of Domitian took place with her knowledge and participation. Intriguing behind the throne, and the manipulation of the emperor himself, brought about the evolution of the rank.

JULIA MAMAEA, the mother of Alexander Severus, did not bear the title of Augusta. Instead she bore the name: "Mother of the Emperor, Camp, Senate and Country," and she was a power behind the throne throughout Alexander's reign (222–235). Her domination was so complete that, in time, the troops revolted and killed them both.

The development of the Eastern Empire following Constantine's construction of CONSTANTINOPLE, and the very real transfer of political stability to this new site, in the fifth century C.E., allowed an increase in the authority of the Augustas of the period. On January 9, 400, Emperor Arcadius's wife EUDOXIA was elevated to the rank and ruled until her death by miscarriage in 404. Her daughter, Aelia Pulcheria, acquired the title in 414, ousted the Praetorian Prefect Anthemius and, though only 15 years old, served as regent to the emperor, Theodosius II, who was two years younger. She issued coinage, arranged his marriage to Athenais (Aelia EUDOCIA), and was a central figure at the court and in the empire, both in the East and West.

The name was also given to a number of COLONIES and townships that were begun during the reign of Augustus and hence were dedicated to him.

> **Augusta Praetoria** (Aosta) Founded in 24 B.C.E. by Emperor Augustus, who donated the land to several thousand Praetorian Guard veterans. Aosta was previously occupied by the Salassi, of Gallia Cisalpina, who were vanquished by Varro around 25 B.C.E. The town subsequently became a center of communications and extensive Roman building. Extant remains include an arch and the large city gates.
>
> **Augusta Raurica** (Augst) Founded in 44 B.C.E., shortly after the defeat of the Raurici, a Gallic people, by Munatius. Augusta Raurica became one of the colonial foundations for Roman communication in southeastern Gaul, Germania, and Raetia. In the second century C.E., much of the city was rebuilt, with a temple, a Capitolium, a basilica, and a large forum. In 260, the Alamanni attacked Augusta Raurica, but the presence of considerable remains gives evidence of economic prosperity.
>
> **Augusta Taurinorum** *See* TURIN.
>
> **Augusta Treverorum** *See* TRIER.
>
> **Augusta Vindelicorum** (Augsburg) Founded in 6 C.E. in the province of Raetia. According to Tacitus, Vindelicorum was important as an economic and government center for the province, remaining so until the period of the late empire. Very few remains are extant.

Augustans A unit of soldiers formed by Nero in 59 C.E. and numbering approximately 5,000. The Augustans were a special corps, with one purpose—to lead the applause at the performances of the emperor. The Augustans were used at all public events of importance to cheer, applaud and shout their approval, thus intimidating everyone else present to do the same, regardless of the mediocrity of performance or display. The Augustans were favorites of Nero, traveling with him to Greece in 66 C.E. They were recruited mainly from the Equestrian Order, chosen for their youth, physique, and willingness to participate in the debaucheries of the emperor. Reportedly arrogant and haughty, they proposed in 67 to cast a gold statue of Nero, to weigh a thousand pounds. The rest of the Equestrians were forced to help defray the cost of the statue.

See also CLAQUEURS.

Augustine (Aurelius Augustinus, St. Augustine)
(354–430 C.E.) *Father of the church, writer, philosopher, and key figure in the development of Christianity*
Born in the Algerian town of Thagaste, son of a landowner and a devoutly Christian mother, Saint Monica, Augustine was educated at Carthage. He eventually taught and came to the attention of the pagan philosopher SYMMACHUS. Educationally, he aspired to be a man of letters, terminating a marriage and abandoning a son for more ambitious associations. When he was 18, he followed his intellectual curiosities and read Cicero's *Hortensius* (now lost). He tried to follow the Manichaeist sect, which promised wisdom in a Gnostic fashion, but it proved ultimately unsatisfactory. As a teacher in 384, he traveled to Rome but finally settled in Milan where he began a long relationship and friendship with the local bishop, the formidable AMBROSE. Two years later Ambrose introduced him to the wide circle of Christian Neoplatonists of the city.

Augustine found a spiritual home. Although he still lacked the capacity to differentiate Christian theology and Neoplatonic thought, in August of 386 he was baptized by Ambrose. As he wrote in his *Confessions,* it was through Neoplatonism that he came to a full appreciation of Christianity. Returning to Thagaste, Augustine attempted to live as a recluse. His reputation among the Christian intellectuals, however, brought about his forced ordination into the priesthood of Hippo in 391. The elderly bishop of that diocese needed an assistant. In 395 Augustine was named as his successor to the see.

Just as Augustine's life was altered by the *Hortensius,* so was the church changed by the new bishop. Writing and continuing his scholarship, he spearheaded the spread of Christianity in Africa, in the face of paganism and numerous heretical sects. The Manichaeans fell before him; the Donatists were condemned at Carthage in 411; he reproached Pelagianism in 412.

Augustine was a prolific writer. His *Confessions,* an autobiographical account of his youth that recounted everything until the death of his mother in 387, was a demonstration of his intense curiosity and quest for knowledge. *De Doctrina Christiana* (397) examined scholarship and the manner in which it was to be pursued from the perspective of Christianity and the Scriptures. Philosophy and thought were to be studied only to achieve a greater understanding of the Gospels and the meaning of God's Will. His greatest work, *The City of God* (413–426) defended the Christianization of Rome, refuting paganism's ancient claim to the city. *The City of God* extended its concerns to the next world, where the elect and the doomed would be separated. Augustine is ranked with Ambrose, Gregory I, and Jerome as one of the Four Fathers of the church.

Augustodonum
Capital of the Gallic tribe, the Aedui. Augustodonum was built by the Aedui following their defeat by Julius Caesar in his Gallic Wars, circa 56 B.C.E. The previous capital was the stronghold of Bibracte but with Caesar's victory it was abandoned, and Augustodonum was built in its place. It was also called Autun. In 21 C.E., the Gallic rebel, Sacrovir, used the city as his headquarters for his unsuccessful rebellion against Rome. Augustodonum was located in the Aedui territory near the Loire River.

Augustus (Gaius Octavian) (63 B.C.E.–14 C.E.) *First emperor of Rome and founder of the Roman imperial state*

> I found Rome a city of bricks and left it a city of marble.
>
> Augustus

Gaius Octavian was born on September 23, 63 B.C.E., to C. Octavius and Atia, a niece of Julius Caesar by his sister Julia. The family of Octavian was a good one, but its alliance to the Julians was far more important, and Octavian came under their direct influence when his father died in 59 B.C.E. Atia raised him and ensured his education by grammarians and philosophers, but it was Caesar who would have the most impact upon Octavian, and who presented him with the greatest opportunities.

In 53 B.C.E., at the age of 12, Octavian delivered the funeral oration (the laudatio) for his grandmother Julia, and several years later served in a priesthood. Caesar came to dominate his life's direction. He saw his uncle's triumph in Rome in 46 B.C.E. and in 45 journeyed to Spain to be with him on campaign.

Octavian was never strong physically, suffering from a variety of complaints that plagued him throughout his life. The trip to Spain was arduous, along dangerous roads. He also suffered a shipwreck and was in a sorry state when he arrived at Caesar's camp. But his uncle recognized something unique in him, rewarding his efforts with military training.

After a time Octavian was sent to Apollonia, in Epirus, to study philosophy and the arts of war. He took with him his two dearest friends, Marcus Agrippa and Marcus Rufus. His studies were cut short by the assassination of Caesar in Rome.

Octavian was only 18 years old, but the will of his uncle declared him his chief heir and adopted son. His position in Rome was now radically different and bound by the obligation to avenge Caesar's death. Octavian traveled to Rome and found that cautious deliberation would be far more useful than rash action, a characteristic that would mark his later years.

Marc ANTONY was in Rome, and Octavian found him unwilling to relinquish control of Julius Caesar's property or assets. Octavian immediately began a defensive action against Antony. Cicero, Antony's bitter foe, was befriended, and Octavian presented the *ludi Victoriae Caesaris*, the Victory Games of Caesar, to the people. The Senate, anxious to snub the ambitious Antony and his claims, made Octavian a senator and asked his aid in the wars that had begun as a result of the assassination.

Octavian defeated Antony's legions at Mutina in April of 43 B.C.E. As a result, Octavian's troops demanded that he be given the rank and the powers of a consul. Reluctantly the Senate agreed, and, as Caesar's adopted heir, he took the name Gaius Julius Caesar Octavianus.

Realizing that he had to reach a truce with Antony to achieve wider aims, Octavian formed a SECOND TRIUMVIRATE with him and Marcus Lepidus on November 27, 43 B.C.E. Octavian thus ruled Africa, Sicily, and Sardinia. He also benefited from the fact that Caesar had been elevated to the status of a god. Antony was joined to him as well, in the common ambition of defeating Brutus, Cassius, and the party of the LIBERATORS, a task accomplished at the battle of Philippi in 42 B.C.E. Octavian was not present, however, being too ill.

Antony was given control of the East as a result, while Octavian worked to strengthen his hold on Italy, sensing that Rome was where the ultimate power rested. Officially he still held Africa, but in Italy he fought with Antony's brother Lucius and Fulvia in 41 B.C.E., in the

PERUSINE WAR, and then began gaining the good will of the legions by distributing land to the veterans of campaigns.

Political maneuvering next involved him in a marriage with Scribonia, a relative of Sextus Pompey, the son of Pompey the Great, but he divorced her and married the formidable Livia Drusilla, who remained with him until his death. Antony still troubled him, and a certain relaxation of tension was accomplished by the treaty of Brundisium in 40 B.C.E.

The triumvirate was maintained and extended by the treaty of Tarentum in 37 B.C.E.: Octavian ruled the West, Antony the East, and Lepidus took Africa. Marc Antony married Octavia, Octavian's sister, but found life in the East too compelling, falling in love with Cleopatra VII of Egypt and thus dooming the marriage. Octavian could not take action against his brother-in-law as Sextus Pompey, a pirate with a vast fleet and a reputation for cruelty, still plagued Rome. Marcus Agrippa, however, waged a brilliant campaign against Sextus Pompey, and in 36 B.C.E. Sextus was defeated at the battle of Naulochus.

Lepidus then attempted to revolt against his fellow triumvirs, but his legions were taken away from him by Octavian, who sent him into exile at Circeii. This left only Octavian and Antony, dividing the Roman world between them. Octavian took the title of Imperator as he waged campaigns in Illyricum and Dalmatia (35–33 B.C.E.), after which he proclaimed to the Romans that their frontiers were safe. With that proclamation came a beautification program for the city, under the direction of Agrippa. His popularity thus ensured, Octavian was prepared to meet Antony for the final confrontation.

In October of 32 B.C.E., the western provinces swore their allegiance to Octavian. War was inevitable, and on September 2, 31, the battle of ACTIUM was fought off the west coast of Greece, with Octavian facing Antony and Cleopatra. Through Agrippa's brilliant leadership, Octavian won the day and gained mastery over the Roman world. He conquered Egypt in 30 and generally pacified the East along the lines begun by Antony.

As the "foremost citizen" of the Republic, Octavian exercised power beyond that of his predecessors. Unlike his uncle, Julius Caesar, he had no intention of declaring himself the master of the people, the ruler of the state— the dictator. Octavian recognized that by maintaining the Republican institutions and ensuring the prosperity of all Roman traditions, he could help Rome achieve its destined greatness.

He served as consul from 31 to 23 B.C.E. In 30 he was granted tribunician power, and in 29 began his reforms of the army. The plunder of Egypt was used to pay off his troops, and many veterans were given lands to farm and colonize. The legions were thus reduced, but Roman influence in the provinces was ensured.

Soon the once ponderous 60 legions were reduced to 28, although they were supplemented by large formations

A silver denarius of Augustus, struck before he was granted the title of Augustus in 27 B.C.E. The coin was struck to commemorate Augustus's formal possession of Egypt a year after Actium in 30 B.C.E. *(Courtesy Historical Coins, Inc.)*

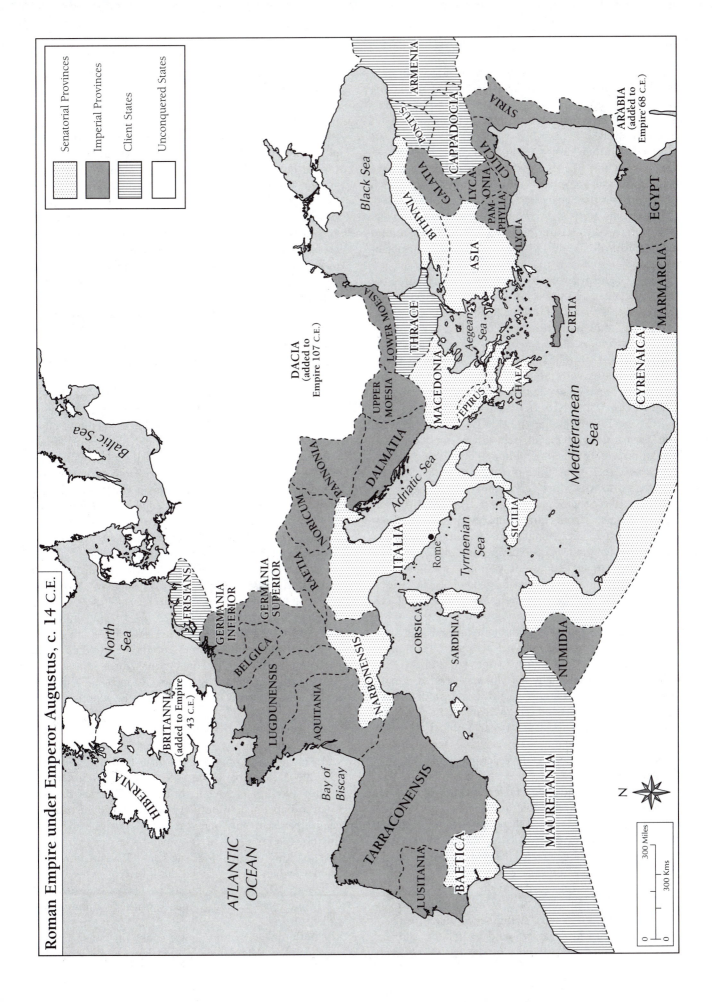

Roman Empire under Emperor Augustus, c. 14 C.E.

Senatorial Provinces
Imperial Provinces
Client States
Unconquered States

ATLANTIC OCEAN

HIBERNIA

BRITANNIA (added to Empire 43 C.E.)

FRISIANS

North Sea

Baltic Sea

Black Sea

Bay of Biscay

TARRACONENSIS

LUSITANIA

BAETICA

AQUITANIA

LUGDUNENSIS

BELGICA

GERMANIA INFERIOR

GERMANIA SUPERIOR

NARBONENSIS

RAETIA

NORICUM

PANNONIA

DACIA (added to Empire 107 C.E.)

UPPER MOESIA

LOWER MOESIA

DALMATIA

ITALIA

Rome

CORSICA

SARDINIA

Tyrrhenian Sea

SICILIA

Adriatic Sea

MACEDONIA

EPIRUS

ACHAEA

THRACE

Aegean Sea

ASIA

BITHYNIA

PONTUS

GALATIA

CAPPADOCIA

ARMENIA

LYCA-ONIA

PAM-PHYLIA

LYCIA

CILICIA

SYRIA

ARABIA (added to Empire 68 C.E.)

EGYPT

CRETA

Mediterranean Sea

CYRENAICA

MARMARCIA

NUMIDIA

MAURETANIA

300 Miles
300 Kms
0
0

N

of auxiliaries. None of these legions were allowed in Italy, and for his own protection Octavian created something new—the PRAETORIAN GUARD. Later a treasury department, the *aerarium militare,* was created for better organization of military finances.

Octavian then turned to the Senate and in 28 B.C.E., armed with the title of PRINCEPS SENATUS and with the help of Marcus Agrippa, conducted a census. Through this maneuver the Senate was reduced in number to 800. Certain of his AUCTORITAS, or unquestioned position, Octavian prepared to return his power to the Senate and to the people of Rome, thus gaining for all time their obedience.

The Senate received back its powers to control the state on January 13, 27 B.C.E. In return, Octavian was granted for 10 years control of Spain, Gaul, and Syria, centers of frontier defense, and controlled the appointment of governors. These were thus imperial provinces, and the Senate controlled the rest. This system was seemingly Republican, with the added safeguard that no governor of any province would dare to go against Augustus's wishes.

On the 16th of January in 27 B.C.E., he received the title *Augustus,* signifying his semi-divine, or more than human, nature. By 23 B.C.E., although no longer a consul, Augustus received the titles of IMPERIUM MAIUS and TRIBUNICIA POTESTAS, which gave him control over the provinces, the Senate, and the state. His response was typical; Augustus concentrated on reviving Roman religion. He created great temples to Mars and Apollo and ordered the temple of Capitoline Jupiter. In 12 B.C.E., he succeeded Marcus Lepidus as pontifex maximus, the highest priesthood of Roman religion. The ARVAL BRETHREN were revived, and the ranks of the Vestal Virgins were filled.

He built the Forum and the temples and supported any wealthy citizen who followed his lead. Most notable were the ever-faithful Marcus Agrippa and Marcius Philippus. Organizationally the city was divided into 14 wards under his direction. Police duties were performed by the Urban Cohorts, and order was maintained over the often unruly mobs. Above the Urban Cohorts, however, and above the population, the Senate, and, eventually, the emperors themselves, stood the Praetorian Guards.

Administrative changes were made in finances and bureaucracy. The Equestrian Order and Freedmen were brought into the government, and the civil system was born, a unit that maintained the empire for the next 500 years. The provinces contributed to the tax system, and laws were reformed or created, extending from adultery, treason, and bribery to marriage.

Augustus was concerned with the preservation of the frontiers, their certification, and, where possible, expansion. Spain and Gaul were strengthened and urbanized. Egypt's borders were organized, and in 20 B.C.E. a formal peace was signed with Parthia in the East. The treaty

affirmed Roman dominion over Armenia and pointed to one of Augustus's focal points of policy: the utilization of existing client countries in the East—Armenia, Commagene, Cappadocia, Galatia, and even Syria—as buffers toward Parthian expansion. Augustus did not realize all of his ambitions. Germany was occupied, and steps taken toward colonization and pacification, but in 9 C.E., the general Varus was annihilated by Arminius and Germans in the Teutoburg Forest. All hopes of achieving Roman supremacy there were abandoned.

As PATER PATRIAE, Augustus stressed the importance of the Roman family and institutions. In 18 B.C.E., he pushed for the acceptance of the *lex Julia de adulteriis,* which punished adultery, and the *lex Julia de maritandis ordinibus,* which required marriage and also the remarriage of the widowed. Only one person, the Lady Antonia, was given dispensation. Augustus honored family life and was always devoted to Livia, but his domestic affairs, and especially his constant search for a successor, dominated and strained his later years.

A successor to Augustus was not necessarily expected as there were no imperial precedents. Although Augustus searched constantly for an heir, Suetonius commented that twice the ruler thought of stepping down (after Antony's death and when he fell seriously ill, probably in 23 B.C.E.). But finding a suitable successor was not easy, for few men in the Roman world would have been able to maintain Augustus's equilibrium between the republican traditions and imperial realities. As the years passed, family tragedies and disappointments reduced his options until only one figure remained.

In the early years there was a battle of wills between Marcus Agrippa and Augustus's nephew, Marcellus (29–23 B.C.E.). Marcellus was the husband of Augustus's daughter Julia, but he died in 23. As a result, Julia was married to Agrippa. Although not eligible for the throne himself because of his common origin, his children could become emperors. Julia bore Agrippa three sons: Gaius, Lucius, and Agrippa Posthumus. Agrippa and his two sons, Gaius and Lucius, were officially adopted in 17 B.C.E.

Augustus needed administrative help, but his three adopted grandsons were too young. He turned to his wife Livia's sons by her former husband, Tiberius Claudius Nero: Tiberius and Nero Drusus. Nero Drusus died on the Elbe in 9 B.C.E.; in 6 B.C.E., Tiberius was elevated to imperial assistant, with a share in Augustus's *tribunicia potestas.* Only one year later, Gaius was given the title of PRINCEPS IUVENTUTIS, joined by Lucius in 5 B.C.E., thus marking them as the true heirs. Tiberius moved to Rhodes, where he remained until 4 C.E., when tragic events brought him to Rome again. Lucius had died in 2 C.E., followed by Gaius. And Agrippa Posthumus was exiled.

With the heirs of his choice gone, Augustus faced yet another blow. His daughter Julia had caused a terrible scandal in 2 B.C.E. and was exiled. This left Augustus with only Tiberius to aid him, something that Livia had always desired. In 3 C.E., Augustus accepted 10 more years of rule. The fact that Tiberius was destined to succeed him became evident in 13 C.E., when he was granted full *tribunicia potestas* and *imperium proconsulare*. Augustus placed his will with the Vestal Virgins and fell ill in 14, dying on August 29. Tiberius, who was on his way to Illyricum, was summoned back to assume the position of PRINCEPS. On the 17th of September, Augustus was deified by the Senate of Rome.

Octavian, or Augustus, was a figure of immensely human proportions, despite his *auctoritas* and eventual divinity. Suetonius wrote that he was remarkably handsome, of graceful gait but often less than immaculate appearance. His teeth were decayed, and his messily tended hair was yellow. Although he was only five feet, seven inches tall (perhaps less), he was elegantly proportioned. His health was always a concern. There was a weakness in his left hip and right forefinger, and ringworm was probably present. More importantly, Augustus fought terrible bouts of illness: abscessed liver, influenza and seasonal complaints. The worst came in 23 B.C.E., when it was generally believed that he would die. His private physician, Antonius Musa, managed to heal him.

A practical man, no great luxuries were kept in the palace, and his furnishings, like his diet and dress, were simple. He mistrusted the mob, disliked large crowds, and once, during the Civil Wars, had to be rescued by Marc Antony from a group of rioters.

Augustus was educated in rhetoric and studied with Apollodorus of Pergamum, from whom he learned Greek. Areus, a philosopher, and his sons Dionysius and Nicanor also provided elements of Augustus's education. Although he never mastered Greek, he was a patron of Greek poetry and intellectuals in general, especially writers and philosophers. He himself possessed literary aspirations.

Most of Augustus's writings are not extant. Only the famous *Res Gestae*, which listed his achievements, was preserved, in inscriptions, from antiquity. Augustus also penned an attack on Brutus's *Eulogy of Cato*, a philosophical treatise and an autobiography of 13 books. Attempts at poetry and tragedy were made in his short poem, *Sicily*, and in his *Epiphanus* and *Ajax*. He destroyed *Ajax* himself. His style was simple but idiomatic, with numerous peculiarities of grammar and spelling.

Suggested Readings: Baker, G. P. *Augustus.* New York: Cooper Square Press, 2000; Southern, Pat. *Augustus.* New York: Routledge, 1998; Bowersock, Glen W. *Augustus and the Greek World.* Oxford: Clarendon Press, 1965; Braund, David. *Augustus to Nero: A Sourcebook on Roman History 31 B.C.–A.D. 68.* London: Croom Helm, c1985;———. *The Early Principate: Augustus to Trajan.* Oxford: Claren-

don Press, 1982; Reinhold, Meyer, ed., *The Golden Age of Augustus.* Toronto: S. Stevens, 1978; Gurval, Robert. *Actium and Augustus: The Politics and Emotions of Civil War.* Ann Arbor: University of Michigan Press, 1998; Millar, Fergus, and Erich Segal, eds. *Caesar Augustus: Seven Aspects.* New York: Clarendon Press, 1984; *The Power of Images in the Age of Augustus.* Translated by Alan Shapiro. Ann Arbor: University of Michigan Press, c1988; Raaflaub, Kurt A., and Mark Toher, eds. *Between Republic and Empire: Interpretations of Augustus and His Principate.* Berkeley: University of California Press, 1990; Suetonius *The Twelve Caesars.* Translated and with an introduction by Michael Grant. New York: Penguin, 1979; Tacitus, Cornelius. *Empire and Emperors: Selections from Tacitus' Annals.* Translated by Graham Tingay. New York: Cambridge University Press, 1983; ———. *The Annals of Imperial Rome.* Translated and with an introduction by Michael Grant. New York: Penguin, 1964; ———. *Annales.* Edited by Henry Furneaux. Oxford: Clarendon Press, 1965.

Aurelian (Lucius Domitius Aurelianus) (c. 215 C.E. 275 C.E.) *Roman emperor from 270 to 275 C.E.; as a general in the field, one of the most successful of third-century rulers*

Aurelian probably came from Sirmium, or perhaps Moesia, although his roots were obscure. He did become a leading officer during the reign of Emperor Gallienus, and in 268, when the general Aureolus revolted, he assumed that officer's command of the cavalry corps at Mediolanum (Milan). During the reduction of the city, Aurelian became embroiled with Marcus Claudius (Claudius Gothicus) in an imperial intrigue. Gallienus was murdered, and Claudius became emperor, with Aurelian serving as Master of the Horse.

A series of campaigns against the Goths followed, but in January 270, Claudius died of the plague in Sirmium. His brother Quintillus aspired to the throne, but Aurelian gained support of the army and was elevated to the throne. Quintillus killed himself.

The state of imperial affairs was pitiful when Aurelian came to power. Barbarians threatened the frontiers while usurpers divided the Roman world. General Tetricus was on the Rhine, and Zenobia, the queen of Palmyra, stood with various generals and pretenders in her camp. Aurelian took the only course of action open to him. The empire had to be strengthened and unified. With the nickname *Manu ad ferrum*, "Hand-on-hilt," this burly, coarse but gifted soldier aspired to the title *Restitutor Orbis*, the "Restorer of the World."

He marched first against the Germanic Juthungi, who had invaded the province of Raetia and thus threatened Italy. Aurelian forced the barbarians into a retreat and routed them on the Danube. The Juthungi sued for peace, and Aurelian allowed them to return home. Journeying to Rome, Aurelian received the imperial powers begrudgingly. He could not enjoy them in peace for long. An urgent request came from Pannonia, where the Vandals were on the attack. Aurelian crushed them in 270–271 but had to face the Juthungi again in Italy, this time allied with the Alamanni and the Marcomanni. The tribes ambushed Aurelian near Placentia, defeating him and forcing a retreat into northern Italy. However, the Germans were too disorganized to follow up on their victory, and Aurelian used the time to bolster the defenses of the north. He marched against them a second time and exterminated them at Metaurus, Fanum Fortuna, and Ticinum, winning the so-called JUTHUNGINE WAR.

Returning to Rome in 271, Aurelian had to pacify a terrified city. He halted the rioting and put up new defense walls (the Aurelian Walls). The minters of Rome had also revolted, and Aurelian was forced to trap and execute them and their allies, some of senatorial rank, in a terrible battle on the Caelian Hills. Thrace was reconquered and freed of the Goths, who were pursued over the Danube. But imperial frontiers had proven impossible to defend, and the province of Dacia was abandoned entirely. A battle near the Orontes River ended the revolt of Palmyra in the East, as Aurelian defeated General Zabdas and his forces.

In 274, Aurelian marched into Gaul to attack the usurper Tetricus and his Gallic empire. At the battle of Campi Catalaunii, near Chalons, Tetricus abandoned his troops and surrendered. The empire had been pacified, and a triumphant return to Rome ended senatorial resistance to Aurelian's claims.

The currency of the empire had been reduced in value, causing inflation, and Aurelian reformed the system using the sestertii. Informers were punished, debts cancelled, bread and corn rationed fairly, and religious devotion to the sun god, Sol Invictus, encouraged. Aurelian attempted by these means to develop a universal deity to unite the pagan world. In the process he started persecution of the Christians again.

With his internal reforms accomplished, Aurelian returned to the East in the summer of 275 with ambitions toward Mesopotamia. A harsh disciplinarian, he caught his secretary, Eros, in a lie during the campaign and promised dire punishment. Eros, expecting to die, went to the Praetorian Guards and said that Aurelian planned to kill them too. A plot sprang up immediately, resulting in the assassination of Aurelian a short time later.

Aurelius, Marcus See MARCUS AURELIUS.

Aurelius Victor (fl. late fourth century C.E.) *Historian whose main work was a brief account of the emperors, writ-* *ten around 360 C.E. and covering the period from the reign of Tiberius to Constantius II*

Aurelius Victor was, by his own admission, a man of humble African origin. Following the publication of his book, *Caesars*, he was honored by Julian with the post of governor of Pannonia Secundae in 361 and was later the Prefect of the City of Rome (c. 389). A pagan, Victor wrote in the style of Sallust. The *Caesars* was a large collection of stories but was only the most important of several histories. A second imperial annal was an *Epitome* to the time of Theodosius I. Although similarities exist between the two, the apparent differences in sources rendered them both unique. A record of the earliest period of Rome was found in *Origo gentis romanae* (Origin of the Roman nation) and the era of the Kings and the Republic was treated in his *De viris illustribus* (On famous men), using as its sources Hyginus and Livy.

Aureolus, Manius Acilius (d. 268 C.E.) *A cavalry commander under Gallienus (253–268 C.E.)*

From Dacia, Aureolus came to the attention of the emperor sometime during 257, when Gallienus was searching for a commander for his new central cavalry corps. Aureolus was given the post and a force of horsemen stationed in Mediolanum (Milan) for use as a flying detachment for the frontiers. In 258, the baptism of fire for this unit came in the campaigns against the Alamanni, who threatened Italy itself, invading through Raetia. Just outside of Mediolanum the barbarians were routed.

In 260, two usurpers were crushed, Ingenius in Pannonia and then Regalianus in Upper Pannonia. Aureolus now received considerable liberty in his command, for a subordinate, Domitianus, was dispatched to crush the family of the quartermaster in Thrace, Macrianus, who were in revolt. In 268, while Gallienus was away on campaign, Aureolus rebelled while in charge of the Italian defenses. Gallienus marched back to face him, laid siege to Mediolanum, but then was assassinated. Aureolus surrendered to one of the assassins, M. Aurelius Claudius, but was executed immediately.

Aureus Imperial coin of Rome; its standard issue gold currency from the time of Julius Caesar to the reign of Constantine the Great. Caesar introduced the coin around 49 B.C.E., and it developed a value approximately equal to 25 denarii and 100 sestertii. After Constantine the Great, the aureus declined in worth as a gold piece and was replaced by the solidus.

Ausonius, Decimus Magnus (fl. fourth century C.E.) *Poet, consul and governor of Gaul*

Ausonius grew up in Burdigala (Bordeaux), receiving his education in rhetoric and grammar while studying in his native area and Tolosa (Toulouse). His teaching became renowned, and Emperor Valentinian I sought his aid in tutoring his son and heir, Gratian. Ausonius became a powerful adviser, and in 375, when Gratian succeeded to the throne, he was given a Praetorian prefectship with control of Gaul, followed in 379 by a consulship. Ausonius remained a fixture at court but was eventually challenged for imperial attention by St. Ambrose. With Gratian's murder in 383, Ausonius retired to Bordeaux and to his poetry and correspondence. He was a prolific poet and writer. There were poems, often collected (*Ephemeris* and *Parentalia*) or individual (*Mosella*). His other notable works included the *Ordo Nobilium Urbium*, a collection of articles on great cities.

Auxiliaries   *See* LEGIONS.

Avaricum, Siege of   Bloody event in 52 B.C.E., during Julius Caesar's GALLIC WARS, that was a temporary inconvenience to the Romans in the conquest of Gaul. During an uprising in unpacified Gaul, led by the chieftain Vercingetorix, Caesar moved quickly to crush all opposition. One of his targets was the Biturigan city of Avaricum. The local tribes decided to resist openly and prepared the city for a siege. With around two legions, Caesar skillfully broke attempts to raise his attack and then ruthlessly brought the city to its knees. Nearly 40,000 Biturigans died for nothing, as Caesar lost only time.

Averni (Arverni)   A tribe in Gaul that was long opposed to Roman imperialism and was a bitter enemy of another major people, the Aedui. The height of their power in Gaul was in the middle of the second century B.C.E., when their king was Luernius and they occupied all of the territory from the Rhone to the Atlantic. Such a kingdom was not to be allowed by the Romans.

The Aedui joined Rome in a war with the Averni, who had the Allobroges as allies. The Roman generals Fabius Maximus and Cn. Domitius Ahenobarbus crushed the Averni and their King Bituitus, son of Luernius, in a battle in 121 B.C.E.

The power of the Averni was effectively shattered, and the Aedui were preeminent until about 80 B.C.E., when Celtillus ruled them. The GALLIC WARS (58–52 B.C.E.) gave the Averni their last chance for greatness. Vercingetorix, their king, was young but gifted, and under his leadership most of Gaul joined a revolt against Rome. Julius CAESAR ended any hopes for the Averni's future at the siege of ALESIA in 52 B.C.E. The Averni capital of Gergovia was renamed Augustonemetum by Augustus, and the Averni were reduced in status. In the fifth century C.E., their lands were taken by the Visigoths.

Avidius Heliodorus   (fl. early second century C.E.) *Philosopher, secretary, and associate of Emperor Hadrian*

Heliodorus acquired a reputation of philosophical and oratorical brilliance as a member of Hadrian's intellectual circle. His official position was that of secretary of correspondence (*see* EPISTULIS, AB). Later he served as prefect of Egypt, a reward for his speeches. His son was Avidius Cassius, the general of Marcus Aurelius.

Avidius Nigrinus, Gaius   (d. 118 C.E.) *A member of the wealthy and influential Avidius family who held numerous posts during the reign of Trajan (97–117 C.E.)*
Nigrinus was a tribune in 105, consul in 110, and, at a later time, a governor in the recently conquered Dacia. As a legate in ACHAEA, he probably participated in Trajan's attempt to reorganize and stabilize the administration of the financially troubled province. By the succession of HADRIAN in 117, Nigrinus commanded considerable political respect and was seen as both a leading general and the probable heir. Suddenly, in the summer of 118, he and three others were put to death by order of the Senate for conspiring against Hadrian, probably due to Nigrinus's differing position on the imperial policy, as well as his longstanding friendship with Trajan.

Avidius Quietus, Titus   (fl. late first century C.E.) *Consul in 93 C.E.*
A successful military and social figure Quietus served as proconsul of Achaea and governor of Britain in 98. His brother was AVIDIUS NIGRINUS (consul 110 C.E.) and he was a friend of both PLINY THE YOUNGER and PLUTARCH.

Avitus   (d. c. 456 C.E.) *Emperor of the West (455–456) whose career in the service of the empire outmatched his brief and unsuccessful reign*
Marcus Maecilius Flavius Eparchius Avitus came from a noble family in Gaul, where he was favored with the posts of *magister militum* and Praetorian prefect for the province. He was known mostly for his association with the Goths, especially the Visigoth King Theodoric I. In 437, Avitus had joined the powerful *magister militum* AETIUS in his fight against the Goths and had personally persuaded King Theodoric to accept a peace. In 451, Avitus once more proved useful to the Western cause by persuading the king to join in the fight against Attila the Hun. Victory was attained, but Theodoric was killed. His son Theodoric II was, however, a friend of Avitus, and in 455 this association proved to be of tremendous political value.

Petronius Maximus reigned as emperor for less than four months in 455. When his death was reported to him at Tolosa, Avitus was approached by Theodoric with the idea of the prefect succeeding to the throne. On July 9–10, 455, Avitus was hailed as emperor by the Goths, and several weeks later was invested at Arles. He entered

Italy and assumed the consulship for 456. Although he was accepted by Marcian, the emperor of the East, he had trouble convincing the Roman Senate and the people that he should be emperor. He chose the *magister militum* RICIMER to defeat the Vandals who were threatening Italy, and the Romans chose to make Ricimer's triumphs personal. Avitus, snubbed in this manner, found his own imperial position deteriorating. The Senate despised him and the mobs of Rome were enraged by his handling of a famine. In an attempt to ease the situation, Avitus dismissed his contingents of Gothic and Gallic troops but paid them off by stripping Rome of its bronze statues. Horrified, the people rebelled, forced Avitus out of the city and accepted the return of Ricimer and the other imperial candidate, Majorian.

Avitus was defeated in 456, probably in September of that year, at Placentia and was allowed to step down to seek a religious life. The Senate sentenced him to death, despite his being consecrated a bishop in late October. He fled to Gaul but died suspiciously on the way.

Axona   At the Aisne River, between Laon and Reims; site of a battle between Galba, king of the Suessiones (Soissons), and Julius Caesar in 57 B.C.E. Galba led the Belgae with a force of about 75,000 men but was defeated. Caesar, as a result, marched northward into Belgica.

Axum   African kingdom in the region of Abyssinia.

B

Baalbek City in the province of Syria, near the cities of Tyre and Berytus, that boasted one of the empire's finest temple precincts and public buildings. In existence since before the sixth century B.C.E., when the first great temple structures were built, Baalbek figured in the stabilizing of the frontiers during the early years of the reign of AUGUSTUS (ruled 27 B.C.E.–14 C.E.). Marcus AGRIPPA reorganized the East and chose Baalbek and Berytus as two important Roman colonies. Henceforth Baalbek was a thoroughly Roman city in the midst of Syria, and its name was changed eventually to Heliopolis. Not only did Baalbek serve Roman interests in Syria, it also helped maintain a buffer against PARTHIA and PERSIA, a difficult task as the imperial frontier became weak.

The new colonists brought their new gods, and the result was a spectacular series of buildings erected between the first and third centuries C.E. Collectively, the edifices were called the Sanctuary of Jupiter. The Temple of Jupiter dominated the complex. Nearby rose the Temple of Bacchus, constructed in the second century, which survives in remarkably good shape and so offers excellent archaeological and artistic details from the period. Known as Bacchus's temple, but most likely the Temple of Venus-Atargatis, it was heavily decorated and supported by Corinthian columns.

Bacchus Roman god of wine, a conversion of the Greek god Dionysus, the son of Zeus (Jupiter) and Semele. He was considered boisterous, and his festival, the wild, orgiastic Bacchanalia, was suppressed in 186 B.C.E. Bacchus remained popular into the empire, and his impersonation was attempted by Emperor GAIUS CALIGULA. Around 211 C.E., Emperor Septimius SEVERUS

constructed a temple at Rome in Bacchus's honor. The city of Baalbek also contained a temple, known as Bacchus's temple, erected between the first and third centuries.

See also GODS AND GODDESSES OF ROME.

Bactria A territory of PARTHIA, also called Bactriana, stretching to the east of Parthia proper. Bactria was situated near the mountains of the Hindu Kush. The region played little part in the affairs of Rome, although the Bactrian king did send envoys to Hadrian to establish relations. It apparently was custom for the Bactrians to remain fiercely independent, as they refused to support the Persian ruler SHAPUR I in 259 C.E. when he defeated Emperor VALERIAN. The Bactrians even offered to attempt to rescue Valerian after his capture.

Baetica The name used by the Romans for the region of Andalusia in Spain.

See also HISPANIA.

Bagaudae The name given to a tribe (really a loose group of peasants) in Gaul during the late third century C.E. Crushed under the weight of the imperial tax system and disenfranchised by the barbarian invasions, many Gallic farmers and peasants banded together to form brigand communities. In 286 they put forth two leaders, AMANDUS AND AELIAN, as imperial aspirants. Emperor Diocletian, testing out his new form of government through trusted aides, sent his colleague MAXIMIAN to Gaul to crush the rebellion. Swiftly, but mercifully, the Bagaudae were eliminated and their leaders faded.

See also GALLIA.

Baiae Town in the Campania district of Italy; on a beautiful bay near Naples, just across from the city of Puteoli. The region was one of the most lovely in Italy, with natural springs and baths in abundance. For centuries the elite of Rome, including senators and emperors, built homes, estates, and palaces along the water. Baiae gained increased notoriety during the reign of NERO (54–69 C.E.), who spent much time at the villa of Gaius Calpurnius PISO, who became the center of the famed PISONIAN CONSPIRACY. It was proposed that Nero be murdered there but Piso refused. In 138 C.E. Emperor HADRIAN, his health deteriorating, left Rome and traveled to Baiae where he died on July 10. SEVERUS ALEXANDER was fond of the town, building a palace and a pool for his use as well as many public works of which most have been lost to the sea.

See also BAULI.

Balbillus, Tiberius Claudius (fl. mid-first century C.E.) *Astrologer for the emperors Claudius, Nero, and Vespasian*
Probably the son of THRASYLLUS (for many years the astrologer for TIBERIUS and from whom he learned his trade). Balbillus was a friend of Claudius, traveling with him to Britannia. A political career followed, including a procuratorship in Asia and a prefecture in Egypt. During the reign of Nero, Balbillus became an astrological adviser to the emperor and his mother. When a comet passed across the sky, in either 60 or 64, signalling the death of a great personage, Balbillus tried to calm Nero's fears by noting that the usual solution was to murder prominent citizens and thus appease the gods. Nero agreed, killing many nobles. Balbillus died in the late first century C.E. He was also known as Barbillus.

See also ASTROLOGY.

Balbinus (d. 238 C.E.) *Senator and coemperor in 238 C.E.*
According to the unreliable *Historia Augusta*, Decimus Caelius Calvinus Balbinus was an aristocrat while his colleague was of more humble origins. Like PUPIENUS, Balbinus had a long and distinguished career before his membership on the Committee of Twenty in 238 C.E. In terms of military skill, however, he was apparently the inferior to his co-ruler, for Pupienus was named chief of operations against Maximinus. The wild reception given to Pupienus upon his return to Rome was irksome to Balbinus, who also resented the German bodyguard retained by his colleague.

The two emperors began disagreeing on policy to the extent that, when the Praetorians stormed the palace only 99 days after their accession, Balbinus refused to allow the Germans to be summoned. Both were subsequently killed by the Guard and replaced by Gordian III. They were one of the last achievements of the Roman Senate in exerting its independence from the imperial palace.

Balbus, Lucius Cornelius (1) (fl. mid-first century B.C.E.) *An ally of Julius Caesar in Rome, eventually serving Augustus's cause in the capital as well*
Of Spanish descent, Balbus came from Gades; his reportedly tremendous wealth earned him the friendship of POMPEY THE GREAT from whom he received Roman citizenship in 72 B.C.E. Henceforth Balbus lived in Rome as a friend of Pompey and especially Caesar, whose interests he increasingly managed. These relationships proved invaluable in 56, when he was prosecuted for receiving his citizenship illegally. Pompey and Crassus both testified upon his behalf, and Cicero delivered one of his finest extant speeches, resulting in full acquittal. When the Civil War erupted, Balbus remained outwardly neutral, although he was Caesar's representative in personal matters; he joined Gaius Oppius, especially after the battle of PHARSALUS in 48, as a powerful political figure. Caesar's death in 44 diminished his influence, but as an agent of Octavian (AUGUSTUS), he served the consulship in 40 B.C.E.

Balbus, Lucius Cornelius (2) (fl. late first century B.C.E.) *A nephew of Lucius Cornelius Balbus (1)*
Balbus gained more power under AUGUSTUS than his uncle and returned to his home in Gades and rebuilt it. Like his relatives, he gained Roman citizenship and worked actively for Caesar in the Civil War (49–45 B.C.E.). He held the rank of proquaestor in Spain (HISPANIA) and was later a consul under Augustus. In 21 B.C.E., he received his greatest opportunity when he was named proconsul in Africa. In 19 B.C.E., he fought and defeated the African tribes of the Garamantes and had the distinction of being the last general to receive a TRIUMPH in Rome—who was not a member of the Imperial House. Making the most of his victory, Balbus built a theater in Rome, dedicated in 13 B.C.E.

Balbus, T. Ampius (d. after 48 B.C.E.) *Legate and proconsul in Asia*
A supporter of Pompey during the Civil War between POMPEY THE GREAT and Julius CAESAR in the mid-first century B.C.E., T. Ampius Balbus raised troops for the Pompeian cause. After the battle of Pharsalus (48 B.C.E.) he was exiled by the victorious Caesar. Ampius was brought back to Rome with the help of Cicero. In his work on Caesar, SUETONIUS acknowledged Balbus's reliability as a source, especially his recording of Caesar's comments on the Republic.

Balearic Islands A series of islands off the Spanish coast. The two largest were known to the Romans as Superior and Inferior. Recognized as a property of Rome as early as 202 B.C.E., the islands were occupied briefly by the forces of POMPEY THE GREAT when, after defeats of Pompeian armies by Julius CAESAR, he was forced to retreat from Spain. Pompey used the islands as a rallying center for the disheartened units of the Pompeian cause.

Ballista (fl. mid-third century C.E.) *Praetorian prefect (260–261 C.E.) of Emperor Valerian and the usurper Macrianus*
In 260 Valerian was defeated and captured by SHAPUR I, king of Persia, throwing the imperial succession into chaos. Ballista, one of Rome's most successful soldiers, proposed that FULVIUS MACRIANUS, another general, and his sons should take the throne. Despite throwing his considerable military skills behind Fulvius's sons Macrianus and the younger Quietus, defeat could not be averted at the hands of ODAENATH, king of Palmyra, in 261. Both Macrianus and Quietus were killed. There is some question as to Ballista's fate. According to the dubious *Scriptores Historiae Augustae*, Ballista may have been pardoned or settled on land in the Antioch area. More likely he was executed.

Barbia Orbiana (d. after 227 C.E.) *Empress from 225 to 226 C.E. and the wife of Severus Alexander*
Sallustia Barbia Orbiana was probably the daughter of the nobleman Seius Sallustius Barbius. In 225 Julia Mamaea, the mother of Severus Alexander, arranged for her son to marry Orbiana. Ever jealous of sharing her power or her control with her son, Mamaea treated her daughter-in-law cruelly and persecuted Orbiana's father. Although Severus Alexander opposed his mother's actions, Mamaea eventually had Macrinus put to death and compelled her son to divorce Orbiana. The empress was sent to Africa in 227, where she lived in exile.

Barbillus *See* BALBILLUS, TIBERIUS CLAUDIUS.

Bar Cochba, Simon (d. 135 C.E.) *The leader of a Jewish revolt in 132–135 C.E.*
After visiting Palestine in 130, HADRIAN desired to erect temples to Jupiter and Zeus and planned to place a Roman colony, Aelia Capitolina, on the site of JERUSALEM's destroyed walls and streets. Fulfilling the prophecy in the Book of Numbers, Simon son of Cosba (or Kosba) declared himself leader of the resultant uprising, taking the promised name Bar Cochba or "Son of Star." Using guerrilla tactics, Bar Cochba's warriors defeated sizable Roman detachments and then disappeared into the hills. Hadrian sent JULIUS SEVERUS to Palestine with a large army; according to Dio, 50 outposts and 985 villages were destroyed. The rebels were driven into caves and, from his base at Engeddi, Bar Cochba wrote of their sinking morale. As the Romans closed in, the Jews retreated to the Dead Sea caves and to Bethar. It was in Bethar that the last battle was fought, and Simon Bar Cochba was killed. So ended the revolt, but Judaea was devastated. Severus was given a triumph by Hadrian.

Accounts of the revolt were made by Dio, and Eusebius in the *Ecclesiastical History* noted the letters of the teacher Basilades referring to Bar Cochba. In letters recently unearthed in the Dead Sea caves, Bar Cochba is called Prince of Israel, a title also used on coinage he issued.

Bardasanes of Edessa (154–222 C.E.) *A heretic from Armenia*
Bardasanes denied the resurrection of Christ, and the resurrection of the body after death. He wrote the *Book of the Laws of the Nations* in defense of his anti-GNOSTICISM.

Bargoia, Simon (d. 70 C.E.) *Also called Simon Bar Giora; leader of the Jewish revolt put down by Titus in 70*
Defending the Great Temple of JERUSALEM from the besieging Romans, many of the rebels, including Bargoia, were captured. As he was the leader, only he was chosen for execution by Titus.

Barnabas (fl. first century C.E.) *Saint*
Also referred to as an Apostle, although he was not an original Apostle of Jesus. Barnabas was originally a Jew from Cyprus. Known as Joseph, he was later given the name Barnabas by the Apostles, a name said by St. Luke to mean "son of consolation." It was Barnabas who introduced St. Paul to the Apostles after Paul's conversion and vouched for Paul to the Christians of Jerusalem. Barnabas was sent to Antioch to look into the affairs of the growing church there. He later fetched Paul from Tarsus and, with him, embarked on the first of the famed missionary journeys, initially to Cyprus. Barnabas is thus considered the founder of the Cypriot Church. At the Council of Jerusalem, he defended the membership of Gentile Christians but later split with Paul over the issue of his cousin the Evangelist John Mark. Barnabas probably continued his travels and was martyred, according to legend, in 61 at Salamis, although nothing of this is recorded in the New Testament. The work called *Epistle of Barnabas* was not written by him.

Basil the Great (c. 329–379) *Bishop of Caesarea, one of the great defenders of Christian orthodoxy against Arianism*
With his brother St. Gregory of Nyssa and St. Gregory of Nazianzus, Basil is one of "The Three Cappadocians." Basil was the son of St. Basil the Elder and Emmelia, the daughter of a martyr, and was one of 10 children, three of whom—Basil, Gregory, and Macrina—became saints. Largely raised by his grandmother, Basil studied at Caesarea, his native town, and at Constantinople, where he developed his long friendship with Gregory of Nazianzus. Having obtained a superb education, he returned to Caesarea as a teacher. He soon also underwent a profound spiritual transformation, embarking on a journey in 357 to the monasteries of Egypt, Palestine, and Mesopotamia.

After his return, he founded a monastic community near Annesi, where his sister Macrina had already established a religious house. Basil's innovations within the monastic community, especially his rule, earned him the title Father of Eastern (or Oriental) Monasticism. The Rule of St. Basil is still followed by religious where Orthodox Christianity is practiced.

In 360, Basil was finally convinced to depart his hermitage and take part in a council at Constantinople. Subsequently ordained with great reluctance, he played a major role in the administration of the diocese of Caesarea under Bishop Eusebius, so much so that the two entered into a dispute. Basil withdrew to his monastic community but was recalled in 365 at the insistence of Gregory of Nazianzus. In 370, he was chosen to succeed to the see of Caesarea that had by now acquired the status of metropolitan. His appointment was a great pleasure to ST. ATHANASIUS, bishop of Alexandria, but was greeted with suspicion by the ardent Arian emperor Valens. Over the next nine years Basil was conspicuous for his care of the poor, his efforts in the defense of ecclesiastical rights, and most of all, for his steadfast opposition to heresy, especially Arianism. When defending himself before Valens, Basil was so fiery that a courtier questioned his nerve, to which the saint gave his famous reply: "Perhaps you are not familiar with a proper bishop." Basil died on January 1, 379, at a time of terrible upheaval in the Roman Empire both politically (because of the Goths) and religiously (because of the Arians). His funeral was attended by a large crowd, including Christians, Jews, and pagans.

Some 366 letters are extant, most from after his elevation to the episcopacy. His other writings included a treatise, *On the Holy Spirit*; three books against Enomius, an outspoken Arian Bishop of Cyzicus; and a compilation, with Gregory of Nazianzus, from the works of Origen in the *Philocalia*. He is also the ascribed formulator of the Liturgy of St. Basil, still used on certain days in the liturgy of the Greek Orthodox Church.

Basilianus (d. 218 C.E.) *Supporter of Emperor Macrinus* Basilianus was named governor of Egypt in 218. While a loyal associate of the short-reigning emperor Marcus Opellius MACRINUS, Basilianus fell a victim of the rampant political instability of the empire. A revolt against Macrinus erupted in the East, and representatives of the imperial claimant Elagabalus were sent to Egypt to enlist Basilianus against his patron. Basilianus ordered the emissaries put to death, only to learn a short time later that Macrinus, and Macrinus's son Diadumenianus, had been defeated. A panic ensued in Egypt and Basilianus fled to Italy. There he was betrayed into the hands of supporters of Elagabalus, taken to Nicomedia, and executed.

basilica Roman structure with architecture similar to the Greek *stoa*. The basilica was a large, heavily decorated meeting place or public center, used for various purposes. Basilicas served most often to house the meetings of governmental groups or commissions. In the Western Empire, virtually all major structures were erected to accompany the edifices of a FORUM. Architecturally most basilicas, even those in the outer provinces, shared a number of characteristics: ornate columns, open areas fronting the forums of which they were an integral part, and spaces within that were designed to provide not only room but also air. In the empire, four of the most important basilicas were the Aemilia, Julia, Maxentius, and Ulpia.

Basilica Aemilia The basilica in the FORUM ROMANUM that was rebuilt in 14 B.C.E. by Augustus. It was located across from its sister building, the BASILICA JULIA, and was surrounded by the Temple of Antoninus and the CURIA JULIA. Built before the time of Julius Caesar, the basilica was repaired with elaborate artifices and opulence during the Augustan Age. It was damaged in 12 B.C.E. from the ravages of the same fire that burned the Julia but was not repaired until 22 C.E., by Emperor Tiberius. There was a special chapel, called *sacrarium*, within the basilica, in honor of Gaius and Lucius, the grandsons of Augustus. In his *Natural History*, PLINY THE ELDER wrote of its beauty.

Basilica Julia Begun by Julius CAESAR in 54 B.C.E., the Basilica Julia was finished by Augustus early in his reign. In the space once occupied by the Basilica Sempronia, built in 170 B.C.E., the new edifice was part of the great FORUM ROMANUM, parallel to the Rostra and surrounded by the TEMPLE OF SATURN and TEMPLE OF CASTOR AND POLLUX. In 12 B.C.E. it was damaged by a fire. Augustus

The remains of the Basilica Aemilia, with the Curia Julia in the background *(Courtesy Fr. Felix Just, S.J.)*

dedicated the new marble works and additions to his designated heirs, his grandsons Gaius and Lucius, but the use of the name Julia continued. Another fire in 283 C.E. caused more destruction, but DIOCLETIAN had the basilica repaired. Originally, the basilica housed the board of the *centumviri;* the 180 court members worked in a building over 110 feet long and 53 feet wide.

Basilica Maxentia   A massive project undertaken during the reign of the usurper MAXENTIUS (306–312 C.E.); the last great architectural endeavor of Classical Rome. Maxentius, who ruled for six war-plagued years, desired a structure radically different from the Roman basilicas. Also called the Basilica Nova, the structure rested on the Velian Hill and relied upon the baths of the period for inspiration, rather than the other basilicas. Thus there were three vaults in the structure, and the nave was triple vaulted as well. Eight Corinthian columns supported the vaults. Maxentius died before the building was complete, and Constantine altered the original design by having the entrance front the Sacred Way. He also placed an immense statue of himself, carved from stone, in the apse. This basilica measured 92 feet in length and was 27 feet wide.

Basilica Ulpia   Constructed during the reign of TRAJAN (98–117 C.E.), this basilica was larger than any other structure of its time and influenced later Christian architecture. The basilica relied upon two rows of columns and contained a central nave, with two apses. The high roof, made of timber, allowed windows with clerestory lighting. Later Christian basilicas, especially those constructed in the time of Constantine the Great (306–337 C.E.), copied the plans of this monument. In LEPCIS MAGNA, the Basilica Severiana followed the basic theme, proving that such constructions were not only possible outside of Italy but also could be achieved with great sophistication.

Basilides   (fl. second century C.E.) *Syrian theologian who became the founder of the Alexandrian school of Gnosticism*
Basilides taught at Alexandria probably in the second quarter of the second century, during the reigns of the Roman emperors HADRIAN and ANTONINUS PIUS. His writings are preserved only in fragments, but these include psalms, odes, an otherwise unknown work entitled "The Gospel," and a biblical commentary, in 24 books, called the *Exegetica.* The doctrine he apparently espoused was a combination of Neoplatonism, Gnostic teachings, Persian dualism, and traditions derived from the supposed teachings of Sts. Peter and Matthias.

Basiliscus   (fl. fifth century C.E.) *Usurper in the Eastern Empire who ruled from 475 to 476 C.E.; brother of the Empress Verina, wife of Leo I*

In 468, Verina convinced her husband to appoint Basiliscus commander of the large fleet setting sail from CONSTANTINOPLE against the Vandal kingdom of GEISERIC in Africa. With 1,113 ships and over 100,000 men, Basiliscus sailed to Africa, forming the main blow of a three-pronged attack from Constantinople, Egypt, and Italy. CARTHAGE might have fallen but Basiliscus failed to follow up on initial successes, and Geiseric mustered a fleet of fire ships and put the galleys of Constantinople to rout. Returning to the capital, the failed commander hid in the Church of St. Sophia and then returned to Heraclea. When Leo died in 474, Verina adamantly opposed the rightful successor, ZENO, and enlisted her brother's aid in usurping the throne for PATRICIUS, an Isaurian master of the palace and her lover. Instead, Basiliscus seized control himself. Zeno fled the city as Basiliscus elevated his wife Zenonis to the rank of Augusta and his son to that of Augustus. Patricius was killed.

Upon Zeno's departure, however, rioting began in Constantinople, and fire destroyed the Basilica of Julian and the Palace of Lausus. The situation grew more serious as the emperor turned away from Orthodoxy and various ministers of the city urged Zeno's return. Zeno thus set out from his hiding place among his native Isaurians and entered the city amid the support of the state officers. Basiliscus, his wife and children, were exiled to Cucusus in Cappadocia and there starved to death.

Bassianus   The name originally given to two Roman emperors, CARACALLA and SEVERUS ALEXANDER.

Bassus, Aufidius   (d. after 54 C.E.) *Roman historian who helped lay the ground work for the later efforts of Cornelius Tacitus and Roman historiography*
Philosophical by nature, Bassus wrote several ambitious books including *Bellum Germanicum,* a history of the German Wars, praised by the critic Quintilian. Bassus also wrote a history of Rome, furthering Livy's writings on the same subject. It is generally accepted that Bassus's history of Rome began with 44 B.C.E. and probably terminated with the reign of CLAUDIUS in 54 C.E. Only fragments of the *Bellum Germanicum* are extant.

Bassus, Caesius   (fl. first century C.E.) *Lyrical poet Highly honored in his day, especially by Quintilian*
Bassus was also known to be a long-time friend of the satirist Persius. Bassus's main contribution was a manual on poetic meter, extant only in abbreviated form. All other works were lost or appeared under different names.

Bassus, Betilinus   (d. 40 C.E.) *A victim of Emperor Gaius Caligula*
In 40 C.E., Bassus was ordered executed by imperial decree, and his father Capito was compelled by Caligula to watch the event. When Capito asked to close his eyes,

he too was condemned to death. Knowing that he would perish, Capito stated that he was part of a conspiracy, and promised to disclose his accomplices. Having already murdered others for plotting against him, the emperor listened as Capito named all of the courtiers who had most abetted Caligula in his crimes. Capito thus died knowing that he had sown discord in the court. Within a year, Caligula was a victim of assassination by the PRAE-TORIAN GUARD.

Bassus, C. Julius Quadratus (d. after 118 C.E.) *Soldier of the emperor Trajan*

Bassus was a leading general in Trajan's war on Dacia (101–106) and served on the imperial staff both during that war and the subsequent Parthian campaign (114). He managed DACIA (117–118) for the empire and emerged as a powerful friend of Trajan, receiving the governorships of CAPPADOCIA (107–112) and SYRIA as well (113–117). Despite his death and honorary funeral at Pergamum, there remained great controversy among scholars as to details of his life.

Bassus, Junius (fl. fourth century C.E.) *Prefect of the Praetorian Guard under Emperor Constantine the Great and consul*

Junius Bassus was a loyal servant of CONSTANTINE and served as prefect for Italia for 13 to 14 years before obtaining a consulship in 331. He was responsible for the construction of a basilica of a pagan artistic nature on the Esquiline Hill in Rome. Such a style matched his own personal tendencies, for he was comfortable with the old pagan socio-political order even as he readily embraced the new Christian reality. He may have become a Christian, but a reference in Prudentius places doubts on the possibility.

Bassus, Quintus Caecilius (fl. first century B.C.E.) *An officer of Pompey the Great during the Civil War (49–45 B.C.E.)*

Bassus took part in the battle of PHARSALUS in 48, which forced him to flee for safety. When a rumor of Caesar's defeat in Africa caused a mutiny, a large portion of the Caesarean forces joined Bassus in Syria. Antistius Vetus, a legate of Julius Caesar, besieged Bassus at Apamea during 45, but with the help of the Parthians the mutineers survived. Eventually CRASSUS arrived in Syria and the soldiers in Apamea joined him, while Bassus escaped into anonymity.

Bassus, Saleius (fl. late first century C.E.) *Poet who specialized in epic poems*

Listed by QUINTILIAN among the epic writers, Bassus attained the friendship of VESPASIAN but then died at an early age. TACITUS mentions him with Vespasian.

Bassus Theotechnis, Junius (317–359 C.E.) *Son of Junius Bassus*

While his father served as Praetorian prefect, Theotechnis became prefect of Rome in 359, but died soon after. In death he acquired his greatest fame, for his sarcophagus is one of the finest examples of Roman Christian art. According to Ammianus Marcellinus, the year of his death was 358 but he probably died in 359. PRUDENTIUS noted that he was the first Christian in his family (suggesting that his father was not a Christian himself).

Batavi

A people of Germanic or of Celtic origin, the Batavi lived along the Rhine River in an island-like territory formed by the Rhine, the Waal and the Maas and known to contemporaries as *Insula Batavorum*. Related to the hostile Germanic tribe of the CHATTI, the Batavi joined the Romans as allies around the first century C.E. In 12 B.C.E. they aided Drusus in his campaign in Germany and in 16 C.E. assisted GERMANICUS in his seeking of revenge for the loss of Roman legions in 9 C.E. (in which the Batavi played no part). The historian TACITUS spoke of the reckless courage of their chief Chariovalda who dashed across the Weser with his warriors to attack the Germans. The awaiting CHERUSCI severely mauled the Batavi and Chariovalda was killed. Roman cavalry rode to their rescue, after which their loyalty was unquestioned. By 69 C.E., they not only composed auxiliary formations in the Roman legions but were also a horse guard and a personal bodyguard to emperors. A Batavian unit played a critical role in the first battle of BEDRIACUM (69 C.E.). Their obedience ended in 69, for the Batavian CIVILIS used his command of Vespasian's supporters on the lower Rhine to launch what became a massive, Batavian-led revolt. Caught in the ambitions of Civilis, the Batavi fought valiantly but were crushed finally by the emperor Vespasian's legate Petilius CERE-ALIS around 70. Thereafter the position of the tribe was greatly weakened, and its importance to Rome decreased. The Batavi were eclipsed completely by the arrival of new peoples from the East.

Bath *See* AQUAE (SULIS).

baths

The baths of the Roman Empire were one of the most common types of building and came to represent luxury, community, recreation, and, in the provinces, an association with Rome. Any city aspiring to greatness would have possessed baths (or *thermae*). The baths first appeared in the Italian region of Campania, and the best preserved examples of the early types are in POMPEII. There the Stabian Baths of the first century B.C.E. were used, although they tended to be darker, smaller, and more primitive than their later imperial counterparts.

Any large bath consisted of a number of rooms: the *apodyterium* (the changing room), *frigidarium* (cold room), *tepidarium* (warm room), *caldarium* (hot room), *laconicum* (dry sweating room), and an area for swimming, a *natatio*. Heat was provided to the *caldarium* from braziers or with ducts and hypocausts or underfloor heating. The better the bath, the more luxuries and amenities would be provided. The *caldarium* might be supplied with a *schola labri,* a basin of cold water, for example. Other additions were libraries, private suites (in public baths), gardens, and especially a gymnasium with an exercise area, the *palestra.*

It is not surprising, then, that baths were popular centers of local activity. Nowhere was this more true than in Rome itself. Marcus AGRIPPA, around 20 B.C.E., constructed the first major baths in the city, in the area of the Campus Martius. The baths that bore his name stood until 80 C.E. when they were consumed in the fire that destroyed much of the Campus Martius. The GOLDEN HOUSE OF NERO was described by SUETONIUS as having running sea water and sulphur water. Perhaps based on the Golden House, TITUS constructed a large series of rooms that included a bath with all of the essential elements plus two *palaestrae,* although it lacked a *natatio.* The much larger Baths of Trajan were begun in 104 C.E. and took five years to complete under the architect APOLLODORUS. He brilliantly placed the *frigidarium* in an elevated middle position, allowing everything else to revolve around it, including the extensive *natatio.* These baths, situated on the Esquiline and utilizing much of the Golden House, were the largest structure yet built and remained so until CARACALLA's reign.

The vast Baths of Caracalla, completed by his successors, represented the height of bath architecture. There were libraries, gardens, gymnasiums, and cisterns. The *natatio* was large and positioned to maximize the sky overhead; further, screens and walls semi-enclosed its area. Vaster in size was the *frigidarium,* which was

The Roman baths in Bath, Somerset, England *(Hulton/Getty Archive)*

supported by cross vaults and surrounded by small pools. The *caldarium* was moved away from the interior of the baths and set in its own position with a magnificent dome, some 35 meters high. Caracalla's Baths remained in excellent condition for centuries and have preserved even into the 20th century their scale and ambition.

DIOCLETIAN was next to order new baths for Rome, finishing in 306 the work begun by MAXIMIAN in 298. They resembled Caracalla's baths but were simpler in design, though they were certainly well built, for they stand today.

The provinces and cities of the empire adapted these designs. In Africa, in LEPCIS MAGNA and CARTHAGE baths were erected. Lepcis Magna offered both the Baths of Hadrian and the smaller Hunting Baths of the late second century C.E. Carthage boasted the extensive Antonine Baths (mid-second century C.E.) near the ocean, pointing to the economic success of both city and province. Tivoli, the resort of Hadrian, possessed two *thermae,* a small and a large. The Small Baths were probably the emperor's personal area and were a twisting amalgam of shapes and sizes. The Large Baths were very conventional, with cross vaults over the *frigidarium.*

Bathyllus (fl. early first century C.E.) *Pantomime actor from Alexandria*
Bathyllus was the freedman of Gaius MAECENAS, who was his patron and most ardent admirer. Through his influence, Bathyllus became, with Pylades, one of the leading actors of his time.

Bato (1) (d. 9 C.E.) *Chief of the Breucian tribes of Pannonia*
In 6 C.E. used the departure of the governor of ILLYRICUM and Pannonia, Valerius Mesallinus, who meant to aid Tiberius in his German campaign, as a suitable time to lead his people in a revolt. The Breucians marched against Sirmium but were severely checked by Caecina Severus, governor of Moesia, who had moved swiftly to defend Illyricum and Pannonia. Defeated but not broken, Bato the Breucian allied himself to Bato the Dalmatian, and their combined armies took refuge in the mountainous territory of Pannonia. The two Batos were again defeated, this time by King Rhoemetalces of Thrace, but again survived annihilation. Using guerrilla tactics they ravaged Illyricum and even broke into MACEDONIA. Germanicus was dispatched by Augustus to the Danube frontier. But victory still eluded Rome, and Bato the Breucian was undone only because of the suspicion of his ally. Bato the Dalmatian disliked the Breucian's taking of hostages from the tribes, trapped him and put him to death.

Bato (2) (fl. early first century C.E.) *Chief of the Dalmatians who led a major revolt in Illyricum and Pannonia*

In 6 C.E., reluctantly assembling his warriors for use by the Romnas in Tiberius's campaign against the Germans, Bato decided instead that he had enough troops to rebel, especially in the absence of the governor Valerius Messallinus, who was away with Tiberius. The Dalmatians marched on the city of Salonae but Bato was wounded. He dispatched a column to the coast, threatening Tiberius's communications with Italy. Messallinus marched to give battle; although outnumbering the Romans, Bato was defeated.

An alliance was formed shortly thereafter with Bato the Breucian (*see* BATO [1]). After receiving another blow at the hands of Rhoemetalces of Thrace, the allies nevertheless ravaged Illyricum and threatened Greece via Macedonia. Sometime in 8 C.E. Bato the Dalmatian fell out with Bato the Breucian and had him killed, whereupon the Breucians broke the alliance and were easily conquered by Caecina Severus, governor of Moesia. Bato fled into Pannonia. Tiberius and Germanicus besieged him at Andetrium, a fortress near Salonae. Seeing his garrison reduced, Bato fled but eventually surrendered after receiving a pledge of his safety. Tiberius asked him why he had revolted, and his answer cut to the heart of a problem underlying the imperial system of provincial government: Rome, he said, sent as protectors of its flocks, not dogs or even shepherds, but wolves.

Bato (3) (d. 212 C.E.) *Popular gladiator during the reign of Emperor Caracalla*
CARACALLA had an obsession with gladiatorial combat and was once struck by the idea of seeing how many opponents one gladiator could defeat in one bloody session. The gladiator chosen was the gifted fighter Bato, of whom nothing else is known. Bato was able to defeat (and hence slay) two consecutive opponents, but fatigue led to his defeat and death at the hands of the third. CARACALLA gave Bato a lavish funeral.
See also COMMODUS.

Battarius (d. after 170 C.E.) *Leader of a tribe in Pannonia*
In 169–70, at the age of 12, Battarius went before MARCUS AURELIUS to request an alliance with Rome. The emperor granted his request. In return for gold, Battarius also agreed to convince the tribes along the Danube frontier, especially the Tarbus, to cease their hostilities with the empire.

Bauli A small community near the towns of BAIAE and Misenum; composed of the estates of the most powerful figures in Rome. Like Baiae, the area was for centuries a retreat for senators and emperors. This, and its location directly across the bay from Puteoli in Campania, made Bauli susceptible to the bizarre plans of GAIUS CALIGULA.

The astrologer THRASYLLUS, servant of Tiberius, once prophesied that Gaius had as much chance of becoming emperor as he did of riding dryshod across the Gulf of Baiae between Puteoli and Bauli. To prove the prediction false, Caligula ordered in 39 C.E. a bridge of boats be thrown across the bay. Every boat in Italy was commissioned, causing starvation and food shortages, and other boats were built on the spot. A massive project, the historian Dio reported that there were rooms, resting places, and running water on the bridge. Dressed like Alexander the Great, Caligula for days paraded his friends and his Praetorian Guard from shore to shore as he rode in a chariot, with Darius, a prince of the Arsacids, at his side.

Bauto (d. c. 388 C.E.) Magister militum *under Emperor Valentinian II*

Bauto was one of the first and most powerful generals of the late empire. He both interfered in imperial policies and directed their course through his daughter, Aelia EUDOXIA, who became the wife of Eastern emperor Arcadius.

According to Zosimus, Bauto, a Frank, was sent by Gratian, the emperor of the West, to aid Theodosius on the Balkan and Danube frontiers after the disastrous battle of ADRIANOPLE in 378 C.E. As a general he was valued by Valentinian II, who brought him back to defend Italy against the attack of the usurper Magnus MAXIMUS. Henceforth, Bauto influenced Valentinian's policy in the West, working as an ally or as a neutral with AMBROSE, the bishop of Milan. He achieved the consulship in 385, serving with Arcadius, who married his daughter in 395. His control over Valentinian ended, however, around 388, and it can be assumed that he died in that year. His wife was probably a Roman, and his daughter was given a Roman education.

Bedriacum A town in northern Italy, located on the Via Postuma, between the cities of Cremona and Verona. In 69 C.E. it was the site of two major battles. The first confrontation was on April 15; it brought to an end the brief reign of Emperor OTHO, at the hands of the army of VITELLIUS. Otho had begun his reign with the assassination of Galba but discovered immediately that the German legions were in revolt, having declared their commander, Vitellius, emperor of Rome. Two legates, Aulus CAECINA ALIENUS of the IV Legion and Fabius VALENS of the I Legion at Bonn, assumed control of Vitellius's army and set out for Rome with approximately 70,000 men.

In Rome, Otho cultivated popular support and garnered the oaths of legions in Pannonia, Dalmatia, and Moesia, and that of the commander VESPASIAN in Judaea, but he could not muster more than 25,000 men for the campaign. Although additional legions were marching to his aid, the bulk of his troops were from the reliable PRAETORIAN GUARD. His generals included the aged Marius Celsus, the Praetorian Prefect Licinius Proculus, Sue-

tonius Paulinus and Annius Gallus. Vitellius's legions breached the Alps and fought several inconclusive skirmishes in northern Italy with the Othonians. The first large battle took place at PLACENTIA, between Caecina and several contingents of Otho's Praetorians. Although outnumbering the Othonians, the veterans of Germany did not fare well.

By April, Otho was reinforced by the first troops from the Danube legions. Paulinus, Celsus, and Gallus called for patience. Victory could be won with additional forces. But Proculus and his brother, who possessed Otho's ear, counseled bold action, citing Otho's military genius. As Tacitus noted: "Such was the language of flattery. They made their position palatable, and no man presumed to administer an antidote." Otho commanded his army from the town of Brixellum, some miles from Bedriacum, while his legions grew despondent and fatigued.

Otho's generals entered the contest with the I Adjutrix, the XII Pannonian, gladiators, and the Praetorian Guard in the center position. The XIV Legion from Britain stood as a reserve. They were opposed by the XXI Legion, the V Alaudae, the cohorts of Batavians, and the I Italian, which faced the Praetorians directly.

The I Adjutrix plowed into the XXI, and the Vitellians lost their eagle. Recovering quickly, the German veterans launched a brutal counterattack, and the Othonian I Adjutrix broke apart, its young cohorts disintegrating. Vitellius's other legion, the Alaudae, routed the XII Pannonian, and then put the XIV from Britain to flight as well. Only the Praetorians refused to yield ground, bloodily dueling the I Italian Legion to a standstill. The Batavians, however, tipped the scales against them, finishing the rout of Otho's wings. Facing retreat or total annihilation, the Praetorians withdrew.

The next morning, Otho's camp at Bedriacum lay open to Valens and Caecina. The Praetorians pulled back to Brixellum to be with the emperor. Otho killed himself at dawn on April 17, 69. Vitellius marched to Rome to become emperor. His reign did not last much longer than Otho's, however, for Vespasian was also on his way to Rome and would claim the throne for himself. Accounts of the battle were written by Tacitus, Suetonius, Dio, and Josephus.

A second military engagement was fought at Bedriacum—actually at Cremona, some miles distant—on October 27, 69 C.E., between the legions of Emperor VITELLIUS and the army of Antonius PRIMUS, who represented the cause of VESPASIAN. After crushing the Othonians in April, Vitellius had proceeded to Rome and there humiliated the Praetorian Guard by replacing it with new members; incensed the Danube Legions with cruel treatment; refused to allow the dead at Bedriacum to be buried; and then demonstrated a pernicious avarice and gluttony. The discontented legions chose Vespasian, general of the legions in JUDAEA, to remove Vitellius from power.

Titus, Vespasian's son, Mucianus, the governor of Syria, and Tiberius Julius Alexander, the prefect of Egypt, urged Vespasian to accept the throne. The balance of the legions joined in his crusade. Tiberius Alexander administered the oath of allegiance to the troops on July 1, and plans were begun for a march on Rome.

Meanwhile, Antonius Primus, the legate on the Danube, and Cornelius FUSCUS, the procurator of Pannonia, stirred up the Danubian Legions and were soon joined by the disbanded Praetorian Guards, by now a ferocious enemy of Vitellius. These three western legions set out for Italy, even before Vespasian's eastern legions could begin their march. Vitellius sent his legate, Alienus Caecina, with six legions to the north to confront Primus. Intending to defect to Vespasian, Caecina ignored orders from Rome and dispatched the bulk of his forces to Cremona, while a large detachment moved to Hostilia, a city on the Po River. Primus moved southward across the Alps, investing Verona and using it as the center of his operations—unaware that Vespasian had ordered that no troops cross the great mountains, preferring to leave the war to the hard-marching Mucianus. Letters from Caecina to Primus set the groundwork for betrayal, and Caecina, with the backing of the fleet in the Adriatic, proposed to his legions that they join the Flavian cause. His plans were dashed when his own soldiers placed him in chains. From Cremona the legions marched out to give battle to the waiting Primus.

The now-leaderless Vitellians formed up from right to left, cavalry and auxiliaries, XXII, XVI, I, V, and IV Legions, with more auxiliaries and cavalry. The British Legions, the IX, II, and XX, stood in reserve. Opposite them, near the crossroads of the Via Postuma, were Primus's legions, from right to left: cavalry, auxiliary cohorts, the III, VIII, XIII, VII Galbiana, and VII Claudia, with more auxiliaries and cavalry. The Praetorians formed a powerful reserve. Altogether, 100,000 soldiers took part.

The Vitellians were numerically superior, but, as Tacitus noted, the soldiers of the emperor had grown soft during their days in Rome. Tacitus wrote that "The battle lasted through the night with great slaughter on both sides, and alternate success." The eagles were lost, retaken and lost again. The dead piled up on the field. Slowly the Vitellians gained the edge but then lost it as Primus threw in the fanatical cohorts of the Guard. A rout was started, but then prevented, as the Vitellians dragged up siege engines and opened fire with great effect on the Flavians. Two soldiers saved the battle by cutting the ropes on the engines. Nature then turned on Vitellius as the moon rose high in the sky, shining on his soldiers' faces and shrouding Primus's legions. According to Tacitus, Primus exhorted the Praetorians: "Now is your time to conquer, or renounce the name of soldiers." At dawn the Flavian legions from Syria cheered the new day. The Vitellians, knowing nothing of this tradition from Syria, believed reinforcements had arrived and fled the scene.

Cremona was pillaged, looted, and burned to the ground. Vitellius, in Rome, could only wait the arrival of Primus, Mucianus and Vespasian, the next emperor of the Roman Empire. Accounts of the battle were written by Tacitus, Suetonius, Dio, Josephus, and Plutarch.

Belgae   A people, probably of German extraction, living in GALLA Belgica, the most northern area of Gaul, near the Rhine, the North Sea, and the Sequani. Because of their location they not only fought with the BATAVI but, at the time of Caesar's GALLIC WARS, were also the most "uncivilized" Gallic people. They were reportedly hard, cruel, and vicious in battle, the hardest to subdue, and even extended their influence into Britain. The Belgae penetrated the southeastern coast of Britain in the early first century B.C.E. and intervened there is subsequent years, although direct control was not possible. These ties remained until Julius Caesar destroyed the Belgae on the continent and thus put an end to their holdings in Britain.

Belgica   *See* GALLIA.

Bellona   A goddess of the Roman pantheon, generally associated with war. Her temple stood in the Campus Martius and formed a relationship with the god Mars, her temple resting near his altar. She was later associated with the Cappadocian goddess Ma.

beneficiarii   Soldiers in the legions who held the rank of *principales* (noncommissioned officers) and who were given added administrative duties by a high-ranking officer or official. Their title was derived from the *beneficium,* or promotion, bestowed upon them by a commanding officer, and the specific rank and prominence of the *beneficiarius* depended upon the rank of their commander. Thus, there were *beneficiarii procuratoris, beneficiarii legati legionis,* and *beneficiarii tribuni.* As the imperial era progressed, the number and prominence of the *beneficiarii* increased. New grades were created (*cornicularii* and *commentarienses,* for example) and the *beneficiarii* began to wield more and more power. It also became common in the later empire for *beneficiarii* to hold a post that included nonmilitary duties.

Beneventum   Town in the south-central region of Samnium in Italy, along the Appian Way. Beneventum was one of the oldest towns in Italy, but for many years was called Maleventum, because of its bad air. During the empire it saw heavy traffic bound to and from southern Italy and thus depended upon good roads. Nerva planned to improve the roads, but it was not until Trajan's era that serious work was accomplished. The emperor completely rebuilt the circuit from Beneventum to Brundisium. In gratitude, the stretch was renamed the Via Traiana and the famed Arch of Trajan (*see* ARCHES) was constructed in

117 C.E. to mark the start of the road. A temple dedicated to Isis, the patron of Beneventum, was built during the reign of Domitian.

Berenice (b. 28 C.E.) *Jewish princess*

Berenice was the daughter of Agrippa I and a sister of King Agrippa II of Judaea. She was first married to the brother of Tiberius Julius Alexander, the prefect of Egypt, and then, in 46 C.E., to her uncle Herod of Chalcis, a minor prince by whom she had two sons. Herod died in 48, and she moved back with her brother Agrippa, sharing in the rule of Judaea. In 50, she also ruled Chalcis, when Emperor Claudius granted Agrippa control of the region too.

Her relations with the populace of Judaea were never good. Rumors abounded that she carried on incestuously with her brother. A marriage to a Cilician priest-king, sometime around 54, neither lasted nor improved her standing with the Jews. In 67, Titus arrived in the province and fell in love with her, an affair that lasted for years.

When Agrippa visited Rome in 75, he brought Berenice with him, and she moved into the palace, living openly with Titus. According to various sources, she expected to marry Titus one day. The Romans took little pleasure in the thought of another Eastern princess involved in the imperial politics; with the name "Cleopatra" floating through the city, Titus was compelled to send Berenice away.

Berytus

City in Phoenicia (later Syria), long prosperous under the Seleucid kings and the Roman Empire. In 32 B.C.E., Berytus played a role in the Civil War between Octavian (later Emperor AUGUSTUS) and Antony and Cleopatra, by revolting against the Egyptian queen. It declared its independence and issued its own coinage. As part of Augustus's reorganization of the East, Marcus Agrippa settled veterans in the area, converting Berytus into a Roman colony. This transformation in 16 B.C.E. not only helped establish the city as part of the empire, but also provided the colony with territory stretching all the way to Baalbek.

Berytus was located on the major trade routes traversing Syria and drew the attention of others, such as Agrippa I of Judaea, who gave the people art works and an amphitheater. Romanization was complete by the second century, and, aside from the textiles for which the entire province was famed, Berytus's reputation increasingly depended upon its school of law. Students from all over the empire traveled to the city to be instructed in law, and Berytus greatly influenced Roman legal development. Courses were given in Latin, not Greek. As a center for higher learning, the city remained integral to imperial education until at least the fifth century.

Betriacum   *See* BEDRIACUM.

Bibracte

Capital of the powerful Gallic tribe, the Aedui, Bibracte was situated on a hill (now Mount Beuvray in east-central France) in Gallia Lugdunensis. A battle was fought there in July of 58 B.C.E., between Julius CAESAR and the migrating Helvetians. After defeating the Helvetians at the battle of ARAR, Caesar took up a defensive position in the face of an enemy counteroffensive. He had at his disposal some 30,000 legionnaires, 2,000 Gallic auxiliaries and about 4,000 cavalry. Although the Helvetians had some 70,000 warriors, their attack was a disaster. Caesar's legions stood firm and then shattered the increasingly confused barbarians. An all-out Roman assault ensued, driving the Helvetians back into their camp, where their women and children became entangled in the massacre. More than 120,000 Helvetians died on the site, and those who survived retreated into their homelands. The site was abandoned after the Gallic Wars in favor of AUGUSTODONUM.

Bibulus, Lucius Calpurnius (d. 32 or 31 B.C.E.) *Son of Marcus Calpurnius Bibulus and Porcia*

Bibulus followed in his father's footsteps, espousing anti-Caesarean beliefs and joining his father-in-law, Marcus Brutus, against Marc ANTONY at the battle of PHILIPPI in 42 B.C.E. Although proscribed and eventually captured by Antony, he entered his service and over time reached an accord with the general. As Antony's lieutenant, Bibulus acted as a messenger between the triumvir and his comrade Octavian (*see* AUGUSTUS) and then looked after his own affairs in Syria, where he died. Bibulus was noted for a history of Marcus Brutus and was a prose writer in the last Republican period.

Bibulus, Marcus Calpurnius (d. 48 B.C.E.) *Roman politician in the late Republic*

Bibulus was one of Julius Caesar's early partners and served with him in the aedileship (65 B.C.E.), praetorship (62 B.C.E.), and the consulship (59 B.C.E.). He believed in the aristocratic party and looked disapprovingly on the growing powers of the FIRST TRIUMVIRATE. He was forced by violence to abandon his intentions of blocking Caesar's agrarian laws, and thereafter withdrew from all public or political activities and fought Caesar's legislation by viewing the stars for omens. His absence, it was said humorously, created the consulship of Julius and Caesar.

In 52 B.C.E., Bibulus took up the cause of Pompey, proposing him for the consulship. As the civil wars erupted, he first governed Syria for Pompey and then commanded the Adriatic fleet, where he worked himself to death. He was married to Porcia, who gave him a son, Lucius Calpurnius BIBULUS. Dio noted that so great an admiral was Bibulus that Antony had not dared to sail from Brundisium.

Bithynia   Roman province in ASIA MINOR, bordered by ASIA, Galatia, and the Black Sea. Bithynia was a pivotal territory in the empire, for it served as the geographical, economic, and cultural bridge over the Bosporus for East and West. Its importance, moreover, increased as imperial power shifted eastward in the fourth century C.E.

In 74 B.C.E., Nicomedes IV, a Mithridatic king, bequeathed to Rome his kingdom along the Black Sea, and when Augustus established the empire, Bithynia was classified as a senatorial province, under a PROCONSUL. Bithynia shared in the development of economic wealth that characterized the entire region of Asia Minor. Located on direct trade routes, the communities benefited from a local economy based on agriculture, timber, and iron. Its major cities included such metropolises as NICOMEDIA, NICAEA, and Prusa. It was governed as a senatorial province, with the seat at Nicomedia on the Black Sea, though the Nicaeans repeatedly tried to gain that advantage.

Beginning with Trajan, special legates, based in Nicomedia, were appointed to aid in the administration of Bithynia, rooting out corruption among civil servants, auditing city accounts, and suppressing political movements and Christianity. Bithynia's political environment is understood more clearly than virtually any other province because of the writings of PLINY THE YOUNGER, who served as the first legate from 109 C.E. Pliny constantly communicated with Rome, especially with Trajan, and proposed building a canal for Nicomedia, along the coast, and a series of aqueducts, though neither project was ever completed. The legates in Bithynia exercised greater imperial control and were given the right to examine the accounts of the free cities of Anisus and CHALCEDON, a temporary but significant authority. Marcus Aurelius finally redesignated Bithynia as an imperial province. Another famous Bithynian politician was the philosopher Dio Chrysostom (DIO COCCEIANUS), who represented his native Prusa in a delegation to Trajan at his accession in 98 C.E. He requested from the emperor the right to a larger city council, permission to redevelop the city and a waiver on taxes, which was denied, not surprisingly.

Bithynia was not immune to the decline of imperial power in the third century. Starting in 256 C.E., a terrible seaborne invasion of GOTHS devastated much of the province. Chalcedon, Nicomedia, Prusa, and Nicaea were all captured and plundered. By the late third century, Diocletian rejected the Roman establishment and made Nicomedia his capital for a time. Constantine the Great, however, was most responsible for Bithynia's role in the Eastern Empire. He created CONSTANTINOPLE and favored Nicaea, where he held the great council in 325 C.E.

Nicaea was the appropriate location for a Christian council. Bithynia was the gateway for Christianity into Europe, and Pliny had written of the new sect in his province. Its popularity increased, and with Constantine was legitimized. During the era of the Christian Empire, the Bithynian bishops were involved with the Arian heresy (see ARIANISM). Because of the territorial grants made by Nicomedes, the province was also known as Bithynia-Pontus. Of note is the terrible earthquake that flattened Nicomedia on August 24, 358 C.E. Under the late empire, Bithynia was part of the Eastern provinces and was spared some of the ravages that befell the West.

Black Sea   Body of water that stretched from the northern shores of the province of BITHYNIA to the rest of Asia Minor, to the Caucusus, Thrace, Moesia, and Scythia. The Black Sea was of considerable importance to the Romans because of its location and because of the economic activity centered upon it.

Seaborne goods ranging from cloths to wine and agricultural products crossed the Black Sea. The most important was grain from the kingdom of the BOSPORUS, whose fields in southern Russia supplied Bithynia and Asia. Roman fleets also scoured the Black Sea in search of pirates. The fleet operating out of NICOMEDIA was effective and increased the influence of the empire along the northern costs. Determined military alertness was essential, given the presence of the hostile SARMATIANS and Scythians. By the third century, with the arrival of the GOTHS, Rome's domination was seriously opposed. Starting in 254, the Bosporus nations were compelled to supply ships to the Goths, and the barbarians swept over the Black Sea and pillaged Asia Minor. ARRIAN wrote *Circumnavigation of the Black Sea*; the Latin name for the sea was Pontus Euxinus (a Latin transliteration of the Greek, meaning "hospitable sea").

Blaesus, Quintus Junius   (d. 31 C.E.)   *General and governor of Pannonia and Africa*
Blaesus's military career of successes and failures was ended by association with his nephew, the Praetorian Prefect SEJANUS. Blaesus was the governor of Pannonia in 14 C.E., a very important frontier post, but when Emperor Augustus died, his three legions, the VIII Augustus, IX Hispania and XV Apollinaris, mutinied. Under the urgings of a soldier Percennius, the troops erupted, demanded better service conditions, tried to kill Blaesus and tortured his slaves. Blaesus sent envoys to the new Emperor Tiberius, informing him that the frontier was now virtually defenseless. Drusus, Tiberius's son, arrived with several cohorts of the Praetorian Guard, and only by the good fortune of a lunar eclipse was order restored. Blaesus had lost control of his legions, but by 21 C.E. was supported by the powerful political arm of his nephew, Sejanus. He became proconsul of Africa in 21, where he conducted himself well; and his command was extended. He soon after achieved his greatest success, defeating the famed African pirate TACFARINAS. In 22, Tiberius granted him the title of IMPERATOR. When Sejanus fell from

power, however, Blaesus was one of the first on Tiberius's long list of victims. In 31, Blaesus was killed, and his two sons committed suicide.

Bolanus, Vettius (d. after 71 C.E.) *Governor of Britannia in 69 C.E.*

Bolanus first appeared as a legate under General Gnaeus Domitius CORBULO (2) in his campaigns in Armenia in 62. Seven years later he was in Rome as part of the court of the new emperor, VITELLIUS, when word arrived that the governor of Britannia under GALBA, Trebellius Maximus, was evicted from his post by his own troops and sought refuge with the new emperor. Bolanus was sent to take his place.

As governor he did nothing personally to aid Vitellius and remained inactive as far as administering Britannia was concerned. His forces were reduced sharply due to demands for troops in the Civil War in Rome. He was recalled by VESPASIAN in 71 but later served as proconsul in Asia.

Bona Dea

Roman goddess worshiped in festivals attended exclusively, with one famous exception, by women. She was traditionally the wife or daughter of Faunus, hence her other name, Fauna, and her role as the patroness of chastity. The VESTAL VIRGINS conducted her festival on the first of May, always in the home of the chief consul or praetor, with his wife presiding. A sow was sacrificed to her. It was long a tradition that no male was allowed at the sacrifices, made on behalf of the Roman people. On one occasion this custom was violated. In 62 B.C.E., CLODIUS PULCHER entered the house of Caesar dressed as a woman and thus committed a great outrage against the tradition and the religious ideals of the nation.

Boniface (fl. early fifth century C.E.) *Also Bonifatius, a magister militum in Africa*

In 421, Boniface was assigned the task of aiding the general and *come domesticorum,* CASTINUS, in his campaigns against the VANDALS in Spain. Already a noted soldier, Boniface quarreled immediately with Castinus and departed for Africa. Castinus's subsequent defeat was blamed on Boniface and the influence of the empress, Galla Placidia, wife of Emperor Constantius III. When the powerful Honorius exiled Placidia in 422, Boniface sent Placidia money and in 423–425 defended Africa loyally for her and her son, Valentinian III, against the usurper John. John's defeat simply opened the door for the more cunning *magister militum,* AETIUS.

By 427, Boniface was strengthening his own hold over Africa. He was a close friend of St. AUGUSTINE but isolated himself politically with a marriage to an Arian woman named Pelagia. Under the influence of the *magister utriusque militiae* Felix, Galla Placidia recalled Boniface to

Ravenna. He refused and then defeated the armies sent to subdue him. In an effort to strengthen his position, he invited the Vandals to invade. In 429, GEISERIC, the Vandal king, led the entire Vandal nation across the Mediterranean. Galla Placidia sought Boniface's support through an intermediary named Darius, and Boniface once more represented imperial interests but was soundly defeated by the Vandals and besieged for a year at HIPPO in Africa in 431. The city was sacked and effective resistance in Africa collapsed. Galla Placidia welcomed Boniface, and, faced with two great generals, she removed Aetius and elevated her favorite to the patricianate. Outraged, Aetius gathered an army and stormed over the Alps. At Arminium the two met, and Aetius was defeated. Though victorious, Boniface was wounded and died three months later. Aetius left Italy, gained the alliance of RUGILA, the king of the Huns, and returned to negotiate with Galla Placidia. Boniface's wife was compelled to marry Aetius and thus to deliver up the army of Boniface to him.

Bordeaux   *See* BURDIGALA.

Bosporus kingdom

Domain located on the north shore of the Black Sea and one of the most important buffer states for Rome. The Bosporus kingdom controlled the region opposite Asia Minor and was closely connected to PONTUS, which it once ruled. The kingdom was of interest to the Romans for several reasons. The fields of the Ukraine and southern Russia (Crimea), though populated by the nomadic SARMATIANS, provided the bulk of the agricultural resources for Asia Minor. More important were the geopolitical realities of the Black Sea area. The Bosporus buffered the Roman provinces from potential invasions by the Sarmatians and the SCYTHIANS, who inhabited all of the Crimea and much of the Steppes. Parthian expansion was also checked there.

After the battle of ZELA in 47 B.C.E., Asander, the slayer of MITHRIDATES OF PERGAMUM, gained the throne and ruled for the next 30 years. In 17 B.C.E., Emperor AUGUSTUS desired greater control and assigned to AGRIPPA the task of finding a reliable king. Agrippa compelled Dynamis, the daughter of Pharnaces, who was defeated by CAESAR at Zela, to marry Polemo of Pontus. The marriage proved unsuccessful, and Polemo was ousted in favor of Dynamis and her new husband, the Sarmatian Aspurgus.

After Emperor GAIUS CALIGULA gave the Bosporus lands to Polemo II of Pontus, Emperor CLAUDIUS, in 39 C.E., decided upon one of Aspurgus's two sons, MITHRIDATES (2) (the other was Cotys). Mithridates, however, had to share his rule with a Thracian stepmother, Gepaepyris (the natural mother of Cotys). COTYS (2) alerted Claudius in 44 or 45 C.E. that Mithridates planned rebellion. Didius Gallus, the governor of Moesia, removed Mithridates and installed his brother on the throne.

Mithridates, however, found Sarmatian allies but was defeated in battle and sent to Rome.

By 62 C.E., the coinage of Cotys ceased being issued, an indication of the loss of independence. NERO, planning to conquer the Sarmatians, annexed the kingdom. Cotys was dead, deposed, or reduced to a figurehead. Roman occupation of the region lasted until Nero's fall in 68 C.E., and Cotys's son Rhescuporis regained a client status. Semi-independent once more, the Bosporus continued its trade with Asia Minor, despite the arrival in the first century C.E. of the ALANS. Although the Scythians were aggressive and threatening, relations with the Sarmatians were so favorable that by the second century a Sarmatian influence dominated the kingdom.

Boudicca (d. 61 C.E.) *Also called Boadaecia or Boadecia; leader of one of the most famous and bloody revolts ever mounted against Rome*

Boudicca was ruler of the powerful tribe, the ICENI, with her husband PRASUTAGUS. They reigned in an area north of Cambridge and Colchester, in what is now Norfolk and Sussex in Britain. In 61 C.E. Prasutagus died and left his kingdom to Emperor Nero, believing that client status would assure its survival. The imperial response was, according to Tacitus, appalling: Roman legionnaires plundered the realm, flogged the queen and ravished her daughters. CATUS, the procurator of Britain, fomented the revolt further by demanding funds back from the Iceni, given by the Romans in the past as gifts. SENECA also called for the return of 40 million sesterces he had forced the Britons to accept as a loan.

Boudicca gathered her warriors and with the blessings of her DRUIDS called for a war against Rome. While the legate of the local legions, SUETONIUS PAULINUS, was away on a campaign to subjugate the Druids on Anglesey Island, the queen's force grew to some 120,000 men.

The strength of Boudicca's attack was compounded by surprise. Suetonius had made no preparations for a revolt. CAMULODUNUM (Colchester), the center of Roman administration, was undefended as Boudicca stormed it easily, burning it to the ground. The Iceni collided with the legions of Petillius CEREALIS, and the cohorts were destroyed, retreating to LINDUM; Catus fled to Gaul. When Paulinus received word of the rebellion and returned, Boudicca was threatening Lincoln, and more importantly, LONDINIUM (London). Paulinus was forced to abandon London; the city fell to Iceni, and its inhabitants were massacred. Verulamium was captured next, while the Romans regrouped for war.

Suetonius had assembled his troops near Verulamium (St. Alban's), where he awaited the Iceni. With their wives and children in nearby wagons to watch, the warriors of Boudicca swept forward, screaming as they came to grips with the enemy. The Romans held firm, however, and then counterattacked, smashing the Briton forces. Boudicca's troops broke but were hemmed in by

their own wagons, and men, women, and children were thus annihilated by the vengeful cohorts. Tacitus put the number of Iceni dead at 80,000, a suspicious number. The losses were unquestionably high, however, and Boudicca's power was crushed. Rather than face Roman retaliation, she returned to her home and committed suicide.

Boudicca reportedly wiped out 70,000 colonists and townsfolk, ending imperial policies of colonization without fortifications. Dio described Boudicca in some detail, stating:

> In stature she was very tall, in appearance most terrifying, in the glance of her eye most fierce, and her voice was harsh; a great mass of the tawniest hair fell to her hips; around her neck was a large golden necklace; and she wore a tunic of diverse colours over which a thick mantle was fashioned with a brooch.

Brigantes   The most populous and powerful tribe in Britain until the era of Emperor VESPASIAN (69–79 C.E.). Brigantian influence stretched from the River Tyne to the Trent, and included such cities as Isurium (Aldborough), Olicana (Ilkley), Mancunium (Manchester), and the legionary fort at EBURACUM (York). Not one specific people like the CELTS, the Brigantes were actually a confederation of tribes acting in mutual cooperation. The Romans first encountered the Brigantes during the era of P. Ostorius SCAPULA, in 50 C.E., when they joined the ICENI in an assault. The Brigantes were driven off, and circa 51 the queen of the Brigantes, Cartimandua, signed a treaty with Emperor Claudius, bringing a short-lived peace. When the queen parted violently from her husband Venutius, civil war resulted in his exile. A counterattack threw her off the throne. Remembering that she had handed over the British rebel, Caratacus, Claudius supported her cause. She was reinstated by the Roman army and ruled over a divided people. In 68, Venutius, who had reconciled with Cartimandua, was again ousted from the palace, and Vespasian intervened. CEREALIS led the campaign to establish Roman domination in 71, driving the Brigantes northward and establishing superiority all the way to Eburacum. His work was carried on by AGRICOLA, who pacified the region and established roads and forts.

The Brigantes had not surrendered, however, and in 138, the WALL OF HADRIAN was breached and they attacked Roman areas. The new governor, LOLLIUS URBICUS, beat the tribes back beyond the wall and then established a new perimeter of defense, the WALL OF ANTONINUS, farther north. The tribes attacked again in 154, and the Antonine Wall did not stem their invasion. Legions from Germany were dispatched to the scene to restore order. By this time, however, the strength of the Brigantes had been sapped.

Britain   *See* BRITANNIA (1).

Britannia (1) The British Isles, also called Albion; the focus of numerous Roman invasions and colonization.

ROMAN RULE

Britannia (or Britain) was originally known as *Insulae Britannicae* and contained several cultures of interest, the most important being that of the CELTS, transplanted from Gaul (*see* GALLIA). Celtic society was isolated by the now-English Channel in many respects. Thus DRUIDISM, a cornerstone in the life of the Celts, developed more richly than in Gaul and was far more powerful. It was only in the first century B.C.E. that new waves of people crossed the water and attempted to establish themselves in Britain. The BELGAE took over much of the countryside in the southwest, while maintaining strong ties with their homeland in Gallia Belgica. In 55 B.C.E., as a sidebar campaign to his GALLIC WARS, Julius CAESAR crossed the Channel. Sailing with two legions, he landed at Dover on August 26 and moved on to Kent. Fierce battles ensued with the local inhabitants. Victory was delayed because of further uprisings and a storm that wrecked many of the Roman transports. After putting down the last of the Kentish tribes, Caesar left Britannia in September.

The following year, in July, the Romans began a second invasion. This time 600 transports, five legions, and around 2,000 Gallic horsemen arrived in Kent to discover no unified opposition from the local tribes. A quick advance could have concretized Caesar's position, but another storm wrecked many of his ships and allowed time for the chieftain CASSIVELLAUNUS and his chariot-driving Belgae near the Thames to organize. The chieftain was beaten in a pitched battle. Mandubracius, leader of an oppressed tribe, the Trinovantes, then joined Caesar's cause. These tribesmen helped the legions subdue Cassivellaunus and shared in the subsequent treaty. Because the Gallic peoples, in his absence, had started another revolt, Caesar retreated to Kent and set sail from Britain for the last time.

Caesar had done little to convince the Britons of Roman supremacy in arms. Cassivellaunus probably never paid his promised tribute, and no doubt conquered the Trinovantes. A strong kingdom was established in southern Britannia, centered at Lexden near CAMULO-DUNUM (Colchester), under Cassivellaunus and his son Tasciovanus. They were joined by the Gallic chief COMMIUS, who had fled Gallia Belgica during Caesar's war against VERCINGETORIX (52 B.C.E.). An extensive Belgian influence was consequently felt throughout the island's southern domains. By Augustus's era, CUNOBELLINUS, son of Tasciovanus, ruled much of the isles, coexisting with the kingdoms of the ICENI, the BRIGANTES and the Silures. Cunobellinus ran his affairs most intelligently. Local Britons were never so oppressed as to revolt, and his organization was strong enough that an actual invasion by the Romans would have been a massive and precarious undertaking. AUGUSTUS refused to mount any expedition, considering such a venture wasteful, although Dio reported that he planned twice to invade, once in 34 B.C.E. and again in 27 B.C.E. He was prevented by more pressing matters in the empire. Division ripped the Colchester kingdom, meanwhile, as Cunobellinus's sons differed over policy. Amminius favored Rome, while CARATACUS and Togodumnus despised the Romans. Amminius fled and promised the realm to GAIUS CALIGULA, who made a rash display of Roman power along the coast to receive Amminius. He then wrote to the Senate that all of Britain had surrendered. When Cunobellinus finally died c. 41 C.E., his two remaining sons pledged their hatred of Rome. In 43, CLAUDIUS put forward the plan for conquest that Caesar had envisioned so long ago.

General Aulus PLAUTIUS sailed to Kent with some four legions and auxiliaries. Plautius landed unopposed and defeated first Caratacus and then Togodumnus, who died in battle. When Claudius himself arrived, with elephants no less, Caratacus's kingdom collapsed. The fallen domain became a province, with Plautius as its first governor. In 47, P. Ostorius SCAPULA took over the governorship and pacified all of the old territories of the Belgae. Caratacus, however, refused to yield, and stirred up the Silures in Wales, leading a revolt. When it was crushed, Caratacus fled to CARTIMANDUA, the queen of the Brigantes, who by treaty handed him over to the Romans for punishment. PRASUTAGUS, the king of the Iceni, opposed the new frontier of 47 and was suppressed. Upon his death the Romans seized his lands and caused the dangerous revolt of BOUDICCA, his widow. SUETONIUS PAULINUS defeated the rebellion, but the position of the occupying Roman forces had been seriously threatened.

The FLAVIANS initiated a series of campaigns in Britain. Beginning in 71, the commander Petillius CERE-ALIS destroyed the power of the Brigantes, marching past EBURACUM (York). His successor, FRONTINUS, subjugated much of Wales and the hard-fighting Silures. AGRICOLA conquered the rest of the Welsh lands and the island of Mona, the Druid stronghold. The advance units of Agricola entered Scotland, as he penetrated into the Grampian Mountains and CALEDONIA. Forts were established along the Forth and Clyde, and a Roman presence permeated the entire country. In six short years (78–83/84 C.E.) Rome had annexed vast amounts of territory. The province of Britannia was called Britannia Romana, while the wild north was Britannia Barbara.

Three legions were subsequently allotted to the new governor, and Roman policy assumed a far more defensive approach. The wild tribes were again pressing the frontiers, and a retreat was made to the Tyne-Solway line. Around 120, this new boundary was fortified by the WALL OF HADRIAN, 80 miles long. A few years later, the shorter WALL OF ANTONINUS was built.

Roman Conquest of Britannia, 54 B.C.E.–100 C.E.

North Sea

Irish Sea

Eburacum (York) 77 C.E.

Deva (Chester) 77 C.E.

Lindum (Lincoln) 47 C.E.

Viroconium Cornoviorum (Wroxeter) 47 C.E.

Isca Silurum (Caerleon) 75 C.E.

Glevum (Gloucester) 50 C.E.

Londinium (London)

North Downs Trackway

English Channel

N

GAUL

→ Route of Julius Caesar's expedition 54 B.C.E.

╌╌ Roman advances 43–83 C.E.

■ Roman fort with date of foundation

0   50 Miles

0   50 Kms

In 196, CLODIUS ALBINUS attempted to seize the throne from Emperor Septimius SEVERUS. He took his legions in Britannia to Gaul, leaving the province unprotected. The Caledonians beyond the walls burst through the perimeters. Massacres and devastation ensued, and Emperor Severus himself went to the isles. He repaired Hadrian's Wall and constructed a new one, just a short distance to the north, called the Severan Wall. A campaign began in Scotland, and in 209, several battles relieved the pressure on the frontier. The Caledonians still threatened, when Severus died at Eburacum while preparing for another attack. After his death the province was fortified again and made secure. Henceforth, Britannia was divided into two provinces, as the emperor could not trust a sole governor with three legions.

The next years witnessed the preservation of Roman rule, but two important new developments as well. SAX-

ONS were beginning to harass the coasts, and the empire found itself increasingly unable to recover from such assaults. The usurper CARAUSIUS proved that a usurper could wreak havoc among the provinces, gaining the support of the Britons while doing it. DIOCLETIAN and CONSTANTIUS I CHLORUS eventually defeated him and his murderer, ALLECTUS, restoring Roman dominance in 297. The provinces were divided yet again, as a result, into four separate regions. CONSTANTINE THE GREAT launched his bid for rule from Eburacum in 306. As he pursued his goal, the walls in Britain stood unmanned; the PICTS and Scots plundered by land and the Saxons ravaged by sea. In 407, the usurper CONSTANTINE III withdrew the remaining isle troops for use in Gaul, effectively ending Roman rule in Britannia.

CULTURE AND COLONIZATION

Britannia's culture was Celtic in origin. Throughout the southernmost regions there were Belgae Gallic influences, but the Celtic character remained predominant (an ancient lifestyle once enjoyed by the Gauls as well). The Celts painted themselves blue, the sacred Druid color, and HERODIAN wrote that tattoos were also common. He described the Britons as savage and warlike, armed with spears and shields, and with swords suspended from their waists. They also used chariots to great effect.

Roman imperial civilization began in Claudius' reign, when Camulodunum (Colchester) fell in 43 C.E. Subsequent occupation saw the construction of harbor settlements near modern Fishbourne, just outside of Colchester; in 49, an actual colony was begun. Roman veterans helped establish the *colonia*, building a town with a provincial cult, a theater and baths. By the middle of the first century small towns were populating the Roman possession. Camulodunum was the capital, while other influential towns like VERULAMIUM (St. Alban's) and the trading center of LONDINIUM (London) sprang up. As with the other major towns and fledgling homesteads, London could not defend itself, a fact that became catastrophically evident in 61 C.E., during the revolt of Boudicca. Sweeping across the countryside, the vengeful Britons sacked Colchester, St. Albans and London, as well as every farm and estate in between. Although Tacitus' figure of 80,000 dead was high, losses were severe enough to ensure that all subsequent building was fortified.

After the campaigns of Cerealis, Frontinus and Agricola from 71 to 84 C.E., towns were walled and economic prosperity increased. London came to serve as a vital link in the military control of the south and had a garrison, while more veterans arrived to establish colonies, such as those of Lincoln and Gloucester. In urban areas, Latin was used, and native art and culture waned. Outside of the cities, farming was an essential way of life, and the Romans relied upon this agricultural base. Considerable gentry holdings, the villas, ensured that agricultural products were pumped into the cities. But in the country, even in the villas, elements of Celtic culture endured.

An excellent road system connected cities, which now sported public baths and temples, including ones to the IMPERIAL CULT. By Hadrian's reign (117–138 C.E.) many municipalities used street grid systems to expand. Under Cunobellinus the economy had fared well, and the Roman occupation following his reign merely tapped into that abundance. Agriculture, supported by the villas, was the source of Britannia's wealth. Wheat was grown to feed the natives and the legions and was used as an export. Aside from its verdant fields, the province boasted numerous mineral deposits. Tin was important in the first century C.E., and again in the fourth century, when Rome was forced to seek new resources to sustain itself. Iron exports helped the economy of the empire as a whole, and administrators in Britannia mined it extensively. The geographer STRABO noted Britannia's economic wealth and exports in corn, cattle, gold, iron, and silver.

In the balance of trade, Gaul supplied pottery, manufactured goods and art, while Britannia exported minerals and agricultural products. There was little incentive for developing other industry, and the quality of life in the province was better than in many other imperial domains.

While the Britons appeared highly Romanized, Celtic culture persisted, especially in the rural areas. Druidism was pervasive and hence viewed as dangerous; Suetonius Paulinus attacked the island of Mona, a Druid stronghold, and the Druids were massacred. Christianity faced the same resistance, and upon its arrival, which coincided with the decline of Roman power, it struggled to attract vast numbers of followers in the isles.

Suggested Readings: Allason-Jones, Lindsay. *Women in Roman Britain.* London: British Museum Publications, 1989; Arnold, C. J. *Roman Britain to Saxon England.* Bloomington: Indiana University Press, 1984; Askew, Gilbert. *The Coinage of Roman Britain.* London: Seaby Publications, 1980; Birley, Anthony. *The People of Roman Britain.* Berkeley: University of California Press, 1980; Campbell, J. B. *Roman Britain.* London: Jonathan Cape, 1963; Collingwood, R. G. *Roman Britain.* New York: Barnes & Noble in cooperation with Oxford University Press, 1994; Coulston, J. C. *Hadrian's Wall West of the North Tyne and Carlisle.* Oxford, U.K.: Published for the British Academy by the Oxford University Press, 1988; Dark, Petra. *The Landscape of Roman Britain.* London: Sutton Publishing, 1997; Frere, Sheppard Sunderland. *Britannia: A History of Roman Britain.* 3rd ed. London: Routledge & Kegan Paul, 1987; Hanson, William and Maxwell, Gordon. *Rome's Northwest Frontier: The Antonine Wall.* New York: Columbia University Press, 1983; Hingley, Richard. *Rural Settlement in Roman Britain.* Lon-

don: B. A. Seaby, 1989; Holder, P. A. *The Roman Army in Britain.* London: B. T. Batsford, 1982; Johnson, Stephen. *Later Roman Britain.* New York: Scribner, 1980; Jones Michael. *The End of Roman Britain.* Cornell: Cornell University Press, 1996; Manning, William H. *The fortress excavations, 1968–1971.* Cardiff: University of Wales Press, 1981; Marsden, Peter R. *Roman London.* New York: Thames and Hudson, 1981; Marsh, Henry. *Dark Age Britain.* New York: Dorset Press, 1987; Milne, Gustav. *The Port of Roman London.* London: B. T. Batsford, 1985; Morgan, Kenneth, ed. *The Oxford History of Britain: Roman and Anglo-Saxon Britain.* Oxford: Oxford University Press, 1992; Peddie, John. *Conquest: The Roman Invasion of Britain.* London: Palgrave, 1997; Place, Robin. *The Romans: Fact and Fiction. Adventures in Roman Britain.* Cambridge, U.K.: Cambridge University Press, 1988; Salway, Peter. *A History of Roman Britain.* Oxford, U.K.: Oxford University Press, 1997; Salway, Peter. *The Oxford Illustrated History of Roman Britain.* Oxford: Oxford University Press, 1993; Scullard, H. H. *Roman Britain: Outpost of the empire.* London: Thames and Hudson, 1986; Stead, Ian M. *Verulamium, the King Harry Lane site.* London: English Heritage in association with British Museum Publications, 1989; Webster, Graham, ed. *Fortress into City: The Consolidation of Roman Britain, First Century A.D.* London: Batsford, 1988.

Britannia (2)   The name given to a coin minted by emperors HADRIAN (117–138 C.E.) and ANTONIUS PIUS (117–161 C.E.) to celebrate their victories in Britain. The coin was decorated with the personified figure of Britannia. Its value was that of a sestertius.

See also COINAGE.

Britannicus (41–55 C.E.) *Son of Emperor Claudius and Messalina and the legitimate heir to the throne*
Britannicus lived under a cloud from birth, being the offspring of MESSALINA, whose scandalous life had shocked Rome and resulted in her death. His position as heir was thus questioned and was hampered even further by the arrival of AGRIPPINA as CLAUDIUS's new wife, together with her son NERO. Britannicus appears to have done little to ingratiate himself with his stepmother and adopted brother. He refused the goodwill of Agrippina, referred to Nero by his original family name "Domitius" and later, in 55 C.E., went so far as to accuse Nero of being a usurper.

With Claudius's death and Nero's claim to the throne supported by the Praetorian Guard and the Prefect BURRUS, Britannicus was left politically impotent. Already sensitive to the inflammatory accusation of usurper hurled at him. Nero plotted to remove Britannicus and charged a tribune of the Guard, Pollio Julius, with the task. The poison administered proved ineffective, and LUCUSTA, who had arranged the poison, died as a result.

A second attempt worked perfectly. Britannicus, dining with the court, became ill, and many fled the scene in horror. Nero commented to the onlookers that Britannicus was subject to epileptic fits.

Bructeri   Germanic people living near the Ems and Lippe rivers; fought extensively in the wars against Roman expansion along the northern Rhine. In 4 C.E., TIBERIUS, campaigning in Germany, forced them to accept his domination, and in 14–15 C.E., Roman supremacy was certified in the defeat the Bructeri suffered from CAECINA SEVERUS, the legate of GERMANICUS. Although Germanicus thus avenged the annihilation of VARUS in 9 C.E. at the hands of ARMINIUS, the Bructeri simply waited for another moment in which to strike at the Romans. In 69 C.E., when Julius CIVILIS led the BATAVI in revolt, the Bructeri joined in the fray but were put to flight by Petillius CEREALIS. Undaunted, the Bructeri priestess Veleda became the heart of the Bructeri resistance, and the target of Roman operations.

In 75–78 C.E., RUTILIUS GALLICUS successfully crushed the Germans with several sorties, one of which captured Veleda. The Bructeri then ousted one of their kings, who fled across the Rhine and convinced the Romans, under Vestricius SPURINNA, the governor of Lower Germany, to force his people to take him back. Subsequent fighting supposedly cost the Bructeri some 60,000 men. Following the disaster, the Bructeri were subdued, eventually joining with the migratory FRANKS.

Brundisium   City in the Calabria region of southern Italy, on the Adriatic; it became one of the most important ports and harbors in the empire. With its natural port facilities and location, Brundisium was the gateway for shipping activity in the southern Adriatic, in Greece and in much of Asia. Commerce and trade to all of Italy started through the city and moved along the VIA APPIA, which stretched northward. Roman domination of the sea lanes relied upon Brundisium as a naval cornerstone, along with RAVENNA, AQUILEIA and MISENUM for the eastern Mediterranean. In the Civil War between Caesar and Pompey in 48 B.C.E., Marc Antony used it as the launching point of an invasion of Asia.

Brundisium, Treaty of   Pact signed in the later part of October 40 B.C.E. between Marc ANTONY and Octavian (AUGUSTUS), after the battle of PHILIPPI in 42 C.E., in which the forces of the SECOND TRIUMVIRATE had defeated the LIBERATORS led by CASSIUS and BRUTUS.

Following Philippi, great tension remained between the forces of Antony and Octavian, with all of Italy prepared for war. The death of Antony's troublesome wife FULVIA paved the way for peace. Two envoys, Asinius Pollio representing Antony and Maecenas representing Octavian, hammered out an accord. Marcus LEPIDUS (1) was to

remain in Africa as the impotent third triumvir, but the rest of the Roman world was split between Antony and Octavian. Antony received the east, and Octavian the west, the boundary line running through DALMATIA, with Italy accessible to both. They could both appoint consuls, and Octavian ceded Antony five legions belonging to CALENUS. Individuals proscribed by both parties were pardoned. The two triumvirs embraced. Antony then warned his new ally of a plot against him instigated by Salvidienus Rufus, Octavian's general in Gaul, while Octavian gave Antony his sister OCTAVIA in marriage—a union doomed to failure. As the men grew distant, so did the spirit of the treaty. Though reaffirmed in 37 B.C.E., with the Treaty of TARENTUM, Antony's infatuation with the East, and Octavian's increasing power in the West, propelled them into conflict that was finally resolved at the battle of ACTIUM in 31 B.C.E.

Bruttidius Niger   (d. c. 31 C.E.) *Aedile, or administrator, during the reign of Tiberius (14–37 C.E.)*
Niger was responsible, with Mamercus Scaurus and Junius Otho, for the persecution of the proconsul of Asia Gaius Silanus, on charges of *maiesta,* or treason. Niger was a student of Apollodorus and was both a rhetorician and historian. His friendship with Lucius Aelius SEJANUS, prefect of the Praetorian Guard, was a powerful aid in his career, but, like for so many others, in 31 C.E., that friendship cost him his life.

Brutus, Marcus Junius   (d. 42 B.C.E.) *One of the prime movers in the assassination of Julius Caesar in 44 B.C.E. and a champion of the Republican cause*
Brutus was the son of Marcus Junius and Servilia, the half sister of CATO UTICENSIS, and was brought up in a staunchly Republican environment. Though his father had been killed by POMPEY in 77 B.C.E. Brutus allied himself to the general in 49 B.C.E., at the outbreak of the CIVIL WAR against CAESAR, who was at the time his mother's lover. The battle of PHARSALUS in 48 B.C.E. brought him once more into contact with Caesar, who expressed faith in him, appointing Brutus the governor of Cisalpine Gaul in 46 B.C.E. In 44 B.C.E. he was made praeter and was promised not only the governorship of Macedonia but the consulship in 41 as well.

Brutus, however, suffered a change of heart while in Rome in 44 B.C.E., coming under the influence of CASSIUS, who worked on his desire to ensure the survival of the Republic. On the Ides of March, the LIBERATORS, as they called themselves, murdered Caesar. Brutus had underestimated the sentiment of the Roman people and was forced to flee the city and eventually to abandon Italy altogether. The Senate gave him a command in the Balkans, and in 43 B.C.E. he was put in charge of the provinces of Greece-Macedonia. Brutus demanded tribute from the provinces in Asia Minor, earning their enmity.

With Caesar's deification by the Senate in January of 42 B.C.E., the campaign against all of the Liberators began. By October of that year the forces of the SECOND TRIUMVIRATE were pressing the attack at PHILIPPI, and on October 23, the Republican forces fell to Antony and Octavian. In defeat, Cassius and Brutus committed suicide and with them perished the Republican cause. Brutus was known as a literary man, writing numerous now lost histories, and was a friend of CICERO. His second wife was the beautiful PORCIA, daughter of Cato Uticensis.

Brutus Albinus, Decimus Junius (d. 43 B.C.E.) *One-time officer under Julius Caesar who joined in the conspiracy to assassinate his former commander*
Brutus Albinus had had a successful military career with CAESAR as his legate in the GALLIC WARS and then his supporter in the CIVIL WAR (49–45 B.C.E.). He served as propraetor in Gaul from 48 to 46 B.C.E. and was promised a proconsulship in the area of Cisalpine Gaul. But before he took up the position, the conspirator CASSIUS drew him into the plot. Presumably in the belief that a true Republic would be reinstated, he joined in the murder. He then fled to Cisalpine Gaul, pursued by the avenging Marc ANTONY, who besieged him at MUTINA. In April of 43 B.C.E., Brutus Albinus was rescued by the combined legions of Hirtius, Pansa, and Octavian. Octavian turned against him, however. Fleeing to Gaul, and hoping to make his way to Macedonia and his coconspirator Marcus BRUTUS, he was trapped by Antony and slain.

Bucolici Tribe of herdsmen and nationalists living near the Nile Delta just northeast of ALEXANDRIA in Egypt. In 172–175 C.E., they revolted against Rome in a widespread uprising. Under the leadership of the local chief Isidorus, a priest, the Bucolici first killed Roman troops stationed nearby in Alexandria, then defeated larger forces sent against them. Fearing the loss of such an important city as Alexandria, the governor of Syria, Gaius Avidius Cassius, marched into Egypt. His war on Isidorus was aided by dissension among the tribesmen, and by 173 C.E. the region was pacified and the rebels crushed. Dio remarked on their bravery. They were also called the Bucoli, and the Boukolai.

Bulla Regia A town in the Roman province of Africa Proconsularis, in what is now Tunisia. The region was taken by Rome after the Third Punic War (149–146 B.C.E.) and was again claimed by Pompey in 81 B.C.E. It developed an imperial atmosphere sometime during the reign of Tiberius (14–37 C.E.), when buildings of an Italian design began appearing. Such construction came as part of the peaceful and prosperous development of Africa, in which the community shared. The archaeological remains of Bulla Regia display homes built both above and below ground, with ancient lighting and fountains.

Burdigala A major city, modern Bordeaux, in the province of Gallia AQUITANIA. Burdigala may have been the provincial capital. The importance of the city did not begin with the Roman occupation of Gallia in 51 B.C.E. Burdigala, located on the Garonne River, was the center of activity for the fierce people of the region, the Aquitani. After Caesar's conquest of Aquitania through his legate, Publius Crassus, pacification commenced, and in 27 B.C.E., Augustus declared the area a Roman province.

Burdigala was probably the administrative capital, although Saintes and Poitiers have both been identified as possible seats. Clearly, however, the emperor Vespasian gave it a municipal standing, and the city produced several senators, as did the province.

In the third century a wall was built around Burdigala to protect it from the increasingly dangerous migrations and invasions of the time. The construction apparently proved valuable, for in the later fourth century the poet Ausonius returned to Burdigala, his native city, and retired there in great comfort. Ausonius wrote of his own land and about his colleagues in the schools of the city.

In the later period of the empire, however, as Roman power collapsed, several Gothic kings conquered the city. Athaulf seized and then burned the city in 415. As part of a compact between Constantius and Wallia, the Gothic kingdom gained the city.

Burebista (d. 44 B.C.E.) *King of Dacia responsible for the aggrandizement of his land from 60 to 44 B.C.E.*
With the aid of his adviser, a prophet-priest named Dekaineos (of Decaeneos), Burebista changed much in the country, and then launched an assault on those neighboring peoples who either threatened DACIA or proved detrimental to his royal ambitions. In succession Burebista crushed the Boii, a race of Celts, and the Taurini, moving into Thrace and facing the entire Danube frontier, which endangered Roman control and led to direct involvement in Roman politics. In 48 B.C.E., Pompey the Great sought Burebista's aid, but Caesar ended any hope of an alliance at the battle of Pharsalus. Caesar had been aware of the Dacian king since his days governing Illyricum. After Pharsalus, Caesar planned to relieve the pressure on the Danube with a massive campaign against Burebista, really a preparatory move for the greater military programs planned against Parthia. Burebista was assassinated in 44 B.C.E. His rapidly created empire broke apart at his death, but whatever long-term plans Caesar had for Dacia were also cut short, as he too was murdered.

See also DECEBALUS.

Burgundians A Germanic people originating in the region of the Vistula River, who possessed considerable power in Gaul in the fifth century C.E. The Burgundians first appeared around 250 C.E., in the vanguard of the

Goths, with whom they shared a common ancestry. Settling in the region of the Main, they then faded from view, resurfacing again in 406, when they seized the lands directly on the Rhine. By 413, the Burgundians had crossed the great boundary and were in control of Germania Superior. Emperor Honorius was forced to accept their presence and concluded a treaty with them, by which they became allies. A kingdom was born, centered on Worms and ruled by Gundohar. In 436, the realm of Worms was crushed by the Huns, with Gundohar and thousands of his men slain. The remnant of the Burgundians moved into Savoy and were settled there by 443. They aided the *magister militum* AETIUS in his campaign against ATTILA, marking a resurgence. The Burgundians were finally overwhelmed by the Franks in the sixth century.

Burrus, Sextus Afranius (d. 62 C.E.) *Prefect of the Praetorian Guard during the reigns of Claudius and Nero*

Burrus was an important adviser and key figure in NERO's era. An inscription claims that he came from Vasio in Gaul. His military career prospered from the start, as he served as a tribune, then as a procurator in some private capacity for the Empress LIVIA and later for TIBERIUS and CLAUDIUS as well. Through Claudius he met AGRIPPINA THE YOUNGER. The empress found him useful and trustworthy, and in 51 C.E. recommended him as sole prefect of the Guard. The prefect pursued Agrippina's interests, especially her desire to promote her adopted son Nero as Claudius's heir over his own son, BRITANNICUS. Thus, in 54, on the death of Claudius, Burrus presented the prince to the cohorts of the Praetorians.

Early in Nero's reign, Burrus settled into the role of adviser, together with Seneca. The two men managed to preserve the empire from Nero's eccentricities and to break Agrippina's hold on her son as well. In 59, Agrippina was murdered by her son, and the influence of Burrus and Seneca weakened. Burrus had already faced one charge of plotting against the throne, in 55, and had escaped the charge. In 62, he tried to dissuade Nero from divorcing OCTAVIA. He became ill, with a swelling in his throat and difficulties breathing, and suspected poison. When Nero visited him, Burrus reportedly turned his face away, saying only "With me all is well." At his death soon after, he was replaced by TIGELLINUS, whom Nero had been grooming for some time.

Tacitus wrote that Burrus was an officer of high reputation, and he was generally considered a gifted soldier and brilliant administrator and an honorable man. Dio wrote of his frankness, that when the emperor once asked him a second time for his opinions, Burrus responded: "When once I have spoken, do not ask me again."

Byzantium

A city founded by Dorian Greeks in the seventh century B.C.E. that was transformed by CONSTANTINE in November of 324 C.E. and became his capital in 330. Modern Istanbul occupies the site today.

See also CONSTANTINOPLE.

C

Cabiri Spirits of the underworld, perhaps of a volcanic nature; they formed the heart of a cult centered in Asia that grew to immense popularity in the late empire. They were said to protect mankind against storms and hence were beneficial to all travelers. The cult appealed to all walks of life, and its centers of worship were mainly in Asia. Pergamum possessed an altar in their honor, although Samothrace was known as an important site, even the capital of the sect. Boeotia was a favorite place for the faithful, as were Phrygia and Thessalonica. Mysteries and initiations were widespread, and all classes were eligible. By 400 C.E., the Cabiri had faded.

See also RELIGION.

Caecina Alienus, Aulus (d. 79 C.E.) *Legate of the IV Legion on the Rhine; in 69 C.E., with Fabius Valens, led the movement to install Vitellius as emperor*
Caecina was born at Volaterrae, serving in Boeotia as a quaestor. He acquired the patronage of Galba and soon was promoted to legate. Galba convicted him for misappropriation of funds, but he gained a command from Nero on the Rhine.

From the start of Galba's brief reign in 69 C.E., Caecina and his loyal troops were reluctant to support the new emperor. Soon his statues were broken, and open rebellion ensued. Vitellius, it was decided, should be emperor, and the legions along the entire Rhine frontier set off for Italy. Otho, meanwhile, succeeded the assassinated Galba and in turn became the object of the legion's mutiny. While Valens pillaged much of Gaul, Caecina crossed Switzerland, encountering troubles with the local tribes. The Helvetii were massacred in the thousands, and only Vitellius himself prevented the destruction of Aven-ticum, the Helvetian capital. By March the legions of Caecina had descended the Great St. Bernard Pass. On April 15, at the battle of BEDRIACUM, the Vitellians won the empire. Caecina shared in the subsequent division of spoils.

Self-aggrandizement ceased, however, as the legions in the East declared for Vespasian. Caecina doubted that Vitellius would survive, and conspired to hand over the army to Vespasian's oncoming forces. He met at Ravenna with the admiral of the fleet, Lucius Bassus, who easily convinced his sailors, and Caecina drew in several officers. The bulk of the legions, however, refused to defect and threw Caecina into chains. The second battle of Bedriacum followed, and Vespasian's followers won the day. Under the Flavians Caecina was rewarded for his efforts, but in 79, he was executed for conspiracy.

Caecina, Paetus (d. 42 C.E.) *Official, proconsul in Asia*
Paetus Caecina was more famous for the manner of his death than his governorship. In 42, he conspired against CLAUDIUS but was discovered and condemned to die. He lacked the courage to kill himself, and his wife, Arria, seized the dagger, stabbed herself, and told him: "It does not hurt, Paetus."

Caecina Severus, Aulus (fl. early first century C.E.) *Also called Aulus Caecina Severus; a legate of Moesia in 6 C.E.*
During the uprising of local tribes in Dalmatia and Pannonia under the two BATOS, Caecina marched swiftly to rescue the city of Sirmium, checking Bato, the chief of the Breucians. When the Sarmatians and the Dacians threatened his own province, Caecina hurried home. In 7 C.E.

he again participated in Roman operations against the Pannonians and Dalmatians, seeing a conclusion to these matters. The highlight of the campaign was his victory near Sirmium. Command in Germania Inferior came in 14 C.E., when Caecina faced a mutiny in his troops following the death of Augustus. Germanicus helped him restore order in his legions and then put him to use in a campaign against the Germans. During the fighting in 15 C.E., he was caught by the army of Arminius while crossing the Long Bridge over swampy terrain near the Ems River. He assumed a defensive posture awaiting the dawn. That night he dreamed that the ghost of the defeated Roman general VARUS emerged from the swamp, beckoning to him. He did not follow Varus's path to destruction. The legions broke through and drove Arminius from the field. Caecina reportedly served for 40 years and had six children, despite his personal belief that provincial governors should not be allowed to take their wives with them.

Caelian Hill   *See* HILLS OF ROME.

Caelius Rufus, Marcus (d. 47 B.C.E.) *Politician, correspondent, and rabble-rouser; friend and associate of the most important men of his time*

He was introduced by his father to Crassus and CICERO, developing a friendship with the latter. Already in politics by 56 B.C.E., as a member of the council in his home town, he joined the group surrounding the seductive CLODIA, replacing Catullus in her affections. This liaison proved unprofitable, and Cicero defended Caelius in the subsequent and famous trial. Henceforth, Caelius, probably older than Cicero, served as the eyes and ears of the politician in Rome, while Cicero was in Cilicia. Caelius's letters to Cicero were humorous, often malicious, but generally accurate accounts of current events in the city. With the outbreak of the Civil War in 49 B.C.E., debts forced Caelius to join with Julius Caesar, who made him a praetor in 48. After fighting in Spain, he returned to Rome where differences with Caesar surfaced. Caelius desired sweeping legal changes and found himself evicted from the capital. He fled to Campania, teaming with Titus Annius MILO in 47 to start a revolt in which both were killed. Caelius was reportedly fond of luxury and immoral conduct, all of which Cicero went to some pains to ignore.

Caenis (d. 75 C.E.) *Concubine of Vespasian who had a very long service in the imperial household*

Caenis was the friend and servant of the Lady Antonia, in whose service she acquired the reputation of possessing a perfect memory. It was said that she helped Antonia write the letter warning Emperor Tiberius in 31 C.E. about Sejanus's plot. VESPASIAN (ruled 69–79 C.E.) was enchanted with her, making her his concubine. Rewards and gifts were acquired naturally, but Caenis also exer-

cised tremendous influence at court with respect to monetary matters. Vespasian, unable to overcome habits from his lean, Judaean years, allowed governorships, military posts, priesthoods and even statues of himself to be sold. Caenis handled all such transactions. Condemned prisoners could also buy their own lives. Caenis, though clearly loved by the emperor, amassed untold wealth in this fashion.

Caesar, Gaius (20 B.C.E.–4 C.E.) *Son of Agrippa and Julia*

Born in Rome and groomed with his brother Lucius to the imperial throne, he was adopted by Augustus in 17 B.C.E. The following year Gaius received the *toga virilis.* Membership in the Senate and the promise of a consulship in 1 C.E. were further symbols of his status. A marriage to Livilla in 1 B.C.E. aided in creating an environment for dynastic stability. Augustus sent Gaius to the East in 1 B.C.E. as a proconsul; there his advisers were men of considerable promise and power, including SEJANUS and QUIRINIUS. He returned to the East in 2 C.E. and met with the king of Parthia, installing a pro-Roman candidate on the Armenian throne. A revolt ensued, and at the siege of ARTAGIRA Gaius was wounded. On February 21, 4 C.E., he died in Lycia, on his way back to Rome. His death was a severe blow to Augustus. Suetonius wrote that the emperor had supervised personally the education and upbringing of Gaius and Lucius Caesar. Lucius had died in 2 C.E. in Massilia.

Caesar, Julius (Gaius Julius Caesar) (100–44 B.C.E.) *General, politician, statesman, orator, and writer who laid the foundation of the Roman Empire*

Gaius Julius Caesar belonged to the family Julia, a patrician household supposedly descended from the son of Aeneas Iulus. According to tradition, he was born on July 12, 100 B.C.E., during the consulship of the great MARIUS. Connections with the famous consul were cemented by the marriage of Caesar's aunt JULIA to Marius; and in 83 B.C.E., Caesar himself married CORNELIA, the daughter of CINNA, a lieutenant of Marius and the organizer of the Marian party. In the Rome of dictator SULLA, such affiliations could be fatal. When Sulla ordered him to divorce Cornelia, he refused and fled to the Sabinian region. Sulla allowed him to return, but gave the warning to "never forget that the man you wish me to save will one day be the ruin of the party, there are many Mariuses in him!"

A return to Rome would be safe only temporarily, so the young Caesar chose a military career. He traveled to Asia as an aide-de-camp to Marcus Thermus in 81 B.C.E., helping in the capture of Mytilene in 80, where he was rewarded with a civic crown for saving a soldier's life. Sulla's death in 78 B.C.E. brought Caesar back to Rome, but he fled again after unsuccessfully prosecuting Dolabella. To improve his oratorical skills he sailed to Rhodes to study under Apolonius Molo. On the way, pirates kidnapped him, holding him for a ransom of 12,000 gold pieces. Caesar vowed during his imprisonment to hunt down his captors and stayed true to his word, crucifying every one of them.

When he returned to Rome, every effort was spent to gain the goodwill of the people through the reversal of Sullan legislation and by lavish displays of generosity. His rise was rapid: QUAESTOR in 69 B.C.E., in which he served in Spain as an assizer for Rome; AEDILE in 65 B.C.E., spending large sums on games; and PONTIFEX MAXIMUS in 63 B.C.E. A praetorship followed in 62 B.C.E., then military exploits in Spain, which provided him a way to gain both fame and fortune, while evading his creditors in Rome. (He had spent vast amounts to secure votes for the position of pontifex maximus.) After defeating the Lusitanians and pacifying the province, he returned to Italy.

Caesar and the wealthy Lucius Lucceius conspired to bribe Caesar's way into the consulships of 59 B.C.E. Alarmed, the aristocratic party ordered its candidate Marcus BIBULUS to spend even more money. Both Caesar and Bibulus were successful. Caesar then called upon two allies, the formidable CRASSUS and POMPEY THE GREAT. Crassus stood as a rich, powerful figure, while Pompey had grown estranged from the aristocratic party, which feared his conquests in Asia Minor. Caesar resolved their differences (they had disagreed bitterly during their consulships) and then suggested that the state be divided among them so long as each defended the interests of the others. Out of this arrangement came the FIRST TRIUMVIRATE. Caesar moved with confidence against the aristocratic party, ignoring the presence of Bibulus to such a degree that the joint consulship was called that of "Julius and Caesar." Radical measures were passed by the sheer force of his will or threat by arms; his agrarian laws and the cancellation of the farmers' debts infuriated the opposition but cheered the populace. Further acts ensured Caesar's support among the poor, the Equestrians and with Pompey. He married CALPURNIA, the daughter of his successor in the consulship, LUCIUS PISO, and then betrothed his own daughter JULIA to Pompey.

Caesar looked to the Roman provinces for areas where he could not only gain a successful command but also insulate himself from possible prosecution for his unorthodox consulship. He first chose GALLIA CISALPINA and ILLYRICUM. In Cisalpine Gaul he commanded three legions and held the post of proconsul in both provinces for five years. Gallia Transalpina was added to his holdings, and the next nine years (59–50 B.C.E.) were spent campaigning in the GALLIC WARS to pacify Gaul and subdue the native tribes. In 55 and 54, he launched two sorties into BRITANNIA, after renewing his authority over the provinces with the help of Pompey. His ally's aid came in the face of threats from Lucius DOMITIUS AHENOBARBUS (1), who threatened to replace him.

Success in the field strengthened his reputation, now the rival of Pompey's, and his fellow triumvir came to view him with some apprehension. Crassus' death in 55 at the battle of CARRHAE accentuated the growing tension, and his daughter Julia's death in labor in 54 severed the cordiality between Caesar and Pompey, who returned to the aristocratic party.

Caesar desired the consulship in 49, but could not be elected in absentia by senatorial decree. He agreed to resign if Pompey did the same. The Senate, however, proposed a resolution on January 1, 49 B.C.E., ordering Caesar to disband his legions or be declared an enemy of the Republic. Despite the veto of Marc ANTONY and CASSIUS, the resolution passed, and Antony and Cassius allied themselves with Caesar.

Caesar's army, with which he had subdued Gaul, was superior to any opponent in the Roman world. The troops were superbly trained, experienced, and generaled by a master military mind. Taking an advance guard with him, Caesar rode to the Rubicon, the river separating Italy from the provinces. Suetonius reports that he called out: "Let us accept this as a sign from the gods, and follow where they call, in vengeance on our treacherous enemies. The die is cast." With that he rode across the Rubicon and civil war began.

Caesar discovered the Italians welcoming his advance toward Rome. City gates were opened to his soldiers, and the troops of Pompey deserted to him in large numbers. In the face of an underestimated enemy, Pompey and the leaders of the Senate and the Republic fled the capital to southern Italy, then Greece. Caesar chose not to pursue them, campaigning instead against the Pompeian strongholds elsewhere. He said, "I am off to meet an army without a leader, and when I come back, I shall meet a leader without an army." His victory at MASSILIA followed, as well as an easy conquest at ILERDA in Spain. Returning to Rome, he set out at once for Greece and an encounter with Pompey. His armies were stayed by the impenetrable walls of the city of DYRRHACHIUM in Epirus. In subsequent maneuverings, however, the two armies finally collided. Total victory was Caesar's, at the battle of PHARSALUS on August 9, 48 B.C.E.

Pompey escaped to Egypt, and Caesar followed him. Caesar arrived in ALEXANDRIA to discover King PTOLEMY XIII feuding with his sister, Queen CLEOPATRA. A gift of the murdered Pompey's head, from Ptolemy, did little for the king or his cause. The small Roman expedition found itself under siege in the city. Brilliant handling of his limited forces staved off defeat, and reinforcements provided Caesar with the means to destroy Ptolemy in the battle of the NILE.

Caesar then went to Pontus to defeat PHARNACES, the son of MITHRIDATES THE GREAT. Pharnaces, an ally of Pompey, was put to rout at the battle of ZELA (where the famous "veni, vidi, vici" was supposedly uttered). Rome greeted its returning hero in September of 47, but Caesar was soon bound for Africa, where two more allies of Pompey fell—Scipio and King Juba—at the battle of THAPSUS. At MUNDA in Spain the resistance of the Pompeians ended, and five great triumphs were staged in Rome.

In control of Rome, Caesar proved magnanimous, pardoning many of his enemies. From 49 B.C.E. onward the increasing powers of a dictator were granted to him, and he held successive consulships. He instituted a new CALENDAR in 46 and was revered by the people as semidivine. Marc Antony offered him the crown, but Caesar refused it, fearing the adverse reaction of the mob. Despite conciliatory gestures toward the aristocratic party, many ardent Republicans conspired against him. Some, headed by BRUTUS and Cassius, were the most serious threats, forming the party of the LIBERATORS. The ancient sources claimed that omens preceded his death, but Caesar ignored them and fell beneath the daggers of his assassins on the Ides of March, in 44 B.C.E. The Republican form of government did not outlive its supposed enemy.

Julius Caesar was said to have been tall and muscular. He forgave his enemies easily, even those who fought openly against his cause, and bore a grudge only toward CATO, whom he hunted across the deserts of Africa. And once dictator, he denigrated the Republic and questioned the logic of his old enemy, Sulla, in resigning his dictatorship. His first wife Cornelia bore him Julia. He divorced his second wife, POMPEIA, the granddaughter of Sulla, because of her affair with CLODIUS. He remained with his third wife, Calpurnia, until his death.

His oratorical skills placed him in the ranks of the finest speakers of his age, and even CICERO admired his wit, vocabulary, and style. He wrote poetry, works on grammar, letters, and commentaries on the Gallic and Civil Wars, which Cicero and Hirtius (who may have finished the *Gallic Wars*) praised. In fact, these campaigns were recorded by numerous other writers, including: Appian's *Civil War;* Suetonius's *Julius Caesar;* Dio; Plutarch's *Caesar;* and the assorted letters of Cicero. Caesar's varied works included:

Bellum Africum probably was authored by someone other than Caesar; although tradition gives credit to Hirtius, it was not him. This record centered on the war in Africa (47–46 B.C.E.). *Bellum Alexandrium* examined various aspects of the Civil War, especially the long siege of Alexandria. Hirtius, according to Suetonius, authored this work (and others).

The Civil War certainly was begun by Caesar, who commented on his victories starting in 49 B.C.E. It included three books, treating events to the start of the Alexandrian conflict. *The Gallic Wars* contained seven books covering seven years of campaigning. Hirtius probably finished it, but this work proved the most enduring and popular of Caesar's commentaries.

Anti Cato was written in response to Cicero's panegyric, *Cato.* Cicero's defense of Cato Uticensis prompted Caesar to respond with an interesting record of the degree of hatred and spite to which he went in defaming his most ardent Republican foe.

Suggested Readings: Bradford, Ernle. *Julius Caesar: The Pursuit of Power.* London: H. Hamilton, 1984; Dodge, Theodore. *Caesar: A History of the Art of War Among the Romans Down to the End of the Roman Empire, With a Detailed Account of the Campaigns of Gaius Julius Caesar.* New York: Da Capo Press, 1997; Gelzer, Matthias. *Caesar: Politician and Statesman.* Translated by Peter Needham. Cambridge, Mass.: Harvard University Press, 1985; Julius Caesar. *The Civil War.* New York: Penguin, 1967; Julius Caesar. *The Conquest of Gaul.* New York: Penguin, 1982; Meier, Christian. *Caesar.* New York: HarperCollins, 1997.

Caesar, Lucius (17 B.C.E.–2 C.E.) *Son of Marcus Agrippa and Julia, grandson of Augustus*
One of the obvious choices as heir to the throne, with his brother, Gaius, until his death. Lucius was adopted (with Gaius) by Augustus, to stop any plots. The brothers were subsequently raised in the emperor's house, where Augustus personally supervised their education and their upbringing. Augustus was only partially successful, for both succumbed readily to flattery, and Lucius especially was spoiled.

In 2 B.C.E., Lucius received the title PRINCEPS IUVENTUTIS, one year after Gaius, a clear sign that both were the designated heirs to the throne. Augustus then gave them the right to dedicate all public buildings, and they managed the Circensian Games. Finally, both brothers were chosen for more important tasks; Gaius going to the East and Lucius traveling to Spain to receive military training. He never reached the legions there, dying of a sudden illness at Massilia in 2 C.E. His death was a blow to Augustus, who suffered another, more serious disaster two years later when Gaius failed to recover from injuries received in Armenia. Rumors were rampant that LIVIA was at the bottom of the deaths, for her son Tiberius returned to Rome a short time later.

Caesar, Ptolemy (47 B.C.E.–30 B.C.E.) *Son of Julius Caesar and Queen Cleopatra of Egypt*
Following his father's assassination in 44 B.C.E., Ptolemy Caesar was placed on the Egyptian throne as his mother's coruler. In 34 B.C.E., Marc ANTONY arrived in Alexandria and declared that Caesarion (as he was known by the Alexandrians) was CAESAR's legitimate heir. Antony decreed that he should be called the "King of Kings," with full powers inherent with sharing the throne with CLEOPATRA. His rule proved to be brief: Octavian (AUGUSTUS) won the battle of ACTIUM in 31 and Ptolemy Caesar was slain in 30.

Caesarea Large seaport on the Mediterranean Sea shore of PALESTINE, in the region of Samaria-Galatia. Originally called Stratonis Turri, or Strato's Tower, in 63 B.C.E., as part of the reorganization of the East by POMPEY, it was removed from the control of the Jews and placed with the province of SYRIA. Octavian (AUGUSTUS), after repairing relations with HEROD THE GREAT, restored the city to him in 30 B.C.E. Under the rule of Herod, a mammoth building program was initiated in the city, and the name Caesarea was adopted in honor of Augustus. A wall was built around the city, and construction lasted for some 12 years (22–10 B.C.E.). Hellenistic designs dominated, while the new harbor system became the gateway for the seaborne trade of Palestine. Augustus donated 500 talents, out of his own accounts, in genuine gratitude, and then sent AGRIPPA to visit JERUSALEM as an act of good will.

Being a port of international standing, like ALEXANDRIA, Caesarea was a gathering point for many races, including Greeks, Syrians, and large numbers of Jews. Jewish demands for citizenship in 60 C.E. caused riots; Nero refused, however, to grant their demands. Six years later, Jews in Caesarea were murdered by non-Jews, and the governor of Syria, CESTIUS GALLUS, intervened. After 70 C.E., Caesarea served as home for the legates of the province. Vespasian designated Caesarea a colony, although for many years it was not given a colony's immunity from all forms of tribute. Archaeological work continues in Caesarea, most notably just off the coast and centering on Herod's Harbor.

Caesarion *See* CAESAR, PTOLEMY.

Caledonia Name given to the region of northern Britain beyond Roman control. As the Roman legions pressed to the north of the island, the BRIGANTES moved into what is now Scotland. From around 80 C.E., this wild territory was called Caledonia, also Britannia Barbara. Caledonians were a mix of races whose opposition to the Roman presence and dense population brought about massive assaults on the frontier. In 208 C.E., Septimius SEVERUS threw them back beyond the WALL OF HADRIAN. Punitive expeditions were then launched directly into Caledonia by the Romans. The Caledonians withdrew before Severus's cohorts, pulling them further into dense forest and swamps, where impure water waged a very efficient war of attrition.

A signed treaty with the Caledonians was the only victory that the emperor could claim. He left Caledonia, with the local inhabitants unpacified. Dio described in some detail not only the campaign by the Romans but also the unbearably harsh conditions of the region.

Caledonians See CALEDONIA.

Calenas, Q. Fufius (d. 40 B.C.E.) *General and consul during the civil wars of the first century B.C.E.*
Under Caesar, Calenas commanded a body of troops in Greece, where he harassed the Pompeians. While unable to storm ATHENS, Calenas did take Piraeus and laid waste the Athenian environs. In 48 B.C.E., after the death of Pompey the Great, the city surrendered to him. The Megarians apparently resisted, and the general put them down with great force but then sold the captives back to their relatives for small fees. After Caesar's assassination, Calenas sided with Marc Antony in 43 B.C.E., defending him in a spirited oratorical rebuttal of CICERO. After the battle of PHILIPPI in 42, Antony gave Calenas 11 legions to command in Gaul, relying on him to keep the real threat, Octavian (AUGUSTUS), out of the province. Calenas's death was a cruel blow to Antony's cause, for not only was Gaul lost, but also, by the terms of the TREATY OF BRUNDISIUM, he had to surrender five of Calenas's legions. Calenas was also a friend of CLODIUS, saving him in 61 B.C.E. from condemnation after he violated the festival of BONA DEA.

calendar The Roman calendar was originally based on a 10-month year that reflected the agricultural priorities of the Roman people. It ran from March to December for 304 days and then had an uncounted four-month gap, as during the winter months there were few agricultural concerns. The first day of the year commenced on March 1. By the sixth century the calendar had changed to a 12-month year, using lunar months. This meant that each month had roughly 29.5 days. The solar year is about $365\frac{1}{4}$ days long, so there was a discrepancy of 11 days in the solar year compared to the lunar months. Not surprisingly, the Romans realized the difficulty and so added occasionally an extra month to adjust to the solar year, a process called intercalation.

What was actually involved in intercalation remains somewhat unclear, but it would appear that the Romans added 22 or 23 days (termed Intercalaris or Mercedonius) to every other February. This added more time to the calendar than was needed for the solar year, resulting in $366\frac{1}{4}$ days per year. By the time of Julius Caesar, intercalation had created so many extra days that the civil calendar (which began on January 1, 153 B.C.E.) was three months ahead of the solar year.

To fix the inadequate system, Julius Caesar, then dictator of Rome and an accomplished astronomer in his own right, introduced reforms to the calendar. He wiped away the old calendar and extended the year 46 B.C.E. to a length of 445 days to bring the civil calendar in line with the solar year. The new 12-month year, consisting of 365 days began on January 1, 45 B.C.E., with each month having the number of days that are presently in practice. To make the system even more precise, Caesar created a leap year by adding an extra day between February 23 and 24; originally, the leap year was used every three years, but this was modified to every four years in 8 B.C.E. Technically, the Julian calendar, as it came to be called, is 11 minutes longer than the solar year, but it served so admirably the purposes of the Romans that it remained the official calendar for Western civilization until the introduction of the Gregorian calendar in 1582 by Pope Gregory XIII.

The Roman year was divided into twelve months with varying numbers of days. The names of several months changed over time, but the final list of names was set by the middle of the first century C.E. They were: Ianuarius, Februarius, Martius, Aprilis, Maius, Iunius, Iulius, Augustus, September, October, November, and December. Iulius was originally Quintilis and was counted as the fifth month. It was changed in 44 B.C.E. to Iulius in honor of Julius Caesar. Augustus was also originally called Sextilis, the sixth month. It was renamed Augustus in honor of Emperor AUGUSTUS in 8 B.C.E. The names of the months reflected in part the original 10-month calendar of the Romans: Quintilis (fifth month), Sextilis (sixth month), September (seventh month), October (eighth month), November (ninth month), and December (tenth month). After the adoption of a 12-month year, these were, of course, no longer reflective of their proper month, but the names were retained.

The days of the month were not counted in sequence (as from one to 30 or 31, or one to 28 or 29 for February). Instead, all of the months except February (which had its own system of reckoning) were divided into three parts: the Kalends, the Nones, and the Ides. The Kalends always fell on the first day of the month. The Nones began on the ninth day before the Ides and fell on the seventh day of the month in March, May, July, and October, and on the fifth day in all of the other months. The Ides fell on the 15th day of the months of March, May, July, and October, and the 13th in all other months. Days were thus calculated by the span in days before (*ante diem*) the Kalends, Nones, and Ides. The day right before one of these named days was termed *pridie*. For example, the first day of the month of December was termed the *Kalendas Decembribus*; December 2 was called *ante diem* (or simply *a.d.*) *IV ante Nonas Decembres;* December 5 was *Nonis Decembribus;* December 13 was *Idibus Decembribus* (*Idus*); December 30 was *pridie Kalendas Ianuarius* (or *Kal. Ian.*). For February, the 24th day of the month was termed IV *ante Kalendas Martias*, with the leap year added to the calendar with a *posteriorem*.

See also FESTIVALS.

Calends   *See* KALENDS.

Caligula   *See* GAIUS CALIGULA.

Callistus (d. 222 C.E.) *Former slave and eventually bishop of Rome*

Callistus was at the heart of a bitter and divisive feud within the Church of Rome in the late second and early third centuries C.E. Most of what is known about him comes from the oppositional writings of the Roman presbyter HIPPOLYTUS, in his *Refutations of the Heresies,* written around 222 C.E. The poisonous nature of the work raises questions of accuracy, but generally Hippolytus is accepted for biographical purposes. The servant of an official of Emperor Commodus, Callistus impressed his master Carpophorus with his skills in finance and was given capital to establish a bank. When it failed, apparently from embezzlement, Callistus fled, trying to sail away from Pontus. He jumped into the sea but was fished out. Freed by Carpophorus to repay the terrible debts, Callistus chose to incite an anti-Jewish riot. The city prefect, Seius Fuscianus, sent him to Sardinia.

As a Christian, Callistus was able to have himself included in the general amnesty of Commodus in 192 C.E. that was directed at all Christian prisoners. He returned to Rome a free man. In 199, Zephyrinus was named bishop of the city, and Callistus entered his service. Ordained, he became a new archdeacon and ran the diocese's administrative affairs and its cemetery. Essential to the diocese in this and other capacities, Callistus succeeded Zephyrinus, who died in 217. As the new leader of the Roman Christians, Callistus espoused views that were contrary to those of many of his clergy and other important figures. Chief among these foes were Hippolytus and Tertullian. The disagreement was bitter, but the direct activity of Callistus was ultimately brief. Nearly 60 when he assumed the see, he died in 222. His successor was Urban, accompanied by Pontian, both of whom carried on a religious war with Hippolytus.

See also CHRISTIANITY.

Callistus, Gaius Julius (d. c. 52 C.E.) *Imperial freedman during the reigns of emperors Gaius Caligula and Claudius*

Under Gaius, Callistus began using his office to enrich himself, but the emperor's increasing madness forced him in 40 C.E. to join in the large group of conspirators plotting to kill the emperor. The assassination took place on January 24, 41, and Callistus was able to ingratiate himself immediately with CLAUDIUS, Gaius's successor. As the A LIBELLUS, or secretary of petitions, to Claudius, Callistus worked with other freedmen, such as Narcissus, Pallas, and Polybius, eventually exercising tremendous influence over both the emperor and the court.

Calpurnia (fl. mid-first century B.C.E.) *Third wife of Julius Caesar*

Calpurnia helped establish a political alliance between CAESAR and her father, Lucius Piso Caesoninus, in 59 B.C.E. Piso gained a consulship because of the marriage.

Calpurnia was very loyal to Caesar, even though in 53 B.C.E. he considered divorcing her in favor of Pompey's daughter. It is reported that she dreamed of Caesar's impending assassination and tried to prevent his departure from the house on the day of his death. No one came to comfort her after Caesar's death, except her father. Antony did visit, to claim Caesar's papers and all available money.

Calpurnius Siculus, Titus (fl. 50–60 C.E.) *Bucolic poet, author of seven pastoral poems covering a wide variety of topics, including the amphitheater in Rome, singing contests, and the speeches of Nero*
In style, Calpurnius greatly emulated the pastoral works of Virgil, although he also imitated Ovid. Calpurnius is a figure of some scholarly debate. Even his name could be questioned, for it is unclear whether it denoted his origins (Siculus, or Sicily), or referred to his style in writing, similar to Theokritos (the third-century B.C.E. Syracusan poet). The greatest mystery, however, surrounds his poems and those of Menesianus. Until 1854, the poems of these two authors were always published together leading to a dispute as to which poem was penned by Calpurnius and which by Nemesianus. Calpurnius, hence, may not have written the *Laude Pisonis*, a panegyric to the famed conspirator of the Neronian era.

Calvinus, Gnaeus Domitius (fl. mid-first century B.C.E.) *Consul in 53 and in 40 B.C.E. and a supporter of Julius Caesar and Augustus*
Calvinus served as a tribune during Caesar's consulship and then ran for the post himself in 54 B.C.E. In some of the worst election campaigns of the era, Calvinus gained his seat by corrupt methods. During the Civil War, he chose the side of Caesar against POMPEY THE GREAT. As a legate in Thessaly during the Dyrrhachium campaign of 48 B.C.E., he helped defeat the forces of Pompey in that region. After the battle of Pharsalus in that same year, Caesar ordered him to send two legions as support to Alexandria. Meanwhile, with only one legion and some auxiliaries at his disposal, Calvinus tried to stop the advance of Pharnaces, the king of the Bosporus, but was beaten at Nicopolis. Following Caesar's assassination, Calvinus granted his allegiance to Octavian (Augustus), taking over affairs in Spain around 40 B.C.E.

Calvisius (fl. mid-first century C.E.) *Accuser during the reign of Nero*
JUNIA SILANAS, a one-time friend and then bitter enemy of empress AGRIPPINA THE YOUNGER, attempted in 55 C.E. to ensnare the empress in false accusations. Two of Junia's clients, Calvisius and Iturius, spread the story that Agrippina was planning to elevate Rubellius Plautus to the throne because Nero, her son, had spurned her.

Upon hearing of the supposed plot, Nero was ready to murder both his mother and Plautus. Burrus, the prefect of the Praetorian Guard, restrained Nero's rage and proposed to allow the empress to clear herself of the charges. She did so, and Junia Silanas was banished. Calvisius and his partners both suffered self-imposed exile, returning to Rome in 59.

Calvus, Gaius Licinius Macer (82–47 or 46 B.C.E.) *Son of the annalist and praetor Licinius Macer*
An ADVOCATUS and an erotic poet, he was born on May 28, 82 B.C.E., Calvus displayed early on a gift for oratory and at the age of 27 challenged Cicero in his prosecution of Vatinius. A long career seemed to stretch ahead of him but he died at the age of 35 or 36, in either 47 or 46 B.C.E. Calvus also distinguished himself as a poet. Influenced by the Alexandrian School, he wrote numerous poems, specializing in erotica and the epic, although his lampoons of Caesar were so sharp as to require a formal reconciliation. None of his works are extant.

See also POETRY.

Camillus, Furius Scribonianus (1) (d. 42 C.E.) *Father of Camillus (2), and consul in 32 C.E.*
As legate in Dalmatia, Camillus conspired with such notables as Caecina Paetus, Annius Vinicianus, and Pomponius Secundus to overthrow the emperor. He composed a letter to Claudius, threatening him with civil war if he did not abdicate. His two legions, however, refused to follow him, and either killed him or forced him to commit suicide. He was married to Vibia.

Camillus, Furius Scribonianus (2) (d. c. 52 C.E.) *Son of Furius Scribonianus Camillus (1)*
Like his father, Camillus was destroyed politically during the reign of Claudius. He probably fell prey to the jealous alertness of Agrippina. In 52 C.E. he was charged with the use of magic (by consulting Chaldaean astrologers) to curse the emperor. As a result, Camillus and his mother Vibia were exiled. He died soon after, possibly of poison.

Cammuni A tribe of Helvetians who revolted against Rome in 16 B.C.E. Given their location in the Alps relative to Italia, Roman authorities took immediate steps to suppress the tribe. The brief campaign was conducted by Publius Silius.

Campania District in southern Italy surrounded by the region of Latium, Samnium, and Lucania; one of the most beautiful areas of Italy, possessing several famous cities and natural points of interest. For centuries Campania was a select retreat for the nobility. Under the empire such Campanian communities as Baiae and Bauli maintained an atmosphere of leisure and exclusivity. Fertile soil allowed crops to be grown three times a year, and vineyards produced a fine wine. Oils, metalwork, and cloth were other products, while the port of Puteoli provided a gateway for seaborne trade, but was suppressed by Ostia in the second century C.E. POMPEII and HERCULANEUM were burgeoning metropolises preserved as time capsules for the future by the explosion of Mount Vesuvius on August 24, 79 C.E. The principal city of the region was CAPUA.

Campus Agrippa   Area within the boundaries of Rome named after Marcus AGRIPPA. A number of construction projects were developed within its perimeters, including a portico, built by his sister, Polla, and a race course. In 7 B.C.E., Augustus declared the Campus open to the public.

Campus Martius   Large plain named after its altar to Mars; located just outside of the original walls of Rome near the northwestern bend of the Tiber River. The plain was surrounded by the Capitoline, Quirinal, and Pincian hills and for centuries served as the gymnasium area for youths and military drilling. Temples and altars multiplied there during the days of the Republic, but under the empire a strenuous building program on the property never ceased. Emperor Augustus sponsored a temple to Neptune in 32 B.C.E., and the first stone amphitheater, of Statilius Taurus, was erected in 29 B.C.E. Marcus Agrippa laid out an ambitious program: the *Saepta* of Julia, the Baths of Agrippa, and the PANTHEON. Other buildings were constructed over the next centuries. During the reign of Domitian (81–96 C.E.), a stadium housed athletic shows. It rested on a solid foundation of concrete. Entertainment could also be found in the Theater of Marcellus, dedicated in 13 or 11 B.C.E., and the Theater of Balbus, dedicated in 13 B.C.E. Hadrian placed the basilicas of Marciana and Matidia in the Campus Martius and was memorialized by Antoninus Pius with his own temple in 154 C.E. In turn, Pius was honored with a column of beautiful classic sculpture, depicting the Marcomannic War.

The Campus Martius also served as the final resting place of many notable Romans. In 12 B.C.E., Agrippa was placed in a mausoleum there. Drusus, Tiberius's brother, joined him in 9 B.C.E. Augustus (d. 14 C.E.) had his own elaborate mausoleum. In 193 C.E., Septimius Severus used the burial of the murdered Emperor Pertinax to eulogize the deceased and to further his own firm hold on the throne. Gardens, an aqueduct, a sun-dial (added in 10 B.C.E.) and the famous Ara Pacis, the Altar of Peace, made the Campus Martius popular. It was officially added to Rome when the WALL OF AURELIAN was constructed.

Camulodunum   One of the leading cities of Roman-occupied BRITANNIA, situated in modern Essex. For years prior to the invasion by Aulus Platius, Camulodunum (modern Colchester) served as the capital of the Belgae in Britain, under the rule of Cassivellaunus and his son, Tasciovanus. The court there during the reign of Cunobellinus was a center of strong rule but increasing disagreement on policy toward the Roman Empire. Claudius's conquest of the isles focused strategically on Camulodunum, and its fall in 43 C.E. signalled the end of Belgae power.

The new Roman province of Britannia, under Aulus Plautius, had Camulodunum as its capital. Colonists followed, settling in the former Belgae lands. Town life emerged after the official declaration in 49 C.E. of the colonial status of the region. Near Fishbourne, just outside of the city, a harbor was constructed. Veterans continued the expansion of the colony, with baths, a forum, theaters and a remarkable temple. This temple, originally dedicated to Claudius, emerged as the seat of the IMPERIAL CULT in the province. By the end of the first century C.E., Camulodunum had been surpassed in importance by Londinium (London). The administrative center of the Roman occupation remained in the city until the revolt of Queen BOUDICCA in 61 C.E.

Candidus, Tiberius Claudius   (fl. late second century C.E.) *General and senator*
Candidus was an accomplished officer serving in the army of Emperor Marcus Aurelius. He possessed the favor of Emperor Commodus, who made him a senator, and was eventually the general of Emperor Septimius Severus. He commanded an army in Illyria from 193 to 197 C.E., proving invaluable at the battles of Cyzicus, Nicaea, and the Issus, against the claimant Pescennius Niger.

Candidus Crassus, Publius   (d. 30 B.C.E.) *Legate of Marc Antony*
Candidus served as Antony's principal agent and general in preparing for his war with PARTHIA in 36 B.C.E. Crassus arrived in ARMENIA sometime in 37 to bring its King Artavasdes back into the sphere of Roman influence. A quick battle was followed by Armenia's submission; Crassus, with Antony's prodding, took Artavasdes at his word. With no guarantees, the legate marched away into the Asian kingdom of Iberia and conquered its ruler, Pharnabazus. He then joined Antony for the Parthian invasion, completely ignorant of the fact that Armenia could not be trusted. Marc ANTONY's war on the Parthians ended in disaster, and when he left his retreating columns to join Cleopatra, it was up to Crassus and his fellow officer, Domitius Ahenobarbus, to bring the broken army back to Syria.

Unlike many soldiers and politicians who saw Octavian (*see* AUGUSTUS) gaining the upper hand, Crassus chose to remain with his leader. In 31, when the final battle at ACTIUM was about to start, Crassus was appointed the commander of Antony's land forces. With the legions on shore he awaited news of the titanic struggle taking place on the sea. Within hours he knew that the destiny of Antony had been sealed. His troops refused to escape to Egypt and settled into negotiations with the agents of Octavian. Crassus wisely fled but was captured. After the deaths of Antony and Cleopatra in 30 B.C.E., Octavian pondered Crassus's fate and deemed him too loyal to the dead. Crassus was put to death, one of but a few executed by the new, sole ruler of Rome.

Cantabri   People of the Cantabri region of northern Spain. Like the native Spaniards in the early days of Roman occupation, the Cantabri did not accept subjugation or pacification until they were utterly defeated by Emperor Augustus's generals. In 35 B.C.E., Augustus waged war in Spain and, though successful against surrounding tribes, he could not subdue the Cantabri. They revolted again in 22 B.C.E., as part of a wider uprising, but were defeated by the governor, Gaius Furnius, with many prisoners sent into slavery and others committing suicide. The tribes rose up yet again in 19 B.C.E. Their cause was championed by former warriors who had been enslaved but who had slain their masters and returned home. The Roman legions were victorious, and their general Agrippa took severe steps. All Cantabri of military age were massacred, and the rest were forced to live on the area's plains.

Capella, Martianus   (fl. fifth century) *Encyclopedist*
Born in Africa prior to the Vandal invasions, Capella composed an encyclopedia of the seven arts, forming nine separate volumes. Subject matter ranged from rhetoric, geography, mathematics, and music. His sources included Pliny the Elder, Salinus, and Varro, whom he imitated in poetic form and style. His work was written in prose-poetical way, presenting personified types of learning.

Capellianus   (fl. mid-third century C.E.) *Governor (of senatorial rank) of Numidia, who in 238 C.E. proved the personal undoing of the imperial aspirations of the Gordians*
Capellianus had been appointed governor by Maximinus and remained loyal to him. During his tenure of office he had even entered into a lawsuit with the governor of Africa, GORDIAN. In 238, when the Gordians seized the throne, Capellianus sided with Maximinus. The Numidian governor marched on Carthage with the III Augusta Legion and its auxiliary cohorts. Gordian's hopes were crushed, despite the popular support of the Carthaginians. Gordian II fell in the battle, and his father, Gordian I, killed himself.

Caper, Flavius   (fl. early second century C.E.) *Grammarian of the era of Trajan (97–117 C.E.)*

Caper was the author of two treatises: *de orthographia* and *de verbis dubiis*. Little is known about his personal life.

Capito, Cossutianus   (fl. 57–66 C.E.) *Governor of Cilicia c. 57 C.E.*
Famed for his role as an accuser during the reign of NERO, Capito served in Cilicia and earned the enmity of the local populace by shamefully extorting them. Prosecuted for this crime, he returned to Rome and began to accuse others. His first victim was the praetor, Antistius, who was accused in 62 of treason for reading a libelous verse against Nero at a banquet. Capito found allies at court and was elevated to the rank of senator by his father-in-law, the infamous Praetorian Prefect Tigellinus. The pair soon began to blackmail the rich and powerful of the city, gaining the wealth of Annaeus Mela, the father of the poet Lucan, after Mela killed himself in 66. Capito bore one Thrasea Paetus a grudge for aiding the Cilicians in 57 C.E., and in 66, after Thrasea had made the mistake of not honoring Empress Poppaea, listed a battery of charges against him. Thrasea was prosecuted, and Capito received five million sesterces.

Capito, Gaius Ateius   (34 B.C.E.–22 C.E.) *Jurist of the early Augustan era*
Capito represented the conservative monarchist perspective in the reigns of Augustus (27 B.C.E.–14 C.E.) and Tiberius (14–37 C.E.). Although from a nonaristocratic family (his father was a praetor), Capito was famed for his oratorical skills and was placed second only to M. Antistius Labeo as a noted jurist. He lived in Rome as a favorite of Augustus, who made him a consul in 5 C.E.; he also served on the influential *cura aquarum* from 13 to 22 C.E.

Capitoline Hill   *See* HILLS OF ROME.

Cappadocia   Strategically important province in eastern ASIA MINOR that was a buffer along the wild and unpredictable frontier separating the empire and the Parthian-Persian empires. The province offered a fertile environment for various cereals and fruits but was more suited to grazing herds of cattle, sheep, and horses. Severe winters and inhospitable terrain prevented the Cappadocians from developing as fully as their neighbors in GALATIA, Paphlagonia, and Lycaonia. Thus the region was governed for centuries by kings overseeing a feudal, horse-based culture that changed very little, despite contact with Hellenic and later Roman influence. Cappadocia's position in Asia Minor ensured political involvement with Rome. POMPEY THE GREAT helped rebuild several cities following the Mithridatic wars (c. 65 B.C.E.), installing a line of client kings who ruled only briefly. Antony replaced them with the far more reliable ARCHELAUS, but by 17 C.E. the Romans were in control of the country.

Roman occupation not only dictated Cappadocian policy from then on, but allowed the empire to acquire as well a considerable portion of the province's tax revenues. Cappadocia served as a procuratorial province until 72 C.E., when Emperor VESPASIAN deemed its strategic location to be too important. Henceforth, until the time of TRAJAN, Cappadocia was attached to Galatia, guarded by legions and run by a legate. Trajan preferred a more aggressive frontier policy and severed the connection with Galatia, replacing it with PONTUS sometime before 113. This organization remained intact for centuries.

Stability within Cappadocia's borders allowed the province to keep its traditional territorial divisions. Urbanization came slowly and remained limited throughout the area. Once the frontiers were strengthened with legions, and with the addition of roads, Cappadocia participated, albeit slowly, in the trade system of the empire. Several cities were constructed, but only a few could be called developed in comparison with the other cities of Asia Minor. Two of the more important urban centers were Caesarea and TRAPEZUS (modern Trebizond). Caesarea served as the provincial capital. Originally called Mozaca, it was rebuilt by Archelaus. Trapezus, a port on the Black Sea, was a trading post for the northern provincial lands. The Romans also founded large estates, the work of colonists. Formed from confiscated or purchased properties, these estates helped the economic strength of the province and were tiny islands of culture in a wild land. It is known that the Roman emperors maintained their own stud farms for horses in the province, controlling large sections of land into the fourth century.

In the middle of the third century Cappadocia witnessed a decline of imperial influence and a major shift of power in the East. In 251–252, SHAPUR I, king of Persia, invaded Armenia, Syria, and Cappadocia. For the next years the province was a battleground for Persia and Rome. Emperor Valerian's forces fell to Shapur in 259. From then on the Romans had only a fragile hold on the province, and CHRISTIANITY was persecuted severely.

Capri   Also called Caprae; an island south of Naples, just off the coast of CAMPANIA. Long held to be a beautiful island retreat, Emperor AUGUSTUS spent some time there, and his successor TIBERIUS chose the site for his self-imposed exile from Rome. He took it from the Neapolitans in 27 C.E. but reimbursed them with other territories. From 27 to 37 C.E., the emperor lived on Capri. The stories told of his lifestyle there, the murders, debaucheries, and orgies, overshadow the considerable architectural achievements of his Villa Jovi. Capri lost its appeal to the Roman emperors after Tiberius. COMMODUS (ruled 177–192 C.E.) banished his wife and sister there. Tacitus described the island as isolated, with no harbors, mild in the winter and charming in the summer. A stun-ning view of Mount Vesuvius can still be seen from atop the hills of the small bay.

Capua   Chief city of the CAMPANIA district of ITALY. It was located northeast from the coast, along the Via Appia and near the river Volturnus. Capua played a significant role in the Roman trade in metal goods and pottery. Small factories of the area manufactured vessels of silver, and these were distributed throughout the empire.

Caracalla (Marcus Aurelius Antoninus) (188–217 C.E.) *Ruler of Rome from 211 to 217 C.E.; the son of Septimius Severus and Julia Domna*
Caracalla's original name, Julius Bassianus, came from the Syrian side of his family, although he was born in Gaul. In an attempt to strengthen his own imperial line, SEVERUS, in 195 C.E., appointed his son to the rank of Caesar (or junior emperor), two years before Caracalla's great rival, his brother GETA, would receive that same honor. In 197 Caracalla became emperor-designate as well, and in the following year received the powerful title of Augustus. All of this led to palace intrigues, and Caracalla and Geta became bitter enemies, despite the efforts of Julia to keep the peace.

The Praetorian Prefect GAIUS PLAUTIANUS conspired to improve his already considerable powers by wedding his daughter Plautilla to Caracalla in 202. Caracalla resisted the marriage and then treated his bride coldly, all the while plotting against her father. Accounts varied as to the manner by which Plautianus fell in 205, but the death of the prefect was greeted with joy by Caracalla, who exiled his wife and now waited for his father to die as well.

Severus campaigned in Britain from 208 to 211, but because of his father's ill health, Caracalla was forced to conduct many of the campaigns in his place—earning the loyalty of the troops on the field. The name "Caracalla," in fact, came from the hooded cloak that he wore. The troops followed him faithfully, and he turned to them when Severus died at Eburacum (York) in 211. However, the Guard and the legions swore their oaths to both sons of the dead emperor. HERODIAN noted that the two brothers proposed to divide the empire between them. Caracalla found a more permanent solution by assassinating Geta on February 12, 212, in their mother's apartment. To stem any problems with the legions and the Praetorian Guard, Caracalla immediately gave them better pay.

As emperor, Caracalla proved harsh, cruel, and obsessed with the fulfillment of his martial dreams, as evidenced by his constant style of dress—that of a simple soldier. Where his father had disliked the SENATE, Caracalla displayed an outright hatred of the members of the legislative body. Those aspects of the empire in which

Caracalla did meddle soon suffered greatly. When PAP-INIAN, the jurist and prefect, was hacked to pieces by the Guard, Caracalla merely commented that the killer should have used an ax instead of a sword. The provincial distribution of the legions was changed so that no more than two could be stationed in any province, an indication that Caracalla feared revolt.

Caracalla was forced to take money from the imperial treasury to pay his military units and was compelled to use other means as well. He issued a new COINAGE to debase the currency; the AUREUS was reduced and the ANTONINIANUS was introduced. In 212, to gain further revenues, Caracalla decreed the Constitutio Antoniniana bestowing citizenship on nearly everyone in the Roman world. While it must have had limitations (slaves were automatically ineligible and others must have been excluded for various reasons), its immediate benefit was the considerable TAXES that could be collected on inheritances and emancipation. Other methods of raising money were also employed. Dio noted that Caracalla spent freely on his soldiers but excelled in stripping, despoiling, and grinding down the rest of humanity. New taxes were instituted and old ones increased. Cities had to build him houses, amphitheaters, and race tracks whenever he visited. Of course, not every ounce of the collected gold went into the military coffers. Caracalla admired Alexander tremendously, seeing himself as the reincarnation of the Greek conqueror. He tried to be a general, emperor, and builder, with the result that Rome saw the creation of one of the grandest monuments in the city's history. The BATHS of Caracalla epitomized the grandiose vision of the emperor, putting into architectural splendor his material expectations.

In 213, he marched to the Danube and Rhine frontiers, defeating the barbarian confederation of the ALA-MANNI on the Main River and adding forts to strengthen the LIMES (frontier). Beginning in 214, he planned to conquer the East, much as Alexander had in his own time. Sweeping triumphantly through Macedonia, he recruited a 16,000-man phalanx, similar to the ancient Macedonian phalanx. Illness prevented serious campaigning, and Caracalla retraced Alexander's route to Egypt, where, in 215, he slaughtered many of Alexandria's hostile inhabitants. So many died at his hands that he could not even write to the Senate the exact number. By 216, his eastern preparations were complete, and he set out again for Mesopotamia. Wintering in Edessa, Caracalla suffered a bout of paranoia. MACRINUS, one of the Praetorian prefects, watched as many of his companions died as the result of an imperial whim. A seer, the Egyptian Serapio, who openly predicted the emperor's death and the succession of Macrinus, was thrown to the lions, survived and was slain. Caracalla confirmed his growing fear of the prefect in dispatches, which Macrinus managed to discover. With tribunes of the Guard, Macrinus killed Caracalla on April 8, 217 C.E., at Carrhae and became his successor.

Emperor Caracalla *(Hulton/Getty Archive)*

Caracalla, despite his growing mental instability, formalized the increasingly international stature of the empire. He favored the Gallic cloak, the German-style wig and certainly displayed the influences of his Syrian origins. His decree, the *Constitutio Antoniniana,* confirmed the changes taking place in the Roman world. Caracalla's family would return to power in the person of Bassianus (218 C.E.)

Caratacus (fl. mid-first century C.E.) *King of the Catuvellauni from 41 to 51 C.E.*

The British ruler Caratacus, also called Caractacus, resisted the conquest of his kingdom by Rome for eight years. He was the son of King Cunobellinus, along with Togodumnus and Amminius. At court Caratacus and Togodumnus championed the anti-Roman sentiment, in opposition to Amminius. In 41, Amminius fled the isles to Gaius Caligula, the same year in which Cunobellinus died. Claudius, in 43, determined that the time was right and invaded Britain with four legions under General Aulus Plautius. The brothers made the mistake of not opposing the Roman landing. They were soon defeated in the field, and Togodumnus died in battle. Claudius ended British resistance with his elephants, and Caratacus fled into Wales to stir up the tribes in that region. In 47, he lost another battle, this time to the general Ostorius Scapula. Only Cartimandua, queen of the Brigantes, could help him, but in keeping with her treaty with Rome, she handed him over to the enemy. He was taken to Rome and brought before Claudius, where, according to Tacitus, he delivered a speech of such force that the emperor gave him his life.

Carausius, Marcus Aurelius Mausaeus (d. 293 C.E.)

A major usurper during the late third century C.E., who controlled Britain and much of modern Gaul

Carausius had humble origins in Messapia but won fame in the campaigns of Emperor Maximian against the Franks and the Bagaudae in 286. Looking for a competent officer to eradicate the Frank and Saxon pirates in the Channel, Maximian chose Carausius.

He proved a brilliant admiral but was accused of keeping recovered plunder for his own use and of pressing captured pirates into his own fleet. Sentenced to death, he sailed to Britain in late 286 or early 287, declaring himself independent of imperial control. The Britons greeted him cheerfully and helped him to consolidate his power. Carausius soon began to seize large parts of the Gallic coast. In April of 289, Maximian finally moved against him, only to suffer defeat at Carausius's hands. The emperor was reduced to making a treaty with him instead. Carausius declared his triumph, issuing at first an irregular and then an imperial coinage, with the presumptuous words: "Carausius and his brothers, Diocletian and Maximian." Ironically, Carausius provided the TETRARCHY exactly what it needed in Britain. He resisted the incursions of the Picts, repaired Hadrian's Wall, and kept the regions secure. His independence, however, could not be tolerated, and Diocletian waited until the time was ripe to strike.

In 293, Emperor Constantius I Chlorus, Diocletian's junior, launched a massive assault on Carausius's holdings in Gaul. The port of Gesoriacum (Boulogne) was blockaded by Constantius, while Carausius's main fleet remained in Britain to repel an invasion. The city fell, but just barely; reinforcements were prevented from arriving by a great mole stretched across the harbor. These initial setbacks were compounded as Constantius cleared the entire region of Gaul. Having lost his continental territories, Carausius suffered other political difficulties as well, until his chief minister, ALLECTUS, became disenchanted and killed him in 293, taking over his ships, troops, and his claim to supremacy in Britain.

Caria

One of the districts of the Roman province of ASIA.

Carinus, Marcus Aurelius (d. 285 C.E.)

Joint emperor with his brother Numerian (late 283 to November 285)

Ruler of the West until defeated by the claimant DIOCLETIAN, CARUS ascended the throne in 282. His two adult sons, Carinus and Numerian, assumed leading roles in his reign. In early 283, Carus set off with Numerian for a campaign against Persia, while Carinus took up the reins of power in Rome, to maintain control of the West. He received the ranks of Augustus and coemperor later in the year. When Carus died, Carinus and Numerian became joint emperors, Carinus in the West and Numerian in the East.

He proved himself successful in the field against the Germans but did not inspire the legions in the East. Thus, when Numerian died, they chose Diocletian. Carinus prepared for civil war, defeating first Julianus, the rebelling governor of Venetia, before turning to the real threat. In a pitched and hard-fought battle in the Margus Valley of MOESIA, Carinus's recently experienced troops had the upper hand. One of the emperor's officers, however, chose that moment to exact revenge for Carinus's seduction of his wife, and he killed him. Diocletian, as a result, became undisputed master of the empire.

Carna

Roman divinity who, as her name would suggest (*caro*, flesh), was the protectoress of health and well-being. Her festival was on the 1st of July.

See also GODS AND GODDESSES OF ROME.

Carnuntum

Town in Upper PANNONIA, east of Vindobona (modern Vienna); originally settled by a Celtic people, under later Roman occupation it became a strategically based colony. Its location was prized, not only because of its roads but also because legions could be stationed there in defense of the entire frontier of the Danube. As colonists from Rome, mostly veterans, established themselves in the region, Carnuntum boasted the largest amphitheater in Pannonia.

carpentum

A two-wheeled cart. Due to the congestion of wheeled traffic in the city of Rome, strict limitations were made on all such vehicles. The *carpentum* was no exception, and only a few very special people could ride in one during daylight hours. These included Vestal Virgins, priests on special days, and women of great distinction.

Carpi

A sizeable group of free Dacians who lived outside of DACIA after the conquest of their homeland by TRAJAN in the early second century. The Carpi led waves of barbarians who molested the Roman province throughout the third century and eventually regained much of their old lands in 271 C.E.

Carrhae

Town in Mesopotamia, south of Edessa; site of the crushing defeat of CRASSUS (1) at the hands of the Parthians in 53 B.C.E. In 217 C.E., Emperor CARACALLA was assassinated near here, and in 296, GALERIUS faced a setback on the same site, in his campaign against the Persians.

The battle that took place in early May of 53 B.C.E., between the forces of the Triumvir Marcus Licinius Crassus (1) and the army of PARTHIA, under the command of General SURENAS, was one of the worst defeats ever inflicted on the Roman legions.

In 55 B.C.E., the Parthians were being torn apart by internal conflict. The sons of PHRAATES IV, Orodes and Mithridates, had murdered their father in 57 B.C.E. and were warring against each other. Orodes forced Mithridates to flee to Syria. Its Roman governor, Aulus GABINIUS, provided troops, and Mithridates marched back to Parthia, but was defeated and died in 54 B.C.E. Crassus sensed an opportunity to conquer the Parthians while this internal disorder worked to his advantage. Despite the opposition of many in the Senate, the triumvir set out, crossing the Euphrates in late spring of 53 B.C.E. with about seven legions, cavalry, and auxiliaries totaling approximately 36,000 men. His lieutenants were his son, Publius CRASSUS, and the future assassin CASSIUS. Orodes gave command of his Parthian forces to General Surenas. His units were smaller in number than the Romans, but the Parthian cavalry, legendarily accurate bowmen, gave Surenas a distinct superiority.

With ample room to encircle the enemy, Surenas ambushed the Romans in the arid region of Carrhae. Responding in the traditional manner, Crassus's troops formed into a square. Publius was dispatched on a charge at the enemy to ensure enough time to dress the line completely. Surenas, however, cunningly withdrew as Publius pursued him. Isolated from the main body, the detachment was cut to pieces, and Publius literally lost his head. The remaining Parthians rode across Crassus and his men, raining down arrows on their heads. That night Crassus withdrew, abandoning 4,000 wounded to certain death. The Parthians continued their pursuit, and, with discipline collapsing under the heat of the Mesopotamian sun, Crassus was forced to agree to negotiations. He was killed during a meeting with Surenas, and his entire force was slaughtered. Crassus's death was never fully explained. PLUTARCH argued that a Parthian, Pomaxathres, killed him, but Dio wrote that a servant stabbed him to avoid his capture. Surenas sent his head to Orodes and held a mock triumph with a Roman prisoner named Gaius Paccianus dressed to resemble Crassus.

Carrhae was a disaster of monumental proportions. Only 5,000 to 10,000 soldiers returned to Syria. Another 10,000 had been captured while the rest had died horribly. Parthia had destroyed one of the armies of the triumvirate and had gained the eagles of the fallen legions. No revenge was forthcoming from Rome, embroiled in its CIVIL WARS, nor until the time of AUGUSTUS was any treaty made with the Parthians to return the symbols of legionary power.

Carthage Major city on the Mediterranean coast of AFRICA, at the tip of a peninsula near modern Tunis; eventually the capital of the Roman province of AFRICA PRO-

CONSULARIS. For centuries Carthage had stood as the great rival to Rome. But after the conquest of the city in 146 B.C.E. by the Roman military leader Scipio Aemilianus, its walls were destroyed, and only a ruin identified its location. Carthage remained in this devastated condition for 30 years, until late in the second century B.C.E., when colonists began to repopulate the region. These inhabitants could reclaim the city only partially. Julius CAESAR sent more colonists to Carthage and launched an extensive rebuilding program in 44 B.C.E. Emperor AUGUSTUS, sometime around 29 B.C.E., continued the improvements. The proof of his success was documented with the fact that during his reign the capital of the province was moved from Utica to Carthage.

From that point on the city established its dominance over all of Africa. The only legion in Africa outside of Egypt was placed under the proconsul there, a policy changed by GAIUS CALIGULA in 37 C.E.; he established the III Augusta Legion under a separate legate. This legion moved farther west in 200 C.E. to become part of the African province of NUMIDIA. The economic health and the relative security of Carthage made the presence of a legion there unnecessary. Roads brought all of the major communities and outposts of the province right to the gates of the city. The economic base of the region was agricultural, and Carthage was able to provide the manufactured wares. Rome took much of the wealth of Africa for its own treasury, but enough remained in Carthage for massive construction programs and extensive building.

Little of the city survived the empire, but those sites uncovered as ruins show a major effort at Romanization of the territory. The best example of such Romanization is the Antonine BATHS. Built between 145 and 162 C.E., they rivaled the Baths of Caracalla in size and in architectural beauty. Carthage thus reflected the growing importance of Africa to the empire. Annually the region exported some 500 million tons of corn to Rome. The schools of Carthage, especially those dedicated to law, produced *advocati* (courtroom lawyers) of considerable skill.

In 238 C.E., GORDIAN I, the governor of Africa, proclaimed himself emperor from his seat at Carthage. CAPELLIANUS, the governor of Numidia, who was loyal to Emperor MAXIMINUS, marched on Carthage to dispute the claim. Though the citizens of the city remained loyal to Gordian and his son, they could not prevent their defeat. In 308, the prefect of Africa, Domitius ALEXANDER, also revolted against Rome, threatening the imperial corn supply. MAXENTIUS sent the Praetorian prefect Rufus VOLUSIANUS to crush the rebels, and he not only defeated them but also sacked and pillaged the city in the process. CONSTANTINE rebuilt Carthage in the 320s.

CHRISTIANITY became entrenched successfully in Africa after 180 C.E., but persecution followed. TERTULLIAN was one of the first writers to detail the persecution and survival of the church in Africa. His successor proved a brilliant leader of the Christians; CYPRIAN, who became bishop of Carthage, carried on the propagation of the faith in the face of outrages committed at the order of Emperor DECIUS in the mid-third century.

Carthage proved a center of dogmatic controversy as well. Disagreements between the Carthaginian presbyters and the Roman Church surfaced. AUGUSTINE proved a powerful spokesman for orthodoxy, but the city was receptive to the heretical movements of the fourth and fifth centuries. The Donatists (see DONATUS AND DONATISM) differed with Rome, and the church thus split apart. PELAGIUS and his theories next surfaced in the region. Pope ZOSIMUS assembled a large council on May 1, 418, in Carthage, to bring about the end of Pelagianism there. His successor, CELESTINE, further crushed the movement but also listened to the Carthaginian presbyter, Apiarius, in his complaints about his fellow Christian clerics.

In 429, the VANDALS led by GEISERIC invaded Africa. On October 19, 439, Carthage fell. Geiseric made the city his capital. Old landholders were stripped of their property and reduced to serfdom. More importantly, with an air of total independence, the Vandal kingdom elevated the status of ARIANISM. The orthodox Christian creed and clergy were abolished.

Cartimandua (fl. mid-first century C.E.) *Queen of Britain's Brigantes*

Her client status with Rome preserved her power for a time but eventually cost Cartimandua the kingdom. Following the conquest of southern Britain in 43 C.E., she opted for a treaty relationship. The Romans, who were always eager to nurture buffer client states, agreed. For the most part both sides remained faithful to the agreement.

In 51, the rebel King Caratacus fled to Cartimandua, but she offered him up to the Romans. Anti-Roman sentiment, however, grew to such an extent that her own marriage was threatened. Venutius, her husband, broke with her, and direct intervention by Rome was required on two occasions, between 52 and 57, to keep her on the throne.

She finally divorced Venutius and married Vellocatus, resulting in a Brigantian revolt. The BRIGANTES sent Cartimandua into exile in 69. With Rome involved in its own civil war, help was not immediately forthcoming, although the queen was eventually given a haven and sanctuary. Rome's best ally in Britain having fallen, however, Vespasian eventually sent Petillius CEREALIS to crush the Brigantes.

Carus, Marcus Aurelius (d. 283 C.E.) *Roman emperor from 282 to 283*

Probably from Narbo in Gaul, Carus rose through the ranks until 276, when he was elevated to PREFECT OF THE PRAETORIAN GUARD by Emperor PROBUS. He remained loyal to his imperial master in 282, even when the troops mutinied against protracted and harsh service conditions. Commanding the legions in the province of Raetia, while Probus was away preparing for another campaign, Carus tried to prevent his own elevation to the throne by the disgruntled legions. When even the detachment sent to him by Probus defected to his cause, Carus had little choice in the matter. Mercifully, Probus died at the hands of his own men, sparing the nation a civil war. The SENATE was informed but not asked for its blessing, as the days of such influence were long past. Carus accepted the throne and arranged for the deification of Probus.

A dynasty seemed to be developing with the accession of Carus, as he had two able sons, CARINUS and NUMERIAN. Both received the title of Caesar; Carinus ruled the West, and Numerian campaigned with his father. The SARMATIANS and QUADI were pushing across the Danube into Pannonia, and Carus crushed them in the field, slaughtering thousands. Early in 283, he and Numerian, along with the prefect of the Guard Arrius APER, marched east against the Persians. Seleucia fell and then Ctesiphon, the nation's capital. Mesopotamia was recovered and restored to the Romans, and Carus assumed the title of Parthicus Maximus. At the behest of Aper, another war in the East was planned.

Mysteriously, the night following a violent storm near Ctesiphon, Carus was found dead in his bed. Accounts vary as to the nature of his demise. Disease may have taken its toll, though lightning was blamed by others. Aper, who already called himself Numerian's father-in-law, may have had something to do with Carus's passing. Numerian did not long survive his father.

Casca, Gaius (d. after 44 B.C.E.) *Tribune in Rome in 44 B.C.E.*

Casca issued a public statement to the effect that he was not in any way related to the other Gaius Casca, one of the assassins of Julius Caesar. He claimed to be a supporter of Caesar and was justifiably worried after Gaius Helvius CINNA, who had been mistaken for another of Caesar's assassins, Lucius Cornelius CINNA, was murdered. Casca's disavowal spared him from death.

Casca, Servilius (d. 42 B.C.E.) *One of the assassins of Julius Caesar in 44 B.C.E.*

It was said that Casca struck the first blow. Octavian (AUGUSTUS) allowed him to serve as tribune in 43 B.C.E., but when the future emperor marched on Rome, Casca fled the city. After the battle at PHILIPPI, Casca killed himself to avoid punishment.

Cassian, John (Eremita, Johannes Cassianus, Johannes Massiliensis) (360–435 C.E.) *Christian saint, monk, and ascetic writer*

Generally considered the first monk to introduce the Eastern styles of monasticism into the West, Cassian was born possibly in the region that is modern Romania. The ecclesiastical historian Gennadius of Marseilles wrote that Cassian was "natione Scythia." While still a young man, he entered a monastery in Bethlehem, but soon he departed for Egypt, where he received eremitic training (i.e., training to be a hermit) from Egyptian ascetics. By 399, he was at Constantinople, where he served as a disciple of the patriarch St. John Chrysostom. When Chrysostom was deposed illegally by Theophilus, patriarch of Alexandria, and exiled by Empress Eudoxia, Cassian was sent to Rome by partisans of Chrysostom to make an appeal before Pope (later St.) Innocent I. During this Roman period, Cassian was ordained in 405, receiving the strong support of the pope. In 413, he founded at Massilia (Marseilles) the monastery of St. Victor, where he was abbot until his death. While at St. Victor (c. 420–429), he authored two important works, *Institutes of the Monastic Life* and *Conferences of the Egyptian Monks* (or *Collations of the Fathers*). The *Institutes* presented basic rules for monastic life and was an important source for St. Benedict in the creation of his rule; the *Conferences* gathered conversations of the foremost figures of Eastern monasticism, the Fathers of the Desert. Around 430, he also authored *De Incarnatione Domini*, against the heresiarch Nestorius, for Pope Leo I the Great. He was also a leading exponent of the heresy of Semi-Pelagianism and is considered its founder.

Cassius (Gaius Cassius Longinus) (d. 42 B.C.E.) *Prime mover in the assassination of Julius Caesar in 44 B.C.E. and the leader, with Brutus, of the Liberators*
Cassius marched to war against Parthia under CRASSUS, holding the rank of quaester. In 53 B.C.E. he participated in the battle of CARRHAE, watching as Crassus was annihilated. He assumed control of the pitiful remnants, returning in 52 and in 51 to defeat the Parthians, especially at Antigoneia. In 49, as a tribune, he joined POMPEY THE GREAT against CAESAR, commanding as an admiral and losing his flagship in one engagement. In 48 B.C.E., Caesar pardoned Cassius after defeating Pompey at PHARSALUS. Like BRUTUS, Cassius received the praetorship and command in Syria and was consul designate for 41 B.C.E.

By 44, conspiracies were widespread throughout Rome, with Cassius emerging as the leader of the most dangerous of the plots against Caesar. Like his fellow murderers, Cassius fled Italy in April. Instead of Syria, he was given the province of Cyrene by the Senate. He went to Syria anyway, defeating the appointed governor, Dolabella, and then plundering the provinces of Asia Minor. In 42, he joined Brutus in Greece, where they prepared for war with the triumvirs Octavian (AUGUSTUS) and Marc ANTONY. The battle of Philippi ended Cassius's ambitions. After being routed by Antony he instructed his freedman to kill him. His wife was Brutus's half sister, Junia Tertulla.

Cassius, Gaius Avidius (d. 175 C.E.) *General under Emperor Marcus Aurelius and unsuccessful usurper*
Of Syrian origin, Cassius was the son of an Equestrian. He joined the army, rising through the ranks and gaining the attention of the emperor. Marcus put him in charge of the sadly demoralized and ill-disciplined legions in Syria, where he earned the nickname "Marius," alluding to the cruelty of the Republican Consul Marius. Soldiers were burned, bound with chains and thrown into the sea, had their hands chopped off, their legs broken, or died of fright. By 163, the once unstable legions stood fully prepared for hardship and war.

In 164, the general marched against PARTHIA as part of the great Roman offensive in that region. He captured Seleucia, subdued Mesopotamia, and claimed Ctesiphon, the great capital, as well. The total conquest of Parthia seemed possible, but a plague broke out in the legions. Retreat followed in 165–166, although MARCUS AURELIUS realized the magnitude of his victories and Cassius was promoted from governor of Syria to commander of the East. Cassius crushed the BUCOLICI in 172 in Egypt, and held his provinces as the Romans faced increasing frontier troubles in the West. The emperor was also deteriorating. Cassius perhaps contemplated a move for power in the face of such opportunity, but it was not until 175 that he became amorously entangled with Empress FAUSTINA, a relationship that prompted him to take political steps.

With all of Syria and most of the Eastern region behind him, Cassius heard that Marcus had died. He proclaimed himself emperor, appointed a prefect, and pulled together a court, where he received the allegiance of Syria, Judaea, and Cilicia, as well as Egypt. Only Bithynia and Cappadocia, under Martius Verus, held firm to Rome. Wider support never materialized. The Senate refused to recognize him—especially as Marcus still lived. All hopes vanished when the emperor returned to Rome. A centurion murdered Cassius, removed his head and brought it before the throne. The remains were buried as Verus crushed the remnants of the rebellion in preparation for a conciliatory visit from Marcus in 176. Cassius was described as sometimes stern, often gentle, a devotee of Venus and well loved by his own people. As a result of Cassius's rebellion, a law was passed forbidding all governors to be appointed in their own provinces of origin.

Cassius Longinus, Gaius (fl. mid-first century C.E.) *Jurist, governor, and one of the most sober figures in the empire during the reigns of Gaius Caligula and Nero*
A descendant of the famed Cassius of the same name, Cassius Longinus served as governor of Syria in 45, or perhaps earlier. He authored 10 books on civil law as well as other forms of law, and he helped shape the legal evolution of the school of Ateius CAPITO, eventually having adherents of his scientific system who called themselves the Cassiani. In 58, he criticized NERO for having too

many honors, later vehemently supporting the policy of slaughtering the slaves belonging to a murdered owner. In 65, charged with revering too greatly the memory of his ancestor Cassius, he was banished by Nero to Sardinia. He returned to Rome under VESPASIAN and lived out his days in great popularity. He reportedly went blind at the end of his life.

Cassius Longinus, Lucius (d. after 44 B.C.E.) *Brother of Gaius Cassius Longinus, one of Julius Caesar's assassins*
Disagreeing with his brother, who joined the Republican cause, Lucius remained a faithful supporter of Julius CAESAR during the Civil War. In 48 B.C.E., he assumed command of troops in Greece at Caesar's instruction and reached the rank of tribune in 44. Following Caesar's assassination, he again parted with his brother politically, stating publicly that he had no role in the murder of Caesar. He then cast his future with Octavian in the struggle with the Liberators. He was, however, later reconciled with Marc Antony.

Cassius Parmensis (d. 31 B.C.E.) *A member of the conspiracy against Julius Caesar in 44 B.C.E.*
Cassius Parmensis fled to Asia in 43 and took up a command there. Apparently he was never on very good terms with Octavian (AUGUSTUS). His letterwriting style imitated that of Cicero, and he composed poetry. After Actium in 31 B.C.E., Cassius Parmensis was put to death by Octavian. He was called Parmensis because of his origins in Parma.

Cassius Severus (d. 34 C.E.) *Orator of the Augustan age (27 B.C.E.–14 C.E.) feared for his brilliantly biting wit*
He spoke exceptionally well and took to his pen only reluctantly. His works were publicly burned as libelous. Cassius Severus faced banishment around 12 B.C.E., and later received Seriphus in the Cyclades as his place of exile. The fact that he made many enemies is attested to by the references of his contemporaries and historians. Caligula posthumously rehabilitated his works.

Cassivellaunus (fl. mid-first century B.C.E.) *King of the Britons and ruler of the Belgic confederation in Britain at the time of Caesar's expedition in 54 B.C.E.*
The British realm stretched across the Thames River region into Essex, after the Trinovantes, under Mandubracius, were subdued. Caesar's landing pushed Cassivellaunus into the forefront of British chiefs as he organized an effective resistance. He tried first to win in the field but lost. Guerrilla tactics followed but were ineffective against the Roman advance, especially when Mandubracius joined Caesar. When an attack on the flotilla of Roman ships failed, the king agreed to terms. Caesar demanded a tribute and the promise to leave the Trinovantes in peace. As the Roman legions sailed away,

however, Cassivellaunus immediately marched on Mandubracius and conquered the Trinovantes. Around 20 B.C.E., he established a new community near Camulodunum (Colchester). More importantly, Cassivellaunus certified his rule and ensured the continuation of Belgic influence in the isles for the next 60 years.

Castinus (fl. early fifth century C.E.) *Magister militum*
A one-time *comes domesticorum* in the time of Emperor Constantius, he became MAGISTER MILITUM around 421, the year of Constantius's death. Castinus assumed command of an expedition against the Vandals in Spain, differing immediately with the *magister militum* Boniface on its conduct. Boniface departed for Africa while Castinus finished off any chances for a Roman victory by alienating his Visigoth allies. He claimed the defeat to be the responsibility of Boniface and Galla Placidia, the mother of the imperial aspirant, Valentinian III. Through his efforts Emperor Honorius exiled Galla Placidia from the court, and he obtained the consulship in 424, from Theodosius II. In 423, however, Galla Placidia, now in Constantinople, worked her way into a friendly relationship with the politically invincible Theodosius. Sensing that Valentinian might be elevated to the Western throne, Castinus opted for a radical solution, pushing for a usurper, a civil servant named John. Theodosius could not accept John and sent the *magister militum* Ardaburius and his son Aspar against Italy. In 425 the army of Theodosius under the command of Aspar, entered Ravenna, John's capital. The usurper was put to death and Castinus exiled, his gamble having failed.

Castra   *See* LEGIONS.

Castra Peregrina   Large military camp on the Caelian Hill in Rome, probably built during the reign of Emperor Septimius SEVERUS (193–211 C.E.). Its purpose was to house non-Italian troops stationed in the city. A temple to Jupiter was kept in the camp, and it stood as late as 357 C.E.

Castra Praetoria   The military camp of the PRAETORIAN GUARD in Rome. Founded in 23 C.E. by the infamous prefect of the Guard, SEJANUS, the Castra Praetoria stood as the physical manifestation of the Guard's strength for nearly 300 years. Sejanus convinced Emperor Tiberius that the cohorts of the Praetorians should be organized into one camp to ensure discipline and to allow a more rapid response to crises in the city. The camp was constructed on the heights in the northwest just within sight of the city walls and some 450 meters beyond the area called the Agger of Servius. Its design was similar to that of a regular army camp, but was permanent; the buildings were splendidly colored, constructed of pink and red bricks. After the struggle in Rome in 69 C.E., repairs were made with yellow bricks. Emperor Caracalla later raised the main walls and redesigned the interior, organizing and improving the living quarters. Marcus Aurelius elevated the walls even further.

The Castra assumed considerable importance in imperial affairs. In 41 C.E., after the murder of Caligula, Claudius spent several days there while the Guard debated his fate. Nero was certified on the throne by going to the camp with the Prefect BURRUS to ensure the loyalty of the Praetorians. In 69, the assassination of Galba was followed by a grotesque ceremony in the Castra in which Otho received the imperial purple, while Galba's head was paraded around on a spear. Later the new Praetorians of Vitellius were besieged and then massacred by the old Guard, and much of the camp was destroyed. In 193, following the murder of Emperor Pertinax, Sulpicianus and the Senator Didius Julianus went to the Castra. Julianus stood inside and Sulpicianus outside, each man shouting the price he would pay for the throne, with Didius Julianus gaining the Praetorians' support. Senator Gallicanus led the citizenry in a siege of the Praetorians. The walls of the camp proved too strong, and

hundreds died in the fighting as the Senate called in troops from all over Italy. A second siege also failed, and in desperation the citizens of Rome cut off the water supply of the camp. The Praetorians responded by charging into the mobs, burning buildings and looting much of the city. The crowds surrendered, in the face of an ongoing fire that was destroying vast sections of the metropolis.

Having provided protection for the Praetorians for so long, the Castra was finally destroyed in 312. After Constantine the Great won the battle of MILVIAN BRIDGE, he marched on Rome, rode to the Castra Praetoria and decreed its destruction. Brick by brick the walls were torn down, with very little remaining for archaeological exploration.

catacombs Underground cemeteries composed of passages and tomb-chambers, with recesses in the walls for interring bodies. While catacombs are found throughout the Mediterranean world, they are most associated with the burial grounds near Rome used by Christians during the imperial era. The name is of uncertain origin, but it was first applied to the Basilica of St. Sebastian on

A fresco of St. Paul, from the Catacomb of San Gennaro, Naples *(Hulton/Getty Archive)*

the Via Appia, about three miles south of Rome, and came into use especially in the fourth and fifth centuries C.E. Saints Peter and Paul were buried there. In all, there are approximately 40 known catacombs, stretching for some 350 miles in a circle near Rome, located along the main roads leading to the city and positioned parallel to pagan cemeteries. Among the notable Christian catacombs are St. Priscilla, St. Callixtus, and St. Praetextatus.

Catalaunian Plain (northeastern Gaul) Site of a battle in 451 C.E. between ATTILA and the combined armies of the *magister militum* AETIUS and his allies. In early 451, Attila launched his invasion of Gaul, sweeping through Gallia Belgica, with his ultimate object being Orleans. Aetius could not allow such a catastrophe and consequently asked the aid of the local barbarian kingdoms, the BURGUNDIANS, FRANKS, CELTS, and the VISIGOTHS of King Theodoric. Sometime between late June and early July the two armies clashed on the road to Troyes, near the Catalaunian Plain.

If accounts of the historians Jordanes, Hydatius, and Isidore are accurate, a terrible slaughter resulted in a draw. King Theodoric died in the fray, but Aetius did not press for a conclusive victory. Attila, meanwhile, had placed himself in a large, easily defended encampment. Aetius supposedly visited the Hun king there, warning him of the supposedly dangerous position in which the Huns found themselves. Attila believed him and rode off to Italy. Aetius maintained his control over Gaul as well as the equilibrium among the demanding kingdoms of his region. While the HUNS were not defeated, their failure to capture Gaul accelerated the invasion of Italy—with severe consequences for Aetius, who was seen as the man responsible for allowing Attila to escape. The battle of Catalaunian Plain has also been called Mauriac, Troyes, and, most often, Chalons.

Cato Uticensis, Marcus Porcius (95–46 B.C.E.) *Praetor in 54 B.C.E.; a descendant of the great Cato and a champion of Republicanism in Rome*
In 63 B.C.E. Cato differed with Caesar on the question of executions in the Catiline Conspiracy and helped prosecute many of the conspirators. This was the first of his many disagreements with Julius Caesar. The next dispute involved the Agrarian Laws of 59. M. Calpurnius Bibulus, Cato, and others in the Senate opposed the measure supported by the eventual members of the FIRST TRIUMVIRATE: Caesar, Crassus, and Pompey. Cato strenuously spoke out against the measure, continuing even after he had received death threats. In 58, a political bully in Rome, CLODIUS PULCHER, nominated Cato to receive the governorship of the recently acquired island of Cyprus. Unable to oppose such a post, the senator reluctantly departed and was absent from Rome during the next two eventful years. He returned with a record of having gov-

erned effectively, but was slightly diminished in influence in Rome.

Battles with Caesar erupted almost immediately, and each one attacked the other before the Senate. Cato served as praetor in 54, while his brother-in-law, L. Domitius Ahenobarbus, gained a consulship. In 52, Pompey served as sole consul. Cato failed to be elected to the office, although his reputation for fairness and honesty was unsullied.

Cato never wavered in his hatred for Caesar. As a figure in the Senate, he aided in creating the atmosphere that made civil war inevitable. Distrusting Pompey but needing his military might, Cato joined the Pompeians, and, after the loss at Pharsalus in 48 B.C.E., fled to Africa. When Caesar triumphed at Thapsus, Cato returned to Utica, with Caesar in pursuit. There, around February 10, 46, he killed himself, denying his enemy the pleasure. Cicero dictated a panegyric to him, *Cato,* and Caesar wrote *Anti-Cato.*

Catullus (fl. mid-first century C.E.) *Writer of mimes, probably during the reign of Emperor Gaius Caligula*
Catullus (the name may be a corruption) authored several works, including *Phasma* and *Laureolus. Laureolus* was performed shortly before Caligula's assassination. The end of the play included a crucifixion of the lead player, a highway bandit. According to Roman writers, one of the performances provided an omen about the impending murder of the emperor. At the crucifixion scene, overexcited understudies poured blood all over the stage.

Catullus, Gaius Valerius (87–54 B.C.E.) *One of the foremost poets in Roman history*
Catullus came from Verona and his father had some affiliation with Julius Caesar, but details of his life are few. He stood in some regard with the writers of his own age. He visited Bithynia with the governor, Gaius Memmius, Helvius Cinna, and others, staying there from 57 to 56 B.C.E. On his return he made a pilgrimage to the tomb of his brother in Troas. In Rome he continued his affiliations with Cicero and Cornelius Nepos, and remained close friends with Cinna and Calvus.

The most notable involvement in his life was with "Lesbia," probably CLODIA the sister of P. Clodius Pulcher. Unhappily married to Metellus Celer, Clodia seemed to have carried on a torrid romance with Catullus, the passion of which influenced his love poems. Again the details remain obscure, including the intrusion of Caelius into the affair. Politics held no interest for him, despite his definite views on certain matters. He wrote against Julius Caesar and his adherents, especially the engineer Mamurra, whom he called "Mentula."

The works of Catullus were varied and extensive. He openly imitated the Alexandrine school but showed his own special brilliance with his short poems. A collection of his work, including a dedicatory poem to Cornelius Nepos, probably saw publication in 54 B.C.E. The poet received acclaim at the time but died before any concomitant wealth could be garnered. The collection, as it has come down through the ages, was apparently organized in three parts. Part one presented short iambic and melic poems. Part two had long poems, including *Peleus and Thetis*. Finally, part three contained elegiacs (epigrams).

See also POETRY.

Catus Decianus (fl. mid-first century C.E.) *Procurator of Britain*

Catus was an unpopular governor who was responsible in part for the rebellion of BOUDICCA in 61 C.E. As Roman policy in the province turned harsher, the death of Prasutagus, king of the Iceni, prompted the direct seizure of his territory, the claims of his wife Boudicca and his daughters notwithstanding. Catus also demanded the repayment of large sums given to the dead king by CLAUDIUS. Such outrages pushed the Britons too far, and they revolted. Catus, in charge of military affairs while Suetonius Paulinus was away on campaign, sent only a handful of soldiers to defend against the onslaught of the queen's forces. Frightened by the defeat of the IX Legion, the procurator fled to safety on the continent. He was replaced by Julius Classicianus.

Catuvellauni

A leading tribe in Britain that reached ascendancy in the southern part of the isles between 55 B.C.E. and 43 C.E. They were a part of the large influx of the BELGAE into Britain, occupying much of the Thames region. In 54 B.C.E., under their King CASSIVELLAUNUS, they resisted the invasion of Julius Caesar. Warfare conducted by the Catuvellauni was in a style traditionally Celtic that used chariots, long abandoned on the mainland of Europe. Forced to accept treaty terms with Rome, the tribe waited only until Caesar's departure to reassert its dominance, and the Trinovantes fell under their power. Cassivellaunus established a strong kingdom around CAMULODUNUM (Colchester) and VERULAMIUM (St. Alban's), composed of the Belgic tribes, of which the Catuvellauni were the heart. A line of kings established by Cassivellaunus included TASCIOVANUS, CUNOBELLINUS, and CARATACUS. Under Caratacus, in 43 C.E., the tribe fought against the massive invasion of Aulus Plautius and Claudius. Despite hard fighting, the warriors broke before the Roman legions. The territory of the Catuvellauni became the Roman province of BRITANNIA.

Celer, Caninius (fl. second century C.E.) *Orator and rhetorician*

Celer served as a tutor to Emperor Marcus Aurelius and Lucius Verus.

Celer, Publius (d. c. 69 C.E.) *Philosopher during the reign of Nero (r. 54–68)*

Celer profited from accusing a former pupil, Barea Soranus, of using magic. Nero, who was looking for an excuse to murder Soranus, prosecuted him and put him to death. Publius received rewards and honors for the deed, and according to Tacitus this had not been his first service to the imperial household. In 54, he reportedly helped poison the proconsul of Asia, Junius Silanus, the great-grandson of Augustus, at the behest of Empress Agrippina the Younger. In 69, after the fall of Nero and Vitellius, Musonius Rufus prosecuted Celer on the grounds of perjury in the Soranus case. Accusers were out of fashion in Rome under the Flavians, and the conviction was obtained.

Celer and Severus (fl. first century C.E.) *Two architects*

Commissioned by Emperor NERO to rebuild Rome after the terrible fire of 64 C.E., Severus and Celer rebuilt much of the devastated city at great cost and then laid out grand designs for Nero's new palace, the Domus Aurea, the GOLDEN HOUSE, to replace the burned DOMUS TRANSITORIA.

Celestine I (d. 432) *Pope from 422–432, Christian saint*

Celestine was traditionally held to have come from Campania and was a deacon at the time of his election to the papacy on September 10, 422, to succeed Boniface I. He soon undertook to continue the efforts of his predecessor in combating the various heresies that were plaguing the church. In 429, he sent St. Germanus of Auxerre to Britain to counter the teachings of Pelagius in the isles. He also wrote letters condemning the Semi-Pelagianism being propagated by John Cassian in southern Gaul. Celestine launched a campaign against Nestorianism by condemning its author, Nestorius, at a Roman synod in August 430. St. Cyril of Alexandria was then ordered to excommunicate and depose the troublesome patriarch of Constantinople, Nestorius, if he did not submit. Nestorius refused, and, on December 7, 430, the sentence by Cyril was delivered to Constantinople in a set of 12 anathemas.

Celestine also consecrated St. Palladius at Rome in 431 and sent him on his short-lived mission as bishop of the Christians of Ireland.

Celsus (fl. second century C.E.) *Platonic philosopher*

Celsus wrote (177–180 C.E.) one of the first comprehensive and intellectual attacks on Christianity. The actual work is lost, but large parts of it are preserved in the reply written by the theologian ORIGEN (246–248). Celsus's attack utilized a series of progressively logical questions and answers, demanding such information as why should God come to Earth or why should he visit the Earth in the shape of Jesus and why in Palestine. He dismissed

Christ as the illegitimate child of Mary and a Roman soldier and said that he was no better than an Egyptian magician. Despite Origen's ardent defense of Christian thought, subsequent pagan Neoplatonists used Celsus's polemic in their own attacks on the growing church.

Celsus, Aulus Cornelius (fl. first century C.E.) *Encyclopedist, probably during the time of Tiberius (ruled 14–37 C.E.)*

Celsus composed a large encyclopedia, *Artes,* that was similar to those of Cato the Elder and VARRO. His subjects included war, farming, law, oratory, philosophy, and medicine. The only extant books are 6 to 13, on medicine, clearly influenced by Hippocrates and including general therapy, internal illnesses, pharmacology, and surgery. Celsus's work on farming was used by Julius Graecinus and his compilation on war by Vegetius. Celsus was respected well past the Middle Ages.

Celsus, Marius (fl. first century C.E.) *General and consul-elect in 69 C.E.*

At the start of Galba's reign; Celsus stood firm in his loyalty to the emperor, despite the turbulence of that emperor's reign. Following the death of Galba, Celsus refused to disavow his previous fealty and stood in danger of execution. Otho had to arrest him to protect him from the angry Roman citizens and soldiers, pardoning him as part of a larger amnesty to cement his control of the throne. Henceforth Celsus obediently served Otho, even in the face of scheming fellow generals, such as the Praetorian Prefect Licinius PROCULUS. When word arrived that the legions on the Rhine had revolted and were marching on Italy, Otho appointed Celsus one of his leading generals, along with Proculus, L. Otho, and Suetonius Paulinus. He conducted himself well in the early skirmishes but advised against an all-out effort against the Vitellian units, being joined in this counsel by Paulinus. Otho, however, listened to Proculus and to his own brother. At the battle of BEDRIACUM on April 15, 69, Celsus went into battle faithfully and lost, trying afterward to rally the broken and fleeing Othonian legions. Emperor Vitellius allowed him to serve his consulship.

Celsus, L. Publius (d. 117 C.E.) *Senator and friend of Emperor Trajan who also served as consul in 113*

Celsus belonged to a group of four respected advisers, which included A. Cornelius Palma, L. Junius Ursus Servianus, and Lusius Quietus. As supporters of Trajan, Celsus and his companions opposed Hadrian as heir to the throne and greeted his rise with jealousy and concern for the future imperial policies. Each was murdered, however, at the start of Hadrian's reign, ending what may have been a conspiracy but beginning the emperor's reign in an unpleasant manner.

Celsus, Publius Juventius (fl. first century C.E.) *Lawyer*

The son of P. Juventius Celsus, he attended the Proculian School and served HADRIAN, attaining the consulship around 129 C.E. He may also have been a member of the Consilium Principis. Various works were credited to him, including a digest, a legal commentary, and letters.

Celts

One of the dominant peoples of the Iron Age. The Celts spread across all of the region now termed modern Europe, settling in Iberia, GALLIA CISALPINA in Italy, Britain, Illyricum, Macedonia, Galatia, Gallia Belgica, and along the Danube. They ruled uncontestedly until the second century B.C.E., when faced with pressures from Italy and the East. Rome seized southeastern Gaul in 121 B.C.E., and the Teutonic tribes drove the Celts away from the Rhine. With their original dominions shrinking, the main bastions of Celtic culture became Gaul and Britain.

Throughout Gallia Lugdunensis and Gallia Belgica, the Celtic tribes banded together to form large political confederations. This practice was in place during the campaigns of Julius CAESAR (59–51 B.C.E.). Working against Celtic unity was the competition between local chiefdoms, which very often destroyed any hope of presenting a popular front against intruders. The AEDUI, AVERNI, NERVII, and others never fully trusted one another, and chiefs such as COMMIUS of the Trebates would serve as allies with Rome for a time and then desert the Roman cause. In the ensuing internal quarrels the Celts proved easy prey for Roman LEGIONS bent on avenging the Celtic sack of Rome in 390 B.C.E. The Celts had maintained anachronistic military ways. Their nobles and kings went into battle with cavalry, while the infantry fought in the horde-like fashion of the past, without real discipline and lacking military complexity. Even when the Celts were victorious against the legions they suffered terrible losses, such as at ARAR and throughout Caesar's GALLIC WARS.

The Celts of Gaul preserved their old beliefs in DRUIDS AND DRUIDISM but grew more influenced by the Roman gods and goddesses, which in time supplanted or stood as equals to the Celtic originals. After Caesar's conquests (and even before) assimilation and Romanization began. Druidism was stamped out violently, and even the capital of the Aedui fell in favor of a new one, AUGUSTODONUM. The Celtic arts, enduring from the La Tene Culture, ceased to flourish, and only in Gallia Belgica and eventually just in Britain did Celtic life continue. This prompted Rome to exercise a tremendous effort, starting with its crushing invasion in 43 C.E., to stamp out all Celtic culture. In 60–61, SUETONIUS PAULINUS campaigned on Angelsey Island to annihilate the Druids. ROADS were laid and cities were constructed along Roman colonial lines. But Britain changed culturally only on a superficial basis, and even during the period of Roman dominance the Romanization of the isles extended only to the limits of townships, legionary forts or colonies. When the Romans left the isles, the Celtic culture, so long kept under foot, sprang once more to life.

See also BRITANNIA.

censor An important office during the days of the Republic. The censors were responsible for keeping the citizen lists, conducting any needed CENSUS and holding the rolls of the members of the SENATE. They thus possessed the right to strike all senators who might act immorally or in opposition to the law. As magistrates of a key Republican institution, the censors came under attack by Sulla, who curtailed their influence, a process furthered by the emperors. It became policy for the masters of Rome, from AUGUSTUS onward, to assume for themselves the powers of the censors, the *censoria potestas.* They appointed senators, purged the senatorial ranks of unqualified members and controlled enactments. Other, more mundane functions passed from the hands of the censors in time. The water supply of Rome had long been under their jurisdiction, but in 12 B.C.E. Augustus required that a water board, called the *curatores aquarum,* henceforth care for the city's supplies. DOMITIAN took the final step in terminating censorial powers by assuming the *censoria potestas* for life.

Censorinus (fl. mid-third century C.E.) *Writer*
Censorinus was a grammarian whose main work, *De die Natali,* is extant.

census A registration method used irregularly in the Republic and in the early empire to calculate population statistics in Rome, Italy, and the provinces in order to determine taxation in Rome's territories and to provide a register for military service among Roman citizens. The census conducted by the CENSORS was generally held by a provincial administrator, although Emperor Augustus put it to tremendous use. The emperor called for a census three times, and in Gaul alone the dates of a register were 27 B.C.E., 12 B.C.E., 14 C.E., and 61 C.E.

Normal procedure involved the listing of the names of males and their families and property owned (especially farmed lands, but including all other property as well as slaves). Taxes could be collected as a result, increased or decreased according to the figures provided. Based on the divisions established by Julius Caesar in Gaul, 40 million gold pieces were collected. The census was thus an important source of revenue. The census required forced migratory registration, which caused great discontent and often violence. In Judaea, the famous census of 6 C.E. provoked a harsh reaction from the Jews. Pannonia, Noricum, Raetia, and Dalmatia made census taking difficult, because of their unpacified nature. Most of Asia Minor presented few problems, and in Egypt a very systematic census routine was in place from the time of the Ptolemies. Every 14 years a census was taken in Egypt, and every city and town provided complete information, street by street, in an impressive display of efficiency. Vespasian ordered the last known census in Italy.

centuriation Process by which Roman colonists or provincial administrators sectionalized land previously undelineated or uncultivated. A system popular in Italy, centuriation was especially liked in the provinces, where COLONIES were being founded. One of the best examples of the process can be found in Africa. There the members of the III Augusta Legion helped carve up all of the available territories. The resulting development yielded 500 communities, with 200 cities. The centuriated land is still visible by air in its original checkerboard design. A *centuria* was composed of 100 *heredia,* with each *heredium* equaling two *iugera* or approximately two *actus,* a plot of 120 square feet (by Roman measure).

See also COLONIES.

centurion *See* LEGIONS.

Cerealia The festival of CERES, goddess of agriculture. This celebration was held every year on the 12th of April and went on for eight days, with lavish ceremonies in the deity's temple in Rome. On the last day, according to tradition, foxes were released from her temple on the Aventine Hill, with burning brands attached to their tails. The story was told that a fox one day tried to steal hens, was caught and wrapped in straw to be burned. The animal got loose while on fire and burned crops as he ran for his life.

Cerealis (Quintus Petillius Cerealis Caesius Rufus) (fl. first century C.E.) *Prominent general during the Flavian era and brother-in-law of Emperor Vespasian*
Cerealis probably hailed from Sabine country. His first notable appearance was as a legate in Britain during the revolt of BOUDICCA in 61 C.E. As commander of the IX Hispania Legion, he had the misfortune of being routed by the British queen, losing much of the legion in the process. Eight years later, Cerealis took part in Vespasian's battle for the throne. Part of Antonius Primus's army, he took charge of the cavalry. Outside of Rome, however, he learned of the death of Vespasian's brother, Flavius Sabinus, and, like the soldiers in the army, demanded an immediate conquest of the city. He shared subsequently in the rewards but was sent out immediately to put down the rebellion of the Treveri and the Batavians under Julius CIVILIS. The general Annius Gallus took charge of Germania Superior while Cerealis attacked the rebels directly.

He marched on Mainz and then crushed Treveri resistance at Rigodulum, which was followed by the capture of Treves, the tribal capital. Cerealis moved in for the kill but ended up negotiating a peace with Civilis and the former Roman ally, Julius Classicus. In 71 C.E., Cerealis received a second opportunity in Britain. A legate there for three years, he advanced Roman conquests in the north, destroying the Brigantes.

Ceres Goddess of agriculture, patron of Roman farmers and a powerful figure in the Roman pantheon, with its emphasis on crops. Originally worshiped at Cumae, a temple was dedicated to her in 496 B.C.E., after a famine, and her statue showed her holding ears or corn. Ceres was worshiped by several colleges of priests, and measures of corn went by the name *mensores frumentarii cereris.* Her temple rested upon the Aventine Hill. There pigs were sacrificed to her, and the goods of traitors condemned by the Republic were stored in her complex. It also became traditional for Senate decrees to be deposited in the temple of this goddess. Her festival fell on the 12th of April and for eight days after (*see* CEREALIA). Ceres corresponds to the Demeter of Greek mythology.

See also GODS AND GODDESSES OF ROME.

Cerretani A tribe in the Pyrenees that was well known throughout the imperial era for the quality of its hams.

Cervidius, Scaevola Q. (fl. second century C.E.) *Teacher of Papinian and one of the leading jurists of the second century C.E.*
Cervidius belonged to the consilium principis of MARCUS AURELIUS and later taught Septimius SEVERUS. His *Digest,* begun under Marcus Aurelius, served as an invaluable textbook for later legal students, including his own opinion on the law.

Cestius Gallus (fl. first century C.E.) *Governor of Syria during the early part of the Jewish rebellion in Palestine, in 66 C.E.*
Cestius was sent to the East around 65 to replace the famous CORBULO (2) as administrator of SYRIA. While he controlled the legions of the province and had bureaucratic mastery over JUDAEA, his powers were limited compared to those of his predecessor. He arrived at a time when Jewish nationalistic feeling was running high, but he lacked both the vision to see his danger and the means to suppress that danger. The procurator of Judaea, Gessius Florus, had acquired a terrible reputation for corruption. When the Jews complained to Gallus during a visit to Jerusalem in 65, he naturally sided with his underling.

The following year war erupted. Gallus gathered all available troops (the XII Legion) and marched on Palestine. He pushed his way to the very gates of Jerusalem but realized too late that Roman rule was being ignored

in all other locations. Hoping to salvage his position strategically, Gallus ordered a retreat. Marching in the heat and under constant attack, the withdrawal deteriorated into a rout, and Gallus was put to flight. The Jewish victory spurred on the rest of the country and further reduced imperial control. He did take steps to restore order in Galilee (*see* JOSEPHUS) but apparently died, perhaps from exhaustion or possibly due to recognition that his career was over. His replacement—VESPASIAN—was far more competent.

Cestus, Gallius (fl. mid-first century C.E.) *Consul in 35*
Cestus helped to prosecute Quintus Servaeus (a friend of Germanicus) and Minucius Thermus (a former client of Sejanus) for Tiberius in 32. Tacitus decried his prosecution as the beginning of a calamitous practice in which all words uttered by a person could be used against that person, no matter how innocently spoken or how long ago stated. Cestus was apparently the same senator who in 21 C.E. convicted one Annia Rufidla for fraud. She fled to the Capitoline Hill to seek sanctuary, and Cestus decried the mockery inherent in hiding behind a statue of the emperor. Drusus, Tiberius's son, agreed, and she was hauled away to prison.

Chaerea, Cassius (d. 41 C.E.) *Tribune of the Praetorian Guard and assassin in 41 C.E.*
A career officer, Chaerea was first mentioned as a soldier in 14 C.E., in the Rhine legions that revolted against their legate, Aulus Caecina, and their centurions. Chaerea cut his way through the unruly mob surrounding Caecina, and his devotion apparently earned him a reward. During the reign of Tiberius, Chaerea earned a posting to the Praetorian Guard, eventually rising to the rank of tribune. Chaerea later dealt daily with GAIUS CALIGULA not only witnessed his peculiar habits but also suffered increasingly cruel jokes at Caligula's hands. Suetonius reported that the emperor persistently teased Chaerea for being effeminate. When asked for the watchword, Caligula would respond with the names Priapus or Venus, two fertility deities; and, while being thanked for a favor, Caligula gave Chaerea his middle finger to kiss, while wagging it obscenely. The humor became unendurable when his fellow tribunes joined in the torment.

Chaerea's pride injured, he looked for partners in a plot to be rid of Caligula. He had no trouble finding accomplices. Arrecinus Clemens, a prefect; Cornelius Sabinus, a fellow tribune; Annius Vinicianus, a senator; Callistus, the imperial freedman; and others were eager to join him. On January 24, during the *ludi Palatini,* the assassins struck. Although historical versions differ, all agree that Chaerea struck the first blow. In the panic that followed the assassination, Chaerea forgot his own Praetorian command, receiving instead the thanks of the Senate. He announced a new watchword, given by senators for the first time in a hundred years: "Liberty!" While he celebrated liberation with the Senate, the Praetorian Guard installed Claudius on the throne of Rome without Chaerea's knowledge. Chaerea, with Sabinus and Julius Lupus, a tribune and the murderer of Caligula's wife and daughter, were handed over for execution to protect the institution of the emperor.

Chalcedon   City in the province of Bithynia, across the Bosporus from the city of Byzantium and predating the building of Constantinople. Chalcedon was the site of a major church council in October of 451 C.E., in which the dual nature of Christ's divinity and humanity was accepted. More importantly, the theological battle between the sees of Alexandria and Constantinople ended, with Constantinople victorious. Alexandria faded, and Byzantine CHRISTIANITY emerged supreme in the East.

Chalcedon, Council of   The fourth general (or ecumenical) council in the history of the Christian Church, held from October 8 to November 1, 451, in the town of Chalcedon, in Asia Minor, just outside of Constantinople. A major council in the history of Christology, it asserted the orthodox doctrine concerning the nature of Christ; namely, that he is one person with two distinct natures, divine and human. It brought to an end furious theological debate and controversy that had raged for much of the fifth century.

The Council of Chalcedon was convened by Emperor MARCIAN to deal with the pressing crisis of the Eutychian heresy (an extreme form of MONOPHYSITISM), which argued that Christ had two natures but that these were so intimately connected that they became one, thereby resulting in the human nature being absorbed by the divine. The chief spokesman for this was Eutyches, the archimandrite of a monastery just outside of Constantinople.

The controversy over Eutychian's doctrine had been exacerbated by the Second Council of Ephesus (449), the Latrocinium (or Robber) Council that was manipulated by Dioscorus, patriarch of Alexandria. Dioscorus had deposed Flavian, the patriarch of Constantinople, restoring Eutyches in his stead and refusing to allow the reading of the *Epistola Dogmatica* by Pope (later Saint) Leo I, the so-called TOME OF LEO, which elucidated the orthodox doctrine on the Incarnation. While condemned by the pope and opposed by most of the church, the work of the Latrocinium Council stood unrepealed as long as Theodosius II, a patron of Eutyches, sat on the imperial throne. His sudden death in July 450, however, changed the situation, as his sister Pulcheria succeeded him, marrying Marcian (r. 450–457). Both were enemies of Eutyches and Dioscorus and thus sent to Pope Leo their approval for a new council to address the heresy.

The council opened at Chalcedon on October 8. In attendance were around 600 bishops (Pope Leo wrote that there were 600; other sources say 520 or even 630). All were from the East except two who had come from Africa and two papal legates, Boniface and Paschasinus, bishop of Lilybaeum (who also presided). The sessions were held in the Church of St. Euphemia Martyr, across the Bosporus from Constantinople. The work of the council was clear from the start and resulted in a complete triumph for the orthodox position. The decrees of the Latrocinium Council were annulled; Eutyches was condemned; Dioscorus deposed; and the Tome of Leo given full approval. The council delegates said of the epistle: "This is the faith of the Fathers and of the Apostles. This we all believe. Peter has spoken through Leo . . . anathema to him who teaches otherwise. . . ." In the fifth session (October 22), the dogma of the Church was formulated: "One and the same Christ, Son, Lord, Only-begotten, known in two natures, without confusion, without change, without division, without separation." All of the canons were acceptable to the pope except for Canon 28, which proclaimed the see of Constantinople to be a patriarchate second only to Rome. Initially opposed by papal legates, the canon was rejected by Leo on the grounds that it was an insult to the older patriarchates; there were also political considerations involved, as the see of Constantinople had long harbored ambitions of eventual equal status with Rome.

Chalcis   A small kingdom in Syria, ruled originally by a family of Ituraean princes. In 40 B.C.E., King Lysanias lost the domain to Marc Antony, who gave it to Queen CLEOPATRA as part of his reorganization of the East. After the battle of Actium in 31 B.C.E., Octavian (AUGUSTUS) restored the family to the throne. Lysanias's son, Zenodorus, ruled what Augustus hoped would be a reliable state buffering the Parthian Empire. Zenodorus proved so greedy and incompetent that in 24 B.C.E. he was deposed. The kingdom was given into the control of Herod, and remained Herodian for some time. Claudius placed Herod, brother of Agrippa, in charge but, after Herod's death in 48 C.E., gave it to Agrippa's son in 50. The Flavians seized Chalcis in 92 C.E., and from that time the domain belonged to the province of SYRIA.

Chaldaea   An ancient province of Babylonia, located along the Euphrates River. "Chaldaea" assumed historical significance in later Roman eras as a seat of magical and mystical lore. Chaldaeans were honored as the creators of astrology. Their works, appearing in inscriptions and books, such as the *Chaldaean Oracles,* greatly influenced subsequent Greek and Roman thought on such subjects as astronomy and related fields. Strabo held them in great esteem.

Châlons, Battle of *See* CATALAUNIAN PLAIN.

Charisius, Aurelius Arcadius (unknown) *Jurist*
A little-known jurist of the early fourth century C.E., probably during the reign of Emperor CONSTANTINE THE GREAT. He authored several works on law.

Charisius, Flavius Sosipater (fl. late fourth century) *Grammarian*
Charisius probably came from Africa and gained historical notoriety through the compilations of other authors made within his own works. His *Ars grammatica* survives only in large fragments, the first, fourth, and fifth books (out of five) all containing gaps. Charisius mentioned as sources and citations such writers as Remmius Palaemon, Ennius, and Cato, although the commemorations within the broad outline of his book were haphazard.

Charon Mythical boatman of the Roman Underworld. Charon was a ferryman for the deceased, who would transport the dead over the river STYX—if he was paid. The Romans thus devised the custom of putting two coins over the eyes of their corpses.

Chatti Major Germanic tribe that resided in the region of the Weser and Rhine rivers in modern Hesse. The Chatti fought the Romans bitterly for most of the first century C.E. and gained superiority over their neighbors, especially the Cherusci. Julius Caesar may have referred to them as the Suebi, indicating that he had contact with them, but the tribe's greatest struggle came during the reigns of Augustus (27 B.C.E.–14 C.E.) and Tiberius (14–37 C.E.). In 12 B.C.E. Drusus launched punitive expeditions against them, returning on two other occasions, in 10 and in 9 B.C.E., before his death. The Chatti refused to submit and joined with the Cherusci in destroying General Varus in 9 C.E. Roman vengeance took six years. Germanicus marched against the Chatti in 15 C.E. His victories climaxed with the burning of the Chatti capital at Mattium, somewhere north of the Eder River.

The loss of the tribal center did not terminate Chatti aggression or power. The next few years were spent wearing down their immediate foes, again the Cherucsi, who ceased being a major factor in Germania. In 50 C.E., Pomponius Secundus, legate of Germania Superior, beat back a Chatti incursion into the region. Subsequent imperial attempts to manipulate the Cherusci, and the stronger tribe of the Hermunduri, into war against the Chatti reduced pressure along this Roman frontier.

Again resilient, the Chatti were known again in Rome in 69–70 C.E., when they participated in the rebellion of Civilis. Although they were beaten back, Roman forces reached the conclusion that a permanent solution had to be found. In 83, Emperor Domitian marched into Chattian territory with a large force to defeat the Chatti and to ensure their submission. Columns of Roman auxiliaries and legionaries carved up the Chatti lands with roads, barricades and water towers. The Chatti were forced to make a treaty at the end of Domitian's campaign, guaranteeing the tribe's recognition of the empire. The Chatti, however, joined in the general upheaval on the Danube and Rhine frontiers in 169 C.E. Marcus Aurelius repelled the Chatti invasion, but by this time the frontier tribes were in the throes of change. Migrations were taking place throughout the region. The Chatti were unable to cope with the new pressures and faded from view.

Tacitus wrote of the Chatti with great admiration. They differed from other Germanic tribes in that discipline was maintained in battle, their commanders were obeyed and organization was used by them intelligently. Each Chattian warrior carried his own provisions and digging tools, much like the Roman soldier, and a system of supply followed large-scale troop movements.

Chauci A Germanic people who lived along the North Sea, between the Ems and Elbe rivers. The Chauci earned the title of noblest and most just of the Germans from the historian Tacitus. In 12 B.C.E., when their lands faced conquest at the hands of Drusus, they elected to make peace with the empire. The Chauci did not join in the destruction of General Varus at the hands of their neighbors, but they did war with Rome in 41 C.E. Crushed by Publius Secundus, they again offered peace but also launched raids into Gaul by sea. As subjects of the Romans, the Chauci stayed quiet as long as the might of the legions could not be contested. By the middle of the second century C.E., however, the Rhine frontier had collapsed, and the Chauci seized parts of Gallia Belgica in 170. The emperor Didius Julianus quelled their ambitions, and the Chauci slipped as a power and were eventually subjugated and absorbed by the Saxons.

Chersonese City in Thrace that came into the possession of Marcus Agrippa. In 12 B.C.E. he died and left it in his will to Emperor Augustus, who took ownership. Chersonese remained a private city of the emperors even when Thrace became a province in 44 C.E.

Cherusci Not the most powerful German tribe in the early days of the empire, but certainly the most famous of Rome's Germanic foes. The Cherusci, both the tribe and the loose confederation of which it was the head, dominated the region between the Weser and Elbe Rivers, to the north of the Chatti, their hated enemy. They fought Rome for control of the frontier along the Rhine and Ems rivers. In 12 B.C.E., Drusus inflicted a defeat upon them, and in 1 B.C.E. L. Domitius Ahenobarbus constructed the Long Bridges over the marshes in the area to make them more accessible to legionary control. Tiberius extracted their submission in 4 C.E., but the Cherusci simply waited for their moment, which came in 9 C.E.

No military event in the early empire captured the Roman public's imagination or sense of horror like the annihilation of General VARUS and his legions in the TEUTOBURG FOREST (on the southern edge of Lower Saxony) by ARMINIUS, the Cheruscan king. The Romans were pushed back to the Rhine, and Arminius carved a place for himself in Teutonic folklore. More importantly, Roman vengeance took six years to organize and prepare. Germanicus defeated Arminius in 15 C.E., but the victory of the Romans was not a total one. The Cherusci faced two more powerful, and ultimately insurmountable, foes: the Chatti and the pressure of internal discord. Arminius and his tribes defeated Varus and almost snatched victory from Germanicus, but in doing so they fought without the widespread support of the other Germans. Further, in 15, the Cherusci had been divided into two camps: those of Arminius and his father in law, Segestes, who joined the Romans. With Arminius's death in 19, fortunes turned from bad to worse. The Chatti made inroads both in territories and in numbers. By the late first century C.E., the Cherusci were having their kings chosen by the emperor in Rome. As pawns of the empire the Cherusci played the part of allies, used continually to sap Chatti strength at their own expense. The Cherusci had declined by the second century.

China   The relationship between two of the greatest states of the ancient world—Rome and China—was made possible by two seemingly unrelated events. The first was the foundation, from about 138 to 119 B.C.E., of the famed Silk Road, which was intended to connect China with the rest of the trading world. The chief Chinese figure in the development of the Silk Road was a general and diplomat of the Han Dynasty (206 B.C.E.–220 C.E.), Chang Ch'ien (Zhang Qian), who traveled to Central Asia to form military alliances. Chang Ch'ien's assistant journeyed to Iran and India and gave encouragement to representatives of those countries to establish trade relations with China.

The second event was the Roman conquest of Egypt in 30 B.C.E. From the time of Emperor AUGUSTUS, Roman traders and merchants were provided access to the Red Sea and the vast spice trade of the East. Gradually, the Romans came into contact with the goods that journeyed along the Silk Road, especially the silk of China.

As the goods were carried across thousands of miles and made numerous stops between China and Rome, there was little direct contact between either government. Not surprisingly, then, neither people knew much about the other, and the Romans were ignorant of how exactly the magnificent garments of the East were made. Pliny the Elder, in his *Natural History*, theorized that silk came from trees, with the down removed gently from the leaves with the help of water.

Direct contact between China and Rome was attempted around 97 C.E. when Pan Chao (Ban Chao), a general of the Han Dynasty, defeated the Hsiung-nu (Xiongnu) and took control of the Tarim basin region and its trade routes. The general commanded that an ambassador journey along the Silk Road and then across Ta Chi'en (Daqin; the name given by Chinese to the Roman Empire) to Rome. The ambassador, Kan Ying (Gan Ying), reached the Persian Gulf and would have sailed for Rome had he not been discouraged by the Parthians, who worried that any formal contact between the Romans and Chinese might threaten their lucrative positions as mercantile mediators in the trade route.

The first successful diplomatic mission did not take place until c. 166 when Emperor MARCUS AURELIUS sent a representative from the Persian Gulf to China. The trip was made easier by the defeat of the Parthian Empire by Rome and was accomplished by an ocean voyage. The mission marked a new and immensely profitable era for trade both along the Silk Road and by sea. With the Roman Empire at its zenith of size, the provinces of the empire were a massive mercantile market. Goods and wares from the East were extremely desirable, but the chief commodity was silk. The patricians of Rome and the nobles of the provinces had an insatiable appetite for silk, exemplified by the decadent Emperor Elagabalus (r. 218–222) who wore nothing but silken robes.

Silk was never cheap, and a typical bolt of silk could cost as much as a soldier's pay for a year. The price did not slow the appeal of the fabric, and by the fourth century, Romans of all classes were able to wear silk, as noted by Ammianus Marcellinus. The positive impact of the craving for silk was to widen the trade networks with the East, but it proved a serious drain on Roman currency. Roman denarii and sesterces traveled east, out of the empire to fill the coffers of the cities on the Silk Road and in China. While it was hardly the sole cause of the decline and destabilization of the Roman imperial economy from the third century C.E., the silk trade was nevertheless a factor in the debasement of Roman currency.

See also CLOTHING, TRADE AND COMMERCE.

Christianity   The rise of Christianity from a minor sect of Judaism to the most dominant religious body in the lands of the Roman Empire took place almost entirely within the borders of imperial civilization. The Christian Church was long viewed as one of the most dangerous threats to the stability of the empire and was persecuted with varying vigor by emperors from Nero in the first century to Diocletian in the early fourth century. The struggle proved one of the most fruitless ever waged by the empire, and from the time of Emperor Constantine the Great (d. 337), Christianity was the chief religion of Roman life and culture. The following article covers the spread of Christianity throughout the Roman world and the development of the internal structure of the religion.

GENERAL HISTORY

Christianity began as a minor sect of Judaism, at a time when great pressures were crowding upon the Jewish people, concomitant with the supremacy of Rome. The Jewish religion was strongly nationalistic but nevertheless enjoyed certain benefits under Roman law, a fact of some importance in the formative period of Christianity. At first the teachings of Christ, called the Word by believers, were given to Jews only, but it proved inevitable that the gentiles should be included in the missionary work and be converted. This inclusion was a heated question in the middle of the first century C.E., resolved unsatisfactorily in the minds of many "Jewish-Christians" by the greatest of the early missionaries, Saul or St. Paul.

Paul chose to preach to the gentiles without demanding that such new converts conform formally to Judaic law and religious practices. He found himself opposed by his fellow Jews on the subject, especially in Jerusalem. With its population of gentiles, the city offered fertile ground for Paul, and there he preached of the more universal nature of Christ's message. James the Apostle headed the Chris-

tian Jews in Jerusalem at the time. He fought with Paul over the issue of conversions, but James died in 62, a martyr of Christianity. Peter, the head of all Christians, had struck a middle ground, placating both parties.

The issue of whether Christianity should remain within the religious fold of Judaism or evangelize among the Gentile populations of the Roman Empire was resolved officially in 49 at the Council of Jerusalem. The first council convoked by the leaders of the church, the gathering was under the authority of Peter and was directed by the Apostles. Two parties within the church had formed. There were the so-called Judaizers, those Christians who argued that Jewish customs (e.g., circumcision, dietary restrictions, and other rituals) should be retained as essential for all Christians. The other party favored a broader appeal and opposed any Jewish traditions for new converts. The council decided against the Judaizers and declared that there should henceforth be no difference between Jew and Gentile in the eyes of the church. The council's decisions were then sent to the other Christian communities in Cilicia and Syria, making

A mosaic of Christ, from the Cathedral of Il Salvatore, Cefalú, Sicily *(Hulton/Getty Archive)*

Coins from the Christian era of the empire *(Courtesy Warren Esty)*

the declaration essentially universal and the appeal of Christianity equally so.

After the Romans under General Titus conquered and humiliated all Jewish lands in 70 C.E., Jewish Christianity would decline as the creed moved outward to Asia Minor and Greece. There the labors of Paul took hold.

But Christianity had already fallen under increasing attack by the Jews, who resented the religion's growing popularity and its continued protection under Roman law. Magistrates and officials throughout the East were generally tolerant, continuing to understand that Christians were within the Jewish fold.

It was only until the reign of NERO (c. 64 C.E.) that Rome perceived Christianity as a unique entity, different from Judaism. Romans usually greeted with mixed emotions the arrival of new religions into their city. Most were tolerated, but many, Judaism and Christianity included, were connected in the Roman mind with the strange and occult religions of the East and followers were accused of practicing peculiar rites (*see* CYBELE). The historian Tacitus thus referred to Christians as adherents of a "detestable superstition," who came even to Rome "where every horrible and shameful iniquity, from every quarter of the world, pours in and finds a welcome." In 64, following the great fire in Rome, Nero chose this new religion as his means of satisfying the anger of the mobs at losing large parts of the city. His decision to persecute the Christians was a natural means of escape. Christians did not preach revolution and taught in the finest Jewish tradition a higher moral and philosophical ideal by which to live on Earth. The cult of Rome and the emperors (*see* IMPERIAL CULT) was abhorrent to them, as were most precepts of paganism, despite its tremendous claim to the classical world so admired by all thinking persons. These characteristics left Christianity open to attack.

Paul had provoked a riot in Ephesus when preaching against Artemis, giving Nero an impetus for his murder of the Christians. Such outbursts of violence were limited, however, and after the Neronian pogrom such methods were curtailed. The next years were spent attempting to deal with the Christians from a purely legal standpoint. Some definition had to be made of their status and rights, particularly because the Christians could no longer claim to be Jews, a title that the Jews themselves would not allow them. A clearer legal identification was made when it became a crime punishable by death to practice faith in Christ. The only way to escape such a fate was to sacrifice to the gods or to the emperor. There remained, however, wide avenues of discretion on the part of provincial governors; despite the ardent attempts of local bigots and detractors, Christians for the most part lived in comparative safety.

Individual martyrdoms took place, of course. Domitian exiled Domitilla and executed Flavius Clemens in 95 C.E. for supposed involvement with the religion. Popular Roman rumors depicted Christians as cannibals, incestuous devils and murderers, alleged crimes found to be untrue by the governor of Bithynia, PLINY THE YOUNGER. He wrote to Emperor Trajan (c. 111–112 C.E.) that he could find no evidence to support the wild accusations of the times but saw in the religion dangerous creeds capable of destroying Rome. Thus he ordered the deaths of unrepentant Christians when they were brought before him, a practice agreed upon by Trajan.

Hadrian and Antoninus Pius left the pattern of legal action intact; the general prosperity of the era also allowed the Christians to propagate their faith. Marcus Aurelius, the philosopher emperor, allowed informers to be used against the Christians, and in his time Asia was the heart of anti-Christian sentiment. Philosophers, Marcus included, had strong intellectual disagreements with the Christian religion, even if they did not believe the gossip and spurious attacks.

The Christians were quick to take advantage of any lull in persecution, adapting themselves to various enterprises and services in order to increase their membership. Bishop Polycarp of Smyrna and Bishop Melito of Sardis furthered the Christian cause while assuming honored positions in the eyes of their local governments. The church spread beyond Asia Minor, Palestine, and Rome into Gaul. Egypt and Africa were missionary fields where Christianity soon rivaled the major cults of Rome and the Roman state religion.

Emperor Severus placed a legal restriction on the propagation of both Judaism and Christianity. In 212 C.E., Caracalla ensured further harassment by granting his *Constitutio Antoniniana*, the edict by which all residents of the empire were granted citizenship and could therefore be expected to offer sacrifices to the emperor. The result of such legislation could have been devastating to the

Christians, but they weathered the storm and emerged from the period intact.

The next years (217–249 C.E.) were filled with alternating bouts of quiet and persecution. Throughout, the organized church grew in temporal power and influence, especially in Africa, and the supremacy of the Christians, ready in the late second century to burst forth, seemed once again on the verge of exploding. Events were to prove otherwise, as the very survival of the Roman Empire seemed in doubt with the crises of the middle third century. Trajanus Decius seized the throne in the summer of 249. He saw Christianity as a symptom of the general decline of imperial culture. While he campaigned aggressively against the Goths along the Danube, orders were issued to begin a very serious effort against the church as well. Bishops were arrested and martyred, including Pope Fabian. Another edict cleverly ensnared Christians by demanding that sacrifices be made to the gods. Commissioners handed out certificates to prove that all proper rituals had been performed by individual citizens. Tremendous upheaval was caused by the edict, which forced the Christians to wrestle with their own consciences and the views of their fellow church members. Violent disagreements would plague the Christian community after the end of the purge in 251, when Decius died in battle. Many of the certificates issued at the time still survive.

After a brief respite, Valerian became emperor in 253, and he initiated another wave of persecution four years later, presumably to divert attention from his own problems and to seize for himself part of the considerable wealth of the Christians. As with the other attacks, Valerian concentrated on executing the leaders and all Christians of note. Hence, thinkers and writers like CYPRIAN of Carthage were tried and slain, and many martyrs joined him over the period of 258–259. Valerian was equally concerned with wars in the East. He made war upon Shapur I of Persia, and in 260 lost a major battle, was captured and eventually put to death by his foe. This event was providential, for his son Gallienus ended all anti-Christian declarations.

From 261 to 303, Christianity made more progress than at any other time. In Africa, the East, and in parts of the West, the pagan gods were slowly rooted out and replaced. Christianity became the religion not only of the great cities of Carthage, Antioch, and Alexandria but attracted the farmers and workers of the fields as well. Once the seeds planted in the provinces took root, there was no way the emperors could rid themselves and Rome of the faith. This fact, unfortunately, was understood only after a long struggle.

Diocletian became emperor in 284, setting himself the task of repairing the shattered framework of the Roman world. In time he would be aided by his tetrarchs (*see* TETRARCHY), Maximian and Constantius I Chlorus in the West, and Galerius with himself in the East. Galerius was the most anti-Christian of all the rulers. Using all of his influence with Diocletian, he called for a wide and severe edict against the creed. Fearing perhaps the already considerable temporal power of Christianity, Diocletian agreed. On February 23, 303, all churches of the Christian religion were ordered destroyed. Clerics were arrested, and, in 304, general sacrifices by citizens were commanded; but the horrors of Decius and Valerian were not repeated at this time. No longer could the imperial might so easily crush the Christians. There were now too many of them in the empire, even among notables in the government.

Failure was admitted at last by Diocletian, who abdicated in 305, putting an end to the anti-Christian campaign in the West. Galerius would not surrender for another six years, and then only because he was about to drop dead of a terrible cancer, which was reported with gleeful detail by the hostile chronicler, Lactantius. Maximinus, his successor, made a half-hearted attempt to continue the persecution, but he, too, failed. Meanwhile, Constantius had died in 306, and his son became the great champion of Christianity. CONSTANTINE the Great won the Western Empire from Maxentius in 312, and the following year issued the EDICT OF MILAN with the co-Emperor Licinius. In 325 he held the Council of NICAEA, and Christianity was given legal status as a religion of the Roman Empire.

CHRISTIAN HIERARCHIES

Christ left as his representatives his Apostles, headed by the Rock, Peter. As each of them spread out through Judaea, Palestine, and beyond, they traveled as the unquestioned leaders of the new religion. They were the first followers of Jesus, having lived with him, talked with him and having shared in his mission. They also emulated his life and his death. This last point created the first major question for the new church. After the deaths of the Apostles, who would guide the faithful? Among the Jews there had always been a question about the Apostles' authority, but the Gentiles brought a different perspective to the situation. They viewed the problem of succession as one with a possible solution. Paul was an important figure in concretizing the notion that a chief could be appointed with full powers when the need arose. Thus a hierarchy was established within the Christian communities.

There were *diakonoi* ("attendants"), or deacons, who aided the regular clergy, the *presbyteroi* ("elders"), or priests. These priests were responsible for caring for their congregations, including baptisms, a very important element of the religion, giving aid to the poor, and educating the faithful with the doctrinal decisions of their superiors, the *episkopoi* ("overseers"), or bishops. Every congregation possessed a chief shepherd, who, by virtue of his wisdom and acceptance by other bishops, served as the prelate empowered to ordain and declare positions on

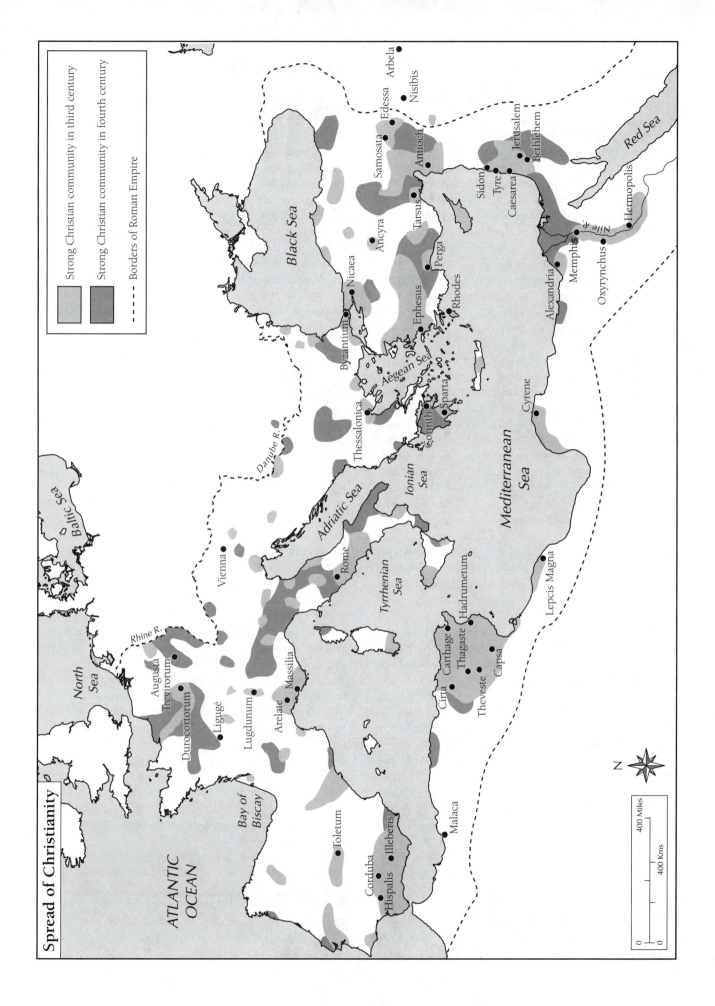

Spread of Christianity

Strong Christian community in third century

Strong Christian community in fourth century

Borders of Roman Empire

ATLANTIC OCEAN

North Sea

Baltic Sea

Black Sea

Red Sea

Mediterranean Sea

Aegean Sea

Adriatic Sea

Ionian Sea

Tyrrhenian Sea

Bay of Biscay

Rhine R.

Danube R.

Nile R.

Arbela

Edessa

Nisibis

Samosata

Antioch

Jerusalem

Bethlehem

Tarsus

Caesarea

Tyre

Sidon

Ancyra

Perga

Rhodes

Hermopolis

Memphis

Alexandria

Oxyrynchus

Nicaea

Byzantium

Ephesus

Sparta

Corinth

Thessalonica

Cyrene

Rome

Vienna

Lepcis Magna

Hadrumetum

Capsa

Theveste

Thagaste

Carthage

Cirta

Malaca

Illeberis

Hispalis

Corduba

Toletum

Arelate

Massilia

Lugdunum

Ligugé

Durocortorum

Augusta Trevirorum

N

0   400 Miles

0   400 Kms

theology. Each bishop kept in touch with his associates in the surrounding area. By the end of the first century C.E., Clement, the bishop of Rome, could claim correctly that the church's system was based on that of the bishops. In the East, the bishops were more numerous, with virtually every township possessing such a prelate. In the West, where Christians followed the Roman Empire's provincial system, the bishoprics, or sees, were separated by greater distances and thus wielded greater influence, especially in their own communities, where the congregations had nowhere to go for aid and no one else to whom they could turn.

This pattern changed slightly in the third century. First, the bishops of those cities serving as provincial capitals in the empire came to occupy a higher position in the eyes of the church—a precedent of some note, as Christianity was henceforth inextricably bound to the government seeking so eagerly to destroy it. This new office was called a metropolitan see, and the archbishop occupying that office took control of the consecration of the bishops in his particular province, as well as the institution of their nominations (a practice that ensured each archbishop had suitably loyal and like-minded associates). Second, while other cities, like Antioch and Alexandria, were significant in the Roman world, Christians early on recognized the importance of Rome itself. Peter had perished there in 64, and Paul had preached in the Eternal City before dying on the road to Ostia. The bishop of Rome assumed a very special status as a result of his veneration, and Stephen, in the middle third century, even proclaimed his supremacy as a successor to Peter. Such an assumption would be disputed for centuries, especially in other sees, but in the time of persecution the Christians sought only unity.

CONFLICTS WITHIN THE
CHRISTIAN COMMUNITY/LATER HISTORY

Attempts by the emperors to expunge the Christians from the empire were only partially successful at any given time. Such persecutions, however, succeeded in tearing apart the delicately woven fabric of Christian solidarity, especially in the face of a diversity of views on doctrine and theology. Disputes in the Christian movement were not new and could often be settled only at a high price. In the early church disagreements had raged over the Gentile question, and by the second century more serious movements, deemed heretical by many, were being born. GNOSTICISM appealed to the less learned Christians, who saw the world around them as corrupt and evil. This doctrine offered a personal sense of salvation and self-discovery and ran counter to the avowed Christian belief in appointed ministers and representatives of Christ. Attacked by every orthodox see in Christendom, the movement lasted for some time. Next came the Phrygian prophet and ascetic Montanus, who, from 156–157 or perhaps 172, called for all Christians to pre-

pare for the arrival of the New Jerusalem. His appeal was to those of an equal asceticism, notably in Africa, where he earned the devotion of TERTULLIAN, who was himself attempting to defend Christians with his great intellect and his gifted writings.

The outrages of Decius in the years 249–251 caused a bitter rift in the Christian community. Many Christians, priests included, had recanted their faith and had made sacrifices to the pagan gods and to the emperor. The church had to consider what was to be done with such people. The debate raged as to whether or not they should be allowed to return and to receive forgiveness. Many rigorists said no—once a sinner, always a sinner—and felt such people should be excluded from the church. Others, with greater foresight and more moderate natures, argued for readmission on the basis that all people were sinners, and the power to forgive them had been granted to the clergy by Christ himself. Chief among the rigorists was NOVATIAN. Unable to endure the return of the lapsed Christians into the fold, he established his own schismatic group in 251, taking many adherents with him. His sect would endure for many years. Cyprian, bishop of Carthage, was the main opponent of the Novatian movement. As it was, the church survived the persecutions and martyrdoms (both Novatian and Cyprian would die in the reign of Valerian), and it would grow in size and in importance in the empire.

The Christian Church became politically and socially prominent, to the point that many felt it was advantageous to know Christians. In 306, Constantine the Great followed his father's custom and tolerated the church. By 312 he firmly believed in the cause, issuing the Edict of Milan in 313.

Constantine did more than ensure the survival of Christ's church. He became its patron and its greatest supporter. Throughout the Roman Empire Christianity was encouraged, fostered and protected. From 325 and the Council of Nicaea, there could be no doubt as to Constantine's intention. His creed and faith would rule the hearts and minds of every citizen in the world.

Services were held in private homes until the third century, when Christians were secure and prosperous enough to erect buildings. One of the most interesting archaeological discoveries was at Dura, where a BASILICA was uncovered. Such a general design became synonymous with Christian structures. Constantine founded many great churches in Rome and elsewhere, culminating in his finest achievement, the new Rome, the Christian capital of CONSTANTINOPLE.

There he took up residence, surrounded by what would become the largest collection of churches in the world, the greatest of which was the Church of Saint Sophia. Constantinople also received the prestigious title of metropolitan, befitting its general importance. The archbishop, close to the emperor and the empress, could directly shape church policy.

Constantine took a firm hand in guiding the organization and evolution of Christianity in his era. The faith assumed imperial status, with territorial authority resting in the hands of patriarchs in Constantinople, Rome, Jerusalem, Antioch, and Alexandria. Furthermore, even though the bishops were theoretically elected in their own territories, the patriarchs and the emperors exercised the right to intervene wherever and whenever they felt it was necessary to ensure orthodoxy of the creed or the maintenance of their personal views. This was very necessary in the face of the doctrinal heresies so rampant in the fourth and fifth centuries.

The heresy of Novatian in 251 was part of the debate within the church concerning intellectual and spiritual matters. One of the first of such arguments emerged in 313, actually born out of the Novatian movement. Cyprian believed that the sacraments of the church could not be administered by an unclean priest, a view shared by many African Christians. One advocate of Cyprian's beliefs was the bishop of Carthage, DONATUS. While Rome held that the sacraments were inviolate, pure, and powerful in their own right, to the point that any minister, even an immoral one, could not taint them, Donatus and his followers disagreed. Constantine, fretting over the crisis, convened the Council of Arles in 314, but the North Africans persisted in their viewpoint, even in the face of an imperial decree. St. AUGUSTINE, the bishop of Hippo from 395 to 430, argued brilliantly against the logic of Donatus, but he too could not bring such dissidents back into the fold. In desperation, the church turned to more violent methods.

Augustine, a great figure, fought as well against the heretic PELAGIUS. This British monk preached that God's grace was not wholly responsible for man's actions; humanity bore much credit for its behavior. Augustine differed, and Pelagius was condemned, although some of Augustine's personal beliefs on matters such as predestination fell out of favor or were never adopted as church doctrine. While Pelagianism endured for some time, it could not compare to the far reaching and divisive heresy of ARIANISM.

No church debate ever caused such lasting bitterness or harsh treatment as did Arianism. Begun by ARIUS, the Alexandrian presbyter, in the early fourth century, the doctrine held that the only true godhead was the Father, who created all things and all persons, including Jesus Christ. The Son was therefore like, but second to, the Father. Unquestionably, Christ was the pivot of salvation, but the Father remained unique. The outcry resulting from this thinking drew in the entire religio-political framework of church and state.

In 325 Emperor Constantine the Great convoked the Council of Nicaea which condemned the heresy. Arianism, however, proved resilient, thanks to the efforts of several Eastern bishops and the sympathy of Constantine's own sister. Gradually, Arian adherents were rehabil-

itated and permitted back into the palace. The heresy was given formal imperial support by one of Constantine's successors, Constantius II, and thus was positioned to triumph at the Church councils at Seleucia and Ariminum in 359. St. Jerome wrote that the councils made the "world groan and wonder to find itself Arian."

From the start, Arianism was opposed by virtually the whole of the Western Church and all of the orthodox theologians and most of the church leaders of the East. The heresy's final defeat was largely secured by the efforts of several significant so-called church fathers, including St. Athanasius and the great Cappadocian theologians Gregory Nazianzus, Basil of Caesarea, and Gregory of Nyssa. Theodosius I, a devout orthodox Christian, and his coemperor, Gratian, began moving the empire toward a permanent reinstatement of the faith. Finally repudiated at the Council of Constantinople in 381 under Emperor Theodosius I, the heresy endured only in small pockets and among the Germanic tribes (in particular the Goths and Vandals).

The Arian struggle accentuated the temporal status of the church in the Roman world and the often close relationship between the institutional church and the imperial throne. Under Constantine the eventually pervasive practice of Caesaropapism was first given shape, so that henceforth the emperors—especially in the Eastern Empire—involved themselves directly in the affairs of the church. Their interference frequently created a charged political atmosphere for discussions of matters of faith, with emperors willing to expend political will and even brute force to settle purely doctrinal controversies. One of the earliest demonstrations of this political will was under Constantine when he used imperial troops to bring an end to the Donatist controversy in Africa. Caesaropapism continued as common imperial practice throughout the life of the Eastern and then Byzantine Empire.

A concomitant of Caesaropapism was the tendency on the part of some clergy to scheme for advantage and advancement in the church through political patronage. This was exemplified in the fourth and fifth centuries by the competition that developed among the Eastern patriarchies of Alexandria, Jerusalem, Antioch, and Constantinople. The rivalry was exacerbated by the efforts of the patriarchs of Constantinople to assume a position of supremacy over the East following the Council of Chalcedon in 451. In Canon 28 of that ecumenical council, the patriarch of Constantinople was given a position second only to that of Rome, a claim resisted by the Holy See and opposed strenuously by the other patriarchates. The question of relative authority in the Eastern Church became irrelevant after the seventh century and the conquest of the ancient sees of Antioch, Jerusalem, and Alexandria by the armies of Islam. Henceforth, virtually all ecclesiastical authority in the lands of the Byzantine Empire fell to the patriarchs of Constantinople.

The authority of the patriarch of Constantinople was itself second in the capital to the emperors and their wives or regents. Caesaropapism requires that the patriarchs of the imperial capital of the Eastern Empire be subject to the will and the whim of the emperor. It was partly for this reason that St. John Chrysostom proved so intractable in his dealings with Empress Eudoxia. The patriarchs were appointed by the emperors, followed their wishes in most matters ecclesiastical, and gave their prestige to the preservation of the imperial machinery of state.

This intertwining of church and state had far-reaching implications in the West, for with the collapse of imperial authority only the bishop of Rome, the pope (*see* PAPACY), could have an impact on the broad and terrible events of the time, e.g., the barbarian invasions. When the emperors of the West died out altogether in 476, the pope stood as the figure of prominence, a guide and shepherd in the lives of Christians for the next 1,500 years.

Sources for Christianity are varied. Of great importance are the four Gospels, especially the Synoptic of Matthew, Mark, and Luke. The New Testament on the whole is an excellent account of early Christianity, in particular the *Acts of the Apostles*.

For the opinions of the early historians before the time of Constantine, see Dio, Suetonius, Tacitus, and Josephus. *See also* Pliny the Younger, *Letters*. Later historians include Ammianus Marcellinus, Aurelius Victor, and Zosimus. *See* as well the *Ecclesiastical Histories* of Philostorgus, Socrates, Sozomen, Theodoret, and Eusebius. Eusebius and Lactantius (*De Mortibus Persecutorum*, most notably) provide fairly detailed records of the struggle and final victory of Christianity. Eusebius also wrote on other aspects of the triumphant church.

As for writers of the evolutionary Creed, see the epistles, teachings, and writings of Athanasius, Athenagoras, Augustine, Clement of Alexandria, Cyprian, Dionysius of Alexandria, Epiphanius, Hilary, Ignatius, Irenaeus, Jerome, Origen, Philo, Porphyry, Tertullian, and Theophilus.

Suggested Readings: Augustine of Hippo. *Selected Writings*. Translated by Mary T. Clark. New York: Paulist Press, 1984; Barnes, Timothy. *Constantine and Eusebius*. Cambridge, Mass.: Harvard University Press, 1981; Baus, Karl. *From the Apostolic Community to Constantine* (Vol. 1 of *History of the Church*, edited by Hubert Jedin and John P. Dolan. New York: Crossroad, 1982; Bausch, William. *Pilgrim Church: A Popular History of Catholic Christianity*. Mystic, Conn.: Twenty-Third Publications, 1989; Bokenkotter, Thomas. *A Concise History of the Catholic Church*. Rev. ed. New York: Doubleday Image Books, 1990; Bonner, Gerald. *St. Augustine of Hippo: Life and Controversies*. Norfolk, New Zealand: Canterbury, Press, 1986; Brown, Raymond. *The Church of the Apostles Left Behind*. New York: Paulist Press, 1984; Brown, Raymond, and John P. Meier. *Antioch and Rome*. New York: Paulist Press, 1983; Brown, Raymond, Karl Donfried, and John Reumann. *Peter in the New Testament*. Minneapolis: Augsburg Press, 1973; Brown, Peter. *The World of Late Antiquity, A.D. 150–750*. New York: W. W. Norton, 1989; Chadwick, Henry. *The Early Church*. New York: Penguin Books, 1988; Chadwick, Owen. A History of Christianity. New York: St. Martin's Press, 1995; Cook, Michael. *The Jesus of Faith*. New York: Paulist Press 1981; Cwiekowski, Frederick J. *The Beginnings of the Church*. Mahwah, New Jersey: Paulist Press, 1988; Dodds, E. R. *Pagan and Christian in an Age of Anxiety*. New York: Cambridge University Press, 1991; Frend, W. H. C. *Martyrdom and Persecution in the Early Church*. Grand Rapids, Mich.: Baker Book House, 1981; ———. *The Rise of Christianity*. Philadelphia: Fortress Press, 1984; Gonzalez, Justo L. *The Story of Christianity*. 3 vols. San Francisco: HarperSanFrancisco, 1984; Grant, Michael. Constantine the Great. New York: Scribner's, 1994; ———. *Peter*. New York: Scribner's, 1994; Hazlett, Ian, ed. *Early Christianity*. Nashville: Abingdon Press, 1991; LaPorte, Jean. *The Role of Women in Early Christianity*. New York: E. Mellen Press, 1982; MacMullen, Ramsay. *Christianizing the Roman Empire C.E. 100–400*. New Haven, Conn.: Yale University Press, 1986; McGinn, Bernard. *The Foundations of Mysticism: Origins to the Fifth Century*. New York: Crossroad, 1991; O'Donnell, James J. *Augustine*. Boston: Twayne Publishers, 1985; *Oxford Dictionary of the Christian Church*. Edited by F. L. Cross. Oxford, U.K.: Oxford University Press, 1983; *The Oxford Illustrated History of the Christian Church*. Edited by John McManners. New York: Oxford University Press, 1990; Senior, Donald. *Jesus: A Gospel Portrait*. Rev. ed. New York: Paulist Press, 1992; Streeter, Burnett H. *The Four Gospels: A Study of Origins*. Rev. ed. New York: Paulist Press, 1983; Tyson, Joseph B. *The New Testament and Early Christianity*. New York: Macmillan, 1984.

Chrysanthius (1) (fl. fourth century C.E.) *Neoplatonic philosopher*

Chrysanthius studied under Aedesius in Pergamum and was a friend and colleague of Maximus of Ephesus and taught Emperor Julian. When this pupil became emperor, he was twice summoned to the court (c. 362 C.E.) but declined because of unfavorable omens. Julian made both Chrysanthius and his wife Melite high officials of the religious cult in Lydia; Chrysanthius proved mild toward Christians. He died at the age of 80 and was remembered by his student EUNAPIUS, who composed his *Lives of the Sophists* at Chrysanthius's suggestion.

Chrysanthius (2) (d. 419 C.E.) *Vicarius of Britain c. 395 C.E.*

Chrysanthius served first in the court and then as the administrator of a province in Italy, from 389–395, under Emperor Theodosius I. From 395 until sometime before

412, he was the vicar of Britain, one of the last Roman governors of the isles. Chrysanthius retired to Constantinople, hoping to become an urban prefect but was consecrated a bishop of the sect of Novatianists, succeeding Sisinnius. His father had been a bishop as well. He served in that capacity for seven years.

Cicero, Marcus Tullius (1) (106–43 B.C.E.) *One of the most important Roman orators, who wielded enormous philosophical, intellectual, and political influence in the final years of the Republic*

Cicero was, by far, the most famous of the Republican leaders and was noted for his voluminous writings. The son of an Equestrian, Cicero came from Arpinum and, along with his brother, Quintus, was well educated, receiving instruction from Archias of Antioch, a noted poet. He also studied under SCAEVOLA, PHILO of the Roman Academy, PHAEDRUS the Epicurean, and Molo of Rhodes. He came to public attention in 81 B.C.E., speaking for P. Quintius. This was a property dispute that is noteworthy as Cicero's opponent was Hortensius. Like Julius Caesar, Cicero offended Sulla and left Rome for Greece and Rhodes, returning in 77. He then served as QUAESTOR in Sicily (75 B.C.E.), as AEDILE in Rome (69), and as PRAETOR (66). His skills in law and oratory were at first in support of the popular party, and he defended the *lex Manilia*, which granted unlimited powers to Pompey. As a lawyer of reputation, and with the support of the populace, he was elected CONSUL in 63 B.C.E.

The aristocratic party in Rome attracted Cicero, and he forsook his previous political affiliations. He opposed agrarian reform and then began his efforts to hound populist Catiline, who was crushed and finally executed on Cicero's orders. The Senate praised Cicero and gave him honors, including the title of *Pater Patriae*, but the populists despised him and feared his influence, while the aristocrats viewed him as an upstart. Though opposed, Cicero could not prevent the formation of the FIRST TRIUMVIRATE of Julius Caesar, Pompey, and Crassus.

In 58 B.C.E., CLODIUS PULCHER, a personal enemy, influenced a law that exiled all officials found guilty of executing any Roman without a trial, implicating Cicero for his role in the Catiline conspiracy, and Cicero fled to Greece. Pompey urged his return in 57 B.C.E. By now, however, his carefully cultivated political reputation had been irreparably damaged. Pompey gave him several tasks, including the defense of T. Annius Milo, and in 52 B.C.E., Cicero received a proconsular seat in Cilicia.

He returned to Rome in January of 49, just in time for the eruption of the Civil War. Owing Pompey, Cicero joined reluctantly his cause. He sailed to Greece and was present in the Dyrrhachium Campaign (48 B.C.E.). After the battle of PHARSALUS (48 B.C.E.), the victorious Caesar not only pardoned Cicero but also met him personally, treating him with respect and allowing him to return to Rome.

Seemingly retired, Cicero spent the next years hard at work writing, a respite that ended on the Ides of March, 44 B.C.E. With Caesar dead, he emerged again as the champion of the Republic. Cicero tried but failed to win over Octavian (AUGUSTUS) but did deliver his finest addresses, aimed at Marc ANTONY, the *Philippics*. So vicious and biting was his oratory that on November 27, 43 B.C.E., when a new triumvirate was signed, Cicero's name appeared prominently on the lists of those who were condemned to die. Once again he fled. Soldiers found him, however, and his head and hands were chopped off, carried to Rome, and nailed to the Rostra.

His works are varied in scope and in imagination. A survey follows:

oratory Cicero possessed no equal in speechmaking. Of his orations, 57 or 58 are extant, starting with *pro Quinctio*, in 81 B.C.E. In all, he defended an amazingly diverse clientele, dealing with the issue of slaves (*pro Q. Roscio comoedo* in 76), inheritance (*pro Caecina* in 69), citizenship (*pro Archia* in 62), and bribery (*pro Cn. Plancio* in 54), as well as causes such as the Catiline Conspiracy, which he attacked in four speeches in November of 63. He also countered Caesar's command in Gaul (*see* GALLIA) in 56 and, of course, directed the *Philippics* at Marc Antony in 43.

rhetoric Cicero's main extant works on rhetoric are: *Rhetorica*; *De oratore*, a dialogue between two great orators and the training involved, written at the request of his brother; *Brutus*, a history of Roman oratory; *Orator ad M. Brutus*, his examination of oratorical ideals, written in 46; *Topica*, on themes taken from Aristotle; *De partitione oratoria*, a dry analysis of rhetorical answers and questions; and *De optimo genere oratorum*.

philosophy Cicero returned to philosophy around 46, writing extensively between then and 44. He favored the New Academy but was eclectic in his own tastes, using Latin as the medium of expression, a bold decision for the time and one perfectly suited to display his brilliance in the language. His writings in political philosophy include *De republica* (54–51) and *De legibus* (*On the laws*, c. 52–46, never completed), which were both dialogues. In moral philosophy he authored a number of treatises, including *De natura Deorum* (*On the Nature of the Gods*), *On Fate*, *On Ends*, *On Duties*, and the *Tusculanae disputationes* (the *Tusculan Disputations*).

poetry Cicero used poetry as a source of experimentation and translations. He transcribed the Greek poem *Phaenomena* by Aratus but earned a poor reputation for himself because of his habit of presenting episodes in his own life as epics of note, *On His Consulship* and *On His Own Times*. He was devoted mainly to Hellenistic verse.

letters   A great letter writer, some 931 messages and examples of correspondence from Cicero were preserved in four main collections: *Letters,* a compilation in 16 books, which covered his writings from 62 to 43; *Letters to Atticus,* also preserved in 16 books, which made evident the author's private thoughts and were probably published much later, perhaps during the reign of Nero; *Letters to Quintus,* showing Cicero addressing his brother; and the *Correspondence Between Brutus and Cicero,* demonstrating his opinions on the war in 43 B.C.E.

Most of Cicero's works, especially his letters, orations, and a biography of him, were published or written by his freedman and friend, M. Tullius Tiro. Cicero married twice, to Terentia, whom he divorced in 46, after 30 years of marriage, and then briefly to Pubilia, a wealthy woman much younger than himself. By Terentia he had two children: Tullia, who died in 45, and Marcus.

Suggested Readings: Cicero, Marcus Tullius. *Selected Political Speeches.* New York: Penguin, 1969; ———. *The Letters to His Friends.* Translated by W. Glynn Williams. Cambridge, Mass.: Harvard University Press, 1927–1929; ———. *The Verrine Orations.* Translated by L. H. G. Greenwood. Cambridge, Mass.: Harvard University Press, 1966–67; ———. *Tusculan disputations.* Translated by J. E. King. Rev. ed. Cambridge, Mass.: Harvard University Press, 1971; Rawson, Elizabeth. *Cicero: a Portrait.* Ithaca, New York: Cornell University Press, 1983; Fuhrmann, Manfred. Translated by W. E. Yuill. *Cicero and the Roman Republic.* Oxford, U.K.: Blackwell, 1992.

Cicero, Marcus Tullius (2) (b. 65 B.C.E.) *Son of Cicero and Terentia*

Like his father, Marcus Tillius Cicero opposed Julius Caesar, and, when the dictator perished in 44 B.C.E., he joined the LIBERATORS and served under BRUTUS in Greece. After the battle of PHILIPPI in 42, Marcus sailed to Sicily and worked with SEXTUS, the son of Pompey, in the Mediterranean. In 39 B.C.E., Sextus signed a treaty with the SECOND TRIUMVIRATE, and Marcus returned to Rome and met with Octavian (AUGUSTUS), one of the triumvirs who had sentenced his father, the great Cicero, to death. A reconciliation was made between the two, and Marcus shared the consulship with Octavian but died shortly after.

Cicero, Quintus Tullius (102 B.C.E.–43 B.C.E.) *The brother of Cicero*

Well educated, Cicero earned positions as an AEDILE in 67, PRAETOR in 62, and propraetor of Asia from 61 to 58

B.C.E. He served under Julius CAESAR in Gaul, from 55 until he joined his brother in Cilicia as legate, in 51.

During the CIVIL WAR, he supported Pompey, but after the battle of PHARSALUS in 48, Quintus received a full pardon from Caesar. In 43, again like his brother, his name was placed on the death list of the SECOND TRIUMVIRATE. He died that year. Quintus Cicero translated works by Sophocles, wrote original verse and authored a missive to Cicero, *Commentariolum petitionis,* a guide on campaigning for the consulship composed in 64 B.C.E.; but he never rivaled his brother in fame.

Cilicia

Imperial province stretching across virtually the entire southern coast of ASIA MINOR. Cilicia was surrounded by the Mediterranean Sea and the ranges of the Amanus and Taurus mountains, which divided the region into Cilicia Aspera and Cilicia Campestris, in the west and east, respectively. Although the two geographical divisions were united in the creation of the imperial borders in 72 C.E., they differed greatly in landscape and in culture.

With its location so close to SYRIA and the east-west trade routes, Cilicia Campestris attracted the Romans in 102 B.C.E., when pirate activity led to Roman occupation. In 67 B.C.E., POMPEY subjugated the region and it became a province. Cyprus was added in 58 B.C.E., and the province was joined to the territory of Syria for administrative and security reasons.

The rugged, mountainous Cilicia Aspera remained the provenance of client kingdoms well into the first century C.E. Marc ANTONY granted much land to CLEOPATRA, but in 25 B.C.E. Octavian (AUGUSTUS) proclaimed ARCHELAUS OF CAPPADOCIA, a reliable ally of Rome, as king, and his son succeeded him. In 38 or 41 C.E., GAIUS CALIGULA or CLAUDIUS placed ANTIOCHUS OF COMMAGENE on the throne. In 72, Emperor VESPASIAN liquidated that realm, along with all of the other smaller kingdoms, such as OLBA. Vespasian stripped Cilicia Campestris from Syria and united it with Aspera to form the new province of Cilicia.

A more diverse province did not exist in the empire. Aspera was mountainous, with wild territories and people. Campestris, on the other hand, offered fertile plains and thus contributed to the economy of the East. Exports included wheat, olives, fruit, and wine, while Aspera produced timber. Cities sprang up on the coast and then farther inland. TARSUS was the provincial capital, with its meeting place of the local assembly, and the schools there were of note. Other cities included SELEUCIA, in Aspera; and in the second century C.E. Anazarbos rivaled Tarsus as a great metropolis deep in the province. Christianity spread quickly through Cilicia, from Syria and Asia Minor. STRABO visited Cilicia and Tarsus, and CICERO in 52 B.C.E. fled Rome to take up a position as proconsul of the province.

Cilo, Lucius Fabius (fl. late second–early third century C.E.) *Consul in 193 and 203*
A friend of Septimius SEVERUS and tutor to CARACALLA, Cilo came from Iluro in Raetia and served as governor of Bithynia and of Moesia in 195–196. He was also the governor of Pannonia and urban prefect of Rome. In 212, the new Emperor Caracalla, who had once called Cilo "father," plotted his death. The soldiers sent to murder him plundered his home, disfigured his face, and carted him off to the palace for execution. The reaction of the crowds who witnessed the assault broke Caracalla's resolve, and he was forced to execute the offending soldiers, protecting Cilo with mock sincerity. In 193, Cilo may have buried COMMODUS after the emperor was assassinated.

Cinna, Lucius Cornelius (fl. mid-first century B.C.E.) *Praetor in 44 B.C.E.*
A member of the plot to kill Julius CAESAR, Cinna stood among the assassins on the Ides of March.

Cinna, Gaius Helvius (d. 44 B.C.E.) *Friend of Catullus and a poet in the period of the Late Republic*
Cinna traveled with Catullus in the suite of Praetor Memmius of Bithynia and knew most of the notable literary figures of his time. His main work was the poem *Smyrna*, written in an Alexandrine style over a period of nine years. His other poems and writings included erotica, hexameters and an epigram. Following Caesar's assassination in 44 B.C.E., an angry mob murdered him, confusing him with one of Caesar's assassins, Cornelius CINNA. Cinna may have been a TRIBUNE as well during his career.

circus   A stadium designed for the presentation of great races, rivaling the amphitheaters as a major gathering place for Romans in pursuit of entertainment and sports. Because of their cost, Rome boasted the finest arenas, including the famed CIRCUS MAXIMUS. As with basilicas and baths, a circus could be an indicator of the wealth and degree of Romanization of a province. Any territory capable of affording a circus was prosperous and presumably stable. Throughout much of Gaul, a number of archaeological sites provide details of their number: They stood in LUTETIA (Paris), ARLES, LUGDUNUM (Lyons), and Saintes. Elsewhere they are found in CARTHAGE and in cities of Spain.

Circus Agonalis was erected by DOMITIAN around 86 B.C.E., on the present site of the Piazza Navona. This circus was a smaller structure than the CIRCUS MAXIMUS and could hold only some 30,000 spectators. Circus Flaminius was a structure within the CAMPUS MARTIUS, popular during the days of the Republic. Because of the prime location, other edifices were built nearby. Julius Caesar began construction of the nearby THEATER OF MARCELLUS, completed by Augustus in 17 B.C.E. Circus Gaius was constructed upon

Vatican Hill to honor Emperor GAIUS CALIGULA. The obelisk of this circus is presently in the Piazza San Petro.

See also GLADIATORS; *LUDI*; THEATERS AND AMPHITHEATERS.

Circus Maximus   The most famous race course in the Roman Empire, situated between the Palatine and Aventine Hills in Rome. Originally built by King Tarquin in the seventh century B.C.E., the circus fell into disuse during the Republic but was restored by Julius CAESAR to supersede the Circus Flaminius, and Augustus put it to great use during his reign. The circus was 700 yards long and 135 yards wide. Three tiered, covered porticos stretched along three sides, the fourth being left open for the competitors to assemble. Accommodating 150,000 spectators, much of the stadium had wooden seats, while the lower benches were cement. At one end stood a rampart of pink and gray granite, called the *oppidium;* opposite was the victor's gate. Until the time of TRAJAN a special box was used by the emperor, and senators and knights always sat in their own areas. Statues of heroes and deities dotted the circus, and an altar to the goddess Murcia, a local divinity equated with Venus, looked down from the *oppidium.* Vendors and merchants operated shops as close as possible to the massive structure. In time these wooden shacks became attached to the outer wall as the city and population surrounded the area. In 36 C.E., a fire broke out; the establishments of the merchants were destroyed and a section of the circus along the Aventine was damaged. After the great fire in 64 C.E., NERO rebuilt the burned sections and added his own touches of adornment.

Cirta   Chief city of the province of NUMIDIA; designated a colony during the reign of CONSTANTINE and renamed Constantius. Cirta was situated upon a large hilltop on the road from CARTHAGE, surrounded by the Ampsagas River. Cornelius FRONTO came from Cirta, a product of Africa's intellectual flowering within the empire.

citizenship, Roman   The possession of formal Roman citizenship was the source of great privilege in the Roman Republic and Empire until 212 C.E. when Emperor Caracalla issued the Constitutio Antoniniana, which bestowed citizenship upon all free inhabitants of the empire. Originally, Roman citizenship depended upon the birth of the person; ideally, both parents should be citizens, although it was permitted to have one parent who was a member of the *peregrini* (foreigners). Citizenship could also be bestowed upon a person or community by either the People of Rome (in the Republic) or by the command of the emperor, *princeps,* during the imperial age.

Possession of citizenship entitled the holder to definite rights and privileges, including *conubium* and *suffragium,* the rights to participate in government and to vote (except women, who did not possess suffrage). Theoreti-

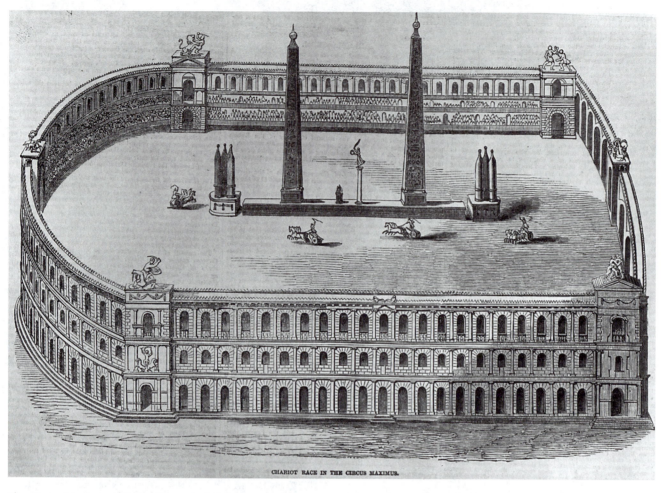

The Circus Maximus *(Hulton/Getty Archive)*

cally, the citizen also had a claim to the process of *honores* (the ability to be elected to a magistracy). In reality, however, due to the division of the Roman social structure into clear classes of wealth, nobility, and influence, access of the average citizen to the system of *honores* was limited, and the rights of *suffragium* were curtailed as the imperial era progressed. Equally, citizenship brought obligations, expressed in the *munera,* the duties of the citizen to the state. These included the payment of taxes, supporting the maintenance of city streets and public works, and above all, compulsory military service. The latter (termed the *munus publicum* in the Republic) became less important when the Romans adopted voluntary military service in the legions on the third century B.C.E. The *munera municipalia* remained, namely, the specific obligations on the part of a citizen to their local city, or *municipium*. In the later empire, a form of the *munus publicum* was reinstituted. It was less concerned with compulsory military service than the collection of taxes. Local municipal magistrates became liable for the collection of all taxes, with the added demand that any shortfalls in collection be met from their own funds. This

created not only a system of oppression but rendered government service less than desirable, with calamitous effects on the stability of the imperial government.

The extension of the Roman franchise to other communities reflected the growth of Roman influence across Italy and then beyond the Italian frontiers. The typical process of adoption into the Roman franchise involved several stages. A community would first fall under Roman influence, with its members serving as allies or subjects of the Republic or Empire. A community might then receive an intermediary status, the *civitas sine suffragio* (citizenship without voting rights), followed by the *ius Latii*, the granting of Roman rights. The final granting of Roman citizenship meant as well that there could be no other fealty given to any other state or ruler and that all inhabitants of the *municipium* accepted their duties under the *munera*. There were still certain local rights retained by the *municipium*, the details of which depended upon the specific circumstances of local government.

Citizenship spread from Rome itself to the surrounding communities and then to the whole of Italy. As the empire extended outward and established *colonia, ius Latii* and citizenship were granted to increasing numbers of cities throughout the Mediterranean and across conquered provinces. In 212, the Constitutio Antoniniana granted the Roman franchise to all inhabitants of the empire. It did not, however, change the formal status of the communities across the Roman world, and it tended to reduce the once desirable aspects of citizenship. Romans living in the provinces were no longer exempt from the often crushing taxes of the provincial governments; the *suffragium*, long in decline, was curtailed further by the demise of many forms of local representative government. Citizenship remained a useful legal status, with guaranteed rights and privileges.

This evolution of the definition and spirit of citizenship was a decisive influence in the process of Romanization of newly conquered territory in that the benefits of citizenship encouraged the adoption of Roman customs, culture, and language. Above all, extending citizenship to all of its subjects helped the empire cement the concept of *Romanitas* in all the corners of the empire. As a symbol of Roman unity, it had a value in holding together the many disparate cultures and peoples of the Roman world at a time when the stability of the empire was falling into question.

Civilis, Gaius Julius (fl. first century C.E.) *Chieftain of the Batavi, led a large-scale revolt of tribes against Rome in 69–70 C.E.*
Civilis had long dealt with the empire, serving as the captain of a Batavian cohort in the auxiliaries, but never earning the trust of his supposed allies. Fonteius Capito, the governor of Germania Inferior, executed a Batavian chief, Julius Paulus, and sent Civilis in chains to Nero, under a charge of rebellion. Galba subsequently released Civilis, who, understandably, harbored resentment thereafter.

In 69, while Vitellius fought for his throne, Antonius Primus wrote Civilis to ask for cooperation, a request echoed by Hordeonius Flaccus, the governor of Germania Superior and a supporter of Vespasian. Civilis supported the Flavians against Vitellius openly, while planning a massive rebellion. His warriors began working against Vitellian garrisons, and as successes grew, the other local tribes joined, including the Bructeri. Civilis marched on the camp and headquarters of the V and XV legions at Castra Vetera, calling on them to surrender to the cause of Vespasian. Alarmed by the vigor of his supposed ally, Flaccus sent a legionary force under Dillius Vocula to keep Civilis in line. The force was attacked by Civilis instead.

When Vitellian hopes died at the second battle of BEDRIACUM, the pretense was over. Vetera's garrison broke through Civilis's siege, linking with Vocula. The Romans had only one emperor now. Civilis faced a dangerous situation. Although he was unable to generate enthusiasm among the general population of Gaul, three tribal leaders did join him: Julius Classicus and Julius Tutor, of the Treviri, and Julius Sabinus of the small Gallic tribe, the Lingones. At a meeting in Cologne it was agreed that the defeat of the legions on the Rhine should be followed by the declaration of an *Imperium Galliarum*. Vocula, meanwhile, tried to conduct operations but was murdered, his legions defecting or being massacred.

In Rome, Vespasian's representative Mucianus wasted no time in dealing with the crisis. Annius Gallus and Petilius Cerealis were dispatched north. Gallus pacified Germania Superior while Cerealis took on Civilis. Gallic cooperation failed to materialize, and the *Imperium Galliarum* fell apart. Civilis's wife and sister were captured, and despite late-hour heroics on the part of the one-eyed chief, he saw defeat unavoidably approaching. Civilis agreed to meet with Cerealis on a bridge; the uprising was ended with favorable terms for the Batavians and their allies.

civil service The cornerstone of the Roman civil administration. Under the Republic the government was run by elected magistrates, while the provinces were administered by officials and governors. There was no wide organization to regulate government affairs; Augustus, assuming the reins of empire in 27 B.C.E., recognized the need for a competent service. He began by appointing his governors from a pool of senators on whom he could rely. More importantly, the Augustan Principate (27 B.C.E.–14 C.E.) marked the political ascendancy of the EQUITES. Augustus appointed them to many posts, including the prefectship of the PRAETORIAN GUARD.

This class was beholden to him and reliable as an instrument of his will. Imperial freedmen were placed in court positions and in financial offices, but their influence would not be felt completely until the reign of Claudius. Local provincial governments stood autonomous, and cities ran their own affairs.

It was widely held by contemporary writers and Roman historians that Claudius was dominated by freedmen. Clearly, CALLISTUS, NARCISSUS, and PALLAS exercised great influence, but they also provided the means by which the emperor could rid himself of tiresome administrative tasks. Claudius elevated his freedmen and improved administration of the FISCUS or imperial treasury. Provinces saw their officials, especially the procurators, rise in power, pre-figuring the increased imperial dominance of later years.

In his brief reign in 69 C.E., Vitellius returned to the Augustan policy of giving precedence to the Equites. They replaced the freedmen in such positions as the secretariat, the *fiscus*, and the court. This policy became the norm during the next regimes, culminating with the changes initiated by Hadrian. The long, influential period of Hadrian's reign saw the Civil Service appear to Romans as a legitimate career choice. Previously, positions in the service were part of a regular imperial career, including military commands. Henceforth, a candidate had his choice of careers: the military or administration. Such a development had great impact on imperial government, as the split between bureaucracy and legions created, in time, a tremendous influence for both.

Meanwhile, another figure was emerging. The PREFECT OF THE PRAETORIAN GUARD had long been amassing posts as part of the policy of AMICI PRINCIPIS. Septimius Severus elevated by prefecture even further by granting to the holders of the office broad legal authority: PAPINIAN and ULPIAN served both as prefects and as jurists. They were unable to overcome, however, the difficult palace politics, and both were murdered by their own guardsmen.

With barbarian invasions and internal strife, the Civil Service fell into a state of decline and disarray. Diocletian came to the throne in 284 and immediately established a new system. A strong centralization characterized this age. New offices of secretary, adviser and chief legal administrator assisted the head of the civil services, the *MAGISTER OFFICIORUM*. Other notables in the imperial court were the COMITES, or counts, a civil nobility of sorts. The prefects continued to be important, and after Constantine terminated the last military tasks of the prefecture, they served as the great conduit of imperial control over the numerous provinces.

With the establishment of separate Eastern and Western empires, the bureaucracies were answerable to the rulers in the two great territories. The governors of the provinces exercised great power on behalf of the government and were often tyrannical figures. Centralization brought domination, and the constant desire to bring all of the regions into line with imperial policy.

The empire was divided into prefectures, including Britain (Britannia), Gaul (Gallia), Spain (Hispania), Viennensis, Italy, Pannonia, Moesia, Thrace, Pontus, Asiana (Asia), Africa, and Oriens. Prefects conducted the affairs of their districts with the help of deputies, or VICARII. Governors were in control of local administration, and the cities, once semi-independent, were regulated even down to the councils. Finances were placed under the control of the agents of the emperor.

Late imperial Civil Service was authoritarian, efficient, and professional. It grew distant from the army and people, however, and this separation of the military and the one-time leaders of the legions from the state ensured the rise of the generals, the *MAGISTER MILITUM*, who intimidated and conspired against the imperial households in the East and in the West.

Civil War, First Triumvirate

Military and political contest (49–45 B.C.E.) that struck a mortal blow to the Republic and made Julius CAESAR master of the Roman world. The Civil War commenced on January 11, 49 B.C.E. With the words, "The die is cast," Caesar crossed the Rubicon from his province in northern Italy in direct disobedience to the orders of the SENATE. Caesar possessed eight legions and auxiliaries totaling 60,000 men, one of the finest fighting forces in history. Against him, POMPEY THE GREAT and the Senate had two legions in Italy and seven in Spain, with about eight more being recruited. More troops would be available in the provinces, but isolated and separated from each other as the senatorial forces were, quick marches by the Caesareans could negate any numerical advantages.

Caesar dealt with Italy first. He marched on Rome, forcing Pompey and the Senate to flee to Epirus, and then consolidated his hold on the capital. With his choice of theaters, Caesar marched to Spain claiming, "I am off to meet an army without a leader, and when I come back I shall meet a leader without an army." Caesar sent Gaius TREBONIUS to besiege the Pompeian city of MASSILIA (Marseilles), and by September, Pompey's general there, DOMITIUS AHENOBARBUS, was defeated and the city fell.

The legions of Caesar, 37,000 strong, forced their way into Spain across the Pyrenees. They faced AFRANIUS and PETREIUS, hounded them and finally trapped their army in ILERDA. On July 2, Ilerda surrendered, and with it, Spain. Shortly after this victory, Curio lost Africa to the Pompeians under Attius VARUS and King JUBA of NUMIDIA. The loss of Africa did not seriously affect Caesar's position in Italy, however, and he was declared dictator in October. With the provinces of the West firmly in his grasp, he turned to Pompey in Greece. Allies and recruitments had swelled Pompey's ranks to a number exceeding 100,000. His army, though, lacked the discipline and experience of Caesar's.

In early December, Caesar sailed from Brundisium to Greece with seven legions equaling between 25,000 and 30,000 men. He was joined by the trusted Marc ANTONY, with another 20,000. Pompey, allowing Caesar to seize the initiative, did not force battle and even endured a siege by Caesar's numerically inferior legions at DYRRHACHIUM and later drove off the enemy. By June 48, Caesar was on the move again, and this time Pompey, outnumbering him by nearly two to one, sought an open battle. At the battle of PHARSALUS, on August 9, Caesar lost several hundred men while Pompey fled the field, leaving 15,000 dead and 25,000 prisoners.

Caesar had little time to savor his triumph, however, as Pompey sailed to Egypt. In August, he moved in pursuit of Pompey, catching up with his body in ALEXANDRIA. With only 4,000 legionaries on hand, Caesar found himself fighting an immediate war with PTOLEMY XIII. For nearly four months a vicious siege raged, and the Romans could not gain the upper hand until January 47, when MITHRIDATES of Pergamum arrived with aid. The battle of the NILE in February gave Caesar complete control of Egypt. After remaining some time with Queen CLEOPATRA, Caesar marched to Asia Minor to avenge the defeat of CALVINUS at the hands of PHARNACES, the king of PON-

TUS. His claim *"veni, vidi, vici"* ("I came, I saw, I conquered") expressed his easy win at ZELA in May. Mithridates received Pharnaces's realm and the East was reorganized.

In early February 46, the battle of THAPSUS decided the allegiance of the region. METELLUS SCIPIO and Juba lost some 10,000 men, but many fled to Spain, where Gnaeus and Sextus POMPEY were rallying their father's broken armies. Caesar moved quickly against them in December of 46, with 40,000 soldiers against the Pompeian 60,000. By March 45, he had cornered the enemy, and on the seventeenth fought the most closely contested and harshest battle of the civil war at MUNDA. Victorious at last, Caesar returned to Rome to assume his position of power.

Civil War, Second Triumvirate

The conflict resulting from the assassination of Julius CAESAR in 44 B.C.E. and lasting until 31 B.C.E. Into the political vacuum caused by Caesar's death stepped Octavian (AUGUSTUS), Marc ANTONY and the ringleaders of the murder plot: Gaius CASSIUS and Marcus BRUTUS. Each jockeyed for power, and Octavian, trying to eliminate Antony, allied himself with BRUTUS ALBINUS, the Republican in Gallia Cisalpina, as the fighting broke out.

Antony chose to attack Brutus at MUTINA, besieging him from December 44 to April 43 B.C.E. When reinforcements under HIRTIUS and PANSA arrived, Antony defeated and killed Pansa but was routed by Hirtius at the battle of FORUM GALLORUM on April 14. On April 21, Antony again faced defeat and retreated to Gaul. Octavian marched to Rome, where he became consul in August. He realized that an alliance with Antony was more useful than facing the Republican generals, so, in November of 43 B.C.E., the triumvirate of Octavian, Antony, and Marcus LEPIDUS was born—and turned on the assassins of Julius Caesar.

Brutus and Cassius had fled to Greece and, after pillaging the provinces of Syria, Greece, and Asia Minor, raised armies for the inevitable conflict. In September 42, Antony and Octavian moved from Brundisium to Epirus, mirroring Caesar's campaign against Pompey in 49. The two armies, both numbering around 80,000 infantry, collided at PHILIPPI in Macedonia, about 10 miles inland from the Aegean Sea. Cassius and Brutus killed themselves when they saw defeat.

Antony and Octavian immediately began to differ. The PERUSINE WAR between Octavian and Antony's wife, FULVIA and her brother Lucius, only aggravated the situation. Fulvia's death eased the tension, and in 40, the two triumvirs signed the TREATY OF BRUNDISIUM, reaffirming it in 37 with the Treaty of TARENTUM. Peace between the two rivals lasted for four years, while Antony grew obsessed with the East and launched his disastrous Parthian invasion. Octavian solidified his position in the West, using Marcus AGRIPPA in Gaul and on the Rhine to quell revolts. Agrippa also battled against Sextus POMPEY, the son of POMPEY THE GREAT, who had become a sea pirate and menaced supply-lines.

By 33 B.C.E., Antony divorced OCTAVIA, the sister of Octavian, and was living openly with Queen CLEOPATRA of Egypt. Lepidus's power as a triumvir had waned, and civil war erupted again for supremacy over the Roman world. The struggle ended on September 2, 31 B.C.E., at the battle of ACTIUM, with Octavian victorious. He entered triumphantly into Rome in 29 B.C.E. to become Augustus, ushering in the imperial period.

Civil War, 69 C.E.   *See* 69 C.E.

claqueurs   Professional applauders hired for various performances or events during the time of NERO (54–69 C.E.).

Clarus, C. Septicius   (fl. early second century C.E.) Prefect of the Praetorian Guard under HADRIAN (ruled 117–138 C.E.); succeeded the long-serving Sulpicius Similis at the start of the emperor's reign (c. 118). Clarus was a friend of SUETONIUS, who dedicated his *Lives of the Caesars* to him, and was an influence on PLINY THE YOUNGER, convincing him to publish his *Letters*.

Classicus, Julius   (fl. first century C.E.) A cavalry commander and leader in the rebellion of CIVILIS in 69–70 C.E. A tribal potentate of the Treviri, Classicus took a troop of cavalry to Italy during the civil war of 69 C.E. As part of the army of Fabius Valens, he defended Gallia Narbonensis against a sortie of the Othonians. He reappeared in Germania as a representative of the Treviri, along with Julius Tutor, at the meeting of the rebellious chiefs at Cologne. There he helped established the *Imperium Galliarum*, but proved inactive in the face of the Roman counterattack along the Rhine frontier. His daughter was captured, and he laid down his weapons when Civilis agreed to meet with the legate Petilius Cerealis to end the war.

Claudian (Claudius Claudianus)   (c. 370–c. 404 C.E.) Last great Roman classical poet; lived and wrote in an age of tremendous activity and declining imperial power. Little is known about his life. He probably came from Alexandria in Egypt, and wrote about his native land with poems concerning the Nile, Memphis, and the Phoenix. His early writings were in Greek, and he did not use Latin until 395, about the same time as his arrival in Rome. He had friends in Rome, the two most powerful being the consuls Probinus and Aubrius, the sons of Petronius Probus, to whom he had written from Mediolanum (Milan). Claudian remained at the court in Milan for five years. There he became poet in residence for the MAGISTER MILITUM, STILICHO. Poems and panegyrics showed the state of the imperial palace during the period.

An unfinished poem to Urban Prefect Frontinus meant that the official fell out of power.

On January 3, 396, a panegyric praised Emperor Honorius. That same year saw Claudian mark Honorius's fourth consulship and the marriage of Honorious to Stilicho's daughter, Maria. These efforts joined others, including compositions on the Praetorian Prefect Rufinus and the rebellion of Gildo in Africa. In 399, he viciously attacked the eunuch Eutropius, chamberlain to Arcadius, and then offered a panegyric to Flavius Theodorus.

Early in 400, Claudian returned to Rome, where he praised Stilicho with a poem on his consulship. Two years later he again praised the *magister militum* for his victory over the Goths, receiving a statue in his honor from Honorius, a gift that he repaid with a poem dedicated to the emperor on his sixth consulship and his defeat of the Goths in 403. In 404, Claudian married, wrote two last poems to his new wife and died. Claudian was a remarkable writer for his age, with a flair for Latin born of intense study of the classical age. He wrote historical epics, as well as notably descriptive and stylized mythology, such as *The Rape of Proserpina*.

Claudius (Tiberius Claudius Drusus Nero Germanicus) (10 B.C.E.–54 C.E.) *Emperor of Rome from 41 to 54 C.E.*

Born at Lugdunum (Lyons) to Drusus the Elder and Antonia, his life was troubled with illness from infancy. He was so beset with physical problems, such as a stammer, that his family believed any public career would be impossible for him. He suffered humiliation at the hands of his relatives, and his own mother called him "a monster." Discussing another person, Antonia was heard to remark: "He is a bigger fool than even my son Claudius!" During Augustus's entire reign (27 B.C.E.–14 C.E.) the only post that Claudius received was to the College of Augurs. In the emperor's will, Claudius was given 1,000 gold pieces and treated as an heir in the sixth part, a place for non-relatives.

Beneath the terrible social manners, stuttering and clumsiness, there lurked the mind of a scholar and orator. He authored several histories, including one on Carthage and on Etruscan matters, and earned the respect of the Equestrian class. The knights rose, for example, and removed their cloaks out of respect every time that Claudius entered the theater. Even Augustus could be surprised by him, writing to Livia of Claudius's skill in oratory. Despite these glimpses of his true character, TIBERIUS and then GAIUS CALIGULA considered his mental capacities defective, thereby safeguarding him, because he posed no threat to their ambitions. Claudius thus survived while other members of his family and his circle of friends suffered death or exile at their hands. He served as consul for Caligula and was once thrown into the Rhine by him.

So decimated was the imperial family by 41 C.E. that, when Caligula fell to the blades of assassins, the Praeto-

A silver tetradrachm of Claudius struck at Ephesus *(Courtesy Historical Coins, Inc.)*

rian Guard had a difficult time in finding a qualified replacement. They chose Claudius and forced Rome to accept him. The legions agreed, happy to have the brother of Germanicus on the throne. The Senate had little choice, with the Praetorians bent on their candidate and threatening violence. As for Claudius, he never forgot who was responsible for his elevation, granting the Guards a sizable DONATIVUM.

The snickers accompanying his arrival quickly disappeared as the new emperor assumed the greatest power of any Roman ruler to date. He furthered the decline of the Senate both in the manner of his rule and in his resurrection of censorial privilege. He used the powers of CENSOR in 47–48 to bring the Senate to its knees, and infuriated the senatorial class further with his constant pleas for them to assume a greater role in government. The senators considered Claudius boorish and deserving of little respect, thus ensuring a political breach and the birth of conspiracies.

Claudius endured six such plots against his life, from lone dagger-wielding assassins to a large-scale attempt by M. Furius Scribonianus to lead a revolt of the legions in Dalmatia. Execution of the conspirators often included senators, which did little to heal the relationship between the throne and the Senate. In their place as servants and advisers, the emperor relied upon two other classes, the Equestrians and the imperial FREEDMEN. The knights found Claudius grateful. He made advancement in the government and in the military easier for the members of this class. Real progress toward influence was made by the imperial freedmen. Claudius surrounded himself with these able-bodied secretaries to alleviate his work load, and he turned to the freedmen to assume tasks of a bureaucratic nature. While he kept the major decisions for himself throughout much of his reign, near the end of it the freedmen dominated the civil service and the palace. Furthermore, the leading freedmen amassed considerable wealth and a say in policy, which even a major friend of Claudius, such as Lucius Vitellius, could not match.

The emperor paid great attention to detail, especially with regard to judicial matters. He sat in court and delivered judgments he thought were fair, even if the actual statutes differed with his view. His decisions could be annoying to the legal experts, and many stories were recorded of lawyers and defendants encroaching severely upon his goodwill and his time, out of a lack of respect (and a sense of frustration). But Rome profited from his attentions. He tried earnestly to maintain the grain imports and constructed aqueducts to improve the water supply. In Ostia, Claudius built a new harbor and port and handed out large gifts to the population at various times, including games. As a result of Claudius's reign, the empire was stabilized, especially when compared to the eccentricities of Caligula. In 50, Claudius granted Herod Agrippa the kingdom of Chalcis and the tetrarchy of Philip Archelaus. Thrace was annexed and declared a province. The greatest achievement in foreign policy came in 43, however, when Claudius finally embarked on an invasion of Britain. General Aulus Plautius landed on the isle and defeated the kings of the Catuvellauni—Caratacus and Togodumnus. Claudius soon claimed the victory personally, as much of southern Britain fell to his legions. He declared the conquered region a province.

He returned to Rome but soon had to face a major crisis. Empress Valeria MESSALLINA committed adultery frequently and with such ardor that her murder had to be ordered in 48. For Claudius this disastrous marriage was but one of four unsuccessful relationships, culminating in his union with AGRIPPINA THE YOUNGER. This marriage brought a formidable figure into the palace and sacrificed the claims of Claudius's other children, his daughters Octavia and Antonia and his son Britannicus. Nero moved in with his mother, marrying Octavia in time. Once her son stood unquestionably as the heir to the throne, Agrippina poisoned Claudius with a plate of mushrooms, and he died on October 13, 54, at the age of 64.

Although his rule often left much to be desired, as a writer he was considered by his contemporaries to be remarkable. His works were histories (not extant) of Carthage and the Etruscans, an autobiography and a study of the alphabet.

Suggested Readings: Levick, Barbara. *Claudius.* New Haven, Conn.: Yale University Press, 1990; Momigliano, Arnaldo. *Claudius, the Emperor and His Achievement.* Translated by W. D. Hogarth. New York: Barnes & Noble, 1961; Suetonius. *Claudius.* Edited and with an introduction and commentary by J. Mottershead. Bristol, U.K.: Bristol Classical Press, 1986.

Claudius, Freedmen of   Members of the court who were generally held to dominate Claudius's life and palace. These servants also made themselves tremendously wealthy during his reign. Some of these freedmen were Posides, a eunuch who was awarded a headless spear after the British campaign; Felix, who rose to the governorship of Judaea; Harpocras, a noted host of entertainments, who rode in a special litter; and the imperial mentor of literature, Polybius. The three most powerful of the freedmen, however, were Callistus, Narcissus, and Pallas.

Claudius, Wives of   Women who were married to Claudius before and after his ascent to the throne of Rome. He married four times: to Plautia Urgulanilla, Aelia Paetina, Valeria MESSALLINA, and AGRIPPINA THE YOUNGER. Urgulanilla he divorced for adultery. Aelia Paetina was also divorced. Valeria Messallina proved even more wanton, and after her death in 48 C.E., Claudius swore to the Praetorian Guard that if he ever remarried they should kill him. Urgulanilla bore Claudius two children, Drusus and Claudia. Drusus died in childhood and Claudia was illegitimate, the daughter of the Freedman Boter. Messallina gave him Octavia and Britannicus. Antonia is considered the daughter of Aelia Paetina.

Claudius II Gothicus (Marcus Aurelius Valerius Claudius) (c. 214–270 C.E.) *Emperor from 268 to 270 C.E.*
Probably from Upper Moesia, Claudius served as a tribune under Trajanus Decius and Valerian, becoming for the latter the chief of the legions in the troublesome province of Illyricum. Details reported in the *Scriptores Historiae Augustae* are unreliable.

In 268, Claudius joined the army of Gallienus, as one of his generals, helping to besiege the rebel Aureolus in Mediolanum (Milan). Gallienus died at the hands of assassins during the siege, and the army faced with the task of finding a successor. They chose Claudius over Aurelian. He immediately put down a mutiny in the troops, promising a *donativum* (a money-grant to each soldier). He then continued the siege, worked out a cease-fire with Aureolus and had him put to death. The emperor moved quickly to push back an Alamanni invasion and turned his attention to the dangerous Goths along the Danube frontiers and in the Balkans. In a series of smashing victories the barbarians were routed, earning him the title "Gothicus."

More invasions followed, this time by the Juthungi, who crossed the Danube in 270. Aurelian was given charge of finishing off the Goths while Claudius marched to Sirmium, where he succumbed to the plague. Claudius II Gothicus left behind him a number of crises. Postumus and Victorinus, usurpers in Gaul, and Zenobia of Palmyra were yet to be subdued. The Juthungi, Vandals, and

Goths still threatened the frontiers, and Aurelian, unloved by his legions, took over an uncertain empire. Claudius supposedly founded the family of Constantine the Great.

Cleander, Marcus Aurelius (d. 186 C.E.) *Phrygian freedman, and from 186, prefect of the Praetorian Guard under Emperor Commodus*

Cleander plotted against Perennis, the prefect who constantly interfered with his ambitions. With his fellow freedmen, Cleander worked for his foe's destruction and eventually succeeded in causing his death. Perfectly suited to manipulating COMMODUS's many weaknesses, Cleander assumed for himself broad powers, including the stewardship in the palace and control of the legions in the empire. He also hoarded the grain of the city (*see* ANNONA) in order to use it to feed the army and public in the event of a famine. Public outrage erupted in violence as a mob charged Commodus's estate near Rome. Cleander unleashed the cavalry on them, dispersing them cruelly. Commodus remained ignorant of these events until his sister, possibly named Phadilla, finally alerted him to the truth. The emperor summoned Cleander to the palace, where his head was severed and presented to the vengeful mobs. His children died brutally, as did his friends, their bodies dragged away and thrown into sewers.

See also PAPIRIUS DIONYSIUS for a variation on Cleander's end.

Clemens, Arrecinus (d. c. 81 C.E.) *Prefect of the Praetorian Guard under Emperor Vespasian*

Clemens was the son of the Prefect M. Arrecinus CLEMENS. His sister had been married to Titus, and this relationship to VESPASIAN made him a candidate for the prefecture in 70. Clemens was well suited to deal with the reconstructed PRAETORIAN GUARD and had the backing of the Senate, as he was a member of that legislative body. He knew and befriended Domitian, but when Domitian succeeded to the throne, the prefect was charged with some offense and executed.

Clemens, Flavius (d. 95 C.E.) *Consul in 95 C.E. and a relative of Domitian*

Not only a cousin of the emperor but also married to Domitian's niece, DOMITILLA, Clemens succeeded in having his two sons, named for the emperors Vespasian and Domitian, declared as eventual successors to the childless Emperor Domitian. Such imperial favor was difficult to maintain. Shortly before leaving office in 95, Clemens was called to answer charges of impiety. He and his wife were charged with neglecting the state religion and of favoring both Christianity and Judaism. It is possible that they were converts to one of these religions. Clemens was executed, and Domitilla was exiled from Rome.

Clemens, M. Arrecinus (fl. mid-first century C.E.) *Prefect of the Praetorian Guard under Gaius Caligula*

Replaced by the fallen MACRO in 38 C.E., Clemens was involved in the plots against the emperor in 41, but found himself stripped of his post by Claudius's new wife, Agrippina. His son was Arrecinus CLEMENS.

Clement of Alexandria (Titus Flavius Clemens) (c. 150–203? C.E.) *Christian theologian from the Egyptian community*

Ranked with ORIGEN as a Church Father, Clement called himself an Athenian and a pagan by birth. He came to Alexandria, enrolling in the famous Catechetical School and studying under Pantaenus, whom he succeeded in 190. As the head of the school, Clement authored several notable works. In *Protrepticus* (Exhortation to the Greeks), he argued the natural attraction and superiority of Christianity. *Paidogogus* observed the many facets of Christian doctrine. *Stromateis* was concerned with the philosophical basis of Christian intellectual thought. He opposed pagan beliefs but accepted them as a logical progression toward the enlightenment of Christ. In *Stromateis* he wrote that philosophy to the Greeks prepared them for Christianity, while the Jews were prepared by the law. Paganism as part of a process could be tolerated if, in its own cultivated manner, it accepted Christ as the true, final, enlightened vision of cosmic order. In 202, Clemens left Alexandria because of the persecutions conducted by Septimius Severus. He lived out his days in Palestine. His successor in Alexandria as the head of the Catechetical School was Origen.

Clement I (Clement of Rome) (d. 97 C.E.) *Christian saint and pope*

The third successor to St. Peter as bishop of Rome, Clement served as pope from c. 88 to 97 C.E. In official lists, he is the successor to St. Anacletus (r. 76–88), although according to both Tertullian and St. Jerome, he was the immediate follower of St. Peter and was consecrated by him. Clement was possibly a onetime slave in the household of Titus Flavius Clemens, the cousin of Emperor Domitian. Origen and others identified him with the Clement mentioned by St. Paul: ". . . they have labored side by side with me in the gospel together with Clement and the rest of my fellow workers, whose names are in the book of life" (Phil. 4:3). Other stories about his life—such as his banishment to Crimea and martyrdom by having been thrown into the sea with an anchor tied around his neck—are unreliable. He was the subject of numerous legends and the reputed author of a considerable body of work, the so-called Clementine Literature. This apocrypha includes the Second Epistle of Clement, Apostolic Constitutions, Homilies, *Recognitions*, the *Apocalypse of Clement*, and two Epistles to Virgins. He was most likely the author of the very notable First Epistle of

Clement, considered the most important church document, outside of the New Testament and the *Didache,* of the first century.

Written around 96, the epistle was addressed to the Christians of Corinth, where there had been severe strife in the community and several presbyters had been deposed. Clement calls upon the Corinthians to repent, to reinstate the presbyters, and to accept their commands, emphasizing that the Apostles were the ones who established the order of succession in the church by appointing bishops and deacons. He then stresses the role of these clergy in the offering of gifts, meaning the Eucharist. Much read and deeply respected in the early church, the First Epistle of Clement was publicly proclaimed at Corinth with the Scriptures and was even combined with or added to the New Testament. It provides historians an excellent picture of the conditions in the church during this era, especially in Rome.

Cleopatra (d. 30 B.C.E.) *Last queen of Egypt (ruling 51–30 B.C.E)*

Of Macedonian descent, Cleopatra was the eldest daughter of Ptolemy XII Auletes. When growing up in the palace of Alexandria, she learned court intrigue and also developed a loathing for her ambitious brother Ptolemy. In 51 B.C.E., Auletes died, leaving Cleopatra and Ptolemy (now Ptolemy XIII) as corulers of the kingdom of EGYPT. Cleopatra was 17 years old. A feud started instantly, and with the aid of his mercenary advisers, Ptolemy expelled Cleopatra from the throne. He relied upon such men as Pothinus and Achillas to assume the burden of administration. Cleopatra, in turn, raised an army to counter the forces of Achillas and was about to battle Ptolemy when Julius Caesar arrived in Alexandria in October of 48 B.C.E. The head of POMPEY was delivered to Caesar as a gift from Ptolemy, an act that offended the Romans and even Caesar, who had been Pompey's father-in-law. Caesar declared his intention to settle Egyptian affairs as the official representative of Rome on the scene. After charming Caesar, Cleopatra was installed on the throne and, after Ptolemy XIII's death, she elevated her youngest brother, Ptolemy XIV, as her royal consort. But she was the true power in Egypt, and, supported by Caesar, bore him a son, Caesarion (*see* Ptolemy CAESAR). Cleopatra subsequently traveled to Rome and stayed there until 44 B.C.E. No longer welcome after Caesar's assassination, she returned to Egypt. In 41 B.C.E. she met Marc ANTONY in Cilicia, and the two became lovers.

Her status and that of her country grew in the East as Antony became centered more and more on his possessions there. In Rome, Octavian (AUGUSTUS) anticipated civil war, starting propaganda campaigns against the couple on the Nile. Their open alliance gave him more than enough scandalous material, and in 31 the conflict erupted for control of the Roman world. Antony was financed by Cleopatra but even with such support could

A relief of Queen Cleopatra of Egypt *(Hulton/Getty Archive)*

not win the battle of ACTIUM. The queen's premature retreat from the battle had an impact on the loss. Cleopatra sailed to Alexandria, where Antony joined her. Trying to salvage her realm and Antony's life, she negotiated with Octavian to no avail. Antony killed himself. After failing to win Octavian's affection, Cleopatra joined her lover in one of the most celebrated suicides in history. She died at the age of 39; her desires and ambitions proved the undoing of Marc Antony and ensured the supremacy of Augustus. With her death the line of the

Ptolemies came to an end. Egypt was seized and became just another Roman province.

client states   Regions used by the Roman Empire as territorial buffers along the troubled frontiers, or as pawns in the destruction of powerful enemy kingdoms. Most of these client states reflected Roman policy, and most of the domains were controlled by old dynasties or by tribes newly arrived in an area. Others were friends or servants to the emperors. This was especially true in the days of the early empire, when Augustus left intact many of Marc Antony's clients or awarded them to his own associates. Clients received more than the blessing of Rome. They probably did not have to pay taxes, could depend upon the Roman legions for support in the event of an attack, and could rule domestic affairs as they pleased. Very often, however, such kingdoms were corrupt, dynastically exhausted, and destined for annexation.

An administrator could be named to watch over their affairs, as was the case with the governor of Syria and the small domains of Cilicia. Furthermore, the foreign policy of the emperors had to be followed, because failure to comply meant direct intervention. The kings of the client states thus traveled a narrow road, placating their own national concerns of religion, politics, and social organization, while holding fast against an insane Roman emperor or a demanding, long-term strategic policy. Few client states survived.

In the eastern regions and provinces were found most of the ancient dynastic kingdoms. They had been reorganized in the era of the Republic and were maintained by both Antony and Augustus. Some, such as Armenia and Armenia Minor, were constantly receiving new rulers from Parthia or Rome—as the previous ruler was murdered, driven out or, rarely, died of natural causes. These states were:

Arabia
Armenia
Armenia Minor
Bosporan Kingdom
Cappadocia
Cilicia
Commagene
Judaea
Olba
Palmyra
Pontus

In Africa, Egypt could be considered a client state, under Ptolemy XII Auletes and Cleopatra, but its status was always special to Rome, given its prime strategic location and its grain exports. After 30 B.C.E. it was a province. Mauretania became a Roman province after Caligula murdered the dynasty of Juba in 40–41 C.E.

Numidia was seized by Augustus and incorporated into Africa.

In the West, with the exception of the British kings of the Brigantes and the Iceni, and Thrace, the allies of Rome were most often barbarian peoples and used against a more powerful frontier threat. The Cherusci, for example, and the Hermunduri, fought as counterweights to the Chatti.

League of Achaea
Britannia
Brigantes
Burgundian Kingdom
Chauci
Cherusci
Hermunduri
Iceni
Thrace

See individual entries for complete details about each kingdom or group.

Clodia (b. c. 94 B.C.E.) *Famous sister of P. Clodius Pulcher*
Known as one of the most beautiful women in Rome, Clodia was unhappily married to Metellus Celer in 60 B.C.E. and became a widow one year later. She was possibly involved with the poet CATULLUS, in an affair that became well known in the city. Entranced by her wit and skills in love, Catullus devoted most of his passionate poetry to her charms. Their relationship seems to have lasted from 61 to 58 B.C.E., despite his unsuccessful attempts at freeing himself of her during that time. In his poems, Catullus names Clodia as "Lesbia." Catullus was replaced in her affections by the friend of Cicero, CAELIUS RUFUS. He surrendered himself to her circle but grew distant and was taken to court by Clodia in 56 B.C.E. Defended by Cicero, he was acquitted, but a lasting enmity developed between Clodia and Cicero as a result. The writer and statesman countercharged her with incest and the murder of her husband.

Clodius Albinus, Decimus (d. 197 C.E.) *Governor of Britain and a leading figure in the civil war of 193*
Albinus was from wealthy background and made a name for himself in Germany (*see* GERMANIA), under the command of Commodus, and in Dacia, before assuming his first post in Britain. The unrest in Rome, the result of the murder of Emperor Pertinax by the Praetorian Guard in 193 and the subsequent auctioning off of the empire to Didius Julianus, compelled Albinus to rise up against the infamous deeds.

Upon assuming the title of emperor, Severus tried to protect his rear while engaged against the claimant Pescennius Niger in the East; he offered Albinus the post of Caesar, the second highest office in the empire. Severus routed Niger at Issus, while Albinus held his own forces in check. His legions clamored for Albinus to take the title, while the Senate approved of his connections to Rome. In 196, at the head of an army, Albinus crossed into Gaul to rally the support of the German legions. He failed and was crushed by Severus at Lugdunum in 197, committing suicide. His followers in Rome followed him into early graves.

Clodius Pulcher, Publius (d. 52 B.C.E.) *Violent and ambitious figure in the final years of the Republic*

Clodius achieved legendary status in 62 B.C.E. by profaning the mysteries being held in the home of Julius Caesar for the BONA DEA. Forbidden to males, Clodius dressed as a woman and violated the festival. Brought to trial, he provided an alibi that Cicero refuted by stating on the witness stand that Clodius had been with him for only three hours on the night in question. As Clodius held the rank of *quaestor* at the time of the trial, he was able to bribe the judges. Still he never forgave Cicero, and the two of them became the most vicious enemies of the period. It was a possibility that his arranged adoption into a Plebeian family formed part of an elaborate plot against Cicero. Using this new position, he became a powerful tribune of the plebs in 58 B.C.E., throwing his lot in with the FIRST TRIUMVIRATE members, Crassus, Pompey, and Caesar.

With their help he persecuted Cicero and Caesar's enemy, Cato Uticensis. In 58, both of these politicians were exiled from Rome, and Clodius proceeded to extend his own influence over the city and the assemblies. Despite gaining an aedileship in 56, Clodius was on the decline. He could not prevent the return of Cicero, and his decision to intimidate Pompey proved fatal. His gangs roamed the streets to enforce his will, and in 57 he used these tactics on Pompey but found a foe with the resources to counterattack. Pompey summoned Annius MILO and turned him loose on Clodius. The resulting struggle was a physical and legal bloodbath. Squads of roaming thugs inflicted injury on one another while the two officials sparred in the courts. In 52, Clodius ran for the praetorship and Milo for the consulship. A fierce battle ensued on January 20, 52, on the Appian Way. Clodius died, and his supporters erupted as a result. They burned the house of the Senate and caused such civil strife that Pompey was appointed sole consul.

clothing

Textile production, aimed primarily at the manufacture of cloth for use in clothing, bags, rugs, and other needed fabrics, was one of the most important industries in all of the Roman provinces. Roman clothing was expensive for both rich and poor owing to the limitations that existed in raw materials and also because of the length of time required to make even one roll of cloth.

The Romans used wool, flax, cotton, and cultivated silk. Wool was sheared using iron shears and purified in a manner of combing that remained commonly accepted until modern times—the flat iron comb. Flax was harvested from flax plants and retted by soaking either in running or stale water for about three weeks. Other fibers included goat hair and rabbit hair.

Silk was imported from Asia, principally cultivated silk from China and wild silk from India. The use of silk increased in Roman territories with the spread of trade routes and emerged as a significant drain on the imperial economy through the loss of Roman money flowing out of the empire to China and India.

Associated textile industries to fiber cultivation were spinning and weaving, both largely cottage industries. Romans used the spindle and distaff for spinning, and weaving was dome chiefly by the vertical loom.

For dyeing and fulling, it was common to use vegetable dyes. Other dyes were produced from shellfish and lichens. As many dyes required a mordant, dyers would treat pre-dyed fabrics with iron salts or alum. To complete cloth manufacturing, fullers placed the cloth in a vat or tub with decayed urine or fuller's earth (alkaline clay). Other finishing, touches included raising and cropping the nap of some fabrics.

The dress of Romans differed depending upon the social class of the wearer, but there were several common elements that applied nearly to everyone. The principal basic unit of attire was the tunic (the *tunica*), which was worn by both Plebeians and Patricians. In general, the tunic was a simple shift, tied at the waist, and with either a short sleeve or no sleeve at all. The tunic for men was cut to a little below the knees. It was tied at the waist by a rope or a belt.

Women also wore a *tunica*, adapted from the Greek *chiton*. Like their male counterparts, they wore a *tunica* that was usually knee-length, but over this they wore a *stola*, which was a kind of dress that went from the neck to the feet or ankles. It had a high waist, was fastened at the shoulders, and often had careful and attractive pleating. It also had a border around the neck. As stitching was often poor owing to the low qualities of needles and thread, the typical Roman relied on *fibulae*, safety pins, to fasten outer clothing and even to hold together some of their undergarments. The *stolae* were usually white, brown, or gray. It became fashionable for wealthy Roman women to buy *stolae* of very bright colors, thanks to a healthy application of vegetable dyes. To complete the basic dress, a woman might wear a shawl, called a *palla*. The *palla* was wrapped around the shoulders and arm, or it could be draped over the head when a woman went out, as was the custom.

For men, a *tunica* with long sleeves, such as the one Caesar often adopted, was considered effeminate. Men also did not wear long, hemmed *tunicae*. In cold weather, it was the practice to put on three or four tunics. For common people, including slaves, herdsmen, and laborers, the *tunica* was made of less expensive cloth, usually dark in color and coarse. The tunic worn by Patricians was made from white wool or linen and decorated with stripes to indicate social position. Senators wore a *tunica* with a wide purple stripe, while members of the Equites wore a *tunica* with a thinner purple stripe. This was then complemented by the TOGAS they wore, which were also adorned with similar stripes. Military tunics were normally shorter than those worn by civilians to provide greater freedom of movement. The *tunica* evolved from a sleeveless or short-sleeved garment into a long-sleeved shirt with ornamentation. Termed the *dalmatic*, it became a common element in subsequent centuries in the vestments of the Christian Church. The stole likewise became a vestment for the clergy.

The principal heavier garment of the Roman upper class was famed toga. So ubiquitous did the toga become among the upper classes that it was possible to tell the status of a person by his toga. Members of the lower class normally wore a cloak as their chief outer garment.

For many centuries, some of the most unacceptable of all fashions were trousers. Woolen trousers (*braca*) were considered suitable only for the barbarians beyond the frontiers of the empire. As late as 397 C.E., Emperor Honorius proclaimed laws that made it a crime for any Roman to wear trousers within the Eternal City. Only soldiers, who used trousers in extremely cold climates and for cavalry, were excepted. Leather breeches were adopted by the Equites to facilitate their hard riding in the field.

When Romans needed heavier clothing than the toga, they had a number of choices, including the *paenula*, a cloak made from thick wool, although laborers and hunters in cold climates adopted a leather version; the *lacerna*, a light hooded cloak often popular with wealthy young Romans, including Marc Antony, who earned a rebuke from Cicero for wearing a *lacerna* instead of a toga; the *cucullus*, a short cape with a hood; and the *paludamentum*, an ornate version of the *cucullus* that could be worn only by generals.

The Romans' undergarments are less well known than their other garments, owing to the scarcity of direct references in writings. It is believed that Roman men wore a form of loincloth. Women probably wore a similar loincloth, with a band of soft leather that covered the breasts. It is likely that Romans also wore types of socks and stockings for additional warmth.

Children wore clothing that was similar in most respects to their parents'. Children of patricians varied their attire depending on their age, especially with regard to the toga. For most of their childhood, both boys and girls wore the *toga praetexta*, a toga decorated with a distinctive purple stripe. On reaching maturity, boys were granted the *toga virilis*, and girls were permitted to wear the *stola*, the dress of a woman. Children of the middle classes wore a white toga and lower-class children a tunic

with cloaks. However, in the later empire children of these less powerful classes started adopting the *toga praetexta* as well. The adoption of the *toga virilis* was marked with celebration and ceremony. For girls, there was often a ceremony in which her toys and her toga were laid aside as things of the past.

Like the toga, footwear was a means of displaying the social status of the wearer. Nearly all males wore sandals, save for those in military service. Variations of sandals were the *carbatina*, *solea*, and *soccus*. Members of the patrician class wore red sandals. Senators wore brown sandals, with black straps wound up the leg to mid-calf, where the straps were tied. To make their status plain, consuls wore white shoes. Women wore a closed shoe, a *calceus*, that was tied by laces. They were decorated in various colors, including white, yellow, or green.

Soldiers in the legions most often wore the *caliga*, a heavy sandal with a strong upper leather secured by thongs and a hobnail leather sole. This was the shoe that was used by the legions to march across the Roman world. For difficult terrains and especially colder climes, the soldiers were permitted to wear hose and leather boots. This was an adaptation made through contact with barbarian tribes, since boots and shoes, some made of wood, proved useful for battle.

Cleaning clothes at home was difficult because the typical Roman could not afford the proper cleaning equipment and was not able to use the requisite large amounts of water. It fell to the fullers to perform the vital task of cleaning clothes for the upper classes, a task documented in wall paintings, which show fullers treading clothes in water with their feet. The fuller placed clothes in large vats and marched and trod on them to expel dirt and grime. Finer woolens were bleached in a process using burning sulfur and urine from the public lavatories. This work was hazardous to the respiratory systems of the fullers, as well as the cause of assorted skin diseases from constant contact with chemicals and human waste. After treatment, the cloth was washed once more and brushed with a comb, sometimes made of the skins of hedgehogs. The nap was raised and then trimmed with shears, with the fibers snipped away used to stuff pillows and cushions. A final treatment involved a last washing with water, although fullers regularly applied the water by taking a swig of water and spitting it on the fabric.

Suggested Readings: Adkins, Lesley and Roy Adkins. *Handbook to Life in Ancient Rome.* New York: Facts On File, 1994; Balsdon, J. P. V. D. *Life and Leisure in Ancient Rome.* New York: McGraw-Hill, 1969; ———. *Roman Women: Their History and Habits.* London: Bodley Head, 1962; Boren, Henry C. *Roman Society: A Social, Economic, and Cultural History.* Lexington, Mass.: D. C. Heath, 1977; Brown, Peter R. L. *Society and the Holy in Late Antiquity.* Berkeley: University of California Press, 1982; Carcopino, Jerome. *Daily Life in Ancient Rome.* New

Haven: Yale University Press, 1968; Cowell, F. R. *Life in Ancient Rome*. New York: G. P. Putnam's Sons, 1961; Dupont, Florence. *Daily Life in Ancient Rome*. Translated by Christopher Woodall. Oxford, U.K.: Blackwell Publishers, 1992; Houston, M. G. *Ancient Greek, Roman, and Byzantine Costume and Decoration*. London: Adam & Charles Black, 1947; Lindsay, Jack. *Daily Life in Roman Egypt*. London: F. Muller, 1963; Potter, D. S., and D. J. Mattingly, eds. *Life, Death, and Entertainment in the Roman Empire*. Ann Arbor, Mich.: University of Michigan Press, 1999; Sitwell, Nigel H. *The World the Romans Knew*. London: H. Hamilton, 1984; Wilson, L. M. *The Roman Toga*. Baltimore: Johns Hopkins Press, 1924.

Cogidubnus, Tiberius Claudius (fl. first century C.E.) *King of the Britons, and a client of Rome in Britain*
Cogidubnus surrendered voluntarily after the fall of the Catuvellauni at Roman hands in 43 C.E. He subsequently received the blessings of Claudius to rule his own territory with the added title of *rex*.

In 47 C.E., when the governor, Ostorius Scapula, encountered opposition from the local tribes for incursions, Cogidubnus chose to remain loyal. Scapula rewarded him with several additions of territory. However, his kingdom was eventually annexed as part of the Roman province of BRITANNIA.

cohort *See* LEGIONS.

coinage Basis of a monetary system that existed for centuries and served as a unifying element of imperial life. The coins surviving in modern times serve as important sources of information about the eras in which they were minted. Much remains unclear, however, and new discoveries yield new questions. It is not possible to examine here every aspect of Roman coinage, but a general analysis will examine the place of the coins in Roman history, their types, and the Roman mints.

Under the Republic, the Senate oversaw the nation's coinage, and the mint at Rome turned out its monetary needs. The years of civil war, however, put an end to senatorial control. Generals and governors throughout the provinces used the smaller mints at their disposal to strike enough money to pay troops and conduct campaigns. Coinage, once depicting Roma and a sturdy ship, now displayed references to personal achievements, as in the case of POMPEY THE GREAT, or portraits of leaders, as in the case of Julius CAESAR. Inflation was rampant in the provinces and in Rome, and leaders in widely separated regions produced their own coins. As a result, the great mint in Rome was closed in 40 B.C.E. After winning the battle of Actium, AUGUSTUS returned to Rome to assume imperial powers in 31 B.C.E.

Augustus first stabilized the coinage by retaining the main coin types: the AUREUS, DENARIUS, *SESTERTIUS*, and

Early imperial coins. *(Courtesy Warren Esty)*

others. He then established across the empire numerous imperial and local mints, all to be strictly controlled. From 19 to 12 B.C.E. the mint at Rome was reopened and struck the gold and silver coins that were dispersed to the provinces. The Roman mint was later abandoned, for some reason, and Augustus chose a new site for the operation in Lugdunum (Lyons). Over the next years in his reign (27 B.C.E.–14 C.E.), and indeed throughout all of Tiberius's era (14 B.C.E.–37 C.E.), the gold and much of the silver coinage came from Lugdunum. Other silver coins were struck in the East or in special mints. Bronze tokens, used everywhere, were the responsibility of smaller, provincial mints, and were struck with the letters "S.C.," for SENATUS CONSULTUM, a recognition by the emperor of the Senate's historical role in coinage and an example of Augustus's desire to work with this legislative body for the good of Rome.

A change was made under GAIUS CALIGULA. Sometime between 37 and 41 C.E., the main coining operation returned from Lugdunum to Rome. Claudius, most likely, kept the mint at Rome, and Nero followed suit. The young emperor, however, decided that the Senate should be granted a say in the striking of gold and silver. The letters "EX S.C." appeared on coins for a time, but the senatorial privilege was revoked in 64, reviving Lugdunum's mint—which burned down later that same year.

Following the civil war of 69 C.E., the new regime of the FLAVIANS, especially Vespasian, took steps to reinstate Rome's lost grandeur and supremacy. Provincial mints were severely limited as a result, and for the next century only the silver mints in the East could claim any kind of independence; in Trajan's reign they were combined under one roof in Cappadocia. Emperors Nerva, Trajan, Hadrian, Antoninus Pius, Marcus Aurelius, and, presumably, Commodus, all followed the tradition of the Roman monetary dominance.

New civil wars from 193 to 197 allowed the provinces at long last to strike coinage of all types. Pescennius Niger, a rival for the throne, poured out money from the East and possibly from Byzantium (CONSTANTINOPLE). The eventual victor for the throne, Septimius Severus, used provincial mints as well, in Laodicea, perhaps in Emesa and possibly in Antioch. When he became emperor he chose to continue this new policy. Henceforth, Roman coins were joined by those struck elsewhere.

The beginning of the third century witnessed a deterioration of the value of money, the near collapse of the frontiers, a terrible financial crisis and rampant inflation. Debasement reduced the value of several coins, especially the denarius. This silver denomination dropped drastically so that by the time Caracalla came to the throne in 211, it had a value of some 5% of its original. To offset such reductions, Caracalla issued a new coin, the Antoninianus, worth $1\frac{1}{2}$ or two denarii. The Antoninianus was dropped by Severus Alexander but restored by Balbinus and Pupienus, and was used until the great reforms of Diocletian as the replacement of the denarius.

Knowledge of late third century coinage is very limited because of the chaos of the era. Sometime between 270 and 275, Aurelian withdrew all existing currency and struck new models. His two copper-based silver coins, while serving his immediate needs, were of dubious value. The empire was faced with a multitude of mints, issuing badly debased coins. Reforms were needed, not only in financial matters, but also in government and in administration.

In 284, Diocletian became emperor and labored to stabilize the Roman world. Around 293 or 294, he began to reorganize the coinage types. Within two years the old debased currency had been replaced by gold aurei and by silver, copper, and other, lighter tokens. Only those mints specifically chosen for imperial service struck coins of legal tender. These mints, some 15 in all (see page 134), ranged across the provinces and marked their coins to show their source of origin. All smaller mints on the local or provincial level were closed, including those of the usurpers Carausius and Allectus in Britain.

The system of weight and value adopted by Diocletian remains a source of some doubt, as are the actions of his eventual successor, Constantine. Aureus (gold) coins at the time were very pure, and none more so than the new gold piece, the SOLIDUS. The solidus became the primary means of paying taxes, and it was traded in for other minor coins, the *pecunia*. Their metallic composition remains a mystery. Little silver was minted for a time, until around 330. The bronze coins lost much of their value during the reign of Constantine, although the basic systems remained intact for some years.

Constantius II, circa 348, issued two new coins of varying value: the miliarense and the centenionalis. The former was probably silver or part silver, and the latter could have been a form of denarius. Julian, the emperor from 355 to 363, ordered another series of reforms. But the system established by Diocletian and Constantine remained relatively intact until the middle of the fifth century.

With the rise of Constantinople as capital of the Eastern Empire, the minting of coins was secure, especially in comparison to the mints of the Western Empire, which suffered conquest, destruction, or seizure by the barbarians dominating Germany, Gaul, and Spain. In time only the mints of the Italian districts and of Rome were still functioning. Henceforth, the barbarian peoples would develop their own systems of money.

The coins of the Republic most often contained phrases or even small pictures. Later, generals placed small commemoratives upon them, and Julius Caesar even adorned his coinage with the picture of a man. Under Augustus, the propaganda of the empire was furthered by the currency. The Pax Romana was celebrated, as was the magnificence of the emperor and his state.

Middle imperial coins. *(Courtesy Warren Esty)*

Late imperial coins. *(Courtesy Warren Esty)*

All coinage could be classified into several artistic types. Some were designed to honor the gods, such as those minted at Lugdunum. Others displayed events, battles, campaigns, or building programs. Commemorative coins honored individuals, groups (such as the medals struck by Claudius for his Praetorian Guard around 41 C.E.) and events. For the most part, the coins stressed the rulers themselves. Every emperor wanted to display his own likeness or those of his wife, mother, or other relative.

This aspect of the currency provides a wealth of historical information, establishing chronologies and tracing the internal affairs of the empire. For example, Nero began his reign with coins prominently displaying his mother Agrippina the Younger. As his reign progressed her portrait ceased to appear; her fortunes followed suit.

COINAGE TYPES AND VALUES

Throughout the years of the Roman Empire there was a constant effort to maintain distinct species of coinage with their own values. The following were the main coins used from the days of the Late Republic until the end of the empire, circa 476 C.E.:

antoninianus   Coin issued during Caracalla's reign (211–217 C.E.). After 256 C.E., it became the main silver coin of the realm, replacing the denarius. Its value declined steadily in the third century.

argentus   An invention of Diocletian in 296 C.E., given the value of the denarius and replacing the antoninianus in popular use.

as (sing.) or **asses** (pl.)   Coin issued by the Republic. It was the principal form of currency for years before being reduced to a mere measurement of weight.

aureus   Gold coin of general currency from the era of Julius Caesar to that of Constantine. By the fourth century its value had been debased and it was replaced by the solidus.

centenionalis   Form of currency issued around 348 C.E., as part of the new coinage of Constantius II. It may have been a variation on the denarius, but many questions remain as to its value and purpose.

denarius (sing.) or **denarii** (pl.)   Silver coin of the republican and imperial eras, until the late fourth century C.E. Its value declined steadily through the first and second centuries C.E., and by the third century it was replaced by the antoninianus. Diocletian revived its issue around 294–296, but under the name "argentus."

dupondius   Republican currency equal to approximately two asses. The coin depreciated to such an extent that, like the as, the dupondius became a weight.

miliarense   Probably a silver coin issued as part of the coinage of Constantine in the early fourth century C.E. Its content and overall purpose are difficult to calculate with any accuracy.

pecunia   Currency issued to replace the solidus; a mixture of silver and bronze.

pecunia maiorina   Name often given to the centenionalis.

quadrans   Old coin from the days of the Republic, made of bronze.

quinarius   Silver-based currency equal to one-half the denarius. The value fluctuated with that of the silver in the denarius, especially in the late years of the third century C.E. It formed part of the general breakdown of the denarius and represented five asses. The gold quinarius equalled approximately one-half the aureus.

semis   Part of the republican form of currency, made of brass and originally some six ounces in weight. As was the case with many of the coins, its value fell severely.

sestertius   One of the lesser breakdowns of a denarius, with a silver content equivalent to one-quarter of a denarius. Of all the coins in the empire, the sestertius achieved the widest distribution and was also called the nummus. It ceased to be minted in the middle of the third century C.E.

siliqua   Coin of silver that stood as a lesser equivalent of the denarius and, in the later Roman Empire, the solidus.

solidus   The most important and valuable coin in the empire from the time of Constantine. It was normally exchanged for pecunia and thus could be returned to the mints as payment of taxes.

The general values of the coinage changed from age to age, but several patterns can be deduced.

AUGUSTAN VALUES

1 aureus = 25 denarii = 100 sestertii
1 quinarius = $12^1/_2$ denarii = 50 sestertii = 200 asses
1 denarius = 4 sestertii = 16 asses
1 silver quinarius = 2 sestertii = 8 asses
1 sestertius = 4 asses
1 dupondius = 2 asses
1 as = $^1/_4$ sestertius
1 quadrans = $^1/_4$ as

CONSTANTINE VALUES

1 solidus = 24 siliquae = 1,000 silvered bronze = 2,000 denarii

CONSTANTIUS II VALUES

1 solidus = 12 miliarensia = 2 siliquae

1,200 centenionales = 2,400 half-centenionales = 12,000 nummi or smallest units

THE IMPERIAL MINTS

As we have seen, the mints were divided originally between the emperor and the Senate. Augustus had control over the gold and silver, while the Senate managed the bronze coinage. Under later rulers even this courtesy was ended, and total fiscal and currency powers resided in the hands of the emperors and their imperial administrators.

Aside from the mints of the provinces, under the control of governors, and the Senate's own mint, run by the *praefecti aerarii,* the currency of the empire was struck under the direction of the A RATIONIBUS, the head of the Roman FINANCES.

Clearly, for a time the two mints in Rome were kept in different buildings. On the Capitoline Hill stood the temple of Julia Moneta; within it was the Senate's mint, the emperor's being somewhere else, perhaps near the Baths of Trajan. In time they came together. Precisely how they functioned is hard to say, as many bits of knowledge are lost, especially with regard to the bullion and how it was acquired and stored, among many other factors. What is clear is the fact that the mints formed the backbone of Roman financial stability. After Constantine, the mints were under the control of the RATIONALES of the *comes sacrarum largitionum.*

The following is a list of the mints of the empire during several historical periods, excluding the smaller, provincial shops or those opened by usurpers.

IMPERIAL MINTS

Western Provinces	Eastern Provinces
Italy	Syria
Rome	Antioch
Mediolanum (Milan)	Emesa
Ticinum	Laodicea
Aquileia	Bithynia
Gallia	Cyzicus
Lugdunum (Lyon)	Nicomedia
Treveri (Trier)	Cappadocia
Macedonia	Caesarea
Thessalonica	Africa
Thrace	Carthage
Heraclea	Egypt
Illyricum-Danube	Alexandria
Serdica	
Siscia	

Spain

Germania Inferior

    Cologne (Colonia Agrippina)

Suggested Readings: Askew, Gilbert. *The Coinage of Roman Britain.* London: Seaby Publications, 1980; Carson, R. A. G., P. V. Hill, and J. P. C. Kent. *Late Roman Bronze Coinage.* New York: Sanford J. Durst, 1989; De White, J. *Atlas of the Ancient Coins Struck by the Emperors of the Gallic Empire.* Chicago: Ares Publishers Inc., 1989; Harl, Kenneth W. *Civic Coins and Civic Politics in the Roman East, A.D. 180–275.* Berkeley: University of California Press, 1987; King, C. E. *Roman Silver Coins, V. V: Carausius to Romulus Augustus.* London: Seaby Publications Ltd., 1987; Klawans, Zander H. *Reading and Dating Roman Imperial Coins.* New York: Sanford J. Durst, 1982; Klawans, Zander H., and K. E. Bressett, eds. *Handbook of Ancient Greek and Roman Coins.* Racine, Wisc.: Whitman Publishing Co. Inc., 1995; Mattingly, Harold. *Roman Coins from the Earliest Times to the Fall of the Western Empire.* New York: Sanford J. Durst, 1987; Pearce, J. W. E., Harold Mattingly, C. H. V. Sutherland, and R. A. G. Carson, eds. *The Roman Imperial Coinage.* London: Spink & Son Ltd., 1968; Sayles, Wayne G. *Ancient Coin Collecting.* Iola, Wisc.: Krause Publications, 1996; Sutherland, Carol H. V. *Roman History and Coinage, 44 B.C.–A.D. 69: Fifty Points of Relation from Julius Caesar to Vespasian.* New York: Oxford University Press, 1987; Van Meter, David. *The Handbook of Roman Imperial Coins: A Complete Guide to the History, Types, and Values of Roman Imperial Coinage.* Nashua, N.H.: Laurion Numismatics, 1991.

Cologne Also known as Colonia Agrippina or Agrippinensis; one of the leading cities in the West, serving for centuries as the provincial capital of Germania Inferior. Cologne was an unimportant site on the Rhine until the time of Augustus (ruled 27 B.C.E.–14 C.E.). His lieutenant Marcus Agrippa moved the Roman-allied tribe of the Ubii across the great river for protection and settled them there. In time, they were joined by a legionary detachment camp.

The name given to the tribal center was Oppidum or Civitas Ubiorum, and settlers from Italy began arriving there. Agrippina, the wife of Claudius, was born to Germanicus and Agrippina the Elder while in the camp. This birthplace proved important, for in 51 C.E. Agrippina convinced Claudius to declare the community a colony, with forts for protection and veteran colonists sent to populate it. Success seemed evident, for Cologne was considered essential to the victory of the Rhine revolt in 69 C.E. The city fell to CIVILIS but then rose up and expelled the rebels, precipitating Civilis's defeat. An indication of the hostility felt by the colonists toward the Germans was given shortly afterward. All of the natives in the town died cruelly.

Cologne became attached to the province of Germania Inferior, and Domitian decreed it to be the capital as well. With this new status, large efforts were made to redesign the city and construct suitable edifices. So effective were the city's planners that the original design remained visible into the 20th century. Baths, government buildings, and temples to Mercury and the imperial cult dominated the architecture. Industry began as well. From Gaul, glass-blowing and manufacturing were imported and pursued vigorously. By the late second century C.E., Cologne rivaled Aquileia in the distribution of glass, pottery, and fine goods. Famous glass markets in Africa and Alexandria were driven completely out of the Western provinces as Cologne formed the heart of Rome's economic thrust into northern Europe. In the third century C.E., Emperor Gallienus conducted many of his campaigns from Cologne. He also resided there, and in 257 decided to move the imperial mint to the city.

Colonia Agrippina   *See* COLOGNE.

colonies   The creation of *coloniae* allowed Rome to extend its people, culture, and control over the hostile, foreign, or desired territories, all the while meeting the demands of the empire's growing population.

During the early Roman times and during the Republic, colonies were established in ITALIA (Italy) with their own constitutions and organization, enabling Rome to bring all of Italy under its domination. Special privileges were accorded to colonists, who considered themselves extensions of Rome itself, although in time all of the inhabitants of the Italian districts enjoyed full citizenship. The Senate was against foreign colonization and opposed even small settlements in Africa and Gaul, especially the colony established in 118 B.C.E. in GALLIA NARBONENSIS. Few further attempts were made until two figures arrived on the scene: Julius CAESAR and AUGUSTUS.

Caesar extended land grants to many of his veterans, and land in Africa and Italy was set aside for retired legionaries. Specifically, he settled his ex-soldiers in Campania (Italy), Carthage (Africa), and in Corinth (Greece), saving allotments of territory in Gallia Narbonensis and Gallia Transalpina for his VI and X Legions. Caesar made other colonial attempts overseas by moving large elements of the crowded Roman population into a variety of settlements from Corinth to Spain. Two types of colonist emerged: army veterans desirous of finding land on which to settle; and the unemployed, often poverty stricken Romans and Italians who were willing to go anywhere for better circumstances. Colonies thus gave the empire both short- and long-term solutions to its problems. First, ex-soldiers could be satisfied, and the overpopulation at home could be resolved. Furthermore, once established, new colonies could provide economic power for Roman interests abroad. Finally, as it was policy not to recruit from native peoples for the army, the established Roman communities in Gaul, Spain, Africa, and in the East could produce the needed recruits for centuries to come.

Augustus certainly understood this, for he pursued an aggressive process of colonization. He created settlements in the West and focused on Asia Minor to establish veterans in lush regions that were also troubled areas. Under Claudius, parts of Germania were appropriated at the expense of the local tribes. Other *coloniae* sprang up at least until the reign of Hadrian. From that time, new colonies were rare.

Essentially, a colony came into being when a group of Roman citizens, be they veterans or civilians, received from the state a grant of land in a province (or in Italy). The amount allotted to each colonist followed the regular plotting used as the standard throughout the empire (CENTURIATION). Once measured, all the colonists' land received the prized status of IUS ITALICUM, in which no tribute was demanded because they were all citizens.

By the middle of the third century C.E., imperial requirements for manpower were such that the provinces produced soldiers for the army. Cities in existence prior to Roman preeminence began to request the right to change their status. Non-Roman territories could rise to a better status in the provinces by acquiring the rank of *colonia*. Hadrian agreed to grant colonial privileges to Italica in Spain, his native home, and other *municipia* received not only the honorable IUS LATII but also the more valuable *ius Italicum*.

An improved title did not necessarily guarantee full freedom, however. Thus when Caesarea became a colony under Vespasian, only its poll tax (*tributum capitis*) was dropped. It did not initially claim the *ius Italicum,* and very few cities ever would. Caesarea finally gained its *ius* status under Titus, and Utica, Carthage, and Lepcis Magna were so blessed by Caracalla. Equally, the designation *coloniae civium Romanorum* made such a district part of the provincial elite, ahead of the title MUNICIPIUM, and certainly superior to the communities of the PEREGRINI, or foreigners. The advantages were obvious, and in an Empire where commercial, social, and administrative competition was fierce, it helped to have every conceivable edge.

Colosseum   The greatest structure erected during the age of the Flavian emperors (69–96 C.E.) and arguably the finest architectural achievement in the history of the Roman Empire. The Colosseum was originally called the Flavian Amphitheater, but it became known as the Colosseum after a colossal statue of Nero that once stood nearby. Its origins are to be found in the desire of the Emperor VESPASIAN to create for the Romans a stadium of such magnitude as to convince both them and the world of Rome's return to unquestioned power after the bitter civil war.

Construction began in 72 or 75 C.E. Vespasian chose as the site a large plot between the Caelian and Esquiline Hills, near the lake of Stagnum Neronis and the GOLDEN HOUSE OF NERO. His intent was obvious—to transform the old residence of the despot Nero into a public place of joy and entertainment. He succeeded admirably, and his achievement would be supplemented in time by the Baths of Titus, built in order to use up the rest of the Golden House. The work proceeded feverishly and the tale that 30,000 Jews were pressed into service persists. Yet Vespasian did not live to see its completion. Titus took up the task in his reign, but it was Domitian who completed the structure sometime around 81 C.E. The official opening, however, was held on a festal day in 80. Titus presided over the ceremonies, which were followed by a prolonged gladiatorial show lasting for 100 days.

The Colosseum seated at least 45,000 to 55,000 people. Vespasian chose an elliptical shape in honor of the amphitheater of Curio, but this one was larger. There were three principal arcades, the intervals of which were filled with arched corridors, staircases, supporting substructures, and finally the seats. Travertine stone was used throughout, although some brick, pumice, and concrete proved effective in construction. The stones came from Albulae near Tivoli. The elliptically shaped walls were 620 feet by 507 feet wide at their long and short axes, the outer walls standing 157 feet high. The arena floor stretched 290 feet by 180 feet at its two axes. The dimensions of the Colosseum have changed slightly over the years, as war and disaster took their toll. Eighty arches opened onto the stands, and the columns employed throughout represented the various orders—Doric, Ionic, and Corinthian—while the fourth story, the top floor, was set with Corinthian pilasters, installed with iron to hold them securely in place.

The seats were arranged in four different sections on the podium. The bottom seats belonged to the tribunes, senators, and members of the Equestrian Order. The second and third sections were for the general citizenry and the lower classes, respectively. The final rows, near the upper arches, were used by the lower classes and many women. All of these public zones bore the name *maeniana*. Spectators in the upper seats saw clearly not only the games but were shaded by the *velaria* as well, awnings stretched across the exposed areas of the stadium to cover the public from the sun. The canvas and ropes were the responsibility of a large group of sailors from Misenum, stationed permanently in Rome for this sole purpose.

The Flavian Amphitheater, or Colosseum, photographed around 1890 *(Hulton/Getty Archive)*

Every arch had a number corresponding to the tickets issued, and each ticket specifically listed the entrance, row and number of the seat belonging to the holder for that day. There were a number of restricted or specific entrances. Imperial spectators could enter and be escorted to their own box, although Commodus made himself an underground passage. Routinely, the excited fans took their seats very early in the morning and stayed throughout the day.

The stories told of the games and of the ingenious tricks used to enhance the performances and to entertain the mobs could rarely exaggerate the truth. Two of the most interesting events were the animal spectacles and the famed staged sea battles of Titus, both requiring special architectural devices. In the animal spectacles the cages were arranged so expertly that large groups of beasts could be led directly into the arena. Domitian added to the sublevels of the arena, putting in rooms and hinged trapdoors that allowed for changes of scenery and the logistical requirements of the various displays. As for the sea fights, while Suetonius reports that they were held instead in the artificial lake of Naumachia and not in the amphitheater, Dio's account disagrees. The Colosseum did contain drains for the production of such naval shows, although they were not installed until the reign of Domitian. The abundance of water nearby made the filling of the Colosseum possible, although architecturally stressful. The drains routinely became clogged, causing extensive rot in the surrounding wood. The year 248 C.E. saw the last recorded, sea-oriented spectacle called a *naumachia*. (For more on the events held in the Colosseum, *see* GLADIATORS and *LUDI*.)

A number of other practical features were designed for the comfort of the thousands of spectators. Spouts could send out cool and scented streams of water on hot days, and *vomitoria* (oversized doors) were found at convenient spots for use by those wishing to relieve themselves of heavy foods. Aside from the statues adorning the arches, the Colosseum was solid, thick, and as sturdy as the empire liked to fancy itself. The structure was Vespasian's gift to the Romans, whose common saying remains to this day: "When the Colosseum falls, so falls Rome and all the world."

Columella, Lucius Junius Moderatus (fl. first century C.E.) *Agricultural writer who was a contemporary of Seneca*
From Gades, he served in the legions but then embarked on a career of writing on horticulture and nature. His first notable effort was *De re rustica (On Agriculture)*. In twelve books he examined the field, using Virgil's *Georgics* as a source and as an inspiration.

columns Columns were erected by the Romans to honor and revere an individual or his achievements. Although they were not as popular as other commemorative monuments (*see* ARCHES), during the Republic they appeared frequently. During the empire, several rulers designed massive columns, including:

Column of Trajan
Erected sometime between 108 and 113 C.E. to honor the emperor's great victory over the Dacians (101–106). Aside from a number of extant references in the *Dacian Commentaries* and DIO, the column is the invaluable source of information on the conflict. It stood in the new FORUM TRAIANO and was some 100 feet high. In a spiraling design, the entire campaign unfolded through elaborate carvings and reliefs, cut from the finest available marble. Scenes of soldiers, Dacians, the Danube, and battles dominated the curving outside of the structure, while Trajan's ashes were placed in the interior of the podium. A set of stairs led up to the top of the column, on which stood a statue nearly 30 feet high. Two libraries were constructed on either side of the column, one Greek, the other Latin.

Column of Antoninus Pius
Placed in the Campus Martius; a monument that adhered closely to Antoninus's firm belief in the preservation of classicism in art.

Column of Marcus Aurelius
Dedicated in 193 C.E. and built by order of the emperor's son, COMMODUS, the column was placed in what is now the Piazza Colonna. It resembled very closely the Column of Trajan, although its base is considered to be better proportioned. Like Trajan's monument, the column was carved with a series of magnificent reliefs spiraling along the shaft and depicting the wars raging along the Danube from 167 to 179. The battles grimly represented involved hardship and blood, with fallen legionaries alongside barbarians. The story of the "Miracle Rain" was carved into the column, the thunderstorms that proved to be so providential and beneficial to the Romans during one of these battles. Marcus himself appeared in the same harsh, somber relief as the rest of the figures. The monument came to be known as the Antonine Column. The column's base was repaired in 1589 C.E.

Comana (1) Town in CAPPADOCIA whose importance derived from its temples and the power of its high priests. These clerics ruled land and faithful, but the town attracted merchants and markets. In time the influx of new people helped break the priests' hold, and under VESPASIAN, Comana received a charter as part of a province.

Comana (2) City in the kingdom of PONTUS. Comana was the seat of the state religion, and the high priest there exercised considerable power. The strength of the religion faded after Pontus was annexed by Rome in the reign of Augustus (27 B.C.E.–14 C.E.).

Trajan's Column *(Courtesy Fr. Felix Just, S.J.)*

comes Title given to a high-ranking military or administrative figure in the late empire. As the court developed in size and in influence, the emperors established a casual practice of appointing loyal servants to various posts. This process has already been utilized elsewhere, as with the PREFECT OF THE PRAETORIAN GUARD and the AMICI PRINCIPIS. As the imperial system expanded, however, new offices were needed and centralization demanded change. The result was the creation of the rank of "comes" or count.

The *comites* (counts) became the leading officials of the Roman Empire. They wielded posts of every description, from the army to the civil service, while never surrendering their direct links and access to the emperors. Constantine took the final step of certifying the posts so that they were permanent fixtures of imperial government. The following is a list of the various types of *comes*:

> **comes Africae** Count in charge of the defense of Roman Africa.
> **comes Avernorum** Count in charge of the defenses of part of Gaul (GALLIA).

comes Britanniarum Count in charge of the defense of Roman Britain (BRITTANIA). This post presumably died out circa 410 C.E., when the last Romans in the isles sailed away forever.

comes dispositionum A deputy to the very powerful MAGISTER OFFICIORUM (master of offices); responsible for organizing the imperial calendar and preparing the correspondence for distribution to the proper offices for transcription.

comes domesticorum Head of the DOMESTICI, the imperial bodyguards of the emperor who were stationed in the palace. This count controlled both the horse and foot units.

comes Hispaniarum Count in charge of the defense of Roman Spain (HISPANIA).

comes Orientis Actually a member of the VICARII, this count had control of the large diocese of ORIENS.

comes privatae largitionis Official in charge of the privy purse, answerable and subordinate to the *comes rerum privatarum*.

comes rerum privatarum Powerful imperial official responsible for the private estates or holdings of the emperor and his family (RES PRIVATA). The count maintained the properties and collected all money from rent, of which most went to the public funds and some to the privy purse administered by the *comes privatae largitionis*.

comes sacrarum largitionum Master of the sacred Largesse, this count operated the imperial finances. He controlled all of the mints, collected senatorial taxes, custom duties, and some of the land taxes. He was also responsible for the yields of mines. The count provided budgets for the civil service and armies and supplied all uniforms.

> *See also* FINANCE; FISCUS; RATIONALIS; and RATIONIBUS, A.

comes sacrae vestis Count in charge of the wardrobe of the emperor.

See also PRAEPOSITUS SACRI CUBICULI.

Comitatenses One of the divisions of the army of the Late Roman Empire, forming a strong mobile force at the disposal of the emperor. In effect, these were field troops, as compared to the LIMITANEI and PALATINI, the border and bodyguards respectively. For a detailed examination, see LEGIONS.

Comitates Names given to the retinue of the emperor when he was in the field. These were the troops who actually accompanied the ruler on military campaigns. Service was distinctly more enjoyable than that on the frontiers. Composition of the *comitates* came from the COMITATENSES.

See also LEGIONS.

comites See COMES.

Comitia Tributa Venerable Republican institution empowered for centuries with the right to elect magistrates and to pass laws. It remained in existence into the imperial age but lost influence with the increasing authority of the emperors and eventually ceased to exist.

Commagene Small Euphrates-based kingdom of Seleucid origin, located between Armenia and Cilicia. Commagene survived the fall of the Seleucids in Syria and came to the attention of Rome in 63 B.C.E., when POMPEY THE GREAT reorganized the East. Antiochus I, the ruler of Commagene, was allowed to remain on the throne as a buffer between the Parthians and the Romans. His position, however, drew his kingdom into the wider conflict between those powers. Antiochus leaned toward PARTHIA, and in 36 B.C.E., during Marc Antony's ill-fated campaign, he gave aid to the retreating Parthians. Antiochus was thus deposed by the Romans in favor of his brother, Mithridates II.

Roman influence in the kingdom grew over the next decades. Mithridates and another notable monarch, Antiochus III, reigned over a troubled land as parties both internally and externally called for imperial annexation. In 17 C.E., Antiochus III died, and Commagene was placed under the control of praetors by Emperor Tiberius —Quintus Servius being the first. In 37 C.E., GAIUS CALIGULA returned the realm to its rightful claimants. Antiochus IV received back his kingdom, to which was added parts of Cilicia and Lycaonia, plus the sum of 100 million sesterces. Caligula proved an unreliable patron. In 40 he expelled the cruel Antiochus, not out of disappointment with his rule (he liked him) but because he wanted his money back. Claudius reinstated Antiochus, and the entire kingdom supported Rome in its next war against Parthia in 57. Emperor Vespasian decided to return to Tiberius's policies toward Commagene. In 72, he annexed small domains in the region and Commagene was among them. It was attached to the province of SYRIA.

Commius (fl. first century B.C.E.) *King of the Trebates, the Belgic tribe also called Atrebates*
Commius owed his kingship to Julius CAESAR and was, for as long as possible, his trusted ally. The Belgae had both communications and colonies in Britain, a fact not lost on Caesar as he planned his expedition to the isles in 55 B.C.E. Commius received a request to sail across the Channel to encourage the local British tribes to submit peacefully to Rome. His mission was a disaster, however, and Commius found himself imprisoned by the tribes in the region of Kent. Caesar landed, fought and won a few victories before Commius was released. He returned to his own land.

Much of Gaul planned to revolt against Rome. Commius joined the organizers, intending to bring with him the entire nation of Gallia Belgica. Labienus, Caesar's able lieutenant, discovered the plot and tried to remove Commius through murder. The Roman assassination failed, but Commius suffered a grievous injury, which aborted the involvement of his people in the uprising. Following the conclusion of the Gallic revolt, circa 51 B.C.E., Caesar aided a Belgic warlord, Correus, in stirring up dissent among the tribes of Gallia Belgica, although Correus is best known for his later opposition to Caesar. He died in an ambush during a revolt of the Belloraci. Caesar moved quickly against them, forcing Commius to settle with his old Roman ally. By 50 B.C.E. Commius was resolved to leave the land of Roman occupation. Commius sailed across the Channel again, this time as a free king in search of a domain. Commius settled near the Thames River and founded a dynasty in southern Britain, in coordination with the other Celtic tribes already there.

Commodian (fl. third century C.E.) *Christian poet*
Commodian authored two long poems, in loosely written hexameters but varying in quality and in accent. He probably came from Gaza and was a convert to Christianity, accepting the faith with great fanaticism.

Commodus (Marcus Aurelius Commodus Antoninus) (161–192 C.E.) *Emperor from 180 to 192 C.E.*
Aurelius Commodus proved to be an unworthy successor to his illustrious father, MARCUS AURELIUS. Born at Lanuvium as one of a pair of twins to Faustina (his brother died in 165), he was named Commodus after the original name of his adoptive uncle Lucius Verus. His education was the finest available for an imperial heir and, beginning in 166, Marcus Aurelius groomed him for the throne. In that year he was made Caesar (junior emperor), 10 years later imperator and in 177, Augustus (coruler of the empire).

From 177 to 180, Commodus studied under his father the art of statecraft in the field. Marcus Aurelius was managing the mammoth affairs of the empire while conducting a war with the Marcomanni on the Danube. The aged emperor's health finally collapsed, however, and on March 17, 180, Commodus succeeded to the throne at Vienna. At only 19, the new ruler at first wisely listened to the advisers of his late father but then started to give in to the flattery and intrigue of those courtiers who wanted to abandon the campaign and return home. The result was Commodus's first major, independent decision. He suspended the war along the Danube, which also meant that Rome's territorial ambitions had to be curbed. Commodus opted for a triumphal entry into Rome. Despite the pleas of his father's counselors, he returned to the capital, buying off the Marcomanni and other Germanic tribes with tributes and concessions, a policy that proved successful for a time.

A coin from the reign of Commodus; on the obverse side is a testament to Britannia. *(Hulton/Getty Archive)*

Shortly after his arrival in Rome, Commodus uncovered supposed plots against him, all hatched within the palace and even within his own family. His sister, Annia Lucilla, her cousin, Ummidius Quadratus, and her nephew-in-law, Quintianus, were all accused of conspiracy. Quadratus and Quintianus died immediately. Lucilla was exiled to Capri and later executed. Commodus was not satisfied with these deaths and became convinced that one of his two prefects of the PRAETORIAN GUARD, Tarrutenius Paternus, had also been a member of the conspiracy. Paternus joined the others in death.

The trend of Commodus's reign was set with Paternus's fall, for the successor in his power and rank was Tigidius PERENNIS, who had been his coprefect. Perennis was the first of several court officials who would gain considerable influence over the unstable emperor. Perennis allowed his master to indulge his taste for games and suspicion while he ran the empire virtually unchallenged. His sons received posts in Pannonia, while the prefect himself came to be hated by his court rivals. Inevitably he perished, in 185, along with his sons.

Marcus Aurelius CLEANDER followed him in imperial favor. A freedman, Cleander outmaneuvered his fellow prefects and tried to elevate himself even further by hoarding imperial grain. Riots broke out in Rome, and an indication of Commodus's casual rule was demonstrated by his near total ignorance of the city's upheavals. Alerted finally by his sister, Phadilla, his response was simple. He cut off Cleander's head and gave it to the crowd on a stick. Following Cleander's decapitation in 186, Aemilius Laetus took control of the Guard and watched Commodus deteriorate steadily. Dio called him a greater curse upon the Romans than any plague, and the Senate especially felt his hatred and suspicions. Commodus killed its members and seized their property at every opportunity, extorting money in return for keeping accused persons alive. The imperial treasury was being drained, and he found extreme means of refilling his purse.

He loved games of every sort and once ran 30 races in two hours. His true passion, however, was for gladiatorial exhibitions and athletic prowess. Animals of every description were slaughtered in groups; his excesses culminating in a 14-day bloodbath of races, gladiators, and massacres. For Commodus the games were a great personal triumph, fostering his own belief in his superiority.

Commodus believed himself to be Hercules reincarnated and a fighter worthy of heroic legend. Rome was renamed Commodianus, and the legions became known as Commodian. Another plot was formed against Commodus as a result. This time Laetus and the Chamberlain Eclectus were involved. Buoyed by Commodus's declaration that at his inauguration as consul on January 1, 193, he would march in full gladiatorial costume (he normally wore a lion skin and carried a club), even his concubine, Marcia, joined in the plot. They attempted to poison him but he showed every indication of surviving that attack. A wrestling companion was then brought to him to put an end to his life and reign. The companion, Narcissus, strangled Commodus in his bath on the night of January 31, 192.

The main historical event of his reign took place in Britain, where, in 184, the Antonine Wall was breached by the Caledonians. Ulpius Marcellus had to campaign three times in order to evict the invaders. Commodus's body was placed in the mausoleum of Hadrian as the Senate greeted the news of his death with glee. The first natural heir to succeed to the throne, Commodus bequeathed chaos to coming generations. Pertinax followed him as emperor, but only a short time later the empire would be auctioned off to the highest bidder.

communication See CURSUS PUBLICUS, MANSIONES, TRANSPORTATION, VIA; *see also* LITERATURE and WRITING INSTRUMENTS.

concilia The councils (singular, *concilium*) of each province, established to keep Rome informed of regional needs and problems and to propagate the cult of Rome and the emperors. Under the Republic the occupied territories had no voice with which to express opinions or complaints, except for infrequent and ineffective delegations of local officials. The first emperor, Augustus, desired channels of communication with the provinces when his reign began (27 B.C.E.). He took steps to ensure that most provinces possessed a board or congress of some sort, and the result was the *concilia*.

The *concilia* fulfilled two major functions. Augustus believed that the empire should be efficient, yet allow a certain amount of native self-expression in a given region, coupled with participation in the grand imperial framework of events and policies. The *concilia* in each territory provided both the voice of the province and the means by which the IMPERIAL CULT could be fostered.

The *concilia* (or *koina* in the East) were not wholly new. They had existed in some form in various kingdoms of Asia Minor, and even Julius Caesar had summoned notable tribal chiefs to participate in a conference in Gaul. In the West, however, the form of councils was less known and hence more malleable to Roman influence.

One of the first *concilia* in the West originated in 12 B.C.E. in Gallia Comata. By the time Vespasian ruled the Roman world (69–79 B.C.E.), all of the various parts of the empire had councils. Exceptions to this were Egypt and those groups of provinces (such as in Gaul) where one congress represented a broad stretch of interests and concerns along racial or cultural lines, rather than political ones.

Delegates from each city traveled to a major center and elected its *concilium* and an officer to serve as president. The council head administered secular affairs and directed the annual grand festival, with games, in honor of Rome and the emperor. Regular business would also be conducted and dispatches to Rome drafted. Such dispatches proved invaluable in the first century C.E. in providing an accurate assessment of the provinces. Also, governors found themselves suddenly answerable to the Senate and the emperor for administering affairs incorrectly or harshly. In 23 C.E., for example, Lucilius Capito, procurator of Asia, was accused and tried for overstepping his authority. The *concilia* lacked basic powers, however. The members could not enact legislation and relied upon imperial goodwill in all matters. When the emperor became isolated or absent, as in years of crisis, the role of the *concilia* declined.

Condianus, Sextus Quintilius *See* the QUINTILII BROTHERS.

Condrusi Germanic people residing in Gallia Belgica. They were clients of the TREVIRI.

conductores *See* FARMING.

congiarium Name (plural: *congiaria*) for the gifts of oil, wine, or other goods distributed to the general populace by public officials. During the empire it became the custom for rulers to make most gifts in money upon the occasion of a great victory, an imperial birthday, or some other public celebration.

Consilium Principis Name given to the Council of State, the body of advisers who helped the emperors decide important legal and administrative matters until the beginning of the fourth century C.E. A tradition actually starting in the Republic and carried on by the emperors, Augustus made it a habit to call together senators, Equestrians, and friends (*amici Caesaris*).

Tiberius had his own board, which appealed to him to hand over PISO to the Senate in 20 C.E. He also added several legal experts, a precedent followed by Claudius. It

was Hadrian, however, who widened the legal jurisdiction of the Consilium and opened it to greater membership on the part of jurists. Legal technicians such as Julian, Papinian, and Ulpian found their roles expanded in direct proportion to the judicial demands of the growing imperial administration. Severus Alexander (ruled 222–235 C.E.) further organized his consilium by having a regular number of 70 members, including senators, Equestrians, and some 20 priests. The Equestrians played a major role, no more so than in their most important officeholder, the Praetorian prefect. Not only were the prefects powerful legal administrators (Ulpian and Papinian were officeholders), but by the middle of the third century C.E. they ran the affairs of the consilium by virtue of their political positions and their special role of *amici principis*. Diocletian changed the entire council when he created the Consistorium.

Consistorium The council of advisers during the reigns of Diocletian, Constantine, and their successors. The Consistorium evolved out of the CONSILIUM PRINCIPIS of the early and middle empire but differed in several ways from its predecessor. In the past, appointments were made in an ad hoc fashion; members were summoned to deal with a crisis, and their powers lasted only for the duration of that emergency. The new council had fixed members with permanent roles. This policy reflected the purposeful reorganization of the imperial court.

Members of the Consistorium included all major officers of the empire. There were the MAGISTER OFFICIORUM (master of offices), the *comes rerum privatarum* (master of the privy purse), the *praefectus praetorio praesens* (Praetorian prefect of the capital), the PRAEPOSITUS SACRI CUBICULI (grand chamberlain), the *comes sacrarum largitionum* (master of the sacred largesse), the QUAESTOR SACRI PALATII (imperial legal adviser), and minor officials. The emperor normally presided over the meetings, but in his absence the quaestor was in charge, reporting to the emperor all decisions and inspecting the minutes taken down by the NOTARII. Membership was influential, and the name *consistorians* was granted to each one. Constantine called the council the Sacrum Consistorium to differentiate it from the Consilium Principis. As the name would indicate, the Consistorium stood in the emperor's presence while the old Consilium sat.

Constans, Flavius Julius (320–350 C.E.) *Emperor of Italy, Illyricum, and Africa from 337 to 350 C.E.*
The youngest son of Constantine the Great and Fausta, he shared in the division of the empire into three parts, with his brothers Constantine II and Constantius II as partners. His designated territory included Italy, Illyricum, and Africa, although for a time he also controlled Greece and Constantinople. Constans's brother, Constantine II, coveted Italy, and in 340 marched against

the capital while Constans was away. The conflict between the two had been growing; Constans had even given Constantinople back to his other brother, Constantius, in 339 in hopes of winning his support. It proved unnecessary, for the legions of Constantine were crushed near Aquileia in 340, and Constantine died.

Two brothers now owned the world, and trouble flared between them immediately. They quarreled bitterly over Christian doctrines, with Constantius favoring the Arians and Constans the tenets of the Nicene Creed. Constans championed the anti-Arian cause of Athanasius, especially at the Council of Serdica in 342. A reconciliation was made in 346.

Constans kept busy with campaigns and with travels throughout his lands. He crushed the Franks in 342 and visited Britain in 343, the last emperor to do so. His reign, according to the historian Aurelius Victor, was tyrannical and unpopular, especially among the military. In 350, an officer named Magnentius rebelled, and Constans fled. Soldiers caught up with him and put him to death.

Constantia (fl. early fourth century C.E.) *Wife of the co-emperor Licinianus Licinius, from 313 to 325 C.E.*

Constantia was the daughter of Emperor Constantius I and Theodora, and the sister of CONSTANTINE the Great. Her marriage to LICINIUS came about as a result of political expediency, as Constantine and Licinius united against the influence of the other emperors of their era, Maxentius and Maximin Daia. The betrothal was made in 310 and the wedding was held at Mediolanum (Milan) in 313.

Little is known of her marriage. A child was born to the couple, but great events overshadowed its life. In 323–324, war erupted between Licinius and her brother, culminating in Constantine's victory at the battle of ADRIANOPLE. Constantia pleaded for her husband's life, and Constantine relented, exiling Licinius to Salonica. A year later Licinius was put to death. His son was killed in 326. Constantia henceforth lived in the palace as a widow. Her relations with Constantine were good; she convinced him to hear Arius (she was one of his followers) and to accept her confessor, an Arian, as part of a deathbed wish.

Constantina (d. 354 C.E.) *Known also as Constantia, the daughter of Constantine the Great*

Constantina was the wife of her cousin, King Hannibalianus (335–337), and then wife of another cousin, Gallus Caesar (351–354). After the end of her marriage to Hannibalianus, who was the king of Armenia and Pontus, she returned to the West and played a part in the events following the death of her brother Constans in 350.

Fearing the rise of Magnentius in Gaul, Constantina persuaded the aged MAGISTER PEDITUM, Vetranio, to help contain the usurper. Subsequently she was married to Gallus Caesar, recently elevated to that title by Constantius II. The new couple traveled east to maintain the Syrian region for Constantius while he moved against Magnentius.

Gallus proved to be cruel and incompetent, and Constantina earned the reputation of being a wicked abettor of his crimes. Ammianus Marcellinus called her one of the Furies, insatiable for blood, and an expert in causing harm and unhappiness. Appalled at events in the East, Constantius recalled Gallus Caesar after a palace revolt. Constantina set out to defend her husband but died in Bithynia in 354, before she could help. Gallus soon joined her.

Constantine ("the Great" Flavius Valerius Constantinus) (c. 285–337 C.E.) *Joint emperor from 306 to 323 and sole emperor from 324 to 337*

Flavius Valerius Constantinus transformed the Roman Empire and helped shape the future course of Western civilization.

Constantine was born at Naissus in Upper Dacia, to CONSTANTIUS I CHLORUS and an innkeeper's daughter, Helena. He received a good education and served at the court of DIOCLETIAN after 293, when Constantius became a Caesar (junior emperor) in the TETRARCHY. As a soldier he displayed some skill and joined the other Caesar, GALERIUS, in his campaigns against the Persians. Galerius kept Constantine attached to his staff as a comfortable hostage until 305, when the two AUGUSTI (senior emperors), Diocletian and MAXIMIAN, abdicated in favor of the two Caesars.

In 306, trouble in Britain caused Constantine to travel to join his father in Gaul; they crossed the Channel and made war on the Picts. Constantius died at Eburacum (York) on July 25, 306, and with the legions on hand, Constantine was declared his heir. Galerius received word and with little choice accepted Constantine's rise. He insisted that Constantine be elevated only to the rank of Caesar, however, not that of Augustus. The new Caesar maneuvered around the title by marrying FAUSTA, the daughter of the retired Emperor Maximian, and gaining his blessing to be Augustus over Britain and Gaul.

In 306, Maximian's son, MAXENTIUS, usurped control of Rome, and Constantine made an alliance immediately as a counter to the considerable influence of Galerius in the East. Three years later he was dragged into the quarrels between Maximian and his son, granting sanctuary to the father in Gaul when he was evicted from Italy.

After an unsuccessful conference at Carnuntum in 308, at which time Galerius tried to strip him of his title, Constantine launched several expeditions against the Alamanni and the Franks along the Rhine. Further campaigns in German territory were cut short when word arrived that Maximian had tried to seize power and was cornered in Massilia. Constantine immediately besieged him, compelled him to surrender and probably put him

A gold medallion of Constantine I, the Great, struck early 327 at Thessalonica *(Courtesy, Historical Coins, Inc.)*

to death in 310. After disposing of his father-in-law, Constantine felt the need to rehabilitate his family origins. He decided that a direct, hereditary line to Emperor CLAUDIUS II GOTHICUS would supply the needed legitimacy; this claim was perpetuated by the vast imperial machine. Maximian's demise was joined in 311 by that of Galerius. Four main potentates now ruled the world: Constantine in Gaul and Britain as well as in Spain; Maxentius in Italy and parts of Africa; LICINIUS in the Danube area; and Maximin Daia (Maximinus II Daia) in the East.

Constantine and Licinius formed an uneasy alliance against Maximin Daia and Maxentius, and in 312 hostilities erupted when Constantine took the chance of marching against Maxentius. His legions pressed over the Alps, and in a series of victories he pushed Maxentius to the very gates of Rome. There, in a bloody struggle, the future of the empire was decided on October 28 at the battle of MILVIAN BRIDGE. Constantine proved victorious and entered the Eternal City. Licinius greeted the success of his ally with enthusiasm. In 313 he married Constantine's sister CONSTANTIA and set out with an army to destroy Maximin Daia. Two emperors now controlled the East and the West, but even this proved one too many.

By 316, new struggles gripped the Roman world as Constantine and Licinius vied for control of the Balkans. Victory for Constantine in one battle was not followed by a string of successes, and a temporary peace established new frontiers. In 323, Constantine made war upon the Goths in the Danube area, using his pursuit of the enemy as an excuse to openly violate the borders. The following year a final campaign was launched, and Constantine and Licinius collided at ADRIANOPLE on July 3, 324. Licinius's army broke; after losing at sea on September 8 of that year, he surrendered. The Roman Empire was now in the hands of one man.

Diocletian had started the many processes of centralization, and Constantine first embraced them and then expanded on them. First he subjected the bureaucracy to a massive overhaul. All ministries were under the command of the MAGISTER OFFICIORUM (master of offices), who supervised the rapidly centralized government. Although this trend had been toward a greater imperial authority, under Constantine's direction the bureaus grew even weightier, more demanding but more efficient.

Officers of the civil service rose in rank to wield influence and titles. Finances were administered by the *comes sacrarum largitionum* (count of the sacred largesse) and the *comes privatae largitionis* (count of the privy purse) *(see comes)*. In legal matters Constantine relied upon the Jurists and his QUAESTER SACRI PALATI (chief legal adviser). All of these reforms found body and substance in the altered CONSILIUM PRINCIPIS, now called the CONSISTORIUM. This council of permanent magistrates and ministers framed the legislative enactments of the imperial will and brought all of the provinces under control. The regions of the empire were still under the authority of prefectures, but the prefects themselves were more answerable to the imperial house, and the functions of these offices were altered.

Following the battle at Milvian Bridge, Constantine destroyed the CASTRA PRAETORIA, the centuries-old barracks of the PRAETORIAN GUARD. The Praetorians were disbanded and their prefects stripped of military duties. They retained their political and legal powers, however, overseeing the DIOCESE of the prefecture. In the place of the Guard, the DOMESTICI of Diocletian, along with the PALATINI, emerged as the military powers.

Now Constantine recognized the need to make a parallel military structure that would mirror the improved governmental body. He thus organized the army into two main classes, the COMITATENSES and the LIMITANEI. The Comitatenses was the emperor's mobile army. The Limitanei stood as the static frontier troops, ready to defend the imperial domains. This military machine was entrusted by Constantine to very reliable officers: the MAGISTER MILITUM (master of soldiers), the MAGISTER PEDITUM (master of infantry), and *magister equitum* (master of cavalry). Although supposedly under the watchful eyes of the rulers, in the late fourth century and during the fifth century, the *magister militum* would seize unequaled supremacy in the Western Empire and considerable power in the Eastern Empire.

Constantine thus succeeded in concretizing the separation between his government, or administration, and the military and sought a new capital city in the East to secure his enlarged frontiers. Constantine settled upon a site that was well situated both east and west. It possessed a splendid harbor and rested on the great continental dividing line, the Bosporus. The city was Byzantium, and between 324 and 330, it changed into the great Christian city, CONSTANTINOPLE. According to legend, Constantine walked out the dimensions of the city personally, with the Spear of LONGINUS in hand, stopping only when the voice of God told him he had measured enough area. Such stories maintained Constantine's personal sense of debt to the God of the Christians. In 312, his conversion had already begun, and he attributed his victory at Milvian Bridge to this deity's intervention. The imperial world henceforth would be a Christian one.

In 313, Constantine had agreed with Licinius to cease all persecution of Christians. With his great EDICT OF MILAN, a more comprehensive decree than the Edict of Serdica, Constantine became a patron of Christianity and, in many ways, its head. It was he who influenced the proceedings of the council at Arles in 314, and especially that at Nicaea in 325, and it was he who fought the heresies of DONATUS and ARIUS. Christianity was encouraged in the government, the masses and the army. Great edifices were constructed in Rome and in Constantinople, and this new city represented the temporal power of the creed. Finally, in May of 337, Constantine himself was baptized.

Constantine's personal life was troubled. With his wife Minervina he had a son Crispus, and then with Fausta had three more sons: CONSTANTINE II, CONSTANTIUS II, and CONSTANS. In 326, Constantine executed Crispus at Pola, while on his way to Italy, and a little later put Fausta to death by suffocation for allegedly having an affair. The question of succession, however, plagued him.

With three sons, civil war after his death would have been unavoidable, hence the division of the empire into three parts, a move that only delayed the inevitable conflict among the siblings. Furthermore, Constantine's death in 337 touched off a pogrom in the palace; much of his family faced extermination to reduce the number of groups of influence so common during his reign. Constantine's institutions, however, were so solid and so organized that they would survive civil wars, barbarian invasions, theological conflagrations, and incompetent emperors. In the West the empire would last another century, while Constantinople stood for a millennium.

Constantine was described as pious, intelligent, and dignified by his biographer EUSEBIUS. He certainly excelled intellectually, not necessarily in philosophy or theology but in the ways of war and in the art of leading others. A ruthless character was tempered by the Christian doctrine. A complex personality, Constantine stood as the cornerstone of a new age.

See also CHRISTIANITY; for other reforms, see also COINAGE; FINANCE.

Suggested Readings: Barnes, Timothy D. *Constantine and Eusebius.* Cambridge, Mass.: Harvard University Press, 1981; Baus, Karl. *From the Apostolic Community to Constantine.* Vol. 1 of *History of the Church* edited by Hubert Jedin and John P. Dolan. New York: Crossroad, 1982; Bowder, Diana. *The Age of Constantine and Julian.* London: Elek, 1978; Burckhardt, Jacob. *The Age of Constan-*tine the Great. Berkeley and Los Angeles: University of California Press, 1983; Eusebius. *Life of Constantine* Clarendon Ancient History Series. Oxford, U.K.: Oxford University Press, 1999; Grant, Michael. *Constantine the Great.* New York: Scribner's, 1994; Jones, A. H. M. *Constantine and the Conversion of Europe.* Toronto: University of Toronto Press, 1979.

Constantine II (317–340 C.E.) *Joint emperor from 337 to 340 C.E.*
The son of CONSTANTINE the Great and Fausta, the eldest of three, Constantine II was born at Arles. Named a Caesar and eventually sharing in the division of the empire upon his father's death in 337, he joined his brothers CONSTANTIUS II and CONSTANS as masters of the world. He received Gaul, Britain, Spain, and a small part of Africa. He was never fully satisfied, coveting the territories of Constans in Italy and Constantius in the East. In 340, Constantine II marched on Constans but suffered defeat in a battle near Aquileia and died.

Constantine III (d. 411 C.E.) *The third usurper proclaimed by the legions of Britain in 407 C.E.*
Constantine III was a common soldier with a fortuitous name. He succeeded the murdered Marcus and Gratian as leader of the legions in the isles. Hoping to ensure his own position, he sailed to Gaul with a large army. Without any competent general in Gaul to resist him, he seized both the region and the troops. His rule over Gaul proved competent, inflicting defeats upon the local barbarians and negotiating agreements with the Alamanni and probably the Burgundians. HONORIUS, emperor of the West, finally took notice when the major city of Arles fell to the usurper, who then marched on Spain. The only response Honorius could make was to accept an offer to legitimize Constantine's claim to rule his conquered lands. An attempt to enter Italy proved unsuccessful, and in 411, Constantine's trusted general in Spain, Gerontius, rebelled. Gerontius elevated his own candidate for emperor, Maximus. He then invaded Gaul, killing Constantine's first-born son Constans at Vienne and besieging Constantine and his other son, Julian, at Arles. Honorius took up the siege, sending his MAGISTER MILITUM, Constantius, to take command. Hoping to save himself, Constantine fled to the sanctuary of the church, was ordained a priest and surrendered to the mercy of Honorius. Disregarding the clerical robes, the emperor put Constantine to death in September of 411.

Constantinople Capital of the Eastern Roman Empire; replacing Rome as the heart of imperial power, it maintained influence and stability in the face of the decline of the West.

In 324 C.E., CONSTANTINE the Great defeated rival emperor LICINIUS at the battle of ADRIANOPLE, laying claim to sole mastery over the entire Roman Empire. He recognized the need for a new capital to replace Rome, which could no longer serve as the center of defense for the widely spread frontiers on the Rhine and Danube and in the East. A new location had to be found, one easily fortified and centrally situated. In addition, Constantine planned not only to expand Diocletian's sweeping reforms but also envisioned an entirely new world for mankind and planned to overcome the dangerous influences of Rome, which had destroyed other emperors, by establishing a new model for the empire. At the same time, Rome stood for the paganism of centuries, and Constantine's faith demanded a new setting, where Christianity could flourish.

Bithynia and Nicomedia and other places in Asia had appeal, but none could be defended adequately, and some even presented themselves as targets for Persian attack. Constantine decided on Byzantium, a small city on the edge of the Golden Horn, on the Strait of the Bosporus, a bridge between East and West. Legendary accounts state that Constantine arrived there in November of 324 to march off the measurements for the extended building program, his yardstick being the "Hand of God." Using the Lance of LONGINUS, the relic that was reported to have pierced the side of Christ while he was on the cross, the emperor started walking from Byzantium; when he stopped two miles later, he gave orders to start construction. Constantinople had seven hills and 14 quarters, as did Rome, and like that city it could not be built in a day. Six years of work followed its founding, and it was not until May 11, 330, that Constantine could declare the construction completed, and officially renamed the city, although changes and modifications never ceased.

Byzantium had been a small community set on a promontory between the Golden Horn and the Sea of Marmara. In 194, the town had become embroiled in the war between the imperial claimants Septimius SEVERUS and PESCENNIUS NIGER. After a long and bitter siege, Severus took the walls, and the town fell and suffered the humiliations of defeat. Constantine chose the site, in part because the rocks along its southern shore crushed vessels attempting to land outside the harbor, and the currents of the Bosporus made navigation difficult and sinkings frequent. About $3^1/_2$ miles at its widest, the cir-

An engraving representing Christian Constantinople *(Hulton/Getty Archive)*

cumference of the city was some 15 miles. Constantine erected his new edifices around the original structures, eventually called the Augusteum, in honor of his mother Helena.

As the most prominent part of the jutting land mass and the most easily defended, the Augusteum became the spoke in a circle of urban growth that housed the most important offices of state. Nearby were the imperial palaces, the hippodrome and several of the great forums. The emperors and their families resided in the palaces, accompanied by government bureaucrats and ministers, the SCRINARII. Also, the CONSISTORIUM met there, and close by the Senate convened. The hippodrome served as the entertainment center for all residents. Smaller than the Circus Maximus, on which it was based, the hippodrome offered great games, chariot races, and lavish spectacles, and seated more than 60,000.

In the finest Roman tradition, several forums were erected to allow public assemblies and shopping areas, and no expense was spared in bringing the finest artisans and intellectuals to the city. As in Rome, columns adorned the skyline. In the Forum of Constantine the emperor was made eternal, with his own head mounted on top of a statue of Apollo at the peak of a column. In the Forum Tauri (from the reign of THEODOSIUS I), one of the emperor's columns towered above the landscape. Other monuments in the city included those dedicated to ARCADIUS, Aelia EUDOXIA, and MARCIAN, as well as those of JUSTINIAN, of a later era. Near the Forum Tauri was the city's seat of learning, the Capitolium. There young from the various provinces studied under the foremost rhetoricians, grammarians, philosophers, and academicians of the time. In 425, THEODOSIUS II certified the University of Constantinople, which rivaled those of Antioch, Alexandria, and, of course. Athens.

Three periods of growth took place within its borders. The first, from 324 to 330, was when Constantine's Wall established the perimeters from the Propontis to the Golden Horn. The second was from 330 to about 413, when the population expanded beyond the walls and into the adjoining eastern districts. The last period of growth was from 413 to a time well beyond the fall of the Roman Empire in the West, when the walls established newer and wider borders.

Access could be gained through the ports, harbors, or gates. The Golden Horn entrances included posts along the seawall and in the harbor of Prosphorion. Two main harbors served Propontis, the Theodosius and the Julian. Chains could be used to seal off the mouths of these harbors. As for the walls, the grand portal of Constantine's Wall was the Golden Gate. Built by Theodosius I, the gate commemorated his victory over Maximus the usurper in 388. A second Golden Gate loomed at the southern end of the Anthemian Walls (eventually renamed in honor of Theodosius). In the wider series of fortifications, the gates could be used either by the civil-

ian population or the military, depending upon classification. There were five entrances for the army and numerous ones for everyone else.

Entering the Golden Gate, a traveler would proceed north along the Middle Way, the road cutting through the city all the way to the Church of Saint Sophia. It crossed the Lycus River near the harbor of Theodosius and passed through most of the forums and many of the other buildings of importance, including the hippodrome and the Great Palace and the Palace of Hormisdas, constructed during Constantine's reign to house a Persian prince.

As the center of the Eastern Roman Empire, Constantinople had a population to rival Rome's—anywhere from 500,000 to 800,000 people. Aqueducts supplied the water needs, and Egypt's fields provided the food. When the number of inhabitants began to outgrow the original boundaries of the city, towns such as Chrysopolis and Chalcedon could assume some of the population burdens. But a more permanent solution had to be found. At the same time, Constantinople needed even more defensive strength in the fourth and fifth centuries C.E., as barbarians pillaged in the West and turned on the eastern borders.

Thus, in the first years of the reign of young Theodosius II, his Praetorian prefect ANTHEMIUS took upon himself (c. 408–414) the task of creating the strong fortifications still standing today. Anthemius placed the new wall approximately one mile to the west, along a wider line. Towers and gates, both civil and military, and fortified positions dotted this new structure.

Cyrus, a popular Praetorian prefect and prefect of the city (439–441), extended the northern wall. No longer relying upon the Blachernae Palace for an anchor, it was linked to the seawall, defending the approaches to the city along the entire coastline. In the middle of the fifth century, a violent earthquake (not uncommon) shook the walls, and a Praetorian prefect by the name of Constantine ordered repairs to be made immediately. Another, smaller outer wall was added. The capacity to withstand attack became essential during the chaotic era of the fourth century. The Huns remained as a constant threat to Constantinople, as did other barbarian tribes. But the city served as a constant bulwark throughout the late Roman Empire.

Constantine had built his city as a point from which Christianity could spread to the entire world. Thus the city became a center of churches, reflecting the changes within the Roman Empire. The greatest religious structure was Saint Sophia's Church. Finished around 360, it represented the ideal of Great Wisdom. The church stood until the time of Justinian (ruled 527–565), when the Nika Revolt destroyed it. Its successor was greater than the original. Other magnificent churches included (through the ages) the Holy Apostles, St. Euphemia, Theotokos, St. Irene, St. Thomas, St. Laurentius, St. Diamed, and Theotokos Hodegetria, among others.

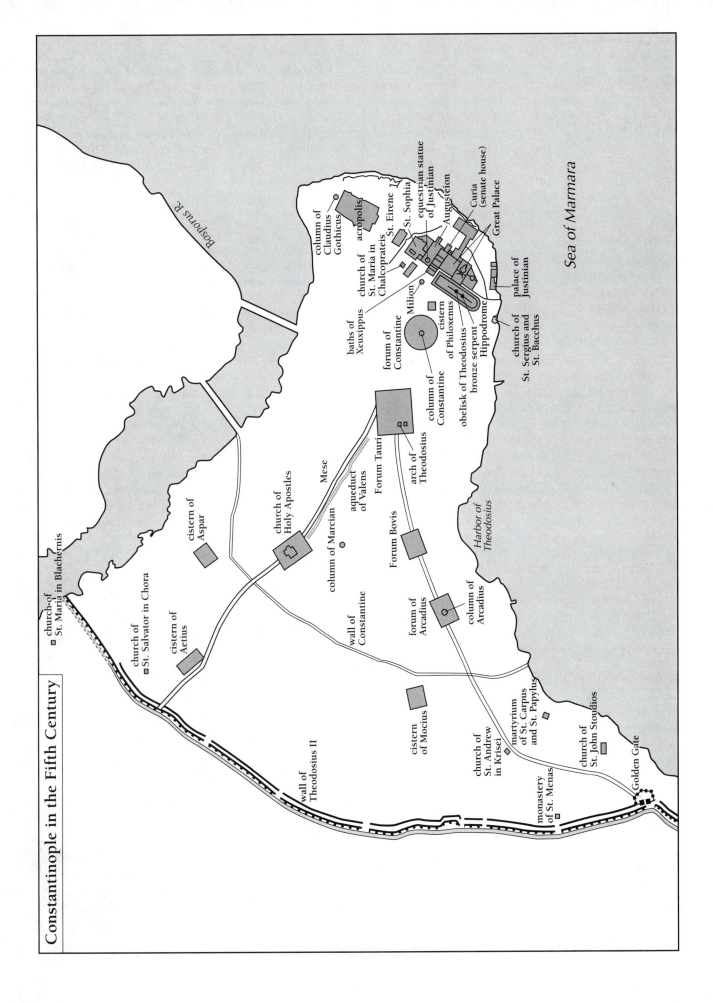

Constantinople in the Fifth Century

Bosporus R.

Sea of Marmara

church of St. Maria in Blachernis
church of St. Salvator in Chora
cistern of Aetius
cistern of Aspar
column of Claudius Gothicus
acropolis
baths of Xeuxippus
church of St. Maria in Chalcoprateis
St. Eirene
St. Sophia
equestrian statue of Justinian
Augustéion
Curia (senate house)
Great Palace
palace of Justinian
church of St. Sergius and St. Bacchus
Milion
cistern of Philoxenus
column of Constantine
forum of Constantine
obelisk of Theodosius
bronze serpent
Hippodrome
church of Holy Apostles
Mese
aqueduct of Valens
column of Marcian
Forum Tauri
arch of Theodosius
Forum Bovis
Harbor of Theodosius
wall of Constantine
forum of Arcadius
column of Arcadius
cistern of Mocius
church of St. Andrew in Krisei
martyrium of St. Carpus and St. Papylus
monastery of St. Menas
church of St. John Stoudios
wall of Theodosius II
Golden Gate

A bastion of spiritual authority, Constantinople played a significant role in the evolution of Christian doctrine. From its thrones the emperors and empresses directed the implementation of Christianity as the religion of the state. And in bitter theological feuds with such heresies as ARIANISM, Donatism, and Novatianism, the patriarch of Constantinople vied for influence with the emperors, as Antioch, Alexandria, and Rome formed joint and competing alliances.

Theodosius I summoned the Council of Constantinople in 381 to reaffirm the Nicene Creed. Theodosius II listened to both sides of a dispute over the nature of Christ but succumbed to the bribes and threats of CYRIL OF ALEXANDRIA over the Nestorians.

Constantinople remained the capital of the Eastern Empire until the fall of the West circa 476, and served as the home of the Byzantine rulers until 1453. In that year, it was finally captured by the Turks.

Constantius I Chlorus (d. 306 C.E.) *Joint emperor in the West from 293 to 306 C.E.; one of the founders of the new imperial system of Diocletian (the Tetrarchy)*

Constantius probably came from the Danube region and was not a descendant of Claudius II Gothicus, as would be claimed by his self-legitimizing son, CONSTANTINE the Great. Embarking on a career in the army, Constantius I became the governor of Dalmatia and then, sometime around 293, PREFECT OF THE PRAETORIAN GUARD. He was chosen for even higher office and had moved toward that ambition by removing his first wife, Helena, an innkeeper's daughter, in favor of Theodora, daughter of Diocletian's coemperor Maximian.

In 293, as part of the tetrachy system, Diocletian named Constantius to be Caesar (junior emperor), assisting Maximian in the West, while Galerius served Diocletian in the East. His territory included Gaul and Britain. His first task was to deal with a usurper, the dangerous admiral CARAUSIUS, who controlled northern Gaul and Britain. Constantius blocked part of the admiral's fleet at Gesoriacum (Boulogne); in 293, Carausius died at the hands of his minister, Allectus. In 296, Constantius sailed to Britain with his Praetorian Prefect ASCLEPIODOTUS. While he tried unsuccessfully to land, Asclepiodotus destroyed Allectus in battle. Constantius seized the opportunity and celebrated in great triumph.

Diocletian abdicated in 305, as did Maximian. Their successors were Constantius and Galerius. Galerius ruled the East while Constantius possessed Spain, along with Gaul and Britain. The tetrarchy so carefully established was showing signs of strain, and Galerius clearly had the advantage. Not only did he dominate the East, but Constantius's son, Constantine (the son of Helena), was at his court as a hostage. Only the barbarian invasions of Britain (*see* PICTS) gave Constantius an excuse to have his son returned to him. Constantine fled to his father, and in 306 they repelled the Picts. On July 25, 306, Constan-

tius I Chlorus died at Eburacum (York), leaving Constantine to face Galerius alone. He did not depart without having left his son considerable resources. Constantius had proved himself to be an able if not beloved emperor. He strengthened the Rhine frontier and did extensive building at Treviri (*see* TRIER). Further, his son was bright, well-educated, and supported by experienced and devoted legions.

Constantius II (317–361 C.E.) *Joint emperor from 337 to 350 C.E. and sole emperor of Rome from 350 to 361*

Constantius was the most gifted son of CONSTANTINE the Great and FAUSTA. He was born in Illyricum, named Caesar (junior emperor) in 324 and given Antioch to administer in 333. Upon his father's death in 337, he played a major part in the massacre of all parties of influence in the imperial family; the empire was then partitioned among himself and his two brothers, Constans and Constantine II. He received the East, minus (briefly) Armenia and Constantinople, which belonged for a time to HANNIBALIANUS, Constantine's nephew, and to Constans, respectively.

The first years of independent rule were filled with campaigns against the Persians under Shapur II, but, starting in 350, his attention turned to the West. In 340, the triple division of the empire ended when Constantine II died while trying to overthrow Constans in Italy. Until 350, the two remaining brothers ruled the world; in that year, however, the usurper Magnentius killed Constans.

Emperor Constantius I Chlorus *(Hulton/Getty Archive)*

Tension gripped the domain of Constantius, for the whole West, with its legions, could have hailed Magnentius as emperor. Fortunately, Constantina, daughter of Constantine and Constantius's sister, convinced the MAGISTER PEDITUM, Vetranio, to allow himself to be hailed as Augustus, as a counterweight to Magnentius. The move, obviously calculated to aid her brother, proved very successful. Magnentius lost momentum, and Vetranio stepped down, retiring to Prusa in Bithynia. Strengthened by the addition of the legions along the Danube, Constantius crushed Magnentius in battle (*see* MURSA MAJOR) in 351. The usurper committed suicide in 353, leaving Constantius the undisputed master.

He returned to campaigning, defeating the Sarmatians and the Quadi on the Danube frontier. Persia saw further action, and in 359, he attacked Mesopotamia. Clearly, as a general, Constantius II possessed remarkable skills, defeating the Frankish king Silvanus, the Suevi, the Sarmatians, the Quadi, and the Persians all in a span of several years.

Constantius recognized the need to appoint a Caesar who could aid him in ruling regions that he could not visit. His first choice, Gallus, married the emperor's sister Constantia in 351, but was tyrannical as the ruler of Antioch and had to be put to death in 354. Constantine then appointed JULIAN, Gallus's half-brother, to be Caesar in the West, marrying him to his sister Helena. Julian was competent and loved by the army. When Constantius sent orders for him to dispatch reinforcements in 360 to help in the Persian wars, the legions in the West revolted, declaring Julian their ruler. Despite his triumphant entry into Rome in 357, Constantius knew that the threat to his reign was legitimate. He organized an expeditionary force and headed toward a confrontation with Julian. While marching through Cilicia, Constantius II succumbed to a fever near Tarsus, dying on October 5, 361.

Constantius believed in the cause of ARIANISM. He protected the Arians from the start and then differed vehemently with his orthodox brother Constans on the future of Christianity. At the Council of Serdica in 342, some differences were resolved, but no substantial harmony could be achieved until 346, when war nearly erupted. Constantius received a free hand in theological matters following Constans's death in 350. Henceforth the Arians dominated religious affairs at court. Athanasius, the anti-Arian champion, was removed from his seat as the bishop of Alexandria in 356, and the emperor named many Arian prelates to succeed to the major sees in Christendom. Ammianus Marcellinus, who lived and served in the army of that era, wrote extensively of Constantius's character and achievements.

Constantius III (d. 421 C.E.) *Joint emperor in the West in 421*

Constantius III was a *MAGISTER MILITUM* who rose to claim the throne, albeit briefly. Born in the Danube region, he entered upon a military career and by 411 had earned the *magister militum* rank under Emperor Honorius. For the next 10 years Constantius administered most of the Western Empire, dealing with the crises of the period. In 410, he became the primary factor in the destruction of the usurper Constantine III, marching into Gaul with his lieutenant, Ulfilas, and besieging Constantine at Arles. In 411, he crushed an African-based rebel, Heraclianus, before turning to the pressing problem of the Visigoths in Gaul and in Spain.

Athaulf, successor of Alaric as king of the Visigoths, had established a domain in Gaul and had not only refused to return Honorius's sister, GALLA PLACIDIA, but also set up Priscus Attalus as an imperial claimant and married Placidia in 414. Constantius crushed Attalus in southern Gaul. By 415, Athaulf was dead, and the new Visigoth king, Wallia, negotiated a peace with Honorius. Galla Placidia returned to her brother. Out of political need she was married early in 417 to Constantius. Despite her reluctance, she bore him two children, one of whom became Valentinian III, emperor from 425 to 455. With such a union, and in recognition of the overwhelming power at his disposal, Honorius elevated Constantius to the rank of co-emperor or Augustus on February 8, 421. He ruled only from February to September.

Constantius, Julius (d. 337 C.E.) *A half-brother of Constantine the Great*

The son of CONSTANTIUS I CHLORUS and his second wife, Theodora, Constantius suffered from court intrigues and retired in semi-exile to Toulouse and Corinth but profited from political rehabilitation in 335. CONSTANTINE made him a patrician and a consul in that year, and he emerged as leader of one of the numerous factions formed in the palace just before the emperor's death. Constantius married twice. His first wife, Galla, gave him two sons. The younger, Gallus, became Caesar but was killed by Constantius II in 354. Basilina, his second wife, produced Julian, the eventual emperor. In 337, after the death of Constantine, Constantius intended to share in the division of power between all of the major family members and sons. A massacre of the parties formed in the court took place instead, instigated by Constantius II and supported by his brothers, Constans and Constantine II. Julius Constantius died at the hands of soldiers, along with his eldest son.

constitutiones The term used to describe the legal enactments and edicts of the Roman emperors. The *constitutiones* did not appear in great number until the fourth century C.E.

Emperor Augustus and his immediate successors certainly passed laws, but their actions were based on two principles: (1) they possessed the IMPERIUM PROCONSULARIS, giving the right to issue edicts; and (2) all proposed legislation was brought to the Senate, where the emperor requested through an *oratio* (speech) that the august legislative body of the empire pass them. In this system there existed supposed limits on power. The Senate could refuse him if it so desired; and the IMPERIUM ended upon the emperor's death.

Furthermore, those pronouncements actually made by the emperors were seldom original. Virtually all such statements could be classified as either *rescripta* (rescripts) or *decreta* (decrees). Rescripts were answers to questions on law made by members of a ministry or by a litigant. They explained or interpreted the law. The *decreta* were actual decisions made in trials over which the emperor presided. As Suetonius showed with the verdicts of Claudius, such pronouncements could be debatable, changeable, even nonsensical.

What an emperor intended to be an explanation, however, very often became an authoritative basis for subsequent legislation. This was especially true in the second century C.E. Senatorial power fell as imperial dominance of the administration took place. The permission from the Senate was no longer sought actively by the emperors, and then the *constitutiones* themselves automatically became binding law. Thus the rulers could have a tremendous influence over the entire framework of law, as CARACALLA demonstrated in 212 C.E., with his Constitutio Antoniana, granting citizenship to all free persons in the empire.

With the broadening of political power came a recognition on the part of the emperors that increased knowledge and expertise were also necessary. Jurists joined the great advisory boards of the palace, the CONSILIUM PRINCIPIS, and Hadrian relied upon lawyers to aid him in framing his *constitutiones*. Quite often it was the CONCILIA that authored the greatest legal reforms and advances, with the Jurists responsible for fine details. In the fourth century the emperors faced no hindrances to legal enactments, and then the *constitutiones* went unquestioned, for the benefit or peril of the empire.

Consualia Great FESTIVAL of the god CONSUS, celebrated twice every year, on August 19 or 21 and on December 15, in the Circus Maximus. According to legend, the Consualia was begun by Romulus and the Rape of the Sabines took place at the first commemoration of the festival. Lavish games were held in the Circus, supervised by the emperor, while sacrifices to the god were made by the VESTAL VIRGINS and the FLAMENS. The day also included the rare unearthing of Consus's statue from beneath the Circus Maximus, so that the deity might witness the day's events.

consul The supreme office of power during the Roman Republic and a position of honor but decreasing political value in the days of the empire. In the year 510 B.C.E., the kings of Rome were expelled and in their place the

Romans chose a government of dual magistrates who were equal in power and in influence. Elected by the *comitia centuriata,* the consuls, for some four centuries, fulfilled the political role of royal authority, bringing all other magistrates into the service of the people and the city of Rome. The tasks of a consul were varied. Their laws could be appealed by the people, vetoed by the TRIBUNES, and severely curtailed by any appointed dictator. They could, however, control their own administrations, decide civil and criminal cases in the legions, and prepare resolutions to become law. In Rome, consuls had the right to summon the SENATE and the *comitia* and to nominate and conduct the elections of dictators and members of the *comitia.* Over the years certain other powers were lost: Civil jurisdiction within the city passed to the PRAETORS, and the census fell to the CENSORS.

As the consuls were to be equal, the actual governing was shared; with each holding greater influence on a monthly rotational basis. In the field, each wielded two legions; military strength maintained a unique equilibrium. The Senate encroached yearly upon the operation of the Republic, while the consuls' position of preeminence outside of Rome ensured a proper balance. Thus the dictator Sulla sought to curb this strength by stripping the consular office of its military base, the IMPERIUM. Sulla insisted that the term of the consul, one year, be spent in Rome.

As civil wars erupted in the Republic in the first century B.C.E., the consuls lost all control of their office. The FIRST and SECOND TRIUMVIRATES held the true reins of power; the office was even altered in 52 B.C.E., when POMPEY THE GREAT held it alone. With the founding of the empire under Augustus in 27 B.C.E., further reductions in the status of consul were inevitable. Augustus worked to preserve the Republican facade in his new imperial system, thus, while still a great honor, consulship also meant little influence. Augustus even held the consulship himself, and the emperors who followed him did the same. Family members, friends, and associates also served, for the ruler had full control over nominations and, hence, the election returns. The old process provided for resignation and death by having replacement consuls available, with those who were the original consul for a year (inaugurated on January 1) bearing the name *consules ordinarii* and their successors, *consules suffecti.* The practice naturally evolved that the *consules suffecti* finished out each year. By the middle of the first century C.E., the actual holding of the consulship by anyone for the entire year became very rare.

A consul's new duties, while not significant, were nonetheless interesting. Certain criminal trials were supervised, with the final judgment resting in the hands of the consul, as did civil authority, including questions concerning slaves. Another task of considerable prestige was that of presiding over the games (*LUDI*) and the many FESTIVALS celebrated in Rome.

Aside from the emperor himself, the consul held one of the most glamorous offices in the empire. Their insignia included the *toga praetexta, sella curculis* (a ceremonial chair) and the right to be surrounded by the LIC-TORES. These 12 guardians normally walked before the consul officiating for the month and walked behind his associate. Usually, the inauguration of a consul took place on January 1, by a law passed in 153 B.C.E. (Previously, the inauguration was held on March 15, as decreed in 222 B.C.E.) The candidates marched to the capital with the senators, members of the Equestrians and other important figures. Prayers were offered solemnly, as were the oaths. To the Romans, the entire ceremony was serious and even the thought of offending tradition was fraught with dread. Thus, when Emperor COMMODUS proposed to go to his inauguration dressed as a gladiator on January 1, 193 C.E., the group plotting his assassination was so horrified that they murdered him the night before his oath-taking.

There can be little doubt that the rulers of the empire dismissed the consuls easily. TIBERIUS sent the consular robes to CLAUDIUS as a joke and grew angry when his lame relative pressed him for the office's full powers. GAIUS CALIGULA also appointed Claudius, his uncle, to the office, both as a humorous distraction and to gain popularity. Family members routinely served, many under-age. From the time of Cicero no one under 43 (or perhaps 42) could be consul, a regulation frequently ignored.

With the division of the empire into East and West, the consulship was equally divided, sometime in the late fourth century C.E. The emperors in Constantinople assumed the title *consul perpetuus*, and in the West the consuls disappeared altogether in 534 C.E.

Consus   An Italian god of several identities whose festival, CONSUALIA, was held on the days of August 19 or 21 and December 15. Consus may have been associated with corn or with the harvest, although his altar stood in the Circus Maximus. The fact that this altar was placed underground, covered with dirt, probably implied an association with the underworld; corn was also planted in the earth and stored in subterranean holds. As a result of the games held during the god's festival, Consus was also known as Neptunus Equestrius to Livy.

Conventus   Name given to the small associations of Roman citizens living abroad but outside the COLONIES. It was quite common for Romans in the provinces to associate freely with each other, given their generally superior legal status. Groups of them came together to form boards within their own towns, to discuss problems or issues of interest. They elected their own committee head, a *curator*, and kept in touch both with Rome and with other such organizations throughout the empire. Another kind of *conventus* was the judicial summons

made in the provinces when the governor or magistrate paid a visit to a town, city or large community so chosen for the honor. A provincial head would arrive on the scene and normally be greeted by artificially enthusiastic crowds. He would then conduct all necessary legal business before departing for the next *conventus*. For smaller, non-colonial townships and cities, the reception of the title *conventus* brought considerable prestige and wealth because of the number of visitors lured to the scene to have cases heard.

Corbulo, Gnaeus Domitius (1) (fl. mid-first century C.E.) *Praetor, master of the Roman roads and father of the famed general, Gnaeus Domitius Corbulo (2)*
In 21 C.E., Corbulo called attention to the deplorable condition of the roads in Italy. He argued that corruption among magistrates and contract workers was such that no remedy could be found unless drastic measures were put into effect. Corbulo consequently received a commission to watch over each officer in charge of a road, the *curator viarum*. He administered the roads for much of the reign of Tiberius, and in 39 C.E., Caligula drafted him to help acquire funds. All former highway repairmen, alive or dead, were fined for obviously embezzling some of the money used on roads. Caligula took his share, and presumably so did Corbulo. In 43 C.E., Claudius put an end to the fines. Corbulo was then forced to return some of his reward money to help reimburse those who had endured previous punishments.

Corbulo, Gnaeus Domitius (2) (d. 67 C.E.) *Roman general who preserved Roman supremacy in Germania and in the East*
Corbulo was probably the son of the head of the roads during the reigns of TIBERIUS and GAIUS CALIGULA (*see* CORBULO [1]) and early on achieved some success as a military officer. In 47 C.E., he received the rank of legate for Germania Inferior and took command of Roman troops in the face of the invading Chauci. He won a series of engagements over the Germans, including a battle of the Rhine, using triremes rowed up the great river. Once the Chauci were repulsed, Corbulo disciplined the legions of the province. Known as a strict and stern general, he not only brought the legionaries back to full strength and morale but also shattered the resolve of the surrounding tribes, especially the Frisii.

Corbulo regretted, however, his lack of free movement as a general; Germania, in his view, was ripe for subjugation. When Claudius forbade any actions in that direction, he remarked: "How happy must have been the generals in older days!"

Corbulo's reputation was enhanced by his reception of the triumphal insignia from Claudius. When Nero, therefore, searched for an officer to salvage Roman policy in ARMENIA in 54 C.E., he turned to Corbulo. After arriving in Cilicia, he found the governor of Syria, Ummidius Quadratus, waiting for him. Eager not to lose power or prestige, Quadratus insisted on sharing in all major decisions; not surprisingly, a bitter fight erupted between them. Nero settled the dispute by having laurels placed on the imperial *fasces* or insignia, as a credit to each man. Corbulo then repeated his work in Germania, where the legions were relentlessly and mercilessly drilled and beaten into shape. The pleasant climate and good living in Syria ended in 58, when the reformed troops finally set out to reclaim Armenia from the Parthians.

Since the occupation of the kingdom by Parthia in 54 (and by its King Vologases I), Armenia had been ruled by the pro-Parthian Tiridates. Corbulo now besieged him militarily and politically, using the client states of Iberia, Cappadocia, and Commagene to pressure his borders. When the Armenian ruler and his Parthian masters refused to yield during negotiations, the Roman general marched on the capital of Artaxata, capturing it in 58 and then netting the other major city of TIGRANOCERTA as well. Tiridates, ousted from the country, tried to reclaim the dominion but could not; Corbulo pacified all of Armenia.

In 60-61, Nero chose to place a new client on the throne, TIGRANES. Corbulo was ordered to assume the governorship in Syria, as Quadratus had died. Tigranes proved an incompetent monarch and in 61 attacked a small region of Parthia, Adiabene; he soon called for help from Syria when Vologases moved against him. Despite the strong possibility that Corbulo may have approved of the sortie, his position in Syria gave him no powers in dealing with the Armenian question. Thus, Rome sent out the appallingly bad general, Caesennius Paetus, to annex all of the region, as Tigranes could not hold the throne. Paetus bungled his task. Corbulo did not march from Syria. The Parthian king and the ousted Tiridates, instead, agreed to Roman terms. Armenia would be a client to Rome once more. Nero ordered Paetus to return to Italy, and Corbulo received the position equal to his skills. He obtained the *maius imperium,* the power over all of the adjoining provinces and the client states therein. He continued to administer most of the East until 66, when a conspiracy surfaced in Rome.

Plots against Nero were common. When Annius Vinicianus began his, Corbulo naturally was implicated. Vinicianus had married Corbulo's daughter; as the foremost military figure of the time, Corbulo's name surfaced as a successor to the tyrant. In 67, Corbulo received a summons to Greece. Joining several other governors, namely the SCRIBONII BROTHERS, the loyal general bowed before his emperor and heard the imperial command for him to commit suicide.

Cordius (Gordius) (d. after 221 C.E.) *Charioteer and imperial favorite*

A charioteer during the reign of Emperor Elagabalus (218–222), Cordius reportedly taught the emperor to drive a chariot and subsequently became one of his favorite courtiers. In Elagabalus's series of eccentric appointments, Cordius received the post of Prefect of the Watch, to the consternation of the Praetorian Guard, who considered him wholly unqualified. Late in 221, he was included in a list of officials removed from office at the demand of the Praetorians.

Corduba   Also called Corduva, the provincial capital of the senatorial province of Baetica in Spain. Very little of the ancient city survived the Islamic period, although the organization of the city reportedly was based upon the original design. The capital contained all of the necessary Roman structures, including a forum and baths.

Cordus, Aulus Cremutius (d. 25 C.E.) *Writer a highly respected figure of the early first century*
Cremutius Cordus authored *History,* in which he commended Marcus BRUTUS and Gaius CASSIUS. The work was elevated by AUGUSTUS, who may have accorded Cordus the honor of having him read from it out loud in the palace. By 25, Cordus had reached considerable age but had lost none of his wit. A determined opponent of the notorious prefect Lucius Aelius SEJANUS, he commented upon a statue of Sejanus in the Theater of Pompey, saying: "Now Pompey's theater is truly destroyed." In 25, Sejanus accused Cordus of improper writings in his *History,* especially with regard to Brutus and Cassius. Cordus was found guilty. He subsequently returned home and starved himself to death. The books of Cordus were then burned by the *aediles,* although his daughter, Marcia, hid many copies. GAIUS CALIGULA later rehabilitated him posthumously.

Corinth   City in Greece. Once one of the great trading centers of the ancient world, Corinth was reborn under the empire. For centuries the city served as the heart of Hellenic commercial ties with the world, and its buildings, stretching across the Isthmus of Corinth, were magnificent. Not surprisingly, the Republic sought to include the city in its list of second century B.C.E. conquests. In 146 B.C.E., L. Mummius laid siege and brutally destroyed Corinth. The population saw no means of rebuilding, and the city became a deserted shell.

In 46 B.C.E., Julius CAESAR looked for a means of reducing the population of Italy and needed a place to settle his many retired and discharged legionary veterans. His solution, colonization, soon benefited many regions of Roman occupation, Corinth among them. Colonists arrived sometime after Caesar's assassination in 44 B.C.E., choosing to rebuild in a style very Roman. They succeeded brilliantly, and their efforts produced a capital for the eventual province of Achaea.

Architecturally, Corinth received a massive transfusion from Rome. With the exception of the Temple of Apollo, the usual Agora (Forum) and the various stoas, the city was more Roman than Greek—a characteristic very pleasing to the appointed proconsul, who administered the province from his office near the Forum. To provide the bureaucratic organization befitting a capital, four basilicas were constructed as well. They were grouped around the Forum and stood close to the stoas and merchant centers in the city. Early on, the colonists had realized that Corinth, just as before, had to be based on commerce. Thus the city life was centered on trade and economic growth.

In a reflection of the wealth brought in by the merchants, no expenses were spared in decoration or in public entertainments. The original Greek theater was changed to a Roman structure, complete with a changeable arena for games and gladiatorial contests. A small Odeum was added to provide yet another alternate amusement. To display the city's religious sincerity, six temples were completed sometime in the second century C.E., the same time as Herodes Atticus made his generous gifts to Greece. Corinth received a beautiful fountain from him. Reliant upon trade, Corinth was very susceptible to changes in the economic health of the empire. When the strength of Rome began to fail in the third century C.E., the effects were felt first in Corinth; then the entire *colonia* began to decline.

Archaeologically, Corinth is extremely interesting, with excavation work still proceeding on the site. The most bizarre episode in its history surely came in the reign of Nero. In 66 C.E., the emperor went to Greece on a grand tour. When visiting Corinth he conceived of a plan to cut a canal across the isthmus and gathered together the Praetorian Guard to begin digging. He joined them with a shovel, filling a bucket of dirt, which he carried away on his back. Fortunately for both the Corinthians and the abused guards, Nero lost interest in the project. In the empire, the original name for Corinth was Colonia Laus Julia Corinthus.

Cornelia (1) (fl. first century B.C.E.) *First wife of Julius Caesar*

Cornelia was the daughter of the four-time Consul Cinna. The dictator Sulla opposed the marriage and demanded that CAESAR divorce her. When Caesar refused, Sulla stripped him of his priesthood and her dowry. She bore Caesar a daughter, JULIA.

Cornelia (2) (fl. first century B.C.E.) *Fifth wife of Pompey the Great and stepmother of Sextus Pompey and Gnaeus Pompey*

Cornelia proved a kind and caring mother and was known for possessing a combination of beauty and intelligence. She knew literature, music, philosophy, and mathematics.

Cornelia supported her husband during the CIVIL WAR with Julius Caesar. After the Dyrrhachium campaign, POMPEY sent her back to the city of Mitylene, on the island of Lesbos. He was apparently concerned about the coming battle with Caesar and had Sextus join her. The battle of PHARSALUS fulfilled his fears. After a rout of his army at Caesar's hands, Pompey fled to Lesbos, and Cornelia and Sextus boarded his ship of escape. Rhodes and Antioch would not allow them to land. With no other choice, they sailed to Egypt after taking on a small troop at Cyprus. On September 29, 48 B.C.E., they reached Egypt and tried to land the following day. Before Cornelia's horrified eyes, Pompey was murdered on the orders of Ptolemy XIII. With the scene still firmly in her mind, Cornelia and her shocked stepson landed at Tyre. After the Civil War, the magnanimous Caesar made peace with her.

Cornelia (3) (d. 90 C.E.) *The ranking Vestal Virgin during the reign of Domitian*

Cornelia and several of her fellow Vestals were involved in a scandal and were eventually put to death. Domitian believed firmly in religious devotion and when word arrived that the Vestals had broken their vows of chastity he looked into the matter personally. Domitian found them all guilty and was far more angry with Cornelia than with the others. The two sisters of the Oculata family and another, Varonilla, were executed in 83 C.E. Cornelia, however, suffered the traditional punishment of burial alive. Her lovers were then beaten to death in public view.

Cornelius (d. 253 C.E.) *Pope and Christian saint*

In 251 Cornelius was elected the successor to the martyred St. Fabian during a lull in the intense persecutions of the emperor Decius, ending the vacancy in the papacy that had lasted for some 14 months. His pontificate was noted for the controversy over the church's position toward the *lapsi,* those who had lapsed from the faith during the persecutions. Novatian, leader of the rigorist party in the church, took his followers to schism to protest what they felt was Cornelius's lax attitude. The pope was supported, however, by synods at Rome and Carthage and by bishops in the East; a major support came from St. Cyprian of Carthage. Several letters from Cornelius to Cyprian have survived. When the Christian persecutions under Gallus resumed in 252, Cornelius was exiled, traditionally dying as a martyr at Centumcellae (modern Civitavecchia). He was buried at Rome, in the crypt of Lucina; his tomb contains the inscription "Cornelius Martyr."

Cornificius, Lucius (fl. first century B.C.E.) *A supporter of Octavian (Augustus) during the civil war*

Cornificius helped prosecute Brutus for Caesar's assassination and then joined the forces of Octavian during the struggles for power (*see* CIVIL WAR, SECOND TRIUMVIRATE). In 36 B.C.E., he commanded a sizable detachment in Sicily and was besieged by the dangerous Sextus POMPEY. His situation grew increasingly desperate as his casualties mounted and provisions became scarce. Marcus Agrippa arrived to relieve him in time. Cornificius forever afterward commemorated his good fortune by traveling to dinner on the back of an elephant. Octavian granted him a consulship in 35 B.C.E., during which Sextus Pompey met his end. He also held a proconsulship in Africa with considerable success.

Cornutus, Caecilius (d. 24 C.E.) *Roman Praetorian falsely implicated in a conspiracy against Tiberius*
The son of the similarly accused Vibius Serenus brought the charge. Unable to bear the suspense of a trial and despairing of justice, Cornutus killed himself. It was then suggested that as Cornutus had committed suicide, the prosecutors should not receive their customary rewards. Tiberius, however, disagreed and ruled that regardless of the disposition of the accused, all informers should be paid. It was a serious decision by the emperor that encouraged the spread of the *DELATORES*.

Cornutus, Lucius Annaeus (fl. first century C.E.) *A philosopher and writer*
Born in Lepcis around 20 C.E., Cornutus was a freedman to Seneca, or perhaps a relative. In the mid-sixties he was exiled, perhaps as part of the conspiracy of G. C. PISO, but there is debate concerning this. Cornutus may also have returned to Rome at a later time.

correctores   Special agents employed by the emperors in certain provinces or territories to examine finances, supervise administrative affairs or simply to represent imperial will where the ruler desired it to be stressed. Most *correctores* were appointed from the ranks of praetors or ex-praetors, and thus they could wield power and influence comfortably. The *correctores* proved tremendously useful in Achaea. Appointed by Trajan, they worked to reorganize the bureaucracy in the province and to salvage the desperate financial situation in Athens in the early second century C.E. By the third century, they had also been appointed to the Italian districts, where the local townships needed administrative supervision. In the late Roman Empire, the office evolved into the regular functions of the provincial governors. Diocletian granted increased power to his heads of provinces, and financial control gave the imperial government more authority.

Corsica   Large island in the Mediterranean Sea between Italy and Gaul; first seized from the Carthaginians around 227 B.C.E. by Rome. In establishing the imperial system, Augustus (ruled 27 B.C.E.–14 C.E.) placed Corsica under a Praetorian consul but in 6 C.E. named the island as a part of the territories governed by the procurator of SARDINIA. Corsica was never fully settled, despite its harbors, and it remained a wilderness. On the eastern side there were two colonies—Aleria and Mariana. Aleria served as the local center of government and came the closest to achieving the standards and quality of life expected by the imperial domination. The most popular export of Corsica was wax. The island also served as a popular place for exiles (Domitian sent one Mettius Pompusianus there in 91 C.E.). Corsica also served as a stopping-off point for those unfortunate Romans being sent to the island of Planasia.

Cotta, Lucius Aurunculeius   *See* ADUATUCA.

Cotta Messalinius, M. Aurelius (fl. first century C.E.) *Consul in 20 C.E.*
Also known as M. Aurelius Cotta Maximus, Cotta was the son of MESSALLA CORVINUS, the writer, Cotta was one of the most despised figures of the reign of Tiberius (14–37 C.E.). He sat in the Senate, ever prepared to accuse and to prosecute any poor victim chosen by the emperor. In 20 C.E. he led the attack on Piso, and in 29 tried to have Agrippina the Elder and her son Nero (son of Germanicus) condemned. After the fall of SEJANUS in 31 C.E. created a difficult environment for imperial henchmen, Cotta found himself facing charges. When the Senate would not protect him from these prosecutions, he appealed to Tiberius, who wrote a long letter in his defense. Tacitus wasted no opportunity to attack Cotta in the *Annals*. In 24 C.E., however, Cotta did propose one sensible piece of legislation. Governors of the provinces, he argued, should be held accountable for the crimes of their wives, an idea considered insulting by Tacitus.

Cottiaen Alps   Mountain range (also called Alpes Cottiae) between the Maritime Alps of the French-Italian seacoast and the Graiaen Alps of northwestern Italy. Originally inhabited by a native people, the area was subjugated by Augustus sometime around 8 B.C.E. Its king COTTIUS (after whom the mountains were named) became a client of Rome; subsequently, the Cottiaen Alps benefited from imperial attention. Roads were built and an arch placed at a conspicuous point to honor Augustus. The Romans used the passes to maintain communications with Gaul.

Cottius (fl. first century C.E.) *King of the Ligurians*
Cottius earned the honor of having a part of the Alpine range named after him—the Cottiaen Alps. Cottius very wisely submitted to Augustus and sometime around 8 B.C.E. signed a peace treaty with Rome. His domains

included most of the surrounding regions and peoples, and as a client he was reliable. He built roads and allowed his territory to serve as a launching site for at least one expedition during the reign of Tiberius. An arch for Augustus was also constructed. In 44 C.E., Claudius recognized the claims of the king's son, Marcus Julius Cottius. This new king sat on the throne until some time during the reign of Nero, when he died. With his passing his realm became part of the Roman territories.

Cotys (1) (fl. first century C.E.) *King of Armenia Minor*
Grandson of Polemo, king of Pontus, Cotys received the rule of Armenia Minor in 38 C.E. from GAIUS CALIGULA. He was a friend of the emperor from the days of his youth. Claudius certified his control over the Armenian kingdom, although he was one of the last possessors of the throne before the annexation of the country under Vespasian.

Cotys (2) (d. before 62 C.E.) *King of the Bosporus*
Son of Aspurgeus of the Bosporan kingdom and his second wife, the Thracian Princess Gepaepyris, Cotys was the half-brother of Mithridates, son of Aspurgeus and Queen Dynamis. In 37 or 38 C.E., the king died, and GAIUS CALIGULA named Polemo II of Pontus as the ruler. Gepaepyris and her stepson Mithridates took effective control. Claudius affirmed Mithridates's claim in 41 C.E. Cotys, meanwhile, waited for his half-brother to grow ambitious. Sometime around 44 or 45, the prince revealed to Claudius that Mithridates planned a revolt. The grateful emperor gave Cotys the throne. After overcoming his brother's attempted usurpation (Cotys relied upon the help of Roman troops under the command of Julius Aquila), Cotys administered the kingdom until his death, sometime before Nero seized it in 62. A number of other Bosporan kings bore the same name.

Cotys of Thrace (fl. early first century C.E.) *Son of the Thracian King Rhoemetalces*
Cotys became part of the struggle for the throne of THRACE in 19 C.E. When Rhoemetalces died in the reign of Augustus (27 B.C.E.–14 C.E.), the Thracian realm was divided between his son Cotys and his brother, Rhescuporis. Cotys ruled the civilized and abundant regions, while his uncle controlled the wilder, mountainous territories.

A peace existed between the two rulers for several years, but by 19 C.E. the marauders of Rhescuporis had developed into outright military columns. Emperor Tiberius sent a centurion to warn them, and a treaty was to be negotiated. Instead, Rhescuporis trapped Cotys and put him to death. Unable to tolerate such actions, Tiberius ordered Pomponius Flaccus to bring Rhescuporis to Rome. There he was accused by Cotys's widow, the greatly respected Antonia Tryphaena, a relative of

Marc Anthony. Cotys was avenged, and his sons shared in the distribution of power in Thrace.

Crassus, Canidius *See* CANDIDUS CRASSUS, PUBLIUS.

Crassus (1), Marcus Licinius (c. 115–53 B.C.E.) *A member of the first triumvirate and a leading figure in the final days of the Republic*
Crassus was known as one of the wealthiest men in Rome. His family had long been involved in politics, and his father served as consul in 97 B.C.E. before warring against Marius with Sulla, a struggle resulting in the father's death in 87 B.C.E. The young Crassus immediately enlisted with Sulla, after returning from the safety of Spain. Loyalty to Sulla was rewarded when large amounts of confiscated property fell under his control after Sulla became the master of Rome. He continued his accumulation of wealth and rose in political power. Money he amassed from his estates, from the slave trade and silver mines. Political strength came from his popularity carefully cultivated over the years. He became *praetor,* earning eventually a proconsular position over several legions, putting down Spartacus and his slave army in 72–71 B.C.E.

Military achievements were not to be his road to supremacy in the Republic. Another, more able general emerged—POMPEY THE GREAT. Crassus had watched with growing alarm as Pompey first seized martial fame with his own exploits and then stole Crassus's glory in 71 B.C.E. by crushing the pitiful remnants of Spartacus's forces. From that moment on Crassus worked against Pompey, although serving in the consulship of 70 with him. They argued and debated every issue, rendering the time of their consulships absolutely useless. Crassus did finance a huge festival with 10,000 tables for the citizens.

The Catiline affair next dominated Rome in 63 B.C.E. Many officials of note fell, and as Crassus had served with Catiline in the censorship, he too came under suspicion for a time. He was saved by Julius CAESAR's ambitions for the consulship and for greatness. Caesar desired to increase his powers and needed allies. With Crassus and Pompey so bitterly opposed to one another, Caesar sought a reconciliation between them. In 60 B.C.E., Crassus agreed to join a triumvirate with Pompey and Caesar. Each shared in the full benefits of the state.

Crassus found his situation virtually unchanged. Pompey had grown in the view of the optimate party in Rome and Caesar amassed victories in Gaul, while Crassus did little to improve his personal fortunes. In 56 B.C.E. a conference was held at LUCA to change this situation. Crassus, it was decided, would share a consulship again with Pompey, and Caesar would remain in Gaul to finish his conquests. For Crassus, however, such gains were not enough.

Aside from his defeat of Spartacus, for which a triumph had been celebrated, Crassus was no match for the reputations of his fellow triumvirs. He resolved to establish himself militarily and demanded the territory of Syria. Despite his age, which was 60, and deafness in one ear, Crassus put together an army for the invasion of Parthia. Two years of planning and meticulous preparation preceded one of the worst disasters ever inflicted upon Roman arms, in 53 B.C.E. In the deserts of Mesopotamia, near a town called CARRHAE, the would-be general allowed his troops to be surrounded by the Parthians. Under a hail of arrows and the relentless sun, Crassus watched as his army disappeared. Accounts varied as to his death. Plutarch reported that a Parthian named Pomaxathres killed him, and Dio wrote that he died at the hands of one of his men in order to avoid capture. His head and right hand were sent to the king of Parthia, Orodes. That monarch reportedly poured molten gold into Crassus's mouth, saying: "Satisfy yourself with the metal for which in life you were so greedy."

Crassus (2), Marcus Licinius (fl. last first century B.C.E.) *General and one-time follower of Sextus Pompey and Marc Antony*
Crassus served with Octavian as consul in 30 B.C.E., a sign of Octavian's goodwill toward members of the various political parties in existence before ACTIUM. In 29 B.C.E. he was sent to Macedonia to repel an invasion of the Bastarnae (*see* SCYTHIANS). After crushing these wild people, he pursued them into MOESIA, subdividing the country along the way. The Scythians turned to give battle, and Crassus launched a devastating attack upon them, personally killing their King DELDO. He then finished the Scythians before marching against the Moesians. Winter was coming, and Crassus retired to Thrace but had to launch another expedition against the Scythians, who were seeking vengeance upon the few Roman allies of that region. The victories of Crassus were celebrated by the Senate. He could have received the *spolia opima* for slaying Deldo (the honorific dedication of his armor to Jupiter Feretrius) had he possessed the title of IMPERATOR, but Octavian kept that for himself, perhaps preferring to deny such an honor to a former lieutenant of Antony.

Crassus, Publius Licinius (d. 53 B.C.E.) *A legate during the late Republic*
Crassus served both Julius CAESAR and his father Marcus Licinius CRASSUS (1). Crassus was an officer of Caesar's army in Gaul. He was used for a number of missions conducted with a considerable freedom of operation. Caesar sent him with a legion into Normandy and Brittany in early 57 B.C.E.; he conquered the tribes there. Later that year he sailed across the Channel conducting a reconnais-sance in force, part of the preparation for Caesar's expeditions two years later.

Crassus achieved his greatest success at the expense of the tribes in Gallia Aquitania. In 56 B.C.E., as Caesar labored to maintain his hold over Gaul, Crassus was sent with 12 cohorts and cavalry to invade all of Aquitania. His advance was absolutely triumphant, and the region became pacified very quickly. A year later, Caesar gave Crassus a cavalry command under his triumvir father. Publius Crassus arrived in Syria in time to embark with his father on the ill-fated Parthian invasion in 53; he was given the right flank of the advancing Roman host. The ensuing battle of CARRHAE was a disaster. The Roman army marched into the dry lands away from Euphrates, and there the legions were surrounded by the Parthians under the command of SURENAS. As the enemy rained down arrows, Publius tried to charge the enemy in order to buy time for the main body to form into a defensive square. His frontal assault was initially effective, but soon he and his men found themselves isolated from their comrades. Publius and his cohorts were cut to pieces; the young legate's head was placed on a spear and displayed by the Parthians who rode gleefully around the remaining Romans. Morale perished with Publius, and Marcus Licinius Crassus suffered one of the worst defeats in Roman history. According to Plutarch, Publius admired Cicero and his oratorical skills.

Cremona   *See* BEDRIACUM (second battle).

Cremutius Cordus, Aulus (d. 25 C.E.) *A writer and highly respected figure of the early first century C.E.*
Cremutius Cordus authored a *History* in which he commended Marcus Brutus and praised Gaius Cassius. The work was honored by Augustus, who may have not only read it but also accorded Cordus the honor of having him read out loud in the palace. SEJANUS accused him of improper writings in his *History*, especially with regard to Brutus and Cassius. He was found guilty, returned home, and starved himself to death. The books of Cordus were then banned and burned by the AEDILES, although his daughter Marcia hid many copies. Gaius Caligula later rehabilitated him, posthumously.

Crescentia, Cannutia (d. 213 C.E.) *One of the four Vestal Virgins sentenced to death by Caracalla in 213.*
Cannutia Crescentia earned the displeasure of the emperor, and he ordered her to die. While her sisters, Clodia Laeta, Pomponia Rufina, and Aurelia Severa, were all buried alive, Cannutia threw herself off a roof.

Crete and Cyrenaica   Two formerly different territories—Cyrenaica on the North African coast, west of

Egypt, and Crete, an island in the Mediterranean some 200 miles north of Cyrenaica—combined by the Republic in 67 B.C.E. to form one province. In his reorganization of the Roman world, Emperor Augustus chose to certify the union once more, as control had waned during the troubled years before his rise. The union was convenient in governmental affairs only, however, for neither half could ever be so organized as to warrant independent provincial status. Under normal circumstances it was a senatorial province under a proconsul.

Piracy and its assault on the general sea routes of the Mediterranean first attracted the attention of Rome in or around 67 B.C.E. In that year, Caecilius Metellus landed and easily captured the island of Crete. Henceforth it belonged firmly to the Romans, who brought it under further control with the use of colonists, former soldiers in search of land.

Roman life, however, never took firm root in Cretan soil. Only one real colony was granted full status, Knossus (Colonia Julia Cnossus), and the people of native origin remained unchanged for centuries. They retained their own tribal systems, had magistrates and continued to use Greek as the language of choice. To them Latin remained a strange tongue, used only by those of great power who had arrived to change all aspects of life. The Cretans were not violently opposed to Rome; on the contrary, they benefited handsomely from Rome's gifts of money and labor. They just did not surrender their way of living. For the imperial officials given the task of working with the residents of Crete, the fulfillment of duty was not easy. These Romans, however, chose to aid the Cretans in the areas that they understood best, namely economics and architecture.

Fertile fields naturally made agriculture the financial base of Cretan stability, and the colonists introduced better farming and harvesting techniques. But the intrusion of government into such matters dissipated the benefits to some degree, for large tracts of land were taken over by the Italians, especially families from Campania, who received rights to estates from Augustus.

Builders arrived on Crete as well, to expedite both a series of construction programs (especially in the second century C.E.) and to effect repairs on the towns all over the island. An earthquake in 46 C.E. flattened most of the cities, and administrators for the next century worked to overcome the terrible damage. Despite such natural disasters, the Cretans spent the entire imperial era in isolation. The only cities of note on Crete were Knossus and Gortyn. Knossus, of course, captured the imagination of the Romans with its fabled past. Gortyn, in contrast, was a thoroughly modern site and consequently served as the provincial capital.

Cyrenaica formed a diverse but beautiful stretch of land directly east of the Gulf of Sidra and the provinces of Africa and Numidia. Cyrenaica stood isolated from the rest of Africa by deserts and by the terrible sun. Greek colonists settled there in the seventh century B.C.E., when they founded the Pentapolis or five colonies: Barea (later Ptolemais), Hespera (later Berenice), Teuchira (later Arsinoe), Cyrene, and Apollonia.

For a time Egypt occupied the country through the Ptolemies, but in 96 B.C.E., the Republic took control of the dead Ptolemy Apion's royal lands, which was followed by the region's complete annexation in 74 B.C.E. Thought surely was given to combining Cyrenaica with other African areas, such as Tripolitana, but the difficulties inherent environmentally and geographically necessitated a different solution, in 67 B.C.E.

Wars raged along its arid borders for most of the early reign of Augustus, as Sulpicius Quirinius waged several campaigns against the nomadic tribes from 6 B.C.E. until 2 C.E. Augustus then dealt with the terrible economic and administrative problems. Although the pirates had been cleared from the seas, more pillaging was done by the governors. Augustus and his successors took swift action, which resulted in charges and prosecutions. Men like Pedius Blaesus, the provincial governor who in 59 C.E. was ousted from the Senate for bribery, soon learned that the position could not be abused.

As a result, Cyrenaica became a model of Roman efficiency, for the state not only protected the citizen's rights and culture, limiting colonization, but also helped the economy to develop and prosper. Engineering projects, improved irrigation, roads, communication, and district organization became commonplace as magistrates and administrators cared for the legal and governmental needs of the cities and the estates.

Starting with Cyrene, all of Cyrenaica blossomed, and while its wealth was never vast, by the start of the second century the province could lay claim to true prosperity. Much of the credit had to be given to the special legates appointed by the emperors to organize the land allotments. From the time of Claudius to the reign of the Flavians, officers such as L. Acilius Strabo and Q. Paconius Agrippinus worked hard in the service of the province and its people.

From 115 to 117 C.E., the Jewish revolt caused chaos in Cyprus, Egypt, and Cyrenaica. Cities were destroyed and thousands massacred. Cyrene was ruined utterly. Emperor Hadrian instituted a major building program, restoring damaged communities and granting the status of coloniae to Cyrene and Arsinoe. He also created Hadrianopolis. With this aid, however, came the unavoidable Roman cultural influences. Too much had taken place in the region to restore the original morale and prosperity of the inhabitants. The result was an uncomfortable mixture of the old and the new.

Crispina (d. 182 C.E.) *First wife of Emperor Commodus*
Marcus Aurelius, Crispina's father-in-law, apparently regretted the union of 178 C.E. but had little choice because of the demands of state. Crispina suffered at the

hands of Commodus's sister, LUCILLA, who resented her status as empress, a seat of honor she held once herself as the wife of Lucius Verus. When Commodus deteriorated mentally, Crispina's situation became precarious. In 182, believing her guilty of adultery, Commodus exiled her to Capri, along with his sister, who had been exposed as a member of a plot against his life. Both women were subsequently executed.

Crispinilla, Calvia (fl. first century C.E.) *A mistress of Nero*
Crispinilla succeeded, as did most of the imperial favorites, in amassing great power and influence. In 67 C.E., she possessed the title of caretaker of the imperial wardrobe and also was charged by Nero with watching over his eunuch while the emperor journeyed to Greece. In the fulfillment of her duties she managed to plunder Rome. Nero later used her as an emissary to the rebelling legate of Africa, Clodius Macer, but she was unsuccessful in preventing an uprising.
   See also HELIUS; POLYCLEITUS.

Crispinus, Rufrius (d. 66 C.E.) *Prefect of the Praetorian Guard in the reign of Claudius (41–54 C.E.)*
With his coprefect, Lusius Geta, Crispinus was removed in 51 by Empress Agrippina, Claudius's wife. He had been appointed coprefect sometime before 47, for in that year he was sent to Baiae to arrest Valerius Asiaticus on the charge of conspiracy against the emperor. Although the real reason for the arrest had been the hatred of Empress Messallina, Crispinus received the Praetorian insignia.

   Crispinus remained at his post for the next four years, watching Messallina die and be replaced by the powerful Agrippina. He had apparently been loyal to Messallina as had Geta, and the new wife of the emperor could tolerate no one who might disagree with her or prevent her domination in the palace. On the pretext that the Praetorian Guard needed one commander only, she convinced Claudius to remove both Crispinus and Geta in 51.

   His fortunes continued to decline under Nero. His wife, Poppaea, one of the most beautiful women in the empire, set upon an adulterous affair with the handsome and influential M. Junius Otho, the eventual emperor. Leaving Crispinus and her son behind, she married Otho and then found Nero. Aware of Crispinus's one-time union with Poppaea, Nero banished him in 65 to Sardinia, where he lived in exile until the following year. In 66, Nero ordered him to die.

Crispinus, Tullius (d. 193 C.E.) *Prefect of the Praetorian Guard under Emperor Didius Julianus*
Crispinus served in his post (along with the coprefect, Flavius Genealis) for a brief period in 193. After buying the Roman Empire in an auction conducted by the Prae-

torian Guard, Didius Julianus allowed the cohorts to choose their own prefects, and Crispinus and Genealis were their favorites. The reign of Julianus proved brief, for the legions of Septimius Severus marched on Italy. Crispinus was sent to block the arrival of Severus at Ravenna, but when the fleet fell into Severus's hands and many officers joined his cause, Crispinus returned to Rome. Desperately trying to save his throne, Julianus once more dispatched Crispinus, this time to meet and negotiate with Severus in the hope of securing an agreement to share the rule. Again Crispinus was unsuccessful. Fearing that he may have been ordered to commit murder, Severus put the prefect to death on the advice of Julius Laetus.

Crispus, Flavius Julius (305–326 C.E.) *Oldest son of Constantine the Great and his first wife, Minervina*
Crispus received an education from the family friend, Lactantius, while living in Gaul. In March of 317, he received the title of Caesar (junior emperor), which he shared with his brother Constantine. Crispus served in the army of his father and commanded part of the fleet used in 324 to destroy the emperor of the East, Licinius, at the battle of ADRIANOPLE. He then traveled to Rome with his father but somehow fell out of favor on the way. Early in 326, at Pola, he was executed on Constantine's order, perhaps for committing adultery with his stepmother Fausta, although the exact reason remained unclear.

Crispus of Vercellae, Vibius (10–90) *First century orator*
Crispus acquired the respect and friendship of Emperors Nero, Vitellius, Vespasian, and Domitian. A native of Vercellae, he served as consul under Nero, Vespasian, and Domitian. He was never very popular with the average Roman, but he cultivated excellent relations with the rulers of his time and managed to survive the considerable political upheaval in Rome during the period. In describing the excessive orgies of Vitellius, he noted after our especially lavish banquet, "If I had not become sick I surely would have died."

Ctesiphon   One of the two great capitals of the empire of PARTHIA, situated in Babylonia along the east bank of the Tigris River, near modern Baghdad. Under the Parthians the large city was used as a winter residence of the kings, while Echatana was the royal summer home. When the Persians seized control of the entire empire, Ctesiphon remained the seat of power. Situated on the great trade lane from the east, the city provided a rest point for caravans and merchants traveling back and forth from as far as Spain and China. Ctesiphon was reportedly very large and can actually be called an amalgamation of two cities, Ctesiphon and Seleuceia. The Persian kings liked Ctesiphon because of its central location, especially with relation to Roman Syria and Armenia, and SHAPUR I (214–272 C.E.) built himself a grand palace there.

Strategically, however, the capital was exposed, and any advance down the Euphrates, through Mesopotamia, produced a serious threat. The Parthians and the Persians lost Ctesiphon on several occasions. In 115–116 C.E., the Emperor Trajan not only captured the city but also used the victory to award himself the title of *Parthicus*. Avidius Cassius, Marcus Aurelius's great general, burned down the palace of Vologases III; in 197, Septimius Severus allowed his legions to plunder the city and to massacre its inhabitants. With the coming of the Persians, many things changed. ARDASHIR I around 224 C.E. named Ctesiphon his home, and the dynastically vigorous successors defeated Rome several times in wars launched from the site. The Roman military recovery late in the third century once more imperiled Ctesiphon. For a time several emperors marched around Babylonia, virtually unmolested. These included Carus in 283 and more importantly, Galerius in 296, whose victories were never forgiven and caused the incessant wars of Shapur II for much of the fourth century.

Cuicul Military colony created in the late first century C.E. (c. 96). Cuicul was one of the numerous Roman colonies in North Africa (*see* THAMUGADI; THUGGA; THYSDRUS), specifically in NUMIDIA. The original walls of the colony were outgrown by the middle of the second century C.E., and the city emerged as one of the most interesting sites in Africa. Cuicul possessed all of the normal buildings associated with Roman colonies, including baths and various basilicas. It also had a Senate chamber, a forum of some size, and a theater. The colonists, however, were blessed with two other notable structures, the Temple of the Severans and the Arch of Caracalla. The arch was erected in 216 C.E., as part of a large effort by the city to honor the family of Septimius Severus. It stood just north of the Severan temple and near the square named after the family. The temple was completed around 230 and contained all of the normal elements found in classical Roman religious buildings. Cuicul also became known as Djemila.

Cunobellinus (d. 42 C.E.) *King of the Catuvellauni, a powerful tribe in Britain, from about 5 C.E. to 41 or 42 C.E.*
He was the son of the powerful leader Tasciovanus and took over the throne with an eye toward solidification and expansion. Thus he conquered or acquired dominance over most of southeastern England. Ruling from CAMULODUNUM (Colchester), Cunobellinus furthered the economic growth of the islands and ties with the BELGAE on the Continent. The Romans knew him as the king of the Britons. He had three sons: CARATACUS, Togodumnus, and Amminius. Caratacus and Todogumnus agreed with their father's anti-Roman policies, but Amminius favored improved relations and eventually fled to the Romans. Cunobellinus died shortly after, and the stage was set for the invasion by Claudius in 43 C.E.

cura annonae The original board charged with the supply of corn for Rome, its name meaning "care for the harvest." The task of this group's members was handed eventually by Augustus to the newly created office of the *praefectus annonae*.
See also ANNONA.

cura aquarum Board that maintained the water supply and the aqueducts of Rome. The three members were appointed by the emperor, with a presiding officer and the pay and full rights of public officials. Augustus founded the board in 11 B.C.E. but acted in coordination with the Senate. The first presiding officer of the *cura aquarum* was Messalla Corvinus.

curae palatiorum The board overseeing residences of the emperors during the late empire. They were under the care of the PRAEPOSITUS SACRI CUBICULI.
See also DOMUS.

curatores Agents of the imperial government who oversaw the finances of the various cities of the empire. The institution probably began under Emperor TRAJAN, who sent out reliable officials, some of senatorial rank, to examine the accounts of the cities. Eventually he appointed them to other provinces as well, such as BITHYNIA. Their original role was as advisers and to stem corruption. However, they provided the emperors with a means of bureaucratic control and could dominate a community by virtue of their special status. Increased centralization was the inevitable result.

curia The meeting house of the SENATE, specifically, and the name also applied to a meeting place generally. Senatorial proceedings were held throughout Rome's history in several buildings: the CURIA HOSTILIA, CURIA POMPEY, and the CURIA JULIA. Tradition dictated that *curia* be prominently positioned with access to the sky to observe omens.

Curia Cornelia The *curia* begun in 52 B.C.E. by Faustus Sulla, the son of Sulla the dictator. It was intended to restore the CURIA HOSTILIA, but Julius CAESAR ordered construction to cease in the mid-forties, in favor of his own CURIA JULIA. A lingering dislike for Sulla led the Romans to destroy the work and to replace it with a temple.

Curia Hostilia The first great *curia* and the meeting place of the SENATE for centuries. According to tradition, the CURIA had been built by King Tullus Hostilius in the seventh century B.C.E. for his own use but was taken over by the new Republic. Finally succumbing to violence in 52 B.C.E., the *curia* was burned in riots following the death of CLODIUS. Faustus Sulla, the dictator's son, began an effort to rebuild it as the CURIA CORNELIA, but Julius CAESAR halted the work to ensure the completion of his own CURIA JULIA. The Curia Hostilia was the stage on which some of the finest orations of Rome were made, including those of Caesar and Cicero. The structure stood prominently in the FORUM ROMANUM.

Curia Julia The new home for the SENATE, begun by Julius CAESAR in place of the CURIA HOSTILIA and finished by AUGUSTUS. It was dedicated in 29 B.C.E. Its location, as conceived by Caesar, reflected the decline of the Senate. Instead of a prominent site in the FORUM ROMANUM, the CURIA now stood next to the BASILICA AEMILIA along a different axis from the original Curia Hostilia, actually near the Forum Julium. In 94 C.E., DOMITIAN reconstructed the Curia Julia slightly in order to position it along the cardinal points of the compass, retaining Caesar's original plan. In 283 C.E., during the reign of CARINUS, a fire destroyed much of the structure. DIOCLETIAN repaired the structure using concrete and stucco. The renewed curia survived and provided the clearest glimpse of the environment in which the Senate of Rome functioned. Two aisles led to the seats of the CONSULS, while on either side the senators in the benches were arranged according to importance and seniority. The more powerful senators sat comfortably in the front, while the junior members stood crowded at the top. The curia was 27 feet by 18 feet, and tremendous congestion must have been commonplace.

Curia Pompeia A *curia* situated in the entrance of the Theater of Pompey. It was reportedly small but served during the construction of the CURIA JULIA as the meeting place of the SENATE. The Senate met in the Curia Pompey on the fateful Ides of March in 44 B.C.E., and Julius CAESAR died at the base of Pompey's statue, which stood in the midst of the building. The *curia* was located near the Tiber, in the area of the Circus Flaminius.

curialis The title given to a member of the city councils (the *curiae*) throughout the Roman Empire; an inherited position. The *curiales* (plural) worked as the local representatives of the imperial government. Their duties included assisting in the administration of estates and offices and, most importantly, in the collection of duties, levies, and taxes. Local agents thus assumed considerable power in their own regions. As the principle representatives of imperial TAXATION, the *curiales* earned the dislike of a city's inhabitants. They acted as workers for the state without real compensation or rewards. Thus only the wealthiest of the social classes in a region could afford service but were initially unwilling to do so, for obvious reasons. Exemptions were made for a number of categories, and senators and Equestrians avoided it because of their duties in Rome, while others were exempted, including the clergy, doctors, and caretakers of imperial grounds. All landowners not eligible for inclusion on the exemption list, all those possessing 25 Roman acres or more had to join the *curia;* their children were compelled to follow.

By the fourth century, as the central bureaucracy under DIOCLETIAN and CONSTANTINE grew in autocratic strength, serving as a *curialis* became unbearable. The *curiales* were seen as tyrannical and cruel oppressors of the poorest classes, while the higher social strata avoided all association with them. Great effort was exerted by individuals to escape the *curiae,* and decrees of the fourth and fifth centuries indicate that they were no more popular with the emperors than they were with the taxed populace. During the time of Diocletian members could not received honorific offices, but under THEODOSIUS II, the Codex Theodosianus (428–439 C.E.) restricted any departures from the land, exacerbating the already unpleasant restrictions. The members were forced to pay tax deficiencies out of their own pocket and were beaten for disobeying imperial decrees. The inevitable collapse of the middle class took place as the *curiales* went bankrupt or fled their land holdings. This social demise worsened the already decaying economic situation in the provinces and contributed to the demise of the Roman Empire.

See also ECONOMY.

cursus honorum Circuit of appointments by which a Roman magistrate could rise to increasingly powerful positions in government. Normally, an individual would assume the offices of: TRIBUNE (military service); QUAESTOR; AEDILE; PRAETOR; CONSUL; and CENSOR. Other forms of the *cursus honorum* existed in the imperial government, including one for the Equestrian Class (EQUITES).

cursus publicus Courier service of the Roman Empire, created by Emperor AUGUSTUS for the purpose of transporting messages and officials from one province to another. A series of forts and stations were spread out along the major road systems connecting the regions of the Roman world. These relay points (or *stationes*) provided horses to dispatch riders, usually soldiers, and vehicles for magistrates or officers of the court. The vehicles were called *clabulae,* but little is known of them. A *diplomata* or certificate issued by the emperor himself was necessary to use the roads. Abuses of the system existed, for governors and minor appointees used the *diplomata* either to aid themselves in transport free of charge or to avail their families; forgeries and stolen *diplomata* were also used.

The *cursus* operated in Italy and in the more advanced provinces. There was only one in EGYPT and one in ASIA MINOR, as Pliny's letters to Trajan attest. It was common for a village to exist every 12 miles or so, and there a courier might rest at large, privately owned *mansiones*. Operated by a *manceps*, or business man, the *mansiones* provided food and lodging, and care and a blacksmith for the horses. The *cursus* also used communities located along the imperial highways. These towns very often provided food and horses to messengers of the LEGIONS, theoretically receiving reimbursement, and were responsible for the care of their section of the Roman ROADS. Disputes arose naturally, and for a time the central administration participated more directly.

Costs for the *cursus publicus* were always high, and its maintenance could not always be guaranteed. Around the time of Nerva, in the late first century, the general cost was transferred to the FISCUS (treasury). Further centralization came during the reign of Hadrian, who created an actual administration under a prefect, who bore the title *praefectus vehiculorum*. Provinces were always in touch with Rome and one another. The Imperial Post gave to the legions the capacity to summon reinforcements and provide status reports before any situation deteriorated too badly. The average citizen sent letters and messages to friends across the sea through slaves and traveling associates. Most news reached its destination eventually.

Cybele The Great Earth Mother of Asia, she found a large and passionate following both in Rome and throughout the empire. The goddess of nature, the mountains, and fertility, she had been known to the Romans through Hellenic influence. In 204 B.C.E., the Senate chose a moment of crisis during the Punic War to bring Cybele to Rome from her cultic center at Pessinus in Phrygia. An embassy brought her black betyl stone of odd shape to the Temple of Victory, and there P. Scipio Nasica installed it. The black stone, made supposedly of meteoric rock, represented Cybele's throne. The great games of MEGALESIA were then held in her honor. In 191 B.C.E., the goddess received her own temple on the Palatine Hill. When Phrygian priests arrived to conduct orgiastic and bloody ceremonies, a law was passed by the Senate to prohibit direct involvement by citizens in the rituals of Cybele, although support of her brotherhoods was allowed. Phrygian clerics became a fixture in the city, with their magnificent attire, and during the reign of Claudius (41–54 C.E.) a more lax attitude toward the cult was adopted.

Cybele's legendary lover Attis, of whom CATULLUS wrote his 63rd poem, began to be honored in Rome under Claudius. With the arrival of this deity the Romans

The Round Temple of Cybele, in Rome, from the Forum Boarium *(Courtesy Fr. Felix Just, S.J.)*

could join the cultic priesthood freely, although the entire cult fell under the jurisdiction of the QUINDECIMVIRI. A new series of holy days in his honor began the spring cycle. Already popular in ASIA MINOR, the cult of Cybele spread out from Rome to the provinces. The goddess was associated with forms of ARTEMIS and VENUS, and cults grew in MACEDONIA, THRACE, AFRICA, HISPANIA, and throughout GALLIA and all of Italy. As a pagan form of worship, Cybele was attacked vehemently by the Christians, and of all the cults in Rome and elsewhere, hers took the longest to die in the Christian era.

In 392 C.E., Emperor Eugenius allowed Cybele to return from exile, having been sent away in 363 under Christian influence. Rome was treated once more to the Megalesian games, and her statue received the obligatory centuries-old washing. The Christians successfully reasserted their dominance in time.

See also GNOSTICISM; GODS AND GODDESSES; RELIGION.

Cynegius, Maternus (fl. late fourth century C.E.) *Praetorian prefect in the East from 384 to 388 C.E.*
Cynegius was a proponent of strict Christian orthodoxy, especially in dealing with the remnants of PAGANISM. Emperor Theodosius I charged him with the task of closing all of the pagan temples in which sacrifices were conducted. Cynegius took to his mission with fanaticism, touring Asia and Egypt and setting off other, more punitive actions by monks who destroyed completely the Serapeum at Alexandria and the temple of Edessa. Cynegius was opposed by LIBANIUS. He also served as consul in 388.

Cynics Members of a philosophical school of the ancient world, probably founded by Diogenes of Sinope (c. 400–325 B.C.E.). In principle, Cynicism called for the ruthless purging of materialism and the development of a sense of ethical selflessness, valuing poverty and the freedom to speak one's mind. The development of the Cynic philosophy was hampered by its own lack of organization; although considerably popular in the fourth and third century B.C.E., it faded in the next 200 years. A rebirth of the movement took place in the first century C.E. Cynics in the Roman Empire were easily identified, because they wandered the cities in rags, preaching their doctrines. They were vocal opponents of authority and government, especially under Vespasian.

Unconventional, demanding, and mocking, the Cynics attacked the emperor and all forms of tyranny, led by DEMETRIUS THE CYNIC. Vespasian at first ignored them, calling Demetrius "good dog," a reference to the Greek *kuon*, or dog, the original term for the Cynics. So harsh did the group become, however, that the normally even-handed emperor first banished them in 71 C.E. and then turned to harsher measures. Although Demetrius was executed, other compatriots later denounced Titus's relationship with the Jewish Princess BERENICE, forcing him to abandon his long-term plans with her. Pseudo-Cynics emerged in the first century C.E. as well, who carried on in their ragged habits while secretly living in comfort and ease. They were condemned by the real Cynics.

Famous Cynics of the first and second century included DIO COCCEIANUS, Peregrinus Proteus, and Demonax. The school remained very popular both in the public imagination and in the minds of the well educated. Remarkable similarities emerged between the Cynics and the early Christian ascetics. By the sixth century C.E., the philosophers had been absorbed completely into the Christian community.

Cyprian of Carthage (Thrascius Caecilius Cyprianus) (d. 258 C.E.) *Bishop of Carthage and an important early Christian theologian*
Born at Tunisia, Cyprian studied law and was a pagan rhetorician prior to his conversion to Christianity about 246. Elected bishop of Carthage around 248, he was soon forced to flee in 249 when the persecutions of Emperor Trajanus Decius began. Cyprian remained in communication with his former diocese by correspondence and, upon his return in 251 to Carthage, he was reestablished as bishop.

He then faced a controversy that would trouble the church for years to come. During the years of persecution many Christians had lapsed from the faith or had purchased *libelli pacis* certificates stating that they had made sacrifices to the Roman gods when in fact they had not. Now they were being welcomed back into the fold with no consequences. Cyprian opposed such lax discipline, but allowed the so-called *lapsi* to return to the church after suitable penance, thereby rejecting the Novatianists, who refused the idea of rebaptism altogether. He supported Pope Cornelius (r. 251–253) in his struggle against Novatian. Cyprian was supported by the African bishops, but the controversy was cut short by the persecution by Emperor Valerian, during which Cyprian was martyred at Carthage on September 14, 258.

A theologian of deep learning, Cyprian authored numerous letters and treatises. His correspondence, providing a clear picture of the times and the horrors of the persecutions, consists of 81 items, 65 from Cyprian and 16 in response to him from others. The treatises include: *De Catholicae Ecclesiae Unitate* (or simply *De Unitate*), discussing the nature of unity in the church and the ideal of equality among the bishops; *De Lapsis*, detailing the conditions by which the lapsed could be readmitted into the church; and *Ad Quirinam* (or *Testimonia*), a compilation of biblical proof texts. He was much influenced by Tertullian and coined a number of remarkable statements such as "You cannot have God for your Father, if you cannot have the Church for your mother."

Cyprus Roman province on the large Mediterranean island off the coast of SYRIA and south of ASIA MINOR. Cyprus came under direct Roman control in 58 B.C.E., when it was attached to the province of CILICIA. In that year, however, political feuds in Rome made its status unclear. CLODIUS sought to remove the troublesome CATO UTICENSIS from the city and so named him administrator of Cyprus. Cato fulfilled his duties, ironically aiding the island in the process. Later and for a brief time, CLEOPATRA owned Cyprus, as a gift from Marc ANTONY. AUGUSTUS reclaimed it and declared the entire stretch of land an imperial province once more, though control probably passed into the hands of the SENATE, appointing a proconsul. Cyprus was dominated by two major cities, Paphos and Salamis. When the massive Jewish revolt broke out in 115 C.E., it spread to Cyprus. By the following year virtually all of Salamis had been destroyed, and its non-Jewish residents had been massacred. When peace was restored, a decree was enacted, banning all Jews from the province and condemning any found on the island to death. Paphos served as the seat of administration during this and other periods, but a terrible earthquake forced the movement of the pro-consul's seat to Salamis in the fourth century C.E.

Known originally as a fertile and abundant island, the province served as a source of copper for some time and helped to promote trade throughout most of the empire. It was said as well that the worship of Aphrodite (VENUS) arrived in Cyprus through Phoenician traders. Christianity took over the island quickly, and the Church of Cyprus won its temporal and theological independence from ANTIOCH as a result of the Council of Chalcedon in 451.

Cyrenaica   *See* CRETE AND CYRENAICA.

Cyrene   A large and prosperous city in North Africa, between ALEXANDRIA and CARTHAGE. Originally a Greek colony, Cyrene belonged to the province of CRETE AND CYRENAICA. The city was located about 10 miles from the coast on the top of the Cyrenaican Mountains, some 2,000 feet above sea level. For some years Cyrene was in the hands of the Ptolemies, and the Republic allowed it to remain so until the early first century B.C.E. Control was then granted to Greek cities, but in 74 B.C.E. all of Cyrenaica reverted to Rome, and Cyrene joined the newly formed province. Under the early empire it grew in size and in wealth, though never boasting great economic power. From 115 to 117 C.E., the Jewish revolt raged across much of Africa, Egypt, and Cyprus, and its flames reached the city. The Greek populations was massacred, temples burned, and roads destroyed. Hadrian assumed the task of rebuilding and repairing, especially the temples of Zeus and Apollo. A number of other monuments and buildings dominated the city, including a temple to Augustus near the Forum of Proclus, a structure erected in the early first century C.E. Baths were also built during the reign of Trajan, though not as impressive as those in Rome or in major provincial capitals.

The economy of Cyrene was based upon agriculture, although horses were bred and raised there as well. Cereals and corn were the main exports after the decline of silphium, a medicinal plant that became nearly extinct.

Cyrene's agora housed several inscriptions dating from the time of Augustus and detailing the enactments of the emperor. The first four inscriptions, dated from 7 to 6 B.C.E. dealt with Crete and Cyrenaica specifically and covered such issues as criminal procedures, treatment of Roman citizens, and the rights of the Greeks. The last decree, issued in 4 B.C.E., covered the judicial powers of the Senate. Cyrene later received colonial status from Hadrian.

Cyril of Alexandria   (d. 444 C.E.) *Bishop of Alexandria from 412*
An influential theologian, Christian saint, and one of the most outspoken figures in the church during the fifth century, Cyril was born in Egypt. He was the nephew of Bishop Theophilus of Alexandria, whom he succeeded in 412. A devoted Orthodox Christian, Cyril spoke out against paganism and heresy. His role in the brutal death of the Neoplatonic philosopher Hypatia in 415 (she was flayed alive with a whip made from abalone shells) is still

questioned by scholars, and he helped expel the Jews from Alexandria after Christians were attacked by members of the Jewish community. Cyril's principal focus, however, was against Nestorius, bishop of Constantinople and founder of the heresy of Nestorianism. Cyril represented the Alexandrian theological position, arguing for the unity of two natures in Christ against Nestorius's theory that Christ had two separate and distinct natures, divine and human. Cyril entered into the severe conflict with Nestorius specifically over the former's adherence that the Virgin Mary be honored with the title Theotokos (Greek for "bearer of God"), a name opposed by Nestorius, who saw Mary as the mother only of the human nature in Christ. Beyond the theological dispute, itself enough to alarm Alexandrian theologians, the dispute had religio-political ramifications, since it represented the potential rise of Constantinople as one of the most important sees in all of Christendom, a development that threatened and was much opposed by the Alexandrians. Both sides attempted to gather supporters, political maneuvering that culminated with the Council of Ephesus in 431.

Wielding the firm approval of Pope (later Saint) Celestine I (r. 422–432), Cyril served as president of the council, securing the condemnation of Nestorius, moving so precipitately that he did not wait for the arrival of a number of bishops from the East. As most of these prelates were allies or supporters of Nestorius, they convened on their own and condemned Cyril. While Nestorius was exiled, a breach had opened between Cyril and the see of Antioch, a disagreement resolved only in 433 with a compromise declaration on the nature of Christ. Cyril remained bishop until his death. He made important contributions to Christian theology, especially the Trinity and the nature of Christ. His brilliant writings included letters and anathemas, and a refutation of the work *Against the Galileans* by Emperor Julian the Apostate (r. 361–363). This defense of Christianity is the last of the great apologies for the faith in the Roman era.

Cyril of Jerusalem   (c. 315–386 C.E.) *Christian saint and bishop of Jerusalem during the troubled era of the Arian Controversy*
A native of Jerusalem, Cyril became bishop in Jerusalem around 349 or 350, succeeding Maximus. He was exiled in 357 from his post by the Arians because of his opposition to their cause, the first of three separate periods of exile; of the thirty-five years he spent as bishop, Cyril was in exile for sixteen. The last period was from 367–378 when he was banished by the Emperor Valens. He returned to Jerusalem in 378 after Valens's defeat and death at the terrible battle of Adrianople (378). Jerusalem was in a state of severe moral decay and was plagued by spiritual and social disorder. Cyril thus spent his last year

bringing reforms and revitalization. Possibly suspected himself of heresy (he did not like the term *homoousios,* of one substance, concerning the nature of Christ, because it was man-made), he went to the Council of Constantinople in 381 and recited the creed used at Jerusalem, which contained *homoousios.* He survived the reign of Julian the Apostate without banishment. Cyril's primary surviving work is the *Catecheses,* 18 instructional addresses for baptismal candidates during Lent and five for the newly baptized after Easter. The last five are known as the *Mystagogic,* as they are concerned with mysteries.

Cyrus, Flavius (fl. fifth century C.E.) *Praetorian prefect of the East (439–441) and Prefect of the City of Constantinople (439)*
From Panopolis in Egypt originally, Cyrus studied architecture and art and wrote poetry. Although generally considered a pagan, he attained influence in the court at CONSTANTINOPLE and the friendship of Empress EUDOCIA, wife of THEODOSIUS II. As Praetorian prefect, he proved both successful and, until 441, immensely popular. Cyrus issued decrees in Greek, rather than Latin, and effected numerous civic improvements, completing the walls of Anthemius, restoring buildings, and installing street lighting. In 441, however, his influence faded with Eudocia's fall from power. Apparently converted to Christianity, he was then named to the see of a small town in PHRYGIA, where his first sermon contained a mere 37 words.

Cyzicus City in the province of BITHYNIA, located at the neck of a peninsula jutting into the Sea of Marmara.

Cyzicus traditionally served as a major port in the Bosporus region because of its two harbors and its ingenious defense measures. The isthmus could be flooded to halt sieges or attacks from pirates, an event that took place in 21 C.E. The city was a haven for the combatants of the civil war between Antony and Octavian (Augustus). Its increasing power in trade brought merchants into conflict with other parties in time. In 20 B.C.E., Cyzicus temporarily suffered the loss of its rights (*Libertas*), apparently because of the murder of several traders from Rome. Claudius established a mint at Cyzicus, and Hadrian build a large temple, affirming the city's status as a metropolis. By the third century C.E., its influence stretched throughout Bithynia and into Mysia. Antonia Tryphaena, the widow of the murdered COTYS OF THRACE, lived in Cyzicus.

Cyzicus, battle of An engagement in the fall of 193 C.E. between the legions of Septimius SEVERUS and the governor of Asia, Asellius Aemilianus, who supported NIGER in the battle for the throne of Rome. When Severus marched from Rome, Aemilianus tried to stop his advance on the west side of the Bosporus, at Byzantium, failing in his efforts. The governor doubled back to meet the enemy, being ferried to the eastern shore. Near Cyzicus the two armies clashed, and Aemilianus was crushed. He died on the field of battle, as did Bithynian support for Niger.

See also ISSUS; NICAEA, BATTLE OF.

Dacia A rugged, mountainous land located north of the Danube River in the areas of present-day Transylvania and eastern Hungary. Dacia became a target for Roman strategic interests and, despite the fierce opposition of its native people, served as an imperial province from around 106 to 271 C.E.

AN INDEPENDENT KINGDOM

The Dacians probably came from a Thracian stock and moved into the region sometime in the seventh or sixth century B.C.E. They were joined by the Getae, with whom they shared certain cultural and linguistic similarities. The Dacians warred with their neighbors, especially the Getae, but a certain geographic isolation allowed them to survive often catastrophic struggles and to retain dominance. Situated south of the Carpathian Mountains, they developed an identifiable culture, and by the first century B.C.E. they were the leading tribe of the region. A stable leadership was all that the Dacians required for greatness.

Around 61 B.C.E., Burebista emerged as the king of the Dacians. He organized and improved the socioeconomic coalition of the people and launched a vast campaign of conquest against the surrounding chiefdoms and clans. Burebista destroyed the Boii, the Taurisci, and the Bastarnae before ravaging Thrace and threatening the entire Danube and Black sea territories. His success brought Dacia not only to the attention of Rome but also into direct involvement in its politics, when Pompey sought the king as an ally in 48 B.C.E. Julius CAESAR was certainly aware of the growing menace presented by Burebista and planned an expedition against him. Both rulers were assassinated, however, in 44 B.C.E. The Dacian king-

dom fell apart amid turmoil and civil strife. Octavian (AUGUSTUS) nevertheless worried about the frontier and possible alliances between Marc ANTONY and the Dacians. He too plotted an expedition around 35 B.C.E; because of Antony, he had to propose a marriage with the daughter of Cotiso, the new Dacian king. The war with Antony prevented the completion of such designs, and no settlement of the Dacian question was forthcoming during Augustus's reign.

Despite several small conflicts, no serious campaigns were mounted, and Augustus had to content himself with simple containment of the state. He claimed in his *Res Gestae* that the Dacians had been subdued. This was mere propaganda, because Dacian troops frequently crossed the Danube to ravage parts of Pannonia and Moesia, especially during the winter when the river froze. During Tiberius's reign (14–37 C.E.) efforts were made to maintain the established frontier, but even he had to move allied people away from the Dacian reach, especially the Iazyges and the Roxolani. These tribes were transported to Moesia during the years of Nero. In 69 C.E., even more serious inroads were made in Moesia as the Roxolani feuded with the Dacians. No Roman retribution was immediately forthcoming, but a collision was inevitable as the new king of Dacia made his move in 85 C.E.

Sometime between 69 and 85, a powerful and gifted warrior named DECEBALUS gained undisputed mastery over the Dacians. He proved to be an excellent ruler, rebuilding the unity of the land and improving the already formidable military strength of the army. The governor of Moesia, Oppius SABINUS, found himself beset by an invasion in 85 and was defeated and killed with much of the V Alaudae Legion. The war between Rome

An engraving of the Dacian Wars during the reign of Trajan (98–117 C.E.) *(Hulton/Getty Archive)*

and Dacia had begun. Emperor DOMITIAN hurried to Moesia with reinforcements. He pushed the Dacians out of the imperial territory and then returned to Rome. Cornelius Fuscus, Prefect of the Praetorian Guard, remained to launch a campaign into Dacia itself. He suffered a rout and death as the entire Danube was again threatened. The emperor returned to gain a victory at Tapae, near a pass called the Iron Gates. Decebalus accepted terms for a temporary peace in 89, knowing that he was unchallenged in the field.

For a time Decebalus accepted his role as a client of Rome, but Dacian interests propelled his people into another war. TRAJAN began the greatest series of battles in Dacia's history in March 101, and by 106, all of Decebalus's realm was vanquished. Decebalus died by his own hand. With all of Dacia in his control, Trajan made the momentous decision to declare it an imperial province within the Roman Empire.

For the next 164 years the remnants of the Dacians lived under the rule of outsiders and endured the arrival of foreign colonists. Those Dacian refugees who fled their homeland or were expelled kept alive their traditions and culture. Starting in the third century C.E., they became the extremely dangerous barbarian force of the CARPI. As imperial power collapsed in the provinces in the face of the Goths and others, the evacuation of Dacia became necessary, and in 270–271, the Dacians were reunited as a nation, witnessing the return of their culture.

As a people, the Dacians pursued the traditional Geto-Dacian way of life, with agriculture and cattle rais-

ing, but also developed a Celtic/Thracian style of mining and superb metal crafting arts. The Carpathian Mountains were abundant in gold, silver, and iron, and the Dacians profited handsomely from the wares forged and carved out of these natural resources. Later economic ties provided the wealth so essential for the rise of cities and nationalism.

Mines, treasures, and unity of purpose attracted other peoples, and by the first century B.C.E., foreign cultural influences could be seen. The Germanic-Sarmatian tribes surrounding Dacia, subdued and controlled by Burebista, nevertheless played a distinct role in Dacian culture, especially in fostering anti-Roman sentiments.

AN IMPERIAL PROVINCE

The Roman occupation of Dacia first aimed at reducing the inevitable resistance through a program that called for the garrisoning of troops throughout the province and the use of the LIMES, the defensive system proven in other regions. Rome moved quickly to make its occupation permanent. In 118–119, Hadrian divided Dacia into Superior and Inferior and divided the Superior region again in 124 C.E., forming a Dacia Porolissensis. Three provinces thus prevented a national uprising, and the presence of one governor to watch over all three kept intelligence well in hand.

The major source of imperial influence, however, came not from the legions or legates but from simple colonists and merchants. From all over the empire, especially from the Danubian provinces, farmers and founders of *coloniae* arrived to receive tracts of land and to take up residence in Dacian territories. Sarmizegethusa was declared a *colonia* to exemplify its status as a provincial capital.

Colonial communities made cultural life in Dacia a very mixed and decidedly cosmopolitan affair. The Dacians retained their names and their own ways in the midst of the newcomers, and the region continued to exhibit Dacian characteristics. Outside the province, however, those Dacians who had fled their homeland bided their time, watching the Romans drain their native territory of gold while rebuilding and improving their cities. Workers labored in the mines of Dacia to bring out the gold, silver, and other metals desired by the emperors. The Dalmatians were noted for their mining skills, and Trajan erected many buildings in Rome with resources stripped from Dacia. Cities in the Dacian provinces did gain as a result of Roman interest. The greatest of these, aside from Sarmizegethusa, was Apulum. The one-time camp of the legions grew in size until it achieved both municipal and colonial rank. When Dacia was separated into several provinces, Apulum served first as the chief community of Dacia Superior. Later the governor of the entire region resided there.

From the start the Roman Empire faced problems with Dacia. Strategically the stable line of defense had always rested upon the Danube, and the Dacian kingdom extended well north of the Danubian provinces. Its borders fronted such troublesome groups as the Roxolani, the Sarmatians, and worst of all, from a Roman perspective, the Goths. Maintaining the frontier proved increasingly difficult as the Carpi and the Goths pushed into Transylvania. Their organization and strength increased at the same time that Rome was beset by the crisis of the mid-third century C.E. AURELIAN, who headed the relatively successful military recovery, nevertheless decided that the Dacian holdings were far too exposed. He made the decision to evacuate all of Dacia. Parts of Moesia were seized in order to form yet another province for the evacuees, but the prize of Dacia was surrendered to its native peoples forever.

Dalmatia   *See* ILLYRICUM.

Dalmatius, Flavius (d. c. 337 C.E.) *Half-brother of Constantine the Great, by Constantius I Chlorus and Theodora*
As a relative of the emperor, Dalmatius had various positions of authority, including a censorship and consulship in 333. From 334 to 335, he held a command in the Eastern Empire, where he put down a revolt of Calocaerus, whom he put to death in Tarsus. In 335, he saved ATHANASIUS from persecution at the Council of Tyre but died, probably in 337, as part of the terrible massacre instigated by the heirs of CONSTANTINE, following that ruler's death.

Dalmatius, Flavius Julius (d. 337 C.E.) *Son of Flavius Dalmatius and nephew of Constantine the Great*
Reportedly a favorite of his uncle, Dalmatius received an education at Toulouse. On September 18, 335, he was granted the title of Caesar and was no doubt included in the intended division of the empire at CONSTANTINE's death. His territories, according to the will, were to include Thrace, Macedonia, and Achaea. CONSTANTIUS II was apparently jealous of him, and in 337, after the death of Constantine, a massacre took place within the family and palace. Dalmatius was put to death along with his father and many other relatives.

Damascus   Large, ancient city in southern Syria on the banks of the Chrysorrhoas River, east of Phoenicia. Damascus has stood for millennia as one of the great centers in Syria and dates to the era of Abraham. It was, however, overshadowed in Roman times by ANTIOCH, the capital of the imperial province, and by PALMYRA. Damascus was directly on the frontier with the Parthian, and later Persian, Empire, and thus was positioned perfectly to receive and distribute the trade coming from the east and from Palmyra. Caravans crossing the arid lands of southern Mesopotamia found the many comforts of the city inviting; under the empire, trade was abundant, despite the bitter wars with the Parthians and the Sassanids. During the Late Roman Empire, Damascus served with Antioch and Edessa as an arms factory, acquiring a reputation for manufacturing exquisite blades. Its position was always threatened, as Rome lost control over its frontiers.

Damasus (c. 304–384 C.E.) *Bishop of Rome and pope, from 366 to 384*
Of Spanish descent, Damasus entered the service of LIBERIUS, his predecessor as bishop, and became a deacon of the Christian Church. Most of the clergy and the laity supported Damasus, but a small and powerful minority chose Ursicinus as a candidate for the bishopric. Both men were elected in rival churches, and fighting erupted in the streets, causing the death of some 137 people. Having worked for Liberius, Damasus had made many friends in the government, and Emperor Valentinian I stepped into the dispute. The emperor exiled Ursicinus and declared Damasus to be pope. The archives of his predecessor were carefully maintained, several new churches were built and steps were taken to honor the martyrs. The tombs of the martyrs were elaborately decorated with poems written by Damasus and carved by the famous Filocalus. Damasus also worked against the rampant heresies of the time, corresponding with Basil of Caesarea, with an eye toward eliminating ARIANISM. He was reportedly fond of stylish attire.

damnatio memoriae   A severe element in the penalty for *MAIESTAS* (treason). According to its terms, the name (*praenomen*) of the charged was to be expunged, thus ensuring that the name would not be passed on to a next generation. Additionally, the name was scratched off all inscriptions, and any statues or images of the condemned were destroyed. Several emperors were subject to the *damnatio memoriae*, such as Nero and Didius Julianus.

Danube   One of the great rivers of the Roman Empire, serving for centuries as the northern frontier of imperial territory. The river bore two names: The Upper Danube, from its source in Germania to the city of Vienna, was called Danubius, and the Lower Danube, from Vienna to the Black Sea, was known as the Ister. Virtually every province from the Alps to Asia bordered the river, including RAETIA, NORICUM, PANNONIA, ILLYRICUM, MOESIA, and THRACE. Emperor Augustus (ruled 27 B.C.E.–14 C.E.) determined that the Danube would be a natural border between the provinces and the barbarians of the north. As he plotted the means by which he could unite the regions of Greece and Macedonia with Italy and Gaul, he launched several punitive expeditions over the Danube into DACIA, to reduce the pressures from the tribes there. Thus Lucius Domitius Ahenobarbus attacked from 7 to 2 B.C.E., as possibly did M. Vinicius. In 6 C.E., a more concerted effort was headed by TIBERIUS, whose operations were cut short by a massive revolt in Illyricum and Pannonia.

The uprising pointed to a perennial weakness in the entire frontier. Tribes on both sides of the Danube were unstable and unreliable; Rome stationed anywhere from seven to 12 legions on the Danube at any given time. Auxiliary troops probably were first used in support of these legions. A fleet sailed the river well into the fifth century, when the Praetorian prefect of Constantinople, ANTHEMIUS, reorganized the ships and boats and made them far more effective. Strategically essential to Roman supremacy, the Danube inevitably became a battleground between the empire and the ever-changing peoples of Dacia and beyond. TRAJAN, from around 100 to 106 C.E., waged a large war against DECEBALUS of Dacia, based on the Danube. He subsequently made Dacia a province and eased the burden on the Danubian line. Trajan's dream would not last beyond the third century C.E., for the sheer length of the frontier made defense difficult in the face of an organized or massive foe.

After the death of Emperor Marcus Aurelius in 180, and in the face of the reluctance of his heir, Commodus, to carry on conquests, instability was inevitable. Throughout the century the Goths threatened the province, and in 249, KNIVA, the king of the Goths, caused havoc. In 251, Emperor Trajanus Decius fell in battle near the Danube, and from 254 to 261 the once secure border to the north was overrun. Although Constantine would campaign effectively, the problems inher-

ent with the river were a contributing factor in the decision to create a new Roman capital, closer to this chronic theater of operations. But even Constantinople could not halt the march of the Goths, and in 378, pushed by migratory peoples farther to the east, these hard-fighting barbarians settled across the Danube. That same year they crushed Emperor Valens at ADRIANOPLE, ending forever imperial hopes of ruling the region. The Danube was worshiped by the local tribes, such as the Getae, Thracians, Marcomanni, and Dacians, as a living god of nature.

Daphne   A Greek deity worshiped by the Greeks and Romans. It was said that Apollo saw Daphne and fell madly in love and eagerly pursued her. But she refused his advances, and when he did not stop his attentions, she called out to her divine mother, Gaia, Mother Earth, for aid. She transformed her into a laurel tree. To the Romans Daphne epitomized the virtue of virginity. Her symbol was the laurel wreath, as Apollo honored her by wearing one himself. In Antioch there was a grove named Daphne, where stood a temple of Apollo.

See also GODS AND GODDESSES OF ROME.

Datianus   (d. after 365 C.E.) *Consul, senator, and comes under Constantine the Great and Constantius II*
Datianus had considerable influence in the imperial court at Constantinople. He was the son of a bath attendant who made the most of his opportunities. He learned to read and write, mastered the shorthand of the period and became one of the NOTARII. In 337, Constantius became emperor, and Datianus served as one of his closest advisers. Over the next years his offices and power increased. He became a senator of Constantinople, a COMES circa 345, consul in 358 and a patrician sometime before 360. He was the one who wrote to Athanasius, bestowing upon him the right to return to Alexandria, and his status in the court clearly did not die with Constantius in 361. Datianus was a member of the confidential circle of Emperor Jovian, and when Jovian died in 364, he wrote to the imperial ministers at Nicaea, trying to find a new ruler and heartily recommending Valentinian.

Dea Dia   Ancient Roman goddess whose special area of divine concern was the fertility of the annual crops. Her sacred residence was a grove, and her ministers, the ARVAL BRETHREN. The Arval Brethren performed the worship rituals of Dea Dia in May, as part of their regular priesthood duties. The festival took place over a four-day period (actually three days, with one day separating the ceremonies of the first and second days). Opening rites included prayers at the home of the head of the brethren, the magister. The second ritual was held at the grove. At dawn the prayers of honor and adoration were sung. Later, bedecked in wreaths of corn ears, the actual sacrifices, the *agna opima* were made. Feasts concluded the proceedings, as Rome celebrated the abundance of Dea Dia's gifts.

See also GODS AND GODDESSES OF ROME.

death Considered a source of incredible bad luck (to the living) by the Romans, who were great students of fortune and ill. Death was a temporary curse, a *funestum* that could be overcome with certain traditions and rituals, and the passing of a family member was a solemn occasion. Immediately after the death, the survivors performed the *conclamatio,* or wailing and crying, accompanied by the blowing of horns, which announced the parting of a loved one. Each family member then gave his or her final farewells, the *extremum vale.* The corpse was washed and anointed, dressed in suitably splendid raiment, according to the person's station in life, and placed upon a bier. Until the period of mourning was ended, no priestly official of Jupiter could approach the house of the deceased or touch the body. A cypress was placed in front of the residence to warn clergy, especially the PONTIFEX MAXIMUS, to stay away.

On the day of the funeral, the body was carried to the final resting place, a location of some importance. The procession included many torchbearers, although cremation was not always the final means of disposal. Cremation was the most common means, however, and bits of bone were retained after the ritual burning. Such remnants were buried, for it was considered essential that the earth cover some part of the body. After the rituals, several days, usually nine, or even weeks passed before the priests declared the burial complete. The ceremonies accompanying the funerals, burials, and cremations of the Romans were equally crucial. A pig was sacrificed on occasion, and the purifying prayers were recited for the house. Further sacrifices were also offered to the LARES.

Nine days later, eight after the funeral, offerings were made on the *novendiale sacrificium* or the final day. Wax masks were hung on the walls, depicting the faces of those who had died. These could be used in the funeral processions as well, worn by actors who played the parts of ancestors who walked with the dead and ushered them into the next world. These rites of parting were called the *iusta facere.* They had to be performed correctly or the consequences for the departed and the living would be spiritually grievous. If left without burial, or if buried improperly, the spirit of the deceased would walk the earth in an evil mood and might even return to its former abode. Precautions were taken to avoid that possibility, but when necessary, other steps could be taken to keep the dead from causing trouble. Purifications of the house helped, as did the practice of taking the deceased out of his residence feet first.

More extreme forms of exorcism took place at the somber festival of the dead, the Lemuria, held every May. A ghost could be repulsed by spitting out black beans, and by uttering: "With these you and I are redeemed." Ovid described the Lemuria as a terrible event of three days, filled with the LEMURES and demons roaming the city. The Lemuria was certainly reflective of an ancient view of death, and it was opposed by the newer, more pleasant philosophy behind the Parentalia or Feast of Souls, held from the 13th to the 21st of each February. The Parentalia was a beautiful ceremony, designed to help recall the deceased, be they mother, father, daughter, or son. These deceased came not as terrible spirits but as loved ones not to be feared. As such they were honored relatives.

The state used this day to commemorate all dead ancestors, the founders and builders of the greatness that was Rome. There was none of the dread so infused into Ovid's description of the Lemuria. Instead, the Romans faced the prospect of death with an optimism that reasoned that the deceased had been successful in reaching their final goal. A soul or spirit journeyed into the Underworld, and, if all went according to practiced traditions, it would enter there and live with the other transformed spiritual entities, the MANES. The exact structure or landscape of the region remained suitably vague. Christianity, of course, changed Roman concepts about death and the afterlife. Like the pagan gods, the *lemures* and the *manes* and their eternal abodes faded or were absorbed into the new religious tenets.

Decangi A tribe in Britain that probably resided in the area of modern Cheshire. The Decangi (or Deceangi) were victims of the campaign of Ostorius Scapula in 50 C.E. Their lands were ruined and most of their wealth seized outright, a prize of some value considering the lead mines nearby. The newly created province of BRITANNIA would eventually include the Decangi.

Decebalus (d. 106 C.E.) *King of the Dacians; ruled in Dacia from sometime before 85 C.E. until his death*
Decebalus proved an excellent king and a brilliant general, avoiding personal defeat at Roman hands until the reign of TRAJAN. After the fall of Nero in 69 C.E. and several Dacian incursions into the Danubian provinces, the often strife-torn domain of DACIA witnessed the emergence of the warrior Decebalus. He seized the throne and laid claim to the entire country. Under his guidance the once great army was restored to its level in the era of BUREBISTAS, who had ruled from circa 60 to 44 B.C.E. As a result, the unity of Dacia was unquestioned.

In 85 C.E., Decebalus resolved to defeat his great enemy, Rome. He launched a campaign into Moesia, where he crushed and killed its governor, Oppius Sabinus. Emperor Domitian marched to the province and, after bitter fighting, drove the Dacians back across the Danube. In 86, the Praetorian Prefect Cornelius Fuscus invaded Dacia, only to be annihilated. The Romans returned with reinforcements, driving far into the region and winning a victory at Tapae, near the mountain pass called the Iron Gate, in 88, under the command of Tettius Julianus. Domitian himself returned to take part in the final surrender. Decebalus sued then for peace and in time a treaty was enjoined between Rome and Dacia. Domitian was caught by an uprising in Germania and had to accept terms for a general peace in the area. He recognized Decebalus as a client in return for a promise not to engage in anti-imperial activities. Reasonably satisfied by this arrangement, Rome and Dacia agreed to the pact in 89.

However, the agreement was broken and war broke out in 101. Trajan intended to reduce the pressure along the Danube and Dacia. With hopes of luring the Romans to their destruction, as he had done to Cornelius Fuscus, Decebalus permitted an uncontested advance and then attacked at Tapae—a stalemate. Decebalus used the winter to counterattack, this time in Moesia. His gamble failed, and Trajan won more victories in the spring of 102. To save his capital and to spare his people more hardships, Decebalus capitulated. Trajan allowed him to keep his throne, and Decebalus plotted revenge. In 105, he threw off the cloak of obedience and client status and made war upon the Roman ally, the Iazyges. Accompanied by a vast army, Trajan swept into Dacia, reducing the opposition until at last the great Dacian city of SARMIZEGETHUSA was his. Decebalus fled north in 106 with the few trusted servants he had maintained over the years, finally killing himself in order to avoid capture. As a trophy for the Senate and for the people of Rome, the king's head was dispatched to the Eternal City, and his kingdom became an imperial province.

The historian Dio wrote that Decebalus hid his vast treasure by diverting the course of the Sargetia River, burying the wealth in a large pit, covering it with rocks and then allowing the river to return to its normal path.

Decius, Gaius Messius Quintus (Trajanus) (d. 251 C.E.) *Emperor from 249 to 251 C.E.*

Originally from Pannonia and born around 190 C.E., Decius held various posts in Rome and was probably prefect of the city in 248, when Emperor PHILIP I, plagued with troubles all over the empire, looked for a suitable general to restore imperial supremacy along the Danube frontier. He chose Decius, who departed for Moesia.

Decius proved an able administrator and general. The Danubian legions were brought back under control and, in a series of engagements, repulsed the invading Goths. As was typical for the age, his success convinced the troops under his command that he should be given the throne. What Decius thought of this initially is unknown, and he may have intended to surrender to Philip eventually. As it was, Philip marched to northern Italy to meet the legions of Decius in September of 249. He lost a battle at Verona, died on the field, and his young son Philip was put to death. A generally obedient

Senate granted the new emperor the title of Trajanus. Two major issues dominated the rest of Decius's brief reign: the deliberate and organized persecution of CHRISTIANITY and the war against the Goths.

Beginning in 250, Decius initiated a series of harsh measures against the Christians. Their leaders were arrested, imprisoned, and executed. Sacrifices were then ordered, and all citizens of Rome had to make offerings to the gods and in return received certificates guaranteeing their actions and their safety. The Christian Church was thrown into a state of panic, and under relentless pressure Christians everywhere recanted their faith. The death of the religion, however, was prevented by the far greater crisis on the Danubian frontier. In 249, Decius left his post to begin his campaign against Philip—offering KNIVA, the king of the Goths, a golden opportunity. He struck at Moesia. Decius named his son Herennius as Augustus and sent him to Moesia to prepare the way for his own campaigns. Decius arrived in 250 and inflicted a defeat upon Kniva but was then severely checked and forced to flee for the safety of Roman territory at the Danube.

In 251, Decius chose to attack the Goths. In June, near Abrittus, both Decius and his son perished in a disastrous encounter. Trebonianus Gallus succeeded him. Christianity witnessed a softening on the part of the empire, and the Goths poured into the Balkans. Decius was notable for originating one of the first great persecutions of Christians and for being the first emperor to fall in battle.

declamatio   A declamation; originally a Greek form of oratory, it developed under the Romans into an oratorical exercise, customarily about some abstract or artificial subject. The two types of *declamatio* were the *suasoria* and the *controversia*. The *suasoria* was a discussion held by a person with himself on a given topic, usually historical in nature. The *controversia* was a mock legal proceeding to improve a lawyer's presentation in court. Quintilian noted that this exercise was often taken to extremes, with the orator becoming proficient at speaking on any subject the moment that it was first proposed.

decuriones   Senate members in municipal towns and colonies. They received their positions as town councillors for life and eventually passed them on as hereditary titles and duties. Former magistrates were chosen according to their wealth and age, coming together to oversee the administrative life of their communities. They became the unhappy and despised classes of the *curiales* in time.

See also CURIALIS.

Deiotarus (fl. first century B.C.E.) *Ruler of Armenia Minor and part of Galatia for much of the Late Republic*
Deiotarus was placed in power by Pompey in 63 B.C.E., as part of his settlement of the East. From the start he

evinced ambitions toward his neighbors in Asia Minor but remained generally reliable as a Roman ally, although he became embroiled in the politics of the Republic. In 59 B.C.E., the powerful politician P. Clodius Pulcher stripped him of part of his Galatian territory. Deiotarus later chose the wrong side in the CIVIL WAR between Julius Caesar and Pompey (49–45 B.C.E.), siding with the Pompeians. After the battle of Pharsalus in 48 B.C.E., he apparently pledged himself to Caesar and used his troops to aid Caesar at the battle of Zela in 46. Caesar was aware of his past record, however, and returned his realm to him with marked reductions in size and territory. Mithridates of Pergamum received eastern GALATIA, and Ariobarzanes of Cappadocia was given the throne of ARMENIA Minor. Deiotarus's survival was reportedly due to the intervention of Cicero, a friend whom he had assisted when the famed figure was serving as a governor in Cilicia in 52 B.C.E. The soldiers of Deiotarus were considered some of the best in his area of the empire.

delatores The informers and accusers of Rome, the professionals who profited from the fall of the great. In the early empire legal bias and political desire conspired to make an informer's job both easy and useful. Any accuser would receive one-quarter of the property of the victim if he or she were prosecuted, and certain laws existed in such vague terminology that virtually anyone could come under suspicion.

Two laws formed the foundation of the *delatores*, the *lex Papia Poppaea* and the *lex Iulia de maiestate*, the law of conspiracy and the law of treason (MAIESTAS). Created by Emperor Augustus for the good of the state, they were open to ridiculous and terrible interpretations by those seeking to intimidate or annihilate a victim. The *delatores* provided evidence and testimony. There was a lure of promised riches for the creative informer, especially if he could be used by the servants of the state to bring down wealthy or powerful nobles, generals, senators, and even members of the royal family.

Tacitus in his *Annals* bemoaned the development of what he called a steady system of oppression, crediting Emperor Tiberius with the first fostering of its hideous effects in Rome. His reign had not begun with cruelty, and he lent a certain air of common sense to legal proceedings in the beginning. As his reign progressed, however, and as the ambitions of SEJANUS, the Prefect of the PRAETORIAN GUARD, grew, no one was safe from accusation or attack. One of the first *delatores* mentioned by Tacitus was Romanus Hispo. In 15 C.E. he accused Granius Marcellus, the *praetor* of Bithynia, of treason and improprieties in his post. Although Granius was acquitted, the entire affair convinced many unscrupulous men of the opportunities awaiting.

More saw the possibilities following the trial of Drusus Libo in 16 C.E. Of the Scribonii, Drusus fell prey

to ambitious friends who convinced him to celebrate his heritage, especially his kinship with Pompey. They then brought evidence to Tiberius of treasonable activities. Informers provided the often fanciful details, and Drusus was put on trial before committing suicide. Chief among the *delatores* who testified at the trial was Fulcinius Trio. He impeached Libo himself and then gained both politically and financially from Libo's demise. Trio's career epitomized the successful *delator.* Tiberius used him in 20 against Piso, in the famous affair following the death of Germanicus, and then again in 31, to ferret out and crush the supporters of the dead Sejanus. For his efforts, Trio received the consulship of 31.

But just as Tiberius turned on Sejanus in 31, so did the informers themselves face torment and even death. Many associates of the prefect were executed and others died because Tiberius found them no longer useful to his plans. Fulcinius Trio was haunted by the prospect of dying through torture or starvation in a dungeon and killed himself in 35.

Although Claudius launched a program against the *delatores* in 42, his wife, Empress Messallina, and the leading freedman, Narcissus, gathered slaves and other freedmen into a network of informants who would spy on their owners and superiors. The result was a terrible rebirth of the *delatores* during the years of Nero and his Praetorian Prefect Ofonius Tigellinus.

The climate for the *delatores* changed when the Flavians took the throne in 69. Titus disliked informers of every kind and banished them altogether in 79, an act repeated by his stern brother, Domitian, in 81. Their actions were based certainly upon a respect for the rights of the Romans but also upon the improved means of state control and intelligence gathering. Suetonius wrote that Titus would send out detachments of the Praetorian Guard to arrest and murder those he feared or disliked. His assassins were the dangerous SPECULATORES of the guard, the agents, spies, and killers of the Praetorian ranks. The *speculatores* served as one of the early Roman intelligence units, and with the later, far larger and better organized FRUMENTARII, rendered the concept of the *delatores* obsolete. From them on, all informers were paid by the government, dependent upon imperial spy masters for their wages.

Deldo (d. 29 B.C.E.) *King of the migratory tribe of the Bastarnae (Scythians), who led a people long accustomed to warfare*
The Bastarnae had marched into the Danube region in the middle of the first century B.C.E. There they fought with the Triballi and Moesi, achieving some success. By 30 B.C.E., however, Deldo looked south to the pastures of northern Macedonia. He launched a sortie over the Haemus Range, thereby attracting the local Roman legions under the command of Marcus Licinius

CRASSUS (2). With a sizable army (possibly four legions), Crassus repulsed the Bastarnae in 29 B.C.E. Deldo then made the mistake of asking to negotiate. By a clever ruse, Crassus maneuvered Deldo and his entire host into a disastrous position on the Cedrus River, a tributary of the Danube. A massacre ensued, and Deldo suffered the unfortunate distinction of being killed in battle by Crassus himself.

Demetrius (fl. third century C.E.) *Bishop of Alexandria and the man responsible for the rise of Origen in the Egyptian Church*

Needing catechists in the face of the severe persecutions of the period, Demetrius chose ORIGEN to teach in the Alexandrian school. While there, Origen began to acquire his reputation for brilliance, and he traveled to Rome to hear Hippolytus. Demetrius preferred to keep Origen in Alexandria and recalled him to help administer the educational programs of the diocese. Origen gathered increasing renown as a theologian, receiving request for visits from as far away as Arabia; he also preached in Caesarea and Jerusalem. Demetrius, angered by the actions of an underling who had not even been ordained, sent several priests after him.

Around 225 C.E., Origen's writings began to appear, especially his theological and doctrinal treatise on the principle of Christianity. In 230, Origen departed again from Egypt, this time going to Athens. On the way he was ordained a presbyter by the bishops of Jerusalem and Caesarea. Demetrius finally had had enough, and in the following year he excommunicated Origen, a condemnation that Origen refused to accept without debate. At first Origen was successful, as the Eastern prelates supported him and refused to acknowledge Demetrius's jurisdiction. In 232, the formidable Julia Mamaea, the mother of Severus Alexander, granted Origen imperial protection. Defeated, Demetrius administered his see for several years before being succeeded by Heracles, a pupil of Origen.

Demetrius the Cynic (fl. first century C.E.) *Leader of the popular movement of Cynics*

Demetrius was one of the most outspoken members of the school of philosophy already famed for its harsh attacks on authority. He was a friend of Seneca and Thrasea Paetus, and was present when Paetus received the order from the Senate that he had to die. Demetrius's activities and associations caused him to be exiled by the Praetorian Prefect Ofonius Tigellinus in 66 C.E.

He returned to Rome in time to see Vespasian upon the throne and immediately returned to his CYNIC tactics. He added his formidable skills to the efforts of other Cynics and Stoics, who were heaping abuses on the new emperor. Vespasian at first responded with good humor, but Musonius Rufus convinced the emperor to expel the troublesome philosophers. Demetrius was sent to an island. While others yielded to such threats, the Cynic merely converted his words to paper and continued his war against the monarchy. Vespasian responded to one such attack, saying: "You are doing everything you can to make me kill you, but I do not kill barking dogs." Finally, Demetrius did enough to coerce the emperor, and died at the hands of Roman executioners.

denarius One of the principal silver coins issued both by the Republic and the empire. Its name was derived from its use as an exchange equivalent for 10 ASSES (*a denis assibus*). The denarius was first issued circa 269 B.C.E.

During the period of the empire, the denarius served as the silver coin of general issue and bore a portrait of the emperor. From the time of Augustus its value decreased as its weight was diminished by the use of bronze. In time it was valued at only one-eighth of its original value, in effect a useless bronze monetary unit. An effort was made at the start of the third century C.E. to revive the worth of the denarius through the striking of a new silver denomination, the ANTONINIANUS, a coin issued by Caracalla. This currency remained in circulation until the time of Diocletian. Around 296 C.E., the denarius was reborn under the name of *argenteus*.

See also COINAGE.

Densus, Sempronius (d. 69 C.E.) *Centurion of the Praetorian Guard*

Densus was noted by both the historians Dio and Tacitus as being one of the few loyal soldiers in Rome on January 15, 69, when Galba was assassinated by the Praetorian Guard in favor of Otho. There are two different accounts of Densus's death. Dio's account declares that Densus

Samples of the denarius *(Courtesy Warren Esty)*

died while defending Galba from assassins. Tacitus claims that Galba sent Densus to protect his designated heir, Piso. Densus faced the appointed killers of the heir with a dagger while Piso fled for the safety of the Temple of Vesta. Densus was then killed, his death proving to have been in vain, for Piso was murdered later that day.

Dentheleti Known as the Dentheletae, a tribe living in THRACE along the Strymon River. By 29 B.C.E. they were an ally of Rome under the leadership of their blind King Sitas. In that year the Bastarnae (SCYTHIANS) broke across the Danube and ravaged part of their territory, giving CRASSUS (2) the pretext needed to crush the Bastarnae and drive the barbarians out of the Dentheleti area.

Dexippus, Publius Herennius (fl. third century C.E.) *Historian and prominent figure in Athens*
Born to a wealthy and influential Athenian family, Dexippus became the head of the magistrates in the city, although he did not pursue a career in Roman government. He lived in an era of war and rampant instability on the frontiers. In 267 C.E., the barbarian Heruli broke into the East and ravaged first Cyzicus and Asia and then all of Achaea, including Athens. Dexippus, as the leading citizen of Athens, organized a fighting force and rode to battle. With the very fate of Athens resting on their shoulders, they put the Heruli to flight in a desperate flight.

As a historian, Dexippus authored numerous works of which three are extant, although only in fragments. *Scythica* recounted the terrible events of the Gothic and Scythian invasions of the mid-third century C.E.; Dexippus chose Thucydides as the model for *Scythica*. His main effort, aside from *Scythica* and *On Alexander*, was a history or chronicle. This long work began with Rome's mythical origins and followed the empire to 268 C.E., or the start of Claudius II Gothicus's reign. Written in 12 books, the work was used quite extensively by authors of the *Scriptores Historiae Augustae*.

Diadumenian (Marcus Opellius Antoninus Diadumenianus) (d. 218 C.E.) *Son of Emperor Macrinus*
Diadumenian served his father briefly as Caesar (junior emperor) from 217 to 218 C.E. and as Augustus in 218. He had little time to enjoy his position or to learn anything from its opportunities because the legions of Syria revolted and declared Elagabalus ruler of the empire. When Macrinus was defeated on June 8, 218, at Antioch, Diadumenian followed his father in death. According to the *Scriptores Historiae Augustae*, Diadumenian emulated Macrinus in tyranny. He called upon his father not to spare any who might oppose them or who made plots. His head was cut off and presented to Elagabalus as a trophy.

Diana Goddess of hunters, an ancient divinity to the Romans; originally considered a goddess of the forest, whose sacred grove stood near Aricia. She was the patroness of hunters, and King Servius Tullius built her a temple on the Aventine Hill, where she became associated both with light (*dies*, "day") and Artemis, the Greek sister of Apollo. Festivals held in honor of Diana were Greek in fashion, although she developed cultic aspects at other functions as well. Just as Artemis had many incarnations—Artemis Arcadia, Artemis Tauria, Artemis Ephesia—so did Diana serve as the goddess of a cult in Ephesus. Her statues displayed her concern for fertility, with a multitude of carved breasts. In Rome she joined with Janus, a god of light and the sun, serving as a consort and depicting the light of the moon.

See also GODS AND GODDESSES OF ROME.

dictator One of the most powerful offices of the Republic and one that did not endure into the empire. The dictator was a Roman magistrate granted extraordinary authority during time of public need or crisis. Once approved and legally elected, the *magister populi*, as he was known, held his office for six months but could be elected again if the problems of the time had not subsided. Traditionally, however, a dictator resigned before the expiration of his tenure.

As dictator, a state official was considered the equal of the kings of old but one who ruled by the good wishes of the Romans and was thus tolerated instead of despised. He wore a purple robe and sat upon a throne, the *curule* chair. Twenty lictors also accompanied him with the FASCES, a bundle of rods enclosing the traditional axe, the *securis*. A dictator had control over life and death and could be opposed only by the tribunes of the Plebeian. His sentence was one from which there could be no appeal, and decisions of peace and war were his to make alone.

In time the position of dictator became troublesome. The bad decisions of some and the possible cruelties of others prompted the passing of the "Law of Duillius," a law forcing all dictators to place their enactments before the people for acceptance or refusal. Passed in 451 B.C.E., the law proved ineffective against the two greatest dictators of the Roman Republic: Cornelius Sulla and Julius Caesar.

Sulla's term was important as a model for later generals and ambitious politicians, who looked to him as a legalizing precedent to justify their own activities. Such recourses to precedent, however, normally failed to sway a cautious Senate. In 52 B.C.E., after terrible riots and bloodshed following the murder of P. Clodius Pulcher, the CURIA HOSTILIA of the Senate was burned. POMPEY stood ready as proconsul to march into the city and restore order, if such services were requested. M. Calpurnius Bibulus, however, successfully thwarted Pompey's reception of a dictatorial mandate by having the Senate make him consul for 52 without a colleague. Pompey conducted himself accordingly, and the trials of Annius Milo and his fellow murderers went forward.

In 49 B.C.E., Julius Caesar was absent from Rome, fighting against the Pompeians. He desired a consulship, considering that position most useful under the circumstances, but considered the dictatorship as well. M. Aemilius Lepidus, as praetor, summoned the people and they voted Caesar into the office of dictator. When his term was ended, he laid down the office, but without surrendering any of its benefits or rights. Two years later, after the battle of Pharsalus, Antony came back to Rome (in October of 47 B.C.E.) with news of Caesar's triumph over Pompey and his desire to be dictator for a second time. He probably received two more terms: in 45, after his African campaign, and in 44, after settling the civil wars. Caesar received the title of dictator for life, with the privilege of wearing the laurel wreath and the use of a throne.

The trappings of glory convinced jealous senators and ardent supporters of the Republic that the dictator would soon become a king. They murdered him to avoid what they believed would become a disaster. Marc Antony, following Caesar's assassination, forced through a law that abolished the position of dictator, although its very nature was evident in the later role of the emperors.

See also CENSOR; IMPERATOR; PRINCEPS.

Didius Julianus (Marcus Didius Severus Julianus)

(133–193 C.E.) *Emperor from March 28 to June 1, 193 C.E.; famed not for his reign but for the fact that he came to power by buying the crown*

Born into a senatorial family of Mediolanum (Milan) and raised in the house of Domiitia Lucilla, the mother of the future Emperor, Marcus Aurelius, Didius held a praetorship in 162, a governorship in Gallia Belgica (170–175) and a consulship with Pertinax in 175. Over the next 15 years more governorships came his way, in Illyricum (176–177), Germania Inferior (178), Bithynia (189–190), and in Africa (190–192). In the meantime he was charged and acquitted of membership in the conspiracy of Publius Salvius Julianus in 182.

Didius Julianus was back in Rome in March 193, during the brief reign of Pertinax, and on March 28, when the PRAETORIAN GUARD murdered the emperor, he hurried to the Castra Praetoria, where the prefect of the city, T. Flavius Sulpicianus, was inside bidding for the throne. Julianus began to make his own offers from outside the wall. Each man thus raised the amount that they were willing to pay to the Praetorians for the throne. Although the prefect had the strategic advantage inside, Julianus raised his bid by 5,000 sesterces and so won the day, promising each man 25,000 sesterces. The gates of the *Castra* were thrown open, and Julianus was proclaimed emperor of Rome.

After assuming the purple, Julianus was confronted with the realities of ruling. Support for him was nonexistent in Rome. The mobs disliked him, and the Praetorians were disenchanted by the delays in payment of their DONATIVUM. The Senate waited to see the response of the provinces, and generals elsewhere seized the moment to declare their own ambitions. Three in particular declared themselves, Pescennius Niger in the East, Septimius Severus on the Danube, and Clodius Albinus in Britain. Albinus and Severus reach an accord, and Severus marched first on Italy.

Julianus tried to organize the defense of Rome but lacked the support of any legions, even of the Marines from Misenum. Choosing to protect its interests and to placate Severus, whom they knew to be the ultimate victor, the Senate deposed Julianus and ordered his execution, declaring Severus emperor. Final attempts at negotiations with the advancing Severus failed, and on June 1 or 2, a soldier entered the palace and slew Julianus, who had reigned only 66 days.

Dio Cassius (b. 155 C.E.?) *Historian*

Born to a Roman senator of Nicaea in BITHYNIA, Dio traveled in 180 to Rome, embarking on a successful political career. He became a senator and held two consulships, in 205 and 229. Septimius Severus appointed him to his CONSILIUM PRINCIPIS, and Macrinius made him a curator in Pergamum and Smyrna. He later governed Africa, Illyricum, and Upper Pannonia, successively, from 223 to 228. He retired to Campania after his second consulship (with Severus Alexander) before returning home to Nicaea, where he died.

Dio authored several no longer-extant works, including a history of the struggle for the throne from 193 to 197 and an analysis of dreams. His main contribution was a very ambitious and partly extant history of Rome in 80 books, covering the period from the legendary Aeneas to 229 C.E. Books 36 to 54 are preserved, detailing the period roughly from Pompey to the death of Marcus Agrippa in 10 B.C.E. Parts of book 55 to 60 and 79 to 80 exist; the last books help paint a clear picture of the time in which Dio lived.

As for the lost books in the history, summaries and epitomes made by later generations, especially Xiphilinus (11th century C.E.), offer the only information. Unquestionably, Dio's efforts were remarkable in his use of sources and authorities and proved invaluable to successive historians. He spent the years from about 200 to 210 C.E. compiling all of his sources and then another 12 years in the actual writing of the history. His book on dreams pointed to the omens that Septimius Severus would become emperor. When Dio sent a copy to him, Severus wrote a long and complimentary letter in return.

Suggested Readings: Dio Cassius. *The Roman History: The Reign of Augustus.* London: Penguin, 1987; ———. *Roman History: Books LXI–LXX.* Cambridge, Mass.: Harvard, 1985; Gowing, Alain M. *The Triumviral Narratives of Appian and Cassius Dio.* Ann Arbor: University of Michigan Press, 1992; Millar, Fergus. *A Study of Cassius Dio.* Oxford, U.K.: Clarendon Press, 1964.

diocese Name given to the 12 new territorial divisions of the Roman Empire in the provincial reforms of Diocletian. The problem of the provinces had long troubled the rulers of Rome, as governors had rebelled and had seized the throne, while the Senate had not relinquished its own, albeit dwindling, influence with its own provinces. Diocletian resolved to end all such chaos, starting reforms sometime around 293 C.E.

The number of provinces was doubled from 50 to 100, preventing any governor from amassing enough personal power to contemplate a revolt. To further ensure the loyalty of the governors, all provinces ceased to be either imperial or senatorial and henceforth would be grouped into large units called dioceses. Each diocese contained several provinces, and each provincial head was answerable to the official of the diocese, the *vicarii praetectorum praetorio*, or just VICARII. Each of the *vacarii*, in turn, reported to one of the four PRAETORIAN PREFECTS assigned to the four members of the tetrarchy, an Augustus and a Caesar, both in the East and in the West.

Thus, no government official was ever isolated or endowed with enough strength to ponder the possibilities of an uprising. Further, the dioceses facilitated Diocletian's desire for increased centralization and the aggrandizement of the central imperial government at the expense of the Senate and provinces. The dioceses stretched across traditional geographical, hence cultural, borders. Oriens contained Mesopotamia, Syria, Palestine, Egypt, and Libya, while Hispania contained all of Spain and part of Africa, namely the small coastal province of Mauretania Tingitana.

Italy, previously held sacred and separate from the empire as a bastion of elitism, lost its special status. Not only was it now placed under direct imperial supervision, it was also cut in half to make two dioceses. Finally, as the Roman world had been divided into East and West, the numerical discrepancy of eight dioceses in the West, as compared to five in the East, was offset by the reality that economic superiority rested with the provinces of Greece, Asia Minor, Egypt, and Syria.

See also entries for the various provinces of the Roman Empire for a detailed account of the evolution of the provincial system.

DIOCESES OF DIOCLETIAN

Name	Territories
East	
Oriens	Aegyptus Herculia, Aegyptus Iovia, Arabia, Augusta Euphratensis, Augusta Libanensis, Cilicia, Cyprus, Isauria, Libya Interior, Libya Superior, Mesopotamia, Osrhoene, Palaestina, Phoenica, Syria Coele, Thebais
Pontus (Pontica)	Armenia Minor, Bithynia, Cappadocia, Diospontus, Galatia, Paphlagonia, Pontus Polemoniacus
Asia (Asiana)	Asia, Caria, Hellespontus, Lycia and Pamphylia, Lydia, Phrygia I, Phrygia II, Pisidia
Thrace (Thraciae)	Europa, Haemimontus, Moesia II, Rhodope, Scythia, Thrace
Moesiae	Achaea, Dacia, Dardania, Epirus Vetus, Macedonia, Moesia I, Praevalitana, Thessalia
West	
Africa	Byzacena, Mauretania Caesariensis, Mauretania Tabia, Numidia Cirtensis, Numidia Militana, Proconsularis, Tripolitania
Hispaniae	Carthaginiensis, Baetica, Gallaecia, Lusitania, Mauretania Tingitana, Tarraconensis
Viennensis	Alpes Maritimae, Aquitanica I, Aquitanica II, Narbonensis I, Narbonensis II, Viennensis
Galliae	Belgica I, Belgica II, Germania I, Germania II, Lugdunensis I, Lugdunensis II, Sequania
Britanniae	Britannia, Maxima Caesariensis
Italia	Aemilia, Alpes Cottiae, Alpes Graiae, Campania, Corsica, Flaminia, Liguria, Raetia I, Raetia II, Sardinia, Sicilia, Tuscia and Umbria, Venetia and Istria
Pannoniae	Dalmatia, Noricum Mediterraneum, Noricum Ripense, Pannonia I, Pannonia II, Savia

Diocletian (Gaius Aurelius Valerius Diocletianus) (d. 316) *Emperor from 284 to 305 C.E., best known for his persecution of Christians*

Diocletian was born to a poor family in Dalmatia (ILLYRICUM) in the mid-third century, under the name Diocles. Entering military service, his intelligence and competence earned him promotions. By 284 he was a member of the army of Carus and then head of the elite *protectores domestici* upon the succession of NUMERIAN to the throne. This was a stroke of good fortune because, during the brief term of his command, Diocletian earned the trust of the legions in the imperial army stationed near Nicomedia. Thus, when Numerian died under very suspicious circumstances, it was to Diocletian that the soldiers turned in their search for vengeance. Years before a druidess had predicted that he would become emperor, but first he would have to slay the boar (*aper*). The man charged with murdering Numerian was Prefect of the Guard Arrius Aper. He was brought before Diocletian, who pronounced a sentence of death upon him and ran him through.

Having slain the "boar," Diocletian was proclaimed ruler by the troops. He then crossed over the Bosporus to wage war upon Numerian's brother, Carinus, in the West. Victory came in 285, and Diocletian ruled the entire world. From the start Diocletian assumed the utmost grandeur of the office, elevating his own status beyond mortal dimensions. Henceforth the imperial house was to be heart of the empire instead of Rome. He worked over the next years to bring this policy to fruition. Diocletian named his own friend, the reliable MAXIMIAN, to be first his Caesar (junior emperor) and then Augustus in 286. Maximian aided the emperor in all matters, and the next six years were spent in repairing the frontiers and in restoring honor to the Roman Empire.

Diocletian took as his patron the god Jupiter or Jove, and Maximian had Hercules. In their names wars were fought in Moesia, Pannonia, Gaul, and Syria. Stability returned, and in 293 he was able to initiate the next step in his broad program of imperial reform. Two emperors became four. Joining Diocletian and Maximian were two Caesars, GALERIUS and CONSTANTIUS I CHLORUS. Diocletian and Galerius would rule the East, and Maximian and Constantius the West. The empire was still one entity, but from now on the administration (under a tetrarchy) would be far better organized, and the succession uncluttered by rival claimants, as Galerius and Constantius would be the eventual Augusti and would then name their own Caesars.

The TETRARCHY established, Diocletian turned to the vast task of transforming the imperial government and military. LEGIONS were changed to fit the adjustments in the provinces. Each ruler—the two Augusti and the two Caesars—wielded a field army or the COMITATENSES, along with cavalry, and a guard, the SCHOLAE PALATINAE, who replaced the now reduced Praetorian Guard. This field force traveled with the emperor and was used specifically to bolster the frontier troops watching the borders, the LIMITANEI. Any invasion, even if successful in piercing the frontier defenses, would be destroyed by the Comitatenses and any Limitanei deployed temporarily for the crisis.

Such military formations reduced the often paralyzing effect of legions summoned by an emperor and then revolting on behalf of their own general. Their effectiveness was seen in the numerous and successful campaigns launched during Diocletian's reign: against Persia in 296, Achilleus in Egypt, and Carausius and Allectus in Britain.

Assisting the legionary reforms was the new provincial system. The number of provinces was doubled, and each was included in the larger, DIOCESE units under very powerful governors who, in turn, were answerable to one of each emperor's four Praetorian prefects. This style of rule would be in place for many years, making the central administration more efficient and objective and avoiding potential tyranny.

Italy was added to a diocese, ending its unique, centuries-old status. Diocletian wanted something new and to avoid the sociopolitical traps so common in Rome. Ravenna served as the capital of the West, and for himself Diocletian chose Nicomedia in Bithynia as his initial residence, before moving to Antioch at the start of the tetrarchy. He did not visit Rome until 303 and then only to celebrate the anniversary of his accession. While the Eternal City played no part in his grand plans, he nevertheless gave to it many gifts, including a new *curia* and baths of great beauty. Indeed, throughout the empire he worked

hard to return a sense of grandeur and high culture. Schools were encouraged and opened, building programs completed, and Latin reborn as the first language of the realm.

In the face of crushing taxation caused by Diocletian's policies, the common people were given an edict in 301 to fix a maximum for goods and services. At the same time, Diocletian honored the citizenry by having coinage of bronze called a "follis" struck with the inscription "GENIVS POPVLI ROMANI," or the "Spirit of the Roman People." Dedicating his house to Jove and that of Maximian to Hercules, coupled with a reprise of pagan classicism, Diocletian did not bode well for CHRISTIANITY. The faith had grown considerably in the years before his reign. Galerius found Diocletian very responsive to suggestions about renewed persecutions against the religion, and in 303 they issued an edict beginning the last great period of martyrdom and suffering for the followers of Christ. Just as Diocletian revived the old Roman imperial order, so did his fight against the Christ epitomize the struggle of the ancient and the new. Assemblies were forbidden, churches were destroyed and the Scriptures burned. Eventually sacrifices to the imperial cult were required of all citizens, especially the Christian priests, who were arrested when they refused. Diocletian's lack of success in stamping out Christianity was one of the great disappointments of his life and contributed directly to his retirement in 305.

Suffering an illness one year earlier, he was convinced that it was time for him to relinquish his powers. On May 1, 305, he abdicated, convincing the hesitant Maximian to join him. Galerius and Constantius followed as the two Augusti. Content that affairs were in good hands, Diocletian retired to an estate of great luxury in Illyricum, at SPLIT. There he spent most of his time in his gardens, growing his favorite vegetables.

From Split, however, he learned to his dismay of the rifts developing between the joint emperors. In 308, he traveled to Carnuntum to repair the situation, but to no avail. Diocletian's last years were spent in frustration and isolation as Constantine, Maxentius, and others slaughtered one another in the name of ambition. He died in 316, quite probably from a broken heart. Diocletian was responsible, however, for beginning a process of change that would find its fullest expression in the reign of CONSTANTINE the Great. He proved himself a superb administrator, an excellent general and the initial architect of the survival of imperial power into the fifth century.

Suggested Readings: Barnes, Timothy D. *The New Empire of Diocletian and Constantine.* Cambridge, Mass.: Harvard University Press, 1982; Burckhardt, Jacob. *The Age of Constantine the Great.* Translated by Moses Hadas. Berkeley: University of California Press, 1983; Williams, Stephen. *Diocletian and the Roman Recovery.* London: B. T. Batsford, 1985.

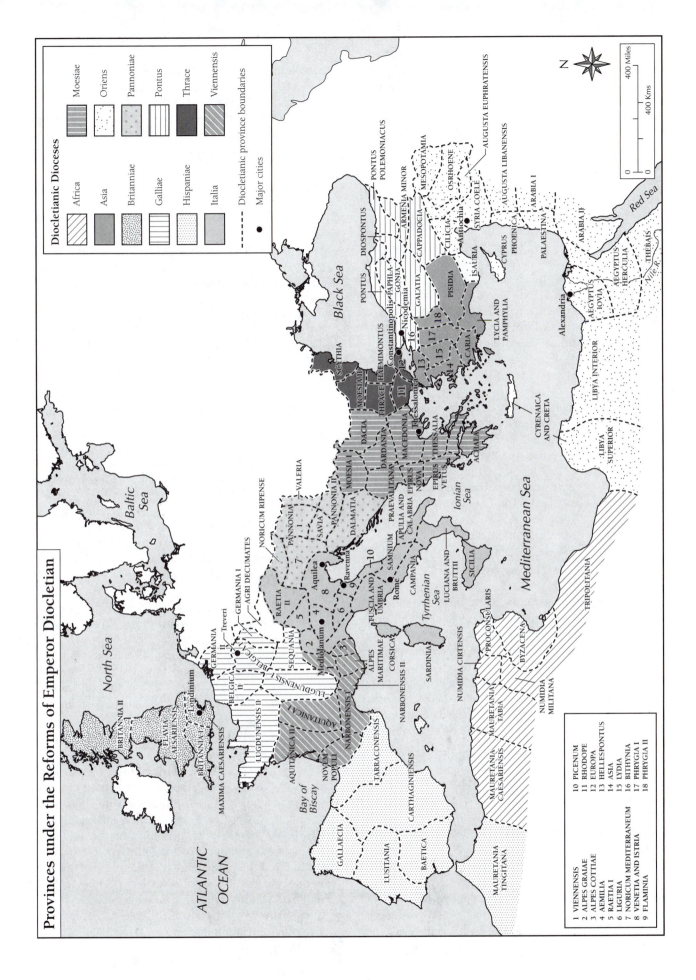

Provinces under the Reforms of Emperor Diocletian

Diocletianic Dioceses

Moesiae | Oriens | Pannoniae | Pontus | Thrace | Viennensis

Africa | Asia | Britanniae | Galliae | Hispaniae | Italia

- - - Diocletianic province boundaries
- Major cities

1 VIENNENSIS
2 ALPES GRAIAE
3 ALPES COTTIAE
4 RAETIA I
5 LIGURIA
6 NORICUM MEDITERRANEUM
7 NORICUM RIPENSE
8 VENETIA AND ISTRIA
9 FLAMINIA

10 PICENUM
11 RHODOPE
12 EUROPA
13 HELLESPONTUS
14 ASIA
15 LYDIA
16 BITHYNIA
17 PHRYGIA I
18 PHRYGIA II

ATLANTIC OCEAN

North Sea

Baltic Sea

Black Sea

Mediterranean Sea

Tyrrhenian Sea

Ionian Sea

Bay of Biscay

Red Sea

BRITANNIA II
FLAVIA CAESARIENSIS
Londinium
BRITANNIA I
MAXIMA CAESARIENSIS

GERMANIA II
Treveri
GERMANIA I
AGRI DECUMATES
BELGICA II
BELGICA I
LUGDUNENSIS II
LUGDUNENSIS I
SEQUANIA
AQUITANICA II
AQUITANICA I
NOVEM POPULI
NARBONENSIS I

GALLAECIA
TARRACONENSIS
LUSITANIA
CARTHAGINIENSIS
BAETICA
MAURETANIA TINGITANA

MAURETANIA CAESARIENSIS
MAURETANIA SITIFIA
NUMIDIA MILITANA
NUMIDIA CIRTENSIS
PROCONSULARIS
BYZACENA
TRIPOLITANIA

NORICUM RIPENSE
VALERIA
RAETIA II
PANNONIA I
SAVIA
7
1
5
4
6
2
3
8
Aquileia
Mediolanum
Ravenna
9
10
ALPES MARITIMAE
CORSICA
NARBONENSIS II
SARDINIA
TUSCIA AND UMBRIA
Rome
CAMPANIA
LUCIANA AND BRUTTII
SAMNIUM
APULIA AND CALABRIA
SICILIA

PANNONIA II
DALMATIA
MOESIA I
DARDANIA
PRAEVALITANA
EPIRUS NOVA
MACEDONIA
EPIRUS VETUS
THESSALIA
ACHAEA
DACIA
II
III
Thessalonica

SCYTHIA
MOESIA II
THRACE
HAEMIMONTUS
Constantinopolis
Nicomedia
16
12
13
17
15
18
14
CARIA
LYCIA AND PAMPHYLIA
PISIDIA
GALATIA
PAPHLAGONIA
DIOSPONTUS
PONTUS POLEMONIACUS
ARMENIA MINOR
CAPPADOCIA
MESOPOTAMIA
OSRHOENE
CILICIA
ISAURIA
Antiochia
SYRIA COELE
AUGUSTA EUPHRATENSIS
AUGUSTA LIBANENSIS
ARABIA I
CYPRUS
PHOENICE
PALAESTINA
ARABIA II
LIBYA INTERIOR
CYRENAICA AND CRETA
LIBYA SUPERIOR
Alexandria
AEGYPTUS IOVIA
AEGYPTUS HERCULIA
THEBAIS
Nile R.

N
400 Miles
400 Kms

Dio Cocceianus (c. 40/45–c. 114 C.E.) *Also called Dio Chrysostom and Dio of Prusa, the "golden mouthed" philosopher and writer*

Dio was born at Prusa in Bithynia and learned rhetoric from his family before going to Rome as a Sophist. During the reign of Domitian (around 82 C.E.), his association with philosophers and his outspoken oratory brought him exile from Rome and his native land. He then wandered around the empire, especially in Illyricum and the surrounding provinces, working and speaking.

In 96, Domitian was assassinated, and Nerva invited Dio to return to Rome. Furthering the attentions of the emperor, he received permission to travel to Prusa. There he put to use the considerable knowledge he had acquired in his days of exile. His speeches there covered a wide variety of topics, including politics, morality, and philosophy. Dio owned vineyards and land and fought to improve conditions in Prusa. He joined a delegation to greet Trajan on his accession and to ask for a larger city council and improved self-determination in taxes and in legal jurisdictions. He also planned extensive building programs for his city but earned the enmity of his fellow citizens who resented his harsh and demanding style. As an orator and Sophist, Dio Chrysostom delivered some 80 extant speeches. Some of these were comical, especially the First Oration in Tarsus, but many stood as biting attacks on the era, such as his oratory on the nature of god. Dio Cassius may have been a descendant.

See also RHETORIC and SOPHISTRY.

Diodorus, Siculus (fl. first century B.C.E.) *Historian from Agyrium in Sicily*

An author of considerable industry, Diodorus journeyed throughout ASIA MINOR and Europe researching his mammoth work, the *Bibliotheca Historica* (Historical library). These travels brought him to Rome, where he remained for many years. The *Bibliotheca Historica* covered the period from darkest antiquity to the age of Julius Caesar, ending approximately in 54 B.C.E. with the beginnings of Caesar's GALLIC WARS. Originally in 40 books, only 15 have survived; the rest exist in fragments. Much of his chronicle was both derivative and very unreliable.

Diogenes, Laertius (fl. third century C.E.) *Writer and philosopher*

Diogenes's main work was a long *History of Greek Philosophy*, in which he wrote about the philosophers in biographical form. Little is known of the details of his life.

Diomedes (fl. late fourth century C.E.) *Grammarian who authored the Ars grammatica in three parts*

Diomedes's writing was notable for several reasons. He was well organized in his presentation and relied upon early grammatical sources, although he never actually named them. Secondly, his best section (Book III) in the *Ars grammatica* contained a preserved work of Suetonius, *de poetis*. Diomedes's book very closely resembled the similar effort of Flavius Sosipater Charisius, although it was better constructed and authoritative. The *Ars grammatica* was dedicated to someone named Athanasius.

Dionysius, Papirius (fl. second century C.E.) *Prefect of grain during the reign of Commodus*

In 189, Dionysius played some kind of role in the downfall of the ambitious and corrupt Prefect of the Praetorian Guard Cleander. Cleander had been hoarding much of the grain supply for use by Rome's citizens and army in times of famine, but in so doing earned the enmity of the mob.

A famine did occur in 189, but Dionysius held back the grain on hand, thus exacerbating an already inflammatory situation. The Roman crowds turned on Cleander, and COMMODUS murdered him as the mob set out on a rampage. Whatever ambitions Dionysius may have harbored were never known, for he died in that same year by imperial decree. Dio is the main source for Dionysius's plottings.

Dionysius of Alexandria (d. 264 C.E.) *Bishop who had been a student of Origen and head of the Catechetical School of Alexandria (c. 233)*

Dionysius was elected bishop in 247, just in time to serve as shepherd over the Egyptian Christians during one of the darkest hours of Christian history. Trajanus DECIUS instigated severe persecutions, and in 250, Dionysius, as bishop of Alexandria, fell into imperial hands. He managed to escape from his captors and went into hiding until 251. As a prelate, he became involved in the dispute over whether or not to readmit those Christians who had abandoned the faith during the crisis. He struck a middle ground theologically, accepting all sincere sinners back into the church. He opposed, however, the various heretical sects of the time. In 257, Dionysius went into exile during Valerian's persecutions but later died at his post.

Dionysius of Halicarnassus (d. 8/7 B.C.E.) *Greek rhetorician and historian of the first century B.C.E.*

Dionysius lived in Rome during the Augustan age (27 B.C.E.—14 C.E.) and regarded Roman history as a worthy subject of study. In honor of his hosts he wrote a 20- or 22-volume history of Rome entitled *Roman Antiquities*. The books covered the period from the founding in 753 B.C.E. to the Punic Wars. Only half of the work is extant but displays his sense for pedantic analysis, rhetorical discourses, and an obvious lack of humor. He also authored various criticisms of Greek classical writers. Dionysius served for years as the chief spokesman for the Atticist movement in Rome.

See also LITERATURE.

Dionysius the Areopagite (fl. mid-first century C.E.)
Convert to Christianity

Dionysius was brought into the church by St. Paul at Athens, as recorded in Acts (17:34): "But some men joined him and believed, among them Dionysius the Areopagite and a woman named Damaris and others with them." According to Dionysius of Corinth, he became the first bishop of the Christian community of Athens. He was later identified in the ninth century with Dionysius of Paris and his name attached to the theological writings of Pseudo-Dionysius (Dionysius the Pseudo-Areopagite).

Dionysius the Great (d. c. 264) *Bishop of Alexandria from 247 and leading opponent of the heresy of Sabellianism*

Dionysius was a native of Alexandria and a pupil of Origen, whom he succeeded as head of the Catechetical School of Alexandria from around 233. As bishop of Alexandria, he was forced to flee the city in 251 during the persecutions of Emperor Trajanus Decius, going to the Libyan Desert. Another period of exile lasted from 257 to 260, during the persecutions by Emperor Valerian. Back at Alexandria, he faced plague, civil unrest, and famine, as well as the controversy over the rebaptizing of lapsed Christians. He did not demand harsh penalties for apostates, favoring readmission for all penitent Christians. His dispute with the Sabellians, who taught that the Trinity was indivisible, caused him to be accused of tritheism (the Trinity as three distinct deities), a dispute eventually brought before Pope Dionysius in a Roman synod, the so-called affair of the two Dionysii. In his *Refutation* and *Apology*, Dionysius of Alexandria secured formal vindication, and the entire incident set the stage for the Council of Nicaea in 325. While greatly respected for his writings, especially by the theologians of the Byzantine Church, his work is preserved mostly in fragments or extracts by Eusebius of Caesarea, St. Athanasius, and other ecclesiastical writers. Dionysius also denied that St. John the Evangelist was the author of both the Fourth Gospel and the Book of Revelation.

Dionysus *See* BACCHUS.

Dioscorides (fl. first or second century C.E.) *Writer on medicine*

Dioscorides came from Anazarba in Cilicia and was an army physician. His *Materia Medica*, an excellent study of medicine, was at least partly derived from Pliny the Elder's *Natural History*.

Dioscuri
Castor and Pollux, sons of JUPITER; Castor was noted for his horse skills and Pollux for his boxing. In Greek mythology, the *Dioscuri*, as the sons of Zeus, were participants in great heroic deeds and naturally captured the imagination of the Romans, especially in their incarnation as the Gemini. According to Roman legend, the brothers came to the aid of the dictator Postumius Albinus against the Latins in the battle of Lake Regillus in 494 B.C.E. Not only did the dictator promise them a temple in gratitude, but he also had their faces and stars (of Gemini) depicted on one of the earliest forms of the denarius. The Temple of Castor and Pollux was situated in the Forum, near the circular Temple of Vesta. There, every July 15, the Equestrian Order (EQUITES) held a great festival in the temple to celebrate the patronage of the *Dioscuri*. The brothers were also known as the *Castores*.

See also GODS AND GODDESSES OF ROME.

diplomata
Imperial certificates granted to certain individuals under specific circumstances or for a set purpose. Traditionally the *diplomata* were actually two bronze plaques tied together and inscribed with a record, message, or decree. Many are extant and provide a major source of information concerning the bureaucratic and administrative systems, both in the legions and in the government. *Diplomata militaria* were the certificates given to retiring legionaries of 25 years' service in the *auxilia*. They granted full citizenship to the veteran, along with his children. Furthermore, any woman he might choose to marry would be accepted as being wed in the full light of Roman law, and all children born of such a union would be Roman citizens.

In the Praetorian Guard the *diplomata* were presented to a soldier, normally a *principales*, of 16 years' service. A very elaborate ceremony was held with demonstrations of gratitude. The *diplomata* was written in the imperial first person, signed by the emperor and dedicated "to the soldiers having courageously and loyally finished their service."

The other kind of *diplomata* were those signed by the emperor for the CURSUS PUBLICUS. All persons using the imperial post had to receive a *diplomata*, which granted the right to travel and to benefit from the horses and superb transport system of the empire. These were the certificates to which Pliny the Younger referred in his letters to Trajan while serving as the special legate in Bithynia. *Diplomata* unfortunately fell into the hands of functionaries who did not deserve them or were not entitled, while others were forged.

Dis, king of the Underworld *See* PLUTON.

divination *See* AUGURS AND AUGURY; AUGURIUM CANARIUM.

Dolabella, Publius Cornelius (fl. first century B.C.E.)
A profligate and ambitious young aristocrat

A member of the wealthy patrician family of Cornelia in 51 B.C.E. Dolabella married Cicero's daughter Tullia, over her father's protests. He served as a legate to Caesar during the Civil War and fought at the battle of PHARSALUS in 48 B.C.E. Caesar rewarded him with a consulship in 44 B.C.E. but was assassinated soon after. After Caesar's murder, Dolabella allied himself with Marc Antony, using his power as consul to crush the turbulent mobs throughout the city. Through Antony's patronage he became governor of the province of SYRIA in 43 B.C.E. Marching east, he plundered Greece, Asia, and most of Asia Minor, earning the enmity of the Senate. Cassius sailed to Syria, amassed as many legions as possible and awaited the arrival of the appointed governor. Dolabella was blockaded at Laodicea and, defeated, he committed suicide.

dolphin Small, toothed whale long held to be sacred by both the Greeks and the Romans and protected by various divinities.

domestici, protectores The personal bodyguard of rulers in later eras of the Roman Empire. Composed of two different formations, they were also called *protectores et domestici*. After CONSTANTINE eradicated the old PRAETORIAN GUARD in 312 C.E., he instituted the SCHOLAE PALATINAE and the *protectores et domestici* to assume Praetorian duties. Constantine granted the greatest privileges of the Praetorians to the *protectores domestici,* and they stood in higher rank than the *scholae.* Their commander was the *comes domesticorum,* and their division into smaller units followed the pattern of the *scholae:* 10 cohorts of around 50 men. The *protectores domestici* possessed considerable social status, similar to the TRIBUNES or high-ranked officers of the earlier years of the empire.

Their responsibilities included personal attendance to the emperor, especially in the field. Just as the Praetorian guardsmen might have been sent on missions to the provinces, so were the soldiers of the *protectores domestici.* Any possible task could be given them, from delivering messages to governors or generals to being seconded to the staff of a MAGISTER MILITUM for a period of time. They were generally well paid.

Domitia (d. 59 C.E.) *Aunt of Emperor Nero*
Sister to Domitia LEPIDA, Domitia was the mother of Claudius Empress MESSALLINA. Domitia was a formidable person within the imperial palace and the most bitter of the many enemies of AGRIPPINA THE YOUNGER. When Domitia Lepida was sentenced to death in 54 C.E., Domitia lost an ally but soon found another in Junia SILANA, who used two clients, Iturius and Calvisius, to accuse Agrippina of plotting against her son Nero. Domitia's freedman Atimetus immediately informed the famous actor PARIS, a favorite of Nero who related the accusation to the emperor. Agrippina barely escaped execution. By 59, Domitia had fallen from favor and was seriously ill. Nero poisoned her, intending to lay his hands on her vast estates near Ravenna and Baiae. Domitia was also involved in a legal case surrounding the freedman Paris, who claimed that he had been born free and should thus receive back the money given to buy his freedom. When a court examined the case, Nero, who not only admired Paris but was also distrustful of Domitia, instructed the magistrate to find in favor of the actor.

Domitia Lepida *See* LEPIDA, DOMITIA.

Domitia Longina (fl. late first century B.C.) *Empress from 81 to 96 C.E.*
Wife of DOMITIAN and daughter of the famous general, Gnaeus Domitius Corbulo, Domitia was originally married to Lucius Aelianus Lamia, but Domitian forced her to divorce him in 70 C.E. She subsequently lived with the emperor at his estate near Mount Alban, although he eventually married her. She bore him a daughter and a short-lived son in 73. Domitian was insanely jealous of his wife's rumored affairs. His brother TITUS supposedly had committed adultery with her, and the actor PARIS was slain in the street because of the same suspicion. Domitia was divorced sometime around 83. She would have been murdered by Domitian but for the influence of the adviser Ursus, who counseled a separation instead. Domitian then involved himself with his niece JULIA (7) but could not bear to be away from Domitia. Although he hated her, a reconciliation was made in 83. Domitian continued his relationship with Julia at the same time.

By 96, her life was in constant danger, as Domitian executed anyone that he suspected of disloyalty. According to the historian Dio, Domitia found her name on a list of those to be destroyed. She took the list to her own allies, people plotting the emperor's assassination. Armed with the names, the conspirators were able to accelerate their plans. Domitian died soon after. Domitia lived on for many years, held in high esteem by the Romans.

Domitia Lucilla *See* LUCILLA, DOMITIA.

Domitian (Titus Flavius Domitianus) (51–96 C.E.) *Emperor from 81 to 96 C.E.; the son of Vespasian and the brother of Titus, both emperors in their own time*
As a ruler, Domitian was grim but proved himself an able administrator and a surprisingly competent general. He was born on October 24, 51 C.E., in Rome to Flavia Domitilla and VESPASIAN, who was the consul-elect at the time. Most of his youth was spent in poverty, and he remained at home when Vespasian and TITUS marched off to command the East.

In 69, VITELLIUS, recently placed on the throne, faced a revolt of the legions under Vespasian. At first Vitellius refused to make use of Domitian as hostage, but his position deteriorated late in the year, and he ordered Domitian's arrest. Domitian fled with his uncle Flavius and was put under siege, escaping a second time when the emperor's soldiers broke through his defenses. Domitian finally made his way to the advancing units of Vespasian's army, under the command of Antonius PRIMUS. He returned to Rome in triumph after Vitellius's death and was subsequently embroiled in arguments with Vespasian's representative, MUCIANUS, over control of the city. Domitian tried to make personal appointments and was prevented from riding to Germany to put down the revolt of CIVILIS.

Throughout Vespasian's reign, Domitian was given little honor, while Titus grew in fame and stature as both a general of renown and Vespasian's aide. When Titus succeeded Vespasian in 79, Dio reports, Domitian complained that his father had actually intended the power to be shared by the brothers and even charged that Titus had forged the will. Domitian's role in imperial affairs increased and, upon Titus's death in 81 C.E., he was bequeathed the throne. There has been some speculation as to Domitian's part in Titus's demise, but his accession to the throne marked the beginning of his attempts to outdo his brother and father in grandeur.

Domitian launched a campaign against the CHATTI in 83, crushing the tribe and making the Roman presence in GERMANIA felt to a greater degree. In 85 he moved quickly to MOESIA to aid the province against an invasion by the Dacians, under DECEBALUS. Domitian led the counterattack, which drove off the enemy and returned to Rome to celebrate the double triumphs. While he was rejoicing, however, his Praetorian Prefect Cornelius FUSCUS was routed and killed, and only a victory at the battle of TAPAE in 88 by Tettius Julianus regained Roman supremacy. Domitian returned to the Danube frontier only to be denied final victory over Decebalus because of the revolt of Lucius Antonius SATURNINUS, commander of the legions in Germania Superior. The legate in Germania

Inferior, Lappius Maximus, marched against Saturninus and killed him, thanks in part to the absence of Saturninus's German allies, who could not cross the Rhine because of an early thaw.

Under Domitian the lot of soldiers improved, their pay was increased and the bureaucracy of the legions reformed. As a general, Domitian conducted intelligent campaigns, especially against the Chatti, using forts and massive defensive foundations to curb unrest and to secure the Roman advances. Domitian was popular with his troops in the field and started wearing military costume even when in Rome. An admirer of Tiberius, Domitian was suspicious of plots around him, and senators, freedmen, and others were arrested, tortured, and executed on charges of conspiracy, including the one-time prefect of the Guard, Arrecinus Clemens. This massacre of the nobles and the Senate made Domitian feared by the Romans and contributed to his eventual assassination.

During his reign, Domitian held many games, finished the COLOSSEUM and constructed several temples at great expense. He also built the DOMUS FLAVIA, the palace of the emperors until the reign of Diocletian. Festivals were provided to entertain the mobs, where various forms of the CONGIARIUM, or largess, were given out. Public morals were also strictly supervised, and Domitian ordered several VESTAL VIRGINS put to death for impurity. Jews were treated harshly, and Vespasian and Titus were reduced in the public memory while Domitian elevated himself in various ways. September and October were briefly renamed after him, and he held 17 consulships, a record.

DOMITIA LONGINA, Domitian's wife, had been declared an Augusta in 81, and was subsequently divorced and reinstated. Aware of Domitian's suspicious nature, she was compelled to join a conspiracy with the prefects NORBANUS and Petronius SECUNDUS. The assassin chosen for their ends was a former slave named STEPHANUS, who stabbed the emperor repeatedly but died in the struggle. Domitian died of his wounds on September 18, 96. His body was taken away by his old nurse, Phyllis, who cremated him and then mixed his ashes with those of Julia in the Temple of the Flavians on the Quirinal Hill.

Domitian was treated harshly by most of the writers and historians of Rome. Dio called him treacherous and secretive. PLINY THE YOUNGER wrote of his extreme nervous condition, while TACITUS was equally hostile, due mainly to Domitian's recall in 85 C.E. of his father-in-law, Agricola, from his triumphant campaigns in Britain. SUETONIUS wrote that he was tall, with a ruddy complexion, and was quite conscious of going bald. Domitian had a tendency toward laziness and had a peculiar habit of trapping and killing flies with his pen. He was a diligent reader of law.

Silver denarius, Domitian, struck in 87–88 in Rome *(Courtesy Historical Coins, Inc.)*

Suggested Readings: Jones, Brian W. *Domitian and the Senatorial Order: A Prosopographical Study of Domitian's*

Relationship with the Senate, A.D. 81–96. Philadelphia: American Philosophical Society, 1979; ———. *The Emperor Domitian.* London: Routledge, 1992; Southern, Pat. *Domitian: Tragic Tyrant.* New York: Routledge, 1997; Suetonius. *The Twelve Caesars.* Translated by and with an introduction by Michael Grant. New York: Penguin, 1979; Tacitus, Cornelius. *Empire and Emperors: Selections from Tacitus' Annals.* Translated by Graham Tingay. New York: Cambridge University Press, 1983; ———. *The Histories.* New York: Penguin, 1989.

Domitianus, Gaius (fl. third century C.E.) *A usurper circa 270 C.E.*

Mentioned in several sources as the victor over MACRIANUS, another usurper. Domitianus apparently set himself up as a pretender to the imperial power. He claimed descent from DOMITIAN and struck his own coinage in Gallia Aquintania, of which one piece has been found.

Domitilla, Flavia (1) (d. before 69 C.E.) *Wife of Vespasian*

Daughter of Flavius Liberalis, a quaestor's clerk, who pleaded successfully to give his child full Roman citizenship instead of a Latin one, she was, for a time, the mistress of an Equestrian from Africa, Statilius Capella, but married VESPASIAN sometime before 41 C.E. Flavia had three children: TITUS in 41; DOMITIAN in 51; and Flavia DOMITILLA (2). She died perhaps during the reign of Claudius or Nero. Vespasian then lived with his mistress, CAENIS, who was disliked by Domitian.

Domitilla, Flavia (2) (d. before 69 C.E.) *The daughter of Vespasian and Flavia Domitilla (1)*

Sister of TITUS and DOMITIAN, little is known about Domitilla's life, except for the fact that she was married, bore three children, and the noted rhetorician and writer QUINTILIAN was the tutor to her two sons. Her daughter was given the same name and became famous in the reign of Domitian for aiding Christians.

Domitilla, Flavia (3) (d. c. 95 C.E.) *Granddaughter of Vespasian*

Daughter of Flavia DOMITILLA (2), Domitilla was the niece of Emperor DOMITIAN. Her connection to the royal family was strengthened by her marriage to Flavius CLEMENS, a first cousin of Domitian. Domitilla is thought to have supported and possibly converted to CHRISTIANITY. In 95, Flavius Clemens and Domitilla, as well as several of their friends, were accused of impiety and favoring Christian and Jewish festivals. Domitian executed Clemens and exiled his niece to the island of Pandateria. Her two sons, designated as successors to the throne, had their names changed by the emperor to VESPASIAN and Domitian.

Domitius Ahenobarbus Name of the Roman family whose members achieved considerable notoriety and success in the years of the Republic and the empire. Legend provided a source for the appellation of Ahenobarbus, or "Red Beard." The DIOSCURI, Castor and Pollux, promised to one of the earliest Domitians victory in the battle of Lake Regillus over the Latins in 494 B.C.E. To prove the veracity of their word they placed a hand on the black beard of their client, turning it red. Men of the Ahenobarbus clan were perpetually known as rough, harsh, arrogant, and cruel. NERO, who displayed many of these characteristics, was the son of Domitius Ahenobarbus. The family tombs were prominently displayed on the Pincian Hill.

Domitius Ahenobarbus (1), Gnaeus (d. c. 31 B.C.E.) *A consul in 32 B.C.E. and a participant in the Civil Wars of the terminal period of the Republic*

The son of Lucius DOMITIUS AHENOBARBUS (1), Domitius stood with his father at Corfinium in 49 B.C.E. and observed the battle of PHARSALUS in 48 B.C.E. Returning to Italy in 46, he was pardoned by Julius Caesar but was later accused of participating in the murderous plot against the dictator and condemned. The historian Suetonius wrote that he was not a member of the conspiracy; he nevertheless traveled with Marcus BRUTUS to Macedonia and took command of the sizable fleet from the first CIVIL WAR. As its admiral he reorganized the ships and proved an able strategist in the campaign for control of the Adriatic. In 40, however, he negotiated to bring his fleet over to Antony. The price of his allegiance was a full pardon. Of all of the condemned officials under the *lex Pedia*, which prosecuted the murderers of Julius Caesar, Ahenobarbus alone escaped punishment.

For the next nine years he served as a loyal officer to Antony, participating in the political spoils after the TREATY OF BRUNDISIUM and receiving a governorship in Bithynia. In 36, he joined Antony in his Parthian war and then fought against the pirate Sextus POMPEY, with Furnius, the governor of Asia. His political career culminated in the consulship in 32 B.C.E. By 31, however, as a client of Marc Antony, Ahenobarbus was unsafe in Rome. He fled to Antony and served on his staff until offered a command in the forces of Antony and Cleopatra. Terminally ill, Ahenobarbus left Antony's cause and went over to the side of Octavian (AUGUSTUS), leaving one son, Lucius DOMITIUS AHENOBARBUS (2).

Domitius Ahenobarbus (2), Gnaeus (d. 40 C.E.) *Consul in 32 C.E.*

The son of Lucius DOMITIUS AHENOBARBUS (2) and father of the future Emperor NERO, Domitius was detested by his contemporaries and vilified in histories. He began his career on the staff of Gaius CAESAR in the East but was dismissed for murdering a freedman for refusing a drink.

When he returned to Italy he rode down a boy on the Appian Way for amusement and gouged out the eyes of an Equestrian for criticizing him. He also swindled bankers and deprived winning charioteers of their just prizes. Nonetheless, in the Rome of Emperor Tiberius, Ahenobarbus gained not only the consulship but the praetorship as well. By 37 C.E., however, the aged emperor had charged him with adultery, incest, and treason. He was spared by Tiberius's death, and Caligula pardoned him. He died three years later of dropsy in his home at Pyrgi. A marriage had been arranged for him in 28 C.E. with AGRIPPINA THE YOUNGER, who bore him Nero. According to Dio, Ahenobarbus very accurately predicted his son's nature (while giving insight into his own), when he said: "It would not be possible for a good man to be born from me and my wife."

Domitius Ahenobarbus (1), Lucius (d. 48 B.C.E.)
Grandson of the great Republican general, Gnaeus Domitius Ahenobarbus
Domitius married the sister of CATO UTICENSIS, Porcia, and thus found an ally in Cato against the rising power of the FIRST TRIUMVIRATE, especially Julius Caesar and Pompey. As PRAETOR in 58 B.C.E., Ahenobarbus proved himself an opponent of Caesar, summoning him to the Senate. Later, in 56 B.C.E., he openly threatened to terminate Caesar's control over Gallia Transalpina, which had been pacified by his grandfather. As a candidate for the consulship of 55, he proposed a measure aimed directly at the triumvirate by promising to have Caesar stripped of his territories, allowing Pompey a chance to crush his rival. Instead of the bloodbath expected, the triumvirs coolly summoned the CONFERENCE OF LUCA in 56. They reconfirmed the tenets of their shared power and thus forced Ahenobarbus to postpone his consulship until 54 B.C.E. The inevitable war between the forces of Caesar and Pompey erupted in 49, and Ahenobarbus became master of Gaul. He headed north, contrary to Pompey's orders and fought Caesar at Corfinium (in central Italy), where he was defeated and captured. Pardoned by Caesar, he immediately rejoined the Pompeian cause. He played a role in the siege of MASSILIA and then took command in 48 B.C.E. of Pompey's left wing at the battle of PHARSALUS, where he was killed. Suetonius noted that Ahenobarbus believed that all Romans must choose sides in the Civil War, that anyone professing neutrality was an enemy and deserving of death.

Domitius Ahenobarbus (2), Lucius (d. 25 C.E.) *Consul in 16 B.C.E. and grandfather of Nero*
Noted for his arrogance and cruelty, as an AEDILE in 22 B.C.E., Domitius ordered the censor, Lucius Plancus, out of his way; and his animal shows and gladiatorial contests were so bloody that Augustus himself rebuked him. Nonetheless, Lucius gained the consulship, aedileship,

and praetorship and success in the provinces. From 15 B.C.E. to 2 B.C.E. he held various posts, including that of proconsul of AFRICA and legate in ILLYRICUM and GERMANIA.

As legate along the Danube, he marched to the Elbe and penetrated farther into barbarian lands than any general before him, setting up an altar to Augustus on the Upper Elbe. In Germania he surpassed this achievement by crossing the Rhine and building the so-called *Pontes longi*, or Long Bridges, over the marches near the Ems River. These constructions were used for years by the legions and their commanders, including GERMANICUS in 15 C.E. He returned to Rome, where he lived until his death. He was married to the elder ANTONIA (2).

Domitius Domitianus, Lucius (fl. late third century C.E.) *One of the leaders of the revolt of Achilleus in Egypt in 297 C.E.*
Domitius may have been one of the founders of the uprising or may have emerged as a rival for the leadership of Achilleus, though sources ascribe the rebellion to Achilleus, not Domitius.

Domitius Ulpianus (fl. third century C.E.) *One of the last jurists*
Domitius preserved the writings of his predecessors through his compilations and commentaries, especially those of Papinian. His own treatise helped establish the entire character of later imperial codes.

domus The home of a wealthy patrician during the Republic and the empire; large estates, normally occupied by members of the upper classes, especially the senatorial and Equestrian orders. They were based originally on the homes of the kings of Rome, especially the famous "Domus Publica" of ancient days. Under the empire, a *domus* assumed a more specific meaning as the residence or the palace of the emperor.

Domus Augustana Name given to the private portion of the palace of DOMITIAN.
See also DOMUS FLAVIA.

Domus Aurea *See* GOLDEN HOUSE OF NERO.

Domus Flavia Palace of Emperor DOMITIAN; built during his reign (81–96 C.E.) on the Palatine Hill and replacing previous imperial residences. It was so beautiful that the emperors of Rome until the reign of Diocletian (284–305 C.E.) resided there. Domitian's palace, designed by the architect Rabirius, was actually two structures: the Domus Flavia, an imposing edifice on the crest of the Palatine, used for official purposes, and the DOMUS AUGUSTANA, the private residence of the ruler. The

A domus in Herculaneum, the House of the Surgeons
(*Courtesy Fr. Felix Just, S.J.*)

Romans called both structures the Domus Flavia. The official building was composed of rooms for ceremonies and an imposing throne room decorated with marble and statues. Marble was used again in the courtyard, while granite from Egypt adorned the great dining hall. A LARARIUM (a household shrine), fountains, and numerous private bedrooms and guest quarters completed the architectural design. Attached to the Domus Flavia, and sloping down one side of the hill, was the Domus Augustana. Below the opening rooms, an illuminated stairway led to the personal suites and recreation areas of the imperial family. Large pools designed with multi-colored mosaics reflected light and illuminated the entire structure.

The Domus Flavia thus provided grandeur and beauty, combined with practicality. Martial, in his *Epigrams,* described both the palace and the architect Rabirius. Constructed very near the old home of Augustus and the traditional residential site of Romulus himself, the Domus was a suitable link to the past.

Domus Tiberiana   Palace built by Emperor TIBERIUS, sometime after his succession to throne in 14 C.E.; a marked contrast to the modest quarters on the Palatine Hill of his predecessor Augustus. The Domus Tiberiana was designed in all probability along the normal atrium styles so common for the period. Tiberius, however, spent much of his time in his palaces in Campania and on Capri. Though it was later incorporated into Nero's DOMUS TRANSITORIA, nothing remains of the palace.

Domus Transitoria   Nero's palace created to connect the main imperial palace on the Palatine Hill with the estates and gardens of Maecenas on the nearby Oppian Hill. It was begun sometime before or during the early part of 64 C.E. Architecturally, the domus was a combina-

tion of the old and the new. On the Palatine the DOMUS TIBERIANA stood prominently, and close to that, on the Esquiline Hill, was another palace as well. The Domus Transitoria connected these buildings but provided innovations in light and in space. In 64 C.E., in the massive conflagration that engulfed much of Rome, Nero's palaces were not spared. The Domus Transitoria was utterly ruined, with only a fountain and some vaulting surviving. But the rubble was cleared and Nero began planning his GOLDEN HOUSE.

Donatism   Schismatic sect that originated in North Africa during the early fourth century. The Donatists derived their name from Donatus, the second schismatic bishop of Carthage. The members of the sect evolved from the rigorists within the African Christian community, who were vehemently opposed to the so-called *traditors* (traitors)—those Christians who had handed over the Scriptures to Roman officials during the terrible persecutions under Emperor Diocletian. Their focus became centered on Caecilian, bishop of Carthage, who was consecrated in 311 by Felix of Aptunga. The rigorists refused to accept Caecilian on the grounds that Felix had been a *traditor,* thereby rendering him incapable of administering the sacraments validly. In support of this position, Numidian bishops consecrated Majorinus, thus setting him up as a rival bishop for the Carthaginian see. Majorinus was soon succeeded (in 313) by Donatus, who emerged as the leader of the movement. An appeal was made to Pope (later Saint) Melchiades in 313, but the commission looking into the matter found against the Donatists, whereupon they turned to the Council of Arles (314) and then to Emperor Constantine the Great (316). Both appeals were unsuccessful, although the sect continued to grow. It found fertile ground among African Christians who resented the interference of the Roman Church in what they felt was an internal matter of the independent African Church.

Efforts to convince the Donatists to return to the church on the part of Constantine were made from 316 to 321 but were abandoned in the face of rigorist recalcitrance. Many Donatists, however, turned to violence, forming roving bands of raiders known as *circumcelliones.* The imperial government responded by launching an intervention in 347. The repression continued for some years, ceasing under Emperor Julian (r. 361–363). Within the church, opposition to the Donatists was spearheaded by St. Augustine, who elucidated the important doctrinal truth concerning the sacraments: The true minister of the sacraments is Christ and thus the unworthiness of any other minister does not in any way affect the efficacy of a sacrament. Further repression began in 405, leading to a formal declaration against the schism in 411 at a conference at Carthage. The subsequent persecution weakened the movement, but it survived in North Africa until the extirpation of much of the church in Africa by the Muslims in the eighth century.

donativum The name (plural, *donativa*) given to the gifts of money or largesse distributed to the soldiers of the LEGIONS or to the PRAETORIAN GUARD by the emperors. The purpose of a donativum varied as some were tokens of gratitude for favors received, and others bribes for favors expected. *Donativa* were normally rendered at the start of each new emperor's reign. In the second and third centuries C.E., this bribe became crucial to the success of any rule. Such was the case with many of the soldier-emperors from 235 to 248 C.E. The Praetorian Guard, so close to the emperor's person, was an even greater threat. The cohorts stationed in Rome were difficult to appease and quick to commit assassination. The *donativum* thus provided a perfect means for buying the Praetorians' support.

Augustus (ruled 27 B.C.E.–14 C.E.) left the Praetorians a sum in his will, but it was not until Tiberius's reign (14–37 C.E.) that gifts of money were thought necessary. The Guard, for example, received gifts for standing by when SEJANUS, their prefect, fell from power. Each Praetorian received 10 gold pieces for withholding from Sejanus's defense. In 41 C.E., after the assassination of Caligula, the soldiers supported Claudius, and a short time later the Senate learned that the Guard had installed him on the throne. Claudius gave them 150 gold pieces, or some 3,750 denarii, to which 100 sesterces were added annually to commemorate Claudius's accession. The inevitable result of the custom of the *donativum* was the Praetorians' auctioning of the empire to DIDIUS JULIANUS in 193 C.E.

See also CONGIARIUM.

Donatus, Aelius (fl. fourth century C.E.) *Grammarian*
Donatus taught in Rome around 350 C.E. and claimed as his pupil St. JEROME. Of his numerous works two survive. The *Ars* covered grammar in two parts, an *Ars minor*, which examines the parts of speech, and the more extensive *Ars major*, in three books. His commentary on Terence survives in an altered form. As for his other work, the most notable is his analysis of Virgil; only the excerpts used by Servius and the preface and introduction remain.

Donatus, Tiberius Claudius (fl. late fourth century C.E.) *grammarian*
Donatus's principal claim to fame was a very extensive commentary on Virgil and the *Aeneid*, the *Interpretationes Vergilianae*, written for his son, Donatianus.

Doryphorus (d. 62 C.E.) *A freedman of Nero*
Doryphorus came to power as the secretary of petitions. As was typical of the era, NERO gave him vast control over the treasury, once granting him 10,000,000 sesterces.

IMPERIAL *DONATIVA* TO THE PRAETORIAN GUARD 14–193 C.E.

Year	Emperor	Provocation	Denarii
14	Augustus	Last will	250
31	Tiberius	Loyalty in Sejanus crisis	1,000
37	Caligula	Upon accession	500
41	Claudius	Upon accession	3,750
Annually	Claudius	Anniversary of accession to the throne	25
54	Nero	Accession	3,750
		Pay for assassinations	500 or less
69	Galba	Promised by Nymphidius Sabinus, but not paid	7,500
69	Otho	Promised	1,250
69	Vitellius	Promised	1,250
69	Vespasian	Regular *donativum*	unknown
79	Titus	Regular *donativum*	unknown
81	Domitian	Considered doubling the *donativum* but opted for regular sum	unknown
96	Nerva	Regular *donativum*	unknown
98	Trajan	Regular *donativum*	unknown
117	Hadrian	Double normal sum	unknown
138	Antonius Piso	Regular *donativum* and upon daughter's marriage	unknown
161	Marcus Aurelius	Joint rule with Verus	5,000
180	Commodus	Regular *donativum*; second promised but unpaid	unknown
193	Pertinax	Force to pay *donativum* of Commodus	3,000
193	Didius Julianus	Purchased the throne	7,250
193	Septimius Severus	Promised a *donativum* but paid less	250

According to Dio, AGRIPPINA, hoping to show the emperor the ridiculousness of his gift, had the sum piled up before his throne; Nero reportedly ordered the amount doubled, saying: "I had no idea that I had given him so little." It was said that Nero had Doryphorus poisoned in 62 C.E. for opposing his union with POPPAEA.

Doura   City east of PALMYRA and the Syrian desert, situated upon the Euphrates River. Doura was probably founded by the Macedonians; by the time of the Roman Empire it stood within the borders of the Parthian Empire as a self-governing and semi-independent community. Local government rested in the hands of a feudal nobility. Given its proximity to SYRIA, Doura became unavoidably embroiled in the struggle for supremacy between PARTHIA and Rome. In the campaign of Emperor Trajan (115–116 C.E.), Doura fell to the legions, and Trajan erected a triumphal arch in the city to celebrate his victory over the Arsacids of Persia.

Its importance, however, was primarily due to its location on a trade route. From the first century B.C.E., trade had passed through Doura on its way from the East to Palmyra. Later, caravans used the city as a starting point of trips into the Parthian realm or into Asia proper, including India and even China (*see* SILK ROUTES). With trade came other influences, including Judaism and Christianity. By the third century the Christians were firmly entrenched, building themselves a small hall for services. The city again became a hotly contested battleground in the third century, with the Persians regaining control. Archaeological remains at Doura have yielded much information on trade with Palmyra, the early Christian community and the sieges of the Roman-Sassanid wars. Doura was also known as Europus or Doura-Europus.

drama   *See* THEATER.

Druids and Druidism   The religious and philosophical system of the CELTS, especially in Gaul and Britain. Druids were a target for eradication by the Roman Empire throughout the first century C.E. Druidism is of unknown origin and was considered ancient even in the time of Aristotle (fourth century B.C.E.). Some said the original Druids were Phoenicians or Egyptians, but the system took root particularly among the Celts, led by the Druid priests, specifically the Druids, Vates and Bards.

The Druid beliefs provided an expression for the nationalistic fervor that so often dismayed the enemies of the Celts. Everywhere that Druid beliefs were dominant, a sense of unity prevailed, especially in Gaul, Britain, and Ireland, although in other places, such as Germany, Russia, and Thrace, the Druid influence was felt.

Rome thus found Druidism a formidable opponent as it moved to conquer the Celtic territories. Julius Caesar,

who wrote extensively about the priests, smashed the Gallic tribes in his campaigns. The subsequent Roman occupation attempted to curtail all Druid ceremonies, although Augustus did not condemn the Druids to death as long as they did not foment revolt. Roman citizens, naturally, were not allowed to be Druids. Tiberius attempted to destroy the elements of Druidism, but his campaign of persecution proved only marginally successful. Claudius shared the opinion of Tiberius and pursued Druids with some energy.

On the continent, Druidism existed only in secret until the time of Vespasian (ruled 69–79 C.E.). In Britain and Ireland, however, the inhabitants followed their priests faithfully. Roman legions arrived in Britain in 43 C.E., under the command of Aulus Plautius, and in 61 the final war against Druidic power began. The Arch-Druid, the sacred groves of Britain, and the hierarchy of the faithful were housed on the island of Mona (modern Anglesey, off the coast of northwestern Wales). General Suetonius Paulinus landed there with an army, slaughtered the inhabitants and hacked down the famed trees. As the Roman province of BRITANNIA was established, the colonists imported their own gods into the region. In time, Christianity would prove to be the final enemy of Druidism. The Council of Arles in 452 C.E. condemned any worship of trees, and stories from Britain detailed the harsh and ruthless slaughter of the Druids over the next centuries. One Welsh legend claimed that in later years the Arch-Druid and his followers were made bishops of the Christian Church.

Writers of the Roman era appear to have been fascinated with Druidism, as numerous references are made to it. Julius Caesar described them in his GALLIC WARS, though his account is meant to ensure the sympathy of his readers for his own cause, the subjugation of the Gallic people. PLINY THE ELDER, in his *Natural History*, painted a very vivid picture of Druidic life, especially those facets of interest to a naturalist and scientist. Other accounts are given by DIODORUS SICULUS, LUCAN (in *Pharsalia*) and STRABO. Later authors, like AURELIUS VICTOR and DIOGENES LAERTIUS (in his *Lives of the Philosophers*), refer to them as an extinct people. Ammianus Marcellinus and the *Scriptores Historiae Augustae* mentioned several Druid seers who predicted various fates for the emperors, including Severus Alexander and Aurelian. A Druidess also prophesied that DIOCLETIAN would become emperor only after slaying the boar (*aper*). In 284 C.E. Diocletian executed the Praetorian prefect Arrius Aper, and became emperor.

Drusilla (1), Julia   (d. 38 C.E.) *Daughter of Germanicus and Agrippina the Elder*
Drusilla had an incestuous relationship with her brother GAIUS CALIGULA, and achieved a position of prominence when he became emperor in 37 C.E. The honors accorded Drusilla included the right to command the respect nor-

mally reserved for the VESTAL VIRGINS and to attend the Circus. After her death, she was deified, Caligula ordering that she be considered the equal to Augustus. In 38 C.E., her birthday was celebrated in the Circus with two days of entertainments held under the gaze of her statue, which was borne into the arena at the start of the games by elephants.

Drusilla (2) (d. after 79 C.E.) *Wife of the procurator of Judaea, Felix*

Drusilla shared in her husband's corrupt rule of the territory. She was present at the trial of St. Paul in 60 C.E. before the procurator. Accounts of her origins are conflicting. TACITUS reported that she was the granddaughter of Antony and Cleopatra and thus claimed kinship with CLAUDIUS. JOSEPHUS wrote that Drusilla was a daughter of Herod AGRIPPA I and a sister of BERENICE, the one-time lover of Titus. Drusilla supposedly had been married to Azizus, the king of Emesa, but FELIX fell in love with her and unlawfully put an end to that marriage. She was at the time enduring the cruelties of Berenice, who was jealous of her beauty, so the offer from the Roman official was accepted. She later gave birth to a son, Agrippa, and both escaped from the eruption of Mount Vesuvius in 79 C.E.

Drusus (1), Nero Claudius ("Drusus the Elder") (38–9 B.C.E.) *The brother of Tiberius and son of Livia and her first husband, Drusus Claudianus Livius*

Drusus was born in the house of Augustus, however, three months after the future emperor had compelled LIVIA to become his wife. Drusus proved more popular to the Romans than his brother and was famed for his belief in the ideals of the Republic. Nonetheless, his marriage to Lady ANTONIA produced two great imperial figures, GERMANICUS and CLAUDIUS. In 19 B.C.E., Drusus embarked on a public career and, starting in 15 B.C.E., served in the provinces in campaigns that would dominate the adult years of his life. He joined TIBERIUS in a war against the Raetians, who had pushed their way out of Noricum and threatened parts of Italy and Gaul, crushing their advance and embarking on a general invasion of RAETIA. In 13 B.C.E., he prepared in GERMANIA for a series of thrusts ito barbarian lands. From 12 to 9 B.C.E., he not only reached the Elbe and Rhine rivers but also dug a canal to the Rhine and sailed through it to the Atlantic.

In 9 B.C.E., he invaded the lands of the CHATTI and the SUEBI, despite severe thunderstorms portending ill omens for his consulship that year. His victory in this region drove him on against the CHERUSCI, but sufficient warnings and bad omens stopped his campaign. On the way home, he fell from his horse and fractured his leg. Augustus sent Tiberius to him, but Drusus died soon after. All of Rome mourned, and after a huge funeral ceremony in the Forum, Drusus was laid to rest in the CAMPUS MARTIUS.

Drusus (2) (d. 33 C.E.) *Son of Germanicus and Agrippina the Elder*

Drusus was a target, along with his brothers GAIUS CALIGULA and NERO, of the ambitious Prefect of the Praetorian Guard, Lucius Aelius SEJANUS. Sejanus worked for years to destroy Agrippina, her family and the entire party of GERMANICUS. He used their weaknesses against them, and found that Drusus had a fierce temper and a jealousy of his brother Nero, who managed to command their mother's attentions. Drusus thus stood by when Agrippina and Nero were arrested, and imprisoned or exiled. Around 29 C.E., Drusus married the unfaithful and cruel Amelia LEPIDA, who immediately turned against her husband in favor of Sejanus. Drusus was soon dismissed by Tiberius and fell under the treason accusations of Cassius Severus. Declared a criminal, Drusus was sent to a dungeon on the Palatine to die. Tiberius realized in 31 C.E. his error in trusting Sejanus so completely and considered presenting Drusus to the Senate and to the mob. The emperor concluded that the youth had been imprisoned too long to be released. Drusus remained in his cell, near starvation, until his death. The Senate was shocked to read Drusus's diary, recounting his days of agony and isolation.

Drusus (3), Julius Caesar ("Drusus the Younger") (13 B.C.E.–23 C.E.) *Son of Emperor Tiberius by his first wife, Agrippina*

Drusus grew up in the imperial palace and married LIVILLA, the daughter of the Lady Antonia. As his father rose to prominence in Rome, so did he, especially after TIBERIUS was adopted and granted full tribunician power in 13 C.E. Augustus also allowed Drusus honors and position. In 11 C.E. he received the rank of *quaestor* and in 13 was named to serve as CONSUL in 15 C.E. By the year 14, he was an heir to the throne when Tiberius succeeded Augustus, carrying the will of the dead emperor into the Senate. In 14, Drusus was sent to PANNONIA to quell the mutiny of the legions there, which had revolted at Augustus's death. Aided by an eclipse and foul weather, Drusus brought them to order. He then returned to Rome to take up the duties of his consulship.

He greeted with alarm the adoption of GERMANICUS, son of Tiberius's brother Drusus (*see* DRUSUS [1]) but maintained good relations with him and with the entire party of Germanicus in Rome. In 19 C.E., however, Germanicus died, and Drusus faced a more formidable and ambitious rival, the Prefect of the Praetorian Guard Lucius Aelius SEJANUS. Sejanus had accompanied Drusus to Pannonia in 14 and had subsequently come to possess the ear and the trust of Tiberius. The two, Drusus and Sejanus, were naturally bitter enemies, as Drusus saw the officer as a grasping upstart. He complained about Sejanus to his father and even struck him on one occasion. Drusus was called hot-tempered, licentious, and cruel (the sharpest of Roman swords were called Drusian after him). Tiberius grew so angry with his behavior that, according to Dio, he shouted: "You will commit no act of violence or insubordination while I am alive, nor when I am dead either."

Drusus served as consul again in 21, with his father, which had come to be considered an omen. All others who had served in that office with Tiberius had suffered horrible deaths. Sejanus used Livilla and the eunuch Spado to introduce into Drusus's system a slow-acting but deadly poison. He finally died in 23 C.E. The aging emperor would rely increasingly upon Sejanus.

Drusus (4) (fl. first century C.E.) *First son of Emperor Claudius (ruled 41–54 C.E.) and his first wife, Plautia*
Drusus was betrothed to the daughter of SEJANUS but died before the wedding, choking to death on a pear.

***duumviri* (1)**   The magistrates in Rome who presided as judges over criminal cases. They ranked just below the PRAETORS in political influence.
See also LAW.

***duumviri* (2)**   Also called *duumviri municipales;* two magistrates appointed in the Roman colonies and in municipal communities to serve as the highest officials of the local government. The Roman colonial systems mirrored the central government in organization, and as the local CURIA, or council, and DECURIONES and CURIALES were miniature Senates and senators, so were the *duumviri* the colonial equivalents of consuls, responsible for many of the same tasks as the consuls in Rome. The *duumviri* oversaw the functions of the local council and ensured that Roman law and order were maintained. Normally their terms of office were for one year, as in Rome. One of the more interesting variations of the office was that of the *duumviri honorarii.* The title of head of the city could be bestowed upon a visiting dignitary; Trajan, for example, was made *duumvir honorarius* of the city of Byzantium.

Dyrrhachium   Seaport in Illyricum located on a peninsula in the Adriatic; originally called Epidamnus by the Greeks. The city served as a major port on the Adriatic and received most of the seaborne traffic out of BRUNDISIUM, about 100 miles away on the Italian coast. In 48 B.C.E., Dyrrhachium was the site of a major battle between Julius CAESAR and POMPEY THE GREAT, during the CIVIL WAR OF THE FIRST TRIUMVIRATE. After crushing the armies of Pompey in Spain and at MASSILIA, Caesar returned to Italy and Rome to begin preparations for a final confrontation with the Pompeians. On January 4, 48 B.C.E., Caesar set sail from Brundisium with seven legions, equaling some 20,000 men. He left another 20,000 behind, as Marc ANTONY was to transport them.

Pompey, meanwhile, had raised an army of some 100,000 men, although the quality of these troops was suspect.

The Caesarean legions crossed the Adriatic, evading the ships of Pompey and landing in Epirus to allow for maneuvering room in the face of the enemy's superiority in numbers. After several marches, however, Pompey failed to move directly against Caesar, electing to defend the town of Dyrrhachium instead. Caesar sent strict orders for Antony to move with his legions by sea as soon as possible, for no successful conclusion would be reached without him. Furthermore, winter was ending; without the Adriatic storms, Antony's galleys would be easy prey for the Pompeians. Antony set sail in late February, barely scraped past the Pompeian fleet and landed on the present-day Albanian coast, north of Dyrrhachium.

Pompey was in the middle, between Antony and Caesar, and set about crushing the lieutenant and his newly arrived forces. But Caesar marched to join Antony and offer battle with their combined units. Pompey declined the confrontation and hurried to prevent other Caesarean elements from reaching Dyrrhachium. He failed, arriving at the port only to have Caesar bar his entry into the city. An advance guard of Pompey's succeeded in taking some advantageous high ground south of Dyrrhachium, and soon Pompey's entire army was surrounded—minus the sizable garrison of the port, which Caesar could not afford to besiege but which was unable to join Pompey. With less than a quarter of Pompey's strength, Caesar built fortifications around the enemy camps on the coast. Caesar's army had to forage on a plain that had been reduced to dust. Pompey had the advantage, and could be supplied by sea.

Throughout the month of April the two sides built vast fortifications. Caesar was spread thin trying to maintain vigilance on his walls and forts, and food grew very scarce. His legions searched for supplies in desperation, surviving through sheer force of will. By late June, Pompey was compelled to act. The crops outside were ready for harvest, and malaria was soon to break out in his camp. In early July an attack was made. Luring Caesar away from his fortifications, Pompey struck hard along the lines and very nearly broke through, but was stayed by the Legate Sulla. A more straightforward assault was then tried, one designed to use the superiority of numbers. A small sortie engaged Caesar in the north, while a half-dozen legions threw themselves into an attack in the south. Caesar countered, but more and more of Pompey's troops burst across the line.

Caesar terminated the siege and ordered a general retreat to the south, Pompey followed but without enough enthusiasm to compel the rattled legions of Caesar to turn and fight one last battle. Caesar had lost 1,000 men, Pompey fewer. Caesar escaped into Thessaly with his army intact. In August, at PHARSALUS, Caesar and Pompey would meet again.

E

Eburacum (York) Town in the north of Britain (BRITANNIA); originally belonging to the BRIGANTES but conquered by the Roman General AGRICOLA in 78 C.E. He made Eburacum into a powerful fort, stationing a legion there and launching his campaigns into the far north from that new post. Subsequent Roman conquests stabilized the region, and Eburacum achieved the status of *colonia* and eventually became a *municipium* as well. It was the leading city in Roman Britain next to LONDINIUM (London), and it was the most important military post in the isles. When the numerous breakthroughs on the frontier by the Caledonians threatened the city's survival in the second and third centuries C.E., the counterattacks of Septimius SEVERUS were based in Eburacum. In the late third century, CONSTANTIUS chose the site as his personal residence, and on July 25, 306, he died there, as had Septimius Severus a century before. Constantius's son, CONSTANTINE, was hailed as emperor by the legions of Eburacum shortly afterward.

Eburones People of German origin, who crossed into Gallia Belgica to settle there sometime in the second or first centuries B.C.E. They were a leading party in the revolt against Julius Caesar in Gaul in 54 B.C.E. Under their King AMBIORIX, the Eburones successfully lured out and destroyed Caesar's legate, Q. Titurius Sabinus, at ADUATUCA. The Eburones participated in the unsuccessful general uprising following Aduatuca but were isolated by Caesar's deliberate policy of reducing the mutinous tribes one by one in the spring of 53 B.C.E. The Eburones were the last, and during that year the Roman legions marched into Gallia Belgica. Ambiorix fled over the Rhine, and his people ceased to be a vital entity.

Ecbatana Now called Hamadan (in northwestern Iran), an ancient city situated in Media (Persia) and supposedly founded by the first king of the Medes, Deioces, around 700 B.C.E. Its beauty and location made the capital prominent in Media, and it was used by the Persians and Parthians as the summer residence of kings while CTESIPHON housed the court during the winter.

Eclectus (fl. late second century C.E.) *Court chamberlain serving emperors Commodus and Pertinax*
Eclectus came from Egypt and entered into the service of Emperor Lucius VERUS as a freedman, staying until the emperor's death in 169 C.E. Eclectus then became a chamberlain to Commodus, originally working under the formidable Cleander. When Cleander was put to death in 189, Eclectus filled the power vacuum and earned the trust of the young emperor. As Commodus grew increasingly unstable, Eclectus joined the Praetorian prefect Aemilius LAETUS and the emperor's mistress, MARCIA (who also was Eclectus's wife or lover), in a conspiracy—after Marcia read a tablet listing their names as the next courtiers to be executed. The plotters hurriedly set about murdering Commodus in 192. Eclectus then urged the prefect of the city, Pertinax, to assume the throne. The chamberlain held power in the new regime but was killed in 193 when the PRAETORIAN GUARD revolted against Pertinax and massacred most of the palace staff.

economy *See* AMPHORA, CHINA, CLOTHING, COINAGE, FINANCE, FOOD AND DRINK, FURNISHINGS, INDIA, INDUSTRY, NUMBERS, SHIPS, TRADE, TRANSPORTATION, WEIGHTS AND MEASURES, and under individual provinces.

For Suggested Readings, please see under TRADE AND COMMERCE.

Edessa City near the upper reaches of the Euphrates River; from 137 B.C.E. to 216 C.E., the territorial seat of the small and often disputed client state of the OSROENE. In 260 C.E. the disastrous battle of Edessa was fought nearby between Emperor VALERIAN and Persian King SHAPUR I. (Sources vary as to the details of the struggle and it is possible that there was no battle at all.) In 260, Shapur had conquered Roman holdings in MESOPOTAMIA. Valerian, whose legions had been decimated by a plague, attempted to counter by assuming a defensive posture near Edessa. Naturally Shapur offered a fight, but the deplorable condition of Valerian's troops forced the emperor to negotiate a pact. He may then have been captured by the enemy or faced a mutiny in his own ranks. He died horribly, and the Roman army received a blow from which it could not easily recover.

education The two primary influences for the development of the Roman education system were the Greeks and the Etruscans. The Romans especially utilized Greek educational methods, perfected them for their own uses, and then added several areas of special concerns of their own—rhetoric and law. The Middle Ages subsequently inherited from Rome both the *quadrivium* (arithmetic, astronomy, geometry, and music) and *trivium* (grammar, rhetoric, and dialectic), termed the Seven Liberal Arts by Martianus Capella.

By custom, Roman children received rudimentary education under their mother's instruction, in a practice termed *gremio matris*. At around the age of seven, a boy was permitted to begin learning at his father's side, accompanying him on his duties, especially if a father was serving as a magistrate, praetor, or other public official. This familial apprenticeship entailed a boy's joining his father at meetings with clients, public speaking, and dinner engagements. Once the boy assumed the *toga virilis* at maturity, he began an internship, a period called the *tirocinium fori*. After gaining political experience, the youth began the *tirocinium militiae,* military training. This method of education opened the way for future advancement in the *cursus honorum.*

This less standardized method of education endured even into the empire. It was replaced gradually, however, by schools, tutors, and schoolmasters. Cicero noted that there was no fixed system of education, and Rome never developed any kind of imperial education system. Nevertheless, there were schools, based on the Greek system of primary and secondary schools. It is quite notable that within Roman education, both girls and boys were granted access to learning. The quality of education depended upon the talents and the methods of the schoolmasters or individual tutors. The level of learning thus varied from person to person, even among the patrician class. In the later empire, at the urging of emperors and provincial governors, enough standard qualities had been introduced that it was common for most Roman children to have received at the very least an elementary ability to read and write and perform basic mathematical computations.

A teacher or schoolmaster (a *litterator* or *ludi magister*) was poorly paid, earning during the late Republic around 15 denarii a month or 180 denarii a year. In comparison, the typical soldier earned around 225 denarii a year, with his equipment, food, and clothing all provided by the military. Private tutors were normally Greek slaves who had been bought because of their abilities to read, write, and do mathematics.

A Roman youth of the imperial age would be handed over at an early age to a teacher, embarking upon a long and arduous period of study. The chief concern was training in Latin and, when possible, Greek. It was considered desirable to be trained in Greek, as that was the language of culture. The writer QUINTILIAN, in fact, preferred that children begin with Greek, as Latin would be acquired in daily life. He thus urged, as did Tacitus, that the child's nurse or slaves be trained in proper Latin grammar, as they would be the primary linguistic influence on children. Children spent more time with nurses and slaves than with their own parents.

From about the age of 12, a child passed from the instruction of the *litterator* to that of the *grammaticus.* The two principal subjects of instruction now were grammar and literature, with ancillary subjects. The day was spent in the delivery of a *praelectio,* an introductory explanation by the teacher, followed by a *lectio,* the reading aloud of passages; the *enarratio,* a word-by-word explanation of the passage in question and other concerns such as grammar; and *iudicium,* the final judgment of the passage and student. All other subjects, such as music and mathematics, were also taught by the *grammaticus,* although it was possible for a student to advance toward a specialization in rhetoric, music, or mathematics. Legal experts were trained in specific schools. Originally, legal training was started during the *tirocinium fori,* but the development of law in the late Republic required the presence of experts in jurisprudence. Such *iurisprudentes* accepted students and thus established a line of training that received formal recognition during the second century C.E.

One of the most notable characteristics of the Roman school system was its brutality. Aristotle observed that "all learning is painful," and a Roman *litterator* was quite willing to use corporal punishment on students who failed to grasp lessons or misbehaved. Caning and floggings were used, as observed by Quintilian in the first century C.E. He claimed that he had no use for flogging, as it only hardened the student, much like a recalcitrant slave.

See also RHETORIC.

Egypt Eventually a Roman province, Egypt attracted the attention of Rome for many reasons. The entire country was immensely fertile, producing most of the wheat and agricultural goods for the world. The Nile offered a magnificent system of transportation far inland, and included Alexandria, the great port of the Nile Delta, on the Mediterranean Sea. Alexandria's position both in Africa and near Palestine, made it accessible to virtually every known trade route. To the historically minded Romans, Egypt represented a past glory, fabled riches and the most illuminated and stunning culture in the ancient world. When the opportunity for conquest presented itself, the legions were dispatched by Emperor Augustus.

Alexander the Great occupied Egypt in the fourth century B.C.E., leaving behind the foundations of Alexandria. Later, his General Ptolemy returned and established his own dynasty of essentially Greek design. Although the Ptolemies would come to own larger territories in Africa and elsewhere, the base of Egypt was both pleasing and disappointing to them.

Its agriculture and natural wealth were obvious, but the inability of the Hellenic civilization to alter in any serious fashion the area beyond Alexandria and the few Greek-oriented cities, prevented the Ptolemies from validating their claim to the rule of the land. Every effort to Hellenize Egypt met with failure, because the nation was steeped in a culture that was centuries old. Furthermore, the Egyptians at the court began to influence and alter the Greeks soon after the dynasty was started.

Greek culture established only a thin veneer, as the Ptolemaic kings proved inept and unstable over the centuries. By the middle of the second century B.C.E., and with the death of Ptolemy VI Philometor in 145 B.C.E., the rulers of this royal clan had lost not only a position of supremacy in the Mediterranean but also were forced to bribe the local population in order to maintain the throne.

Rome, recently a victor over the Carthaginians, looked upon Egypt as a great prize, even though the Republic, as a rule, declined such overseas expansionism and allowed the Ptolemies to rule unmolested. When Marcus Licinius Crassus became jealous of the conquests of Pompey in the East, he proposed to oust the reigning Ptolemy XII Auletes and to seize the formidable treasury and granaries for Rome in 64 B.C.E. Cicero's oratory and senatorial opposition halted Crassus's plans (*De Rege Alexandrino*). Clearly, however, the domestic trouble besetting Egypt, coupled with Roman ambition, made annexation inevitable.

The deterioration of internal Ptolemaic organizations climaxed with the death of Ptolemy XII in 51 B.C.E. He left as his heir his daughter CLEOPATRA and his son Ptolemy. His will contained a codicil that placed Egypt in the hands of the People of Rome, perhaps to safeguard it from the heirs or from outside influence. Cleopatra and Ptolemy warred upon one another, and she was exiled from the palace. She prepared an army and marched back to do battle just as the Roman Civil War (*see* CIVIL WAR, FIRST TRIUMVIRATE) was decided at PHARSALUS in 48 B.C.E.

Pompey fled to Egypt, only to be cruelly murdered on September 28 on the order of Ptolemy. Julius CAESAR, unknowing, pursued Pompey by sea, arriving in Alexandria in early October.

After a brief and bitter war with Ptolemy, Cleopatra was installed upon Egypt's throne. Through her, Egypt's Greek rulers made one last effort at restoring the moribund greatness. At the battle of ACTIUM in 31 B.C.E., Octavian (AUGUSTUS) proved Roman invincibility, and marched on Egypt in 30. He laid claim to the region and was greeted by the populace as a mighty king.

Augustus recognized the special nature of Egypt from the start. He gave the territory to the Roman People, as was customary, but then he took pains to see to it that he had personal mastery over the land. The status of Egypt was unique in the Roman Empire. Instead of being classified as an imperial or senatorial domain, the region became the personal estate of Augustus. Ostensibly the land belonged to Rome, but it remained always the province of the emperors. Corn and foodstuffs were so abundant, and the treasury of the nation was so vast, that no regular system of administration was practical. Instead of a legate, proconsul, or procurator, Augustus appointed as his reliable representative a prefect, chosen from the ranks of the Equestrian Class (*see* EGYPT, PREFECT OF and EQUITES). The prefectship of Egypt was one of the highest offices attainable by the knights.

To ensure the sanctity of Egypt from meddlesome senators and Equestrians, Augustus further decreed that no members of either class could enter the land without permission of the emperor. In 19 C.E., Germanicus traveled to Egypt and then up the Nile. Tiberius censured him for violating the rule of Augustus. Tacitus added that the cause for such a rebuke was grounded in the reality of Egypt's strategic importance to the sea routes of the Mediterranean and the land-based traffic from Africa to Asia. He later wrote that Vespasian seized Egypt in his campaign of 69 C.E. because *Aegyptus claustra annonae* (Egypt held the key to the granary).

The prefect of Egypt sat in Alexandria. His tasks were to ensure the flow of corn, protect the frontiers of the south against Ethiopia, dispense justice to the populace and maintain domestic harmony—while Romanization continued. At the disposal of the prefect were three legions, a very large force. In Tiberius's reign (14–37 C.E.) the command was reduced to two legions; ultimately only one stood ready, although the territory demanded the use of many cohorts and auxiliary units.

Ethiopia's incursions into southern Egypt began in 25 B.C.E., during the absence of Prefect Aelius Gallus, and this made the weaknesses of the borders evident. Gaius Petronius reconquered all of the lost districts, including Philae and the Elephantine, and henceforth a close watch was maintained on Ethiopia. Borders wars, while inconvenient, were only part of the problems facing Rome on the Nile.

Provincial rule of Egypt was based on centuries of traditions. Many titles applied during earlier periods were retained, including those of *diocetes, idiologus,* and *epistrategus.* The new Roman occupation, however, demanded a more centralized form of government. Old positions of authority in Egypt were therefore stripped of all military duties, which were given to the legions. Equestrians replaced many Egyptians and Greeks in posts, thereby streamlining provincial bureaucracy.

Three districts were created in Egypt: the Delta, including Alexandria, Nicopolis, Canopus; the Faiyum, with Arsinoe and the ancient nomes or territories; and Upper Egypt, including Philae and Elephantine.

The prefect journeyed to each district to carry out his legal duties in the local courts. Hearing cases and accepting petitions not only helped create the illusion of local participation in the government but also brought the prefect into contact with lower administrative officials. A magistrate in each community, called *epistrategus* for the nomes, *gymnasiarch* or *ethnarch,* held sway, especially with their own associates or local inhabitants. They collected taxes just as their counterparts did throughout the empire (*see* CURIALIS and DECURIONES). Egypt's incomparable organization in terms of village and city registration for the CENSUS made taxation easier and hence more burdensome for the people.

From the start the Egyptians recognized the fact that Rome had singled them out for special treatment, not out of affection but in the hopes of draining every ounce of natural wealth and human industry possible. In turn, the special status brought few benefits. Augustus ordered irrigation improvements to increase harvests, and Alexandria profited handsomely from its continued operation as one of the empire's leading ports. But throughout the first three centuries of Roman occupation, the historically impressive vitality of the land was stripped and exported virtually out of existence. Taxes grew heavier and, as was the case elsewhere, the middle class forming most of the various regions was forced to pay any deficiencies between what was expected and what was delivered. This middle class soon collapsed under the weight of its burdens.

Tiberius Julius Alexander, prefect in the late first century C.E., initiated a number of reforms to maintain prosperity, but in the second century strife injured Egyptian economic life. The Jewish revolt caused terrible damage to Alexandria, and other uprisings took place in 153 and 173 C.E., with resulting depopulation.

To stem the inevitable decline of Egypt, Septimius Severus (ruled 193–211 C.E.) made several changes. A new finance minister, a *rationalis,* was appointed, and the Prefect Subatianus Aquila tightened his grip even further. The emperor also granted to Alexandria and many other communities their own senates. Such new councils, unfortunately, could not stem the tide or do anything to help the gradual poverty, which destroyed entire provinces.

Like their Ptolemaic Greek predecessors, the Romans struggled perpetually to imprint themselves upon Egypt and discovered it was easier to revive the Hellenic styles of earlier eras. Several emperors established cities along Greek architectural lines. Hadrian, for example, founded Antinopolis, joining other metropolises such as Naucratis and Ptolemais. Greek literature and culture were openly favored. In Alexandria this program met with some success, but in the countryside, as in Britain, life was untouched and unchanged. Latin failed as anything but the enforced language of government. Tensions increased. The Greeks, Jews, and Egyptians fought continually in the streets of Alexandria, agreeing only that the true enemy was Rome. Christianity grew in popularity in the Greek cities, but the tempestuous manner of living so characteristic of Alexandria produced such controversial church figures as Arius and Athanasius, and a truly remarkable Christian, St. Anthony.

As part of the reorganization of the imperial system, Diocletian (c. 295 C.E.) broke apart the large provinces of Egypt and created three smaller ones: Aegyptus Iovia, Thebais, and Aegyptus Herculia. All were under the control of the DIOCESES of Oriens. For the next two centuries imperial mastery remained in some form, but never again would Egypt serve as the jewel of the Roman Empire.

Suggested Readings: Bagnall, Roger S. *Egypt in Late Antiquity.* Princeton, N.J.: Princeton University Press, 1993; Bowman, Alan K. *Egypt after the Pharaohs 332 B.C.–A.D. 642: From Alexander to the Arab Conquest.* Berkeley: University of California Press, 1986; Chauveau, Michel. *Egypt in the Age of Cleopatra: History and Society under the Ptolemies.* Translated by David Lorton. Ithaca, N.Y.: Cornell University Press, 2000; *Cleopatra's Egypt: Age of the Ptolemies.* Brooklyn, N.Y.: Brooklyn Museum, 1988; Lewis, Naphtali. *Life in Egypt under Roman Rule.* Oxford, U.K.: Clarendon Press, 1983; Lindsay, Jack. *Daily Life in Roman Egypt.* London: F. Muller, 1963; *The Oxford Encyclopedia of Ancient Egypt.* New York: Oxford University Press, 2001; Rowlandson, Jane, ed. *Women and Society in Greek and Roman Egypt: A Sourcebook.* New York: Cambridge University Press, 1998.

Egypt, prefect of The title used by the governor of the unique and important province of EGYPT. Emperor Augustus recognized the need for the imperial office to maintain control over the ports and trading centers of Egypt and so decreed that a special office would be created to serve as the head of all administrative duties. A prefect was chosen, a member of the Equestrian Class, and the prefectship of Egypt, along with that of the Praetorian Guard, was considered the highest political achievement open to a Roman knight.

Elagabalus (Varius Avitus Bassianus Marcus Aurelius Antoninus) (204–222 C.E.) *Emperor from 218 to 222*
Born to the Syrian Varius Marcellus and to JULIA SOAEMIAS, the niece of Emperor Caracalla's formidable mother, JULIA DOMNA, Elagabalus grew up in the imperial family but was dominated by the Syrian environment of his hometown of EMESA and by his ambitious and scheming female relatives. In Emesa he became, at a young age, the chief priest of the Emesian cult of the sun-god, Elah-Gabal—principally because of his mother's connections and his own good looks.

In 217, the assassination of Caracalla set off a series of events that changed his life dramatically. Caracalla's successor, MACRINUS, ordered Julia Domna's sister and Elagabalus's grandmother, JULIA MAESA, to leave Rome and to retire to Emesa. Vowing revenge, Julia Maesa bought or stirred up the legions in Syria to revolt and put an end to her enemy. When Macrinus fell, these same legions elected Elagabalus, who wrote to the Senate and was accepted as the son of Caracalla and given the throne. Macrinus died a short time later, and the young emperor, with his entourage of courtiers, set off for Rome.

Throughout Asia and BITHYNIA, Elagabalus outraged the traditionalists with his behavior and stunned Rome with his religious ceremonies, his lifestyle and his loathsome companions. He occupied the imperial palace in late 219 but left the imperial government in the hands of Julia Maesa and the Praetorian Prefect Comazon, preferring to indulge himself in his cult and in his strange sexual habits. The great sun-god, physically identified with a large black stone, was brought to Rome from Emesa, and Elagabalus supervised the building of the deity's temple. There he held lavish rites, forcing all senators and persons of prominence to attend the divinity. He is rumored to have displayed as well sexual excess, transvestism, and self-mutilation.

In 221, Julia Maesa persuaded Elagabalus to name as Caesar her cousin, SEVERUS ALEXANDER, on the grounds that he could devote more time to his cult if he had such a trusted aide. At first he agreed, but later, as his cousin grew in popularity, he tried to have Severus removed. The Praetorian Guard revolted in March 222, forcing the emperor to the Praetorians' Castra Praetoria, with his mother and Severus. That night he rather foolishly made threats against his enemies, and on the next day, March 12, he was slain. The bodies of Elagabalus and his mother were mutilated, and both corpses were thrown into the public sewer. Severus Alexander was proclaimed emperor.

Three women were married to Emperor Elagabalus during his reign: Julia Paula, Aquilia Severa, and Annia Faustina. He was married first to Julia Paula but divorced her to pursue Aquilia Severa, a Vestal Virgin whom Elagabalus raped and then married in 220—to unite, as he explained it, the Elagabalus of the East with the Minerva of the West. He divorced her in 221 and was married to Annia Faustina, who tried unsuccessfully to stabilize the regime and was divorced in 222, when Elagabalus returned to Aquilia Severa. It is possible that he had other wives as well.

Elegira A city in the north of ARMENIA, situated on the farthest edges of the Euphrates. In 162 C.E., following the death of the emperor ANTONINUS PIUS, a Parthian host invaded Armenia to place its own candidate on the throne of that country. The governor of CAPPADOCIA marched to Elegira to halt the Parthian advance but was defeated and slain, setting off a series of wars that would rage for the next four years.
See also PARTHIA.

Emesa City in the Roman province of Syria, on the Orontes River. It was centuries old when the Romans conquered it, and was the center of the great Emesian cults of the god Baal and the sun god, Elah-Gabal. Emesa gained notoriety in the third century C.E. when its powerful family was the Severans. Following the death of Emperor CARACALLA in 217, his aunt, JULIA MAESA, retired to her home in Emesa and there plotted the destruction of Caracalla's murderer and successor, MACRINUS. By 218, the city was at the heart of a revolt among the Syrian legions, and from Emesa, Julia Maesa's grandson, ELAGABALUS, came to the throne. The cult moved to Rome with Elagabalus, where resentment quickly flared. SEVERUS ALEXANDER maintained Emesa's influence when he became emperor, but his assassination in 235, and the decline of the family of JULIA DOMNA, led to the city's downfall in status and power.

emperors of the Roman Empire *See* APPENDIX 1: EMPERORS OF THE ROMAN EMPIRE 27 B.C.E.–476 C.E.

Empiricus, Sextus (fl. third century C.E.) *Physician*
Empiricus was a contemporary of GALEN and wrote several treatises on MEDICINE.

engineering The Romans were the foremost engineers of the ancient world, with the possible exception of the ancient Egyptians, whose architectural achievements remain some of the most significant ever attempted. The Romans, however, attained engineering triumphs in a wide range of areas, including the construction of buildings, bridges, aqueducts, baths, and roads, and military engineering. They are perhaps best remembered for their colossal public works, including the Pantheon, the Forum Romanum, the Colosseum, and Baths of Caracalla. The roads of the empire, the aqueducts that fed water to the cities, and the feats of military engineering also garner the Romans attention from history.

It has been written that the Romans did not invent many of their technological achievements. Rather, they acquired ideas from others and modified them for their own purposes, often finding new ways to apply an existing technology. They also carried their engineering achievements to the many corners of the empire as part of their deliberate policy of forging a sense of *Romanitas* —"Roman-ness." Roads, for example, were essential in pacifying a region because they allowed legions to march freely throughout a province and later, colonists and merchants to create a permanent Roman presence there. Likewise, Roman aqueducts, bridges, and buildings put a perpetual Roman stamp on an area or city, as can be seen even today in southern France at Nîmes and Arles.

It is generally held that the father of Roman engineering was the censor Appius Claudius Caecus, who undertook the construction of the Appian Way (the Via Appia) and the first of the great aqueducts of Rome in 312 B.C.E. Two other great Roman engineers were Sextus Julius Frontinus and Vitruvius. Frontinus was in charge of building and maintaining the massive series of aqueducts that supplied water to Rome in the late first century C.E. Vitruvius, chief architect of the Augustan age, was also a talented military engineer. Traditionally, the Romans accorded great honor and respect to engineers, especially those who had demonstrated their skills in the field or the city.

BUILDINGS

The Romans were a civilization of builders. As the city of Rome could attest, there was an incessant process of construction, from *insulae* (apartment blocks) to new fora to new temples. It is a testament to the skills of architects, engineers, and construction crews that so much of the architectural patrimony of ancient Rome remains standing today. Among the most notable engineering feats that made their buildings possible were the use of arches, vaults, and domes, and the addition of *pozzolana* to their mortar to create a new and durable cement.

Arches permitted the Romans to depart from the use of the post and lintel by removing the chronic problem of the weight being placed upon the middle of the frame. The Roman arch, termed by architects a voussoir arch (from the tapering on pointed design) and inherited from the Etruscans, used a keystone to balance the distribution of the weight. The keystone was fitted into the very top of the arch. This type of arch became one of the centerpieces of Roman architecture and was the decisive element in the construction of bridges. Similarly, the voussoir arch made possible the application of the vault, an arch-shaped support for a ceiling or roof or the ceiling itself. Romans were able to build variations on the basic arch design, including the groined and the barrel vault. The limited spans of barrel vaults, in fact, hastened the development of the dome. Designed to be a spherical vault resting upon a round base wall, the dome became one of Roman architecture's most remarkable legacies, with supreme examples including the Pantheon, built by Marcus Vipsanius Agrippa in 27 B.C.E.

One of the keys to the success of Roman engineers was access to materials, and the Romans could take credit for a truly unique invention: concrete. Knowledge about artificial stone, or concrete, had been in existence since the time of the Egyptians and Mesopotamians, but the Romans created an additional ingredient to the traditional mixture of lime and sand. A fine, dark volcanic ash, called *pozzolana* (or *pozzuolana*) was added to the mortar. The ash had the positive effect of making the concrete harder and far more durable, especially in water. Bridge piers were thus rendered virtually impervious to the eroding effects of running water. The tougher form of concrete thus played a major role in the construction of arches, vaults, and domes and in the transformation of Rome from a city of huts to the foremost city of the Roman Empire.

BRIDGES AND AQUEDUCTS

As noted, the first AQUEDUCT built in Rome was around 312 B.C.E., the Aqua Appia, designed by Appius Claudius Caecus. Aqueducts were essential to the very survival of Roman civilization, as they guaranteed that freshwater could be supplied to cities and communities. The importance of water was demonstrated by the sheer scale of the aqueduct projects that were financed by the Roman state and that might involve hundreds of civil engineers and thousands of workers and artisans. As the population of the city of Rome reached and then eclipsed 1 million residents at the start of the imperial era, the flow of water guaranteed not only water for drinking and bathing but was one of the linchpins of social order and harmony. Likewise, it was important to be able to carry water out of the cities. Aqueducts and tunnels helped to remove sewage and wastewater from the underground sewers and prevent epidemics. Also, aqueducts relieved threats of flooding by providing drainage of floodwaters and excess water from storms. For construction, engineers relied on the most up-to-date building materials and techniques, placing many of the largest aqueducts on arched causeways.

The first bridge that is known to have been built by the Romans was thrown across the Tiber in the time of King Ancus Marcius (r.c. 642–617 B.C.E.) and was called the Pons Sublicus. Typical Roman bridges were made of wood and were initially simple in design, using post-and-lintel construction. These were, of course, not especially durable, and the rise of the voussoir arch in the fourth century B.C.E. with its much sturdier keystone, permitted the construction of increasingly elaborate bridges. The application of *pozzolana* also allowed engineers to span large rivers, although the single greatest attempt at crossing a body of water was probably the elaborate scheme of Emperor Nero (r. 54–68) to cross the Gulf of Baiae via a series of pontoon bridges made of ships lathed together.

The combination of the arches and the *pozzolana* made the arched bridges extremely durable and capable of supporting great weights, including the siege engines and supply wagons of the legions and the heavy wagons of the Roman merchants, thereby maintaining the commercial routes and the communication lines of the empire.

ROADS

Much as bridges served to help unify the Roman Empire, so too were the Roman roads a decisive element in maintaining imperial civilization. The first Roman road was the famed Via Appia, which connected Rome with Capua and southern Italy and meandered for 132 miles. It was built, as noted, by the censor of 312 B.C.E., Appius Claudius Caecus. From this first route, the Romans constructed more than 372 roads across the empire. The *viae* were not merely a means for travel from one province to another; they were a part of the grand strategic system of the legions, military conquest, and the planting of enduring *Romanitas* in far flung provinces and recently pacified regions. For those reasons, roads were always a priority in administration, and the chief authorities in their construction were the engineers of the legions, supported by the hard-working legionnaires.

A typical road used a series of layers to provide durability. First the engineers placed a bed of mortar or sand. On top of this was poured *statumen*, stones placed into a bed of clay or concrete. The *statumen* layer was not used if the road was built upon a rock foundation. The next layer was called *rudus* or *ruderatio*, a layer of concrete mixed with small stones, crushed tile or brick, or gravel. A final layer was made up of lava or silica (*silex*) and was termed the *summa crusta*. On the sides of the road, crews installed a stone curb, an *umbo,* supported by side gutters or ditches to permit drainage for rain. Constant repairs were done by work crews in the provinces when warranted.

MILITARY ENGINEERING

Engineers were also considered an indispensable part of the personnel of the legions, both because of their abilities as architects and supervisors of construction and as experts in siege warfare. As such, a typical engineer had knowledge of a variety of construction techniques as well as familiarity with a host of different weapons and tactics for besieging cities and camps in various environments. Training for a military engineer was provided through an apprenticeship, by traveling with a legion and studying under experienced engineers. There was much to learn, as the engineers had to be able to build roads, bridges, and set up camps as well as design siege works.

Siege works entailed a strategy of circumvallation in which an enemy location was surrounded by the Roman army. The engineers created a series of camps or forts at key locations around the enemy city, and the camps were then linked by ramparts, trenches, and nearly impassable barriers. A second line of works was erected that surrounded the Roman siege lines and pointed away from the besieged city. Its purpose was to prevent any enemy relief forces from breaking the siege. These lines also had stout barriers, with pits and booby traps. Typical traps might include deep pits lined with stakes that were camouflaged with brushwood. Along the perimeter of the second siege line were towers and archer stations, as well as interior ramparts and communication lines. The latter were important to permit a general to move troops back and forth within the siege lines.

Classic Roman sieges were conducted in several distinct stages. The engineers first surveyed the city to be attacked and its topography. They then began construction of the siege lines, designed to make best use of the terrain. Once the circumvallation was complete, a direct assault on the city was made to try and end the siege as quickly as possible. If that failed, the siege shifted into a long campaign to starve out the enemy. The most famous example of this kind of siege was at Alesia in 52 B.C.E. Julius Caesar attempted to starve out the Gauls under Vercingetorix while repulsing numerous sorties from a Gallic relief army and attempts to break out of the city by Vercingetorix's own troops.

Military engineers also had responsibility for building camps and forts. The Roman *castra,* or camp, was constructed along well-established lines, with engineers essentially laying down miniature cities. Normally, an engineer chose a site that was easily defended on open or raised ground, that was near water, and that offered little opportunity for a hidden or sudden attack by an enemy. Within the camp, the most important first location was the *praetorium,* the tent of the commanding general. From this central spot, the engineer used a surveying tool, the *groma,* to plan out the rest of the camp. The camp soon took on a customary appearance of tents, temporary stables, ramparts (for easy walking in poor weather and defenses).

See also ART AND ARCHITECTURE, LEGIONS.

Suggested Readings: Bidwell, Paul T. *Hadrian's Wall Bridges.* London: Historic Buildings & Monuments Commission for England, 1989; Brodribb, Gerald. *Roman Brick and Tile.* Gloucester, U.K.: Sutton, 1987; Casson, Lionel. *Ships and Seafaring in Ancient Times.* Austin, Tex.: University of Texas Press, 1994; Edmondson, J. C. *Two Industries in Roman Lusitania: Mining and Garum Production.* BAR International Series, 362; Oxford, U.K.: BAR, 1987; Forbes, R. J. *Studies in Ancient Technology.* Vol. 2. Leiden: E. J. Brill, 1966; Hodges, Henry. *Technology in the Ancient World.* London: Allen Lane, 1970; James, Peter, and Nick Thorpe. *Ancient Inventions.* New York: Ballantine, 1994; Lewis, A., and Timothy Runyan. *European Naval and Maritime History 300–1500.* Bloomington, In: University of Indiana Press, 1990; Macaulay, David. *City: A Story of Roman Planning and Engineering.* Boston: Houghton-Mifflin, 1974; Starr, Chester G. *The Influence of Sea Power* *on Ancient History.* New York: Oxford University Press, 1989; White, K. D. *Greek and Roman Technology.* London: Thames and Hudson, 1984.

Ennia Thrasylla (d. 38 C.E.) *Wife of Macro, the ambitious Prefect of the Praetorian Guard*

Ennia's role in her husband's rise was considerable, although the three main sources for the period disagree as to her specific actions. Tacitus wrote that Macro convinced her to have an affair with the next emperor, GAIUS CALIGULA, in 37 C.E., so that he might benefit. Dio recorded that Macro talked Caligula into the liaison, and Suetonius argued that Caligula himself took a liking to Ennia. Macro, nevertheless, proved instrumental in the early days of Caligula's reign, but Ennia and her husband fell out of favor and were ordered to Egypt, where Macro was to take up the prefectship. Before their departure, however, an imperial order commanded that they kill themselves.

Epagathus (fl. early third century C.E.) *Freedman*

Epagathus served during the reigns of CARACALLA, MACRINUS, and SEVERUS ALEXANDER; his power in the imperial courts lasted from about 215 to 228. He was of unquestionable authority in the later years of Caracalla, and in 228, he urged the Praetorian Guard of Severus Alexander to murder their own prefect, the great jurist ULPIAN. Out of fear of reprisals, Severus Alexander ordered Epagathus to be prefect of Egypt but had him taken to Crete to be murdered instead.

Epaphroditus (1) (fl. first century B.C.E.) *Freedman of Octavian (Augustus)*

Epaphroditus was a messenger between his master and CLEOPATRA in her final days in 30 B.C.E. He was given the task of watching the queen carefully during Octavian's negotiations with her and was specially ordered not to allow her to kill herself. It has been surmised that Octavian secretly acquiesced to her plans of suicide, for Epaphroditus was allowed to leave her side to deliver a final letter to Octavian, at which time Cleopatra successfully sought death in the sting of an asp.

Epaphroditus (2) (fl. first century C.E.) *One of the most loyal freedmen in the service of Nero*

He attained the post of secretary of petitions (A LIBELLUS) sometime before 68 C.E. and then helped NERO escape from Rome when the emperor's reign collapsed. Nero was soon pursued by horsemen, and Epaphroditus helped him commit suicide, delivering the final, fatal blow. He survived the next years of war only to be arrested and executed by Domitian in 95, for failing to stand and defend Nero in the last hours of his life.

Ephesus

One of the leading cities in the province of ASIA. Located on the Ionian coast south of SMYRNA, Ephesus was founded many centuries before Rome and once was a part of the 12-city League of Ionia. As one of the cities of Asia Minor, Ephesus competed with Pergamum, where the governor was seated, though the treasury for the province remained in Ephesus. The harbor was excellent, and its road led to the Harbor Baths, which were beautiful in layout and followed a general Greek design instead of the Roman style, with columns and a prominent gymnasium. Nearby was the theater, capable of seating over 20,000 spectators.

The Library of Ephesus, called the Library of Celsus, was a second-century C.E. creation with a second story and a facade with columns. The massive temple of Domitian was given a new name in honor of Vespasian, after Domitian's murder in 96 C.E. Hadrian built a smaller temple following Syrian artistic innovations. The ancient Temple of Artemis (Diana), erected in the sixth century B.C.E., was one of the wonders of the ancient world. By the late third century C.E., Christianity had gained a firm hold in Asia, and PAUL OF TARSUS wrote his *Epistles* to its inhabitants. The city was also visited by St. John.

Ephesus, Council of

The third general (or ecumenical) council in the history of the Christian Church, held at Ephesus in 431 with the aim of bringing an end to the crises caused by Nestorianism. The specific cause for the need of the council had been the power granted St. Cyril of Alexandria in August 430 by Pope Celestine I to excommunicate Nestorius, bishop of Constantinople, should he not recant his heretical position that there were two separate natures in Christ, the divine and the human. Using his influence to prevent his immediate condemnation, Nestorius convinced Emperor Theodosius II to summon a general council. Organized with the full approval of the pope and under the presidency of Cyril, the council convened on June 22, 431, at Ephesus. In attendance were some 200 bishops. Celestine was to be represented by two legates, Bishops Projectus and Arcadius, and the Roman priest Philip, but Cyril did not wait for their arrival before beginning the proceedings, nor did he delay for very long while awaiting the Syrian bishops under John, patriarch of Antioch, whom Cyril knew to be favorably disposed to Nestorius. Acting with the full authority as president and "as filling the place of the most holy blessed archbishop of the Roman Church, Celestine," Cyril maneuvered the majority of bishops into condemning Nestorius. The heresiarch was excommunicated and deposed, his doctrines formally condemned, and the Nicene Creed upheld.

The Eastern bishops, who had arrived and were immediately at odds with the council, were soon joined by a number of prelates, such as Theodoret, bishop of Cyrrhus, also unhappy with Cyril's driving the deliberations to such a precipitate conclusion. The rival bishops

The library of Ephesus *(Hulton/Getty Archive)*

haled their own council, at which Cyril was excommunicated. Protracted negotiations followed, resulting in a compromise in 433 that brought a reconciliation between Cyril and John. Ephesus, however, had been a triumph for orthodox Christianity. Through its seven sessions, Nestorianism had been clearly defeated in favor of Alexandrian theology, especially with the definition of the hypostatic union and the endorsement of the Marian title Theotokos, or "bearer of God."

Epicharis (fl. first century C.E.) *Freedwoman*
In 65 C.E., Epicharis was involved in the PISONIAN CONSPIRACY against Nero.

Epictetus (c. 55–135 C.E.) *Stoic philosopher*
Epictetus's teaching influenced prominent figures of later eras, including ARRIAN and Emperor MARCUS AURELIUS. He was born in Phrygia in the town of Hierapolis and grew up as a slave of Nero's freedman EPAPHRODITUS (2). He attended the lectures of Musonius Rufus in Rome. After Epaphroditus awarded Epictetus his freedom, he immediately began teaching in the capital. When Domi-

tian exiled all philosophers from Rome in 89 C.E., Epictetus took up residence in Nicopolis, in Epirus, where he remained for the rest of his life. Like other Stoics, he taught an indifference to the vagaries of fortune, and that the world reflected a divine providence. His thoughts were preserved by his leading student, Arrian, in eight books, called the *Discourses* (of which four survive). He also authored a *Manual*.

See also STOICISM.

Epicureanism Philosophical school founded many centuries before the empire by the great Greek philosopher Epicurus (342–270 B.C.E.). Epicureans stressed the physical world over a providential one and believed that the senses were the source of pleasure. They advocated a life of simplicity, retreat from the affairs of the world, and prudence as a sound means of achieving happiness. To the Romans, Epicureanism offered the opportunity to remove oneself from the often fatal affairs of the era, and by the second century C.E. most Epicures had virtually disappeared from public view. The great Roman Epicure was Lucretius (c. 95–55 B.C.E.), the author of *De rerum natura (On the Nature of Things)*; the last was Diogenes of

Oenoanda (second century C.E.), who wrote a series of inscriptions for his own town.

Epiphanius (c. 315–403 C.E.) *Bishop of Salamis from 367 to 403 C.E.*

An ardent supporter of Christian orthodoxy, Epiphanius was born in Palestine, he entered a monastery and in 367 was elected bishop of Salamis. He opposed Hellenism and attacked the rampant heresies of his era, cataloged in one large book, the *Panarian,* or *Refutation of All the Heresies* (374), in which he discussed all of the contemporary deviations from the accepted dogma of CHRISTIANITY, as established by the NICENE CREED, and their "cure." From 392 he worked against Origen, allying himself with anyone who would aid him in his cause. He also established many monasteries.

Epirus
Roman province in northwestern Greece, on the coast of the Ionian Sea. The Epirote people were a loose amalgam of ethnic cultures. Settlers arrived in Epirus from Achaea, Macedonia, Thessaly, and Illyria; it was devastated by the Macedonian wars of the second century B.C.E. In 31 B.C.E., Octavian (AUGUSTUS) arrived in the area and established his headquarters at NICOPOLIS, a small Greek community. Octavian won the famous battle against Antony at ACTIUM, just to the north. The future emperor completed the city of Buthrotum, planned by Julius Caesar, but, despite the presence of hardworking Roman colonists, no foundation of wealth was established.

Greater success was achieved at Nicopolis, where a Greek style of life was pursued and a permanent memorial for Augustus's victory was erected. In addition to the influx of new residents, vast numbers from the villages of southern Epirus were moved to Nicopolis, which provided local administration for the southern part of the region. To the north, however, where there were higher numbers of non-Greeks, most of the inhabitants lived in the broken down remnants of earlier towns. Hadrian or Antoninus Pius decreed that Epirus would be removed from the jurisdiction of Achaea and made an individual province. A procurator was installed at Nicopolis, and new towns were founded, most notably Hadrianopolis, in the Epirote wilderness, where trade and manufacturing were attempted unsuccessfully. A panegyric delivered in the time of Constantine, at the start of the fourth century, spoke of Nicopolis's state of deterioration.

epistulis, ab
Title given to the secretaries of correspondence in the palaces and courts. The *ab epistulis* handled all letters for the emperors. In the early empire the post was held almost exclusively by freedmen, but Hadrian transferred responsibility for such affairs to the Equestrian class. By the late second century C.E. the size of the imperial staff warranted the division of the office into two separate groups: secretaries for correspondence in Greek and secretaries for correspondence in Latin (*ab epistulis Graecis* and *ab epistulis Latinis,* respectively).

See also NOTARII.

Eprius Marcellus, Titus Clodius (d. 79 C.E.) *Consul in 60 and 74 C.E. and one of Nero's most trusted and able accusers*

Eprius Marcellus came from rude origins but nevertheless made his way into imperial favor. He served out the term of Lucius Silanus as *praetor,* though for only one day, and then provided his oratorical skills for Nero, becoming an immensely successful speaker, as was noted in Tacitus's *Dialogues de Oratoribus.* In 57, Eprius held the rank of legate in Lycia but the following year was attacked by the Lycians for misappropriation of funds, though his influence was such that many of the visiting accusers were exiled. His ties to Nero brought him in conflict with Helvidius Priscus, and in 66 he played a major role in the condemnation of THRASEA PAETUS, one of Nero's enemies. Eprius survived the fall of Nero, insinuating himself into the good graces of Vespasian, and earned the consulship for 74. In 79, however, he conspired against Vespasian and was condemned. He killed himself by slashing his throat with a razor.

Equites (Equester Ordo, Equestrians, or the Knights)
One of the social ranks or estates of Rome. During the Republic the Equites served as the middle class, situated socially between the Senate and the common Roman citizen. During the empire they were reorganized and used to occupy an increasing number of posts in the imperial bureaucracy. The Knights originated in the days of the kings, who recruited them for the army and then mounted them as a cavalry force. The units survived into the Republican era, but they were no longer mere soldiers. Henceforth their duties were often nonmilitary, providing service as officers of the state and as governors abroad. This new mission became certified in the late second century B.C.E., when the Equestrians finally assumed the position of an actual social class. While senators were forbidden to join them, a certain amount of flexibility characterized the general admission into their ranks. A candidate had to possess property that totaled more than 400,000 sesterces, or 4,000 gold pieces.

Power slowly gravitated to the Equestrians, who assumed positions of prominence, especially under the Gracchi, Tiberius and Gaius, in the early first century B.C.E. The two brothers of the Gracchus family granted the Knights the right to sit on juries and to wield control over the QUAESTIONES (civil courts). They naturally gained considerable wealth and were in a position to oppose the SENATE politically. Sulla temporarily reduced the number and strength of the Equestrians through bloodshed and by adlecting into the Senate (*see*

ADLECTIO). Cicero, in the mid-first century B.C.E., helped the Equestrians to regain their lost ground and then to lay claim to a sizable role in the affairs of the Republic. Cicero used both his ties to the Equites and the senatorial class to improve relations between the two and to foster ties instead of antagonisms. His efforts thus certified their position and their organization.

Throughout the Republic the Equestrians were divided into units, called centuries, 18 in number, along with the *equites equo publico* (knights granted a public horse). While many younger Knights formed a major source of the officer corps in the legions, two trends had developed by the end of the Republican era. First, the order itself stepped away from active involvement in military life; they preferred to find advancement in sociopolitical circles and thus were able to make their positions hereditary. At the same time, however, the decline of the powers of the CENSOR in Rome and the general chaos of the first century B.C.E. allowed many unworthy landowners or recently enriched individuals to gain entry into the knighthood.

Julius Caesar appointed several Equestrians to serve as his personal agents, and Augustus found them similarly loyal. Their propensity for obstructing reforms, however, coupled with their general anarchic behavior, demanded changes. When Augustus initiated his transformation of the Roman government into an imperial system, he singled out the Equestrians. He stripped them of all political strength as his opening move, offering them, instead, very real incentives for their continued obedience. Augustus had rewarded his friends with posts in the administration and expanded the role of the Knights. They now filled offices throughout the empire, including those of the prefectures of the VIGILES and ANNONA. He resurrected its martial connections by allowing long-term centurions, of the empire mainly, to retire into the Equites and to hold commands in the *Eques militia*.

Such a policy, coupled with admissions from the provinces and from the ranks of the FREEDMEN, added even more sources for imperial appointments. Augustus followed the tradition of tribunes being of the equites, sending them all over the empire and also naming many Knights as procurators. In Rome the *iudices* for the *decuriae* were composed of some 3,000 Equestrians, to aid in the courts. A CURSUS HONORUM consequently developed, whereby an Equestrian could rise through various offices. The two highest commands, the pinnacles of service, were the prefectships of EGYPT and the PRAETORIAN GUARD.

Egypt was a very special province, being classified as neither an imperial nor a senatorial territory. Instead, the emperors kept close watch on what Tacitus called the key to Rome's granaries. As his personal representative, Augustus appointed a loyal Knight, who served as prefect of Egypt. This prefect had three legions (initially) under his control and no senator or other member of the Eques-trians could arrive in Alexandria without imperial permission.

The Praetorian Guard, the Imperial Guard of the emperors, was headed by a prefect. This office was the grandest of any class. Originally, the prefect was head of nine cohorts of well dispersed and pliant troops. In time, however, the Praetorian prefect emerged as the chief bureaucrat in Rome, in control of the Guard, the finances and eventually even the legions. By the third century C.E., the previously unthinkable ambition of a prefect of this class becoming emperor, was reality. Aggrandizement of the Praetorian prefect proved symptomatic of the increased attentions lavished upon the Knights. Hadrian reorganized them and improved their *cursus honorum*, and Marcus Aurelius granted them membership in his CONSILIUM PRINCIPIS. Posts held by the Senate and freedmen—the census taking, *ab epistulis*, *a libellis*, and legal advisement—were handed to the Knights. Formal titles came into use to describe their roles: *vir clarissimus*, or "honored man," *vir egregius*, *vir perfectissimus* (for prefects), and *vir eminentissimus* for the Praetorian prefect.

Diocletian ended the separation of provinces as senatorial and imperial. His new governors were almost exclusively Knights, and soon more seats in both the state and military machines were held by them.

The Equestrians aided in the new central government of the fourth century, but such advancement came at a price. The old order of classes had been swept away. Ironically, the Equestrians had contributed to the social transformation by allowing anyone of wealth and competence to be admitted to their ranks. Such a watering down process caused the use of titles to lessen as well, which brought about the ultimate demise of the class by the fifth century.

One of the more interesting rituals associated with the *Equester ordo* was the *travectio equitum*, held every July 15. Augustus used the rebirth of this long abandoned ceremony as part of the reorganization. In the *travectio* (also *transvectio*) a large number of Knights, more than 5,000 in number, paraded before the emperor either on horseback or on foot. All those over 35 could resign their *equus publicus* and so spare themselves possible embarrassment, and Augustus also used the occasion to perform his own *recognitio* or *probatio* of the membership. For the *travectio* the Equestrians were divided into six squadrons (*turmae*) under the command of a *sevir equitum Romanorum*, a senatorially descended younger man.

See also CIVIL SERVICE.

Erato (d. after 1 C.E.) *Queen of Armenia; daughter of King Tigranes II and one of the last hereditary rulers of her nation*
Tigranes had been installed on his throne by Augustus, but after a brief reign, he died around 6 B.C.E. His two children, Erato and TIGRANES III, were chosen to succeed him. They were both anti-Roman and were not the

choices of Augustus. When Tigranes III and Erato were wed, the Romans responded by expelling both from their thrones and putting ARTAVASDES in their place. This proved an unsuccessful ploy, for sometime in 1 B.C.E., a Parthian expedition drove the new king out of Armenia and returned Erato and her brother to power. When Tigranes sent good wishes and submission to Rome, he was allowed to remain. While the two rulers no longer worried about Roman interference, they infuriated their own subjects. Tigranes was killed fighting tribesmen, and Erato abdicated in 1 C.E., leaving behind war and chaos.

Ermanaric (fl. c. 450–471 C.E.) *Third son of the powerful magister militum, Aspar*
Circa 450, Ermanaric played a part in Aspar's move to seize power in the Eastern Empire and in 465 may have served as a CONSUL in Constantinople with BASILISCUS, the son-in-law of Emperor LEO I. When the massacre of Aspar and his family was ordered by Leo in 471, Ermanaric was away and escaped his relative's fate. He probably was aided by ZENO, Leo's eventual successor, and lived in safety for a time in Isauria before returning to Constantinople.

Erucius Clarus, Sextus (fl. early second century C.E.) *Consul and legate*
Erucius Clarus served under Emperor TRAJAN in 116 during the Parthian War. During the campaign, he captured the town of Seleucia. As a reward and because of his friendship with PLINY THE YOUNGER (a friend of the emperor), Erucius Clarus received the consulship of 117. He subsequently served as the prefect of the city and then consul for a second time in 146. He was also highly respected by the literary community in Rome, including the orator Cornelius Fronto and the writer Aulus Gellius.

Esquiline Hill *See* HILLS OF ROME.

Essenes Very strict communal sect of JUDAISM, flowering in the arid regions of Palestine from around the second century B.C.E. to the second century C.E. The name Essenes was translated from the Aramaic as "holy ones," and they were honored for living a highly disciplined and ascetic life at a time of upheaval and chaos in the Jewish world. Membership in the community was highly restricted. A candidate would undergo rigorous training and hardship until he had achieved an understanding of what JOSEPHUS called the willingness to leave all things in God's hands. Only the simplest ways of living were allowed, mainly through agriculture. Considered one of the major schools of philosophy among the Jews, the Essenes were praised by Josephus in his works, *Jewish Antiquities* and the *Jewish War,* and were also mentioned by PHILO and PLINY THE ELDER.

Ethiopia Land to the south of Egypt; ruled by a king throughout the years of the Roman Empire. The nation stood as one of the fringe states with which Rome had dealings on an irregular basis. In 25 B.C.E., the Ethiopian Queen Candace (probably not an accurate name) used the absence of Prefect of Egypt Aelius GALLUS, on a campaign to conquer Arabia, to attack Egypt. The Ethiopians advanced to the Elephantine Island and to Philae before encountering Governor Gaius Petronius. Petronius repelled them and then marched to Ethiopia, where he crushed the queen's army and then seized Napata, one of the leading cities in the realm. In 21 B.C.E., Candace sued for peace and, after unsuccessfully assaulting Petronius's positions, sent envoys to Emperor Augustus. A peace was signed circa 21, and Rome did not treat Egypt's borders lightly thereafter. Nero planned an expedition to subjugate Ethiopia around 64–66 C.E., and sent a small body of soldiers to scout the terrain. Revolts and imperial crises prevented any serious effort, and Ethiopia passed out of the sphere of Roman interest. Pliny the Elder's *Natural History* is the best source for Roman intelligence concerning the region.

Etruria Area of central Italy stretching northward from Rome and the Tiber to the Apennines. For centuries Etruria was the heart of Italian culture, as embodied by the Etruscans. As Rome grew in power, the Etruscans withdrew and were finally defeated by the Romans in 283 B.C.E. Colonies were then founded throughout the region, and full Romanization brought an end to the Etruscan era. Throughout the years of the empire, Etruria was known for its sculpture.
See also ITALIA.

Eubulus, Aurelius (d. 222 C.E.) *Fiscus (head of imperial finances) during the reign of Elagabalus (c. 220–222)*
Eubulus was originally from Emea, as were many of Emperor Elagabalus's appointees. Eubulus was singular in his debauched lifestyle, even by the standards of the imperial court of the time. In 222, after the emperor's assassination, Eubulus was murdered by a mob that had stormed the palace.

Eucherius (d. 408 C.E.) *Son of the powerful Stilicho, who served as magister militum, or master of the soldiers, from c. 394 to 408, and Serena, a niece of Emperor Theodosius I*
Eucharius was a pawn in Stilicho's scheme to dominate the Western Empire. Stilicho proposed to wed Eucherius to Galla Placidia, the half-sister of the Western emperor Honorius. As Maria, Stilicho's daughter, was married to Honorius, the union would have sealed his ties to the imperial family, making some of his descendants eligible for the throne. Eucherius, however, was murdered in 408 as part of the imperial court's retribution against Stilicho.

Eudocia, Aelia (d. 460 C.E.) *Wife of Emperor Theodosius II and empress of the Eastern Empire from 421 to 441 C.E.*

Aelia Eudocia was the daughter of a pagan philosopher, Leontius. Her beauty was renowned, and she was both educated and energetic, having received an intellectual upbringing. While staying in Constantinople, she came to the attention of Empress PULCHERIA, who was, at the time, looking for a suitable wife for her brother, Theodosius. Pulcheria deemed her suitable. Eudocia became a Christian and wed Theodosius on June 7, 421. A child was born sometime in 422, named Licinia EUDOXIA, and a son was also born to the couple, dying in infancy. In January 423, Eudocia received the title of Augusta, and despite interests in poetry and religion, became a force within the imperial palace. This status brought her into conflict with Pulcheria, and to ease the inevitable strains of the relationship, Eudocia made a pilgrimage to Jerusalem in 438, thrilling the people of Antioch when she visited there by giving them a superb oration.

Upon her return to Constantinople in 439, she relied heavily upon the influential Praetorian prefect Cyrus of Panopolis, who fell from power in 441; he was accused of maintaining his pagan beliefs and took holy orders to dispel the charges. His relationship with Eudocia, although never proven to be an adulterous one, contributed to her eventual downfall. The ambitious eunuch chamberlain Chrysaphius first managed to rid the court of Pulcheria, with Eudocia's help, and then he turned the traditionalists of the palace against her. Amid accusations of adultery (accusations that joined her name to that of Cyrus and the MAGISTER OFFICIORUM, Paulinus) Eudocia in 443 moved from Constantinople to Jerusalem. There she lived in relative comfort, working hard for the betterment of that city.

Eudoxia, Aelia (d. 404 C.E.) *Wife of Arcadius and empress of the Eastern Empire from 395 to 404*

The daughter of the MAGISTER MILITUM BAUTO, she used her considerable will to dominate both her husband and affairs of state. Her education had been typically Roman (her mother probably came from Rome), and the eunuch Grand Chamberlain Eutropius decided that she should marry the emperor—instead of his wedding the daughter of the ambitious Praetorian prefect Rufinus. Arcadius agreed, and the wedding took place on April 27, 395. By 400, Eudoxia was the Augusta, deciding most of the empire's issues, as Arcadius was given to laziness and weaknesses in the face of her dominant spirit. Being a pious Christian, she aided in the destruction of all facets of paganism, especially in Egypt, where she aided Porphyry.

The persecution of the pagans in Gaza exacerbated her relationship with St. JOHN CHRYSOSTOM, the bishop of Constantinople. Originally friends, the two of them started a feud in the first years of the fifth century. They were antagonists on a variety of subjects, including Eudoxia's tendency toward opulence and her interference in religious affairs. When Theophilus, patriarch of Alexandria, was brought before a council in Constantinople in 403, Eudoxia ensured that his case was heard and that his counterattack against Chrysostom was successful. The bishop of Constantinople was deposed, although a recall and a temporary reconciliation took place. Eudoxia was successful in bearing an heir for Arcadius—Theodosius II, born in April of 401 and baptized by John Chrysostom—and a daughter, Pulcheria. Another child caused her death in a miscarriage. Arcadius survived her only until 408.

Eudoxia, Licinia (fl. mid-fifth century C.E.) *Daughter of Theodosius II and Eudocia; empress of the West as the wife of Valentinian III, whom she married on October 29, 437*

Eudoxia remained with VALENTINIAN until his death in 455. Eudoxia was then forced to marry the Praetorian prefect and consul Petronius, who thus ascended to the Western throne. Finding her new situation impossible, Eudoxia sent a plea to GEISERIC, the king of the Vandals, asking him to come to her aid. Petronius reigned for only two months, and in May 455 was deposed and probably murdered. Eudoxia did not benefit from her treachery. Geiseric placed her and her two daughters, EUDOCIA and Placidia, on his ship bound for Africa. Eudocia was married to the Vandal ruler Huneric; Eudoxia in 461 received her freedom and with Placidia traveled to Constantinople.

Eugenius, Flavius (d. 394 C.E.) *One-time teacher in Latin who in 392 became a usurper in the West*

The *magister militum* ARBOGAST was searching for a suitable replacement for the recently deceased Valentinian II in the late spring of 392. He needed to install a man on the Western throne, one who was reliable and reasonably intelligent but absolutely incapable of opposing his own martial supremacy. After looking at possible candidates, Arbogast decided upon Eugenius, a professor of Latin, a civil servant and a Christian. Theodosius I, the powerful emperor of the East, at first ignored Eugenius, but in 393 elevated his son, Honorius, to share the empire, making his opinion of the usurper obvious. Theodosius marched into battle in Italy, and after winning at FRIGIDUS on September 5–6, 394, captured Eugenius and executed him. The reign of Eugenius was notable for being the last effort to organize PAGANISM in the Roman Empire. Eugenius, although a Christian, was at first tolerant of all pagans. After Theodosius refused to recognize his imperial claims, however, Eugenius declared the restoration of paganism in Rome. The Altar of Victory found a place of honor once again, and Arbogast rode into the conflict with Theodosius as the last champion of the old gods of Rome.

Eumenius (fl. late third century C.E.) *Teacher, rhetorician, Magister Memoriae and chief legal adviser to Constantius I Chlorus*
Eumenius's family came originally from Athens, but his grandfather had taught in Rome and then settled in Autun, where he was born around 250 C.E. (perhaps in 246). Eumenius studied rhetoric and later taught it, coming to the attention of Constantius in Gaul. He became his MAGISTER MEMORIAE in 293. In 297 he returned home to assume a professorship along with the post of director of Autun's schools. So ruined had they become through war that, in a speech in the spring of 298, Eumenius promised to donate his very large salary to their repair. He is most remembered for his many *Panegyrics*.

Eunapius (c. 346–after 414 C.E.) *Historian and rhetorician from Sardis; born to a poor family*
Eunapius's education was in the classics, under Chrysanthius. Athens beckoned to him in 351–352 C.E.; for the next five years he studied the finest orators and historians of the time. Returning to Sardis he took up a position teaching rhetoric and then began his career as an author. Two major works dominated his career: *Vitae Sophistarum* (Lives of the Sophists) and *Historia* (History). *Vitae Sophistarum* was written around 396; his *Historia* was a continuation of the efforts of DEXIPPUS. He began chronicling in 270, where Dexippus had left off, and carried the account to 404.

Euphrates River   The great waterway of the Fertile Crescent, flowing through Babylonia, Media, and parts of Armenia. The Euphrates rises in the mountains of Armenia and then unites with the Tigris before emptying into the Persian Gulf. Few rivers were of equal importance, except for the Nile, in the formation of Western civilization. The Euphrates, even in the days of the Roman Empire, served as one of the main lifelines of the Parthians, and later of the Persian realm. Its fertility and strategic importance made it the center of operation for numerous wars among Rome, the Parthians, and the Persians in the third century C.E.
   See also PARTHIA; PERSIA.

Euric (d. 484 C.E.) *King of the Visigoths in Gaul and Spain from 466 to 484 C.E.*
Euric was largely responsible for the final demise of the Roman Empire in the West. He was the brother of the Visigoth King Theodoric II, and in 466 murdered him to claim the throne. Henceforth, he sought the aggrandizement of his own position in Gaul, at the expense of the Romans. Conquest and war soon followed, as Euric marched into GALLIA AQUITANIA, seized Arles and then devastated the Rhone Valley. Auvergne fell next, and Emperor Julius Nepos had to recognize the supremacy of

the Germans throughout most of Gaul and in Spain. More fighting brought Massilia (Marseilles) and Provence under his power in 476. For the next years of his reign, Euric was the unquestioned master of Gaul and Spain and the surrounding nations of the Goths. Heruls, Franks, and Burgundians paid him tribute or made peace. Even Persia sent him messages of friendship. He took steps to ensure the continuation of Visigoth domination, especially in Spain. He was a champion and a fanatical supporter of ARIANISM, still very popular with the Germans. He also aided civilization by lending his name to a series of laws for the Goths and Romans who lived in Gothic lands, the Codex Euricianus. The principal source for his life and successes is Sidonius Apollinaris.

Eusebia (d. c. 361 C.E.) *Empress and second wife of Constantius II, from 353 to 360 C.E.*
Eusebia came from Thessalonica and was probably the daughter of the consul of 347, Eusebius. Her brothers, Fl. Eusebius and Fl. Hypatius, were consuls in 359. Around 353–354, Eusebia wed CONSTANTIUS II while he was in Germany. The marriage proved genuinely happy, for Eusebia was well educated and a very good influence on her husband, whom she counseled toward compassion and fairness. Eusebia used her importance as an adviser to push for the supremacy of Arianism and the rise of JULIAN. Through her efforts, Julian went to Athens to study (in 354) and then was named Caesar in 355.

Eusebius (d. 361 C.E.) *A eunuch and chamberlain (Praepositus Sacri Cubiculi) during the reign of Constantius II*
One of the most important advisers to the emperor from 337 to 361, Eusebius had served in the imperial court of Constantine the Great, and in 337, at the death of the old ruler, hid the will. His actions precipitated the palace massacre by Constantine's sons. As chamberlain, Eusebius took part in further intrigues. He brought down Gallus Caesar, conspired to have the MAGISTER MILITUM Ursicinus recalled in 359, and then worked for the cause of ARIANISM. As an Arian, Eusebius interviewed Liberius of Rome in 354 and then schemed with the Arian bishops to remove Athanasius. His power remained unquestioned until 361, when Constantius died. Later that year the Commission of Chalcedon condemned him, and he was executed.

Eusebius of Caesarea (d. 260–340) *Father of the church, one of the most important of all Church historians, and bishop of Caesarea*
Eusebius was born in Palestine. He studied in Caesarea under the notable scholar Pamphilius, who died in 310 during the severe persecution of the church. Eusebius fled, first to Tyre and then to Egypt, where he spent some time in prison. Returning to Caesarea, he became bishop

around 315. In the ensuing Arian controversy that confronted the church, Eusebius struck a moderate position. He at first gave some support to Arius but, after his efforts at organizing a compromise failed, he accepted the Nicene Creed at the Council of Nicaea (325) and attended the Council of Tyre (335), which condemned Arianism. A friend of Emperor Constantine the Great, he delivered an honorific speech to the ruler in 335 and composed a panegyric at the emperor's death in 337, the *Vita Constantini* (Life of Constantine).

A prolific writer, Eusebius was the author of the *Praeparatio Evangelica* (Preparation for the Gospel); *Demonstratio Evangelica* (Demonstration of the Gospel); *Against Hieracles; Chronicle* (covering from Abraham to Eusebius's own era, translated by St. Jerome from the Greek); *Theophany,* on the Incarnation; and *De Solemnitate Paschali,* a treatise on Easter. His most famous work was the *Historia Ecclesiastica* (Ecclesiastical history). Covering the events of the church from its origins to 324, the history was a perfect demonstration of Eusebius's own view of the faith as the inevitable creed of the Roman Empire. While poorly written, it relied upon a host of valuable sources, including the Acts of the Apostles and Josephus and remains the most important source for the history of the church from its beginnings until the fourth century. It was written in 10 books, the last three focusing on Eusebius's own era. It was first translated from the Greek into Latin by Rufinus of Aquileia (d. 410), the scholar and monk who also extended the coverage to 395.

Eusebius of Nicomedia (d. c. 342 C.E.) *Leading figure in the fourth-century Arian movement, whose followers took the name Eusebians in his honor*

Eusebius was probably a fellow pupil of Arius (the founder of Arianism) under the instruction of the martyr St. Lucian of Antioch. He served as bishop of Berytus and then Nicomedia (c. 318). When around 323 Arius was deposed by Alexander, the bishop of Alexandria, Eusebius responded to his call for aid by granting him sanctuary and convening a synod in Bithynia (October 323), which attempted to nullify Arius's excommunication. Influential within the royal court and family (he baptized Constantine on his deathbed in 337), Eusebius succeeded in elevating the Arian controversy into an empire-wide dispute. His connections with the imperial family assisted him in his labors against the orthodox Athanasius and his supporters; however, at the Council of Nicaea (325), he signed the Creed after his own proposal had been rejected as too Arian. Eusebius refused, however, to sign the anathema condemning the Arians. In the subsequent years, he continued to promote Arian doctrines, securing the deposition and exile of St. Athanasius of Alexandria. In 339, he was moved from Nicomedia to the see of Constantinople by order of Emperor Constantius II.

Eustathius of Antioch (Eustathius the Great) (d. c. 337) *Christian saint, bishop of Antioch from 324, and an opponent of Eusebius of Caesarea*

A native of Side, in Pamphylia, Eustathius was appointed bishop of Beroea (c. 320) and several years later was transferred to Antioch. After the Council of Nicaea (325), he pursued the removal of Arians with much vigor, eventually entering into conflict with Eusebius of Caesarea. Through the machinations of the pro-Arian bishop of Caesarea, Eustathius was deposed by the Synod of Antioch and exiled to Thrace by Emperor Constantius the Great. There he died, but his supporters at Antioch, who called themselves Eustathians, formed the basis for the Melitian Schism. The author of numerous works, Eustathius's writings are known today only in fragmentary form, with the exception of the *De Engastrimutho,* an attack on Origen.

Eustathius of Sebaste (d. c. 377) *Christian saint and bishop of Sebaste in Pontus who influenced the development of monasticism*

Born the son of a bishop, Eustathius studied at Alexandria under Arius. It was there that he was introduced to the heretical doctrines of Arianism, propositions about which he would vacillate throughout much of his life. While condemned in 343 by the Council of Gangra, he nevertheless accepted the Nicene Creed (which established the orthodox doctrine of faith) and was on good terms with Pope Liberius (r. 352–366). In 357, despite his checkered theological past, Eustathius was made bishop of Sebaste. In his earlier years, he had focused extensively on monasticism, adhering to a very severe idea of asceticism. His student, St. Basil the Great, was almost certainly much influenced by him, although ultimately the two had a parting of the ways over Eustathius's adoption of semi-Arian teachings that took shape in the so-called Macedonian heresy.

Eutherius (fl. mid-fourth century C.E.) *Chamberlain (praepositus sacri Cubiculi) to Julian the Apostate*

Eutherius served from circa 356 to 360 and earned a reputation as one of the most loyal and honest imperial chamberlains in history. Eutherius was born to free parents in Armenia but was kidnapped by tribesmen, castrated, and sold to Roman slave merchants. He then entered the palace of Constantine, growing up in the courts, where he astounded his contemporaries with solutions to difficult problems and with his remarkable memory. Eutherius passed into the household of Constans before becoming grand chamberlain for Julian, then

Caesar to Constantius II. He freely criticized Julian but always with good reason. In 360, he retired to Rome.

Eutropia (fl. late third century C.E.) *Wife of Emperor Maximian*

She was from Syria and had been married once before, perhaps to one Afranius Hannibalianus, by whom she bore Theodora. By MAXIMIAN she had two children: Fausta, who married Constantine the Great, and Maxentius, emperor in Rome from 306 to 312.

Eutropius (1) (fl. fourth century C.E.) *Historian and consul (in 387)*

A native of Bordeaux, Eutropius served in Julian's campaign against the Persians in 363 and then held numerous posts in the reigns of Julian, Valens, and Theodosius I. He then became MAGISTER MEMORIAE under Valens, from circa 369 to 371, when he held the proconsulship of Asia. As proconsul he rebuilt the area of Magnesia but was then tried for treason by his successor, Festus, in 372. Acquitted because of the faithfulness of the philosopher Pasiphilus, he later visited the court of Gratian and received the titles of Praetorian prefect in Illyricum from 380 to 381 and consul in 387. The greatest achievement of Eutropius's literary career was the very extensive *Digest* of Roman history (*Breviarium ab urbe condita*). It began with Romulus and covered most of the history of Rome until the death of Emperor Jovian in 364. Numerous historians relied heavily upon the *Digest*, including Festus, Hieronymus, and Orosius. Eutropius was a pagan.

Eutropius (2) (d. c. 399 C.E.) *Powerful eunuch and grand chamberlain (Praepositus Sacri Cubiculi) from 395 to 399 during the reign of Arcadius (395–408 C.E.)*

Probably from Armenia, he insinuated himself into a key position of trust in the court of Theodosius I. From this position he countered the power of the Praetorian Prefect of the East Flavius RUFINUS by convincing the next emperor, ARCADIUS, to marry EUDOXIA in April of 395, instead of Rufinus's daughter. For the next four years Arcadius was the prisoner of Eutropius, who succeeded in alienating most of the political forces in Constantinople. He sold offices, crushed possible rivals and abused his power. In 399, he assumed the consulship, the first time that a eunuch had ever attempted such a violation of tradition, although his name was not entered in the consular records (*Fasti*). STILICHO, the ambitious MAGISTER MILITUM, dispatched a trusted lieutenant to Constantinople. Eutropius, outnumbered and defeated by Eudoxia for Arcadius's attentions, fell from power. He was exiled to Cyprus, with his property confiscated. He probably died by the sword there.

Eutyches (c. 378–c. 451) *Progenitor of the heresy of Eutychianism*

Eutyches was the archimandrite (an Eastern type of abbot or monastic superior) of a monastery at Constantinople. Educated under the influence of Cyril of Alexandria (d. 444), he vigorously opposed the doctrines of Nestorianism, particularly as embodied by Nestorius, the patriarch of Constantinople from 428. This disagreement led in 448 to an accusation by Eusebius of Dorylaeum that Eutyches held the heretical positions of confusing the natures of Christ. Specifically, Eutychianism supported an ultra-Monophysite position by stressing the virtual exclusive divinity of Christ. Eutyches was summoned before Flavian, by then patriarch, and the Synod of Constantinople. There, he declared the maxim "two natures before, one after the Incarnation," expressing the Monophysite idea that Christ's human nature was subsumed by the divine one into a single essence. Deposed by Flavian, Eutyches nevertheless used friends at the imperial court to secure a new trial. At the Latrocinium (the Robber Council of Ephesus), in 449, he was acquitted; in 451, at the Council of Chalcedon, however, he was once more condemned and was exiled. After his exile, Eutyches disappeared from prominence. His followers remained as adherents of Eutychianism, and he is ranked as one of the most important figures in the rise of Monophysitism.

Eutychianus, Valerius Comazon (d. c. 222 C.E.?) *Dancer and specialist in buffoonery*

In 218 C.E., Eutychianus was named by Emperor ELAGABALUS to be PREFECT OF THE PRAETORIAN GUARD. Part of the very eccentric court of Elagabalus, Comazon typified the appointments of that ruler's reign so infuriating to the Rome establishment. Utterly unqualified to hold the prefecture, Comazon also received appointments to the consulship and the prefectship of the city, viewed by the Romans as disastrous. Elagabalus gave his friend the right to serve as city prefect twice more, in violation of all precedent. In 222, Comazon's open corruption played a part in the murder of Elagabalus and his mother, Julia Soaemias, by the Praetorian Guard. He may have survived the ensuing massacre, but he probably died with his patron.

Evagrius Ponticus (346–399) *Writer*

One of the more important ascetical writers of his time, Ponticus, named after Pontus, the place of his birth, was ordained a deacon by St. Gregory of Nazianzus. He emerged as a preacher of high repute in Constantinople. He accompanied Gregory to the Second Council of Constantinople (381) but ultimately departed the city and went first to Jerusalem and then to the Nitrian Desert. There he devoted himself to an ascetic life, studying under the monks of the desert and evolving his mystical theology. He became famous for his ascetical writings, including *Monachos,* on the spiritual life of the monk; and a treatise *On the Eight Evil Thoughts*, both in Greek.

His writings, however, were attacked by Jerome as suffering from Origenism, including his teachings on the pre-existence of souls. They were later condemned by the sixth, seventh, and eighth ecumenical councils. Translations into Latin were done by Rufinus and Gennadius.

Evocati   Hand-picked corps of bodyguards and advisers for the emperors. The Evocati, or "Recalled," were veterans of the legions who had retired but were ordered or summoned back into imperial service. In 44 B.C.E., Octavian (AUGUSTUS) looked for all possible reliable troops and thus issued calls to former legionaries of Julius Caesar, now living in Campania on granted lands. He paid them 2,000 sesterces each and instructed them to march with him. In the subsequent campaigns they proved invaluable, lending their experience and opinions as well as their stabilizing influence on raw recruits hastily assembled for the war. Augustus made the Evocati an important formation in his reign. Their numbers were never large, but the acceptance of a retired centurion into the corps was very prestigious. Their pay was good, they saw the emperor every day, and they had the right to carry a rod, just as the regular army centurions did. The Evocati were still in existence in 217 C.E., when one of their number, Julius Martialis, took part in the assassination of Caracalla.

Excubitors   Imperial bodyguard established around 470 C.E. by the Eastern Emperor LEO I. His aim was to counter the Germanic influences at the court of Con-stantinople. Leo's solution was to recruit a large standing army from his Greek and Anatolian provinces. For the Excubitors he chose the fierce hillsmen of ISAURIA. His hopes were more than fulfilled, for his new guard served with loyalty and skill. The Excubitors became a fixture of Byzantine life in the following centuries.

Exploratores   Military units composed of lightly armored and foreign-based soldiers who bore the title of scouts. Exploratores were very useful on campaigns to patrol the regions around an advancing LEGION. On the frontiers they were also used in maintaining watch on troublesome tribes or on other kingdoms. In the fifth century C.E., they formed an actual branch of the imperial army (COMITATENSES).

Exsilium   Form of self-imposed banishment used largely by a person on trial for various offenses in the late Republic and early empire. Under initial imperial law, a court was not empowered to exile a citizen, but throughout a trial the accused could always voluntarily depart from Rome. In return for sparing the life of the accused, such a citizen would accept condemnation and a decree prohibiting a return, the so-called fire and water (*aquae et ignis interdicto*). In later years the emperors did use another form of punishment by exile, the *deportatio in insulam*, or deportation to an island. This was one of Tiberius's favorite forms of punishment.

See also LAW; *RELEGATIO*.

F

Fabatus, Rubrius (d. after 32 C.E.) *Senator during the reign of Tiberius*

In 32, Fabatus, despairing of genuine political and moral reform in Rome, decided to flee to the Parthians. He was caught, returned to the capital, and forced to remain there for the rest of his life. His case demonstrated the ancient law forbidding members of the Senate from traveling beyond Italy and (starting in 49) Gallia Narbonensis, without the permission of the emperor.

Fabian (d. 250 C.E.) *Bishop of Rome and leader of the Christian community there from 232 to 250*

Fabian divided the city into seven regions or districts to improve the spiritual administration. In 250, when Emperor DECIUS launched his terrible persecutions, he had the distinction of being the first martyr.

Fabianus Papirius (fl. first century C.E.) *Roman philosopher*

Probably born in the late first century B.C.E. he studied rhetoric before speaking and teaching on his own. His most famous pupil was SENECA, who ardently defended his writings by claiming that in style and philosophy Fabian was surpassed only by LIVY, CICERO, and Asinius POLLIO. Fabianus also wrote on natural history and was quoted by PLINY THE ELDER in his *Natural History*.

Fabiola (d. 399) *Famous Roman Christian noblewoman and saint*

According to tradition, Fabiola was the founder of the first public hospital in the West, the result of her desire to do penance for her divorce and improper second marriage. She adopted an austere life and distributed her vast wealth; her charitable works included funding a hospice for pilgrims, supporting various monasteries, and establishing her hospital. Much influenced by St. Jerome, she journeyed in 395 to Bethlehem, following Jerome to the Holy Land. There she lived for a time with Sts. Paula and Eustochium. Fabiola returned to Rome in 396, in large measure because of the imminent invasion of Palestine by the Huns and in part because of her personal difficulties with the severe asceticism of the community in Bethlehem. Back in Rome, she resumed her charitable efforts.

Falco, Sosius (fl. late second century C.E.) *Consul in 192 (with Erucius Clarus)*

For a brief time in 193, Falco was proposed as a replacement for the short-reigned PERTINAX, but never received popular support.

farming Rome began as a community of farmers and shepherds, as with other cultures throughout the Mediterranean. The Romans, however, made farming a major economic support of their imperial endeavors. Farming was for centuries the gauge of prosperity, both in Italy and in the provinces, and its decline signaled the true deterioration of imperial power and vitality. Although the Greeks, Egyptians, and other cultures increased the efficiency of growing crops throughout the Hellenic and later Seleucid eras, the innovative Roman farmers did much to improve the entire system. Crop rotation, amelioration, fertilization, and harvesting were all adapted to Italian lands, and agricultural output was vast. Colonies were founded in Italy, especially in such regions as Sicily (SICILIA), as former army veterans ploughed and reaped the benefits of the fertile soil.

At first a farmer worked hand in hand with slaves, using the profits to buy more slaves. As Rome grew as a political entity, estate holders not only distanced themselves from the workers but also added to their properties. By the end of the Punic Wars, massive farms had come into existence, as many small farmers fled war-ravaged Italy and struck out for the colonies. Rome's colonial expansion introduced Roman agricultural techniques to other peoples.

In Italy, meanwhile, the great estates (the latifundia) of the Patricians and rich slave owners grew in size, while poor farmers, unable to support themselves, were reduced to desperation. They were saved only by the inability of the slave trade to supply the demand for workers and by the government's refusal to allow the gentry to amass great armies of slaves. When attempts at reviving the smaller farm system proved unsuccessful, a compromise of some importance took place. Tracts of arable land were parceled out to tenant farmers, and thus was born the colonus or sharecropper. A colonus received a private but leased domain from large landholders, including Patricians, or drew it straight from the *ager publicus*, the public areas owned by the state or the imperial household. Thus an emperor's holdings (RES PRIVATAE), which might include any number of plots, would be partly managed by freedmen or wardens (*vilici*), and, in the late empire, by the *comes rerum privatarum* (commissioner of private estates). Most of such lands were leased to the *coloni*. A tenant would pay rent first in money and then in crops. As it was in the best interest of the owner to squeeze as much profit as possible from the land, all tenants received the most modern equipment possible.

By the late first century B.C.E., no wealthy citizen could claim prestige without a villa and surrounding fields. However, colonization had caused a depopulation of Italy, and the provinces were beginning to out-produce the farms of the Italians. EGYPT had long been a vital key to feeding Rome; by the second century C.E., AFRICA joined Greece and the East in providing wheat, oil, olives, and other grains. The imperial province of Egypt received the personal attention of the emperors, who governed it with a prefect. Thus many *latifundia* existed throughout Egypt, and these were joined by other acquisitions for the *res privatae*. The tradition continued of improving local farming techniques, and so even more competition was created, adding to other problems such as soil exhaustion, overproduction, and social instability.

The Italian colonus lost his unique status with the economic death of the middle class, the CURATORES. TRAJAN tried to repopulate Italy with veterans, and his successors were only partially successful.

Internal chaos and barbarian invasions created the first conditions of feudalism. Many farmers departed from their fields to the cities, where they could earn a good living in industry and under safer conditions, free of ravaging Goths. Those who remained barely raised enough food to survive.

Taxation became difficult because of constant migration. Thus, foreign and conquered peoples from Gaul, Germany and elsewhere were settled on the land, and land was declared hereditary. Like the *curatores* and *delatores,* all *coloni* were forbidden from forsaking their responsibilities. DIOCLETIAN placed severe restrictions on the movement of farmers as part of his broad aggrandizement of the central imperial administration. Registrations were required, fixing citizens to their places of residence. CONSTANTINE extended Diocletian's limitations in 332 C.E. by declaring runaway tenants of equal status with fleeing slaves. They could be tracked down and brought back to their homes in chains, remaining shackled there if necessary. Such radical steps were deemed essential and ensured the survival of agriculture even when the Western Empire collapsed.

Farming was one of the subjects most frequently examined by Roman-era writers, showing clearly its importance both as a profession and as a way of life. Mago, a Carthaginian author on agriculture, was translated into Latin after the Punic Wars, and Cato's *De Agricultura* was published in the second century B.C.E. In the age of the empire, VARRO (c. 37 B.C.E.) wrote a treatise on agriculture in three books, *Res rusticae,* VIRGIL acquired greater fame in the late first century B.C.E. as one of history's finest pastoral writers. He composed the *Bucolics,* poems on herders, but his *Georgics* were far more important. Completed in 29 B.C.E., these four poems were tributes to Varro that described farming and livestock, with an enthusiasm born out of love for the earth.

A wide number of agricultural implements were required to cultivate the rich variety of soils that were found in Italy. As was true with the Greeks before them, the early Roman farmer used primarily two implements for tilling the soil, the hoe (*bidentes* or *rastra*) and the spade (*bipalium*), although farmers developed many versions of both. The development of the plow, or ard, drawn by one or two animals—especially oxen—made farming more efficient, but the often heavy soils required cross-plowing, in which the plow was run over the furrowed earth at a right angle to guarantee that the soil was turned over completely. Early plows were also unable to dig into the heavier soils in Italy and elsewhere, requiring the use of a heavier plow, with a sturdier coulter and a moldboard that could turn over the furrowed earth. Even late into the imperial era, there were many areas where the plow was impractical, so farmers retained the spade and the hoe.

The harvesting of crops also necessitated the use of several specialized implements. The Romans inherited from the Greeks the balanced sickle (*falx messoria*) and made numerous improvements in its design. They also used a well-designed sickle (*falx veruculata*) for harvesting. The chief versions of a harvesting machine, the *vallus* and the *carpentum,* were pulled by an animal and permitted the farmer to push them through crops to gather up the stalks and grain, pass them through pointed blades inside, and then gather up the harvested grain inside a hopper. Mentioned by PLINY THE ELDER and PALLADIUS, the *vallus's* design is well-known today by the image of its sculpted onto a slab that was discovered in 1958.

Threshing was performed by another originally Greek implement, the *tribulum,* a threshing sledge, and a Carthaginian-designed implement, the *plostellum poenicum.* The *tribulum* was a heavy board with flints embedded on the underside, which was dragged across the corn. The *plostellum poenicum* improved upon this design by adopting a set of toothed wheels instead of the indelicate flints. Where the *tribulum* and *plostellum poenicum* could not be used, there remained the traditional and back-breaking method of spreading the grain on the floor and then flogging it with flails. It was also common to have heavy animals tread back and forth over the grain. The task of separating the grain from the chaff was accomplished by winnowing. The grain was repeatedly tossed into the air with a winnowing shovel or basket until the chaff was separated from the wheat. The chaff then blew away in the wind while the valuable wheat was saved.

As the Romans created advanced orchards, they utilized specific implements for pruning and lopping. The most basic instrument was the *falx putatoria,* a *basi* bill hook. Later, the *falx vinitoria* was used, a more advanced type of vine-dresser's knife that had multiple uses for the farmer.

Suggested Readings: Balsdon, J. P. V. D. *Life and Leisure in Ancient Rome.* New York: McGraw-Hill, 1969; Boren, Henry C. *Roman Society: A Social, Economic, and Cultural History.* Lexington, Mass.: D. C. Heath, 1977; Bradley, K. R. *Discovering the Roman Family. Studies in Roman Social History.* Oxford, U.K.: Oxford University Press, 1991; Bradley, K. R. *Slaves and Masters in the Roman Empire: A Study in Social Control.* Bruxelles: Latomus, 1984; Carcopino, Jerome. *Daily Life in Ancient Rome.* New Haven, Conn.: Yale University Press, 1968; Clark, G. *Women in the Ancient World.* Oxford, U.K.: Oxford University Press, 1989; Cowell, F. R. *Life in Ancient Rome.* New York: G. F. Putnam's Sons, 1961; Dupont, Florence. *Daily Life in Ancient Rome.* Translated by Christopher Woodall, Oxford: Blackwell Publishers, 1992; Garnsey, Peter. *The Roman Empire: Economy, Society, and Culture.* Berkeley: University of California Press, 1987; Potter, D. S. and D. J. Mattingly, eds. *Life, Death, and Entertainment in the Roman Empire.* Ann Arbor, Mich.: The Univ. of Michigan Press, 1999; White, K. D. *Agricultural Implements of the Roman World.* Cambridge, U.K.: Cambridge Univ. Press, 1967; ———. *Country Life in Classical Times.* London: Elek, 1978; ———. *Farm Equipment of the Roman World.* Cambridge, U.K.: Cambridge Univ. Press, 1975; ———. *Roman Farming.* London: Thames and Hudson, 1970.

fasces The bundle of rods and axes carried and traditionally used by the lictors (LICTORES) of Rome. The birch rods were tied together, with an axe (*securis*) projecting from the middle. They were symbolic of the power of the magistrates but also of the kinds of punishment inflicted by officers of the state. The rods reminded wrongdoers that a crime, for which they were beaten with rods, could be forgiven. The axe told them of the ultimate penalty of the law. While within the city limits of Rome, the *securis* was removed.

Faunus Originally an Italian divinity associated with agriculture and herds. Faunus became synonymous with the Greek god, Pan, taking on his lecherous form of half-goat and half-man. The festival of Lupercalia was held every year in his honor.

See also FESTIVALS; GODS AND GODDESSES OF ROME.

Fausta, Flavia Maxima (d. 326 C.E.) *Wife of Constantine the Great (with the title of Augusta) from 307 to 326*
She was the daughter of the Augustus Maximian and Eutropia and was raised in Rome with her brother MAXENTIUS, who usurped the throne of Italy and Rome in 306. To cement the family's position, she was married to CONSTANTINE in March 307. She was the stepmother of CRISPUS Caesar and possibly Constantine II and the mother of Constantius II and Constans. Her family proved difficult for her husband. Maximian feuded with Maxentius and sought safety with Constantine. In 308, while Constantine was away, the old emperor tried to reclaim his title, but Fausta informed Constantine of the crisis, and he returned in force to crush his father-in-law. Four years later, Fausta saw her brother die at the battle of MILVIAN BRIDGE. In 326, she became embroiled in palace intrigue and had a hand in the execution of Crispus by his father. Later that year, under suspicion of adultery, Fausta was put to death by Constantine's order, suffocated in a steam bath.

See also HELENA.

Faustina (1), Annia Galeria ("the Elder") (d. 140 C.E.) *Empress of Rome (138–140) and wife of Antoninus Pius (c. 110–140)*
Faustina was the daughter of the Consul Marcus Annius Verus and Rupilla Faustina and was born in Rome sometime before or during the reign of Trajan. In 110 she married T. Aurelius Fulvius Boionius Arrius Antoninus, who would become the heir designate of Hadrian, succeeding him in 138. Faustina was immediately granted the title of Augusta and held it until her death. The reputation she acquired was not entirely pleasant. While the veracity of the rumors about her remain questionable, Antoninus cared deeply for her and went to some pains to quiet the stories. Upon her death she was honored with a temple in the Forum, later called the Temple of Antoninus and Faustina. She was the mother of four children, two sons and two daughters. Her sons were Marcus Galerius and

Marcus Aurelius Fulvius. One daughter, Aurelia Fadilla, married Lamia Syllanus. All three of these children were dead by 138. The fourth child was Annia Galeria FAUSTINA (2), who would marry Emperor Marcus Aurelius.

Faustina (2), Annia Galeria ("the Younger") (d. 176 C.E.) *Empress (161–176) and wife of Marcus Aurelius (145–176)*

Her father was Antoninus Pius, and her mother was Faustina the Elder (Annia Galeria FAUSTINA [1]). By the wish of Hadrian, she was betrothed to Lucius Verus sometime near the end of Hadrian's reign, but Antoninus, as the new ruler, decided that Verus was too young, and in 145 Faustina wed MARCUS AURELIUS instead. Faustina possibly held the title of Augusta even before her husband became emperor in 161. As empress, Faustina spawned more rumors and stories than her mother had, including an accusation that she had a hand in Verus's death and that she encouraged the noted general, Avidius Cassius, to rebel.

Her supposed infidelities included affairs with sailors and gladiators, but when Marcus Aurelius was pressed to divorce her or put her to death, he commented that to send her away would mean a return of her dowry—the empire. In 176, while traveling through Syria to join her husband, Faustina died in a little town called Halala, in the Taurus Mountains. Marcus Aurelius, disregarding her reputation, asked the Senate to grant her a divine tribute, erecting a temple to her and naming her the "Mother of the Camp." He also decreed the area around Halala to be a colony.

Favonius Eulogius (fl. mid-fourth century C.E.) *Writer and pupil of St. Augustine in Carthage*

Favonius was most noted for a treatise on the stars and their impact, the *Disputatio de somnio Scipionis* (Disputation on the dream of Scipio), which influenced the work of Macrobius. This work, *Cicero's Dream of Scipio,* was penned in the late fourth or early fifth century.

Favorinus (c. 80–150 C.E.) *A rhetorician of some note in the court of Hadrian*

Favorinus was born in Arles and was educated in southern Gaul probably at Massilia, before heading east to gain fame in Greece and in Asia. He subsequently taught such notable figures of the second century as Cornelius Fronto and Aulus Gellius, who made constant references to Favorinus in his *Noctes Atticae.* Favorinus came to the attention of Emperor Hadrian, who appointed him to the court. There he was accounted one of the greatest of the emperor's intellectual circle, once refusing to debate with Hadrian the use of a specific word, on the grounds that surely the most learned of men was the one who possessed 30 legions. Feuds developed between Favorinus and Polemo of Smyrna. For some reason he fell out of favor around 130 and was exiled from Rome, until the more agreeable Antoninus Pius brought him back.

Felicitas

Goddess of luck; honored in the second century B.C.E. with a temple on the Velabrum. The face of this Roman goddess was used on coins, and her form normally appeared as an older woman with a cornucopia and the staff of Mercury.

See also FORTUNA; GODS AND GODDESSES OF ROME.

Felix, Flavius Constantius (d. 430 C.E.) *A magister militum who rose from unknown origins to wield great political and military power in the Western Empire from 425 to 429*

Galla Placidia appointed Felix magister in 425, with the hope of defending Gaul from barbarian invasions, specifically, the Germans. From 427 to 429, Felix reorganized and rebuilt the declining imperial presence in Gaul, but from that point on he was faced with the intrigues of two lesser officers: AETIUS and BONIFACE.

Aetius assumed control of the armies in the region, attaining such influence that he probably compelled Galla Placidia into sacrificing Felix by promoting him to the Patrician class. In 430, Felix attempted to regain his lost status but was executed by his successor, Aetius.

Felix, Marcus Antonius (fl. first century C.E.) *Procurator of Judaea from around 52 to 60 C.E.*

As the brother of the powerful imperial freedman, PALLAS, Felix possessed influence in the court—a useful connection given both his corrupt and vindicative nature and the unpleasant posts that he held. He originally served as the freedman of Lady Antonia, using his position to secure for himself the rank of procurator. In 52 C.E., he received the procuratorship in Samaria and later the one in Judaea. As the head of the Roman government in the territory, he did little to stamp out the chronic unrest and even helped increase the resentment of the inhabitants. He attacked Jewish brigands, trapping their leader Eleazar through deception and bribing them to assassinate the High Priest Jonathan. After years of misgovernment, the Jews of Caesarea sent a deputation to charge him with various crimes in 60. Felix had already been replaced by Porcius Festus; through his own reputation and that of his brother, he was acquitted of any wrongdoing. Felix was also noted for marrying, DRUSILLA (2), sister of Berenice, who was reputed to be one of the most beautiful women in the world. He also presided over the trial of St. Paul. Suetonius wrote that Claudius held him in high esteem; Tacitus accused him of indulging in every kind of cruelty and immorality.

Felix, M. Minucius (fl. second century C.E.) *One of the earliest of the Christian intellectuals*

Felix authored a brilliant dialogue, the *Octavius,* in which the philosophical and popular arguments against Christianity were cleverly and systematically destroyed.

Fenestella (52 or 53 B.C.E.–36 C.E.) *Scholar and annalist who wrote during the Augustan Age (27 B.C.E.–14 C.E.)* Fenestella followed VARRO as a source for style and was subsequently mentioned by both Pliny the Elder and Asconius. His principal effort was a long annal of Roman history, from Julius Caesar (c. 57 B.C.E.) to his own age. Most of the history was lost and exists only in fragments.

Festivals of the Roman Year *See* GODS AND GODDESSES OF ROME and individual listings of deities; ARVAL BRETHREN; FLAMINES; *LUDI*; PRIESTHOOD; RELIGION; TIME.

Festus, Porcius (fl. first century C.E.) *Procurator of Judaea from 60 to 62 C.E.*

FESTIVALS OF THE ROMAN YEAR

Month	Date(s)	Festival
January (month of Janus)	9	Agonalia (Janus)
	11	Carmentalia (Carmentis)
	15	Carmentalia (Carmentis)
February	13–21	Parentalia (Feast of Souls)
	15	Lupercalia (Faunus)
	17	Quirinalia (Quirinus)
	21	Feralia
	23	Terminalia (Terminus)
	24	Regifugium ("Flight of the King")
	27	Equirria (Mars)
March (month of Mars)	14	Equirria (Mars)
	15	Anna Perenna
	17	Liberalia (Libera)
		Agonalia (Mars)
	19	Quinquatrus (Mars and Minerva)
	23	Tubilustrium (Mars)
April	4	Megalesia (Cybele)
	15	Fordicidia (Tellus)
	19	Cerialia (Ceres)
	21	Parilia (Founding of Rome)
	23	Vinalia (Venus)
	25	Robigalia (Robigus)
	28–May 3	Florales (Flora)
May (month of Maia)	9, 11, 13	Lemuria (Lemures)
	14	Tiber
	21	Agonalia
	23	Tubilustrium (Vulcan)
June (month of Junius)	9	Vestalia (Vesta)
	11	Matralia (Mater Matuta)
July (month of Julius [Caesar])	5	Poplifugia (Jupiter)
	19, 21	Lucaria
	23	Neptunalia (Neptune)
	25	Furrinalia (Furrina)
August (month of Augustus)	17	Portunalia (Portunus)
	19	Vinalia (Venus)
	21	Consualia (Consus)
	23	Volcanalia (Vulcan)
	23	Lightness to Darkness (Venus)
	25	Opiconsivia (Ops)
	27	Volturnalia (Volturnus)
October	11	Meditrinalia (Jupiter)
	13	Fontinalia (Fons)
	19	Armilustrium (Mars)
December	11	Agonalia (Sol)
	15	Consualia (Consus)
	17	Saturnalia (Saturn)
	19	Opalia (Ops)
	21	Divalia (Angerona)
	23	Larentalia (Larunda)
	25	Sol Invictus (Mithras)

Festus succeeded the corrupt Marcus Antonius FELIX as procurator, perhaps in 60, inheriting an unsettled province with its political and religious problems. Festus immediately had to deal with the outlaws called the Sicarii, who plundered villages, and with a false prophet who promised happiness. Festus next involved himself in a dispute between King Agrippa II and the Jews over the Temple. In 62, he died suddenly. His most famous action was to carry on the trials of St. Paul, before sending that famous Christian to Rome.

Festus, Rufius (d. 380 C.E.) *Historian and imperial official who authored a Breviarium of Roman history*
Originally from Tridentum (Trent) and of a common-born family, Festus entered government service. He attained various posts, including that of MAGISTER MEMORIAE in 369 to Emperor Valens. Festus probably wrote his digest during this period. From 372 to 378, he was proconsul of Asia, persecuting numerous pagan philosophers throughout the province. Dismissal came in 378, following the demise of Valens. Festus returned to Asia to defend himself against charges and was acquitted. He died of a stroke in the Temple of Nemesis.

See also MAXIMUS OF EPHESUS.

Festus, Sextus Pompeius (fl. late second century C.E.) *Grammarian who was the author of a glossary or dictionary in Latin*
Only half of the work is extant, and it was based upon the original lexicon of M. Verrius FLACCUS, who had lived in the reign of Augustus (27 B.C.E.–14 C.E.). It was probably in the introduction or early part that Festus explained that his effort was, in fact, an abridgement or version of Flaccus's original. In the end, his own writing stretched into some 20 books. Ironically, Festus was himself abridged by Paul the Deacon in the eighth century C.E.

Fidenae, Amphitheater of Built by a freedman, Atilius, in the Sabine town of Fidena. By 27 C.E., because of the restrictions placed on all games and contests by Tiberius, Fidenae had become very popular as a source of entertainment. In that year, however, the faulty construction used by Atilius was made obvious when the entire structure collapsed during one of the heavily attended games. According to Tacitus, thousands died in the disaster (probably an exaggeration), but the sheer horror brought changes from the Senate. Henceforth, no one could hold games unless they owned more than 400,000 sesterces, and an amphitheater could be constructed only with the use of careful guidelines, which included the use of solid ground. Atilius was exiled from Italy.

See also THEATERS AND AMPHITHEATERS.

Fides Roman goddess of faith, especially good faith. Fides was considered the personification of faithfulness and hence was used on the coins of the empire to symbolize the trust placed in the government or the legions. Her temple was situated on the Capitoline Hill, near the Temple of Jupiter.

See also GODS AND GODDESSES OF ROME.

Figulus, Nigidius (c. 98 B.C.E.–after 46 B.C.E.) *A noted and successful scholar of the late Republic*
Figulus became a PRAETOR in 58 B.C.E., after which he was one of the greatest supporters of POMPEY THE GREAT against Julius CAESAR. In 46 he was exiled after the defeat of the Pompeian cause. Figulus was a follower of PYTHAGORAS and he pursued all of the Pythagorean interests, including the occult and the Orphic mysteries. His writings included the natural sciences, grammatical commentaries, astronomy, religion, and zoology; some of his work has survived in fragments. He was an associate of CICERO and was eventually overshadowed by VARRO, who had all of his brilliance without his proclivity for the esoteric. According to the historian Suetonius, Figulus cited the stars at the moment of Augustus's birth, declaring "The master of the world has just been born."

finance For centuries the monetary affairs of the Roman Republic had rested in the hands of the SENATE, which was steady and fiscally conservative. The AERARIUM (state treasury) was supervised by members of the government rising in power and prestige, the QUAESTORS, PRAETORS and eventually the prefects. With the dawn of the Roman Empire, a major change took place, as the emperors assumed the reins of financial control. Augustus initially adopted a system that was, on the surface, fair to the Senate. Just as the world was divided into provinces designated as imperial or senatorial, so was the treasury. All tribute brought in from senatorially controlled provinces was given to the *aerarium*, while that of the imperial territories went to the treasury of the emperor, the FISCUS.

Initially, this process of distribution seemed to work, although the legal technicality did not disguise the supremacy of an emperor or his often used right to transfer funds back and forth regularly from the *aerarium* to the *fiscus*. The *fiscus* actually took shape after the reigns of Augustus and Tiberius. It began as a private fund (*fiscus*, meaning purse or basket) but grew to include all imperial monies, not only the private estates but also all public lands and finances under the imperial eye.

The property of the rulers grew to such an extent that changes had to be made starting sometime in the early third century C.E., most certainly under Septimius Severus. Henceforth the imperial treasury was divided. The *fiscus* was retained to handle actual governmental revenue, while a *patrimonium* was created to hold the private fortune, the inheritance of the royal house. (There is a considerable question as to the exact nature of this evaluation, involving possibly a RES PRIVATA so common in the late empire.)

Just as the Senate had its own finance officers, so did the emperors. The head of the *fiscus* in the first years was the RATIONALIS, originally a FREEDMAN due to Augustus's desire to place the office in the hands of a servant free of the class demands of the traditional society. In succeeding years the corruption and reputation of the freedmen forced new and more reliable administrators. From the time of Hadrian (117–138 C.E.), any *rationalis* hailed from the Equestrian Order (EQUITES) and remained so through the chaos of the third century C.E. and into the age of Diocletian.

With Diocletian came a series of massive reforms, and total control over the finances of the empire fell to the now stronger central government. Under Constantine this aggrandizement continued with the emergence of an appointed minister of finance, the *comes sacrarum largitionum* (count of the sacred largess). He maintained the general treasury and the intake of all revenue. His powers were directed toward control of the new *sacrum aerarium,* the result of the combination of the *aerarium* and the *fiscus.*

The *comes sacrarum largitionum* was a figure of tremendous influence. He was responsible for all taxes, examined banks, mints, and mines everywhere, watched over all forms of industry and paid out the budgets of the many departments of the state. To accomplish these many tasks, he was aided by a vast bureaucracy. Just below the *comes sacrarum* were the *comites largitionum,* positioned in each diocese. They acted as territorial chiefs, sending out agents, the *rationales summarum,* to collect all money in tribute, taxes, or fees. They could go virtually anywhere and were the most visible extension of the government in the fourth and fifth centuries C.E.

Only the MAGISTER OFFICIORUM and the *comes rerum privatarum* could counter the political and financial weight of the *comes sacrarum largitionum.* The *magister officiorum* (master of offices) made all of the major decisions concerning military and intelligence matters, receiving a budget of monumental size, over which the *comes sacrarum largitionum* probably had only partial authority.

Given the increased size of the imperial estates and holdings, the *res privata* not only survived but was also officially divided into two different treasuries, the *res privatae* of actual lands and the *patromonium sacrae,* or imperial inheritance. Both were under the jurisdiction of the *comes rerum privatarum.* He also took in any rents or dues from imperial lands and territories.

See also CIVIL SERVICE; COINAGE; TAXATION; and *TRIBUTUM.*

Firmicus Maternus, Julius (fl. fourth century C.E.)
Writer and astrologer
Originally considered two individuals, one Christian and the other pagan, Firmicus Maternus is now generally believed to have been one person. The works of Firmicus,

however, were so different in character that the confusion was understandable, the result of his conversion to Christianity. Firmicus was born in Sicily, where he received his education as a lawyer. His writing began sometime during the reign of Constantine the Great (306–337 C.E.), with the *Matheseos* or *Mathesis.* The *Matheseos* was a guidebook to astrology written in Latin and relying upon many sources. It offered a very thorough system, along Neoplatonic lines, with an inherent bias toward Christianity, including criticisms of the destruction of pagan temples. Around 347 he produced his second work, *De errore profanarum religionum* (On the error of profane religions), a virulent attack against paganism. Firmicus called for the complete extermination of pagan culture. Whereas his first book was quiet and contemplative in style, the second was rabid and harsh, a tome in which he praised the pillaging of non-Christian shrines.

Firmus (fl. third century C.E.) *Rebel leader in Egypt during the reign of Aurelian (270–275 C.E.)*
The account of his life in the *Scriptores Historiae Augustae* is generally unreliable, although Zosimus and the life of AURELIAN make references of Firmus. Zosimus, however, does not refer to him by name. Sometime around 272, while Aurelian was on campaign in Thrace, Firmus, who may have been an imperial officer, declared Egypt an independent state. As an ally of the powerful and ambitious Queen ZENOBIA of Palmyra, Firmus may have entered into her service. Aurelian marched on Palmyra, eliminated Firmus's associates and swept into Egypt. Alexandria was pacified, and Firmus disappeared from history.

Firmus, Plotius (fl. first century C.E.) *Prefect of the Praetorian Guard during the brief reign of Otho in 69 C.E.*
Firmus began his career in Rome as a soldier in a cohort of the Praetorians. By 69 he was head of the VIGILES, the city's police and firefighting force, and an ardent supporter of Otho, long popular as an imperial aspirant. He was counted as a member of Otho's circle, even before the assassination of Galba. After Otho was installed as emperor, the Praetorians were given the right to elect their own prefects, and they chose Firmus and Licinius Proculus. Both men helped to restore order in the Guard when it marched on the imperial palace, fearing a murder attempt on the emperor. Later, after the defeat of the Othonians at the battle of BEDRIACUM on April 15, 69, Firmus begged Otho not to leave his vanquished army, but he failed in preventing the doomed ruler from killing himself.

fiscus
Name applied to the personal treasury of the emperors of Rome. The word is literally translated as "basket" or "purse" and was used to describe those forms of revenue collected from the provinces (specifically the imperial provinces), which were then granted to the emperor. Its existence pointed to the division of power in

the early era of the empire between the imperial court and the Senate. In subsequent years, as the emperors assumed greater control over the finances of the Roman world, the size of the *fiscus* increased. Juvenal satirized the entire treasury by writing that a turbot of great size caught in the Adriatic had to be sent to Rome as part of Domitian's *fiscus.* For details of the working of the *fiscus,* see also FINANCE; *AERARIUM.*

Flaccilla (fl. late fourth century C.E.) *Empress during the reign of Theodosius I (the Great, 379–395)*
Flaccilla was different from the other leading women of that age in that she never attained great power in the imperial court, even as the mother of Theodosius's two sons and successors to the Eastern and Western thrones—Arcadius and Honorius. Despite the very weak nature of Arcadius, Flaccilla refused or was unable to gain ascendancy over him. Little else is known of her.

Flaccus, A. Persius (fl. 34–62 C.E.) *Noted satirist in Rome*
Flaccus was influenced by HORACE and was a friend of the famed writer LUCAN. In his lifetime Flaccus achieved little fame through his work, but his satires, especially his expositions on Stoicism, gained him respect posthumously.

Flaccus, Verrius (fl. early first century C.E.) *Freedman and a learned teacher and lexiconist of the Augustan Age (27 B.C.E.–14 C.E.)*
Flaccus earned note as the author of a large work on Roman and Latin linguistic antiquities, *De verborum significatu (On the Significance of Words).* Flaccus taught Gaius and Lucius Caesar and was thus known to Augustus. *De verborum significatu* was divided alphabetically, with quotations from numerous authors highlighted, and explained the proper use of a word. The entire manuscript, containing a large number of books, was completed probably after or around 10 C.E. Flaccus's greatest achievement survived into the second century, only through an abridgment and subsequent additions and alterations of Sextus FESTUS. Other portions of the lexicon were saved by Paul the Deacon in the eighth century C.E.

Flaccus, C. Valerius (d. c. 90 C.E., but not after 92) *A contemporary of the rhetorician Statius*
C. Valerius Flaccus Setinus Balbus was the leading poet of the time of Vespasian. His main interest was the mythological epic, and the influence of VIRGIL was obvious. That Flaccus lived during the time of the Flavians is demonstrated by his introduction to the *Argonautica,* in which he mentions Vespasian and the capture of Jerusalem in 70 C.E. by Titus, who was not yet emperor. The chief work of Flaccus was the *Argonautica,* compiled in more than eight volumes, retelling of Jason along the lines of Virgil but without his predecessor's smoothness

of organization. He was little known by his own literary community, although some of his writings were later imitated.

flamens One of the most influential groups of priests in Rome. The flamens (or flamines, priests) were given the task of honoring the 15 major and minor deities of the Roman state cult. Numbering 15 also, each of the flamens was assigned his god. It was the responsibility of the priest to honor that divinity, to make sacrifices, and to perform all necessary actions and ceremonies. The 15 flamens were divided into two groups: 12 *minores* of lesser deities and three *maiores,* the priests of the greater gods of Rome. Jupiter, Mars, and Quirinus were the major deities, and their flamens were the Flamen Dialis of Jupiter, the Flamen Martialis for Mars and the Flamen Quirinalis for Quirinus.

Of the 12 *minores* only 10 are known with certainty, and the precise order of importance is still debatable. They were:

Deity	Flamen
Carmentis	Carmentalis
Ceres	Cerealis
Falacer	Falacer
Flora	Florialis
Furrina	Furinalis
Pales	Palatualis
Pomona	Pomonalis
Portunus	Portunalis
Volcanus (Vulcan)	Volcanalis
Volturnus	Volturnalis

The three flamens of Jupiter, Mars, and Quirinus each possessed tremendous power and influence; their areas of jurisdiction stretched even into the cults of the other gods. The Flamen Quirinalis, for example, presided over the feast of ROBIGUS, the Robigalis, each year.

Jupiter commanded the Roman pantheon, and the Flamen Dialis wielded a parallel importance. The Flamen Dialis had many complicated duties and ceremonies to fulfill, including the celebration of the Ides of each month with a procession along the Sacred Way, up to the capital. The Flamen of Jupiter was a relic of an ancient kingship and traveled with a lictor, wore a purple-trimmed toga and sat in a curule or throne-like chair. The life of the Flamen Dialis was surprisingly demanding. Marriage was a requirement, and the wife, the Flaminica, could not divorce him. If she died, he had to step down. Children were also required; if a union had proven barren, the Flamen Dialis had to adopt those provided for him. A long list of taboos (bad omens, habits, words, and foods that could not be used or said within his presence, could not be brought near him or touched to his person) ruled his life. He was also restricted from approaching the house of a recently deceased person (*see* DEATH), and nothing that resembled a chain, a fastening, or a lock could be placed near him.

Mars's priest, the Flamen Martialis, faced similar restrictions, but for the servants of the god of war, life was not so difficult. The same was true for the Flamen Quirinalis. Aside from the celebration of the Quirinalia on February 17 of each year, he had little to do (as information available points to few duties). He served as the chief priest for the ceremonies of Robigus and possibly for Consus and Larentia as well. Whatever their duties or regulations, the *flamines* were important throughout the entire structure of Roman religion.

Under the empire and with the development of the IMPERIAL CULT, new *flamines* were appointed. Julius Caesar was declared divine in 42 B.C.E., and many rulers were subsequently deified. A flamen was named for each new divine emperor. Augustus received one, and the cult of the emperors could thereby magnify itself in importance.

Flavians   The family and political supporters of VESPASIAN and his two successors, TITUS and DOMITIAN. Vespasian's family, or gens, originated in the Sabine town of Reate, where the Flavii came to occupy positions of some local importance. Vespasian's complete name was Titus Flavius Vespasianus, and in 69 C.E. he launched his successful bid to gain the imperial throne. "Flavian" came into use that time to describe all of the adherents of his cause. Thus Danubian legions under the command of Antonius Primus were called Flavians, even though they were not yet under Vespasian's direct command. In designating the dynasty of the family of Vespasian, the term assumed a complimentary nature. The Flavian administrations, including that of the austere and stern Domitian, were considered enlightened, stable, and liberal, with programs of building, domestic tranquility and a return to imperial greatness. The three Flavian emperors were Vespasian (69–79), Titus (79–81), and Domitian (81–96).

Flavianus, Virius Nicomachus (334–394 C.E.) *Praetorian prefect of Italy from 390 to 394, a consul in the West in 394 and one of the last great pagans of the Roman Empire*
Flavianus was born to a pagan family of the senatorial class. He was a friend of SYMMACHUS, profiting from an association with that influential philosopher. He held the posts of consular official in Sicily, vicar of Africa, and *quaestor* under Emperor Theodosius I. In 389 he received the appointment of Praetorian prefect of Italy.

While in that office, Flavianus supported the revival of paganism in the Western Empire and joined the cause of EUGENIUS, the usurper appointed head of the West by the *magister militum* ARBOGAST. After initial attempts at conciliating Theodosius in Constantinople failed, Flavianus led the movement in Rome to reinstate all forms of pagan belief, gaining popular acclaim and both the consulship of 394 and the appointment of his son as a member of the prefecture of the city. Eugenius's Praetorian prefect promised victory from the gods. The war with Theodosius was disastrous. After Eugenius and Arbogast were defeated on September 5, 394, Flavianus killed himself.

Flavius (fl. first century C.E.) *A prince of the powerful tribe of the Cherusci, of Germania*
Flavius was the brother of ARMINIUS, the famed destroyer of the Roman general Varus at the Teutoburg Forest in 9 C.E. Just as Arminius had once served in the army of Rome, so did Flavius, but he chose to remain in the employ of the emperors. He proved a gifted, loyal, and hard-fighting soldier, who lost an eye in battle for Emperor Tiberius. In return, Flavius was given money, gold bracelets, and a residence in Rome. In 16 C.E., the prince joined the legions of Germanicus marching against Arminius. The historian Tacitus recorded fancifully a meeting between Flavius and his brother on the banks of the Weser. There, Arminius upbraided Flavius for being a traitor, accepting pitiful gifts from the Romans while working against his own people. They very nearly came to blows, but Flavius was restrained by his aides. He never saw Arminius again. Returning to Rome, Flavius apparently settled down in retirement. He married the daughter of Actumerus, chief of the Chatti, the most hated enemy of the CHERUSCI. In 47, ITALICUS, the son of Flavius, was sent by Claudius to be king of the subdued Cherusci.

Flora   Roman goddess of flowers and spring. She was perceived as a happy, bright, and merry deity. Her festival was the Floralia, held each April 28 and presided over by the Flamen Florialis.

See also FLAMINES; GODS AND GODDESSES OF ROME; LUDI.

Florentia (Florence)   Originally a small community in Etruria, Florentia began to grow during the early years of the empire and may have been a colony. It could not compete with the other cities and *coloniae* (COLONIES) of Italy, however, and throughout the next four centuries contributed almost nothing to commerce, industry, or culture. A fortress was erected near its main river, the Armes, in the fifth century C.E., but Florentia's era of greatness lay far in the future.

Florianus, Marcus Annius (d. 276 C.E.) *Emperor of Rome from April to June 276*
Florianus was perhaps the half-brother of Emperor Tacitus (2), although that relationship remains unclear, nor was his early career ever chronicled. He was an able soldier, for Tacitus appointed him PREFECT OF THE PRAETORIAN GUARD and used him to repulse the massive Goth

invasions along the Black Sea frontier in Asia Minor. As he gained the upper hand, however, word arrived that Tacitus was dead, either by fever or by assassination at Tyana. Florianus immediately seized the throne and informed both the legions and the Senate. Within weeks he found recognition from every province in the empire, with the exception of Syria and Egypt. There the troops had risen to declare PROBUS emperor. Believing that he could defeat Probus, Florianus chose to deal with the crisis personally and marched toward his enemy, who was encamped near Tarsus. No battle was forthcoming, as Probus maneuvered Florianus's hot and exhausted legions into frustration and then into mutiny. They slew Florianus in the summer of 276.

Florus, Gessius (fl. first century C.E.) *Procurator of Judaea in 64–66 C.E.*
Florus succeeded Albinus and was the last Roman provincial leader before the great Jewish revolt began in 66. He came originally from Clazomenae in Asia Minor, but owed his position to his ambitious spouse, Cleopatra, who was a friend of Poppaea, the wife of Nero. Through Cleopatra, Florus was named governor of the increasingly troubled region. He did nothing to ease tensions and instead set upon a suicidal spree of mismanagement, corruption, and wanton cruelty, supposedly using the chronic presence of bandit gangs in the area to help his plundering. Complaints sent to the governor of Syria, Cestius Gallus, failed to calm the situation. Tacitus, in his *Histories,* wrote that "the Jews could bear oppression until the time of Gessius Florus when war broke out." Open hostilities were brought about by Florus's confiscation of funds (17 talents) from the great temple, and the brutal response of the Roman troops sent in to quell the enraged Jews. Under intense and mounting violence, Florus departed from JERUSALEM, evacuating most of the JUDAEA.

Florus, Julius (d. 21 C.E.) *Tribal leader of the Gallic Treviri*
In 21 C.E., Florus joined Julius SACROVIR of the Aedui in starting a revolt in Gallia Lugdunensis and Gallia Belgica. According to Tacitus, he was descended from a noble family, and both he and Sacrovir probably held Roman citizenship. Slowly Florus and his fellow conspirators prepared for war, but they underestimated both the loyalty of the Gallic levies to Rome and the capacity of the Romans to respond to a crisis. The legate of Gallia Lugdunensis, Acilius Aviola, aided by Visellius Varro, the governor of Germania Inferior, quickly crushed the rebellion. Florus, meanwhile, unsuccessfully tried to convince his own Treviri, especially those warriors trained in the legions, to massacre Roman traders. His revolution crumbling, he fled into the wilds, was pursued by the cohorts of Aviola and killed himself to avoid capture.

Florus, Publius Annius (fl. c. 117–138 C.E.) *Author, rhetorician, and poet who could actually have been two or even three separate individuals*
Florus was known as Julius Florus or Annaeus Florus but was probably P. Annius Florus, mentioned in the late first and early second centuries C.E. He traveled to Rome, having been born in Africa in the late first century, and visited Spain and the city of Tarraco or Tarragona. Florus was back in Rome by the time Hadrian ruled and was counted one of his most gifted courtiers. Both master and servant were famed for the barbs they routinely exchanged with one another. As an author Florus composed several notable works. His *Vergilius orator an poeta* (Virgil, orator or poet) asked whether Virgil deserved greater merit for his orations or poetry. He also penned a survey of Roman history, *Epitome Bellorum* (Epitome of wars). Very little of his work is extant.

food and drink, Roman Given the vastness of the Roman Empire at its height, there was considerable variety among the different provinces and peoples in terms of what was consumed as a regular part of the diet. Among the Romans, however, there was a typically frugal diet for the lower classes and a far more diverse, even flamboyant, array of culinary options for the upper classes. Such was the excessive luxury enjoyed by the nobility willing to spend appropriate amounts of money on their banquets of many courses that the simple fare of the poor and middle classes was often overshadowed in the historical memory.

A great deal of knowledge has been preserved about the Roman diet and cooking customs. Evidence is found from a number of sources, including literary works, mosaics, and especially archaeological excavations. Other valuable sources are Roman cookbooks, such as the famous and influential guide by Apicius, the *De Re Coquinaria* (On cooking).

Normally, the Romans ate three meals each day, although only one was a major dinner. Breakfast (*ientaculum*) was taken at sunrise, or at the first hour. The main meal (*cena*) was eaten at midday at around the ninth or 10th hour, which would vary depending upon the time of year. During the winter, the ninth and 10th hours were around 1:30 P.M. to 2:30 P.M.; in the summer, they were from 2:30 P.M. to 3:30 P.M. A final meal (*vesperna*) was taken in the evening. Over time, the Romans changed their practice of eating *cena* at midday, preferring to dine later in the day. In the place of *cena*, they ate *prandium,* a lighter lunch, followed around sunset by the main meal. In this way, the Romans adopted the practice of consuming a light breakfast, a light lunch, and then their main meal.

Breakfast consisted of bread or biscuits, flavored with honey, salt, olives, or dates, and eaten with water or wine. On rare occasions, meat and cheese was eaten as well. The larger meals depended heavily upon the financial means of the diner. For the poor, meals were primarily made from grain, oil, and wine. Husked wheat was used to make a porridge (*puls*) that was rescued from its monotonous blandness by the flavors added to it. Later, species of wheat (*frumentum*) were cultivated and used to make bread, offering possibilities for additional flavorings and spices. This main dish was supplemented with meat, fish, vegetables, and fruits if they could be acquired or afforded. Vegetables included lettuce, beans, lentils, beets, garlic, onions, asparagus, and cabbage. All Romans flavored their meals with spices, herbs, and sauces. The most common of sauces was *garum* or *liquamen*, a spicy, salty sauce made from fish or a murky mixture of brine and fish by-products. A traditional way of making *garum* was to gut a fish and place its entrails into a jar of brine, allowing it to ferment for weeks.

For the wealthy, there were virtually unlimited options for a meal. A typical meal was of three courses, described as *ab ovo usque ad mala* (from eggs to apples). The first course, *promulsio* or *gustatio,* was a kind of appetizer course, offering choices of salads, mushrooms, radishes, eggs, and oysters. Diners then enjoyed *mulsum*, a cleansing desert wine sweetened with honey. The *cena* might have as many as six or seven courses (or more). The dishes were limited only by the budget of the host and the imagination of the cooks. Aside from poultry and meat, there might be fish, eels, oysters, and shellfish. The poultry itself might include ducks, partridges, peacocks, pigeons, doves, ostriches, cranes, and pheasants. Meats ranged from pork and beef to lamb, venison, hare, and mouse.

Following the main course, it was custom for the diners to take a moment and allow the hosts to make an offering of wheat, wine, and salt to the household gods. This sacrifice was followed by the last course, desert (*secunda mensa*), made up of sweet cakes and fruit. The meal was made more festive by quantities of wine, music,

A warehouse and store in Herculaneum; the counter contained large ceramic jars with wine and foodstuffs (*Courtesy Fr. Felix Just, S.J.*)

and often elaborate—or possibly grotesque—entertainments, such as dwarfs, acrobats, and dancers.

The *vesperna*, while it was still taken, was a far simpler meal than the *cena*, but its particulars depended entirely upon the diner. The same was true of *prandium* when it was adopted. Normally, both meals were accompanied by water, hot wine, and *mulsum*.

Roman writers, including Horace and Columella, document the Roman fondness for wine. Romans normally preferred not to drink undiluted wine, as it was considered distinctly uncivilized. Instead, they cut wine with spices, honey, and, especially, water. Variations included, *acetum, posca, must,* and *mulsum. Acetum* was a cheap, bitter wine that tasted like vinegar. *Posca,* another drink adopted by the poor, was a watered down version of *acetum. Must* was a combination of water and wine concentrate made from the residue of the crushed grapes in wine making. *Mulsum* was said to be good for digestion, improving the appetite, and promoting a long life.

An oven in a house in Herculaneum (*Courtesy Fr. Felix Just, S.J.*)

foricae The *foricae* were a kind of latrine, normally associated with the public baths in a Roman community or town. The typical *forica* was little more than an open sewer covered by a line of wooden or stone seats. There were no partitions between the seats, with Romans never suffering from shyness and sitting next to each other in a communal gathering. Waste water from the nearby baths was used to flush the sewer. Personal hygiene was maintained by the use of a sponge stick and continuous running water flowing through a gutter placed before the seats. The water flowed from the *forica* and emptied directly into the sewer in the nearby street.

In many homes, a private lavatory was beyond the means of the owners. They relied instead upon a nearby *forica*, while in the winter or especially during inclement weather, a chamber pot was used. For those able to afford a private lavatory, the *foricae* system was retained in essentials, except for the number of seats and the obvious communal aspects. The water for the private latrine was delivered from an aqueduct to a distribution tank and from there sent to individual houses by means of pipes made of lead, clay, or even wood. The owners of the houses had to pay for the water, with rates determined by the diameter of the pipes, the standard measuring unit for pipes was the *calix*, the nozzle.

Formulus (fl. first century C.E.) *Painter*
Formulus attained his greatest prominence during the reign of Nero (54–69 C.E.). He was considered to be the finest artist of his era. Nero was so pleased with his skills that he paid him to paint the walls of the GOLDEN HOUSE OF NERO.

Fortuna Goddess of Fortune, known to the Greeks as Tyche; a deity worshiped with considerable enthusiasm in Rome. Fortuna was originally a fertility goddess, who declined in importance until an association with Tyche was developed. Henceforth her role in the pantheon of Rome's divinities was assured. She was depicted in various forms: standing upon a wheel (the symbol of the changing tides of luck), holding a rudder to guide the ship of fate, wielding ears of corn, and offering a cornucopia of goods and bounties (a return to her status as protector of the harvest). Rome was filled with her statues, and monuments were erected in her honor, but the great centers of worship for her cult were at Antium and at Praeneste, just outside of the limits of Rome. At Praeneste a famous shrine and oracle were symbols of her divinity; only the terrace of that temple remains. Her other shrines were divided into male and female sanctuaries, the *Muliebris* for women and the *Virilis* for men.
See also GODS AND GODDESSES OF ROME.

forum An area of open space in many Italian and Roman colonial cities that served as a place of public assembly and as an economic center for vendors and businesses. In the Republic, the greatest forum in the Roman world was the FORUM ROMANUM. Forums constructed under the empire were of varying ambition and purpose and included the FORUM AUGUSTUM, FORUM CAESARIS, Forum Pacis (TEMPLE OF PEACE), FORUM TRANSITORIUM and the FORUM TRAIANI. The provinces naturally imitated Rome, and forums were common throughout the cities and colonies of the Roman world. The two most notable were in Augusta Raurica (Augst) and in LEPCIS MAGNA (Africa).
See also ART AND ARCHITECTURE.

Forum Augustum In 42 B.C.E., Octavian made a vow that if victorious in the battle of PHILIPPI against Brutus and Cassius, he would erect a great temple to Mars Ultor. The Forum Augustum was the result of that oath. Dedi-

cated in 2 B.C.E., it was placed just north of the FORUM ROMANUM and his other effort at reconstruction, the FORUM CAESARIS. The original design was symmetrical and enclosed in order to complete the illusion that the entire series of buildings was one temple, cut off from the rest of the city. Augustus was only partially successful in the fulfillment of that plan, as he could not bring himself to evict the poor tenants who would have had to abandon the site if the geometrical form was enforced. Nevertheless, the Forum Augustum was suitably grand. Columns of marble stood with two stories of porticos, decorated with notable Roman historical figures. The statues depicted the millennium from Aeneas to Julius Caesar, whose sword was kept in the heart of the Forum, at the TEMPLE OF MARS ULTOR.
See also ART AND ARCHITECTURE.

Forum Caesaris Built by Julius CAESAR to ease congestion in the FORUM ROMANUM and to enlarge its capacity for business and commerce. In 54 B.C.E., Caesar purchased land just to the north of the Forum Romanum, spending some 60 million sesterces. The area was situated near the Capitoline and Quirinal Hills in a stretch of territory that would be dominated by other imperial fora over the centuries. To build his new structure, Caesar displaced the old Comitium (assembly house), the Rostra (speaker's podium) and the CURIA HOSTILIA (Senate chamber), which was destroyed in 52 B.C.E., in the terrible riots following the death of CLODIUS PULCHER. Caesar proposed building a new *curia* on a different axis. The new forum was rectangular, with double columns on three sides and an ornate entrance to the south. Stores (*tabernae*) were located on the west. The entrance opened onto the main attraction, the beautiful TEMPLE OF VENUS. This shrine helped establish the subsequent pattern for later forums. Caesar dedicated his project in 46 B.C.E., A fire cause terrible damage, but the structure was restored by TRAJAN and rededicated in 108 C.E. Another fire took place in 283, in the reign of CARINUS, and repairs were made later by DIOCLETIAN.
See also ART AND ARCHITECTURE.

Forum Gallorum Village in northern Italy where a battle was fought on April 14, 43 B.C.E., between the forces of Marc ANTONY and the legions of the Republic under the overall command of Pansa, aided by HIRTIUS and the untested Octavian (AUGUSTUS). After months of negotiations between the Senate and Antony did little to settle the questions of power and government after Caesar's assassination, this conflict became unavoidable.

Antony had Brutus confined in position around Mutina, just south of the Po River on the Via Aemilia. Pansa was sent north from Rome to link with Hirtius and Octavian in order to provide Brutus with aid. Antony, seizing the central position, hoped to deal with the enemy in piecemeal fashion, destroying the columns one at a time.

On April 14, Antony's legions collided with those of Pansa, in the village of Forum Gallorum. Pansa's troops were routed and the general severely wounded. Jubilant, Antony called off the pursuit of the broken army but was then astonished to see Hirtius crashing into his own exhausted ranks. The victory was turned into a disaster, and Antony pulled back, having lost the initiative and the battle. Another conflict would take place six days later, at MUTINA.

Forum Julium   Also known as Forum Julii; a colony in GALLIA NARBONENSIS founded by Julius CAESAR in 44 B.C.E. as part of his broad program of Roman colonization in the provinces. Presumably founded for its economic potential, its location on the coast aided its growth. Following the battle of ACTIUM in 31 B.C.E., AUGUSTUS made the colony a naval base and improved its colonial status. Now called Frejus, Forum Julium was the birthplace of AGRICOLA.

Forum Pacis   *See* TEMPLE OF PEACE.

Forum Romanum   Also called the Great Forum; the chief marketplace of Rome and, during the empire, the main seat of government containing the greatest of the city's BASILICAS. The site was also famed for its beautiful temples (Concord, Divus Julius, Saturn, Castor and Pollux, and the round Temple of Vesta). It was located on marshy ground in a valley between the Capitoline, Oppian, Quirinal, and Palatine Hills that had been used by early inhabitants as a cemetery.

According to legend, the Forum had its origins in the days of Romulus and Tatius, who supposedly designated the area as the meeting place of the Romans. After the Cloaca Maxima (the main sewer) drained the marshes in the sixth century B.C.E., the site served as the central place of public assembly. Starting in the mid-second century B.C.E., it was the seat of the Comitium and the Rostra, where the classes of Rome heard their speeches. Originally, low-class vendors were allowed on the site, but they were driven out in time, in favor of money-changers and more respectable businesses befitting the growing prominence of the forum. No other section of the city reflected more clearly the rise of Rome. As the lands and conquests of the Romans increased, much of the seized treasure and gold went to pay for the statues, monuments, and basilicas of the forum.

Julius CAESAR initiated numerous constructions in the Great Forum, most of them completed by AUGUSTUS. The BASILICA AEMILIA was rebuilt, and he began the BASILICA JULIA in place of the Basilica Sempronia from the time of Triberius Gracchus. Augustus finished the Basilica Julia and the new CURIA, erected the TEMPLE OF DIVUS

The remains of the Forum Romanum *(Courtesy Fr. Felix Just, S.J.)*

JULIUS and a triumphal arch in 29 B.C.E., at the place of Caesar's funeral pyre; a newer one was installed in 19 B.C.E. Equally, Augustus remodeled, refurbished, and improved various other buildings with the aim of furthering their grandeur, including the TEMPLE OF CASTOR AND POLLUX, the TEMPLE OF SATURN, and the TEMPLE OF CONCORD. The Temple of Castor and Pollux was dedicated in 6 C.E. and the Concord Temple in 10 C.E.

DOMITIAN rebuilt the Curia but also constructed the Temple of Vespasian, dedicated in 81 C.E. Septimius SEVERUS placed his magnificent triumphal arch on the sloping end of the forum in 203.

See also ART AND ARCHITECTURE.

Forum Traiani   Situated to the north of the FORUM AUGUSTUM between the Capitoline and Quirinal hills; the grandest achievement of Emperor TRAJAN's reign, rivaling even the FORUM ROMANUM for organization and architectural perfection. The design was conceived and executed by the noted architect APOLLODORUS of Damascus, although construction may have begun at the time of Domitian. It was completed in 114–115 C.E. and was paid for with the vast treasure taken as plunder in the Dacian Wars. This was deemed appropriate, for not only did the forum resemble a large military camp but it also housed

Trajan's Column, the carved monument detailing the great wars with DECEBALUS.

An ornate gate allowed entrance from the Forum Augustum into a flat area with curving sides and double porticos. At the far end sat the BASILICA ULPIA, the largest building of its kind in that era. Behind the basilica was Trajan's Column, with its statue of the ruler, flanked by two libraries, one in Latin and one in Greek. Trajan's successor, HADRIAN, created the Temple Divi Traiani (Divine Trajan) beyond the libraries, constructed of Egyptian granite.

See also ART AND ARCHITECTURE.

Forum Transitorium Also known as the Forum Nervae; begun by DOMITIAN but completed by NERVA and dedicated in 97 C.E. The term *transitorium* came from both the location and the purpose of the construction, namely to connect the FORUM ROMANUM (Great Forum) with the forums of VESPASIAN on the right and AUGUSTUS on the left. Two gates opened onto the forum from the Great Forum, facing the large TEMPLE OF MINERVA.

Franks A Germanic people who came to occupy all of Gaul by the end of the Western Empire in 476 C.E.; the founders of the realm that would later be France. "Franks" (or Franc or Franci) was translated as "Free Men" and symbolized a loose confederation of German tribes on the Lower and Middle Rhine. Such a league of communities was inevitable in the face of the deterioration of the CHERUSCI as a power in Germania and the increasing pressure of migratory peoples from the East.

They appeared as a major threat to Rome only in the middle of the third century C.E., and even then a disunity within their ranks prevented them from attacking as one people. The Romans faced fractured entities known as the Salian Franks and the Ripaurian Franks. Attacks made in Gaul convinced the Romans to take action. Probus routed the Franks and other Germans, forcing them back against the Rhine.

Constantine the Great made another war upon them in 313, and in 355 Julian crushed the Salian Franks and then took steps to ensure their pacification. A large stretch of territory was granted to them in Gallia Belgica, allowing them to exist under Roman leadership in association with the empire.

Here they remained until about 425, growing in the region of Thuringia and biding their time. Under their ambitious King Chlodius, the head of the noble house of the Merovingians, the Salian Franks launched an expansionist campaign into the now feebly defended Gaul. After taking vast territories in the once proud imperial province, Chlodius was vanquished by the *magister militum* AETIUS. The Franks returned to the status of allies to the empire, but the government, unable to mount the sorties needed to recapture the lost cities, allowed the Franks to keep their conquests.

Although they were never considered the strongest of the Germanic peoples, the Franks proved reliable contributors to the defense of Gaul. In the wake of the continued collapsed of the Western Empire, the Franks became the heirs to the supremacy of all that is now France.

freedmen Former slaves, called the *libertini* (sing., *libertus*). During the early empire, a large number of freedmen attained positions of social and political prominence while in the service of the imperial household. According to tradition, the owner of a slave could at any time choose to release him. Such a release was wholly arbitrary but was recognized by law, the ex-slave probably receiving some kind of certificate of manumission. Ceremonies were conducted in some instances to mark the occasion. With freedom came complete citizenship, and all future children were citizens as well. A freedman owed to his or her former owner a certain obligation. The owner became a patron and could expect loyalty and respect. Often a freedman took up a paid office in a former estate or was taken into another house with a recommendation. Most lived fairly comfortable lives, but not elegant ones, while a fortunate few passed into higher and grander circumstances.

From the start of his reign, AUGUSTUS (ruled 27 B.C.E.–14 C.E.) recognized the need to find servants outside of the normal classes of government and society and more loyal to his vision and policies. He placed freedmen from his own court in numerous positions, especially the early imperial CIVIL SERVICE. The most notable freedman of the Augustan Principate was Licinius, who served as procurator in Gaul. Tiberius continued using the freedmen, most often in the civil service, but also in provincial administrations as procurators.

Wealth inevitably came into their hands, and under emperors Gaius Caligula, Claudius, and Nero, the freedmen achieved the acme of their influence and prestige. The imperial palace fell under their sway, offices in the empire were handed out on their word and vast fortunes became a mark of their ambition and level of corruption. Agrippina the Younger, it was said, was made the wife of Claudius only after the imperial freedmen around the aged emperor decided in her favor.

From the time of the Flavians (69–98 C.E.), the freedmen were reduced in the imperial system of government. This decline came as a result of the rise of the Equestrian Order (EQUITES), and this ultimately more reliable class replaced the *libertini* in the civil service and in the provinces. Juvenal wrote bitterly about the freedmen in his *Satires*.

See also CALLISTUS; CLAUDIUS; PALLAS; and NARCISSUS.

Frigidus River in the Julian Alps, east of AQUILEIA, where a battle was fought on September 5–6, 394 C.E., between THEODOSIUS I and the Western usurper EUGENIUS, who was supported by the powerful MAGISTER MILI-

TUM ARBOGAST. In 392, Valentinian II had died and the throne of the Western Empire fell vacant. Arbogast, the real ruler of the West, looked for a suitable replacement, choosing the ex-school teacher Flavius Eugenius. Both magister and usurper tried to gain the approval of Theodosius in Constantinople, but by 394 his decision against them was made clear. War erupted.

Arbogast chose to defend Italy by preventing Theodosius and his Eastern host from entering the country. His strategic base was set at Aquileia. He placed his soldiers just at the lip of the Julian Alps and there awaited Theodosius, with the hope of ambushing him. Theodosius had gathered together every possible ally, using 20,000 Visigoths to form the van of his army.

On September 5, 394, the units of the East reached the pass near Aquileia and found Arbogast and his troops prepared for battle, with their back to the Frigidus River and their pagan banners displaying the figure of Hercules waving in the brisk wind.

Theodosius resolved to attack immediately, ordering a brutal and rather unimaginative frontal assault. The result was a bloody struggle in which neither side managed to do more than survive. By evening, Theodosius had lost 10,000 men. To the West, victory seemed won, and celebrations were ordered by Eugenius. Theodosius, however, refused to retreat from the field. September 6 brought another day of battle, and once more the toll was dreadful. No decision could be reached until a great gust of wind, called the Bora, blasted through the pass, blinding Arbogast and his soldiers. With that divinely sent event (if it happened at all) the battle was won by the Christian army of Constantinople.

As his men died around him, Arbogast fled into the hills and killed himself. Eugenius was captured and executed. While the battle of Frigidus proved the supremacy of the Eastern Empire in imperial politics, it became known as the final victory of the Christian religion over the old Roman gods.

See also PAGANISM.

Frisii A tribal people who lived on the continental edge of the North Sea, from the Rhine to the Ems Rivers. The Frisii were of Germanic stock and had dealings with most of the other tribes in Germania, especially their closest neighbors to the south, the Bructeri. In 12 B.C.E., DRUSUS, Tiberius's brother, came into contact with the Frisii as part of his campaigns and may have established good relations initially. A tribute was paid each year to Rome, but as the tribe was very poor, Drusus made them present only hides.

By 28 C.E., the Frisii were administered by a centurion of the primipilate, a very cruel soldier named Olennius. He demanded that the very rare hide of the wild ox be paid, eventually bankrupting the tribe. Outraged at the greed of the imperial officials, the Frisii rebelled and slaughtered all of the tax collectors, inflicting a defeat upon the governor of Germania Inferior, Lucius APRONIUS.

Because of their victory, the tribesmen earned a reputation for ferocity and also gained independence for the next 19 years. The famous general Domitius Corbulo brought them back under Roman control in 47 C.E. Freedom was not easily forgotten by the tribe, and in 58, they moved across the Rhine, only to be ordered back to their original homeland. Sending two of their kings to Rome, Verritus and Malorix, the Frisii pleaded their cause before Nero (or, according to Suetonius, Claudius), although they still had to return to their homeland. The story was recorded that the two Frisii rulers visited the Theater of Pompey and were seated in the common section. Noticing that the ambassadors of Persia and Armenia were with the senatorial class, the kings were informed that only the loyal and brave allies of Rome sat there. The rulers moved to the senatorial section and claimed their own places, insisting that there was no nation more loyal or brave than the Germans. The rebellion of Civilis (69–70) proved once more that Germanic pride was still rampant in the tribe. Their activities over the next years were typical for the people in the region, and they may have joined in the confederation of the Franks, starting in the third century. In the fifth century, the Frisii took part in the Saxon invasion of Britain.

Fritigern and Alavius *Two kings of the Visigoths*
Fritigern and Alavius played major roles in the Eastern Empire in 378 C.E., especially Fritigern. In 376, Valens, emperor of the East, was informed that the VISIGOTHS under these two kings were asking permission to migrate into the region of the Lower Danube, as their own lands were being inundated with Huns.

Fritigern made an excellent presentation to Valens at Constantinople and returned to his people with the imperial permission. Certain demands, such as the taking of hostages and the surrender of weapons, accompanied the permission, and the kings agreed.

All of Thrace, however, was thrown into chaos by the arrival of the similarly pressed Ostrogoths, under Alatheus and Saphrax. Roman rule became harsh and war erupted. Alavius was slain in an ambush, and Fritigern took sole command, leading his people to the most startling barbarian victory in the history of the Roman Empire, the battle of ADRIANOPLE. Valens died in the battle, and Constantinople was threatened. Fritigern did not take advantage of his victory, for he was slain in 380, as a result of power struggles within his own ranks.

Frontinus, Sextus Julius (c. 40–103 C.E.) *Consul, governor, general, and writer*
Frontinus served as a *praetor* in 70 and as *consul suffectus* in 73 or maybe 74. Shortly afterward, perhaps in 74 or 76, Frontinus succeeded Petillius Cerealis as governor in Britain (BRITANNIA). He waged several successful campaigns against the Silures there until 78, when he was replaced by the famed Agricola. Returning to Italy, Fron-

tinus retired to his estates in Campania, where he began to write. In 97, Nerva brought him back to Rome. The emperor appointed him *curator aquarum,* and in 98 he held a second consulship. He also took up the office of *augur.* His services were retained by Nerva's successor, Trajan, and a third consulship was achieved in 100. Frontinus died in 103, and his position as an *augur* was filled by no less a personage than PLINY THE YOUNGER, who wrote of Frontinus.

His political career served as the basis for many of his notable books. During the reign of Domitian he completed a two-volume treatise on agronomy, of which only fragments survive. His military experience helped in the writing of *De re militari,* a book on war and a major source for VEGETIUS's efforts; only the portion called the *Strategemata* is extant. This section was designed for the use of officers and included such matters as preparing for battle, sieges, and battles themselves. Overall, Frontinus offered advice through the use of historical examples culled from Livy, Caesar, and Sallust, although the fourth book's pomposity, moralizing and style differences separate it from the others.

As a result of the demands of his office as *curator aquarum,* Frontinus resolved to examine the entire AQUE-DUCT and water system of Rome in his *De Aqua Ducto* (On the conveyance of water). Here, in great detail, the history, construction of, care of, and uses for aqueducts were researched. Written around 97, Frontinus based the work on the regulations of the era, using his own reports, documents, and on-site inspections as his sources.

Fronto, Marcus Cornelius (c. 100–166 C.E.) *Rhetorician and teacher*

One of the most famous and respected intellectual figures of his time, Fronto was born in the Numidan town of Cirta and attained some posts in the imperial government before declining the proconsulship of Asia because of poor health (probably gout), a psychosomatic problem that would forever plague him. Fronto did serve as consul in 143. His fame, however, came from his oratory and his teachings. He spoke in the courts of Hadrian and Antoninus Pius, delivering addresses on law and politics, earning the title of the foremost Roman in speaking before such an assembly. He was appointed the tutor of both Marcus Aurelius and Verus. Marcus Aurelius never forgot his teacher, and both master and pupil had a genuine friendship and concern for the other, including a familiarity to such a degree that Fronto felt comfortable chiding the emperor that he should not neglect rhetoric in favor of philosophy.

Fronto was faithful and kind, devoted to Roman literature, especially Cato, Sallust, Lucretius, and Plautus. But at times he could be arrogant and demanding, as his letters indicate. His correspondence, in fact, was his greatest contribution to history, for it included letters from Marcus Aurelius, Verus, and Antoninus Pius and provides a glimpse into the very private and family natures of some of Rome's greatest emperors. Marcus wrote in his *Meditations* that from Fronto he learned what envy, deceit, and hypocrisy meant in a tyrant.

frumentarii

The imperial secret service. It had been a long-standing policy of the Roman legions and armies of occupation to utilize informers and spies, but never in an organized fashion, even in the city of Rome, with its whispers and endless conspiracies (*see* DELATORES). Titus used the special messengers and assassins of the PRAETORIAN GUARD to carry out executions and liquidations (the *SPECULATORES*); however, they belonged only to the Guard and were limited in scope and power.

By the second century C.E. the need for an empire-wide intelligence service was clear. But even an emperor could not easily create a new bureau with the express purpose of spying on the citizens of Rome's far-flung domains. A suitable compromise was found by HADRIAN. He envisioned a large-scale operation and turned to the *frumentarii.* The *frumentarius* was the collector of corn in a province, a position that brought the official into contact with enough locals and natives to acquire considerable intelligence about any given territory. Hadrian put them to use as his spies, and thus had a ready-made service and a large body to act as a courier system. The story was told that the *frumentarii* read a letter addressed to a man in government in the provinces who, according to his wife's correspondence, loved only baths and pleasures. When the official requested a furlough, Hadrian was able to tell him not to be so fond of leisure.

The *frumentarii* quickly earned the hatred of society. In the third century, association with the heads of the service could produce severe repercussions. In 217, Macrinus appointed Marcus Oclatinus Adventus, the former head of the *frumentarii* and the prefect of the Praetorian Guard, to the Senate. With one decision, Macrinus alienated most of the Roman establishment and made his own political destruction inevitable—so much were the *frumentarii* resented. DIOCLETIAN terminated the *frumentarii* because of their abuses and loathsome reputation. The emperor's decision netted him great popularity, but a short time later the equally sinister and far better organized *agens in rebus* made an appearance.

Fulvia (d. 40 B.C.E.) *Wife of Marc Antony and one of the most disliked figures in the last years of the Roman Republic*

Fulvia was the daughter of Marcus Fulvius Bambalio and married first Scribonius Curio and then CLODIUS PULCHER, who was murdered in 52 B.C.E. She then married Marc ANTONY. Antony could find no more fanatical supporter but also could hold no sway over his wife.

Fulvia started in 43 B.C.E. to acquire power in Rome, as the Senate and the survivors of the turbulent assassination of Julius Caesar struggled for advantage. As Antony was away, she served as his main agent in the capital, but after the battle of Philippi in 42 and the creation of the SECOND TRIUMVIRATE, her schemes proved dangerous. The young Octavian (AUGUSTUS) had received Italy as his share of the triumvirate and thus found himself locked in a battle of wills with Fulvia. The contest erupted into war in 41 B.C.E.

Without Antony's approval, but acting in his best interest, Fulvia opposed Octavian's land program in Italy by uniting with Antony's brother, Lucius, and starting the so-called PERUSINE WAR. Octavian surprised her with the ease of his victory; she and Lucius fled to Athens. Antony had been aware of the trouble between Fulvia and Octavian, but he could not imagine that an actual war would break out. Learning of the Perusine struggle in Asia Minor, he quickly crossed over to Athens and demanded to know what she had done. Her explanation met only with condemnations, and she grew more ill by the day. Fulvia retired to Sicyon and died. Her demise brought an immediate cessation of hostilities, and at Brundisium the two triumvirs, Antony and Octavian, made a peace that would last until the conflict in 31 B.C.E. Historians were generally unkind to Fulvia for her opposition to Octavian. Octavian had married, for a time, Claudia, Fulvia's daughter by Clodius.

Furnilla, Marcia (fl. first century C.E.) *Second wife of Emperor Titus (ruled 79–81 C.E.)*
She married him after the death of Arrecina Tertulla, his first wife. *Titus* later divorced her.

furnishings   Roman houses and villas were remarkable for being sparsely furnished beyond meeting the most basic needs of the homeowners. While there were gradual and inevitable changes in tastes and styles, the spare use of furniture remained a Roman tradition, unwavering even among the different classes. The chief differences might be found in the quality of the furniture that separated that of the upper and lower classes, the ornate decorations used for the furniture, and the continuing presence among the poor and laboring classes of implements and tools of their work, such as agricultural implements and weaving frames. Roman furniture was mainly influenced by the Greeks, who provided prototypes for chairs, beds, sofas, and assorted forms of lighting, as well as by the Etruscans.

Chairs were considered one of the most important forms of furniture because of their many uses in the home. The typical Roman chair, the throne or *solium,* was reserved, on formal occasions, for use by those wielding authority in the household, as well as magistrates and women. Chairs with backs and arms, *cathedra,* were used chiefly by women and the aged or infirm, as well as honored guests. The most common seat was the wooden stool, the *sella,* which was used by children and many

workers, such as cobblers and other craftspeople. However, the piece of furniture that was probably the one most used in the house was the couch (*lectus*). When relaxing, the men of the household reclined on the couch. It followed several designs, including the Greek model, which had no back, and one with a back more reminiscent of the modern sofa.

The Roman bed was based on the original Greek design—simple, with a mattress stuffed with wool or straw placed upon a frame of leather and with wooden headboards and footboards. In the homes of the wealthy, and especially in the palaces of the nobility and imperial families, beds became far more ornate, with decorations of gold, ivory, and assorted precious stones. The mattresses also became more comfortable, with additional padding and expensive cushions.

Throughout the house, there might also be tables (*mensae,* sing., *mensa*), cupboards, and bookcases, holding scrolls, chests, and wax tablets. Such additional pieces of furniture were never in abundance, however, and Romans preferred to spend their money on quality pieces rather than stuffing their rooms with excessive possessions. Tables and chairs were particular objects of lavish spending, with Cicero once paying 1 million *sesterces* for one citron wood table. Value was determined by the quality of the carving and decorative materials, such as gold and ivory, but equally important was the wood used for the manufacturing. Two of the most valuable were cypress and cedar.

Floor decorations were rare because of the preference for mosaic floors and the Roman dislike of the eastern habits of using carpets. Rugs were imported nevertheless, but they were used chiefly as bed coverings and also as draperies. Other decorative items varied depending upon the tastes and status of the owner. There might be stat-

The interior of a house in Herculaneum *(Courtesy Fr. Felix Just, S.J.)*

A mosaic floor in Herculaneum *(Courtesy Fr. Felix Just, S.J.)*

ues, vases, and heirlooms from travels, or even mementos from military campaigns.

One of the most important furnishings for every Roman house no matter how poor or wealthy was lighting. The basic lighting implement was the oil lamp, a flat, earthenware container with a spout at one end and a handle at the other. It was filled with olive oil, with a wick jutting out of the spout. Wicks were made of fiber, papyrus, or flax. Lamps came in a variety of shapes and sizes, including hanging lamps, lampstands, and simple flat saucers. Another form of illumination was the candle, a largely Roman invention, that was made of tallow fat rolled around a twisted wick. They were displayed in early forms of the candelabrum or ornate candlesticks.

As is obvious, the more lamps and candles that were in a house, the more light was produced. This meant that only the wealthy had homes that were brightly illuminated, as the poor could scarcely afford the amounts of olive oil or tallow to brighten their homes. Candles were chiefly used by the poor, especially as olive oil was an expensive commodity that was far more practical for cooking and eating than being burned for fuel. As a rule, the typical Roman spent evenings out of their home in an inn or tavern, used few candles or lamps, and went to bed early. Little candles or lamps were also used to honor the household gods and were placed in the small shrines that adorned corners of houses.

Except for those villas or *domi* that were constructed with internal heating facilities, home heating relied upon the hearth fire or braziers. Poor families huddled around their hearth fire in the kitchen for warmth, making it important for the family to maintain the fire, especially during the winter. For those who could afford more mobile heat sources, charcoal braziers were used. The brazier was often elegantly designed, but it also posed a constant risk of fire, just as lamps were a potential fire hazard because of the flammable oil.

Suggested Readings: Adkins, Lesley, and Roy Adkins. *Handbook to Life in Ancient Rome.* New York: Facts On File, 1994; Carcopino, Jerome. *Daily Life in Ancient Rome.* New Haven, Conn.: Yale University Press, 1968; Dupont, Florence. *Daily Life in Ancient Rome.* Translated by Christopher Woodall. Oxford, U.K.: Blackwell Publishers, 1992; Lindsay, Jack. *Daily Life in Roman Egypt.* London: F. Muller, 1963.

Furrina One of the minor deities of Rome's state religion. This goddess was honored by the Flamen Furinalis.

See also FLAMINES; GODS AND GODDESSES OF ROME; RELIGION.

Furtius (fl. second century C.E.) *King of the Quadi*
A Germanic people they resided near the Danube River. In 172–173 C.E., internal troubles developed among the QUADI, and Furtius, who had established peace by a treaty with Marcus Aurelius, was ousted from the throne. ARIOGAESUS was chosen in his place, setting off a series of retributive actions by Rome.

Fuscus, Cornelius (d. 86 C.E.) *Procurator of Pannonia in 69 C.E.*
Fuscus joined with the legate Antonius Primus in a revolt against Emperor VITELLIUS. Fuscus came from a good family of senatorial rank. Eager to make a fortune and to gain political success, he quickly resigned from his station in the Senate and joined the imperial service (in the EQUITES). In late 68, with the fall of Nero, Fuscus assumed the leadership of his own community and called for the accession of Galba. As a reward, the young man was given the procuratorship of Pannonia, where he was answerable to the governor of the territory.

The historian Tacitus wrote that Fuscus enjoyed excitement, drama, and risks. He cared little for Vitellius and in the late spring or early summer of 69 joined the Flavian cause. Antonius Primus did what he could to bring the legions on the Danube frontier into open revolt, and Fuscus supported his every move. The war that followed saw Fuscus one of the most active of the generals of Vespasian. He took command of the fleet at Ravenna, defeating Vitellius and helping to coordinate several sea and land attacks aimed at capturing vital cities on the march to Rome. Fuscus was rewarded with a praetorship and embarked upon a new career with a new administration.

By 85, Fuscus was the PREFECT OF THE PRAETORIAN GUARD under Emperor Domitian. That year the Dacians, with their gifted ruler DECEBALUS, smashed across the Danube into Moesia. With Fuscus at his side, Domitian rode immediately to the threatened frontier with an army. A series of battles repulsed the invaders, and the emperor chose Fuscus to lead the counter-invasion into Dacia itself. Fuscus had probably lost the skills that he displayed in 69, for his sortie proved disastrous. With virtually his entire army the prefect was routed and killed, losing an imperial eagle, probably that of the Praetorian unit.

G

Gabinius, Aulus (d. 48 B.C.E.) *Legate, tribune, and consul in 58 B.C.E., and a loyal supporter of Pompey*

Gabinius proposed in 67 B.C.E. that POMPEY should receive greater powers to crush the pirates so common in the Mediterranean region. From 66 to 63 B.C.E. he served as a legate of Pompey and in 58 secured for himself a consulship, aiding CLODIUS in the exile of CICERO. In 57, Gabinius was given the powerful governorship of Syria, where he ruled effectively until 54. The supremacy of Jerusalem was ended when Gabinius broke apart the Jewish territories into five districts, with equal capitals at Jerusalem, Amathus, Jericho, Sepphoris, and Gazara. He next aided the Parthian claimant MITHRIDATES III of Parthia in his battle with his brother Orodes, but soon turned to restore PTOLEMY XII AULETES to the Egyptian throne. Ptolemy promised a rich reward for Gabinius's aid, and the governor marched into the Egyptian kingdom and forced the inhabitants to take back the ruler that they had just expelled.

In 55 B.C.E., Gabinius refused to step down from office in favor of a legate of CRASSUS, one of the triumvirs, and soon came under attack from opponents in Rome. His administration in Syria had earned him enemies, and the bribe supposedly paid him by Ptolemy made him liable for trial on the charge of MAIESTAS, or treason. Pompey demanded that he be defended by Cicero, his enemy. Gabinius was initially acquitted of the charges but was convicted and exiled in 54. At the outbreak of the CIVIL WAR Gabinius found a new patron in Julius CAESAR, who gave him command over land forces. Gabinius took control of Salonae, holding it against the Pompeians for some time. He was killed in 48 B.C.E., in a plague that ravaged the city.

Gabinius, P. (d. after 41 C.E.) *Legate during the reign of Emperor Claudius*

Gabinius defeated the Couchi, a little known Germanic tribe, in 41 C.E. This victory was important because it coincided with the victory by Sulpicius Galba over another Germanic tribe, the Chatti. During his campaign, Gabinius recovered the last imperial eagle taken by the Germans in 9 C.E. in the Teutoburg Forest, where the Cheruscan leader Arminius inflicted a devastating defeat on the Roman army.

Gaetulia Region in AFRICA, just south of Mauretania and Numidia, extending westward to the Atlantic. In 46 B.C.E., Gaetulia belonged to the kingdom of JUBA I, but Publius Sittius invaded the region and thus halted the ruler's planned march to join the Pompeian remnants in their battle against Julius Caesar. The Gaetulians honored Caesar and joined in his cause. Juba turned back, and Caesar proved victorious. Augustus returned the territory to JUBA II in 25 B.C.E. In 6 C.E., however, the Gaetulians revolted against the king and cried for Roman occupation, and brought war to the neighboring communities. Cornelius Crassus subdued them, and henceforth Gaetulia was under Rome's control. The Gaetulians were probably the first of the Berbers.

Gaius (c. 110–180 C.E.) *One of the earliest imperial Jurists*

Gaius authored numerous important legal works that became influential in the later years of the Roman Empire. He probably came from the East, either Greece or Asia, going to Rome later, perhaps during the reign of Hadrian (117–138 C.E.). He seems to have had a vast knowledge of Asia Minor and Greece but became a noted instructor in Rome. Gaius composed treatises on civil law, including *Rerum cotidianarum* in seven volumes, and examinations of other legal topics. His greatest contribution was the *Institutes,* four books on all of the laws governing men and society. Although completed circa 161, the books did not bring him honor among his contemporaries, and he was all but forgotten until the fifth century, when his writings served as the basis for the *Institutes* of Justinian. Gaius's *Institutes* survived nearly intact in a manuscript discovered in Verona in 1816.

See also LAW.

Gaius Caligula (Gaius Julius Caesar Germanicus)
(12–41 C.E.) *Emperor of Rome from 37 to 41 C.E.*
Gaius was born at Antium, the third son of GERMANICUS and AGRIPPINA THE ELDER. Most of his early years were spent with his family on the Rhine frontier. The popularity of his father with the legions was transferred to him, and the soldiers affectionately called him "little boot"— Caligula. After the death of Germanicus in 19 C.E., Gaius returned to Rome from Syria and lived with his mother and his great-grandmother, LIVIA. After Livia died in 29, he moved in with his grandmother, ANTONIA (1). She was able to shield him from the plottings of Praetorian Prefect SEJANUS, a protection she was unable to provide for her daughter-in-law and other grandchildren. The annihilation of the family and friends of Germanicus by Sejanus and TIBERIUS was greeted by Gaius with remarkable passivity. He did nothing to fight against the exile of his mother and the arrest of his brothers. Instead, he ingratiated himself with Tiberius and survived to see the fall of Sejanus in 31.

In 32, Gaius moved in with the aging emperor at Capri, and from that point on he was groomed to be the successor, with a grandson, Tiberius Gemellus. Gaius possessed little experience in government, but Tiberius, sharing the debaucheries with his nephew and indulging his every vicious habit, once remarked that he was nursing a viper for the Roman people. Tiberius died in 37, and while historians have charged Gaius with his murder, it is unlikely, considering the aged emperor's state of health. Gaius, however, had long prepared for the event, and his trusted Praetorian Prefect Macro immediately went before the Senate to invalidate Tiberius Gemellus's part in the imperial rule. Gaius was proclaimed emperor.

Initially, the Romans greeted the new administration with relief. Gaius honored the memory of his family, recalled all exiles, dismissed a multitude of criminal charges lodged during the reign of Tiberius against innocent persons. All of this behavior changed rather quickly, due partially to his unstable personality and because of an illness in October 37. By 38, Gaius Caligula had assumed the role that history would assign to him forever. A bloodbath soon followed: Macro was ordered to commit suicide, Tiberius Gemellus was beheaded, and those suspected of crimes or disloyalty were executed, some at Caligula's whim. Other peculiar schemes followed. A bridge of boards was stretched across the Bay of BAULI so that Gaius could parade back and forth over the water for days. In September of 39 he embarked on his self-proclaimed German campaign, marching with the Praetorian Guard. Instead of slaying Germans, he ordered the death of LENTULUS GAETULICUS, the governor of Germania Superior. After demonstrations on the Rhine and on the Channel, he wrote to the Senate that Britannia had been subdued and then he returned to Rome.

Once home his mammoth games and enjoyments emptied the treasury, forcing him to seek radical methods of increasing revenue. Every form of taxation was introduced, including the murder of those who had willed him their estates. It was a capital crime not to bequeath him everything. The activity of prostitutes was declared taxable, and a fee had to be paid on virtually every good or service. Tax regulations were posted, maintaining a semblance of legality, but they were printed in such small letters and plastered on such high pedestals that no one could read them. Gaius Caligula also demanded that he be worshiped as a god, and he once placed his own horse INCITATUS among the ranks of the Senate. As anyone suspected of any crime was instantly killed, the court and especially the Praetorian Guard grew increasingly restive. The result was a widespread conspiracy among the Guard, the Senate, the Equestrian ranks and the noble classes. On January 24, 41, Cassius CHAEREA, an embittered tribune of the Praetorians, aided by several other officers, assassinated Caligula during the *ludi,* slaughtering his wife, Caesonia, and infant daughter as well.

The most detailed account of Gaius Caligula's life comes from Suetonius, who describes him as tall, hairy, and bald, with a forbidding face, made even more so by grimaces, which he practiced before a mirror. Even Suetonius believed him to be deranged, listing his many crimes and manias, adding that his reign of terror had been so severe that the Romans refused to believe that he was actually dead.

See also CLAUDIUS; DRUSILLA; and JULIA. (6).

Suggested Readings: Barrett, Anthony. *Caligula: The Corruption of Power.* London: Batsford, 1989; Balsdon, J. P. V. D. *The Emperor Gaius (Caligula).* Oxford, U.K.: The Clarendon Press, 1966; Ferrill, Arthur. *Caligula: Emperor of Rome.* New York: Thames and Hudson, 1991; Hurley, Donna W. *An Historical and Historiographical Commentary on Suetonius' Life of C. Caligula.* Atlanta, Ga.: Scholars Press, 1993; Suetonius. *The Twelve Caesars.* Translated and with an introduction by Michael Grant. New York: Penguin, 1979; Tacitus, Cornelius. *Empire and Emperors: Selections from Tacitus' Annals.* Translated by Graham Tingay. New York: Cambridge University Press, 1983; Tacitus. *The Histories.* New York: Penguin, 1989.

Galatia Roman province; a region of Asia Minor surrounded by the territories of PAPHLAGONIA, PONTUS, CAPPADOCIA, LYCAONIA, PHRYGIA, and BITHYNIA. Galatia was a wild, harsh, and unsettled land, first occupied in the third century B.C.E. by wandering Gallic invaders, who not only lent their name to the country but also left a permanent imprint of Celtic culture. Subsequent populations introduced Cappadocian and Hellenic elements, creating a diverse racial stock. By the first century B.C.E., Galatia controlled much of its surroundings, and one ruler, DEIOTARUS, proved helpful to Rome in the Mithridatic Wars, assuming the status of king and Roman client. Augustus at first chose to retain Galatia as an ally, but in 25 B.C.E. its sovereign, Amyntas, died, and the region became the imperial province of Galatia. Administered originally by an imperial legate of Praetorian rank, the province was both important and large, containing portions of Lycaonia, Isauria, and, later, sections of Paphlagonia.

Provincial status was necessary as Armenia and the Parthian frontier were nearby, requiring firm control, stability and the presence of troops ready to defend Cappadocia, Armenia, and Syria from possible attack. Further, the Celtic tribes of Galatia were unsettled and Augustus placed at the legate's command enough troops to ensure security. The emperor also founded numerous colonies of former soldiers, the most important being ANTIOCH in PISIDIA. This network of communities tamed much of the wilderness, providing roads, communications between Syria and Asia, and a basis for future provincial developments. To better administer the Armenian border area, in 74 Vespasian elevated the governor of Galatia to consular rank, aided by three legates and two legions, with authority over Cappadocia and Armenia Minor. He then tightened jurisdiction by creating a new province, Lycia and Pamphylia, which included parts of Galatia.

In 110, Trajan placed the rule of Galatia in the hands of Cappadocia's Praetorian legate. Further reductions in status were probably made under Hadrian and Antoninus Pius, with the province losing Lycaonia and Isauria. Thus, from his seat at Ancyra (now Ankara), the governor no longer sent out generals but, instead, procurators to each district.

A number of significant cities developed in the region. Antioch achieved the status of metropolis, and it became the focus of Roman influence. Celtic culture survived into the fifth century in the tribes of the Tobistobogi, with their capital of Pessenus; the Trocmi, in Tavium; and the Tectosages, in Ancyra. But the tribesmen, in time, served as soldiers in the Roman army. Ancyra, because of its central location, was one of the best fortified points in Asia Minor, thus enduring the invasions and ravages of the third century far better than other sites. Baths, dating to the early third century C.E., have been uncovered; and a temple to Augustus has walls adorned with two copies of the *Res Gestae Divi Augustus,* the testament of Augustus's achievements, one in Greek and the other in Latin. Finally, Galatia attained prominence in the history of CHRISTIANITY because of Paul's work among its inhabitants. Many early Christians were Jewish converts, earning the enmity of the local Jewish population, and persecution was severe.

Galba (1) (fl. mid-first century C.E.) *Ruler of the tribe of the Suessiones in Gallia Belgica*
In 57 B.C.E., the BELGAE had grown alarmed by the crushing of the Germanic chief ARIOVISTUS at the hands of Julius Caesar. Eager to avoid the same fate, Galba allied himself with the surrounding tribes and prepared for war. Caesar marched into his territory, and Galba tried to oppose him with all available troops. A pitched battle ensued, and the king was defeated at the battle of AXONA.

See also GALLIC WARS.

Galba (2), Servius Sulpicius (3 B.C.E.–69 C.E.) *The first of four emperors who occupied the throne in 69 C.E.*
Galba was a member of the venerable Sulpicii family, born to Mummia Achaica and the partially humpbacked patrician, Gaius Sulpicius Galba. He received an excellent education and married Lepida, who bore him two sons. When she died, he embarked on a career in the legions and in the government. With the support and patronage of AUGUSTUS, LIVIA, TIBERIUS, GAIUS CALIGULA, and CLAUDIUS, Galba rose quickly. He was governor of Gallia Aquitania and a consul in 33. Gaius Caligula appointed him legate of GERMANIA Superior, where he acquired his reputation as a merciless disciplinarian. In 45 he served as proconsul of Africa, before assuming the post of governor in Hispania Tarraconensis for eight years during Nero's reign. He was severe at times (once he ordered a corrupt money changer's hand to be cut off and nailed to the counting table) but largely inactive, claiming (according to Suetonius) that Nero could not remove him for "no one can be held accountable for doing nothing."

In 68, Vindex, the legate in Gallia Lugdunensis, called for Galba to overthrow Nero. He at first declined, but in a declaration issued at New Carthage in Spain in April, he proclaimed himself the spokesman for the Senate and the people of Rome. After several weeks of doubt, word arrived that Nero was dead and that the Senate had named him emperor. Furthermore, the Praetorian Guard, led by Nymphidius SABINUS, had joined his cause.

Galba set out for Rome with his legions and on the way quickly began to alienate both the Guard and the Roman public. Sabinus was removed as prefect and replaced by Cornelius Laco. Knights and senators were murdered at whim; once installed in Rome, Galba listened only to Titus VINIUS, the freedman ICELUS, and Laco—unfortunate advisers who added to the emperor's rapidly increasing unpopularity. A dispute over monies was ultimately responsible for Galba's death. When the Praetorian Guard demanded the DONATIVUM that had been promised them by Sabinus, Galba responded: "I am used to levying troops, not buying them." The Praetorians then plotted against him, joined by OTHO, a onetime friend of Nero who as governor of Lusitania had supported Galba. When Galba overlooked Otho as the imperial heir in favor of Lucius Calpurnius Piso Licinianus, Otho led the plot to slay the emperor. On January 15, 69, the assassins struck. Both Galba and his heir were killed, their heads cut off and paraded around the *Castra Praetoria,* where Otho was proclaimed the master of Rome. VITELLIUS was already on the march with the Rhine legions, however, and the bloody civil wars of 69 began.

Galba was the first emperor not from the Julio-Claudian line and was yet another victim of the Praetorian Guards. The historians were not kind to his memory. Tacitus wrote of him as an aged and sick man, and Suetonius added that his fame and power were far greater as he assumed the purple than they were after he had it for a time.

Galen (Claudius Galenus) (c. 129–c. 200 C.E.) *One of the ancient world's most famous physicians and writers on medicine*

Galen was born in Pergamum, the son of an architect named Nicon, who dreamed one night that his son should become a doctor. Galen studied at Pergamum and then in Smyrna, Corinth, and Alexandria; his work with the anatomists of Alexandria may have been responsible for instilling an appreciation of the human form that would last for the rest of his career. In 157 Galen returned to Pergamum and began to work as an attendant to the gladiators of that city. By 162, with a growing reputation, he went to Rome to establish a practice. There he came to the attention of MARCUS AURELIUS. Galen served for a time as physician to Marcus and treated other notable political figures. Galen returned home to Pergamum again, but around 166–167 a plague broke out in Venetia in Italy, and Marcus sent for him. He remained in Rome for the next 30 years, where he was court physician to the emperors Marcus Aurelius, Lucius Verus, Commodus, and Septimius Severus, as well as to many other prominent men.

Galen's surviving works outnumber those of the other Greek doctors and were the main source for physiological and anatomical knowledge well into the 16th century. An early work on philosophy, *On Medical Experience,* written in 150, survived in Arabic. His later treatises on medicine were so numerous that he spent several of his last years trying to catalog his own books on anatomy, physiology, pathology, diagnosis, and pharmacology. His major works include *De methodo medendi* (The method of healing), *On the Movement of the Muscles, On the Natural Faculties,* and his greatest effort, *On Anatomical Procedure.*

Galerius (Gaius Galerius Valerius Maximianus) (d. 311 C.E.) *Coemperor from 293 to 311*

Galerius served in both the first and second tetrarchy and was one of the most ardent opponents of CHRISTIANITY in Roman history. As a youth he had been a herdsman but entered the army of AURELIAN and made his way through the ranks until 293, when he was chosen by DIOCLETIAN to form the tetrarchy; as Caesar, he was Diocletian's deputy in the East, while CONSTANTIUS I CHLORUS was Caesar to MAXIMIAN in the West. To ensure his position, Galerius divorced his wife and married VALERIA, Diocletian's daughter.

In 294–295, he worked to restore order on the shaky Danube frontier, which demanded constant fighting in Pannonia. In 296 he was ordered by Diocletian to Syria, where Narses, the Persian ruler, had launched a major assault against Rome. An initial counterattack was a disaster, but Galerius attempted another one in 298 and captured Armenia and Mesopotamia as well as one of the Persian capitals, Ctesiphon. Galerius was honored and returned to the Balkans, where THESSALONICA was transformed into a suitable metropolis for his residence, complete with an arch commemorating his victory over the Persians.

With his victory behind him, Galerius took steps to improve his position in the tetrarchy. He became more active in Diocletian's decision-making, according to the historian Lactantius, and successfully demanded the most severe persecutions of Christians, supported by his mother, Romula, an ardent pagan. The edicts of persecution, especially the third and fourth, destroyed churches and books and enforced a death penalty on Christians.

In May 305, Diocletian and Maximian formally abdicated in favor of their deputies. Galerius now shared power with Constantius but actually commanded true imperial supremacy by holding all of the East and much of the West. Furthermore, the two new Caesars, Maximin Daia and Severus II, were clients. Constantius died in 306 at Eburacum (York), and Galerius named Severus Augustus, elevating Constantius's son CONSTANTINE to the rank of Caesar to form a new tetrarchy. This political maneuver was defeated by Maximian's son MAXENTIUS, who seized Rome, Italy, and part of Africa, declaring himself the rightful heir to the throne of his father. Severus tried to crush Maxentius but failed, and even Galerius himself was repulsed. Maxentius put Severus to death, and only the ultimately unsuccessful Conference of CARNUNTUM staved off the demise of the tetrarchy.

Galerius remained in full control of the East until an illness struck him in 311. Lactantius recorded in vengeful detail the extent of Galerius's suffering, describing the slow, agonizing deterioration of his health, replete with sores and hideous stinking worms. Amid this "heaven sent" death, Galerius signed a new edict, joined by his fellow tetrarchs, rescinding all previous anti-Christian proclamations. Henceforth, Christianity was to be tolerated and allowed to propagate freely in the empire. Eusebius, Lactantius, and other writers ascribed his remorse to divine intervention. Galerius succumbed at Easter, 311, and was buried in his hometown of Romulianum.

Galilee

The most northerly of the three main districts of Roman-occupied PALAESTINA, containing such notable cities as Capernaum, GISCHALA and Nazareth. Its population was composed of Phoenicians, Syrians, Greeks, and Jews, making it not only a difficult place to rule but also a land subject to terrible internal strife, as the Jewish population disliked its northern neighbors. Galilee served as a territorial pawn on numerous occasions. It was part of the tetrarchy of HEROD ANTIPAS, bequeathed to him by HEROD THE GREAT and granted to him by Augustus as well. In 40 C.E., Gaius Caligula stripped Antipas of his entire tetrarchy, handing it to Herod Agrippa I, who ruled it until his death in 44 C.E., when a procurator was appointed to administer JUDAEA. Herod Agrippa II eventually took over the domain of Herod of Chalcis, and Nero added a large portion of Galilee as part of his Trans-Jordan realm in 61 C.E. For the next five years the Roman procurators earned the enmity of the Jews, and in 66 their rage erupted into the Jewish rebellion. The troubles in Galilee were recorded in some detail by the official sent to lead the Jews there, Flavius JOSEPHUS. Galilee was overrun by the legions of Vespasian in 67. From the time of Hadrian in the mid-second century C.E. the entire area was possessed by Syria-Palestine.

Galla, Satria (d. after 65 C.E.) *Wife of C. Calpurnius Piso, the famed conspirator against Nero*

Galla had been married to Domitius Silo, a friend of Piso, but he had induced her to leave her husband and become his wife. In 65, as the plot to remove Nero was exposed, Piso committed suicide and, out of love for his wife, wrote a flattering letter to Nero imploring mercy for her. Nero granted clemency to Galla.

Gallia

Roman name for the province of Gaul, roughly embracing modern France and the Low Countries; one of the largest areas under imperial control in the Roman Empire. In 50 B.C.E., Julius CAESAR departed from Gaul, embroiled in the Civil War with POMPEY THE GREAT, leaving behind him a country broken in will and subdued (*see* GALLIC WARS). The sizable conquests he had made for Rome brought whole populations under Rome's control. He named this new territory Gallia Comata but initiated several administrative changes over the next few years. While Gallia Transalpina (GALLIA NARBONENSIS) was at first a part of Gallia Comata, in 44 B.C.E. he separated it, recognizing that it was too Romanized. What was left he split into two parts under legates controlling the Rhine frontier and watching the troublesome tribes there, especially the SUEBI. This done, he then founded the first of the Italian colonies at LUGDUNUM (Lyons) and at Augst.

This arrangement, however, lacked an effective or logical organization, combining very different cultures under one legate. AUGUSTUS, coming to power after the battle of ACTIUM in 31 B.C.E., took upon himself the task of establishing a better policy. He was aided by Marcus AGRIPPA and the census taken among the Gallic tribes around Lugdunum in 27 B.C.E. To the SENATE he gave authority over Gallia Narbonensis in 22, taking for himself the rest and breaking it into three imperial provinces, formed along the lines of race, language, and community. In the south was Gallia Aquitania, with its more Iberian or Spanish people. Next came Gallia Lugdunensis, the home of the CELTS in Gaul, and then Gallia Belgica, with its mix of Celtic and Germanic nations.

The most southern of the three imperial provinces, Aquitania was initially conquered in 56 B.C.E. by the legate of Julius Caesar, Publius Crassus (*see* AQUITANIA). When Gallia Aquitania was established as a province, its boundary was set along the geographic limits of the Pyrenees, the Atlantic and the two rivers, the Loire and the Rhone. Provincial administration was probably conducted from BURDIGALA, the heart of Aquitania, situated on the Garonne River, although Poitiers and Saintes were thriving economic centers. In time, Aquitania sent its own senators to Rome.

The most Romanized of the three provinces, Lugdunensis was centered around the important city of Lugdunum (Lyons). A mint was also situated there, and the city served as the seat of administration for the legate. Boundaries for the province were established to the east and south by three rivers: the Loire, Saône, and Seine. Aside from Lugdunum, other notable cities were AUGUSTDONUM, the famous ALESIA, and LUTETIA (Paris). In the first years of Rome's rule, this province was watched most closely because of the traditionally fierce and powerful tribes of the AEDUI and AVERNI.

Gallia Belgica was the most northern province of Gallia, stretching from the Seine to the Rhine, and as far south as the Saône. With its location so near the Rhine, Gallia Belgica was considered the cornerstone of the regional imperial policy. Provincial government was centered at RHEIMS, while other officials chose TRIER (Treveri) as their headquarters, most notably the procurators of both Belgica and the two Germanies. The original inhabitants, the BELGAE, were a less civilized culture, mixing the Druidic-Celtic way of life with the Germanic dislike of Rome. They developed into *civitates* of remarkable wealth, with cities such as Amiens and Bavay.

By Italian standards Gaul was appallingly underdeveloped and primitive, untouched by outside influences, and even unlike other Celtic lands, most notably Britain (BRITANNIA). Romanization was only marginally successful in Gaul, and the Celts not only survived but also, with a number of compromises, actually flourished.

The Romans put great importance on the rise and use of large towns and cities, fostering economic life and political control. The Celts transposed their cantonal constitutional governments (self-sufficient districts) into towns, thus perpetuating the status of local nobility. While Rome, especially under Caesar and Augustus, tolerated the cantonal pattern, two major steps were later taken to curb its nationalistic tendency and to bring it under imperial administration. First, the number of cantons was reduced from the hundreds of tribes during the Gallic Wars to a more sensible 64. For the Roman magistrates such a number, divided into three provinces, was more manageable, and the number continued to drop over the succeeding years. Each of these cantons, redesignated a *civitas* (city-state), was invested with the full privileges handed out to communities all over the empire. Roman government therefore existed, with all of its requirements and bureaucracy, in conjunction with the original and semi-independent Gallic communities. What was needed was a larger unifying creed to tie the Gauls directly to the Roman imperial state.

Throughout the provinces Augustus initiated the IMPERIAL CULT, the idea of worshiping the emperors and Rome, which was propagated in the CONCILIA, the councils of each province conceived to maintain communication between the ruler and the actual people of the many lands that he commanded. Julius Caesar had found such a group useful in Gaul, summoning together major chieftains to hear their opinions and to receive their adulation. The idea was virtually unknown in the West in the early imperial epoch. The first of the *concilia* was initiated around 12 B.C.E., with the help of TIBERIUS's brother DRUSUS. Each *civitas* sent a delegation to Lugdunum, and there elections were held to supply members for a *concilium*, including a president. The *concilium* conducted minor secular affairs (preserving a veneer of self-government) but was wholly responsible for holding the annual festival in honor of the emperor and Rome. People from all four Gallic provinces traveled to Lugdunum to see the games, ceremonies, and feasts, described in a lengthy report sent to Rome.

Each canton or *civitas* endeavored to achieve success and prosperity, fostering both the betterment of cities and the continued economic growth of an already bountiful country. The provinces of Gallia produced wheat, olives, oil, wine, cheese, ham, fruits, vegetables, and corn. They kept the legions on the Rhine well fed, with a surplus that required, for a time, restriction on exports from the provinces in order to allow the Italians to absorb the economic input. The old Celtic skills in metallurgy and carving were maintained, and Gallic workmanship in jewelry and art was known throughout the provinces. Long periods of peace allowed strides in industry, so that textile, wood, and glass manufacturing developed. Especially noted were Gaul's potters, who eventually exported their wares, and its wine.

Aiding the economy was an advanced network of communication and transportation. Ports in Brittany, at Gesoriacum, Bordeaux (Burdigala), Massilia, Narbo, and Forum Julium loaded ships with items sent from along the many waterways traversing the provinces. The Seine, Loire, Garonne, Rhone, Saône, and Moselle Rivers all contributed to the waterborne commerce, supplementing an extensive road circuit.

The general success of Rome in the provinces of Gaul served only to heighten their prime strategic importance. Just beyond the heavily guarded frontier lay the seething tribes of Germany. A legate in Gallia Belgica supervised the border until the seriousness of the Germanic frontier convinced DOMITIAN, around 90 C.E., to transfer the responsibility to a Roman legion and establish provinces in GERMANIA as well. Still, evidence of the role that Gaul played in the safeguarding of the early empire can be found in the list of its early commanders: Agrippa, Augustus himself from 16 to 13 B.C.E., Tiberius, Drusus, and the famous GERMANICUS, from 12 to 15 C.E. The LEGIONS, however, were never stationed in Gaul, so peaceful had the region become. A form of the URBAN COHORTS, or local police, proved sufficient for centuries, although the tribes supplied large numbers of recruits for the legions and the *auxilia*.

Until the decline of the empire in the West, Gaul knew little hardship or war, and the use of Latin became commonplace. In the first century C.E., the attempted revolts of SACROVIR, VINDEX, and Julius CIVILIS all failed because the tribes on whom they depended for support refused to join them or were split by their loyalties to Rome and knew what a barbarian invasion would mean. The Imperium Galliarum established by the usurper POSTUMUS (c. 261–268) was the product of an ambitious general and not the longing of the Gallic peoples. In fact, throughout the catastrophes of the third century C.E., Gallia survived better than many regions by virtue of its location as the gateway to Britain, Germany, and Spain. Its craftsmen and artists furthered their economic monopoly of foreign markets because war ravaged other areas.

Unfortunately their excellent position ensured that the barbarian invasions of the fifth century would slash and burn through the heart of the Gallic people's domain. In late December, 406, the VANDALS, ALANS, BURGUNDIANS, and Suevians poured across the Rhine. With the Roman Empire of the West in shambles, opposition came only from the usurper CONSTANTINE III, but he was defeated eventually, and the hordes just kept coming. Its cities destroyed, fields burned, economy in ruins, and culture annihilated, the province was broken. The Vandals who seized Aquitania and Narbonensis pillaged even the lovely city of Bordeaux. The Franks eventually emerged supreme, and Gallia entered the next stage of its history, the era called the Dark Ages.

Suggested Readings: Caesar, Julius. *The Conquest of Gaul.* Translated by S. A. Hanford. New York: Penguin, 1982;

Ebel, Charles. *Transalpine Gaul: The Emergence of a Roman Province*. Leiden: Brill, 1976; Drinkwater, J. F. *Roman Gaul: The Three Provinces, 58 B.C.–A.D. 260*. Ithaca, N.Y.: Cornell University Press, 1983; King, Anthony. *Roman Gaul and Germany*. Berkeley: University of California Press, 1990; Van Dam, Raymond. *Leadership and Community in Late Antique Gaul*. Berkeley: University of California Press, 1985.

Gallia Cisalpina   Name given to the region of northern Italy and in use for centuries prior to the foundation of the Roman Empire. Geographically, Gallia Cisalpina was surrounded by GALLIA NARBONENSIS, the Alps, Raetia, Noricum, and Illyricum to the west, north, and east. To the south were the Italian sections of Etruria and Umbria. Traditional dividing lines between the territory and the other provinces were the Alps and the famed RUBICON River, marking the beginning of Italy proper.

Gallia Cisalpina was originally the home of the Etruscans and other Italian peoples, most notably the Umbrians and Ligurians. They were expelled by the Gauls, who desired their land because of its natural beauty and fertility but were in turn subdued by the Romans in the third and second centuries B.C.E. Henceforth, Gallia Cisalpina was a province under Roman control, but its tribes, such as the Taurini, Cenomani, and Insubres, were not fully mastered for some years.

When final Roman mastery was achieved, the implantation of colonies commenced. The sense of foreignness could be removed quickly, and the province remained part of the strategic line of defense, protecting Italy from invasion; Cisalpine, aided by Gallia Transalpina (Narbonensis) and Illyricum, formed a strong corridor of provincial safety. When Julius CAESAR received his five-year commission to govern the Gallic world, included in his command were these three holdings. The great general himself wintered in Gallia Cisalpina each year so as to remain alert to Italian and Roman political developments. In 50 B.C.E., when he had finished his GALLIC WARS and was marching on Rome, it was through this region that he went. The boundary of the Rubicon then assumed momentous importance.

Throughout the CIVIL WARS of the First and Second Triumvirates, Gallia Cisalpina was the scene of troop movements and political appointments. BRUTUS ALBINUS received the province to govern in 44 B.C.E., but he was delayed in taking up his post because of his participation in Caesar's assassination. When he did finally try to assume command, Marc ANTONY involved him in battles around Mutina, and he later died. In the agreements of the Second Triumvirate, Octavian (AUGUSTUS) held Cisalpine Gaul until after Actium, in 31 B.C.E., when he became emperor. In 25 B.C.E., as part of his general reorganization of the Roman world, Augustus declared Italy to be a special province and placed Gallia Cisalpina within its jurisdiction. Of note, the Po Valley bisected Gallia Cisalpina and formed two distinct areas within it: Gallia Transpadana to the north of the river and Gallia Cispadana to the south.

Gallia Narbonensis   Originally called Gallia Transalpina; one of the four large provinces of Gaul (GALLIA), along with Gallia Aquitania, Lugdunensis, and Belgica. It was the oldest and most important Roman possession in Gaul. The province was bordered by the Pyrenees, the Mediterranean, the provinces of *Tres Galliae*, the Alps, and the Rhine. In the earliest days of Roman expansion, Gallia Transalpina attracted Rome's attention, especially with its Greek colony at MASSILIA and its prime location between Italy and the growing Roman possessions in Spain. The need for stable lines of communication, protection of the trade with the Gallic and Helvetian tribes, and its sheer financial potential, prompted annexation around 121 B.C.E. From that time until the fifth century C.E., Gallia Narbonensis was a permanent and reliable territory.

A small degree of Romanization was felt during the initial years of occupation, but not enough to reduce the importance of Hellenic Massilia or to warrant comparisons with Spain, which bore a deep Italian imprint. Julius CAESAR, who arrived in 58 B.C.E., began the real cultural transformation of the land, called in his own annals simply "the province." He launched his GALLIC WARS from there and not only founded new colonies that would become major metropolises but also resurrected any older colonies that had declined.

The colony of NARBO, formed probably under the Gracchi in the late second century B.C.E., was given a new breath of life. Other new *coloniae* (COLONIES) , formed with stout veterans and artisans, were FORUM JULIUM (Frejus) and ARLES. AUGUSTUS carried on Caesar's policies but also expanded and improved upon them. As part of his reorganization of the Roman Empire, he declared the province a senatorial possession, under the administrative concern of a proconsul. Gallia Narbonensis flowered both as an economic entity and as a unique transplant of Roman culture and lifestyle. The capital was Narbo, to which were added many new cities and colonies, especially in the Rhone Valley. The old Greek and Celtic ways surrendered to the new, in return for the benefits that Rome offered. Native communities, most importantly Nîmes (Nemausus), first received municipal status and Latin rights (IUS LATII) and finally full colonial privileges. Arles, Orange (Arausio), Vienne, and Vaison were only a few of the Roman-transformed cities, joined by Ruscino (Roussillon), Aquae Sextiae (Aix), and Avennio (Avignon). Latin emerged as the language of government and preference. Roman and Italian architecture dominated, and the Latin community and local system of government replaced the Celtic cantons. Gallia Narbonensis surpassed Spain in assimilation.

Being very Mediterranean in climate and environment, the province produced fruits in abundance. Agriculture was the mainstay of the local economy, with wines of high quality and excellent olives. There were cereals as well. Its pottery, made by skilled artisans, traveled throughout the world. Even the regional trade was enhanced by the improvement of the Rhone Valley waterways and the continued development of the Roman ROADS.

While incentives and Romanization played major roles in the continued vitality of Gallia Narbonensis, it benefited from centuries of peace. No invasion or major disaster came to its precincts from the time of Augustus until the fourth century C.E. Only the economic collapse of the empire in the third century C.E. and the chaotic state of the Western lands in the fourth and fifth centuries opened up the province to occupation and destruction. Then, with its defenses stripped away, ATHAULF took control in 415 and ravaged much of northern Narbonensis on his way through Aquitania and into Tarraconensis. In the subsequent disintegration of the imperial machine, the province received the same treatment as other lands at the hands of a multitude of conquerors.

Such catastrophes were many years in the future when Augustus became emperor, and Gallia Narbonensis not only earned a reputation for wine but also achieved actual fame for its local citizens. In the first century C.E., there were Domitius AFER and MONTANUS, ASIATICUS, and the Praetorian prefect Sextus Afranius BURRUS. In the second century, the province achieved its highest moment when ANTONINUS PIUS, born to a family from Nîmes, ascended the throne in 138. By the end of the century his native city was the foremost center of provincial life, replacing Narbo, which never recovered from a fire (c. 150). Antoninus Pius epitomized Pliny the Elder's comment that Gallia Narbonensis and Italy were one and the same.

Gallia Transalpina *See* GALLIA NARBONENSIS.

Gallicus, Julius (fl. mid-first century C.E.) *Orator (Advocatus) during the reign of Claudius*
In 53 C.E. Gallicus was defending a case before the emperor with such vigor that *Claudius* became angry and had him thrown into the Tiber. When one of Gallicus's clients, seeking a new legal representative, went to the famous speaker AFER for help, Afer responded: "Who told you that I could swim better than he?"

Gallic Wars Conflicts between the Roman LEGIONS under the command of Julius CAESAR and the many tribes of Gaul (GALLIA); waged between 58 and 51 B.C.E. These wars demonstrated the genius of Julius Caesar, the skills of the legions, the indomitable spirit of the Gauls and the damage that could be inflicted on cities, territories, and entire populations in Rome's drive to world domination.

In 60 B.C.E., the FIRST TRIUMVIRATE was formed among Caesar, POMPEY THE GREAT, and CRASSUS. Although Caesar had been largely responsible for the rise of this political union, Pompey was considered the greater general and the foremost politician. Caesar recognized that, just as Pompey had attained power and fame by subduing and claiming the East, he too needed to find glory in the field. His eyes turned to Gaul.

Marius, his uncle, had defeated the marauding tribes in the provinces of GALLIA CISALPINA and Gallia Transalpina. Furthermore, from Gaul he would always be capable of marching immediately to Italy in times of crisis and could be apprised of news from Rome. Thus, in 59 B.C.E., a tribune of Caesar's own party, Vatinius, made the proposal to the Senate that Caesar be granted the governorship of ILLYRICUM, Gallia Cisalpina and Gallia Transalpina for five years. At his disposal were a quaestor, 10 legates and four legions. With this army, totaling around 35,000 men, the general set out to make history.

In his account of the Gallic Wars, Caesar wrote that Gaul was divided by three: the Belgae, the Aquitani, and the Celtae tribes, different from each other in language, government, and laws. Early in 58 B.C.E., these tribes were threatened by the Helvetii, the people of HELVETIA (modern Switzerland), who were on the march in vast numbers toward southern Gaul, as part of a wider pattern of migration and resettlement. Gathering together all available troops, Caesar surprised the advancing horde at the ARAR River. A battle followed, in which some 30,000 Helvetii were annihilated. In July of that year another engagement took place at BIBRACTE; the Helvetians struck first, but they were repulsed, pushed back into their camp, and massacred. Some 130,000 to 150,000 men, women, and children were slain. Only 110,000 Helvetians were left to begin the long march home, and Caesar noted that he had earned the acclaim of Gaul's many chieftains.

By August Caesar turned his attentions to another foreign threat, this time from the Germanic King ARIOVISTUS. In modern Alsace, Ariovistus and his warriors were conducting a campaign of terror among the local tribes, especially the AEDUI and the AVERNI. Caesar wished for no other masters in Gaul and accepted a Gallic request for assistance. Only one battle was necessary, and Ariovistus was thrown across the Rhine, having lost most of his army. Satisfied that external problems were eased, Caesar entered winter quarters to plan his next move.

The year 57 B.C.E. began with disturbing news from Gallia Belgica. Local tribes had risen and were united into a strong anti-Roman coalition. To prevent their movement out of Belgica, which would promote a widespread rebellion in the region, the legions were ordered to march. The Romans pushed into Belgica in late spring, defeating an army at AXONA under King GALBA (1). This victory, however, was not enough to convince the other people of Belgica about Roman superiority, and the Nervii ambushed Caesar at SABIS in July; a bitter, bloody battle took place until legionary discipline won out. Following up on his triumph, Caesar besieged and captured the important city of ADUATUCA, ending all effective resistance in Gallia Belgica. The BELGAE had lived up to Caesar's description of them as the greatest warriors in Gaul.

Caesar rested in Gallia Cisalpina for the winter and early in 56 B.C.E. set out against the tribes of western Gaul. The VENETI of Armorica (modern Brittany) fell under assault while Publius CRASSUS subdued AQUITANIA. A sea battle between BRUTUS ALBINUS and the ships of the Veneti helped seal Armorica's fate. Crassus was also successful, joined by Titurius SABINUS, who had seized Normandy by vanquishing the Venelli. These notable achievements symbolized the near total ownership of Gaul by the Romans, but they were offset by Caesar's inability to pacify two tribes of Belgica, the Morini and the Menapii. Hampered by foul weather and the on-slaught of winter, Caesar contented himself with the destruction of their villages, forests, and fields before going into winter quarters.

Further steps to establish Roman rule over the reign were delayed because of a major crisis in 55 B.C.E. Ger-manic tribes, the USIPETES and the Tencteri, pushed by the stronger SUEBI, crossed the Rhine and tried to settle in Gaul along the Meuse River. Perhaps half a million Ger-mans were living in the area, and Caesar, facing a poten-tial crisis of staggering importance, first tried to negotiate with them, in vain. When war ensued, Caesar allowed his soldiers to wipe out the tribes, slaughtering hundreds of thousands. Those who survived asked to be placed under his protection.

To impress upon the Germans the futility of crossing the Rhine, Caesar constructed a large bridge over the river in June of that year. He then ordered his men across to intimidate the people on the other side. This demon-stration ended, Caesar started his invasion of Britain (BRI-TANNIA), returning to Gaul to maintain a watch on the increasingly mutinous nations there.

Logistical problems and food shortages forced the legions in Gaul to winter in eight scattered camps. This strategic error invited the Gallic communities to rebel. AMBIORIX, leader of the Eburones, organized around 100,000 men and launched an assault against Titurius Sabinus near Aduatuca. In the subsequent conflict, Sabi-nus was destroyed, and the Gauls moved against Quintus Cicero but were repulsed. Caesar marched into Belgica, forced a battle on unequal terms and suppressed Ambiorix. Meanwhile, his lieutenant LABIENUS defended his camp and repelled Indutiomarus. He then joined Cae-sar as the Roman troops united to face what was antici-pated as a vaster revolt the following year.

At the start of 53 B.C.E., all Gaul erupted. Caesar decided to take the war to the enemy, and with some 10 legions crushed the NERVII, Senones, Carnutes, Menapii, and the TREVERI. Another sortie over the Rhine convinced the Suebi to curb any impulse toward entering the fray; once back in Belgica, Caesar pursued and harried the Gauls into submission, driving Ambiorix from the region.

As soon as one Gallic chieftain was vanquished, how-ever, another appeared. Throughout late 53 B.C.E., the leader of the Averni, VERCINGETORIX, prepared his army, supplied it, trained it, and used discipline and organiza-tion to make it formidable. At the start of 52 B.C.E. he struck, knowing that Caesar was in Italy. By the time the general returned, he faced hostile country between him and Labienus, to the north near LUTETIA (Paris). Pushing ahead, Caesar swept the field, taking Villaunodunum Cenabum (ORLEANS), and Noviodonum.

A siege of AVARICUM netted Caesar a brilliant victory. However, his momentum was lost in May, when he hur-riedly tried to capture GERGOVIA, the capital of the Averni, and suffered defeat and an enforced withdrawal. Labienus was able to extricate himself from the north, uniting with Caesar as he was making countermoves. Caesar swung into the Aedui and then punished Vercingetorix at Vingeanne. Unable to rout the Romans, the Gauls retired to ALESIA to await a siege. From July to the fall of 52 B.C.E., Caesar conducted a masterful opera-tion in siege warfare enduring massive sorties from within the city and from outside forces. Starving, Vercingetorix surrendered. Caesar accepted the submis-sion of the Aedui and the Averni, effectively ending all Gallic resistance. In another year, the entire region was pacified and given the new name of Gallia Comata.

For nearly eight years Julius Caesar fought the peo-ple of Gaul. He was responsible for the deaths of as many as one million people, furthering the spread of Roman might and prestige. So thoroughly did he accomplish his task that, with the exception of a few notable rebellions (*see* CIVILIS and VINDEX), the vast region of Gaul became one of the most loyal in the empire.

Caesar's own commentary, *The Gallic Wars*, is the most detailed account of the campaign.

Gallienus, Publius Licinius Egnatius (d. 268 C.E.)
Emperor from 253 to 268

Gallienus ruled the Roman Empire during an era of politi-cal, military, and social crisis. The son of VALERIAN, he was living in Rome at the time of his father's accession in 253 and received the title of Caesar from the Senate after it confirmed Valerian as the new emperor. He was elevated to Augustus or coruler when his father reached Rome later in the year. While Valerian labored to restore order in the East, Gallienus worked from 254 to 260 to bolster the sagging West, fighting with the GOTHS, CARPI, Germans, MARCOMANNI, QUADI, FRANKS, and ALAMANNI along a wide frontier that stretched from the Rhine to the Danube.

Word then arrived in 259–260 that Valerian had been defeated and captured by the Persian King SHAPUR I. Gal-lienus was unable to respond, while Valerian was humili-ated and tortured to death. The ensuing political chaos gave birth to usurpers in every corner of the empire, including one INGENUUS, the governor of PANNONIA, who was put down and killed by Gallienus himself, aided by his cavalry commander, AUREOLUS. REGALIANUS, governor of Upper Pannonia, revolted next and his elimination was followed by the rise of General POSTUMUS in Gaul. Postumus besieged Gallienus's heir SALONINUS at COLOGNE, forcing him to surrender and then putting him to death. Gallienus could not respond because of his own wounds and the exhausted state of his legions. The rebellions of the general in the East, MACRIANUS, and his sons were ended by ODAENATH of PALMYRA, who proved an able and reliable friend of Rome, fighting for years to push back the Persian menace from SYRIA, ARMENIA, and MESOPOTAMIA.

The Goths and the Heruli entered imperial territory, ravaging Asia Minor and Greece in 267. In 268, Gallienus met and destroyed most of the HERULI at Naissus, only to find out that behind him, at Mediolanum (Milan), his lieutenant Aureolus had taken the city and had declared himself emperor. Gallienus's position was precarious, because Aureolus commanded an elite cavalry force formed with the express intention of defeating the barbarians. Aided by his generals, Gallienus besieged Aureolus, but conspiracies developed, and in 268 he was assassinated by his Praetorian Prefect Heraclianus and a group of officers including AURELIAN and CLAUDIUS II GOTHICUS, who both would become emperors.

For 15 years Gallienus was involved in incessant warfare, trying to stem the tide of disaster and decline. At his death the Roman Empire was little more secured. Odaenath was killed in 267, and his realm fell into the hands of his ambitious wife, ZENOBIA. Postumus controlled Gaul, and the frontiers were precarious. Economically, the provinces suffered from a debasement of currency. The sources, most notably the *Scriptores Historiae Augustae*, treated his reign with contempt. Nonetheless, the achievements of his reign included an end to the persecution of Christians begun by his father, the development of a formidable cavalry and a patronage of culture and the arts.

Gallio, Junius (d. 32 C.E.) *Senator*

Reputed in his time to be a brilliant speaker, Gallio was an associate of Lucius Aelius SEJANUS but survived the bloody fall of the prefect in 31. However, in 32 he made an ill-advised suggestion concerning the Praetorian Guard and was accused of treason against Tiberius. Temporarily exiled to Lesbos, Gallio was returned to Rome and placed under permanent imprisonment. The writer Quintilian mentions him but criticizes his oratorical skill.

Gallio, Lucius Annaeanus Junius (d. c. 65 C.E.) *Son of Seneca the Elder*

Brother of the great philosopher SENECA THE YOUNGER, Annaeus Novatus was adopted by the senator and orator Junius Gallio. He held the proconsulship of ACHAEA (51–52 C.E.) and presided over the famous trial of St. PAUL in CORINTH, uttering the line that he "cared for none of these things" (*Acts*, 18.12). In 65, following the death of his brother, Gallio was accused of conspiracies and denounced by Salienus Clemens. Although acquitted, he received only a temporary reprieve.

Gallus, Aelius (fl. late first century B.C.E.) *Prefect of Egypt during the reign of Augustus (27 B.C.E.–14 C.E.)*

Most noted for his unsuccessful expedition to conquer the country of ARABIA Felix in 25 B.C.E., Gallus's had hoped to establish Roman dominion over all of Arabia and use it as a powerful and financially rewarding base of trade between Egypt and the Far East. He received permission from Augustus and made his preparations, launching his campaign from the Suez-area city of Arsinoe. Delays of various sorts hampered progress, and it was not until early 24 B.C.E. that Gallus and his force of some 10,000 men actually started out. The march through the desert was terrible, even with the help of the king of the Nabateans, a Roman ally named Aretas. Arabia Felix stretched on and on, and after reaching the major city of Mariba, Gallus had to retreat because of a lack of water. He admitted defeat and marched home to Alexandria to find that in his absence the Ethiopians had attacked southern Egypt. Some good came from the campaign, however, for the natives of Arabia Felix soon established relations with Rome, impressed by Gallus's audacity.

Gallus, Appius Annius (fl. mid-first century C.E.) *General who distinguished himself in the campaigns of the year 69 C.E.*

Annius Gallus joined the cause of OTHO, who had helped to murder Galba and then succeeded him on the throne. The legate was given immediate opportunity to display his loyalty, being sent to northern Italy by Otho, with Vestricius Spurinna and a large forward guard, to defend against the advancing legions from the Rhine who supported VITELLIUS. While Spurinna held Placentia, Gallus moved across the Po with several contingents and took up a defensive position around Mantua. He was thus free to aid Spurinna when the Vitellian general, A. Alienus Caecina, tried to storm Placentia. Gallus was little needed, for the defense of that city was fierce.

By April the armies of Otho and Vitellius were maneuvering for strategic advantage, and Gallus prepared his men to march to the main camp at BEDRIACUM. A fall from a horse impaired him, however, and he was unable to attend the final council of war personally. He sent a messenger with the advice to delay battle, as the Othonians were seriously outnumbered. Gallus missed the battle of Bedriacum on April 15, 69, but rode to the area afterward to try and organize Otho's shattered legions. He could not prevent the emperor from committing suicide.

After Vitellius came to power in Rome, Gallus temporarily disappeared from the public eye. Vitellius fell in December of 69, and Gallus was summoned by C. Licinius Mucianus, the representative of the victor, VESPASIAN. Mucianus asked for Gallus's help, and he gave it. Julius Civilis, a one-time Roman soldier and the leader of the Batavi, had started a revolt on the Rhine. Gallus was sent with Petilius Cerealis to stamp out the rebellion; the province of Germania Superior to be his command while Cerealis had the tougher assignment of facing Civilis. Within months the tribes were subdued, and Gallus possessed the goodwill of the new Flavian regime.

Gallus, Aulus Didius (fl. mid-first century C.E.) *Governor of Britain (Britannia) from 51 to 57 C.E.*

Gallus first came to imperial attention around 41 C.E., when Claudius used him to depose the unreliable ruler of the Bosporus kingdom, Mithridates. Gallus was probably the legate of Moesia at the time, and his garrison remained until 49, when Mithridates tried unsuccessfully to oust his successor, Cotys. In 51–52, Gallus was appointed to fill the position of the legate P. Ostorious Scapula, who had died, probably of exhaustion. The new governor of Britain did little to improve upon the work of his predecessors, preferring to maintain the province's status quo. His tenure of command was eventually extended into 57, when he was replaced by Q. Veranius.

Gallus, Cestius (d. c. 66 C.E.) *Governor of Syria during the early phases of the Jewish rebellion in 66*

Cestius was sent to the East c. 65 to replace the famous Gnaeus Domitius Corbulo as administrator of Syria. While he controlled the legions of the province and had bureaucratic mastery over Judaea, his powers were limited when compared to those of his predecessor. That proved unfortunate, as Gallus was unprepared to deal with the impending crisis in Judaea, demonstrating his incompetence when approached during a visit to Jerusalem in 65 by Jewish leaders with complaints about the corrupt procurator of Judaea, Gessius Florus.

The following year, the Jewish rebellion was launched, and Gallus gathered the XII Legion and marched on Palestine. Reaching the gates of Jerusalem, Gallus realized too late his untenable strategic situation, as most of Judaea had overthrown Roman garrisons and rule. The retreat deteriorated in the Judaean heat into a full rout, and Gallus hastened the full rebellion in the region. Gallus took steps to restore order in Galilee but died soon after from illness or exhaustion. He was replaced by the future emperor Vespasian.

Gallus, Gaius Asinius (d. 33 C.E.) *Senator and consul in 8 B.C.E.*

The son of the famous orator C. Asinius Pollio, Gallus followed his father's style of blunt speaking and was the object of intense dislike on the part of Emperor Tiberius for his decision to marry the emperor's former wife, Vipsania. Gallus first offended Tiberius by his determined calls for lavish funeral arrangements for the deceased emperor Augustus. Gallus then wed Vipsania (whom Tiberius had been forced to divorce in order to marry the adulterous daughter of Augustus, Julia, and so secure his connection to the throne) and cultivated friendships with known enemies of the emperor, most notably Agrippina the Elder.

Summoning Gallus to Capri in 30, Tiberius arrested him, put him in chains, and then placed him in prison. For three years, Gallus was tormented and slowly starved to death, finally dying sometime in 33. Tiberius then permitted a decent funeral, commenting that he had not been given a chance to try Gallus properly. According to Tacitus, Augustus had described Gallus as a man harboring ambitions for the throne but lacking in the intelligence necessary to achieve such a lofty position. Of Gallus's five sons, three became consuls of Rome.

Gallus, Gaius Cornelius (70–26 B.C.E.) *Poet, soldier, and the first prefect of Egypt*

Born in the town of Forum Julii, Gallus eventually became a member of the Equestrian Order (EQUITES). Early on he joined the cause of Octavian (AUGUSTUS) and received commands in the CIVIL WAR of the Second TRIUMVIRATE. He took over control of the Antonian legions of L. Pinarius Scarpus in 30 B.C.E., using them to march on Egypt. Showing daring and initiative, Gallus took control of the city of Paraetonium, holding it against Marc Antony and thus ensuring Octavian's victory and the end of Cleopatra.

As a reward for his exploits and his friendship, Augustus appointed him the prefect of Egypt, a highly prized position. Noted for his merciless suppression of Egyptian opposition Gallus also erected statues of himself all over the new province and carved self-proclaiming inscriptions at Philae and on the pyramids. Augustus punished him for such ingratitude by refusing him friendship. Always eager to accommodate the emperor, the Senate condemned him, and in 26 B.C.E., Gallus killed himself. He was reportedly a long-time friend of Virgil, once saving his estates from government seizure. Gallus was the first poet of Rome to adopt the Alexandrine style of erotic elegy. Written in honor of Lycoris or Cytheris, the mistress of Marc Antony, Gallus's poems were widely read and admired by Virgil. Other friends included Asinius Pollo and Ovid.

Gallus Caesar (Flavius Claudius Constantius Gallus) (c. 326–354 C.E.) *Nephew of Emperor Constantine the Great and half-brother of Julian*

The son of Julius Constantius and Galla, Gallus grew up amid the numerous palace intrigues synonymous with the last years of CONSTANTINE's reign. Because of poor health, he was not included in the annihilation of the palace family following the old emperor's demise in 337. Surprised by his survival, the new rulers decided to send him to Cappadocia, where he remained with JULIAN. In 351, Constantius II needed a relative to serve in the East, and Gallus was made Caesar with control over Antioch and much of Syria and Palestine, while Constantius dealt with the troubles in the West. Ammianus Marcellinus wrote of his cruelty and the endless spite and ambition of his wife, Constantia, sister of Constantius, whom he had been forced to marry. His outrages included the murder of courtiers and the massacre of Antioch's senate. Constantius sent one of his generals, Domitianus, the Praetorian Prefect of the East, to Antioch to ask Gallus to return to Italy. When Domitianus treated the Caesar with little respect, he was killed. Finally, in 354, Constantius listened to the warnings of his advisers. Gallus was brought before constantius, tried, convicted, and executed.

Gamala Town in the Gaulanitis region of the Palestinian district of GALILEE. It was situated in rugged hills, and a tall, imposing fortress was built there. In 66 C.E., at the start of the great Jewish rebellion, Gamala remained loyal to Rome through the efforts of the representative of King Herod Agrippa II, an officer named Philip. Eventually, however, the city fell into rebel hands, and in the fall of 67, Vespasian stormed the city. The historian JOSEPHUS described in some detail the efforts to capture the walls of Gamala. Several attempts were necessary, but on November 10, 67, the citadel fell, and Gamala's population was massacred.

games *See* LUDI.

Gannascus (d. c. 47 C.E.) *A chief of the Chauci tribe*
In 47 C.E., Gannascus led a series of punitive raids into GERMANIA Inferior. Gannascus had served in the auxiliaries of Rome but was now working against Roman domination of Germany. He amassed a large fleet of small, fast vessels and struck at Gaul, where the pacified Aedui were easy prey. Domitius Corbulo arrived in Germania Inferior determined to put an end to Gannascus and his activities. The Roman general first unleashed a flotilla of triremes on the Rhine, quickly decimating the naval power of the CHAUCI. Unable to transport his warriors by water, Gannascus retreated. Corbulo then whipped his legions into shape and used terror as a weapon, intimidating the neighboring tribes and conniving with the Chauci to murder their leader in return for peace. He succeeded. The death of Gannascus, however, earned Corbulo and Rome the eternal hatred of the Germans, who waited for the chance to exact vengeance.

Gannys (d. after 218 C.E.) *Tutor of Emperor Elagabalus*
In June of 218, Gannys was instrumental in causing the legions of Syria to rise up in favor of ELAGABALUS against Emperor Marcus Opellius Macrinus. This teacher took command of the army, and on June 2, 218, personally defeated what was left of Macrinus's rapidly declining forces. Just as he had done for most of Elagabalus's young life, Gannys assumed control of all matters of government, working with the powerful matrons Julia Maesa and Julia Soaemias in a close manner. He lent a certain amount of stability to the emperor's bizarre court, proving a capacity for efficient administration while the new ruler was in Bithynia. His capable fulfillment of his office, however, alienated Elagabalus, who resented the severe restrictions that his tutor put upon his actions and personal habits. Elagabalus thus killed him, supposedly delivering the first blow. From that point on the new regime sank into dissipation.

Ganymedes (d. c. 48 B.C.E.) *Egyptian eunuch who was the tutor of a sister of Cleopatra, Arsinoe*
When Julius Caesar arrived in Alexandria in late September of 48 B.C.E., he found the Egyptian kingdom torn apart by civil war between Ptolemy XIII and Cleopatra, his sister. During the subsequent palace intrigues, ARSINOE, the forgotten sibling, embarked upon her own plans for seizing the throne. She enlisted the aid of the reliable general Achillas and that of her own teacher, Ganymedes. Caesar was besieged in Alexandria, but Achillas was slain by the ambitious princess. Ganymedes aided her in this treachery. The instructor then took over the siege, displaying a firm understanding of war. He destroyed Caesar's water supply by pouring in sea water, fought a bitter battle in the harbor against several Roman ships and very nearly trapped Caesar on Pharos, the famed dictator having to jump for his life and swim to safety. Caesar, however, received reinforcements and, with Mithridates of Pergamum, annihilated Ptolemy in the battle of the Nile. Alexandria fell, and Arsinoe with it. She was forced to join Caesar's triumph in Rome. Ganymedes was probably murdered.

gardens The landscaped areas in Rome were divided into two categories: those created to fulfill a productive purpose and those designed for pleasure and set on estates, both private and public. In most farms and villas, garden produce helped feed the residents. Fruits and vegetables were grown, sometimes in such abundance or on plots so large that additional money could be made by selling produce at the local market. Vineyards and orchards were very often sumptuous or aesthetically enhanced. More formal gardens were a legacy of the Greeks, and the inventive Romans took the idea and improved upon it. There were small gardens attached to a house or villa, holding collections of trees, shrubs, and fountains. Public gardens were vaster examples of the same, including fountains and other adornments. While there were many gardens in Rome, some of the finest preserved examples are found in Campania, especially in POMPEII and in HERCULANEUM.

See also entries on specific gardens.

Gardens of Antony   A series of gardens situated along the Tiber River in Rome. They were very close to the GARDENS OF CAESAR.

Gardens of Asiaticus   Name given to private gardens in Rome owned until 47 C.E. by Asiaticus. Situated on the Pincian Hill, the gardens were first built by Lucius Lucullus, the victor of the Mithradatic Wars (74–66 B.C.E.) and were the first of their kind in Rome. The scale was vast, stretching along the Pincian's southern slope with views of the CAMPUS AGRIPPA, CAMPUS MARTIUS, and Quirinal Hill. Asiaticus purchased the gardens and set upon a personal program of beautification. The collection of fountains, sculptures, trees, and shrubs was so stunning that Empress Messallina, coveting the gardens, had Asiaticus accused of treason and forced to commit suicide. He ordered his pyre built in the midst of his trees, so situated as to cause no harm to any of them. Ironically, in 48 C.E., Messallina fled to the grounds to escape from the Praetorian Guardsmen ordered to execute her for her repeated adulteries. She died surrounded by the same trees that had borne witness to Asiaticus's funeral.

Gardens of Caesar   These gardens were privately owned by Julius Caesar but left to the citizens of Rome in his will. They were located somewhere along the Tiber, very close to the GARDENS OF ANTONY. In 32 C.E., Tiberius made his entrance to Rome from the gardens, following the massacre of Lucius Aelius Sejanus.

Gardens of Lucullus   *See* GARDENS OF ASIATICUS.

Gardens of Sallust   The former Ludovisi Gardens, purchased and redesigned by the historian SALLUST. The gardens stood along the southern edge of the Pincian Hill and included part of the Quirinal Hill as well. As they were near the equally lovely GARDENS OF ASIATICUS, the Pincian came to be known as the Collis Hortorum or Collis Hortulorum, the Hill of Gardens. According to Dio, Vespasian favored the gardens more than the palace and actually held most of his audiences there, particularly with the Roman citizenry. In later years the Baths of Diocletian were constructed just south of the gardens, and for centuries the Agger of Servius to the east was dominated by the CASTRA PRAETORIA.

Gaul   *See* GALLIA.

Gavius Maximus, Marcus   (d. after 158 C.E.) *Prefect of the Praetorian Guard and an important adviser to Emperor Antoninus Pius*

Little is known of Gavius prior to 129 C.E., except that he came from Picenum and was, as his career would attest, a member of the Equestrian Order (EQUITES). In 129, Emperor HADRIAN appointed him procurator in Mauretania Tingitana, a post that he maintained until circa 132, when he received the procuratorship in Asia. When ANTONINUS PIUS succeeded Hadrian to the throne in 138, he elevated Gavius to the command of the PRAETORIAN GUARD, along with Marcus Mamertinus. His reception of the Praetorian leadership may have come earlier, but his retirement was in 158, which was recorded as his 20th year of service. His position must have been one that involved more than the Praetorians, as his advisory skills were used by the emperor as well. From 143 on, however, he had sole charge of the Guard. Upon his retirement, Gavius received full consular honors. Antoninus Pius continued Hadrian's policy of enriching prefects with consulships and wealth. Gavius, however, was singled out for attention. His tenure as prefect had been long, given the dangers and the demands of the office.

Geiseric   (d. 477 C.E.) *The greatest king of the Vandals from 428 to 477*

In 428, the "King of the VANDALS and the Alans"—Gunderic—died, leaving control of Spain and parts of the Mediterranean to his half-brother, Geiseric. This new king proved a superb successor. The historian Jordanes wrote of him as intelligent, a man who hated luxury and was highly adroit at predicting the intentions and the actions of others. Born to a slave woman, he became Gunderic's half-brother, despite being partially lame from falling off a horse, and eventually shared the throne of the Vandals. His accession could not have come at a worse time. Internal struggles and political conflicts faced BONIFACE, the *magister militum* and count of AFRICA, who wrestled with Ravenna for power in the West and with the Goths for supremacy in Africa. Despairing of any reasonable solution, Boniface decided to ask Geiseric to enter Africa and to maintain it as part of his realm. He offered Geiseric half of the lands there.

Unable to resist such an opportunity, Geiseric ordered his people across Spain and Gibraltar and swept into Mauretania. With reckless abandon the army of the Vandals pushed across Africa, destroying and burning everything in its path. Boniface instantly regretted his invitation. He tried to stop Geiseric but was defeated and then besieged at Hippo throughout much of 430. Geiseric crushed Boniface's reinforcements, sent to the continent under Aspar in 431. He took Hippo and furthered his conquest of Numidia, going all the way to Carthage, one of the last major cities left under imperial command.

The war had been fought with brilliance, and the Vandal king elected to consolidate his holdings. On February 11, 435, he signed a treaty with the empire in which he received total ownership of Mauretania and a large slice of Numidia. Within five years he violated that agreement and captured Hippo and Carthage in 439, setting off a series of wars that would last for 30 years. Geiseric created a large fleet and used it to menace the commercial lanes of the East and West. Another treaty in 442 merely delayed the inevitable conflict. Around 455, the Vandals broke all pacts and took the rest of Africa. Unopposed, Geiseric broadened his ambitions and answered the call for help from Empress Licinia EUDOXIA, who was being menaced by Petronius Maximus, the brief-reigning Western emperor. Although this plea was probably an historical fiction, the Vandal king did sail with a host from his own capital at Carthage, and in early June 455 he entered Rome. After pillaging the city of everything of value, the barbarians returned home with Licinia Eudoxia and her two daughters, one of whom was subsequently married to Geiseric's son, Huneric.

Direct interference in the imperial succession soon followed, as Geiseric demanded that the nobleman OLY-BRIUS, husband of Eudoxia's second daughter, Placidia, be placed on the Western throne. The emperor at Constantinople, Leo, resolved to deal the Vandals a blow. A large fleet was assembled in 468 at Constantinople under the guidance of the incompetent Basiliscus. It was to sail and fight in conjunction with a second fleet from Italy. A three-pronged attack, using elements of both empires, East and West, developed with some initial success, as the Vandals faced invasion from several directions at once. Geiseric's military genius, however, coupled with Basiliscus's ineptness, ended Roman hopes. Through the use of fire ships and a favorable wind, Geiseric smashed Basiliscus, driving his defeated vessels all the way to Italy. The last great effort of the combined domains of the Roman Empire had failed. Geiseric had beaten them both, and Leo was left close to bankruptcy.

While his position in Africa had been threatened by the Roman assault, Geiseric emerged both victorious and solidly in place as ruler of the Vandal territories. His domain received his attention then, as he sought to make it whole and independent of the influences of both Rome and Constantinople. He stripped his leading city of Carthage, and indeed all of Africa, of its Roman character. ARIANISM served as the religion of state and orthodox Christians suffered persecutions. The old African social order was toppled, and a purely Vandal system of government was adopted. His nation emerged as a potent political force, an economic power and a legitimate player in the political future of the Mediterranean.

Gellius, Aulus (fl. second century C.E.) *Grammarian, archaicist, and author of a collection of knowledge, the* Noctes Atticae *(Attic nights)*
Gellius was born sometime around 130 C.E., but nothing survives to give information about his early years. He went to Rome circa 146, while still young, and he studied under such literary greats as Sulpicius Apollinaris and Erucius Clarus and probably was an associate of Cor-

nelius Fronto. Rhetoric was taught to him by Antonius Julianus, and Favorinus had a marked effect on his subsequent development. Gellius then worked for the government in the judiciary before moving to Athens. There he was tutored by Herodes Atticus, Peregrinus Proteus, and Calvenus Taurus. He remained in Athens for one year before returning to Rome to take up a legal career, which he apparently did not pursue. That he was married can be deduced from his references to his children in the *praefatio* of the *Noctes Atticae*.

His life's great work was begun perhaps in 160, while he was still in Athens, and took many years to complete. It was not published until sometimes between 175 and 180. Gellius's *Noctes* was written to present information on a variety of subjects, including law, grammar, philosophy, history, and gossip. Its organization was deliberately haphazard, divided into 20 books, of which 19 more or less have survived. Recalling his days in Athens, the work abounds with tales of Herodes Atticus. He also relied upon archaic authors to supply his material and preserved vast amounts of literature, both Latin and Greek, that would otherwise have been lost. Later authors used his collection, especially Nonius, Macrobius and Ammianus Marcellinus. Gellius was known even in the Middle Ages.

Gemellus, Tiberius (d. 37 C.E.) *Grandson of Emperor Tiberius by Drusus (3) the Younger and Livilla*
Tiberius Gemellus was never loved or liked by his grandfather, who considered him the product of LIVILLA's adultery, and was included in Tiberius's loathing along with the sons of Germanicus. After 33 C.E., any hope for improving relations between them was ended as GAIUS CALIGULA became Tiberius's favorite. In a testament to the old man's cleverness, however, his will named both Gaius Caligula and Tiberius Gemellus as heirs to the throne. Gaius Caligula, aided by the prefect of the Guard, Macro, had the will rescinded and assumed power by himself. Tiberius Gemellus, still young, was politically impotent but did eventually receive the *toga virilis* and the title PRINCEPS IUVENTUTIS, marking him as the heir. The worsening mental condition of Caligula, however, made the lad's death inevitable; in 37, Tiberius Gemellus was murdered. Caligula's excuse was that Tiberius had been taking a preventative dose of poison, his breath smelled of it, so a tribune of the Guard decapitated him, allegedly before he could poison the emperor. The medicine was probably a remedy for a nervous cough. Gaius had commented on it, saying: "Can there be an antidote for Caesar?"

Gemonian Stairs The Scalae Gemoniae, the Stairs of Sighs, a series of steps leading from the capital (*see* Capitoline Hill, in HILLS OF ROME) to the FORUM ROMANUM. Its name came from its role in some of the saddest and bloodiest events in Roman history. Tradition dictated that any public figures who fell from power should have their statues dragged to the stairs and thrown down. In 20 C.E., for example, Gnaeus Calpurnius Piso was declared an enemy and his likeness was destroyed by the mob upon the stairs. As the empire declined in moral vitality, the *Scalae* served the same purpose as before, only now the actual bodies of the fallen were hurled down them. In 31 C.E., Lucius SEJANUS, the ambitious PREFECT OF THE PRAETORIAN GUARD, was crushed by order of Tiberius. He was taken to the main dungeon near the stairs, the TULLIANUM, while his statues were destroyed. Later he was strangled, and his body kicked down the Stairs of Sighs, where many citizens added insults. His children, a young girl and boy, were executed viciously and also catapulted down the stairs. The Scalae Gemoniae probably played a part in the final act of the Sejanus drama. In 33 C.E., Tiberius ordered that all of the prefect's allies and political clients who had been held for nearly two years in prison were to be massacred. The result was one of the worst days in Roman history and one of the most lurid pages written by Tacitus in his *Annals.* Not surprisingly, the stairs never lost their sinister reputation.

Geneva   One of the leading towns of HELVETIA. Geneva was a possession of the once powerful tribe of the Allobroges but later became a Roman possession. It was useful to the Romans mainly because of its location on the Rhone, serving as a staging point for Roman campaigns into Gaul.

Genialis, T. Flavius (fl. late second century C.E.) *Prefect of the Praetorian Guard with Tullius Crispinus in 193 C.E.*
They were appointed by DIDIUS JULIANUS, who had just purchased the imperial throne from the Guard. In the face of Julianus's rapidly deteriorating political position, Genialis remained utterly loyal, both to the emperor and to the Praetorians, who had forced his nomination. He could not prevent the Senate from condemning or executing Julianus. There is evidence that Genialis held his office into the reign of Septimius Severus, Julianus's successor.

genius   Originally corresponding to the Greek *daemon,* the "genius" was a spirit with varying roles, although throughout Roman history it was associated closely with the man-spirit and Hercules. Each family (and each family member) had its own genius (or founder or protector) responsible for the initial creation of the line and hence its endurance. The connection with a masculine spirit was obvious. Its female equivalent was identified with Juno. Each Roman house honored the genius with a bed, the *lectus genialis,* kept near the door. No human ever slept in it and other, often bloodless, sacrifices were made in its honor, accompanied by festivals and drinking, especially on birthdays.

Throughout the years of the Roman Empire, specific genii were honored. The genius of Emperor Augustus was revered as having begun the family that would raise Rome to unparalleled greatness. Subsequent imperial cultic practices made the genius a legitimate part of their programs. Aurelian tried to combat Christianity with it, and under Diocletian the Genius Populi Romani was his attempt at restoring the very life essence of the Romans (*see* RELIGION). The concept of a genius helping and protecting its charge was founded in the Egyptian belief of the Ka, and later found new attention in the Christian system of the angelic orders.

George of Cappadocia (d. 361 C.E.) *Bishop of Alexandria from 357 to 361*
One of the most feared and despised figures in Christendom, George was reputed to be cruel and violent by nature. He was appointed to the see of Alexandria by Arian bishops in 357, to replace the exiled Athanasius. George immediately exceeded even the hardline expectations of the Arians by opposing everyone with non-Arian beliefs, including moderates in his own theological camp. He thus earned the enmity of every group in Alexandria and on December 24, 361, was torn to pieces by a mob. Emperor Julian offered only slight regret for the church's loss.

See also ARIANISM; CHRISTIANITY.

Gergovia   City in southern Gaul (GALLIA) that served as one of the major centers of the AVERNI (Arverni). Gergovia was situated near the Elaver River upon a high hill and had been built as a fortress of considerable strength, as Julius Caesar discovered in 52 B.C.E. In that year all of Central Gaul rose in revolt under the command of VERCINGETORIX. Caesar immediately launched a campaign into Gaul and in March captured the large city of AVARICUM. His desire at that point was to crush the uprising quickly before it had a chance to spread in the region. Gergovia, an important town of the rebel Averni, thus became his next target. A series of marches brought Caesar and his legions to the site in April, but Vercingetorix was already there. Word then arrived that other tribes were in revolt. Caesar ordered an attack, only to be repulsed. Roman losses had been heavy, and Caesar could not waste time on a fruitless siege. A retreat was ordered, to unite his forces with those of his lieutenant, Titus Labienus. Caesar had received one of the few setbacks of his career.

Germania   One of the most important territorial acquisitions of the Roman Empire, providing the main defense of Gaul north of the Danube. Germania at one time included the territory east of the Rhine, all the way to the

Elbe. Eventually the term referred to the western bank of the Rhine, where two provinces existed: Germania Inferior and Germania Superior, or Lower and Upper Germany.

Julius CAESAR was the first Roman general to cast his eye toward the vast untamed wilderness and tribes of the barbarian world beyond the Rhine. During his GALLIC WARS, in 58 B.C.E., Caesar put an end to the power of the Germanic tribes in Alsace by destroying ARIOVISTUS and then, in 55 B.C.E., actually crossed the Rhine, via a bridge that he had constructed. He convinced the tribes there, most notably the SUEBI, not to interfere in events in Gaul. In 53 B.C.E., he journeyed across again, during his oppression of the rebelling Gallic peoples. Aside from these two minor sorties, the great Roman dictator left the Germans in peace, establishing the Rhine as the natural boundary between the growing territories of Rome and the outer lands. Caesar soon became embroiled in the CIVIL WARS and, following his murder in 44 B.C.E., political struggles erupted to determine the leadership of the empire.

With the dawn of the Roman Empire, from five to six legions were used to pacify Gaul from 27 to 15 B.C.E., and even then unrest continued as the gradual process of Romanization began. Finally, from 16 to 13 B.C.E., AUGUSTUS himself remained in the provinces of Gallia, furthering the changes in the imperial domains. He departed in 13 but the next year DRUSUS THE ELDER dedicated the great altar at LUGDUNUM (Lyons) and then completed preparations for a massive invasion of Germania. Throughout much of 12 B.C.E., Drusus probed across the Rhine, establishing the presence of the legion there. In 11 he pushed farther into what the Romans called Germania Barbara, and from 10 to 9 B.C.E. he smashed the many tribes opposing his advance, such as the CHATTI, FRISII, Sugambri, and BATAVI. The fighting was fierce, but the poorly organized and disjointed nations could not match Drusus's superior generalship or the iron discipline of his legions. By 9 B.C.E., Drusus had reached the Elbe, swinging north to defeat the CHERUSCI and then beginning his march home, dying en route as a prophetess had predicted.

TIBERIUS succeeded his brother in the campaign, waging many small wars from 8 to 7 B.C.E., before leaving the area in the hands of legates, who remained to establish good relations (whenever possible) with local tribes. Encouraged by their successes, Augustus pressed forward for full provincialization of the area, sending Quinctilius VARUS to command the legions in 7 C.E. But the Romans had greatly overestimated their position and the willingness of the Germans to accept pacification. Led by the chieftain ARMINIUS, an officer in the pay of Rome and both a Roman citizen and a client, the Cherusci, aided in part by other surrounding communities, fell upon Varus while he marched through the impossible terrain of the Teutoburg Forest. Varus and his three entire legions were wiped out, prompting Augustus to exclaim: "Varus, bring me back my legions!" The destruction of Varus terminated Rome's expansion to the Elbe, despite the belated punishment handed out to the Germans by GERMANICUS in 15 C.E., and the Rhine once more served as the frontier.

The defeat of Varus and the concomitant independence of the tribes in Germania necessitated a rethinking of the frontier defense. Ten legions were moved to the Rhine, under the immediate command of two legates but answerable to the governor of Gallia Belgica. Frontier defense remained the main activity of the Rhine legions until 69 C.E., when they moved from their posts and placed VITELLIUS on the throne. In their absence a massive revolt broke out under CIVILIS, involving tribes such as the traditionally loyal Batavi, the Frisii, and BRUCTERI. A swift resolution to the crisis was reached when Vespasian and the Flavians gained power in 69–70. Civilis was defeated, and the tribes were punished. Further expeditions were conducted to subdue the Bructeri, led by RUTILIUS GALLICUS and Vestricius SPURINNA.

The Flavians strengthened the line of protection by improving the forts, adding new auxiliaries, and rotating the legions in Upper and Lower Germany; an important campaign was begun to terminate local plots and to shorten the line of communication from the Rhine to the Danube. Emperor DOMITIAN, in 83, continued these actions by striking out against the dangerous Chatti and then extending the line of the imperial border into the fertile and strategically useful territories of Taunus, Odenwald, the Main River, and the Neckar, linking them to Raetia and the Danubian provinces. Around 90 Domitian removed the two Germanias from the authority of Gallia Belgica. Henceforth, the two independent imperial provinces of Germania Inferior and Germania Superior were under the command of legates.

As the province resting upon the Lower Rhine, Germania Inferior, or Lower Germany, bolstered the frontier stretching from the North Sea to the Moselle. A careful watch was maintained over the local tribes. The Batavi and the Canninefates lived to the extreme north, near the troublesome Frisii. To the south were the Cherusci, who had fallen in stature by the time the province was founded around 90. The Ubii were settled on the west bank, with their capital at COLOGNE. The Roman provincial government was based in Cologne, the one-time Colonia Agrippina. Dealings with Gallia Belgica were extensive, and the borders throughout the years remained relatively unchanged. Germania Superior played a greater strategic role on the frontier than Germania Inferior, for it bordered Raetia and the vital Danubian base line. Changes took place continually on its borders. The acquisition of the Agri Decumates gave the province extensive holdings, all ruled from the ideally located city of MOGUNTIACUM (Mainz), the capital.

Along with provinces were created the famous *LIMES* (pl., *limites*) or defensive network of forts, stations, camps, and roads. They began in Germania Superior, stretching south for some 230 miles through Taunus and along the Main down to the vicinity of modern Stuttgart, where they joined the Raetian *limes*. They functioned to keep the barbarians from crossing into the imperial province and helped to reduce the vast amounts of ground to be patrolled, as well as the incessant fear of barbarian invasion. Legionary camps became unnecessary and were soon replaced by more permanent cities. It may have been Emperor TRAJAN who cut the legions of Upper Germany to two, when he needed as many as possible for his campaigns elsewhere. HADRIAN also bolstered the *limes* by adding a palisade to the entire outer wall, in keeping with his policy of isolation, sealing off the empire from the world with ramparts and bastions. His successor, ANTONINUS PIUS, maintained and extended the Main works for better strategic position.

All of these fortifications would prove necessary by the end of the reign of Antoninus Pius, and the accession of MARCUS AURELIUS. For may decades the Rhine had been calm, undisturbed except by infrequent raids by the Chatti or the CHAUCI. Then, in the middle of the second century C.E., the migrating peoples from the East applied pressure on the Germans. Starting around 170, the Chauci, Chatti, and their neighbors pierced the Roman frontier, adding to the chaos and devastation along the Danube. During the MARCOMANNIC WARS, years of fighting were necessary before the tribes could be dislodged from Germany and Raetia, not to mention, Italy itself. By 175 the borders were reestablished, but the destabilization of Germany had begun.

The third century marked the turning point in the Roman era of domination. In 213, Emperor CARACALLA fought a war with the newest arrivals to Upper Germany, the ALAMANNI. From then on, no peace would last for long, and the empire ceased to be the aggressor, using tribute paid to the barbarians as a legitimate form of diplomacy. As the Roman Empire sank into civil strife and internal political struggle, the recently risen FRANKS advanced, finding little resistance. GALLIENUS tried to stem the tide but was unsuccessful, his catastrophic reign serving as a low point in imperial history. All of the Roman cities and towns on the east bank of the Rhine were devastated, until finally, around 263, the Agri Decumates (the Black Forest area) fell and territories were lost. With the soldier emperor PROBUS, the Rhine was reclaimed, at least as a useful frontier, and remained so into the time of DIOCLETIAN. In that ruler's reorganization of the Roman world, the two provinces were renamed Germania I and II, and they received overall command from the vicar of the diocese of Galliae.

However, no amount of reorganization by Diocletian, Constantine or their successors could prevent the internal deterioration of the Roman Empire. The shift of imperial strategic emphasis from Rome to CONSTANTINO-PLE only served to demoralize an already failing vitality. From the fifth century C.E., the Rhine served no longer as a barrier to invasion.

ROMAN AND GERMAN CULTURE

The first Romans in Germania were the legions, their auxiliaries and camp followers. They found a multitude of people descended from mixed Indo-Germanic and Celtic stock: tall, muscular, and skilled in war. Tacitus states in his account *Germania* that their kings were greatly esteemed but all loved liberty and would fight to the death to keep it. They had lived in their lands for centuries but were markedly inferior to the Gauls in civilization, industry, and sophistication. The Romans assumed a willingness of the tribes to assimilate the elements of Roman life, but the legions left only a shallow mark upon the Germans between 12 B.C.E. and 9 C.E., one quickly erased by Arminius.

When eight legions arrived on the Rhine, however, the lack of Germanic unity allowed a massive influx of Roman culture, accelerated by sheer weight of numbers. With the soldiers came women, children, traders, merchants, and the ever present followers who were eager to benefit from the activities of the empire. As was typical of provincial policies, Rome moved to establish COLONIES, cities centered around native tribes, and allowed permanent legion camps with houses to be set up, the *canabae*. The camps and *canabae* served as magnets for settlers who eventually took over the adjoining lands, fostering the growth of cities and ensuring a supply of auxiliaries and soldiers for the army. Early colonies included Augustus Raurica, Augusta Vindelicorum, and Cologne. Trajan began his busy reign by inaugurating such new *coloniae* as Ulpia Noviomagus and ULPIA TRAIANA, while Aurelia Aquensis, Cologne, TRIER, Lopodonum, and Moguntiacum grew prosperous. Along the colonists, Germania absorbed the Roman language and law and the best exports of Gaul, the storehouse for the German legions—and possibly the Graeco-Roman religion. The precise degree of this Romanization process remains a source for continued archaeological research.

At the same time as the empire grew, most notably in the West, it became a more and more highly Germanized state. After the Marcomannic Wars, Cologne, Mainz, Trier, and other cities were settled with Germanic tribes, following the Roman policy of accepting migratory peoples and refugees into the boundaries of the provinces. In time, the officers and highest officials in government came from German territories, until even Emperor CARACALLA astounded his tribal clients from the Rhine by his clothing style and his hair, both traditionally Germanic.

By the time of CONSTANTINE, the soldiers of the army were descendants of the first legionaries and had spent their entire lives in Germania. Constantine relied upon German officers, establishing the trend of the late fourth

and early fifth centuries C.E. in which the MAGISTER MILI-
TUM was always German. When the terrible invasion of
HUNS came pouring across the Rhine, they found inhabi-
tants not dissimilar to those they had already known.

Suggested Readings: King, Anthony. *Roman Gaul and
Germany.* Berkeley: University of California Press, 1990;
Todd, Malcolm. *The Northern Barbarians, 100 BC–AD
300.* New York: B. Blackwell, 1987; Schutz, Herbert. *The
Prehistory of Germanic Europe.* New Haven, Conn.: Yale
University Press, 1983; Wells, C. M. *The German Policy of
Augustus: An Examination of the Archaeological Evidence.*
Oxford, U.K.: Clarendon Press, 1972.

Germanicus Julius Caesar (15 B.C.E.–19 C.E.) *Son of
Drusus (1) the Elder and Antonia; a noted general and political figure of enormous popularity*
As a grandson of AUGUSTUS, Germanicus was raised in the
imperial palace with his brother Claudius, where he
received a good education and was the more favored of
the two by their mother. After the deaths of Lucius CAE-
SAR (2 C.E.) and Gaius CAESAR (4 C.E.), Germanicus was
groomed for high office and became a member of the
Senate, and he was adopted by TIBERIUS at the same time
that Tiberius was adopted by Augustus. From 7 C.E.
onward, Germanicus was on campaign with Tiberius,
first in PANNONIA and DALMATIA (7 to 10 C.E.) and then in
Germany (11 to 12 C.E.). In the field he showed considerable strategic prowess, and when Tiberius departed for
Rome, Germanicus was left in command of the German
legions. Because of his popularity, Germanicus was feared
by Tiberius and his mother LIVIA. Further, Livia engaged
in a long-running feud with Germanicus's wife, AGRIPPINA
THE ELDER. However, in 14 C.E., when Augustus died and
Tiberius laid claim to the throne, Tacitus wrote that Germanicus simply worked harder for the emperor. He took
an oath of loyalty himself and then administered it to all
of the surrounding tribes.

A mutiny erupted in the legions of Germany and
Illyricum at this time, and Germanicus relied upon the
support of his troops to quell it. As proof of the restored
discipline, he took to the field again and made war in
Germany from the Rhine to the Elbe, all the way to the
North Sea, against the Chatti and especially the Cherusci,
under the command of the King ARMINIUS. In a series of
hard-fought battles, Germanicus did much to restore
Roman supremacy and honor among the tribes responsible for the annihilation of General VARUS in 9 C.E. in the
TEUTOBURG FOREST. In 17 C.E., Tiberius ordered him back
to Rome, where he celebrated a great triumph. Then the
emperor, sensing his growing strength among the
Romans, ordered Germanicus to the East, granting him
the title *maius imperium,* master of all of the eastern
provinces. While he clashed with Gnaeus Calpurnius
PISO, appointed by Tiberius governor of Syria, Germanicus achieved numerous successes and was hailed

throughout the major cities of ASIA MINOR, SYRIA, PALES-
TINE, and even in EGYPT. CAPPADOCIA was organized into a
province with the help of the legate Quintus Veranius.
Troubles in Armenia were temporarily eased with the
crowning of POLEMO of Pontus as its king. Parthian relations were improved. A famine in Alexandria was
relieved. Tiberius viewed all of this with jealousy, even
censuring Germanicus for traveling through Egypt without imperial permission.

From the start Germanicus and Piso disliked each
other, and even the normally generous Germanicus was
pushed too far. When he returned from Egypt, he fell ill
but recovered, only to collapse again. On October 10, 19
C.E., he died. Antioch went wild with grief, joined soon
by the entire empire. It was generally held that Germanicus had been poisoned (a fact assumed by Tacitus and
Suetonius), and Piso instantly received the blame. When
Agrippina returned to Italy, she openly charged Tiberius
and Livia with the crime, and the emperor sacrificed Piso
rather than face even greater public outrage. As an orator
Germanicus showed himself gifted and even authored a
translation of an astronomical poem by Aratus. His children were nine in number. The six survivors of childhood
were Agrippina the Younger, Livilla, Drusilla, Drusus,
Nero and, of course, Gaius Caligula, who would be Germanicus's legacy.

Germany *See* GERMANIA.

Geta (1), Lucius Septimius (198–211 C.E.) *Son of
Emperor Septimius Severus and Julia Domna and the brother
of Caracalla*
Born under the full name of Publius Lucius Septimius
Geta, he was younger than his brother by only one year.
He traveled with his family to the Parthian War in 197
and the following year became Caesar, while his brother
received the greater title of Augustus. For the next six
years Geta visited various parts of the empire, and in 205
served in the consulship with CARACALLA. What had been
a rivalry degenerated into outright hatred at this point,
especially after the murder of the PREFECT OF THE PRAE-
TORIAN GUARD, C. Fulvius PLAUTIANUS. SEVERUS did what
he could to ease the situation, but his sons lived with
recklessness and certain depravity.

After another consulship with Caracalla in 208, Geta
set out with his brother and parents for a campaign in
Britain. He served as administrator of the provinces in
the isles, with the title of Augustus, while Severus and
Caracalla made war upon the Caledonians. The imperial
family remained in Eburacum (York) until 211, when the
emperor died, imploring his heirs to make peace
between themselves. Their hatred had existed for too
long, however, and with the control of the world as the
prize, both refused to yield. The imperial will had stipulated that they would serve as corulers. They worked in

this fashion, never speaking and never discussing events or issues.

After returning to Rome, the palace had to be split in half physically to avoid open hostilities. A proposal was then made to have the empire divided between them, something that their mother would not allow. Slowly Caracalla gained the upper hand, acting as sole ruler without any consultation. He dismissed Geta's aides in the court and plotted to kill him. After ending one such plan, Caracalla agreed to meet his brother in his mother's apartment, asking for this as a point of reconciliation. There he had his soldiers attack Geta and watched as his brother died in Julia Domna's blood-stained lap. The sole ruler of the empire, Caracalla gave Geta a funeral and then removed his name from the records and inscriptions and massacred all of his followers.

Geta (2), Lusius (fl. mid-first century C.E.) *Prefect of the Praetorian Guard during the reign of Claudius (41–54 C.E.)*

Lusius Geta served with Rufrius CRISPINUS and was appointed sometime before 47 C.E., probably through the graces of Messallina. The first great crisis of his command came in 48, when Claudius summoned him to the palace for advice on what fate should befall the adulterous Messallina. Despite the power of his office, Geta was known to be a man of weak will, easily swayed. For this reason Claudius did not trust him with the empress's execution. The next years were spent by Geta watching the steady rise of Messallina's successor, Agrippina. Both Geta and Rufrius Crispinus were reportedly loyal to Messallina's memory and her surviving children. The new empress could not tolerate this and made plans to have them removed. She complained to Claudius that the two prefects were unable to maintain discipline and that the Guards would be better off with only one prefect. In 51, as a result, both officers were removed. Their replacement was Burrus.

Getae

One of the more populous tribes of THRACE, who lived in the area of the Danube and its tributaries. Their power was markedly reduced by the Roman imperial era, and they relied upon aid from Rome for their defense, as was seen in 29 B.C.E., when General Marcus Licinius CRASSUS helped them against an invasion of the Bastarnae.

Gildo (d. 398 C.E.) *African-born general of the imperial army in Africa (c. 386–398); the son of King Nubel of Mauretania*

When the king died in 371, the realm was shaken by internal strife among his children. One brother, Firmus, murdered the pro-Roman son, Sammac, gaining the support of the other brothers, Duis, Mauca, and Mascezel, and a sister, Cyria. Gildo remained loyal to his imperial officers, aiding Count THEODOSIUS against Firmus. As a reward he received from Emperor THEODOSIUS I the rank of *comes et magister utriusque militiae per Africam,* or count and commanding general of AFRICA.

In autumn of 397, however, he feuded with officials in the West and in the ensuing political struggles, he halted the shipment of grain to Rome and was declared a public enemy by the Senate at the instigation of the MAGISTER MILITUM STILICHO. An army was sent to Africa under the command of Gildo's brother, Mascezel, who had supported Firmus and whose children Gildo had had executed. On July 31, 398, Gildo was defeated and killed. His property was confiscated and was reportedly so great that a special official was named to act as caretaker.

Gischala

Town in the northern regions of Galilee, to the west of the Jordan River. In the Jewish uprising of 66 C.E., Gischala was one of the centers of popular resistance to Rome. The Roman general, VESPASIAN, moved against the cities of Galilee, and, after reducing GAMALA, sent his son TITUS, with legionary attachments, against the rebels of Gischala, sometime in November. Knowing of the terrible slaughter that had taken place at Gamala, Titus was anxious to avoid a similar occurrence. He therefore implored the city to surrender, rather than endure a destructive siege. JOHN OF GISCHALA, the rebel commander, asked for one day's grace and used it to escape. The next day Gischala opened wide its gates. Titus made a token gesture of conquest (a wall was thrown down) and then left a small garrison. Gischala was thus spared the ravages of the uprising.

gladiators

One of the most famous elements of Roman society and entertainment. A unique product of Rome and Italy, gladiators came to epitomize the socially decadent nature of the Romans, with their taste for blood sports. Gladiators emerged among the Etruscans as a form of the traditional blood sacrifice held at funerals, when teams of warriors dueled to the death. When the early Romans fell under the domination of ETRURIA, many prisoners of war were offered up in this manner, a ceremony repeated in 358 B.C.E., when 307 captives were sacrificed in the Tarquin Forum. Inevitably, the Romans accepted many Etruscan rituals; in 264 B.C.E., the family of M. Brutus solemnly celebrated his funeral with gladiatorial battles.

From that time on, burials honored by bouts between gladiators became both common and grand. The gladiatorial schools, the type of combatants and their place in society were all fully developed. The final aggrandizement of gladiators came in the last stages of the Republic, when candidates staged large shows for public enjoyment and political influence, culminating with the election of Julius CAESAR as an AEDILE in 65 B.C.E. He held a massive celebration, complete with over 300 dueling pairs. Henceforth, the contests became an important part of the imperial control of the Roman mobs, satisfying the Romans' thirst for action and directing their frustrations and energy.

Gladiatorial shows were not a major part of the LUDI, the public games held many times throughout the year in Rome. Rather, the combats were staged privately, especially by the patronage of the ruling family. Rulers were expected to provide entertainments equal to the grandeur of their reigns and were careful not to disappoint the mobs. AUGUSTUS started the so-called extraordinary games, displays with no official function other than amusement for the people. Eight separate shows were put on in his name or in the names of his children. CLAUDIUS followed his example, entering into a shouting match with the contestants on one occasion.

TITUS opened the COLOSSEUM (c. 80 C.E.) with elaborate ceremonies and a gladiatorial spectacle lasting 100 days. TRAJAN, celebrating in 107 his triumph in the Dacian Wars, used 5,000 pairs of gladiators in the rings. Trajan loved to mount displays, and his reign was noted for its shows. HADRIAN, like GAIUS CALIGULA, actually took part for a time in the sport, as did CARACALLA and his brother GETA. COMMODUS, son of MARCUS AURELIUS, displayed such a passion for gladiatorial life-styles that the story was told that his true father, in fact, was one. He fought in the ring and seemed far happier in the presence of the other combatants. He was slain to deter him from entering the consulship of 193 with a parade from the gladiator barracks. DIO wrote in detail of his obsession for the arena.

By the fourth century C.E., and with the rise of CONSTANTINE the Great, gladiators were vehemently opposed by Christians as being a part of the wide practice of PAGANISM. Many earlier writers and political figures, such as SENECA, who epitomized the philosophical view, held that such exhibitions were monstrous and needlessly cruel. (The Christian bishop of Tagaste, ALYPIUS, once watched gladiators and was disturbed to find himself caught up on the excitement of the carnage.) In the face of Christian leaders who were aware of the fact that martyrs of the faith had been slaughtered for centuries in the arenas, gladiators could do little to prevent the growing restrictions and then final abolishment. Constantine gave the Christians a taste of blood vengeance by throwing German prisoners to the wild animals, but he took steps in 326 to curtail the shows through the Edict of BERYTUS.

Such measures were only partially successful because of the popularity of the entertainment. Throughout the fourth century harsher laws were passed, until around 399, when HONORIUS ordered the last of the actual schools closed. The cause of this vigorous action by the emperors was the relentless writing and preaching of Christian officials. St. AUGUSTINE, St. JOHN CHRYSOSTOM, PRUDENTIUS, and, earlier, TERTULLIAN condemned the fighting. Public outrage was also turned against the gladiators, following the murder of the Eastern monk Telemachus by a crowd enraged at his interference in a match (held either in 391 or 404).

There had always been a large number of willing participants in the grim life of combat and death, which was viewed as a haven for the desperate. Candidates for the schools were originally found among slaves and captives; prisoners of war, with nothing to lose, joined. But the popularity of the sport soon demanded other avenues of supply. Slaves were bought and then condemned prisoners used, the *damnati,* as well as members of the lower classes, the *humiliores.* During the empire two other trends developed. First, many noblemen were sent by the various emperors into the ring to fight, for committing many, sometimes imaginary, crimes. Once, when Gaius Caligula fell ill, a courtier vowed to fight in the arena if he should recover. When Caligula returned to good health, he forced the courtier to fulfill his pledge, paying careful attention to his swordplay. The courtier survived the arena.

Later, the imperial citizens, freedmen, even members of high society, entered the class of the *auctorati,* those who abandoned themselves to the gladiatorial lifestyle for a wage, by giving an oath of service for a period of time. Changes in political or economic fortune also prompted this recklessness. Those reduced to poverty signed up to escape debtors and to administer to themselves a kind of purgation for profligate living. Gluttons, the so-called Apicians, would spend vast fortunes on banquets and lavish foods, go bankrupt and either kill themselves or become gladiators; in rare cases, Apician females would become fighting women.

A prospective candidate was trained at a school (*ludus*), either privately or publicly operated. Rome had probably four such schools, although the best were found at CAPUA and POMPEII. Capua was a center of training that dated back to the era of the Etruscans. The treatment of such candidates was harsh, so difficult in fact that it produced the revolt of Spartacus in 73 B.C.E. Horrified at the public threat posed by such warriors, special care was afterward taken to prevent serious uprisings, although some politicians used gladiators for their own campaigns. Julius Caesar owned one of the best schools in Capua and planned another in RAVENNA. He allowed his gladiators to serve as a wordless threat to opposition in Rome.

A *lanista,* or drill instructor, relentlessly exercised the gladiators in the schools. Gymnastics and strength building were first emphasized. The student then practiced with a wooden sword (*lusoria arma*) until proficient with it, and then progressed to harder training with a variety of weapons. This study continued until the gladiator was master of them all. He then chose his special weapon and style, assuming the character that would remain uniquely his until his death or his retirement. Specialists instructed each fighter on a specific weapon.

There were five classes of gladiators: *eques, essedarii,* Galli, Thraeces, and *etiarii.* The *eques* was a horseman, the *essedarii* were charioteers and the *Galli* were heavy fighters, further divided into several types. The Mirmillos (*myrmillones*) and Samnites fought with short swords, long shields and large helmets. A *secutor* was a variation on the Samnite, although in later years the Greek term *hoplomachi* was applied to all heavy fighters. The Mirmillo (identified by the fish crest on his helmet) was often put into combat against the lighter armed but mobile Thracians. Thracians carried long scimitars and bucklers or smaller shields. Their armor was normally tight leather (*fasciae*), fastened around a leg. The least protected of all, but perhaps the most famous, were the *retiarii* or the net-and-trident duelers. They wore no armor at all, holding instead a net and a trident. Quickness was their only hope, for once cornered or separated from their weapons, they were easy prey for the heavier classes. Gladiators learned never to rely upon the mercy of the spectators to save them.

Suggested Readings: Auguet, Roland. *Cruelty and Civilization: The Roman Games.* New York: Routledge, 1994; Futrell, Alison. *Blood in the Arena: The Spectacle of Roman Power.* Austin: University of Texas Press, 1997; Grant, Michael. *Gladiators.* Harmondsworth, Middlesex: Penguin Books, 1971; Köhne, Eckart, and Cornelia Ewigleben, eds. *Gladiators and Caesars: The Power of Spectacle in Ancient Rome.* London: British Museum Press, 2000; Kyle, Donald G. *Spectacles of Death in Ancient Rome.* New York: Routledge, 1998; Wiedemann, Thomas E. J. *Emperors and Gladiators.* London; New York: Routledge, 1992.

gluttony The excessive and obsessive enjoyment of food was taken to absurd and even physical or financial extremes throughout Roman history. Romans had always enjoyed a rich variety of game, fish, meat, vegetables, and desserts. For the rich gourmand the kitchens of the city could provide virtually any meal or dish. Banquets were sumptuous affairs lasting for hours and introducing many courses. Various species of duck, goose and fish, pork, rabbit and oyster, sausages, breads, eggs, and wines were suitable for the average dinner, called *tempestiva convivia.* But for many of the wealthy and the ostentatious upper classes, gluttony was an expression of power, and no expense was spared.

Gluttons, or gourmands, could spend anywhere from 200,000 (a middle-class fortune) to 100 million sesterces on food. Chairs of solid silver, gold gifts of immense value, and such dishes as peacock brains, flamingo tongues, and elephant ears were served as parts of a feast that could contain as many as 100 courses. When one had eaten too much, a *vomitorium* permitted seclusion to allow removal of the ingested food; a long feather was provided to induce the process. A guest could empty his stomach, rest for a time and then start dining again.

Gluttonous revelries began in the Late Republic and reached their peak in the first and second centuries C.E. The notable glutton Marcus Gavius APICIUS lent his name to the practice. He lived in the early first century C.E. and reportedly spent 100 million sesterces on his dinners; eventually he was reduced to suicide when his vast fortune dwindled and he could not indulge his appetites lavishly. Another famous gourmand was the brief-reigning VITELLIUS, emperor in 69 C.E. According to the historian SUETONIUS, he lived for food, banqueting three or four times a day, routinely vomiting up his meal and starting over. His visits to friends required meals of such expense that imperial associates went bankrupt trying to satiate him. In one dinner, 2,000 fish and 7,000 birds were consumed. To Vitellius this meal was ordinary, for he preferred the rarer pike livers, pheasant brains, flamingo tongues, and lamprey milk.

The so-called Apicians survived into the later years of the empire. Ammianus Marcellinus criticized the nobles who hovered over cuts of cooking meat, drooling in anticipation of the repast to come. Other satirists and observers were merciless in their condemnations, including JUVENAL and HORACE, as well as PLINY THE ELDER.

Glycerius (fl. late fifth century C.E.) *Emperor of the West from March 473 to the late spring of 474*
One of the last rulers of the Western Roman Empire Glycerius was the newly appointed commander of the *protectores domestici* with the title *comes domesticorum* when the Burgundian *magister militum*, GUNDOBAD, chose him to fill the vacant throne of the recently deceased OLYBRIUS. Glycerius, a puppet of Gundobad, diverted the invasion of the OSTROGOTHS to Gaul. This was the sum of his reign, for Emperor LEO at Constantinople refused to recognize him and sent his own choice, JULIUS NEPOS, with a fleet to enforce Leo's will. Abandoned by Gundobad, Glycerius stepped down at Ravenna and was ordained the bishop of Salona.

Gnosticism The beliefs of a sect that splintered from CHRISTIANITY, taking shape in the second century C.E. Gnosticism first appeared as a very unorthodox form of spirituality in numerous Christian schools, which were influenced by Neoplatonism and views held by previous pagan philosophers. Such associations made the creed's development within the church both difficult and chaotic. Essentially, the Gnostics believed that spiritual salvation came through the revealed knowledge of God, the gnosis. This gnosis poured from the words of the Apostles and from specially chosen instruments, including the founder of the sect itself. The world was rejected as being foreign to the nature of God, who created all things. Some faithful believers were said to receive from this source of all life the special flame of the spirit. They were the great spokesmen of Gnosticism, but their own views often differed widely from one another, and hence the philosophy assumed a variety of incarnations and included those who took part in esoteric and orgiastic ceremonies. Opposition to Gnosticism was intense and extensive. Such writers as IRENAEUS and TERTULLIAN attacked the Gnostics with Christian orthodoxy and assaulted the group's habit of accepting many pagan myths and tenets.

See also MONTANUS AND MONTANISM.

gods and goddesses of Rome *See* individual entries for the deities listed in the table below.

See also RELIGION; IMPERIAL CULT; PRIESTHOOD.

GODS AND GODDESSES OF ROME

Name	Title
Anna Perena	Goddess of the Year
Apollo	Various
Bacchus	God of Wine
Carmentis	Unknown
Carna	Goddess of Health
Ceres	Goddess of Agriculture
Cybele	Great Mother
Daphne	Goddess of Virginity
Dea Dia	Goddess of Agriculture
Diana	Goddess of Hunters
Dioscuri (Castor and Pollux)	Sons of Zeus
Dis (Pluton)	King of the Underworld
Falacer	Unknown
Felicitas	Goddess of Luck
Fides	Goddess of Faith
Flora	Goddess of Flowers
Fortuna	Goddess of Fortune
Furrina	Unknown
Janus	God of Doors, the Past and the Future
Juno	Goddess of the Earth
Jupiter	God of the Sky
Juventas	Goddess of Youth
Lara	Wife of Mercury
Lares	Sons of Mercury
Luna	Goddess of the Moon
Mars	God of War
Mercury	God of Merchants
Minerva	Various
Neptune	God of the Sea
Ops	Goddess of the Harvest
Pales	God of the Flocks
Penates	Gods of the Household
Pluton	God of the Underworld
Pomona	Goddess of Fruit Trees
Portunus	God of Communications
Priapus	God of Fertility
Proserpina	Goddess of the Underworld
Quirinus	Various (Deified Romulus)
Robigus	God of Wheat-Rust
Roma	Goddess of Rome
Saturnus	God of Agriculture
Venus	Goddess of Love
Vesta	Goddess of the Hearth
Volturnus	Unknown
Vulcan	God of Volcanos

Golden House of Nero Famed palace built by NERO, stretching from the Palatine to the Esquiline hills in Rome. In 64 C.E., much of Rome was destroyed by a terrible fire. Included in the destruction was the DOMUS TRANSITORIA, the imperial residence on the Palatine. Nero had never been pleased with the residence, viewing it as an ugly artistic and architectural compromise, and in its place he planned a far more suitable estate, the Golden House (Domus Aurea). Begun in 64 C.E. and not finished until 68, the Golden House stood as a magnificent, if excessive, achievement in Roman architecture, the proud accomplishment of the imperial architects, CELER AND SEVERUS. The historian TACITUS wrote that these two tried to drain away the resources of the empire on a project that nature had declared impossible. But their use of light, space, and open air was revolutionary and would be seen in other structures through subsequent Roman architectural history.

Suetonius provided the most detailed account:

> Much of the palace was overlaid with gold and decorated with priceless jewels and mother-of-pearl. The many dining halls had a ceiling with sliding ivory panels that allowed flowers or perfume to rain down on guests from secret pipes. The great dining room was built in a circular design, with a rotating roof to show the sky during the day and at night. Baths provided running sea water and sulphur water. When all of these constructions were finished in this opulent manner, Nero dedicated the palace, adding only that he could "at last start to live like a human being."

Within a year, Nero was overthrown. When VESPASIAN took control of the empire in 69 C.E., he decided that the Golden House was not only too grand for his tastes but also an insult to the Roman people. He filled up the vast pond and used this part of the grounds to build his gift to the city, the COLOSSEUM. This mighty stadium, in fact, earned its name from a statue of Nero that had once stood there and had been called the Colosseum because of its size. TITUS furthered the destruction of the Golden House by erecting his Baths over much of the original structure.

Gordian I (Marcus Antonius Gordianus Sempronianus) (c. 159–238 C.E.) *Emperor (with his son, Gordian II) from March to April 238*

Born to a family of obscure and debated origin, Gordian achieved some notable political success with a career in the Senate and a consulship in 222 C.E. Later he became governor of the southern province of Britain, perhaps in the reign of Caracalla. Despite his advancing years (he was near 80) and his extensive property and estates, either Emperor Severus Alexander or Maximinus appointed him proconsul of Africa in 237–238.

At the time of his arrival, the tax collectors of Maximinus were ruthlessly seizing property from wealthy Africans. Unable to survive financially, many young Africans banded together and convinced Gordian to declare himself emperor. In March of 238, the aged governor proclaimed a new imperial era and sent a deputation to Rome and the Senate for approval. The Senate agreed quickly, and Maximinus was condemned.

Despite the general acceptance of Gordian's claim (and that of his son as coemperor), not all of Africa surrendered so easily. Gordian, it seems, had once sued the governor of nearby Numidia, CAPELLIANUS, who chose this moment to exact revenge. Declaring for Maximinus, he marched his legion against Carthage. A brief battle ensued, and Capellianus routed the hastily assembled army sent against him, under the command of Gordian II. The young Gordian died in battle, and Gordian I hanged himself. Capellianus massacred the followers of the dead emperor.

Gordian II (Marcus Antonius Gordianus Sempronianus Romanus Africanus) (d. 238 C.E.) *Emperor (with his father, Gordian I) from March to April 238*

Gordian II served as governor of Achaea and held a consulship under Severus Alexander before traveling with his father to Africa in 238. There he had the position of deputy to the proconsul, his father, at Carthage. In March of that year he joined GORDIAN I in proclaiming themselves the new emperors and was, by April, acknowledged by the Senate as the coruler of the empire. When the governor of Numidia (CAPELLIANUS) launched his legion against CARTHAGE, Gordian II helped organize Carthaginian resistance. In the ensuing battle, the cause of the Gordians was defeated and Gordian II died as well. His body was never found, and Gordian I killed himself after a brief reign.

Gordian III (Marcus Antonius Gordianus) (225–244 C.E.) *Emperor from 238 to 244 C.E.; the grandson of Gordian I by a daughter*

He received an education in Rome, presumably staying behind when his grandfather and uncle (GORDIAN II) went to Africa in 238. When word arrived that both Gordians had assumed the imperial rank and had died in April of that year, their two successors, Balbinus and PUPIENUS, first finished Emperor Maximinus and then took control of the Roman state. To satisfy the mob, which had come to adore the Gordians, Balbinus, and

Pupienus raised the young Gordian to the rank of Caesar. Neither ruler lived out the year because the Praetorian Guards murdered them both and elevated Gordian to the throne. He was only 13 years old at the time. Gordian III's administration was placed in the hands of the Senate, palace officials, and especially his mother. He remained under their power until 241, when a new figure of prominence emerged—TIMESITHEUS. This PREFECT OF THE PRAETORIAN GUARD took upon himself all matters of importance, and so completely did Gordian trust him that he married his daughter, Tranquillina.

In 242, Gordian and his prefect set off to wage war upon the Persians led by SHAPUR I. A highly successful operation provided for the rescue of all of Syria and the repulse of the Persians along the entire frontier. Further campaigns into Persia itself were disastrously aborted by the death of Timesitheus in late 243. Gordian appointed Philip, called the Arab, as the new Praetorian prefect. Within weeks the officer had prepared the legions for mutiny, and in February 244, the young ruler was probably murdered by soldiers unwilling to serve a child. Philip took over the empire.

Gotarzes II (d. 49 C.E.) *King of Parthia, son of Artabanus III and ruler for the troubled years from about 38 to 49 C.E.*

When Artabanus died around 38, Gotarzes embarked upon a campaign to remove all possible rivals. Toward this end he murdered his brother, Artabanus (who may have been Artabanus IV), and the prince's wife and family. This liquidation provided some safety for a number of years. In 47 C.E., another brother, Vardanes, attempted to usurp the throne, and civil war raged across the Parthian provinces. The large country was divided. To avoid destruction of the entire kingdom, Gotarzes stepped down in his brother's favor. Within months he had regrets, however, and the battle raged again. This time Gotarzes prevailed and remained in control despite an attempt in 49, backed by Rome, to install a son of a Parthian hostage of the empire, Meherdates, on the throne. Gotarzes once more proved victorious and died of natural causes in that year, a rare feat for the monarchs of his royal line.

Goths

A powerful group of Germanic people who played a major role in the crises besetting the Roman Empire from the third century C.E. They came originally from the far northern edges of the Vistula River system, around the Baltic Sea. There, Gothic culture developed, but in the late second century C.E. they departed from their lands and migrated south to the frontiers of the Roman Empire. The reasons for the move, which must have involved hundreds of thousands of men, women, and children, were probably the growing unrest in the East, the increasing weakness of border defenses, and the rumor of great plunder and riches available. Their hopes of finding the watch on the border lax were confirmed, and some time in the reign of Severus Alexander (c. 231–232), they burst through the Danubian line. By 238 the Gothic position was so threatening that Emperor Maximinus bought them off with tribute. His aim was to secure time to organize a proper offensive. He was defeated, however, by internal imperial rivalries, and within four years the first raids had begun along the Danube.

The Gothic King Argaithius was simply waiting for his chance, and in 248 the invasion began in earnest. Philip I, the Arab, fought hard against the barbarians, and he seems to have achieved some success. But Philip died trying to fight off his successor, Decius. Trajanus Decius found the Goths his main enemy in 249, for under a new king, KNIVA, the Goths poured over the Danube. Decius beat them back at first but they returned later in the year, better organized and allied with many other enemies of Rome, including the Dacian Carpi. War raged in Moesia, Dacia and even in Thrace, while the main body was preparing a descent into the region of the Black Sea.

The legions of Decius fought valiantly, but in 250, at Beraea, in Thrace, he was severely beaten by Kniva. A year was spent reorganizing; the Goths were attacked again in 251. This time Decius was not only beaten but also slain in battle. The Goths were now the masters of the entire Danube territory, all the way to the Black Sea. The new Emperor Trebonianus Gallus could do nothing to unseat them. Illyricum and Thrace were plundered and burned, and in 253 the Goths set sail along the Black Sea. Asia Minor was wide open for pillage and treasure. Roughly from 256 to 270, the Gothic tribes, under their kings, carried on expeditions in Asia Minor and the Balkans. Chalcedon was burned and Bithynia ravaged, with the cities of Ephesus and Nicomedia especially devastated. Lydia, Phrygia, parts of Asia, Cappadocia, and even Galatia were subject to attack and destruction. These incursions spurred on other hordes, such as the Heruli, the Carpi, and the Bastarnae. More ships sailed throughout the Black Sea, landing, killing, and adding to the growing despair of the area. Gallienus did what he could, which was little despite a notable victory at Naissus in 268 over the Heruli.

Far more successful was Aurelian, the emperor who began the task of restoring Roman pride and strength. Aurelian did not merely fight the Goths, he demolished them. In a series of engagements the Gothic warriors were driven out of the Balkans and into DACIA, while the Black Sea defenses were improved. Instead of pursuing the barbarians into the Roman province of Dacia, Aurelian pulled back; the new border was once again the Danube. This decision left Dacia in the hands of the Carpi and the Goths. Subsequent evolution in the Gothic nation saw it quickly dividing into two distinct groups, powerful states that would bring about the end of the Roman Empire in the West. Sources on the Goths in the third century are highly fragmentary.

See also OSTROGOTHS; VISIGOTHS.

Graecina, Pomponia (fl. mid-first century C.E.) *Wife of the noted general Aulus Plautus*
In 57 C.E., Graecina was accused of impiety and belief in foreign superstition. According to the ancient traditions, her family sat in judgment to determine her guilt or innocence and they found her not guilty of the charges. What cult or alien belief to which she supposedly belonged has never been discovered, although it has been suggested that she may have been a Christian, an unlikely notion. Pomponia Graecina was also noted for her style of clothes. In honor of Julia, daughter of Drusus, Tiberius's son, she wore only clothes of mourning. Julia had been executed on the order of Messallina in 43 C.E. Claudius never punished Pomponia for this obvious act of disloyalty.

Gratian (Flavius Gratianus) (359–383 C.E.) *Emperor of the West from 367 to 383*
Born at Sirmium, Gratian was the son of Emperor Valentinian I and Marina Severa. He held his first consulship in 366 and was named Augustus, or coruler, in 367, although he was only eight years old at the time. On November 17, 375, Valentinian died, leaving Gratian as his heir, until his younger half brother, Valentinian II, was proclaimed his assistant through the influence of the MAGISTER MILITUM Merobaudes. Because of the ages of the two emperors, a bitter struggle took place for mastery of the palace, with the gifted politician and poet AUSONIUS emerging supreme with the title of Praetorian Prefect in Gaul, Italy, and Africa. Merobaudes continued to exercise influence as well, especially in military matters.

Wars on the frontiers demanded his immediate attention, and in 377–378 he campaigned against the Alamanni and then, in 378, received word that his colleague in the East, Valens, was preparing for war against the Gothic tribes. Though Gratian marched quickly, he failed to reach Valens in time, and most of the Eastern army was destroyed, including the emperor, at the battle of ADRIANOPLE. The crisis of the century had occurred. Gratian elevated Theodosius I in January 379 to the throne of Valens, to manage the damaged affairs of that part of the empire while he retained the western regions. They joined a year later, fighting successfully against both the Alamanni and the Goths in the Danubian regions.

By 383, further operations were planned against the Alamanni, but Gratian had to deal with the usurper, Magnus Maximus, a general in Britain who had been named emperor by his army. Discontent in the ranks caused massive defections from his own units, and Gratian found himself without military or political support. He tried to flee, only to be assassinated by one of his own officers, Andragathius, on August 25, 383, at Lugdunum (Lyons). Ammianus Marcellinus wrote that Gratian was a youth of remarkable character, destined for greatness had he not succumbed to a war-like demeanor and an inclination to appalling behavior, unrestrained by his intimates. Nevertheless, he passed from the control of Ausonius to that of AMBROSE and thus worked to further the Christian cause against paganism. He was the first Roman ruler to step down as pontifex maximus, and, under pressure from Ambrose, ordered that the pagan Altar of Victory be removed from the *Curia,* an act considered impious by the old senatorial traditionalists.

Grattius (fl. early first century C.E.) *Didactic poet from the time of Augustus*

Grattius's sole surviving work was notable among that of the poets of the Augustan Golden Age. As a result of his being ignored by his contemporaries, almost nothing is known of his life, except that he was an Italian. Grattius's only extant work is *Cynegetica,* a long and highly technical poem about hunting. He focused on such subjects as the hunter's equipment, traps, and especially dogs. The first and only extant book was composed of some 540 hexameters. Some toward the end have been lost.

Gregory of Nazianzus (St. Gregory Nazianzen) (c. 330–390) *Christian theologian who helped defeat heretical doctrines in the fourth century*

Born at Arianzus, near Nazianzus, in Cappadocia (a Roman province in Asia Minor), Gregory was the son of the bishop of Nazianzus. After studying in Athens, he returned to Cappadocia and entered the monastic life, joining the community that had been established by St. Basil in Pontus. Ordained against his will in 362, he worked for the next years to assist his father, continuing to do so after his own consecration around 370 as bishop of Sasima Cappadocia. He did not take possession of his see, remaining an auxiliary bishop to his father. After his father's death in 374, however, Gregory retired to a monastery in Seleucia until 379, when he was summoned to Constantinople. There, he emerged through his preaching as the main leader of the orthodox party in its struggle with Arianism. By his oratorical skill, Gregory was able to revive resistance to the Arians, prompting the summoning of the Council of Constantinople in 381 and the triumph of the Nicene Creed. Named bishop of Constantinople during the council, he was quickly so appalled by the schemes and intrigues of those around him that he resigned his see and retired to Nazianzus. A little later he returned to Cappadocia, where he spent his last years in prayer and contemplation. Ranked with Sts. BASIL the Great and GREGORY OF NYSSA as one of the Cappadocian Fathers, Gregory played an important role in the final defeat of Arianism. While shy and retiring, he nevertheless accepted responsibility for using his consid-

erable oratorical skill on behalf of Christian orthodoxy. Among his writings were poems, letters, and treatises such as the five *Theological Orations* and the *Philocalia,* which contained excerpts from ORIGEN.

Gregory of Nyssa (c. 335–395) *Christian saint and one of the Cappadocian Fathers (with Basil and Gregory of Nazianzus)*

Bishop of Nyssa, brother of St. Basil the Great, Gregory was born at Caesarea, in Cappadocia, Asia Minor, Gregory was intended for the religious life, but he temporarily abandoned his calling, becoming a rhetorician and marrying a woman named Theosebeia. At the urging of St. Gregory of Nazianzus, however, he was convinced to devote himself to the church, being consecrated around 371 as bishop of Nyssa by his brother. After being charged with improper use of church property by the local governor, Gregory was deposed in 376 and exiled for two years. The real cause of the deposition was the offense taken by the Arians at his strong adherence to the Nicene Creed. Gregory returned to his see after the destruction and death of the pro-Arian emperor Valens in 378. The next year he attended the Council of Antioch, where he gained prominence as an outspoken opponent of Arianism. Elected in 380 to be bishop of Sebaste, he protested the appointment. At the Council of Constantinople (381) he was a leader of the orthodox party, emerging from the council as a deeply respected orthodox theologian, one of the most influential in the Eastern Empire. He apparently died a short time after participating in the Council of Constantinople (394) under Nectarius, patriarch of Constantinople and successor to GREGORY OF NAZIANZUS.

Gregory of Nyssa was a remarkable theologian, philosopher, and writer. Philosophically, he sought a harmony between Christian teaching and the tenets of Platonism and Neoplatonism. He was the author of numerous theological treatises, the most famous being the *Catechetical Orations* in which he examined the Trinity and the Incarnation, as well as baptism and the Eucharist. He also wrote against the heretical leaders Apollinaris and Eunomius. His ascetical works include *On Perfection, On Virginity,* and *On the Christian Life.* Aside from sermons, homilies, and letters, he also composed numerous works on Sacred Scriptures, his exegetical writings covering the life of Moses, a *Treatise on the Work of the Six Days,* and an explanation of the titles of the Psalms.

Gregory the Illuminator (257–332) *Apostle and patron saint of Armenia*

Called the Illuminator because of his preaching of the Christian faith to the Armenians, Gregory was not the first to preach the Gospel in Armenia (that honor is traditionally held by the Apostles Bartholomew and Jude

Thaddeus), but he was responsible for convincing the ruler of the Armenians, King Tiridates III, to accept Christianity as the national religion. Details about his life are complicated by the general unreliability of accounts written by Armenian chroniclers, such as that of Agathangelos (penned after 456), who embellished their narratives with fantastic tales and legends. It is likely, however, that Gregory was originally a Parthian prince who was raised as a Christian at Caesarea, in Cappadocia. He married and had two sons but then went to Armenia during the persecution of the church in that country under King Tiridates. Gregory succeeded not only in converting the ruler but inspired him to such devotion that the king sponsored the church throughout his realm. The Armenian nobles and people quickly followed suit. Gregory then returned to Caesarea, where he was ordained and consecrated bishop of the Armenians by Leontius of Caesarea. He continued to preach among the Armenians, establishing bishops and extending Christian influence into surrounding regions, including the Caucasus Mountains. Upon retiring, he was succeeded by his son Aristakes who, in 325, attended the Council of Nicaea. The position of bishop (or *katholikos*, also *catholicos*) was for a long period hereditary, remaining in Gregory's family. The many letters and sermons attributed to him are not considered genuine.

Gundioc (fl. mid-fifth century C.E.) *King of the Burgundians*

Gundioc distinguished himself by his successful dealings with the Western Empire, from which he probably received possession of Lugdunum (Lyons). He also played a part in the meteoric rise of the *magister militum* RICIMER, by marrying his sister. The child resulting from that union was GUNDOBAD, who would succeed him.

Gundobad (fl. late fifth century C.E.) *King of the Burgundians (after 474) and* magister militum

Gundobad was the son of King GUNDIOC, who was wedded to the sister of the MAGISTER MILITUM RICIMER. From the start of his political and military career, Gundobad relied upon his uncle, Ricimer, both for protection and for advancement. Thus, while his father continued to reign over the Burgundians, he aided Ricimer in attaining mastery over the Western Empire. In 472 he helped besiege Emperor ANTHEMIUS in Rome, and, after finding the defeated and disguised monarch, beheaded him personally on July 11, 472. As a reward for his loyalty and service, Ricimer elevated Gundobad to the rank of *magister militum*. When Ricimer was murdered in 472, Gundobad naturally succeeded him, assuming control over the affairs of the West. He personally approved the appointment of Glycerius to be emperor on March 25, 473, but did nothing to ensure the acceptance of his decision by Constantinople. The rejection of Glycerius by Leo and the subsequent naming of Julius Nepos to be emperor mattered little to Gundobad, because he was already returning home. His father died around 474, and Gundobad followed him on the throne. He was king at the time of the demise of the Roman Empire in the West.

H

Hadrian (Publius Aelius Hadrianus) (76–138 C.E.)
Emperor from 117 to 138 C.E.

Hadrian was born the son of Publius Aelius Hadrianus Afer and Domitia Paulina. The date of his birth was reported as January 24, 76, in Rome, although his family came from Picenum in Italy and had lived in Italica, a town of Hispania Baetica. Connections to the imperial palace came from the marriage of his grandfather, a senator, to Ulpia, the aunt of TRAJAN. Thus when Hadrian's father died in 85, the lad fell under the care of his guardians, Trajan himself (not yet emperor) and Acilius ATTIANUS, both of whom would prove influential in his subsequent development.

During his education, Hadrian displayed an intense fondness for all things Greek, earning the nickname "Greekling." Through Trajan's influence he entered into government service and held the powerful rank of tribune, with posts in Pannonia, Moesia, and Germania Superior. During this last posting, with the XXII Legion, the Primigenia Pia Fidelis, word arrived in October of 97 that Nerva had died. Trajan succeeded him. Hadrian hurried to give him congratulations and never ceased to enjoy the emperor's favor, journeying with him to Rome. There Hadrian married Trajan's grandniece, Vibia Sabina.

Wars followed as Hadrian saw duty in the First and Second Dacian Wars (102–103 and 105–106). He became a quaestor, legate, and praetor during the conflicts and then governed Pannonia in 107. A consulship followed in 108, along with the governorship of Syria in 114. A second consulship was set to be his in 118, but Trajan died on August 8, 117, in Cicilia.

Hadrian was at Antioch at the time of Trajan's death. He may not have been the emperor's first choice as successor, but through Attianus and the Empress Pompeia Plotina, Hadrian's adoption was announced on the ninth, two days before the official pronouncement of Trajan's demise. Despite such a suspicious beginning, the new emperor assumed power immediately. He terminated Trajan's attempts at expansion by pulling out of Mesopotamia, installing clients there instead. Urgent matters then summoned him to Moesia, where the Sarmatians and Roxolani were suppressed. Despite a promise not to execute members of the Senate, four senators were slain, an act that horrified the senatorial class and started Hadrian's reign badly. His association with the Senate would never assume any warmth.

The cause of the alleged plottings had been fear of Hadrian's changes in the imperial foreign and domestic policies. Many officials feared a weakening of the empire as a result. Hadrian abandoned military conquests, deeming them far too expensive, and instead centered on the frontiers. The borders were strengthened, new cities and

A coin from the reign of Hadrian; on the observe side is a testament to Britannia *(Hulton/Getty Archive)*

communities encouraged, legions made stationary in the provinces, and a broader system of static walls and fortifications adopted. Thus, in Raetia and Germania Superior, the *limites* were improved with palisades. In Britain (BRITANNIA) the incursions of the northern tribes were opposed by the Great Wall erected between Tyne and Solway (*see* WALL OF HADRIAN).

With a new, inward focus, Hadrian paid most of his attention to the provinces. He traveled more extensively than any of his predecessors, listening to the inhabitants of each territory. From 120 to 132 he never ceased his wanderings, journeying to Gaul, Britain, Spain, Asia, Greece (*see* ACHAEA and ATHENS), Sicily, Africa, Asia Minor, Cappadocia, Syria, and Egypt, where his favorite courtier, ANTINOUS, died in the Nile. The CURSUS PUBLICUS, or imperial post, was placed under central imperial administration. Athens he loved, giving it new buildings and favors and sitting as president of its public games. Throughout Asia and Asia Minor temples were dedicated. Rome was not forgotten, for there he built a new PANTHEON in the Campus Martius, to replace Marcus Agrippa's old structure. The Pantheon was a mammoth achievement, the highlight of a golden age in the empire.

While touring the provinces, Hadrian made it a point to win and hold the loyalty of his LEGIONS, for he had plans for them as well. Despite his gifts and constant sharing in the drudgery of their camp life, Hadrian demanded better discipline and more training. The legions were now rarely moved from their posts, and relied upon smaller detachments, the *vexillationes,* to provide patrols and communications between camps.

Hadrian was aided in these frontier and legionary adjustments by a period of calm. DACIA, subjugated by Trajan, was converted into a Roman territory of three provinces, and virtually everywhere else the imperial peace was maintained. Only in JUDAEA was there yet another episode in its bloody history of Roman occupation. In 132, the Jews under Simon BAR COCHBA rebelled, taking Jerusalem and forcing a war of two years' duration.

Two other areas of concern for Hadrian were government and law. The Equestrian Order (EQUITES) was advanced in importance, taking over the major burden of the civil service and amassing secretariat positions. The Equestrians were also placed on Hadrian's board, the CONSILIUM PRINCIPIS. This commission advised him on various matters, including legal questions. The edicts passed throughout the previous years were systematically organized with the help of experts in law and the judiciary. Judges were appointed in place of the traditional role of the Senate, adding further to the increased centralization of the state, including the development of the FRUMENTARII, the imperial Secret Service.

As was obvious from his grasp of the role of government on a vast scale, Hadrian was an intellectual of some stature. He surrounded himself with the finest minds of the time, encouraged Hellenic art styles, literature, and culture, and was himself an author of poems and an autobiography. To live in a retreat from Rome, he built a private estate just outside the city at TIVOLI.

His many gifts, which included a superb memory, were offset by a ruthless nature and a capacity to indulge in tyrannical behavior. His *frumentarii* would never be popular, and the frequent executions at the start and the end of his reign caused widespread dislike. The last murders were a part of the emperor's attempts to provide Rome with a proper heir. His first choice was Lucius Aelius Caesar, for he had no children himself; but Aelius dropped dead in January of 138. Another successor was found, ANTONINUS PIUS, who adopted Aelius's one son, Lucius Verus, and MARCUS AURELIUS. To simplify the succession, Hadrian killed his brother-in-law, Julius Ursus Servianus, and Servianus's grandson. The murders were prompted by a desire to avoid political strife and were evidence of the emperor's increasing harshness in the face of worsening illness. Suffering from numerous ailments, Hadrian reportedly had a desire to be killed, pleading with those around him to do so. He left Rome, finally, for a villa at Baiae, where he died on July 10, 138, having ruled Rome for 20 years and 11 months.

Spartianus authored an unreliable biography of Hadrian, using the emperor's own autobiography, and included it in the *Scriptores Historiae Augustae.*

Suggested Readings: Birley, Anthony. *Hadrian: The Restless Emperor.* New York: Routledge, 1997; Boatwright, Mary Taliaferro. *Hadrian and the City of Rome.* Princeton, N.J.: Princeton University Press, 1987; Lambert, Royston. *Beloved and God: The Story of Hadrian and Antinous.* London: Lyle Stuart, 1988; Perowne, Stewart. *Hadrian.* Dover, N.H.: Croom Helm, 1986.

Hannibalianus (d. 337 C.E.) *Nephew of Constantine the Great and ruler, briefly, of the kingdoms of Pontus, Armenia, and Cappadocia (335–337)*
The son of Flavius Dalmatius, Hannibalianus was the brother of Flavius Julius Dalmatius, with whom he was educated at Toulouse by Exsuperius. CONSTANTINE considered him worthy of participation in the succession, marrying him in 335 to his daughter Constantina and granting him the rank of *nobilissimus,* then appointing him to the throne of Pontus. Hannibalianus proved to be an able ruler and general, driving the Persians out of Armenia before taking over the rule of the country. He then took the title of King of Kings, with control over ARMENIA, PONTUS, and CAPPADOCIA. After the death of Constantine in 337, the successors, especially CONSTANTIUS II, grew wary of his power, and he was included in the palace massacre at Constantinople.

harpax Roman word for the Greek *harpagos,* or grappling hook, used by the Roman NAVY. One of the superb tactical innovations developed by Marcus AGRIPPA, the *harpax* was designed to be fired from a catapult at an approaching enemy ship, smashing into a hull to connect the two vessels. The Romans then reeled in the foe, smashing their oars and making them susceptible to attack by the highly skilled Imperial MARINES. The *harpax* enjoyed its greatest hour at ACTIUM, on September 2, 31 B.C.E., when the fleet of Octavian (AUGUSTUS) routed the ships of Antony and Cleopatra. Using the lighter Liburnian vessels, Agrippa, Octavian's admiral, moved around Antony's heavier ships, pinning and boarding them.

Haterius, Quintus (d. 26 C.E.) *Orator of the early first century* C.E.

Haterius came from a senatorial family and showed an early gift for speaking. According to Tacitus, however, this reputation did not survive his death because it was more the result of natural inclinations and skills than of study and discipline. His speeches were always aimed at acquiring the good will of Emperor TIBERIUS.

Hatra Fortress city situated in the harsh desert of MESOPOTAMIA, south of Nineveh and west of the Tigris. Its principal source of income was the trade routes that stretched from the East to Antioch and Palmyra and near Hatra. During the Roman Empire, the city was Parthian at first and then Persian, although it identified with the Arabs.

Hatra was involved in several of the Roman-Persian wars, using its many advantages to thwart capture. In 117 C.E., Trajan struggled to take the city but failed. It happened again in 199–200. Septimius Severus spent 20 days of incessant fighting but could produce only a shattered wall and no breaches in Hatra's defenses. Later, in the sweeping conquests of Ardashir, the first Sassanid king, the city still held out, and it would not be until 244 C.E. that Ardashir's son, Shapur, overcame the independent garrison. By the 360s it was in ruins.

The reasons for Hatra's invincibility were described in some detail by the historian Dio. He wrote that Hatra was neither large nor prosperous but used its location in the arid desert to exercise a terrible advantage over foes. The sun proved merciless to encampments, water dried up in the region and swarms of flies infested the invading troops. Storms frequently appeared as well, sent by the Sun-god, to whom the area had been consecrated. Trajan, having attempted to take Hatra, fell ill from the unpleasant conditions there and never recovered.

Hegesippus (fl. second-century C.E.) *Christian historian and saint*

Hegesippus was the author of five books of memoirs, in Greek, against the Gnostics and on the true tradition of apostolic preaching. He is known only through fragments, mostly preserved in Eusebius's *Ecclesiastical History*. Although the work was supposedly found in several libraries in Europe during the 1500s and 1600s, such copies are now lost. In the surviving portions, Hegesippus is concerned with the church in its early days in Jerusalem. He also compiled an important succession list of the Roman bishops. Originally probably from Palestine, he seems to have journeyed to Corinth and Rome, where he met several bishops as recorded in Eusebius.

Helena (Flavia Julia Helena) (c. 250–330) *Mother of Constantine the Great, Augusta from c. 325–330, and a renowned patron of Christianity*

Helena was born in Bithynia to a poor family of little social status. She was working as a servant when she met Constantius I Chlorus (d. 306). As he was not yet prominent politically, their relationship was not discouraged, and their subsequent union resulted in the birth of Constantine around 285. In 293, however, Constantius became Caesar (junior emperor) and found it politically expedient to divorce Helena, marrying Theodora, stepdaughter of Emperor Maximian. Helena withdrew from public life until 306 when her son succeeded Constantius in the imperial system of the tetrarchy. Converted to Christianity, Helena came to enjoy considerable prestige within the empire, especially as her son became sole ruler in 324. The following year, Helena was given the honorific title of Augusta and wielded much influence in the government, with control over part of the imperial treasury. In 326 she went on a pilgrimage to the Holy Land. While there she helped finance the building of churches, especially the Churches of the Holy Sepulchre, the Nativity, and the Ascension. She was also reported to have found the True Cross. After returning to Rome in 330, she died a short time later at the age of 80, one of the most venerable figures in the Roman Empire. Her tomb was installed in the basilica of Via Labicana. According to later traditions, she was attributed, incorrectly, a background and lineage based in England.

Heliodorus, C. Avidius (fl. mid-second century C.E.) *Philosopher, secretary, and associate of Hadrian*

C. Avidius Heliodorus acquired a reputation for philosophical and rhetorical brilliance as a member of Hadrian's intellectual circle. His official position was that of *ab epistulis*. Later he served as prefect of Egypt, a reward for his speeches. He was the father of Avidius Cassius, a future general under Emperor MARCUS AURELIUS.

Helius (d. 69 C.E.) *Freedman*

Helius amassed great power during the reign of Nero (54–69 C.E.). He may have held a procuratorship in Asia during the reign of Claudius, helping to launch the Neronian age with the destruction of SILANUS in 54 C.E.; he and Publius Celer poisoned Silanus. As a freedman of Nero, Helius received the emperor's trust and emulated his corruption and vices. In 67, the emperor traveled to Greece, leaving Helius virtually in control of the empire. He murdered at will but found that the responsibilities of the office were too great. He begged Nero to return, and eventually went to Greece to so alarm Nero that he would go back to Rome. Helius claimed that conspiracies were everywhere. He was accurate, because Nero fell from power in the next year. In 69 C.E., Galba, Nero's successor, ordered Helius put in chains, marched through the streets of Rome and then executed.

Helix, Aurelius (d. after 220 C.E.) *Famous Roman athlete*

Helix became one of the most popular athletes in Rome in 219–220. During the *ludi Capitolini*, he won both the wrestling and the *pancratium,* a type of violent boxing match. While performing at Olympia, he so frightened his opponents that no one entered the ring with him, fearing that he was the "eighth from Hercules."

Hellenism

One of the most pervasive and influential cultures encountered by the Romans was that of the Hellenic civilization, which reached its zenith in the fourth- and fifth-centuries B.C.E. and left its imprint on virtually the entire Mediterranean world. The Romans found in Greek culture the qualities and skills that they could emulate. Rome thus adopted and Latinized elements of Hellenic civilization, including its pantheon of gods and key facets of literature, art, and science. The acceptance of Hellenism came slowly, but its embrace made possible its place in the cultural inheritance bequeathed by the Romans to Western civilization.

The earliest influences of Hellenism on the Romans can be traced to the eighth century B.C.E. Greek colonies were established in southern Italy and Sicily, and the Etruscans bore a distinct Hellenic cultural imprint. The Romans, rustic farmers long suspicious of foreign influences, were reluctant to accept Greek customs, seeing them as contrary to traditional Roman values of family life and simple country habits. This opposition declined gradually following the overthrow of the last king of Rome in 509 B.C.E. and the foundation of the Republic. As Roman influence was extended across the Italian Peninsula, Greek literature, philosophy, art, and social practices became evidenced in Etruria, as did the use of Greek language. The continued expansion of Rome throughout the Mediterranean and the conquest of Greece and Sicily ultimately led to the adoption of Hellenic civilization by the Romans themselves in the third century B.C.E.

There followed an anti-Hellenic intellectual and cultural backlash led by Cato the Elder (234–149 B.C.E.), who saw Hellenism as a threat to Romanitas, the self-perception of being Roman and part of Roman culture. His sober call—like that of other Romans'—found little sympathy among the Roman upper class, who, as they grew more affluent, preferred the refinement, luxuries, and artistic sensibility of the Greeks to their own previous rusticity. Greek thus became the cultural benchmark for the elite of Roman society.

The Hellenic cultural imprint was advanced further by the four Macedonian Wars fought between Rome and the kingdom of Macedonia from 214–148 B.C.E. The conflicts ended in the reduction of Macedonia to the status of a Roman province and the perpetual involvement of Rome in the affairs of the Greeks and the Hellenized East. The war also brought a steady influx of Greek and Hellenized slaves and prisoners to Rome, marking a significant social change. Many of the prisoners became tutors to the children of the powerful of the city, teaching the future leaders of the empire Greek, philosophy, literature, and rhetoric. Inevitably, Greek became one of the mandatory languages of the upper classes, and ignorance of Greek intellectual arts was considered a genuine social failing.

Hellenism was embraced subsequently by the Romans in virtually every significant aspect of their culture. Its influence was felt in the fields of education, art and architecture, literature, and philosophy, and nearly every notable Roman intellectual had some association with the Greeks. Cicero and Julius Caesar both studied in Greece; Lucretius acknowledged openly the superiority of the Greeks; and Emperor Hadrian was unquestionably more of a Greek in outlook than he was a Roman. Marcus Aurelius wrote his correspondence in Greek, not in Latin.

Beyond the confines of Rome and its social classes, Hellenism exercised perhaps its greatest influence on the peoples of the eastern provinces of the Roman Empire and upon the sociopolitical system utilized by the Romans for the maintenance of their far-flung empire. Thanks to the conquests of Alexander the Great and domination of the Mediterranean world by his immediate successors, Hellenism was firmly planted across the many lands of the East well before the Roman legions marched upon their frontiers.

The inhabitants of what became the eastern provinces of the Roman Empire were thus already united in a number of ways by Hellenic civilization. The first and most ubiquitous forms of cultural unity was the presence of a common tongue, a lingua franca: Greek, in the form of colloquial language termed *koin*. Colloquial Greek was spoken from the Italian peninsula to parts of Africa to Egypt and Alexandria, across Palestine, and over the whole of Asia Minor. It was the language of commerce and of most local government. The Romans did not change this system, finding it useful as a centralizing language, as they lacked the resources and the bureaucratic personnel to staff every form and level of government administration.

Equally, the presence of established cities and urban centers based upon the traditional Greek structure of the *polis*, offered to the Romans a ready-made arrangement for government. The local administration was left in the hands of those administrators on the scene, but they were gradually absorbed into the wider imperial system of the *colonia* and *municipia,* which offered many advantages. The most favored status possible for a community was the granting of Roman citizenship, a privilege that necessitated the abandonment of the earlier *polis* in favor of the colonial and then municipal status. Nevertheless, *koin* remained the lingua franca and the adoption of Roman law was uneven, with long-standing Greek law and local customs enduring long after a city was declared a *municipia.*

The Hellenization of the Roman Empire was marked in the late third century, with the decline of Rome and the division of the empire by Diocletian. As Rome proved strategically indefensible to the threats on its frontiers, the heart of the empire gravitated eastward, culminating in the decision of Constantine the Great to build his capital at Byzantium, the city renamed Constantinople. The Eastern Empire, based in Constantine's metropolis, began along Latin lines but within a few centuries was fully imbued with the Hellenic flavor of the region and its historical sensibilities. The Latin culture that had forged the empire deteriorated in the West and was amalgamated with the even more vital Germanic peoples that were overrunning it. In the East, the fading Latin culture received a major strengthening by grounding itself further in Hellenism, which it earlier had admired grudgingly and had adopted gradually. Greek life and traditions allowed the Eastern Empire to reject outright the Germanic influences so dominant in the West during the later imperial era, thereby granting a stay of execution to the Roman Empire itself. While the Western Empire ended in broad terms in 476, the Eastern or Byzantine Empire endured until 1453. The words of HORACE (*Epist.,* 2.1.156–57) proved prophetic indeed: *Graecia capta ferum victorum capit et artes; intulit agresti Latio.*

See also ART AND ARCHITECTURE, EDUCATION, LITERATURE, PHILOSOPHY.

Suggested Readings: Aries, Philippe, and Georges Duby, eds. *A History of Private Life 1: From Pagan Rome to Byzantium.* Cambridge, Mass.: Belknap Press of Harvard University Press, 1987; Athanassiadi-Fowden, Polymnia. *Julian and Hellenism: An intellectual biography.* Oxford: Clarendon Press, 1981; Balsdon, J. P. V. D. *Life and Leisure in Ancient Rome.* New York: McGraw-Hill, 1969; Balsdon, J. P. V. D. *Roman Women: Their History and Habits.* London: Bodley Head, 1962; Bertman, Stephen, eds. *The Conflict of Generations in Ancient Greece and Rome.* Amsterdam: Gruner, 1976; Boren, Henry C. *Roman Society: A Social, Economic, and Cultural History;* Lexington, Mass.: D.C. Heath, 1977; Bradley, K. R. *Slaves and Masters in the Roman Empire: A Study in Social Control.* Brussels: Latomus, 1984; Bradley, K. R. *Slavery and Rebellion in the Roman World, 140 B.C.–70 B.C.* London: B. T. Batsford, 1989; Brown, Peter R. L. *Society and the Holy in Late Antiquity.* Berkeley: University of California Press, 1982;

Carcopino, Jerome. *Daily Life in Ancient Rome.* New Haven, Conn.: Yale University Press, 1968; Clark, G. *Women in the Ancient World.* Oxford: Oxford University Press, 1989; Cowell, F. R. *Life in Ancient Rome.* New York: G. F. Putnam's Sons, 1961; Cunliffe, Barry. *Greeks, Romans and Barbarians: Spheres of Interaction.* London: Batsford, 1988; Dupont, Florence. *Daily Life in Ancient Rome.* Translated by Christopher Woodall. Oxford, U.K.: Blackwell Publishers, 1992; Finley, M. I., ed. *Classical Slavery.* London: F. Cass, 1987; Garnsey, Peter. *The Roman Empire: Economy, Society, and Culture.* Berkeley: University of California Press, 1987; Hallett, Judith P. *Fathers and Daughters in Roman Society: Women and the Elite Family.* Princeton, N.J.: Princeton University Press, 1984; Raaflaub, Kurt A., ed. *Social Struggles in Archaic Rome: New Perspectives on the Conflict of the Orders.* Berkeley: University of California Press, 1986; Rawson, Elizabeth. *Intellectual Life in the Late Roman Republic.* Baltimore: Johns Hopkins University Press, 1985; Trager, James. *The Women's Chronology: A Year-By-Year Record from Prehistory to the Present.* New York: Henry Holt, 1994; Veyne, P., ed. *A History of Private Life 1. From Pagan Rome to Byzantium.* Cambridge, Mass.: Harvard University Press, 1987.

Helvetia Correctly called *Ager Helvetiorum* (Land of the Helvetians); the territory occupied by the Helvetii, a fierce people living in the western part of modern Switzerland. In the late second century B.C.E., and throughout the first, according to Caesar, this territory was surrounded by the Rhine, the Jura range and both Lake Geneva and the Rhone. As a consequence, the Helvetii lived a crowded existence, making expansion difficult and war inevitable.

Their first experience with Rome came around 107 B.C.E., when they invaded Gaul and later Italy, only to be routed by Marius in 101. The cramped circumstances under which they lived were not improved in 58 B.C.E. when Julius CAESAR took control of Gaul (*See* GALLIC WARS). Under their chief, ORGETORIX, they planned to leave their homes and settle in the more fertile and expansive regions of southern Gaul (GALLIA NARBONENSIS). After Orgetorix died, the Helvetii set out on their quest.

It was unfortunate for them that Caesar had power over Gaul at the time, for there they met an enemy that they could not defeat. At Arar and Bibracte, they suffered devastating setbacks and were compelled to return home. Subsequent Roman domination brought colonies and legionary camps, subduing the Helvetii and, in time, Romanizing them.

The capital of the Helvetii was Aventicum, joined by such cities as Vindonissa and Noviodunum. They remained pacified and quiet for over a century and then, in 69 C.E., suffered the misfortune of being in the line of march of the legions of aspiring-emperor VITELLIUS. Believing that Galba was still emperor, they refused to accept Vitellius's claims (they had not even heard of Otho). Alienus Caecina, Vitellius's general, launched an attack against the Helvetii in retaliation. Thousands of the Helvetians were killed and most of the country was pillaged and burned. Aventicum was spared only by abject surrender and by the acceptance of humiliating terms.

Helvetii *See* HELVETIA.

Helvidius Priscus (fl. first century C.E.) *Stoic philosopher*
The son of a centurion, Helvidius became a Stoic and had a long, distinguished career ahead of him when he married the daughter of THRASEA PAETUS. Unfortunately, in 66, his father-in-law was destroyed politically through the machinations of EPRIUS MARCELLUS. While Thrasea Paetus was forced to commit suicide, Priscus was exiled from Rome to Apollonia, Syria.

When Galba succeeded to the throne in 69, Priscus returned to Rome, eager to avenge the death of Thrasea upon Marcellus. He was prevented from this by Galba and the division of the Senate. In 70 he was praetor, greeting the new emperor Vespasian by his own name. This act of rudeness was only the start of a long campaign of dissension and effrontery, culminating in his banishment from Rome again. Vespasian reportedly ordered his death reluctantly, sending an order of pardon as well, but accidentally allowing it to be withdrawn when a report reached him that Priscus was already dead. He thus died in the same Stoic manner as his father-in-law. Tacitus, in the *Histories*, wrote that Priscus discharged his duties as senator, husband, and son-in-law with propriety, always demanding the truth and firm in the face of danger.

Hera *See* JUNO.

Heracleus the Eunuch (d. 455 C.E.) *Official in the court of Valentinian III*
Heracleus helped to murder the *magister militum* AETIUS on September 21, 454. Heracleus held the post of chamberlain (*PRAEPOSITUS SACRI CUBICULI*), using his skills to secure palace control. Toward this end he convinced the emperor that Aetius was dangerous and had to be removed. Valentinian, in agreeing to the murder, removed from the scene the only man capable of halting the barbarian invasions of the era. Once Aetius was gone, Heracleus secured his own position by opposing the nominations of any successors, including PETRONIUS MAXIMUS. Maximus, however, was equal to the occasion and convinced former officers of Aetius to remove not only Heracleus but Valentinian as well. They died only months after Aetius's murder, in 455.

Heraclianus, Aurelius (d. 268 C.E.) *Prefect of the Praetorian Guard (267–268)*
Heraclianus served in the army of Emperor GALLIENUS and was a prime player in the conspiracy against him in 268. He first appeared in the records as the general in command of an expedition against the Persians, defeated by the Palmyrenes of Queen Zenobia. This story is highly unlikely. Heraclianus plotted to remove the emperor, whose reign had been marked by seemingly endless disasters, political and military. His coconspirators were Claudius and Domitius Aurelianus (both later emperors) and, presumably, numerous other generals and staff officers. For whatever reasons, Heraclianus killed himself after the assassination.

Herculaneum City in CAMPANIA situated between Neapolis and POMPEII that achieved everlasting fame as the sister city of Pompeii covered by Mount VESUVIUS on August 24, 79 C.E. Herculaneum was founded either by local inhabitants or as a trading post by the Greeks. Its development followed closely that of nearby Pompeii, and, like it, the city was captured by the Romans in 89 B.C.E. Unlike Pompeii, the city did not receive colonial status but, instead, municipal rank (*see* COLONIES and MUNICIPIUM). Throughout the late Republic and in the early years of the empire, Herculaneum became the opposite of Pompeii, with residences, villas, and little industry. Where Pompeii relied upon trade and business to survive,

The remains of Herculaneum *(Courtesy Fr. Felix Just, S.J.)*

the inhabitants of Herculaneum put their hopes in the smaller taverns and shops and in the gold of the wealthy owners of the villas. Thus, in 62 C.E., when an earthquake caused severe damage in Campania, repairs went much faster in Herculaneum. Any previous disasters were as nothing compared to the eruption of Mount Vesuvius. Herculaneum, Pompeii, and Stabiae were buried by lava and ash. In this city, the ash was as deep as 100 feet, sealing for centuries the entire community. When discovered in 1720, and through many long years of excavation, Herculaneum emerged as an almost complete city. It contained a theater, a basilica, baths, and temples to Isis and Magna Mater. Its value, historically, and archaeologically, has increased with each new discovery.

Herennia Etruscilla (Herennia Cupressenia Etruscilla (fl. mid-third century C.E.) *Wife of G. M. Q. Decius; empress from 249 to 251 and Augusta from around 250*
Herennia joined her husband as ruler of the Roman Empire and supported his persecution of Christianity. She also supervised the education of their son, Herennius Etruscus, who became Caesar in 250 and Augustus in 251. She was elevated to Augusta around this time to aid her position in Rome while DECIUS was away on campaigns. In June 251, the emperor was annihilated with his son at Abrittus by the Goths under KNIVA. His successor was Gallus, who worked to placate the political elements in the capital by leaving Herennia in her position as Augusta and by placing her younger son, Hostilian, in the role of co-emperor. Gallus did not last past 253, and Herennia faded into obscurity.

Herennius Etruscus (Quintus Herennius Etruscus Messius Decius) (d. 251 C.E.) *Son of Decius and Herennia Etruscilla*
Herennius received the traditional education of the court and, when his father became emperor in 249, was made a prince. In 250 he was appointed heir designate of the throne, with the title of Caesar, and in 251 he became Augustus. Herennius joined his father in the wars on the frontier against the Goths, after leading troops himself into Moesia to protect the Danubian provinces. The fighting was fierce. Herennius apparently was at his father's side in every engagement, including the last one, the disaster at Abrittus in June of 251. This terrible battle, fought with the Goths, cost the empire its ruler and the designated heir, for Herennius died beside his father.

Hermes   *See* MERCURY.

Hermes Trismegistos   A mystic author, generally associated with the Egyptian god Thoth, whose works, collectively known as the *Corpus Hermeticum,* were divided into 18 books and played a major role in the subsequent evolution of European occultism, hermetic magic, and pseudo-mystical alchemy.

Hermogenes (d. after 138 C.E.) *Physician of Emperor Hadrian (r. 117–138 C.E.)*
Hermogenes was unable to cure HADRIAN of dropsy, an ailment that plagued the emperor toward the end of his life. According to the historian Dio, Hermogenes participated in Hadrian's efforts to end his life prematurely because of his illness. Hadrian summoned Mastor, an IAZYGES, and instructed Hermogenes to show him where to strike at the heart for a quick death. Hermogenes began the instructions, but Mastor recoiled in terror from the deed. Hadrian then supposedly ate dangerous foods and finally died, saying, "Many doctors have killed a king."

Hermunduri   One of the major tribes of southern Germany (GERMANIA), who occupied the region between the Main and the Danube rivers. They were strategically placed between two traditionally hostile people, the CHATTI to the north and the MARCOMANNI to the south. The presence of such enemies and the geographic position of the Hermunduri made an alliance with Rome both desirous and inevitable.

According to the historian Tacitus, the Hermunduri were friends of the Roman Empire to an unusual extent. They could cross borders and enter freely into Germania Superior and Raetia. Commerce between them and the provinces was heavy. In 58 C.E., the Hermunduri fought a summer-long battle with the Chatti for control over several important salt springs. The Hermunduri gained victory. Later, Emperor Domitian probably received their help against the Chatti during his campaign in Germany. By the middle of the second century C.E. the Hermunduri had joined the ranks of the Marcomanni and their German allies. They made unsuccessful war against Marcus Aurelius, were defeated and subsequently became only one element of the wider barbarian cataclysm growing just beyond the Roman world.

Herod Antipas (d. after 39 C.E.) *Son of Herod the Great and his Samaritan wife Matthace*
Herod Antipas was king of Galilee and Peraea from 4 B.C.E. to 39 C.E. He was one of the fortunate sons of HEROD THE GREAT, surviving childhood and his father, who died in 4 B.C.E. As an heir, he aspired to the throne of Judaea but had to be satisfied with Galilee and Peraea, ruling as a tetrarch, appointed by Emperor Augustus. Herod did what he could to improve his domain, emulating his father in the construction of cities. Tiberias was founded and Sepphoris improved, although it was intended to be subordinate to Tiberias, where Herod lived in a palace erected for his pleasure. In Peraea he also repaired Betharamptha, renaming it first Livias and then Julias.

Domestically, Herod was not popular with his subjects, inheriting the same local problems that had plagued his father. He compounded these by divorcing the daughter of Aretas IV of Nabataea and marrying the famous HERODIAS. She urged her new husband to ambitious projects but could do little to prevent his suffering a damaging attack in 37 C.E. at the hands of his estranged father-in-law, Aretas, who exacted revenge for his daughter, an act left largely unpunished by Rome.

Tiberius used Herod to negotiate a treaty with Parthia in 36 C.E., but his success in this venture was short-lived. Herodias continued her ambitions, and in 39, Herod made the mistake of asking the new emperor, GAIUS CALIGULA, for the right to rule as an independent king, with ambitions toward the realm of Herod Agrippa I. Caligula deposed him in favor of his friend Herod Agrippa I. Herod Antipas and his wife were sent into exile in Lugdunum (Lyons), his removal probably the result of Herod Agrippa's plotting. Ironically, Herod Antipas never recovered politically from the two major events of his long reign. First, he was responsible for the arrest and execution of John the Baptist. Later, PONTIUS PILATE sent him a prisoner to be tried, but the tetrarch would have nothing to do with such a religiously prominent figure, Jesus Christ.

Herod the Great (c. 73–4 B.C.E.) *King of Judaea from 37 to 4 B.C.E.*

Herod was the son of ANTIPATER of Idumaea, then a minister of state for the family of Jannaeus Alexander. As his father grew in power and influence in the kingdom, Herod and his brother Phasael attained positions in government. By 47 B.C.E. he was governor of GALILEE, while his brother served as governor of JUDAEA. Both were Roman citizens. Antipater was assassinated in 43 by the religio-political party of Malichus, and Herod immediately destroyed the group, making himself indispensable to the ethnarch of Judaea, the weak Hyrcanus. The next three years were spent by Herod in cementing his position as the successor to Antipater in the kingdom. When Antigonus, the son of the disenfranchised Prince Aristobulus, arrived to start a civil war, Herod defeated him and compelled Hyrcanus to give him a share in the royal house, including a marriage to his granddaughter Mariamne.

Herod was certainly working toward the succession when, in 40, the Parthians invaded Palestine. Hyrcanus was captured, Phasael forced to kill himself and Antigonus placed in control of Jerusalem. Unable to win without allies, Herod retreated to the mountain fastness of MASADA, set its defenses and then journeyed to Rome to ask for the aid of Marc Antony. The general gave him full support and the rights to the throne of Hyrcanus, as ethnarch of Judaea, and the family home of Herod, Idumaea. Three years of fighting followed, including a siege of Jerusalem to evict Antigonus. Finally, with the help of

the Roman legions, Herod was firmly in place. He wisely maintained excellent relations with Antony, now master of the East as a member of the Second TRIUMVIRATE, but avoided losing the kingdom to Cleopatra, who was amassing vast territories for Egypt. Such an association eventually proved ill-advised, when Octavian (AUGUSTUS) won the battle of ACTIUM in 31 B.C.E.

Herod was able to convince the new emperor that he was trustworthy, and Augustus fitted the Judaean realm into his general plan for the eastern clients of the empire. Not only was Herod confirmed in his role, but also new cities were added to his possessions. Such gifts did nothing to improve his standing with his own subjects, however, for they disliked his Idumaean origins and his policies toward Gentiles, despite the fact that they resulted in prosperity.

The economics of Palestine were improved. Herod built CAESAREA on the coast and granted gifts to foreign communities, especially the Greeks, whom he admired and emulated. The Hellenic character of his court inflamed the conservative Jewish population. His citizens found little joy in his rebuilding of the Great Temple, preferring to focus on his foreign tastes and his harsh and despotic government, so openly answerable to Rome. Herod was beset by domestic troubles and by his own violent nature. Unrest was chronic throughout all of Palestine, and the more ruthlessly the king suppressed it the more widespread it became. Equally, Herod carried his willingness to shed blood into the privacy of the palace. In 30 he murdered his predecessor, Hyrcanus, and the following year executed his wife Mariamne.

His sons were fortunate to survive him, and on some occasions lucky to survive dinner parties. Two sons, ARISTOBULUS AND ALEXANDER, were tried and killed in 7 B.C.E., and another died in 4 B.C.E., just before Herod himself expired after a bout with a terrible illness much like that which later infected Emperor GALERIUS. Augustus commented that it was safer to be one of Herod's pigs than one of his sons, making note of the Jewish ban on the handling of pork. Following his demise in 4 B.C.E., Herod's vast realm was divided among his heirs: Antipas, Archelaus, and Philip. Never again would Rome allow such independence on the part of a king of Palestine.

Herodes Atticus (Lucius Vibullius Hipparchus Tiberius Claudius Atticus Herodes) (c. 104–178 C.E.) *Sophist, political figure, and a patron of extreme wealth*

Herodes was born in the famed city of Marathon but taught in Rome and gained a considerable reputation for rhetoric. Atticus became the tutor of Marcus Aurelius and Lucius Verus. Made a CONSUL in 143 and having amassed tremendous riches, Atticus was also heir to the fortune of Hipparchus of Athens, as his grandson. He turned this legacy into a series of gifts to his native land, especially to the city of Athens. In time his generosity overcame his reputation as a sophist. Athens received buildings and other gifts from Atticus, as well as aqueducts, which were erected at Olympia. Atticus also constructed the Odeion of Athens, in honor of his wife who died in 160.

Herodian (d. c. 250 C.E.) *Historian and writer*

Born in Syria, Herodian joined the civil service according to his own account. Little else is known of his early or private life, except that his work displays a strong sense of patriotism toward the empire and a stern moral streak. His lasting achievement was a history of the emperors, from Marcus Aurelius to the accession of Gordian III (180–238 C.E.). Its value is limited until the narrative reaches a more contemporary account, for Herodian ignored chronology, historical facts, and events. As a younger associate of DIO, Herodian was overshadowed in his own generation by this great historian. His own history reflected Dio's mammoth effort, relying upon it for many details but, at times, supplementing Dio's own writing.

Herodias (d. after 39 C.E.) *Famous wife of Herod Antipas and daughter of Berenice and Aristobulus, son of Herod the Great*

Herodias watched her father being murdered at the order of Herod the Great and then married the half-brother of HEROD ANTIPAS, another Herod called Philip in the account of the Gospel of Mark. Herod Antipas apparently fell in love with his niece and proposed to her. Seeing that his fortunes were rising faster than her husband's, Herodias accepted his hand. Antipas divorced his first wife, the daughter of Aretas IV of Nabataea, and took Herodias as his wife upon his return from Rome, sometime before the murder of John the Baptist.

The marriage was received with animosity by the people, who accused the royal couple of adultery and incest. Further, Aretas IV launched a retaliatory attack upon Herod in 37, with an invasion of Peraea, a strike that Rome did not avenge. Herodias was depicted as harsh, demanding, and scheming. She was supposed to have driven her husband into the ambitious plans that eventually cost him his throne. In 39, she convinced Herod to ask for greater control of Galilee and Peraea, which resulted in the two of them being charged with treasonous conspiracies. They were deposed and exiled to Lugdunum (Lyons) by Gaius Caligula.

Herodion Fortress built by Herod the Great, 60 furlongs south of JERUSALEM, upon an artificial hill; served as one of his major defensive sites in JUDAEA. During Herod's war of reconquest against the Parthians (40–37 B.C.E.), he defeated a Parthian force near the hill. To commemorate this triumph a new fortress was constructed there. Ever ambitious, Herod perhaps exceeded his own hopes, when the Herodion (Latin, *Herodium*) was completed. The

Herodion was generally hidden from view by its artificial mound, tremendous in size but invisible until a visitor actually ascended the 200 steps of white marble leading to the summit. Round towers and high walls provided an architecturally impressive defense. Within, its beauty was centered in the sumptuous palaces inhabited quite often by Herod. There were apartments, baths, gardens, and a synagogue, as well as areas for friends and staff. Water had to be brought in from outside sources.

In 14 B.C.E. Marcus Agrippa visited Judaea and was entertained at the Herodion. Ten years later the fort served as Herod's tomb. He was reportedly buried there, although his body was never discovered. The history of the site did not prevent the Jews from seizing it in 66 C.E. in the JEWISH REBELLION against Rome.

The Herodion, however, was no Masada. It fell to the legate Lucilius Bassus and his forces. During the time of the uprising of Simon BAR COCHBA (132–135), the Herodion was reoccupied by the Jews but once more fell to the Romans.

Heruli One of the more powerful of the barbarian peoples. The Heruli or Heruls migrated originally from Scandinavia, perhaps Sweden, to follow their Gothic neighbors south. They branched off into two main hosts, one continuing on toward the Rhine, the other toward the BLACK SEA. Both arrived during the critical third century C.E. to join in the terrible invasions of the time.

The Rhine Heruli found a place along the southern stretch of the river where they came into immediate contact with the Romans, some time around 286 C.E. They soon entered into the service of Rome, supplying auxiliaries for the army in Germany (GERMANIA). Their separated cousins took a very different path. These Heruli reached the Black Sea in the middle of the third century C.E. and were allied to the major nation of the Goths. As they were familiar with ships and sailing, the Heruli were put in charge of the vessels extracted from the kingdom of the BOSPORUS and used to launch the invasions of Asia Minor, Thrace, and Greece in 267. The Heruli-guided fleets ravaged Bithynia, Byzantium, and much of the Black Sea coast. Gallienus, that same year, fought a bloody battle against the Goths at Naissus. The Heruli contingents under King Naulobotus surrendered, and Naulobotus received a client status from the emperor. But two years later the Heruli ships were again on the prowl.

At first the Heruli settled on the Black Sea, establishing for themselves a small territory. As the eastern hordes continued to arrive, they pushed westward, arriving finally in Pannonia. Relatively peaceful cohabitation followed with their Gothic neighbors, but by the middle of the fifth century, a new, potent race had taken control of a vast stretch of land from the Steppes to the Danube. The Huns became slave masters of the many smaller tribes across much of Europe, using them as fighting servants. Thus, in 451, when Attila set off to conquer Gaul, the

Heruli were in his host. The Hunnic empire, however, was destined to be brief. Attila died in 454. One year later a union of the Germans smashed the Huns in Pannonia at the battle of Nedao, breaking them so thoroughly that they never again troubled Europe in any organized fashion. Heruli warriors participated in the battle against the Huns and reaped the rewards of freedom. They took over a part of Pannonia and there grew in size and in strength. By the end of the Western Empire, in 476 C.E., the mighty Odoacer, the first barbarian king of Italy, may have deposed Romulus Augustulus with the help of the Heruli.

Hesychius of Jerusalem (fl. early fifth century) *Greek presbyter and exegete, author of numerous biblical commentaries, saint in the Greek Church*
Little is known of Hesychius's life, although he was probably a monk in his early years and, according to Theophanes the Confessor, a presbyter in Jerusalem in 412. His writings have been lost in part, but many were preserved in edited form and passed on under other names. Thus, the commentary on the Psalms attributed to St. Athanasius was probably the work of Hesychius. He apparently wrote commentaries on the entire Bible and was the author of a lost church history. Hesychius should not be confused with Bishop Hesychius of Jerusalem, a contemporary of St. Gregory the Great.

Hibernia Roman name for Ireland; also called Iverna or Juverna after one of the tribes upon its southern coast. Ireland never suffered subjugation by Rome, although it was known to the Romans, including Julius Caesar and Agricola. Tacitus, in *Agricola,* wrote of the country:

> This island is less than Britain, but larger than those of our sea (the Mediterranean). Its soil, climate, and the manner and dispositions of its inhabitants, are little different from those in Britain. Its ports and harbors are better known, from the concourse of merchants for the purpose of commerce.

Agricola, the great general of Rome in Britain, was of the opinion that all of Ireland could have been conquered and held by one legion and some auxiliaries. But the inability of the legions in Britain to keep those islands safe from invasion precluded any new acquisitions of territory.

Hierocles (1) (d. 222. C.E.) *Most decadent of the courtiers in the service of Emperor Elagabalus*
Hierocles earned the title of "husband" to the ruler. Hierocles was a slave from Caria, living in Rome and earning his living as a chariot driver. One day he took a spill just in front of the royal box. His golden hair and beauty attracted ELAGABALUS immediately, and within days Hierocles was installed in the palace, amassing tremendous power over the court and the emperor. Elagabalus, by

220, was absolutely enamored of him. The slave's mother, also in servitude, was brought to Rome and given a place of honor. Elagabalus tried to raise Hierocles to the rank of Caesar and enjoyed being beaten by him for "adultery." Not surprisingly, the Romans, and the Praetorian Guard especially, greeted such behavior as revolting and demanded Hierocles' dismissal with other, equally offensive officials. Elagabalus first agreed but then reinstated Hierocles, an act that hastened the emperor's assassination by the Guard in 222. Hierocles was included in the ranks of those massacred after the death of the emperor.

Hierocles (2), **Sossianus** (fl. early fourth century C.E.) *Governor of Bithynia and Egypt and the instigator of persecutions against the Christians*
Hierocles tried to use an intellectual, philosophical, and imaginative response to CHRISTIANITY. He preferred to compel Christians to recant rather than seek martyrdom by execution. Punishment for those who remained steadfast, however, could take a unique turn. He once confined a virgin to a brothel, an act for which he was beaten with a stick by the philosopher Aedesius. Hierocles also authored a treatise attacking the basis and logic of Christ and the Christian Creed. Eusebius responded with his *Contra Hieroclem* (Against Hierocles).

Hieronymian Martyrology Famous martyrology, known in Latin as the *Hieronymianum,* that was probably compiled in the fifth century in Italy. Its name was derived from a statement in the (apocryphal) correspondence that precedes the text that lists St. Jerome as the author of the work. The martyrology gives the date on the calendar year, followed by the name of a saint commemorated on each day, where the saint might be buried, entombed, or venerated, and any appropriate details related to the particular saint.

Hilarianus, Q. Iulius (fl. early fourth century C.E.) *Chronologist*
Hilarianus was the author of several works on chronology. The most notable of these works was *De duratione mundi* (On the duration of the world).

Hilary (1) (**Hilary of Arles**) (403–449) *Archbishop of Arles who became a catalyst in the extending of papal authority over the church in Gaul*
From a family in northern Gaul, Hilary became a monk in Lérins, succeeding St. Honoratus in 428–429 as archbishop of Arles. A supporter of reform, he presided over several councils, including those of Orange (441) and Vaison (442). In 444, he took the important step of deposing Bishop Chelidonius of Besançon and irregularly replacing him with another. This act exceeded his authority as a metropolitan, and the entire measure was rescinded by Pope St. Leo I. The pontiff then deprived

Hilary of his metropolitan powers and obtained from Emperor Valentinian III recognition that Rome had supreme jurisdiction over the church in Gaul. Hilary submitted to the papal acts and was not removed from his see. He also authored a still extant biography of Honoratus and other minor works.

Hilary (2) (Hilary of Poitiers) (c. 315–367) *Bishop of Poitiers, theologian, leading opponent of Arianism*

Called the Athanasius of the West, Hilary was raised as a pagan, receiving an education centered around Neoplatonism. Converted to Christianity, he was elected bishop of Poitiers around 353. A short time later, he emerged as the main defender of orthodoxy in the West against the Arians. He was condemned for his stand by the Council of Biterrae in 356 and exiled to Phrygia for four years by Emperor Constantius III. In 359, he returned to prominence at the Council of Seleucia, where he spoke out eloquently on his own behalf. His oratorical skills were matched by his lasting contributions to the faith through his writings. Aside from his commentaries on the Old and New Testaments, particularly the Psalms, his chief works are *De Trinitate* (On the Trinity) and *De Synodis* (On the Synods).

Hilary (3) (Hilarius) (d. 468 C.E.) *Saint, pope from 461 to 468*

Probably a native of Sardinia, Hilary served for a time as archdeacon to Pope Leo I and was one of his legates with Julius, bishop of Puteoli, at the Latrocinium, the Robber Council of Ephesus in 449. There he protested the condemnation of Flavian, patriarch of Constantinople, and fought for the rights of the Roman see. He was forced to flee the city because of the violence that erupted there, barely escaping unharmed and attributing his safe journey to John the Evangelist, in whose burial site just outside Ephesus Hilary had hidden himself. Elected successor to Leo in November 461, he pursued the policies of his illustrious predecessor, devoting particular attention to Gaul (France) and Spain, where he resolved a number of ecclesiastical disputes and consolidated the authority of Rome. His synod at Rome in 465 is the oldest Roman synod for which extensive minutes have been preserved. In his dealings with the Eastern Church, Hilary circulated a decretal confirming the Councils of Nicaea (325), Ephesus (431), and Chalcedon (451).

Hills of Rome

Tradition held that King Servius Tullius in the sixth century B.C.E. erected a fortification around the growing city of Rome, including within his walls the seven hills that became so much a part of Roman history and legend. These hills were the Palatine, Capitoline, Quirinal, Caelian, Aventine, Viminal, and Esquiline. Other hills surrounding the city included the Pincian, Janiculum, and Vatican.

Mons Palatinus The Palatine Hill was situated just south of the Quirinal Hill and the CAMPUS MARTIUS. Throughout the Imperial Age it was the abode of the emperors. Augustus lived upon it in a small house, and his successors built increasingly lavish palaces. The DOMUS TIBERIANA was eventually connected to the GOLDEN HOUSE OF NERO by the DOMUS TRANSITORIA, which stretched across the Velia to the valley beneath the Esquiline. Domitian constructed the Domus Domitiani and the DOMUS AUGUSTANA, with its own stadium. There were, as well, several arches surrounding the hill, including those of Titus and Constantine.

Mons Capitolinus The Capitoline was actually two hills with a depression between them, the Capitol and the Arx. Its name was derived from the magnificent temple adorning its summit, the Temple of Jupiter Optimus Maximus. Here was the very heart of the Roman Cult of State and in time the religious center for the pagan world. The SIBYLLINE BOOKS were kept in the temple, and TRIUMPHS for generals were routed past it.

See also TEMPLE OF JUPITER CAPITOLINUS.

Collis Quirinalis One of the largest hills of Rome, the Quirinal is adjacent to the Campus Martius and just south of the Pincian Hills. It also formed a valley with the Viminal, the *vallis Quirini*. Aside from the GARDENS OF SALLUST (Horti Sallusti), rightfully belonging to the Pincian Hills, the Quirinal contained two spectacular structures: the Baths of Constantine and the sumptuous Baths of Diocletian (*see* BATHS). Along the base of the southern end of the Quirinal was the area of the city called the Subura.

Mons Caelius The most southeasterly of the seven hills, the Caelian was connected to the inner workings of the city mainly by its northwestern tip. Here the jutting portions were used in part by Emperor Nero for his Golden House. Later, the Flavians created the COLOSSEUM in that area, filling the valley between the Caelian, Palatine, and Esquiline hills. After the death of Claudius, Agrippina began the TEMPLE OF DIVUS CLAUDIUS. Nero tore down its walls, but Vespasian restored them. Because of its isolated position, relatively speaking, the Caelian Hill served as a useful site for several military and semi-political units. The Castra Nova Equilum Singularium housed the horse soldiers of the PRAETORIAN GUARD until 312 C.E. Two other camps were used as the headquarters of the FRUMENTARII (the Imperial Secret Service) and the PEREGRINI (foreign soldiers barracked in Rome).

Mons Aventinus The Aventine Hill was roughly parallel to the Caelian Hill in the southern sections of the city. It was the gathering place of residences and displayed the considerable differences among the classes of Rome. Along the lower areas of the Aventine lived the plebeians and the foreigners. At the top were the villas of the wealthy.

Collis Viminalis The Viminal was situated between the large Quirinal and Esquiline hills. It contained a hill and a wider expanse of territory to the east, the Campus Viminalis. On that site were two barracks, the *castra* of the *cohortes urbanae* (URBAN COHORTS) and the CASTRA PRAETORIA, the camp of the Praetorian Guard from 23 to 312 C.E. The Urban Cohorts were maintained with the Praetorians until the time of Emperor Aurelian. They were then moved to their own camp in the Campus Martius.

Mons Esquilinus A large hill like the Viminal, the Esquiline contained the Campus Esquilinius. The Esquiline was covered with a number of beautiful GARDENS—the Horti Pallantiani, Horti Maecenatis and Horti Lamiani—and several grand buildings were constructed upon it. The major portion of the Golden House rested along its southern slope, and, because of the popularity of the Esquiline, the Flavians chose to erect the Baths of Titus there, using the Golden House of Nero as a starting point. Later, Trajan erected his baths just northeast of Titus's.

Collis Hortorum Pincius The Pincian Hills were not within the original boundaries of Rome, but the city nevertheless grew around them. Originally, Collis Pincius, or Pincian Hills, was used, but this changed as private estates were founded upon its crests, villas with the lavish GARDENS OF ASIATICUS and GARDENS OF SALLUST. The family of the Domitii also owned a series of tombs there, where Nero was buried in 68 C.E.

Mons Janiculus A hill across the Tiber from Rome, which served originally as a fortress facing the Etruscans and protecting the Romans from invasion. Later, the hill became one of the building sites for those foreign deities that were not allowed to be honored in the pantheon of the Roman gods or the city. The Syrian gods who had a following were worshiped there. Estates and villas also sprang up, as the view of Rome was impressive from the hill's heights.

Mons Vaticanus *See* VATICAN HILLS.

Hippo Also called Hippo Regius, a city on the Mediterranean coast of Numidia. Hippo was an old metropolis, in existence long before the Romans came to control AFRICA. It was situated between the towns of Bulla Regia and Cirta and was part of the line of communications running along the coast from Carthage. Hippo achieved notoriety twice in the fifth century C.E. St. AUGUSTINE, a doctor of the Christian Church, was consecrated a bishop in the city, remaining its chief prelate from 396 to his death on

August 28, 430. Ever after he was known as St. Augustine of Hippo. On the very day that Augustine died, the Vandals were besieging the city. Under Geiseric, their king, the Vandals had entered Africa, sweeping across the frontier and laying siege to Hippo from May to June of 430. In the wars that followed the Vandal settlement in Africa, Hippo endured terrible suffering as did all of the Roman holdings in the region that fell into Geiseric's hands.

Hippolytus (c. 170–236) *Theologian, saint, writer; antipope in the early Christian Church*
A presbyter in Rome, Hippolytus emerged a controversial and inflammatory figure in the Eternal City, largely because of his opposition to a number of popes, most notably Zepherinus (199–217) and Callistus (217–222), as well as their successors Urban (222–230) and Pontianus (230–235). Hippolytus particularly resisted the teachings of Callistus, possibly establishing himself as an antipope. His struggles with the popes ended only in 235 when, during the persecution of the church under Emperor Maximinus Thrax, Hippolytus and Pontianus were exiled to Sardinia. Hippolytus died there, possibly in 236 but apparently after reconciling himself with the Roman Christians, for his body was returned to Rome in 236 and given a proper burial. Hippolytus authored a number of works, including commentaries on Daniel and the Song of Songs, a treatise on the Apostolic tradition, and his greatest writing, *Refutation of All Heresies*, of which Books 4 to 10 are extant. A list of all his works was discovered on a statue of him in Rome in 1551; the statue was probably made during Hippolytus's lifetime. One of the greatest theologians of the West in the third century, he was all but forgotten for many centuries, largely because of his troubles with the popes.

Hirtius, Aulus (d. 44 B.C.E.) *Author, consul in 43 B.C.E. and an avid supporter and officer for Julius Caesar*
Aulus Hirtius was one of the young, bright leaders who flocked to Caesar, serving in his legions during the GALLIC WARS and in the CIVIL WAR OF THE FIRST TRIUMVIRATE. As a result of Caesar's goodwill, he became a praetor in 46 and was scheduled to be a consul in 43. After the assassination of Caesar in 44, Hirtius chose to follow Octavian (AUGUSTUS) and commanded an army with PANSA against Marc ANTONY. At Mutina he defeated Antony but was then killed in action. His death may have been caused by Octavian, who feared his skills and wanted sole control of the troops during battle. The loss of Hirtius was severe, for reasons that went beyond his usefulness militarily. When Caesar died, leaving his *De Bello Gallico* (*Gallic Wars*) unfinished, Hirtius completed its eighth book (as written in the *praefatio*) and quite possibly authored Caesar's *De Bello Alexandrino* (*Alexandrine War*). He had plans, it may be assumed, to write the

accounts of Caesar's other campaigns, *de Bello Africa* (*African War*) and *de Bello Hispaniensi* (*Spanish War*), but died before he had the opportunity. The authorship of these two histories remains an important question. While Suetonius states that Hirtius completed *De Bello Gallico*, the African and Spanish accounts are far too poor in style and organization, as well as in grammar, to be his efforts.

Hispania Roman province of Spain, one of the most successful in imperial provincial history. In Hispania, Rome founded three of its most profitable provinces: Baetica, LUSITANIA and Tarraconensis. While these lands were the first in the West to be acquired by the Republic, they proved very difficult to subdue and took many years to Romanize.

The first inhabitants were known as the Iberi and lived throughout modern Spain and just over the Pyrenees. In time, a large Celtic migration brought the Celtiberi into the region, who took over the central zones east of the Guadarrama Mountains and south of the Ebro River. The Celtiberi and the Iberians often united, but in the north, from the Pyrenees to the Minius River, there were Iberians who retained their cultural independence. These tribes evolved into the Astures and the fierce CANTABRI.

For many centuries Spain had the reputation of being rich in minerals, jewels, and, most notably, in gold. Phoenician traders arrived and, around 500 B.C.E., the Greeks established colonies on the eastern coast, naming the region Iberia; west of Gibraltar (the Pillars of Hercules), they named it Tartessus. The colonies brought in new populations, which resulted in a mixture of native peoples. Such was the situation in 238 B.C.E., when the Carthaginians invaded the region and Spain became a battleground in the bitter Punic Wars between Rome and Carthage. The Romans won mastery of the Mediterranean territory, and in the second Punic War (218–201 B.C.E.), the Carthaginians were driven out of Spain entirely, forced to surrender their cities of Gades and Carthago Nova.

Rome thus inherited the problems of the region. Spain was totally primitive and required centuries of incessant warfare for pacification. The two most independent tribes were the Lusitanians and the Cantabri. Living in the southwestern sections, the Lusitanians refused to accept Roman domination and demanded the presence of some of Rome's most gifted military commanders: BRUTUS ALBINUS, Scipio Aemilianus and, finally, Julius CAESAR, who vanquished the tribe in 60 B.C.E. The Cantabri to the north, and to a lesser extent the Astures, required frequent campaigns in the first century B.C.E., all conducted by the local governors in order to maintain the peace. Six different generals launched wars against them between 44 and 27 B.C.E., with only temporary results. AUGUSTUS himself arrived in 27, thereby opening up all of Hispania for provincialization. Although victory was gained and many Cantabri enslaved, the resulting tranquility proved illusory. The slaves escaped, returned home, and started

another insurrection. Marcus AGRIPPA, in 19 B.C.E., burned their mountain cities, forcing them to live on the plains. This policy broke the will of the tribespeople and gave birth to the new era of Romanization.

After its initial conquests, Rome divided Spain into two relatively equal provinces, Hispania Citerior and Hispania Ulterior, or Nearer and Farther Spain, originally under the command of two proconsuls. This arrangement neglected to take into account the considerable differences in geography, culture, and economic potential of the various Spanish regions.

As part of the Roman Empire, Hispania was seen as a province of potential by the first emperor, who wanted it run efficiently, with an eye toward bringing out its vast wealth and Romanizing it with cities and colonies. He thus ordered the creation of three provinces, two of imperial status and one of senatorial rank. Lusitania and Tarraconensis he kept for himself, knowing that wars were inevitable there, while in the south, Baetica was ceded to the Senate, largely because of the territory's reputation for harmony. Its boundaries were formed by the Anas and the Baetis rivers, the latter giving the province its name.

A governor, normally a proconsul in rank, administered Baetica's affairs from his office at Corduba, although Hispalis is also named as a possible seat of government. Baetica contained the old Carthaginian colony of Gades, a reminder of the connections to Africa, the continent lying just to the south. The line of communications of the empire ran through Baetica to Mauretania, specifically to Tingitana. In the second century C.E. the Moors from the Rif made incursions into Baetica, ravaging coastal towns and sailing up the Baetis to Italica.

Augustus retained Lusitania as an imperial province because of the prolonged unrest caused by the natives. The province occupied the area of modern Portugal, with its borders resting along the Douro and Anas rivers. Its capital was at Merida (Emerita), situated on the Anas. The location was chosen to allow the governor to rely upon Baetica in the event of a major rebellion among the local tribes.

Tarraconensis was the most important of the three provinces in Spain, for it controlled not only the Pyrenees leading to Gallia Aquitania (GALLIA) but also watched over the tribes of the Cantabri and the Astures. These considerations influenced the size of the province, stretching its borders from the northwest coast all the way down to the Baetis River, including all of the mountain tribes and the Celtiberi cantons. To assist in administering the province, the governor was initially provided with three legions (eventually reduced to one). The capital of Tarraco on the coast served as the strategic center for Spain and the major port on the Mediterranean for the three provinces.

From the start Spain was prosperous, relying upon several staple products for its economic health. Foremost of its exports were minerals; it supplied the empire with most of its gold, silver, lead, iron, copper, and tin. PLINY THE ELDER wrote of the production capacities of Galicia, Lusitania, and Asturia, where there were many mines. Lead flowed in from Baetica, silver from Carthago Nova, tin from Lusitania, and copper from Lusitania and Marianus. As a result, Hispania emerged as the mineral capital of the empire, and from the earliest days of imperial rule the focus of administration was on exhausting the supply and developing the surrounding countryside to aid in distribution and transportation. The many well designed and intricate road systems were built originally to combat rebellion and were then used to move the precious minerals from the provincial capitals of Tarraco, Corduba, and Merida.

The other major export was agriculture. Much of Spain was fertile, with rivers and valleys offering an environment for produce in such abundance that the Spanish could feed themselves and then supply Italy and Rome. The types of food represented the diversity of the local climates. Spain sent Rome wheat, olive oil, wine, fruits, and vegetables. Large cattle herds provided beef, and the coasts offered another type of harvest, fish.

Development of so many industries, including manufacture of goods, was made easier by the stability that Hispania enjoyed for centuries under the empire. Surrounded on three sides by water and the Pyrenees guarding the fourth, few frontier crises ever took place, except for the arrival of the MOORS. Tarraconensis originally had three legions, but VESPASIAN found little use for such a waste of good troops and moved two out of the province, a decision reflecting the extent of pacification and the degree of Romanization that had been accomplished. Peace reigned until the demise of the empire in the West in the fifth century C.E.

Augustus had initiated the influx of Roman and Italian culture. Twenty-one colonies were founded in Hispania, ultimately superceding the ones established by the Phoenicians, Greeks, and Carthaginians. Many of these were added to the long list of cities given a part in the Latin franchise. Because of these holdings, and because of the long years of Roman presence, Spain was the most Romanized group of provinces in the world, more so than even GALLIA NARBONENSIS. The thorough intertwining of Italian and Celtiberian and Iberian ways of life resulted in the same separation of classes and culture seen in other lands, especially in Britain. The cities and larger communities were very Roman, while the greater mass of miners, peasants, and lower-class workers were touched only in language, currency, and military service.

Hispania provided the Roman legions with soldiers of remarkable stamina, bred in the mountains and fields. Two functions of Spanish recruiting were to supply the legions and auxiliaries in Tarraconensis and to provide troops for other regions. By the middle of the second century C.E., however, such recruitment was difficult because of urban development. Secondly, the evolution of these centers, out of the traditional Celtic cantons, made the Iberians and Celtiberians reluctant to march off to war in the service of Rome.

The upper classes and the Romanized families, meanwhile, produced brilliant intellectuals and writers who impressed the empire. The teacher of OVID, Marcus Porcius Latro, SENECA THE ELDER, SENECA THE YOUNGER, Pomponius MELA, Lucius COLUMELLA—all came from Baetica. There were many others, the most famous of whom was QUINTILIAN, the first-century C.E. rhetorician and historian. In politics, citizens from Hispania assumed positions of greater power, attaining the consulship under CORNELIUS BALBUS and ultimately the throne. The emperors HADRIAN and TRAJAN were from Hispania.

Suggested Readings: Curchin, L. A. *Roman Spain. Conquest and Assimilation.* London: Routledge, 1991; De Alarcão, J. *Roman Portugal: Introduction and Gazeteer.* Warminster, U.K.: Aris & Phillips, 1988; Keay, S. J. *Roman Spain.* London: British Museum Publications, 1988.

Hispo, Romanus *See* DELATORES.

Historia Augusta *See* SCRIPTORES HISTORIAE AUGUSTAE.

Honoria Augusta (Justa Grata Honoria) (417/418– after 451 C.E.) *Sister of Emperor Valentinian III and daughter of Constantius III and the formidable Galla Placidia*
In 425 Honoria received the title of Augusta, shortly after her brother's elevation to the throne. Honoria entered into an affair with one of the stewards, Eugenius, in 449, a liaison that was discovered and terminated by her lover's execution. Betrothal followed to an utterly nonambitious senator, Flavius Herculanus. Desperate, Honoria looked for a barbarian champion whom she could recruit, choosing the most dangerous of them all, ATTILA the Hun. The "Scourge of God" received her ring and her plea. Finding it convenient to support her, Attila interpreted the ring as a proposal of marriage. In the spring of 451, therefore, he set out with his army, invading Gaul. When the Huns were repulsed at the Catalaunian Plain in the summer of 451, Attila turned on Italy and arrived there in the following year, demanding the hand of Honoria. Valentinian refused to surrender his sister, and only the famed intervention of Pope Leo, and perhaps the presence of a deadly plague, prevented the Huns from repeating on Rome the total destruction they had wreaked on Aquileia. The ultimate fate of Honoria remains a mystery.

Honorius, Flavius (383–423 C.E.) *Emperor in the West from 395 to 423*
The son of THEODOSIUS I and Aelia Flavia Flaccilla, Honorius reigned at a time marked by the rapid deterioration of the Western Empire. He was given the title of Augustus

at Constantinople in 393; two years later, Theodosius died, leaving the empire to be divided between Honorius in the West and Arcadius in the East. From the start of his rule, Honorius was dominated by his powerful *magister militum*, STILICHO, whose daughter MARIA married the emperor in 395. Unfortunately, Stilicho was little concerned with the welfare of the West, but consumed instead with an overwhelming desire to rule both empires. He interfered with the internal court policies of Constantinople, effected assassinations and plotted to snatch up Illyricum, a territory taken by Theodosius and possessed at the time by Arcadius.

These aspirations, coupled with a regrettable familiarity with the Gothic hosts of Alaric, caused a stagnation of frontier defenses. On the last day of 406, the Alamanni, Alans, Burgundians, Vandals, and their allies poured over the Rhine, burning Gaul and Spain. The Roman holdings in these lands would never be the same. Stilicho failed to produce effective countermeasures, and soon Alaric demanded tribute from Honorius, as usurpers rose up in the provinces, most notably CONSTANTINE III. Honorius's only solution was to murder his leading general on August 22, 408. The death of Stilicho led to further Visigothic inroads, culminating in 410 with Alaric's capture of Rome. This catastrophe was the lowest point of Honorius's impotent reign, for shortly thereafter Alaric died, and the emperor discovered a new and reliable officer, CONSTANTIUS III. Constantius defeated Alaric's successor, Athaulf; after negotiations, the hostage Galla Placidia (Honorius's half-sister) was surrendered in return for the Visigoths' right to settle in southern Gaul, near Tolosa (Toulouse), in 418. The Visigoths thus enjoyed their own state within imperial boundaries.

Constantius died in 421, depriving the battered army of a commander, and Galla Placidia, unable to bear the peculiar advances of Honorius, left Italy for Constantinople in 423. She took the young Valentinian, Honorius's successor, with her. Honorius was now alone and childless, for Maria had given him no heirs. A second marriage to Stilicho's second daughter, Thermantia, also proved barren. Honorius died, a failure in many respects, on August 15, 423. In 402, however, he moved the imperial center at MEDIOLANUM (Milan) to the marshy, easily defended city of RAVENNA, which for more than a century would be the home of the emperors and their Gothic successors.

Horace (Quintus Horatius Flaccus) (65–8 B.C.E.)

One of the greatest poets in Roman history

Born on December 8 at Venusia, Horace was the son of a freedman tax collector or auctioneer. He was educated in Rome, where he studied under Orbilius, who enjoyed flogging his pupils. Eventually Horace traveled to Athens (c. 45 B.C.E.), where he continued his studies. In 44, he joined the army of Marcus Brutus, achieving the rank of TRIBUNE. He fought at the battle of PHILIPPI in 42,

fleeing with the rest of the Republican army after its defeat. He lost his family estates and forfeited all political ambitions, but was pardoned and took a position as a clerk in the offices of the QUAESTOR (treasury) and wrote poetry.

In 39 B.C.E., he was introduced by Varius and Virgil to the literary patron Gaius MAECENAS. A friendship developed quickly between them, and Maecenas became Horace's benefactor, giving him funds and the means to journey with him, especially to Brundisium in 37. Maecenas's greatest gift to Horace was a villa in the Sabine hills, near Tivoli (Tibur). Horace mentions his villa in his works and spent much of his time there, often in the company of his patron. Through his association with Maecenas and because of his writing, Horace knew the most influential and important figures of the era. AUGUSTUS himself honored Horace with his favor and with the offer of a post as secretary. His prestige continued after Maecenas's death in 8 B.C.E., his patron requesting in his will that the emperor be "as mindful of Horace as of himself." Horace was buried next to Maecenas when he died himself later that year.

Horace described himself as short and fat, with a stomach so large that even the emperor remarked upon it. He was reportedly a cheery individual who enjoyed the company of friends, though he was the subject of critical attack and literary feuding as well. He was inclined to live frugally.

The works of Horace are numerous, displaying a knowledge of philosophy (EPICUREANISM), a vast vocabulary and a reliance upon common sense. His efforts can be divided into several genres.

Epodes Written around 31–30 B.C.E., these poems, based upon Archilochus, are among the earliest political verse in Rome. They could be bitter and harsh, critical even of Maecenas (No. 3), whom Horace chides for the use of garlic.

Satires Horace chose not to use moral outrage but humor as the basis of his two books of satires, published in 30 B.C.E. The 18 poems are filled with his opinion, comedic touches, and observations on such subjects as food, sex, friends, and success. Through them all he wove genuine artistic flair and style, achieving his intent to "laughing tell the truth."

Odes The *Carmina*, or *Odes*, were published together for the first time in 23 B.C.E. They followed closely the style of the Alexandrine poets and other Greek lyric forms, although Horace justly laid claim to the distinction of being the first Roman poet to use such refined Hellenic techniques in Latin. These 103 poems were written during a period of maturity and thus represent Horace at the peak of his form, revealing vast learning in mythology, religion, and the verse of other periods.

In 17 B.C.E., his long ode, the *Carmen Saecu-lare*, was published. Commissioned by Augustus for the *ludi Saeculares* (games), Horace used the style to honor not only the gods but his imperial patron as well, recounting his noble deeds. The *Carmen Saeculare* was followed by other poems, forming a fourth book of odes.

Epistles   The *Epistles* of Horace were published in two books, the first in 20 B.C.E. and the second in 17 or later. He wrote to a vast number of people, including Augustus, Maecenas, and LOLLIUS. Although less significant and (some would argue) inferior to the Satires, Horace injected his letters with his own philosophy and opinions on social problems, etiquette, and questions of morality. His method was informal, convivial, and filled with flashes of vision.

Ars Poetica   Although probably composed as part of the Epistles, the *Ars Poetica* (Art of Poetry) was separated from the original collection. It was a letter, written to two members of the Piso family. The *Ars Poetica* presented a criticism of the art and stood as Horace's longest poem. Its dating is hard to determine, appearing first in the time of Quintilian; he may have finished it around 18 B.C.E. Another name for the *Ars Poetica* was *Epistula ad Pisones*.

The principal sources for details of Horace's life are his own works and a biography by Suetonius.

See also POETRY.

Hormazd Ardashir (d. c. 272 C.E.) *King of Persia, also called Hormazd I; son of the great Shapur I*

Throughout much of SHAPUR's reign, Hormazd served as governor of the territory of Khorasan, bearing the title of Great King of Kings of the Kushans. When Shapur died in 272, Hormazd succeeded him but died after a brief time on the throne. He probably served with his father in the war against Rome and witnessed the capture and humiliation of Valerian in 259–260.

See also SASSANID DYNASTY.

Hormazd II (d. 309 C.E.) *King of Persia and ruler of the Sassanids from 302 to 309*

Sometimes called Hormizd II, Hormazd succeeded his father Narses to the throne in the wake of a Persian defeat. Narses had lost the war with Rome in 296–298 and had signed an unsatisfactory treaty, ceding control of Armenia to Rome. Hormazd could do little to reinstate the glory of the Persian army and appears to have contented himself with internal affairs. His reign was marked, however, by domestic unrest, and he may have died prematurely. An infant son, Shapur II, followed him in 309.

Hormazd III (d. 459 C.E.) *King of Persia for two years, 457–459*

Hormazd succeeded Yazdagird II and was followed by Peroz, the mighty king who ruled from 459 to 484.

See also SASSANID DYNASTY.

Hormisdas (fl. mid-fourth century C.E.) *Sassanid prince and the son of the Persian King Hormazd II; brother of Shapur II, who succeeded Hormazd in 309*

Hormisdas fled Persia in 324 to offer himself to the Roman Empire. He was welcomed by Constantine or Licinius Licinianus. Constantius II made him a cavalry commander and companion on a trip to Rome in 357. Julian the Apostate then gave him another post in his army, which was headed for the East in 362. He took him along on his Persian expedition of 363, where the Roman cavalry once again came under Hormisdas's control. The prince took insults from his countrymen in this campaign but did manage to convince a Persian garrison to surrender. Julian may have planned to install Hormisdas on the Persian throne after conquering the country. The imperial army, however, failed to take Ctesiphon, and Julian died in battle a short time later, ending any ambitions. Back in Constantinople, Hormisdas lived in a palace. His son, also named Hormisdas, entered into the service of the Roman Empire.

Hosius (c. 257–357 C.E.) *Also called Ossius; bishop of Cordova*

A prelate who played a major role in the Christianization of the Roman Empire and in the early Arian controversy, Hosius was elected a bishop in 296. He suffered in the persecutions of Maximian but survived to take part in the Council of Elvira in 306. From 313, Emperor Constantine relied upon him as an adviser, requesting a report on the Arian controversy. Traveling to Alexandria, Hosius returned with conclusions so certain that the emperor convened the Council of Nicaea. Hosius may have served as the president of the council and may have been the one to introduce the theological term *homoousios* (*see* ARIANISM). The next years were spent in ardent opposition to the growing Arian movement. He took part in the Council of Sardica in 343 and was exiled to Sirmium in 355 for supporting St. Athanasius. In a letter from exile, written to Constantius II, he called for a delineation between church and state, a very unique view for the time. In 357, at a synod, he finally agreed to sign a pro-Arian declaration, regretting and repudiating his signature upon his death bed at the age of 100.

Hostilian (Gaius Valens Hostilianus Messius Quintus) (d. c. 251 C.E.) *Younger son of Decius and Herennia Etruscilla, and the brother of Herennius Etruscus*

In 251, Herennius was appointed Augustus, and Hostilian received the title of Caesar. While his brother and father were away on campaign against the Goths, Hostilian remained in Rome with Herennia. In the summer of 251, word came that DECIUS and his son had been massacred at Abrittus by Kniva and the Goths. TREBONIANUS GALLUS became emperor but placated the Romans by leaving Herennia as Augusta and by appointing Hostilian as his coruler. The young emperor died a short time later of the plague.

Hostilianus (fl. first century C.E.) *Cynic philosopher of Rome*

Hostilianus was an associate of the more famous Demetrius the Cynic. Both were exiled from the capital as part of the campaign to remove philosophers from Rome in 71–75 C.E.

Huneric (d. 484 C.E.) *King of the Vandals from 477 to 484, the son of King Geiseric*

Huneric joined his father in his conquest of Africa in 429, at the invitation of the *MAGISTER MILITUM* BONIFACE. After six years of bloodshed, a treaty was signed with Valentinian III in 435. As part of the pact, Huneric was sent to Rome to live there as a hostage, but he returned home before 439, as his father began to exert his influence over all of Africa. Back with GEISERIC, Huneric was married to the daughter of the Gothic ruler, Theoderic, to form an alliance between the Visigoths and the VANDALS. By 449, however, Geiseric wished to make a different union, and a reason was found to invalidate the marriage contract. Huneric allowed his wife to be charged with attempting to poison Geiseric. Her nose and ears were cut off, and she was sent back to a horrified Theoderic. This mutilation and dismissal made possible the wedding between Huneric and Eudocia, the daughter of Licinia EUDOXIA, in 455. Eudoxia and her two daughters, Eudocia and Placidia, had been taken from the sacked city of Rome by sea to Carthage and had been useful in the bargaining between Geiseric and Emperor Leo. When an agreement was reached in 461, allowing captives to be released, Huneric kept Eudocia as his wife. He succeeded Geiseric in 477 as the king of the Vandals.

Huns The most famous and most feared of all of the barbarian hordes to ravage the Roman Empire. Known originally as the Hsiung-nu, the Huns developed as a disjointed confederation in Central Asia. In the third century B.C.E. they were already nomadic and on the move into China. The Great Wall was erected to hold them at bay, and so the Huns turned west. Culturally, the Huns were united by a sense of perpetual danger and by an instinct for self-preservation, uniting against a common foe. They relied upon leaders who ensured that no enemy ever matched them in ferocity or in martial skills. The cheeks of infant males were slashed to form scars, pre-venting long beards. Their diet consisted of milk products and meats when available, made tender by being placed under the saddle during riding. Physically they were very stout, with thick legs and muscular frames. Though invariably outnumbered, their proficiency with weapons made one Hun a match for many of his foes. Opposition was reduced by outright cruelty toward subject populations. While traveling to Europe the Huns annihilated everything in their path, destroying the Slavs on the Steppes and pillaging their way across the Ukraine.

In the middle of the fourth century C.E. the first screaming horsemen descended upon the ALANS, OSTROGOTHS, and HERULI. Within years the Huns dominated the ways between the Black Sea and Dacia, burning everything in their wake. For whatever reason, perhaps a struggle between rival chieftains, a period of quiet followed.

By the middle of the fifth century, however, the Huns once more stood ready to make war. Their first ambitious chief was ULDIN, who was defeated by an army of Theodosius, somewhere in Thrace. Uldin had failed to hold together the various elements of his nation. The Hunnic population was then split into three camps, the two most powerful being led by Rugila and Mandiuch. Rugila received tribute from Theodosius and may have supported him against the Goths, for more land in Pannonia. When he died shortly after 433, his brother Mandiuch took over the majority of the clans and was succeeded by his own sons, Bleda and ATTILA. Attila proved the most capable ruler that the Huns would ever know. He pushed to the East and seized the Caucasus, solidifying his own position before murdering Bleda in 444. Sitting alone on the throne, Attila embarked on a strong campaign of war. In 447 he invaded the Danube frontier, threatening Constantinople. Marcianopolis fell, and more tributes of money and land resulted in a treaty by which he agreed to respect the Danube.

In 451, Attila and the Huns set out for the Rhine. They pierced Germany and poured into Gaul. Total victory seemed within his grasp when the Huns suffered a reverse at the battle of the CATALAUNIAN PLAIN in the summer of 451. After this defeat, Attila turned on Italy. AQUILEIA was besieged and utterly ruined. The Hunnic horsemen next moved on Rome. Pope Leo, aided by a plague and by an Italian famine, forced a Hunnic retreat. Attila was dead within the year.

Attila's empire did not long survive him. His sons proved incapable of holding together the fabric of the united clans, and in 454, at the NEDAO River in Pannonia, the long-enslaved Goths, Alans, Heruli, and their allies rose up. The Hun holdings were lost, and their clans were driven in every direction. For nearly a century the Huns had been the strongest barbarian nation and the greatest rival of the Roman Empire in the north. Their realm stretched at one point from the Ukraine to the Rhine. By holding the Goths and many others in check, they provided the cities of the Eastern and Western Empires time to prepare for the inevitable onslaughts, and compelled many tribes to join with the Romans against a common foe. Ammianus Marcellinus wrote of them in some detail.

Hydatius (c. 400–470 C.E.) *Christian chronicler in Spain in the fifth century*
Hydatius became bishop of Aquae Flaviae in 427. His great work, the *Chronicle,* was a continuation of Jerome, extending the history to his own time, up to the year 469. It is one of the few extant and contemporary examinations of the invasions of Spain in that century.

Hyginus, Gaius Julius (c. 64 B.C.E.–17 C.E.) *Freedman, scholar, and librarian of the Augustan Age (27 B.C.E.–14 C.E.)*
Hyginus may have come from Spain to enter the service of Augustus, under whose patronage he came to be the head of the library on the Palatine Hill. As a writer, Hyginus was prolific, following VARRO in style. He was a friend of OVID and authored an examination of famous figures in Roman history, commentaries on Cinna and Virgil, and compiled extensive surveys on agriculture and bees. The writings of two other men under the name Hyginus, one on legal boundaries, are sometimes ascribed to him.

Hypatia (c. 375–415 C.E.) *Neoplatonic philosopher of Alexandria*
Hypatia suffered the rare distinction of being a pagan martyr. She was the daughter of Theon, receiving an education in Alexandria, where she soon gained fame as the leading Neoplatonist. Among her students was the Christian, SYNESIUS, who became bishop of Ptolemais. Hypatia had poor relations with the Christian leaders of her city. In 415, a mob grabbed her and physically tore her to pieces. Some legends state that she was flayed alive with whips made of abalone shells. Those responsible were never punished.

Hyrcanus (d. 30 B.C.E.) *Son of the Hasmonaean King Alexander Jannaeus and Alexandra Salome, and the brother of Aristobulus*
When Alexander died, leaving his wife to rule his Jewish domain, Alexandra assumed power for the years 76 to 67 B.C.E., with the help of the cunning minister, ANTIPATER OF IDUMAEA. In 67, Alexandra died, and the throne passed to her sons. Hyrcanus immediately fell under the influence of Antipater, who allowed the rivalry between the brothers to erupt violently. With Antipater's aid, Hyrcanus gained the upper hand in the civil strife, relying upon King ARETAS III, the Nabataean of Arabia, to besiege Aristobulus at Jerusalem in 65. A Roman army under the command of Marcus Scaurus, a lieutenant of Pompey, prevented total victory. Antipater convinced Hyrcanus to address Pompey directly, to ask for the throne. Pompey gave him the traditional high priesthood and a reduced territory to rule, not as a monarch but as a prince or ethnarch. Henceforth, although Hyrcanus bore a title, Chief Minister Antipater held the true power, even gaining the favor of Julius Caesar. By 43, Hyrcanus was a virtual puppet of his minister and the minister's two sons, Phasael and Herod (the Great), the governors of Jerusalem and Galilee, respectively.

Domestic unrest culminated in Antipater's assassination in 43. Hyrcanus was then placed under the control of Phasael and, especially, Herod. The ethnarch had little choice but to support Herod against Antigonus, the son of his dispossessed brother ARISTOBULUS. Once Herod defeated Antigonus, Hyrcanus had to give him a share in full royal authority, including the hand of his daughter Mariamne. In 40, Antigonus found an ally in the Parthian Empire. The Parthians swept into Palestine, placed Antigonus in control, forced Phasael to commit suicide and captured Hyrcanus. The aging ruler was led away in chains, as Herod escaped to Rome. When Hyrcanus returned in 37 to Judaea, he found that Herod had been installed in his place. From that time on, Hyrcanus was used by Herod as a symbol of Jewish unity, but he was murdered in 30. The pretext was that Hyrcanus was trying to remove Herod.

I

Iamblichus (c. 250–319/325 C.E.) *Neoplatonic philosopher and theurgist*

One of the most noted writers and pseudo-mystics of his time, Iamblichus was born in Coele-Syria to a family of Chalcis. Porphyry influenced his education at Rome, where he developed a knowledge of NEOPLATONISM, a subject that he later taught, perhaps at Apamea. Iamblichus earned his fame as both a writer and a mystic. His extant works include a *Vita Pythagorae* (Life of Pythagoras), a defense of magic (*De Mysteriis*), several mathematical treaties, a book on rhetoric, and *Protrepticus,* using other authors. He is reported to have written commentaries on Plato and Aristotle (not extant) and a work on the oracles of Chaldea. As a mystic, Iamblichus supposedly possessed the power to perform miracles and to levitate. He displayed an interest in theurgy (supernatural or divine intervention in human affairs), ritualistic magic, and ceremony. He differed with Porphyry in his disdain for Plotinus and his Neoplatonism.

Iazyges Tribe of Sarmatians who settled on the Danube frontier and had dealings with Rome from the first century C.E. They were probably among the first of the Sarmatians to advance from their original homes around the Sea of Azov, being driven westward through southern Russia along the Dnieper. After several migrations the Iazyges reached the area along the Danube and the Theiss, where the plains afforded room and the surrounding mountains defense. The Iazyges were counted among the client states of the Roman Empire from the time of the Flavians into the third century, with a number of incidents proving that imperial control was not always effective. During Domitian's wars with Dacia, the Sarmatians joined their Germanic neighbors in raids followed by a full-scale invasion of Pannonia in 92. They defeated the local legion, the XXI Rapax, and required the personal efforts of the emperor in order to be subdued.

Other battles took place mainly as a result of the general chaos on the borders during the wars of Marcus Aurelius (*see* MARCOMANNIC WARS). The Iazyges also considered the Dacians as bitter enemies and attempted to seize Dacian territory even when the country had been converted into an imperial province.

Iberia Kingdom in the Caucasus, situated between the Caspian and BLACK SEAS. It was known for its beauty and fertility, while the Iberians themselves were noted for their civilization, especially when compared to their barbaric neighbors to the north and to the Armenians in the south. Connections were made with the Roman Empire and the Parthians through trade and agriculture. Pompey the Great launched an expedition against the Iberians in 65 B.C.E.; according to the historian Tacitus, the three kingdoms of the region, Albania, Iberia, and Colchis, were protected in the name of Rome. Tiberius later requested Iberian aid against the Parthian King Artabanus. The domain was still in existence during the reign of Caracalla (211–217 C.E.), when its king Pharasmanes visited Rome. Iberia was frequently confused in the ancient histories with the kingdom of the BOSPORUS, which was also located near the Black Sea.

Icelus (d. 69 C.E.) *Freedman of Rome*

Icelus was one of Emperor Galba's former slaves who won his freedom as a reward for service and for being a long-time lover of the aging general. He took the name of Marcianus as a free man and became a key adviser to Galba when the general was governor of Hispania Tarraconensis. According to Suetonius, he may have been imprisoned in Rome just before the fall of Nero, but was released in time to allow the dead ruler to be buried properly and to prepare Rome for Galba's triumphant arrival. Throughout Galba's reign, Icelus fought with two important state officers: Cornelius LACO and Titus VINIUS. He differed with his rivals on virtually every issue, especially that of the succession. When Icelus was unable to put forward a candidate, Piso was named Galba's heir (Laco's choice). Otho then conspired to take the throne, and Icelus was included on his list of condemned. He died by public execution.

Iceni A leading tribe of Britain (BRITANNIA), living in the far northeast (modern Suffolk and Norfolk); their capital was called Venta Icenorum (Caistor) and was located near Norwich. The Iceni were one of the first allies of Rome, following the invasion of Britain by Claudius in 47 C.E., a decision they regretted almost immediately, as the ruthless and expansionist imperial policy was revealed by the governor appointed in 50 C.E., Publius Ostorius Scapula. The Roman advance into the tribal regions of Britain caused fighting, and the call came from Scapula even to clients of the empire to surrender all weapons. Proud and resenting this dishonor, the Iceni revolted, only to be routed.

Peace returned for the next 11 years as the Iceni king Prasutagus and his wife BOUDICCA ruled their people without major incident. In 61, Prasutagus died, bequeathing his domain to Caesar in the hopes of avoiding annihilation. The Romans jumped at the chance to take over the Iceni lands. Centurions pillaged the kingdom, flogged Boudicca and outraged her daughters. Unable to endure these and other cruelties, the Iceni revolted under the command of the queen. They were eventually defeated by General Suetonius Paulinus, and their territory, conquered by Rome, was added to the province of Britannia.

Ides Name given to the middle day or days of the Roman month. According to tradition, these days were normally placed under the care of the god Jupiter and were celebrated in his name. The one exception of this custom was March, for its Ides was celebrated to honor both Jupiter and Anna Perenna.

See also CALENDAR.

Idumaea District of JUDAEA to the south of Jerusalem, stretching from Gaza to the Dead Sea and including a small part of Arabia Petrae; known in the Old Testament as Edom. Its inhabitants, called Edomites, made incursions into Judea, and for centuries afterward the Jews of Judaea considered the Edomites to be foreigners, a fact of some importance during the years of the dynasty of Antipater of Idumaea.

It was as Idumaea, the Greek form of Edom, that the region was included in the territory of Roman-occupied Judaea. Idumaea achieved supremacy in Jewish affairs with the rise of ANTIPATER OF IDUMAEA in the middle of the first century B.C.E. This minister of state became the power behind the throne, propping up the moribund Hasmonaean line. Antipater's son, HEROD THE GREAT, first served as governor of Galilee and then, in 40 B.C.E., retreated to Idumaea to establish a line of defense against the invading Parthians. His cornerstone of defense was the mountain fortress of MASADA, the strongest citadel in Palestine.

After Herod died in 4 B.C.E., his vast kingdom was carved up and granted to his sons by Augustus. Archelaus, one heir, received Judaea, Samaria, and Idumaea, where he ruled as an ethnarch. His successor was Agrippa I, whose administration became unpopular, owing to his reputation and to the continued unwillingness of the Jewish people to accept the family of Antipater. In the following years, Idumaea suffered as the JEWISH REBELLION (66–70 C.E.) ravaged much of the province. Masada once more proved strategically essential, enduring a long siege.

Ignatius (St. Ignatius) (c. 35–107 C.E.) *Bishop of Antioch; one of the earliest Christian martyrs, whose letters on the road to Rome and whose death left an impression on the second-century church and beyond*
According to the theologian Origen, Ignatius was the pupil of St. John and the second bishop of Antioch. According to the historian Eusebius, however, he was the third, following Euodius, although Euodius is generally ranked as the first bishop of Antioch. As bishop of Antioch, Ignatius was arrested and sent for execution to Rome. On the way he began writing epistles to the Christian communities, in which he reaffirmed the honors of martyrdom, the greatness of Christ and the need to remain steadfast in the face of unorthodox elements and influences. These letters were the subject of intense scholarly debate during the Middle Ages and in the 19th century.

See also CHRISTIANITY.

Ilerda Spanish city that was the site of a series of battles fought from April to July in 49 B.C.E., between the legions of Julius CAESAR and the Pompeian generals, Lucius Afranius and Marchus Petreius, in the Civil War of 49–45 B.C.E. After setting out from Italy in March with the declaration, "I am off to meet an army without a leader and when I come back I shall meet a leader without an army," Caesar hoped to destroy the forces of POMPEY in the West. He trapped Lucius Domitius Ahenobarbus in MASSILIA and then moved on Spain with an army of 37,000. With lightning speed the Caesareans captured the important passes of the Pyrenees ahead of the Pompeians, who withdrew, hoping for a better opportunity to use their 60,000 men to advantage.

Caesar chose to pursue them cautiously and both sides maneuvered, refusing to give battle. Afranius and Petreius were less skilled than Caesar and were soon forced to retreat to Ilerda with their larger legions. Once trapped there, the Pompeians watched as Caesar surrounded the city, cut off the water supply and starved them into submission. On July 2, Ilerda surrendered. Caesar was able to recruit thousands of soldiers as a result, while destroying bloodlessly one of Pompey's largest field forces. A mere demonstration was all that would be necessary to pacify the rest of Spain.

Illyricum (Dalmatia) Territory stretching from northeastern Italy to Macedonia, and from the Danube along the Moesian border to Epirus. In the days of the Roman Empire this vast region on the east shore of the Adriatic was divided into two provinces: Illyricum (also called Dalmatia) and Pannonia. While PANNONIA evolved into a major frontier province along the Danube, all of Illyricum provided a land route for imperial trade and communications with Greece and Asia Minor.

Rome's interest in Illyricum had existed since its first political and economic expansion in the third century B.C.E., when it came into contact with the peoples of the Illyrian kingdom and at the Celticized tribes of the Delmatae. When their pirate activity interfered with Roman shipping, direct intervention resulted in the so-called Illyrian Wars in 228–227 and in 219 B.C.E. In time, the Illyrians became allies of Rome, siding with them against the Carthaginians and especially against Macedonia in the Second Punic War.

Future relations were less pleasant, as another conflict in 168 B.C.E. proved the general supremacy of the Roman army and the fall of the Illyrians. Local destabilization occurred when the Danubian tribes assumed a greater importance in strategic affairs. Several expeditions kept them in line, but the Delmatae remained a major factor, especially at the time of Julius Caesar's acquisition of the governorship of Illyricum in 59 B.C.E.

Caesar visited Illyricum during the winters of his Gallic Wars, spending time at Aquileia, but his attention was focused on Gaul from 58 to 51, and he left the Illyrians and Delmatae unmolested. Because of their proximity to Pompey's political bases in Greece, most of the Illyrian tribes fell under Pompey's influence. When the Civil War erupted between Pompey and Caesar, they sided with the Pompeians, defeating Caesar's lieutenants in 51 and in 48–47 B.C.E. Furthermore, the Illyrian threat was considered in the planning of the Caesareans for their campaign against Pompey in 49–48, during the CIVIL WAR, FIRST TRIUMVIRATE.

Following the defeat of Pompey in 48, Caesar first concluded a peace with the Delmatae but then, in 45–44, unleashed P. Vatinius in combat. His successes against the tribe were extended by Octavian (AUGUSTUS) in the years 35–33 B.C.E. These sorties were very limited, however, and aimed solely at certifying Roman ownership of the area. In 27 B.C.E. this mastery was confirmed as Illyricum was added to the provinces of the empire.

The senatorial province status of Illyricum would not last long. Warfare raged across the land as Tiberius fought the *Bellum Pannonicum* (the Pannonian War) from 13 to 9 B.C.E., in which he seized Pannonia, suppressed the Illyrians and punished the Delmatae. Sometime around 11 B.C.E., Illyricum was proclaimed an imperial province to ease in defense and the provincial administration. Every resource available to the Danubian legions was needed in 6 C.E., when the Delmatae and their neighboring tribes rose up again (*see* BATO [1] and BATO [2]). Bitter fighting characterized this three-year struggle in all parts of Illyricum. By 9 C.E., however, the power of the Delmatae was broken, and all resistance shattered. To be certain of this, Augustus divided the large province; henceforth there were Illyricum Superius and Illyricum Inferius, known in the time of Vespasian as Illyricum (Dalmatia) and Pannonia.

As an imperial province, Illyricum was placed under the authority of a legate, who maintained order initially with two legions. His seat was at SALONA, and the boundary of the province ran from the edge of Italy and the Save River on the north, to MACEDONIA in the south. In the west was the Adriatic, with Salona on the coast, and to the east was MOESIA.

The importance of Illyricum rested in its key location on the communication lane from the East to Italy and as a support for the provinces on the ever troubled Danube frontier. Thus, Romanization and pacification proceeded there at an accelerated rate. The legions and their auxiliaries introduced Latin culture. Latin proved supreme over native dialects, and cities slowly replaced the villages and Celtic communities, except in the Dalmatian highlands, where the old ways died slowly. Roads were begun by Augustus and continued by Tiberius, who made Illyricum's links with Pannonia, Moesia, Macedonia, NORICUM, RAETIA and the Italian city of Aquileia one of the key elements of the Danubian line of defense.

By the middle of the first century C.E., one legion was removed and sent to Moesia. During Domitian's reign a second was found to be unnecessary. While some garrisons were vital, the process of Romanization created an environment of suitable social harmony.

Legions throughout the empire found the province an excellent source for recruits. Throughout the second century C.E. the tough, intelligent, and reliable Illyrians injected a new vitality into the legions. They became a source of stability in military affairs and formed the principle pool of officers in the third century. This was the final political achievement of Illyricum and, indeed, the growing provinces of the Danube. With the third century came the great crises of economic decline, internal anarchy, and barbarian invasions. Generals emerged as emperors, marching against other generals and usurpers. Few years of Roman history were as black as the middle of the third century, as rulers fell in battle or were overwhelmed by the sheer enormity of the tasks facing them.

The Illyrian and Danubian officers of the army were the ones to stabilize the situation. CLAUDIUS II GOTHICUS (268–270), AURELIAN (270–275), and PROBUS (276–282) were born to Illyrian families, and each helped to repair the damage of war, disease, and financial ruin. More importantly, they laid the foundations for the reign of an emperor born to a poor Dalmatian family, Diocletian.

He redesigned the entire empire, resurrecting its fortunes and setting it upon a path of order that would last for another century. His gift to Illyricum was to retire to his estates at Split, near Salona. Under the new imperial provincial system, Illyricum was included in the diocese of Pannonia.

It was unfortunate that a province so influential to the imperial rebirth in the third and fourth centuries should suffer so severely in the fifth. Illyricum was ravaged by the barbarians and also served as the cause of a disagreement between the Eastern and Western Empires. The debate was over jurisdiction, an issue made irrelevant by the demise of the West.

imagines Masks made of wax and other materials as portraits of deceased Romans; kept by the family and descendants for use in other funeral processions. At the time of a funeral, all *imagines* were taken from their shrines and given to actors who had been hired for the occasion. During the funeral procession the actors would surround the bier of the corpse, wearing the masks and representing the spirits of those who had gone before. This ceremony was considered essential and socially important to ensure a proper burial.

See also DEATH.

immunitas The freedom granted to a colony, community, or individual from paying taxes, local or imperial, seeing service in the legions, or performing other required duties. During the time of the Republic, the *immunitas* was granted by the Senate to many cities as an addition to their *libertas*. It was also given to allies and to members of the Italian Confederacy. During the period of the empire, the emperor and the Senate determined the granting or revocation of the *immunitas*. Nero, for example, gave it to Greece, along with its freedom, but Vespasian rescinded it. Other cases involved full exemption or temporary declarations. The island of Cos (Kos) was given *immunitas* by Claudius in 54 C.E. because of its great mythological history and because of the intercession of a native son, Xenophon, who was the imperial physician at the time. Byzantium also received a five-year right to be spared from tribute in order to ease its financial problems. As was obvious, *immunitas* followed no fixed pattern and could be adjusted to meet the demands of a specific situation. Roman colonies were not immediately included, although they usually benefited from the IUS ITALICUM. Individuals also held *immunitas*, normally as a result of special status with Rome. Such a person or group would reap the inscribed benefits; depending upon the imperial decree, or *lex senatus consultum,* such rights could become hereditary.

See also IUS LATII; TAXATION; TRIBUTUM.

imperator Originally, an honor paid to a general who had won a great victory; later conferred upon the supreme head of the empire. In the days of the Republic, a victorious general received the title with the cheers (SALUTATIO) of his soldiers until he celebrated his TRIUMPH. The Senate could also grant such a tribute, as conferred upon Sulla, Pompey, and Julius Caesar. Sulla and Pompey received the honor more than once, and Caesar used it permanently. Augustus was given the title in 29 B.C.E. by the Senate, and it was incorporated into his name and was claimed by his successors, despite the fact that they had no military honors or victories. In 69 C.E., Otho took the throne by assassination, with the acclamation of the Praetorian Guard, and assumed the dignifying title, while Vespasian claimed it for the imperial household. Tradition developed that a ruler was given the imperator for the individual successes of his generals. (Claudius was, by the end of his life, Imperator XXVII.) The title was also claimed by proconsuls and governors. Junius Blaesus, the proconsul of Africa, was the last to hold the position of imperator without royal rank, in 22 C.E. A rebellious general might also use the traditional SALUTATIO of the legions to lay claim to the throne. Imperial coinage remains the best evidence for the title in practice.

Imperial Cult Also, Cult of the Emperors; the systematic religio-political practice of honoring the emperors and the Roman state. Viewing the emperors as divine and worthy of prayers and honors, the cult was of considerable political value, enhancing the status of Rome within the provinces and ensuring the obedience of all imperial subjects. The notion of ruler-worship was pervasive in the ancient world; it was traditionally observed in most Asian nations and exalted to a high degree in Egypt. The Hellenic world followed the custom, adding a pantheon of highly anthropomorphic deities, to the extent that certain royal men were seen as gods. Alexander the Great used such cultic practices, and Ptolemy was deified by his own heir. Initially, the Romans rebelled at such an excess, but Roman generals had become associated with gods and goddesses by the second century B.C.E., after major triumphs. The conquered tribes in the provinces took up the custom of calling the senators of Rome their "saviors" and looked upon them as gods. Pompey the Great, Marc Antony, and Julius Caesar all attained a semi-divine status.

AUGUSTUS, however, exploited the full potential of deification of the emperor in order to deal with the expanse of the empire and the diversity of its inhabitants. In Egypt, Greece, and parts of Asia Minor and in Gaul, as well as in Africa, the imperial cult was fostered in the name of Roman et Augustus. Roman supremacy and unity were the result, and out of this early practice came the Cult of the Emperors.

After Caesar's death in 44 B.C.E., Octavian (Augustus) officially proclaimed him a god, Divus Julius, and in 27 B.C.E., Octavian received the auspicious title of divi filius. Public holidays henceforth were proclaimed on his birthday, his house was dedicated to Jupiter, and in 12 B.C.E. prayers and oaths were given to him. Finally, his funeral was dramatized as the scene of his resurrection and immorality.

This Imperial Cult evolved along two different paths in the empire. In the East, the Romans were able to adapt to the traditional forms of divine kingship, while in the West, where no such practice existed, Rome invented one. Romans and Italians accepted the cult as part of the Roman state religion, but with little enthusiasm. Throughout Asia, Bithynia, Greece (Achaea and Macedonia) and in most of Asia Minor, temples to the divine Julius and Roma were constructed. At the same time, the koinon, or city assemblies, were joined into CONCILIA to administer the cultic ceremonies and to act as local provincial councils. The concilia in the Asian provinces were granted a wide latitude in the form and style of worship ceremonies. Pergamum, Ephesus, Smyrna, and Tarsus erected the earliest temples to Rome and Augustus and to succeeding rulers and empresses, including Tiberius, Livia, and Hadrian.

In the West, the concilia were used to impress Roman culture upon the subjugated peoples. In Gaul, Britain, along the Danube, and in Germany, the concilia acted as the leading proponents of intensive Romanization. In 12 B.C.E., Drusus the Elder consecrated the altar of Roma et Augustus at LUGDUNUM (Lyons), and from that point on the city was the cult center for the Gallic provinces. Another altar was erected before 4 C.E. in Oppidum Ubiorum for all of Germania. By the end of the first century more altars appeared in Gallia Narbonensis and in Spain, Africa, Dacia, and throughout the Danubian frontier.

Just as the concilia did not survive the changes of the second and third centuries, the Imperial Cult suffered from the isolation of the emperors from the provinces and the instability of many regions. Local gods became more attractive to the populace in the distant realms of the empire's Eastern provinces, while the West had been so Romanized that such a cult was superfluous.

imperium   The ancient term used to describe the powers possessed by the supreme administrative authority of the Roman state. Imperium extended to matters of life and death, as well as law, military command, and all decisions of policy. Its bestowal on an individual conveyed a supreme but temporary power. By tradition the first kings of Rome held the imperium, but after their removal and the acceptance of the Republic, such authority passed into the hands of elected officials. Consuls, praetors, and specially chosen officers could be granted the imperium for a set time period, normally one year or the time necessary for the completion of a particular task, such as Pompey's military commission in 67 B.C.E.

Throughout the Republic, the nature of the imperium evolved. The privileges of such an office might be withheld by dictators such as Sulla, or the amassing of foreign holdings might require that governors be given an imperium to administer their own territories. Such an imperium, however, ceased at the borders of their region, and the imperium had no power within the boundary (pomerium) of Rome itself. In 27 B.C.E., Augustus reformed this system in such a way that he ultimately gained control over the entire Rome Empire when he worked out an agreement with the Senate to divide the Roman world between imperial and senatorial provinces. He retained control, as proconsul, of those regions on the frontier that required legions, extending his imperium outside of Rome and within as well. In 23 B.C.E., when Augustus resigned the consulship, he was allowed to maintain this in perpetuity. At the same time, he was granted control over the imperial provinces above that of the governors (IMPERIUM MAIUS). Augustus was now master of the most important provinces and the very heart of the imperial administration. The imperium was voted to Augustus for five years in 18 and 13 B.C.E., and for 10 in 27 and 8 B.C.E. and in 3 and 13 C.E. Subsequent emperors received their imperium from the Senate upon gaining the throne, although approval was probably pro forma.

imperium maius   Also, maius imperium; a term denoting the special power conferred upon certain individuals to conduct a mission with an authority superior to a governor's (IMPERIUM PROCONSULARES) in a given region or in the entire empire. During the Republic, the Senate had the exclusive right to grant the imperium maius, but during the empire the rulers not only possessed it in perpetuity but also shared it with the others. Such authority was granted rarely during the Republic, and Pompey was denied the privilege in 57 B.C.E. In 43 B.C.E., however, Brutus and Cassius were given that rank in the East. Augustus was voted the imperium maius in 23 B.C.E. as part of his settlement with the Senate over the division of the Roman Empire (*see* IMPERIUM); Augustus's *maius* extended over every province under imperial jurisdiction. On occasion he shared the *imperium maius* with a reliable lieutenant, such as Marcus Agrippa in 18 B.C.E. and again in 13 B.C.E., when Agrippa traveled to the Pannonian area to settle its affairs. Tiberius assumed the *imperium maius* in 13 C.E. as the designated heir of Augustus. Others granted this power in the first century C.E. were Germanicus in 17 and Corbulo in 63, both assigned to the troublesome East.

imperium proconsulares A type of the IMPERIUM pertaining to the powers of a PROCONSUL in charge of a province. In principle, such an imperium gave a governor administrative control over the territory under his command, with two major restrictions. First, the *imperium proconsulare* of one proconsul could not be greater than that of any other unless the emperor provided him with a special status (*see* IMPERIUM MAIUS). Secondly, all authority of the imperium ended when the official crossed the POMERIUM, or the sacred boundary of Rome. Any official visiting Rome was subject to the laws and magistrates of the city.

Incitatus The horse of Emperor GAIUS CALIGULA. The emperor treated the chariot horse with his usual excesses, allowing him to live in a marble stable, to sleep in an ivory stall and to wear purple blankets and jeweled collars. Incitatus was given furniture, slaves, and guards who were ordered to patrol the nearby streets and enforce quiet among the human residents so that the animal could sleep in peace. Caligula frequently had the horse to dinner, feeding him golden barley and toasting his health with golden goblets. He even promised to make Incitatus a consul but was assassinated before he could do so.

India Originally, the name applied by the Romans to all the nations of modern Asia, but in time designating the land that carried on extensive trade with the empire. India was known to the Romans from accounts about Darius (the Persian ruler), Alexander the Great, and Seleucus I, all of whom sent embassies or traveled to India personally. Inevitably, economic ties developed, as the region possessed many rare, exotic, and fabled items. Trade was disrupted, however, by the rise of the hostile Parthian Empire and the attempts by the tribes of Arabia Felix to dominate trade. Under the empire, relations with the Parthians improved. The expeditions of AELIUS GALLUS, though largely unsuccessful, reduced Arab reluctance to trade, and land routes were improved in the north and south. Aqaba served as a port for these ventures.

In 20 B.C.E., envoys from India arrived in Rome to make overtures of friendship, which resulted in a treaty. According to Dio, the gifts from the Indians included

tigers, an animal never seen by the Romans, and an armless boy, who performed marvelous feats with his legs and toes, presumable due to a mastery of yoga. For the next two and one-half centuries a lucrative and busy system of exchange was in existence. From India, Rome received spices of a wide variety, silk from China, perfumes and many precious stones and gems. Caligula wore a robe with Indian jewels when he crossed his boat bridge at Bauli, and Septimius Severus used an altar adorned with ivory and stones from India in his ostentatious funeral procession for Pertinax in 193 C.E. In return, the Romans sent metals, cloth, glass, and, most importantly, gold, silver, and copper. In fact, so much coinage was exported during the first century C.E. that its effect upon the economy is still debated; one theory argues that this mammoth exportation of currency brought about the third century collapse and played a role in the general demise of the empire two centuries later, which further weakened trade. As the eastern frontiers closed with the rise of the Persian SASSANIDS, the links with India were terminated.

See also SILK ROUTE; TRADE AND COMMERCE.

industry The first Roman industry of any significance began in the second century B.C.E. as a result of the Roman victory in the Punic Wars against Carthage. The victory in the war brought expansion of Roman influence over Spain, Greece, and parts of Africa and Asia Minor and the acquisition of cheap labor in the form of slaves and prisoners. The capture of skilled workers made possible the development of key industries in Italy that were discovered in other markets of the Mediterranean. Specialization in crafts and industries allowed Roman merchants to become competitive throughout the Hellenic world and in turn facilitated the rise of trade networks that eventually reached to Asia in the first century B.C.E., including China and India. To assist their work, craftspeople and traders formed guilds (*collegia*). The *collegia* wielded some influence, but their tendency to involve themselves in politics led to their suppression.

The networks of trade that spread outward from Rome and that grafted themselves onto pre-existing trade routes marked one of the distinguishing characteristics of Roman industry. Industries located on the Roman provinces, ranging from glass and agriculture to metalworking and pottery became so numerous and prosperous that they overshadowed the industries of Italy. This decline of Italian industry was hastened by the decision on the part of the later Roman government to depend on provincial industries for needs in weapons, goods, and materials for administration. At the same time, government centralization, increases in taxes, and strict requirements that sons follow their fathers in the family trade, compelled Italian craftspeople to revive the long dormant custom of guilds in the first century C.E. In time, the renewed *collegia* were able to wrest from the government enough privileges and

An olive press in Pompeii *(Courtesy Fr. Felix Just, S.J.)*

economic advantages that the Italian craftspeople were able to protect their work and ensure the survival of many forms of industry after the demise of the Roman Empire in the West.

While *collegia* played a major role in industrial output, the darker reality of Rome's craftwork was that in many industries—such as mining—most of the work was performed by slaves or condemned criminals *ad metallum* (to the mine). Other slaves were used as craftspeople because of their specialized skills. However, the majority of craftspeople were Roman citizens or freedmen who grew up learning their trade at the sides of their fathers and other members of the same craft guilds. The *collegia* provided a social milieu for craftspeople, ensuring not only employment but funeral services and care for surviving family.

Individual provinces became noted for certain industries, encouraged by both provincial administration and the increasingly centralized imperial bureaucracy. There was metalwork from Gaul, luxury items from the East, and agriculture throughout the West, Egypt, and Africa. Syria profited from its glassmaking and weaving and from its prime location on the trade routes with the East. Spain provided glassware and the mineral needs of most of the empire, including gold, silver, and copper for currency. Individual artisans produced pottery, leather, metal, bricks, glass, and other goods in provincial centers, while the economies of independent cities in Asia, Achaea, and Italy were supervised by the *correctores.*

Britain and Gaul perhaps best epitomized the blend of imperial and provincial industry. In Britain, agriculture and minerals were used locally but were also exported to the Continent. Small industries produced pottery and metalwork for domestic use. The province was thus vital as a self-sufficient entity and as a minor player in the economics of the empire. Because of Gaul's strategic location

as the western gateway to Britain, Spain, and especially Germany, it developed multi-provincial ties. Its agricultural produce fed Germanic legions and the inhabitants of the camps on the Rhine, while workshops and factories pursued traditional Gallic crafts, including woodworking, silversmithing, pottery making, glasswork, and the forging of iron. Gallic pottery was highly regarded throughout the empire. Local commerce provided a smaller, secondary market.

Suggested Readings: Casson, Lionel. *Ancient Trade and Society.* Detroit, Mich.: Wayne State University Press, 1984; D'Arms, John H. *Commerce and Social Standing in Ancient Rome.* Cambridge, Mass.: Harvard University Press, 1981; Duncan-Jones, Richard. *Structure and Scale in the Roman Economy.* Cambridge, U.K.: Cambridge University Press, 1990; ———. *The Economy of the Roman Empire: Quantitative Studies.* Cambridge, U.K.: Cambridge University Press, 1982; Finley, M. I. *The Ancient Economy.* second edition. London: Hogarth, 1985; Frayn, Joan M. *Sheep-rearing and the Wool Trade in Italy During the Roman Period.* Liverpool U.K.: F. Cairns, 1984; Greene, Kevin. *The Archaeology of the Roman Economy.* Berkeley: University of California Press, 1986.

informers *See* DELATORES.

Ingenuus (fl. third century C.E.) *Governor of Pannonia and a usurper in 260*
Following the defeat and capture of Emperor Valerian by the Persians, Ingenuus challenged Valerian's son and successor, Gallienus, and declared himself emperor at Sirmium with the help of his legions from Moesia. His attempt was short-lived, however, as Gallienus defeated him that same year at the battle of MURSA MAJOR.

Ingiuomerus (fl. early first century C.E.) *Uncle of the chieftain Arminius and a leader of the Cherusci*
Ingiuomerus acquired a formidable reputation as an enemy of Rome and formed a union with Arminius in 15 C.E. to oppose the advances of the Roman troops of GERMANICUS. Ingiuomerus lived up to his reputation in battle but was wounded after leading an assault on Germanicus's camp. In 16 C.E. both Ingiuomerus and ARMINIUS narrowly escaped capture, evading the enemy with the help of their CHERUSCI, who allowed them to get away. The following year the Germans themselves divided as MAROBODUUS struggled with the tribes not under his control. Ingiuomerus deserted his nephew and joined Maroboduus, sharing in his defeat at the hands of Arminius and the Cherusci and SUEBI.

Innocent I (d. 417 C.E.) *Pope from 401 to 417*
Innocent was born at Albano, Italy, and was possibly the son of St. Anastasius I. He served Anastasius as his dea-

con and was elected his successor on December 21, 401. A pontiff of considerable ability, personal strength, and morality, Innocent proved an important figure in establishing the primacy of the Roman see. He demanded, for example, that all disputes within the church be settled by him, setting important precedents in jurisdiction and authority. In 404, he called for the restoration of St. John Chrysostom as patriarch of Constantinople and later he secured ecclesiastical control over Illyricum, which had passed under Eastern jurisdiction in 388. The heresy of Pelagianism was condemned in 417, and its founder, Pelagius, was excommunicated. Innocent also emerged as a formidable political figure, working to have Emperor Honorius issue decrees against the Donatists. In 410, however, Innocent could not prevent the sack of Rome by the Visigoths, despite his efforts at Ravenna to negotiate a settlement. Returning to Rome in 412 after being spared the horrors of the invasions, his absence was considered providential. Innocent is considered by many historians to be the first pope, with his predecessors who ruled with less authority, being counted as bishops of Rome.

insula   A series of houses formed into blocks of rooms and used in those major cities of the empire where the Italian influence was predominant. In ROME the *insula* was the main style of living quarters and developed as a response to the crowded population of the capital. *Insulae* normally had the same outward appearance, that of a tall, square set of floors; within, however, some variety in architectural planning could be exhibited. There might be a large mansion covering many rooms, which could be sublet. By law they were limited in height to 70 feet. Other internal styles included many small apartments; one room or more; even whole floor suites. While *insulae* were both necessary and inevitable, they contributed to the massive overpopulation of Rome and to its filthy, squalid, tenementlike nature. What was worse, any small fire would quickly spread from one connected *insula* to anther, as happened in 36 C.E. on the Aventine and, of course, in the great fire of 64. The inhabitants of these buildings had very little hope of escape from such fires because of their height and the poor quality of the structures.

See also DOMUS.

Ionia   Famous area of Asia Minor; included in the province of Asia in the Roman Empire. The area occupied the central west coast on the Aegean and included such cities as Ephesus and Smyrna.

See also ASIA.

Ionian Sea   *See* ADRIATIC SEA.

Ireland   *See* HIBERNIA.

Irenaeus   (c. 130–200 C.E.) *Bishop of Lyons and one of the first theologians in early Christianity*
Probably born in Smyrna, Irenaeus listened as a boy to the profound Christian message of Polycarp. Subsequently St. Irenaeus studied in Rome, entered the clergy and became a presbyter at Lyons. In 177 he was sent to Rome, narrowly missing the initial persecution of Christians in Lyons, which claimed the local bishop, Pothinus. Irenaeus returned the following year and was chosen to succeed the martyred prelate as leader of the Lyons Christian community, a position that he held until the end of his days. From his see, he served as a defender of orthodoxy in Christian doctrine, composing *Adversus omnes Haereses* (Against All Heresies), a brilliant attack upon GNOSTICISM. This work was translated from the original Greek into Latin, Armenian, and other languages. He may have suffered martyrdom, a common fate of major figures in the church at that time.

Isaac the Great (St. Sahak)   (c. 350–439) *Saint and famed* katholikos (*also* catholicos, *or head*) *of the Armenian Church*
Isaac was very important in promoting Armenian cultural independence and a sense of national literature. The son of St. Narses, he was a descendant of St. Gregory the Illuminator. Isaac was educated at Constantinople and, after the death of his wife, he became a monk. In 390, he was appointed *katholicos* of Armenia, the 10th to hold the office. He fostered monasticism among the Armenians, converting his residence into a monastery, and secured the recognition by Constantinople that the Armenian Church had patriarchal rights, thereby freeing Armenian Christianity from the control of the Greeks. Isaac was crucial in organizing a group of scholars, with the help of his auxiliary bishop, Mesrop Mastots, that translated Greek and Syriac works, especially the Bible, into Armenian. It is possible that he also composed Armenian hymns and, perhaps, the Armenian liturgy. Deposed by the Persians in 425, he was able to regain his see in 432 through popular insistence. He is known as St. Sahak in the Armenian Church.

Isauria   A region of Asia Minor situated roughly between PISIDIA and CILICIA, to the west of the Taurus Mountains and comprising a part of that range's western slope. Traditionally the Isaurians were a fierce people, specializing in robbery. They were initially defeated by Lucius Servilius Vatia in 75 B.C.E., their territory subsequently falling under Roman rule. Isauria passed into the jurisdiction first of CAPPADOCIA, but under Antoninus Pius it was given to Cilicia. Two small cities served as the local economic centers: New Isaura and Old Isaura.

Although supposedly subjugated, the Isaurians refused to surrender their old ways. In 6 C.E., they resumed their marauding of surrounding communities and were again defeated. Two centuries later, in the reign of Severus Alexander (c. 222), the Isaurians rose up briefly, continuing to make trouble into the reign of Probus, who had to build a fortress in order to keep them pacified in 278. So resilient did they prove that they were mentioned in 404 C.E. by St. John Chrysostom in his letters from his place of exile in the Taurus Mountains. A campaign had to be mounted and lasted three years (404–407), but was wholly insufficient to stop them.

Emperor Leo found the best way to end their threats. In order to put the Isaurians to constructive use and to counter the same Germanic military influence that overwhelmed the West, Leo recruited native peoples in the East to serve in his army. The Isaurians were probably chosen to fill the ranks of the newly created Palace Guard, the EXCUBITORS. Leo married (c. 466) Ariadne, the daughter of Tarasicodissa, a chief of the Isaurians. Tarasicodissa took the name ZENO and played a major role in court politics. In November of 474 he succeeded to the throne when Zeno's grandson, Leo II, died. The Isaurians, who now controlled the palace, were very unpopular because of their reputations and previous crimes. A palace revolt led by Basiliscus ousted Zeno, who simply retired to Isauria as its king. Basiliscus proved even more unpopular, and in 476, Zeno returned and ruled the empire until 491.

Isidorus   *See* BUCOLICI.

Isis   One of the most popular and enduring goddesses of the ancient world. Isis was originally one of the great deities of Egypt. She was the sister and consort of Osiris, and put him together after he had been dismembered by his evil brother, Set. She was later impregnated by the dead Osiris, giving birth to Horus, who took revenge upon Set.

Isis evolved as a fertility goddess and as a universal Mother figure. By the second century B.C.E., traders and sailors were carrying her cultic influences throughout the known world. Within the Greek domains Isis became identified with Demeter, her statues assuming the usual Grecian motif. They soon appeared in the cities of Africa, Asia Minor, and Spain. Before long she arrived in Italy and entered Rome toward the end of the Republic.

Popular resistance to foreign cults had always been a part of the Roman makeup (*see* APOLLO and CYBELE), but Isis was more successful than other deities. Her followers moved from Pompeii, and sometime before 50 B.C.E. a temple in her honor was erected in Rome. The great moment of Roman acceptance came in the reign of Gaius Caligula, who built a large temple to her in the Campus Martius. She thus earned the title of *Isis Campensis*.

As was true of most of the highly popular cults in the Roman Empire, the temple of Isis offered elaborate ceremonies and complex mysteries. Her highly disci-

plined priests, dressed in white linen garments, performed beautiful rituals, accompanied by music. A well organized spiritual structure made Isis's devotional doctrines even more exciting and easily propagated. Isis endured for many centuries, replaced only by the Madonna of Christian belief. An interesting example of the Hellenization of Isis is found in a novel of the late first century C.E., by Xenophon of Ephesus. He combined the character of Apollo and Isis into one story of two lovers who evade hardships through her constant intervention.

See also RELIGION.

Issus   Small town, near the northeastern corner of the Mediterranean, where a battle was fought in 194 C.E. between the legions of Septimius Severus and Pescennius Niger for control of the Eastern provinces of the empire. After assuming the purple in Rome in 193, Severus, with his Pannonian legions, passed into Asia Minor, winning the battles of CYZICUS and NICAEA. By 194, Severus was marching toward Syria, when Niger himself arrived with reinforcements.

The location of this final confrontation was the same as at that historic battle of 333 B.C.E. between Alexander the Great and Darius the Persian. Just as earlier, the invader, Severus, was outnumbered by his opponents, for Niger possessed a vast host. While Niger commanded his troops personally, however, Severus entrusted his troops to P. Cornelius Anullinus.

According to the historian Dio, the battle initially favored Niger because of his superior numbers and would have gone against the Severans had a storm not erupted. Lightning struck and rain drenched the field. Niger's troops were more adversely affected because of the wind. Unable to overcome both nature and the enemy, these troops began a retreat that quickly degenerated into a rout. Some 20,000 soldiers died on Niger's side as Severus proved triumphant. Niger tried to flee but was slain outside of Antioch. Severus could now turn his attention to Clodius Albinus, his opponent in the West.

Istria   Also called Histria; a land at the north of the Adriatic, between VENETIA on the Timavus River and ILLYRICUM on the Arsia. The Istrian territory extended into the Julian Alps. The Istri were reputed to be a fierce, warlike and territorially possessive people. They resented the founding of AQUILEIA by the Romans, and war was common until C. Claudius Pulcher defeated them in 177 B.C.E. Although there would be small insurrections in the future, Istria became part of the important province of ITALIA, and Aquileia served as the largest port on the Adriatic.

Italia   Homeland of the Romans, for centuries distinguished by special status, honors, and rights. Originally,

"Italia" referred only to the southern half of the peninsula, where the Italians or Vitalians resided. In succeeding years, however, the territorial possessions of the Romans increased so greatly that by the time of the empire, "Italy" stretched from Sicily to the ALPS, including the once barbarian GALLIA CISALPINA.

Although the Romans came to dominate the Mediterranean and beyond, Italia itself was not easily acquired and was composed of numerous peoples, some never fully assimilated, and a complex internal social strata. Indeed, the final organization and pacification of Italy did not occur until the late first century B.C.E. Even then, many tribal complexes remained. The oldest people known to ancient tradition were the Pelasgians or Siculi, who came from a Greek line and could be called the first inhabitants. More famous were the Etruscans, who mastered the lands between the Tiber and the Alps. There were also the Umbrians, the Latini, Sabines, Apulians, and a host of smaller clans, including the Volsci, Baeligni, Marsi, Hernici, and Sallentini. Far to the south there lived as well Greek colonists. All were defeated and subjugated by the Romans through many wars.

In recognition of the tapestry of Italia's cultures, Augustus, in 27 B.C.E., established a system of 11 districts:

    I. Campania and Latium
    II. The region of Calabria, Apulia, and the Hirpini
    III. Lucania and Bruttium
    IV. Samnium (The region of the Marsi, Frentani, Marrucini, Paeligni, Vestini, and Sabines)
    V. Picenum
    VI. Umbria
    VII. Etruria
    VIII. Gallia Cispadana
    IX. Liguria
    X. Eastern Gallia Traspadana, Venetia, Istria (Aquileia), and Carnia
    XI. Western Gallia Transpadana

ROME was excluded from the jurisdiction of the districts. All land within Italia benefited from the full protection of law and participated in the IUS ITALICUM. Such advantages allowed inhabitants to live in considerable prosperity but fostered economic expansion as well.

Since the second century B.C.E., Italy had grown from a primitive country to the leading financial power in the empire. Its industries enjoyed a monopoly in the first century C.E., and its merchants controlled trade everywhere. Equally, Italia was blessed with abundant beauty, agricultural goods, and a fortunate location. Exports included metalworks from CAMPANIA, silver from CAPUA, and pottery from PUTEOLI, Cumae, and Campania. If Rome was the political center of the world, Italy was the industrial one. Wealth allowed the cities of POMPEII, Capua, AQUILEIA, and others to achieve considerable prestige. The villa system of the Republican age endured, as well as the great figures of the time who built these retreats from the world. They fled to luxurious estates in Campania, at BAULI, and BAIAE, and life throughout the region was generally good.

In the second century C.E. Italia's status changed. The decline of the region was rooted in numerous events, all of which reflected upon the state of the empire itself. Economic decentralization threatened Italian supremacy, peace in Asia and Africa reduced the number of slaves and cheap labor available for Italia's industries, and thousands of Italians had departed for better lives in the colonies, bringing a crisis of depopulation. No longer were the Roman LEGIONS Italian, and by the second century, even the emperors were of foreign birth.

Most serious of all was the philosophy of the central imperial government that the Roman Empire was a united fabric of provinces. HADRIAN had already set a wider perimeter by traveling for most of his long reign (117–138 C.E.) to the cities of the West, the East, and of Africa. Economic production elsewhere was encouraged. COLOGNE soon made better glassware, Africa better lamps, and the Gallic artisans proved superior in pottery and metal goods. Sensing the need to respond to the demands of a new era, the cities in northern Italia, Aquileia, and MEDIOLANUM (Milan), adapted to meet the needs of new markets in Raetia, Noricum, Pannonia, and Illyricum, and thus survived by supplying wine, glass, and weapons to the legions on the Danube. Southern Italy showed no such initiative. Ominously, the north suffered a prefiguring of the fifth century when, around 170 C.E., the QUADI and MARCOMANNI burst across the Danube and besieged Aquileia while ravaging parts of Gallia Transpadana and Istria.

Caracalla (ruled 211–217 C.E.) then dealt two crushing blows to Italian pride. He appointed the financial officers of the state, the CURATORES, to the cities of Italia. Each CURATORE supervised the finances of a municipality, determining if the funds were being used properly. The passing of the *Constitutio Antoniniana* ended Italia's unique legal and social status forever by granting citizenship to every inhabitant of the empire. Under the next emperors and throughout the third century C.E., the duties of the CORRECTORES expanded as their jurisdiction came to encompass geographical boundaries instead of legal matters only.

DIOCLETIAN, however, was responsible for the administrative decline. In reorganizing the provinces of the empire circa 300 C.E., Italia was declared part of the diocese of Italiae, under the governorship of two VICARII, one in the north and the other in the south. Aside from the loss of prestige, tax rights, and political independence, Italia suffered as well by being ignored by both Diocletian and his eventual, powerful successor, CONSTANTINE THE GREAT. Diocletian refused to live in Rome, preferring Nicomedia, and visited Italy only in 303, after he had

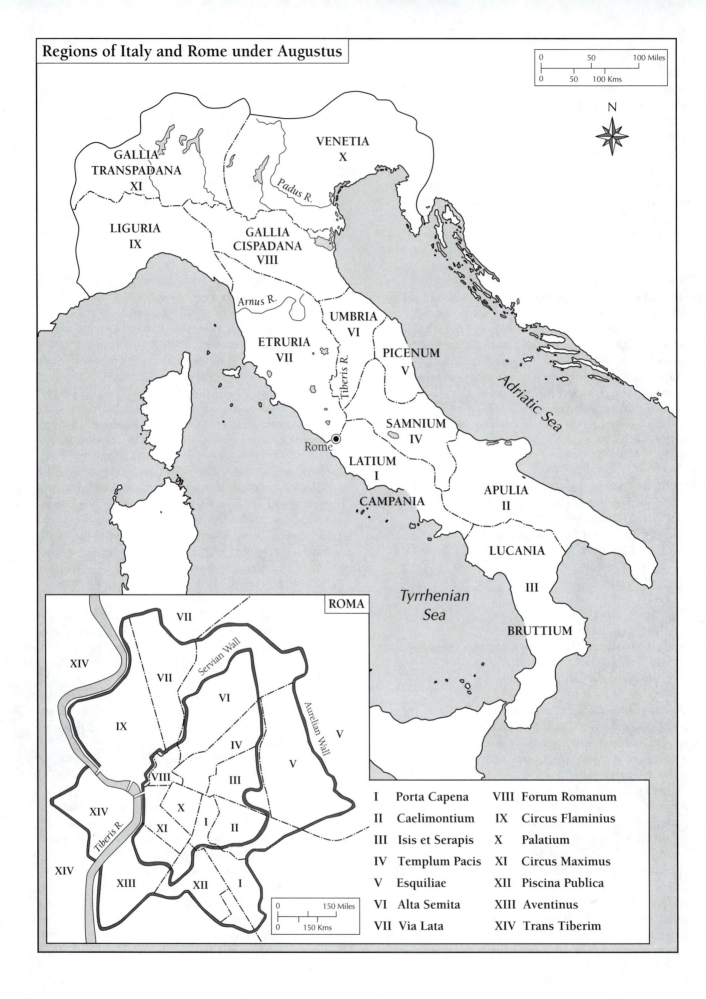

Regions of Italy and Rome under Augustus

0   50   100 Miles
0   50   100 Kms

N

GALLIA TRANSPADANA XI

VENETIA X

Padus R.

LIGURIA IX

GALLIA CISPADANA VIII

Arnus R.

UMBRIA VI

ETRURIA VII

PICENUM V

Tiberis R.

SAMNIUM IV

Adriatic Sea

Rome

LATIUM I

CAMPANIA

APULIA II

LUCANIA III

Tyrrhenian Sea

BRUTTIUM

ROMA

VII

XIV

Servian Wall

VII

IX

VI

IV

VIII

Aurelian Wall

V

V

III

XIV

X

I

II

XI

XIV

I

XIII

XII

Tiberis R.

0   150 Miles
0   150 Kms

I	Porta Capena	VIII	Forum Romanum
II	Caelimontium	IX	Circus Flaminius
III	Isis et Serapis	X	Palatium
IV	Templum Pacis	XI	Circus Maximus
V	Esquiliae	XII	Piscina Publica
VI	Alta Semita	XIII	Aventinus
VII	Via Lata	XIV	Trans Tiberim

been on the throne for 20 years. Constantine, born in Serbia, conquered the Italians in 312 when he defeated MAXENTIUS at the MILVIAN BRIDGE, but he chose Serdica as his initial headquarters before building his new capital, CONSTANTINOPLE. This city on the Bosporus became the heart of the empire.

Italy remained the home of the emperors of the West, who lived in Rome, Mediolanum (Milan), and eventually RAVENNA. Such attractions drew the VANDALS and the HUNS, who poured into the province. With the fall in 476 C.E. of ROMULUS AUGUSTULUS at the hands of ODOACER, the barbarian king, Italia came under the rule of foreigners.

See also COLONIES, ETRURIA, HERCULANEUM, POMPEII, TIBER, UMBRIA, VESUVIUS, *viae.*

Suggested Readings: Clarke, J. R. *Houses of Roman Italy 100 B.C.E.–C.E. 250.* Los Angeles: University of California Press, 1991; Clayton, Peter *Treasures of Ancient Rome.* New York: Random House, 1986; Grimal, Pierre. *Roman Cities.* Translated and edited by G. Michael Woloch. Madison: University of Wisconsin Press, 1983; Harris, William V. *Rome in Etruria and Umbria.* Oxford, U.K., Clarendon Press, 1971; Neeve, P. W. de. *Peasants in Peril: Location and Economy in Italy in the Second Century* B.C.E. Amsterdam: J. C. Gieben, 1984; Potter, T. W. *Roman Italy.* London: British Museum Publications, 1987; Salmon, Edward Togo. *The Making of Roman Italy.* Ithaca, N.Y.: Cornell University Press, 1982.

Italicus (fl. mid-first century C.E.) *Son of the Cheruscan Prince Flavius and a Chatti princess, and nephew of the famous leader of the German Cherusci, Arminius*
Italicus was born in Rome, as his father had been unable to return home because of his loyalties to the Romans. In 47 C.E., CLAUDIUS gave Italicus an escort and gold, sending him to take over the vacant throne of the CHERUSCI. A civil war had decimated the aristocracy, and Italicus was welcomed initially as a suitable chieftain. However, his imperial associations made the establishment of a permanent sovereignty difficult, for elements in the Cherusci refused to accept him. A battle ensued, and Italicus and his followers were victorious. For a number of years he remained the head of the tribe, but, growing arrogant, he was eventually expelled. With the aid of the LANGOBARDI, Italicus returned but reigned as a notoriously bad king.

Italy *See* ITALIA.

itineraria Maps or guides that provided lists of stations along a road, distances to various points, and other useful information that might be of value to the Roman traveler. The *itinerarium* was the land equivalent of the *periploi,* which provided similar details for ocean travel. Carved on stone or bronze tablets, or written on papyrus or parchment, the *intineraria* were quite com-

mon throughout the empire and could often be consulted in libraries.

It is likely that itineraries were first developed in early Roman history, but the surviving examples date from the first century C.E. A few notable examples have survived, but the most notable is the *Itinerarium Antoninianum,* also called *Itinerarium Provinciarum Antonini Augusti* (Antonine itinerary). Dating probably to the late third century, the *Itinerarium Antoniniarum* collected 225 routes, mainly for troop movements, along the major roads of the empire. It offers details on where to stop at *mansiones* along the routes of the *cursus publicus,* with a variety of proposed intineraries, although there is clear information on the shortest route that might be taken between two locations. The longest route described is that between Rome and Egypt and was perhaps included in the plan of Emperor Caracalla's proposed journey to Egypt in 214–15. Included with the *Itinerarium Antoniniarum* was the *Imperatoris Antonini Augusti itinerarium maritimum,* an itinerary on sea travel.

The *Ravenna Cosmography,* a compilation by an 11th-century monk that was originally the work of a cleric in Ravenna around 700, made use of earlier Roman documents from as far back as the fifth century. It provides a list of stops, river names, and other information for travelers. Copy errors are abundant, however.

In the later empire, *itineraria* were created to provide Christian pilgrims with maps and routes to the holy city of Jerusalem. Among the best known of these are the *Itinerarium Burdigalense sive Hierosolymitanum* (Jerusalem or Bordeaux itinerary) and the *Peregrinatio Aetheriae* (Journey of Aetheriae). The Bordeaux itinerary gives details to pilgrims journeying from Bordeaux to Jerusalem, with stops at Milan, Constantinople, and Antioch and with an alternate return route home. The text offers descriptions, annotations, and distances between the sites. The *Peregrinatio Aetheriae,* also called the *Itinerarium Egeriae,* dates to 400 and is an account of a nun who made a pilgrimage to the East, with visits to Constantinople, Egypt, and Edessa. The nun wrote the book for her fellow sisters in Hispania. Aside from its great value in terms of Roman cartography and travel, the *Peregrinatio* also preserves details on the liturgical life of the Holy Land during the period, as well as examples of Late and Vulgar Latin.

See also NOTITIA DIGNITATEM and PEUTINGER TABLE.

Iuga The Roman name for JUNO, as the goddess of marriage.

ius civile Roman civil law. The *ius civile* denoted the laws, statutes, and regulations governing Roman citizens, which were different from those applied to foreigners (the IUS GENTIUM). In the first century B.C.E., SCAEVOLA organized the *ius civile* into a mammoth collection of 18 books, while Servius Sulpicius a short time later amassed the sum of Roman legalism into 180 books. The *ius civile* was frequently amended and clarified by the edicts of the PRAETORS and by the JURISTS throughout the era of the empire.

ius emphyteuticum   A form of lease used in the later years of the Roman Empire. By its terms, a renter leased an estate of unused or deteriorated land with the promise of returning the soil to a usable condition. Rents, taxes, and other fees were reduced for a period, usually for several years. At the end of that time the rates returned to normal, on the assumption that the lessee had restored the grounds to a profitable condition.

ius gentium   The laws governing the dealings of Rome with foreigners, the PEREGRINI. As Roman conquests and territorial acquisitions brought many new peoples into the boundaries of Roman dominion, it became necessary to formulate a legal system that could accommodate the wide-ranging differences between Roman law, the IUS CIVILE, and the laws for foreigners. Trade, economic ties and close alliances with other states forced the Romans to acknowledge legal systems of the *peregrini* and that the *peregrini* were entitled to legal protection. To handle cases involving foreigners, the *praetor peregrini* was appointed. With his pronouncements, and with the increased international nature of the Roman Empire, there was born a vast system of statutes, regulations, and guidelines that was eventually applied to Romans and non-Romans. A blurring was inevitable between the *ius civile* and the *ius gentium,* an intertwining later rendered redundant by the passing of the Consitiutio Antoniniana by Emperor CARACALLA, making all inhabitants of the empire citizens of the empire. Henceforth, there would be one law for all people.

ius honorum   *See* PRAETOR.

ius Italicum   Term used to describe the legal status of Roman land, either as part of Italia itself or in an Italian colony. In essence, the *ius Italicum* declared a parcel of land or area to be legally considered Italian soil, superceding the designation IUS LATII. Thus cities in Spain and elsewhere became Italian. Beyond the prestige associated with the *ius Italicum,* there were specific advantages. Such land was capable of individual ownership (*optimo iure Quiritium*), passed out of direct taxation (the *tributum capitis*) and stood outside the jurisdiction of the provincial governor. The special status of the *ius Italicum* was thus costly to Rome in lost revenues and in reduced authority and was not given easily. Augustus allowed the *ius* to only a few colonies, mainly in ASIA MINOR, where the colonists needed the financial support to compensate for the hardships of life. With the decline in outright colonization, the *ius* was very rarely granted to municipalities, either as a reward or as a means of furthering Romanization. Septimius Severus elevated his own home land of AFRICA, LEPCIS MAGNA, CARTHAGE, and UTICA. All such distinctions ended with the declaration of the Constitutio Antoniniana in the reign of Caracalla (211–217 C.E.), making all inhabitants of the provinces Roman citizens.

ius Latii   The Latin rights or privileges granted to individuals and communities as members of the Latin community. Originally, the *ius Latti* was enjoyed by the Latins, who had developed a special relationship with Rome. Over the succeeding years they became full citizens of Rome. The principle of the *ius Latii* remained, however, as part of the process by which a municipality achieved Roman citizenship and the IUS ITALICUM. Latin rights, with only few exceptions in AFRICA, were granted in the West. The rights included participation in the *ius civitatis* (right of citizenship) and in the commerce of Italy. Most importantly, the possession of the *ius Latii* meant eventual citizenship.

J

James (d. c. 62 C.E.) *Leader of the Christians of Jerusalem, called the Lord's brother*

James is often confused with St. James the Less (Son of Alphaeus) and shares with that James and with St. Philip the feast day May 3. According to St. Paul, James received a singular appearance of Christ after the Resurrection, subsequently becoming a prominent leader among the Christian community of Jerusalem with St. Peter. His prominence is attested by the mention made of him by Paul in Galatians and the fact that he presided over the crucial Council of Jerusalem concerning Paul's preaching to the Gentiles. His authority was only heightened after the departure of Peter from the city to escape Herod Agrippa I and the beheading of St. James the Greater by that same king. He was also visited by Paul on his last visit to Jerusalem. While not described as such in the New Testament, James is traditionally considered the first bishop of Jerusalem on the basis of a report by Clement of Alexandria as recorded by Eusebius of Caesarea in the *Ecclesiastical History*. Clement calls him the Just, perhaps because of his desire to adhere to some element of Jewish law. He was apparently put to death by the Sanhedrin in 62. The second-century historian HEGESIPPUS described his death, preserved in the *Ecclesiastical History* of Eusebius. According to him, James was thrown off a tower in the Great Temple of Jerusalem and then beaten to death. The Jewish historian Josephus in the first century wrote that James was stoned. James's symbol in art is a club or heavy staff.

James's name was attached to a number of apocryphal writings. Among these are the Apocalypses of James, two works found in the codices of the Nag Hammadi, texts on Christian gnosticism written in the Coptic language; an Epistle of James, also found at Nag Hammadi; the Liturgy of St. James, traditionally ascribed to him; and the so-called Infancy Gospel or the Book of James, also known as the *Protoevangelium,* from the 16th century, that was based on the Gospels of Mark and Luke. James was also proposed as the author of the New Testament Epistle of James.

James the Greater (James the Great) (d. 44 C.E.) *Son of Zebedee, brother of St. John, and one of the Twelve Apostles*

James is called the Greater to distinguish him from James the Less, the name not denoting any ecclesiastical or honorific superiority but simply implying that he was older than James the Less or of greater height. A native of Galilee, he became a follower of Christ.

He was the first Apostle to suffer martyrdom, being beheaded at the command of King Herod Agrippa I of Judaea in 44. His death, recorded in Acts (12:2), is the only one pertaining to the Twelve Apostles to be reported in the New Testament. According to Spanish tradition, James was able to preach there before his death, and thus became one of the most popular Spanish saints. It is generally accepted in Spain that his body was translated to Santiago de Compostela, a foremost pilgrim site.

James the Less (d. 66 C.E.) *Apostle and early leader in the Christian Church*

Son of Alphaeus, James is called the Less or the Lesser to distinguish him from James the Greater, who was older or taller. James is often confused with James, the "Lord's brother," although there is a certain tradition that they might be one and the same person. He is mentioned several times in the Gospels. As the son of Mary, a woman, who, with Mary Magdalene, stood and witnessed the Crucifixion. Little else is known of him, unless the possibility of his being the aforementioned James is accepted.

Janus The Roman god of doorways, beginnings, the past, and the future. Janus was an original Roman creation, not taken from any other pantheon. According to tradition, he was established in Rome by King Numa, who also built the so-called Temple of Janus. In times of war the temple gates were opened, and closed only when there was peace throughout the Roman world. So rare was this occurrence (Livy wrote that up until Augustus's own day it happened only three times) that commemorative coins were issued with the head of Janus imprinted upon them. Janus's visage normally showed two heads (*Janus bifrons*), one looking forward and the other behind. Such was the god's function in Rome. He was invoked even before Jupiter to protect the beginning of all endeavors. A festival took place on New Year's Day in which people gave gifts and coins of Janus to welcome another year. The first entire month of the calendar was under his auspices. An association with the past and the future made him the god of doorways.

See also GODS AND GODDESSES OF ROME.

Javolenus Priscus, Gaius Octavius Tidius Tassianus Lucius (fl. second century C.E.) *Leading jurist* Javolenus was the head of the Sabinian School of Law and a legate in Britannia, Germania Superior, and Africa and proconsul of Africa. Among his writings were *Epistulae* (Letters) and extensive analyses of previous legal experts. Salvius Julianus was his most famous student.

See also LAW.

Jericho Very ancient city mentioned in the Old Testament as the place of the Canaanites. It was situated on a tributary flowing west from the Jordan River. During the early years of the empire, Jericho belonged to the kingdom of JUDAEA. HEROD THE GREAT owned balsam gardens and probably spent time in a palace there. During his reign the unrest that occurred in parts of Judaea caused the palace to be burned. Archelaus, as ethnarch, rebuilt it.

Jerome (Eusebius Hieronymus; "St. Jerome") (c. 345–420 C.E.) *Biblical Scholar, translator and noted outspoken Christian*
St. Jerome was born at Stridon near Aquileia. He studied in Rome, learning rhetoric and Latin literature prior to becoming a Christian. After baptism he traveled to Gaul and elsewhere in the West before returning to Aquileia to devote himself to an ascetic's life. Jerome (c. 374) embarked on a trip to the East, stopping at Antioch, where he dreamed that Christ spoke to him, condemning his preference for Roman literature to Christianity, with the words: *"Ciceronianus es, non Christianus"*—"Thou art a Ciceronian, not a Christian." The deserts of Syria seemed a suitable place to repent, and there, living as a hermit for four or five years, he mastered Hebrew. Ordination came while visiting Antioch, followed by a trip to Constantinople.

Further journeys brought Jerome to Rome in 382, where he came to the attention of Pope Damasus, serving as his personal secretary and gaining wide popularity with the Roman nobility, particularly with the ladies. Friendships developed with such noblewomen as Marcella and Paula and the latter's two daughters, Blaesilla and Eustochium. Marcella, Paula, and Eustochium were later canonized, proving the innocence of his relationship with them.

Damasus died in 385, and Jerome departed for the East. In the company of Paula and Eustochium, he made visits to Antioch, Palestine, and Egypt. In 386, he settled in Bethlehem. The rest of his life was spent in strict study and in scholarly pursuits. In his writings, Jerome used every lesson in his early education to carve for himself a place of high intellectual honor within the early church. His translation of the Bible, commenced at the suggestion of Damasus, was the highlight of his career. He translated the Bible into Latin, revising and improving translations already in existence in a series of versions. The Four Gospels and the *psalterium vetus* were transcribed, followed by the protocanonical sections of the Old Testament, from the original Hebrew and at a cost of some 15 years' labor (c. 390–405). The church later recognized these efforts as essential to the writing of the Vulgate.

Other works were numerous. There were commentaries on the Old and New Testament, in which he displayed his knowledge of Hebrew and tradition, and a continuation of the *Ecclesiastical History* of Eusebius, brought down to 378. *De viris illustribus*, compiled in 392, examined the ecclesiastical writers of the Christian past. Jerome's letters were sent to the most important church figures of the time. He involved himself in the fiercest controversies of the day, battling with Jovinian and Vigilantius and entering the heated debates on ARIANISM. ORIGEN's theology and PELAGIANISM also received his attention. Though he once called Rome a Babylon, its sacking by Alaric in 410 caused Jerome terrible sorrow, marking as it did the death of the Roman world. He lived on another 10 years, continuing to write until his death.

Jerusalem The sacred city of Judaism, and later of Christianity as well. Jerusalem was the very heart of the Jewish world. Its destruction in 70 C.E. ensured the dispersal of the Jews within the Roman Empire, and its rebirth as a Christian center ushered in a new age for the Holy Land.

"I shall wipe Jerusalem as a man wipeth a dish, wiping it and turning it upside down."

Chronicles, Book I, 16:41.

Jerusalem was an ancient city, built, it was said, by the Canaanite tribe of the Jebusites. In 1050 B.C.E., King David captured it and made it his great capital. The name came from *Hierusaleme,* or "Holy City," and Jerusalem was, for the Jews, truly sacred. Their kings, including Solomon, lived within its walls until 588, when King Nebuchadnezzar besieged it and wholly enslaved the Jewish nation. Although Cyrus granted in 538 B.C.E. to the Jews the right to rebuild the city, the next centuries brought new masters and new hardships. Finally, an independence of sorts was gained by Judas Maccabaeus (167–164 B.C.E.) and the Hasmonaean line of high priests. Internal debate led to civil war in 63 B.C.E., when the sons of the Hasmonaean King Jannaeus Alexander, Aristobulus, and Hyrcanus, used Jerusalem as a battleground for supremacy.

Appropriately, given subsequent dealings, Rome's first introduction to Jerusalem was in a siege. POMPEY THE GREAT, newly arrived in the region, immediately besieged the city in 63 to end the civil strife. Jerusalem fell and never again would know complete freedom. Hyrcanus was allowed to remain high priest, but within the city political power was held by ANTIPATER OF IDUMAEA, the royal minister who not only achieved personal supremacy in Judaea but also had one son, Phasael, named governor of Jerusalem and another son, HEROD THE GREAT, appointed governor of Galilee. This Idumaean won the trust of Julius Caesar and was granted the right to fortify the city walls in circa 47 B.C.E.

Strong walls could not prevent Caesar's assassin, CASSIUS, from plundering the temple to fund his campaign against Marc ANTONY nor could they keep the Parthians from launching an invasion of Judaea in 40. Jerusalem fell to the Parthians, who placed the Hasmonaean claimant Antigonus on the throne. Herod fled to Rome, returning with Roman legions, and in July of 37 B.C.E. took back Jerusalem and became the king of the Jews.

Just as the entire Judaean realm was given new cities and defensive constructions, so was Jerusalem fortified, including the Tower of Antonia. Relations with Rome were generally cordial at the beginning of Herod's reign, but deteriorated as he grew repressive and estranged from his people. The Jews disliked having an Idumaean as a monarch, and riots broke out in the streets. The problems did not end with Herod's death in 4 B.C.E., for Augustus named his son Archelaus as ruler of a much reduced kingdom (JUDAEA, IDUMAEA, AND SAMARIA). More unrest and violence, most notably in Jerusalem, attracted Roman attention, and in 6 C.E. Augustus acquiesced to Jewish requests that Archelaus be removed. Henceforth, Judaea was an imperial province.

Jerusalem and the Temple of Solomon, from a 16th-century engraving *(Hulton/Getty Archive)*

Caesarea became the administrative seat of the procurators for the province because Jerusalem, with its multitude of religious groups, its volatile nature and long history of violence, was not the best place for a Roman overseer. However, Roman government was unpopular everywhere in the region, and in 66 C.E., despite the presence of legions, Jerusalem was once again the scene of rebellion. The actual conflagration began here, when Gessius Florus, procurator of Judaea, seized part of the temple treasury and then stood by while his troops plundered a part of the city. Florus wisely withdrew, allowing Agrippa II to try to stem the tide. When Jerusalem started a revolution, however, Palestine joined in, and the governor of Syria, Cestius Gallus, with the XII Legion, was defeated outside the city gates. This encouraged the rebels.

Jerusalem's leaders now took command of the war, appointing Ananus, a former high priest, and Joseph, son of Gorion, to be co-leaders. They faced both internal and outside foes, as the ZEALOTS and inveterate haters of Rome took over key posts and filled the city with their followers. General Vespasian pacified most of the territory during a hard-fought period from February 67 to June 68. He was preparing to lay siege to Jerusalem, actually, when the civil war in Rome called a halt to all other activities.

The delay in Rome's conquest of Palestine aided Jerusalem very little, for the ambitious John of Gischala used gangs of Zealots to massacre any moderates or opponents. Matters were made worse by the arrival of two more factions, those of Simon Bar Giora (Bargoia) and Eleazar, son of Simon. Vespasian became emperor in late 69 and in spring of 70, his son TITUS assumed control over the Palestinian legions. Jerusalem soon fell under attack, and the first of the city's three great walls fell to Rome siegemasters by the end of May. In June, the Romans relentlessly drove on, smashing into the Tower of Antonia and moving against the Great TEMPLE. According to Josephus, Titus was firm against the destruction of the Temple, but he had no control over the disaster.

On August 30, 70 C.E. (9 Ab on the Jewish calendar, the date of Nebuchadnezzar's burning of the earlier Temple), soldiers of Titus's legions engaged in a struggle with the insurgents just outside of the Temple. One of the Romans, caught up in the fray, threw a firebrand into the building, and a fire broke out; quite probably Titus had ordered the burning. The following day, anyone caught within the boundaries was killed, and the treasury, gates, and porticos were also set on fire. All the valuables salvaged from the blaze were confiscated to be displayed in Rome for Titus's triumph.

Still the defenders would not surrender, especially John of Gischala, who fled to the defenses of the Upper City. Titus allowed his troops to sack and demolish the Lower City, and on September 8 launched his final assault. By the 26th, all of Jerusalem was on fire. Titus entered the ruined city a short time later, marveled at the magnificent towers and ordered that everything except the forts be demolished. The wrath of Rome was thus appeased, and the ancient city of Jerusalem was no more.

The Flavians refused to allow the rebuilding of the Temple, and the ruins of the city were left untouched, except for the areas directly around the site, which were farmed out to the followers of the legion, the X Fretensis, stationed in a camp there. The absence of the Temple had a profound effect upon the nature of Judaism. The Jews never forgot the Temple and never forgave the Romans for destroying it.

Thus, in 132, conspiracies were formed when a rumor was circulated that Hadrian intended to build a pagan city on the ruins of the ancient capital and Temple. The Jews were willing to pay their temple tax of two drachmas to Jupiter Capitolinus, but they would not tolerate a Roman building defiling the capital. Simon Bar Cochba led an unsuccessful war from 132 to 135 and was crushed by Julius Severus, Hadrian's legate. The city was renamed Colonia Aelia Capitolina as a result of this revolt. A temple to Jupiter Capitolinus was erected on the site of the old Temple, and all Jews were forbidden entry into its perimeters. It stood in place for two centuries, while around it the Roman Empire changed.

Earliest Christianity found an audience in Jerusalem, where Sts. Peter and James led the community. From the time of Christ until the transformation of the Roman Empire into a Christian domain, Jerusalem attracted pilgrims who were eager to walk in Christ's footsteps. As a result, there was a curious mixture of creeds, for the Jewish origins of the city could not be removed easily. There were pagans, soldiers, merchants, and Christians living among the Jews. Aelia Capitolina in the third and fourth centuries was probably neither a pleasant nor a safe place. Constantine the Great did little to change the overall status of the city directly. His Christianization of the world, however, led to larger numbers of pilgrims and a return to the name "Jerusalem." Caesarea remained the administrative capital. Although there was an old church in Jerusalem, the patriarchs of Antioch and Alexandria and the bishop of Caesarea steadfastly opposed any ecclesiastical adornments for the see, if it meant a decline of their own powers. Jerusalem remained a mere bishopric, but a popular one, visited by thousands.

Two events in the fifth century changed the history of the city for all time. Juvenal, the bishop of Jerusalem (422–458), had worked for his entire episcopal career to aggrandize his position. He supported Cyril of Alexandria but turned on Cyril's successor. Dioscorus, because he believed that would aid his cause. He was successful in this venture; at the Council of Chalcedon, Jerusalem received patriarchal rights equal to those of Antioch.

The city still needed financial support and imperial attention. That came with the visit of Aelia Eudocia, the wife of Theodosius II, in the spring of 438. She visited the city as an intellectual pilgrim and, when forced to depart Constantinople in semi-disgrace circa 444, she asked to live in Jerusalem. For the last years before her death in 460, she spent vast sums of money and great effort to improve the city. Hospitals, churches, monasteries, and the Basilica of St. Stephen were all erected because of her, and even a new wall was completed. Jerusalem finally offered an appearance of beauty and grandeur equal to its lofty spiritual position, a status it never lost, even in the face of new invaders and conquerors.

The best description of Jerusalem was written by Josephus in his *Jewish War;* he had examined the city prior to its destruction in 70 C.E. Aelia Capitolina would differ greatly from the original, and the Jerusalem of the fifth century and beyond changed once more. Jerusalem was located within the province of Judaea to the west of the Jordan River and the Dead Sea (by some 20 miles) and east of the Mediterranean Sea by about 35 miles. It was built upon two major hills, along a valley separating them. The greater of the hills was called King David (Mt. Zion), on which rested the original city, and to the southeast was Acre. Tyropoeon (the Valley of the Cheesemakers) was the name given to the valley. The hills placed Jerusalem in a strategically superior position, with steep ravines and tall cliffs on nearly every side. What nature made difficult to capture, the Jews made virtually impregnable, for upon the hills stood three mighty walls, reinforced by a stout system of towers.

The first wall, built to encompass the entire Lower and much of the Upper City, used the Hippicus and the Xystus Towers as its anchors. The second wall was shorter, enclosing only part of the northern sections. It no doubt began at Hippicus or Phasael Towers and stretched in a northerly direction to the Antonine Tower; perhaps it marked off the area of the city called Bezetha. Farther to the north was the third wall. It began also at Hippicus and formed a perimeter to Psephinus Tower, and then east, along the Damascus Gate to the Valley of Kedron.

Agrippa I, who intended it to protect the city, might have added an extension to the north for better defense, but he was discouraged from such construction because Emperor Claudius was already suspicious of his intentions. Archaeological evidence points to the possibility that Agrippa made better headway then previously believed in this regard. The towers of support included Psephinus in the north, with three towers built by Herod the Great: Hippicus, which spanned 80 Hebrew cubits and was quadrangular; Phasael, a duplicate of the Hippicus reaching 90 cubits (serving as the headquarters of the rebellion of 70 for John of Gischala); Mariamme, along the interior of the first wall, containing many luxurious living quarters, and 55 cubits. Another tower, the Xystus, is no longer evident. Finally, there was the Antonia Tower, or Castle, named after Marc Antony and built by Herod in the high area just above the Temple. It was spacious, with many rooms, baths, and courtyards. The *Acts of the Apostles* called it a castle. Its strategic value was obvious to the Romans, who permanently quartered a garrison of one cohort within it to watch for trouble within the Temple and in Bezetha.

The actual city of Jerusalem was divided into five sections: the Lower City, the Upper City, the Temple, Bezetha, and the area between the second and third walls. Acra was the hill upon which stood the Lower City, and it included aqueducts, the pool of Siloam, and the Ophlas. Through the Zion Gate one passed to the Upper City. Here could be found more exclusive residences, including Herod's Palace and the Palace of Agrippa. Just to the west was the large complex of offices and religious rooms, the Great Temple. Beyond that and its guardian, the Antonia Tower, was Bezetha, a very high part of the town, encroached on by new neighborhoods. Lastly, the district between the second and third walls opened outward upon the great Damascus Gate—the first part of the city to fall to Titus.

Jewish Rebellion See JERUSALEM and JUDAEA.

Johannes See JOHN THE USURPER.

John (fl. first century C.E.) *Probable author of the Fourth Gospel, three Epistles, and the Book of Revelation, known as The Beloved Disciple*
John was a Galilean, the son of Zebedee, brother of JAMES THE GREATER, with whom he was called Boanerges (Sons of thunder) in Mark. John was originally a fisherman and was probably a follower of John the Baptist before becoming a disciple of Jesus. Among the disciples he, James, and Peter, formed the inner circle around Jesus.

According to tradition, John traveled and took up residence in Ephesus. He was eventually exiled to Patmos. This exile took place during the reign of Emperor Domitian (81–96). It was here at Patmos that he wrote Revelation, subsequently returning under Emperor Nerva (96–98) to Ephesus, where he wrote the Gospel and Epistles. The church has long upheld the authorship of John concerning the Gospel, although debate has taken place in modern times among scholars who question the identity of John as author. Its apostolic nature, however, is not suspected. He apparently died at Ephesus of old age, the only disciple known with some reliability not to have been martyred, although some experts point to inconclusive evidence that he may have been put to death with St. James.

John Chrysostom (c. 347–407 C.E.) *Bishop of Constantinople and a leading figure in early Christianity*
St. John Chrysostom was born in Antioch, studying law under LIBANIUS the pagan orator. He tried to become a monk but was prevented by the health of his mother and then by his own deteriorating physical condition, the result of excessive asceticism from living as a hermit (c. 373–381). He elected, instead, to serve as a deacon in Antioch and in 386 was ordained a priest and began to preach to the Christians. He had found his true calling, for his sermons established him as the foremost Christian orator of his time, hence, the "Golden-mouthed," a title that would distinguish him for all time. His homiletic topics varied from the Bible, to conscience to the moral reformation of the world.

He refused but was finally consecrated bishop of Constantinople in 398, entering the morass of intrigues and plots with an eye to spiritualizing the people. The Byzantine commoners adored his sermons about morality, but the local nobles, especially the ruthless Empress EUDOXIA, viewed the orations as personal attacks. When a rival, THEOPHILUS, the bishop of Alexandria, plotted to depose John in 403, the empress convened a council furthering Theophilus's attacks by placing an overwhelming number of his allies on the panel. His supporters carried the day for him; John Chrysostom was condemned by the council and removed. A reconciliation with Eudoxia in the following year allowed him to return to Constantinople, but their feud soon erupted again. John was banished in June of 404 to Isauria in the Taurus Mountains, where he wrote letters to summon aid from the church. Pope Innocent I tried to help him, but Eudoxia prevailed. John lingered for years, despite the harsh conditions of his exile and his own physical frailties. Finally, in 407, he was moved to Pontus, forced to travel during bad weather. He died on September 14.

John of Gischala (d. after 70 C.E.) *One of the leaders of the Jewish rebellion of 66–70 C.E.*

John, the son of Levi, was mentioned by the historian JOSEPHUS in less than kind terms, for he was a political rival. He commanded brigands in Galilee and represented the war party of the ZEALOTS. Assigned to order the defenses of Gischala, John spent most of his time opposing the position of his superior, Josephus. When the local bands proved incapable of defeating the Roman units pursuing rebels in the districts of Judaea, John fled to JERUSALEM. Once in the city, he reassumed his place within the Zealots, engaging in bitter intrigue to remove all moderates and political opponents. Murder and terror were used to bring Jerusalem under his control. When the less fanatical elements tried to organize themselves, Idumaeans were admitted through the city gates. More bloodshed followed until Simon BARGOIA arrived to act as a counterpoint. The inhabitants of Jerusalem initially rejoiced at Simon's intervention, but they soon realized that yet another internal struggle had begun.

Jerusalem's tribal disputes could not take precedence over the fact that Titus was at the city gates with his legions. John could not prevent Roman invasion of Jerusalem and was subsequently captured. Unlike Simon, he did not face execution, but was imprisoned for life, perhaps out of recognition that his ambitions had ensured a Roman victory.

John the Usurper (d. 425 C.E.) *Emperor of the West from 423 to 425*

John, also called Johannes, came to the throne as a result of the internal power struggles in the Western Empire. Honorius (emperor from 395 to 423) had suffered under the influences of two rivals: The *MAGISTER MILITUM*, CASTINUS and the imperial half-sister, Galla Placidia. In 423 Castinus won the war between them by having Placidia driven from Ravenna. His victory was short-lived, however, for Honorius died suddenly in August of that same year. To avoid the return of Galla Placidia from Constantinople with her young son (the eventual Valentinian III), Castinus chose to support a usurper, John.

John was of Gothic origins and was a civil servant before attaining the rank of *primicerius notariorum,* or chief notary. He was thoroughly unmilitary and thus represented no threat to Castinus, who elevated him to the throne in September 423. John immediately attempted to win the approval of Theodosius II, but he already supported the claim of Valentinian. Any doubt was removed by the proclamation of Valentinian as Caesar. An army under the command of Ardaburius and ASPAR set out from Constantinople to remove John. On his side, the usurper claimed the support of Aetius, the magister who would become a major force in the near future. Initial successes against Ardaburius proved useless, for John could not follow them up against Aspar. Castinus, meanwhile, had disappeared entirely. In 425, Ravenna fell to

Aspar before John's Hunnic allies could arrive. He was taken to Aquileia, condemned to death by Galla Placidia and executed early in the summer of 425, after first being separated from his right hand, stuck on a donkey and paraded around a circus.

Josephus, Flavius (c. 37–c. 100 C.E.) *The most famous Jewish historical writer of the Roman imperial era*

Josephus earned the favor of Roman emperors but also authored two very useful and important histories of his own people. He was born in Jerusalem and came to support Rome and its supremacy in Palestine. Ties to his native land compelled him to join the cause of the Jews in the early stages of the JEWISH REBELLION (66–70 C.E.) He became an officer in charge of Galilee. His command was questioned and undermined by jealous rivals, preventing better defense of Jotapata in Galilee, which fell in 67, allowing Vespasian to capture him. Josephus was known to the conquering general and his son Titus. Vespasian spared Josephus, who predicted that one day he would be emperor. For the rest of the campaign Josephus remained at Titus's side, watching the fall of Jerusalem in 70. He then traveled to Rome, receiving the freedom of the city and long-lasting imperial favor. He joined the Flavian family (hence the "Flavius") as a client, enjoying the attentions of Vespasian, Titus, and Domitian.

While in Rome, Josephus wrote his two major works: the *Jewish Antiquities* and the *Jewish War*. The *Antiquities* covered Jewish history from the earliest times to 66 C.E. and the start of the rebellion. Organized into 20 books, it was finished in 93 or 94. His *Jewish War* was actually two books in one, a brief chronicle of events from about 170 B.C.E. to 66 C.E. and then a long, precise analysis of the war from 66 to 73 C.E. This history was first completed in 73 in Aramaic and rewritten in 75–76 in Greek. As there was much interest in such a contemporary topic, Josephus went to great lengths to stylize the narrative and to display his knowledge of Greek literature. The result was entirely successful, although in his seven books comprising the *Jewish War*, he chose to ignore the source material used and shown in the *Antiquities* several years later (93–94). Because of his involvement with Rome and his reputation, Josephus was attacked by other Jewish writers and figures of note (*see* JUSTUS). As a response to these critics he penned an autobiography. Further, to refute rampant anti-Semitism, he also composed the *Contra Apionem* (Against Apion), completed very late in his life.

Jotapianus (fl. third century C.E.) *A usurper during the final years of the reign of Philip I (the Arab) (c. 248–249)*

Jotapianus may have been a relative of Emperor Severus Alexander and probably was a native of Syria. During the incompetent administration of Philip's brother Gaius Julius PRISCUS as governor of Mesopotamia, Jotapianus rose up in Commagene to declare himself an emperor.

Although he was quickly defeated, his usurpation pointed to the growing crisis within the Roman Empire.

Jove *See* JUPITER.

Jovian (Flavius Jovinus) (c. 330–364 C.E.) *Emperor (363–364) of Rome*

Flavius Jovinus was born at Singidunum (modern Belgrade), the son of Varronianus, the *comes domesticorum* of Constantius II. He entered the *protectores domestici*, serving both Constantius and Julian the Apostate, and by 363 was the COMES of the PROTECTORES and held a position of some influence in Emperor Julian's court, despite the fact that he was a Christian.

In June 363, while on campaign against Persia, Julian died. The army looked for a successor, and Jovian was chosen in a compromise agreement by officers. His first task as emperor was to bring his exhausted army back to Syria. Shapur II attacked, forcing a treaty that may not have been necessary. Jovian surrendered parts of Armenia and Mesopotamia. With an unsatisfactory peace concluded, Jovian arrived in Antioch, repudiating Julian's pagan supremacy policy. Christianity was once more declared the religion of the empire. This done, and with oaths of allegiance from various parts of the empire, he set out for Constantinople. He never reached the city. Somewhere between Galatia and Bithynia, he was found dead. The cause of his death was unclear, although he possibly suffered asphyxiation from poisonous charcoal in February. Ammianus Marcellinus described him as very tall, amiable, and careful in his appointments.

Jovians and Herculians Name given to the new bodyguard created by Diocletian as part of his general reduction of the political importance of the PRAETORIAN GUARD. They were founded with the SCUTARII and *protectores domestici* to serve as an imperial guard while the Praetorians were left to their own devices in Rome. Diocletian chose to recruit the Jovians and Herculians from his Illyrian legions (*see* ILLYRICUM), known for their martial skill and intense loyalty. Their title came from the deities to which the two houses of the coemperors were dedicated: Diocletian to Jove and Maximian to Hercules. The guard was easily recognized by the color of its shields: red for the Jovians and black for the Herculians. Both of these shields (*scutum*) were oval, with rings and eagles.

Jovinus (d. 413 C.E.) *Usurper in Gaul who ruled briefly from 412 to 413*

In the chaos of the Western Empire, it became the habit of the barbarian kings to elevate their own candidates for the throne of the West. In 412, two of these rulers, Gundohar the Burgundian and Goar the Alan, supported a Gallic candidate, Jovinus. His reign was brief, notable only for the advancement of his brother Sebastian as co-emperor—and the unwillingness of the Visigoths to accept a monarch in the West whom they did not control. King Athaulf of the Visigoths marched against Jovinus, killed his brother, besieged the usurper in Valence and captured him. He was executed in 413.

Juba I (d. 46 B.C.E.) *King of Numidia during the final years of the Roman Republic and throughout the Civil War of the First Triumvirate (49–45 B.C.E.)*

From the start of the war, Juba sided with Pompey, proving instrumental in the defeat of Caesar's legate Gaius Curio in Africa in 49 B.C.E., at Bagrada. When Caesar was able at last to turn his attention to the Pompeians in Africa in 46 B.C.E., Juba aided Q. Scipio, the leading general in Africa of the dead Pompey. Juba, however, could not save his allies from defeat at THAPSUS. He fled to Zama, despairing of retaining his realm, and there had a slave kill him. A part of his kingdom was taken by Caesar to form the province of Africa Nova.

Juba II (d. c. 19 C.E.) *King of Mauretania and the son of King Juba I of Numidia*

Taken as a child to Rome in 46 B.C.E., following the death of his father, Juba lived there under the protection of both Caesar and Octavian (AUGUSTUS) and received a Roman education and the reputation of being one of the most learned men in the world. He became a supporter of Octavian in his war against Antony and Cleopatra. In 30 B.C.E., after the conquest of Egypt, Juba was married to Cleopatra, the daughter of Antony and the Egyptian queen. To stabilize Africa, Augustus sent the prince to rule his own people. In 25, however, Augustus traded him NUMIDIA for MAURETANIA. Juba held Mauretania, including Gaetulia, as a loyal client of Rome. His reign was noted for its intellectualism and for Juba's reliance upon Rome's aid to keep his throne in the face of public unrest.

Judaea The southern region of Palestine, surrounded by the Dead Sea, Arabia, Gaza, Samaria, the Jordan River, and Peraea, a Roman province. Judaea was the home of the largest concentration of Jews in the Roman Empire and, with such sites as JERUSALEM, JERICHO, and MASADA, was one of the most turbulent regions in the world. Judaea had long been the heart of the kingdom of the Jews and was still so in 63 B.C.E., when POMPEY THE GREAT and his legions marched into Palestine. He found the realm divided by a civil war being fought between HYRCANUS and Aristobulus, the sons of the dead king, Jannaeus Alexander. Pompey stormed Jerusalem and named one son, Hyrcanus, the high priest and ethnarch of Judaea, Samaria, Galilee, and Peraea. GABINIUS, Pompey's lieutenant, later seized the ethnarchy and transformed it into five districts. But when ANTIPATER OF IDUMAEA rendered aid to Julius CAESAR during the siege of

The destruction of Jerusalem, commemorated on the Arch of Titus *(Courtesy Fr. Felix Just, S.J.)*

ALEXANDRIA (48–47 B.C.E.), Caesar rewarded his loyalty by returning the territory to its status prior to Gabinius.

Antipater and his immediate successors emerged as the most prominent Jewish leaders over the next century. Hyrcanus was ethnarch, but Antipater had the power and named his sons, HEROD THE GREAT and Phasael, as governors of Galilee and Jerusalem respectively. Antipater was murdered in 43, but the brothers continued to exercise political influence and even gained the goodwill of Marc Antony, despite Herod's excellent relations with Cassius, the assassin of Caesar. So effective was their diplomacy that Antony made them both ethnarchs.

Judaean history took a new direction in 40 B.C.E., when the Parthians invaded and temporarily established the claimant Antigonous on the Jewish throne. Phasael committed suicide, Hyrcanus was captured and Herod organized the defenses of Idumaea before fleeing to Rome for aid. Roman prestige in the area demanded prompt action, and the Parthians were evicted by an imperially assisted Herod during fighting in 39 and 38 B.C.E. In July 37, Jerusalem was recaptured with two Roman legions, and Judaea passed under Herod's control as part of his kingdom. From 37 to 4 B.C.E., Herod ruled over the Judaeans, who hated his tyranny, his Hellenism and his Idumaean background, sparking revolts and unrest. His death, therefore, was a cause for massive celebrations. His son ARCHELAUS was named by Augustus as Herod's heir, but as an ethnarch, not as a king. This was part of Rome's deliberate policy of breaking up the Herodian domain. The Jews sent a delegation to Augustus in the hopes of having the monarch removed entirely, but Augustus chose to rely upon his clients, and Archelaus, Philip, and Antipas were set upon their own thrones.

Judaea erupted as the PROCURATOR Sabinus, assigned by Augustus to aid in the administration, tried to ease local troubles. He could not manage to do so, and Varus, the governor of Syria, sent in troops. By 6 C.E., Augustus was willing to listen to the delegations. The Jews wanted theocratic independence but were willing to settle for the

removal of Archelaus. Augustus agreed. Archelaus was sent to Gallia Narbonensis, and Judaea was constituted a province under a procurator, answerable to the Syrian governor but with wide latitude, financial and judicial, within the boundaries. Judaea actually comprised Judaea proper, Idumaea, and Samaria. The seat of the Roman administration was at Caesarea.

Roman hopes of tranquillity were dashed immediately. Few territories under Rome's control were marked by such intense dislike, on both sides, as Judaea. The Jews resented foreign masters who cared nothing for their traditions, and the Romans found Jewish stubbornness cause for severe intolerance. The initial census provoked serious outbreaks of violence, which were never fully eased until 70 C.E. Successive procurators contended with local brigands, violent pseudo-religious groups, the ZEALOTS, and uprisings in entire districts. Pontius Pilate (c. 26–36 C.E.) not only tried Jesus Christ but also massacred large sections of the Samartian population, an act for which he was removed by Vitellius, the governor of Syria. Procurators very often were deliberately difficult, and others who actually tried to do good were unable to please their charges. Such was the case when Pilate expropriated funds from the Temple of Jerusalem (the *shekalim*) for use on an aqueduct project. The resulting riots were bloody affairs and cruelly suppressed. On other occasions the imperial policy itself brought upheaval, as in 39–40 C.E., when Gaius Caligula ordered his own statues to be placed in the Temple, a suicidal gesture narrowly avoided by Petronius, the legate in Syria.

An admission that Roman hopes were unfulfilled came in 41 C.E., when Claudius placed Judaea back in the hands of a king. AGRIPPA I worked for the easing of tensions, but his reign lasted only three years (41–44), and Cuspius Fadus marched back in as procurator. The next decades were marked by continued ineptitude and greed on the part of the local Roman authorities and by the growth of rebel parties and widespread acceptance of their tenets. Hatred peaked under Gessius Florus, and the Jewish Rebellion began.

All of Palestine was aflame instantly, with the battles between Jews and non-Jews. Slaughters took place and panic spread among the military command. In February 67, Nero appointed the general VESPASIAN with full powers to end the rebellion. He proved capable, reducing opposition in Galilee and, by June 69, in most of Judaea as well. The Civil War of 69 (*see* 69 C.E.) interrupted operations, and in spring of 70, a new general took command, sent by the new emperor, Vespasian. TITUS finished off the rebels in Judaea and then captured Jerusalem, ending the war. The province, minus the city of Jerusalem, which had been totally destroyed, was once again reconstituted, although a legion, the X Fretensis, remained in permanent garrison at the legionary camp in the ruined city. Its legate had supreme administrative powers, even over the procurator.

Still, the Jews would not submit, and in 115–117 another revolt took place, crushed this time by Lusius QUIETUS. In 132, one more attempt at Jewish nationalism was made on a grand scale. Simon BAR COCHBA (Son of Star) put up a fierce resistance, involving most of Judaea in the process. With Hadrian's victory in 135, the province ceased to be called by its original name and henceforth bore the title of Syria-Palentina. Trouble continued under Antoninus Pius, Marcus Aurelius, and Septimius Severus, but throughout the third and fourth centuries the chaos of the Roman Empire and the ascendancy of CHRISTIANITY overshadowed traditional local unhappiness. During the reforms of Diocletian, the province was part of the Diocese Oriens and was known as Palaestina. In the Christianized empire, all of Palestine and Judaea became the Holy Land.

PROCURATORS OF JUDAEA (6–66 C.E.)

Coponius	6–9 C.E.
Marcus Ambibulus	9–12 C.E.
Annius Rufus Tineus	12–15 C.E.
Valerius Gratus	15–26 C.E.
Pontius Pilate	26–36 C.E.
Marcellus	36–41 C.E.
Marullus	37–41 C.E.
Era of Agrippa	41–44 C.E.
Cuspius Fadus	44–46 C.E.
Tiberius Julius Alexander	46–48 C.E.
Ventidius Cumanus	48–52 C.E.
Felix	52–60 C.E.
Porcius Festus	60–62 C.E.
Luccerius Albinus	62–64 C.E.
Gessius Florus	64–66 C.E.

Josephus's *Jewish Antiquities, Jewish War, Vita,* and *Against Apion* are the best sources for events in Judaea from 63 B.C.E. to 73 C.E.

Judaism Term denoting the ancient religion of the Jews. Originally, the Jews possessed a unique place and status in the Roman Empire. But their fiercely independent spirit led to some of the most violent revolts in Roman history. The response of the emperors and the imperial government destroyed the Jewish state as a political entity.

It is impossible to examine fully within the scope of this book every fact of historical Judaism, especially with respect to the complex subjects of Jewish law, traditions, and Hebraic eschatology. The people of Judaism, however, have been treated in many other entries. For the history of the Jews from the early days to 73 C.E., see Josephus's *Against Apion, Jewish Antiquities,* and *Vita;* the *New Testament;* the *Codex Theodosianus* for later laws; and Tacitus's *Histories.*

See also JERUSALEM and JUDAEA; AGRIPPA I; AGRIPPA II; ALEXANDRIA; ANTIOCH (2); ANTIPATER OF IDUMAEA; ARCHELAUS; ARETAS III; ARISTOBULUS II; ARISTOBULUS AND ALEXANDER; ASIA; BAR COCHBA, SIMON; BARGOIA, SIMON; CHRISTIANITY; CRETE AND CYREMAICA; CYPRUS; CYRENE; EGYPT; GALILEE; HEROD ANTIPAS; HEROD THE GREAT; HERODIAS; IDUMAEA; JERICHO; JOHN OF GISCHALA; JUDAEA; JULIAN; MASADA; PHARISEE; QUIETUS, LUSIUS; RELIGION; SADDUCEES; TEMPLE OF JERUSALEM; TITUS; TURBO, MARCIUS; VESPASIAN; and ZEALOTS.

Suggested Readings: Edwards, Douglas R. *Religion & Power: Pagans, Jews, and Christians in the Greek East.* New York: Oxford University Press, 1996; Lieu, Judith, John North, and Tessa Rajak, eds. *The Jews among Pagans and Christians: In the Roman World.* New York: Routledge, 1992; Momigliano, Arnaldo. *On Pagans, Jews, and Christians.* Middletown, Conn.: Wesleyan University Press, 1987; Whittaker, Molly. *Jews and Christians: Graeco-Roman Views.* New York: Cambridge University Press, 1984.

Julia (1) (d. 51 B.C.E.) *Sister of Julius Caesar by C. Julius Caesar and Marcia*
Julia married M. Atius Balbus and bore Atia, the mother of Augustus. At the age of 12 (in 51 B.C.E.), Octavian (AUGUSTUS) delivered an oration at her funeral.

Julia (2) (c. 83 B.C.E.–54 B.C.E.) *Daughter of Julius Caesar and his first wife Cornelia (daughter of Cinna)*
Although originally betrothed to Servilius Caepio, an ally of her father, Julia instead married POMPEY THE GREAT in 59 B.C.E. This union cemented the ties between the two triumvirs for the next five years. Julia was able to influence both figures, convincing them to settle their differences and to preserve the peace. In 54 B.C.E., Julia died in childbirth; the child died, too, a few days later. Her death was a personal tragedy for both men and a political catastrophe for Rome. Pompey and CAESAR grew estranged, a parting unsettled by Caesar's offering of his grandniece Octavia in marriage. Julia received a massive public funeral befitting her place among Roman women. Caesar held a gladiatorial show and a banquet in her memory, an unprecedented act. She was buried in the Campus Martius.

Julia (3) (39 B.C.E.–14 C.E.) *Only child of Augustus and his first wife, Scribonia*
Julia became the center of the greatest scandal of Augustus's long reign. After a normal upbringing, she married Marcus Claudius MARCELLUS in 25 B.C.E. When he died in 23, she next married Marcus Vipsanius AGRIPPA (c. 21 B.C.E.), by whom she had five children: Gaius and Lucius Caesar, Agrippa Posthumus, Julia (4), and Agrippina the Elder. She remained with Agrippa until his death in 12 B.C.E., although, according to the historian Suetonius, she

was already lusting after Tiberius. In 11 B.C.E., Augustus ordered Tiberius to divorce his beloved wife Vipsania and marry Julia. Tiberius greeted the union with an intense hatred, unable to bear the loss of the woman he loved. The marriage went from cold to hostile. After one child was stillborn at Aquileia, Tiberius would have nothing further to do with her, and in 6 B.C.E. departed for Rhodes.

Abandoned, Julia kept her good humor and reputation for kindness, but she also entered into a number of adulteries, with such wantonness that virtually everyone in Rome, except for Augustus, was aware of her actions. He could not bring himself to believe the rumors, but in 2 B.C.E. he was finally convinced by an investigation that uncovered her affairs with a large group of men, including various tribunes and Iullus Antonius, the son of Marc Antony. Julia was banished from Rome and sent to PANDATERIA, with her mother Scribonia joining her there. She lived on Pandateria until 3 C.E., when public outcry compelled Augustus to transfer her to Rhegium, where her life was eased somewhat. But the emperor stated in his will that, upon her death, she was to be left out of his mausoleum. When Tiberius came to the throne in 14 C.E., he decreed that Julia's comforts should cease. All gifts were forbidden, and the small allowance that Augustus had granted her was stopped. She died of exhaustion and malnutrition, probably in late 14.

Julia (4) (19 B.C.E.–28 C.E.) *Daughter of Julia (3) and Marcus Agrippa*

Granddaughter of Augustus—as much a disappointment to him as to her mother, Julia was born around 19 B.C.E. and later married the noble and respected Lucius Aemilius PAULLUS. She soon followed in her mother's footsteps and carried on adulterous affairs. In 8 C.E., Augustus banished her, but not to Pandateria, where he had exiled Julia, his daughter; he had her placed on Trimerium (Trimerus), a small island off the coast of Apulia. Julia survived there for nearly 20 years, aided by the secret support of Livia. The two Julias and the exiled AGRIPPA Postumus were sources of intense personal grief for Augustus. He referred to them as the three boils, reciting the line of the *Iliad:* "Ah that I never had married and childless could die."

Julia (5) (d. 43. C.E.) *Daughter of Drusus Caesar (the son of Emperor Tiberius) and Livilla*

In 20 C.E., she was married to Nero, son of Germanicus, but by 30 he had been banished to Pontia and a new betrothal was arranged with SEJANUS, the ambitious PREFECT OF THE PRAETORIAN GUARD. After his execution in 31 by order of Tiberius, she wed Rubellius Blandus (c. 33). At the instigation of the jealous Empress MESSALLINA, she was put to death by Claudius in 43.

Julia (6) Livilla (18–c. 41 C.E.) *Daughter of Germanicus and Agrippina the Elder*

Born on the island of Lesbos, Julia was the youngest of Germanicus's many children. In 33, at the age of 15, she was betrothed to Marcus VINICIUS (2) but supposedly carried on an indiscreet affair with Aemilius Lepidus; she was also linked to her brother, GAIUS CALIGULA. Caligula banished her to the Pontian islands with her sister Agrippina, the mother of Nero. Following Caligula's murder in 41 C.E., both Julia and her sister returned to Rome by order of Emperor Claudius. Known to be beautiful and given to spending much time with her uncle, Julia was hated by Empress MESSALLINA. Later in 41, Messallina brought false charges against her, and Claudius was eventually persuaded to order her execution.

Julia (7) Flavia (65–91 C.E.) *Daughter of Titus by his second wife; later married to her cousin, Flavius Sabinus*

Julia remained with Flavius until his execution in 84 by order of Emperor Domitian. It was rumored that at an early age she was offered to Domitian, but he had no interest in his niece until his own marriage with Domitia Longina. By then Julia was wed. Sabinus was duly executed, and Julia moved into the palace with the emperor, becoming pregnant by him. She died in 91 as a result of an abortion that he forced upon her. Domitian deified her.

Julia Domna (d. after 217 C.E.) *Empress from 193 to 211*

The second wife of Septimius Severus, she was matriarch to the dynasty that would see four successive emperors of Rome. Julia Domna was born in Emesa, Syria. In 187 she married Severus, then a general, and bore him two sons: CARACALLA (in 188) and GETA (in 189). She then aided her husband in his ambitions for the throne, which he gained in 193. As an empress, Julia was noted for both her beauty and her intelligence. She brought together the finest minds and philosophers of her time to invigorate the climate of the court. Among her guests were Galen, Philostratus, and Ulpian. She feuded bitterly with the PREFECT OF THE PRAETORIAN GUARD, Plautianus, and was in political eclipse during his years of power (c. 200–205). Unable to defeat him, she retired to a life of philosophy and study, returning to her influential position in 205, when Plautianus fell from his office.

Julia joined her husband and two sons on the British campaign in 208 and was with Severus when he died in 211 at Eburacum (York). Although he was no longer empress, she tried desperately to reconcile the many differences between Caracalla and Geta. Geta reportedly died in her arms after being stabbed by one of Caracalla's centurions in her apartment in 212. Throughout Caracalla's reign she continued to take part in government, advising her son when possible and serving as AB EPISTULIS for both his Latin and Greek correspondence. In

217, she was at Antioch when word arrived that Caracalla had been assassinated and that Macrinus was now emperor. Although she did not care for Caracalla, her status as Augusta was preserved for as long as he lived. She either died naturally or killed herself.

Julia Drusilla *See* DRUSILLA.

Julia Livilla *See* JULIA (6).

Julia Maesa (d. 226 C.E.) *Sister of Julia Domna and grandmother of two emperors, Elagabalus and Severus Alexander*
Julia Maesa was married to Julius Avitus, a consular official of Syria, by whom she bore two daughters, JULIA SOAEMIAS and JULIA MAMAEA, the mothers of ELAGABALUS and SEVERUS ALEXANDER respectively. She lived in Rome with her sister for all of Caracalla's reign but was allowed by Macrinus to retire to her home at Emesa in 217. Once back in Syria, Julia Maesa masterminded the conspiracy in the provinces to ensure the destruction of Macrinus and the elevation of Elagabalus to the throne. Through her efforts, Macrinus fell, and her grandson was proclaimed emperor in 218. She received the title of Augusta, working with her tutor Gannys to maintain order in the imperial government.

Faced with a bizarre and disliked grandson, Julia tried to curb Elagabalus's sexual habits. Failing in this, she supported her other grandson, Severus Alexander. Through her influence he was elevated to the rank of Caesar, adopted and protected from the jealousies of Elagabalus. When, in 222, Elagabalus and his mother were murdered in the Castra Praetoria, she again proved instrumental in securing an acceptable replacement, Severus Alexander. Her place in his administration was even greater. She headed the CONSILIUM PRINCIPIS and guided every decision with a steady hand. Already aged, she died in 226.

Julia Mamaea (d. 235 C.E.) *Daughter of Julia Maesa and mother of Severus Alexander*
Julia held the rank of Augusta from 222 to 235. She was married to a Syrian knight, Gessius Marcianus, by whom she had Severus. When Elagabalus became uncontrollable as emperor, even to his own mother, JULIA SOAEMIAS (Julia Mamaea's sister), Severus was elevated to the rank of Caesar and groomed to succeed him. In 222, Elagabalus and his mother were murdered in the Castra Praetoria. SEVERUS ALEXANDER was proclaimed his successor, and Julia Mamaea the Augusta. Her influence over the government and her son was at first heavily restricted by the presence of Julia Maesa. When she died in 226, however, Mamaea assumed virtual control of the empire. Unfortunately, she dominated the young emperor to the point that no one could curb her avarice for gold, titles,

and treasures. Even Severus Alexander remarked that her greed was relentless. She drove all opposition from the palace, including her son's wife, Barbia Orbiana, in 227. During the campaigns of 231–232, Julia interfered with Severus's decisions; and in the German campaigns of 234–235, her domination of the monarch earned her the resentment of the LEGIONS. A general named Maximinus used Julia as the means for causing a mutiny, and the soldiers murdered her and Severus Alexander, bringing the Severan line to an end.

Julia Soaemias (fl. third century C.E.) *Daughter of Julia Maesa, mother of Elagabalus, and Augusta from 218 to 222*
Julia Soaemias married Sextus Varius Mercellus, a Syrian knight from Apamea, by whom she had her son. Through the conspiracies of her mother, in 218, Julia witnessed the defeat of Emperor Macrinus and the elevation of ELAGABALUS to the throne. From the start she displayed a total ignorance of conservative Roman customs. She lacked, as well, any control over her son. Thus he outraged Rome with his religious practices and with his bizarre sexual tastes. To restore order, JULIA MAESA forced her daughter to accept the elevation of Severus Alexander and his mother JULIA MAMAEA (her sister). When the Praetorian Guard became violent over Elagabalus's jealous treatment of Severus Alexander, Julia Soaemias and her son went to the Castra Praetoria to put down the rebellion. They failed and were murdered there. Both were decapitated, stripped, carried through Rome, and dumped, Elagabalus in the river and Julia Soaemias on the side of the road.

Julian the Apostate (Flavius Claudius Julianus) (c. 332–363 C.E.) *Emperor from 361 to 363*
Julianus was the last pagan ruler of the Roman Empire and rivaled the greatest of his predecessors in intelligence. He was born at Constantinople, the son of Julius Constantius, half brother of Constantine the Great, and Basilina, daughter of the governor of Egypt. Basilina died just after his birth, and his father was murdered in the palace massacre following the death of Constantine in 337. Julian was spared only because of his age, and he and his half-brother Gallus were the only survivors.

For several years he studied grammar and literature under the tutor Mardonius in Constantinople. In 342, however, the cautious CONSTANTIUS II moved both Julian and Gallus to Nicomedia and then to a villa in Macellum, in Cappadocia. Education there followed Christian traditions, but Julian developed a taste for pagan literature. Despite serving as a reader in the Christian Church, he continued his pagan preferences privately. Sometime around 348, Constantius allowed Julian to return to Constantinople; he returned to Nicomedia in 351. There he was able to travel and follow his own pursuits in Neoplatonism and pseudo-mystical or magical PAGANISM. He studied with Maximus of Ephesus and turned away from the Christian Church in secret. Through the intercession of Constantius's wife Eusebia, Julian first traveled to Mediolanum (Milan) and then to Athens, where he completed his study of pagan literature. Another summons arrived in 355, however, and he was informed that he had been chosen by Constantius to be elevated to the rank of Caesar. Gallus Caesar had once held that position but had been tried and executed for treason. On November 6, 355, Julian was invested and then married to Helena, Constantius's sister.

Julian was sent to the frontier to repel the invasions of the Franks and Alamanni in Gaul. With surprising skill and adroit strategic sense, the young prince inflicted serious defeats upon the barbarians, most notably at Strasbourg in 357. Further expeditions reestablished Roman supremacy on the Rhine and earned Julian the respect of his soldiers and of the civilian population.

Constantius had desired success, but not to the degree displayed by Julian. Listening to his courtiers, he commanded Julian to send his best troops to the East, to be used in the upcoming war with Persia. The command was useless, because Julian's men mutinied and in February 360, at Lutetia (Paris), declared him emperor. Despite negotiations, both Constantius and Julian knew that war was inevitable. In 361, Julian set out against the imperial forces, but Constantius died of a fever near Mopsucrene in Cilicia, and Julian entered Constantinople in December of that year, unopposed.

He began his reign by throwing off his Christian background, thus earning himself the historical title of "Apostate." He declared that all religions in the empire were to be tolerated and gave generous donations to pagan groups. The aim of Julian was to resurrect the traditional Roman paganism, if necessary, at the expense of Christianity. He thus dismissed Christian teachers, put an end to state subsidies and organized pagan worship in all of the provinces.

Personally, Julian added to the new pagan emphasis by authoring several works displaying his own philosophy and spirit. He wrote *Hymn to the Sun God*; a praise to the *Mother of all the Gods*; *To a Priest,* a work extolling the virtues of pagan priesthoods; and, most importantly, *Against the Galileans,* an attack on Christianity. Julian was clearly unimpressed with the effects of Christianity on the empire. Christians had slaughtered most of his family and had proven totally incapable of defending the borders.

There was little support for his return to paganism, despite his efforts. Also, the Romans disliked his attempts to improve the lot of the Jews in the empire, including his plans to rebuild the Great Temple in Jerusalem. He turned then to the economic condition of the empire and began to institute reforms in its vast bureaucratic world. Finances were tightened and inflation was curbed as a result. Aid was also given to the provinces, mainly in the East, where he had the greatest support.

Julian believed that a long war with Persia was necessary and began preparations for yet another struggle with the Sassanids in 362. Many omens were visible throughout the empire. A famine struck Antioch as a result of drought, a crisis left unrelieved by the local council, which protested Julian's insistence on their attendance at a pagan ritual. The temple of Daphne there was struck by fire, which made the attendance unnecessary.

Undaunted by the opposition and the signs, Julian set out with his army of some 65,000 infantry and cavalry in March of 363. He crossed the Syrian desert and descended the Euphrates, capturing small cities and winning a large battle over the forces of Shapur II. Ctesiphon was reached in June but could not be stormed. Aware of his dwindling food supply and harassed by Shapur's light cavalry, Julian ordered a tactical retreat up the Tigris. On June 26 he was wounded in a skirmish and died a short time later. A general, Jovian, assumed the purple and extricated the army from its precarious position. Julian's body was taken back to Constantinople.

Aside from his pagan works, he also wrote the *Beard-Hater,* a satire on the discourteous people of Antioch; *The Caesars,* a humorous review of the previous emperors; as well as many panegyrics, eulogies, and letters. His *Consolation* was written in sorrow at the departure of Saturninus Sallustius Secundus, his friend, from the court.

A bronze *majorina* of Julian the Apostate, struck in late 326–363, at Sirmium *(Courtesy Historical Coins, Inc.)*

Julianus, Salvius (Lucius Octavius Cornelius Publius Salvius Julianus Aemilianus) (c. 100–169 C.E.)

Last known head of the Sabinian School of Law

Julianus earned his reputation in Hadrian's reign (117–138 C.E.) as one of the foremost JURISTS in Roman history. He came originally from Hadrumetum, Africa, studying under Javolenus Priscus. Entering into the service of Hadrian, one of his first tasks was the collecting of the Edicts of the Praetors, editing them and publishing their final version under imperial sanction. Julianus belonged to Hadrian's CONSILIUM PRINCIPIS and served in a wide variety of imperial posts throughout the emperor's reign and in the reigns of Antoninus Pius and Marcus Aurelius. He was a tribune, *praetor, praefectus* of the *aerarium Saturni, praefectus* of the *aerarium militare,* consul in 148, and governor, successively, in Germania Inferior, Hispania Citerior, and Africa. His legal works were unmatched in their originality and imagination. The most important of these was his *Digest,* organized into 90 books detailing virtually every facet of civil and praetorian law. Preserved mainly in subsequent codes, especially in that of Justinian, the *Digest* advanced the theory and nature of Roman classical legalism, and Julianus ensured his place as one of Rome's greatest jurists.

Julius (fl. fourth century C.E.) *Bishop of Rome (c. 337–352) and an opponent of Arianism*
Julius became the protector of those priests condemned or exiled by the Arians when they achieved a short-lived supremacy in the mid-fourth century C.E. He thus gave aid to MARCELLUS of Smyrna and St. Athanasius. In 342, Julius helped convene the Council of Sardica, uniting the West against ARIANISM and helping to establish the powers of the PAPACY.

Julius, Clemens (fl. first century C.E.) *Centurion of the Pannonian legions in 14 C.E.*
Following the death of Augustus, the army in Pannonia revolted, driving out their tribunes and centurions. Most of the centurions hid themselves to avoid death, but one was kept back as a hostage, Julius, a soldier noted for his wit. He became the envoy from the rebels to the authorities, conveying their demands: discharge after 16 years, better pay and improved conditions for veterans. When Drusus, Tiberius's son, negotiated the legionaries into confusion and disunity, Clemens Julius played his part, asking them if they intended to kidnap the heir to the throne or overthrow the government. These words had their effect because the uprising ended soon after.

Julius Africanus, Sextus (d. c. 240 C.E.) *Christian writer, the author of* A History of the World *in Greek*
Julius is considered a father of Christian historiography. Probably a native of Jerusalem, Julius enjoyed the favor of the Severan dynasty of the Roman emperors, most notably Elagabalus (r. 218–222) and Alexander Severus (r. 222–235). Under the latter, he played a major role in the creation of a public library in the Pantheon of Rome. His main work was the aforementioned world history, dated to perhaps between 212 and 221. It attempts to unite the account of the Bible with Roman and Greek history, carrying events from the creation (5499 B.C.E. by Julius's calculations) to 221 C.E. The first effort at Chris-

tian historiography, the work is quite important, particularly as it was the basis of Eusebius's *Ecclesiastical History* and a vital source for later Byzantine historical writings. It is now known only in fragmentary form. Julius also wrote the *Embroidered Girdles,* an encyclopedic guide to miscellaneous sciences, natural history, and medicine, dedicated to Severus Alexander, in 24 books.

Julius Gabinianus, Sextus (fl. late first century C.E.) *Teacher of rhetoric during the reign of Vespasian (69–79 C.E.)*
Julius Gabinianus lived in Gaul and attained such a reputation as an instructor that many of his contemporaries called him a second Cicero, equating subsequent rhetoricians as *Cicerones Gabiniani.*

Julius Victor, Gaius (fl. fourth century C.E.) *Writer*
Julius was noted for his *ars rhetorica,* a work following that of QUINTILIAN very closely. Ironically, his own *ars* was equally plundered in a later *disputatio.*

Junia (d. 22 C.E.) *Wife of Gaius Cassius, niece of Cato and sister of Marcus Brutus*
Junia was the daughter of the Consul D. Junius Silanus (62) and Servilia. As her connections and relationships to the LIBERATORS were deep, she lived a life of protest during the principates of Augustus (27 B.C.E.–14 C.E.) and Tiberius (14–37 C.E.). Her death came some 64 years after the battle of PHILIPPI, which had ended the last vestiges of the Republic and resulted in the deaths of her husband and brother. A last insult to the emperors was made in her will. She made great gifts of her vast fortune to most of the Roman nobility but ignored Tiberius totally. The normally vindictive ruler tolerated such an intentional oversight, but at the funeral, when Junia's family origins were displayed, the names of CASSIUS and BRUTUS were absent.

Junius Otho (fl. first century C.E.) *Praetor during the reign of Tiberius (14–37 C.E.)*
Originally taught as a schoolmaster, by 22 Junius had achieved some political success, owing to the patronage of Praetorian Prefect Lucius Aelius SEJANUS. In that year he joined Mamercus Scaurus and Bruttedius Niger in the persecution of Gaius Silanus, proconsul of Asia, for further advancement and imperial favor. For his involvement, Tacitus commented that Junius Otho added a further blemish to his lowly origins. He survived the fall of Sejanus in 31, for mention was made of him in 37. Seneca had more respect for him as a rhetorician and author.

Juno Called Hera by the Greeks and Uni by the Etruscans; the Roman queen of heaven and hence one of the most important deities of the Roman pantheon. One of the oldest goddesses for the Romans, she evolved into many forms. According to tradition, she tried to prevent the sailing of Aeneas from Troy to Italy, but was introduced into Rome by the Etruscan city of Veii in the early fourth century B.C.E. Her name has been the source of considerable debate. It may have come from *iu* (*iuventis*, or "young"), or perhaps from the same root as Jupiter, or even as a derivation of *iuno*, to equal the GENIUS of man.

As JUPITER was the king of heaven and guardian of males, so Juno was the celestial queen and protectoress of women. It was as the guardian of females that she developed many incarnations. As Matrona or Virginalis, she journeyed through life with every woman, and her great festival was on March 1 each year, the Matronalia. Other roles were Sororia (puberty), Luga (marriage) and Natalis, or as someone's birthday. One other name was used in connection with Juno, not as a female goddess, but rather as the patroness of Roman finances, and then she was called Moneta (literally "the Reminder"). The worship of Juno was traditional, and temples dedicated to her cult under various titles were common throughout the empire. In Lanvium there was a temple to Juno Sospita, and on the Capitoline stood the TEMPLE OF JUPITER CAPITOLINUS, where the mint was located and where Juno was revered as Moneta. Her presence in the Capitoline temple resulted from her being grouped with Jupiter and Minerva as one of the three most important divinities. Hellenic traditions prompted this association. From the beginning, Jupiter was connected to the Greek Zeus, Juno to Hera, and Minerva to Athena.

The calends of each month were dedicated to Juno, with sacrifices and prayers. And June was named after her and considered the best month for marriages, a custom that outlived the Roman Empire.

See GODS AND GODDESSES OF ROME; MINERVA; ROMAN RELIGION.

Jupiter Supreme god of the Roman pantheon. Jupiter protected Rome and ruled heaven as the father of the gods. His introduction to Rome was traditionally attributed to the Etruscans, who gave the Romans Jupiter Optimus Maximus (the Best and Greatest). They also built the first temple of his cult, dominating the Capitoline Hill; the TEMPLE OF JUPITER CAPITOLINUS subsequently became the very heart of the IMPERIAL CULT of state and of the Roman Religion. Once he was accepted by Rome, Jupiter's cult was enlarged and aggrandized.

Jupiter was originally a sky god who controlled the weather, heaven, agriculture, justice, war, peace, treaties, and light. Each of these areas warranted a special title and specific characteristics (see below). Temples were also constructed to honor him in his various forms. As a god of agriculture, festivals honoring him were held on each August 19, the VINALIA, or the Festival of Wine. December 23 was the date of the transformation of darkness into light, the winter solstice, and Jupiter was worshiped on

that day. He could predict the future and worked with the god Janus to successfully initiate undertakings.

It was, however, in his role of supreme god of the Roman Empire that Jupiter attained his highest station. The state religion of Rome honored him as its patron and used his cult to further the religious grandeur of the empire. In Rome the worship of Jupiter was the duty of the Flamen Dialis (*see* FLAMENS), who performed all of the proscribed rituals. On the Ides of each month the flamen sacrificed a ewe lamb upon the Capitoline, wearing white always and presiding over all events that were in the jurisdiction of the god. These might include sacrifices and prayers offered up by new consuls, the triumphs held by victorious generals, and games such as the *ludi Capitolini* or *ludi Romani* (*see* LUDI).

THE TITLES OF JUPITER

Capitolinus	Head of the Capitoline and the Ludi Capitolini
Divis pater or Diespiter	Father of Heaven
Feretrius	Epithet of Jupiter
Fulgurator	Sender of Lightning
Fulminator	God of Lightning
Imperator	Emperor of Heaven
Invictus	Invincible
Latialis	Head of the Latin Feast
Opitulus	Sender of Aid or Help
Optimus Maximus	Best and Greatest
Praedator	The Hunter
Pluvius	God of Rain
Prodigialialis	Sender of Prodigies or Omens
Stator	Stayer (invoked by Roman soldiers in battle)
Tonans	Sender of Thunder
Tonitrualis	God of Thunder
Triumphator	The Victor

See also GODS AND GODDESSES OF ROME; JUNO; MINERVA; PAGANISM.

jurists Legal experts who played leading roles in the formation of Roman imperial LAW. Their contributions helped to organize and standardize the legal enactments for future generations, and most were honored in their own day. The greatest jurists of the imperial period were:

Gaius A second-century C.E. lawyer, whose greatest contribution was the *Institutes,* in four books, detailing law with regard to persons, items, and actions. He also wrote various commentaries on Edicts and the Law of the Twelve Tablets.

Salvius Julianus A second-century C.E. head of the Sabinian School of Law, the last one. His impact on Roman legalism was great because he collected the Edicts of the Praetors and then wrote the *Digest,* a massive treatise (in 90 books) on virtually every aspect of law up to his time.

M. Antistius Labeo   One of the earliest jurists (first century C.E.), and an innovative lawyer who wrote the first commentary on the Edicts.

C. Cassius Longinus   A first-century C.E. jurist who authored 10 commentaries on law, including the *ius civile.* He was very successful in the political field and helped to form the school of the Augustan lawyer, Ateius Capito.

Aemilius Papinian   A late-second century C.E. jurist, chosen to serve as the PREFECT OF THE PRAETORIAN GUARD in the reigns of Septimius Severus and Caracalla. He wrote commentaries on many aspects of legalism. His two most notable efforts were *Opiniones* and *Responsa.* His mastery over both public and private law earned him a reputation as one of Rome's greatest jurists.

Julius Paulus   Mainly of the third century C.E.; serving on the CONSILIUM PRINCIPIS of Severus Alexander and using his position as adviser and lawyer to influence Roman law with philosophical outlooks. In the *Digest* of Justinian, Paulus is quoted extensively.

Proculus   A little known first-century C.E. lawyer who lent his name to the Proculean School of Law and attained notoriety in the reign of Nero.

Masurius Sabinus   A first-century C.E. lawyer whose name became associated with the school of Ateius Capito. His name was used as well in the commentaries of Ulpian and Paulus (*ad Sabinum*) as a result of his own work on civil law.

Domitius Ulpianus   One of the last jurists (third century C.E.); preserved the writings of his predecessors through his compilations and commentaries, especially those of Papinian. His own treatise helped establish the entire character of later imperial codes.

See individual entries for further details; *See also* PROCULEANS and SABINIANS.

Justina (d. c. 388 C.E.) *Empress from 370 to 375, the wife of Valentinian I*
From a noble family, she married while quite young the usurper Magnentius, but after his fall was given to VALENTINIAN I to be his wife. She bore him four children: Valentinian II, Iusta, Grata, and Galla. Valentinian I died in 375, while Justina was away at Sirmium. When she returned, she became a major figure in the court of her son. Her greatest rival was St. Ambrose, who opposed her vehemently for declaring publicly her ARIANISM and her support for pro-Arian legislation. Still alive in 387, Justina and her son fled Italy for Thessalonica when Max-

imus entered Italy. Only through the granting of Galla's hand to Theodosius could she be given the support of the Eastern Empire. She probably died in the following year, before Maximus's defeat.

Justin Martyr (c. 100–165) *Early Christian theologian and a foremost apologist*
Justin was born in Flavia Neapolis in Samaria to a pagan family. After spending many years of his life studying paganism, he grew dissatisfied and, at the age of 30, found Christianity. A teacher at a school in Ephesus, he engaged around 135 in a famous debate with Trypho the Jew, the basis for Justin's later work, *Dialogue with Trypho the Jew.* Moving to Rome, he opened a place of learning for Christians, claiming as one of his pupils the theologian Tatian. By now a learned Christian, Justin began to defend his faith in clear and brilliant fashion, utilizing his extensive familiarity with pagan teachings to provide an educated Roman audience with reasoned arguments for the moral and intellectual superiority of Christianity. His *First Apology* (c. 155) was written for ANTONINUS PIUS, MARCUS AURELIUS, and Lucius VERUS, defending the faith against various charges and accusations. The *Second Apology* was written for the Senate and again refuted assorted charges. Around 165, the imperial government finally took action against him. He and several followers were arrested, ordered to make sacrifices, and, upon their refusal, were scourged and beheaded. The greatest of the early apologists, Justin was remarkable for his effort to unite Christian faith with reason. An extant account of his death is the *Martyrium S. Iustini et Sociorum.*

Justus (first century C.E.) *Jewish leader from Tiberias and a rival of Josephus during the Jewish rebellion of 66–70*
Justus helped start the revolt of the Jews in Tiberias and was eager for war with Rome. He fought with JOSEPHUS over his command in Galilee (66–67), working to cause desertions among the populace. Justus fled from Tiberias and was arrested by Vespasian. Handed over to Agrippa II, he was merely detained and given his freedom, becoming the king's secretary. He subsequently authored a history of the war, considered by Josephus to be prejudiced and inaccurate.

Justus, Cantonius (d. 43 C.E.) *Coprefect of the Praetorian Guard with Rufrius Pollio*
Justus was put to death by Empress MESSALLINA in 43 C.E. because he knew of her adulteries and indiscretions. His replacement was either Lusius Geta or Rufrius Crispinus.

Jutes   Teutonic people who probably lived in the northern European region of Jutland. They took part in an invasion of England in the years between 450 and 455 C.E., joining the Angles and the Saxons. Their kings were

Hengist and Horsa, and the Jutes subsequently played a role in the Dark Ages of England.

Juthungi   *See* MARCOMANNI.

Juthungine War   A bitter conflict fought over northern Italy between Emperor AURELIAN and a barbarian horde in 270 C.E. Convinced that Roman power was sufficiently weakened, a large Marcomannic-based nation, the Juthungi, invaded Italy. The new Emperor Aurelian hurried from his campaign against the Goths to evict the marauders, a task that proved difficult. Aurelian arrived at Placentia and demanded that the Juthungi surrender. He tried to follow this with a smashing victory but was ambushed and beaten. A retreat was called, and a historian of the *Scriptores Historiae Augustae* wrote that the empire of Rome was nearly destroyed. A threat to the Eternal City was averted only by the desire of the Juthungi to plunder the northern regions of Italy, while Aurelian reorganized his shattered army and bolstered Italian defenses. Once his preparations were complete, Aurelian descended upon the barbarians, and crushed the Juthungi at Metaurus, Fanum, Fortuna, and Ticenum. The Juthungi retreated across the Alps in complete disarray. Surviving elements in Italy were hunted down and exterminated.

Juvenal (Decimus Junius Juvenalis) (fl. early second century C.E.) *Greatest of the Roman satirists*
Few details of Juvenal's life are available, except for infrequent references to himself and mention by MARTIAL. He probably came from Aquinum and achieved notoriety in his later years (c. 110–227) as Rome's most gifted and eloquent satirist. Juvenal's satires were superb essays decrying the state of his times, examining scathingly the moral abnormalities of Roman society, and ridiculing the more inane facets of daily life and government. His righteous indignation was probably more effect than reality, for no historical period could have been as hopeless as the one he portrayed. Nevertheless, they were clear, insightful, and humorous, and they fulfilled the demands of satire beyond the level of any previous works.

Juvenalia   The Games of Youth, established in 59 C.E. by Nero to celebrate the cutting of his beard as part of the coming of age ritual practiced in Rome. As was typical of the emperor, he could not resist turning the event into an offensive display of excess. Nobles and even women (contrary to dramatic traditions) were forced to perform plays in Greek and in Latin. Booths for wine and food were set up to feed the guests, who had to purchase vast amounts, and a general atmosphere of debauchery prevailed. Nero, himself, finally serenaded the crowd with his songs, accepting the adulation of the AUGUSTANS or paid applauders (CLAQUEURS). Thrasea Paetus, the philosopher, was put to death in 66 on the pretext that he had refused to attend the Juvenalia (among other charges). The Juvenalia was still held in the reign of Domitian (c. 95).

Juvenalis, Flavius (fl. late second century C.E.) *Prefect of the Praetorian Guard (c. 193–197)*
Juvenalis may have been appointed to the post by Emperor Didius Julianus to serve as the third prefect with Tullius CRISPINUS and T. Flavius GENIALIS. When Septimius Severus assumed the throne in 193, he named Juvenalis as prefect, perhaps upon the death of Crispinus. He eventually was joined in his post by C. FULVIUS PLAUTIANUS. Juvenalis was replaced by Aemilius Saturninus, a fortuitous event, because Saturninus was murdered by Plautianus (c. 200) who became sole prefect.

Juvenal of Jerusalem (d. 458 C.E.) *Christian prelate from 422–458*
Juvenal worked to improve the church's political status and that of his own see. Juvenal hoped to have JERUSALEM elevated to the rank of a patriarchate even though that would mean a decline for Caesarea and Antioch. Toward this end he supported CYRIL OF ALEXANDRIA against Nestorius at the Council of Ephesus in 431, but failed to receive recognition. He later aided Cyril's successor Dioscorus, but changed sides in 451 after Dioscorus was condemned at the Council of Chalcedon. He finally earned the rank of patriarch and returned home, where he was greeted by a revolt of his own priests, who had favored Dioscorus.

Juvencus, Gaius Vettius Aquilinus (fourth century C.E.) *Christian poet*
Juvencus authored a hexameter verse on the Four Gospels based on Matthew in 330 C.E. as an alternative to traditional pagan poetry.

Juventas   Also called Hebe, the daughter of Jupiter and Juno and the goddess of youth. She served as the protectoress of the young and poured the nectar of the gods at the great divine banquets, at least until the emergence of Ganymedes.

See also GODS AND GODDESSES OF ROME.

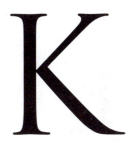

Kalends The first day of each month of the Roman calendar. According to tradition, these days were difficult to foretell, as the seers claimed that they came too early for an accurate prophesy.

See also CALENDAR, ROMAN; IDES; NONES.

Kanus, Julius (d. 40 C.E.) *A Stoic philosopher during the reign of Gaius Caligula (37–41 C.E.)*
Kanus was executed by the emperor as part of Caligula's general persecution of philosophers in Rome, especially the Stoics. His friends included Antiochus of Seleucia and RECTUS.

See also STOICISM.

Knights *See* EQUITES.

Kniva (d. after 253 C.E.) *King of the Goths during the middle of the third century C.E.*
Kniva not only led his people in an invasion of the Roman Empire but succeeded in destroying an emperor. He appeared suddenly on the Danubian frontier in 249, commanding a massive force. While one column ravaged DACIA, he led another into MOESIA, dividing his army into two forces, one laying siege to Philippopolis and the other, with 70,000 men, assaulting Novae on the Danube. Turned aside by TREBONIANUS GALLUS, then the governor of Moesia, Kniva moved from Novae to NICOPOLIS in the south. Word of the crisis quickly drew Emperor Trajanus DECIUS and his son HERENNIUS ETRUSCUS to the Danubian theater. Decius surprised the Goths at Nicopolis (c. 249) and inflicted upon them a terrible defeat. Kniva retreated over the Haemus Mountains and, despite Decius's attempts to prevent him, joined his troops at Philippopo-

lis. The strategic situation was thus reversed when, at the small town of Beroca at the base of the Haemus Mountains, Kniva surprised the emperor and crushed him. Decius's legions fled in disarray over the mountains to Moesia, where the emperor tried to reorganize.

Kniva pressed on against Philippopolis, capturing it with the help of T. Julius Priscus, governor of Thrace, who harbored ambitions of the throne, while pillaging the Thracian cities. Kniva probably put him to death with thousands of others. By the spring of 251, Decius launched his campaign. It began well, for Kniva suffered several setbacks, but then he devised a trap for the Romans at Abrittus, midway between the Danube and the Black Sea, in June 251. The battle proved an overwhelming triumph for the Goths. Decius and his son Herennius fell on the field, as did most of the imperial army. Countless cities were ravaged by the Goths. Kniva negotiated with Decius's successor, Trebonianus Gallus, to retain their spoils and prisoners, in return for an unharassed march back to the Danube. The frontier and Black Sea provinces were now open to full-scale barbarian invasions. In 253, the Goths demanded more tribute to keep them from crossing the Danube again. The governor of Moesia, Aemilius Aemilianus, refused and tried to wage war over the river but failed, and Goths returned. The remaining years of Kniva's life are unclear.

Koblenz (Coblenz or Coblence) A city probably founded by the Romans in the late first century B.C.E. DRUSUS (1), according to tradition, founded the community he called Confluentes at the meeting point of the Rhine and the Moselle rivers.

See also GERMANIA.

L

Labeo Marcus Antistius (c. 54 B.C.E.–10/11 C.E.) *One of the earliest of the Roman Jurists*
Labeo lived during the Augustan age (27 B.C.E.–14 C.E.). Trained by Cicero and Ciceronian legalist C. Trebatius Testa, he was considered one of the finest legal minds in Rome, despite his firm Republicanism. Labeo became a rival of the other great jurist, G. Ateius Capito, opposing his monarchist tendencies. Augustus, who disliked both Labeo's politics and his sharp wit, passed him over and granted Capito a consulship. Capito thus possessed greater social prominence than his senior, although Labeo was always considered his equal. Labeo authored some 400 books, including an early commentary on the Edicts. Always ready with a quick retort, he placed the name of Lepidus, the ex-triumvir, on a list for the Senate. When Augustus threatened him with a charge of perjury, Labeo responded: "What have I done wrong by naming to the Senate one whom you allowed to remain High Priest?" Later, it was proposed that the senators should protect Augustus as a special guard, to which Labeo replied: "As for me, I snore, and thus should not sleep at Augustus's chamber door."

Labeo, Pomponius (d. 34 C.E.) *Praetor and governor of Moesia for eight years during the reign of Tiberius*
In 34, Labeo and his wife, Paxaea, were accused of taking bribes while in office. Fearing that no possible hope could be offered by a trial, they chose to kill themselves. Tiberius remarked that Paxaea had committed suicide needlessly as she was in no danger of prosecution.

Labienus, Quintus (d. c. 39 B.C.E.) *Son of Titus Labienus, and opponent of Julius Caesar*
Labienus joined Cassius and Brutus, the LIBERATORS. He acted as an envoy for them to King ORODES II of PARTHIA, developing a rapport with the monarch. In 42 B.C.E., when the Republican cause was annihilated at the battle of Philippi, LABIENUS fled to Parthia, offering his services to Orodes. Two years later, Labienus returned to Roman territory but at the head of the Parthian army, invading SYRIA and PALESTINE. He captured Apamea and most of the Syrian cities, except for Tyre, subjugated JUDAEA, carried off the ethnarch Hyrcanus, and installed the Jewish claimant Antigones on the throne. His seizure of Cilicia was his military crowning achievement; but he had considerable influence on Jewish history. It took nearly a year for Marc ANTONY to respond to Labienus's invasion. Publius Ventidius arrived in Asia with several legions, evicted the Parthians and crushed Labienus's own force. Labienus attempted to flee to Parthia but was captured in Cilicia and executed.

Labienus, Titus (d. 45 B.C.E.) *Tribune and gifted lieutenant to Julius Caesar*
Labienus appeared on the political scene in 63 B.C.E., serving as a tribune. In this office he aided Caesar, who was prosecuting the aged Senator C. Rabirius, who had a role in the murder of Saturninus in 100 B.C.E. His connection with Caesar continued during the GALLIC WARS (58–51 B.C.E.), when Labienus held a major post of legate and chief officer in support of the conqueror of the Gauls. He distinguished himself in several campaigns; in 54, an attack by the chieftain Indutiomarus was repulsed, salvaging the Roman victory in Gallia, and in 53 he defeated the Treviri during a major uprising of the Gallic tribes. Labienus was also at Caesar's side in the siege of ALESIA in 52 B.C.E.

At the start of the CIVIL WAR, FIRST TRIUMVIRATE in 49 Labienus chose the Pompeian cause, because of the clear signs of Pompey emerging as ultimate victor. He saw action at the battle of PHARSALUS, and escaped to Africa with the Gallic and Germanic cavalry units. His advice to Cornelius Scipio at the battle of THAPSUS in February 46 was not enough to ensure victory, and he again fled, this time to Spain. In March 45, Labienus fought in the last battle of the wars, at MUNDA. Despite a hard struggle, Caesar proved triumphant and Labienus died, one of the last Pompeian officers to fall.

Laco, Cornelius (d. 69 C.E.) *Prefect of the Praetorian Guard from late 68 until January 15, 69, during the brief reign of Galba*

Laco served originally in Hispania Tarraconensis as a judge's assessor and entered the circle of the provincial governor, GALBA. Described by Suetonius as stupid and arrogant and by Tacitus as the laziest of men, Laco nevertheless became one of Galba's key advisers, competing with Titus Vinius and the freedman Icelus for attention. When Galba ascended the throne in 68, Laco received as his reward the prefectship of the Guard. As prefect he proved absolutely incompetent, infuriating the Praetorians. Not only was the DONATIVUM promised to them by Galba left unpaid, but Laco also spent most of his time plotting against Vinius and Icelus for the right to choose an heir for the emperor. The increasing unpopularity of Galba and the murderous mood of the Guard were ignored until, on January 15, Laco paid for his lack of vision. Galba was murdered by the Praetorians, Otho was elevated to the throne and Laco was reportedly run through by a soldier's sword.

Laco, Graecinus (fl. first century C.E.) *Prefect of the Vigiles (city watch)*

In 31 C.E., Laco became a pivotal figure in the downfall of the Praetorian Prefect SEJANUS. From his island abode at Capri, Emperor Tiberius plotted the death of his ambitious PREFECT OF THE PRAETORIAN GUARD. He wrote a letter to the Senate, destroying Sejanus, and entrusted its delivery and the inevitable massacre to several reliable servants, Sertorius MACRO of the Guard, the consul Memmius Regulus, and Laco. On the morning of October 18, Macro arrived at the Senate's meeting place for the day, the Temple of Apollo, delivered Tiberius's letter and went outside to greet Laco. The prefect of the Vigiles had marched up with a troop of city police, and, by Macro's order, replaced Sejanus's own special detachment of men. Once the Senate condemned Sejanus, Laco led him away to the dreaded dungeons of TULLIANUM, where he was executed. For this act of loyalty, Tiberius elevated Laco to the rank of ex-praetor. Claudius later added further honors, including a governorship in Gallia and the position of ex-consul.

Lactantius (Lucius Caecilius Firmianus Lactantius) (c. 245–323 C.E.) *One of the great Christian apologists*

Originally from Africa, Lactantius entered the service of Emperor Diocletian, receiving from him an appointment as a teacher of rhetoric in Nicomedia. In 300, however, Lactantius was converted to Christianity and, under the laws of persecution of the time, he was removed from office. Later Emperor Constantine named him tutor to his son Crispus. Lactantius authored a number of books to propagate the faith. Between 304 and 311 he wrote the *Divinae Institutiones* (Divine institutions), presenting many facets of Christian doctrine with particular emphasis in attracting Latin leaders; *De Mortibus Persecutorum* (On the death of the persecutors), a very detailed and often lurid account of the death of the persecutors as evidence of divine punishment for their attacks on Christians. The description of the death of Emperor Galerius was notably graphic. Two other books were *De Opificio Deo* (On the existence of God) and *Ira Dei* (The wrath of God).

Laelianus, Upius Cornelius (d. c. 268 C.E.) *Usurper of 268 C.E. against the Gallic Emperor Postumus*

Laelianus attempted his revolt at Mainz but was either defeated and killed by Postumus or died at the hands of his own troops.

Laeta, Clodia (d. 213 C.E.) *One of the four Vestal Virgins put to death by Caracalla*

Clodia Laeta suffered the traditional form of execution for having lost her virginity, that of burial alive. She endured her fate, screaming that Caracalla knew that she was pure.

See also CRESCENTIA, CANNUTIA; RUFINA, POMPONIA; SEVERA, AURELIA.

laeti The name given to large bodies of barbarian prisoners captured in the many wars on the frontiers of the empire and settled on imperial lands. The aim of this resettlement program was to reduce the pressure of invaders in certain areas, especially on the borders, and to make the prisoners productive clients capable of supplying both food and (eventually) troops for the Roman army. Given sizeable areas to cultivate, the *laeti* did become active participants in the defense of the provinces, now their homes, but by their very presence they insured the Germanization of many districts of the Roman Empire.

See the section on Germanic culture in Germania.

Laetus (d. c. 198 C.E.) *Legate in the army of Emperor Septimius Severus; known as either Julian or Maecius*

The details of Laetus's identity remain obscure, except for several mentions in the histories. He was an officer, probably in the Pannonian legions, and thus helped to ensure the elevation of Severus to the throne in 193. In 195, he commanded one wing of the imperial army in its campaigns against the Osroeni, relieving the besieged city of Nisibis. Two years later, Laetus was in charge of the important reserves at the battle of LUGDUNUM (Lyons), between Severus and the imperial aspirant, Clodius Albinus. It was written that he delayed in entering the battle, hoping that both generals would die and he would become emperor. Severus apparently did not forget this. Laetus returned to the East in 198, saving Nisibis once more, this time from the Parthians. His popularity was high among the soldiers. Refusing to allow any rival, Severus put him to death, blaming the deed on others.

Laetus, Quintus Aemilius (d. c. 192 C.E.) *Prefect of the Praetorian Guard in the reign of Commodus (177–192 C.E.)*
Laetus played a major role in the emperor's assassination in 192. Laetus became prefect in 191 and served as an important adviser to Commodus. Through his influence Septimius Severus was made governor of Pannonia Superior in 191; and he may have dissuaded Commodus from burning Rome. In 192, he conspired with the imperial concubine Marcia and with the Chamberlain Eclectus to murder Commodus on the last day of the year. Laetus and Eclectus then secured the elevation to the throne of Pertinax, the prefect of the city. At first happy with his choice, Laetus destroyed the historical reputation of Commodus. Later, he found that Pertinax was not to his liking and thus stirred up the Praetorians, resulting in a cruel death for Pertinax after a reign of only 87 days. What part he had in the subsequent auctioning of the empire is unclear. He was, however, retained in his post by Didius Julianus, until Septimius Severus marched on Italy later that year. To appease Severus, Julianus executed the assassins of Commodus, Laetus among them.

Lamia, Aelius Plautius (d. 33 C.E.) *An imperial office-holder throughout the reigns of Augustus (27 B.C.E.–14 C.E.) and Tiberius (14–37 C.E.)*
Lamia came from an excellent family and served as consul in 3 C.E. before holding a governorship in Africa. Years later, Tiberius appointed him governor of Syria. But it was the emperor's habit never to permit certain officials to leave Rome to take up their duties, so Lamia resided in Rome during his years as governor of Syria. Having earned some popularity from his mock position, Lamia was finally released by Tiberius, who gave him the post of prefect of the city, a position left vacant in 32 by the death of Lucius Piso. Lamia died in 33 and received the funerary honors due a censor, a lavish ceremony normally reserved for censors alone. Horace addressed Lamia in his *Odes*.

Langobardi One of the minor tribes of the Suebi, originally in possession of a small strip of land along the Elbe River. In 5 C.E., they were defeated by Tiberius and forced to retire across the river to the eastern banks. They slowly made their way over barbarian Germania and fell under the control of Maroboduus, the king of the Marcomanni. In 166 C.E., the Langobardi crossed the Danube as part of the widespread crisis along the frontiers. A Roman army crushed 6,000 warriors, driving them back. The Langobardi waited and attacked in 568 with such success that they founded the kingdom of the Lombards. The historian Tacitus described them as never great in numbers and dependent solely upon their military skills.

Laodicea, Canons of Set of 60 canons of the Christian Church dating to the fourth century. They may have been the subject-headings of the canons that were issued by councils earlier in the century, particularly the Council of Nicaea (325) and the otherwise unknown Council of Laodicea. The canons are concerned with such subjects as heresies (Novatianism, Montanism, etc.) and the list of the scriptural books considered canonical. The Epistle of St. Paul to the Laodiceans is an apocryphal Latin epistle, included in many Latin manuscripts of the New Testament from the sixth through 15th centuries. Scholars generally agree that it dates to the fourth or fifth century and was probably written in Greek.

lapsi A Latin term for "fallen" denoting those individuals who had denied their Christian faith during times of persecution by the Roman government. Early church teaching held that apostasy was an unforgivable sin, but, by the third century, the problem of the *lapsi* had grown so acute that a means of finding readmission for the repentant had to be found. St. Cyprian of Carthage (d. 258), confronted by the Decian persecutions (launched by Emperor Trajanus Decius), made the decision to readmit the *lapsi* but only after a suitable period of penance. Cyprian recognized three classes of the *lapsi*; *thurificati*, those who gave incense at pagan ceremonies; *sacrificati*, those who took part in pagan sacrifices; and *libellatici*, those who went so far as to secure certificates that they had conformed to legally required pagan practices. Cyprian's decision was vigorously opposed by the Novatianists, who were unbending in resisting the readmission, opposition that led them to open schism. Several councils took up the issue of the *lapsi*, including Elvira (306), Arles (314), Ancyra (314), and Nicaea (325).

Lara Nymph who became the wife of MERCURY and bore him two sons, the LARES.
See also GODS AND GODDESSES OF ROME.

lararium An altar, dedicated to the LARES and containing their images, which was kept in a special place in each Roman household. According to the custom, a good Roman would offer prayers at the *lararium* each morning.

Statues of the individual Lares could be kept as well, sometimes made out of gold, as were those possessed by Vitellius.

Lares   The sons of Mercury by Lara, according to Ovid. This identification, however, differs greatly from the traditional Roman understanding of these spirits. The Lares began as deities of agriculture and farming before coming to symbolize, at crossroads, a protective force of nature. As such, they were honored with shrines at the meeting places of various roads. Travelers, even sea-goers, declared the Lares to be their patrons. It was thus inevitable that they should become part of the Roman state religion; a division of their nature took place in time, as they became the *Lares domestici* and the *Lares publici.*

The *Lares domestici* represented those spirits of the dead (MANES) within a family who were elevated because of their goodness and importance to a higher spiritual existence, that of the Lares. They protected the family and were headed by the *Lar familiaris* or the founding spirit of the household (GENIUS). Any food that was dropped during a meal was not thrown away but picked up and burned in sacrifice. Other offerings were made, especially of food in the morning, accompanying the prayers made each day at the LARARIUM, the altar devoted to the Lares in every Roman household. Anytime the family moved, special care was taken to transport the *lararium* to the new residence.

The *Lares publici* functioned on a far wider scale. There were two forms: the *Lares compitales* and the *Lares praestites.* The *Lares compitales* protected crossroads in various sections of the city. All of Rome, and presumably the entire empire, was guarded by the *Lares praestites.*

See also GODS AND GODDESSES OF ROME; RELIGION.

Largus, Scribonius (d. after 53 C.E.) *Court physician to Claudius (ruled 41–54 C.E.)*
Largus came from Arminium and served as the doctor to the emperor both in Rome and on all imperial travels, until at least 53, when the medical needs were filled by XENOPHON. Largus was noted for a book of prescriptions published with Claudius's permission in 47. He was an expert in Greek MEDICINE and relied upon many physicians of his time for his prescriptions.

Lateranus, Plautius (d. 65 C.E.) *Nephew of the conqueror of Britannia in 43 C.E., Aulus Plautius*
During his lifetime, Plautius Lateranus became embroiled in two major scandals, first with Empress Valeria MESSALLINA in 48 and then in the Pisonian Conspiracy in 65. Emperor Claudius's chief secretary was aware that Lateranus had become Messallina's lover but did nothing until 48, when the empress actually married Gaius Silius, an act that brought her indiscretions to light. Because of his uncle, Lateranus was spared by Claudius but was ousted from the Senate. In 65, he became one of the ringleaders in a plot to assassinate Nero. He despised the tyrant, despite the emperor's gift to him—the restoration of his rights lost in the Messallina affair. Lateranus thus had much to lose when the plot was uncovered. Lateranus reportedly met his fate with bravery and silence at the Porta Maggiore. Tacitus described him as a big man, firm and resolute in character. Juvenal wrote of his luxurious palace on the Caelian Hill as an example of fleeting wealth.

latifundia   Large agricultural estates that were established in Italy during the second century B.C.E. and that were formed out of the distribution by lease of a portion of the *ager publicus,* or public land. The majority of recipients were members of the Patrician class, and the land distribution came largely at the expense of peasant farmers who were compelled to sell their small plots after it became clear they could not compete with the large productive estates.

The latifundium characteristically had a villa and a population of slaves who could be used to grow crops and raise animals. The estate thus had considerable financial potential because of the capital investment its owner could inject into it. As the peasants on the surrounding smaller farms were forced to sell, the latifundium acquired their fields at low cost. The latifundia spread to the provinces, but they never reached the same size of those in Italy. During the imperial era, the cost of slaves became so high that latifundia were replaced gradually by the *patrocinium,* which was farmed by *coloni.* Still later, in the face of social and political decline in the empire, many of the old estates were abandoned, especially in the provinces.

Latin language   The Latin language belongs to the Italic branch of the Indo-European family of languages and thus has a relationship to Greek, Germanic, and Celtic. It appeared first in the Italian Peninsula around the eighth century B.C.E., most likely penetrating from across the Alps and Appenines. It is certain that other Indo-European languages were spoken in Italy, but these today are little known. Greek was spoken in southern Italy, and Celtic was used in the north. A number of non–Indo-European languages were also spoken, namely Etruscan, which centered in Etruria. Little has survived of the Etruscan language, save for inscriptions, dedications, and epitaphs. While other languages, such as Greek and Italic dialects influenced the development of Latin, Etruscan did not make a substantial impression on the language of Rome.

Latin was originally spoken in the city of Rome and in Latium. As the city expanded its power and influence, the tongue spread into neighboring regions and then into other parts of the Mediterranean as Rome founded *colonia.* Each colony became a Latin speaking urban center, united by language, culture, law, and custom to Rome.

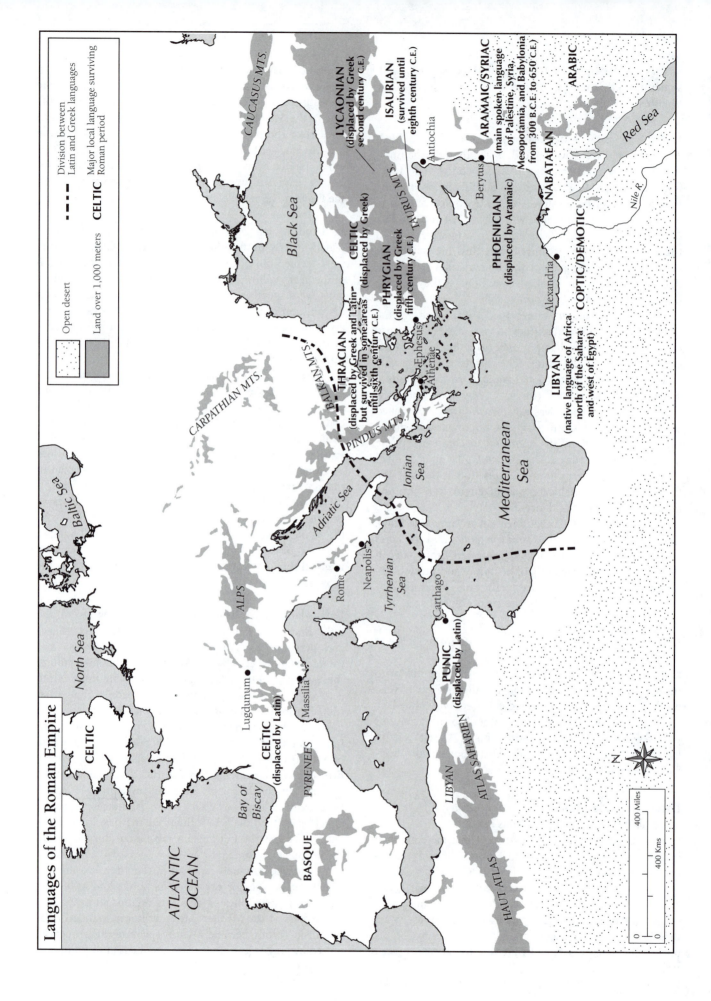

Languages of the Roman Empire

Division between
Latin and Greek languages

CELTIC   Major local language surviving
Roman period

Open desert

Land over 1,000 meters

ATLANTIC
OCEAN

North Sea

Baltic Sea

CELTIC

Bay of Biscay

PYRENEES

BASQUE

Lugdunum

CELTIC
(displaced by Latin)

Massilia

CAUCASUS MTS.

Black Sea

CARPATHIAN MTS.

ALPS

Rome

Neapolis

Tyrrhenian
Sea

Adriatic Sea

BALKAN MTS.

PINDUS MTS.

Ionian
Sea

THRACIAN
(displaced by Greek and Latin
but survived in some areas
until sixth century C.E.)

Ephesus
Athenae

CELTIC
(displaced by Greek)

PHRYGIAN
(displaced by Greek
fifth century C.E.)

LYCAONIAN
(displaced by Greek
second century C.E.)

TAURUS MTS.

ISAURIAN
(survived until
eighth century C.E.)

Antiochia

Berytus

ARAMAIC/SYRIAC
(main spoken language
of Palestine, Syria,
Mesopotamia, and Babylonia
from 300 B.C.E. to 650 C.E.)

NABATAEAN

Red Sea

Nile R.

PHOENICIAN
(displaced by Aramaic)

Alexandria

COPTIC/DEMOTIC

LIBYAN
(native language of Africa
north of the Sahara
and west of Egypt)

Mediterranean
Sea

Carthago

PUNIC
(displaced by Latin)

ATLAS SAHARIEN

LIBYAN

HAUT ATLAS

ARABIC

N

400 Miles

400 Kms

As the empire expanded through conquest, Latin became the primary language of government in all of the provinces and one of the most obvious symbols of Roman domination. Nevertheless, there was no official command for the subjugated peoples to master the Latin tongue, and native languages remained in use, such as Celtic, Syriac, and, of course, Greek. Greek was the primary lingua franca of the Hellenic regions of the empire, termed, *koin*. Among the Romans themselves, Greek was considered the language of culture and was seen as a prerequisite for a true education. With the division of the empire in the fourth century into eastern and western spheres, Greek's ascendancy in the eastern provinces was virtually codified, while in the western provinces, Latin remained the dominant language of culture and the dimming civilization of Rome. Latin held on as the official language of imperial government until the reign of Justinian in the sixth century.

Latin is divided into several eras. Archaic or Early Latin endured until around 100 B.C.E. when it was superseded by so-called Classical Latin. This golden age of Latin extended from 100 B.C.E. to 14 C.E. and the end of the Augustan principate, a period that boasted some of Latin's greatest figures, including CICERO, VIRGIL, and HORACE. The period that followed, from around 17 to 150, is termed the Silver Era. It was marked by a decline in the overall quality of Latin writing in direct comparison to the golden age. There were still notable literary figures, such as SENECA, TACITUS, and SUETONIOUS, but the times were characterized by the florid use of Latin and an obvious effort to emulate a bygone time.

The spoken Latin language used by the Romans varied considerably depending on the level of education and class of the speaker. Colloquial Latin, *sermo cotidianus,* was spoken by the educated. It is demonstrated in the letters of the Romans to each other and in literature and plays. TERENCE, for example, wrote most of his plays in a style of *sermo cotidianus*. Similarly, it was found in Horace's *Epistles* and *Satires*.

In sharp contrast to the *sermo cotidianus* was the language of the streets, the uneducated, and the lower classes. Termed Vulgar Latin, it was used principally in Rome and the cities and districts of Italy. It was a more casual, less structured way of speaking, with less attention to proper declensions. An excellent example of Vulgar Latin in the first century C.E. was preserved in literary form in the *Satyricon* by PETRONIUS; a later example of Vulgar Latin is found in the *Itinerarium Egeriae* (The Itinerary of Egeria, c. 400 C.E.). Graffiti, such as that preserved in Pompeii, is also an excellent source of details on the language of the common people.

The Latin language endured as the chief language of culture in the West even after the demise of the Western Roman Empire in 476 C.E. It had already been embraced by the migratory peoples who were reshaping what became Europe and was essential in providing the structure to the subsequent Romance languages. Latin was also the dominant language of the Christian Church and remains today the official language of the Roman Catholic Church.

Latium   The region of Italy in the middle of the peninsula, surrounded by Etruria, Samnium, and Campania, and bordered to the north by the Tiber River, to the south by the Volturnus. Latium was known for its beauty and fertility, and it was dominated by Mount Albanus, just south of Rome. Originally inhabited, according to the folk traditions, by the Pelasgians, the primitive tribesmen of Italy, Latium eventually became the home of the Latini, the Latins. The Latins were important in the foundation and development of Rome, and their territory, once conquered by the Romans, served as the first area of colonization. During the years of the Roman Empire, Latium was combined with Campania as a district of Italy. It was bisected by two major roads, the Via Appia and the Via Latina.

See also ITALIA.

law   The Roman legal system was founded on two key documents. The first was the Twelve Tables, issued c. 451–450 B.C.E. The second was the Corpus Iuris Civilis organized by Emperor Justinian and promulgated c. 540 C.E., which compiled the entire body of Roman law for the Byzantine Empire. From these two principal sources, supplemented by the Codex Theodosianus of Emperor Theodosius II in 438, almost the whole of Western legal tradition received its foundation.

HISTORY

The Twelve Tables were drafted by a committee of 10 magistrates (the *decemviri legibusscribundis,* or "ten men for writing the laws"). The particulars of the laws are preserved only in fragments or in quotes from extant writings, but it is known that early legal interpretation was left to priests. Over time, the interpretation of laws fell to jurists. The Twelve Tables were never repealed and technically remained in effect until the time of Justinian. The legal system in the early Republic was marked by its formalism and adherence to established norms. These changed gradually in the hands of the PRAETORS, who took upon themselves the task of issuing edicts and, when necessary, making reforms.

Technically, the creation of new laws was the prerogative of the Comitia Centuriata (the main legislative body of the Republic), and the laws (*leges*) that were passed were identified by the names of the magistrates who initially proposed them. From the third century, the chief mechanism for establishing new laws was the *plebiscitum,* laws proposed by the people. From 218 B.C.E., the Comitia only rarely passed new laws, leaving it to magistrates and jurists to decide what was best in terms of their meaning and application. The SENATE was involved chiefly in an advisory capacity, although its advice, in the form of the SENATUS CONSULTUM, did have the binding effect of law. In this way, the *senatus consultum* helped prepare the way for the imperial system that commenced with the Augustan principate (27 B.C.E.–14 C.E.).

From the time of Augustus, the notion of the *plebiscita* and other legal structures of the Republic were gradually curbed and replaced by the imperial will. As a mechanism of the emperors, the Senate emerged as the chief legislative body of the empire, and the *senatus consultum* assumed full legal status. This was not because of an increase in power on the part of the Senate but because it was a useful body for the emperors to use in promulgating new laws.

The emperors themselves also issued decrees that, by the second century, carried the full weight of law. Imperial pronouncements, termed CONSTITUTIONES (constitutions), took various forms, including decrees (*decreta*), rescripts (*rescripta*), and edicts (*edicta*). As interpretation of law became increasingly important, the emperors—assisted by legal experts and assorted secretaries—spent much of their time in legal matters answering and issuing rescripts. These were replies to assorted legal questions that had been raised in the course of legal cases, as well as petitions. Such replies were a key element in the further development of Roman law as it came to be practiced.

Traditionally, the body of Roman laws, the IUS CIVILE, applied only to Roman citizens. Others outside the Roman citizenship, fell under the authority of the *ius gentium* and under the particular laws of their own country or city when permitted by the Roman governors. The sharp differentiation, which was so crucial to many citizens because of its rights of appeal (as in the famous case of St. Paul who made an appeal to the emperor), ended in 212 C.E. In that year, Emperor Caracalla granted universal citizenship. Technically, the differences between the *ius civile* and *ius gentium* should have ceased, but there remained for many years two kinds of justice, one for long-standing citizens and the other for recent ones. Equally, the change in status opened up the *ius civile* to many forms of local interpretation, thereby influencing Roman law in general through appeals and rescripts when local customs were accepted as fully legal and binding on all citizens.

The structure of the imperial system centralized law in the hands of the emperor and so, by extension, the imperial advisers as well. The chief legal figures in the imperial era were the jurists, such as Ulpian and Papinian. Held in high esteem by the Roman courts, their opinions were sought on cases and other legal matters by both emperors and magistrates. Their responses, *responsa*, to questions became important consultative documents in case law.

Relentless centralization of government and power in the hands of the emperor, however, made the value of *responsa* less significant, from the third century onward, in favor of *rescripta*.

From the time of Constantine the Great (d. 337 C.E.), Roman law entered what is termed the age of Vulgar Law. Because of the general decay that crept into the educational system, the quality of legal practice declined steadily. This deterioration was hastened by the political instability in the West from the early fifth century, the loss of a command of the earlier juridical writings, and the wide influence of Germanic peoples settled in the empire. Large elements of Roman law survived the ruins of the Roman Empire in the West thanks to three late imperial developments. The first, was the Codex Theodosianus of 438. Emperor Theodosius II decreed that all *constitutiones* from the time of Constantine the Great be collected and preserved. Second, the successor to the empire in the West, such as the Visigoths and the Burgundians, incorporated elements of Roman law in their own codes (e.g., the Lex Romana Visigothorum). Finally, in the Eastern Empire, a revival of classical learning sparked a renewed interest in earlier Roman law.

The revival in the East made possible the decision of Emperor Justinian to appoint in 540 a commission to amass the entire body of Roman law. Their work was completed in the Corpus Iuris Civilis (Body of civil law), actually a compilation of different collections, including the Digest (a collection of commentaries by earlier jurists) and the Codex Justinianus (a collection of *constitutiones*). The Corpus Iuris Civilis was the code of Roman law that formed the basis of virtually all succeeding legal developments.

LEGAL SYSTEM

The Twelve Tables of Roman law did not establish in any sense a clear set of codes or laws governing criminal offenses. Rather, Roman criminal justice was a largely loosely applied structure, with different courts and jurisdictions each having a role to play. While unorganized by modern standards, Roman justice was harsh in its application, and unmerciful in its punishments. By custom, trials and court cases in early Rome were tried before the kings. Justice was later dispensed by magistrates and then, at the command of the Senate, by officially appointed courts. Under Sulla in the second century B.C.E., criminal courts (QUAESTIONES) were widened to handle such crimes as treason and corruption. Praetors were the chief judges of these courts, although they declined in use during the life of the empire.

The system that became established for much of the imperial era was for criminal cases to be tried in one of several ways. For members of the patrician class, senators, and in special circumstances, the Senate served as a kind of supreme criminal tribunal. The emperor also retained the privilege of trying cases himself, a right that took on grim political ramifications under vindictive emperors such Gaius Caligula and Nero.

The average Romans, of course, rarely found themselves before such exalted judges. Most cases were handled by civil courts or by a number of lower courts under the authority of the urban prefect or the praetorian prefect. Outside of Rome, there were two basic forms of criminal justice until 212 C.E. and the decree of Caracalla making all inhabitants citizens of the empire. For non-Roman citizens, local courts might be permitted to exercise justice according to their agreements with Rome. In most cases, however, cases were handled by the local Roman governors, who would travel throughout the cities and towns hearing various disputes. Cases involving civil law were the purview of local courts, although in neither criminal nor civil law was it permitted for a Roman citizen to be tried anywhere save before a representative of the Roman Empire. The trial of St. Paul is considered a classic example of the rights of appeal of the Roman citizen. St. Paul was tried before the local Roman officials and, as was his right, he appealed directly to the emperor.

Criminal law recognized two distinct types of offenses, private and public. Private offenses were settled through recompense, usually the payment of whatever financial amount was deemed suitable to the injured party. Public crimes were subject to brutal public punishment, varying in harshness depending on the nature of the crime. Assorted minor punishments included public flogging and confiscation of property. Imprisonment was not common, as Roman justice saw it as unlikely that years in a prison would be conducive to reforming a criminal's character. The various forms of banishment were more extreme. These ranged from exile to work in the mines (*deportatio in metalla*), banishment to the gladiator schools (*in ludos*), and *deportatio*, meaning that the criminal was sent away forever from Rome, often to a small and dreadful island, as happened to Julia, daughter of Emperor Augustus, and many of the enemies of Emperor Tiberius. Exile or banishment usually entailed a loss of Roman citizenship. The death penalty (*poena capitis*) was applied frequently, for such crimes as murder and treason, and also for impiety—hence the persecutions of Christians. The most common forms of execution were crucifixion, burning, decapitation, and being thrown to wild animals. The forms of execution used against the Christians were limited only by the imaginations of the Roman authorities throughout the empire.

Suggested Readings: Bauman, Richard A. *Lawyers in Roman Republican Politics: A Study of the Roman Jurists in their Political Setting, 316–82 B.C.E.* Munich, Ger.: C. H. Beck'sche Verlagsbuchhandlung, 1983; Buck, Robert J. *Agriculture and Agricultural Practice in Roman Law.* Wiesbaden, Ger.: F. Steiner, 1983; Cracknell, D. G. *Roman Law: Origins and Influence.* London: HLT, 1990; Crone, Patricia. *Roman, Provincial, and Islamic Law: The Origins of the Islamic Patronate.* Cambridge, U.K.: Cambridge University Press, 1987; Diosdi, Gyorgy. *Contract in Roman Law: From the Twelve Tables to the Glossators.* Translated by J. Szabo. Budapest: Akademiai Kiado, 1981; Frier, Bruce W. *The Rise of the Roman Jurists: studies in Cicero's Pro Caecina.* Princeton, N.J.: Princeton University Press, 1985; Gaius. *The Institutes of Gaius.* Translated by W. M. Gordon and O. F. Robinson. Ithaca, N.Y.: Cornell University Press, 1988; Gardner, Jane F. *Women in Roman Law & Society.* London: Croom Helm, 1986; Honore, Tony. *Emperors and Lawyers.* London: Duckworth, 1981; ———. *Ulpian.* Oxford: Clarendon Press, 1982; *Justinian's Institutes.* Translated by Peter Birks & Grant McLeod. Ithaca, N.Y.: Cornell University Press, 1987; Mommsen, Theodore, ed. *The Digest of Justinian.* Translated by Alan Watson. Philadelphia: University of Pennsylvania Press, 1985; Stein, Peter. *The Character and Influence of the Roman Civil Law: Historical Essays.* London: Hambledon Press, 1988; *Studies in Justinian's Institutes: In Memory of J. A. C. Thomas, ed.,* P. G. Stein and A. D. E. Lewis. London: Sweet & Maxwell, 1983; Thomas, Ph. J. *Introduction to Roman Law.* Deventer, Neth.: Kluwer Law and Taxation Publishers, 1986; Treggiari, Susan. *Roman Marriage: Iusti Coniuges from the Time of Cicero to the Time of Ulpian.* Oxford, U.K.: Clarendon Press, 1991; Ullmann, Walter. *Law and Jurisdiction in the Middle Ages.* Edited by George Garnett. London: Variorum Reprints, 1988; Watson, Alan. *Contract of Mandate in Roman Law.* Aalen: Scientia Verlag, 1984; ———. *The Evolution of Law.* Baltimore: Johns Hopkins University Press, 1985; ———. *The Law of Persons in the Later Roman Republic.* Aalen, Ger.: Scientia Verlag, 1984; ———. *The Law of Property in the Later Roman Republic.* Aalen, Ger.: Scientia Verlag, 1984; ———. *Roman Slave Law.* Baltimore: Johns Hopkins University Press, 1987.

Lawrence (Laurence) (d. 258 C.E.) *One of the most famous martyrs of the early Christian church*
Lawrence was one of the seven deacons of Rome during the reign of Pope (later St.) Sixtus II, dying a mere four days after the pontiff. According to tradition as preserved by St. Ambrose, Prudentius, and others, Lawrence was ordered by the prefect to hand over the treasures of the church, whereupon he gathered the poor and sick, presented them to the Roman official, and said, "Here is the treasure of the church." He was then supposedly executed by being roasted on a grid. Scholars prefer to maintain that he was beheaded like Sixtus II. Lawrence was buried on the road to Tivoli, on the Via Tiburtina, and a chapel was built on the site in the early fourth century, where the church of St. Lawrence-Outside-the-Walls currently stands. He is mentioned in the Canon of the Mass.

legatus **(legate)**   An imperial officer who served as the lieutenant of the emperor and fulfilled a variety of duties, political and military. Legates (Latin plural, *legati*) were invariably members of the senatorial class and had served as PRAETORS in their passage through the CURSUS HONORUM. In the Republic, legates emerged as useful officials for provincial administration, aiding the governors of provinces as loyal deputies, envoys to local communities and as commanders of all troops stationed in the region. This last task became their main duty by the time of Caesar, as they assumed the rank of general in charge of one LEGION each. This system was concretized by the end of the Republic, as Caesar distributed his army of the Gallic Wars to several *legati*, including the gifted Titus Labienus. Throughout the Civil War (*see* CIVIL WAR, FIRST TRIUMVIRATE), the legates grew in number and were such a mainstay of legionary organization that they earned a major place in the imperial establishment of Augustus in 27 B.C.E.

In the Roman Empire, every legion had its own legate, known as a *legatus legionis,* who was answerable to Rome but at times also to the governor of the province in which he was stationed. As legions belonged almost exclusively to the imperial provinces, their commanding officers were normally legates. The position of legate in charge of an entire province was the chief source of aggrandizement for the rank. Known as *legati Augusti pro praetore,* these legates were appointed to each imperial province (with several exceptions) and controlled all troops within the province. Where there was more than one legion, the *legati* were answerable to the *legatus Augusti pro praetore.*

Two provinces did not follow this form of government. In Africa the legion (and its *legatus*) were originally under the proconsul of Africa, as it was a prestigious senatorial province. During the reign of Gaius Caligula, however, the legate was made independent of the proconsul, henceforth patrolling the Numidian region and the African frontiers while the proconsul cared for the legal and economic needs of the province. Around 238 C.E., the Legion, the III Augusta, was disbanded by Gordian III after its chief, Capellianus, had marched on Gordian I and II and killed them both at Carthage. The other special case was EGYPT. Being a crucial economic and strategic possession, Egypt was ruled by a prefect (*see* EGYPT, PREFECT OF), not by a *legatus Augusti pro praetore.* The legions stationed there, of varying number, belonged to his jurisdiction.

Legati were also sent by the emperor on missions to other countries, served as advisers in campaigns, and even acted as lieutenants to proconsuls in senatorial provinces. The legates were unchanged in their positions until the reorganization of the empire by Diocletian, when the differentiation between imperial and senatorial provinces was ended. Later, with the changes made in the army, the rank of legate underwent further transformation.

legions The basic fighting force of the Roman Empire. The legions for three centuries had no rivals for discipline, training, ability, and sheer military prowess. Through its soldiers the empire was able to control vast stretches of territory and entire peoples.

DEVELOPMENT OF THE LEGIONS

From the earliest times the Romans found organization on the battlefield to be a decided advantage over their enemies. At first the army was divided into various classes, according to the ranks of citizenship, the Servian model as established by King Servius Tullius (578–535 B.C.E.). While a further breakdown was made into smaller formations called centuries, these units joined together to form a Greek-influenced phalanx, fighting in the traditional hoplite, or Greek, fashion. The legendary Camillus (early fourth century B.C.E.) instituted reforms by creating the *manipulus* or maniple, a tactical joining of two centuries totaling between 120 and 160 men. Camillus made the legions more efficient by introducing a precise chain of command, with centurions of several grades and officers (TRIBUNES) to command them.

Such was the basic system in place during Rome's expansion throughout the Punic Wars (264–146 B.C.E.). With victory in that long series of struggles, came the inevitable strains of overseas possessions. No longer could the legions of the Republic be kept in the field for a short period and then disbanded. Longer service and permanent legions were necessary. The problems in standardizing such a force were centered in recruiting and in opposition from the upper classes, who found that chronic war was a hindrance to wealth and stability.

The answer was found by the powerful consul Marius, the architect of Rome's legionary superiority. He allowed all classes to join the army, ending the crisis of recruiting while placating the upper social stratas. Previously, a potential soldier was required to prove an estate valued at 4,000 asses. The maniple was reduced to a mere administrative entity. Cohorts now emerged as the standard tactical organization. Ten cohorts, averaging 480 men, added up to a legion, forming in battle into three lines of four cohorts in the first, and three in the second and third. Changes in configuration could be made according to the demands of battle or the brilliance of the general in charge.

Marius's reforms had a long-lasting impact on the legions and on Roman warfare in general. The legions were now flexible and interchangeable, no longer organized by economic class. There remained still a sense of the temporary, for the wars of the Republic gained territory for Rome but drained the financial resources so that legions had to be disbanded. The veterans of these units were turned into colonists and placed on frontier lands to stabilize the regions and to open up new areas of influence. Maintained legions, however, became better fighting forces with each season, developing a definite unity

The Roman legions, from Trajan's Column *(Courtesy Fr. Felix Just, S.J.)*

and loyalty to their commanders, an emotion feared by Rome's political elements.

Julius CAESAR found the Roman army a ready-made instrument for smashing his enemies and achieving greatness. He took over, with the approval of the Senate, the regions of Illyricum, Gallia Cisalpina, and Gallia Transalpina in 59 B.C.E. For the next eight years he conquered the Gauls, made two trips into Britain, crossed into Germany, and generally pacified the Gallic regions in now legendary campaigns. By the time he had finished his GALLIC WARS, the Senate was terrified of his ambitions and of the weapons he had forged through a mixture of incessant combat, discipline, and loyalty.

The ensuing CIVIL WAR (49–45 B.C.E.) proved that Caesar's legions were the finest field army that Rome would ever possess. In the hands of a military genius, no one, not even POMPEY THE GREAT, could hope to defeat it. From 49–44 B.C.E., Caesar crushed the Pompeians all across the Roman world, in Spain, Africa, and Greece. Few generals could ask their troops to eat grass, as Caesar did at DYRRHACHIUM in 48, or withstand a siege by an entire city as he did at ALEXANDRIA in that same year.

The Civil War, however, initiated a new trend. Whereas Caesar utilized a long-standing army, his opponents, most notably Pompey, assembled hurriedly as many legions as possible, so that, by the time that Caesar had decimated the Pompeians in Spain, Pompey had 100,000 men available. Most were unreliable, as was proven at the battle of PHARSALUS in 48, but this proliferation continued until the final settlement of Rome's political future at ACTIUM in 31 B.C.E., with the victory of Octavian (AUGUSTUS).

Besides the many sociopolitical, economic, religious, and financial crises facing him as emperor, Augustus was confronted with a bloated military system and wide frontiers to protect when he came to the throne. At the end of the Civil Wars there were numerous armies and some 60 legions. First he discharged over 100,000 soldiers, sending most to the provinces, where they helped forge colonies. Any troublesome contingents were removed; once fully organized, the 28 remaining legions were sent out to the provinces under his direct supervision. There they remained, watching the borders, maintaining the peace and enforcing Augustus's will.

TRAINING AND EQUIPMENT

One of the secrets to the success of the Roman legions was the masterful job traditionally done in training the troops. Routinely, a centurion handled the drilling, aided by his staff. Discipline, instruction, and preparation were honed, especially in those provinces where active service did not always entail warfare.

In his *De re militari*, Vegetius wrote in considerable detail of the gruelling techniques used to make the *miles*, the common soldier, ready for battle. Aside from camp duties, they were forced to march with heavy packs for great distances and in precise formations. Running and swimming were important; most essential of all was proficiency in weapons.

The legionaries were walking arsenals. Their primary weapon was the *gladius*, or sword. Post exercises involved a wooden or actual sword, used against a post designed to resemble an opponent. When not fighting a dummy, the recruit was given the *armatura* or gladiator drill where two adversaries sparred together. (TRAJAN was an admirer of the *armatura*.) Other weapons included the *pilum*, or javelin. Early versions had a shaft so thick that it could be hurled back at the thrower by his opponent. Modifications made the pointed end snap off on an opponent's shield, rendering the shaft relatively useless.

The uniform of the legions was substantially unchanged for many centuries. A linen undercloth was worn with a tunic or kilt of wool. In cold or very rugged climates trousers (*bracae*) could be worn, while sandaled wrappings and thick soles protected the feet.

Walls, COLUMNS, and the COINAGE of ancient Rome preserved a great deal of information about the body of armor of the Roman legions. Changes in style reflected military fashion for an era, as well as adaptations for purposes of combat. One kind of protection was the *lorica segmentata*, strips of armor with reinforced leather as displayed on Trajan's Column; it was eventually replaced by two newer designs, the *lorica squamata* and the *lorica hamata*. The *squamata* was the scale armor with individual rings woven together, the style illustrated on Constantine's Arch, while the *hamata* was actually heavy mail, far less flexible than those worn previously and a throwback to the days of Julius Caesar. Helmets were normally of bronze or iron, with a neck protector and cheek guards.

The shield (*scutum*) of the legionary was changed considerably from the early days of the empire to the third century C.E. A traditionally oval shape was redesigned to a rectangular form with curved edges, which became straight in time. By the age of the Severan dynasty, an oval shape was used once more, remaining the most common type until the fall of the Western Empire in the fifth century C.E. A number of motifs were used to decorate the shields; the best known was the lightning rod of Jupiter. Each *scutum* was owned personally by the soldier, who put both his name and the name of his centurion inside. The general quality of the equipment declined after the fourth century C.E.

ORGANIZATION

Discipline and training were possible only if organization existed within the legion. While the *miles,* or common soldiers, were the lifeblood of the army, the entire system depended upon the centurions, 60 per legion. Overseeing all centurions in a legion was the *primus pilus* (or primi-pilus), head of the first century of the first cohort. He wielded more actual power than the tribunes. Beneath him were his *primi ordines,* all in the first cohorts, followed by the centurions of the remaining cohorts, serving as *pilus prior, pilus posterior, princeps prior, princeps posterior, hastatus prior*, and *hastatus posterior.* An *optio* or aide, selected for the post, was given to every centurion, and could be promoted to the centurionate if he performed well.

Above the centurions were the tribunes and the *praefectus castrorum,* or the prefect of the camp. The tribunes numbered six in the legion but only rarely saw combat, as they came from the Equestrian class, were young and served in the army only in the hope of bettering themselves politically. The senior tribune, a member of the senatorial class (*tribunus laticlavius*), viewed his time in the legions as a necessary step in the CURSUS HONORUM or government bureaucracy. Whereas the tribunes were at the start of their careers, the *praefectus castrorum* had already labored for many years as a *primus pilus.* As prefect of the camp, he headed the entire legion in the absence of the legate (commanding general) or senior tribune and had the respect of every soldier of every cohort.

The officers of the legion were supported by a large staff. Business and administration was the duty of clerks under the authority of the *cornicularius.* Accounts, pay, supplies, personnel records, and transfers all had to be kept in perfect order, as chaos would result from a major breakdown. Finally, the legions also possessed specialists and cavalry. Special soldiers, who had such needed skills as engineering, writing, and surveying, formed a unique corps within the legions. As they were needed to fulfill the tasks of building roads, selecting camps, or composing reports, from the time of Hadrian they became known as *immunes,* because of their immunity to regular service.

Armor and weapons of Roman legions of the time of Constantine the Great, from the Arch of Constantine *(Hulton/Getty Archive)*

The Romans never used massed cavalry, but every legion had its own corps of riders. Attached probably to the headquarters and under the command of an *optio equitum*, the horsemen numbered some 120. Their value in the field derived from their mobility and skill as scouts. Against heavier or more dangerous cavalry, such as the Parthians, they could be liabilities.

Life for a soldier was never easy, for punishments were always handed out mercilessly, and there was the danger of sudden and unexpected campaigning. Some postings were better than others in the empire. The legions in Syria in 69 C.E. were induced to revolt partly because of rumors that they were going to be transferred from their comfortable Syrian environment to Germany.

Length of service in the first century C.E. was 20 years, as compared to 26 for the navy, 25 for the auxiliaries and 16 for the PRAETORIAN GUARD. Pay was always a point of contention with the soldiers, and mutinies occurred (in 5 and in 14 C.E., for example) as they demanded better reward for incessant fighting. From the first century B.C.E. to the time of Domitian, pay was 225 denarii; from Domitian's reign to that of Septimius SEVERUS, 300 denarii; under Severus around 450 denarii; and under CARACALLA, 675 denarii.

Increased disorder surrounded payments for the remaining imperial era. Centurions received a higher amount according to seniority and rank within the centurionate. Upon retirement, a soldier received a payment (3,000 denarii in the time of Augustus) and a plot of land. Colonies throughout the Roman Empire were populated with former soldiers, each having gained his sum of money from the *aerarium militare* (the military treasury) and the *praemia militiae* (military retirement fund).

LEGIONARY CAMPS

In early Roman history, legions did not serve on a permanent basis and there was thus no need for any permanent encampments. As the empire was established, however, legions became stationed in distant provinces, many of them barely pacified. Longer term camps were soon needed, followed by permanent forts and fortresses. Winter camps (*hiberna*) and summer camps (*castra aestiva*) were used initially, with greater defenses constructed for the winter camps. Eventually, permanent camps were erected, termed *castra stativa*.

There were two basic types of *castra*, the Polybian and the Hyginian. The Polybian camp is so named from the description of Roman *castra* by Polybius in the second century B.C.E. The *castra* he described could accommodate two entire legions, along with cavalry, supplies, and auxiliary troops. In all, it could hold more than 16,000 soldiers and 1,800 cavalry. The Hyginian camp was named after Hyginus, a writer of the imperial era, and his work *De Munitionibus Castrorum* (On the defenses of camps). This type of camp could hold three legions as well as auxiliary troops, for a total of 40,000 troops. While larger and better defended than the Polybian *castra*, the Hyginian *castra* were still very similar in shape and basic design. Both camps were square or rectangular, with the *praetorium* resting at their center and a space between the tents and the ramparts (the *intervallum*) that safeguarded the tents from missile attack should the camp be besieged. The essential requirement for any Roman camp was that it be surveyed and erected with the greatest possible speed and efficiency. For that reason, each camp was largely identical to any other camp, with only minor modifications allowed for geography or specific military circumstances.

The need for the garrisoning of permanent camps in the provinces and especially along the provincial frontiers led to the rise of standing forts and fortresses. The fort was a camp used by auxiliaries and some legionnaires and generally was considerably smaller than a fortress. The latter was used as a garrison for a legion. In the first and second centuries C.E., both types of camps relied upon the traditional square or rectangular shape for the encampment. As the forts and fortresses were intended to be long-standing structures, however, a number of modifications were made in defenses, size, and internal composition.

The permanent camp was given strengthened defenses, including significantly more reliable perimeters. These might include extra pits and stakes, deadly hedges of sticks, thorns, and branches, and additional towers and stronger gates. The towers might also be equipped with *ballistae* and other projectiles. The defenses alone made the capture of a fort or fortress an ambitious undertaking for an enemy, and even a large enemy force faced many challenges in storming a Roman fort that was defended with determination.

Early forts and fortresses were constructed of wood, but practical experience in Germania and Britannia prompted engineers to build forts out of stone. Additionally, tents were replaced by more formal barracks, and warehouses, granaries, storerooms, armories, and prison rooms were all added. The permanent nature of the installation also prompted a change in the living and working arrangement of the commander. While in the *castra* a general might be housed in a *praetorium*, in the fort or fortress, a commander used two sets of quarters. The *praetorium* became his personal residence, and the day-to-day business of the command was centered in the *principia*, or headquarters. The *principia* also housed the standards of the legion, in a shrine, the *sacellum*. Baths were also installed in fortresses for the use of the soldiers, as were amphitheaters. The latter were built for entertainments, but they also doubled as drill yards. When well supplied, the legionary fortress was very much like a self-sufficient city. Examples of these have been found all over Europe, especially in Germany and in Britain. As many of the legions were permanently stationed on some frontier, many veterans chose to retire lived near the camps.

THE AUXILIA

From the days of the Republic, Rome had utilized the armies of its client states and federated tribes, as well as the legions, for the defense of the empire. These troops were the *auxilia*, or auxiliaries, of the imperial army.

Under Augustus, recruitments were a major part of the legionary system in the more reliable provinces, such as Germania, Africa, and the Danube. The possibility of full Roman citizenship after 25 years of service was a great enticement. Basically, the *auxilia* served on the frontiers, patrolling, watching, holding the *limes* (border), and acting as support to the legions in battle.

There were three kinds of unit in the auxiliaries: *alae* or cavalry, infantry, and mixed formations of the two. The *alae* (from the Latin for "wing") normally served on the flanks in an engagement, as the Romans liked to secure their infantry in the middle and then have horsemen available to exploit any break in the enemy line. Auxiliary horsemen numbered 512 per *quingenaria* (unit), divided into 16 *turmae*. Infantry was categorized into bodies of soldiers either 500 strong (*cohors quingenaria*) or 1,000 strong (*cohors miliaria*), broken down into centuries. Here the auxiliaries most closely resembled the legions, for they had centurions and an internal organization like that of the legion. Equipment was similar, as was weaponry, but in a pitched battle with an obstinate foe, no legate would ever risk victory by depending solely upon these troops.

Mixed *auxilia* of infantry and cavalry, the *cohors equitata*, were for an unclear purpose. Aside from the aid that they gave their infantry counterparts, the mounted elements of any cohort were posted with the regular *alae* in a conflict and were less well equipped. Their numbers probably varied, for the *quingenaria* and *miliaria*: 480 infantry and 128 cavalry for the former, and 800 infantry and 256 cavalry for the latter.

At the start of the empire, it was policy never to use an auxiliary formation in its own province, for fear of divided loyalties and poor discipline. While such a prohibition grew lax over the years, it was still common to see Spaniards in the East and Germans in Britannia. As the pool of recruits from the more Romanized provinces dried up, it became necessary to find troops from the more remote areas of the empire. This led to an increased barbarization and Germanization of the Roman world.

THE LATE EMPIRE

Throughout the history of the Roman Empire, the role of the legions in determining the succession and the very direction of Rome's destiny was considerable. Starting in 69 C.E., through the second and third centuries, governors and generals were proclaimed by their troops. Civil wars followed with such appalling regularity that no emperor could hope to rule effectively without the support of the legions stationed in various parts of the Roman world. The third-century crisis was made more severe by the constant upheavals of the soldiery.

DIOCLETIAN and later CONSTANTINE took drastic steps to curb such practices. Along with the massive overhaul of the provincial system, came a reform of the imperial defenses. No longer would the legions be distributed to the provinces under command of a potentially ambitious governor. Henceforth, there were to be two divisions in the army, the LIMITANEI and the COMITATENSES.

The *limitanei* were to watch the frontiers only. They protected the borders, never moving from their area unless specifically ordered to do so in support of some other *limitanei* body that was threatened by attack. While the *limitanei* did not move, the *comitatenses*, the main field army near the emperor or under the command of his prefects, was always on the march. Each *comitatensis* was composed of *legiones palatinae* (the PALATINI) and the *vexillationes palatinae*. The legions, as they had been known, were replaced by the 1,000–1,500-man *legiones palatinae*, grouped five at a time into a *comitatenses*. Joining them was the cavalry, now called the *vexillationes*, probably numbering the same. Their increased importance in Roman warfare reflected the change of tactics in dealing with swarming barbarian horsemen such as the Huns (*see* ADRIANOPLE). Auxiliaries called the *auxilia palatina*, in cohorts of about 500 men, continued to exist.

Discipline in the armies of the later Roman Empire was markedly inferior to that of earlier eras. Germanic troops, chaos in the West and a deterioration of the social system, all contributed to the decline in the capacities of the soldiers. The emergence of the powerful MAGISTER MILITUM aided the breakdown of military unity. As the titles *magister equitum, peditum*, or *militum* passed into the hands of German generals, the fate of the West was sealed. In the East, Emperor LEO made certain that his domain did not fall prey to the barbarians, by recruiting his forces from the provinces of the East and relying upon his Isaurian lieutenant, ZENO, to lead them.

TABLE OF KNOWN IMPERIAL LEGIONS

The following are the legions that are known to have been recruited and to have served during the imperial era. The legions were reorganized at the command of Augustus at the end of the civil wars. There was some confusion in the numbering system, as new legions were often given the same number as already existing ones, so that there might be several legions with the number I or III, for example. If a legion was destroyed, its number was retired permanently. The most famous example of this was the loss under General Varus in Germania at the Teutoburg Forest of Legions XVII, XVIII, and XIX in 9 C.E. These legions were never replaced. The multiplicity of numbers was prevented from becoming impossibly confusing by the use of *cognomina*, or nicknames, for many legions. Some *cognomina* were obvious reflections of locations where a legion served (e.g., *Germanica* for Germania), where it campaigned (e.g., *Parthica*), or as a tribute to some particular service (e.g., *Fretensis*, denoting some action at sea, or action in battle, such as Actium or Naulochus).

I **Adiutrix:** Raised by Emperor Nero in 68 from a force of marines at Misenum, the troops subsequently received formal establishment under General Galba. They fought for Otho at the battle of BEDRIACUM (68) and distinguished themselves by their capture of the eagle of the Legio XXI Rapax. The legion later served in Hispania, Germania, Dacia, and along the Danube. It was also nicknamed Pia Fidelis.

I **Germanica:** A legion first constituted during the civil wars (perhaps by Julius Caesar himself in 48). Originally known as Legio I Augusta, the legion was reformed after a disastrous performance in Hispania in 19 B.C.E. It was disbanded after participating in the revolt of Civilis in 69.

I **Italica:** Raised around 67 by Nero, it was stationed to Gaul in 68 and fought for Vitellius in the civil war. For its misplaced loyalty, it was sent to Moesia.

I **Macriana:** Also titled Liberatrix, it was raised by Clodius Macer in Africa in his revolt against Nero in 68. Following the establishment of Galba as emperor and the death of Macer, the legion was disbanded. It was perhaps reconstituted briefly during the reign of Vitellius in 69.

I **Minervia:** Raised by Emperor Domitian in 83 C.E. and named at first Flavia Minerva, after the ruler's favorite goddess, the legion was first stationed at Bonn. It subsequently received the title of Pia Fidelis Domitiana for loyalty in 89 during the revolt of Saturninus. The titles Flavia and Domitiana were dropped after Domitian's assassination. The legion later fought in Trajan's Dacian War and Marcus Aurelius's Parthian War.

I **Parthica:** Raised around 197 C.E. by Septimius Severus for his campaign in the East.

II **Adiutrix:** Raised by Vespasian from the units of sailors stationed at Ravenna to serve against the armies of Vitellius during the civil war in 69, it was approved officially as a legion on March 7, 70, and was stationed to Britannia. It later served on the Danube, in Pannonia Inferior. The legion also bore the title of Pia Fidelis.

II **Augusta:** Raised probably by Octavian, it served in Hispania and then Germania from 14 C.E. It later served in the Britannia campaign in 43. It bore as its legionary symbol the pegasus, for reasons that are not known.

II **Italica:** Raised around 165 by Marcus Aurelius in Italia for service in Noricum. It also bore the title of Pia Fidelis.

II **Parthica:** Raised around 197 by Septimius Severus for service in the East. It was later posted to Albanum and held the distinction of being the emperor's personal legion. In this capacity it journeyed across the empire.

II **Traiana** *Fortis:* Raised around 101 by Trajan for use in the Dacian War, the legion earned the title Fortis, or strong. Moved to Syria, it was later transferred to Egypt and was posted at Nicopolis.

III **Augusta:** Raised most likely by Octavian c. 41–40 B.C.E. for service in the civil wars, it was posted to Africa.

III **Cyrenaica:** Raised either by Marc Antony or Lepidus sometime before 30 B.C.E., it was posted to Egypt and shared a *castra* (camp) with the Legio XXII Deiotariana at Nicopolis.

III **Gallica:** Raised perhaps by Julius Caesar in 48 B.C.E., it fought at Munda (45) and Philippi (42) and then was posted to Syria, where it was active under Antony until Actium (31). The legion remained in Syria until 68, when it transferred by Nero to Moesia. Its symbol was the bull, an indication that its origins traced themselves to Caesar—owing to Caesar's claim of descent from Jupiter, a god whose symbol was the bull.

III **Italica:** Raised around 165 C.E. by Marcus Aurelius, it was stationed for a very long time in Raetia. In its early history, it was also called Legio III Concors (United).

III **Parthica:** Raised by Septimius Severus around 197 C.E., it was used for his campaign in the East.

IV **Flavia Felix:** The reconstituted IV Macedonica in 70 C.E., after it was disbanded following participation in the revolt of Civilis in 69. It later served in Dacia.

IV **Macedonica:** Raised perhaps by Caesar in 48 B.C.E., it served in Macedonia from 47 to 44 and was then transferred to Italia in 44. During the civil war, it fought initially for Marc Antony and then defected to Octavian during the battle of Forum Gallorum in 43. The battle record was subsequently distinguished during the civil war, and the legion fought possibly at Actium in 31. It was later posted to Hispania and to Germania. In 69, it joined the revolt of Civilis and was disbanded after Civilis's defeat. Vespasian reconstituted the legion as the IV Flavia Felix. Its symbol was the bull, a sign of its origins at the command of Caesar.

IV **Scythica:** Raised perhaps by Marc Antony around 30 B.C.E., the legion served in Macedonia and Moesia. It was moved around 55 to Syria.

V **Alaudae:** Raised by Julius Caesar around 52 B.C.E., it was constituted from among Gallic levies in Narbonensis. The troops fought for Caesar at Pharsalus (48), Thapsus (46) and Munda (45). It was probably disbanded by Antony in 44 and reconstituted, remaining in the service of Antony all the way to Actium in 31. Augustus posted it to

Hispania and then moved it to Germania in 19 B.C.E. In 70 C.E., after participating in the rebellion of Civilis, the legion may have been disbanded by Vespasian. There is a possibility that it was transferred instead to the Dacian frontier and was annihilated in 86 under the command of Cornelius Fuscus.

V   Macedonica: Raised perhaps by Octavian around 41 B.C.E., it fought at Actium in 31 and was posted to Macedonia. In 9 C.E., it was transferred to Moesia. There it probably took part in Trajan's campaign against the Dacians.

VI   Ferrata: Raised probably by Julius Caesar in 52 B.C.E., it served in Gaul and then throughout Caesar's campaigns in the civil war, including action at Phrasalus (48), Alexandria (47), Zela (46), and Munda (45). It was later under Marc Antony until Actium (31). During the civil war of 68–69, it earned the title Fidelis Constans (Firm and Steady) for its loyalty to Severus. The legion was later posted to Syria.

VI   Victrix: Raised by Octavian around 41, it fought for his cause in the civil war and was then posted to Hispania, earning an early title of Hispaniensis. Around 69, it was transferred to the German frontier and was granted the title Pia Fidelis Domitiana for its loyalty to Domitian in 89. Where it received the title Victrix is uncertain.

VII   Raised around 59 B.C.E. by Julius Caesar, the legion had the early title of Macedonica, a reference perhaps to its origins or its posting from 12 to 1 B.C.E. It fought at Pharsalus (48) but was disbanded and reconstituted by Octavian in 45. Throughout the civil war period, it fought in many actions for Octavian. Posted to Dalmatia in 9 C.E., it earned the title Claudia Pia Fidelis for remaining loyal to Claudius in 42 during the revolt of Camillus Scribonianus. It was later transferred to Moesia. The legionary symbol was the bull, a sign of its origins under Julius Caesar.

VII   Gemina: Raised by Vespasian in 70 C.E., it was formed out of the VII Galbiana (or Hispana). It later served in Moesia and Hispania.

VII   Hispana: Raised by Galba in 70 C.E., the legion was initially known as Legio VII Hispana and Legio VII Galbiana. It journeyed to Rome with Galba in 68 and then fought for the Flavian cause under its legate Antonius Primus. The losses it received at Cremona were so severe, however, that the surviving cohorts were disbanded and the legion reconstituted under the title VII Gemina.

VIII   Augusta: Raised by Julius Caesar around 59 B.C.E., it fought in Gaul until 49 and then at Pharsalus in 48 and Thapsus in 46. Disbanded in 46 or 45, it was reconstituted by Octavian in 44 and fought at Forum Gallorum and Mutina in 43 and then

Philippi in 42. Until 31, it served under Octavian and then received posting to Moesia perhaps before 6 C.E. In 70, it was sent to Germania Superior.

IX   Hispania: This legion claimed its origins to the IX Legion that served with distinction under Julius Caesar. The remaining cohorts of the IX were disbanded in 46 or 45 B.C.E., and it remains uncertain whether they were reconstituted into the IX Hispana or whether Octavian recruited an entirely new unit in 41–40 B.C.E. The new legion fought throughout the civil war until Actium (31 B.C.E.) and then earned its title Hispana from a decade of service in Hispania (30–19 B.C.E.). It was then posted to Pannonia, Africa, and Britannia. The later history is obscure, although it is possible it was destroyed during the Jewish rebellion (132–35 C.E.) or in Armenia (161).

X   Fretensis: A legion that claimed roots to the famed X Legion in the army of Julius Caesar. It was formed sometime before 59 B.C.E. and served with nearly legendary distinction in Caesar's Gallic Wars (58–49 B.C.E.) and then in the civil war, with action at Pharsalus (48) and Thapsus (46). Disbanded around 45, it was perhaps reconstituted by Octavian around 41–40 B.C.E. and possibly fought at Mylae and Naulochus, as well as Actium in 31, engagements that would be the basis for the title Fretensis (denoting action at sea) and the symbols of the legion, including a dolphin and galley. From around 27 B.C.E., it was posted to Syria and later fought in the Jewish rebellion (66–70 C.E.) and was stationed in the destroyed Jerusalem.

X   Gemina: Raised by Lepidus in 44 B.C.E., it is possible that this legion claimed descent from the famed X Legion of Caesar that was disbanded around 45 B.C.E. As the name *Gemina* implies, the legion was most likely an amalgamation of cohorts from at least two legions, one of which may have been the X Fretensis. In any event, it served under Marc Antony from 41 to 31 B.C.E., including action at Actium in 31. After the end of the civil war, it was posted to Hispania, remaining there for most of the first century C.E. It was later transferred to Pannonia. The legion also bore the titles of Pia Fidelis Domitiana for remaining loyal to Domitian in 89 and Equestris (mounted).

XI   Raised by Octavian in 41–40 B.C.E., it served in his armies until 31 B.C.E. and the battle of Actium. It subsequently served in Dalmatia and Germania. In 42, it earned the title Claudia Pia Fidelis for its loyalty to Claudius during the revolt of Camillus Scribonianus.

XII   Fulminata: Originally a legion raised by Julius Caesar, it fought in the Gallic Wars from 58 to 49 B.C.E. and then at Pharsalus in 48. Disbanded in 45, it was reconstituted by Lepidus in 44–43 B.C.E. and then fought for Marc Antony until the battle of Actium. It was posted primarily in Greece under Antony. Under Augustus, it was sent to Egypt; later, it was posted to Syria. In 66 C.E., during the Jewish rebellion, the legion lost its eagle, but perhaps recovered it later in the war. The name and symbol of the legion, Fulminata (derived from the Latin for lightning bolt), was taken from the perhaps apocryphal event in 172 during the war against the Germanic Quadi people when the legion was assisted by a sudden rain and lightning storm.

XIII **Gemina:** Raised by Octavian around 41–40 B.C.E. and, as the name implies, formed out of the remnants of two different legions, it served Octavian throughout the civil war and was later posted to Illyricum before 9 C.E. After that it was sent to Germania and then Pannonia, where it took part in the Dacian campaign under Emperor Trajan.

XIV **Gemina:** Probably raised by Octavian in 41–40 B.C.E., it was an amalgamation of the remnants of at least two older disbanded legions. It fought for Octavian through Actium and was then posted to Illyricum sometime before 9 C.E. It was moved to Mainz and then took part in the campaign in Britannia. Posted to the island, it earned the title Martia Victrix for its action against the rebel Queen Boudicca (60–61 C.E.).

XV **Apollinaris:** Raised by Octavian in 41–40 B.C.E., it served throughout the civil war and was perhaps at the battle of Actium. Subsequently stationed in Illyricum, it was transferred to Syria and fought during the Jewish rebellion (66–70) in Judaea. From the early second century, it was posted to Cappadocia.

XV **Primigenia:** This late legion was first raised either in 39 C.E. by Gaius Caligula for his German campaign of around 42 or by Claudius for his campaign in Britannia. The legion was annihilated during the revolt of Civilis in 70.

XVI **Flavia Firma:** The legion reconstituted around 71 C.E. by Vespasian following the disbanding of the Legio XVI Gallica following the revolt of Civilis. The new legion was posted initially to Cappadocia and then to the East, where it took part in the Parthian campaign of Trajan. The name was derived from its origins (*flavia*) and its steadfastness (*firma*).

XVI **Gallica:** Raised by Octavian in 41–40 B.C.E., it was posted after the civil war to the Rhine, around 30 B.C.E. During the reign of Claudius, the legion was moved from Germania Superior to Germania Inferior, where it proved unreliable to the Flavians during the revolt of Civilis in 70. As a result, Vespasian disbanded it and reconstituted it as the Legio XVI Flavia Firma.

XVII: Raised by Octavian around 41–40 B.C.E., the legion was eventually posted to the Rhine. There, with the Legio XVIII and Legio XIX, the XVII was annihilated by the Germans at the Teutoburg Forest in 9 C.E. As was Roman custom, the legion was not reconstituted, especially after the loss of its eagle. The eagle was recovered around 16.

XVIII: Raised by Octavian around 41–40 B.C.E., it was sent after the civil wars to the Rhine. There, in 9 C.E., along with the Legio XVII and Legio XIX, the XVIII was annihilated by the Germans at the Teutoburg Forest. As was Roman custom, the legion was not reconstituted. The eagle of the legion was recovered in 41.

XIX: Raised by Octavian around 41–40 B.C.E., the legion was posted after 30 B.C.E. to the Rhine. There, with the Legio XVII and Legio XVIII, the XIX was annihilated by the Germans at the Teutoburg Forest in 9 C.E. The legion was not reconstituted, in keeping with Roman custom. The eagle was recovered in 15 from the Bructeri.

XX **Valeria Victrix:** Raised by Octavian perhaps in 41–40 B.C.E. or after the battle of Actium, it was posted to Hispania after the civil war and then to Illyricum. Following the disaster of the Teutoburg Forest in 9 C.E., the legion was posted to Germania. It later took part in the campaign in Britannia in 43 and earned the title of Victrix for its actions in the field against Boudicca.

XXI **Rapax:** Raised by Augustus sometime after 25 B.C.E., it was assigned to Raetia before 6 C.E. and moved to Germania in 9 following the disaster at Teutoburg. The legion remained in Germania until around 90, when, as it had proven unreliable in 89 during the Saturninus revolt against Domitian, it was transferred to the Danube. The legion was probably destroyed in 92 while serving on the Dacian frontier. Its nickname was taken from a bird of prey, "grasping" its victim.

XXII **Deiotariana:** Formed sometime before 25 B.C.E. by Augustus, the legion was recruited from the kingdom of Galatia, which had been taken over by Rome, and whose king, Deiotarus, had died in 40. The legion was formally constituted after the formation of the Legio XXI Rapax. It served throughout its history in Egypt, although it took part in the Jewish War of 132–35, during which it received severe losses and was disbanded.

XXII **Primigenia:** A legion raised at the same time as the Legio XV Primigenia, it was created either by Gaius Caligula for his German campaign in 39 or Claudius for his campaign in Britannia in 43. Posted originally to Germania, it was transferred to the Danube frontier following the civil war in 69 for its support of Vitellius against the Flavians. Nevertheless, in 89, the legion remained loyal to

Domitian against Saturninus and was granted the title Pia Fidelis Domitiana.

XXX **Ulpia Victrix:** Raised by Trajan around 101 C.E., the legion was intended to fight in the Dacian Wars. Following the campaign, the troops were transferred to Germania Inferior.

See also ENGINEERING.

Suggested Readings: Blois, Lukas de. *The Roman Army and Politics in the First Century before Christ.* Amsterdam: J.C. Gieben, 1987; Campbell, J. B. *The Emperor and the Roman Army, 31 B.C.E.–C.E. 235.* Oxford, U.K.: Clarendon Press, 1984; Connolly, Peter. *Greece and Rome at War.* Englewood Cliffs, N.J.: Prentice-Hall, 1981; Davies, Roy W. *Service in the Roman Army.* Edinburgh: Edinburgh University Press with the Publications Board of the University of Durham, 1989; Davison, David P. *The Barracks of the Roman Army from the first to third Centuries A.D.: A Comparative Study of the Barracks from Fortresses, Forts, and Fortlets with an Analysis of Building Types and Construction, Stabling, and Garrisons.* Oxford, U.K.: B.A.R., 1989; Evans, Robert F. *Soldiers of Rome: Praetorians and Legionnaires.* Cabin John: Seven Locks Press, 1986; Ferrill, Arther. *The Fall of the Roman Empire: The Military Explanation.* London: Thames and Hudson, 1986; Fitz, Jeno. *Honorific Titles of Roman Military Units in the 3rd Century.* Bonn: Habelt, 1983; Grant, Michael. *The Army of the Caesars.* New York: Charles Scribner's Sons, 1974; ———. *The Fall of the Roman Empire.* New York: Collier, 1990; Isaac, Benjamin H. *The Limits of Empire: the Roman Army in the East.* New York: Oxford University Press, 1990; Julius Caesar. *The Civil War.* New York: Penguin, 1967; ———. *The Conquest of Gaul.* New York: Penguin, 1982; Parker, H. M. D. *The Roman Legions.* New York: Barnes & Noble, 1993; Peterson, Daniel. *The Roman Legions Recreated in Colour Photographs.* London: Windrow & Greene Ltd., 1992; Rankov, Dr. Boris, and Richard Hook. *The Praetorian Guard.* London: Osprey, 1994; Sekunda, Nick, and Angus McBride. *Republican Roman Armies 200–104 B.C.* London: Osprey, 1996; Simkins, Michael, and Ronald Embleton. *The Roman Army from Caesar to Trajan.* London: Osprey, 1984; ———. *The Roman Army from Hadrian to Constantine.* London: Osprey, 1979; Speidel, Michael. *Roman Army Studies.* Amsterdam: J. C. Gieben, 1984; Warry, John. *Warfare in the Classical World.* Norman, Oklahoma: University of Oklahoma Press, 1995; Webster, Graham. *The Roman Imperial Army of the First and Second Centuries A.D.* 3d ed.; London: A & C Black, 1985.

lemures Roman spirits or ghosts of the dead, who played a major role in beliefs concerning death and the disposition of the soul in the afterlife. According to tradition, the lemures wandered the earth to torment the living. They haunted crossroads or returned to the homes in which they died.

The belief in lemures originated from two possible sources: the spirits of wicked persons, called *larvae*, who were condemned to roam the world, or those unfortunate persons who did not receive a proper burial and came back to frighten their surviving relatives. Both forms could be driven off with ceremonies held for that purpose or as part of the festival of Lemuria, which was celebrated every May.

See also DEATH.

Lentulus, Gnaeus Cornelius (d. 25 C.E.) *Consul in 14 B.C.E. and a victorious general during the reign of Augustus (27 B.C.E.–14 C.E.) known to historians as Lentulus the Augur*

Lentulus emerged from honored but poor origins to hold vast riches and considerable influence. After the consulship, he served as proconsul of Asia (2–1 B.C.E.) and later defeated the Getae, earning a triumphal insignia. In 14 C.E., Lentulus accompanied Drusus the Younger to Pannonia, where the legions were in a state of mutiny. It was the hope of Tiberius that he would serve as an adviser and support to the young prince, but his presence infuriated the soldiers, who rushed upon him. Drusus saved him from certain death and pulled him out of harm's way, so Lentulus escaped with only a minor injury. He remained a friend to Tiberius, one of the few that the grim ruler would have in his lifetime.

He received the position of augur and was still in office in 22. Two years later, despite his age, he faced an accusation of plotting to murder the emperor. The Senate was horrified. Lentulus laughed out loud at the charge, and Tiberius paid him the greatest compliment by declaring: "I am not worthy to live if Lentulus hates me as well." Only Seneca had harsh words for Lentulus, calling him rich and greedily stupid, so slow in speech that, miserly though he was, he parted with words with greater reluctance than with money. Dio wrote of his mild disposition and Tacitus of his patience in bearing his early penniless state. He left his money to Tiberius.

Lentulus Gaetulicus, Gnaues Cornelius (d. 39 C.E.) *Consul in 26 C.E. and son of the consul of 1 B.C.E.*

Lentulus served for nearly 10 years as the legate of GERMANIA Superior. He earned the love of his troops with his genuine goodness and with the mildness of his discipline, a favor that spread to the legions of Germania Inferior under the command of his father-in-law, Lucius Apronius. This legionary devotion saved his career and his life. A long-time associate of SEJANUS, Lentulus was indicted in 34 for having supported the fallen prefect. In a letter written to Tiberius, Lentulus defended his alliance with Sejanus as having originated with the emperor, therefore not of his own will. Mindful of Lentulus's position with the Rhine legions, Tiberius halted all attempts at prosecution. Thus Lentulus was the only member of

Sejanus's powerful circle not to be executed. Left unmolested at his post, Lentulus remained in Germany until 39 C.E., when he became involved in a plot to assassinate Gaius Caligula at Moguntiacum (Mainz). Caligula heard of the plot and put him to death. Lentulus was also a writer of erotic poetry.

Leo I (c. 401–474 C.E.) *Emperor of the East from 457 to 474 C.E.; called "the Great"*

Leo emerged from obscurity to rule the East with a firm hand, while the Western Empire faced its final collapse. He was born in Thrace, entering the service of the Alan MAGISTER MILITUM, ASPAR. Under the patronage of this powerful German he eventually commanded the legion of the *Mattiarii seniores*. In 457 the Emperor Marcian died, leaving no heir. While Anthemius was supported by the Senate at Constantinople, he lacked the approval of Aspar, who was searching for a more pliable candidate. He chose Leo, forced the government to accept him, and had him crowned on February 7, at the Hebdomon Palace in the capital. All that Aspar hoped to achieve was soon ruined by this handpicked ruler.

Leo initially allowed Aspar to remain supreme in the court and in the East, as the *magister* had no rival. His son Ardaburius was named *magister militum* for the Eastern Empire as well. Leo, however, had witnessed the catastrophic effect of having Germans and other barbarians in the imperial administration. He was determined to avoid that during his reign and therefore set out against them slowly and carefully. Leo initiated a program to reduce Aspar's influence and to find a suitable counterbalance, understanding the strength of the Germans both militarily and politically in his domain. The provinces in Asia Minor provided the first part of the solution. Leo recruited soldiers from all over Anatolia but focused especially on the wild and dangerous warriors from ISAURIA. They formed the bulk of his new army, and their chief Tarasicodissa (later called ZENO) proved a reliable opponent for Aspar. Leo married Zeno to his daughter Aelia Ariadne (in 466 or 467), and by 468, Zeno was probably a *magister militum* in his own right.

Meanwhile, a massive effort was made against the Vandal King GEISERIC in Africa. This last attempt at a unified war between the Eastern and Western Empires on one side and the Vandals on the other was not entrusted to Aspar but to Leo's brother-in-law, BASILISCUS. The decision to name Basiliscus to this exalted command came as result of the prodding of Empress Aelia Verina and the determination to isolate Aspar. It was a poor selection. Launched in 468, the combined operation was a disaster brought about by Basiliscus's sheer incompetence and by Geiseric's brilliance. The treasury at Constantinople was nearly emptied, and the Western Empire lost its last hope for recovery. The disastrous expedition did not slow the determination of Leo to press ahead with Aspar's fall. Zeno served as consul and was sent to repulse a Hunnic invasion of Thrace sometime in 470. In his absence, however, Aspar insisted that Leo fulfill a long-standing promise, namely, to raise one of his sons, Patricius, to the rank of Caesar and to wed him to Princess Leontia. Leo had to agree but the situation worsened when Aspar's supporters tried to win over the Isaurians. Zeno returned at once from Thrace in 471; sensing danger, Aspar and Ardaburius tried to flee to the safety of the church. They could not manage an escape, and both died at the hands of the palace eunuchs. Patricius got away with only a wound.

With the great Germanic influence removed from Constantinople, Leo was able to recognize the position of Aspar's barbarian allies. He allowed them to hold territories and titles but knew that they no longer threatened his power. Stable as he was, Leo also tried to reorganize the West. He named Anthemius to the throne there in 467 and Julius Nepos in 474. He also defended Christian orthodoxy, using Aspar's Arianism as a useful weapon in bringing about his downfall. Zeno and Ariadne had a son, Leo II. In October 473, Leo elevated that young prince to the rank of Augustus and then died on February 3, 474.

Leo II (467–474 C.E.) *Grandson of* LEO I

The son of the Isaurian MAGISTER MILITUM, ZENO, and Aelia Ariadne, Leo was born in 467 at Constantinople, and in October of 473 was elevated to the rank of co-ruler of the Eastern Empire. When LEO I died on February 3, 474, Leo II was proclaimed his successor and received the crown on February 9. True power rested in the hands of his father, as the throne actually passed into Zeno's hands on November 17, 474, when Leo II died, probably from an illness.

Leo I (d. 461 C.E.) *Pope from 440 to 461 C.E.*

One of the two popes, with St. Gregory I (r. 590–604), to be given the title "the Great." Little is known with certainty about his early years. He was born in Rome, served as a deacon, and was a staunch opponent of Pelagianism. While serving as a deacon, he wielded considerable influence during the pontificates of St. Celestine I (422–432) and Sixtus III (432–440) and was elected the successor to Sixtus while away in Gaul. He was consecrated on September 29, 440, and took as the primary policy of his long pontificate the aggrandizement of the papacy throughout Christendom, the full recognition of the primacy of the bishop of Rome as the successor of St. Peter. He maintained the obedience of those dioceses around him and worked to secure his jurisdiction over the sees in Gaul (France) and Spain. He was also successful in winning the trust of the African bishops by providing them with advice and regulations aimed at curbing various irregularities then afflicting the church there. An important development was Leo's obtaining from Emperor Valentinian III (r. 425–455) a rescript granting him full jurisdiction over the West. He thus received vast powers in the Western Empire, and, although his authority was not recognized in the East, such was the force of his personality and the heightened gravitas of the papacy that Leo was inexorably drawn into the major theological crisis that had erupted in the Eastern Empire over the nature of Christ. He sent his famous Tome to Flavian of Constantinople on June 13, 449, condemning Eutyches and elucidating clearly the important teaching that Christ had two natures in his one Person. Three legates were sent to the Council of Ephesus (449), where the pope fully expected the Tome to be read. Instead, it was rejected; Eutyches was fully restored to favor; and Flavian deposed as patriarch. Leo called the Council of Ephesus the Latrocinium, or Robber Council, and used his full authority to reverse its acts. At the Council of Chalcedon (451), his Tome was read and given full approval; the decrees of Ephesus were rescinded; and the doctrine concerning the Person of Christ formally proclaimed. Chalcedon marked a major triumph for Leo, particularly the declaration by the council members that "Peter has spoken through Leo. . . ." In keeping with his principle concerning the Roman see, however, he rejected Canon 28 of the Chalcedonian decrees granting broad patriarchal rights to Constantinople.

Leo was also of enormous help to the increasingly weak imperial government. When, in 452, Attila the Hun was poised to sack all of Italy, the pope bravely met him at Mantua and convinced him to withdraw. Three years later, the Vandals under King Geiseric invaded, and Leo greeted the king at the gates of Rome. While unable to prevent the sack of the city, he did win from Geiseric the promise not to burn or massacre. Leo died on November 10, 461, and was buried in St. Peter's. Of his writings, there are extant 143 letters and 96 sermons. He may have contributed prayers to both the Leonine and Gelasian Sacramentaries.

Lepcis Magna   Also known as Leptis Magna; this seaport was one of the major cities of Roman AFRICA and, despite a flood in 1987, remains a very significant archaeological site. About 75 miles east of modern Tripoli, Lepcis Magna was founded by Phoenician traders as a colony perhaps around 600 B.C.E. When Rome conquered the Carthaginians in 146 B.C.E., it assumed control over all of Africa, and in 46 B.C.E., after the battle of Thapsus, Julius Caesar seized TRIPOLITANIA outright. Under Emperor Augustus (ruled 27 B.C.E.–14 C.E.) its position on the coast was improved by roads connecting with desert caravan routes into the interior. Carthaginian in origin, the city was allowed to maintain a local council, answerable to the magistrates of Rome.

Attempts were made to Romanize the inhabitants throughout the first century C.E., and a temple (one of three) was erected to *Roma et Augustus*, housing the IMPERIAL CULT. Roman architecture soon dominated, and both Latin and the native Punic tongues were used in official inscriptions. With little stress, Lepcis Magna was transformed rapidly into a Latin community, allowing all of the inhabitants to reap benefits from the resulting imperial favor. The title of MUNICIPIUM was given to Lepcis Magna at the end of the first century C.E. as a result of its prosperity. Continued building programs extended into the first and second centuries C.E., and then the city entered its Golden Age, the reward for having one of its own sons, Septimius SEVERUS, on the Roman throne. The city had a forum, temples, and markets, and economic advancement brought developmental freedom. Earlier, a temple to Magna Mater was built around 72 C.E., and a theater already had been erected by a wealthy citizen named Rufus in 1 C.E., containing columns of limestone (later replaced) and high vaulting.

With the start of the second century C.E. the ambitions of the architects increased to match the sizable capital available. No longer was limestone the normal medium of expression. Marble was imported and put to use. Although the Arch of Trajan (109–110 C.E.) was of limestone, the foremost achievement of the city at this time was the Baths of Hadrian, dedicated in 126/127 and fashioned out of marble. Based on the Trajanic baths in Rome, the Baths of Hadrian used the characteristic arrangement then in vogue. All of the proper rooms were included: the *frigidarium, natatio, caldarium*, and the *tepidarium* (see BATHS). Colonnades, mosaic-covered vaultings, and ingeniously crafted tubes and spaces for cool and hot air added refined touches.

Septimius Severus had left Lepcis Magna in 160 to pursue his political career. Throughout his reign (193–211 C.E.) Severus was generous to Africa and lavishly bestowed favors upon the city of his birth. Lepcis Magna (as Carthage and Utica) received wider rights under the IUS ITALICUM, befitting a Roman colony. Furthermore, his gifts of money and buildings changed the appearance of the city drastically. From the Baths of Hadrian was carved a grand road to the new harbor. Colonnades lined the route, and at an intersection there was a *nymphaeum*, complete with a magnificent fountain. Far larger, however, was the Severan Forum, 656 square feet in size, with high columns and a temple and basilica. The basilica was adorned with Corinthian columns. The small Hunting Baths were also erected in this era, distinct from the others by barrel vaulting. Out of gratitude to their mighty patron, and in honor of his visit in 203, the community hired artisans to carve the famous Arch of Severus, located near the Arch of Trajan. Their debt to Severus was considerable, and never again would the city enjoy such splendor, as the collapse of the empire took its toll.

Lepida, Aemilia (d. 36 C.E.)   *Married to Drusus (2), son of Germanicus, sometime around 29 C.E.*
Lepida proved utterly faithless, succumbing to the advances of SEJANUS, the ambitious PREFECT OF THE PRAETORIAN GUARD, who was plotting the destruction of

Drusus and Germanicus's entire family. Sejanus reportedly seduced Aemilia, and she went to Tiberius and accused her husband of numerous crimes, resulting in his dismissal from service at Capri, eventual arrest, imprisonment, and death (in 33). After the fall of Sejanus in 31 C.E., Aemilia was allowed to remain unpunished because of her family name. In 36, however, she was indicted for adultery with a slave. Knowing that her conviction was assured, she killed herself three years after the death of Drusus. There were references to her in the last books of Tacitus's *Annals*.

Lepida, Domitia (d. 54 C.E.) *Granddaughter of Marc Antony by Antonia (2); mother of Empress Messallina*

Long accustomed to the highest levels of Roman society, her brother was Gnaeus Domitius Ahenobarbus, and she was aunt to Nero, the sister-in-law of AGRIPPINA THE YOUNGER. In 41 C.E., she became the relative of Claudius when he married MESSALLINA. When the empress's scandalous behavior caused her downfall in 48, Lepida journeyed to the Gardens of Lucullus to be with her daughter in the last hours of her life. Although she apparently differed with Messallina over her actions, Tacitus remarked upon Lepida's loyalty during that tragic time. She remained a fixture of palace life during the remainder of Claudius's reign and found in Agrippina a cruel and bitter enemy, loathing her as well. Lepida considered herself the equal of Agrippina in age, beauty, wealth, and temper. To prove her claims she worked tirelessly to gain control of Nero. The battle between the women raged for years, even to the time when he gained the throne. In 54, Lepida was condemned for having used incantations against Agrippina and for threatening the peace with her slave gangs in Calabria. She was executed for her crimes.

Lepidus, Marcus Aemilius (1) (d. 13 B.C.E.) *Son of Marcus Aemilius Lepidus, the consul of 78 B.C.E.*

Lepidus used his family name and influence to reach high positions in the Late Republic. In 49 B.C.E., he served as *praetor* before throwing his support behind Julius Caesar in the Civil War with Pompey. As a reward he held a consulship in 46 and then, in 44, the governorship of Gallia Narbonensis and Hispania Citerior. When Caesar was assassinated in 44, Lepidus emerged as one of the most feared men in Roman politics. He was near Rome at the time of Caesar's murder and immediately allied himself with Marc ANTONY, rendering him great service in stabilizing the city. With Antony's help he assumed the office of PONTIFEX MAXIMUS, long held by Caesar, before returning to his provinces to prepare for the inevitable war.

It came in 43, and Antony, defeated at the battle of MUTINA, fled to Lepidus. Both men gathered together all available legions and marched on Rome. They were met

by Octavian (AUGUSTUS) in northern Italy. The three formed the SECOND TRIUMVIRATE in October of that year, thus dividing the world between them. Lepidus retained control of Gallia Narbonensis and Hispania Citerior but gained Hispania Ulterior and held a second consulship in 42. By that time, however, the true power was in the hands of Antony and Octavian. Thus, after the battle of PHILIPPI in 42, a new separation of the provinces was made. Lepidus lost his European possessions and was granted only Africa. He held these territories until 36, living in the shadow of the other triumvirs.

Octavian had need of him in 36, to bring reinforcements to Italy for use against Sextus Pompey, the pirate son of Pompey. Lepidus arrived a Sicily with 14 legions and helped to negotiate the surrender of a large part of Pompey's army. His activities as a mere subordinate to Octavian galled him, however, and with the troops at hand he made war on his equal. Octavian won the conflict easily, and Lepidus was stripped of his titles, losing both the triumviral and proconsular authority. Only his office of pontifex maximus was left to him, and he retired to his estate at Circeii, enduring harsh treatment from Octavian, who disliked him. After Lepidus died in 13 B.C.E., his office of pontifex maximus was taken by Octavian, who had become "Augustus."

Lepidus, Marcus Aemilius (2) (d. c. 30 B.C.E.) *Son of the Triumvir Marcus Aemilius Lepidus (1)*

Lepidus tried unsuccessfully to murder Augustus in 30 B.C.E. The plot was a disaster, and Lepidus was known as the first would-be assassin of an emperor, which gave Augustus yet another reason to torment and harass Lepidus's father.

Lepidus, Marcus Aemilius (3) (d. 39 C.E.) *Courtier during the reign of Gaius Caligula*

Lepidus became the long-time favorite and lover of the emperor. He was married to Gaius's sister DRUSILLA (1), but shared her with her brother while he engaged in affairs with her sisters, Agrippina and Julia. Lepidus was named publicly as the heir to the throne, but he grew afraid for his life and plotted to assassinate Caligula. The emperor learned of the conspiracy and put Lepidus and LENTULUS GAETICULUS to death. The event was celebrated with gifts of money and three daggers, which were sent to the Temple of Mars Ultor.

Lepidus, Paullus Aemilius (late first century B.C.E.) *Nephew of the Triumvir Marcus Aemilius Lepidus (1)*

During the proscriptions of the Second Triumvirate in 43 B.C.E., both Paullus and his father were on the lists. Eventually forgiven, he became a figure in the Augustan principate. In 22 B.C.E. the emperor appointed him and L. Munatius Plancus to the rank of CENSORS. They were thus the last two holders of censorial powers under the

Republican form. Interestingly, when Lepidus and Plancus ascended the platform to perform one of their duties, the structure collapsed, a sign that all was not well with the office. In time, Augustus, as emperor, assumed most of their duties.

lex   The sophisticated legal system of the Romans (*see* LAW). Among the many enactments of the Romans, who were the supreme legalists of the ancient world, was a broad-ranging series of laws (plural, *leges*), covering many topics and situations. Following is a list of some of those laws that were promulgated in the imperial era or survived from the days of the Republic.

> *Acilia Calpurnia de ambitu*   See *Calpurnia de ambitu* below.
>
> *Aelia Sentia*   Passed in 4 C.E. under the magistrates S. Aelius Catus and C. Sentius Saturninus, the *lex Aelia Sentia* finished the work of the *lex Fufia Caninia* (2 B.C.E.). By this law specific rules were established governing the manumission of slaves, reducing the discretion of an owner to release a slave unless certain conditions could be met. A board of officials examined the suitability of a candidate for release, determining whether or not such an individual should be allowed on moral or social grounds to become a Roman citizen.
>
> > *See also* SLAVERY.
>
> *Annales*   A law setting age limits for all political appointments.
>
> > *See also* CONSUL; CURSUS HONORUM.
>
> *Antonia de actis confirmandis*   Actually a series of enactments decreed under the auspices of MARC ANTONY during his period as a member of the Second Triumvirate. He assumed this authority immediately after Caesar's assassination in 44 B.C.E., using it to abolish the office of dictator, and to make changes in the provincial administrations throughout the Roman world. There were other facets to his power under this law.
>
> *Calpurnia de ambitu*   A legislative reformist, C. Cornelius, succeeded in passing in 67 C.E. a series of acts of which the *lex Calpurnia de ambitu* had far reaching effects. Any magistrate found to be corrupt while in office was subject to a rigorous fine and was banished from holding public office forever. The other Cornelian edict, the *lex Cornelia*, as it was commonly known, proved instrumental in establishing the notion of set law; all judicial officials were answerable to a higher legal authority, the law itself.
>
> *Cassia de plebeis in patricious adlegendis*   According to Suetonius and Dio, Caesar received the right to make changes in the sociopolitical structure of Rome as he saw fit. Among these changes was the authority to appoint new patricians. He used the so-called Cassian law to bring the Senate back to full strength. The legislation was still in effect in 48 C.E., when Claudius used it to add more patricians to the senatorial class.
>
> *Clodiae*   The name used to describe the often arbitrary edicts proposed by P. CLODIUS PULCHER in the violent year of 58 B.C.E.
>
> *Cornelia*   See *Calpurnia de ambitu,* above.
>
> *Fufia Caninia*   Passed in 2 B.C.E., the *lex Fufia Caninia* was designed to curb the mass manumission of slaves by the will of a deceased owner. No longer could a dead slaveholder free all of his surviving slaves at once. From that point on only a percentage of all slaves could benefit from such a posthumous gift. In 4 C.E., a more severe version of this law was decreed; see *Aelia Sentia,* above.
>
> *de imperio Vespasian*   A very important *lex*—only the last section survives on a bronze tablet—delineating in clear, legal terms the authority of Vespasian. It is a landmark document because of Vespasian's assumption of broad constitutional and imperial rights without the natural status established by Augustus.
>
> > *See* AUCTORITAS.
>
> *Gabiniae*   A group of enactments sponsored by then-tribune Aulus GABINIUS in 67 B.C.E. Although Gabinius was the political puppet of POMPEY THE GREAT, several of his laws were genuinely beneficial. First, he proposed that all moneylenders be forbidden from granting loans to the embassies of foreign states or provincials in Rome. They had been using funds to bribe senators and magistrates into hearing their pleas or cases first.
>
> To add further to the legislation, he had another law passed that forbade all delays in the hearing of appeals from foreigners. The period of one month, February, was regulated. Favors were consequently prohibited. Finally, Gabinius helped lay the legal groundwork for the demise of the Republic by having Pompey granted, under the *lex Gabinia de piratis persequendis,* an IMPERIUM to clear the seas of pirates. Pompey's political strength became awesome, and the trend had begun for ambitious men to reach for more than the Republic had to offer them.
>
> *Julia agraria*   The title of Julius Caesar's proposed reform of the agrarian law in 59 B.C.E.; it caused a furor.
>
> *Julia de adulteriis coercendis*   One of the more famous statutes enacted during the time of Augustus, which treated incidents of adultery (*see* MARRIAGE AND DIVORCE). By its stipulation, a man could divorce his wife on the grounds of adultery but had to seek such proceedings within sixty days of the act or his spouse was virtually immune to prosecution.

Julia de ambitu Another regulation on the conduct of public officials. Any corrupt official, as of 18 B.C.E., was required to step down and to remain out of service for five years. In 8 B.C.E., another demand was made that all candidates make a deposit of money that could be lost upon their conviction of wrongdoing.

Julia de maiestate A statute born in the good years of Augustus's reign but twisted into an appalling instrument of tyranny in the reign of Tiberius. The *lex Julia de maiestate* provided the means to prosecute and condemn an individual for treason (MAIESTAS). This was a well known law, gaining fame because of the many trials conducted under its jurisdiction and because of Tacitus's description of the trials in his *Annals*.

Julia de maritandis ordinibus The law resulting (with the *lex Papia Poppaea*) from the concerns of both Caesar and Augustus as to the dwindling population. In essence, the law gave handsome benefits to men who married and reared children, while supposedly inflicting penalties upon those who divorced or remained bachelors. The only widow exempted from enforced marriage was Lady Antonia. The *lex Julia de maritandis,* however, was rendered impractical because of the continued refusal of many of Rome's wealthiest upper strata to get married. Furthermore, it provided the DELATORES, or informers, with yet another means of committing extortion or blackmail and profiting from the destruction of others.

> *See also* MARRIAGE AND DIVORCE.

Junia Petronia One of the laws passed to govern the status of slaves during the early empire. By the *lex Junia Petronia*, whenever a trial was held to determine the question of a slave's freedom, any tied jury would mean a victory for the slave.

> *See also* SLAVERY.

Licinia de provincia Caesaris Passed in 55 B.C.E., this decree was partially the result of the Conference of Luca in 56, between member of the FIRST TRIUMVIRATE: Julius Caesar, Crassus, and Pompey. By the *lex Licinia,* Caesar was allowed to retain his control over Gaul for five more years. It was a defeat for CICERO and L. DOMITIUS AHENOBARBUS (1), while aiding Caesar in his final pacification of the Gallic tribes.

Malacitana The *lex Malacitana* granted the status of the *ius Latii* to the provinces of Spain, by order of Vespasian.

Manciana A law, found on inscriptions and difficult to date, which was passed specifically for Africa, with the intent of encouraging farmers to reclaim wasteland and return it to a fertile condition. The rent was reduced, and other rights were granted, such as hereditary ownership. The basic precepts of the *lex Manciana* were increased by Hadrian in the second century to invigorate all of Africa.

> *See also* IUS EMPHYTEUTICUM.

Munatia Aemilia A special decree passed in 42 B.C.E., giving the members of the SECOND TRIUMVIRATE—Octavian (AUGUSTUS), Antony, and Lepidus—the strength to grant, at will, full citizenship and total exemption from taxes.

Papia Poppaea By 9 C.E., it was clear that the *lex Julia maritandis ordinibus* was not successful in increasing marriages or the birth rate of Rome. Augustus decided to formulate another, clearer statute. The result was the *lex Papia Poppaea*. New categories of celibacy were allowed and the long-held legal view that a childless marriage constituted no union at all (the so-called *orbi*) was eased. Widows and divorced women could now wait to remarry, up to two years for the former and a year and a half for the latter. Other inducements were increased for child bearing and marriage; *see* MARRIAGE AND DIVORCE.

Petronia While the *lex Aelia Sentia* and the *lex Fufia Caninia* restricted the nature of SLAVERY in Rome, the *lex Petronia,* issued perhaps in the middle of the first century B.C.E., tried to protect the lives of slaves. No longer could an owner murder slaves at will or send them against wild animals.

Rufrena A decree, proposed in 42 B.C.E. (if actually accepted as a law in the official sense), that ordered the placing of Caesar's statues in all of the temples and cities in the Roman world. The historian Dio wrote that while Caesar lived his statues were already decorating many buildings and temples. The *lex Rufrena* simply continued the honors already paid to Caesar, while setting him firmly on the path to deification.

Titia The law by which the SECOND TRIUMVIRATE was formed. Signed on November 27, 43 B.C.E., by Marc Antony, Marcus Aemilius Lepidus, and Octavian (AUGUSTUS), the pact lasted until December 31, 38 B.C.E. Although that date should have ended the triumvirate, the group continued.

Vatinius The enactment, sponsored by P. Vatinius in 59 B.C.E., giving Julius Caesar command over Gallia Cisalpina, Gallia Transalpina, and Illyricum for five years. This was a major law, for it sent Caesar to wage war upon the Gallic tribes, thus allowing him to earn a reputation as the foremost military intellect of his era. This, in turn, marked him as the man destined to control Rome.

Libanius (314–393 C.E.) *Greek rhetorician and teacher; one of the most famous pagan intellectuals in imperial history*
Libanius was born to a wealthy family in Antioch, studying in Athens from 336 to 340. After teaching there for a time, he moved to Constantinople, where he offered

rhetorical training (342–343), and then to Nicomedia. His sojourn in that city was brought to an end in 348 by a summons from Constantius II, who offered him the seat of RHETORIC director in Athens. Despite his popularity with the court and with many government officials, as well as gifts of favor from the emperor, Libanius declined. He returned home, instead, to accept the position of professor of rhetoric at Antioch, remaining there for the rest of his life. During his years as a noted intellectual, Libanius came to know many emperors. Julian became a friend during his visit to Antioch in 362–363, and his subsequent death was a bitter blow to Libanius, who had admired the emperor's PAGANISM, even as they differed on the speculative aspects of NEOPLATONISM. Under Theodosius I, Libanius received great acclaim and, sometime during the reign (378–395), was granted an honorary Praetorian prefecture.

Libanius was a traditionalist, cultured and genuinely interested in the freedom of the individual. Through his intervention he saved many political figures and common citizens in Antioch. When fighting an injustice he used his oratorical skills to crush opponents. While a pagan, Libanius trained the finest minds of the next generation, including Christians: St. Basil, St. John Chrysostom, St. Gregory of Nazianzus, Theodore of Mopsuestia and perhaps Ammianus Marcellinus. He poured out a vast amount of written work, including his oratories, which provided a deep, personal, and authentic look at the fourth century's people and events. More than 1,600 letters survive, as well as rhetorical exercises, declamations, and 64 speeches, covering a variety of topics.

See also SOPHISTRY.

libellatici   Name used for those Christians who, during the persecutions under Emperor Trajanus Decius of 249–251, purchased from officials of the Roman state certificates called *libelli pacis* that declared that the holder had made the required sacrifices to pagan idols. Condemned by the church, the *libellatici* were ranked among the *lapsi*, those who had turned from the faith during the persecutions. Their punishment and required penance, however, were lighter than for those Christians who had made actual sacrifices to pagan gods.

libellis, a   An office on the imperial staff that was charged with writing petitions to the emperor from cities, provinces or individuals. The hearing of petitions was an important part of governmental business, and the *a libellis* wielded considerable influence in determining those requests actually heard. In the early empire the post was held by an imperial freedman. From the time of Hadrian, any such official was an Equestrian. During the late empire the *a libellis* was known as the *magister libellorum* or the *libellis respondens*.

Liberators   Term used to denote the party of assassins responsible for the murder of Julius Caesar in 44 B.C.E., thus "liberating" Rome from the tyranny of the dictator. The movement was epitomized by its two leaders: Gaius CASSIUS Longinus and Marcus Brutus. Through the vengeance of Marc Antony and Octavian and the formation of the SECOND TRIUMVIRATE, the Liberators' cause was destroyed and died at the battle of PHILIPPI on October 22, 42 B.C.E.

Liberius   (d. 366 C.E.)   *Bishop of Rome from 352 to 366*
The reign of Liberius was embroiled in the Arian controversy. He succeeded Julius as bishop of Rome in 352 and three years later was banished by Constantius II because he refused to join in the condemnation of St. Athanasius. Under intense pressure, quite probably duress as well, he finally agreed to put his signature on Arian documents in 357 and was allowed to return to Rome. Upon his return he built a large church on the Esquiline Hill, the Basilica Liberiana (now called Santa Maria Maggiore).

See also ARIANISM.

Libitina   First of the names given to the Roman deity later known as PROSERPINA. Libitina as an ancient goddess who was associated with DEATH, especially burials. An undertaker in Rome was called a *libitinarius*.

Libius Severus   (d. 465 C.E.)   *Emperor of the West from 461 to 465*
Libius Severus came originally from Lucania but nothing else of his origins survived. When Majorian died in 461, the formidable German MAGISTER MILITUM, RICIMER ran the Western Empire for three months before finally choosing a suitable heir to the throne, Libius Severus, who seemed a manageable puppet. The Senate naturally agreed with Ricimer, electing Severus emperor on November 19. Nevertheless, he faced insurmountable obstacles in the numerous political factions of the empires, both East and West. LEO I, at Constantinople, opposed his election and used Count (*comes*) MARCELLINUS OF DALMATIA to put pressure on Severus' imperial administrators. The Vandals, meanwhile, under King GEISERIC, were plotting Severus's downfall. Geiseric supported OLYBRIUS, whose wife was Placidia (daughter of Emperor Valentinian III), as his choice for emperor, as the Vandal ruler already had close ties to Valentinian through the marriage of his son, Huneric, to Valentinian's daughter Eudocia.

Such were the circumstances on November 14, 465, when Libius Severus died. His passing was the source of much speculation. Ricimer may have determined that his client had outlived his usefulness, or perhaps he saw the need to improve relations with Leo, and thus poisoned Severus, as was widely reported. Severus himself might have tried to instigate a palace coup and died in the attempt, or, least likely of all, his demise could have been from natural causes, a rare event in that era.

Libo, M. Drusus (d. 16 C.E.) *Great-grandson of Pompey the Great*

A young senator in the reign of Tiberius (14–37 C.E.), Libo became one of the earliest victims of the dreaded informers, the DELATORES, who became so common in the Tiberian principate. In 16 C.E., the dull-witted Libo was led into an involvement in Chaldaean magic and rituals by the scheming *delator*, Firmus Catus, who played upon his naivete. Rather foolishly, Libo celebrated his Pompeian origins and his connections to Scribonia, niece to Scribonia, the first wife of Augustus. Once evidence was accumulated, detailing his supposedly treasonous crimes, Tiberius was informed. With his usual deliberate nature, the emperor led Libo into a false sense of security, promoting him to a praetorship and inviting him to dinner. Then, at the appropriate moment, another informer, Fulcinius Trio, impeached Libo, who was put on trial before the Senate. No one dared defend him as the prosecutor brought numerous witnesses, including his own slaves who had been sold to the treasury and were thus compelled to testify. Despairing of any acquittal Libo killed himself after holding a farewell banquet. Ironically enough, Tiberius later commented that he would have spared him had he not committed suicide. Libo's property was divided up among his accusers. His brother, L. Scribonius Libo, was consul in 16 C.E. M. Drusus Libo may have been the young noble mentioned by Dio. There he was called Lucius Scribonius Libo; he supposedly entered his trial in a litter, committed suicide and had his fortune broken apart. The details of this account match the one of Tacitus.

Library of Alexandria   *See* ALEXANDRIA, LIBRARY OF.

Liburnia   Region of ILLYRICUM situated directly upon the ADRIATIC. The Liburnians were among the first of the Illyrian-Dalmatians to submit to Rome. For centuries they had a remarkable reputation as superb navigators and seamen, and Liburnian vessels roamed the Mediterranean, putting in at all of the major ports. Their light, fast SHIPS, called *liburnicae,* became part of the navy of Octavian (AUGUSTUS) and proved instrumental in gaining victory, under Agrippa, at the battle of Actium in 31 B.C.E. Subsequently, some Liburnians served in the Roman Imperial Navy, while others remained in native waters, some ravaging the Adriatic as pirates.

See also PIRACY.

Licinius, Valerius Licinianus (d. 325 C.E.) *One of the coemperors from 308 to 324*

Licinius was originally chosen as a temporary solution to a political crisis but proved himself an able rival to CONSTANTINE THE GREAT. He was born in Upper Moesia sometime in the middle of the third century C.E. and entered into a long and successful military career. Serving under GALERIUS, Licinius became a trusted lieutenant and a friend, aiding the tetrarch in 297 during the Persian War and as a general defending the Danube frontier. Licinius was soon chosen to stand in line as a successor to the TETRARCHY. But when Maxentius usurped the throne in Italy in 306, the entire system established by DIOCLETIAN was on the verge of collapse. At the Conference of Carnuntum in 308, Galerius used his influence to appoint Licinius to the post of Augustus, with control over the Danube and Illyricum, as well as most of the West.

Although he was now emperor, Licinius was smart enough to realize that his position was not strong. After Galerius's death in 311, his powers were further tested by the ambitious ruler of Egypt and Syria, Maximinus II Daia, who in 312 attempted to conquer all of Thrace and so gain a foothold in the Western provinces. In a fierce battle, Licinius displayed the considerable martial experience that he had learned with Galerius, defeating Maximinus, who retreated to Asia Minor and died in Tarsus in 313. In the West, Constantine routed and killed Maxentius in 312. The Roman Empire was now divided between two men: Licinius and Constantine. A union of the imperial families began in 310, with a betrothal between Constantine's sister, CONSTANTIA, and Licinius, made official by a marriage in 313. Peace between the two emperors was doomed.

The first troubles came in 314, over the choice of successors to the throne, and two years later an actual war erupted. Constantine defeated his rival in two encounters, but he then agreed to terms. Licinius lost his Danubian and Illyrian provinces but retained the East. This treaty, certified by the elevation of Constantine's two sons, Crispus and Constantine II, to the rank of Caesar, along with Licinius's son, Licinius II, proved only temporary.

Differences over consular appointments emerged, and Licinius began to argue with Constantine over the favored status of Christians within the empire. Only a small spark was needed to ignite a general struggle. In 322, Constantine pursued a defeated party of Goths into Licinius's domain, and war erupted again. On July 3, 324, the armies of Licinius and Constantine collided, with Constantine proving triumphant at Adrianople. A short time later, the sea engagement of Chrysolopis ended the hopes of Licinius once and for all. Through the intercession of Constantia, her husband was spared immediate execution. Before the year 325 ended, however, Constantine had put him to death. His son was executed in 327. Licinius had supported (for whatever reason) the Edict of Milan, granting Christianity its political freedom, and continued the edict's policy until his estrangement from Constantine brought a change of heart. Furthermore, Licinius governed with a firm hand

and stabilized the finances of his own territory. His opposition to Constantine and his own liquidation of political rivals, including Diocletian's own widow, Prisca, earned him a reputation for cruelty.

Licinius Macer Calvus, Gaius (82–46 or 47 B.C.E.)
Advocatus and erotic poet

Born on May 28, 82, the son of the annalist and praetor Licinius Macer, Licinius displayed early on a gift for oratory. At the age of 27 he challenged Cicero in his prosecution of Vatinius. A long career seemed to be before him, but he died at the age 35 or 36. Licinius also distinguished himself as a poet. Influenced by the Alexandrian School, he wrote numerous poems, specializing in erotica and the epic, although his lampoons of Caesar were so sharp as to require a formal reconciliation. None of his works are extant.

lictors
Bodyguards, status symbols, and often executioners for the high officials and magistrates of the Roman state. By tradition they were founded by Romulus, who copied the Etruscans in appointing special companions. Recruits were found normally in the lowest or destitute classes, although legally they were considered free men. Lictors walked ahead of a magistrate in a single column, bearing the FASCES. By their very presence they called for attention and respect, and they protected important personages and carried out their instructions. In earliest times, when a sentence was passed, the lictors normally used the axe part of their fasces to decapitate the convicted culprit. Set numbers were used to fill the entourage. A DICTATOR had 24 lictors, a CONSUL 12 and a PRAETOR 6.

Ligur, Valerius (d. after 14 C.E.) *Prefect of the Praetorian Guard during the reign of Augustus (27 B.C.E.–14 C.E.)*

Ligur derived his name from his place of origin and was thus called Valerius the Ligurian. He was one of the earliest prefects. Augustus had appointed the first Praetorian prefects in 2 C.E., ensuring that control of the Guard was in the hands of two men, to prevent the accumulation of too much power by one officer. The original commanders were P. Salvius Aper and Q. Ostorius Scapula. Sometime before 14 C.E., Augustus replaced them with one prefect, Valerius, thus displaying his trust in the man. As a further gift, the emperor ordered that a seat be always available for Valerius whenever the two of them went together to the Senate, an honor granted later by Claudius to his Prefect Rufrius Pollio. Ligur held his post until 14 C.E., when a successor was named, Lucius Strabo, the father of SEJANUS.

Liguria
Region of northern Italy (ITALIA) delineated by the Varus River and the Maritime Alps to the west, the Po River to the north, the Mediterranean Sea to the south, and the region of Etruria over the Macra River to the East. Its importance to the Romans was its strategic location along the lines of communication through Gallia Cisalpina over the Alps to Gallia Transalpina. The inhabitants of Liguria, called Ligyes by the Greeks and Ligures by the Romans, were a widely spread people, short but fierce and very independent. They were defeated by M. Fulvius Flaccus in 123 B.C.E. and by C. Sextus Calvinus a short time later. Pacification soon followed and by the start of the Roman Empire, Augustus had placed Liguria in Italia, declaring it one of the districts of the peninsula. The Alps cut through a large part of the region, and most of the country was rugged and mountainous, contributing to the skill displayed by the natives as mercenary soldiers or in the legions.

limes
From the Latin *limus* or boundary (pl. *limites*); *limes* was an imperial frontier road, used to delineate the boundaries of the Roman Empire and to impede or regulate communications between a barbarian people and those living within a province. The Romans originally used *limes* to mean a straight or clear military road that was traversed by the legions as part of an advance into enemy territory or into battle. As the Roman army relied heavily upon excellent roads for fast communications and for ease of troop movements, the creating of the *limes* was an important first step in conquest and in subsequent pacification of any territory. During expansion of Roman territory under the Republic, the frontier boundary was continually shifting, and the *limes* was the principal way of defining its limits. By the time of Augustus, the legions had succeeded in subjugating great nations in GERMANIA, on the Rhine and on the Danube.

The *limes* used at first to cross enemy lands, was now used to demarcate vast stretches of area, sealing off entire states and running for hundreds of square miles, providing a means of observation and control. The *limes* was not so much a defensive wall as a series of watchtowers, connected by sentinel stations and guarded walkways through which no one passed without authority.

The earliest *limes* was probably used during the Augustan age, when the Roman Empire's frontiers were first defined. The roads marked the extent of imperial progress, and a toll system was installed. According to the historian Tacitus, Germanicus used the *limes* over the Rhine in his campaign in 14 C.E., so its construction was sound enough to fulfill a strategic and tactical role. With the end of the first century C.E. and through much of the second, the *limes* was much used in the wars of Domitian and Trajan; by the time of Hadrian they were synonymous with the endless borders surrounding the entire empire.

In 83 C.E., Domitian launched his massive war on the Germanic CHATTI tribe. His advance was effective, and the lands between the Taunus and Neckar-Danube lines were annexed and formed the so-called Agri Decumates, connecting the Danube and Rhine theaters. *Limites* were then constructed and provided not only a stable environment but also shorter lines of communication. Hadrian emphasized the importance of the frontiers as permanent symbols of the separation between the Roman and the barbarian worlds. His *limites* were actual walls with palisades and towers, erected in Raetia, Germania Superior, Numidia and, most famous of all, in Britannia (*see* WALL OF HADRIAN). Elsewhere, as in Africa and along the Danube and in Dacia, other less formal fortifications were built wherever deemed necessary.

The walls were effective. Local tribes were cut off from their homelands, most notably those forced to migrate because of government order or because of civil strife. More important, these forts freed the legions from border control, which was taken over by auxiliary troops, allowing the building of permanent camps within the provinces. These became cities in time. However, the very stability created by the *limes* contributed to the collapse of the empire in the third century C.E. Although strengthened in the second and early third centuries by Antoninus Pius (*see* WALL OF ANTONINUS), Septimius Severus, and Caracalla, the legions became isolated from the forts and watchtowers along the frontiers they were supposed to defend and support. Less mobile and engaged in civil wars, the legions failed to protect the once vital boundaries of the empire. The *limites* in Germania and Dacia were pierced by the ALAMANNI, the CARPI, and the GOTHS, destroyed in some areas and rebuilt in others. The Agri Decumates was lost in the reign of Gallienus when the *limes* there were destroyed by fire. Germania fell under siege and the *limes* of Germania Superior ultimately fell. In 270 C.E., under Aurelian, Dacia was abandoned in favor of the more defensible Danube. Under Diocletian and Constantine the Great, the borders were strengthened, but the effectiveness of the *limes* had been greatly diminished. For nearly two-and-a-half centuries, however, they had secured the frontier, aiding in the development and Romanization of the provinces.

Limitanei The military formations used in the later years of the Roman Empire as static defense forces on the frontier. Their primary purpose was to patrol the borders and prevent a breakthrough by invading barbarian armies, although they were sometimes absorbed into the COMITATENSES, or mobile field army.

Lindum (Lincoln) City in Britannia (BRITAIN) founded by the Romans, probably in the late first century C.E. but fully developed by the middle of the second century. The territory around Lindum was originally home to the Coritani tribe; following their defeat, a legionary camp was established to pacify the natives and to mark Roman jurisdiction. This camp became the headquarters of the II Legion Adjutrix, around which a city emerged. Strategically, Lindum protected the vital line from LONDINIUM (London) to Eburacum (York). With the establishment of those cities, however, the need for a base at Lindum was diminished, and the fortress was abandoned. The flourishing colony, complete with a siphon aqueduct, existed well into the fourth century. The later "Lincoln" was an evolution of the Roman Lindum Colonia.

literature The Romans produced a genuine literary culture, whose changing nature served as a mirror of their history and of those individuals who made that history and who lived during it. It is fortunate for historians that such a vast amount of the Roman written word has survived.

THE AUGUSTAN AGE

A new era for Rome began with Octavius's victory at the battle of Actium in 31 B.C.E., following the chaos and death of the Civil Wars. Because of Augustus and the nascent sociopolitical system, literature entered a golden age. The emperor was a great patron of the arts, encouraging the finest writers of the time. Encouragement also came from the elite circles of the court and government. Gaius Maecenas was a very old friend of HORACE. Marcus Agrippa not only supported authors but also wrote an autobiography and surveyed the whole empire. Other patronages could be found under Asinius Pollio and Marcus Valerius Messalla.

While the populace on the whole knew little of these artists, among the high and mighty competition for attention was fierce, and genius was often rewarded. The result was a blossoming of the written word in all styles. Oratory may have declined in favor of rhetoric, but even this form of communication was treated brilliantly by the early jurists, especially Antistius LABEO and Gaius CAPITO.

The Alexandrine influence of the Hellenic literary minds of Ptolemaic Alexandria had for many years served as the guiding light for Roman literature. The use of the Greek phrase and Greek traditions was considered the finest of accomplishments. Under CICERO, however, there was a growing change, a turn toward Latin, which became the chosen language during the Augustan Age, as poets used it increasingly. Already a master of the pastoral, epic and didactic forms, VIRGIL's *Aeneid* made him the model for every poet of Rome to come. The genius of another poet, Horace, was seen in his immense output. He authored epodes, satires, epistles, an *Ars Poetica,* and Odes. In his jovial writings he achieved lasting fame and the status of friend to the emperor. Sextus Propertius was an avid composer of the elegiac poem along the expected Alexandrine style, but he did not move on to pursue other fields as did OVID. Ovid was another prolific writer whose interest in a multitude of subjects led him to examine love in all its shapes, mythology, heroes and heroines, and even the desperate loneliness of exile.

There are many minor poets of the Augustan Age. Cornelius Gallus, a close friend of Virgil's, preferred the erotic elegy. Domitius Marsus authored epigrams and the epic poem *Amazonis,* while Albius Tibullus, like Propertius, pursued elegiac poems. Also in Rome were Ponticus, an epic poet; Macer, a copier of the legends of Troy; Rabirius; Largus; and Grattius. The latter was a didactic poet who penned the long, stylistically complex poem *Cynegetica,* about hunting.

In the long peace that followed Actium, interest in the past was once more in vogue. Antiquarians were given their place and many found suitable topics for exposition in the civil wars, while others used all of Roman history to gain fame. Many of the Augustan historians were careful to avoid political insults, and imitations of Sallust, Varro, and the Annalists were common. Pompeius Trogus offered his version of a universal history; the later Fenestella observed Roman social history and manners. All of these figures were overshadowed in historiography by LIVY. His 142-book chronicle of Rome from its foundation to 9 B.C.E. was the acme of historical composition and prose, epitomizing in its dramatic scenes, its rhetoric and idealism, the triumphs of this Golden Age.

THE SILVER AGE

The Augustan Age passed away with its founder in 14 C.E. Unavoidably, Roman literature entered into a period of intellectual decline brought about by tyranny and evidenced by a noticeable lack of originality. Happiness and hope were replaced by brooding tension and introspection. Tiberius, Gaius Caligula, Nero, and Domitian provided the despotism, and Romans the creative stagnation. The reality of imperial grandeur and Roman supremacy supplanted the supposedly unsophisticated Augustan period. Literature reflected this as writers produced overly decorated and exaggerated imitations of what they considered inferior efforts by their predecessors. Finally, there was seen in the literature of the first century C.E. the arrival of men and women of definite brilliance from the province, most notably Spain (*see* HISPANIA). Quintilian, the Senecas, Martial, and Lucan came from Spain—living proof of how effective Romanization could be. Their writings were Roman in every sense, and they were accepted as such.

The first century produced some of the most durable of works. Equally, there was growth in the kinds of subjects chosen and the degree of critical thinking that accompanied them. Thus, throughout the Tiberian, Neronian, and Flavian years there were books on history, knowledge, oratory, satire, and poetry.

Of all the poets in this period, the one who stood above the rest was Lucan, who wrote *Belle Civile,* known as *Pharsalia.* Other notable efforts were authored by Silius Italicus, Valerius Flaccus, and P. Papinius Statius. Perhaps more interesting was the development of satire as a readily available source of artistic commentary on contemporary and historical events. Varro and Horace had played a part in the role of satire, but it found its best practitioners in Persius and Juvenal (*see* SATIRE).

The most influential of the prose writers was Lucius Annaeus Seneca who taught Nero and for many years was a powerful minister of state. He composed tragedies, plays, essays, letters, and other writings now possessed in fragments. Harshly judged by critics for his style and modernistic rejection of the past, Seneca shaped a generation of aspiring artists. Pliny the Elder provided an astonishing collection of scientific, geographical, historical, natural, and medicinal knowledge in his *Natural History,* while the lesser known A. Cornelius Celsus assembled a comprehensive encyclopedia on oratory, farming, and medicine, of which only a little is extant. Pliny the Younger earned a reputation for vanity but in so doing contributed to historical awareness of his era by maintaining a correspondence with the great minds of politics, philosophy, and literature. Other authors included Petronius, Quintilian, and Martial. Petronius gained lasting fame with his *Satyricon;* Quintilian's *Institutio Oratoria* analyzed the education of an orator and preserved his own opinions of the first century's most fertile minds; Martial wrote his *Epigrams* in 15 books, clearly and concisely cutting to the heart of pressing issues.

The first century was a crucial one for Roman and world history, and Rome produced its share of fine historical chroniclers, such as Tacitus and Suetonius. Velleius Paterculus briefly held attention during the rise of the Praetorian Prefect Sejanus. Q. Curtius Rufus, during the Claudian principate, finished a history of Alexander the Great. Tacitus and Suetonius both extended into the second century. Tacitus covered the reigns of Augustus, Tiberius, Gaius Caligula, Claudius, and Nero in the *Annals,* the civil war of 69 in the *Histories,* the Germans in *Germania,* the life of Agricola in his invaluable biography, and oratory in his *Dialogue.* Suetonis authored *The Twelve Caesars.*

THE SECOND CENTURY

Two elements dominated Roman literature throughout the second century: the general stability of the empire and the revival of Greek as a potent literary language. The reigns of Trajan, Hadrian, Antoninus Pius, and Marcus Aurelius were the most solid series of successions the empire would know. They were learned, gifted rulers. The Roman Empire changed under these emperors, especially under Hadrian, when it became increasingly cosmopolitan. In the midst of these reigns, Greek reemerged as the language of literary choice. Authors wrote in Latin and Greek but, as new writers entered the field from Greece and the Hellenized East, the final transformation was made into a civilization composed of many peoples instead of numerous nations dominated by one.

The one mighty rhetorician, teacher, poet, and critic of the Antonines was Marcus Cornelius Fronto, tutor of Marcus Aurelius and Lucius Verus. He also corresponded with his favorite pupil, Marcus, as well as Antoninus Pius and others, and penned a series of treatises on oratory and panegyrics. His associate may have been the grammarian Aulus Gellius who wrote the *Noctes Atticae,* a haphazardly organized mass of facts and stories on law, philosophy, and grammar. At the same time in Africa, the novelist Apuleius was attracting attention and recognition for his *Metamorphoses* (also called the *Golden Ass*). Apuleius authored several other books, *Apologia,* written in his own defense, *De Deo Socratis,* covering Platonic philosophy and demons, *Platone et euis dogmate,* on Plato, and wrote his oratories. Under Hadrian, all facets of law received imperial favor and importance. The writings of the so-called Jurists thus took a major place in the literary production of the Hadrianic reign and that of the Antonines. Gaius, Ulpius Marcellus, and Papinian all contributed to legalism and its documentation.

Finally, Christianity, long growing in popularity, laid claim to its own place in the literary field. Tertullian brilliantly represented the cause of the Christians in his *Apologia.* Minucius Felix, one of the earliest Christian writers, used a dialogue form to destroy the charges being hurled at Christianity. Cyprian, bishop of Carthage, used the pen to organize the church itself. He was a harbinger of the empire's struggles in the third century, and the Christians' growing strength and numbers.

THE THIRD CENTURY

The disastrous third century produced only the notable Dio Cassius and Nemesianus. Trends of the era showed the continuing rise of Christians as legitimate participants in the literature of the empire; continued work by the Jurists; and the composition of excellent histories. Cyprian carried on the tradition of Felix and Tertullian. Arnobius, from North Africa, studied rhetoric and was converted to Christianity by a dream. As proof of his newfound faith he wrote the *Adversus Nationes,* attacking paganism. Finished sometime during the reign of Diocletian (c. 295–303), Arnobius's book was an example of the philosophical and rhetoric skills learned in a pagan environment but put to use to promote a Christian one.

The Christian poet Commodian applied rude verse to two poems. The *Instructiones* was a polemic on Jews, the Resurrection and the Anti-Christ; *Carmen Apologetica* was a plea for more conversions. Nemesianus hailed from Carthage, and his poems were an imitation of Virgil. *Cynegetica* discussed hunting and survived only in part, while his other attempts, including the *Nautica,* were lost. Historiography was advanced in this century by the presence of several chroniclers and chronicles. Dio was the foremost of all of these writers. His history of Rome, from Aeneas to 229 C.E., was well researched and proved of great help to succeeding generations of scholars. Herennius Dexippus, the Athenian historian, detailed the terrible invasions of the Goths in the mid-third century in his

Scythica, partly extant. The Syrian-born Herodian, a friendly contemporary of Dio, followed Dio's pattern in his account of the emperors from Marcus Aurelius to Gordian III. Finally, the *Scriptores Historiae Augustae* (called also the *Historia Augustae*) is a highly suspect annal, covering the empire from Hadrian to the accession of Diocletian in 284.

THE FOURTH CENTURY

Christianity triumphed over paganism and the Roman Empire when it found its champion in Constantine. Henceforth much of the literature was aimed at propagating the proclaimed faith to the world and ensuring that Constantine and his successors were given their rightful places as heads of church and state. Ambrose and Jerome were Christian intellectuals, while Lactantius showed the potential of mixing history with religious fanaticism.

Paganism was now in eclipse, although it could still claim two bright stars, Libanius and Symmachus. Libanius was a rhetorician and a fierce espouser of causes. He believed in logical NEOPLATONISM, defended the rights of pagans and wrote over 1,500 letters. Symmachus used his eloquence and gift for prose in the Senate and to battle for paganism in the face of the Christian onslaught led by Ambrose. He authored panegyrics and appeals.

Historical writers were likewise faced with a different world. Eusebius, bishop of Caesarea, relied upon his own experience to aid him in writing his church chronicle, the *Ecclesiastical History.* Ammianus Marcellinus was the sharpest historian of the century, with a grasp of the wider events occurring within the empire from the reign of Constantius II to Valens. His style was readable and detailed, as well as reliable. Aurelius Victor, Eutropius, and Festus all made contributions; Aurelius Victor offered an examination of the Caesars and an *Epitome* down to Theodosius I; Eutropius chose a far more ambitious subject, the entire span of Roman history in only 10 books, the *Breviarum ab urbe condita.* In poetry, Avienus translated Aratus's *Phaenomena* and Dionysius's *Periegesis* or *Descriptions of the Earth.* His own works were epigrams, poems, and *Ora Maritima* (Maritime shores). Prudentius was a Christian who used Christianity as the basis of his writings. He attacked Symmachus and paganism in *Anti-Symmachus,* lauded martyrs in *Peristefanon,* and joined in the war against heretics with the *Apotheosis* and *The Origin of Sin.*

By the end of the fourth century, the climate of the empire had turned against Roman literature in its long-held form. Constantinople was now the capital of the world and the Christian Church dictated the nature of society, working hand in hand with an increasingly centralized government. Outside, the migrations were bringing the barbarians closer to the very heart of the imperial world. *See* under individuals' entries for additional information; see also under the subject index.

Suggested Readings: Aili, Hans. *The Prose Rhythm of Sallust and Livy.* Stockholm: Almqvist & Wiksell International, 1979; Aristides. *Orationes. Opera Quae Exstant Omnia.* Edited by F. W. Lenz and A. Behr. Lyons, France: Brill, 1976; Baldwin, Barry. *An Anthology of Later Latin Literature.* Amsterdam: J. C. Gieben, 1987; Barnes, Timothy David. *The Sources of the Historia Augusta.* Brussels: Latomus, 1978; Benario, Herbert W. *A Commentary on the Vita Hadriani in the Historia Augusta.* Chico, Calif.: Scholars Press, 1980; Chilver, Guy E. F. *A Historical Commentary on Tacitus' Histories IV and V.* New York: Oxford University Press, 1985; Chilver, Guy Edward Farquhar. *A Historical Commentary on Tacitus' Histories I and II.* New York: Oxford University Press, 1979; Courtney, E. *The Fragmentary Latin Poets.* Oxford: Clarendon Press, 1993; ———. *Musa Lapidaria: A Selection of Latin Verse Inscriptions.* Atlanta, Ga.: Scholars Press, 1995; Craddock, Patricia B. *Edward Gibbon, Luminous Historian, 1772–1794.* Baltimore: Johns Hopkins University Press, 1989; Enos, Richard Leo. *The Literate Mode of Cicero's Legal Rhetoric.* Carbondale: Southern Illinois University Press, 1988; Hawes, Adeline. *Citizens of Long Ago; Essays on Life and Letters in the Roman Empire.* Freeport, N.Y., Books for Libraries Press, 1967; *A Garden of Roman Verse.* Los Angeles: J. Paul Getty Museum, 1998; Kraus, Christina Shuttleworth. *Latin Historians.* Oxford, U.K.: Oxford University Press, 1997; Laistner, Max L. W. *The Greater Roman Historians.* Berkeley: University of California Press, 1977; Lockwood, D.P. *A Survey of Classical Roman Literature.* Chicago: University of Chicago Press, 1982; Luce, T. James. *Livy: The Composition of His History.* Princeton, N.J.: Princeton University Press, 1977; *The Penguin Book of Latin Verse.* Baltimore: Penguin Books, 1962. Studies in Latin Poetry. Cambridge: University Press, 1969; Rawson, Elizabeth. *Cicero: a Portrait.* Rev. ed. Ithaca, N.Y.: Cornell University Press, 1983; Reynolds, Joyce Maire. *Aphrodisias and Rome: Documents from the Excavation of the Theatre at Aphrodisias.* London: Society for the Promotion of Roman Studies, 1982; Walbank, F. W. *Selected Papers: Studies in Greek and Roman History and Historiography.* New York: Cambridge University Press, 1985.

Livia (58 B.C.E.–29 C.E.) *Wife of Augustus, mother of Tiberius and one of the most powerful women in Roman imperial history*

Livia Drusilla was born the daughter of Marcus Livius Drusus Claudius, a nobleman. In 43 or 42 B.C.E. she married Tiberius Claudius Nero. Tiberius was an opponent of Octavian (AUGUSTUS), and in 40 B.C.E. Livia and her young son TIBERIUS, the future emperor, fled with him from his estates in Campania to the protection of Marc ANTONY. In 39 B.C.E., however, immediately after Octavian's wife Scribonia bore him a daughter, Octavian divorced her. The following year, he convinced Tiberius Claudius Nero to separate from Livia so that Octavian could wed her. Despite the fact that Livia was six months pregnant, Tiberius Claudius Nero attended the wedding, going so far as to give away the bride and to sit with friends at the wedding feast. Soon after Livia gave birth to DRUSUS (1). Octavian sent him to his father, while many in Rome joked that "the fortunate have children in only three months."

As the wife of Augustus, Livia proved utterly faithful and devoted both to the emperor and to the state. A woman of renowned virtue and dignity, she assumed her matriarchal role, while covertly influencing Augustus's reign and protecting the interests of her sons, both adopted by Augustus. She was especially devoted to the cause of Tiberius, though her meddling earned her Tiberius's enmity and a reputation as a cunning manipulator. It has been suggested that she murdered MARCELLUS in 23 B.C.E., the nephew that Augustus had been grooming as a successor, as well as Gaius and Lucius CAESAR, also heirs to the throne, in 4 C.E. and 2 C.E. respectively. Livia probably was instrumental in the exile of AGRIPPA POSTUMUS to Planasia. It was written by Suetonius that, although she bore him no children, Augustus loved Livia until his death in 14 C.E. The historian Dio charged that she had poisoned his figs because he intended to bring back Agrippa Postumus and elevate him over Tiberius.

Regardless of the truth of the accusation, Livia's political influence increased after her son's accession in 14. She was given the title of Julia Augusta and exercised power on equal terms with Tiberius, fueling Tiberius's resentment. She may have murdered Agrippa Postumus and then energetically opposed the family of GERMANICUS, engaging in a lengthy feud with his wife, AGRIPPINA THE ELDER. Livia was aided by the fatal illness that killed Germanicus in 19. As a counter to her reputation for ruthlessness, Livia protected GAIUS CALIGULA from harm, helped to raise many children from the families of Rome, saved senators from probable execution and assisted many Roman daughters with their dowries. Upon her death, the Senate decreed all possible honors to her memory, ordering an arch to be built—a singular tribute. Tiberius terminated that proposal by declaring that he would construct it himself, which he never did, and he also refused to deify her, although she was buried in the mausoleum of Augustus. In 42, Claudius elevated her to divine status. Livia lived to be 86, having displayed a methodical and precise pursuit of power that left chroniclers such as Tacitus uneasy.

Suggested Readings: Bartman, Elizabeth. *Portraits of Livia.* New York: Cambridge University Press, 1999; McAfee, Gabriel. *Livia's Garden Room at Prima Porta.* New York: New York University Press, 1955.

Livianus, Claudius (fl. early second century C.E.) *Prefect of the Praetorian Guard during the early years of Emperor Trajan's reign*

Livianus accompanied the emperor in the Dacian Wars (101–102/103–107 C.E.). In 102, Trajan sent him, with the envoy L. Licinius Sura, as the official representatives of Rome to DECEBALUS, king of DACIA. The monarch refused to meet with them, so hostilities continued.

Livilla (d. 31 C.E.) *Sister of Emperor Claudius and Germanicus and wife of Drusus (3) the Younger*

Livilla, also called Livia, was reportedly ungainly in her youth but grew to be a beautiful woman. She married DRUSUS and bore several children, including Julia and a pair of twins. As a wife, however, she proved faithless. SEJANUS, PREFECT OF THE PRAETORIAN GUARD, became her lover sometime in 23 C.E., and subsequently used her in his plot to eliminate Drusus. He and the prince were bitter enemies, so the irony of using Drusus's wife as an instrument of murder was remarkable. How Livilla came to be seduced is not clear, save that Sejanus could be irresistible and she was having poor relations with her husband at the time.

Having prepared the ground carefully, Sejanus poisoned Drusus. Livilla's hopes for marriage to Sejanus, however, were never fulfilled, as Tiberius would not allow the union. Instead, she suffered the humiliation of having her daughter JULIA betrothed to the prefect. In 31, Sejanus was destroyed by Tiberius, and his children, friends and associates were massacred. His wife Apicata, whom he divorced, killed herself after writing a letter to Tiberius in which she accused Livilla of complicity in Drusus's murder. Accounts vary as to the emperor's response. He may have executed her or, as the historian Dio reported, turned her over to her mother Antonia, who starved her to death for her many crimes. By imperial order, all memory of Livilla was obliterated, her statues broken and her name banned.

Livius, Drusus Claudius (d. c. 42 B.C.E.) *Father of Livia*

A member of the ancient and noble house of the Claudians Livius received adoption into the plebeian line of the Livii. He was an ardent Republican, who came out in support of the assassination of Caesar and of Caesar's murderers, Brutus and Cassius. For this loyalty he was proscribed by the members of the SECOND TRIUMVIRATE, most notably Antony and Octavian (AUGUSTUS). Following the defeat of the Republican cause at the battle of Philippi in 42 B.C.E., Livius killed himself. Ironically, Octavian married his daughter four years later.

Livy (Titus Livius) (64 or 59 B.C.E.–12 or 17 C.E.) *Roman historian*

Born at Patavium (Padua), Livy spent most of his days in Rome. Little has survived concerning his private life. He chose to remain apart from the literary society of the Augustan Age, quite possibly because of the resentment and jealousy of his contemporaries. Nevertheless, he enjoyed the long patronage of Augustus, who overlooked his Republican tendencies and even called him a "Pompeian." Livy was also familiar with the imperial family, encouraging Claudius to continue his own writing.

Livy studied rhetoric and philosophy. For his son he composed a rhetorical exercise and later penned a series of dialogues on philosophical matters. As a historian, he was also familiar with some of the Annalists and recent historical authors. These he used in the creation of his mammoth achievement, a history of Rome. Called *Ab urbe conditi (From the Foundation of the City)*, Livy's masterwork covered all of the Roman past, from the earliest days of Rome to the death of Drusus in 9 B.C.E. It contained 142 books in all, of which only 35 are extant. Epitomes helped save elements of the remainder, except for two books, and fragments or inclusions in later works salvaged other valuable pieces. A system of decades (groups of 10 books) was used to organize the overall collection, so that intact were books 1 to 10 and 21 to 45. These examined the establishment of Rome, including its sack by the Gauls, and the wars with Macedonia and Syria.

This history was begun sometime between 27 and 25 B.C.E., and the early books were completed during the first years. Livy subsequently spent the next years adding to his growing collection of finished works: Books one to nine were completed by 20 B.C.E., 10 to 28 after 19 B.C.E. and books 29 to 49 around 18 B.C.E. He continued researching and writing well into the first century C.E. and probably did not complete the entire publication of the Augustan era until after the death of Augustus in 14 C.E. What plans he might have had as far as ending the history are unknown, as the last recorded event in the manuscript was the death of Drusus in 9 B.C.E.

A bronze *dupondius* of Livia, wife of Augustus, struck in the name of Drusus, in 22–23 C.E. at Rome *(Courtesy Historical Coins, Inc.)*

Livy made public readings of his work, while his published sections earned the respect of his associates but also their envy. All agreed that he was eloquent and candid, while admitting that his was the highest level of Roman historiography, a sentiment unchallenged by subsequent generations. Livy was (and is) one of the most examined and discussed authors of the ancient world. While his methods as a historian were decidedly lacking, his genius for composition, narrative, and style reached a level beyond any previously attempted by Roman literary figures. His gift to the Romans and to posterity was a monumental chronicle, bringing to life events of dubious accuracy but unquestionable significance.

Suggested Readings: Aili, Hans. *The Prose Rhythm of Sallust and Livy.* Stockholm: Almqvist & Wiksell International, 1979; Briscoe, John. *A Commentary on Livy.* Books 31–33. Oxford, U.K.: Clarendon Press, 1972; Chaplin, Jane D. *Livy's Exemplary History.* Oxford, U.K.: Oxford University Press, 2000; Dorey, Thomas Alan. *Livy.* London: Routledge, 1971; Forsythe, Gary. *Livy and Early Rome: A Study in Historical Method and Judgment.* Stuttgart, Ger.: Franz Steiner, 1999; Jaeger, Mary. *Livy's Written Rome.* Ann Arbor: University of Michigan Press, 1997; Kraus, Christina Shuttleworth. *Latin Historians.* Oxford, U.K.: Oxford University Press, 1997; Luce, T. James. *Livy: The Composition of His History.* Princeton, N.J.: Princeton University Press, 1977; Miles, Gary B. *Livy: Reconstructing Early Rome.* Ithaca, N.Y.: Cornell University Press, 1995; Moore, Timothy J. *Artistry and Ideology: Livy's Vocabulary of Virtue.* Frankfurt am Main: Athenäum, 1989; Oakley, S. P. *A Commentary on Livy.* Books VI–X. New York: Oxford University Press, 1997.

Lollia Paulina (d. 49 C.E.) *Granddaughter of the famous consul (21 B.C.E.) and general, Marcus Lollius*
Lollia originally married the governor of Macedonia, Memmius Regulus. In 38 C.E., however, Gaius Caligula heard of her beauty and sent for the married couple. The emperor forced Regulus to give up Lollia and married her himself. As was his habit, he divorced her immediately but decreed that she could bed no other men. Following the death of Messallina in 49 C.E., a search was launched to find Emperor Claudius a new spouse. Two candidates were final qualifiers, AGRIPPINA THE YOUNGER and Lollia Paulina. Agrippina won the contest, and ever vindictive, plotted Lollia's destruction as a rival. Thus, in 49, she was charged with having trafficked in Chaldaean magic. Claudius, prompted by his wife, allowed a trial, at which Lollia was condemned. She was exiled and forced to surrender her vast fortune. Unsatisfied with that sentence, Agrippina sent Lollia a letter demanding that she commit suicide, which Lollia performed promptly. Pliny the Elder wrote of her many famous jewels.

Lollius, Marcus (d. c. 1 C.E.) *Consul in 21 B.C.E., governor in Galatia, Macedonia, and Gallia, and a companion of Augustus*
In 25 B.C.E., when the imperial government annexed Galatia, Lollius proved instrumental in its transformation into a Roman province. After his consulship he traveled to Macedonia where he ran the administration from 19 to 18 B.C.E., aiding the local ruler, Rhoemetalces, son of Cotys, during a period of dynastic problems. There followed a period of service in Gallia, where Lollius suffered an apparent reversal at the hands of the Tencteri and Sugambri (two Germanic tribes). The historian Velleius Paterculus described this defeat as a catastrophe of terrible importance, when, in fact, it had no serious or long-lasting effects on Rome's control of the Rhine. Velleius was probably motivated to this exaggeration by Tiberius, who considered Lollius to be one of his most bitter enemies. The setback in 17 did not ruin his career, for in 1 C.E., Augustus appointed him chief adviser to Gaius CAESAR in his Eastern tour, heading the board of experienced ministers surrounding the prince. Perhaps through the Parthians, Gaius learned that Lollius had been accepting bribes from Eastern tribes. He was dismissed immediately and died a short time later.

See also LOLLIA PAULINA.

Lollius Urbicus, Quintus (fl. second century C.E.) *Consul in 138 C.E. and a successful governor of Britain from 139 to 142*
An African by birth, Urbicus attained imperial favor as an officer during the reign of HADRIAN, especially during the Jewish Rebellion of 132–135. He later became governor of Germania Inferior; in 139, ANTONINUS PIUS appointed him legate in Britain, where Urbicus faced a sudden invasion of the province by the BRIGANTES from the north, who poured over the WALL OF HADRIAN. In a swift campaign he defeated the barbarians, and to strengthen the borders of Roman Britain he constructed the WALL OF ANTONINUS PIUS (Antonine Wall) in modern Scotland. After returning to Rome, he served as PREFECT OF THE CITY.

Londinium Modern London; one of the most important cities in Roman Britannia (BRITAIN) and the gateway for all trade in and out of the isles throughout the imperial era. This area of land, about 40 miles upstream from the mouth of the Thames River, served originally as the capital of the Cantii, who lived on its southern, or right, bank. The territory of the north bank belonged to the Trinovantes. Even before the Roman invasion of 43 C.E., traders had started a community at Londinium. In the year of conquest, the advancing Roman legions of Aulus Plautius and Emperor Claudius pursued the retreating Britons over the Thames at the lowest point (where the water could be forded), and used this crossing site as a camp. Londinium was the result.

Roman economic expansion thus centered on the town, and Tacitus made the earliest mention of the site by writing that Londinium was a "town, which though not favored with the title of *colonia* was nevertheless an active spot for trade and for traders." This reference of London in 61 C.E. also discussed the major event of that year, the revolt of Boudicca, the queen of the Iceni. The legate of Britain, Suetonius Paulinus, was forced to surrender London to the Britons in order to recover and reorganize his position within the province. Boudicca captured London and destroyed it utterly, slaying its inhabitants. With her eventual defeat an extensive rebuilding program was undertaken, as the Romans throughout the first century added to their control by fostering Romanization.

By the end of the century Londinium was the heart of the imperial provincial administration. For the first years of occupation, Camulodonum (Colchester) had served as the capital, with its imperial cult and temple, but there is strong evidence to support the theory that after Boudicca's uprising the capital was moved to London. After Claudius subjugated Britain roads were made, starting in London and moving in all directions to the tribal capitals and legion camps. The entire line of Roman communications relied upon the London network, especially after the establishment of such northern bases as Lindum (Lincoln) and Eburacum (York).

Building within London was also extensive, warranting its consideration as an elevated city. Roman London had all of the usual structures: a basilica, baths, a Mithraeum, a forum, government offices, and a formal residence of the governor. Equally, the markets, houses, and shops of the merchants declared that, if nothing else, London (and in time the colony) provided the thrust for financial growth elsewhere in the province. Finally, protection of the inhabitants was maintained by a fortress, a leftover from the days of unrest.

Throughout the second century C.E., Londinium continued to spread outward. Its position as capital, however, was altered by Emperor Septimius Severus around 197. As a result of the departure of Clodius Albinus in 196 for mainland Europe, and because of the struggle for imperial supremacy, Severus resolved to divide Britain into two provinces, with a governor (a legate) administering the VI legion from York. Britannia Superior was a regular province under a consular legate with two legions, and its capital was at London.

Rampant instability in the provinces allowed usurpers to emerge in the late third and early fourth centuries, and in Britain two such were Carausius and Allectus, both of whom used London as their headquarters. Carausius even established his own mint at London. In 296 C.E., however, Constantius I Chlorus and his Praetorian Prefect Asclepiodotus defeated Allectus and entered the city. Constantius's son Constantine sailed from London on his way to conquer the Roman world. An imperial presence remained in London until the start of the fifth-century.

Longinus   A legendary and mystical figure of Christian lore, supposedly the centurion in charge of the crucifixion of Jesus Christ. It was he who speared Christ in the side, thus preventing the traditional breaking of the limbs to induce death. He was in that instant converted, becoming the first of the Romans to accept Christ as the Savior. Longinus was reported to have left the legions to wander, carrying his spear, which became known also as the Lance. This weapon emerged as a powerful relic of Christianity, merging with other legends and taking a multifaceted path into obscurity and occult mysticism. It may have been taken by Joseph of Arimathea to England as part of the Holy Grail treasure, or it could be the Lance presently housed in the Hofburg in Vienna, as part of the Hapsburg regalia. Also called the Maurice or Mauritius Lance, the Hofburg relic was sought by Napoleon in 1805, and was owned by Adolf Hitler for a time because of its reported connections to Christ. Still another Lance was found by the Crusaders in Antioch in 1098, during the First Crusade. With its aid the Crusaders defeated a Muslim host on June 28, 1098, at the Orontes, also known as the battle of the Lance. Longinus himself was associated with the Holy Grail in later stories.

Longinus, Cassius (c. 213–273 C.E.) *Neoplatonic philosopher, rhetorician, and grammarian*
Longinus was a Syrian, son of Fronto, the nephew of Fronto of Emesa. After studying with Ammonius and Origen, he gained fame as a teacher of philosophy and rhetoric at Athens, where he included among his students Porphyry. Around 267, Longinus traveled to PALMYRA, where he met Queen ZENOBIA and entered into her service, either as an adviser and teacher of Greek, or as her *ab epistulis Graecis*. Through his influence she renounced her allegiance to Rome and entered into an unsuccessful revolt against Aurelian. Following Zenobia's defeat in 283, Longinus was put to death. Of his many works, only fragments of his rhetoric are extant; the treatise, *On the Sublime,* was long attributed to his pen.

Longus, Velius (d. early second century C.E.) *Grammarian*
Noted mainly for his precise and well-organized treatise, *De Orthographia,* Longus was considered one of the major grammatical writers in the late first and early second centuries.

Luca, Conference of   A meeting held around April 15, 56 B.C.E., among the members of the FIRST TRIUMVIRATE: Julius CAESAR, POMPEY THE GREAT, and Marcus Licinius CRASSUS (1). The triumvirate that had been formed in 60 B.C.E. was, by 56, showing signs of severe strain. Pompey and Caesar had a relationship that wavered between friendship and hostility, while Crassus envied Pompey's strength in Rome and Caesar's continued successes in the GALLIC WARS. This internal dissension gave hope to opponents, such as Cicero and L. Domitius Ahenobarbus, that a splintering of the coalition was possible. To avoid this, Caesar, who was wintering at Ravenna, traveled to Luca in Gallia Cisalpina and sent requests to his colleagues to join him there. Crassus was already with him, while Pompey arrived late, on the 15th. The conference was understandably brief, but it reaffirmed the original unity of the triumvirate, ensured Caesar control over Gaul and kept Pompey and Crassus politically agreeable. No long-term solution was reached; the rivalries and suspicions remained as Pompey feared Caesar's ambitions. Crassus rode off to die in Parthia, while Caesar prepared his legions for the final battles some six years hence.

Lucan, Marcus Annaeus (39–65 C.E.) *Roman writer best known for his great surviving work, the* Bellum Civile (Civil War), *known also as the* Pharsalis

Lucan came from Corduba in Spain and was the grandson of SENECA THE ELDER and nephew of SENECA the Younger. Raised in Rome, Lucan studied under CORNUTUS the Stoic before embarking on a highly successful career as a writer. His output was prolific in both verse and prose. Emperor Nero granted him honors and imperial favor with a quaestorship. In return, Lucan recited a panegyric to Nero at the Neronian Games in 60 C.E., and the first three books of the *Civil War* were highly flattering to the ruler. However, the emperor grew jealous of Lucan's genius and popularity. By 65, Lucan was barred from publishing his poetry altogether and, unable to stomach Nero's cruelties and deprecations of his work, he entered into the Pisonian Conspiracy. Trapped (as were all of the conspirators), Lucan first betrayed his own mother and then all of his colleagues. Despite the promise of a pardon, Nero ordered him to die. Lucan committed suicide, quoting several lines from his masterwork in which a soldier likewise bled to death.

The *Bellum Civile* was a massive undertaking and stretched the limits even of epic poetry. Errors, both in fact and rhetoric, abound as his own bias toward Pompey and the Republican cause shines through. He relied upon Livy for many details, a source noted for mistakes and casual research. The brilliance of his skill, however, is unmistakable. The work itself detailed the *Civil War* in 10 books, from the start of the conflict to the siege of Alexandria in 48 B.C.E. Books one to three were published by Lucan himself and included praise for Nero. These earlier sections were filled with preferences for Pompey as the champion of liberty, while his later books displayed a growing sense of anger and frustration mirroring his own life.

Books four to nine were published sometime after his death in 65, either by a relative or friends. Book 10, however, was obviously never finished, for it was not perfect nor did it end in any manner, rather, the verses cease during the siege of Alexandria.

Lucania One of the southernmost regions of Italy (ITALIA), surrounded by Campania, Samnium, Apulia, Calabria, and Bruttium, with a coastline on both the Tyrrhenian Sea and the Gulf of Taranto. In the earliest days of settlement, Lucania was the home of Greek sailors and colonists, who competed with the original inhabitants, the Chones. Both cultures were subsequently subdued by the Samnite-based Lucanians, who were, in turn, conquered by the Romans. Lucania was not known for the beauty of its landscape but rather for its pasturelands. Here was the heart of cattle raising in Italy, and Lucanian oxen were especially famous for their size and strength. During the years of the Roman Empire, Lucania was combined with Bruttium to form one of the Italian districts.

Lucian (fl. second century C.E.) *Writer born at Samosata in Syria*

Although Greek was not his native tongue, Lucian became fluent in Greek and worked for a time as an advocate. He may have traveled through Greece in that capacity, later taking up a position in the administration of the procurator of Egypt. His principle work was his *Dialogues,* in which he examined, with irreverence and satire, his own era. He used both seriousness and comedy to drive home his biting examples from every element of society, while displaying not only his own excellent grammar but also his remarkable wit. Lucian's parodic *True History* is often cited as the first science fiction story.

See also SATIRE.

Lucian of Antioch (d. 312 C.E.) *Christian theologian, scholar, and martyr*

A presbyter in Antioch, Lucian authored numerous works on the doctrines of the church and the Bible. His writings in Greek were so respected that they were accepted texts by most of the sees of the East. Unfortunately, little of his output is extant, although it is believed that the second of the four creeds issued by the Council of Antioch (341) may have been composed by Lucian. He also founded the important theological school that claimed as students Arius and Eusebius of Nicomedia.

Lucifer of Cagliari (Lucifer of Sardinia) (d. 370 or 371 C.E.) *Bishop of Cagliari and one of the Church's most outspoken opponents of Arianism*

At the Council of Milan (354) he refused to condemn St. Athanasius and was imprisoned by Emperor Constantius II for several days in the imperial palace before being banished to Egypt. Throughout, he continued his attacks on Arianism in general and the emperor in particular. Released by the general amnesty of Emperor Julian in 362, Lucifer had spent much of his period of exile writing defenses of orthodox Christianity against the Arians. His works included *De non conveniendo cum haereticis* (On his refusal to meet with the heretics); *Pro S. Athanasio,* a defense of Athanasius; and *De regibus apostacisis,* an attack on Constantius. After his release, Lucifer traveled to Antioch and then returned to his see in Cagliari.

Lucilius, Gaius (fl. first century C.E.) *Centurion in the mutinous Pannonian legions in 14 C.E.*

The legions in Pannonia revolted, with various demands, shortly after the death of Augustus, and singled out Lucilius for murder because of his fondness for corporal punishment. He was known as "Another, quick!" for he would shout that out after the rod he was using on the legionaries snapped. Sometimes two or three rods would break before he was satisfied. The soldiers avenged themselves upon him as part of their mutiny.

Lucilla, Annia Aurelia Galeria (c. 148–182 C.E.) *Empress from circa 164 to 169, with the title of Augusta*

Lucilla was the daughter of MARCUS AURELIUS and FAUSTINA and received a comfortable upbringing. For political convenience she wed the coemperor Lucius VERUS, probably in 164. He died in 169, the cause of his death rumored to be poison, administered by either Faustina or Marcus Aurelius. Marcus chose another man for Lucilla, an aging Equestrian whom she did not love, Claudius POMPEIANUS. The match proved unhappy, although they remained together until the reign of Lucilla's brother, COMMODUS. Differences with her brother led Lucilla into a plot against him. It failed miserably, and Commodus witnessed the execution of the ringleaders. Lucilla was exiled to Capri and murdered.

Lucilla, Domitia (fl. second century C.E.) *Mother of Marcus Aurelius*

The family of Lucilla was reportedly well established and owned a factory that made tiles somewhere near Rome. Her marriage to Annius Verus produced two children, a son, MARCUS AURELIUS, and a daughter, Annia Cornificia. Annius Verus died while serving as praetor, and Marcus spent most of his youth in the care of his grandfather. Lucilla also helped raise another eventual emperor, DIDIUS JULIANUS, using her influence to start him on his long career.

Lucina Name given to the Roman goddess JUNO as patroness of childbirth.

Lucius Caesar See CAESAR, LUCIUS.

Lucusta the Poisoner (d. 69 C.E.) *Most famous poisoner of the first century C.E.; also called Locusta*

In 54 C.E., she was hired by Agrippina the Younger to mix the poison that killed Emperor CLAUDIUS, administered in a plate of mushrooms. One year later, Lucusta was convicted of poisoning someone, but Nero sent a tribune of the Praetorian Guard, Pollio Julius, to take her into custody. She was ordered to prepare a new potion to kill Claudius's son, BRITANNICUS. The brew proved ineffective, however, and Nero punished both Julius and Lucusta. A second, more lethal dose was concocted, and Britannicus succumbed almost at once. Lucusta survived Nero but was executed by Galba.

ludi Public games held to entertain the Roman populace. The *ludi* had their analogues in the great festivals of the Greek city-states, where lavish festivals were staged for both a religious and political purpose. In Rome, the *ludi* fulfilled a similar dual function, as expressions of the faith of the Romans in their divinities and in the Roman Cult of State. The games probably began as races honoring Mars and Consus but soon expanded to include the so-called *ludi votivi* or games held for special occasions, which became annual events. Most were established during the era of the Republic, although some of the most interesting were creations of the empire. They helped to provide continuity in imperial rule by maintaining a tangible link to previous glory and stability. This was especially necessary in the third century C.E., when lavish *ludi* were staged to distract the Romans from catastrophes in the provinces. Gallienus, for example, held the *ludi Saeculares* after his father Valerian was captured and murdered by the Persians in 260 C.E.

Originally the *ludi* were organized by the various colleges of priests, but as the games became more state oriented, their organization passed to the consuls and then to AEDILES, and finally, under Augustus, to the praetors. The *ludi* were public holidays and no work would be done, remarkably, considering that in the imperial era over 135 days might be spent either in the theater or in the circus. The games ordinarily started with a parade or a banquet, followed by the demonstrations and performances of the finest actors (*ludi Scaenici*). Near the end of the celebration the exciting chariot races (*ludi Circenses*) were held at the CIRCUS MAXIMUS.

The more than 40 types of *ludi* included:

ludi Apollinares Similar to the Hellenic Pythian Games: established in 208 B.C.E. by senatorial decree. Traditionally, Equestrian events, horse races, and chariot events were conducted at the Circus Maximus. They were held from July 6 to 13.

ludi Augustales Established in 14 C.E., shortly after the death of Augustus, and based on the

Augustalia, held first in 11 B.C.E. to honor Augustus on his birthday and placed in the care of the praetors. The tribunes of the Plebs were to fund the games and were authorized to hold them October 3–12 of each year. A delay marred the first staging of the event because of a quarrel among the main actors, a disagreement that angered Tiberius and may have contributed to his decision to banish all actors from Rome. The *ludi Augustales* was eventually linked to the *ludi Circenses* and *ludi Palatini,* specifically under the patronage of the divine Augustus.

ludi Capitolini Games started in 388 B.C.E. to memorialize the preservation of the capital from the Gauls with the help of JUPITER. It was decreed that special *collegium* to organize the games should be voted from among those who lived on the Capitoline Hill in Rome, although the patricians were eventually excluded. Aside from the regular festivities, the *Ludi Capitolini* boasted an unusual ceremony, in which an old man was paraded through the street dressed as a king. He represented the ancient ruler of one of the Etruscan cities (Veii), who was marched through the city in 396 B.C.E., after the defeat of his people by the Romans.

ludi Ceriales These games were held annually, April 12–19, commencing with the CEREALIA on April 12 in honor of Ceres, the goddess of agriculture. They began in 202 B.C.E.

ludi Decennales Beginning with Augustus, an emperor could celebrate his 10th anniversary on the throne with the *Ludi Decennales,* a demonstration of imperial strength and dynastic vitality.

ludi Florales Begun in 173 B.C.E. to honor Flora, the goddess of flowers and spring. Held from April 28 to May 3, the *ludi Florales* was noted for its excessive celebrations and decadence.

ludi Megalenses Also called the *Megalesii* or the *Megalensia,* the days from April 4 to 10 were devoted to the honor of the Great Mother (Mater Magna) CYBELE. In 204 B.C.E., in the throes of the Punic War, the oracles insisted that the sacred black stone of Cybele be moved from Asia Minor to a temple on the Palatine Hill in Rome. The *ludi Megalenses* was organized to honor her, becoming a fixed part of the year around 19 B.C.E., with most of the performers acting at or near her temple. The Christian Church terminated the use of the name *Megalensia,* but the days remained part of the Christian calendar as a festive period.

ludi Plebeii Series of games first staged in 216 B.C.E., during the Punic Wars, and traditionally held in the Circus. The name was derived from the plebian AEDILES who superintended their productions. At first they were held on a single day, November 15, the sacred Ides of Jupiter, but eventually they were expanded to 14 days, from November 4 to 17. The *ludi Plebeii* lasted into the fourth century C.E.

ludi Pontificales These celebrations were held every fourth year, starting in 30 B.C.E., to commemorate Augustus's victory at ACTIUM. A wide number of events took place, including the rare gladiatorial contests. They were also called the *ludi Actiaci.*

ludi Romani The oldest of the *ludi,* dating back to the days of kings and supposedly founded by the Tarquins in the sixth century B.C.E. Jupiter was honored, and a special procession (*pompa*) marched from the Capitol to the Circus Maximus. Chariots formed part of the parade, each with a driver and a soldier rider. The *ludi Romani* were organized at first only under special circumstances (and were called *sollemnes* rather than *annui* or annual), but by the fourth century B.C.E., more days were later added until at Caesar's death in 44 B.C.E., which was honored by yet another day, the *ludi* extended from September 4 to 19—16 days. In the fourth century C.E. the number was reduced, and the *ludi* was celebrated from September 12 to 15.

ludi Saeculares One of the most solemn festivals on the Roman calendar, born out of legend and held infrequently. These *ludi* were begun shortly after the expulsion of the kings, when a pestilence descended upon Rome and the consul, P. Valerius Publicola, ordered sacrifices made to Pluto and Proserpina. When the plague ended, the date was recorded, and it became the *ludi Terentini* because of the location of the altars in the Terentium. The SIBYLLINE BOOKS then ordered that sacrifice be repeated every 60 years, but Greek and Etruscan influence decreed otherwise. According to Greek mythology, the earth went through various cycles (*saeculae*), beginning anew every 110 years. This belief, combined with the Etruscan practice of making prayers and offerings at the end of their own cycles, was integrated into the *ludi.* In 17 B.C.E., the QUINDECIMVIRI, with the blessings of Augustus, instituted the games, declaring the propitious end of the latest cycle, or *saeculum,* and maintaining that in the past the *ludi* had been celebrated every 110 years.

Claudius allowed the *ludi* in 47 C.E., even though an actor who had participated in the first one still lived, reasoning that 800 years had passed since the founding of Rome. Domitian staged them as well in 87. Emperor Antoninus Pius, in 147 C.E., returned to the Claudian method, honoring Rome on its 900th birthday,

The Hippodrome of Domitian, site of races during the *ludi*
(Courtesy Fr. Felix Just, S.J.)

A hymn was sung by choirs, one of them the *Carmen Saeculare* of Horace, written for Augustus and the first *ludi* in 17 B.C.E.

ludi Victoriae Caesaris A *ludi* held in 46 B.C.E. by Julius Caesar to celebrate the dedication of his temple to Venus, promised at the battle of PHARSALUS in 48 B.C.E. This *ludi* was held from July 20 to 30.

ludi Volcanalici Augustan games staged in 20 B.C.E. to mark the treaty of peace with Parthia and the return of the legionary standards, which had been lost at the battle of CARRHAE by Crassus in 53. The *ludi* took place on August 23, inside the temple of Vulcan but outside of the city of Rome.

Lugdunum Capital city of the province of Gallia Lugdunensis. Now called Lyons, the city was the premier metropolis in Gaul (GALLIA) and the most influential in the process of Romanization. In 43 B.C.E., L. Munatius Plancus established a colony called Copia Felix Munatia at the confluence of the rivers Arar (Saône) and Rhodanus (Rhone). This colony was thriving when Augustus created the three provinces of Gaul—Gallia Aquitania, Gallia Belgica, and Gallia Lugdunensis—around 27 B.C.E. The imperial provincial administration was launched with a census that year of the tribes of the region.

Henceforth, the city assumed increasing importance not only as the local capital but also as the center of the IMPERIAL CULT in Gaul, where in 12 B.C.E. DRUSUS the Elder dedicated an altar to Roma et Augustus, implanting the worship of Rome and its emperors in Gallic life. The *concilia* or provincial councils for Gaul met at Lugdunum each year to hold elections, and for the great annual festival honoring their Roman patrons. Tiberius ordered than an amphitheater and temple be built to supplement the altar. Like the cities in Gallia Narbonensis of Arausio, ARLES and NEMAUSUS (Nîmes), Lugdunum was to serve as the model of Romanization.

Originally, the town had been situated at the base of a high hill near the two rivers. Through large-scale efforts of engineers, and with the support of the legate, whose seat and residence were at Lyons, the *colonia* expanded beyond the hill, until all of the neighboring communities and Celtic tribes had been absorbed. Lugdunum was known for its two theaters, one an *odeum* built to supplement its older and larger companion. There were two forums by the end of the second century C.E. and a capitol overlooking the buildings from the hill. In addition to the altar of the imperial cult, a Temple of Jupiter was erected in the second forum.

Lugdunum, centered on the main lines of communication and trade through Gallia, reaped full financial rewards and economic prosperity. Gallic pottery rivaled that of Italy, and Lyons's glasswork earned a wide reputation. Artisans and merchants worked out of the city's

while Septimius Severus held the *ludi* in 204, 220 years after Augustus's celebration. Philip the Arab, in the year A.V.C. 1000 (247 C.E.) celebrated the *ludi* with splendor. Gallienus ordered a special *ludi* following the defeat and death of his father Valerian in 260 C.E. Finally, Honorius, perhaps in 397, allowed the pagans to organize a *ludi Saeculares*, the last held until the Middle Ages.

The *ludi Saeculares* was very much a pagan ritual. On the appointed day, the *Quindecimviri*, magistrates and senators, dressed in white, were joined by a large throng in the Campus Martius. Purification rites were conducted, and the festival began. On the second day, the *ludi* moved to the Capitoline and the TEMPLE OF JUPITER CAPITOLINUS. On the third day the Palatine was host to the festivities in the TEMPLE OF APOLLO. Throughout, elaborate sacrifices were made to Jupiter, Juno, Apollo, Diana, Pluto, and Proserpina. The emperor and the *Quindecimviri* slaughtered three rams, which were bled and then burned in the midst of revelry. Jupiter was given white bulls and Juno a white cow. Pigs and a white sow were offered, as well as oxen, and, according to legend, dark victims to please the gods of the underworld.

factories and shops, and an imperial mint was established. Herodian was thus able to pay Lugdunum the compliment of writing that, at the start of the third century C.E., it was both large and prosperous. The city was damaged during the revolt of ALBINUS, and in the late fifth century, with the decline of the empire, it became the capital of the kingdom of the BURGUNDIANS. The emperor Claudius was from Lugdunum.

Lugdunum, battle of   Engagement fought on February 19, 197 C.E., between Septimius SEVERUS and CLODIUS ALBINUS for the supremacy of the Roman world. Following the assassination of the emperor PERTINAX in 193, three claimants for the imperial throne emerged; Severus, governor of PANNONIA; Albinus, governor of BRITAIN; and PESCENNIUS NIGER, governor of SYRIA. Severus persuaded Albinus to accept the rank of Caesar, or lieutenant governor, and set out East against Niger. With his powerful Danubian legions, Severus destroyed Niger in the East at ISSUS in 194. Having conquered half the empire, Severus turned against Albinus. In Britain, Albinus made preparations before crossing over to the Gallic provinces with his small British detachment, levying all possible troops to supplement his three legions. A victory over the governor of Germania Inferior allowed further recruiting in Germania and in Gallia Belgica. Albinus next entered Gallia Lugdunesis, settling at LUGDUNUM (Lyons), where he tried to rally the West against the advancing Severus.

Severus ordered the passes of the Alps to be shut while he marched across Raetia and Noricum toward his enemy. Severus gained a strategically superior position and then forced Albinus to fight outside his base at Lyons. The battle involved perhaps 150,000 men on each side and, according to historian Dio, was bitterly fought. The Danubian legions, however, equated themselves well, crushing Albinus's left wing and driving it into the camp. Hours of bloody fighting were necessary before Severus's cavalry commander, LAETUS, made the winning charge. Herodian states that Laetus had hovered, waiting for both leaders to die in the fray so that he could claim the throne. Albinus's legions disintegrated and Albinus himself fled to a small house. Seeing that he was surrounded, he killed himself. His head was removed and sent to Rome, where it was displayed on a pole. Septimius Severus now ruled without a rival.

Luna   Roman goddesses of the moon. She was originally identified with Diana, the Greek deity, although she did not retain Diana's reputation for chastity. Luna enjoyed a number of amorous adventures.

See also GODS AND GODDESSES OF ROME.

Lupicinus, Flavius (d. after 367 C.E.) *Magister militum to Emperor Julian and later Jovian and Valens*

Lupicinus served initially under Julian (c. 359–360) and was sent on a mission to BRITANNIA in 360, where he remained despite the order of Eastern Emperor Constantius II to bring his troops for service in the East. Constantius stripped him of his command, but died soon after, leaving Julian sole ruler of the empire. Julian, however, mistrusted Lupicinus, halting all supplies to Britain and arresting him upon his return to Gaul. Lupicinus survived Julian's reign and in 364 was appointed *magister militum* in the East, a post that he held for three years (364–367). He served as consul in 367 and was credited by the orator LIBANIUS as a patron of philosophy and literature.

Lusitania   *See* HISPANIA.

Lutetia   Modern Paris, originally the capital city of the Gallic tribe, the Parisii, eventually serving as an important Roman site in Gallia Lugdunensis. Located on an island in the Sequana (Seine) River, it was connected to both banks by two large wooden bridges, affording an excellent defensive position. In 52 B.C.E., during Julius Caesar's GALLIC WARS, his legate was forced to fight his way from northern Gaul to rejoin Caesar and to unite their forces against a major uprising of most of the Gallic tribes. Labienus made for Lutetia, but was opposed by the Parisii and their allies. A fight ensued, and the Romans defeated the Gauls but Lutetia was burned and its bridges cut. Following the pacification of the Gauls by Caesar and the incorporation of GALLIA into the Roman Empire by Augustus, Lutetia became a port city in Gallia Lugdunensis. All boat traffic on the Seine traveled from its docks; imperial naval flotillas probably operated from there as well. In 360 C.E., the Emperor Julian was residing there when his troops proclaimed him Augustus and sole ruler of the empire over CONSTANTIUS II.

Lycaonia   Region located in the southeast of Asia Minor, between Pisidia and Cappadocia, in the Roman province of GALATIA; its major cities, Laodicea Combusta, Lystra, and Iconium, developed into thriving economic entities. Lystra was founded by Augustus, with a colony of veterans of the legions, while Iconium was eventually honored with full colonial status by Hadrian. Under Trajan, Lycaonia was separated from Galatia and placed under the control of the governor of CILICIA, although several cities probably remained attached to Galatia. Within the provincial assembly of Cilicia, the Lycaonians were allowed their own council, or *koinon*.

The Lycaonians were said to be independent, fierce in battle, and to excel in archery. To help pacify them, Augustus used his successful colonial solution, establishing two colonies, Parlais and Lystra.

Lycia-Pamphylia Two very different Roman provinces in Asia Minor that were joined together by Claudius in 43 C.E. and Vespasian in 74 C.E. for the purposes of administration. Such a process had already been applied, with some success, in CRETE AND CYRENAICA.

LYCIA

As was true with many parts of Asia Minor, Lycia was an ancient land, situated on the southern coast between Caria and Pamphylia, just south of Pisidia. Before the arrival of the Romans circa 130 B.C.E., it had existed for many years as a remarkable conglomeration of 23 cities, known as the Lycian League. King Attalus III of Pergamum had bequeathed his large domain to Rome, and by 100 B.C.E., all of Asia Minor was under Roman sway. Under the Romans, the Lycians were officially classified as a client state, but little interference was made in the Lycian government. They continued to elect the officials of the league, including the lyciarch, each city retained voting privileges, and the Lycian language and coinage continued in use. Protection was afforded by the fact that the surrounding area was Roman.

Inevitably, Roman traders opened up economic links with the Lycians. Their high mountains provided lumber, their fields produced corn and their harbors offered excellent moorings for ships, though Lycia's harsh climate and rugged terrain prevented its full participation in Asian commerce. Nevertheless, the Lycians proved themselves to be shrewd and ruthless business partners, who would go to extreme lengths to settle affairs.

In 43 C.E., a revolt or feud of some kind prompted the imperial government to seize the cities and to place them under the care of the imperial governor. However, in 69 C.E., Galba returned the province to the hands of the Lycians. In reorganizing the imperial holdings, Vespasian reclaimed Lycia in 74, annexing it to Pamphylia to ease local administration. Government was now centered on the imperial legate and his trusted procurator, although the cities of Lycia continued to provide the provincial assemblies with delegates and now aided as well in the empire-wide system of the IMPERIAL CULT. These CONCILIA kept up with the cult while collecting taxes and overseeing municipal administration, though final authority rested with the governor.

Lycia and Pamphylia continued to enjoy this semi-autonomous existence until the time of Hadrian, when several major changes were made in their domestic affairs. Hadrian passed the provincial duties to the Senate, especially because there had been no serious outbreaks of violence over the years, and the imperial legate was replaced by a Praetorian proconsul. In return, Hadrian received the wealthy province of BITHYNIA from the Senate. That the process succeeded was proven by the total absence of the dreadful CURATORES so common in the East and in Achaea to examine finances. Finally, there was established, perhaps in the time of Marcus Aurelius, a garrison from the I Legion.

In the imperial dispositions of Diocletian, Lycia was attached to the diocese of Asiana. The Lycian metropolises were still thriving in the late fourth century C.E., when the Praetorian Prefect Rufinus punished a Lycian minister named Tatian by publishing an order forbidding all Lycians from serving in public office. This ban lasted approximately one year (394–395), until Rufinus was assassinated.

Lycia was remarkable for maintaining its own culture, style, and nationalistic identity in the empire. Its geography, isolating it from the rest of Asia Minor, contributed to this, but more so its superb league of cities, formed on a Greek model. Like Crete, Lycia proved that there could be Roman government without disastrous consequences for local traditions.

PAMPHYLIA

Unlike Lycia, Pamphylia, on the coast just to the east of Lycia, was wild and undeveloped. Belonging for many years to SELEUCIA, around 189 B.C.E. it was ceded to Rome by Antiochus III. The province was placed first within the jurisdiction of Cilicia and then of Asia, sometime in 44 B.C.E. No permanent solution could be found for Pamphylia. Under Augustus it was included in the province of Galatia when that territory was pacified by the governor, P. Sulpicius QUIRINIUS. It was joined to Lycia in 43 C.E. by Claudius, then was reattached to Galatia by Galba. Colonies of veterans were used to reestablish Lycia-Pamphylia by Vespasian in 74 C.E. Colonial foundations at Comana, Crena, and Olbasa pointed to the fundamental differences between Lycia and Pamphylia, namely that in the former the Romans found, in full force, an already developed and vivacious culture, while in the latter a considerable effort at Romanization was needed.

Claudius improved the road system from the coast to the inland areas, opening up the potential for trade, and the colonies of Roman soldiers, having tamed the inhabitants with the help of the imperial government, finally profited from the rich natural resources of Pamphylia. Throughout the second and third centuries C.E., both the populace and building in the region grew, yielding numerous archaeological sites today. The colony depended on Rome for local government; no *concilia* was ever fully successful and the Imperial Cult failed to gain in popularity with the natives.

Lydia Ancient region of Asia Minor situated between Caria and Mysia. Lydia was, for many centuries, a substantial kingdom in Anatolia and in the Aegean. Its last ruler, Attalus III, bequeathed his holdings to Rome around 133 B.C.E. Lydia then became a district in the province of ASIA, until Diocletian named it a separate province.

M

Macarius (Macarius the Egyptian, Macarius the Great) (d. c. 390 C.E.) *One of the Desert Fathers who helped foster monasticism in Christianity*

Born in Upper Egypt, Macarius retired at the age of 30 to the desert of Scete, or Scetis (Wadi-el-Natrun), where he soon attracted followers. The colony of hermits became a renowned place of monasticism, and Macarius's reputation for sanctity, intelligence, and healing powers quickly spread. Ordained a priest around 340, he was noted by writers of the era as particularly gifted in preaching and offering spiritual guidance. He supported St. Athanasius against the Arians and was banished in 374 to an island in the Nile by Athanasius's successor as bishop of Alexandria, Lucius. Macarius later returned and spent his remaining years in the desert.

While the sources on Macarius mention nothing of his literary output, a body of work is ascribed to him and called at times Macarian literature. The most notable of these is a collection of 50 spiritual homilies. Also attributed to him is the letter "To the Friends of God," addressed to younger monks. Jacques Paul Migne in Volume 34 of the *Patrologia Graeca* preserved the Macarian literature, and many scholars have examined the possible influence upon Macarius and the sources of the so-called Macarian writings.

Macarius Magnes (fl. late fourth century C.E.) *Christian apologist and author of the Apocritica*

Nothing is known concerning Macarius's life, although he has sometimes been identified with Macarius, bishop of Magnesia, who accused Heraclides, bishop of Ephesus, of Origenism at the so-called Synod of the Oak (Chalcedon, 403). The *Apocritica* was a defense of the faith against an unknown pagan philosopher, written in five books in the form of a dispute. The work was used in the ninth century by the Iconoclasts to defend their doctrines.

Macedonia Roman province that, in the time of Philip and Alexander the Great in the fourth century B.C.E., was the most powerful nation in the ancient world. Its armies conquered the Persian Empire, and Alexander's generals, Seleucus Nicator and Ptolemy, created their own kingdoms. The homeland and its armies and generals began to feel the pressure of Rome by the second century B.C.E. Rome terminated Macedonian mastery over Greece by 168 B.C.E., when General Lucius PAULLUS won the battle of Pydna over King Perseus, son of Philip V. Pydna proved for all time that the venerable phalanx of the Macedonians was useless against the legions, and Romans controlled the entire eastern Mediterranean. Initial Roman policy in Macedonia centered on retaining a high degree of self-government. Toward this end, the old realm was divided into four separate republics. This arrangement worked only until 148 B.C.E., when a revolt was started by Andriscus. To improve the administrative deficiencies that had allowed the uprising in the first place, the Romans seized outright the entire country, declaring it a province. At that time it contained most of Greece as well.

All of this changed with Emperor Augustus, who perceived Macedonia's importance strategically when he formulated coherent plans for the region. Augustus's first objective was to remove any chance of local trouble. Macedonia had always been plagued by tribal incursions from Dacia and Thrace. Thus, in 30 B.C.E., the legate M. Licinius Crassus was sent with four legions. In a series of brilliantly waged campaigns, Crassus reduced the strength of the surrounding people, pacified Macedonia and established a buffer zone with client chieftains. By 27

B.C.E. Crassus's work was done. Augustus declared Macedonia a province in the care of the Senate. Its size, however, was reduced as other provinces, Achaea and Epirus, were carved out of it.

This organization remained until 15 C.E., when Emperor Tiberius decided that a complete reappraisal of the Danube frontier was needed. To strengthen the Danubian line, the emperor founded the province of Moesia, placing both Macedonia and Achaea under its legate, C. Poppaeus Sabinus. Claudius, in 44, determined that such an extraordinary command was unwarranted and returned Macedonia and Achaea to provincial independence. The Macedonia known for the next few centuries took form. Provincial boundaries extended from Achaea to Moesia and from Thrace to the Adriatic and Illyricum. A great highway, the Via Egnatia, running from east to west along the north of Macedonia, connected Thrace and the East with Illyricum, Italy and the West. The Via Egnatia ran through the key cities of Philippi, THESSALONICA, Pella, and the historical site of DYRRHACHIUM.

Roman administration was under a proconsul of Praetorian rank, aided by a legate, a quaestor, and a procurator. The government's duties were all bureaucratic, for Macedonia was considered an unarmed province and had no garrison. Aside from the imperial officers, the proconsul had to deal with the Macedonian assemblies and the CONCILIA, allowed and encouraged by Augustus for the propagation of the IMPERIAL CULT. The *concilium* met at Beroea, although the provincial seat was at Thessalonica.

The presence of the Imperial Cult was only one element of a wider program of Romanization. *Coloniae* and *municipia* were used to introduce Italian colonists at Dyrrhachium, Pella, Philippi, Byllis, and Cassandreia, and *municipia* at Denda and Stabi. Intense Romanization was considered crucial as a basis for cultural unification. With Celts, Illyrians, Macedonians, Greeks, and Thracians all living in the same territory, the Roman way of life was used as a common thread to bind them together. The increased use of Latin with Greek, and the large number of Macedonian recruits for the army showed the success of this process.

Economically, Macedonia's geographical variety allowed diversification. Agricultural goods had always been important, as were sheep, but the province found wealth in two other areas as well. Mining was very productive (as in Hispania), and the timber industry was burgeoning. To this was added the prime location of the province on the trade route between East and West, with the Via Egnatia as its lifeline. Macedonia suffered terribly in the third century C.E., for it was defenseless in the face of the massive Gothic invasions and was crossed repeatedly by barbarian hordes eager to ravage Achaea. Subsequently, any threats to the Danube frontiers meant danger to the province. Under the Diocletian reforms, Macedonia was made part of the diocese of Moesia.

macellum A meat market in a Roman city (pl. *macella*). While technically designating a meat market itself, the term eventually came to be applied to the wider hall surrounding the meat market, including the stalls and other shops. Normally the *macellum* was built close to a forum to make it more available to shoppers. The best known of the *macella* of Rome was the so-called Trajan's Market, which boasted in its prime stalls room enough for more than 150 ships.

Macer, Aemilius (d. 16 B.C.E.) *Poet of the early Augustan Age*
Macer was from Verona and probably a friend of Virgil. He authored poems on herbs (*de herbis*) as well as poems on animals, especially birds and snakes. Macer died in Asia. Pliny the Elder used him as a source for his *Natural History.*

Macrianus, Titus Fulvius (d. 261 C.E.) *Officer in the army of Valerian*
In 260 Macrianus commanded the remnants of Rome's army in the East, following the emperor's capture and eventual death at the hands of the Persians. Titus Fulvius Macrianus was a lame soldier who nevertheless secured the ranks of *praepositus annonae expeditionalis* and *procurator arcae expeditionis* from Valerian, and thus was quartermaster general in the ill-fated Persian campaign. When word arrived of the Persian victory, Fulvius Macrianus and a general named Callistus (nicknamed Ballista) initiated a counterattack from the base at Samosata. Ballista defeated Shapur I at Corycus in Cilicia, driving the Persians back to the Euphrates. Roman arms having been avenged and the East temporarily saved, both Fulvius Macrianus and Ballista split from Gallienus, Valerian's son. As neither could claim the throne (Ballista was a commoner and Macrianus too old and too ill), T. F. J. MACRIANUS and T. Fulvius QUIETUS were proclaimed joint rulers in 260. Ballista was made the Praetorian prefect. Quietus and Ballista were left in Syria to maintain the provinces there, while Fulvius Macrianus and his son marched west in 261 to destroy Gallienus. In the area of the Danube their army encountered Gallienus's general, Aureolus. After a brief engagement, their soldiers surrendered and both leaders were killed.

Macrianus, Titus Fulvius Junius (d. 261 C.E.) *Son of General Fulvius Macrianus*
Macrianus reigned with his brother QUIETUS as a usurper in the East from 260 to 261. Following the capture and murder of Emperor Valerian in 260 by the Persians, Fulvius Macrianus and the future Praetorian prefect Ballista, unable to make the throne themselves, agreed that Macrianus and Quietus should be elevated. This was accomplished in 260, and numerous Eastern provinces immediately recognized them as rulers. These provinces

included Syria, Egypt, and parts of Asia Minor. There remained the rest of the Roman Empire, however, and Gallienus, Valerian's son and heir. It was therefore resolved that Quietus and Ballista should remain in Syria to watch the East, while Macrianus and his father marched west to make war upon Gallienus. In 261 they reached the Danube and, somewhere in Illyricum, were met and crushed by Gallienus's general, Aureolus. Both father and son died.

Macrinus, Marcus Opellius (c. 165–218 C.E.)
Emperor from 217 to 218, and a one-time prefect of the praetorian guard under Caracalla

Macrinus was born to a poor family in Caesarea, in Mauretania, and many details of his life have not been verified, but he apparently moved to Rome and acquired a position as adviser on law and finances to the Praetorian prefect Plautianus. Surviving the fall of the prefect in 205, Macrinus became financial minister to Septimius Severus and of the Flaminian Way. By 212, Macrinus held the trust of Emperor Caracalla and was appointed prefect of the Praetorian Guard, sharing his duties with Oclatinus Adventus. Campaigning with Caracalla in 216 against the Parthians, Macrinus came to fear for his own safety, as Caracalla could be murderous. When letters addressed to the emperor seemed to point to his own doom, Macrinus engineered a conspiracy that ended in early 217 with Caracalla's assassination near Edessa.

Feigning grief and surprise, Macrinus manipulated the legions into proclaiming him emperor. To ensure their devotion and to assuage any doubts as to his complicity in the murder, he deified the martially popular Caracalla. Meanwhile, the Senate, which had come to loathe the emperor, granted full approval to Macrinus's claims. The Senate's enthusiasm was dampened, however, by Macrinus's appointments, including Adventus as city prefect and Ulpius Julianus and Julianus Nestor as prefects of the Guard. Adventus was too old and unqualified, while the two prefects and Adventus had been heads of the feared FRUMENTARII.

Real problems, both military and political, soon surfaced. Artabanus V had invaded Mesopotamia, and the resulting battle of Nisibis did not resolve matters. Unable to push his troops, whom he did not trust, Macrinus accepted a humiliating peace. This, unfortunately, coincided with plotting by Caracalla's Syrian family, headed by JULIA MAESA. Macrinus had tried to create dynastic stability, but mutiny in the Syrian legions threatened his survival. The Severans put up the young Elagabalus, high priest of the Sun God at Emesa, as the rival for the throne. Macrinus sent his prefect Ulpius against the Severan forces only to have him betrayed and murdered. He then faced Elagabalus's army, led by the eunuch Gannys, and lost. Macrinus fled to Antioch and tried to escape to the West but was captured at Chalcedon and returned to Antioch. Both Macrinus and his son DIADUMENIANUS, whom he had declared his co-ruler, were executed.

The reign of Macrinus was important in that it was the first time that a nonsenator and a Mauretanian had occupied the throne. Further, he could be called the first of the soldier emperors who would dominate the chaotic third century C.E. As his successors would discover, the loyalty of the legions was crucial, more important in some ways than the support of the rest of the Roman Empire.

Macrinus, Veturius (fl. late second century C.E.) *Prefect of the Praetorian Guard in the reign of Didius Julianus and the era of Septimius Severus*

Macrinus, a supporter of Severus, was appointed to the post of prefect by Julianus in 193 in the hopes that the emperor might gain favor with Severus, who was advancing on Rome with the legions from Pannonia. The attempt failed, and Julianus fell from power. Macrinus, who had already been promised the office by Severus, was retained, serving until 200.

Macro, Quintus Naevius Cordus Sutorius (d. 38 C.E.) *Prefect of the Praetorian Guard (31–38) under emperors Tiberius and Gaius Caligula*

Macro served in the guard, reaching the post of tribune by 31 C.E. In that year he came to the attention of Tiberius, who was seeking the means to destroy the overreaching Praetorian Prefect SEJANUS. Macro was summoned to the emperor at the island of Capri, handed the imperial letter of condemnation and offered Sejanus's post if he would deliver the message to the Senate in Rome. On the morning of October 18, Macro ascended the steps of the Palatine, handed the decree from Tiberius to the Senate and went immediately to the Castra Praetoria to assume command of the Guard. Tiberius did not forget Macro's role in the liquidation of Sejanus. He gave him the rank of expraetor while granting him the position of trusted adviser. For the rest of the aging emperor's life, Macro played a double game. On the one hand he mercilessly perpetuated Tiberius's tyrannies in Rome, arresting, torturing, and murdering the opposition, real or imagined. All the while, however, he was cultivating the trust and good wishes of the next emperor, Gaius Caligula.

Sources vary as to his role in and possible approval of his wife Ennia Thrasylla's affair with Caligula in 37 to ensure that her husband remained in favor. Tiberius noted Macro's preparation for the future by remarking: "You desert the setting and rush to the rising sun." Macro reportedly helped to finished off Tiberius in 37; according to the historian Tacitus, he ordered clothes heaped on the dying ruler and so suffocated him. Other accounts place the actual act in other hands, although Macro was certainly an accomplice. Subsequently, he aided Gaius in receiving the approval of the Senate as emperor; the voiding of Tiberius's will was part of his duties. Tiberius had named his grandson, Tiberius Gemellus, as an equal heir.

Having worked tirelessly to acquire power and prestige, Macro became one of the first victims of Gaius. In 38 he was ordered to step down as prefect, ostensibly to assume new duties as the prefect of Egypt. Before he could leave, however, both he and his wife received Caligula's command that they kill themselves.

Macrobius, Ambrosius Theodosius (fl. early fifth century C.E.) *Writer who probably came from Africa, but little has survived of his private or public life*
Macrobius may have been the Praetorian prefect of Hispaniarum but was most likely Praetorian prefect of Italy. Based upon his writings and associations with Symmachus, Nicomachus Flavianus, and Praetextatus, Macrobius was no doubt a pagan, or at least a supporter of Paganism with a taste as well for Neoplatonism. Two works earned Macrobius considerable fame: a *Commentary* on Cicero's *Dream of Scipio* (*Somnium Scipionis*) and *Saturnalia*. The commentary examined Cicero by applying Neoplatonic philosophy to Cicero's text, including ideas concerning the soul and astronomy. *Saturnalia* presented a three-day dialogue held during the festival of Saturnalia at the home of Praetextatus. In attendance were friends such as Symmachus, Nicomachus Flavianus, Avienus, and Servius. Aside from the individual subjects as part of the conversation, most of the *Saturnalia* revolved around the qualities of Virgil, both good and bad. It is thought that the *Saturnalia* was intended for the education of Macrobius's son in polite manners.

Maeatae One of the two major tribes living north of the Wall of Hadrian in the region of Caledonia in Britain. The Maeatae shared the region with the Caledonians but were not openly warlike (as were their neighbors) until late in the second century C.E. Dio described the two tribes as similar: both inhabiting wild country, living off flocks and game, with a very uncivilized culture. In war the Maeatae drove chariots with small horses, using infantry as well, with shields and spears. They lived closest to the wall, threatening first in 197, with their Caledonian allies. The legate of Britain, Lupus, had to buy them off, as the Roman Empire was engulfed in a civil war between Septimius Severus and Clodius Albinus. In 208, Severus arrived in Britain to subjugate all of Caledonia. His son Caracalla joined him on campaign. In 210 the Maeatae resisted and were dealt with cruelly. The Caledonians then chose to aid their longtime neighbors. Severus planned another march into the north but died in 211, and Caracalla made peace with the tribes.

Maecenas, Gaius Cilnius (74/64–8 B.C.E.) *Trusted friend and confidant of Augustus; also, one of the greatest artistic and literary patrons of the Augustan Age (27 B.C.E. to 14 C.E.)*
Maecenas was born at Arretium, to an Equestrian family; his ancestors were part of the powerful Etruscan clan of the Cilnii on one side and the important line of the Maecenatae on the other. Maecenas became attached to the young Octavian (AUGUSTUS) in 43 B.C.E., gaining his complete faith and emerging as one of his most important advisers, along with Marcus Agrippa. Where Agrippa was the key lieutenant in matters of war, Maecenas was Augustus's intellectual and political adviser, having a brilliant mind and a quiet temperament. He acted as mediator, diplomat, and reconciler between Augustus and the various political factions of Rome. As the official representative of Augustus in Rome and Italy during the Civil War of the Second Triumvirate with Marc Antony, Maecenas helped pave the way for the Augustan principate.

Throughout the early years of imperial rule, Maecenas continued to enjoy the complete favor of Augustus, being noted for his loyalty without conspicuous grasping for status or privilege. He did not join the Senate or aspire to high office, although all were aware of his influence, and wielded authority ever courteously and judiciously in the city. After 22 B.C.E., however, the friendship between Augustus and Maecenas declined. The cause was never made clear, but it probably had to do with the execution that year of Licinius MURENA by imperial order on charges of treason and conspiracy. Maecenas was Murena's brother-in-law and may have felt that Augustus's reign, which was noted for its leniency, was taking a bad turn with this sentence. Maecenas dropped out of the councils of Augustus and retired from public life.

He achieved lasting fame for his work for Augustus but had an equal reputation for his patronage of the arts, especially literature. A longtime friend of HORACE, Maecenas was seldom apart from him and gave the poet a beautiful villa and a farm in the Sabine country. Virgil owed to Maecenas the recovery of his estate and the impetus to write the *Georgics*. Maecenas also aided Propertius and Varius. Augustus greeted the death of Maecenas with understandable grief. They had drifted apart because of the Murena affair and, perhaps, because of an incident involving Maecenas's wife Terentia but in Maecenas's will, Augustus was named as heir with full rights to discharge Maecenas's property as he saw fit. After all, it was to Maecenas's villa that the emperor would go when ill, and it was always Maecenas who could bring Augustus out of rages, sometimes caused by stress. The historian Dio recorded a supposed speech imploring Augustus in 29 B.C.E. to retain the full powers that he already possessed.

Maecianus, Lucius Volusius (fl. second century C.E.) *Jurist and a tutor of Marcus Aurelius*
Maecianus made his name during the reign of Antoninus Pius, joining his staff as a LIBELLUS (secretary of petitions). Other appointments soon followed, including that

of prefect of Egypt (c. 160–161), but writing dominated his activities. Maecianus authored 16 books on legal matters and other topics of interest. Two nonjuridical efforts were a treatise on meteorology and a study of weights and measures. Salvius Julianus may have been an instructor of Maecianus but was certainly an acquaintance.

Magetobriga Unknown site of a military engagement fought in 61 B.C.E. between the Gallic tribes of the Aedui, Averni, and Sequani on one side and the Germanic Suebi, under their king Ariovistus. The Suebi had moved into the region of Gaul comprising modern Alsace and had emerged as a powerful rival to the Gauls on the Rhine. Hoping to evict the unwelcome Germans, the local peoples, headed by the Aedui, confronted Ariovistus in the field. The resulting battle was a display of the martial superiority of the Suebi, for the tribes were crushed. Ariovistus established his rule over much of eastern Gaul. By 58 B.C.E., Rome was willing to listen to the pleas of the Gallic chieftains, and war erupted once again.

magic To the Romans, an elaborate and philosophically complex system, connected to cults, private practice, and even NEOPLATONISM. By their own admission the Romans were a superstitious people, adhering to all kinds of magical beliefs from their earliest times, including astrology, divination, extreme forms of mysticism, and spell casting. Much of what the Romans understood to be magic came from the Greeks, who had definite views concerning magical phenomena. A word such as *magicus* was Greek, conveying the Hellenic dislike for what was viewed as negative or black magic. This stigma was never overcome by magic's practitioners, in Roman intellectual circles. The general public, however, did not subscribe to this skepticism. Over the years certain styles of magic became popular and then faded from view.

Divination was intensely followed by many people of all social levels in Rome (*see* AUGURS and SOOTHSAYERS). Astrologers were used by the emperors, including Tiberius, but even he realized the possibility of fraud or corruption. In 16 C.E., he executed all foreign astrologers while exiling all Italian practitioners of the trade. Claudius banished them all again in 52 C.E., and Vespasian repeated the tradition in 69–70. Astrology could not so easily be destroyed, however, and it remained popular even in the face of CHRISTIANITY.

Distinctions were made between magic that was used for good and for evil purposes. Much as it always had been, magic was applied by individuals hoping to secure a personal victory, gain riches, or ruin an enemy. The means available for such deeds were endless. Curses could be laid upon someone using amulets, spells, dolls, and tablets carrying potent incantations. Those skilled in their use might be nobles, midwives, or the ever-present witches, although witches and sorcerers were most common.

Essentially, applied magic fell into two categories: sympathetic and contagious. Sympathetic magic (*similia similibus*) used the idea of imaging an event—making a wax doll representing an individual and burning it, or performing a ritual of reciprocal action (i.e., striking a spear on a shield to bring rain). This could also be called homeopathic magic. Contagious (*pars pro toto*) magic used some piece of an intended victim's possessions: hair, skin, or clothing. These components were then burned or combined with other ingredients to effect a change—injury or death. Used normally for malicious reasons, contagious magic could, in the eyes of believers, be very powerful.

Its potential to do harm, coupled with a longstanding reputation for evil, made magic a target for attack in literature and by Roman politicians. Virgil described a magical rite in his writings, as did Horace in describing the kidnapping and death of a child. Such scenes depicted the more twisted aspects of magic, while Pliny the Elder, in his *Natural History,* charged all magicians with fraud, claiming that they derived their knowledge from a poor mixture of astronomy and religion. Only Apuleius, in his *Apologia,* attempted to repair the damage done to the practice, although he was not a champion of magic.

Political figures joined the offensive, applying the often false charge of witchcraft to objects of personal hatred. The first notable victim of such an attack was in the reign of Tiberius. M. Drusus Libo was forced to commit suicide because of his involvement with Chaldaean fortune-tellers. Legislation was actually passed, allowing prosecutions of witches and stiff fines, which were applied to anyone who might bring harm to another person, their property, or family.

See also FIGULUS, NIGIDIUS; HERMES TRISMEGISTOS; IAMBLICHUS; JULIAN THE APOSTATE; MAXIMUS OF EPHESUS; PAGANISM; PHILOSOPHY.

magister equitum Master of horse, or master of the cavalry, in Rome. The *magister equitum* was an important military and political office during the Republic and in the late empire. Originally, the *magister equitum* was the deputy to the dictator, appointed by him to oversee various duties. Julius Caesar used reliable *magistri* as his personal representatives in Rome during the Civil War (c. 49–45 B.C.E.). Augustus, however, disliked the relative independence of the office and dissolved it with the founding of the principate. Most of the duties of the office were entrusted to those that became PREFECT OF THE PRAETORIAN GUARD.

By the time of Constantine the Great (early fourth century C.E.) the status of the Praetorian was great. To curb the prefects' power, the emperor reinstituted the office of *magister equitum*. Now it was one of the two generalships in charge of the new army, one for the cavalry and the other for the infantry (*magister peditum*). There was, at first, distinction between the two positions, but by the reign of Constantius II, both *magistri* were called simply *magister equitum et peditum, magister militiae* or, most commonly, *magister militum* (master of the soldiers). *See* also LEGIONS for the nature of the army in the late empire.

magister memoriae Head of the imperial office of the *scrinium* (SCRINII) *memoriale,* or the department concerned with organizing all materials written by the emperors, ministers, and other bureaucrats, as well as the drafting or publishing of replies to these memos, reports, decrees, and petitions. Originally known as the *a memoria,* the post began in the second century C.E. as part of the wider bureaucratization of imperial administration. The associated tasks at first consisted of composing replies to petitions made to the emperor. Thus the office holders required legal training and expertise, filling as well the influential position of chief legal adviser, with the right to sit as a member of any CONSILIUM PRINCIPIS.

By the fourth century, with the reforms made in government, the *a memoria* became a *magister memoriae,* in charge of only one small section of a vast machine of rule. The MAGISTER OFFICIORUM was now the most important legal authority, and the *magister memoriae* was under his command.

magister militum The title possessed by a group of supreme generals during the fourth and fifth centuries C.E. Meaning "master of soldiers," the position was born of the reforms of the early fourth century, and its holders came to occupy an unprecedented place in the affairs of the Roman Empire. In the East they influenced the court at Constantinople, while in the West they ran virtually every facet of government.

It was the decision of CONSTANTINE the Great to reduce further the power of the PREFECT OF THE PRAETORIAN GUARD. Already stripped of certain military authority by DIOCLETIAN, the prefect was removed completely from the field of generalship. To replace the prefect, Constantine appointed two reliable officers: the MAGISTER EQUITUM and the MAGISTER PEDITUM. His intention was to have one lead the cavalry and the other head the infantry. They were to work together in a collegial sense, watched and supported by each other.

Initially this system seemed to work, as the reforms of Constantine covering the entire army of the empire took hold. Toward the middle of the fourth century, however, certain patterns had developed. The *magister peditum* assumed a slightly superior position, born out of the routine appointment of a senior officer at that post. Equally, the wars of the time required that any field force (COMITATENSES) be fully supplied with cavalry and infantry. When both commanders could not be present, the remaining one assumed control over any contingents supposedly under the authority of his colleague. In time, therefore, the actual titles became so blurred that they

fell into disuse. Henceforth a variety of names was used to describe the generals: *magister equitum et peditum, magister utriusque militiae, magister armorum, magister rei castrensis,* and *pedestris militiae rector.* All of these appear in the writings of Ammianus Marcellinus, but common usage reduced them to a simpler title—*magister militum.*

Although Constantine had originally created only two such lieutenants, by the time of Constantius II, there were several in both the Western and Eastern Empires. Constantius himself was responsible for three new *magistri,* in Gallia, the Orient and in the strategically vital Illyricum. Inevitably there was a need for centralization of authority. Two of the *magistri* (one in the East and one in the West) climbed to positions of supremacy in their own territories. The date of this change is unclear, although it probably centered on the special status of certain *magistri* assigned to the imperial palace, with the rank of *magister militum praesentalis* or *magister militum in praesentis.* According to the most reliable source for such matters, the NOTITIA DIGNITATUM, the *magister militum* (at first, *peditum*) *praesentalis* was chief of the combined armies in the West. This was in keeping with the pattern already established concerning the higher place of the *magister peditum* in the command structure. Of note, the *magister equitum praesentalis* was far more important than any regular *magister equitum,* pointing to the reality of life at the courts.

There remains the process by which these *magistri* came to dominate both the armies and their supposed masters, the emperors. The gulf between the government and its military had been growing since the third century C.E., with a stricter differentiation between careers of public and of military service. Where once the two had been entwined in the sociopolitical chain of the *CURSUS HONORUM,* by the time of Constantine, the soldier's life was totally removed from that of the bureaucrat. Barbarians increasingly emerged from the ranks to hold central positions in the army. These men were then chosen to fill the high office of *magister militum.* Their troops, seeing them to be of similar descent, be it Frank, German, Goth, or even Hun, followed them both personally and professionally.

In the West this obedience to the servant and not to the master handed to the competent *magister militum* the potential for vast political strength. Unlike the soldier-leaders of the third century, the *magistri* were no longer trying to elevate themselves to the throne. The Western Empire offered few enticements to a ruler. Rather, the state officials appeared to dominate everything, including the man occupying the throne. From the time of MEROBAUDES, who supported Magnus MAXIMUS against Gratian in 383, no emperor was truly safe from the threat or the machinations of the *magister militum.* A Western monarch might poison his general or have him assassinated, but there would always be another general to take his place, and the vengeance of the martyr's troops often culminated in the death of the emperor.

The struggles between two or more *magistri* helped tear apart the empire in the West, while the personal ambitions of others prevented victory or ensured defeat. In 468, Emperor Anthemius joined in the massive campaign to destroy Geiseric and the Vandal kingdom of Africa. His *magister militum* RICIMER was feuding with the *magister militum* of Dalmatia, MARCELLINUS. As head of the Italian fleet sent to join an armada from Constantinople, Marcellinus was too great a rival for Ricimer. Probably at Ricimer's instigation, several officers murdered Marcellinus. What had been a failed campaign thus degenerated into a total rout, and the last hope of the West died with Marcellinus.

Some years before that, in 451, Attila the Hun drove into Gaul, intending to ravage the entire country. He was met in battle by the *magister militum* AETIUS and his Visigoth allies. The battle of Catalaunian Plain in that year could have resulted in the total destruction of Hunnic ambitions. Instead, Aetius, realizing that such a triumph would make him dependent upon the Visigoths exclusively for his political position, allowed Attila to escape. The Huns, angered at not winning Gaul, turned on Italy. Aetius was blamed for the resulting slaughter.

The Eastern Empire spared itself the chaos of the West. Constantinople proved a deadly place for ambitious generals. LEO I (ruled 454–474 C.E.) provided an excellent example of this. He hoped to spare the East from a heavy reliance upon barbarian levies and thus recruited a new army from his home province, especially from Anatolia and Isauria. From the Isaurians he promoted a chief, Tarasicodissa, renamed him Zeno and put him to use as a counterweight for the potent *magister militum* Aspar. By 471, Zeno was Aspar's relative equal, and Leo put the barbarian general to death. A continued recruitment from the provinces of Asia Minor rescued the Eastern Empire, ensuring its survival long past the fall of the West.

magister officiorum

One of the most important imperial ministers, from the third century C.E. As a result of the reforms in government instituted by Diocletian, all of the departments of public administration were reorganized under military lines. This change allowed the emperor to use the senior tribune of the PRAETORIAN GUARD as the head of the palace servants while reducing the powers of the prefect of the Guard. This reduction in power created an opportunity to elevate another officer of state.

Though actual military service was not required from civil servants, sometime during the reign of Constantine the Great, about 321–323, the rank of *tribunus et magister officiorum* made its appearance—the *magister officiorum* (as it was later known), the chief bureaucrat in the Roman Empire. The master of offices headed all of the bureaus of correspondence, the *scrinii* for dispositions, *memoriae, admissionum*, and petitions. He also command-ed the CURSUS PUBLICUS (imperial mail) and the *agentes in rebus*. As chief of these last two sections of government, the *magister officiorum* not only supplanted the prefect (the previous head) but also assumed control over the two main organs of imperial intelligence and security. He thus wielded vast influence and was the match in intrigue of almost every other potentate in the service of the emperor. Even more powers fell into his hands when the magister was granted the directorship of the arsenals and weapons factories of Italy. For these reasons each master of office was very carefully chosen.

magister peditum

Master of foot (also, master of the infantry); an office created out of the reforms of Constantine the Great in the imperial military system of the fourth century C.E. A *magister peditum* commanded the infantry in the COMITATENSES (mobile field army) of a DIOCESE or group of dioceses. He thus controlled not only his own formations but those of the LIMITANEI (border troops) as well. The MAGISTER EQUITUM was his counterpart with the cavalry. In the East there were five *magistri peditum*, and in the West only one (the same as with the *magister equitum*). By the reign of Constantius II, the *magister peditum* and the *magister equitum* were being called *magister equitum et peditum, magistri utriusque militiae*, or *magistri militum* (masters of the soldiers).

See MAGISTER MILITUM for other details; see also LEGIONS.

magister scriniorum

Also called *magister scrinii*; the head of the imperial secretariat.

See also SCRINII.

Magnentius, Flavius Magnus (c. 303–353 C.E.)
Usurper in the West from 350 to 353

Born in Ambiani (Amiens) to a British father and a Frankish mother. Magnentius joined the army of Constantine the Great, rising through the ranks as a staff officer and then as senior field commander (*comes rei militaris*). What caused him to aspire suddenly to the throne is unclear, but on January 18, 350, he dressed in purple robes and visited a birthday party at Augustodonum, held by the finance minister of Emperor Constans I, Marcellinus. He was acclaimed the emperor of the West. Constans soon lost his army to Magnentius and was killed while trying to escape. Magnentius received the support of most of the Western provinces, although two other usurpers, Nepotianus and Vetranio, required his attentions. Nepotianus was executed, while Vetranio, in the Danube region, joined the cause of Constans's brother and ruler in the East, Constantius II. Knowing that hostilities were inevitable with Constantius, who refused to accept his claims, Magnentius prepared for war, naming as his Caesar his brother Flavius Magnus Decentius.

The first clashes took place in 351, near Noricum, where Constantius tried to advance into Italy. Early fighting was in Magnentius's favor. Hoping to snatch a total victory, he invaded Illyricum, maneuvered behind Constantius and forced battle on seemingly unequal terms. At a site called MURSA MAJOR, a bloody and wasteful engagement was fought on September 28, 351. Magnentius's infantry fought valiantly, but they were no match for the superior cavalry of Constantius. Leaving behind nearly 60,000 dead, Magnentius retreated to Aquileia. Constantius, having reorganized his own reduced army, pushed into Italy in the summer of 352. Unable to resist effectively, Magnentius withdrew to Gallia. Another defeat brought him to Lugdunum (Lyons), where he killed himself on August 10, 353, rather than fall into the hands of his enemy.

For a briefly reigning usurper, Magnentius showed both political and military skills. He may have been a pagan, certainly he leaned toward paganism, but he cultivated as well the Christians in the West. Coinage issued under his name displayed for the first time actual Christian symbols, the Chi-rho emblem (☧) with the words *alpha* and *omega*. Unfortunately for the Roman Empire, the struggle that developed for the throne was far too costly. The battle of Mursa Major caused more casualties than the provinces could afford. With barbarian pressure mounting on the borders, the thousands of dead would be sorely missed.

maiestas The Roman conception of treason; in the first century C.E., a weapon of imperial tyranny. Always patriotic, even nationalistic, the Romans viewed betrayal of their country as a very severe crime, previously calling it *perduellio*, or high treason. From the earliest times, treason was punishable by death, although the nature of such violations of the law was varied. Incompetent generals, for example, could be tried for *maiestas* in the late second century B.C.E. under the *lex Appuleia* (103 or 100 B.C.E.), codified by Sulla around 81 B.C.E. With the dawn of the empire under Augustus, the emperor attempted to clarify treason laws with the *lex Julia maiestatis,* but even this piece of legislation was vague. It might be applied to condemn those who had conspired against Augustus's life (as in the trial of Fannius Caepio in 23 B.C.E.), but also to cases of slander of the emperor, adultery with a member of the imperial family or disrespect for the gods or government. Under Augustus these questions were decided by the Senate, courts and rulers.

By the end of Augustus's life, *maiestas* had passed beyond mere betrayal of the state to treason against the person of the emperor. As the ruler of Rome became the heart of the imperial government, any violation of his honor or any insult directed at him could be viewed as a crime equal to *perduellio,* a policy with unlimited potential for terror in the reign of Tiberius. In 15 C.E., Tiberius demonstrated great leniency and flexibility in the interpretation of the treason law. When two Equestrians were accused of impiety, the new emperor dismissed the proceedings for lack of cause; but inevitably Tiberius sank into despotism, using *maiestas* as his principal means of destroying his opponents. The historian Tacitus wrote that it was a deadly system of oppression, carefully crafted by the emperor. Informers, DELATORES, sprang up to accuse mainly the wealthy and powerful, knowing that upon condemnation they would receive large portions of the accused's estate. Early trials, even when unsuccessful, demonstrated that an effective *delator* was more often believed than not, most notably when the defendant was known to be out of favor with Tiberius or considered a political enemy.

The pages of Tacitus's *Annals* are filled with episodes of injustice and judicial cruelty, demonstrating a will to drive the law into abusive areas. Such direction came from the PREFECT OF THE PRAETORIAN GUARD, Sejanus, who used *maiestas* to annihilate the party of GERMANICUS, the friends of AGRIPPINA THE ELDER and finally Agrippina and her children as well. High and low in Rome were cut down, their most personal utterances or actions repeated faithfully by informers.

Upon Tiberius's death in 37 C.E., Gaius Caligula allowed *maiestas* to be abolished, dealing with his enemies more straightforwardly, as did Claudius. In 62, Nero resurrected the law, applying it with vigor in his own interpretation, and more innocent victims died before Nero's fall in 68 C.E. Domitian revived the *maiestas* in the late first century. With the extensive analysis given to the law in the second century C.E., manipulation of statutes for treason became unfashionable, even to the grim Trajan, who had to admit that he had little taste for it.

Majorian (Julius Valerius Majorianus) (d. 461 C.E.)
Emperor of the West from 457 to 461 who owed his throne to the good graces of a magister militum, *Ricimer*

Majorian was of a good Roman family, his grandfather having been *magister militum* in the service of Theodosius I. He joined the army of the general AETIUS, and, although he acquired the reputation of a gifted military commander, Majorian was dismissed by Aetius, probably because he began to seem like a rival.

In 455, Valentinian III summoned Majorian following the death of Aetius (in 454). Valentinian needed advisers, and he granted Majorian the title of *comes domesticorum.* When the emperor was assassinated a short time later (March 16), Majorian was a leading candidate for the vacant throne, having the support of Valentinian's widow, Licinia Eudoxia. He was passed over, however, for PETRONIUS MAXIMUS (455) and then AVITUS (455–456). Avitus was deposed in October 456, made a bishop and then probably murdered. There followed a period of six months, during which the West was without an emperor.

Majorian probably had a hand in the fall of Avitus, with the help of Ricimer, and now took steps to improve his own political standing. In February of 457 he became a *magister militum* in his own right, while Ricimer was made a patrician. LEO I, successor to MARCIAN as emperor of the East, was persuaded by Ricimer to support Majorian, and on April 1, 457, the ceremony of accession took place.

Facing Majorian were the tasks of pacifying the Gallic nobles, who had backed Avitus, and diminishing the influence of King GEISERIC and his powerful VANDALS in Africa. Majorian marched into Gaul (Lugdunum Princa) and reduced political opposition with the use of threats, promises, and taxes. The VISIGOTHS of King Theodoric II were then defeated in battle by the general Aegidius and convinced to sign a peace agreement. Geiseric was not so easy. With considerable ambition, Majorian assembled a huge army and fleet with the aim of crushing the Vandal kingdom in Africa. In 460, his massive flotilla was discovered and burned by Geiseric at Carthago Nova in Spain. Majorian had to accept humiliating terms from Geiseric. The emperor was forced to abdicate on August 2, 461, and was probably beheaded the same day at Ricimer's orders, though it was reported that he died of dysentery. He had reigned only four-and-a-half years. In that time he had shown flashes of considerable ability and was praised by Sidonius.

Mamertinus, Claudius (d. after 365 C.E.) *Pagan official who held a variety of posts during the reign of Julian the Apostate*

In 361, Mamertinus was appointed *comes sacrae largitionum,* (count of the sacred largesse) and, soon after, Praetorian prefect of Illyricum and later Italy and Africa. He held a consulship in 362 and continued as prefect until 365. Upon assuming his duties as consul, he delivered an extant panegyric at Constantinople, lauding his imperial patron, Julian. Already very old, in 365 or 368 he was accused of embezzlement and replaced.

Mamurra (fl. first century B.C.E.) *Praefectus fabrum (prefect of engineers) in the army of Julius Caesar during the Gallic Wars*

Mamurra was born at Formiae, a member of the Equestrians (EQUITES). As an officer in the war against the Gauls, he amassed great riches and was, for personal reasons, viciously attacked by the poet Catullus, who linked him with Julius Caesar in a scandal. Catullus called Mamurra a glutton, lecher, and mountebank gamester, guilty of stealing uncounted wealth in Gaul and Britain. The biting words of Catullus against Mamurra were taken by Caesar as a personal insult, and a special reconciliation was needed to repair the association between Caesar and Catullus.

Mandiuch (fl. early fifth century C.E.) *Hunnic chieftain and the father of Attila the Hun*

Mandiuch was one of the two most important leaders of the Huns, on equal standing with his brother Rugila. When Rugila died in 433, Mandiuch assumed control over virtually all of the Hunnic tribes. He used his strength and influence to forge the Huns into one nation. Upon his death (date uncertain), his two sons, Bleda and Attila, succeeded him.

manes The Roman spirits of the dead, probably derived from the Latin *manus* or "good" (good folk) or possibly *manēre* for "what remains," and applied to the souls of the departed. According to Roman belief, the kind persons who died passed into the underworld, where, because of their immortal souls, they graduated into a form of minor divinity. In most large cities, most notably in Rome (on the Palatine Hill), there was a large pit, called the *mundus.* A stone, the *lapis manalis,* was used to cover the hole, and legend said that here was a gateway to the land of the dead. Whenever the *lapis manalis* was opened, it signaled a time of deep religious significance, for the *manes* thus left their nether domain and walked the world of the living. Two major festivals were celebrated to honor the *manes:* Lemuria in May, and the Parentalia (culminating with the Feralia) in February. Sacrifices were made to the *manes,* both publicly and in private, with milk, sheep's blood, pigs, oxen, honey, water, beans, eggs, bread, wine, and other foods.

See DEATH.

Manichaeism Pervasive religious sect established by a Persian named Mani (Manes) in the third century C.E. that found considerable success throughout the East and the Roman Empire. Mani (c. 215–276 C.E.) was born at Ctesiphon; little has survived concerning his early life, except that he saw visions that convinced him of his mission. He began preaching a new doctrine very different from the recognized creed of the Persian Empire, Zoroastrianism. Possibly as a result of local religious opposition, Mani departed for India (c. 242), spreading his newly developed creed on the way. Upon his return to Persia, he became friendly with its monarch, Shapur I, who refused to persecute him or his followers. Shapur's successor, Varahran I, viewed Mani differently, arrested and imprisoned him and put him to death. Most of his supporters were exiled. Banishment of his followers led to wider popularity, and by 297, Manichaeism had achieved such notoriety that Diocletian condemned it. The faith was also attacked by the Christians and Neoplatonists. Despite such opposition, Manichaeism attracted believers in Egypt, Africa, the European provinces and finally in Rome itself. St. Augustine was a member for nine years, with the rank of Hearer. Although Manichaeism died slowly in the West, Islam pushed it out of the East and into China, where it survived until the 14th century. There has been some question as to its influence on such later heretics as the Albigensians, Bogomils, and Paulicians.

Mani was a prolific writer, although only fragments of his work survive. The most important were texts discovered in Turfan, in Chinese Turkestan, in the early 20th century, and papyri of Coptic origin discovered in Egypt in 1933. Essentially, the Manichaeans believed in an endless struggle between good and evil, epitomized by darkness and light. Through the intrusion of darkness into the realm of light, there was an intermingling of the divine with the mortal, trapped in matter (specifically, the light was caged in the brain). The sole task of man was to lead an ascetic life, practicing vegetarianism, and becoming "Hearers" who hoped to attain rebirth as the Elect, those who had overcome the need for the transmigration of the soul. These were forbidden material goods and possessions. The Manichaeans believed that Jesus was the Son of God, but they decreed that he came to Earth to save his own soul because of Adam. Buddha, Jesus and all other holy persons were believed to have aided mankind on its path to spiritual freedom.

See also RELIGION.

Manilius (fl. late second century C.E.) *Secretary of correspondence (ab epistulae Latinis) to Avidius Cassius in the East (c. 175 C.E.)*
After the revolt and fall of Cassius, Manilius fled. Around 182–83, however, he was captured and promised to reveal information. Commodus would not listen, and in a rare act of public service, had all of Manilius's papers burned to prevent their further use.

Manilius, Marcus (fl. early first century C.E.) *Poet during the later years of the Augustan Age*
Manilius passed into history leaving virtually no trace but the remarkable poem, *Astronomica*. He was certainly influenced by Lucretius, Horace, and Virgil in that attempt to present, in hexameter verse, the Stoic system or science of astrology. The title is ambiguous as to Manilius's real purpose, since his interest rested in astrology, not astronomy. The dating of *Astronomica* can be placed sometime after 9 C.E. He probably did not finish the last books (4 and 5) until the time of Tiberius, after 14 C.E., since he refers to the emperor in book 4.

mansiones Stations that were distributed along the major roads of the empire to serve as rest spots for the members of the *CURSUS PUBLICUS,* or imperial post. The *mansiones* (sing. *mansio*) were positioned approximately 20 to 30 miles apart on the roads. Each *mansio* offered the runner food, rooms for sleep, bathing facilities, and fresh horses, mules, or oxen. Use of the *mansiones* was generally limited to official personnel, such as soldiers and bearers of the *diploma* (the official document of government service).

Marcellinus, of Dalmatia (d. 468 C.E.) *A magister militum in the middle of the fifth century C.E.*
Marcellinus was a friend of the general AETIUS and a bitter enemy of the powerful RICIMER. Following the fall of Aetius in 454, Marcellinus withdrew to Dalmatia where he established himself as the quasi-independent master of the region, free from the influence of the West, while relying upon the East for political support. By 455 he had become popular with the Western nobility, especially in Gaul, and after the death of Emperor Avitus. His name circulated as an excellent choice as successor. In 458 he may even have been offered the throne, but Majorian eventually became emperor of the West. Marcellinus, eager to deal a blow to the influence of Ricimer, assumed control of the fleet and the army of defense for Sicily against the Vandals. Ricimer greeted his arrival and subsequent success with alarm, for he could not allow a rival to steal the ear of Majorian. Knowing that most of Marcellinus's army in Sicily was Hunnic, Ricimer offered the soldiers a bribe to desert their general, and his money proved too tempting.

Marcellinus departed Italy, refusing to wage a war of money with Ricimer. Instead, he returned to Dalmatia, working closely with Emperor Leo I at Constantinople, who made him MAGISTER MILITUM Dalmatiae. Ricimer was still uncomfortable and petitioned Leo to keep Marcellinus in line while making supposed overtures of reconciliation with Marcellinus. Leo cleverly utilized his Dalmatian ruler by having him named one of the supreme generals in the West, alongside Ricimer. To afford Marcellinus an equal position with Ricimer, Leo probably had his client elevated to the patricianate, although that is uncertain. Marcellinus was considered the partner of Ricimer in the West, both serving the Emperor Anthemius. In 468, when the Eastern and Western Empires joined in a last attempt to destroy Geiseric and the Vandals in Africa, Marcellinus headed the fleet that set out from Italy. His qualities as an admiral were great, but he campaigned under two handicaps: the incompetence of Basiliscus, the Eastern admiral, and the conniving of Ricimer. Basiliscus's fleet was destroyed by Geiseric; before Marcellinus could put things right again, he was assassinated, no doubt by order of Ricimer. Marcellinus's death ensured the collapse of the West. In Dalmatia he was succeeded by his nephew Julius Nepos, one of the last emperors to wear the Western purple.

Marcellus, Lucius Ulpius (fl. second century C.E.) *Consul in 184 C.E. and legate in the service of Emperor Commodus (ruled 177–192)*
Marcellus was sent to Britain in 184 to repel the Caledonians who had burst over the Antonine Wall. In a series of campaigns he ruthlessly crushed the invaders. The historian Dio called Marcellus frugal and temperate by nature, while possessing an amazing constitution. He required little sleep and only small amounts of

food. Marcellus enjoyed keeping his officers alert at all times by writing orders on 12 tablets and having an aide deliver them to different commanders at varied times of night so as to give the impression that he was always awake. Marcellus also suffered from bleeding gums. The jurist Ulpius Marcellus may have been his father.

Marcellus, Marcus Claudius (43–23 B.C.E.) *Son of Augustus's sister Octavia and C. Claudius Marcellus (consul in 50 B.C.E.)*
Known commonly as Marcellus, he was considered the inevitable heir to the throne. He received the finest possible education, and in 39 he was briefly betrothed to a daughter of Sextus Pompey, but an actual union proved unnecessary: by 25, Augustus's favor was obvious, and Marcellus traveled to Spain with Tiberius, where they served under the emperor. A politically monumental step was taken in that same year, when Augustus arranged the marriage of Marcellus to his daughter JULIA (3). His advancement to the rank of *curule aedile* caused the first signs of friction between his supporters and the imperial friend Marcus Agrippa. The rivalry was terminated abruptly in 23 B.C.E. when Marcellus became ill suddenly and died. Grief-stricken, Augustus and all of Rome mourned him. A library and a theater were named after him, but he was only the first of a long line of potential heirs who would not survive Augustus. Virgil and Propertius wrote of his demise.

Marcellus, Nonius (fl. early fourth century C.E.) *Compiler of the extant work Compendiosa doctrina ad filium*
The *Compendiosa* proved an invaluable source for the preservation of numerous quotations and fragments of Roman LITERATURE. Marcellus probably came from Africa but mastered Latin and took an interest in antiquarian matters. His *compendiosa doctrina* is a study of Latin literature. It begins with Plautus and ends with Serenus and Apuleius. In between are such writers as Varro, Sallust, Virgil, Terence, Cicero, and others. Divided into 20 chapters, the book is valued for its many excerpts from the authors in question. These citations are well organized and carefully considered, rendering unnecessary Marcellus's feeble commentary.
    See LITERATURE.

Marcellus, Sextus Varius (d. before 217 C.E.) *Father of Emperor Elagabalus and husband of Julia Soaemias*
Marcellus was a Syrian from Apamea with a long and distinguished career as a member of the Equestrian Order. He held several procuratorships before being elevated to the Senate.

Marcellus, Ulpius (fl. second century C.E.) *Jurist during the reigns of Antoninus Pius and Marcus Aurelius*

He was an adviser to both rulers but probably did not begin writing until after the death of Pius. Many of his legal views were recorded in Justinian's digest.
    See also JURISTS; LAW.

Marcellus of Gaul (fl. late fourth century C.E.) *Writer who specialized in medicine*
Marcellus was probably a *magister officiorum* under Emperor Theodosius I and is mentioned in the Code of Theodosius as a persecutor of pagan officials (he was a devout Christian). An interest in medicine led him to compose the treatise *De medicamentis* in the reign of Theodosius II. Although not a physician, Marcellus assembled cures and medicinal aids for a wide variety of diseases. The book, in 36 chapters, was based in large part on Scribonius Largus, with additions found in superstitious traditions, legends, magic, and Jewish lore.

Marcia (d. 193 C.E.) *Wife of the courtier Quadratus, concubine of Emperor Commodus*
Following the banishment of Empress Crispina, Marcia became the most influential of the imperial concubines. Commodus reportedly trusted her completely, listening to her words of warning in 189 that the powerful freedman Cleander had to die. While she profited from this execution, so did the *cubicularius* (chamberlain) Eclectus, who was possibly her lover. By late 192, Maricia's grip on Commodus was slipping. She entered into the conspiracy of Eclectus and Laetus to murder the emperor, which they accomplished on the last day of that year. They tried to poison him, but when that failed they sent in a wrestler, Narcissus, who finished the job. Marcia no doubt helped her coconspirators choose Pertinax as the successor of Commodus. However, when Didius Julianus purchased the throne in 193, he tried to appease the Roman establishment and put Marcia and Laetus to death. It was reported that she favored Christians and aided them whenever possible.

Marcian (392–457 C.E.) *Emperor of the East from 450 to 457*
The son of a soldier from the Balkans, he also joined the army, serving in a campaign against the Persians and then in the forces of Ardaburius and his son, the eventual MAGISTER MILITUM Aspar. By 431, Marcian was a tribune and was highly respected by Aspar as well as by the entire court, including Emperor Theodosius II. Thus in 450, according to reports, the dying Theodosius declared that it had been revealed to him that Marcian would succeed him on the throne. No opposition was voiced against Marcian, considering the support of Aspar and Theodosius's formidable sister, PULCHERIA. Marcian married Pulcheria and was crowned at the Hebdomon on August 25, 450. Although the union with Pulcheria was purely political (she had taken an oath of chastity), her influence was

felt immediately when Marcian began his reign by executing her longtime rival, the eunuch Chrysaphius ZSTOMMAS.

The removal of Zstommas was one of the few bloody acts of a reign viewed as a happy and peaceful time for the empire. Marcian led the Eastern Empire with an eye toward strength and financial security. He terminated the huge tributes paid to the Huns during the reign of Theodosius, saying that he had for Attila no gold but only iron. By saving these tributes, he refilled the depleted treasury and then added to it by cutting back on expenditures. Tax arrears were paid, administrative reforms instituted and, when necessary, large amounts of money used to repair damage caused by the natural disasters. The total effect of these measures was to make the empire in the East free of the chaos, war, and barbarian invasions shattering the West. While his refusal to aid Italy during the sack of Rome by Geiseric in 455 was not popular in the Western provinces, it ensured that an army from Constantinople was not destroyed in a fruitless campaign.

Marcian also earned the enmity of the Western Church through his most memorable act, the convening of the Fourth Ecumenical Council of Chalcedon in 451. Pope Leo's "Tome" was widely accepted by the delegates to the council, but the patriarch of Constantinople was also able to elevate the status of his patriarchate at the expense of Rome. The papacy could not easily accept the new status of a rival see, and so began the split of Christianity within the empire. Pulcheria died in 453, leaving behind many churches. For advisers, Marcian now leaned more heavily on his *MAGISTER OFFICIORUM,* Euphemius, and on Anatolius, the patriarch of Constantinople. The emperor fell ill in 457 and died, ending the line of Theodosius.

Marciana, Ulpia (c. 48–112 C.E.) *Older sister of Trajan; devoted to her brother and his wife, Plotina*
Marciana married C. Salonius Matidius Patruinus, who died in 78, leaving her and their daughter Matidia. Many honors were given to Marciana both during her life and posthumously. In 105 she accepted the title of Augusta with reluctance, sharing it with Plotina. Trajan founded two colonies in her name: Marcianopolis in Moesia and Ulpia Marciana Traiana in Africa.

Marcianus, Aelius (fl. third century C.E.) *Jurist and one of the last of the Roman classical legal experts*
Marcianus was a prolific writer, authoring some 16 treatises on family law, criminal procedure, and punishments. It has been theorized that he worked in the chancery because of his use of rescripts. The verified dates of his books indicate that his major writings were done after the death of Emperor Caracalla.

See also JURISTS; LAW.

Marcionism A Christian heresy that became quite popular throughout the Roman Empire during the second century C.E. It was developed by the heretic Marcion (d. c. 160), who was originally from Sinope in Pontus, Asia Minor. Around 140 he journeyed to Rome, where he developed his own radical interpretation of Christianity. Marcion distinguished between the God of the Old Testament—the God of the Law—and the God of the New Testament—the God of Love. He rejected the former as cruel and despotic. According to Marcion, Christ descended to earth from heaven to replace the doctrine of the law with the doctrine of love. He did not accept the Old Testament, but he also rejected whole parts of the New Testament because of their Jewish content or influence. He accepted only ten epistles of St. Paul (whom he honored) and portions of the Gospel of Luke. Marcion was excommunicated in 144 for the heresy of dualism. A genuinely gifted preacher and a superb organizer, he traveled throughout the Roman Empire, attracting numerous converts from all social classes. His church was characterized by fanatical devotion to its founder, the practice of stern asceticism, and the maintaining of rigid discipline, including the forbidding of marriage. His success can be seen in the number and the geographical locations of his opponents in the church: TERTULLIAN (in Carthage), Bardesanes (at Edessa), and Dionysius (at Corinth), to name a few. While a threat to the orthodox teachings of the church, by the late third century Marcionism had been absorbed by Manichaeism. Although his writings are not extant, scholars are able to know much about them through the early Christian historians and authors, in particular Tertullian in his *Adversus Marcionem* and *De praescriptione haereticorum;* other sources include Irenaeus, Origen, and Clement of Alexandria.

Marcius, Publius (d. 16 C.E.) *Astrologer*
Marcius did not share in Tiberius's expulsion of all astrologers from Rome to Italy. Marcius was one of the few ordered to die.

Marcomanni One of the larger and, for a time, one of the best-organized of the Germanic enemies of Rome. The Marcomanni were a division of the Suebi, earning their name from their location (men of the "mark," or border). They originally inhabited the region around Saxony, but were forced to migrate under pressure from the Teutons at the start of the first century B.C.E. Subsequently, they settled on the Main River. There they participated in the frequent tribal wars and joined Ariovistus in his invasion of Gaul (c. 61 B.C.E.). They probably fought at Magetobriga in 61 B.C.E. and shared in Ariovistus's defeat in 58 at the hands of Julius Caesar.

In the period between Caesar and the establishment of the empire, the Marcomanni increased both in numbers and in strength, so that in 9 B.C.E. Drusus the Elder was instructed by Augustus to make war upon them. The following year a client king was sent by Rome to assume their leadership. Their new ruler was MAROBODUUS, the first of the great Germanic chiefs. His first step was to move the Marcomanni from the Main to the formidable mountain areas of Bohemia. There the tribes were trained in war along Roman lines, and within a few years were superbly disciplined and stood as the best soldiers in Germania.

Campaigns were launched against their neighbors with such devastating effect that Augustus viewed Maroboduus as a serious threat to regional security. Under Tiberius a new campaign was launched in 6 C.E., and the Marcomanni king was saved only by the sudden revolt against Rome of the tribes in Illyricum-Pannonia. Peace was made with Rome, but in 17, the peoples of Germania, long tired of being dominated by the Marcomanni, revolted. Under Arminius, the Germans fought a terrible battle with Maroboduus. Victory eluded both sides, but, politically weakened, Maroboduus was ousted in favor of Catualda in 19, and then by Vibilius in 20.

Internal feuding and the leadership of chiefs who could rule only with the help of Rome kept the power of the Marcomanni at a low point for many years. By Domitian's time, however, they had recovered their vigor. While the emperor was engaged in his war with the Dacians, the Marcomanni, with their allies, the Iazyges and Quadi, prepared to attack Pannonia. Domitian had warning of their plans because of their refusal to aid him against Dacia. In 89 he put to death the second diplomatic mission of the Marcomanni and ordered a legionary assault across the Danube. The attack met with total failure and more campaigning was necessary by both Domitian and his successor, Nerva, in 97 to restore order on the frontier. The Marcomanni accepted another general peace, but they were as yet unvanquished. Waiting for their moment to strike, the Marcomanni believed it had come in 166, when they became the leading element in the massive barbarian onslaught sweeping through the Danube provinces and into Italy itself. There followed the long and bitter MARCOMANNIC WARS, ended only in 180 by Marcus Aurelius's son COMMODUS, who terminated all operations and entered into a treaty with the Germans.

The failure of Commodus to carry out Marcus's plans left the Marcomanni in a position to participate in the numerous fights of the third century. During the reign of Gallienus (c. 254), they crossed into Pannonia, creating such a difficult situation for the hard-pressed Roman ruler that he had to cede to them part of the province, thus preventing another invasion of Italy. An actual defeat of the Marcomanni was effected by Galerius in 296 or 297; from then on they were mentioned only infrequently.

Marcomannic Wars Series of bitter struggles fought between the Roman Empire and a number of barbarian tribes from circa 166 to 175 and 177 to 180 C.E. The name came from the MARCOMANNI, who acted as the guiding force of the conflict. Major literary sources that examine the wars are lacking. Although the *Historia Augusta* (*see* SCRIPTORES HISTORIAE AUGUSTAE) offers some information, as does Dio, they are not definitive. Other evidence can be found in inscriptions, but they are unclear, as demonstrated by the Column of Marcus Aurelius. Furthermore, a chronology of events is difficult to formulate. What follows, then, is only a broad outline of the fighting.

By the start of the reign of Marcus Aurelius in 161, the pressure along the frontiers was becoming serious. Pushed by the new peoples moving toward the West, those tribes already established along the Rhine and Danube were realizing that their only hope for survival was to break into the provinces of the Roman Empire, to take for themselves the necessary territories. Marcus Aurelius and his coemperor, Lucius VERUS, had watched the trend but had to focus their energies on the East, relying on their governors to delay the Germanic advance through negotiations.

By the summer of 166 or 167, the policy clearly had failed. A small army of the UBII and LANGOBARDI crossed into Pannonia Superior, where they had to be routed in a series of counterattacks. In that same season a full-scale invasion swept across the Danube, as a host of the Marcomanni, under King Ballomar and aided by the QUADI, Langobardi, VANDALS, and other minor tribes, marched toward Italy. A Roman army sent against them was broken, and Aquileia was besieged. The Italians faced disaster.

Marcus and Verus immediately took steps to halt the invasion. The Alpine passes were blocked, defenses improved, reinforcements summoned, and new legions levied. The emperors were hampered by a devastated economy and by a plague that ravaged the cities and legions. By early 168, however, the counterattack was launched. Aquileia was relieved and Illyricum scoured clean of the invaders. Losses were heavy for Rome, including two Praetorian prefects, Furius Victorinus, and Macrinus Vindex, but the Quadi lost their king in the battle.

Around 170, a new torrent poured down on the frontiers, as the Chatti, Chauci, Sequani, and Iazyges tribes made incursions into Germania, Gallia Belgica, and throughout the Danubian theater. Each new threat was met and defeated through hard combat, stubborn will and good fortune. In 175, Marcus Aurelius's legions were hemmed in by the Quadi, who used the summer's heat to induce them to surrender; without water, the soldiers were withering. The story was told of a legion of Christians who prayed to Christ and, miraculously, it began to rain. The battle was won, and Marcus rewarded the soldiers with the title of "Thundering Legion."

Verus had died in 169, and by 175, Marcus was ruling alone and preparing to take the war directly to the foe. His plans were aborted when word arrived that the trusted governor of Syria, Avidius Cassius, had revolted. Two years of delay (176–177) followed as the usurper was crushed. Meanwhile, a temporary peace was fashioned, even though it was doomed to failure.

In 177, Marcus embarked upon his most ambitious operation, with his son COMMODUS at his side. Centering his strategic interests on the Danube, the emperor pursued three years of relentless warfare, destroying the Marcomanni and Quadi. The tribes had been reduced in strength and in number by 180, and their annihilation as a race seemed inevitable.

The imperial plan, as envisioned by Marcus, was to convert the territory of the barbarians into the Trans-Danubian provinces, far stronger than Trajan's Dacia. His hopes were left unfulfilled, as he died on March 17, 180, begging Commodus to finish his campaigns. Commodus chose to return to Rome, make peace with the various nations and end the Marcomannic Wars. Not only did Rome advance into northern Europe during these campaigns and then withdraw, but also thousands of prisoners were allowed to return home. Many thousands more were settled on land in Italy and in the provinces. These immigrants soon participated in the affairs of the empire, while supplying the army with fresh troops. Marcus Aurelius rendered the Marcomannic Wars an eventual success for the barbarians by helping to Germanize the Roman world.

Marcus Aurelius (Marcus Aurelius Antoninus)
(121–180 C.E.) *One of the foremost emperors in Roman history and a gifted philosopher; ruled from 161 to 180*

> This Being of mine, whatever it truly may be, is composed of a little flesh, a little breath, and the part that governs.
> —Marcus Aurelius, *Meditations* II, 2.

Marcus Aurelius was born in Rome on April 26, 121, to a politically active and wealthy family. His grandfather, Annius Verus, was a member of the senatorial class, a praetor, and three times a consul. His parents were Annius Verus and the wealthy Domitia Lucilla, although he knew his father only briefly, for Annius died when Marcus was barely old enough to begin his education (c. 124). The lad was given to the care of his grandfather for his training. Growing up in high Roman society, Marcus came to the attention of Emperor Hadrian, who took an immediate liking to him, becoming his most influential patron. At the age of six, Marcus was enrolled in the Equestrians (EQUITES), and two years later he joined the ranks of the Salian Order of Priests. Hadrian called him "Verissimus," or most truthful, ordering that only the finest tutors be used for his education. Hadrian was thus responsible for the superb intellect that was subsequently created and nurtured.

The teachers of Marcus were a blend of the cultures in the Roman Empire at the time. Early tutors included the expert in geometry, Andro, and the painter Diognetus. Later came the little known Trosius Aper and the famous Tuticius Proculus and Alexander of Cotiaeon. By far his most famous instructor, the man whom he genuinely loved, was Cornelius FRONTO. HERODES ATTICUS also contributed his own talents.

Hadrian had the foresight to make Marcus a part of his plans for the long-range stability of the empire. When, in 136, the aging ruler adopted Lucius Aelius Caesar as his successor, he ensured that Marcus was betrothed to Aelius's daughter. The succession was temporarily wrecked in 138, when Aelius dropped dead and Antoninus Pius was chosen instead. Antoninus soon after adopted into his own house two sons: Marcus and a male child of the recently deceased Aelius, Lucius VERUS. Later that year Hadrian passed away, and Antoninus Pius became emperor. From the start it was clear that Marcus Aurelius was the designated heir. His betrothal to Aelius's daughter was terminated in favor of a union with Annia Galeria Faustina, the daughter of Antoninus. They were wed six years later, and in the meantime Antoninus introduced Marcus into the business of administering the world. He held consulships in 140, 145, and 46. Marcus sat as a member of the CONSILIUM PRINCIPIS, and in 146 received the essential powers of the IMPERIUM PROCONSULARE and the TRIBUNICIA POTESTAS. By March 7, 161, when Antoninus died, putting the empire into his hands, Marcus was ready to assume the burdens of office. Realizing that the task before him was too great for one man, he requested that the Senate elevate Lucius Verus to full status as his colleague. The two were to work together, despite Verus's young age and Marcus's obvious superiority in experience.

Through the long years of the reign of Antoninus Pius, pressures had been building within the empire and along its borders. Three cataclysms broke during Marcus's time, characterizing his era as one of intense hardship, incessant warfare, and financial suffering. In the East, the Parthians chose this moment to launch an invasion of Armenia. The Parthian king Vologases III defeated two Roman armies in 162. Marcus sent out Lucius Verus with all reliable generals and a large army. Heavy fighting ensued as Armenia was recovered, and in 163 a new vassal assumed the crown there. Avidius Cassius, the new governor of Syria, took over the legions in his province in 165. The following year more defeats were inflicted on the Parthians, as Mesopotamia once more fell to Roman might. Lucius Verus was honored upon his return to Rome in October 166.

These triumphs were offset by a second disaster, the sudden outbreak of plague throughout the empire. Brought back from the East by the legions, it may have killed millions. Marcus did what he could, summoning famed physician GALEN to Italy.

A relief of Emperor Marcus Aurelius *(Hulton/Getty Archive)*

In the midst of the crippling epidemic came a serious threat to the provinces of the West. Beginning around 166 or 167, the tribes living along the Danube frontier could no longer resist the pressure of migrating peoples from the East. These border people had to force their way into Roman territory or be destroyed. So began the dreadful MARCOMANNIC WARS that were to occupy the balance of Marcus's life. A host of nations, the Marcomanni, Langobardi, and others, broke into the Danubian provinces, routing one army, then besieging Aquileia as a prelude to an invasion of Italy.

Marcus responded as best he could, with Lucius at his side until 169, when that colleague died. He improved the Italian defenses, summoned reinforcements, and levied troops. Slowly the Romans gained the upper hand, as Aquileia was relieved. In 175, Marcus felt prepared to bring the Marcomanni and Quadi to their knees with an ambitious operation that took the Romans directly into their lands. This great advance was cut short when Avidius Cassius revolted in Syria. Cassius had been granted total command of the East for the duration of the wars. He may have had an affair with Faustina, and when the rumor spread that Marcus had

perished in the field, Cassius naturally declared himself the obvious successor. Marcus returned to Rome, whereupon the usurpation collapsed. En route to the East to reconcile the estranged regions of the empire, Empress Faustina fell ill in Asia Minor and died. Marcus Aurelius had her deified.

Returning to Rome in 176, Marcus made himself ready for his final battles with the nations of the Danube. With his son COMMODUS at his side, he inflicted severe defeats upon the Marcomanni and the Quadi. They were crushed so completely that by 179 they stood on the verge of extinction. Such was Marcus's intention; he was laying the groundwork for the creation of new, trans-Danubian provinces that would have extended Roman dominion into Northern Europe, potentially altering history. Augustus and Trajan had hoped for this adventure; like them, Marcus was to suffer disappointment. Falling ill early in 180, he summoned Commodus, begging him to continue the great work. On March 17, 180, Marcus Aurelius succumbed to his ailments. Not desiring to live in a legionary camp, Commodus returned to Rome after making a hasty peace with his enemies, the first of many reversals of imperial policy.

The Parthian and Marcomannic Wars were not the only crises faced by Marcus Aurelius. Imperial finances were ruined by the chaos of constant campaigning. Revenues dropped, and in 169 the Romans saw their own emperor auctioning off imperial property to help pay for the troops. To ease the situation, Marcus adopted all possible means of increasing his funds. Legal and bureaucratic reforms tended to increase the size of the imperial government, while broadening its jurisdiction at the expense of the local administrations. His other major difficulty came from the domestic scene. Empress Faustina, whom he adored, was notoriously involved with a number of paramours. Cassius was not the only one to profit from a liaison with her. There were Moderatus Orfitus, Tertullus, and Tutilius. When the emperor was told of these indiscretions, as well as of her affairs with sailors and gladiators, he replied typically that to divorce her would mean returning her dowry, namely the empire. Commodus, his son, was probably a greater disappointment. He gave him the same extensive education that he had received, raising him from childhood as the heir to important offices, Caesar in 166, and Augustus in 177. Through it all, the heir designate displayed qualities wholly unsuited to governing.

Principally because of his own writings and the highly favorable reporting of historians, Marcus Aurelius is regarded as a truly great emperor. To his already formidable gifts was added the philosophy of Stoicism, a way of life that allowed him to find strength to carry on in the face of disaster, pestilence, and unremitting brutality. He was introduced to Stoicism in the lessons of a tutor, Apollonius of Chalcedon, and confirmed in his beliefs through the words and example of Claudius Maximus and Junius Rusticus. Much to the dismay of Cornelius Fronto, he adopted it as his own creed. How intensely Marcus accepted Stoic principles is obvious in his *Meditations,* the 12-book record of his personal reflections, maxims, confessions and warnings.

Suggested Readings: Birley, Anthony R. *Marcus Aurelius, a Biography.* Rev. ed. New Haven, Conn.: Yale University Press, 1987; Hadot, Pierre. *The Inner Citadel: the Meditations of Marcus Aurelius.* Translated by Michael Chase. Cambridge, Mass.: Harvard University Press, 1998; Oliver, James H. *Marcus Aurelius: Aspects of Civic and Cultural Policy in the East.* Princeton, N.J.: American School of Classical Studies at Athens, 1970; Rutherford, R. B. *The Meditations of Marcus Aurelius: A Study.* New York: Oxford University Press, 1989.

Maria (d. 408 C.E.) *Daughter of the* magister militum *Stilicho*
Maria was married in 398 to Emperor Honorius to cement her father's political supremacy in the West. When she died, Stilicho wasted no time in having Honorius wed another daughter, Aemilia Materna Thermantia. Maria's cause of death is uncertain. She was placed in a sarcophagus in St. Peter's with full honors.

marines Soldiers used for military service on board ships of the empire. The imperial marines of the Roman fleets were not members of a "marine corps," because of the traditional methods of Roman warfare at sea. In the birth and flowering of the NAVY in the Punic Wars, Rome used its vessels as heavy flotillas transporting units of regular infantry into battle against other ships. The success of this system against Carthage, combined with the lack of subsequent attention to its naval arm, ensured the failure to develop a large, organized marine force. Essentially, the Roman marines, called the *classiarii,* were divided into squads on board imperial ships and were led into combat by a centurion. Above the centurion in rank was probably the so-called trierarch, but the exact nature of this chain of command is unclear. Any fighting done by the vessel in close quarters was usually handled by the marines, although the rowers and most of the crew had experience with hand-to-hand encounters and some weapons training. As marines were part of a larger fleet, they could be used for a variety of tasks when a group of ships was stationed permanently in one of the major ports throughout the empire. By far the busiest of the *classiarii* were those situated at Misenum. Aside from the duties that called them to Rome, including the possibility of work at the Colosseum, in 59 C.E. a detachment was organized by the admiral of Misenum, Anicetus, to commit the most famous murder of Nero's reign, the assassination of AGRIPPINA THE YOUNGER.

Maritime Alps Called the Alpes Maritimae; the western mountain area of the Alps. The Maritimes divided Italy from Gaul but also helped to maintain a line of communications between northern Italian districts and Gallia Narbonensis. Augustus, hoping to ensure long-term stability, annexed the entire region, declaring it a province. He sent out a prefect to care for the administration of the area but eventually replaced him with a procurator. The inhabitants were called the Comati or the "Long-haired" and belonged to Ligurian stock.
See also PROVINCES; LIGURIA.

Suggested Reading: Rankov, Boris. "Fleets of the Early Roman Empire, 31BC–AD 324," in *The Age of the Galley: Mediterranean Oared Vessels since Pre-classical Times,* edited by Robert Gardiner. Annapolis, Md.: Naval Institute Press, 1995.

Marius, Marcus Aurelius (fl. third century C.E.) *Gallic usurper*
Marius proclaimed himself emperor in 268, following the death of POSTUMUS. His reign was both brief and uneventful.
See also THIRTY TYRANTS.

Marius Maximus, Lucius (fl. late second century C.E.) *Prominent political and literary figure*
Marius served as *Legatus Augustus pro praetor* (legate) in Syria and Germania Inferior and probably served as urban prefect in 217–218, under Emperor Macrinus. As a writer, Maximus played a substantial role in the historiography of later years, with his continuation of SUETONIUS's biographies of the emperors. Maximus picked up his research with Nerva and carried the history down to Elagabalus. While this account has not survived, it certainly was the primary source for the so-called *Historia Augusta* (SCRIPTORES HISTORIAE AUGUSTAE). As he did not write of Severus Alexander, it has been presumed that Maximus died sometime before 235.

Maroboduus (d. c. 36 C.E.) *King of the Marcomanni*
Maroboduus proved himself second only to ARMINIUS in fame and in skill as a Germanic leader in the first century C.E. He was of the Suebi nobility by birth, spending most of his childhood in the court of Augustus. In 9 B.C.E., Drusus the Elder had made war upon the Marcomanni in the Main Valley, and Augustus sent Maroboduus to the tribe a short time later, in the hopes of establishing him as their king and thus reducing the tribe to a client state. Maroboduus was accepted immediately but removed his people to the strong, mountainous regions of Bohemia, where he shaped his warriors into the most disciplined soldiers in the barbarian world.

Under his guidance, the Marcomanni launched campaigns to the north along the Elbe, and the Semnones and LANGOBARDI were subjugated. Alarmed by the rise of a potential rival in Germania, Augustus made preparations to isolate and then destroy Maroboduus. In 6 C.E., the Rhine legions marched from the West and from the south came the legions of Raetia, while Tiberius crossed the Danube frontier in the East. The Romans sliced into Bohemia, trapping the Marcomanni, but Maroboduus was rescued by the revolt of the Pannonians and Illyrians. A catastrophe in his rear made Tiberius conclude a quick treaty and then depart. Maroboduus accepted the title of "Friend of Rome" and continued ruling his lands and his people. The Germans, however, had gained a great victory over Rome's legions in 9 C.E. at TEUTOBURG FOREST under Arminius, and by 17 C.E. the domains of the Marcomanni were besieged by their Germanic enemies, as the Langobardi and other tribes joined the confederation begun by Arminius. Though Inguiomerus, Arminius's uncle, switched to Maroboduus's cause, the politically weakened monarch called upon Tiberius for help. In 18 C.E., Catualda, a Suebi exile, toppled Maroboduus with Rome's help. The banished king requested permission to settle in imperial territory, and Tiberius consented, allowing him to go to Ravenna, where he spent the last 18 years of his life, reflecting, according to Tacitus, upon his rise and fall at the hands of Rome.

marriage and divorce   Initially, no formal legal or religious ceremonies were required for a Roman marriage. A man and a woman who established a household were considered married. However, the requirements of marriage became increasingly codified during the course of the Republic and the empire and were particularly reformed by Augustus. Originally, only patricians could marry. This system changed in 445 B.C.E., with the granting of marriage rights to all Roman citizens. Initially, certain restrictions were placed on who could marry—forbidding marriages between members of different social classes or marriages to freedmen, for instance—but eventually these strictures were loosened. There were several forms of legal union, depending upon the status of the couple and whether or not the husband enjoyed *manus* (control over his wife as well as her property). The earliest type of marriage, and the one used by the patricians for centuries, was *confarreatio*. By this religious ceremony, a daughter was given freely to the family of the groom. Care was taken to ensure that the auspices were favorable, and sacrifices were offered to Jupiter in the presence of the Flamen Dialis and the *pontifex*. Normally, *manus* went with the *confarreatio*. Plebeians often entered into the kind of marriage called *usus*. Similar to a common-law marriage, the *usus* was considered binding if the woman spent one year under the man's roof. If, however, she spent three successive nights (of that one year) away from him, she retained full rights to her own possessions. *Coemptio* involved the symbolic selling of a man's daughter to another man. A sum was paid to the bride's family

and a contract was made, often signified by a ring. *Manus* was assumed under such circumstances.

Toward the end of the Republic during the imperial years, *manus* fell out of fashion to such a degree that by the time of Tiberius it was no longer included in the *confarreatio*. This was in part a response to the improved role of women in society but was also due to reforms instituted by Augustus in response to a dwindling birth rate among the Italians. The *lex Julia de maritandis ordinibus*, passed in 18 B.C.E., induced unmarried, divorced or widowed Romans to marry, threatening to inflict severe punishments if they did not. The *lex Papia Poppaea* of 9 C.E. stipulated further restrictions. Together the laws made certain inheritances difficult to secure for unmarried persons or childless couples, while rewarding others for children, especially those with three or more offspring. Augustus' laws were kept in force by his successors in the first century C.E. and endured in spirit until the fourth century.

The date for a wedding was chosen only after detailed consultation with the proper oracles, although weddings were most common in June. The bride wore a white *tunica recta,* and her hair was dressed in six locks and adorned with flowers and a red veil. She was led, with the groom, by a married woman to a sacred altar (normally a public one) where a sacrifice was made. The couple joined hands to symbolize their union, and marriage contracts were signed. The couple and their guests feasted in the bride's home, and then the groom took the bride forcibly from her mother's arms. With torches and flute players accompanying them, the couple embarked on a wedding procession. The bride was attended by three boys, two holding her hand and another walking ahead with a torch. *Versus Fescennini* were sung as the husband threw nuts at nearby youths, showing both his prosperity and the end of his childhood. Once at his abode, the door was sanctified with oil and fat. The groom then carried the bride over the threshold. Further prayers were offered for the success of the union, and the next day a final feast, a *repotia*, was given, introducing the bride to her role as the mother of the family. She wore for the first time the robes of a matron (the *stola matronalis*).

A Roman woman had considerable independence and retained property rights even in a marriage through the *manum viri* (possession by the husband). Though her dowry, or *dos*, was claimed by her husband, it was often returned if the marriage dissolved. A married woman commanded the title *domina* (mistress), and on certain days, especially the Matronalia on March 1, she was honored. The legal termination of a marriage was rare during the early Republic but became more common from the first century B.C.E., particularly as marriages were used frequently to solidify political alliances. A marriage could be ended simply by mutual consent, or by the *repudium* of one spouse. Under Augustus's *lex Julia de adulteriis coercendis,* more formal procedures were introduced.

Faced with adultery a husband would divorce his wife and then bring charges before a special court. He had 60 days to present his argument, while others could put forth evidence for a period of four months. After that time, the adulteress could no longer be prosecuted. The punishment for adultery could include the loss of a dowry or even, under Constantine, death.

The most famous case prosecuted under the *lex Julia de adulteriis* was that of Titidius Labeo and his reportedly profligate wife, Vestilia. Reluctant to divorce her, he was pressured to do so. The Senate, fearful that he would relent, took matters into its own hands, and Vestilia was charged, condemned, and banished to Seriphos.

Roman law did not recognize adultery by a male spouse. However, under Augustus's reforms, the charge of *stuprum* (rape or sexual misconduct) could result in stern punishment. The Christian emperors, particularly Constantine, placed restrictions and penalties on divorce and Justinian forbade it, although his ban was reversed soon after his death.

See also WOMEN IN ROMAN SOCIETY.

Mars   Roman god of war. Mars was second only to Jupiter in power and importance. His origin is uncertain, although he eventually became identified with the Greek god Ares, sharing his patronage of conquest and conflict. He may have started as an agricultural or fertility god, worshiped by the Latins and the Romans. The people of Rome, however, also revered him as the father of Romulus and the son of Juno. As the god of war, Mars aided Rome in its campaigns of expansion. He was known as *Gradivus,* the Strider, and was invoked at the start of all military operations by the commanding general, who shook the sacred spears of Mars with the cry: "*Mars vigila*" ("Mars, awake!"). His symbols were the wolf, the lance struck upon the *ancilia* (holy shield), and the woodpecker.

The cult of Mars was maintained by the Flamen Martialis and the Salii priesthood, who oversaw festivals and all religious rites in his honor. March and October were especially devoted to Mars. In March were several holy days: March 1, *feriae Marti;* March 14, second Equirria; March 17, *agonium Martiala;* March 19, Quinquatrus; and March 23, the Tubilustrium. In October, the sacred horse races, the *October equus,* were held on the Ides (15th), in the CAMPUS MARTIUS, or Field of Mars. A horse from the winning team was sacrificed on the Altar of Mars in the Campus, and its blood was given to the Vestal Virgins for use in later purifications. Blessings were given to the legions on the Armilustrium, October 19, closing the religious year, until the first Equirria on February 27. After his victory over Caesar's assassins, Augustus conferred on the god the title Mars Ultor, Mars the Avenger, and the TEMPLE OF MARS ULTOR in the FORUM AUGUSTUM was dedicated to him in 2 B.C.E.

See also GODS AND GODDESSES OF ROME.

The Temple of Mars Ultor *(Courtesy Fr. Felix Just, S.J.)*

Marsi   A Germanic tribe living in the northwest of GERMANIA, although the exact location of their domain has not been established firmly. The Marsi were closely allied with their more powerful neighbors, the CHERUSCI, aiding them in the defeat of the Roman governor Varus in the TEUTOBURG FOREST in 9 C.E. They shared as well in the retribution of Rome, belatedly delivered by Germanicus starting in 14, when a number of Marsian villages were captured by the Romans and their inhabitants slaughtered. In 15 C.E., Germanicus led an expedition against them and the nearby CHATTI. The chief of the Marsi, Mallovendus, submitted to the Romans in 16 but soon broke the treaty. Another attack was then made against them, and they probably faced the same decline as the Cherusci. Tacitus reported that the Marsi had in their possession one of the eagles lost by Varus.

Martial (Marcus Valerius Martialis) (c. 40–103/104 C.E.) *One of the greatest epigrammatic poets in all of Roman literature*
Born in Bilbilis in Hispania Tarraconensis, the son of Valerius Fronto and Flaccilla, Martial moved to Rome around 64, where he was given support by his compatriots Lucan and Seneca. He achieved no real financial prosperity, though his circle came to include Juvenal, Quintilian and Pliny the Younger. Through his writings and a brilliant capacity to flatter the most powerful figures of his time, he became the client of two emperors, Titus and Domitian. When Domitian was assassinated in 96 C.E., Martial, anticipating Nerva's disfavor, returned to Spain where he remained until his death.

Martial penned more than 1,500 poems, or *Epigrammata,* collected in 14 books, including *Liber spectaculorum* (Book of spectacles), composed in 80 to coincide with the opening of the Colosseum, and *Xenia* and *Apophoreta,* both published in 84–85, catalog appropriate gifts and tokens of friendship. But he is known mostly for his 12 books of epigrams, published between 85 and 103.

Their subject matter is as diverse as life itself, touching on friendship, loss, and, sometimes, obscene human behavior. Martial applied a vicious bite in his style and keen powers of observation.

Martialis, Julius (d. 217 C.E.) *Assassin of Emperor Caracalla in 217*

Julius Martialis was a member of the elite organization of the EVOCATI but bore a grudge against the emperor. Apparently, Caracalla refused to grant him the post of centurion, although the writer Herodian reported that Martialis's hatred was caused by the murder of his brother. In any event, when the prefect MACRINUS was assembling conspirators in 217 to murder the emperor, he found Martialis both a willing accomplice and the obvious one to accomplish the deed. On April 8, Caracalla set out from Edessa to Carrhae but stopped for an instant while on the road, and Martialis chose that moment to kill him with a dagger. He tried to flee but was hunted down and slain. Macrinus had conducted the operation with such subtlety that no one in the army was aware of his complicity. Using the dead body of Martialis, Macrinus rose to the throne with the acclaim of the legions.

Martialis, Q. Gargilius (fl. third century C.E.) *Writer who specialized in husbandry and medicine*

Martialis probably came from Mauretania, serving in the legions. He was, however, highly educated and well acquainted with the major authors of the previous eras. His treatise, *De hortis* (On gardens), covered various aspects of husbandry, focusing on the use of plants and herbs, especially some 60 varieties. Only fragments of these writings are extant. Martialis used as his sources such notables as PLINY THE ELDER, CELSUS, Julius Frontinus, and COLUMELLA.

Martianus Capella (fl. fifth century C.E.) *Encyclopedist*

Born in Africa prior to the Vandal invasions, Capella composed a nine-volume encyclopedia of the seven arts, *On the Marriage of Mercury and Philosophy*. Subject matter included rhetoric, geography, mathematics, and music. His sources included Pliny the Elder, Salinus, and Varro, whom he imitated in poetical form. His work was written as prose-poetry, presenting the types of learning as personages described in pedantic detail.

Martin of Tours (c. 316–397 C.E.) *A patron saint of France and a founder of Western monasticism*

St. Martin, the son of a pagan soldier, was born in Pannonia. Compelled to join the army, probably by his father, he could not overcome a charitable nature. When he shared his cloak with a beggar, a vision struck him. Christ, in this vision, told him to leave soldiering and pursue a religious life. A short time later, Martin left the service and traveled throughout Italy's northern regions and in the Balkans. By 360, he had become associated with HILARY (2) of Poitiers, establishing the first Gallic monastery near Hilary's city. The success of his work in this field led to his consecration as the bishop of Tours in 371–372, although he continued to help develop monasticism in Gaul. He was also influential in converting large number of Gauls to Christianity. Martin commanded deep respect from the imperial officials of Gaul but could not prevent the execution of PRISCILLIAN in 386 by Magnus Maximus. A disciple, Sulpicius Severus, wrote a *Life of St. Martin*.

Masada

Name originally given to a plateau on the western shore of the Dead Sea that was the site of a virtually impregnable fortress. The plateau rose more than 1,300 feet above sea level and was noted for its deep ravines, sheer walls, and treacherous precipices. Only two tracks allowed any kind of easy ascent. The eastern track led from the Dead Sea but rendered large-scale attack from that side suicidal because of jagged rocks, complex paths, and the total absence of safe footing. Appropriately, it was called the Snake Path. From the west came the other route, which was topographically easier. The Jews constructed a mighty tower upon it.

Such was the Masada found by Jonathan Maccabaeus (or perhaps Jannaeus Alexander). Its defensive possibilities were obvious, and a small defensive bastion was constructed upon it sometime in the middle of the second century B.C.E. Even this proved formidable enough to resist capture by the Parthians in 40 B.C.E. In that year, Herod the Great retreated there when the Judaean lands were overrun. His family was safely deposited upon the heights, and Masada remained unconquered during Herod's flight to Rome and his return to reclaim the country.

As was typical of Herod's genius for aggrandizing locations and situations in his realm to his own benefit, the king reorganized Masada, transforming it into the vast fortress still standing today. He enclosed the summit with high walls and 37 towers. This was not to be a mere citadel of stone, for Herod envisioned a refuge of comfort against the armies of Cleopatra or, more likely, those of his own people. It was to be a place of defense where he could remain secure for years if necessary. Toward this end, Herod built lavish palaces with apartments, baths, huge storerooms, water cisterns, and arsenals. Massive supplies of wine, oil, corn, water, and other foods were kept ever at the ready, and plots within the walls were used to grow vegetables. Masada was made both impossible to besiege and self-sustaining.

Herod never had need of his mountain bastion, but in 66 C.E., the Jewish revolt brought the ZEALOTS, or Sicarii, to Masada. They captured the site through the skill of their leader, Eleazar, son of Yair, and hoped to hold it against the Romans. Rome's generals were too preoccupied with subduing the rest of Palestine to worry about Masada until early 73, when General Flavius SILVA arrived with an army.

Though Masada had resisted enemies before, its walls could not stand against the siege masters of the Roman legions. Silva constructed a system of works and circumvallation around the fort, augmented by siege weapons and eight legionary camps. Once all was ready, Silva launched his 7,000 men against the 1,000 defenders. A bitter, bloody struggle followed for six months, until, slowly and unavoidably, the Romans breached the wall of Masada. A fire broke out, destroying many buildings and a hastily built interior wall made of wood. On May 2, 73, Silva's legionaries forced their way through the ruined and burned stoneworks. To their surprise and horror they found that all of the Zealots, including Eleazar, men, women, and children, had killed themselves. Only seven survivors remained, two women and five children. Roman occupation lasted until the second century. Masada has been the center of intense archaeological excavations, verifying the generally reliable written account of Josephus and expanding upon its details.

Massilia Also known as Massalia, modern Marseilles, a city established on the southern coast of ancient Gaul (GALLIA NARBONENSIS) by the Phocaeans from Asia Minor early in the sixth century B.C.E. The port emerged as one of the most important Greek centers in the western Mediterranean. Trade was conducted with Spain (HISPANIA), Italy, Africa, and parts of Gaul, while Hellenic culture and influence spread through both trade goods and the deliberate founding of colonies in Spain and southern Gaul, including the Alpine city of Nicaea. Early in the history of the Roman Republic, Massilia established ties with the Romans. The Massilians (or Massiliotes) retained their influence and economic power while relying upon their friendship with Rome to ensure their military safety. This arrangement was successful for centuries.

Association with Rome came at a price, for in 49 B.C.E., at the start of the civil war between Julius CAESAR and POMPEY THE GREAT, Massilia had to choose sides. The city supported Pompey, after Lucius Domitius Ahenobarbus convinced them that Pompey would be the victor. The result was the brave but ultimately disastrous siege and battle of Massilia, from March to September of 49.

Caesar set out from Italy in March to destroy the armies of Pompey in Spain (see CIVIL WAR, FIRST TRIUMVIRATE), taking with him some nine legions plus cavalry and auxiliaries. Six legions were to be used in Spain, while three were set aside to conduct what could be a protracted siege of Massilia. When Caesar arrived at Massilia, he found the port closed to him. Hastening to Spain as planned, he left the siege to a reliable legate, Gaius Trebonius, with all three legions. This officer was aided by Decimus Brutus, who organized a blockade by sea with a fleet of 12 ships and reliable marines. Despite the tradi-

tional seamanship of the Massilians and the help of a Pompeian flotilla, the city was twice defeated in the water by the more imaginative Brutus. Cut off from help by sea, Massilia's position grew increasingly desperate as Trebonius pressed home his siege. By late August there was talk of surrender, and Caesar accepted their terms, too hurriedly, perhaps, because the Massilians counterattacked with good effect. Trebonius simply went back to work, and on September 6 the city opened its gates. Caesar's requirements were now harsher. Massilia's territorial possessions were taken away, and its economic supremacy over the region was severely curtailed. Subsequently, the Roman development and Romanization of Gallia Narbonensis came at the expense of the more Greek Massilia. Its rival for seaborne traffic was founded at Narbo, and throughout the early years of the empire other important Roman cities were established around it, especially Arles, Nemausus (Nîmes), Lugdunum (Lyons), and Arausio (Orange). Having lost its mercantile strength, Massilia became known as a seat of learning.

Mater Matuta Roman goddess whose precise nature is unclear. Mater Matuta, sometimes called simply Matuta, was connected by the writer Lucretius to the dawn, but in the Greek tradition was identified with Leucothea, a goddess of the water. In other circles she was connected to fertility or nature. The Festival of Mater Matuta was called the Matralia and was held every June 11. Women were always in charge of her worship, running the Matralia and her temple. Interestingly, only free women were allowed to enter the temple. They could bring a slave girl into the sanctuary only if they slapped the slave's face before entering.

See also GODS AND GODDESSES OF ROME.

Mater Regina Name given to the goddess JUNO as queen mother in Rome.

Maternas, Curiatius (fl. late first century C.E.) *Orator and writer of tragedies*
Maternus was immortalized by Tacitus in his *Dialogue.* There has been considerable discussion as to the identity of Maternus; he may have been a retired advocatus who took up poetry and tragedy. Dio wrote that Domitian put to death a Sophist in 91 for giving speeches against tyrants and identifies him with Maternas. The timing of this is late, however, and there is no corroborating evidence. Maternus, it is reasonably certain, composed tragedies during the reigns of Nero and Vespasian, authoring such lost works as *Medea, Cato,* and *Thyestes.*

mathematics The science employed by the Romans as a result of its introduction by the Greeks. Although the Roman imperial epoch was a time of considerable intellectual activity, it could not match the brilliance of the

Hellenic world in its Golden Age. This was especially true in mathematics. The cause for this was exemplified best by the Roman occupation of Egypt. That land, as cited by Aristotle, was the birthplace of the science, and came under Roman control in 30 B.C.E. Its administration proved efficient, but internal strife tore apart much of the social fabric of Alexandria, the capital. With domestic troubles exacerbated by the catastrophic burning of the Library of Alexandria, an environment for the pursuit of mathematics was not present. Greece, under Roman domination since 146 B.C.E., suffered terribly in the civil wars, and it took long years before Athens was restored to a state of relative prosperity.

All of this does not mean that mathematics was dead as a pursuit. Spherical trigonometry was examined by Theodosius of Bithynia who probably invented an improved sundial in the last century B.C.E. His research was used by Menelaus (c. 100 C.E.) in his discoveries regarding the role of arcs in spherical triangles. Claudius PTOLEMY (second century C.E.) established himself as a leading mathematician, writer, astronomer, and intellectual. He applied trigonometric processes to his mammoth astronomical treatise, the *Almagest*.

Mathematics from the third century focused heavily on the aspects of collection, preservation, and teaching of the classical sciences. This endeavor was suited perfectly to the Neoplatonic philosophy so popular among intellectuals of the time and turned out such notable authors as Pappus of Alexandria and HYPATIA. Pappus pursued geometry in spite of its declining popularity, while Hypatia symbolized one of the troubles facing all scientific thought in that era. Many Christian attacked science as being closely associated with NEOPLATONISM and PAGANISM. In 415 Hypatia was murdered quite horribly by a Christian mob.

Fortunately, the collections of these scientists survived persecution, finding a home in the Eastern capital of Constantinople. There the Byzantine scholars, aided by Arab foresight and culture, saved the Greek and Roman traditions from the total collapse of the West, keeping them secure as Europe entered its Dark Ages. In the West, ironically, the church served as the main sanctuary of the sciences, through Latin fragments of ancient Greek thinkers such as Euclid and Aristotle.

Matidia (d. 119 C.E.) *Niece of Emperor Trajan*

Daughter of Ulpia MARCIANA, Trajan's sister, and probably C. Salonius Matidius Patriunus, she was married to L. Vibius, Matidia had a daughter, Sabina, who married the future Emperor Hadrian in 100 C.E., at the urging of Empress Plotina. At the death of Trajan, Matidia traveled with his ashes back to Rome in 117. Her relations with Hadrian were apparently excellent, for he honored her with the title of Augusta. Upon her death, Hadrian deified her, issued coinage with the words *Divae Matidiae Socrvi,* held gladiatorial games, made gifts of spices (saffron and balsam), put up her likeness in temples and delivered her funeral oration.

Mauretania

Area of Northwest Africa stretching from the Atlantic coast to Numidia; contained deserts, jagged ranges, including part of the Atlas Mountains, and subject to fierce storms. The Mauri (MOORS) and other tribes, cunning and gifted in war, roamed its domain, traded with merchants from Spain and with Phoenician colonists along the coast. Eventually, the tribesmen established communities and later small kingdoms. Such was Mauretania, the Land of the Moors.

Rome had only a slight acquaintance with Mauretania, as a result of the Punic Wars, although in the second century B.C.E. the Jugurthine War increased the Roman awareness. Subsequently they supported the local rulers, especially any who had served as allies in the conflict. The greatest of these was Bocchus.

The Moorish domains were still thriving during the CIVIL WAR between Julius Caesar and Pompey. King Bogud joined the Caesarean cause, aiding Caesar with his leadership and expert cavalry at the battle of Munda in 45 B.C.E. As no Moor could claim total sovereignty over Mauretania, Augustus hoped to ensure regional stability in 25 B.C.E. by installing JUBA II, king of Numidia, on a Mauretanian throne. Known as one of the foremost intellectuals of his age, Juba brought civilization and culture to the Moors. He and his Egyptian queen based their laws on those of Rome and their lifestyle on Greek tradition. Although popular with Augustus, Juba relied heavily upon Roman subsidies for his wealth, influence, and manpower. Further aid came from the Italian colonists who had settled along the Mauretanian coast. The Moors nevertheless caused considerable problems during his reign (25 B.C.E.–19 C.E.).

Juba's successor, Ptolemy, ruled Mauretania until 40 C.E., when he was summoned to Rome by GAIUS CALIGULA. The emperor murdered him and annexed his realm. Opposition erupted instantly, as the Moors and townsfolk merged to fight their Roman oppressors. Chief among the rebels was a freedman in the household of Ptolemy, a man named Aedemon. He organized resistance with such skill that years of hard fighting were needed, as well as the generalship of Suetonius Paulinus and Hosidius Geta. Finally, sometime before 44 C.E., Emperor Claudius made an assessment of Mauretania and decided that its interests could be best served by dividing the territory. Thus he formed Mauretania Tingitana (close to Hispania Baetica) and Mauretania Caesariensis, near Numidia. Romanization was far better received than in other parts of the empire, for King Juba's years of work had made the Mauretanians receptive, albeit reluctantly, to foreign concepts.

Numerous towns and cities were rewarded for their loyalty during the civil strife, most notably Volubilis. There, one Valerius Severus had commanded local militia on the side of Rome. He received citizenship, and Volubilis was upgraded to a MUNICIPIUM. Other communities were equally successful—Tipasa, in Caesariensis, for example, with its forum, capitol, and other typically Roman constructions. Administration was officially under two procurators, although at various times only one commanded both provinces. They helped Romanization and economic growth. Mauretania was noted for its dyes but depended upon its wines, flocks, olives, and crops.

The problem with respect to Mauretania's attaining vast wealth was the incessant raiding and pillaging by the Moors. Despite its supposed pacification, Mauretania required a very large garrison, filled by local levies and auxiliaries. These Moorish contingents, used to great effect by the Romans elsewhere, were wholly unreliable in Mauretania, where natural ties with desert brigands could be dangerous on campaigns. To make matters worse, the frontiers were open to the south, and the Rif could not be occupied, preventing direct, overland communications between Caesariensis and Tingitana. The Moors acted with impunity.

From the time of the Flavians the Moors were second only to the Isaurians as clever and resourceful enemies of Rome. As the emperors had seen with the ambitious and cruel LUSIUS QUIETUS, any Moorish chieftain could conduct lethal operations. Domitian had to fight a bitter war with them in the years circa 84–89. Roman strategy then focused on subjugation, using cohorts from Numidia under Velius Rufus; the governor of both Mauretanias was Sentius Caecilianus. Peace lasted only a brief time, for both Trajan and Hadrian faced real difficulties in the region. All of these were minor skirmishes compared to the major confrontation during the period of Antoninus Pius, one of the few episodes of war to mar his generally peaceful reign. The magnitude of the Moorish War was seen in the use of troops from outside of Africa, the VI Ferrata Legion and support units from all over the provinces.

The Roman victory in 152 was celebrated, but any claims of a total triumph were soon forgotten, for around 168 the Moors felt strong enough to launch an invasion of Hispania Baetica. The cooperation of the governors of Hispania Tarraconensis and Mauretania Tingitana was needed before the Moors could be evicted. Frontier defenses were only slightly improved by the erection of a series of fortresses, posts and walls similar to the *limes* along the Rhine-Danube axis, while defenses became common for the cities of both provinces. Such acts did little to deter the Moors, who continued their ways into the fifth century, when Geiseric and his Vandals conquered the province. The Vandals took up residence, bringing about devastation and suffering.

MAURETANIA CAESARIENSIS

This was the larger of the two Mauretanian provinces, situated farther east and thus influenced by Africa and Numidia. Its harsh climate and topography contrasted with Mauretania Tingitana, and most of its roads ended in the western desert, while the eastern roads stretched on into the African provinces. As the city of Iol-Caesarea (Cherchel) had been developed by Juba II along Greek and Roman lines, it was chosen as the provincial seat for the procurator. Iol-Caesarea was probably very impressive, the most beautiful site in the province. It contained a harbor and thus served as a center for trade, while boasting the usual Roman temples, baths, theaters, and an administrative headquarters. Claudius designated it as a *colonia*.

MAURETANIA TINGITANA

Far smaller than its neighboring province, Tingitana occupied a limited area from Gibraltar and the Pillars of Hercules to the Atlas Mountains. In the west it stopped at the Atlantic, and in the east it was isolated by a desert. Culturally, this position prompted a northward gaze, toward Hispania Baetica and the rest of Spain. Ties had existed with Hispania for centuries, and early colonization had taken place on its coasts, with immigrants coming from southern Spain. The Phoenician city of Tingis (Tangiers) just south of Gibraltar, had been granted a Roman franchise because of its loyalty during the civil war with Marc Antony and was under the jurisdiction of Hispania Baetica, until Claudius made it the capital of Mauretania Tingitana.

Administration of Tingitana was easier than in Caesariensis, except that the major cities were most often situated along the coast and the roads reflected this geography. An obvious exception was Volubilis, which was located inland. When Diocletian reorganized the provinces in the late third century C.E., he placed Mauretania Tingitana in the diocese of Hispania.

Mavia (d. after 378 C.E.) *Queen of the wild Arabian tribes of the Saraceni, or Saracens*
Mavia succeeded her husband after his death, sometime in the middle of the fourth century C.E. For several years (c. 373–378) she waged war against Roman power throughout Palestine, using her warriors' stealth and skills in guerrilla warfare to great effect. Peace was made with her sometime around 378, when two conditions were met by Roman authorities. First, her daughter was married to the MAGISTER EQUITUM Victor, then a hermit named Moses was consecrated bishop of the Saracens. As an ally of the empire, Mavia proved faithful, sending a contingent of her soldiers to help defend Constantinople from the advancing Goths after the battle of Adrianople in 378.

Maxentius, Marcus Aurelius Valerius (279–312 C.E.) *Emperor in Italy and Africa from 306 to 312*
Maxentius was born to the eventual coruler Maximian and his wife Eutropia. Despite being raised among the

empire's most powerful figures, he was not chosen to succeed them. In 305, when Diocletian and his father Maximian retired, and Galerius and Constantius I Chlorus became joint Augusti in the TETRARCHY, Maxentius, despite his senatorial rank and his marriage to Galerius's daughter Valeria Maximilla, was not elevated to Caesar (coemperor). Constantius, who died the following year, was succeeded by Severus II, and Maxentius was again passed over, this time by Constantine, Constantius's son. Maxentius promptly instigated a revolt in Rome, aided by the Romans and the forgotten PRAETORIAN GUARD. Rome had recently lost its immunity to taxation and its centuries-old special status, and was thus ready to support anyone who would bring back its traditional privileges. The Praetorians had been replaced by Diocletian's SCUTARII, *domesticii*, and the Jovians and Herculeans (all filling the role of imperial guards without the danger of assassination or mutiny); they became followers of Maxentius.

On October 28, 306, all of Rome joined in proclaiming his emperor. He discovered other allies as well, in Italy and Africa. Galerius, the senior Augustus, was opposed to all efforts to secure recognition of Maxentius's claims. Severus was thus ordered to march on Rome. His advance faced obstacles in enemy agents, incompetence and the continued popularity of the rebel among the soldiers of his father Maximian, brought out of retirement to help his son. Severus's host collapsed, and Galerius was forced to take to the field personally, only to experience the same disaster.

Meanwhile, Maxentius was strengthened through an alliance with Constantine. In return for his acceptance of Maxentius's position, Constantine received in marriage Maximian's daughter Fausta. The political union was strained almost immediately by the defeat of Galerius, for Spain declared itself on Maxentius's side. Then Maximian, jealous of his son, attempted a coup in 308, only to be crushed and forced to flee to Constantine. The actions of Maximian heralded a period of decline in Maxentius's powers. At Carnuntum, later that year, the united masters of the Roman Empire agreed to declare him a public enemy. While his control over Italy was in no way weakened, he lost Africa when the prefect there, Domitius Alexander, revolted and declared the region his own. Alexander cut off the crucial grain supply to Rome, and so desperate was the starvation by 311 that the PREFECT OF THE PRAETORIAN GUARD, Rufius Volusianus, was sent to Africa to recapture both the province and its grain. CARTHAGE suffered the torments of retribution and Alexander died.

These setbacks for Maxentius convinced Constantine that the time was ripe for a final assault. He knew that his enemy had not recovered from the African crisis and could no longer wield his father as a weapon of influence (Maximian had died in 310). Thus, in 312, Constantine marched across the Alps, through Mount Genevre Pass

and into Italy. Maxentius's larger but inferior forces were defeated at Segusis and at Augusta Taurinorum, and Constantine advanced to the Walls of Rome where, as the Christian historians liked to write, the great battle between CHRISTIANITY and PAGANISM took place on the MILVIAN BRIDGE.

Only Maxentius's Praetorian units proved reliable in this battle, and his army was destroyed. As the soldiers retreated back to Rome, a bridge of boats collapsed into the Tiber, and Maxentius fell into the river. Unable to escape from his weighty armor, he drowned with thousands of his followers.

The reign of Maxentius was described by the Christian chroniclers as the era of a wicked pagan tyrant who fell before the bright rays of the new Christian champion. Though he was a pagan, Maxentius actually treated Christians in a generally kind fashion to ensure his popularity.

Maximian (Marcus Aurelius Valerius Maximianus) (c. 240–310 C.E.) *Co-emperor (286–305) with Diocletian and a member of the Tetrarchy*

Maximian was an able general and good administrator but proved to be a jealous and scheming ruler. Born to a poor family in Sirmium, he entered the army and rose through the ranks in the service of the emperors Aurelian and Probus, coming to know quite well the talented officer named Diocletian. In 285, when Diocletian became the undisputed master of the Roman Empire, he named Maximian as his Caesar or junior emperor, with considerable military powers. These were put to the test immediately in Gaul, where local tribes and desperate peasants had created the so-called Bagaudae to resist the crushing imperial taxation and economic drain. In a series of swift but merciless operations, Maximian reduced all opposition, and as a result was promoted to full Augustus by Diocletian. Henceforth the two shared the world between them.

Diocletian took up residence in the East, and Maximian maintained the West; they worked in close harmony and adopted as divine patrons for their houses, Jove, or Jupiter, for Diocletian, and Hercules for Maximian. In severe fighting between about 296 and 298, he warred with the Alamanni and other Germanic tribes on the Rhine and met a rebellion by his Admiral Carausius in Britain. Carausius's superb seamanship brought about Maximian's defeat and the temporary loss of Britain.

Meeting with Diocletian at Mediolanum in 291, the two rulers recognized the fact that two men could not control the sprawling territories of the empire. As a result of this recognition, each man received an aide, a Caesar, in 293. GALERIUS was made Diocletian's assistant emperor, and Maximian nominated the reliable general CONSTANTIUS I CHLORUS, marrying him to his daughter Theodora to cement the political union. The arrangement proved successful, as Constantius patrolled the northern provinces, making war upon Carausius and his successor Allectus, while Maximian campaigned on the Danube against the Carpi and fought the Mauretanians in Africa, all in 297. Ruling the West from his capital at Mediolanum (Milan), Maximian was content, but in 304, Diocletian began working to convince him to retire. Maximian was reluctant and entered Rome in 305 with regret. On May 1, 305, after celebrating their 20th anniversary amid festivals, triumphs, and the unveiling of Diocletian's great Baths, the two monarchs stepped down in favor of Constantius and Galerius. The transfer of power was smooth, but it was doomed to be short-lived.

At Mediolanum, Maximian handed the reins to Constantius, who raised up SEVERUS II as his Caesar. Diocletian's successor, Galerius, opted for his own nephew, MAXIMINUS DAIA. Constantius died in 306, and Constantine, his son, became Caesar to the newly made Augustus, Severus. Angered at being twice ignored, Maximian's son, MAXENTIUS, usurped control of Italy and Africa and brought his father out of retirement to aid his cause. As an Augustus again, Maximian helped to defeat Severus and Galerius and their armies in 307. He made an alliance with Constantine, marrying his daughter Fausta to his new confederate, but then he appeared in Rome in an attempt to turn the troops of Maxentius against him. He failed and fled to Gaul and the safety of Constantine's court in 308. At the Conference of Carnuntum in that same year, the retired Diocletian demanded that Maximian assume a retired status again. Stung in his pride, Maximian waited until Constantine was away and then tried to instigate a palace coup against his son-in-law. Warned of the treachery by Fausta, Constantine returned to Gaul, trapped Maximian at Massilia (Marseilles) and forced him to surrender. The official story was that Maximian died by his own hand, but it is more likely that Constantine had him executed.

Maximinus (d.c. 376 C.E.) *Imperial official*
Born at Sopianae in Valeria, a part of Pannonia, supposedly to parents of CARPI descent. His early career was in law, where he became an advocate and entered the service of the government. Within a few years he was governor of Corsica, Sardinia, and Etruria (c. 364–366) Promotion followed in 368, when Maximinus made himself useful to Emperor Valentinian I as his *praefectus annonae* (prefect of grain). As such, he conducted cruel investigations of senators in Rome on charges of sorcery and immoral behavior. His arrogant and malicious nature was corrupted even more by his elevation to VICARIUS around 370, with instructions to carry on the examinations. He condemned numerous officials to death with the support of a colleague named Leo. Advocates, nobles, senators, and public officials were slain or exiled, as Maximinus was given a free hand. Valentinian gave him further reward in 371, with the post of Praetorian prefect for Gal-

liarum. He carried on in his usual manner for the next five years, but with the death of his patron in 375, his days were numbered. In that same year or in 376, Emperor Gratian had him beheaded.

Maximinus Daia (d. 313 C.E.) *Coemperor from 310–313*
Maximinus was blessed with the opportunities open to him as a result of being the nephew of Emperor GALERIUS. Through his uncle's patronage he received the rank of officer in the army and steady promotion, with the clear possibility of rising to the highest office in the state. In 305, Diocletian and Maximian, colleagues on the imperial throne, retired. Their successors were the two Caesars (junior emperors) in the TETRARCHY system, Galerius and Constantius I Chlorus. Galerius immediately chose Maximinus to serve as his lieutenant, or Caesar, in the East. His area of concern was designated as Egypt, Syria, and much of the East, while Galerius maintained Asia Minor and other Eastern provinces. Although Maximinus retained his region throughout the turbulent years of 306–310, the Conference of Carnuntum in 308 was a bitter disappointment to him because he had hoped for advancement to the rank of Augustus. When, in 310, no such position was offered, Maximinus allowed his troops to proclaim him Augustus.

Between the usurping Maximinus and the usurper in the West, MAXENTIUS, the tetrarchy established by Diocletian collapsed, and open warfare between rival claimants was inevitable. Galerius died in 311. To improve his position over the "legitimate" Augustus in the East, Licinianus LICINIUS, Maximinus marched into Thrace, seizing a portion of the province from Licinius's grasp. Immediate hostilities were prevented temporarily by diplomatic negotiations. Maximinus and Licinius spent the next two years improving their political situations, a race won by Licinius, who gained the goodwill of CONSTANTINE the Great. Maximinus earned from Constantine only an insistence that he cease persecuting Christians and aggrandizing the pagan establishment. Meanwhile, famine struck the East in early 313, bringing economic hardship, chaos, and pestilence. Resolved to destroy Licinius, Maximinus chose this desperate moment and advanced with some 70,000 men into Thrace, where he engaged Licinius in the battle of Tzirallum, or Campus Serenus. Licinius's troops were outnumbered but were fresh and heavily supported by Constantine. The battle was a rout, and Maximinus fled back to Asia Minor, dying there a short time later from fever.

As with Maxentius (who had died in 312), the passing of Maximinus was cheered by Christian scholars, who vilified his name because of his long-term persecutions and anti-Christian activities. During his time as Caesar he went to extreme lengths to harass and crush Christianity, extending the attacks of Diocletian with personal edicts that insisted upon sacrifices by everyone. More decrees were issued in 309, followed by an intensive program of enactments designed to expand the structure and organization of PAGANISM in the empire. When Maxentius's defeat by Constantine heralded a new era of Christian toleration, Maximinus had no choice but to comply with the changes.

Maximinus I Thrax (Gaius Julius Verius Maximinus) (d. 238 C.E.) *Emperor from 235 to 238; neither the most successful nor the longest reigning ruler, but certainly the biggest in Roman history*

Every major account of his life remarked upon his massive build, gargantuan strength, and cruel, barbarous nature. He was born in the latter years of the second century C.E. in Thrace (the historian Zonaras, probably incorrectly, put his birth date as 172 or 173) to a Gothic father and an Alan mother, named Micca and Ababa respectively.

Not surprisingly, he entered the army, serving in the cavalry before attracting attention because of his size, hence receiving a post in the bodyguard of Emperor Septimius Severus and positions of honor under Caracalla. Called "Thrax" because of his origins, Maximinus despised Elagabalus but served as a tribune in the government and was greeted with joy by the new emperor, Severus Alexander, who gave him command of the recruits from Pannonia serving on the Rhine. These troops then murdered Severus in 235 and proclaimed Maximinus as ruler of Rome.

What part he played in the assassination is unclear, but the troops favored him over the matriarchally dominated Severus Alexander. The Senate reluctantly accepted his elevation, but Maximinus committed a grave error by not going to Rome to cement his political base. His presence on the German frontier was considered an insult by the Romans, who waited to welcome him in the traditional style.

After crushing two minor plots to assassinate him, Maximinus launched a major campaign against the Germanic tribes beyond the Rhine. He inflicted severe defeats upon the Alamanni, while ravaging vast stretches of Germania, and by the end of 235 had laid claim to the title of Germanicus Maximus. Troubles on the Danube interrupted whatever other plans he had for that region.

Maximinus fought against the Sarmatians and Dacians from 236 to 238. Total victory was cut short, however, by news that, in Africa, Governor Gordian and his son had usurped the throne—with the approval of the Senate. Naturally alarmed, Maximinus made ready for an invasion of Italy. He set out with his son, now Caesar, Gaius Julius Verus Maximus, when word came that the Gordians were dead. The Senate, however, had chosen two of their own, Balbinus and Pupienus, to succeed them.

Reaching Aquileia, Maximinus found the city barred to him and his hungry army. A siege could not bring about the city's surrender, and with each day the legions grew more mutinous until, on May 10, 238, while resting in the afternoon sun, the emperor and his son were murdered. Maximinus was one of the first soldier-emperors of the third century, a victim both of his lack of education in Roman ways and of the last attempt of the Senate to influence imperial affairs.

Maximus, A. Lappius (fl. late first century C.E.) *Consul in either 95 or 103; legate in charge of Germania Inferior during the reign of Domitian*

Maximus Norbanus was governing his province in January 89, when the legate of Germania Superior, Antonius Saturninus, seized the treasuries of his legions and began a revolt against the emperor. Maximus chose to remain loyal to Domitian and was attacked by Saturninus before any imperial reinforcements could arrive. The odds facing Maximus and his army were considerable, for Saturninus was expecting help from the Chatti, who were to cross the frozen Rhine. A sudden thaw set in, however, and the Germans were prevented from coming to his aid. In the ensuing battle between the legions, Maximus emerged triumphant, aborting the dreams of his colleague. Maximus burned all of Saturninus's papers, thus preventing their future use in blackmail or persecution, an act lauded by the historian Dio.

Maximus, Gaius Julius Verius (d. 238 C.E.) *Son of Emperor Maximinus I Thrax*

Maximus (called in some histories Maximinus) never received the title of Augustus from his father but was made Caesar (junior emperor) in 236, with the title *princeps iuventutis*. He was reportedly stunningly handsome but very indolent. Remaining at his father's side throughout his reign (235–238), Maximus campaigned with him on the Danube and was present at the disastrous siege of Aquileia in 238. Condemned by the Senate, Emperor Maximinus was murdered by his troops outside of Aquileia, and Maximus joined him in death.

Maximus, L. Marius (d. before 235 C.E.) *Prominent political and literary figure of the late second and early third centuries C.E.*

His biography, preserved in inscriptions and as a result of his writings, attest to his powers. He served as *legatus Augustus pro praetor* in Syria Coelae and Germania Inferior and probably served as urban prefect in 217–18, under Emperor Macrinus. As a writer, Macrinus played a substantial role in the historiography of later years by continuing Suetonius's biographies of the emperors. Maximus picked up his research with the reign of Emperor Nerva (96–98 C.E.) and carried the history down to Emperor Elagabalus (218–222 C.E.). While this actual account has not survived, it certainly was the primary source for the *SCRIPTORES HISTORIAE AUGUSTAE*. As his biographies did not include Severus Alexander, it has been presumed that Maximus died sometime before 235.

Maximus, Magnus (d. 388 C.E.) *Usurper and emperor of the West (383–388)*
Of Spanish descent and related to Count Theodosius, father of Emperor Theodosius I, Maximus served under the count in Britain in 369 and later fought in Africa from 373 to 375. A proven military commander, Maximus was appointed COMES or general of the provinces in Britain, where he launched several successful campaigns against the Picts and other tribes from Caledonia.

In 383 his troops proclaimed Maximus rival emperor to Gratian and crossed over into Gaul to overthrow Gratian. Deserted by his own soldiers, Gratian tried to retreat to Lugdunum (Lyons) but was put to death by Maximus's MAGISTER EQUITUM Andragathius in August. With Maximus in control of Britain, Gaul, and Spain, both Theodosius I in the East and Valentinian II in Italy had to accept the reality of the usurper's claims. Maximus assumed the name Flavius, issuing coinage and emerging as a staunch champion of Christian orthodoxy. He executed the Spanish layman PRISCILLIAN for his supposed heresies.

From his capital at Treveri (Trier), Maximus worked to extend his influence. In 387 he raised his young son, Flavius Victor, to the rank of Augustus and then marched on Italy to add it to his list of territories. Valentinian fled to Constantinople. The aroused Theodosius made his preparations, launching an Eastern army in 388. It rolled its way through Illyricum, defeating Andragathius and Maximus himself. The usurper threw himself upon the mercy of Theodosius but was sentenced to die on August 28. Flavius Victor later joined him.

Maximus, Sextus Quintilius *See* QUINTILII BROTHERS.

Maximus, Tattius (fl. second century C.E.) *Prefect of the Praetorian Guard during the reign of Emperor Antoninus Pius (138–161 C.E.)*
Maximus was given the difficult task of succeeding GAVIUS MAXIMUS, who retired in 158 after a tenure of 20 years. Gaius Tattius Maximus served from 156 to 158 as the prefect of the VIGILES before being promoted to command the Guard. Upon his death (date uncertain) he was replaced by two men, Cornelius Repentinus and Furius Victorinus.

Maximus of Ephesus (d. 370 or 371 C.E.) *Leading Neoplatonic philosophers of the fourth century C.E.*
Maximus was a student of Aedesius and thus a recipient of the philosopher Iamblichus's pseudo-mystical and magical variation on NEOPLATONISM. Maximus specialized in theurgy, centering on divination, although his most famous prophecies were either obvious or never came true. Nevertheless, his reputation attracted the young

JULIAN (the future emperor) in the 350s; Maximus and several other pagan philosophical masters became his tutors, introducing the prince to the mysteries of PAGANISM and ensuring his total conversion to the pagan cause. Maximus claimed that it was through the use of divination that he predicted the rise of Julian to the throne.

By 361, in fact, Julian was emperor. The ruler summoned his teacher to Constantinople, where Maximus took up residence as one of the leading non-Christian intellectuals at court, remaining at Julian's side for much of his reign. With Maximus's favorable divinations, Julian set out on his war against the Persians but died during the campaign, with Maximus at his bedside. Julian's demise terminated the favored status of the pagans, although Maximus gained the trust of Emperor Valens for a brief time. In 370 or 371, he was arrested and executed for supposed complicity in a plot against Valens. Eunapius, in his *Lives of the Sophists,* wrote about Maximus.

Maximus of Tyre (c. 125–185 C.E.) *Itinerant Sophist lecturer and pseudo-Platonic philosopher*
Maximus was clearly familiar with the works of Plato, for he quoted him extensively and claimed to be a follower, but his gifts were limited and his originality wanting. Lectures were delivered in Athens, although all of the 41 extant addresses given by Maximus were in Rome during the reign of Emperor Commodus (177–192 C.E.).

Media Atropatene One of the oldest regions of Persia, between the Tigris and the Euphrates rivers on the west and the Caspian Sea on the east; a fertile, heavily populated region, long important to the effective administration of the Parthian and the later Persian Empires. Media was surrounded by key geographical or political sites: Armenia to the north, the Caspian Sea to the east, Assyria to the south, and Mesopotamia to the west.

See PERSIA.

medicine Medicine was bequeathed to the Romans through the traditions of the Egyptians, the Chaldaeans, the Greeks, and the Etruscans. As was true with many other elements of Roman life, the Romans received their first organized introduction to the medical world from Etruria, and later, in a far more constructive sense, from the Greeks. Rome had little original medical knowledge. There was an association of anatomy and disease with the forces of the occult, and thus the care of the sick was left to the soothsayers, the *haruspices,* or the best method of finding relief was determined by consultation with the SIBYLLINE BOOKS.

Two developments caused major changes in Roman medicine. First there was the contact with the Etruscans and especially the Greeks, who brought with them an increased level of sophistication; secondly, with Rome's conquests in the Mediterranean, large numbers of slaves became available (*see* SLAVERY), many of whom knew medicine and practiced it for their owners. This created the image that most physicians were of the lower class. In fact, during the late Republic and into the imperial epoch, Roman doctors, *medici,* emerged as a genuine, albeit small, class of professionals.

Cato may have hated the Greek practitioners of medicine at Rome, but even Caesar eventually called one a friend, the doctor who stayed with him at Pharmacusa while the ransom was collected to pay the pirates who had kidnapped him. Increasingly, private physicians, especially those in the service of great men, were widely respected. The best example in the early days of the empire was Antonius Musa, the author and man responsible for many years of medical service to Emperor Augustus.

Writers in the Greek tradition earned enough money to support themselves by helping to advance the general state of medicine throughout the Roman world. CELSUS, from the early first century C.E., presented encyclopedically the field of medicine. Scribonius LARGUS, practitioner to the Emperor Claudius, centered on prescriptions for all kinds of ailments. PLINY THE ELDER, in his *Natural History,* showed the means by which a doctor could find cures from the world of nature. Above them all stood GALEN. From Pergamum, Galen's career through the second century C.E. stood as a symbol of both his genius and the manner in which medicine had evolved. He studied at Pergamum and at Alexandria, under the foremost Egyptian anatomists before perfecting his skills treating gladiators. His reputation brought him to Rome, where even Marcus Aurelius paid for his services. With Galen came an end to progressive treatment and imagination. Roman medicine had reached its peak and would advance no further.

The education of a physician was a highly individualized matter. A hopeful student had to find a doctor willing to serve as his (or in some cases, her) tutor. This teacher would be someone of high reputation preferably but not so busy as to make instruction a problem. Medicine was still divided into the various areas of expertise: anatomy and physiology, diagnostics, pathology, hygiene, therapeutics, and the veterinary arts. Surgery was an essential part of a practice, especially for the doctors appointed to the legions, an office that was regulated by the time of Trajan in the second century C.E. Because of the obviously irregular nature of the training, mastery of the medical arts must have taken years. The experience gained in the apprenticeship to a great doctor would have been considerable, and the rewards of these many lessons would have been worth the wait for the lucky few. The first Greek physician to set up practice in Rome was Archagathus, who in 219 B.C.E. had his offices paid for at public expense. His business was no doubt excellent, setting the stage for other successful doctors to come to Rome. Asclapio called Cicero his friend, and Eudemus

held a position of trust with Livia, closer in some regards than Antonius Musa with Augustus.

Monetarily, a good doctor in Rome who treated nobility could earn vast amounts of money. According to Pliny, such medical experts as Albutius and Rubrius managed to amass 250,000 sesterces a year. During the reign of Claudius, Quintus Stertinius was granted 500,000 sesterces from the emperor. With his brother, also a physician, Quintus was able to spend a fortune improving Naples and, again with his sibling, still retire owning 30 million sesterces.

Mediolanum   Large city situated on a plain in northern Italy, below the Alps and between the Ticino and Adda rivers; relatively unimportant, despite its location, until the late third century C.E., when it became one of the most prominent metropolises in the Roman Empire. Mediolanum (modern Milan) began as a creation of the Gallic tribes and served for many years as the city of the Insubres in Gallia Cisalpina. It received little attention from Roman historians, save from Polybius, who mentioned it as part of his coverage of the war between Rome and Gaul. In 222 B.C.E., Cn. Scipio and Marcellus captured it, compelling the Insubres to submit. Henceforth, Mediolanum belonged to the Romans, becoming first a *municipium* and then a *colonia.*

Throughout the remaining years of the Republic and into the era of the empire, Mediolanum remained in relative obscurity. The Roman Civil Wars in the first century B.C.E. bypassed the site completely. Slowly, however, economic prosperity became possible because of several key developments. Mediolanum's position in Italy placed it directly along a number of key lines of communication. Gallia Narbonensis, Gaul, the Alps, and Raetia kept in touch with Rome via the city. Further, Mediolanum acted as a support center for Aquileia, the Italian gateway to the Danubian provinces. In the face of economic challenges from the provinces, both communities realized the importance of meeting the threat to Italy's industrial supremacy by adapting to market needs. They thus epitomized the more imaginative response of the northern Italians to the growing wealth of Gaul, Spain, and Africa. Mediolanum and Aquileia began manufacturing glass, wine, and especially (for Milan) weapons. Where the south became stagnant, Mediolanum was rewarded for its ingenuity.

Emperor Diocletian reformed the entire imperial system, downgrading the status of both Rome and Italy. The West of the Roman Empire, though, still needed a capital, one that was strong, ideally close to both the Rhine and Danube frontiers, but one free from the influence of Rome. In 291 C.E., Diocletian met with his colleague Maximian at Mediolanum, and two years later Maximian returned, this time as Augustus (coemperor). The city was to be his new headquarters from which he would rule the Western imperial territories. Maximian improved its general appearance, and from 293 until the early years of the fifth century, all subsequent emperors of the West maintained a residence there. In 404, the Emperor Honorius felt that he could not defend himself adequately there, choosing to move the court to Ravenna, on the Adriatic. There it remained until the end of Roman rule. But Milan continued to wield genuine power. The famous St. Ambrose held his see there (374–397 C.E.), and the Lombard kings later chose it as their capital.

Mediolanum was built on the Lambrus River, in the valley of the Addus and Ticinus. The surrounding countryside, including the Po Valley, was known for its fertility and beauty. Unfortunately, nothing remains of the original city, and only bits of the grand construction of the third and fourth centuries survived the ravages of the fifth and the building programs of the Middle Ages. Maximian put great effort into improving the state of his capital. Extended city defenses included new walls surrounding the palace, baths, theaters, a circus, and the all-important mint. Of these only part of the wall is still standing, with the Torre di Ansperto, an old tower.

Mediterranean Sea Called by the Romans the Mare Internum, this was the most important body of water in the Roman Empire. Over its waters sailed the bulk of the vessels from many nations, and the economic lifelines of entire provinces were dependent upon the merchant ships that moved from port to port. Initially, the Romans were not great seafarers in the tradition of their Etruscan predecessors. Because of the Punic Wars, however, the mighty fleets of Rome were created. Subsequently the Mediterranean became a Roman lake. The military supremacy of their ships was not questioned on a grand scale until the time of Geiseric and the Vandals in the middle of the fifth century C.E., when the Vandal war vessels terrorized Africa, Spain, and Italy.

For details on the many facets of Mediterranean life, see also ACHAEA; ADRIATIC SEA; AFRICA; ALEXANDRIA; AQUILEIA; ASIA; BLACK SEA; BRUNDISIUM; CAESAREA; CARTHAGE; CONSTANTINOPLE; CORSICA; CRETE AND CYRENAICA; CYPRUS; EGYPT; GALLIA; GEISERIC; HISPANIA; INDUSTRY; IONIA; ITALIA; LIBURNIA; MASSILIA; NARBO; NAVY; PIRACY; POMPEY, SEXTUS; RED SEA; RHODES; SARDINIA; SHIPS; SICILIA; TRADE; and VANDALS.

Megalesia Also known as Megalensia; a unique festival in honor of the goddess CYBELE, held annually from April 4 to 10. The Festival of the Great Mother began in 205–204 B.C.E., when Cybele was invited by the Senate to come to Rome from her center at Pessinus in Phrygia. Cybele's arrival in the Eternal City, at a moment of crisis during the Punic Wars, was marked by a grand celebration, the first holding of the Megalesia, then lasting only one day, on April 4. Although Cybele received a temple on the Palatine Hill and the addition of several days to the Megalesia in 191 B.C.E., the strangeness of her cult horrified traditional Roman sensibilities. Not only were her priests eunuchs, but also some participants in the festival very often castrated themselves in fits of ecstasy. The Senate forbade all Romans from physically participating in the Megalesia. The activities of the Phrygian clerics were tolerated and, probably to increase the public enjoyment, the tradition began of staging Roman comedies. In the first century C.E., other changes were made, mainly through the influence of Claudius. The figure of Attis, Cybele's lover, was magnified, and a spring cycle was initiated to add him to the Megalesia. The dates of the Attis festival were March 15–27, while the elaborate rituals of the feast were unchanged. This left the Megalesia still an important religious holiday but tempered its bizarre nature by including it in a broader context.

Meherdates (fl. first century C.E.) *Claimant to the throne of Parthia (c. 47–49 C.E.)*
The son of the Parthian King Phraates, Meherdates had been sent as a child-hostage to the Romans. Raised in Rome, he was still there in 47, when Gotarzes II was embroiled in a bitter struggle with Vardanes for political supremacy. During the trouble the name of Meherdates was mentioned as a possible candidate for the throne but was forgotten when Gotarzes proved triumphant. Two years later, a group of Parthian emissaries arrived in Rome to beg Claudius to send Meherdates to Parthia. They were confident that he could overthrow the tyrannical Gotarzes and rule as a reliable ally to the Roman Empire. Claudius agreed, ordering Gaius Cassius, governor of Syria, to accompany Meherdates to the Euphrates. There the prince was met by a sizable collection of Parthian nobles.

The host should have set out, but delays took place. Meherdates proved fond of drink and banquets. After finally setting forth, the would-be usurper was unable to hold his wavering supporters, who deserted him in large numbers. With the odds more to his liking, Gotarzes attacked, won a victory and had Meherdates brought before him in chains. His ears were cut off before he was displayed to the Parthian crowds as a client of Rome.

Mela, Annaeus (fl. mid-first century C.E.) *Father of the poet Lucan and brother to Junius Gallio and Seneca*
Mela was a member of the Equestrians (EQUITES) who devoted himself almost exclusively to a career in the imperial government. He held various procuratorships, attaining finally the rank of senator, but wielding greater influence through his son. The wealth of Mela was reportedly considerable, increasing after the suicide of Lucan in 65 C.E., when the father assumed the poet's estate. This acquisition attracted the attention of Nero, who, coveting such riches, listened to false charges against Mela concerning his complicity in the PISONIAN

CONSPIRACY. Mela killed himself, bequeathing his fortune to the Praetorian prefect Ofonius TIGELLINUS and his son-in-law, Cassutianus Capito. His wife Acilia was shamefully named by Lucan as an accomplice in the Piso affair.

Mela, Pomponius (fl. first century C.E.) *Geographer during the reign of Gaius Caligula (37–41 C.E.), or perhaps of Claudius (41–54 C.E.)*

Pomponius Mela came from Tingentera, a town near Gibraltar in Hispania Baetica. Based upon a reading of his work, he received training in rhetoric and was influenced by the literary style of Seneca. Mela authored a three-volume treatise on geography, *De situ orbis,* or "On the world's locations." In it he examined the geography of the known world, listing some 1,500 places while providing details about the customs and characteristics of each spot. He used as his resources a variety of writers, especially Cornelius Nepos. PLINY THE ELDER, in turn, used Mela in his *Natural History.*

Melania the Elder (c. 345–410 C.E.) *Roman noblewoman and convert to Christianity*

A symbol (with Melania the Younger) of the eventual success and pervasive nature of Christianity among the Roman upper classes, St. Melania departed from her high place in society to follow the example of St. JEROME in adopting the ascetic life. She left her estates in 372 for the East, establishing a monastery near JERUSALEM on the Mount of Olives before returning briefly to Rome in 397. The attack of the Goths on Italy in the early fifth century forced her to flee to Africa and then to Jerusalem, where she died. St. Melania had a profound influence upon her granddaughter, St. MELANIA THE YOUNGER.

Melania the Younger (c. 383–438 C.E.) *Granddaughter of Melania the Elder*

Another convert to Christian asceticism from the ranks of the Roman nobility, Melania the Younger followed the path of her grandmother by renouncing the world and her vast wealth, embracing the life of an ascetic with her husband Pinianus. She left Italy, which was overrun by the Goths of Alaric at the time, traveling to Tagaste, Africa. Accompanied by her faithful husband, she joined a monastery at Bethlehem before moving to JERUSALEM. There Melania founded a monastery, as had her older namesake, on the Mount of Olives. Pinianus died in 431, seven years before Melania.

Melitius and the Melitians (fl. early fourth century C.E.) *Bishop of Lycopolis in Egypt*

Melitius founded and lent his name to a religious movement that was declared schismatic by the fourth-century C.E. Christian Church. The schism originated as a result of the great persecution of Emperor Diocletian (c. 303–313) throughout the Roman Empire. Many Christians, on pain of torture and death, had given up the faith but later wished to repent. The conditions for their acceptance once more into the church were found by Melitius to be far too lenient. He voiced his complaints and, finding no satisfactory response from his superiors, ordained his own priests. Peter, the bishop of Alexandria (home of Arius [260–336 C.E.] the later heresiarch), excommunicated Melitius only to find that the Egyptian prelate had many supporters. Peter was later executed by the imperial government, and Melitius was sent to work in the mines, a harsh period for him that added to his claims. Interestingly, the Council of Nicaea did not declare the Melitians to be heretics, working instead to integrate them back into the church. Devout followers of Melitius continued to worship separately for centuries and were wiped out finally in Egypt in the eight century, by Islam.

Melitius of Antioch (d. 381 C.E.) *Bishop of Antioch*

Melitius was a source of controversy in the mid-fourth century with regard to the see of Antioch. Formerly the bishop of Sebaste (modern Sivas), Melitius was translated from his see to that of Antioch around 360, at the time when the diocese was still in the throes of considerable theological upheaval resulting from the heresy of Arianism. As Melitius had made promises to both parties in the city before his election, he was soon facing trouble. Of a mild, peaceful, and religious disposition, he was forced to decide his theological loyalties before Emperor Constantius II, who, upon hearing Melitius's orthodoxy, exiled him. There followed a bitter division within the city and, upon Melitius's return under Emperor Julian (362), his claim to the see was disputed, particularly as an opposing claimant, Paulinus, had entered the picture. Banished several more times and censured over questionable theological views, Melitius was finally restored in 378. He died fully reconciled with the church in 381 while presiding over the Council of Constantinople. The followers of Melitius came to be called Melitians and these efforts were denoted the Melitian Schism, not to be confused with the Melitian Schism in Egypt in the early fourth century. The pro-Melitian bishop Flavian was recognized as bishop of Antioch in 398 by Pope St. Siricius.

Menas (Menodorus) (d. 35 B.C.E.) *Freedman and a very unreliable admiral in the service of the pirate Sextus Pompey (38–37 B.C.E.).*

Menas was a trusted servant of Sextus who received command of Sardinia in 38, during the long struggle between Sextus and the combined forces (naval and legionary) of Octavian (AUGUSTUS). Sextus Pompey, however, could never hold the loyalty of his officers, and Menas deserted his cause, transferring his allegiance to Octavian, along with all of Sardinia and three legions. Octavian welcomed him, appointing him to a major command in his fleet. He was to be subordinate to Admiral Calvisius Sabinus in the upcoming campaign against Sextus in Sicily. Menas thus shared the defeat inflicted upon Octavian's ships and the resulting disaster that destroyed half of the fleet. Although Octavian's repaired flotilla was impressive, Menas chafed at holding a secondary rank to Sabinus and went back to Sextus in 36. By July, facing accusations from his fellow commanders, and unable to bear the suspicions of his chief, Menas again deserted. It was a timely betrayal, because on September 3, Marcus AGRIPPA crushed the Sextian fleet at NAULOCHUS. Octavian could no longer trust Menas, and he was given minor positions until he was killed in a battle with the Pannonians.

Mercury God of travel and merchants, a unique Roman divinity who was identified with the Greek god Hermes and later received all of that deity's characteristics. Mercurius, or Mercury, was a late arrival to Rome's pantheon, receiving his own temple near the Circus Maximus in 495 B.C.E. and an altar next to the Porta Capena. As was true with most of the other Roman gods, Mercury had several incarnations. Merchants adopted him as their patron, offering him sacrifices to ensure safe journeys and bountiful commerce. This facet of his nature may have come about as a result of his also being known as the winged messenger of Jupiter. Although he had no festival date on the "calendar of Numa," his special day was May 25, when the merchants visited his altar.

See also GODS AND GODDESSES OF ROME.

Merida (Emerita) Capital of HISPANIA Lusitania and the principal center of Roman influence in the province. It was situated in eastern Lusitania (southwestern Spain) on the Anas (modern Guadiana) River to allow its governor to summon aid from his associates in Hispania Baetica and Hispania Taraconensis in the event of trouble from the unpredictable Lusitanian tribes. Equally, its location allowed the city to participate fully in the extensive economic life of Spain, while ensuring the line of communications for the Roman government throughout the entire region. Merida was founded sometime around 25 B.C.E. by the order of Augustus. As part of his imperial colonization effort, veterans were given land to establish themselves as a colony, and they were totally successful. Merida acquired a reputation as an Italian stronghold, blessed with every Roman architectural wonder and amusement. There were aqueducts, temples, an amphitheater, a circus and the traditional monuments to Rome's greatness, in particular an arch to Trajan.

Merobaudes, Flavius (1) (d. 387 C.E.) *Magister peditum, three-time consul (377, 383, 388), powerful figure in the Roman Empire during the later years of the fourth century C.E.*
Merobaudes was a German, probably a Frank by descent, who served in the imperial armies and attained command

as an officer in the reign of Julian (361–363 C.E.). In 363 he was part of the entourage escorting the dead emperor to Tarsus for burial. Merobaudes received an appointment from Valentinian I in 375 to the office of *magister peditum* in the West. He directed the emperor's last campaign in Pannonia. When Valentinian died that year, the magister ensured that Valentinian's son, Valentinian II, was elevated to the rank of Augustus, while dominating the other heir, GRATIAN. The next years saw Merobaudes as the master of the West. He held consulships in 377 and 383, worked against the influence of the MAGISTER MILITUM RICIMER, and was the key political entity at court, ever eager to increase his sway and authority. A major opportunity presented itself in 383 when the usurper Magnus Maximus, the general of the armies in Britain, crossed the Channel and proclaimed himself emperor. Merobaudes threw his support behind Maximus, retaining in all probability the post of *magister peditum* following Gratian's death in August 383. For the next five years he continued to exercise his will upon the Western provinces and was named to a highly irregular third consulship in 388. Because of the collapse of relations between Maximus and the emperor of the East, Theodosius, Merobaudes committed suicide late in 387, before he could assume his consul duties. The exact reason for this remains unclear, although Maximus took his place as consul.

Merobaudes, Flavius (2) (d. after 446 C.E.) *Christian poet*
Merobaudes probably came from a German (Frankish) family but lived in Spain, studying rhetoric and serving as an army commander (c. 443). He had achieved fame in Rome, where he worked at the court of Emperor Valentinian III, writing PANEGYRICS to his parton, the imperial family and the powerful general AETIUS. For his poems Merobaudes was given a statue in the Forum of Trajan. He followed Claudian in general style, but lacked his polish and ease with words. Mainly fragments of his works have survived, composed in a popular fashion while displaying an obvious Christian perspective.

Mesopotamia The large and ancient region between the Tigris and Euphrates rivers. Surrounded on all sides by important territories (Armenia, Syria, Arabia, and Assyria), Mesopotamia served as a battleground between Romans and Parthians or Romans and Persians. It was also an important route for trade and commerce. The name was derived from the Greek, and came to stand for several divisions of the area. Mesopotamia could include merely its Syrian parts or its Assyrian, or both. During the old Persian Empire it was under the satrapy of Babylonia and later received extensive colonization from the Seleucids. Under the Parthians, however, a new strategic importance was given to it, as it became a wall against

Rome, at such key sites as CARRHAE, HATRA, and NISIBIS. Throughout the long, bitter wars with the Romans, Mesopotamia suffered numerous invasions, counterattacks, and sieges. For Roman generals often chose to assault Babylonia by taking a line of advance along the rivers, and thus wreaked repeated devastation with marches through the invariably contested districts.

In the final years of TRAJAN (114–117 C.E.), Mesopotamia was subjugated by the legions and transformed into an imperial domain, the province of Mesopotamia. HADRIAN, retreating back to the Syrian border, later abandoned the conquests. Lucius Verus (162–165) regained Mesopotamia, and the Romans would not leave until the late third century. Upper Mesopotamia became, by order of Septimius Severus, the imperial province of Mesopotamia and was defended by veteran colonies at Carrhae, Singara, and Edessa, as well as fortresses at strategic locations. The dynastically exhausted Parthians could not mount effective countermeasures but were crushed in turn by the new power in the East, the Sassanids, who resurrected the Persian Empire beginning in 226 C.E. There followed a thunderous series of campaigns to solidify their hold over all of the old Parthian lands. In 230, Mesopotamia was attacked. By 237–238 it had fallen, and years of fighting culminated in 260 with defeat and the eventual death of Valerian at the hands of Shapur I.

Through the efforts of subsequent emperors, a Roman recovery of the East was undertaken, and in 238 Carus reclaimed Mesopotamia. Emperor GALERIUS, in 296, inflicted another crushing defeat on the Persians. So devastating was the loss to Persia that only in the time of Constantius was trouble renewed. The emperor JULIAN, in 363, took to the field once more to defend Mesopotamia but died from wounds received in battle. His successor, Jovian, accepted a humiliating peace, and the Persians triumphantly assumed mastery over the land between the rivers.

Messalla Corvinus, Marcus Valerius (64 B.C.E.–8 C.E.) *Influential figure in the reign of Emperor Augustus*

Respected and well liked, he was a great patron of the arts. Messalla was a member of the old patrician nobility, studying Greek subjects in his youth, while mastering oratory. Subsequently he became one of Rome's leading orators, earning favorable comparison with Asinius Pollio. As a writer he examined grammar, composed bucolic poems in the style of Virgil and may have authored an autobiography later used by historians such as Appian, Plutarch, and Suetonius.

Messalla entered politics on the side of the LIBERATORS, joining Brutus and Cassius and fighting the battle of Philippi in 42 B.C.E. As his reputation was already considerable, he was offered command of the surviving legions of the Republic but declined. The party of Marc ANTONY seemed to him to be the brightest, and so he entered into Antony's circle, aiding the eventual triumvir on several occasions. Antony, however, was too unpredictable for Messalla and was utterly dominated by Cleopatra, Egypt's queen. Messalla thus joined Octavian (AUGUSTUS) sometime before 36 B.C.E., campaigning for him over the next years. He fought the pirate Sextus Pompey in 36 and saw duty in Illyricum, Pannonia in 35–34 and overcame the Alpine tribe of the Salassi in 34–33. Octavian rewarded him with the consulship in 31, the same year in which Messalla joined him in the battle of Actium, where Antony was destroyed.

With an empire to organize, Augustus sent Messalla to the East, then named him proconsul of Gaul. There, on his birthday in 27, he subdued the Aquitani. Henceforth he held various government positions. In 25 B.C.E., Augustus named him the urban prefect of Rome, only to have him resign after six days in protest against the status of the office in regard to the Eternal City, or perhaps because Messalla did not feel up to the task. Later, in 11, he was on the water board of the city, as a *curator aquarum*. Finally, in 2 B.C.E., he made the recommendation that Augustus hold the title of PATER PATRIAE. Aside from his political activities, Messalla spent most of his time engaged in social and artistic endeavors. Tibullus, Ovid, Sulpicia, and others enjoyed Messalla's favor. They, in turn, wrote of him in their panegyrics elegiacs. He also devoted vast sums to public works and buildings, most notably the reconstruction of sections of the Via Latina.

Messalla Messallinus, Marcus Valerius (fl. early first century C.E.) *Son of Messalla Corvinus, who achieved some fame during the reigns of Augustus (27 B.C.E.–14 C.E.) and Tiberius (14–37 C.E.)*

Messalla held a consulship in 3 B.C.E. and was known as a fairly proficient orator in his own right. In 6 C.E. he was legate of ILLYRICUM, assigned to aid Tiberius in his campaign against the Marcommanic king MAROBODUUS. When all of the Dalmatian and Pannonian tribes erupted in the rear of the advancing Roman legions, Messalla was sent back to Pannonia to deal with them. His skills as a general were put to the test. A battle was won and Siscia captured, for which he received a tribute in Rome. As a member of the Senate, Messalla played a role in the early days of Tiberius's rule. His speeches, in part, were preserved. Later he was elected one of the QUINDECIMVIRI, with care over the SIBYLLINE BOOKS.

Messallina, Statilia (fl. first century C.E.) *Empress from 66–68 C.E. and the last wife of Emperor Nero*

Statilia was reportedly a stunning beauty, born to a noble family and descended from Taurus, the triumphant general and two-time consul. This combination of wealth and good looks attracted many suitors. She was married five times in all and had many lovers. In 65, one of her latest affairs was with Nero; therefore, it was considered political suicide for another to interfere in the alliance. M. Vestinus Atticus, consul in 65, made such a blunder by becoming her fourth husband. Jealous, Nero put him to death, wedding the lady in 66. Statilia's associations with the most influential Romans protected her when Nero fell from power. In 69, during Otho's brief reign, he planned to marry her, but he lost the throne before he could do so. Statilia overcame this tragedy as well.

Messallina, Valeria (d. 48 C.E.) *Empress from 41–48, the third wife of Emperor Claudius*

Valeria Messallina was one of the most infamous women of Rome because of her abuses of power and her debaucheries. She came from a noble family, her mother being Domitia Lepida, the daughter of ANTONIA (2). Gnaeus Domitius Ahenobarbus was her uncle, and thus she was related to Nero as well. Claudius, notoriously bad in his choice of women, married her in 41. From the start she exercised a wholly unhealthy control over him, equal to the powers of the imperial freedmen, who dominated palace life during this period. She bore Claudius two children, Britannicus and Octavia, but her principal efforts were dedicated to crushing her opponents and acquiring new lovers. She told most of her lovers that Claudius knew about her affairs, approving of them. Often Claudius would instruct courtiers to do whatever she commanded, so they thought that he condoned her activities. It became clear by 48, however, that the emperor was just about the only person in Rome who did not know of Messallina's encounters and endless indiscretions. A general fear of her, and a worry that the popular actor Mnester might be killed for sleeping with her, kept most of the court silent.

Finally, in 48, Messallina developed such a passion for Gaius Silius that she married him in a mock wedding ceremony. The freedman Narcissus was now able to move against the empress. Using the many members of Claudius's circle, he secured her condemnation at the order of a shaken and terrified emperor. Amazed that her offenses had actually been discovered, Messallina fled to the gardens of Lucullus and there met her death at the hands of a tribune of the Praetorian Guard. She epitomized the political weakness of Claudius's reign and the general decline of Roman morality. Interestingly, Claudius ordered that all mention of her name was to be obliterated from documents, monuments, and inscriptions and vowed never to marry again, though he did during the next year, this time to Agrippina the Younger.

Metellus Celer, Quintus Caecilius *Consul in 60 B.C.E.*

Metellus Celer was a minor player in the drama of the Republic during the years prior to the formation of the FIRST TRIUMVIRATE. He opposed both the political aspirations of CLODIUS PULCHER and the proposed land reforms of Julius CAESAR. Metellus was appointed governor of Gallia Transalpina at the same time that the Lex Vatinia was passed, giving Caesar command of Illyricum and Gallia Cisalpina (c. 59 B.C.E.). But Metellus suddenly dropped dead, allowing Pompey to press the Senate to approve Caesar's command over Transalpine Gaul as well. Caesar was thus able to embark upon his famous GALLIC WARS. For a number of years before his death, Metellus was unhappily married to the infamous Clodia, the sister of Clodius Pulcher, a cousin. The charge was made by Cicero, and often repeated, that Clodia poisoned her husband, having tired of him. He was also counted among the better orators of his time by the historian Tacitus, who wrote that he was one of several successful political figures who achieved greatness through strength of arms and keenness of rhetorical wit.

Metellus Scipio, Quintus Caecilius (d. 46 B.C.E.) *Consul in 52 B.C.E. and a supporter of Pompey the Great during the Civil War with Julius Caesar (49–45 B.C.E.).*

A member of an ancient family, Scipio was a firm adherent of the aristocracy of the Republic and thus found Pompey a useful counterbalance to Caesar. A political alliance was cemented by the marriage of his daughter CORNELIA (2) to Pompey following the death of JULIA (2) in 54. A grateful Pompey then elevated Scipio to the consulship as his colleague, this despite his inability to become consul on his own. With the eruption of hostilities in the Republic in 49, Scipio joined Pompey and was assigned a proconsular command in the East. In 48 he tried to help Pompey at DYRRHACHIUM and the battle of PHARSALUS but could do little. Following the disaster of Pharsalus, he fled to Africa with the Pompeian remnant. There he was one of the leading generals with CATO UTICENSIS, LABIENUS, and King JUBA of Numidia. Caesar arrived and won the battle of THAPSUS in February 46 B.C.E. Scipio killed himself immediately afterward.

Milan *See* MEDIOLANUM.

Milan, Edict of Declaration issued circa 313 C.E. by Emperors CONSTANTINE the Great and LICINIUS, ending the persecution of CHRISTIANITY. It marked the ascendancy of the Christian Church as the dominant religious force in the Roman Empire. Following the battle of Milvian Bridge and the defeat of MAXENTIUS in 312, Constantine was able to pass legislation that went beyond the Edict of Toleration decreed by Emperor GALERIUS in 311. Christians in the provinces under his control were not only granted full rights of worship, they also received certain other benefits. He returned all confiscated monies to them and even opened the coffers of the treasury to the church to meet its financial needs.

Moreover, because of his position as senior emperor in the now disorganized TETRARCHY, Constantine could use his political and military superiority on his supposed corulers, Licinius and the usurper MAXIMINUS DAIA. Licinius agreed immediately to respect Christianity and, searching for an ally against Maximinus in the East, met with Constantine at Mediolanum (Milan) early in 313. There both emperors reached an accord by which Licinius would extend his own toleration to match that of Constantine. The result was the so-called Edict of Milan, which was neither made public there, nor was a real edict.

Maximinus Daia, meanwhile, could not chance a bitter war with Constantine. He thus ceased all persecution of the Christians. The plans to revive organized Paganism also failed with the fall of Maxentius. The inevitable war with Licinius for mastery of the Eastern provinces began in 313 and on May 1, Licinius proved victorious over Maximinus's larger host. Maximinus retreated to Nicomedia, declaring all Christians in his domain to be free, while returning to them all seized property. He died in August.

True to his promise, at Nicomedia in June 313, Licinius published the letter that had been formulated in Milan. It was recorded joyously by the Christian writers Eusebius and Lactantius. Part of it read:

> When I, Constantine Augustus, and I, Licinius Augustus, had made a meeting at Mediolanum and had discussed all matters which pertained to the public good and the safety of the government, amongst all other things that would bring benefit to the majority of men we believed that arrangements were necessary to secure the continued reverence for the Divinity and so toward that end we grant both to Christians and to all men the right to follow freely whatever religion each wished, to insure that thereby any divinity in heaven's seat may be appeased and made propitious towards us and to any who are placed beneath our power.

milestones   Roman milestones gave the distance from a named location to where the milestone stood. In Italy, that location was normally Rome, while in the provinces it was from the provincial capital. Milestones were erected every Roman mile, meaning that they were found every 1,000 paces (*millia passuum*). However, the distances posted on the milestone were expressed in leagues (*leugae*), which equaled 1,500 *passus*, or 1.5 miles.

Milestones in the Republic bore the name of the consul or officials who were responsible for their construction. In the imperial era, milestones were inscribed with the full name and title of the emperor. They were normally cylindrical or oval in shape, resting on a square base and varying in height from 6 feet 6 inches to 13 feet. The engraving was made directly into the stone face, although some were clearly painted. The abundance and value of milestones to the Romans is evidenced by the fact that more than 4,000 survive, with 600 found in Italy alone. They are of great value to historians in that they served to delimit specific territorial units within the empire, especially within the specific boundaries of the provinces.

Miletus   Ancient city near the Aegean Sea coast of ASIA MINOR, situated specifically in Ionian Caria. Miletus early on achieved maritime greatness and expanded colonially along the Black Sea. Its period of unrestricted prosperity ended in 495–4 B.C.E. when the metropolis was destroyed by the Persians. Rebuilt (c. 479 B.C.E.) by its inhabitants, Miletus chose to oppose the advances of Alexander the Great, only to be crushed again. Once more the Miletians resurrected their homes, this time following original plans. By the time the Romans gained control of Asia (130 B.C.E.), Miletus had fully recovered its architectural splendor but not its economic or seagoing might. Nevertheless, the city received heavy assistance from the Roman government, aimed at improving the financial and commercial life of Asia. Miletian artisans and craftsmen benefited reputedly, while the main export of Miletus, wool, found a market in every corner of the ancient world. The sheep of Miletus, for centuries the finest in Asia Minor, produced superb wools, the *milesia vellera*, and were eventually bred in Italy.

In 479 B.C.E., the architect-planner, Hippodamus, a native of the city, had designed Miletus along a grid system. Through the help of the Romans, a more unified artistic theme was developed, with gates to section off parts of the city overlooking the harbor. Thus concealed, and hence more startling upon entrance, were the city's main attractions, a harbor stoa and a larger south stoa reached along a beautifully colonnaded avenue. There was as well the panorama of agora, gymnasium, and temples. The stunning Temple of Apollo was designed to match the other Asian cities and their divinities (Ephesus had Diana, Pergamum had Augustus, Smyrna worshiped Tiberius). Unfortunately for the Milesians, Gaius Caligula heard of the city's plans and in 40 ordered that the new temple be devoted to him. Miletus possessed four harbors, with a group of small islands, and was positioned across the mouth of the Maeander River. But wool and such eccentric natural characteristics were not enough to elevate Miletus into a first-city status in Asia.

Milichus (d. after 65 C.E.) *Freedman to the Senator Flavius Scaevinus*

Milichus was one of the first to inform Emperor NERO of the Pisonian Conspiracy of 65 C.E. Tacitus wrote that it was unclear as to how much Milichus knew of the plot to overthrow Nero, but when Scaevinus told him to sharpen the family dagger and to prepare bandages, he knew that a great event was at hand. The next morning, at dawn, Milichus went to the Servilian Gardens and eventually met the emperor, telling him of the intended attack. This betrayal, aided by the arrests already made of the conspirators, was followed by a period of slaughter. From his betrayal of the plot, Milichus reaped considerable wealth.

Milo, Titus Annius (d.c. 47 B.C.E.) *Military tribune of Samnite origin, and plotter*

In 58 B.C.E., the FIRST TRIUMVIRATE succeeded in ousting its enemy Cicero from Rome, and Pompey felt an increasing apprehension as Julius Caesar installed P. Clodius as his loyal agent, chief bully, and executor of policy. Clodius terrorized the city and caused all opposition to cower—ostensibly on behalf of Caesar.

In 57 B.C.E., Pompey leveled his counterattack. He enlisted the service of the violent Annius to organize a defense against Clodius. Annius performed admirably, and street violence broke out even in the Forum, where bodies piled up everywhere. Meanwhile, Annius and Clodius became dire enemies. Clodius burned down Annius's house in October of that year, and the two sued each other for disturbing the peace, a farce that continued for an entire year.

Finally, on January 18, 52 B.C.E., Clodius was killed on the order of Annius. Due to public outcry, Annius was put on trial by Pompey. The trial was as fair as the triumvirate could make it. Despite a magnificent oration by Cicero, Annius was found guilty and exiled to a comfortable life in Massilia. After Pompey's death in 48 B.C.E., Annius returned to southern Italy and began to make trouble again, enlisting the aid of Caelius, a disgruntled servant of Caesar. Times had changed, and both were killed.

Milvian Bridge   The site of a famous (even legendary) confrontation between the armies of CONSTANTINE the Great and MAXENTIUS, in the last days of October 312 C.E. The battle of Milvian Bridge not only established the political supremacy of Constantine in the West but also ensured the survival and prosperity of CHRISTIANITY. For these reasons the battle assumed the status of a struggle between the forces of light (Christianity) and darkness (PAGANISM).

At the start of 312, relations between the two rival emperors in the West had deteriorated considerably. It was clear that a collision was inevitable, and Constantine, having prepared his army, launched an assault across the Alps to dethrone the man he deemed a tyrant. He had with him the flower of his soldiery, some 40,000 well-trained veterans. Maxentius supposedly counted around 100,000 men for the defense of Italy, although most remained near Rome and the only truly reliable units under his command were the cohorts of the PRAETORIAN GUARD.

Constantine's advance went smoothly over the Mt. Genevre Pass, followed by the storming of Susa, which made a march into northern Italy possible. Maxentius committed a severe blunder by allowing the Alpine passes to fall and had to watch in frustration as his enemy gained followers in each city through a total absence of plundering, and fair treatment for all citizens.

The general of Maxentius, Ruricius Pompeianus, finally engaged Constantine near Turin. Pompeianus used his heavy cavalry to good effect initially, riding through Constantine's center. Having pierced the front lines, however, the horsemen were quickly clubbed off their mounts. Turin was soon surrendered to Constantine's

siege, and Verona was targeted next. Pompeianus brought up reinforcements to break the siege but fell on the field before the city surrendered.

After Modena opened its gates, Constantine found the Via Flaminia totally free, allowing an unmolested line to the gates of Rome. He did not want to lay siege to the Eternal City and was relieved when Maxentius, listening to the oracular SIBYLLINE BOOKS, opted for a military encounter. The first meeting between the forces, at Saxa Rubra, or Red Rock, resulted in a setback for Constantine. It would appear, however, that the once-mighty host of Maxentius was so depleted by the engagement as to remove any hope of exploiting success. For this reason Constantine was able to remain in pursuit to the Tiber and the Milvian Bridge.

Following the Sibylline Books, Maxentius was confident that his foe would be destroyed. Amassing all available troops, he sent them out of Rome, over the Tiber, crossing that river on a bridge of boats erected on the water. His army was by then composed of Praetorian Guards, joined by the Urban Cohorts of Rome, auxiliaries and light cavalry from Numidia and the Moorish lands. He apparently did not enjoy a numerical superiority at this stage, when Constantine discovered that Maxentius's troops were recklessly positioned with their backs to the river.

In late October, perhaps the 28th, the Praetorian Guard dressed for the last time. On the opposite side, Roman legions went into battle for the first time with the Chi-rho (☧) emblazoned upon their shields. True to his dream, Constantine had ordered this symbol of Christ painted upon the shields of his men, hoping that with the sign, he might conquer.

Constantine led his cavalry on the flanks, placing the infantry in the middle. Maxentius, who did not arrive until the opening moments, saw that his dispositions were the same. The cavalry of Constantine burst forward under his leadership, the Gallic riders crushing the lighter Numidians on the right, while their comrades disposed of the enemy on the left. With their flanks exposed, the auxiliaries ran for their lives, joined by the demoralized members of Maxentius's army, save for the Praetorian Guard. The Guardsmen refused to surrender, fighting to the death well into the night. As for the others, they tried to cross the bridges, only to have the boats collapse beneath their weight. Maxentius was among those falling into the water. Unable to remove his armor, he drowned, and his body was not brought out of the river until the next day. Victory for Constantine was total, and he entered Rome as master of the Western world.

Minerva   Known to the Greeks as Athena, an important Roman divinity, ranking behind JUPITER and JUNO. According to legend, Minerva was born fully formed and armed, coming out of Jupiter's head as an emanation of his intellect. The Romans thus honored her as a goddess of reason, wisdom, the arts and intelligence. She received a special chapel in the Temple of Jupiter Capitolinus on the Capitoline Hill, sharing the great edifice with Jupiter and Juno. As her appearance indicated, with her bright helmet, shield, armor, and spear, Minerva was the patroness of soldiers in battle, watching over men's courage, skill, and fortitude. Captured goods or treasures from the enemy were often sacrificed in her temple on the Capitol, or at her altar at the base of the Caelian Hill. The Festival of Quinquatrus, or Quinquatria, was at first wholly unrelated to Minerva, but became attached to her cult over the years.

See also FESTIVALS; GODS AND GODDESSES OF ROME; RELIGION.

minimi   Coins issued by barbarian nations from the third to the sixth centuries C.E., crude, worthless imitations of the Roman imperial currency. Normally, the *minimi* were of bronze, decorated with unsophisticated diagrams and incredibly small in size, hence the derivation from the Latin *minimus,* or smallest.

See also COINAGE.

Misenum   A small promontory jutting into the Tyrrhenian Sea from the coast of Campania in Italy on the Bay of Naples. Misenum was situated in the region of Cumae, BAULI, BAIAE, and PUTEOLI. Its name was derived supposedly from Misenus, the trumpeter of Aeneas, who drowned in the waters of its bay. For many years the Campanians were threatened by pirate sorties out of the Tyrrhenian Sea. These attacks were a leading reason for Pompey's brilliant campaign of 67 B.C.E. against the pirates in the Mediterranean. Misenum's strategic value was clear, and when Augustus reorganized the armed forces of Rome, he chose the spot and its bay to build an excellent harbor. Misenum emerged, with Ravenna, as one of the major ports for the Roman Imperial NAVY in Italy.

Command of the fleet at Misenum was considered a very important step upward in a Roman career. Often marines and sailors could be transferred from Misenum to Rome for special imperial duties or as rigging operators at the COLOSSEUM.

As was true with much of Campania, the community that developed around the bay was a favorite retreat for the most powerful people in Rome. Marius owned a villa there, which passed into the hands of Tiberius. There, in 37 C.E., Gaius Caligula looked on as the aged emperor either died of natural causes or was murdered.

Misenum, Conference of   Meeting held in 39 B.C.E. between the Triumvirs Marc ANTONY and Octavian (AUGUSTUS) on one side, and Sextus POMPEY, the pirate son of Pompey the Great. Sextus had proven a surprisingly successful pirate chief, whose ships commanded much of the Mediterranean, threatening all of the Italian coast as well as the provinces, and wielding the power to cut off vital shipments of grain from Africa to Rome. Following the TREATY OF BRUNDISIUM in 40 B.C.E., both Antony and Octavian had recognized the need to deal with Sextus Pompey. They were, however, not in a position to hound him from the seas and consequently agreed to a discussion. The first encounter at Puteoli ended in nothing, but in the spring of 39, real progress in negotiations led to the Treaty of Misenum. By the terms of this agreement, Sextus promised to leave the corn supply unmolested, to respect the integrity of Italy, return all seized property and to engage in no hostile actions. In return, he received Corsica, Sardinia, Achaea, and Sicily, along with vast sums of money as recompense, and a position in the triumvirate. He was also promised eventual augurship and consulship. His status was thus strengthened militarily and politically, although both of his opponents knew that the treaty would not remain intact.

Mithras   One of the major cult figures in the Roman Empire, popular in large circles of society from the first century C.E. until the fourth century. Mithras was an ancient deity, first established by the Aryans and then included in the Vedas as a god of light. In this incarnation he traveled to Persia, where the Zoroastrians attached him to their pantheon. As a light bringer, Mithras suited perfectly Zoroaster's belief in the duality of light and dark. He became a soldier in the service of Ahura-Mazda, fighting against the darkness of Ahriman. Though subordinated to Ahura-Mazda, Mithras retained such an individuality that he emerged as a unique god with his own cult and special myths. According to his mythology, Mithras came from a rock, born miraculously and then forced to endure two great tasks: a match of wrestling with the sun (they thus became friends) and the capture of the sacred bull of creation. The sacrifice of this animal brought about the blossoming of flowers, plants, and crops.

As the Mithraic cult moved west, it assumed an increasing attachment to sun worship and mystical astrology. Sun connections were obvious, given the long-term relationship with Ahura-Mazda, and the astrology was the result of conversions made in Babylonia and Chaldaea. The god probably entered the Roman world sometime in the middle of the first century B.C.E., taking hold first in the eastern provinces. Plutarch mentions Mithraism in connection with Cilician pirates in his *Life of Pompey.* The cult moved west through the ports of call and in the ranks of the Roman legions. Sailors, merchants, and even pirates brought Mithraism to the docks of Rome, finding support among foreigners and then among the various Roman social groups. Soldiers stationed in Syria became devotees, and the god's rituals found adherents throughout the legions in the empire. Mithras offered soldiers a sense of secret elitism, brotherhood achieved only after a rigorous period of study and occult initiations. Underground chapels filled with incense only added to the mystical nature of their experiences, ensuring both their faith and desire to bring others into the fold. In time, even the jaded members of the Praetorian Guard were counted among the Mithraic ranks.

For most of the first century C.E., the Romans expressed little interest in yet another Eastern cult. But when Vespasian became emperor, the Flavians found themselves presiding over many places suddenly captivated by Mithras. The East was most receptive, while in the West even as far as London he continued to be popular in legionary camps and towns and in commercial centers. Commodus may have been a member of the Mithras cult, although he was charged with having desecrated their services by murdering someone. Nothing was proven because one of the characteristics of the Mithraic ceremony was a kind of mock homicide.

By far the most useful association developed by the cult was that of the invincible sun god, SOL INVICTUS. Already Mithras was known as a god of light, so his identification with Sol was natural and nurtured the popular solar worship in the third and fourth centuries. The coinage of the emperors, most notably Valerian (c. 253–259 C.E.) displayed the Sun prominently, and later minting placed Mithras in the same position. Inscriptions called the god the *Sol Invictus comes,* the Unconquered companion of the Sun, or *Sol Invictus Mithras,* Unconquered Sun.

With acceptance by the IMPERIAL CULT of state, Mithraism grew in wealth, although not necessarily in numbers. Its very nature prevented it from achieving the kind of widespread belief being enjoyed by its closest rival, Christianity. With its ceremonies held in secret grottoes, Mithraism conveyed a sense of subtle mystery that appealed to the legions and the religious innovators but was wholly lost on the social mainstream of the empire.

Nevertheless, Diocletian found it expedient to cite Mithras as one of the leading representatives of the return to grand Paganism in the Roman Empire. Just as the other pagan gods could not overcome Christianity so did Mithras, the Sun, fail before the coming of the Son. The extent of the influence of the Mithraic cult on formative Christian doctrine has long been debated, but by the time of Constantine and the Christianization of the empire, the cult was in decline.

A final attempt was made by Emperor JULIAN (361–363) to revive pagan organization. Mithras was certainly included, again no doubt as Sol Invictus. Julian died before any major steps could be taken. Emperor Gratian took measures in hand and closed all places of Mithraic worship in 377. Remnants of Mithras sanctuaries have been excavated all over the Roman Empire. There was one at Ostia, containing an altar and images of

A shrine to Mithras at Ostia *(Courtesy Fr. Felix Just, S.J.)*

Mithras and the bull. Others were found on the Danube and most interestingly, at Carrawburgh in Britain, part of Hadrian's Wall. Built sometime in the second century C.E., the temple there was the center for a group of Mithraic legionaries in the local garrison. It suffered greatly at the hands of its Christian opponents.

See also RELIGION.

Mithridates (1) (d. 51 C.E.) *King of Armenia from 36–51 C.E. (minus the period of his exile by Emperor Gaius Caligula)*
Mithridates was the son of Mithridates and the brother of Pharasmanes, both kings of Iberia. He was at Rome in 35 C.E. when Emperor Tiberius decided to recover the Armenian throne from the Parthian-backed Arsaces, who had taken over the country in 34. Mithridates was eager for the opportunity of winning a kingdom, using threats and cunning to have his brother aid him in his campaign. Thus, with Pharasmanes' support and troops, Mithridates had Arsaces poisoned before repulsing the inevitable Parthian countermeasures. He was crowned king of Armenia in 36.

Tiberius was pleased because the new king proved a loyal and reliable client. Gaius Caligula, however, undid all of Tiberius's diplomacy by having Mithridates summoned to Rome and then sent into exile in 41. Armenia was deprived of its leader until Caligula's assassination. Claudius, trying to repair the damage done to Roman policy in the East, convinced Mithridates to mount another effort to regain his throne. The time seemed highly propitious, because Parthia was at that moment torn apart by internal struggles. Once again Pharasmanes provided support and troops, and Rome offered political prestige. These two weapons proved successful in overcoming Armenian resistance to the king. He remained on the throne, kept there in part by the absence of Parthian plots and by the presence of a Roman garrison at Gorneae, close to the Armenian capital of Artaxata. In 51, however, various pressures caused everything to unravel.

Pharasmanes' son RADAMISTUS was anxious for his own kingdom, and his father pointed him toward Armenia. He won over various nobles in that court and then marched into the land with an army. Mithridates fled to the Roman garrison under the command of Caelius Pollio. Despite the loyalty of the centurion Casperius, who went to Iberia to call upon the honor of Pharasmanes, Pollio urged Mithridates to settle the matter with Radamistus. The king was reluctant. Radamistus, meanwhile, urged on by his father, induced Pollio with more bribes to have his troops threaten to surrender if Mithridates did not meet with him. Knowing full well what would happen, Mithridates departed with his entire family, only to be massacred by Radamistus. The death of this king was a cruel blow for Roman hopes in the region, for within a year the Parthians were again in control of Armenia.

Mithridates (2) (d. 69 C.E.) *King of the Bosporus kingdom from circa 39–44/5 C.E.*
Mithridates was the son of King Aspurgus and Queen Dynamis. When Dynamis died in 7 or 8 C.E., Aspurgus headed the Bosporan domain until his death in 37 or 38, when control for a brief time passed to his widow, the Thracian Gepaepyris. In 39 (or perhaps in 41) it was decreed by Rome that she share the throne with her stepson Mithridates, and not Gepaepyris's natural son, Cotys. Mithridates assumed sole mastery of the realm a short time later, although the widowed queen retained considerable influence at court, even if her words had little effect upon the king. He refused to heed her warnings, and sometime around 44 made plans to terminate his nation's client status to Rome. He sent Cotys to Rome in the hopes of masking his intentions from Claudius, but Cotys, probably instructed to do so by his mother, told Claudius everything. For his betrayal, Cotys was rewarded with Mithridates's kingdom. The king fled to the tribes of the Sarmatians in 45.

Organizing his allies, Mithridates waited four years and then struck at the neighboring Dandaridae, deposing their chief to place himself in a sound strategic position for an invasion against Cotys. In 49, the governor of Moesia, Didius Gallus, aided by Cotys and his Roman adviser Julius Aquila, and with the complicity of Eunones, the head of the Sarmatian tribes of the Aorsi, embarked upon a thunderous campaign against Mithridates. Defeated, Mithridates was abandoned by his Sarmatian allies to the mercy of Eunones, who petitioned Claudius to spare him. No death penalty was passed. Mithridates, instead, was forced to spend the rest of his life in Rome. He spoke defiantly to Claudius when they came face to face, saying that he had not been brought to the city but had returned. He remained there until 69, when Galba put him to death on suspicion of conspiracy.

Mithridates (3) (fl. early first century C.E.) *King of the Iberians during the early part of the first century C.E.*
Mithridates succeeded by his devious son Pharasmanes, while another son, MITHRIDATES (1), became ruler of Armenia.

Mithridates III (d. 54 B.C.E.) *King of Parthia from 57 to 56 B.C.E.*
In 57, Mithridates and his brother Orodes II murdered their father, Phraates. As he was older, Orodes ascended the throne, only to have Mithridates rise up and seize power. Orodes sought the aid of the able general SURENAS, who recaptured Parthia with his army. Unable to overcome Orodes on his own, Mithridates fled to GABINIUS, the Roman proconsul of Syria, in 55. Gabinius listened to his pleas, agreeing to help, but a short time after his march began against Parthia, he turned away to accept the gold of King Ptolemy XI Auletes, in return for restoring Ptolemy to the throne of Egypt. Forced to lead his own revolution, Mithridates gathered willing allies. Surenas proved too strong, however, besieging Mithridates at Seleucia. The city fell, and Orodes put his brother to death in 54, going on to crush Crassus one year later at Carrhae.

Mithridates IV (fl. second century C.E.) *Probably the coruler of Parthia with Vologases II (c. 128–147)*
The role of Mithridates in Parthian affairs is at present unclear, for all available coinage sources indicate that his domain was actually in the eastern regions of Parthia, perhaps as Vologases's prince or vassal.

Mithridates of Pergamum (d. 41 B.C.E.) *A general and close ally of Julius Caesar during the Civil War of the First Triumvirate (c. 48–47 B.C.E.)*
Mithridates was the son of a wealthy citizen of Pergamum but received the honor of adoption from Mithridates the Great, who earlier in the first century B.C.E. had fought several wars with Rome. The adopted youth changed his name to that of his new father and became a learned practitioner of war and a friend of Caesar's. When Caesar chased after Pompey, following the battle of Pharsalus (48 B.C.E.), he instructed Mithridates to enter Syria and Cilicia and to gather all available reinforcements before setting out for a union with Caesar in Egypt. His efforts, combined with the cooperation of the local governments, produced a sizable army, which was able to arrive in Egypt at the precise moment that Caesar needed help to raise the siege at ALEXANDRIA. The Egyptians had tried to block the advance of Mithridates, but he surrounded Pelusium, a strategic site, and captured it in one day. Setting out immediately for Alexan-

dria, he encountered a large Egyptian force. The resulting battle was brief and bloody, as the Egyptians were no match for the invaders. A short time later, Caesar arrived from Alexandria, and the battle of the NILE, fought between Caesar and King Ptolemy XIII, ended Egypt's resistance.

Mithridates next accompanied Caesar to Asia Minor, where accounts were to be settled with Pharnaces II, king of the Bosporus, who had defeated Caesar's general Domitius and was stretching out his hand toward all of the lands once owned by Mithridates the Great. Mithridates clearly had a stake in Pharnaces' destruction. At the battle of ZELA in May 47, he served as an able lieutenant, aiding in the total defeat of the enemy. As a reward for his victories and his loyalty, Mithridates was granted Pharnaces' old domain of Pontus, as well as a slice of Galatia. Although it was never expressly mentioned, his titles as granted by Caesar made him eligible for other conquests, specifically at the expense of the Bosporan kingdom. However, there Mithridates ran out of luck, for he found himself facing Asander, the ruler of the Bosporus, who crushed him in battle.

Mnester (d. 48 C.E.) *The most famous and popular actor in the reigns of Gaius Caligula (37–41 C.E.) and Claudius (41–54 C.E.)*

Mnester was adored by GAIUS CALIGULA, who showered him with kisses and would beat with his own hands anyone who made even the slightest disturbance during one of Mnester's performances. Despite his arrogance, the actor remained in favor with the imperial court when CLAUDIUS came to the throne in 41 C.E. He soon became the object of intense desire to Valeria MESSALLINA, who had a statue of him cast in bronze. The empress unsuccessfully tried to seduce him and had to resort to having the gullible Claudius instruct Mnester to do whatever she wanted. When Messalina's many indiscretions were finally exposed, Mnester was included on the list of the condemned. It was said that the courtiers had not told Claudius of Messallina's host of lovers out of fear that Mnester would be punished. By 48 there was no way to protect him. Claudius probably would have spared the actor, but his freedmen convinced him that Mnester deserved to die with the others.

Modestus, Domitius (fl. fourth century C.E.) *Consul in 372 and Praetorian prefect from 369–377*

Described as crude, boorish, and wholly unfamiliar with the ancient authors, Domitius Modestus nevertheless became an important minister in the government of Emperor Valens (364–378 C.E.). Arabian by descent, Modestus served as COMES (count) of the Orient under Emperor CONSTANTIUS II and may have been appointed Praetorian prefect by Julian. His influence over Valens was considerable. Through his efforts the crushing tax systems were reduced, but Modestus was even more

remembered for his less than pleasant accomplishments. Valens used him to conduct treason trials, and he persecuted orthodox Christians and cunningly convinced his emperor to cease involving himself personally in legal cases. Consequently, the justice of the imperial court was available for money.

Moesia Large area fronting the Danube and extending all the way from ILLYRICUM to the BLACK SEA. Rome wanted to establish a Danubian frontier and subjugate what was a very unstable barbarian environment. There were at the time of Augustus (ruled 27 B.C.E.–14 C.E.) numerous tribes fighting for supremacy of the Lower Danube, including the Thracians, Dacians, and the native Moesi. In an attempt to occupy both the upper and lower Danube, Augustus, in 30 B.C.E., sent Marcus Licinius CRASSUS (2) and four legions off to war. His campaign overcame MACEDONIA and what was later called Moesia, bringing an irrevocable Roman presence to the area.

During the reign of Augustus, the governor of Macedonia administered the affairs of the territory. By the start of the first century C.E., however, the legions in Macedonia were being moved to Moesia to protect the Danube line and to watch the Black Sea. Active defense of the lower Danube was left in the hands of the Thracian kings until the time of Claudius (ruled 41–54 C.E.), allowing the legions to focus on both the Moesia-PANNONIA area and the troublesome Dacians. Clearly, the early Roman rule was tenuous at best, as was proven by the revolt of the Dalmatians and Pannonians in 6 C.E. Parts of Moesia were destroyed, and an imperial legate apparently took charge.

From then on, Moesia was treated as a separate province from Macedonia, and around 15 C.E., Tiberius took the formal step of including it among the imperial provinces. Although the tribes paid tribute to Rome, continued Thracian aid was needed to control the reaches of the Danube along the Black Sea, especially against the incessant raids of tribes from over the river. Initial progress was made in administration by the gifted legate Poppaeus Sabinus, who governed the possession for many years. Claudius preferred not to have such a vast holding in one general's hands, and in 44 C.E. he reinstated the Macedonians and Achaeans to senatorial control. Two years later THRACE was annexed, its defense entrusted to the legate of Moesia.

The period of Nero witnessed the work of the finest governor that Moesia would ever know, Silvanus Aelianus, legatus from 57–67. He terminated barbarian raids into Moesia by carrying the fight over the Danube, directly to the tribes, while seizing expanses of land right to the mouth of the Danube on the Black Sea. The Roxolani, Bastarnae, and others found him a fair opponent. He allowed them to have their own leaders as long as they respected the will of Rome. More important, he returned to the useful policy of moving entire tribes into semiautonomous zones where they could be watched. Silvanus pursued this strategy on a grand scale, forcing migration of over 100,000 men, women, and children. Finally, to alleviate pressure and to prevent hostilities in advance, Silvanus defeated both the Sarmatians and the Scythians.

The work of Silvanus did much to stave off trouble for many years, but by the time of DOMITIAN, DACIA was ready to erupt as a legitimate world power. Thus, in 85, their king Decebalus led an expedition into Moesia. The governor, Oppius Sabinus, was killed during the fighting, and the province, with the exception of the legionary fortresses, was overrun. Domitian marched immediately to Moesia, fought a series of bitter engagements, and expelled the Dacians.

To make his counterattack more organized, and to have support form the rear, Domitian divided Moesia into two provinces: Superior and Inferior (see below), with two legions in each under a legate. Although each would differ in its role and size, a similar economic and cultural development could be noted in the two. Trade was able to move both by land, through Thrace and into Illyricum-Pannonia, and by water, along the Danube. This flexibility provided great opportunity for wealth, especially given the commerce so prevalent on the Black Sea. It was the Roman intention to exploit the province fully. Moesia boasted vast natural resources, with rich fields, excellent pasturelands, and mineral deposits.

Unlike in the other Danubian provinces, wealth and colonization did not translate into Romanization. Moesia Superior was slightly more Latin in appearance, but both provinces were remarkably barbaric. The cause of this was the constant movement of tribes. Rome annihilated the Moesi and the Bastarnae in great numbers, only to have them replaced by other Trans-Danubian races. Colonization was always limited, with only a few *municipia* and fewer *coloniae*. The traditional source for Roman imprinting was the legions, but they were handicapped by their late arrival in the region and by their frequent absences on campaigns. While Moesia was thus a strong link in the defensive perimeter of the empire, it was never Romanized.

MOESIA SUPERIOR

Moesia Superior (or Upper Moesia) contained the westernmost lands of the two provinces. During the initial years of Rome's occupation, all of the legions stationed in Moesia were in the area that would later become Moesia Superior. For that reason whatever superficial Romanization was made in the provinces was done there. Under the Flavians (69–96 C.E.) Scupi was founded in the south, and because of Emperor Trajan two other colonies were started, Oescus and Ratiaria. Moesia Superior was much larger than its sister province, for it was centered on defending Macedonia and connecting Thrace to Illyricum and Pannonia. Dacian affairs involved it heavily during the late first and early second centuries C.E., and

both Trajan and Domitian launched their campaigns against the Dacians from there. In 270, Aurelian evacuated the province of Dacia because of intense pressure from the Carpi and the GOTHS. With the survivors, he produced the province of Dacia Ripensis (also Dacia Aureliani), principally at the expense of Moesia Superior. Ratiaria and Oescus became the new legionary headquarters for Dacia Ripensis.

MOESIA INFERIOR

Also called Lower Moesia, and composed of the eastern sections of Moesia. It defended Thrace, the vital area of the Bosporus and the imperial interests at the intersection of the Danube and the Black Sea. Here migrations were especially felt, for many of the moving peoples passed along the Black Sea and the Crimea before entering the Roman Empire on this coast.

For this reason Moesia Inferior was first to feel the horrors of the Gothic invasions of the third century C.E. King KNIVA and his Goths in 249 embarked upon a systematic operation of conquest. Moesia Inferior was ruined despite the best efforts of its governor, the future Emperor TREBONIANUS GALLUS and the Emperor DECIUS. In 251, Decius was crushed and killed at Abrittus, just south of the Danube, and the province was once more laid waste. As part of Emperor AURELIAN's plans for resettling the inhabitants of Roman Dacia in 270, slices of Moesia and Thrace were used to establish Dacia Mediterranea, with its capital at Serdica.

Moesia Inferior was far less Romanized than any other Danubian province, and the few achievements in civilization were culturally Greek. Trajan designed new cities along the Greek line, Nicopolis and Marcianopolis, ensuring that Moesia Inferior would be one of the starting points for the empire's Hellenic East. *See also* PROVINCES.

Moguntiacum (Mainz) A strategic site near the confluence of the Rhine and Main rivers. In the early first century C.E., in preparation for an invasion of Germany, Emperor Augustus ordered a fortress to be constructed here large enough to accommodate two entire legions. Once constructed, Moguntiacum became the perennial launching point of all major operations into Germanic territory from Roman-occupied Germany.

As was true with all of the legionary camps founded in the region, a community soon sprang up near the camp at Moguntiacum. The Rhine provided an excellent location, so the town was based between the fortress and the river. By the end of the first century C.E., the settlement had not only become a city but was also declared the capital of Germania Superior—since 19 C.E. protected by two legions, the XIV and XVI Gemina.

The rebellion of Civilis in 69–70 C.E. ravaged most of Germania, and the capture of Moguntiacum was seen by the rebel leader as essential to the collapse of Roman authority in the region. Fortunately for Rome, the city was spared any long-term damage from the siege of several tribes. Petilius Cerealis embarked upon his pacification of Germania Superior from there. To provide better protection in the event of another uprising, the wooden defenses were replaced by stone.

In 89, the attempted rebellion of Saturninus against Emperor Domitian brought a change in the size of the garrison. The XIV Gemina Legion was transferred to Pannonia and the Danube. Never again would two legions be stationed there on a permanent basis, although the bridges over the Rhine at Moguntiacum were still used by numerous campaigning legions, most notably those of the rulers Caracalla and Severus Alexander. The latter emperor was murdered by his own troops near Moguntiacum in 235.

Twenty-five years later the rampant instability of the frontier forced the abandonment of the fortress. Instead of the citizens relying on the legionary citadel, the city itself was fortified. While this should have ensured the continued prosperity of Moguntiacum in the Dark Ages, the capital never achieved the wealth or prestige of other provincial centers and metropolises, especially neighboring Cologne. Full municipal status (*municipium*) did not come until the fourth century. Excavations have uncovered the remains of aqueducts, an immense amphitheater and a monument to either Drusus or Domitian.

Moneta Name given to the goddess Juno as patron deity of finances.

Monophysitism (Monophysism) A heresy of the fifth and sixth centuries C.E. teaching that there was but one nature in the Person of Christ, a divine one. It was opposed to the orthodox doctrine established at the Council of Chalcedon (451) in which the doctrine of two natures in the One Person of Christ was upheld. Stemming in part from a reaction to Nestorianism, which preached two separate natures, Monophysitism was developed in the writings of the monk Eutyches (d. 454), who was condemned by the synod at Constantinople. Condemned at the second Council of Constantinople (553), the Monophysites continued to find support in Syria, Armenia, and especially among Coptic Christians in Egypt. Several attempts were made to effect a reconciliation, such as the efforts of Emperors Zeno (r. 474–491) and Justinian I (r. 527–565), but both the Monophysites and orthodox remained firm. Any hopes of a reunion were ended with the Islamic conquest of Syria and Egypt.

Mons Aurasius Mountain range cutting across part of the province of AFRICA and into NUMIDIA. Several important sites were included in Mons Aurasius: Zama, in Africa; Theveste (also Thevesta), the headquarters of the III Augusta Legion; and the high fortress of the Numidian chief Tacfarinas.

Montanism Heresy that originated in the latter half of the second century C.E. in the region of Phrygia (in Asia Minor). An apocalyptic and semimystical movement, it was started by a prophet from Phrygia named Montanus. He believed that a holy Jerusalem was soon going to descend upon the Phrygian village of Pepuza and, with the help of two disciples, Prisca and Maximilla, he preached intense asceticism, personal purity, fasting, and the desire to suffer martyrdom. Montanists, as the members of the movement were called, accepted the idea that such a lifestyle was essential to prepare for the impending return of Christ and because sins after birth could not be forgiven. While opposed by many bishops in Asia Minor, Montanism spread throughout the region, and by the third century the movement had become organized into a virtual church. It achieved its greatest success in 207 with the conversion of Tertullian to their cause. The leadership was ultimately excommunicated and the movement died out in the third century in most of the Roman Empire. It lingered in Phrygia for several centuries before finally disappearing.

Montanus, Votienus (d. 25 C.E.) *Distinguished member of Roman society in the reign of Tiberius (14–37 C.E.)*
Montanus was accused of slandering the emperor, the charges laid out in detail by a soldier named Aemilius. Tiberius was appalled that he should be so vilified, promising to take steps to clear his reputation. However, Montanus was condemned, one of many who would face death or banishment until Tiberius felt appeased.

Moors A seminomadic people living throughout much of North Africa but centered in MAURETANIA. The Moors (from the Latin *maurus*) were of Arabian-Berber descent. By the second century B.C.E., the tribes had organized themselves into a series of small kingdoms in Mauretania and thus were considered an important element in Rome's organization of the region into a province. Relations between the Romans and the Moors varied from excellent to intensely hostile. Some Moors served in the Roman army, while others were raiders, terrorizing Africa and Spain.

Julius Caesar used the chieftain Bogud as commander of the excellent Moorish light cavalry during several of his campaigns. The Moors proved especially helpful at MUNDA in 435 B.C.E., when Bogud led the charges that swept Gnaeus Pompey's cavalry from the field and then outflanked his legions. During the reign of Trajan, the Moorish leader Lusius Quietus first headed a native contingent and then became a very reliable lieutenant of the emperor. He captured both Nisibis and Edessa during the Parthian War, suppressed the revolt of the Jews in

Mesopotamia and was given the governorship of Judaea in 117 C.E. Moorish cavalry served as important auxiliary formations in the armies of Rome for the next 300 years. There was even a light-horse regiment in the forces of Maxentius at the battle of the MILVIAN BRIDGE in 312.

Unfortunately, not all dealings with the Moors were so successful. Moorish tribes held sizable domains within Mauretania, and many opposed the intense Romanization so characteristic of the occupation of Africa. When Mauretania became an actual province in 400 C.E., several years of fighting were necessary to secure pacification. Even then, battles could erupt at any time, necessitating the erection of fortifications along the southern boundaries of many Roman colonies. From Mauretania Tingitana, closely associated with HISPANIA Baetica and just across from Gibraltar, the Moors proved willing to expand their unrest to Spain as well.

Around 180 they crossed over into Baetica, ravaging much of the province and besieging the city of Singilia Barba. The governors of Hispania Tarraconensis and Mauretania Tingitana had to conduct unified operations to rid the normally peaceful Baetica of the marauders. The Moors withdrew but would be back in force some 600 years later. Never totally defeated, they continued their resistance to Rome throughout the third and fourth centuries C.E., until they became the problem of Geiseric and the Vandals in the fifth century. Emperor Macrinus (217–18 C.E.) was of Moorish descent.

Mucianus, Gaius Licinius (fl. first century C.E.) *Consul suffectus in 64 or 67, 70, and 72 C.E., governor of Syria and chief lieutenant in the cause of Vespasian during the Civil War of 69 C.E.*

Mucianus was reported by the historian Tacitus to be a mixture of good and bad; he could be arrogant and self-indulgent but ever hardworking, even devoted to his duties. A wild private life, however, made his position in Rome difficult. To avoid the displeasure of Emperor Claudius, he retired to Asia in a partially self-imposed exile. Nero, who liked rogues, later reinstated Mucianus to imperial favor, granting him promotions and, finally, the Syrian governorship. In this position he aided Vespasian and his son Titus in their subjugation of the JEWISH REBELLION (c. 66–69), commanding four legions: IV Scythia, VI Ferrata, XII Fulminata, and III Gallica.

Both Mucianus and Vespasian swore their oaths to Galba. When he was assassinated in January 69, they promised obedience to his successor, Otho. However, Vitellius used his German legions to crush Otho, and the foul reputation of this new emperor created a volatile situation in the East and on the Danube frontier. A rival candidate had to be found. Mucianus was a likely candidate to wear the purple, but, as Tacitus wrote, he was a man more likely to make an emperor than to be one. Joined by the prefect of Egypt, Tiberius Julius Alexander,

Mucianus threw his support behind Vespasian. Over half of the Roman Empire declared for Vespasian, including the legions on the Danube, who took matters into their own hands and marched on Italy.

Vespasian, meanwhile, appointed Mucianus as his main general, instructing him to set out for Rome, hoping to pick up support from other legions. The Flavians did not yet know that the Danube had risen against Vitellius, thanks to the legate Antonius Primus. Thus, when Mucianus and his army arrived in the Balkans, they found the provinces quite deserted of troops. A crisis soon developed, for the Dacians, thinking the time perfect for attack, swept across the Danube, only to find an unexpected Roman army marching toward them. The incursion was repelled, and Mucianus continued his advance on Italy.

Crossing the Alps, he learned that the general Antonius Primus had won the second battle of BEDRIACUM in October, defeating the army of Vitellius. Although Mucianus proceeded to Rome as quickly as possible, he could not arrive there until January 70, nearly two weeks after the death of Vitellius on December 20. Mucianus was greeted by the Romans with relief, because Antonius had allowed his men considerable liberties. Antonius and his associates were curbed, order returning under Mucianus's firm hand. He was the master of Rome for the next six months, administering the government as Vespasian's representative, sending troops to crush the uprising of Civilis in Germania and preparing the Romans for a return to stable imperial rule under Vespasian and the Flavians. The new emperor did not forget the work accomplished by Mucianus. He was given triumphal honors as well as consulships. Dio noted that Mucianus was a major influence in the expulsion from Rome of the philosophers, especially of the Stoics. He also authored a book of curiosities, used by Pliny the Elder.

Muliebris, Temple of Fortuna Temple in Rome devoted to the goddess FORTUNA. Here, only women were permitted to worship. Men offered their prayers at the Temple of VIRILIS.

Munda Town in southern Spain that was site of the last battle fought in the great Roman Civil War (49–45 B.C.E.). The battle ended the hopes of the Pompeians and assured the mastery of JULIUS CAESAR over the Roman world. After crushing the forces of Scipio and King Juba of Numidia at Thapsus in February 46, Caesar returned to Rome to establish his political base for what he knew would be the last campaign against the Pompeians, in Spain.

In December of 46, the dictator sailed from Italy to Spain, returning to the legions that he had left in the region following his successful ILERDA campaign in 49. At his disposal were around 40,000 soldiers. Against him were arrayed the remaining legions still faithful to the memory of POMPEY THE GREAT. They numbered some 55,000 men under the command of Pompey's sons, Gnaeus and Sextus Pompey, and Caesar's former lieutenant in the Gallic Wars, Titus LABIENUS.

From January to March 45, Caesar repeated his skillful maneuverings of Ilerda, using long marches, countermarches and small engagements to bring Gnaeus to bear. The Pompeian generals, fearing the worst in a pitched battle with Caesar's legions, refused to accept his terms for a confrontation. By March, however, most of Spain had fallen to Caesar, who was slowly driving Gnaeus farther south. Finally, near the town of Munda, the Pompeians took up an excellent position on a hill, dressed their lines and waited for Caesar's response. Gnaeus doubted that any fighting would take place. Caesar had a different view. Knowing that his legions would counter any tactical advantage of the enemy, he saw the time to be right for the decisive engagement.

Placing his veteran legions, the III and V, on the left, and the superb X on his right, Caesar moved to the attack. So began the battle of Munda on March 17, 45 B.C.E. The Pompeian cavalry was driven from the field, while Caesar's cohorts pushed up the slope to encounter their less gifted counterparts. What Caesar deemed a limited edge proved to be greater than anticipated, and the fighting became a bitter and bloody struggle, one of the fiercest ever conducted by a general. For hours the contest raged, and Caesar had to rush into the center personally to prevent his forces from wavering. Only by the sheer prowess of the X Legion was victory secured. The legionaries collapsed the Pompeian left, and the Caesarean cavalry was unleashed once more. Despite Labienus's attempts to repair the breach, the day was lost, the rout was on, and the hopeless slaughter of his men began in earnest. Labienus fell with 30,000 men. Caesar hunted down Gnaeus and put him to death. Sextus escaped to become a pirate king. Narrowly won, Munda was the final battle of the war, as well as Caesar's last field command. He had suffered only 1,000 casualties, while winning Spain. Although poorly written, the best source for Munda is *De Bello Hispaniensi,* or *The Spanish War,* supposedly authored by Caesar.

municipium Term used to denote a city with a certain type of legal standing within the Roman Empire. *Municipium* (pl. *municipia*) came to denote one of the stages by which a community could advance to full privileges as a colony of Rome. In the days of the early Republic all towns established by Roman colonists were called *coloniae civium Romanorum* and enjoyed total protection under the laws of Rome, for the very land of the colony held the status of actual Roman soil. However, throughout Italy and eventually the provinces, there were a vast number of cities created by the so-called *peregrini* (foreigners) that had to be classified legally. To them was applied the title *municipia civium Romanorum.*

By Roman law these places were considered part of Rome but not entitled to the full benefits available to *coloniae.* The cities of the Latin League had received the IUS LATII or Latin Rights, and so the *municipia* were given these in Italy under the *lex Julia* of 90 B.C.E. When the Roman empire was established under Augustus, this entire system was adapted to help classify all imperial domains. From the time of Augustus (27 B.C.E.–14 C.E.) to Caracalla and the Constitutio Antoniniana in 212 C.E., *municipium* meant that a city was honored with the *ius Latii* and could, if fortunate or worthy, by upgraded to a *colonia.*

The city elevated to a *municipium* enjoyed numerous benefits. There was the *ius Latii,* of course, but the inhabitants shared as well in imperial commerce, attention, and the protection of the legions. Initially, a continuation of local law and custom was tolerated, but under the empire certain changes were forced upon the cities with respect to the nature of the local administration. The East, with its system of the *polis* or highly organized city, needed only a few adjustments to make the *municipia* more responsive to the will of Rome. Western lands, long barbarian territories, were reshaped dramatically, and thus clung closely to the Roman method of self rule. Each *municipium* had its own constitution, council or senate, and administrative officials. The constitution began with the democratic aim of ensuring a voice for the people while creating competent councils and necessary boards. As was first true in the West, however, more and more power passed into the hand of the senators and magistrates, and finally solely into the realm of the appointed executives.

Throughout the first century C.E. the *municipia* were shaped into common form. The local senate was composed of around 100 members, the initial DECURIONES. They were aided by the highly influential *duoviri* or judges, *quinquennales,* the municipal CENSORS, the QUAESTORS and the AEDILES. Each *municipium* became a microcosm of the Roman Imperial Government, following the pattern of reduced democracy and the transfer of real authority from the Senate to the bureaucracy. By the second century C.E., all important duties were borne by the magistrates, chosen from the now hereditary and privileged class of the *decuriones.*

Even though any self-identity would be lost with the attainment of *colonia* rank, it remained the dream of every *municipium* to be blessed with that promotion. The prestige of being even a small part of Rome was as much as any city could want. The rigid separation began to crack during the second century and was ended altogether by Caracalla in 212.

Murena, Licinius Aulus Terentius Varro (d. 22 B.C.E.) *Brother-in-law of Gaius Maecenas by his sister Terentia*
Murena earned the dislike of Emperor Augustus by his forceful, disrespectful, and loud manner. In 22 B.C.E., he

supposedly joined a plot to assassinate Augustus. The conspiracy was discovered, and Murena, without a trial, was put to death. Gaius Maecenas felt that such a sentence by a regime noted for its clemency was severe. Murena's execution was one of the causes for the decline in friendship between Maecenas and Augustus.

Mursa Major   Site in modern Croatia where a battle was fought in 351 C.E. between Emperor Constantius II and the usurper Magnentius. Mursa Major (modern Dsijek, Yugoslavia) was one of the bloodiest battles in Roman history. By 351 the temporary peace between the emperor of the East and Magnentius was at an end. Magnentius, hoping to seize the initiative, gathered his army, including Germanic contingents and totaling around 100,000 men, and entered Noricum to confront Constantius in Illyricum. Constantius, with a like number of troops, accepted battle near Altrans, and received a setback. He retreated, making an offer of an armistice, which was rejected by his opponent.

Seeking to finish off Constantius, Magnentius pushed eastward from Aquileia into Illyricum. By skillful maneuvering he placed his legions behind a surprised Constantius who turned at bay. Organizing quickly, the Eastern emperor put to use his superior cavalry. His horsemen crushed Magnentius's right flank, bringing a decisive victory, but only after an entire day of slaughter. Both sides lost nearly 30,000 casualties each. Magnentius withdrew to Aquileia. Mursa Major proved the devastating effect of massed heavy cavalry, an omen of the terrible battles to come with the barbarians. Further, the 60,000 dead were irreplaceable, at a time when the Roman Empire would need every soldier that it could find.

music   The Romans brought considerable enthusiasm to the pursuit of music but little creative ingenuity. The Latin flute was a Roman product, but all else was inherited from the Etruscans or borrowed from the Greeks. Etruscan composition was based heavily on the flute, so much so that subsequently the Romans made it their principal instrument. King Numa established a guild of flutists, which was used at all public sacrifices. Diversity arrived shortly after the Punic Wars, as Greek culture gained ascendancy in Rome and Italy, introducing stringed instruments. Greek music became very popular, joined by the dance.

Although musical training was part of the education of most Roman youths, the actual performance of the music was always considered a profession suited to foreigners or the lower classes. Slaves, freedmen, and members of the base levels of the social strata were responsible for the preservation of music invariably Greek in taste. They performed at the houses of the wealthy, powerful, and noble, or at concerts that were very popular at the start of the empire. At games (LUDI) and gladiatorial contests, musicians very often provided introductory music or intermission entertainment. A considerable change in the status of music took place during the reign of Nero. He not only fancied himself as a brilliant musician but also patronized the art, staging lavish contests for musicians on the Greek model. Here the emperor would sing, winning every competition easily. His personal involvement left an excellent picture of the harpists of the era. There was a specific form of dress, as well as strict rules of etiquette. A musician, especially a singer, could not clear his throat. Perspiration was to be wiped away only by his own arm, and handkerchiefs were forbidden. Also, no sweat was allowed to drip from the nose of a performer.

It would not have been surprising if the Romans had no desire to hear another note after the tyrannical demonstrations of Nero (trapping people in buildings for days to hear his feeble plays; special gifts to the Greeks). Nevertheless, Domitian ordered an Odeum to be constructed on the Campus Martius, to house his various musical extravaganzas, especially his own musical festival, held first in 86 C.E. and every four years subsequently.

Musonianus, Strategius (fl. fourth century C.E.) *Imperial minister who made himself useful to both Constantine the Great and Constantius II*
Originally called only Strategius, he was a Christian and learned in Greek and Latin. He earned the name Musonianus while aiding Constantine in various ecclesiastical matters. His career blossomed under Constantius, and at the Council of Sardica in 343 he was the emperor's representative, holding the rank of COMES (count). By 353 he had probably served as proconsul of Constantinople and as proconsul of Achaea, where, through his influence, the famed orator Libanius was offered the chair for rhetoric at the university. In 354 he was promoted to Praetorian prefect of the Orient, serving Gallus Caesar until that prince's fall later that year. During his time in the East (354–358), Musonianus passed numerous laws, conducted trials and became a friend of Libanius, receiving from him a panegyric. Constantius replaced him in 358 (around August) for having entered into negotiations with the Persians without imperial permission. Musonianus retired to Constantinople, where he died before 371. Ammianus Marcellinus wrote that he had a reputation for being mild, well-spoken but bent on amassing wealth.

mutationes   Relay stations situated along the major roads of the empire and used by members of the *cursus publicus,* or imperial post. A *mutatio* provided official personnel, such as soldiers and holders of the diploma, the official document of government service, with a change of horses, mules, or oxen. Smaller than the *mansiones,* the *mutationes* did not provide food or a bed for a night.

Mutina A town (present-day Modena) in northern Italy that was the site of a battle in 43 B.C.E. Located upon the Via Aemilia in Gallia Cisalpina, its date of founding is unclear, except that there was an Etruscan presence, and by the late third century B.C.E. the Romans were using it as a strategic base. In 183 B.C.E. Mutina became a colony, basing its economy on a successful wool industry. The town's most famous moment came in 43 B.C.E., when it figured prominently in the early stages of the Civil War with a confrontation between Marc ANTONY and BRUTUS ALBINUS. Following his surprise loss at Forum Gallorum on April 14, 43 B.C.E., Antony returned to Mutina to keep a watchful eye on Brutus, who was trapped there. He found it necessary to defeat the advancing legions of the Republican cause, under the dying Vibius PANSA CAETRONIANUS, Aulus HIRTIUS, and Octavian (AUGUSTUS), to ensure the eventual surrender of the starving Brutus. Thus, on April 21, he gave battle. Despite their excellent central position, Antony's troops lacked the spirit needed to overcome the enemy, and Hirtius and Octavian fought their way through his lines and into his camp, while a sortie from Mutina nearly annihilated Antony and his suddenly trapped army. Forced to quit the field, he withdrew his remnant legions to Gallia Transalpina. No pursuit was mounted. Brutus could not do so with hungry units, and only Octavian remained as general, as Pansa died of his wounds, joined by Hirtius, who fell in the fray. The Senate had won the battle, but lost two consuls in the process.

Mysia Large region of northwestern Asia Minor. Mysia was a very ancient land, figuring in the Trojan Wars and, because of its location, active in virtually every era of the history of the Persian Empire and the conquests of Alexander the Great. The Romans occupied Mysia in 133 B.C.E., making it a district of the province of ASIA. Included in its jurisdiction was the major city of PERGAMUM.

N

Nabataeans An ancient Arabian people who occupied an extensive part of Palestine, stretching through northern ARABIA into areas on both sides of the Red Sea and north to eastern IDUMAEA and the Dead Sea. The capital of the Nabataeans (or Nabataei) was the stone city of PETRA. Founded in the fourth century B.C.E., Petra eventually served as a major trade center. Caravans from the Mediterranean ports moved through the city to the Far East, and the Nabataeans based their wealth on trade in Arabian incense and myrrh, Indian spices, and silk and other textiles from China. In turn, their kings started vast expansion programs along the Red Sea and into JUDAEA and SYRIA. The advance southward was highly successful, as most of the Red Sea coast fell into their hands. Campaigns against Judaea proved both expensive and fruitless. King Aretas II was prevented by the priest-king Jannaeus Alexander from acquiring land in that domain and in Gaza, although Aretas III, in 85 B.C.E., temporarily held Damascus. The inevitable collision with Rome came in 65 B.C.E., when Aretas III was induced by a minister, ANTIPATER OF IDUMAEA, to invade Judaea and support the claim of HYRCANUS for the Jewish throne against Hyrcanus's brother, ARISTOBULUS. Aretas marched into the area to besiege Aristobulus at Jerusalem. Pompey's lieutenant, Aemilius Scaurus, forced Aretas to give up the siege, and the Nabataeans, unwilling to engage the armies of Rome, retired. A formal treaty was signed later between the Romans and Petra, and Nabataea was recognized as a reliable client. The Nabataeans gave slight resistance to the prefect of Egypt, Aelius GALLUS, in his attempted conquest of Arabia and supplied troops for Roman use. When Gaius Caesar traveled to the East for Augustus (c 1 B.C.E.) he reminded them of their obligations. In 106 C.E., under Trajan, Cornelius Palma and his legion conquered the Nabataeans, and the kingdom became the province of Arabia Petraea.

Nacolea Phrygian town that was the site of a military engagement fought on May 26, 366 C.E., between Emperor VALENS and the usurper PROCOPIUS. In 365 Procopius, a relative of the newly deceased emperor Julian and a commander of Julian's forces in Persia, was proclaimed emperor at Constantinople, while the Eastern emperor Valens was away in Bithynia, heading for Antioch. Initial successes gained Procopius not only thousands of deserters from the cause of Valens but also control of the Bosporus. Valens could only await reinforcements but was given a major boost by the arrival of the MAGISTER EQUITUM, ARBITIO, who had deserted Procopius. His defection initiated the wholesale collapse of Procopius's support. The usurper's generals deserted, and at Nacolea virtually the entire army of Procopius refused to carry on the fight. Valens thus proved victorious. Procopius fled, only to be betrayed again and slain.

Namatianus, Rutilius Claudius (fl. late fourth and early fifth centuries C.E.) *One of the last classical Roman poets*
Namatianus witnessed wholesale carnage in Italy during the invasion of the Visigoths (c. 410–412), and these Gothic attacks, including the sack of Rome in 410, left a deep impression upon him. Namatianus was the son of Lachanius, a Gallic imperial officer, possibly the governor of Tuscany and Umbria. Born at Toulouse, he received an excellent education in classical literature and rhetoric. During the reign of Honorius, he held the posts of MAGISTER OFFICIORUM in 412 and of *praefectus urbis* (prefect of

the city) for Rome, sometime during 414. His valuable work, *De Reditu Suo* (On His Return) survives. Composed around 416 or 417, this long elegiac poem covered his journey from Rome to Gaul to visit his devastated estates there. Very detailed, more so than the similar works of Ovid and Horace, *De reditu suo* described clearly life at the time and is a defense of Paganism, sprinkled with personal attacks against ascetic Christianity, the Jews, and Stilicho, who had burned the Sibylline Books. Namatianus was a lucid writer of considerable literary merit.

Narbo Now Narbonne, a small, wine producing town, but once the capital of GALLIA NARBONENSIS and one of the busiest ports in the northwestern Mediterranean. Narbo was already very old when the Romans arrived there in the second century B.C.E. It had served as the local Celtic capital, and its position on the Atax (Aude) River gave it excellent potential for economic growth. Romans were interested both in its navigable river and in its strategic location along the main route of communications between Rome and Spain. Thus, in 118 B.C.E., Quintus Martius founded Colonia Narbo Martius, the first colonial possession of Roman origin in Gallia Narbonensis. Further colonization was made by Julius Caesar, who gave land grants to his legion veterans. Narbo became the provincial capital as well as center of the IMPERIAL CULT. This preeminence was expanded even further by the patronage of Emperor Claudius. The city possessed a forum, amphitheater, capital, and altars for the propagation of the cult of Roma et Augustus. In the middle of the second century C.E., a fire devastated most of Narbo's buildings, and Nemausus (Nîmes) became the provincial capital. Narbo's decline is confirmed by the scarcity of its archaeological remains, especially when compared with Nîmes, and by the silt that accumulated in its port. It was besieged by Theodoric in 436 and captured in 462 by the Visigoths, then besieged by Childebert and his Franks in the 530s.

Narbonensis *See* GALLIA NARBONENSIS.

Narcissus (1) (d. c. 54 C.E.) *Important freedman in the reign of Claudius*
Narcissus held the post of AB EPISTULIS, or secretary for correspondence, but wielded influence well beyond his office. In the early years of Claudius's reign (c. 42–43), he joined with the Empress Messallina and other FREEDMEN in establishing a tyranny over the palace and all of Rome. Claudius put to death many victims on their word. Narcissus was also sent to exhort the troops of PLAUTIUS, the governor of Pannonia, to launch their invasion of Britain in 43.

Messallina alienated Narcissus, and by 48 he had convinced the emperor to put her to death for her adulteries. Following her execution he supported Aelia Patina

as Claudius's next wife, against the claims of LOLLIA PAULINA and AGRIPPINA THE YOUNGER. When Claudius married Agrippina, Narcissus was naturally a target of her enmity. Agrippina poisoned Claudius in 54, when Narcissus had fallen ill and retired to the waters of Sinessa to recover there. Nero succeeded Claudius, and Narcissus was immediately imprisoned, where he died by his own hand after suffering the cruelest of conditions.

Narcissus (2) (d. 193 C.E.) *Slayer of Emperor Commodus in 192 C.E.*
The plot of Aemilius LAETUS, ECLECTUS, and MARCIA to murder the emperor included lacing his dinner with poison. It failed to kill him, however, for Commodus vomited up most of the food. The conspirators summoned a young, powerful athlete, Narcissus, who was sent into the imperial apartment, where he strangled the weakened ruler in the bath. In the following year, Septimius Severus threw Narcissus to the wild beasts.

Narses (Narseh) (d. 302 C.E.) *King of Persia from 293 to 302 C.E.*
Narses was the son of the great Persian king SHAPUR I and great-uncle of VARAHRAN III, who came to the throne in 293. After a reign of only four months, Varahran was deposed by Narses during an insurrection. Narses then assumed total power and restored the Persian Empire's martial and political vitality, mounting an attack on Roman territories in the East. In 296, he invaded Syria, requiring the immediate presence of Emperor Galerius, who was summoned by Diocletian from the Balkans to deal with the crisis. Galerius repulsed the Persians from the Syrian interior but was then drawn into a battle and defeated by Narses's troops at Callinicus. Galerius made a stunning recovery, crushing the Persians in 298 in one engagement, capturing Ctesiphon as well as a huge treasury and the wives and children of the king. Unable to carry on the war. Narses accepted a treaty, which was a humiliation for Persia. Armenia was acknowledged as a Roman territory, parts of the Tigris (five small districts) were also ceded to Rome and Mesopotamia was given up. Nisibis became a trading center for the two states, as a result. In return, Narses received his captured family. This loss had a major impact on subsequent relations between the two empires, while Galerius used his triumph to increase his own political ambitions. Narses died in 302, followed on the throne by his son, Hormazd II.

See also SASSANID DYNASTY.

Nasamones Tribe in Numidia that revolted against Rome in 85–86 C.E. because of unfair taxation. They slaughtered every tax collector they could find; the defeated governor of Numidia, Flaccus, retreated, abandoning his own camp. Celebrating their triumph, the

Nasamones became drunk on Flaccus's wine and were massacred. Few survived, even of the women and children. According to Dio, Domitian proudly declared: "I have ended the existence of the Nasamones."

Nasidius, Q. (fl. first century B.C.E.) *Admiral commanding vessels in the fleet of Marc Antony in 31 B.C.E.*
Nasidius was defeated in an encounter with AGRIPPA during the early maneuverings preceding the battle of ACTIUM. His failure in battle, combined with the defection of Gnaeus DOMITIUS AHENOBARBUS (2) and the incompetence of other officers, made Antony highly suspicious of his entire command during this crucial campaign.

Natalis, Antonius (d. after 65 C.E.) *Member of the Pisonian Conspiracy in 65 C.E. against Nero*
When the first word of the plot to assassinate the emperor was uncovered, Natalis and his comrade Flavius SCAEVINUS were summoned for questioning. Interrogation shattered their resolve, and Natalis began to pour out names and accusations, indicting Piso, Seneca, and others. Nero relied upon Natalis's testimony to force Seneca, his one-time tutor and guardian, to kill himself. Natalis was spared, eventually being released with a full pardon, while his colleagues died.

Naulochus   Roman naval station on the northeast coast of Sicily, whose waters saw the final engagement between the fleets of Octavian (AUGUSTUS), led by his admiral AGRIPPA and the vessels of Sextus POMPEY. The battle at Naulochus (also called Mylae) was fought on September 3, 36 B.C.E., and ended the ambitions of Pompey, clearing the way for the final confrontation between Octavian and Marc ANTONY. From 40 to 46 B.C.E., Octavian and Sextus had been fighting a war of varying intensity for control of the Mediterranean sea lanes, Sardinia, Corsica, and Sicily. By the start of 36, the focus was on Sicily, and both sides fought on land and sea for supremacy. Octavian, gaining the upper hand, trapped Pompey in the northeastern section of the island with his infantry. Relying, however, upon his able fleet, on September 3, he assembled all available vessels and gave charge to Agrippa just off the Sicilian coast. The exact number of men and ships involved is unclear. Pompey probably had more than 200 ships, against a like number for Agrippa. While the legions on both sides watched from shore, their navies grappled.

Naulochus was a closely matched battle, but the invention of Agrippa, the HARPAX, proved lethal to the Pompeian ships. By the end of the day, Sextus's fleet was aflame or captured. Twenty-eight of his best vessels were sunk, and only 17 escaped. Demoralized, his land forces were cut to pieces by the jubilant forces of Octavian. Sextus changed into traveling clothes, fled Sicily and turned to the mercy of Marc Antony.

navy   The fleets built and troops trained by the Romans in order to maintain their world dominance. Unlike the Etruscans, the Romans were not a great seafaring people and maintained an aversion to such activities right until the last years of the empire. For this reason the development of the navy was delayed in favor of the LEGIONS until the emergence of Rome as a legitimate world power necessitated a naval program.

The Punic Wars with Carthage, fought as much at sea as on land, gave Rome a chance to dominate the Mediterranean, an opportunity it nearly lost because of its ignorance in maritime areas and because the remaining navies of Greece were vastly superior in craftsmanship and skill. But the conquest of Greece, Asia Minor, and ultimately most of the East, put at Rome's disposal the extensive shipyards, sailors, and vessels of many foreign fleets. These acquisitions were particularly important in the first century B.C.E., when pirates were preying on commerce throughout the Mediterranean. These brigands sailed in all seasons and kidnapped high-ranking persons, sank one consular fleet and received tribute from coastal cities. By 67 B.C.E., the pirates from Cilicia had become too dangerous. Pompey was granted an extraordinary command to clear them from the sea lanes. He discovered more than 1,000 such pirate ships roaming over vast regions, but pressed into service every available vessel from the Greeks and supplemented these with fleets from the Republic. With strategic genius, Pompey crushed the Cilicians in only three months (Spring 67) and returned home in triumph.

Henceforth the Romans depended heavily upon vessels built by Greeks or other foreigners and manned by them as well. The role of such fleets in the Civil Wars at the end of the Republic was absolutely critical. Caesar used his own fleets to transport his reliable legions from Italy to the theater of operations against Pompey in Illyricum and then sailed after his vanquished foe to Egypt, where again fleets contested control of the harbor of ALEXANDRIA.

Naval engagements were even more important in the years to come. Sextus Pompey commanded a large pirate fleet that briefly brought even Octavian to the bargaining table (*see* MISENUM, CONFERENCE OF). Octavian (AUGUSTUS) turned to his ever reliable Marcus Agrippa and together they shaped an excellent navy, armed with Agrippa's invention, the HARPAX. They destroyed Sextus at Naulochus in 36 B.C.E. and then proved their superiority over Antony and his Greek-Egyptian ships at Actium in 31 B.C.E. As was the case with the post–Civil War legions, Augustus had to reform and reorganize the hundreds of ships left over from the years of conflict. He incorporated most of them into the Imperial Navy.

The tradition against sea travel continued under the emperors. Rome's navel arm was placed under the supervision of the army, and service terms were for 26 years, a period longer than the auxiliaries'. Sailors completing their service, however, were rewarded with citizenship and with an impressive looking DIPLOMATA. These seamen led a hard life, with the exception of the lucky few who were stationed in Rome and given the task of handling the *velarium* or canvas awnings in the COLOSSEUM. The structure of the naval service continued to be Greek, with various commands and organization that have remained unclear. Each ship had a captain (a triearch), with a staff, headed by a *beneficiarius*, a centurion and his own aides. A grouping of vessels formed a squadron under the control of a *navarch*, probably. This rank was the top post attainable through promotion, for the fleets were under prefects (*praefecti*) from the Equestrian Order (EQUITES). From the reign of Claudius until the time of Vespasian there was a habit of appointing freedmen to the prefectures. Initially considered a relatively unimportant posting, by the second century C.E. the office of prefect of a fleet, especially that at Misenum, the headquarters of the Roman imperial navy, was very prestigious. Individual fleets were distributed throughout the ports of the empire, as they were needed, but each so-called *classis* had a home port and an area of patrol.

Misenum   The port at Misenum replaced the one at Forum Julii (Forum Iulii) as the center for protection of the Western Mediterranean. Its ships patrolled the waters around Spain, Gallia Narbonensis, Sardinia, Capri, Corsica, the Balearic Islands, Sicily, and the Italian coast in the West.

Ravenna-Aquileia   Shipping to the Adriatic was of concern to Rome because its waters connected Italy with the Illyrian coast and the Aegean. Piracy also occurred on this coast, mainly due to the superb sailors of Liburnia.

Pannonia   One of the two fleets stationed on the Danube River, the Classis Pannonica, watched the waterways of the Danubian frontier and probably helped in the campaigns fought on both sides of the river. Its sister was the Classis Moesica.

Moesia   Farther east and downriver from Pannonia was the Classis Moesica, and its area of operation was the Lower Danube from the start of Moesia Superior until the river emptied into the Black Sea. The ships of the Classis Moesica were used in campaigns against Dacia and the barbarians who perennially threatened the Danube frontier near Thrace. Depleted by the fifth century, the squadrons were markedly improved by the Prefect Anthemius and subsequently served as one of the first defenses of Constantinople.

Black Sea   The Black Sea squadrons guarded the Roman shipping there, especially the grain ships from the Caucasus. Most of the vessels were taken from the old Thracian fleet and became the Classis Pontica, which operated out of Nicomedia or Trapezus. In the third century, C.E., the Classis Pontica was driven from the sea by the waterborne invasions of the Goths in that area.

Syria   The long, Mediterranean coastline of Asia Minor and the northeast corner of the Mediterranean at Cappadocia and Syria. Included in their jurisdiction was Cilicia, previously the home of the dreaded pirates. The fleet bore the name Classis Syriaca.

Alexandria   Egypt was, arguably, the most important province in the Roman Empire. Its grain supply and strategic location had to be safeguarded. The seagoing responsibility was entrusted to the Classis Alexandrina (or Classis Augusta Alexandrina). It also sailed the waters of eastern Africa.

Britain   Although the Classis Britannica was assigned to roam the coasts of Britain, its ships were docked at the port of Gesoriacum (Boulogne) on the Channel coast of the Continent. When not helping in the subjugation of the British tribes or in defending the provinces there from assault by the northern tribes, the Classis Britannica joined in the watch on the northern coasts of Gaul. Agricola, in his time as governor of Britain (78–85 C.E.), probably used this fleet in his circumnavigation of the isles.

Germania   The waterways of the Rhine River were the province of the Classis Germanica, based at the port facilities of Cologne. It sailed from the southern edges of Germania Superior to Germania Inferior and the dangerous waters at the mouth of the North Sea.

By the third century C.E., the lack of priority given to the navy came back to haunt the empire. Ships and the quality of navigational skills had deteriorated to such an extent that the Black Sea was lost for a time to barbarian vessels. In the fourth century, the fleets were placed under the MAGISTER MILITUM of Italy in the West and ceased to have any organization in the East. The old ports fell into disuse, and any skillful enemy could develop a rival naval force, as happened in the fifth century when Geiseric and the Vandal kingdom of Africa laid claim to stretches of the Mediterranean. The debacle of the attempted sea invasion of Africa by Leo I in 468 proved that the old Roman Imperial Navy no longer existed.

See also MARINES; SHIPS.

Nedao   River in Pannonia near which a vast engagement was fought in 454 C.E. between the Huns and an alliance of GOTHS, Gepidae, ALANS, HERULI, and many others, to decide the fate of the Huns in Europe. Following the death of ATTILA in 453, the Hunnic Empire was torn apart from within by his feuding sons, each demanding an equal share in the dead king's inheritance of tyranny. When rumor of this internal division was circulated among the numerous barbarian kingdoms long enslaved by the Huns, an alliance was formed. At its head was Ardaric, the king of the Gepidae, a small Germanic tribe, but he was joined by the armies of the Goths, Rugi, Alans, Heruli, Hermunduri and a host of unhappy chiefdoms. They combined their forces and gave battle. Not surprisingly, even in disarray the Huns presented a fearsome challenge, and the ensuing struggle at Nedao was bloody. To the astonishment of the Huns, however, Attila's most beloved son, Ellac, was slain. His brothers suffered a terrible defeat, scattering in numerous directions, their domains lost forever.

Nemausus City (modern-day Nîmes) in GALLIA NARBONENSIS that eventually succeeded Narbo (Narbonne) as the capital of the province. West of the Rhine River, between Massilia (Marseilles) and Narbo, it served as the chief community of the Gallic Arecomici until their conquest by the Romans in the first century B.C.E. Extensive Roman settlement was initiated by Augustus in 28 B.C.E. when he made it a *colonia*, settling veterans of his Egyptian campaign there. Subsequently, the city symbol was a crocodile chained to a palm tree. As part of the intense program of Romanization in Gallia Narbonensis, Augustus made certain that Nemausus received the finest architectural creations of the time, as is evident from the superb archaeological finds in the region.

Marcus Agrippa supervised the construction of the famous Pont du Gard sometime between 20 and 16 B.C.E. to supply the water needs of the inhabitants. This aqueduct was part of a water system for the entire city. Inside Nemausus were two other major structures. The amphitheater, designed by the noted architect T. Crispius Reburrus, held over 20,000 spectators and had such a quality of workmanship that the present residents of Nîmes still use it for various entertainments. Another Augustan-era building, erected possibly by Agrippa, was the Maison Carrée, or the "Square House." Placed atop a raised platform, the Maison was a temple devoted to the IMPERIAL CULT of *Roma et Augustus*. Architecturally it relied upon Corinthian columns. Outside of Nemausus, aside from the aqueducts, there were other interesting projects. Baths, a theater, and a temple to Diana were all positioned near a natural spring, guarded by a watchtower on the overlooking hill. In the middle of the second century C.E., Narbo, the provincial capital, suffered a terrible fire that destroyed most of its buildings and wrecked its economy. Nemausus became the new seat of local administration, a status that it would enjoy for the remainder of the imperial epoch.

Nemesianus (Marcus Aurelius Nemesianus Olympius) (fl. late third century C.E.) *Bucolic and didactic poet*
Nemesianus gained considerable fame for his works, including a reference in the history of Carus, Carinus, and Numerian by Vopiscus, appearing in the *Historia*

The Maison-Carrée, in Nemausus (Nîmes), France
(Hulton/Getty Archive)

Augusta. He came from Carthage, and exhibited a fluidity of style and an ease of diction. Of the three didactic poems of Nemesianus, *On Fishing, On Seamanship*, and *On Hunting* (mentioned by Vopiscus), only the third, *On Hunting* (or *Cynegetica*) is extant, and of that a mere 325 lines. The *Cynegetica* was written sometime after the death of Carus in 284 but before the demise of his two sons, for Nemesianus promised Carus and Numerian a poem on their achievements. Also attributed to him were four bucolic or pastoral poems. He mirrored in poetic craftsmanship the works of Calpurnius, and the four were often included with his seven. A comparison was inevitable, just as the *Cynegetica* was examined in terms of Grattius's own effort in hunting.

Nemesius (fl. early fifth century C.E.) *Bishop of Emesa, and a notable Christian philosopher*
Nothing of his life survived except for knowledge of his position and his influential treatise, in Greek, *On Man's Nature*. This book attempted to reconcile the tenets of Christianity with Platonism and was used by Christian theologians in the Middle Ages. It was, at times, confused with a work by Gregory of Nyssa.

Neoplatonism Influential intellectual movement that revived the philosophy of Platonism while injecting it with elements of the greatest philosophies of the Roman

Empire. Beginning in the third century C.E., Neoplatonism was the single most important ideology of organized paganism in the Western world. Neoplatonism's substance and shape were, in large measure, created by the remarkable philosopher PLOTINUS. Through his works, especially the *Enneads,* the entire movement was given a basis of logical development. From this and the efforts of other notable thinkers, such as Ammonius Saccas, PORPHYRY, and Atticus, a diffusion of ideas took place. Neoplatonism became fashionable as a philosophy of the pagan intellectual, both because of its organization and its inherent speculative flexibility.

In essence, Neoplatonism combined Numenius's Pythagoreanism, Stoicism, the Peripatetic School, and extensive parts of mysticism, the occult and the profound. Fused with such ingredients, Neoplatonism took many forms, depending upon the academic institution one visited. Plotinus stressed the rejection of Aristotle while insisting that contemplation (mysticism) and thought could lead to the understanding of the infinite and hence to a total recognition of reality. His student Porphyry took a different path. He accepted Aristotle but centered himself in a more theurgic-spiritual system. For him asceticism and spirituality led to truth. He bitterly differed with Christianity, imprinting this attitude on the schools at Pergamum, Athens, and in the East.

Mysticism found its champion in IAMBLICHUS. This follower of Porphyry developed fully the Neo-Pythagorean side of Neoplatonism. He studied sacred numbers, analyzed polytheism, and laid out an elaborate gallery of spiritual hierarchies for demons, angels and spirits. His metaphysics impacted upon Athenian-centered Neoplatonism, although the theurgists of Pergamum, Neo-Pythagorean by outlook, adhered faithfully to Iamblichus as well. JULIAN THE APOSTATE fell under the spell of the Pergamum philosophers. Meanwhile, in Alexandria, because of Hierocles, there could be found the more conservative voices of philosophy. They pursued the study of Aristotle and would find a common ground with the Christians of Alexandria. Ammonius eventually became a half-hearted convert to the Christian Church, and many Christian intellectuals joined the school. Thus there occurred the initial union of Christ and Platonism that would so deeply influence Christian philosophy.

In Athens the Neoplatonists still detested Christianity, its authors attacking it whenever possible; one such was PROCLUS in the fifth century. Proclus stood at the zenith of Athenian Neoplatonism. In his numerous treatises on Platonism he brilliantly examined Neoplatonism and NEO-PYTHAGOREANISM, both in terms of how he saw them function and from the perspective of pure scholasticism. His codification of Iamblichus's hierarchies was incorporated into the theology of later religions. Even Jewish mystical thought profited from this effort (possibly in Kabbalism and in the *Sefer Yezira*), as did Christianity.

Neoplatonism was absorbed in many respects into Christian dogma. Church theologians found it useful in uniting creed and philosophy. The two once-contrary systems were intertwined. Some Neoplatonists, of course, steadfastly refused to accept Christianity. They persisted, most notably in Athens, until 529, when the schools were finally closed. Platonism lived on in the East (Alexandria) until the time of the Arabs, and even then, as in the West, found fertile ground.

See also HYPATIA; MAGIC.

Suggested Readings: Berchman, Robert M. *From Philo to Origen: Middle Platonism in Transition.* Chico, Calif.: Scholars Press, 1984; Gregory, John. *The Neoplatonists: A Reader.* London: Routledge, 1999; Kenney, John Peter. *Mystical Monotheism: a Study in Ancient Platonic Theology.* Hanover, N.H.: University Press of New England, 1991; Lloyd, A. C. *The Anatomy of Neoplatonism.* Oxford, U.K.: Clarendon Press, 1990.

Neo-Pythagoreanism   A philosophical and pseudo-mystical revival of the old Pythagorean school. Neo-Pythagoreans combined traditional Pythagorean philosophy with a mixture of numerous other schools, including Stoicism and Platonism, and then injected the entire idea with a form of mystical revelation of an Orphic nature. Neo-Pythagoreanism seems to have been centered on intellectual speculation concerning a number of topics, normally occult but ranging from hidden meanings to numbers, to magical rituals and formulas, to the propagation of legends that Pythagoras originated as part of a profound system of belief.

Begun around the second century B.C.E. by philosophers in Alexandria and Rome, the movement found fertile ground among well-educated sophisticates who were looking for a kind of spiritual release. There was no set doctrine, and no two Neo-Pythagoreans would see an issue in exactly the same way, for each brought their own experiences and academic backgrounds. Two notable members were APOLLONIUS OF TYANA and Nigidius FIGULUS. Apollonius was known for his visions (including the death of Domitian) and for his ability to heal the sick. His miracles caused many pagans to offer him up as a rival to Christ during the period of struggle between organized PAGANISM and CHRISTIANITY. Figulus was important because of his interest in all occults matters, thus imprinting on the revived Pythagoreanism a taste for the obscure.

Both figures were cited by the other major school, NEOPLATONISM, and the impact that Neo-Pythagoreanism had on paganism, especially Neoplatonism, was considerable. Although absorbed by the Neoplatonists in the third century C.E., Neo-Pythagoreanism left as its legacy a fascination with the secret and the arcane. Witness MAXIMUS OF EPHESUS who taught Emperor JULIAN to appreciate magic and theurgy. Further, the movement influenced Christianity through GNOSTICISM, the loose theology so much a part of the writings of CLEMENT OF ALEXANDRIA.

Nepos, Cornelius (c. 100–24 B.C.E.) *Prolific and eclectic writer*

Born in Gallia Cisalpina, Nepos was a contemporary of some of Rome's finest intellects. Cicero, Atticus, and his fellow Gaul, Catallus, were considered his friends, but they seemed to hold little professional regard for him. He was not included in Quintilian's list of notable historians, and his few surviving works appear to justify this absence of adulation. Nepos attempted various literary forms, including erotic poems, a chronology (*Chronica*), and a five-book treatise on morality, *Exempla*. These were all lost, although he probably used Varro as his model for the *Chronica*. Three other efforts remain partially extant: biographies of Cato the Elder and Atticus, and one book of his 16-part study of *Lives of Famous Men* (*De Viris Illustribus*). The biographies, better written than the *Famous Men*, possibly contained many others, such as Cicero. His *De Viris Illustribus* tried to compare the lives of famous Romans with their historical parallels in Greece, much as PLUTARCH would later do. The one extant book covers foreign generals and is disorganized, error-filled and lacking in sophisticated style or diction. There has been a question as to its authorship, but the similarity with the Cato and Atticus biographies is such that most collections combine them under the authorship of Cornelius Nepos.

Nepos, Julius (d. 480 C.E.) *Emperor of the West from 473 to 475; in exile circa 477 to 480 C.E.*

Nepos was the son of a MAGISTER MILITUM, Nepotianus, while his mother was the sister of the semi-independent *magister militum* of Dalmatia, MARCELLINUS. As Marcellinus's heir, Nepos assumed the office of *magister* in Dalmatia, eventually marrying the niece of Aelia Verina, wife of LEO I, the emperor of the East. By virtue of his title and his marriage in 473 Leo proclaimed him emperor of the West and sent him to Italy, where he deposed the unrecognized Emperor GLYCERIUS, forcibly removing him to the episcopal seat of Salonae. He gained the support of the Senate by June 474, but could do little to prevent the king of the Visigoths, EURIC, from declaring independence from imperial influence in his Gallic domains. This crisis resulted in the loss of most of Gaul. Meanwhile, Nepos's own *magister militum*, ORESTES, a one-time secretary to Attila the Hun, relied upon the loyalty of his troops to elevate his son ROMULUS AUGUSTULUS to the throne. With the Senate unwilling to help, Nepos fled from Ravenna to his estates in Dalmatia. Romulus Augustulus was himself deposed by ODOACER, the barbarian master of Italy, and Nepos pressed his rightful claim to rule the West before Leo's successor, ZENO. Elevated to the patriciate by Zeno, Odoacer agreed to Nepos's return to Ravenna but never took steps to bring it about. For the next few years Nepos waited in Dalmatia, and on May 9, 480, was murdered by two retainers near Salonae, possibly with the complicity of Glycerius. As Nepos had the blessing of Zeno, it is possible to argue that he, not Romulus Augustulus, was the last Roman emperor in the West.

Nepos, Platorius (fl. early first century C.E.) *Prominent magistrate (consul in 119 C.E.) during the reigns of Trajan (98–117 C.E.) and Hadrian (117–138 C.E.)*

Of the senatorial class, Nepos served as governor of a number of provinces but was most noted for his achievement while in Britain (c. 122–127) when he constructed the WALL OF HADRIAN. For many years he enjoyed the friendship and devotion of Hadrian, but, as was the case with many others in the imperial circle, by the last years of Hadrian's rule Nepos was counted as a bitter enemy.

Nepotianus, Julius (d. 350 C.E.) *Usurper in Rome in June 350*

Nepotianus was the son of EUTROPIA, the sister of CONSTANTINE THE GREAT. With the help of the city's gladiators, the opponents of the future emperor MAGNENTIUS elevated Nepotianus to the rank of Augustus. He was unable to secure the necessary popular support and was murdered by Magnentius's soldiers at the end of June. Magnentius claimed the throne.

Neptune

God of the sea; originally, a minor Roman divinity whose powers were related to fresh water. When Greek influence became pronounced in Rome, Neptune became associated with the far more powerful deity Poseidon. The place of Neptune in Rome's list of deities was always hampered by the Roman's traditional fear of seafaring; but Poseidon's numerous attributes allowed them to worship Neptune in other ways. As the god was said to be drawn over the waves in a chariot pulled by horses with brazen hoofs and golden manes, he served as an equestrian patron who conveyed skill in managing horses and watched over horse races. The festival of Neptune (Neptunalia) was held every July 23. The celebration was based on his early identity and was thus designed to ensure the continued flow of much-needed water. Ceremonies were held in tents (*umbrae*) made out of tree branches. His temple stood in the CAMPUS MARTIUS.

See also GODS AND GODDESSES OF ROME.

Nero (Lucius Domitius Ahenobarbus) (37–68 C.E.) *Emperor from 54 to 68*

Born in December 37 at Antium, the son of AGRIPPINA THE YOUNGER and Gnaeus DOMITIUS AHENOBARBUS (2). His childhood was very unstable. His family was banished by the emperor GAIUS GALIGULA around 39, and his father died when he was only three. Caligula seized the entire family fortune, and the young boy spent many years in poverty. Agrippina raised him with the help of Domitia

Lepida, his aunt. His tutors were reportedly a dancer and a barber. When Claudius succeeded Gaius Caligula as emperor in 41, Agrippina was returned to Rome, and her estate was returned to her. In 49, following the fall and execution of Empress MESSALLINA, Claudius married Agrippina, and the boy's position was changed. Agrippina had already arranged for him to have excellent instructors, but now he was tutored by the famous SENECA THE ELDER. Betrothed to OCTAVIA, Claudius's daughter, Nero was also adopted officially in 50, becoming the probable heir to the throne, over Claudius's son BRITANNICUS who was younger and suffered the disadvantage of having the unlamented Messallina as his mother. Henceforth the young Lucius Domitius was known as Nero Claudius Drusus Germanicus. Having assured herself the title of Augusta, and her son the throne, Agrippina murdered Claudius in October 54. Nero, with the help of the PREFECT OF THE PRAETORIAN GUARD, BURRUS, was accepted by the Guard and became emperor.

The initial period of his reign was characterized by the supremacy of his mother, both in the palace and in the realm of politics. This mastery was challenged covertly by the alliance of Burrus and Seneca, who worked against her by playing on Nero's highly impressionable nature. By 55, he was leaning toward his advisers, and the eclipse of Agrippina was visible first in the murder of Britannicus and then in her disappearance from the imperial coinage, which had previously borne her image as well as that of Nero. With Agrippina removed from the palace in 55, Burrus and Seneca administered the empire successfully. Suetonius writes that there were many achievements in reforming the public abuses. Nero even made liberal proposals such as the abolition of many taxes; such ideas, impractical or potentially dangerous, demonstrated his lack of fitness to rule. When Nero turned to a life of total excess, seeking luxury and debauchery, Burrus and Seneca attempted to limit his adventures by directing him into affairs of a private nature. Such was the case with ACTE, who became his mistress. Nero found his advisers' inhibiting influences unbearable, as were the wiles of his mother to regain her influence, and in 59 murdered her. This personal decline was exacerbated by the death of Burrus in 62, reportedly from a throat tumor, although the prefect believed that Nero had poisoned him.

Burrus's successors were Faenius RUFUS and the ruthlessly ambitious TIGELLINUS. Well-suited to Nero's appetites, Tigellinus gained the greatest power in the court. Seneca, deprived of Burrus as an ally, retired to private life. It was a testament to the efforts of Burrus, Seneca and Roman institutions that the government functioned as long as it did on an even level. In 61, BOUDICCA, the queen of Britain's Iceni, revolted against imperial tyranny. Suetonius Paulinus, Britain's governor, defeated her, but only after serious damage had been done to Roman possessions in the isles. Meanwhile, an attempt was made to regain Armenia, where the great general, CORBULO, campaigned brilliantly; through his efforts the East was stabilized. Nero's reaction to the triumphs of Corbulo was characteristic. He called him to Greece in 67 and ordered him to commit suicide.

Nero had become megalomaniacal and his illness found expression in despotism and in sensual and artistic obsessions. He traveled to Greece solely because it was the home of the culture that he adored. Poetry, singing, games, painting, sculpture, were all cultivated to excess, vying with orgies, parties, and feasts. With the help of Tigellinus, the briefly suppressed class of informers, the DELATORES, was revived, and many were arrested and executed or exiled. The Senate, originally pleased with Nero's promises of a restoration of senatorial privileges, now viewed him with growing antipathy and distrust. The Romans wearied of being locked in theaters and forced to listen to Nero's interminable verses or songs, and the fire of 64 C.E. was symbolic of municipal chaos. In the aftermath, such construction as the huge DOMUS AUREA (the GOLDEN HOUSE OF NERO) drained the finances of the empire.

Finally, in 65, the PISONIAN CONSPIRACY was formed, centered around Gaius Calpurnius PISO and involving numerous noblemen, senators, and others. Tigellinus increased his standing with Nero when he ferreted out the conspirators; the lists of the executed grew each day. Among the victims were Seneca, LUCAN, and THRASEA PAETUS.

While the murders continued, Nero went to Greece. A food shortage and ensuing unrest brought him back to Rome in early 68. However, he failed to recognize the danger that he was in at the time and did nothing to change his lifestyle. In March, VINDEX, the governor of Gallia Lugdunensis, rose up against Nero. He was crushed by the Rhine legions, but soon other provinces were demanding Nero's removal. With Tigellinus ill, Nero lost his will and did nothing to stop the growing rebellion. Giving up hope, the emperor committed suicide with the help of his secretary, Epaphroditus, on June 9, 68. Suetonius writes that, dying, he uttered the words: "What an artist dies with me!" His legacy was an empire torn apart by civil war and a city that would vilify his name. His reign was heavily documented by the historians Dio, Suetonius, and Tacitus.

Suggested Readings: Charles-Picard, Gilbert. *Augustus and Nero.* Translated by Len Ortzen. New York: Thomas Y. Crowell, 1968; Grant, Michael. *Nero.* London, Weidenfeld & Nicolson, 1970; Griffin, Miriam T. *Nero: The End of a Dynasty.* New Haven, Conn.: Yale University Press, 1985; Holland, Richard. *Nero: The Man Behind the Myth.* Stroud, U.K.: Sutton, 2000; Shotter, David. *Nero.* London: Routledge, 1997; Suetonius *The Twelve Caesars.* Translated and with an introduction by Michael Grant. New York: Penguin, 1979; Tacitus, Cornelius. *Empire and Emperors: Selections from Tacitus' Annals.* Translated by Graham Tingay. New York: Cambridge University Press, 1983; ———.

Annales. Edited by Henry Furneaux. Oxford, U.K.: Clarendon Press, 1965; ———. *The Histories.* New York: Penguin, 1989; Walbank, F. W. *Selected Papers: Studies in Greek and Roman History and Historiography.* New York: Cambridge University Press, 1985; Warmington, B. H. *Nero: Reality and Legend.* New York: Norton, 1970; Woodman, A. J., ed. *Velleius Paterculus. The Tiberian Narrative.* New York: Cambridge University Press, 1977.

Nero, wives of Nero married three times, but throughout each marriage he was involved in numerous affairs with women and with men. In 53 C.E., he wed OCTAVIA (2), the daughter of Claudius, whom he later banished to Pandateria. During that time he fell in love with a freedwoman, ACTE, who was the only lover to remain loyal to him, even though she was replaced in his affections by POPPAEA. Poppaea was instrumental in the murder of Octavia in 62, and Nero took her as his wife. Three years later, however, while she was pregnant with his child, he kicked her to death. Statilia MESSALLINA first served as one of Nero's mistresses, but he married her in 66; a gifted survivor, she outlived Nero. To this list must be added the Vestal Virgin Rubria; SPORUS, his freedman; and DORYPHORUS. Nero wed both Sporus and Doryphorus in a mock ceremony. Doryphorus looked exactly like Nero's mother, Agrippina. It was also rumored that Nero had an affair with his mother.

Nero, Julius Caesar (6–31 C.E.) *Son of Germanicus and Agrippina the Elder*
Nero was given high honors by Emperor Tiberius at an early age, much to Rome's pleasure, for it pleased the mob to see a child of Germanicus gain prominence. In 20, he already held a seat as a magistrate and received advancement to the priesthood. That same year he married JULIA (5), daughter of Tiberius's son DRUSUS (3). After Drusus's death, Nero was considered next in line for the throne. By 23, however, the destruction of Agrippina, her sons and the entire party of Germanicus was being pursued actively by the Praetorian prefect SEJANUS. Slowly, Nero was trapped by Sejanus and stripped of the support of Tiberius, who was convinced that Nero stood as a threat to his reign. In 29, Tiberius denounced both Nero and his mother. The Senate condemned him as a public enemy, and he was sent to the isle of Pontia, where he either killed himself or died at the hands of his guards sometime before the fall of Sejanus in 31. His bones were returned to Rome in 37 by order of his brother, the new emperor GAIUS CALIGULA. Nero's brother DRUSUS (2) was also undone by Sejanus.

Nerseh (King of Persia) *See* NARSES.

Nerva, Marcus Cocceius (30–98 C.E.) *Emperor from 96 to 98*
Nerva enjoyed the favor of his predecessors, from Nero to Vespasian, and proved instrumental in establishing the policy of succession that maintained the stability of the Roman Empire throughout most of the second century C.E. Born at Narvia in Umbria, his family was old and honorable, his grandfather (of the same name) having been a friend of Emperor Tiberius, a *curator aquarum* and a noted legal expert. Growing up in a respected household, Nerva became a lawyer but gained advancement in the court of Nero because of his verse and his help in suppressing the PISONIAN CONSPIRACY of 65. Nerva also enjoyed the favor of the stern Vespasian, who named him his fellow consul in 71. He shared another consulship in 90, with Emperor Domitian. When Domitian later consulted astrologers to determine who might succeed him, and Nerva was proposed, he took no action, thinking that Nerva was already very old and unlikely to outlive him. In fact, Domitian was assassinated in 96, and Nerva may have been involved. He was immediately offered the throne.

As a choice for emperor, he possessed a good conservative nature and promised to deal fairly with the Senate, including a pledge never to put any member of that body to death. Nerva kept his oath, but his reign was wracked by two mutinies. In 97, a nobleman, Gaius Calpurnius Crassus Frugi Licinianus, made an attempt at a coup but failed; Nerva refused to order his death. The second, more dangerous uprising was led by the Praetorian Guard. Nerva had attempted to placate the legions and the Guard with favors and *donativa* following Domitian's death, as Domitian had been very popular among them. The Guard forced him to remove their two prefects, NORBANUS and Petronius Secundus, and in their place Nerva named Casperius AELIANUS. Aelianus led the Praetorians in an attack on the palace, demanding the execution of the plotters against Domitian. Nerva bared his own neck, but the soldiers only laughed. Friends and associates were then killed, and Nerva had to thank his Guard for serving justice. This humiliation broke his will, and shortly thereafter he announced that he had adopted TRAJAN, the governor of Germania Superior, as his heir. In January 98, Nerva died. His brief reign was characterized by excellent relations with the Senate, attention to the completion of Domitian's projects, vast spending of sums on securing the public goodwill and a pronounced attempt to increase civilian dislike for Domitian. Most important, Nerva initiated the system of adopting heirs to ensure the succession of the best possible candidates.

Nervii One of the largest and most warlike tribes of Gallia Belgica, prior to Julius Caesar's GALLIC WARS. Caesar described the harsh lifestyle of the Nervii. They would allow no traders to enter their territory and wine and luxuries were forbidden out of fear that the fierce martial spirit of the clans would be weakened. When the Romans entered Gallia Belgica in 57 B.C.E., the Nervii refused to surrender. As their territory extended roughly from the Sabis (Sambre) River, it became a focus for Caesar's strategy of conquest. In the subsequent battle of the SABIS, he routed the Nervii, slaughtering the bulk of their warriors. The remainder sued for peace, only to join in the rebellions of 54 B.C.E. and 52 B.C.E. Following the siege and battle of ALESIA in 52, the Nervii were pacified, eventually contributing six cohorts of auxiliaries to the defense of the province.

Nestor, Julianus (d. 218 C.E.) *Prefect of the Praetorian Guard (with Ulpius Julianus) during the brief reign of Macrinus (217–218 C.E.)*
Nestor and Julianus had previously served together as the heads of the dreaded FRUMENTARII, the imperial secret service agents. Their appointments to the prefectship of the Guard outraged much of the Roman establishment in the East, contributing to the revolt of the legions in Syria. When Macrinus fell in 218, Nestor was put to death by ELAGABALUS.

Nestorius (d. after 436 C.E.) *Bishop of Constantinople, patriarch from 428 to 431*
Nestorius came from Syria, entering a monastery in Antioch, where he studied the doctrines of Theodore of Mopsuestia. Having fully absorbed that popular religious teachers' beliefs, Nestorius earned a name for himself as a brilliant orator and in 428 was chosen by Emperor THEODOSIUS II to fill the vacant see of Constantinople. A short time later the hotly contested heresy of Nestorianism was born. Nestorius preached that the term *Theotokos* (Mother of God) was improperly used in relation to the Virgin Mary, for it implied that Christ had but one nature, as both God and Man. According to him, Christ had two separate and distinct natures and Mary was thus only the mother of the Jesus incarnated as Man. His ideas were immediately attacked by the Orthodox Christians, in particular by CYRIL OF ALEXANDRIA, who joined the anti-Nestorian group, seeing an opportunity to advance his own see over that of Constantinople. In August 430, Pope Celestine held a council in Rome to hear both sides of the controversy. His decision favored Cyril and the orthodox group, and later in the year Nestorius was condemned, a pronouncement reaffirmed by the Council of Ephesus in June 431. Under intense pressure, Theodosius removed Nestorius from his post. Returning to his monastery at Antioch, Nestorius was banished in 436 to the deserts of Egypt, where he died years later.

Nevitta, Flavius (fl. fourth century C.E.) *Germanic officer*
Nevitta served in the army of CONSTANTIUS II in 358, taking part in the defeat of the Juthungi in Raetia. JULIAN found Nevitta useful, appointing him MAGISTER EQUITUM

in 361. A year later he held a consulship with Claudius MAMERTINUS and was a member of the Commission of Chalcedon. During Julian's Persian Campaign (363) Nevitta commanded the Roman right wing. After the death of Julian later in the year, he participated in the debate to find a successor but was dismissed either by Jovian or by Valentinian.

Nicaea   Large city located in the province of BITHYNIA, just east of the Ascania Lake and about 65 miles from Constantinople. It was built originally by the great king of Asia, Antigonus, as "Antigonea." The name Nicaea came into use after King Lysimachus honored the inhabitants with his wife's name. Known for its beauty and fertility, Nicaea enjoyed the favor of both the original rulers of Bithynia and their successors, the Romans. Under the imperial administration, the city was a source of concern to various governors, including PLINY THE YOUNGER during the reign of Trajan (98–117 C.E.), because of its economic mismanagement and provincial disorganization. Part of the problem rested in the bitter feud that raged for centuries between Nicaea and NICOMEDIA, the provincial headquarters for the legate—a position that Nicaea's city council tried increasingly to secure. Toward the later years of the Roman Empire, this effort seems to have brought success. Constantine the Great held his famous council there in 325 (see below), and Julian constructed for his own use a grand palace. Nicaea's most famous citizen was the historian DIO.

Nicaea, battle of   Engagement fought in north-western Asia Minor, probably in early 194 C.E., between the armies of Septimius SEVERUS and PESCENNIUS NIGER, both claimants to the throne. Following the battle of CYZICUS in 193, the Severan forces were able to secure a solid position in BITHYNIA. Niger, anxious to deny them any further advance, moved his troops into the neighborhood of Nicaea, now his headquarters. NICOMEDIA, the longtime rival to Nicaea, opened its gates to Severus. The two combatants grappled in the narrow passes between Nicaea and Ascania. Niger was on hand while Severus left command of his legions to his reliable general, Candidus. Fighting raged for many hours as fortunes swung back and forth. Finally, through the personal courage of Candidus, the Severans gained the upper hand and drove Niger from the field. Niger ordered retreat to Nicaea before withdrawing farther into Asia Minor.

See also ISSUS.

Nicaea, Council of   A council convened by Emperor Constantine the Great (d. 337 C.E.) in 325 with the principal aim of resolving the Arian Controversy, the heresy that questioned the full divinity of Jesus Christ. Recognizing that Arianism had created a major storm in the Eastern Roman Empire, Constantine decided not to leave the matter in the hands of local church councils but to summon bishops from around the empire. While advice was probably given by Hosius, bishop of Córdoba (Cordova), Constantine was most responsible for organizing the council, including the generous gesture of granting free transportation for the bishops who were attending. The site chosen was the imperial summer palace at Nicaea, on the Bosporus, in Bithynia. It was attended by more than 300 bishops, although the names of only 220 are known. The main Western representatives, besides Hosius, were the bishops of Milan, Dijon, and Carthage and the two papal delegates representing Pope Sylvester I (r. 314–335). The traditionally accepted date for the start of the council was May 20, 325. It went on until the end of August. The president was probably Bishop Hosius, although some historians argue that it may have been Eustathius, bishop of Antioch.

After a brief opening statement by Constantine, the council fathers set to work. It would appear that a creed of Arian disposition was proposed by Eusebius of Nicomedia and rejected. Eusebius of Caesarea then offered his own. With the insertion of the term *homoousios* (of one substance) this was adopted, although it was not the creed finally promulgated. Only two bishops, Theonas of Marmarica and Secundus of Ptolemais, refused to subscribe to the final document, the Nicene Creed and its anti-Arian anathemas, and both were deposed. The council then dealt with other pressing topics, including a resolution of the Melitian Schism, the fixing of the date of Easter for the churches in the East and West (thus ending the Paschal Controversy), and the readmission of the Novatianists and Paulinians (followers of Paul of Samosata) to the church. Privileges were also accorded to the sees of Alexandria, Antioch, and Jerusalem. While the council was supposed to bring a close to the Arian Controversy, this hope proved fleeting; the crisis would continue throughout the fourth century. Unfortunately, the acta of the council are lost. The only extant documents are the 20 canons it issued, the creed, and the synodal letter.

Nice   Mediterranean seaport along the western coast of Liguria. It was founded in the fourth century B.C.E. by Greek colonists from Massilia (Marseilles), who defeated the local Gallic tribe for possession of the area. In honor of their triumph they named the community Nikea (or Nicaea) after Nike, their goddess of victory. As a colony of Massilia, Nice was under that city's jurisdiction until the Civil War between Caesar and Pompey. When Massilia was defeated and conquered by Caesar in 49 B.C.E., losing its right to territorial possessions, Nice was freed of its fealty to its Greek founders. Roman occupation fostered extensive development in the hills behind old Nice. Archaeological remains include baths, an amphitheater, and a temple of Apollo. During the imperial era Nice was one of the leading centers of the mountainous region of the Maritime Alps.

Nicene Creed   The creed or establishment of doctrine for all Christianity as issued by the Council of NICAEA in 325 C.E. The Nicene Creed reflected both the triumph of Christian orthodoxy at the council and the personal desires of Constantine the Great. Its substance was the source of considerable debate throughout the proceedings, as the orthodox delegates and those supporting the cause of ARIANISM differed as to the exact nature of Christ. EUSEBIUS OF NICOMEDIA proposed one draft, only to have it rejected as being too Arian. After much discussion a final draft was composed, very similar in style to the Baptismal Creed of Jerusalem, and containing the all-important Greek word *Homoousion* (one substance), meaning that Christ and the Father were one—a direct blow to Arian doctrine. As further reproof of Arianism special anathemas were included specifically against Arianists.

Nicolaus of Damascus   (fl. first century B.C.E.) *Writer, diplomat, and teacher of Greek descent*
Nicolaus entered the service of Queen CLEOPATRA of Egypt, becoming tutor of her children; he eventually joined the court of HEROD THE GREAT. The king made him chief secretary and traveling spokesman for the Judaean realm. In his capacity as a diplomat, Nicolaus journeyed to Rome where he met Emperor Augustus on numerous occasions. AGRIPPA also received him. In 14 B.C.E. Nicolaus pleaded successfully before Agrippa at Ephesus, achieving an improved status for Jews in Asia Minor, though he was unable to obtain the same for the Jews of Cyrene. Nicolaus was a prolific writer. JOSEPHUS relied heavily upon his *Universal History* (in 144 books) for his own *Jewish Antiquities*. The work, while highly moralistic, contained much useful information. Other books included a biography on the youth and training of Augustus and an autobiography. Some of these works have been preserved in fragments.

Nicomedia   Provincial capital of BITHYNIA on the Gulf of Marmara, about 60 miles from Constantinople; one of the most important metropolises in Asia Minor. Nicomedia was founded by King Nicomedes I of Bithynia around 264 B.C.E. Its position of prominence was undiminished when the Romans assumed control of the region in 74 B.C.E., and the Nicomedians could boast of having both the seat of the governor and the center of Roman influence situated within their walls. The *concilium*, the provincial assembly, convened at Nicomedia, and in 29 B.C.E. Emperor Augustus approved the erection of the temple to hold the service of the IMPERIAL CULT. Nicomedia possessed numerous advantages that aided its claim to supremacy. It was located directly on the main trade routes from East to West, running through Bithynia, and the area around the city was very fertile. The harbor on the Propontis helped link it to the maritime commerce in the BLACK SEA and in the Mediterranean, and the Roman navy maintained its fleet in the harbor. A proposal was made to dig a canal from the sea to a lake farther inland, but the plan was never fulfilled. Nicomedia earned the jealousy of other cities in Bithynia, most notably its southern neighbor, NICAEA, which lobbied successfully to have the governors moved there from Nicomedia. This old and bitter rivalry caused Nicomedia to support Septimius SEVERUS in 193 C.E. against PESCENNIUS NIGER, who had Nicaea's backing. Niger lost his bid for the throne, and by the early third century C.E., Nicomedia's favored status was evident. Diocletian chose it as his headquarters in the East. Archaeologically, very little remains of his numerous constructions, partially because of the disasters visited upon the city over the years. In 258 C.E., the Goths poured into Bithynia and Nicomedia was captured and sacked. Earthquakes were also common, the worst striking on August 24, 358 C.E. Nicomedia also suffered from the ineptitude of financial managers. So severe was the problem that Trajan appointed special legates to reorganize the entire administration of Nicomedia and other cities in the province. One of the legates, PLINY THE YOUNGER, attempted to construct a series of aqueducts. Like the canal, the aqueducts were never finished.

Nicopolis (1) In Epirus, the "City of Victory" built by Emperor Augustus in 31 B.C.E. to celebrate his defeat of Antony and Cleopatra at nearby ACTIUM. Nicopolis was opposite Actium on the Gulf of Ambracia and served as his headquarters prior to the climactic engagement just off the coast. Originally a small Greek community, it was expanded along Greek cultural lines at Augustus's order. A permanent memorial of triumph was also created, the *ludi Actiaci,* or Actian games, held every four years. To populate his new community, Augustus encouraged immigrants from Aetolia and elsewhere. He envisioned using Nicopolis as an important administrative center for the impoverished province of Epirus. People from all over southern Epirus were moved to Nicopolis, including villages from Ambracia and Anactorium. Within a short time the city served as an important model of Hellenic life.

Nicopolis (2) In Moesia; a Danube River city created by order of Emperor Trajan in his attempt to colonize and civilize the province and, like Marcianopolis, to inject Hellenic culture into the region. Nicopolis figured in the Gothic Wars during the third century C.E.

Nigrinus, Gaius Avidius (d. 118 C.E.) *A member of the wealthy and influential Avidius family who held several posts during the reign of Trajan (97–117)*
Nigrinus was a tribune in 105, consul in 110, and a governor in Dacia not long after that region was conquered. As a legate in Achaea, Nigrinus probably participated in Trajan's attempt to reorganize and stabilize the adminis-

tration of that financially troubled province. By the time of the succession of Hadrian in 117, Nigrinus commanded considerable political respect and was seen as both a leading general and possible heir should the new emperor die. It came as a considerable surprise, then, that in the summer of 118 Nigrinus and three others in the court were put to death for conspiring against Hadrian. This course of action was probably caused by Nigrinus's opposition to Hadrian's imperial policy, as well as his long-standing friendship with Trajan. He was also father-in-law to Lucius Aelius.

Nile For countless centuries the Nile River has flowed from the heart of Africa through ETHIOPIA and EGYPT into the Mediterranean. When the Romans came to occupy Egypt, they relied heavily upon Egyptian agriculture, aided in the main by the annual flood of the Nile. It was widely believed that the source of the Nile was to be found in the Atlas Mountains in MAURETANIA, the water traveling underground before emerging in Sudan, and this view was echoed by Dio. Nero, with an eye toward conquering ETHIOPIA, sent an expedition of the Praetorian Guard up the river in the fall of 61 C.E. They journeyed extensively through Ethiopia, collecting a wealth of information. Their progress was exceptional, all the way to the White Nile, but because of the marshlands there they could proceed no farther. The journey home took some time, for they did not reach Rome until around 63, having failed to find the source of the mighty river. That was said to have been discovered in the early second century C.E., when the Greek Diogenes traveled into the heart of Africa and discovered two lakes, each fed by snow-capped ranges, the "Mountains of the Moon."

Nile, battle of the The final engagement in Julius CAESAR's pacification of Egypt, fought in February of 47 B.C.E. between the forces of Caesar and his ally MITHRIDATES OF PERGAMUM against those of King Ptolemy XIII. When Ptolemy learned that Mithridates had reached the Nile Delta, the young ruler immediately dispatched an army to prevent the general's union with the besieged Romans at ALEXANDRIA. Mithridates easily defeated the Egyptian Dioscorides's attack, sending a messenger to Caesar that he should come quickly. Ptolemy sent more troops downriver while watching from Alexandria for the Romans, who he knew would be on the march. Caesar, however, sailed around any possible Egyptian sorties, joining Mithridates before Ptolemy could react. Both sides now had around 20,000 men each. Caesar pushed forward against the demoralized Egyptians, routing all who dared oppose him. The legions destroyed an enemy fort, and after heavy fighting stormed the king's camp. Thousands fled, including Ptolemy, who reportedly drowned when his ship capsized. Egypt was now in the hands of Julius Caesar.

Nisibis   A strategically important city in Mesopotamia, between the upper reaches of the Tigris and Euphrates rivers. Nisibis was for many centuries the capital of the district of Mygdonia, situated on the Mygdonius River. Few cities were so bitterly involved in the conflicts between Rome and the empires of PARTHIA and PERSIA. Any advance into Mesopotamia from Armenia would aim for the occupation of Nisibis to allow a further attack against the Tigris or south into Mesopotamia and the Euphrates satrapies. In his campaign against Parthia, Emperor Trajan captured Nisibis in 114 but then lost it in the revolt of 116 that killed his general Maximus Santra. The reliable Moor, Lusius Quietus, was unleashed, and he retook Nisibis as well as EDESSA. Emperor Septimius Severus suppressed an uprising of the Osroene in 194 and created a colony at Nisibis, providing it with a procurator. Upon his return in 198, Severus decreed MESOPOTAMIA a province, with Nisibis as its capital and the seat of an Equestrian prefect who controlled two legions.

Throughout the third century C.E., Nisibis was buffeted back and forth as Rome and Persia struggled against one another. Following the crushing defeat of King NARSES in 298, at the hands of Emperor Galerius, Nisibis enjoyed a monopoly as the trading center between the two realms. In 363, Julian launched an unsuccessful Persian expedition; his successor Jovian accepted a humiliating peace with SHAPUR II. Nisibis became Persian once again.

nominatio   Process used by the emperor in the early years of the empire to decide whether or not a candidate was worthy of election to a given office. Augustus and Tiberius both examined potential magistrates, and the receiving of the *nominatio* from the emperor was considered of the greatest help in being elected. With the *nominatio* very often came the *commendatio,* or the recommendation of the ruler, as well. The entire process became meaningless in 14 C.E. when Tiberius nominated only 12 candidates for the 12 vacancies in the praetorships. He left no choice for the voters and nullified the ability of the comitia to choose another candidate. More important, he transferred the elections from the comitia to the Senate, terminating active democracy in Rome.

Nones   The fifth or seventh day of each Roman month, depending upon its number of days. Each Nones fell exactly nine days before the IDES, and by tradition was used to list the coming festivals. There were, as a consequence, very few holidays prior to the Nones.

See also CALENDAR.

Norbanus (d. 96 C.E.?) *Prefect of the Praetorian Guard*
Norbanus served as prefect with Petronius Secundus during the reign of DOMITIAN and was a member of the conspiracy to murder the emperor in 96 C.E. He may have had a say in the choice of Nerva as the next emperor but was apparently removed from his post by the new ruler shortly after the accession, being superseded by Casperius AELIANUS. When the Praetorian Guard revolted, insisting that the assassins of Domitian be handed over for execution, Norbanus may have been among the numerous officials slain, but there is no record of his death.

Noricum   Roman province south of the DANUBE River and situated to the north of Italy, between RAETIA and PANNONIA. It was instrumental in the defense of Italy and suffered heavily in the barbarian invasions of the fifth century. This mountainous, green and beautiful land was the home of a large number of Celtic tribes, who overwhelmed the Illyrian peoples of the area sometime between the third and first centuries B.C.E. The greatest of the Celtic communities was that of the Taurisci, who became known as the Norici, from their capital at Noreia. A confederation of tribes who issued their own coinage, they supported Julius Caesar in his war against Pompey in 49 B.C.E.

The strategic value of Noricum became obvious to Emperor Augustus, who saw the need to create a strong border along the Danube. Since its position so close to Italy did not recommend it as a client kingdom, starting in 35 B.C.E. pressure was mounted on the Norici to accept Roman supremacy, with direct Senatorial or proconsular government there. Unlike other parts of the empire, the inhabitants of Noricum accepted their fate. In 16 B.C.E., P. Silius Nerva, governor of ILLYRICUM, annexed the entire country, and Noricum became a province. At first Rome probably used a *praefectus civitatum* to run the local administration, but eventually a *procurator* was sent out. Early Roman occupation was centered on the installation and imprinting of Italian culture on the province. In this they were wholly successful. The local tribes were broken apart and, as in Gaul, the Celtic sociopolitical structure of the *civitates* was rooted out. Despite opposition from the Norici, Noreia was destroyed. In its place were created highly Italianized cities, later *municipia,* whose residents were drawn primarily from the provincial population. Urbanization proceeded so smoothly that colonization was unnecessary.

Over time, Noricum became a province with two different cultural patterns. Near the Danube, life was less developed because of the presence of Rome's armies, while behind the frontier the proximity of Italy was very evident. With Italian ways so ingrained, the province became an example, if not a spearhead, of Romanization in Pannonia and elsewhere. The drive to Romanize the rest of the Danubian line would meet with varying degrees of success compared with Noricum. Under initial administrations the provincial seat was at Virunum, a MUNICIPIUM. As a result of the MARCOMANNIC WARS, a permanent garrison was stationed in the province. Its legate became the new governor, running all affairs from the city of Ovilava, while the procurator remained at

Virunum. Ovilava enjoyed municipal status and in the reign of Caracalla was promoted to a *colonia*. Diocletian later divided Noricum along the civilian and military lines that had long existed, creating *Noricum Ripense* in the north and Noricum Mediterraneum in the south.

Economically, Noricum was blessed with a rich natural supply of iron ore. The Alpes Noricae ran through much of the province, its many peaks holding vast deposits, and Noric swords were among the finest available. Citizens of Noricum served in the legions and for many years helped fill the ranks of the Praetorian Guard; Noricum joined Spain, Macedonia, and Italy as a recruiting center for the guard. Noricum was overwhelmed in the general invasion by Germanic tribes in the fifth century.

notarii The imperial corps of notaries, the secretaries and stenographers of the government and army in the later years of the Roman Empire. The *notarii* were under the control of a chief (*primicerius notariorum*). These officers maintained the entire corps, handling promotions and transfers. Each member of the notarii was assigned to the palace, a Praetorian prefecture or the army. Those belonging to the central bureaucracy (the palace or a prefecture) were known as *tribuni et notarii*, while those working for generals were called *domestici et notarii*, although they held no military rank. The most important task of the *notarii* was the keeping of the minutes of the CONSISTORIUM or imperial council. Because of their familiarity with the workings of the state, and ability to keep secrets, the *notarii* stood as a ready pool for potential holders of high government offices. They were used frequently on missions requiring delicate negotiations. Julian tried unsuccessfully to limit their numbers.

See also CIVIL SERVICE; SCRINII.

Notitia Dignitatum A listing of the most important imperial officers in the Eastern and Western empires, compiled sometime after 395 C.E. The *Notitia Dignitatum* is of great value historically because of its thorough presentation of the many officeholders in the huge bureaucracy of the late empire. It examined each office, starting with that of the Praetorian prefect, working its way down the ranks of the provincial governors. With each entry was provided an account of the duties of the offices, the subordinate staff and, where applicable, any military units at their disposal. The insignia of each office was also depicted. In all likelihood, the *Notitia* that was preserved was for use in the West, as the bulk of the information was on Western officials, while that of the East contained fewer specifics. The original of the *Notitia* was lost, the surviving copy was made in 1551.

Novatian (d. c. 257–258 C.E.) *Theologian, presbyter, and founder of the schismatic sect of Novatianism*

Probably a convert to Christianity, Novatian served as a presbyter in Rome and was the author of an orthodox treatise on the nature of the Trinity. A rigorist in matters of readmission for lapsed Christians, he came to oppose vigorously the policy of the church in allowing those Christians who had denied their faith to repent and return to the fold, particularly after the harsh persecutions of Emperor Decius (r. 249–251). When, in 251, St. Cornelius was elected as successor to Pope later St. Fabian, Novatian allowed himself to be elected bishop of Rome as a rival, making him the first of the antipopes. Condemned by Cornelius and a synod of Rome, Novatian died during the persecution of Emperor Valerian (r. 253–260). Novatian's followers persisted, however, in their belief that those who had fallen from the faith should never be allowed to repent because their sin was unpardonable in the eyes of God. Formally condemned by the Council of Nicaea in 325, the Novatianists survived into the fifth century.

Nuceria An old Italian colony situated just east of POMPEII; reportedly conquered by Hannibal during the Punic Wars. In 59 C.E., its inhabitants and those of Pompeii were attending a gladiator show held by Livineius Regulus (who was expelled from the Senate) in Pompeii. A disagreement between the two groups erupted into violence, and soon they were stoning one another and then dueling with swords. The outnumbered Nucerians were slaughtered. Nero ordered a full investigation when word reached Rome, and Pompeii was forbidden as a result to hold any entertainment for the next 10 years; Livineius and the promoters were exiled.

See also FIDENAE.

numerals, Roman The Roman numeral system was based upon a basic series of seven signs that could then be used in combination, repetition, or slight modification to create other numerals. The seven basic numbers were:

I	1
V	5
X	10
L	50
C	100
I⊃ or D	500
∞ or M	1,000

The D in 500 was often written with a middle bar, but it is now used as a basic D. M is also commonly used for 1,000 today, but it was rarely used by the Romans. Its primary use was as an abbreviation of the words *mille* and *milia*, with ∞ as the actual figure. C was the most likely an abbreviation of the word *centum*, while V was most likely chosen to represent the five fingers of the hand. X represented the joining of two hands (or the union of V and V).

Using these seven symbols, the Romans were able to create other numbers, normally through a process of adding numbers (e.g., VI for 6, II for 2, and XXII for 22) or subtracting numbers (e.g., IV for 4, XL for 40, XC for 90). The Romans apparently preferred to add numbers rather than subtract, but both methods were employed. To create a larger number, a smaller number was attached to the right of the larger number, reading from left to right. A smaller number was created by adding a smaller number to the left of the larger number, thereby making it clear that there is a subtraction of value. Both methods could appear in the same number, such as CCXLIV (244).

In order to calculate and represent larger numbers, in the late Republic a superscript bar was adopted to indicate that a number should be multiplied by 1,000. For even larger numerals, lateral lines were employed, such, as $\overline{X}$ to denote 1,000,000. A medial bar was employed as well, to prevent possible confusion between ordinal and cardinal numbers. The symbol for the denarius thus was written as ✳ to denote that it was worth X asses.

A cursive form of Roman writing brought about a number of minor variations in the forms of numbers. Most variations could be recognized easily, but some eccentric versions could be almost entirely indecipherable. Compounding the difficulty of reading numbers was the fact that Roman numeral usage was not always consistent, and variations could be found all over the empire. There is also the notable absence of zero in the Roman numbering system. The zero was not added to the numerical system of the West until the adoption during the Middle Ages of the Arabic numbering system. Scholars in Baghdad introduced the zero around 800, adopting for their own use the Hindu numbers, with the symbol 0.

ROMAN CARDINAL NUMERALS

1	I	unus
2	II	duo
3	III	tres
4	IV or IIII	quattuor
5	V	quinque
6	VI	sex
7	VII	septem
8	VIII	octo
9	IX	novem
10	X	decem
11	XI	undecim
12	XII	duodecim
13	XIII	tredecim
14	XIV	quattuordecim
15	XV	quindecim
16	XVI	sedecim
17	XVII	septendecim
18	XVIII	duodeviginti
19	XIX	undeviginti
20	XX	viginti

30	XXX	triginta
40	XL	quadraginta
50	L	quinquaginta
60	LX	sexaginta
70	LXX	septuaginta
80	LXXX	octoginta
90	XC	nonaginta
100	C	centum
200	CC	ducenti
300	CCC	trecenti
400	CCCC	quadringenti
500	I⊃ or D	quingenti
600	I⊃C	sescenti
700	I⊃CC	septingenti
800	I⊃CCC	octingenti
900	I⊃CCCC	nongenti
1000	⊂I⊃ or M	mille
10,000	CCI⊃⊃	decem milia

ROMAN ORDINAL NUMBERS

first	primus, -a, -um
second	secundus, -a, -um
third	tertius, -a, -um
fourth	quartus
fifth	quintus
sixth	sextus
seventh	septimus
eighth	octavus
ninth	nonus
tenth	decimus
eleventh	undecimus
twelfth	duodecimus
thirteenth	tertius decimus
fourteenth	quartus decimus
fifteenth	quintus decimus
sixteenth	sextus decimus
seventeenth	septimus decimus
eighteenth	duodevicesimus
nineteenth	undevicesimus
twentieth	vicesimus
twenty-first	unus et vicesimus
thirtieth	tricesimus
fortieth	quadragesimus
fiftieth	quinquagesimus
sixtieth	sexagesimus
seventieth	septuagesimus
eightieth	octogesimus
ninetieth	nonagesimus
hundredth	centesimus

NUMERAL ADVERBS

once	semel
twice	bis

three times	ter
four times	quater
five times	quinquies
six times	sexies
seven times	septies
eight times	octies
nine times	novies
ten times	decies
eleven times	undecies
twelve times	duodecies
thirteen times	terdecies
twenty times	vicies
one hundred times	centies

Note: Numeral adverbs ending in -es have an alternative form in -ens.

DISTRIBUTIVES

one each	singuli
two each	bini
three each	terni
four each	quaterni
five each	quini
six each	seni
seven each	septeni
eight each	octoni
nine each	noveni
ten each	deni
eleven each	undeni
twelve each	duodeni
thirteen each	terni deni
twenty each	viceni
one hundred each	centeni

numeri   Term used to describe any formation of barbarians serving in the Roman LEGIONS whose nature was so un-Roman as to prevent its classification among the *auxilia,* or auxiliaries. These troops, known after the start of the second century C.E., might have included elements of wild tribes living along the Danube or in Germania. In the late empire, *numeri* came to signify any body of soldiers, losing its reference to barbarian origins.

Numerian (Marcus Aurelius Numerius Numerianus) (d. 284) *Emperor from 283 to 284*

Numerian was the son of Emperor CARUS and the younger brother of CARINUS. He was advanced to the imperial power in stages behind Carinus and thus received the rank of Caesar in 282, a short time after Carinus was invested. In 283 Numerian set out with his father on his campaign against the Persians, while Carinus remained in the West. When Carus died quite suddenly, Numerian and his brother succeeded to the throne as corulers. Initially Numerian carried on the war against Persia with the ambitious PREFECT OF THE PRAETORIAN GUARD, APER (who probably had murdered his father). Either because he had failed in the field or had found war distasteful, Numerian terminated the expedition and started for home. While on the march he fell ill, complaining that his eyes hurt. Near Nicomedia he rested, away from the view of his troops, while only Aper had access to him. Finally, when the stench coming from his tent was unbearable, the soldiers entered and discovered Numerian long dead and pronounced Aper the murderer. A young officer, DIOCLETIAN, was proclaimed emperor by the troops and slew Aper.

Numerianus (fl. c. 200 C.E.) *The so-called School Master General*

An individual of dubious reality, Numerianus was supposedly a teacher of letters in Rome in 196 C.E. According to Dio, hearing that CLODIUS ALBINUS, governor of Britain, had crossed into the Gallic provinces against Septimus Severus, Numerianus traveled to Gaul and established himself as a rebel leader by claiming to be a senator. Through Numerianus's skill and daring, Albinus's units were defeated in small engagements. Numerianus stole 70 millions sesterces for the Severans. When Severus next met Numerianus, the schoolteacher asked for nothing, living out his days in the country with an allowance that was pressed upon him by the emperor.

Numidia

Roman province situated between MAURETANIA to the west and AFRICA to the east. It was the last territory in the western regions of the Roman Empire to be converted into a province. Numidia was the home of the African nomads, or Numidae, a herding people of Berber extraction who were eventually divided into two major tribes: the Massylians and the Masaesylians. Small chiefdoms were common until the time of Masinissa (c. 221 B.C.E.), when all of Numidia's tribes were united.

Roman interest in the territory had existed after the destruction of CARTHAGE. In 106 B.C.E., the Numidian ruler Jugurtha was crushed in the Jugurthine War, and Numidia fell under Rome's political control, although client kings were left on their thrones, including Hiempsal (106–60 B.C.E.) and JUBA I (60–46 B.C.E.). This latter monarch joined the cause of POMPEY THE GREAT in 49 B.C.E., serving as his most loyal supporter in Africa. He defeated Caesar's representative in Africa, Gaius Gurio, and then helped METELLUS SCIPIO during the campaign against Caesar in 47–46 B.C.E. Juba was routed at the battle of THAPSUS in 46 and died immediately after, his realm being taken over by Caesar, who established the colony of Africa Nova.

In 30 B.C.E., Augustus installed upon the throne JUBA II, the son of Juba I and one of the most learned men in the world. He remained in Numidia for only five years, for Augustus desired the more strategically placed kingdom for Rome. Juba moved to Mauretania in 25, while Numidia was reunited with Africa Proconsularis. Numidia remained part of the senatorial province, headed by a proconsul with one legion. Local troubles flared during the reign of Tiberius, with tribal uprisings and the serious revolt of TACFARINAS. So successful was this brigand that in 20 C.E. the emperor sent out a legion from Pannonia to Numidia, placed first under the command of BLAESUS and then DOLABELLA, who finally killed Tacfarinas in 22. While the legion was removed from Africa, another legion stayed, the only legion on the continent except for the forces stationed in Egypt. Emperor Gaius Caligula decreed that a proconsul should not command such troops and moved them from deep in Africa Proconsularis to the Numidian frontier. They patrolled the loose border, keeping an eye on the wild tribes.

The presence of the cohorts allowed a highly successful program of Romanization as they constructed roads and helped to build a military colony at THAMUGADI. The roads allowed greater economic development within the interior and connected the colonies with Africa's major ports at Carthage and Hadrumetum. Numidia's wealth was based on agriculture and livestock, including olives, cereals, wine, and cattle. Septimius Severus named Numidia an independent province, with a capital at Cirta (later renamed Constantine) in the most abundant part of the country. Along the southern frontier of Numidia, one of the more fluid boundaries of the Roman Empire, a series of fortifications and posts was built, an African version of the *limes* used on the Rhine and the Danube, to protect it from constant threats riding out of the desert.

nummus castrensis   Literally, "coinage of the camps"; a special kind of Roman coin issued by a general to pay his troops while on campaign. The name was derived from the tradition of handing the money out in the *castra*, or military camp, of the legions.

See also COINAGE.

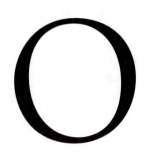

Obodas (d. 9 B.C.E.) *King of Nabataea in the later years of the first century B.C.E.*

The successor of King Malachus, Obodas inherited a country absorbed into the Roman Empire. In 25 B.C.E., Obodas aided Aelius Gallus in his attempted conquest of Arabia by sending a force of 1,000 men to act as auxiliaries. His demise may have been the result of poison, administered by his vizier.

Octavia (d. 11 B.C.E.) *Sister of Octavian (Augustus) and one of the most popular women in Roman history*

Octavia was the daughter of OCTAVIUS and Atia, the mother of Octavian. At an early age she married the CONSUL (50 B.C.E.) Gaius Marcellus, by whom she had three children: a son, MARCELLUS, and two daughters. This union was endangered by Julius Caesar's offering her to POMPEY THE GREAT as a political unifier and then terminated by her husband's death sometime around 40 B.C.E. To cement the alliance between Octavian and Marc ANTONY, Octavia wed the general in 40 and bore him two daughters, the two Antonias, before Marc Antony became enamored of CLEOPATRA. In 32 B.C.E. he renounced the marriage completely. Octavia, very much respected by Rome, was seen as a victim of Antony's ambition. After Antony's defeat and death, Octavia remained loyal to his memory. She cared for all of his children, her own and those of his previous wife FULVIA and of Cleopatra. She lived as a Roman matron, much aggrieved by the death of her son Marcellus in 23 B.C.E.

Octavia, Claudia (c. 41–c. 62 C.E.) *Empress of Rome from 54 to 62; the wife of Nero and the daughter of Claudius*

Though Octavia bore the stigma of having the infamous Empress MESSALLINA as her mother, she was deeply loved by her father. She was betrothed in 49 to L. Junius Silanus, a nobleman and a relative of Augustus, but he was ousted from the Senate as a result of palace intrigue. In 49, she was betrothed to Nero, son of Agrippina the Younger, Claudius's new wife, and they were wed in 53. After Nero succeeded Claudius as emperor, he quickly grew tired of Octavia. By 55 they were estranged, as Nero pursued the freedwoman ACTE. He maintained the marriage for a time because of the legitimacy that Octavia lent to his corrupt rule, but in 62 Nero divorced Octavia, claiming she was barren, to marry POPPAEA. The outraged Roman mob forced her return. This was only a brief respite, for soon charges of treason were made against her, and Octavia was exiled to the island of Pandateria, where, later in the year, she was cruelly murdered and her head delivered to Poppaea.

Octavian *See* AUGUSTUS.

Octavius, Gaius (fl. first century B.C.E.) *Father of Emperor Augustus*

According to the cynical remarks of Marc ANTONY, Gaius Octavius's own father may have been a moneychanger. Certainly he was born into wealth, using it to launch a very successful public career. After serving as a PRAETOR, he became the governor of Macedonia, where as chief administrator he earned the praise of Cicero and proved more than capable. Before 63 B.C.E., he returned home where further political offices were open to him, but he died before reaching the consulship. Gaius was married twice, first to Aucharia (producing a daughter) and then to Atia, daughter of JULIA (1), sister of Julius Caesar. The two children from that union were Octavian (AUGUSTUS) and OCTAVIA (1).

Odaenath (d. 266 C.E.) *King of Palmyra from 260 to 266*

Odaenath was an excellent general and diplomat who used the desperate position of Rome to widen Palmyra's role in the East. As a prince of Palmyra, he had initially looked to establish an alliance with the Persians under SHAPUR I, but was disappointed. In the disastrous mid-third century, with crises on every frontier, the hard-pressed Emperor Gallienus welcomed any aid that Odaenath might offer Rome. The Palmyrene king first avenged the defeat and death of the Roman general, Valerian, by smashing Shapur in battle. When he killed the Roman usurper Quietus in 261, he became the foremost commander of Rome in the Eastern provinces. Having thus proven his worth to Gallienus, Odaenath received the title *dux Romanorum* and *corrector totius Orientus*, granting him broad governmental powers. With every available Roman soldier he marched against Persia, captured Nisibis and Carrhae, swept through Mesopotamia to the very gates of Ctesiphon, the Persian capital, and brought Shapur to his knees. By 264 Odaenath controlled the entire East, from Cilicia to the Egyptian border, including Mesopotamia, while Gallienus was struggling to preserve the West. A fight for Syria and other territories of the East was probably inevitable. In 266, Odaenath was murdered, perhaps by a Roman official appalled at the rise of the Palmyrenes. His death created a vacuum that was filled by his wife ZENOBIA.

Odoacer (d. 493 C.E.) *A Germanic king, responsible in 476 C.E. for the end of the Roman Empire in the West*

Odoacer was a chieftain of a contingent of Sciri (Heruli) in the armies of the PATRICIAN and MAGISTER MILITUM, ORESTES, who in 475 ousted Emperor Julius Nepos from the Western throne in favor of his son, ROMULUS AUGUSTULUS. The basis of the power of Orestes was, as always, the Germanic hosts. They mutinied in 476 over their desire to settle permanently in Italy, a possibility that horrified Orestes. The soldiers found a leader, Odoacer, proclaimed him their king (*rex*) and murdered Orestes. Romulus was deposed but allowed to live in Campania.

Odoacer was determined to end the process of putting politically impotent monarchs in charge of the West. He declared himself king of the Germans but then immediately requested official recognition from Constantinople for his position as *magister militum*. In effect, the West and the East were to be governed from Constantinople as one empire, though his domination would be unquestioned. His claim was challenged by Julius Nepos, the former emperor; Emperor Zeno decided that Odoacer should receive the patriciate while asking that

Nepos be allowed to return. This was never granted, and when Nepos died in 480, Odoacer took over his holdings in Dalmatia as well. Although Constantinople supposedly headed the vast imperial domain, in reality the West was no longer a part of the Roman Empire. Odoacer was slain by the Ostrogoths in 493.

Oea (Tripoli)

One of the leading coastal cities of Tripolitania in Africa; situated west of Lepcis Magna, in modern Libya. Despite its position of importance in Africa, little has survived of it archaeologically, except for the Arch of Marcus Aurelius. Built in 163 C.E., the Arch was architecturally notable because of the dome that covered the top.

Olba

A small client state in CILICIA. Olba was part of the network of kingdoms used by the Romans in the early part of Cilicia's provincial history. It was annexed in 72 C.E. by Vespasian, who renamed the main city of Olba (or Olbia) as Diocaesarea.

Ollius, T. (fl. mid-first century C.E.) *Father of Sabina Poppaea*

A friend and client of the PREFECT OF THE PRAETORIAN GUARD, Sejanus, Ollius held the office of QUAESTOR. He was a victim of that association, dying before he could attain higher office. For that reason Poppaea assumed the name of her grandfather, rather than of her father.

Olybrius (d. 472 C.E.) *Emperor of the West in 472 C.E. and descendant of the noble house of the Anicii*

Olybrius added to his political potential by marrying Placidia, the daughter of Valentinian III. At the same time he was connected to the family of Geiseric, king of the Vandals in Africa, for Placidia's sister Eudocia had wed Geiseric's son Huneric. Geiseric thus favored Olybrius as a possible ruler of the Western Empire. Leo I, at Constantinople, did not trust Olybrius at all.

In an attempt to have Olybrius murdered, Leo sent him to Rome where Emperor Anthemius was feuding bitterly with the MAGISTER MILITUM RICIMER. According to the writer John Malalas, Leo wrote to Anthemius to have Olybrius put to death. Unfortunately, Ricimer learned of the plot and elevated Olybrius to the throne. Anthemius was beheaded in July 472. Leo refused to recognize the claims of Olybrius but did not take any action at first. Ricimer died, followed by Olybrius in November, supposedly of dropsy.

Olybrius, Quintus Clodius Hermogenianus (fourth century C.E.) *Praetorian prefect of various parts of the Roman Empire from 378 to 379*

Olybrius was a Christian and a member of the noble family of the Anicii. He became governor in Campania and then in Africa in 361 and held the urban prefectship from 369 to 370. It was during the reign of VALENS that Olybrius was promoted to the office of PRAETORIAN PREFECT of Illyricum, probably succeeding the influential Ausonius. Emperor GRATIAN, in 379, transferred him to the prefectship of the Orient. Although he was reputedly cruel and hard, Gratian appreciated his military abilities.

Olympiodorus of Thebes (d. after 425 C.E.) *Egyptian historian from the city of Thebes*

Although few of the details of his life have survived, Olympiodorus was known as a poet and journeyer, and was sent in 412 to deal diplomatically with the Hunnic chief Donatus. In all probability he then traveled to the West, as his extant history was centered on the events befalling the western provinces. This work, recording the years 407–425, served as a source for such subsequent chroniclers as Sozomen and Zosimus.

Oppian (fl. late second century C.E.) *Poet*

Oppian's authorship of Greek hexameter poems has been the subject of considerable debate. One or perhaps both of his poems, *Cynegetica* and *Halieutica,* were written either by Oppian of Cilicia or by a namesake from Syria. *Halieutica* was on fishing, while the *Cynegetica* was on hunting, and supposedly was so pleasing to Emperor Caracalla that he awarded the poet one gold piece for every verse.

Oppius, Gaius (fl. mid-first century B.C.E.) *One of the closest friends of Julius Caesar*

With Cornelius Balbus, Oppius managed Caesar's personal affairs. After the dictator's assassination in 44 B.C.E., he joined the cause of Octavian (AUGUSTUS). Oppius came from the Equestrians (EQUITES) and probably had a role in the completion of Caesar's writings on his many campaigns. Books that Oppius wrote included biographies of Caesar, mentioned by Plutarch and Suetonius, of Cassius, no doubt a hostile account, and of Scipio Africanus. For Octavian, and to clear the name of Caesar, Oppius also published a study denying that Ptolemy Caesar (Caesarion) had been the son of Caesar.

Ops (goddess of the harvest)

A Roman deity of fertility, creative forces, and earthly energies. Ops was the wife of the god Saturn, and her festival was held on two days, the *Opalia* on December 19 and the Opiconsivia on August 25. It was said that she could be invoked by sitting on the ground and touching the earth with the hand.

Orange *See* ARAUSIO.

oratory

One of the most important fields of study in Rome. The art of speaking with skill, manipulating the emotions of listeners, and attaining victory because of the logical sequence and delivery of words, was highly regarded by Roman society. Training to become proficient in oratory took many years. Similar to a doctor's medical education, a prospective speaker would attach himself to a noted orator, who would teach by example. Schools of oratory forced students to deliver speeches on matters of pure fiction; CICERO, in *Brutus,* detailed such a course of instruction.

During the Republic, oratory was more skilled and important than during the empire. As the historian Tacitus mentioned in his *Dialogue,* the cause for this may have been the need for a Republican politician to establish his career on the basis of his words, whereas in the empire one was more depended upon the goodwill of the occupant of the throne. Whatever the cause, from the time of Augustus onward, oratory suffered a decline in elegance. *Advocati,* or lawyers, still practiced for a time, but most of the great speeches were made by the emperors themselves, or were panegyrics by grateful courtiers or were made to propose changes in legislation. The last great orator in the Roman Empire was the fourth-century rhetorician, Libanius.

See also ADVOCATUS.

Orbiana, Barbia *See* BARBIA ORBIANA.

Orestes (d.c. 476 C.E.) *Magister militum, Patrician, and the father of Emperor Romulus Augustulus*

Orestes came originally from Pannonia, entering the service of Attila the Hun as a secretary. Using the influence of his position he achieved the patricianate under Julius NEPOS, who named Orestes a *magister militum* in 475. Deciding to usurp the throne for his son, Orestes gathered an army and marched on Ravenna, forcing Nepos to flee to Dalmatia. Romulus was thus given the purple, but his father soon encountered trouble with his German troops. The barbarians wished to settle permanently in Italy, a desire that Orestes opposed. Unwilling to accept such an answer, the Germans chose ODOACER as their king and attacked Orestes at Placentia, putting him to death.

Orgetorix (fl. first century C.E.) *Chieftain of the Helvetii; in 61 B.C.E.*

Orgetorix convinced his people that they should leave their territory in Helvetia to settle in the less populous regions of Gaul. Challenged for the authority of the Helvetii, he fled and soon committed suicide. Orgetorix was nevertheless responsible for the attempted migration of the Helvetians that resulted in their wholesale slaughter by Julius CAESAR.

Oribasius (c. 320–400 C.E.) *Famous and influential writer and physician*

Oribasius came from Pergamum and studied medicine at Alexandria. Among his instructors was Zeno of Cyprus.

After practicing in Asia Minor, he entered the service of Julian the Apostate. As Julian's private physician, Oribasius accompanied him to Gaul in 355, and as a friend and fellow pagan, he was a participant in the movement to have Julian elevated to the throne in 361. Holding a place of high honor in Julian's reign, Oribasius continued to act as the imperial physician. He was with Julian during the Persian campaign in 363, and when the ruler died in that same year he was at his bedside. There followed a period of banishment and disgrace, but Oribasius was eventually recalled by Emperor Valens, who restored his lost property and status. He resumed his practice, married a wealthy woman, had four children, and died sometime around 400.

As a writer, Oribasius authored works on both MEDICINE and his friend Julian. Among his extensive medical books were a non-extant examination of Galen, and the *collectiones medicae,* a vast array of writings by medical specialists through the ages; 25 books from the *collectiones* have survived, while fragments of the others were preserved in such volumes as the *Synopsis ad Eustathium, Ad Eunapium,* and Oribasius's own epitomes. Most of his literary effort was at the request of Julian, and for Eunapius he composed an account of Julian's Persian campaign.

Oriens Diocese created by the reforms of Emperor Diocletian; it included Egypt and most of the East. The provinces included in Oriens were: Pamphylia, Isauria, Cilicia, Mesopotamia, Coele-Syria, Phoenice, Libanensis, Palaestina, Aegyptos, Herculia, Arabia, Thebais, Aegyptus Iovia, Libya Superior, Libya Inferior, and Cyprus.

Origen (Origenes Adamantius) (c. 185–254 C.E.)
Influential teacher, theologian, exegete, and writer
Origen was born probably in Egypt, perhaps Alexandria, to Christian parents. His father, St. Leonidas, taught him the faith and made him memorize passages from the Scriptures. Further education came under the famed teacher Clement of Alexandria, head of the Catechetical School of Alexandria. Around the time of his father's death, who was martyred around 202, Origen succeeded Clement as director of the school, since Clement had been forced into exile by the Romans. He remained in the post for some 20 years, even after the end of the persecution. He taught philosophy, Scripture, and theology but at the same time improved his own knowledge of pagan philosophy by attending lectures by the noted philosopher Ammonius Saccas, founder of the school of Neoplatonism. Origen also adopted a strict asceticism, castrating himself in an extreme interpretation of a passage in Matthew (19:12).

In 212, he traveled to Rome and then to various places in Greece, Palestine, and Arabia. While in Palestine, Origen was invited by several local bishops to preach in their churches. Origen accepted their request, despite being a layman, an action that angered Bishop St. Demetrius of Alexandria, who ordered him to return to Alexandria. On another visit to Palestine around 230, he was ordained a priest by the bishops of Jerusalem and Caesarea. Demetrius, even more angry and feeling that his rights had been violated, held two synods. Origen was exiled from Alexandria and commanded not to exercise his priestly duties. Given sanctuary at Caesarea, he opened another school in 231 and added to his already considerable reputation through his writing and instruction. Sometime in 250, however, he was arrested during the Decian persecution. Imprisoned and tortured, he was shattered physically and never recovered his health after his release in 251. He died a few years later at Tyre.

Origen was the author of a vast corpus of writings. Unfortunately, few of his works have survived, extant mostly in fragments or generally unreliable Latin translations from the original Greek. His scriptural writings include numerous commentaries of the Old and New Testaments and the *Hexapla* (or sixfold Bible), which was used by St. Jerome in his creation of the Vulgate, the Latin translation of the Bible used by the Roman Catholic Church. Other works are *Contra Celsum* (Against Celsus), an apology against the pagan cynic Celsus; *Exhortation to Martyrdom,* a plea to his friends to remain firm in the faith during the persecutions; and perhaps his most important book, *First Principles* (c. 225), an effort to compile a comprehensive manual on dogmatic theology, one of the first in the history of the Christian Church. It is known today only in two Greek fragments and an unreliable Latin version translated by Tyrannius Rufinus (d. 410). This manual became the focus of the Origenist controversy.

Origen was accused by St. Jerome and others of certain heretical tendencies. Others defended him, however, and the majority of the Eastern bishops considered him a defender of the faith. His name nevertheless became attached to a doctrinal system, Origenism, incorporating various unorthodox elements of his teaching. Widely read in the years after his death, Origen attracted many adherents who propagated some of his more adventurous theological speculations (including his notions on the pre-existence of souls), ultimately causing the Origenist controversy of the fourth century. The chief enemy of Origenism was St. Jerome, who helped secure the condemnation of Origen's radical teachings by Pope Anastasius I in 400. Elements of Origenism endured into the sixth century.

Origenes (fl. third century C.E.) A third-century Neoplatonic philosopher often confused with the Christian theologian ORIGEN. Both Origen and Origenes were students of Ammonius Saccas in Alexandria, but Origen died in 254, while Origenes continued writing for many years. He authored two works on NEOPLATONISM in Greek.

ornamenta Two kinds of special rank conferred upon praiseworthy individuals. *Ornamenta* were presented to victorious generals by the grateful people of Rome. (Only emperors could receive the TRIUMPH.) *Ornamenta* were also insignias of status given by the emperor, with the consent of the Senate to indicate a position in the magisterial system of Rome. These *ornamenta* could include the offices of AEDILE, QUAESTOR, and PRAETOR, as well as others.

Orodes II (d. 38 B.C.E.) *King of the Parthian Empire from around 57 to 56 and 55 to 38 B.C.E.*

Orodes was the son of Phraates III and brother of Mithridates III. In 57 he and his brother murdered their father, and Orodes, being older than Mithridates, became the ruler of Parthia. Mithridates then instigated a coup and seized power. Orodes gained the aid of the gifted General SURENAS and recaptured the throne. His brother fled to the Romans, but returned to Parthia and attempted a counterrevolution. Mithridates's failure culminated in 54 with his being trapped at Seleucia and eventually murdered.

Despite having attained total domination of the Parthian Empire, Orodes was seen by the triumvir Marcus Licinius CRASSUS (1) as an easy conquest. Thus, in 53, Crassus embarked upon his doomed Parthian Campaign. While Orodes made war on Armenia, the defense of Mesopotamia was entrusted to Surenas. Crassus was annihilated at the battle of Carrhae, as Orodes took credit for the worst defeat ever inflicted upon the Roman legions to that time. To complete his triumph, and at the same time to remove any potential rivals, Orodes executed Surenas.

Over the next years of his reign, Orodes came to rely upon one of his sons, Pacorus, as his most trusted lieutenant. The prince was entrusted with most of the Parthian operations against Rome, including the disastrous battle in 38 in which Pacorus was slain. The loss of this son broke Orodes's heart. A short time later, Phraates IV, another son, murdered him and took the kingdom as his own.

See also ARSACID DYNASTY.

Orodes III (d. 7 C.E.) *King of Parthia from around 4 or 6 to 7 C.E. and a particularly unpopular ruler*

A member of the royal household, Orodes murdered King PHRAATACES and took the throne, but his reign lasted only a few years. A court intrigue arranged his murder. Orodes was known to be cruel, tyrannical, and paranoid in his relationships.

See also ARSACID DYNASTY.

Oroses (d. 122 C.E.) *King of Parthia from around 110 to 122 C.E.*

Oroses's reign was marked by a terrible civil disorder among the local vassals and by the crushing defeat inflicted upon him by Emperor Trajan. From the start, Oroses attempted to oppose the supremacy of Rome in the East. Shortly after his accession (c. 110) he replaced the new monarch of Armenia, Axidares, with another claimant, Parthamasiris. As Axidares had the support of Rome, Trajan viewed this action as an invitation to war and in 313 embarked upon a massive campaign against Parthia. In a brilliantly waged series of operations, Trajan crushed Oroses's armies, pushed deep into his realm and captured CTESIPHON, his capital. Having lost the city, his actual throne and his daughter, Oroses had little strength to oppose Trajan's direct annexation of Armenia and Mesopotamia.

Oroses was handicapped severely in his struggle with Trajan by serious troubles in his own client states. Satrapies all over the Parthian Empire challenged his direct authority, contributing to his failure against the Romans, while occupying his remaining years with alarms and the need for suppressive measures, thus depriving him of the ability to mount a counterattack against Trajan.

See ARSACID DYNASTY.

Orosius, Paulus (fl. fifth century C.E.) *Christian historian and opponent of Paganism*

Orosius came from Spain, perhaps Tarraco. An ardent Christian, he served as presbyter in Lusitania before fleeing to Africa to escape the invasion of the Vandals (c. 410). This journey to Africa brought him into contact with St. AUGUSTINE, who became a major influence on Orosius, prompting him to join in the fight for Christian orthodoxy and to compose his large history of Christianity. Orosius wrote two treatises against the heretical church movements of Pelagianism and Priscillianism. Far more important was his *Historiae adversus Paganos* (History against the pagans). In this polemic, Orosius chronicled the evolution of Christianity from Adam to 417 C.E., missing no opportunity to ridicule and condemn all forms of paganism. He used as his sources Eusebius, Livy, the Old and New Testaments, Tacitus and others, although the number of references was not as great as he claimed. The hand of Augustine was evident in all of the passages, an association that lent both Orosius and his work an undeserved credence.

See also PELAGIUS; PRISCILLIAN.

Osiris
Egyptian god of the dead and one of the most prominent deities of the ancient Egyptian pantheon. Like his divine wife, the goddess Isis, Osiris fascinated both the Greeks and the Romans and developed a considerable cult following.

See also RELIGION.

Osroene
A strategically vital state situated in northern Mesopotamia, near Syria and Armenia. Osroene (also,

Osrhoene) began as a small kingdom sometime in the second century B.C.E. but fell under the domination of the Parthians. It was included in the list of Parthian vassals and served as a defensive buttress against Rome from the first century C.E. As Rome and Parthia (and later Persia) struggled for regional supremacy, Osroene became a battleground, especially its strong fortress-capital of Edessa. The status of the realm changed late in the third century C.E. after the victories of Lucius Verus and Avidius Cassius. Henceforth Osroene was answerable to Rome, falling under attack in the third century and again at a later time by the Persians.

Ostia The port of Rome, situated at the mouth of the Tiber some 16 miles from the Eternal City. For many centuries Ostia protected the western shore of the Tiber and served as a gateway for vital grain supplies for Rome. Ostia was probably founded as a defensive maritime colony by Ancus Marcius, sometime in the fourth century B.C.E. As the Gallic tribes still ravaged the Italian coast and Greek fleets threatened, a *colonia* at the mouth of the Tiber was essential (*see* COLONIES). Throughout the succeeding years Ostia's value increased as a naval base, in the Punic Wars with Carthage and as a commercial center for the arrival of goods from Spain. Early in the first century B.C.E., in the struggle between Marius and Sulla, the Marians captured and pillaged the town. Sulla put up new walls around all of Ostia.

By the start of the Roman Empire, problems had developed in the harbor. The natural port of the river was now inadequate, too much shipping crowded the harbor and silt was developing. Julius Caesar had hoped to create a better harbor but did not live long enough to complete the project. Augustus (ruled 27 B.C.E.–14 C.E.) improved the city with numerous constructions, and Gaius Caligula (ruled 37–41 C.E.) built a proper aqueduct. It was Claudius who desired a great harbor. Despite the opposition of his advisers, the emperor, in 42 C.E., sponsored a massive engineering project three miles northwest of Ostia—a canal connecting the new harbor to the Tiber and then to the city. Two moles with an ingenious lighthouse marked the dimensions of the new port facilities. Claudius's vision was not matched by reality, for the harbor proved insufficient and unsafe. A storm in 62 destroyed 200 important corn ships while they were in dock. Puteoli remained the harbor of choice for captains.

Trajan (rule 98–117 C.E.) made extensive changes in the Ostian harbor, building a hexagonal foundation within the old site and ensuring the erection of other structures both inside and on the perimeters. The names Portus Romanus, Portus Augusti, and finally *Portus* were used for the port town. Ostia, meanwhile, profited handsomely from the new efforts, as the entire city was rebuilt and expanded. In the reign of Hadrian even more changes took place. Large granaries were established, as were markets, a barracks for a detachment of VIGILES, and the

sumptuous Baths of Neptune. There were eventually 18 baths. As many families moved to Ostia, *insulae* became quite common, replacing the DOMUS as the principal form of housing.

Ostia's greatest prosperity came in the age of the Antonines (late second century C.E.). Puteoli had faded as the favorite harbor, and vast amounts of goods entered Rome from Ostia as a result. However, soon after the zenith came the decline. After the restorative initiatives of the Severans, Ostia began to slip in proportion to the increasing economic chaos of the Roman Empire. Most of the workers moved away, especially to Portus. That competing site first received independence from Ostia and then, in 314, was granted Ostia's old municipal rights.

Religiously, Ostia enjoyed the patronage of Vulcan but also attracted Mithras, Isis and, in the early third century, Christianity. Not even the presence of a bishop, however, could prevent the steady deterioration of the city. By the fifth century it was utterly defenseless, and after a time the surrounding region was contaminated with malaria. In 1938, a massive archaeological program was launched. Most of the old Ostia was excavated, and work is ongoing in other sections. Ostia, even more than Pompeii, was a reflection of Rome's style and tastes. Thus it is invaluable from a historical perspective.

Ostrogoths The GOTHS who penetrated into the Roman Empire in the third century eventually split into two groups, the VISIGOTHS (the Western Goths) and the Ostrogoths (the Eastern Goths). Their destinies, though at times parallel, were from the fourth century quite distinct. The Ostrogoths faded from the Roman view for much of the fourth century, as they focused their attentions on carving out a vast empire from the Don River to the Dniester, and from the Black Sea to the inner stretches of the Ukraine. This was their land, ruled by a king and his organized nobility. The greatest Ostrogoth king was Ermanarich, who routed all competing tribes.

Around 370 C.E., however, there descended upon the West the scourge of the HUNS. The Ostrogoths kept them at bay at first, but were eventually annihilated in battle. Ermanarich fell, and the Ostrogoths surrendered, one of the largest of the Western nations to submit to the Huns. Large numbers of them, under Alatheus and Saphrax, requested permission from Emperor Valens around 377 to settle in the Danubian region, which was free of Hunnic domination. They were refused but crossed the Danube anyway. Both kings joined with the Gothic chief, Fritigern, in Valens's destruction at the battle of ADRIANOPLE in 378. Having achieved total victory over the Romans, the Ostrogoths joined with the Alans in a massive invasion of PANNONIA. Gratian, recognizing the slaughter that would be necessary to subdue the barbarians, allowed them to settle in MOESIA Superior and Pannonia. There they remained, falling under the control of the Huns once more (c. 477) as Attila ravaged the

Danube. In 454 they no doubt shared in the defeat of the Huns at the battle of NEDAO. Subsequently, the Ostrogoths were a dangerous force waiting for a gifted leader. He came in the person of Theodoric the Great.

Otho, Lucius Salvius Titianus (fl. first century C.E.)
Brother of Emperor Otho
Lucius Otho proved more of a hindrance to the Othonian cause in 69 C.E. than a support. Lucius remained in Rome when Otho marched against VITELLIUS in northern Italy. Facing a crisis, Otho sent for him in early April and appointed him a general. With the PREFECT OF THE PRAETORIAN GUARD, Licinius PROCULUS, Lucius ill-advisedly supported an immediate engagement with the Vitellian legions. The resulting battle of BEDRIACUM was a disaster, and the emperor was forced to commit suicide. Lucius was pardoned by Vitellius for what the historian Tacitus called his love of his brother, and his incompetence.

Otho, Marcus Salvius (32–69 C.E.) *Emperor from January 15 to April 16, 69 C.E.*
Otho was born to a family of relative newcomers to political power, elevated to the Equestrian class by Augustus and to the Patrician class by Claudius. He early on acquired a reputation for wildness, using an affair with one of the courtiers of Nero to insinuate himself into a position of favor with that emperor, sharing in Nero's orgies and eccentricities. The two divided as Otho fell in love with POPPAEA, whom he eventually married. Nero, too, fell under her spell and in 58, desiring to take her as his mistress, the ruler gave Otho the governorship of Hispania Lusitania. Poppaea did not accompany her husband to his new post, their marriage was annulled and Nero made her his empress in 62. Three years later he kicked her to death. Otho never forgave him for this, mourning the loss of Poppaea for the rest of his life.

As head of Lusitania, Otho displayed surprising moderation and common sense. In 68, he joined the cause of the imperial claimant GALBA, traveling with him to Rome. Once there he helped to win the support of the Roman establishment, while currying favor with the PRAETORIAN GUARD. Considering himself Galba's heir, he was crushed and embittered by the naming of PISO LICINIANUS as heir. Using his long-time connections in the city, as well as his friends in the Guard, Otho headed the conspiracy that murdered Galba on January 15 and elevated him to the throne. Otho was accepted by the Senate as emperor, but word arrived that VITELLIUS, the governor of Germania Inferior, had revolted with the legions of the Rhine. Vitellius outnumbered Otho by many legions, despite the widespread support for the Othonian cause. Unwilling to wait for help, Otho launched a campaign against Vitellius, who was already marching on Italy. Sending Annius GALLUS and SPURINNA to the Po in March of 69, Otho remained in Rome. In the early stages of the campaign

the Othonians gained the advantage. Heeding the advice of his brother Lucius Titianus and the Praetorian Prefect Licinius Proculus, he gave battle at BEDRIACUM in the middle of April. He was routed and killed himself on April 16. Most historians, especially Tacitus, viewed him as a reprehensible and profligate figure. He was the second of four emperors in 69 C.E.

ovatio A minor kind of triumph given to a victorious general who, for whatever reason, could not claim a smashing defeat of an enemy. It mirrored a regular TRIUMPH or ORNAMENTA in every way except that the victor could not wear a laurel wreath or ride in a chariot. He wore myrtle and either walked or rode on horseback. The expense of the festivities was also smaller. Ovatios were accorded to Octavian (AUGUSTUS) and Marc ANTONY in 40 B.C.E., and Octavian received others in 36 and 20 B.C.E. DRUSUS the Elder received one in 11 B.C.E., and Aulus Plautius one in 47 C.E., while GAIUS CALIGULA refused an ovatio in 39 C.E.

Ovid (Publius Ovidius Naso) (43 B.C.E.–17/18 C.E.)
One of the best-known poets of Rome
Ovid was famed both for the fluency of his composition and his voluminous output. Born at Sulmo in the Apennines, the son of an Equestrian who desired that his offspring pursue a public career, Ovid received the finest education possible. At Rome Ovid was schooled in rhetoric and law, developing a preference for poetry. After finishing his studies at Athens he held posts in the *decemviri* and the *centumviri* but turned away from such a public life to become a poet. Unlike most of the poets of his time, Ovid was eminently successful. He was able to benefit from his reputation, frequenting the best social circles, and was an associate of such writers as TIBULLUS, PROPERTIUS, HORACE, and Cornelius GALLUS.

In 8 C.E., Ovid was mysteriously exiled. The cause of the banishment was never fully explained. He was at the height of his career, a fact that probably contributed to his exile. Ovid had written his *Ars Amatoria (Art of Love)* around 2 B.C.E., exactly the time of the departure from Rome of JULIA (3), Augustus's profligate daughter. A book on love would hardly have pleased Augustus at that time. Later, Ovid apparently committed some offense to the imperial family. In 8 C.E., while visiting Elba, the decree of Augustus reached him. He was to live out his life in Tomi, a small frontier community on the Black Sea, near Constanza in modern Rumania. From 9 until his death in 17 or 18 C.E., Ovid spent his life writing. He described his existence as harsh and primitive, even though people treated him with great kindness in exile. His pleas for forgiveness went unanswered by Augustus and TIBERIUS. Whether in exile or not, the sheer output of Ovid remained vast. He composed mainly in the elegiac style and was influenced by the Alexandrine school. As a poet he wrote with wit, appreciation of beauty, nature, and art, and integrated brilliantly his extensive learning into the chosen literary form. His works were:

Amores   love poetry, written in five books and published around 16 B.C.E.

Ars Amatoria (Art of Love)   in three books, one of his best and most popular works, which defined love as a field of study and research, with the poet acting as instructor. A crafted imitation of the study books of the times, especially the *Ars grammatica*; c. 2 B.C.E.

Epistulae Heroidum (Letters of the heroines)   15 fictitious letters from mythological heroines to their lovers who had abandoned them. Also called simply *Heroides* and very well received.

Remedia amoris (Cures for love)   an effort published after the *Ars* instructing readers how to escape the bonds of love; c. 1 C.E.

Metamorphoses   written in hexameter form. The *Metamorphoses*, composed of 15 books, was a compilation of individual stories, both Greek and Roman, showing the transformation from chaos to order, from the Creation until the time of Julius Caesar's elevation to divine status.

Tristia (Sadness)   letters, contained in five books, addressed to various persons and dating from 8 to 12 C.E. Ovid was able to write to a few individuals while in exile, such as Augustus, Livia and his stepdaughter Perilla, but most of the names were not included because they had to be protected from association with him. The whole is a powerful plea for justice.

Epistulae ex Ponto **(Letters from the Black Sea)**   more epistles in four books, this time from 12 to 13 C.E., sent openly. Like *Tristia*, the correspondence begged for help and pardon.

Fasti **(The calendar)**   an intriguing work on the Roman calendar, including data on legends, rituals and astronomical changes. Only six months of *Fasti* have survived.

Ibis   a curse laid upon someone who was acting against him in Rome. Composed at Tomi, the book was based on a similar poem by Callimachus.

Halieutica   only 130 hexameters have survived of Ovid's poem on fish. The work, based on the author's study of fish in the Black Sea, was known to PLINY THE ELDER.

Nux **(Nut tree)**   one of Ovid's later poems, *Nux* allegorically presented the pitiful plight of a tree subjected to abuse by passers-by, who throw stones.

The last two were perhaps not by Ovid. There were other minor works that were either lost completely or survived only as fragments in the creations of other writers.

Suggested Readings: Kennedy, Eberhard, ed. *Roman Poetry & Prose. Selections from Caesar, Virgil, Livy and Ovid*. Cambridge: University Press, 1959; Ovid. *Ovid in Love: Ovid's Amores*. Translated by Guy Lee. New York: St. Martin's Press, 2000; ———. *Fasti*. Book IV. Edited by Elaine Fantham. Cambridge, U.K.: Cambridge University Press, 1998; ———. *The Art of Love, and Other Poems*. Translated by J. H. Mozley. Cambridge, Mass.: Harvard University Press, 1979; ———. *Metamorphoses*. Book XIII. Edited by Neil Hopkinson. New York: Cambridge University Press, 2000; ———. *Ovid in English*. Edited by Christopher Martin. New York: Penguin Books, 1998; ———. *Ovid in Six Volumes*. Translated by Grant Showerman. Cambridge, Mass.: Harvard University Press, 1986–1988; ———. *The Love Poems*. Translated by A. D. Melville. Oxford: Oxford University Press, 1998; Taylor, A. B., ed. *Shakespeare's Ovid: The Metamorphoses in the Plays and Poems*. Cambridge, U.K.: Cambridge University Press, 2001.

The poet Ovid. *(Hulton/Getty Archive)*

P

Pacatianus, Titus Claudius Marinus (d.c. 249 C.E.)
Usurper in the reign of Philip the Arab (c. 248–249)
Probably of the senatorial class and an officer on the Danube frontier. Pacatianus lost the support of the legions in Moesia and Pannonia and was killed shortly after declaring himself.

Pacatus, Latinus Drepanius (fl. late fourth century)
One of the most gifted rhetoricians of the late empire
Like his friend and older colleague, Ausonius, Pacatus came from Gaul. He served as proconsul of Africa in 390 and as *comes rerum privatarum* under Theodosius I around 393. His panegyric on Theodosius, delivered before the Senate in Rome in 389, displayed a classical upbringing, a blend of Christianity and paganism, and a sense of legend and history.

Pachomius (d. 346 C.E.) *Egyptian saint and founder of Christian cenobitic, or communal, monasticism*
Born near Thebes, Egypt, Pachomius was raised a pagan and served in the Roman legions in North Africa. After leaving the legions in 313, he was converted to Christianity, withdrawing into the desert near Thebes. There he lived for a time as a disciple of the noted hermit Palemon (or Palaemon). He then established a community of monks on the Nile at Tabenissi, in the Thebaid, which soon attracted many followers. Pachomius drew up a rule for the monks that called for a life of work and prayer. It was the first such rule in the history of monasticism and was to prove so remarkable and flexible that by the time of his death Pachomius had founded more than 10 monasteries for both men and women. His rule, further, was to have a major influence on such innovators as St. Basil, St. Bene-

dict, and John Cassian. Pachomius is revered by the Eastern and Western Churches as well as by the Coptic Church.

Pacorus (d. 38 B.C.E.) *Son of King Orodes I of Parthia*
The prince displayed genuine talent in both politics and war and by 41 B.C.E. was probably the joint ruler of the domain, acting as general in all major Parthian operations. Quintus LABIENUS, son of the famed aide to Caesar, arrived in Parthia around 41 and persuaded Orodes to send an invasion force into Syria. Labienus and Pacorus were to direct the attack. Pacorus swept into southern Palestine, installed the claimant Antigonus on the Jewish throne and planned to make his occupation of Syria permanent. Marc Antony sent General P. Ventidius to the East, and he defeated Labienus and then campaigned against Pacorus. In 38, Pacorus assembled his army, attacking Ventidius on Mount Gindarus. The heavy cavalry, the cataphract, of Parthia fell before Rome's organized legions. Pacorus was killed in battle, and the Parthians retreated to the Euphrates. His death was a severe blow to Orodes, who died only a short time later, murdered by another son, Phraates IV.

Pacorus II (d. 114 C.E.) *King of Parthia from around 79 to 114*
Successor to his father, Vologases I, Pacorus may have removed the little-known Artabanus IV. The reign of Pacorus was notable for an increase in tensions between Parthia and Rome. Contact was probably established with the Dacian monarch, Decebalus, in the hopes of undermining influence both in the East and along the Danube. Pacorus certainly interfered with Roman policy in Arme-

nia. This intervention made war inevitable, although he did not live to see it. He was followed by his brother Oroses.

Paetina, Aelia *See* CLAUDIUS.

Paetus, Lucius Caesennius (fl. first century C.E.)
Consul in 61 C.E. and a disastrously incompetent legate
Paetus had the misfortune of having his faults made even more obvious by his brilliant savior, CORBULO (2). In 62, Nero appointed him the legate of Armenia, where he was to relieve Corbulo of some of his burdens. When, later in that year, the Parthians of Vologases I made trouble in Armenia, he gathered his available legions (the IV and XII) and set out at once. His marches were fruitless, his plans ill-conceived. Within months he was forced to retreat, abandoning the East to Corbulo, who completed Rome's dealings with Parthia. Upon Paetus's return to Rome, Nero told him that a pardon was immediately forthcoming, for any general so easily frightened would surely die from prolonged anxiety. Because of Paetus's experience in the Syrian provinces, Vespasian (c. 70) made him governor of Syria. In that capacity he conquered Commagene in 72/3, making it a Roman province. He thus made up for his terrible losses of the past.

paganism   Polytheism, the worship of more than one god, was the reigning form of worship in the ancient world, remaining so throughout the Republic and Roman Empire until its overthrow by CHRISTIANITY. For the Roman government, organized paganism was essential for two reasons: first, it helped to ensure the continued blessings, protection, and patronage of the gods for the empire. Second, it offered a means by which vast populations in the provinces could be brought under Rome's influence. Aside from the Roman IMPERIAL CULT, there were the very old Delphic Oracles and the gods and goddesses of the East, including Mithras, Isis, Osiris, and Asclepius. These other cults became part of what was known to Christendom as paganism.

Christianity presented a fundamental challenge to pagan beliefs. It called for a rejection of the old gods, preached views contrary to the designs of the imperial government and seemed to Roman officials to be antisocial. The bitter hatred evinced between pagans and Christians became so intense that reconciliation was impossible. When Christianity began to propagate, it faced more opposition from JUDAISM than from officials of the Roman state, who viewed the new cult as an offshoot of the Jewish religion. Slowly, paganism perceived the threat from Christian doctrines. There followed two centuries of varyingly intense persecutions and extermination programs, culminating in 3/2 C.E. in the EDICT OF MILAN, granting religious freedom in the empire. With CONSTANTINE THE GREAT and his champi-

oning of the cause of Christianity, the war of the faiths seemed over.

Constantine made a deliberate choice in Christianizing the Roman Empire. He refused, though, to destroy the pagans, as they had tried to do with the Christians in the past. Rather, he promoted the precepts of the Christian Church, making it preferable socially. As virtually the entire imperial establishment, from the farmers in the provinces to the governors and the Praetorian prefects was pagan, Constantine allowed time and the fanaticism of Christian leaders to do their work.

The few laws that had been passed during the reign of Constantine against pagan activities were followed and extended by his sons, especially CONSTANTIUS II. Sacrifices were stopped and, supposedly, all places of pagan worship were to be closed. Such laws, however, were often lamely enforced. Thus, when JULIAN THE APOSTATE reinstated paganism in 361, the old traditions were easily revived. JOVIAN ended this policy in 363, but the temples remained open.

In the second half of the fourth century, emperors such as Gratian, Valentinian II and especially Theodosius the Great acted with ruthlessness in the suppression of the temporal trappings of paganism. Gratian stopped using the title PONTIFEX MAXIMUS (senior priest of Roman religion), ceased subsidies to the Roman cults and dramatically decreed that the pagan statue of VICTORY be removed from the Senate. The appeal to Valentinian II to restore it was defeated by the formidable AMBROSE, bishop of Milan. SYMMACHUS, the gifted orator and philosopher who delivered the appeal, emerged as the foremost spokesman for the old ways. Theodosius then appointed CYNEGIUS, his Praetorian prefect of the East, with the task of closing any temple where sacrifices had been made. This decision inflamed clerics and Christians throughout the East to root out all symbols of paganism. In Alexandria, for instance the famed Serapeum was ruined by a group of monks under the patriarch of Alexandria, THEOPHILUS, in 389 or 391. At the prodding of Ambrose, Theodosius, in 391–392, passed harsh and far-reaching laws aimed at ending organized paganism entirely. It was treasonous to make sacrifices of any kind, all idols were removed and fines were levied on all temple visitations.

The final gasp of large-scale paganism came in 392, when the usurper EUGENIUS, supported by the *MAGISTER MILITUM* ARBOGAST, declared that the old gods were to be worshiped once more. Victory was returned to the Senate house and, with the banners of Hercules leading the way, Eugenius and Arbogast set off in 394 to battle with Theodosius. On September 5–6, 394, the cause of paganism was destroyed at FRIGIDUS. Theodosius instructed the Senate to have Victory removed once more.

Over the next century the Oracle at Delphi was closed, Mysteries of all kinds were ended and pagan temples often converted into Christian buildings. Some pagan movements were more easily absorbed into the

Christian community, especially NEOPLATONISM, while paganism lingered for many years in secret.

See also DIOCLETIAN; GODS AND GODDESSES OF ROME; MAGIC; NEO-PYTHAGOREANISM; PHILOSOPHY; PRIESTHOOD; RELIGION.

Suggested Readings: Benko, Stephen. *Pagan Rome and the Early Christians.* Bloomington: Indiana University Press, 1984; Dowden, Ken. *Religion and the Romans.* London: Bristol Classical Press, 1995; Dumézil, Georges. *Archaic Roman Religion.* Translated by Philip Krapp. Baltimore: Johns Hopkins University Press, 1996; Ferguson, John. *Greek and Roman Religion: A Source Book.* Park Ridge, N.J.: Noyes Press, 1980; ———. *The Religions of the Roman Empire.* Ithaca, N.Y.: Cornell University Press, 1982; Fishwick, Duncan. *The Imperial Cult in the Latin West: Studies in the Ruler Cult of the Western Provinces of the Roman Empire.* New York: E. J. Brill, 1987; Fox, Robin Lane. *Pagans and Christians.* San Francisco: Harper & Row, 1988; Glover, T. R. *The Conflict of Religions in the Early Roman Empire.* Boston: Beacon Press, 1960; Henig, Martin and Anthony King, eds. *Pagan Gods and Shrines of the Roman Empire.* Oxford, U.K.: Oxford University Committee for Archaeology, Institute of Archaeology, 1986; ———. *Religion in Roman Britain.* New York: St. Martin's Press, 1984; Liebeschuetz, J. H. W. G. *Continuity and Change in Roman Religion.* New York: Oxford University Press, 1979; Henig, Martin, and Anthony King, eds. *Pagan Gods and Shrines of the Roman Empire.* Oxford, U.K.: Oxford University Committee for Archaeology, Institute of Archaeology, 1986; Lyttelton, Margaret, and Werner Forman. *The Romans, Their Gods and Their Beliefs.* London: Orbis, 1984; MacMullen, Ramsay. *Paganism in the Roman Empire.* New Haven, Conn.: Yale University Press, 1981; North, J. A. *Roman Religion.* Oxford, U.K.: Oxford University Press, 2000; Smith, John Holland. *The Death of Classical Paganism.* New York: Scribner, 1976; Turcan, Robert. *The Cults of the Roman Empire.* Translated by Antonia Nevill. Cambridge, Mass.: Blackwell, 1996; Wardman, Alan. *Religion and State-craft Among the Romans.* Baltimore: Johns Hopkins University Press, 1982; Watson, Alan. *The State, Law, and Religion: Pagan Rome.* Athens: University of Georgia Press, 1992.

Palaemon, Quintus Remmius (fl. first century C.E.) *A teacher and writer*
Palaemon came originally from Vicenza to Rome, where he made for himself a very successful career as an instructor, claiming as his pupils such notables as QUINTILIAN and Persius. He was also the author of a (lost) study on grammar, *Ars grammatica.* Widely used in its day, the *Ars* became part of the works of the writers CHARISIUS and PLINY THE ELDER. Palaemon also included examples from Virgil and Horace.

Palaestina (Palestine) Name given by the Greeks and Romans to the entire region inhabited by the Jews. It

was a derivation of the Hebrew word for the Philistines, although the Roman term for the actual kingdom of the Jews was JUDAEA. Throughout the years of Rome's occupation of Palestine the region rarely ceased to be troublesome. As a result of the massive Jewish rebellion of 132–135 C.E., Hadrian changed the name of the province of Judaea to Syria-Palaestina, or just Palaestina. By the early fourth century, Palestine was one of the provinces of the diocese of the Oriens.

Palatine Hill *See* HILLS OF ROME.

Palatini The name generally applied to all members of the imperial court during the later years of the Roman Empire. The title *palatini* came to signify a special branch of the government as well. Palatini were agents of the *comites largitionum* and the *comes rei privatae,* who journeyed to the provinces to collect taxes. Their powers and influence increased during the fourth and fifth centuries C.E. to the extent that an attempt by Valentinian II in 440 to curtail their often extortionate activities met with total failure.

Pales A minor deity in the IMPERIAL CULT. Pales was the protector of flocks and shepherds. His festival, the Palilia, was held on April 21 of each year. Its staging and his worship were directed by the Flamen Palatualis.

See also FLAMENS; GODS AND GODDESSES OF ROME.

Palfurius Sura (fl. late first century C.E.) *An orator expelled from the Senate sometime during the reign of Vespasian*
Becoming a Stoic, Palfurius nevertheless retained his exceptional gifts for speechmaking and won the competition of Jupiter Capitolinus during the time of Emperor Domitian. The crowd called for his full pardon, but the emperor would not hear of it. Palfurius subsequently was feared as a dangerous *delator* (informer).

See also DELATORES.

Palladas (fl. fourth century C.E.) *Reviver of epigrammatic poetry*
A Greek schoolmaster living in Alexandria, Palladas was also a pagan and felt increasing pressure and hostility from the new, ascendant Christianity toward PAGANISM. He may have retired in the face of anti-pagan campaigns. As a poet he composed epigrams of intense bitterness. Many of his nearly 150 works were included in the *Greek Anthology.*

Palladius (c. 365–425 C.E.) *Bishop of Helenopolis and historian*
Palladius came probably from Galatia, becoming a monk in Egypt and Palestine. In 400 he was forced to leave Egypt by THEOPHILUS, patriarch of Alexandria, and

journey to Constantinople where the Christian leader JOHN CHRYSOSTOM made him bishop of Helenopolis in Bithynia. Palladius henceforth served as the greatest supporter of Chrysostom, traveling to Italy in 405 for him and accepting exile to Egypt for continuing to back the patriarch. For six years Palladius remained in Egypt, using the time to write his *Dialogus de Vita S. Joannis Chrysostomi (Dialogue on the Life of John Chrysostom)*, a defense of his friend. Allowed to return to Asia Minor in 412, he began work (c. 419) on his famous Lausiac History. Dedicated to Lausus, chamberlain in the court of Theodosius II, the history was a detailed account of monasticism in the early fifth century, derived from experience and written with genuine sincerity. It was finished in 420.

Palladius, Rutilius Taurus Aemilianus (fl. late fourth and perhaps early fifth century C.E.) *Writer on agriculture*
Palladius probably came from Gaul but owned estates in Sardinia and Italy. Little has survived of his life, except that his knowledge of husbandry was vast. He was the author of an extensive treatise on agriculture, the *Opus agriculturae*. Written in 14 books, the work contained an introduction followed by 12 sections, one for each month of the year, and an appendix. Book 14 centered on trees and was dedicated to "Pasiphilus" in elegiac style. Palladius wrote in a very straightforward style, without pretension. Although relying upon years of personal experience, he also used as his sources Columella, Gargilius Martialis, and others.

Pallas, Marcus Antonius (d. 62 C.E.) *Influential freedman in the service of Antonia (1), her son Emperor Claudius, and his successor Nero*
Pallas was originally a member of Antonia's household and was so trusted that he carried her letter to Tiberius warning the emperor against the prefect SEJANUS and became a member of the court of Claudius, holding the position of A RATIONIBUS (financial minister). His position in the government increased greatly with his alliance with AGRIPPINA THE YOUNGER. Perhaps her lover, he advocated very strongly that Claudius marry her instead of the other candidates whom he was considering after the execution of Empress Messallina in 48 C.E. Once successful, he then supported the adoption of Nero to solidify the political base of both Agrippina and himself.

When Nero came to the throne, however, Pallas's fortunes took a downward turn. As was the case with his patroness, Pallas was slowly removed from places of power. Pallas was known to be arrogant and unpopular. In 52 C.E. the Senate gave him an ORNAMENTA and money, but he accepted only the honors. He possessed at the time some 300 million sesterces. Nero forced him to resign his post and, in 62, put him to death because of his vast riches. He was buried on the Via Tiburtina. FELIX, the procurator of Judaea, was his brother.

Palma Frontonianus, Aulus Cornelius (d. 117 C.E.)
Consul in 99 and 109 C.E. and governor of Syria under Emperor Trajan, starting in 105
Palma Frontonianus began the conquest of Arabia Petrae when he arrived in Syria. Using the VI Ferrata Legion, Palma easily subdued the entire region from around 105 to 106. Upon his return to Rome in 108, Trajan granted him a triumphal insignia, a statue in the Forum of Augustus and his second consulship, in 109. Considered very reliable by Trajan, Palma enjoyed imperial goodwill throughout the remainder of his reign. But he was an opponent of Hadrian, and when Trajan was succeeded by him in 117, Palma was put to death on the charge of conspiring to assassinate the emperor. Hadrian claimed to have no knowledge of the order of execution.

Palmyra   "City of Palm Trees," situated between Syria and Mesopotamia on an oasis in the Syrian Desert. According to legend, Solomon was the first to build a city there, calling it Tadmor. The Greeks translated the Aramaic into "Palmyra." From the second century B.C.E., Palmyra increasingly laid claim to the caravan trade between East and West, serving as an obvious resting place for traders. Using the resulting wealth, the Palmyrenes stretched their area of control throughout much of Syria. Roman interests were normally centered on the city's economic value, prompting an urge for political control. Marc Antony made a punitive expedition that proved only preparatory to the arrival of Germanicus in 17 C.E.

Henceforth, Palmyra was tied with Roman interests, especially against Parthia and, later, Persia. A Roman colony was established under Emperor Septimius Severus (ruled 193–211 C.E.), but a certain degree of autonomy was apparently allowed. Thus, the ruling family there emerged as major players in the defense of the Roman Empire in the third century C.E. Under King ODAENATH and Queen ZENOBIA, Palmyra came to rule a domain stretching from Syria to Egypt. This period of greatness was short-lived. Aurelian, in 273, crushed its armies and captured the city itself. Palmyra never recovered.

Culturally, Palmyra was a blend of Aramaic, Hellenic, and Parthian. Other influences inevitably left an impression, as there were caravans from Arabia, China, India, and the Roman world. Both in culture and in architecture the zenith of Palmyra came in the second century C.E., when Hadrian and the Antonines gave the metropolis their full support. Wealth also accumulated after 137 C.E., when duties were levied upon all imported goods. Most of the surviving buildings were constructed around that time and are impressive even after excavation. Most beautiful was the Temple of Bel, dating to the first century C.E. Other remains include columns, temples, arches, and colonnaded streets.

See also TRADE AND COMMERCE.

Pammachius (d. c. 409 C.E.) *Roman senator and friend of St. Jerome*
Following the death of his wife, Paulina, in 397, Pammachius, a devoted Christian, began to wear religious garb and embark on works of charity. Among his noteworthy acts were the construction of a hospice in Porto, at the mouth of the Tiber, in conjunction with St. Fabiola and the founding of the Church of Sts. John and Paul (although this may have been started by his father). St. Jerome dedicated a number of works to Pammachius. Pammachius, however, complained at times about Jerome's vituperative style, especially Jerome's book against Jovinian St. Augustine also thanked Pammachius for a letter to the Africans, in which he called upon them to oppose Donatism.

Pamphylia   *See* LYCIA-PAMPHYLIA.

Pamphylius of Caesarea (d. 309 C.E.) *Martyr and writer*
Pamphylius much admired ORIGEN and was highly respected by EUSEBIUS OF CAESAREA. Probably born in Berytus, Pamphylius studied at Alexandria and finally settled in Caesarea. There he was ordained a priest and established a noted school for the study of theology. Aside from his work copying the Scriptures, Pamphylius was devoted to transcribing and defending the works of Origen. Eusebius, for example, possessed numerous commentaries on Origen that had been compiled by Pamphylius; Pamphylius also composed an *Apology for Origen* in five books (Eusebius added a sixth volume). The *Apology* has only one book that is extant, in a Latin version made by Rufinus of Aquileia. The magnificent library collected by Pamphylius at Caesarea survived at least until the seventh century but was probably destroyed by the Muslims when they captured Caesarea in 638. Pamphylius himself, was arrested in 307 as part of the persecution of the Christian faith in the Roman Empire. He was martyred by beheading in February 309.

Pandateria   Tiny island just off the Campanian coast in the Bay of Naples. Now called Vandotena, Pandateria was the site of several banishments in the early years of the Roman Empire. In 2 B.C.E., Augustus exiled his infamous daughter JULIA (3) there, where she remained for five years. AGRIPPINA THE ELDER was also sent to Pandateria, as was OCTAVIA (2), daughter of Claudius and wife of Nero. Emperor Domitian used the island as a cruel residence for Flavia DOMITILLA (3).
   See also CAPRI.

panegyric   A laudatory address given in praise of the gods and the emperor; another means of flattering the ruler. The panegyric began in ancient Greece as a speech delivered to general assembly (a *panegyris*), such as the Olympic festival. Latin panegyrics possibly originated from the *laudatio funebris* (funeral eulogy) for famous persons. Another type of address was the *epitaphion* (funeral oration) for heroes or great figures.

   It became custom for newly elected consuls to deliver a public thanks (*gratiarum acto*) to the gods and the emperor. Emperor Augustus (ruled 27 B.C.E.–14 C.E.) required this oration through a *senatus consultum*. The foremost Roman panegyricist of the imperial age was PLINY THE YOUNGER whose nomination to the consulship by Emperor Trajan in 100 C.E. prompted a *gratiarum acto* that was preserved in the ancient collection of speeches, the *XII Panegyric Latini*. In the collection, Pliny was considered the model for subsequent orators. It was accepted practice from the third to the fifth century for panegyricists to flatter their imperial patrons. Other notable practitioners of the form were: Claudius Mamertinus, Nazarius, Ausonius, Ennodius, Pacatus, and Eumenius. During the second century C.E., the Greek Aelius Aristides delivered a panegyric on Emperor Marcus Aurelius.

Pannonia   One of Rome's most important provinces along the Danube, eventually divided into separate provinces: Inferior and Superior. The province linked the Danubian frontier with ILLYRICUM, and NORICUM with MOESIA. As was true of most of the lands on the Danube, Pannonia was the home of a varied people, including Celts and Thracians, but the main racial stock was Illyrian, especially in the east and in the south. Dio Cassius, a historian and a governor in Pannonia Superior, wrote that the inhabitants were very brave, bloodthirsty, and high spirited. Some scholars say their name was derived from the habit, peculiar to the region, of cutting up old clothes and sewing the strips together, with the resulting apparel called *pannus*, or patch.

   First Roman contact came in the late second century B.C.E., although long-term Roman policy did not include Pannonia until the time of Octavian (AUGUSTUS). In 35 B.C.E., he launched a punitive expedition against the Pannonians with the aim of subduing some of the local tribes, planting a Roman presence and giving necessary training to his troops in preparation for the inevitable war with Marc Antony. The sortie proved far more difficult than was imagined, and Octavian realized that any return would have to be in force. In 13 B.C.E., Marcus Vinicius was dispatched by Augustus to conquer Pannonia. He was joined in 12 by Marcus Agrippa, who was followed by Tiberius. The eventual emperor marched across the country, reducing the Pannonians tribe by tribe. An uprising in 11 was quickly suppressed, and the entire area seemed so under control by 8 that Tiberius departed, replaced by Sextus Appuleius. The calm was deceiving. Beginning in 6 C.E., three years of bitter fighting saw the Pannonians, under BATO, throw off their allegiances to Rome, setting much of Pannonia and Illyricum in flames. Tiberius returned with a slow, methodical, and highly successful strategy that brought all of the territory once more under the Roman standard. Initially it was planned to place Pannonia under the control of Illyricum, a view that was shattered by the rebellion. Thus, a new province was created to administer the Pannonian section of the Danube. A legate was in charge until the reign of Trajan (98–117 C.E.), when two provinces were decreed (circa 103), Pannonia Superior and Pannonia Inferior.

Throughout the first century C.E., Pannonia was subjected to rigorous Romanization, principally through the presence of the legions, their camps and the eventual surrounding communities, the *canabae*. Colonies of veterans were created to ensure the spread of the Latin language and culture. Typical of these frontier provinces, Pannonia assumed a dual nature. Near the more civilized Noricum, Illyricum and Italy, the degree of Romanization was more pronounced. Those wilder zones right on the Danube, where military life was harder and contact with the trans-Danubian barbarians unavoidable, were less Romanized. This dichotomy was largely solved by Emperor Hadrian (ruled 117–138 C.E.), who promoted such centers as Carnuntum and Aquincum to full municipal standing. Added wealth promoted increased participation in imperial life and affairs.

Economically, Pannonia was never particularly prosperous. With dense forests and harsh mountains, it could boast little agriculture. Grape quality was low, meaning its wines would not sell, and its only lucrative industry was in acquiring wild animals, boars, bison, and bears for the entertainers and circus organizers of Rome. Natural mineral production was another matter, for Pannonian mines produced iron and silver, but it was inferior to competitors' supplies from Moesia and Dacia. Pannonia, however, could boast the largest collection of legions in the entire theater. Strategically, the two provinces were at the crossroads of the Danube. Flowing past VINDOBONA, the mighty Danube turned abruptly south just north of Aquincum, pouring into the Drave River. Troops were needed to watch the entire border. The corridor between the Danube and the easterly Theiss River was a collecting place for barbarian peoples, including the IAZYGES.

PANNONIA SUPERIOR

The larger of the two Pannonian provinces, occupying the west from Carnuntum to Aquincum. Administratively, Pannonia Superior was better organized than its sister province, possessing at its capital the main seat of government for the legate, who was, realistically, the commander of Upper and Lower Pannonia. Carnuntum, his center, possessed theaters, an amphitheater, a basilica, and a forum.

PANNONIA INFERIOR

Smaller than Pannonia Superior, this province administered the river and its islands from, roughly, Aquincum (modern Budapest) to Moesia Superior. Fronting perpetually troubled parts of the trans-Danube, Pannonia Inferior was the starting point for elements of the Roman army in any major operation against the Dacians. One of its important cities was Sirmium.

Pansa Caetronianus, Gaius Vibius (d. 43 B.C.E.) *Consul in 43 B.C.E. and tribune in 51 B.C.E.*
During the civil war between Julius Caesar and Pompey, he joined the cause of the Caesareans (*see* CIVIL WAR, FIRST TRIUMVIRATE). After Caesar's assassination, however, he became one of the leading proponents for the return of the Republic, and was elected consul in 43, with HIRTIUS. The two took command of the senatorial legions, marching north to engage Marc Antony, now an enemy of the Senate. On April 14, 43 B.C.E., the two forces collided at the battle of FORUM GALLORUM. Although the Senate proved victorious, Pansa was wounded and died a few days later.

Pantaenus (d. c. 190 C.E.) *Christian theologian and the first known head of the catechetical school of Alexandria*
He probably came from Sicily but was a convert to Christianity, traveling extensively, perhaps even to India. Among his greatest students was CLEMENT OF ALEXANDRIA.

Pantheon   One of the greatest architectural achievements masterpieces in Roman history; Marcus Agrippa constructed the original Pantheon in 27 B.C.E., to serve as a temple to all of the gods of Rome. The site was in the CAMPUS MARTIUS, but it was decided at the start of Hadrian's reign (c. 117 C.E.) to replace it with a new and better edifice. The result was a vast improvement.

Under the guidance of Hadrian, the new Pantheon was built from 118 to 125, on the same site as that of Agrippa's old structure. As was the habit of Hadrian, he refused to lay claim to the Pantheon, preferring to have an inscription carved on the porch giving credit to Marcus Agrippa. Further repairs or minor adjustments were made by Septimius Severus and Caracalla in the early third century C.E. Agrippa's Pantheon would have fit very comfortably in the temple of Hadrian's time. The cupola's diameter measures the same as its height from the floor, forming half of a perfect sphere. Designed to reflect the few sources of light admitted to the building, the dome or rotunda was a marvel, the largest built by ancient methods. Made of solid concrete, the dome was originally covered with drawings, each being highlighted at various times of the day in the shifting light. Visitors' eyes were inevitably drawn upward to the circular aperture at the crown of the dome.

Ironically, the Pantheon survived only because it was perfectly suited to serve as a Christian church. Pope Boniface IV in 609 C.E. received it as a gift from a Byzantine emperor. Henceforth it was the Church of Santa Maria dei Martiri.

The interior of the Pantheon *(Hulton/Getty Archive)*

papacy The office of the bishops of ROME, the most important church office in the Christian world. Basing their claim to power upon the position of St. Peter, the bishops of Rome claimed supremacy over Christendom.

THE PAPACY (THE BISHOPS OF ROME) 64–483 C.E.

Bishop of Rome	Reign (Year C.E.)
Peter (Saint)	64 or 65
Linus (Saint)	67(?)
Anacletus (Saint)	76(?)
Clement I (Saint)	88
Evaristus (Saint)	97 or 99
Alexander I (Saint)	105 or 109
Sixtus I (Saint)	115 or 119
Telesphorus (Saint)	125(?)
Hyginus (Saint)	136 or 138
Pius I (Saint)	140 or 142
Anicetus (Saint)	155
Soter (Saint)	166(?)
Eleutherius (Saint)	175
Victor I (Saint)	189
Zephyrinus (Saint)	199
Calixtus I (Saint)	217(?)
Urban I (Saint)	222–230
Pontianus (Saint)	230–235
Anterus (Saint)	235–236
Fabian (Saint)	236–250
Cornelius (Saint)	251–253
Lucius I (Saint)	253–254
Stephen I (Saint)	254–257
Sixtus II (Saint)	257–258
Dionysius (Saint)	259–268
Felix I (Saint)	269–274
Eutychian (Saint)	275–283
Gaius (Saint)	283–296
Marcellinus (Saint)	296–304
See vacant	304–308
Marcellus I (Saint)	308–309
Eusebius (Saint)	309 (or 310)
Miltiades (Saint)	311–314
Sylvester I (Saint)	314–335
Mark (Saint)	336
Julius I (Saint)	337–352
Liberius(Saint)	352–366
Damasus I (Saint)	366–384
Siricius (Saint)	384–399
Anastasius I (Saint)	399–401

THE PAPACY (THE BISHOPS OF ROME)
64–483 C.E. (continued)

Innocent I (Saint)	401–417
Zosimus (Saint)	417–418
Boniface I (Saint)	418–422
Celestine I (Saint)	422–432
Sixtus III (Saint)	432–440
Leo I the Great (Saint)	440–461
Hilary (Saint)	461–468
Simplicius (Saint)	468–483

St. Peter, designated as the "Rock" upon which the church of Christ would be built, was martyred in Rome, which attracted the first Christian proselytizers, who viewed the city not only as the capital of the world but also as the core of organized PAGANISM. Just as the Christians adopted the organization of the Roman Empire in establishing their own hierarchy and internal structure, so did Rome emerge as their official headquarters. It was the seat of a bishop, a metropolitan (in control of the bishops of Italy) and the see for the bishop in charge of Italy itself. More important, by the second century C.E., it was considered a more powerful see than that of any other city in the world. Other sites of antiquity, such as ALEXANDRIA and JERUSALEM, even ANTIOCH, had suffered misfortune and decay. There thus existed practical and historical reasons for the supremacy of the see of Rome.

In the second century C.E., IRENAEUS, bishop of Lyon, argued for Rome's primacy in his defense of Christian orthodoxy. Councils throughout the fourth and fifth centuries confirmed the role that Rome would play in the Christianizing of the Roman Empire. The final steps were taken by a pope, whose legal mind and influence with the emperors ensured the aggrandizement of the papacy: LEO THE GREAT, who claimed the rights of St. Peter's heir. He stretched the outright authority of his see to encompass the entire West, gained further concessions from Emperor Valentinian III, and then achieved lasting fame for himself and his office by persuading Attila the Hun to depart from Rome.

Papak (d. before 208 C.E.) **(Pabhagh)** *Ruler of a small client state in the Parthian Empire during the first years of the third century C.E.*
Papak headed a minor kingdom in the province of Persis, while the real power in that region rested with Gochihr, a member of the Basrangi at Stakhr. Through the marriage of his father Sassan to a princess of Basrangi, Papak established a claim to the throne. He murdered Gochihr and became king of Persis. His two sons were SHAPUR and ARDASHIR. Upon Papak's death Shapur succeeded him, only to die himself in 208. Ardashir followed, conquering all of PARTHIA and establishing the SASSANID DYNASTY of PERSIA.

Paphlagonia Region of ASIA MINOR along the south shore of the BLACK SEA, bordering on Bithynia, Pontus, Phrygia, and Galatia. Traditionally a kingdom, Paphlagonia passed into Roman control around 1 C.E. and became attached to the province of Galatia. There followed the usual introduction of Roman colonists, and by the second century C.E. the long-standing capital of the region, Gangra, was replaced by Pompeiopolis. Built further north, just above the Amnias River, the new capital was not only more suited to the tastes of the Roman settlers but also was better situated to share in the extensive economic prosperity of the Black Sea. Paphlagonia was affected by the major reforms of Emperor Diocletian in the late third century C.E.) It was reorganized into an individual province and attached to the diocese of Pontus.

Papinian (Aemilius Papinianus) (c. 150–211 C.E.) *Jurist, prefect of the praetorian guard and a close adviser to Emperor Septimius Severus*
Papinian was an important legalist who left a lasting impression on Roman law. He was born in Syria, probably at Edessa, entering imperial service perhaps as the *magister libellorum,* or head of petitions. Working as a legal assistant to Marcus Aurelius's Praetorian prefects, Papinian made himself indispensable. By the time of Septimius Severus, he was greatly respected, and in 205, following the murder of the prefect Plautianus, the emperor named him one of his two new commanders for the Praetorian Guard. He thus became, as well, vice-president of the CONSILIUM PRINCIPIS and the preeminent legal expert in the court of Severus. Journeying with the emperor to Britain, Papinian was present when the aged emperor died in 211. Following the murder of Geta by his brother Caracalla, Papinian was dismissed from his posts by the new, sole ruler. One year later, Caracalla allowed the Praetorians to kill Papinian, commenting only that the actual killers should have used an axe instead of a sword.

Papinian was the author of many legal works. His most important were 37 books on *Quaestiones* and 19 books of *Responsa.* Justinian in the sixth century C.E. incorporated much of his output into his own collection. As a writer, Papinian was noted for his exactness of wording and his own remarkable fluidity of composition.

Papius Mutilus, Marcus (fl. early first century C.E.) *Consul in 9 C.E. with Quintus Poppaeus Secundus*
Papius Mutilus and Secundus were responsible for drafting the famed marriage law of Augustus, to which they lent their names; *lex Papia Poppaea (see* LEX*).* Ironically, both of them were unmarried and childless.

Parcae The Roman name for the three fates, who were Clotho, Lathesis, and Atropos. Clotho spun the fate, Lachesis chose one for each person, and Atropos determined the fate that no one could avoid.

Paris (fl. mid-first century) *Famous pantomime actor in the reign of Nero*
Paris was a freedman in the house of DOMITIA, Nero's aunt, who became a favorite of the emperor and would entertain him. In 55 C.E., hoping to use this position to destroy her enemy Agrippina, Domitia had Paris play a part in an elaborate plot to bring charges against the Augusta. Although the scheme failed and many were banished or executed, Paris was spared. Nero declared Paris free-born in 56, making it possible for him to demand the return of the sum paid to Domitia to end his slavery. Henceforth a free man, the actor remained in the good graces of Nero until 67. The emperor then asked to be instructed in the art of acting. When the monarch failed to master that craft, he ordered Paris put to death because his ability surpassed that of the emperor. *See also* THEATER.

Another actor of the same name achieved prominence in the late first century C.E. during the reign of Domitian (81–96 C.E.). Empress Domitia Longina fell in love with the performer, and Domitian murdered him in the middle of the street. When mourning Romans brought flowers to the spot, he ordered that they too should die.

Parthamasiris of Armenia (fl. second century C.E.)
Son of Pacorus II of Parthia and nephew of Pacorus's successor in 114 C.E., Oroses
Parthamasiris was nominated by Oroses to be the next ruler of ARMENIA, whose monarch, Exedares, had performed miserably and was, according to Oroses, a disappointment to both Rome and Parthia. Accordingly, Oroses deposed him and placed the diadem of Armenian sovereignty upon Parthamasiris's head. Emperor Trajan, however, had other plans for Armenia. Advancing with his army against Parthia, he received Parthamasiris, who hoped to retain his new throne. Trajan listened to his request but then rejected him, declaring that Armenia was now Rome's to govern. Parthamasiris was sent home to Parthia as Trajan embarked upon his war. The prince disappeared mysteriously on the way home.

Parthamaspates of Parthia (fl. early second century C.E.) *Son of the Parthian general Sanatruces*
A nobleman, Parthamaspates was probably a claimant to the Parthian throne during the war between Parthia and Trajan (c. 114–117 C.E.). According to the historian John Malalas, Parthamaspates was bribed by Trajan to desert his father in return for rewards. Accepting, the young man was made ruler of the Roman-backed government of Parthia, established in 116 at Ctesiphon by Trajan's decree. Parthamaspates was neither strong nor popular. He was rejected by his own people and fell from power in 117.

Parthenius (d. 97 C.E.) *Chamberlain of Domitian*
Called Satur or Saturinus by the historian Suetonius. Parthenius became a leader in the plot to murder the

emperor in 96 C.E. He was greatly favored by Domitian, who allowed him to wear a sword, perhaps in honor of Pathenius's experiences as a gladiator. It was Parthenius who sent in Stephanus to end Domitian's life, and he probably had a role in elevating Nerva to the throne. In 97, Parthenius was handed over for execution when the Praetorian Guard forced Emperor Nerva to have the conspirators in Domitian's assassination brought to justice.

Parthia   A small region of the East, southwest of the Caspian Sea and north of the Persian Gulf, that became an empire, stretching from Syria to India. The Parthians were actually a nomadic people called the Parni and were related to the fierce Dahae who had fought Alexander the Great. Like the Dahae, the Parni were at first subject to the Persians, later falling under the power of the Seleucids. Internal organization seemed to coalesce in the third century B.C.E., allowing them to strike out and seize vast stretches of land in PERSIA, at the expense of their Seleucid overlords. They came to occupy the region called Parthava or Parthia. Dating from 247 B.C.E., their kings established themselves as the heirs of the defunct Seleucids.

Parthia was an amalgam of territories and minor states, all beholden to the Arsacid dynasty, ruling from CTESIPHON and ECBATANA. Politically, the Arsacids drew their power from the noble families of the Pahlavi. The nobles, in turn, wielded administrative rights, such as the appointment of governors and contributions to the armies. In actual government, the Parthians relied upon the readily available system of the Seleucids, meaning that they were heavily influenced by the Greeks. Two councils made major decisions. The first was a board of advisers, the so-called Magi (from the ancient clan of Magus), and the other was composed of the nobility. Any new king of Parthia was chosen by them, a freedom of decision making that often resulted in the most qualified heir, not necessarily the oldest son, being crowned. This system was handicapped by corruption and internal decay, intrigues, murder, and ambition, all of which undermined the dynastic stability of the Arsacids. This deterioration was offset only temporarily by the rise of a fresh line, c. 10 C.E., from Atropatene.

It was a major but unavoidable flaw in the Parthian system that its nobles and vassals were allowed such a free hand in their own rule. The aristocracy, it was hoped, would always be reliable, but even the family of the Surens formed an eastern domain, the Indo-Parthian kingdom. To the south, furthermore, were to be found the kingdoms of the Characene, Elymais, and especially the Persis. The latter, under the Sassanids, were victorious in 226 C.E. over the weakened Parthians.

Culturally, the Parthians brought little to the throne aside from excellent military skills and a willingness to adopt facets of other social systems. Despite speaking the

Coins from the Parthian Empire *(Courtesy Warren Esty)*

Parthian Pahlavi dialect, the Arsacids relied upon Greek as a useful means of organizing the empire and connecting it to the outside world. Thus, councils, titles, literature, philosophy of rule, and bureaucracy were all Hellenic, though superficially, leaving them susceptible to foreign influences, both from the East and the West. Greek practices of warfare, such as the phalanx, bodies of infantry, or balanced attacks of foot and horse were abandoned in the face of the realities of Parthian strength and geographical necessities. The cavalry became the basis of the Parthian military might. They used the heavy cataphract, fast horse archers and other types of mailed horsemen. In their early wars with Rome, this strategy worked perfectly, as was obvious at CARRHAE against Crassus in 53 B.C.E. Wars with Roman legions, however, soon proved costly and disastrous. In war the Romans faced few equals, and Parthia could not match the financial and industrial resources of the Roman provinces.

Economically, the Parthians relied upon trade as their mainstay of expansion. They successfully moved the lines of communication from the Far East to the West through their lands. Caravans traveled from China and India across the Indo-Parthian kingdom to Ecbatana and then to distribution centers such as HATRA, DOURA, PETRA, and ANTIOCH.

While trade brought prosperity, the Parthians contributed few cultural innovations. They had brought their own gods with them, nurtured by their Magi; these deities, becoming eclipsed by Mazdaism, were adopted by the Arsacids as a popular gesture. Religious tolerance was an important policy of the Parthians, and in Persia the ancient faith of the Zoroastrians was still alive, waiting for the day when it could flower and return. Artistically there were perhaps three streams of influence in Parthia; the Hellenic, an Iranian style and the crude form prac-

ticed by the Parni nobles. Each made an impact on Parthian art.

Patavium Important town (present-day Padua) in northern Italy, situated above the Adige River, along the major traffic route from Mutina to Aquileia. Originally founded by colonists from the Venetii, under the Romans Patavium emerged as one of the most successful commercial centers in Italy. It was especially noted for its wool manufacturing and was a major factor in northern Italy's economic recovery in the late third century C.E. Patavium was also the birthplace of the writer LIVY.

Paternus, Tarrutenius (late second century C.E.) *Prefect of the praetorian guard from 180 to 182; was also a legalist, writer and general*
Paternus served as AB EPISTULIS LATINIS (secretary for Latin correspondence) under Emperor Marcus Aurelius, working as an envoy to the Cotini tribe in 169–170; around 179–180 he won a victory in the MARCOMMANIC WARS.

Praetorian prefect for Commodus during the first years of that emperor's reign, Paternus faced political opposition from his coprefect, Tigidius Perennis, appointed in 180. Perennis was victorious, for in 182 Commodus removed Paternus from his post, granting him the status of an ex-consul. A short time after that, however, Commodus charged him with participation in a conspiracy and put him to death. Paternus was the author of *De re militari,* a treatise on military laws used by Vegetius in the fourth century.

Pater Patriae "Father of the Country," an honor bestowed only upon the most important or worthy figures in Rome. Although the title carried no actual political power, it was of lasting prestige. Cicero, following the Catiline Affair in 63 B.C.E., was the first to be granted the name Pater Patriae by a grateful Senate. Subsequently it was given to some, but not to all, emperors. In 2 B.C.E., Augustus became Father of the Country in recognition of his role both as architect of the Roman Empire and heir to Julius Caesar, who had borne the rank himself. The coins of Augustus bore the inscription "CAESAR AUGUSTUS DIVI F. PATER PATRIAE." Unable to compete with his predecessor, Tiberius steadfastly refused the title. Emperors Gaius Caligula and Claudius initially declined but later accepted it. Nero followed their example. Other holders of the title were Vespasian, Nerva, Trajan, and Hadrian.

patria potestas Legal term denoting the rights and powers of the male head of Roman families. Such a head of household possessed all rights to oversee or examine the affairs of his sons and daughters and was able to banish them, send them to another family, even murder them (for just cause). When placed under the care of another *paterfamilias,* or head of a household, such offspring were considered real property, as were estates or slaves.

As autocratic as the *patria potestas* seemed, it was limited both by custom and, later, by imperial law. Cruel treatment or executions were generally determined by a family council. Further, the *patria potestas* could be ended at will by a father through *emancipatio,* or the granting of complete freedom to a son or an unmarried daughter. If a daughter married, she passed into the *familia* of her husband. Other means of breaking the power of a *patria potestas* were the joining of a priesthood, the Flamen Dialis or the sisterhood, the Vestal Virgins. The patria's power ended with his death. With the dawning of the Roman Empire, the arbitrary position of the Roman father was altered, as murder was considered unacceptable punishment. Nevertheless, some elements remained, such as exposure or the deliberate killing of a retarded child. Even this practice was declared illegal in 374 C.E., but continued.

See also MARRIAGE AND DIVORCE.

patriarch Within the Christian Church, the bishop who held special rights and powers by heading the most important sees or designated areas. It was inevitable that Christianity would evolve into a highly structured entity with a clear hierarchy. Existing within the Roman Empire and spreading universally, such an organization was not only convenient but logical. Just as the empire had major cities in the East and West, so did the church.

Initially, there were three patriarchs: at Rome in the West and at Antioch and Alexandria in the East. Rome's bishop had numerous titles, for he was the head of the diocese of Rome, chief prelate for Italy and leader of the Italian bishops. He was also the patriarch of the West and ultimately the pontiff of the entire Christian world (*see* PAPACY). As pontiff, he was above the patriarchs in the East but their equal as a patriarch. Nevertheless, his patriarchal authority was vast. The entire West, specifically the prefectures of Diocletian's provincial reform—Italy, Gaul, and Illyricum—were his domain.

Alexandria and Antioch divided the East (Diocletian's *Orientis*) between them. Egypt and Africa belonged to the patriarch of Alexandria, while Syria and later Asia Minor passed under the control of Antioch. This system was certified with the blessings of CONSTANTINE the Great at the Council of Nicaea in 325 C.E. None could foresee the changes that would take place over the succeeding years.

At the Council of Nicaea, the bishop of Jerusalem, officially under the bishop of Caesarea, was given a place of honor in recognition of Jerusalem's sacred status in Christian history. The see was still subject to Caesarea, but from then on the prelates of Jerusalem lobbied to have the city elevated to the rank of a patriarchy. For over a century they were unsuccessful, but then Juvenal of Jerusalem (422–458) used his political skills at the Council of Chalcedon in 451 to achieve his dream.

With the patriarch of Jerusalem was the patriarch of Constantinople. After Constantine built himself the grand New Rome at Byzantium, the bishop of Heraclea amassed increasing prestige. He not only served the religious needs of the Eastern Empires but also stretched his influence into Thrace and Asia Minor, at the expense of the Roman and Antioch patriarchies. Bitter feuding erupted as the popes worked to curb such a development. They were handicapped by the disorder of the West, however, and in 381 the Council of Constantinople took the important step of giving recognition to the bishop of Constantinople. In 451, at the Council of Chalcedon, Constantinople received its own patriarchal status with total jurisdiction over Asia Minor and Thrace. The popes refused to accept this development, remaining firm in their position until the 13th century.

Patricians The noble class of Rome, the *patricii,* formed the highest social stratum in the Republic and, until the third century C.E., in the Roman Empire. Their origins were obscure, although the name probably was derived from *pater* (father). By the fifth century B.C.E. they were the most important social class, wielding political power, shaping Rome's religious destiny and marrying only among themselves. By the end of the Republic, the Patricians were declining in prestige and numbers. Intermarriage was reducing the size of the class, and the emergence of greater opportunities for the Plebeians led many Patricians to renounce their status through the *transitio ad plebem.* So diminished had their ranks become that both Caesar and Augustus took steps to increase the size of the patricianate through the *lex Cassia* and the *lex Saenia* respectively.

In the fourth century, however, there was a rebirth of the term *patricius,* for Constantine used it as an honorary title, devoid of any governmental duties. It was bestowed very sparingly upon high officials of the state who had distinguished themselves. Later, only former consuls, prefects and members of the *magistri* were eligible. In the fifth century, barbarian holders of the rank MAGISTER MILITUM craved the hallowed position of Patrician as well. Despite the popularity of the rank, it was the rare magister who could hold on to total power while enjoying both, and some emperors tried to force their master of soldiers to retire after being inducted into the Patricianate. A few notable Patricians of the late Roman Empire were Ricimer, Orestes, Felix, and, ironically, Odoacer.

See also SOCIAL CLASSES.

Patricius (d. after 471 C.E.) *Son of the fifth-century magister militum Aspar*

Patricius played a part in his father's attempts to assume total control of the Eastern Empire. Emperor LEO I had promised Aspar to elevate Patricius to the rank of Caesar. Using the absence from Thrace of Leo's Isaurian lieutenant, Zeno, in 469–470. Aspar pressed the emperor to fulfill his promise. Opposition from the orthodox church in Constantinople was immediate, for Patricius was an Arian. The thought of him as a possible heir to the throne was to them horrifying. Their fears were increased a short time later when Patricius married Leo's youngest daughter, Leontia. By 471, Leo was ready to annihilate the entire family of Aspar. Zeno returned to Constantinople to orchestrate the murders. Aspar and his other son, Ardaburius, were slain by eunuchs, and Patricius was severely wounded. Surprisingly, he recovered but had his marriage to Leontia annulled.

Patrick (Patricius) (fl. early fourth century C.E.) *Popular saint, credited with the conversion of Ireland (Hibernia) in the fifth century C.E.*
Patrick is largely a legendary figure, known in direct historical documentation through only two sources: his *Confessio (Confession)*, a kind of autobiography composed in simple Latin, and *Epistola ad milites Corotici* (Letter to the soldiers of Coroticus), an address composed to a British chieftain to complain about the poor treatment of Irish captives. There is also a considerable body of legend and tradition.

Patrick was probably the son of a Christian decurion in Britain, born perhaps near modern Bristol. Leading a comfortable but religiously superficial life, he committed some unrevealed sin (by his own testament) that would come to hurt him politically in later years. At the age of 16, he was taken captive by Irish marauders, who were raiding into Britain, and was transported to Ireland. Sold into slavery, he worked for six years as a shepherd. During this period he was converted to a deep, spiritual Christianity and, after hearing a voice telling him to depart, he escaped to the Irish coast. There he secured passage aboard a ship, sailing away from captivity. After a number of largely unknown and highly debated adventures, Patrick returned home.

After spending some time back in Britain, Patrick had a dream in which a figure, Victoricus, delivered him a letter headed "The voice of the Irish." In the dream he heard the Irish calling to him, one version telling of his hearing the children of the Wood of Voclut; not just the living children but those of future generations. From this point, Patrick was utterly devoted to bringing Christianity to the Irish. Said by tradition to have been ordained by Germanus of Auxerre, Patrick was possibly considered a bishop when sent to Ireland to care for the small but growing Christian community there. It is conceivable that the sin of his youth forced the seniors who decided upon the appointment to choose another. This other was Palladius who had been sent to Britain a few years before to root out the heresy of PELAGIANISM. Palladius's mission lasted only one year (431–32). His untimely death resulted in Patrick's succession to the episcopacy. There was, perhaps, some concern among his

superiors as a result of Patrick's announced intentions: He planned not simply to act as bishop to the Christian community but to labor as a missionary. He expressed grave doubts about his fitness and his skills. In Ireland, however, he worked with zeal and a spiritual devotion to his cause. He enjoyed tremendous success in the field, bringing into the Christian fold many chieftains and kings, the class so crucial to Christianity's flourishing. His work was naturally fraught with danger, as many kings were openly hostile, one casting him into chains. The *Confessio* was penned as a defense of his work in the isle and as a defense against charges that he had sought the office of bishop purely for political and personal gain.

Patruinus, Valerius (d. 211 C.E.) *Co-prefect of the praetorian guard*
Patruinus served as prefect with Papinian and Laetus during the reign of Caracalla. In 211, he was murdered at the same time as Papinian by members of the Guard, and his body was dragged through the streets.

Paulina, Domitia (d. before 130 C.E.) *Sister of Emperor Hadrian*
Married to the consul SERVIANUS. Hadrian was ridiculed after her death, for he waited a long time before paying her honors.

Paulina, Pompeia (d. after 65 C.E.) *Wife of Seneca*
Paulina wished to join her husband in death when he was compelled by Emperor Nero to commit suicide in 65. Although Seneca dearly loved her, he had to agree to her request out of fear of the treatment that might be given to her after his death. They thus had their veins opened at the same time. Upon hearing of the attempt, Nero commanded that Paulina be saved. Her arms were wrapped, and she lived a number of years, serving as the caretaker of Seneca's memory. It was said that she never regained a robust natural coloring, remaining always pale.

Paulinus of Nola (Meropius Pontius Paulinus) (c. 353–431 C.E.) *Bishop of Nola and a Christian poet*
Born at Bordeaux to a wealthy senatorial family, his education was excellent, including a period of study under Ausonius. A long and successful career seemed before him. He was a consul in Rome in 378 and governor of Cisalpina in 381. It came as a surprise to his associates when, in 390, he was baptized by St. Delphinus in Bordeaux. With his wife Therasia, Paulinus adopted an ascetic way of life, giving away his fortune. In 394 he was ordained a priest and in 409 made bishop of Nola, a town in Campania. As a prelate he was in constant touch with some of the most notable Christian figures of his time, including AMBROSE, AUGUSTINE, and MARTIN OF TOURS. When not writing letters, Paulinus was composing

poetry. He excelled as a writer. For Emperor Theodosius I's victory over Eugenius in 394, he penned a panegyric and also wrote several pagan poetical epistles. Upon his conversion to Christianity he became a leading pet of Christendom, on a par with Prudentius. Most of his poems were devoted to the martyr Felix, while others dealt with psalms, prayers, and John the Baptist.

Paullus, Lucius Aemilius (d. 8 C.E.) *Consul in 1 C.E. and husband to Augustus's granddaughter, Julia (4)*
Both Paullus and his wife were disappointments to the emperor, he for engaging in a conspiracy against the throne, and she for following in the footsteps of her scandalous mother. In 8 C.E., Paullus was executed, and Julia was banished. Their daughter Lepida was thus unable to wed Claudius but did marry M. Silanus.

Paul of Samosata (fl. third century C.E.) *Bishop of Antioch in the middle of the third century and a noted heretic*
He came from Samosata and entered the service of Zenobia, queen of Palmyra, probably as a government official. Immensely wealthy, he was named to the see of Antioch around 260. As a bishop his views were greeted by Christian orthodoxy as heretical, most notably his support of Monarchianism, the belief that there was a unity of God, the Word, and Wisdom, and that Jesus Christ was truly human, in the tradition of the Hebrew prophets. At several synods in Antioch Paul was condemned but remained in power through the influence of Zenobia. Finally, in 268 or 270, he was forced to step down.

Paul of Tarsus (St. Paul) (d. 65–67 C.E.) *Apostle of the Gentiles and the figure largely responsible for bringing the Christian message to the Roman Empire*
Paul was born a Roman citizen at Tarsus in Cilicia, the son of a Jew belonging to the tribe of Benjamin. Known originally as Saul, he was educated thoroughly, learning Greek as well as Pharisaic Judaism, with a full appreciation of law and scripture. Being well learned, Paul opposed the Christian religion as a minor sect and assisted in the persecution of early Christians, most notably St. Stephen, who was stoned to death. Following his conversion on the road to Damascus, Paul was baptized by Ananias and traveled to Arabia, returning three years later to Damascus and then to Jerusalem. After initial doubts, he was accepted by Barnabas, emerging as the most eloquent speaker in the ranks of Christ's followers.

The next years were filled with his great journeys in Asia Minor, Macedonia, Cyprus, and Achaea. In each of these areas he found converts among the Gentiles but encountered stiff opposition from pagans, Jews, and Jewish converts to Christianity. The latter especially disagreed with the inclusion of uncircumcised Gentiles in the growing church. Paul's success in convincing St. Peter, St. James, and others at Jerusalem that the Gentiles were also entitled to salvation did much to ensure the widespread propagation of Christianity.

In many of his travels, terrible upheavals took place. At Jerusalem a mob nearly killed him, and only his Roman citizenship kept him from suffering torture at the hands of the Roman authorities. Inevitably, official action was taken by the Sanhedrin, the Jewish council, but through the brilliance of his legal mind he was able to defeat their accusations. An assassination plot compelled the local head of Rome's troops to send him to trial before the procurator, Felix, at Caesarea. This was probably around 57, but the proceedings were not begun until 59 and then under the new procurator, Festus. Again, using his status as a citizen of Rome, Paul appealed to Caesar. After meeting with Herod Agrippa, Paul set sail for Rome but was shipwrecked at Malta. Finally reaching the capital, he spent two years in confinement. After that the details in various sources become unclear. Traditionally, he made further expeditions to Spain and may even have returned to Ephesus, Macedonia, and Achaea. Arrested once more, Paul served as a demonstration of how seriously the Romans took the Christian sect at the time. Taken into custody near Troas, he was transferred to Rome and, between 65 and 67, beheaded in the Neronian persecution. His remains were buried on the road to Ostia.

Paul was instrumental in organizing the young Christian Church. Through his writings, preaching and strength of example, he elevated what could have been a minor and obscure sect of Judaism into a legitimate religious entity. Theologically, his letters and all preserved writings made possible the formulation of Christian intellectual tenets over the succeeding centuries.

Paulus, Julius (fl. third century C.E.) *Prefect of the praetorian guard under Emperor Severus Alexander and a leading jurist*
Like his eventual superior, PAPINIAN, Paulus was a student of the legalist Scaevola Cirvinius, becoming a lawyer and then an assistant to Papinian. He held a seat on the *consilium principis* of the rulers Severus and Caracalla, also serving as MAGISTER MEMORIAE. Elagabalus banished him, but Severus Alexander needed his services, appointing him Praetorian prefect with ULPIAN. Paulus wrote more than 300 books on Roman LAW. Most centered on the codes and were known for their excellent style, brevity, and ease of reading. Large portions were used by Justinian.

Paulus (Catena) (fl. fourth century C.E.) *Member of the Notarii, or imperial secretaries*
Paulus was a native of Spain who came to the attention of Emperor CONSTANTIUS II. The emperor found him a merciless, ruthless, and utterly reliable investigator in cases of treason or conspiracy. Called Catena, or "chain," Paulus used highly inventive means of torture and interrogation. In 353, he was sent to Britain to hunt for

supporters of Magnentius. The following year he was busy questioning suspects in the affair of Gallus Caesar. Constantius sent him to watch over Julian in 358 and then turned him loose in the East, to examine charges of treason in Egypt. Obviously hated, Paulus was condemned by a commission and burned alive in 361/2.

Pausanias (fl. mid-second century C.E.) *Geographer and traveler*

A Greek from Lydia, he was familiar with much of the Roman world, including the East, Egypt, and Rome, but wrote extensively on Greece.

Pax   Pax was originally considered the goddess of peace, with worshipers in Rome and in Athens; the Via Sacra, begun by Claudius and finished by Vespasian, was her temple, in a figurative sense. Her visage and attributes (olive crown, two right hands joined, or a bull) were used by the emperors, especially on coinage, to declare that peace had come to the Roman world. From the time of Augustus (the Pax Augusta beginning with his victory at the battle of Actium in 31 B.C.E.) most rulers claimed such a peace.

The Pax Romana, a term that denoted a period of peace within the Roman Empire, was a very real and powerful sentiment. Rome's greatness stemmed from its ability to maintain peace throughout a world that had never known a cessation of hostilities. Peoples everywhere gave their devotion to the Roman Empire because in return they could live without fear of wars and death. The development of all that was successful in the provinces—trade, culture, agriculture, architecture, and even local forms of nationalism—were possible through the vision of Augustus and, infrequently, its fulfillment.

Pedius, Quintus (cf. 43 B.C.E.) *Grandnephew (or perhaps nephew) of Julius Caesar*

Pedius was the son of an Equestrian (EQUITES), probably the grandson of JULIA (1), Caesar's sister. He entered into the service of his uncle, attaining the rank of legate (LEGATUS) during the GALLIC WARS (c. 56 B.C.E.). At the outbreak of the CIVIL WAR, FIRST TRIUMVIRATE in 49, he joined the cause of Caesar, holding a praetorship the following year. In 46, he and Q. Fabius Maximus headed Caesar's legions in Spain. He was an officer at the battle of MUNDA in 45, earning great praise from Caesar. The dictator included him in his will in 44, and Pedius received one-eighth of his uncle's vast fortune. Octavian (AUGUSTUS), Caesar's true heir, first convinced him to turn over his share of the inheritance, then rewarded him with a consulship in 43 and control of Rome during Octavian's absence while forming the Second Triumvirate. When word spread that the triumvirs had their own proscription lists, a panic erupted, and Pedius died while trying to pacify the city.

Pelagia   (fl. fifth century C.E.) *Second wife of the magister militum, Boniface*

Boniface was solidifying his hold over Africa around 427 when he married Pelagia. Because of her Arian beliefs, his alliance with orthodox Christians was injured, and he suffered an even worse blow when Pelagia induced him to allow his daughter to be baptized into the Arian creed. Having isolated such notables as St. AUGUSTINE, Boniface's position in Africa deteriorated.

Pelagianism   A Christian heretical movement begun in the fifth century C.E. by Pelagius, a lay monk from Britain, but possibly of Irish descent, who traveled to Rome early in the fifth century. Settling there, he acquired a reputation for devotion while gaining a small group of followers who appreciated his views on morality. Around 410, during the Visigoth invasion of Italy by Alaric, Pelagius fled from Rome to Africa. After meeting with St. Augustine, he moved on to Palestine, while Augustus attacked him for what he considered to be heretical opinions. Soon other church officials joined in the assault, and at the synods of Jerusalem and Diospolis (Lydda), in 415, Pelagius had to clear himself of censure, only to have both Augustine and Jerome step up their campaigns with *De natura et Gratia* (*On Birth and Grace*) and *Dialogi adversus Pelagianos* (*Dialogue against Pelagianism*), respectively. Councils in Africa condemned him in 416, a judgment later upheld by popes Innocent I and Zosimus. Pelagius faded from public life after the final condemnation of 418. He probably died in Palestine.

Pelagianism taught that humanity was not subject to predestination toward sin. Salvation was possible through an individual's actions and was not wholly dependent upon divine grace. Man was responsible ultimately for his actions. This belief ran counter to the very heart of St. Augustine's thinking and much of Christian orthodoxy. Unlike other heretical movements, Pelagianism did not find any widespread support after Pelagius's defeats. Carried on by a small group of theologians, by the sixth century it had all but disappeared.

Pelagius   *See* PELAGIANISM.

Penates   The household gods of the Romans. The Penates served publicly as divinities of protection, while in their private nature they helped each household or family. Their name probably came from *penus,* or provisions, hence their images were kept in the heart of the home, and a hearth was always kept lit in their honor. The Penates were similar to the LARES, except the *Lares domestici* were actually family members, while the Penates were gods who watched over the family. The Penates originally had a shrine along the Velia, but it was sacrificed for the Basilica Nova. A temple was dedicated to them sometime in the early fourth century C.E., probably in the time of Maxentius. It was circular and was situated on the Sacred Way.

See also GODS AND GODDESSES OF ROME.

Peponila (d. 79 C.E.) *Wife of the Gallic rebel leader Julius Sabinus*

When her husband was defeated in 70 C.E., she went into hiding with him for nine years, bearing two children. In 79 they were both captured. Taken to Rome, she begged Vespasian to spare her children, but they were put to death with their parents.

Peraea One of the districts of Palestine, situated east of the Jordan River and the Dead Sea and stretching from Machaerus to Pella in Decapolis. While not one of the most beautiful areas of JUDAEA, the Peraeans boasted a plentiful supply of water and the capacity to grow virtually every kind of crop. Its importance, of course, lay in its strategic position. To the south was Arabia, and to the east was *Nabataea.* Any serious Nabataean advance on Jerusalem had to go through Peraea.

Percennius (fl. early first century C.E.) *Soldier in the legions of Pannonia who was largely responsible for their mutiny in 14 C.E.*

Once connected to the theater, he supposedly delivered an oration that convinced his fellow legionaries to revolt after the death of Emperor Augustus. When the mutiny fell apart, with the arrival of Drusus, Percennius was put to death.

peregrini The term used to denote foreigners, those not included in the Latin franchise. According to Roman law the *peregrini* were given unfavorable status for most often their communities were conquered or occupied, and it was up to the local administration in a province to determine how they would be treated. Cases involving the *peregrini* were normally handled by the *praetor peregrinus,* a PRAETOR chosen specifically to preside over foreigners. It was always the hope of the *peregrini* to have their lot improved. They thus adopted Roman ways and replaced their own laws with those of Rome. Foreign troops sent to the Eternal City to be stationed there were barracked in the so-called CASTRA PEREGRINI or "camp of the foreigners."

Perennis, Sextus Tigidius (fl. late second century C.E.) *Prefect of the praetorian guard from 180 to 185, under Emperor Commodus*

Perennis was of Italian birth, a member of the Equestrians (EQUITES) and apparently enjoyed a long, distinguished military career. He was named to the prefectship of the Guard with Tarutenius PATERNUS around 180, but then overshadowed his colleague in prestige and influence. In 182, Paternus was removed from his post by Commodus and was put to death a short time later on charges of conspiracy. Perennis now held command of the Praetorians by himself, and he emerged as the chief instrument of Commodus's autocratic style of rule, coming to run virtually the entire empire. Carefully he fed Commodus's habits but tried to curb some of his most extreme appetites. His methods and the amassing of vast wealth earned him the hatred of both the Senate and the court. Chief among his opponents was the chamberlain Cleander. Through his plottings, Perennis was denounced and executed by imperial order. Accounts vary at to the exact nature of Perennis's fall. The historian Dio wrote that troops from Britain's legions were used to kill him, while Herodian gave a long account of Perennis and his own self-wrought destruction.

Pergamum Leading city of the Roman province of ASIA; in a district of MYSIA called Teuthrania, on the Caicus River, a few miles inland from the Aegean Sea. Probably founded sometime in the fourth century B.C.E., it blossomed in the third century under the Attalid kings, who put the kingdom of Pergamum on a social and economic par with Macedonia, Egypt, and Seleucia. The importance of Pergamum increased when the Romans gave to King Eumenes II (in 190 B.C.E.) control of Mysia, Lydia, Lycaonia, Phrygia, Pamphylia, and Pisidia. For some time the city was a rival of Alexandria. It was the seat of the Roman consul of Asia but, in keeping with the city's intense rivalry with EPHESUS, that center received both the provincial procurator and the treasury. The metropolis of Pergamum, however, wielded considerable power, both because of its political history and its industries. As with Massilia, Pergamum had possession of the entire surrounding area. Further, with its silver mines, parchment production (called *charta Pergamena*), agriculture and textiles, Pergamum was a major player in Roman commerce. Its buildings were improved in the second century C.E. by both Trajan and Hadrian.

Pergamum figured prominently in the religion of the Roman Empire. Under the Attalids, there was an altar of Zeus, and Asclepius was worshiped there in the Asclepium. In 29 B.C.E., Emperor Augustus gave permission for the inhabitants of the city to build a temple in honor of Roma et Augustus; Pergamum thus became the first site in the East for the IMPERIAL CULT, starting in 19 B.C.E. In Christian history, Pergamum was counted as one of the Seven Churches of Revelation, where Satan dwelt.

See also ARISTIDES.

periploi The records of ocean voyages that served as manuals or guides to navigation for future travelers. A *periplus* was customarily a circumnavigation of an enclosed body of water, such as the Black Sea or the Mediterranean, although it could also apply to any navigation of a known coast, or even the explorations of previously uncharted waters. The *periploi* were intended to give details that might be useful to sailors, similar to the *itinerarium*, which was made a guide to travelers on land.

Among the best known of the *periploi* were the *Periplus of the Euxine,* the *Periplus Maris Erythraei, Periplus of the Outer Sea,* and *Stadiasmus Maris Magni. The Periplus of the Euxine* [or Black] *Sea* was written around 132 C.E. by Arrian and was addressed to Emperor Hadrian in the form of a letter. The *Periplus Maris Erythraei* (Periplus of the Erythraen Sea) was compiled in the first century C.E. by an unknown Greek merchant and describes trips along the coastal waters from Egypt to India and along the East African coast; it includes extensive details that would be useful for ship captains and merchants. The *Periplus of the Outer Sea* was compiled around 400 C.E., in Greek, by Marcian of Heraclea Pontica. He describes the waters beyond the Mediterranean, including the Indian and Atlantic Oceans. The *Stadiasmus Maris Magni* survives only in fragments. It was written probably in the second half of the third century C.E. and provides details of the Mediterranean, including distances, sailing directions, and descriptions of specific harbors.

Peroz (d. 484 C.E.) *King of Persia from 459 to 484*
Peroz enjoyed good relations with Emperor ZENO, whose ambassador EUSEBIUS was attached to the Persian imperial court. He was killed in battle with the Huns.

Persia   The land that gave birth to the Sassanids (*see* SASSANID DYNASTY) whose conquered the Parthians in 226 C.E.; originally known as Persis. It was located along the Persian Gulf and Arabian Sea, bordering Parthia, the Indo-Parthian kingdoms and the kingdom of Elymais. Under the Parthians it was granted a considerable amount of autonomy, allowing for the internal development that brought about the Sassanids.

Persians and Athenians   The names taken by two gladiatorial squads who fought in a mock naval engagement in the Saeptia in 2 B.C.E. Their battle was part of the massive Circensian games managed by Gaius and Lucius. As of old, the Athenians won.
    See also LUDI.

Persius Flaccus, Aulus (34–62 C.E.) *Satirist during the age of Nero*
Persius was greatly influenced by Horace and stood as a friend of Lucan. In his lifetime Flaccus achieved little fame with his work, but his satires, especially his expositions on Stoicism, gained him posthumous respect.
    See also SATIRE.

personal appearance   For those with sufficient wealth, need, and slaves, a great deal of time during each day was spent on toiletries, and much effort was given by both genders to personal appearance. There was a vast difference in the personal habits and appearance between the upper classes and the poor or working classes. In both cases, however, there was a fondness for BATHS and bathing that extended across the classes. It is not surprising, then, that Romans possessed a wide variety of toiletries, cosmetics, and beauty aids. The quality of the personal items depended upon the status and the resources of the individual.

A patrician woman regularly awoke and applied a skin paste of flour and milk that was washed off with perfumed water. This was followed by an oral hygiene program that involved brushing the teeth and rinsing the mouth. There was a premium placed by the upper classes on white teeth, especially on the part of young eligible women. Archaeological remains indicate that a typical well-to-do matron had a wide variety of toilet instruments, including tweezers, combs, toothpicks, and razors. There were also face powders, perfumes, lipsticks, and forms of makeup. Strigils were also applied, to remove dead skin and makeup. Cosmetics were often made of charcoal and saffron, while chalk powder was applied to whiten the skin. Romans used mirrors made of polished metals, such as bronze and silver. Most mirrors were of the hand-held variety, but larger, full-size mirrors were not uncommon.

A reflection of the Roman concern for appearance was an acute interest in hairstyle and hair care. The most obvious source of information on varying hairstyles is the abundance of sculpture, especially from the first and second centuries C.E. Specific hairstyles varied across the empire, and unlike the Greeks, there was no classic style of presenting hair, with fashionable trends becoming dominant in some periods and fading in others. Hair care was a priority to the wealthy, with a full head of healthy hair considered a sign of good fortune. Hair colors also passed through fashion trends, with blonde becoming popular during the empire. This color was achieved by hair dyes. There were thus efforts to promote hair growth using assorted ointments, such as animal fat (from bears and sheep). Another remedy for hair loss involved applying a cream made from pepper and crushed rat's heads.

As these methods failed, Romans of both sexes took to wearing wigs, even though writers, such as Ovid, enjoyed poking fun at those forced to wear them. Blonde wigs were popular, made from the hair of Germans captured in the campaigns along the frontier or trimmed from the golden locks of slave girls. Black hair for wigs was also trimmed from slaves across the provinces, or was sometimes imported from as far away as India.

Roman men traditionally wore beards, but this custom changed from the time of Scipio Africanus (d. 184/3 B.C.E.) in the early second century B.C.E. As that famed general was always clean shaven, Romans followed his lead. Beards came back into fashion from the time of Hadrian (r. 117–38). That emperor wore a long and elegant beard, but he adopted it in order to hide a facial blemish. It was custom for a young man to save the hairs shaved for the first time and place them in an ornate box. Men of the lower classes normally kept beards, as shaving was expensive, requiring access to sharp razors on a regular basis and someone, usually a slave, to perform the shaving.

Prosperous Roman men frequented barber shops, especially if they did not have a slave to assist them. Such shops were numerous in Rome, although the quality of the shave varied greatly, as was noted by Martial. He wrote of the threat to life and limb posed by the barber Antiochus, who inflicted scars upon the chin of the poet. As a rule, most razors did not remain sharp for very long and caused nicks and cuts and often left the kinds of scars mentioned by Martial.

Pertinax, Publius Helvius (1) (126–193 C.E.) *Emperor in 193*

The son of a Ligurian freedman, Helvius Successus, Pertinax became a teacher but soon entered the army, where he commanded cohorts in Syria. He also held the same post in Britain and Moesia, and in 168 was given a procuratorship in Italy and another in Dacia. Marcus Aurelius found him useful and appointed him head of troops in Pannonia, where he participated in the MARCOMANNIC WARS. As preparation for further promotion, Pertinax was elevated to the senatorial class and served as PRAETOR. Around 171 he was legate in Raetia and was a consul in 174 or 175. Further offices included governorships in Syria, Moesia Inferior and Superior, and in Dacia.

Commodus, Marcus's successor, stripped Pertinax of his status in 182 because of possible connections to conspiracies. Such was his reputation, however, that the ruler sent him to Britain in 185 to deal with troublesome legions. He remained there for two years and was named proconsul of Africa in 188. A second consulship came in 192. He was PREFECT OF THE CITY in 192 but probably had no part in the assassination of Commodus. Nevertheless, with the help of the Praetorian prefect LAETUS, he traveled to the CASTRA PRAETORIA, where he secured the blessings of the Guard with the promise of a DONATIVUM and was elevated to the throne. Pertinax enjoyed as well the full support of the Senate, which was only too glad to have one of their own adorned with the purple.

He attempted to stabilize the imperial economy, nearly ruined by Commodus, while selling off some of the dead emperor's most valued possessions. Unfortunately, this fiscal conservatism turned the Praetorian Guard against him; he paid only half the sum that he had guaranteed them. Their dislike was accentuated by Laetus, who had regretted his support of Pertinax because the new emperor had proven himself highly independent. Soldiers burst into the palace when spirits ran high, and

Laetus, who had watched, went home when he saw a spear being thrown into Pertinax. The emperor's head was cut off, paraded through the streets and discarded, as the Guard set about auctioning off the empire to the highest bidder. The reign of Pertinax lasted only 87 days (January–March 193). Although considered very imperial in appearance, he declined the Senate's offer to raise up his wife to the rank of Augusta and did not give his son the position of Caesar.

Pertinax, Publius Helvius (2) (d. c. 211 C.E.) *Son of Emperor Pertinax (1)*

Publius was proposed as holder of the rank of Caesar until his father refused him the honor. He survived the assassination of Pertinax in 193 C.E. and was allowed to live by Emperor Didius Julianus. Septimius Severus declared Pertinax a god, and the son held the post of CONSUL in the early part of Caracalla's reign. Unfortunately, Caracalla cared little for him. He was put to death for making a joke about the murder of GETA.

Perusine War

Brief conflict fought in 41 B.C.E. between Octavian (AUGUSTUS) and Lucius ANTONIUS and FULVIA, Marc Antony's brother and wife. While Antony was away in the East, Lucius and Fulvia came to view the party of Octavian as too popular and dangerous. Although Antony and Octavian were equal triumvirs, Octavian was amassing political power in Rome and Italy with his settlement of legionary veterans on granted tracts of land. Feeling that Antony's honor and future were at stake, Lucius initiated hostilities in Italy, aided soon by Fulvia and her chamberlain, Manius.

When a reconciliation failed, war erupted. With some six legions, Lucius opposed Octavian and his lieutenant, AGRIPPA. Where Marc Antony stood in all of this was unclear to his supporters. For that reason, Munatius Plancus, Antony's general in Italy, neglected to involve himself, convincing Antony's other officers to do the same. Lucius thus found himself alone. Chased to Perusia (modern Perugia), northeast of Rome, between the Via Flaminia and Via Cassia, Lucius was surrounded and besieged. After months of unsuccessful breakout attempts and dwindling food supplies, he surrendered to Octavian in February 40. Octavian treated him with kindness, not wishing to antagonize Antony. Fulvia, meanwhile, sailed from Italy to Athens. No soldiers were executed, and Octavian sought to restore peace to the Italian region. Only Perusia was burned and pillaged to serve as a lesson to other towns.

Antony probably did not want any war with Octavian and so was upset to hear of the Perusine struggle; the letters informing him were delayed because of the winter weather. He was angry with Fulvia, and his subsequent treatment of her hastened her death in 40 and made possible the TREATY OF BRUNDISIUM.

Pescennius Niger (Gaius Pescennius Niger Justus)

(c. 135–193 C.E.) *Consul, general, governor of Syria, and in 193 one of the rival claimants for the imperial throne*

Pescennius was born to an Equestrian family in Italy. His successful military career was capped by a smashing victory over the Sarmatians in Dacia in 183. For this he was awarded by Emperor Commodus with elevation to the senatorial class and a consulship in 190 or 191. Niger was then appointed governor of Syria by Commodus, possibly through the influence of someone in the palace, for as the historian Dio stated, Niger was not a man of keen intelligence. As governor, Niger spent huge sums earning the goodwill of the Syrians.

In the summer of 193, when news arrived of the murder of Emperor Pertinax and the rise of DIDIUS JULIANUS, who had purchased the throne, Niger accepted the acclaim of his troops. His position was excellent; he commanded all nine legions of the East and the support of the provinces and BYZANTIUM. Victory would have been assured had he not faced Septimius SEVERUS and the Pannonian legions. Severus gathered together an army and advanced on Asia Minor. After a series of small engagements, all of Niger's trans-Bosporus holdings were either lost or besieged, as was the case with Byzantium. Severus then crossed over into Bithynia. Niger entrusted the fighting to his reliable general, Aemilianus, but was routed at CYZICUS. A short time later, perhaps at the start of 194, Niger's troops were again defeated, at NICAEA.

Niger withdrew into Syria only to learn that the backing of the provinces was deteriorating. The host of Severus continued its march through Asia Minor. Desperate for a victory, Niger gave battle at Issus. The Severans, commanded by Publius Cornelius ANULLINUS (*praefectus urbi* 196 C.E.,), were initially hard pressed in battle but eventually gained the upper hand. With the engagement lost, Niger fled to Antioch, then toward Parthia and sanctuary across the Euphrates. Anullinus took Antioch, and Niger was captured. Severus put him to death, and his head was put on a stick and paraded before his horrified adherents at Byzantium. Dio summed up his life by saying that he "was notable for doing nothing either good or bad, so that one could neither praise nor blame him."

Peter (St. Peter) (d. 64 C.E.?) *Apostle of Christ and the unquestioned leader of the early Christian Church*

Peter, the "Rock" was chosen by Christ to serve as the foundation of the church. His early life was fully documented and commonly known, especially his recognition of Jesus as the Christ. Although he possessed many faults, Peter held the Apostles together after the Crucifixion and Ascension of Christ. Peter was henceforth the primary speaker for the Apostles, appearing before the Sanhedrin with John. Equally, he exhibited the greatest gifts of miraculous healing, so much so that even his shadow was enough to cure the ill. While he allowed the Gentile Cornelius to join his circle, PAUL rebuked him for allowing the Jewish community of Christians to turn away Gentile converts. Of lasting importance to CHRISTIANITY was Peter's early identification as the bishop of ROME. Not only did he apparently head the Roman Church, but also his martyrdom (sometime during the Neronian Persecution, probably 64 C.E.) established forever the supremacy of Rome over the entire Christian hierarchy. Peter, it was said, refused to die in the same manner as Christ. He was thus crucified upside down. Virtually the entire New Testament was his biography, especially Gospels of Matthew and John, as well as the Acts of the Apostles.

See also PAPACY.

Peter of Alexandria (d. 311 C.E.) *Bishop of Alexandria from 300 to 311*

Peter survived the persecutions of Emperor Diocletian and became head of the Christian community in Alexandria. He faced, however, the very important question of what to do with those Christians who had forsaken their faith because of the persecutions. The requirements that he devised were viewed by many, especially MELITIUS, as being far too lenient. The controversy was far from resolved in 306, when Peter had to flee his see in the face of murderous repression. From his place of exile in the desert he continued to write to his flock, only to have Melitius assume control over the Alexandrian Christians. Peter returned in 311, during the brief respite, but was caught and martyred at Alexandria.

Petra

Capital city of ARABIA Petraea; the administrative and commercial center for the NABATAEANS. Petra was founded sometime in the fourth century B.C.E. by the then nomadic people of Nabataea. Located in the Edom Mountains, between the Dead Sea and the Red Sea, its many buildings were accessible only by crossing through sharp, rocky passes, and the city itself was positioned in an easily defended and virtually inaccessible gorge, called Siq. Today, Petra is in Jordan.

From the start, Petra served as an important cog in the trade relations not only of the Nabataean Kingdom but also of the entire East. Caravans from all over the world entered its markets, spread out beneath the stunning sandstone walls. Merchants from India and Arabia, with silks and perfumes, used Petra as a launching point for massive distribution to the Roman world. As its greatest wealth was in the first century C.E., most of the preserved structures in Petra date from that time. Some, of course, were built in earlier eras, displaying a Ptolemaic influence, but Deir, the most famous of the buildings, was from the mid-first century. This tomb relied upon a facade of dramatically placed columns, pilasters, and floors, which inspire visitors with awe and an impression of vastness.

Ironically, the riches of Petra were a contributing factor in Emperor Trajan's decision to send A. Cornelius Palma with troops to annex all of the Nabataean domain in 106 C.E. Petra was replaced as the first city of the region by Bostra, where the VI Ferrata legion and the legate of the new province of Arabia Petraea were stationed. The title metropolis was eventually granted; but from Roman occupation in 106, the city would never again recover its grandeur. Any hopes of resurrecting its economic vitality were ended in the third century with the rise of the city of PALMYRA.

Petreius, Marcus (d. 46 B.C.E.) *Supporter of Pompey the Great during the civil war with Julius Caesar*
A noted soldier, Petreius was responsible for the final annihilation of Catiline's forces in 62 B.C.E., in which supposedly 3,000 supporters of the conspirator were massacred. In 59 he helped CATO UTICENSIS oppose Caesar's agrarian laws, rising from his seat in the Senate and declaring that he would rather be with Cato in prison than in the same Senate chamber with Caesar. This bold move shamed Caesar into releasing Cato.

Ten years later, Petreius threw in with the Pompeians when the war erupted. He traveled to Spain, where he and Afranius were commanders of Pompey's legions there. Caesar chose Spain as his initial target and with five legions defeated and captured Petreius and Afranius at ILERDA in 49. Typical of Caesar, Petreius was forgiven. He refused to retire, but united instead with Pompey's forces in Africa.

From October 47 to February 46, Petreius was a leading general of the Pompeians in the THAPSUS Campaign, with Labienus, King Juba I and Scipio. With Labienus he very nearly defeated Caesar near Ruspina, only to share in the failure of the Pompeians at Thapsus. It was said that he and Juba killed each other rather than face capture.

Petronius (fl. first century C.E.) *Controversial figure in Rome during the reign of Emperor Nero (54–68)*
While well-known to history, Petronius may have been two different people: a courtier in Nero's imperial court and Petronius Arbiter, a famous author best known for writing the *Satyricon*. While it is possible that the two may have been distinct, many scholars are of the opinion that they were one and the same. Based upon Tacitus's description of Petronius and also on his chief work, the *Satyricon*, with one of its surviving fragments, the *Cena Trimalchionis* (Banquet of Trimalchio), the preponderance of evidence does seem to point to Petronius being one person.

Gaius Petronius (or "Titus," according to Pliny the Elder) was famed during the reign of Nero for his indolence and supreme mastery of good taste and pleasure. He specialized in eccentricity and abandon while presenting an air of simplicity. For these characteristics he was admitted into the inner circle of Nero, becoming the emperor's authority on art and culture, with the title *arbiter elegantiae*. As proconsul of Africa and then as consul he displayed utmost vigor, an active nature that he brought to the pursuit of luxury. His favored position with Nero earned him the enmity of the perfect of the Praetorian Guard, TIGELLINUS, who convinced the emperor to have Petronius condemned to death in 66. In a most elegant fashion, Petronius killed himself, but only after composing a letter to Nero detailing the ruler's embarrassing orgies and affairs. Petronius died with the same flair that he used successfully in life.

Tacitus made no mention of any literary ability on the part of Gaius Petronius. For such a historian, however, the content of the noted work could have been considered beneath contempt and thus ignored. The name *Arbiter* (Judge) was rare and can be linked to both the writer and the courtier.

The *Satyricon* was an account of debauchery and outrageous behavior, written in 16 books (*Satyricon libri*). Only fragments are extant, of which the *Banquet of Trimalchio* survived almost intact. Technically, Petronius wrote Menippean satire, using an interwoven verse and prose, while manipulating elements of the Milesian Fables, mainly short stories, into the work. He possessed such a masterful touch that in the *Cena Trimalchionis* he included superb examples of his era's Vulgar Latin, making the novel of great importance to subsequent grammarians. In essence, the story is about Encolpius and Giton, two youths who find love and adventure in southern Italy. It is satirical, biting, and comical, despite the fact that Petronius often abandoned a coherent plot for the sake of inventiveness or imagination.

Petronius Turpilianus, Publius (fl. first century C.E.) *Consul in 19 C.E. and very nearly the last victim of the reign of Gaius Caligula (37–41 C.E.)*
Petronius came from a senatorial family, eventually serving as proconsul of Africa (29–c. 35) and legate of Syria (39–42). As governor of Syria he received orders from Emperor Gaius Caligula in 41 to erect a statue of the monarch in the Great TEMPLE OF JERUSALEM. Torn between his loyalty to the emperor and his fear of a Jewish uprising, he hesitated, while pleading the case of the religious rights of the Jews. Infuriated, Caligula ordered that he kill himself. The decree mercifully was made null by the emperor's assassination in Rome. Petronius was also the co-author of the *lex Junia Petronia*, with M. Junius Silanus.

Petronius Arbiter   *See* PETRONIUS.

Petronius Maximus (396–455 C.E.) *Successor in the Western Empire to Valentinian III in 455*
From obscure origins, but a gifted officer in the imperial government of the West, Petronius held positions as

tribune, *notarius*, and *comes sacrarum largitionum*, all prior to 420. Sometime in that year he was appointed prefect for the city of Rome. A consul twice, once with Theodosius II, Petronius then held the Praetorian prefectship in Italy two times, in 435 and 439. By 445 he was a Patrician. With Valentinian's murder, no male heir was readily available to take the throne. Other choices were considered, but Petronius, with his wealth and offices, seemed the logical choice to receive the purple. But Licinia EUDOXIA, Valentinian's widow, intensely disliked Petronius, holding him responsible for her husband's death. Finding her forced marriage to Petronius unbearable, she appealed for aid from GEISERIC, king of the Vandals in Africa. Only too happy to meddle in the affairs of the West, Geiseric sailed to Italy. Petronius tried to flee from Rome. His bodyguard deserted and the emperor was attacked by a mob. Supposedly he died in a shower of stones, although he may have been hung instead. He had reigned from March 17 to May 31. Geiseric pillaged Rome.

Petronius Turpilianus, Publius (d. c. 68 C.E.) *Governor of Britain in 61–62 C.E.*

Petronius had served as consul in 61 before heading to Britain where he advocated a more peaceful policy than the one pursued by his predecessor. Back in Rome in 63, he held a position as *curator aquarum* for the city and played a role in the massacre that ended the PISONIAN CONSPIRACY. For his loyalty to Nero he received a triumphal insignia in 65. Three years later, Nero ordered him to command the forces sent out against the rebellion. Petronius threw in with Galba but was put to death by that new emperor.

Peutinger Table

The Tabula Peutingeriana, a five-color map of the Roman world, was originally drawn in the fourth or fifth century C.E. It was copied about 1265 by a monk of Colmar, eventually coming into the possession of a scholar named Konrad Peutinger in 1508. The map is 22 feet long and $13\frac{1}{2}$ inches wide and presents much of the then known world, from Britannia to India, although the images are severely stretched as it was intended to serve as a diagram for travelers and was not drawn to scale. The chief feature of the map is the networks of roads of the empire and of the lands to the east beyond the imperial frontier. Details include mountains, rivers, and towns, with annotations on where the traveler might find road stations and baths, and how far the distances are from one point to the next. Unfortunately, part of the map, containing the western regions of the empire, is missing, so that most of Britannia and all of Hispania and Mauretania are lost.

Phaedrus (fl. first century C.E.) *Author of five books of fables, written in the sytle of Aesop*

A freedman, Phaedrus probably came from Thrace or Macedonia, specifically Pieria. He lived in Rome while still young and secured the patronage of Augustus. His first two works on fables were published during the reign of Tiberius but prior to 31 C.E. As Sejanus appears to have been the instrument in some persecution of Phaedrus, the freedman found relief in the fall PREFECT OF THE PRAETORIAN GUARD in 31. Books 3–5 came out later, no doubt in the time of Gaius Caligula. He relied upon iambic senarii in his fables, adding stories or anecdotes about himself or the times. His composition was fluent, delightful, and never verbose. Five books are extant in incomplete form. Few ancient authors made mention of him, considering him to be a minor contributor to the literature of the time.

Phaon (fl. first century C.E.) *Freedmen of the emperor Nero*

Phaon played a part in Nero's last days in 68 C.E. When the emperor has fallen from power and fled from Rome, Phaon offered the use of his own private villa and estates outside the city to which Nero agreed. It was Phaon, however, who sent Nero the letter informing him that the Senate had condemned him to death. Horrified at the prospect of dying by torture, Nero killed himself.

Pharasmanes (first century C.E.) *King of Iberia (modern Kartli, Georgia)*

The son of Mithridates of Iberia and brother of Mithridates of ARMENIA. Pharasmanes succeeded his father on the throne of Iberia sometime before 35 C.E. and was induced to help his brother secure the throne of Armenia. The army of Iberia swept into Armenia as Mithridates replaced its king Arsaces. In the fighting, Pharasmanes defeated a large Parthian force sent against him. Only the threat of a wider war with Rome prevented Parthia from taking direct action against Iberia as a result. Considered a reliable client, Pharasmanes was ordered by Emperor Claudius (c. 49) to aid Mithridates once more in regaining the Armenian crown (he had been exiled by Gaius Caligula). Iberia's troops marched once again into Armenia, and with Roman support, Mithridates resecured the throne. But in 51, RADAMISTUS, son of Pharasmanes, decided that he too wanted to be a monarch. Rather than face assassination, Pharasmanes encouraged his son to subvert Armenia. Relations with Mithridates had never been loving, and Pharasmanes gave his son all of the support that he could. Mithridates was murdered, as Radamistus assumed the sovereignty of Armenia. Rome's governor of Syria, Ummidius Quadratus, was horrified, but the eventual removal of Radamistus did not come at Roman hands. He was ousted by the Armenians themselves and returned to his father. Pharasmanes, fearing for his own kingship, put his son to death in 58 as an act of good faith to Rome. Subsequently, he fought in the long wars between Parthia and the Roman Empire over the fate of Armenia, reportedly enjoying his task of demolishing much of the Armenian landscape.

Pharisees   Members of one of the major theological movements within JUDAISM from the time of the Hasmonaean kings to the fall of JERUSALEM (c. 142 B.C.E.–70 C.E.). The Pharisees ranked with the SADDUCEES and the ESSENES (according to the writer Josephus) as leaders of Jewish thought. Their name probably came from a Greek derivation of the Hebrew *perushim*, or separatists, probably reflecting the view held by the Sadducees of their own teachings. Pharisaism taught that the Law of Moses (the Pentateuch) had to be upheld and, as well, the oral law handed by Moses to Joshua and then to the prophets and finally to the Pharisees. These laws, both oral and written, were given by God to individuals that they might follow his teaching and thus earn eternal life and the resurrection of the body.

The movement originated in the fall of the old Jewish priesthood in favor of the Hasmonaean priest-kings, who came to power with the help of the early Pharisees. Henceforth, the kings of the Hasmonaean line gave their blessings up to the propagation of their doctrines. The Pharisees adopted views especially in two domains, the spiritual and the temporal, that allowed them to deal with the Sadducees and were especially helpful in negotiating for their survival under Roman occupation.

The Pharisees were divided as to the correctness of the Great Rebellion (c. 65–70 C.E.). Many of their leaders worked to stop the revolt, and still others met with Vespasian to convince him to spare the Pharisees as a group. These pleas, coupled with the destruction of the Great Temple, ensured the primacy of the Pharisees in Judaism. Because it was more flexible, fluid and independent of the Great Temple and its stratified priesthood, Pharisaism became the religious heart of the Jews in the Diaspora. Its institution of the synagogue allowed the Jews to live throughout the Roman Empire without losing their religious pride or sense of unity.

Pharnaces   (d. 47 B.C.E.)   *King of the Bosporus*
Also called Pharnaces, king of PONTUS, he was the son of MITHRIDATES VI, who had created the Bosporan domain as a major power in the East, Pharnaces led a revolt in 63 B.C.E. that caused his father to commit suicide. Grateful that such a gifted opponent had fallen, POMPEY THE GREAT allowed Pharnaces to retain his newly gained throne. Ambitious but cautious, Pharnaces waited until the Romans were engaged in the convulsions of their own civil war (49–45 B.C.E.), before embarking upon his campaigns of conquest. Using the absence of any major opponents, especially Deiotarus of Galatia, Pharnaces made war upon Caesar's legate CALVINUS, defeating him at the battle of NICOPOLIS in October 48 B.C.E., while Caesar was in Alexandria. After negotiations failed to gain him a Roman pardon, Pharnaces gave battle at Zela in May 47. He was routed and later murdered by a governor, Asander.

Pharsalus   Greek town in eastern Thessaly, site of the great confrontation between Julius CAESAR and POMPEY THE GREAT on August 9, 48 B.C.E. Pharsalus ended the political fortunes of Pompey. Although years of fighting lay ahead, Caesar's victory earned him a justified status as foremost general in the Roman world. Following the Pompeian victory at DYRRHACHIUM in May 48, Caesar retreated into Thessaly, where his troops were able to recover and to forage for food. Pompey was confronted with two choices: He could leave Greece and move to Rome to gather more political and senatorial support, or he could hunt down Caesar and force a decision. He opted for the second method, as his men were confident, with high morale. Pompey also could not leave Caesar intact, able to crush the Pompeians in the East. As for Caesar, once his men were fed and rested, he eagerly waited for battle.

Throughout June and July, both sides maneuvered for position, trying to pin down the other's detachments or main body and thus seize a strategic or tactical advantage. Finally, knowing that he had much greater numbers, Pompey selected a hill near the plain of Pharsalus and ordered his lines of battle, placing his right flank on the nearby Enipeus River, giving Caesar the option of fighting. Caesar naturally accepted. Pompey possessed 60,000 infantry and 7,000 cavalry, while Caesar commanded around 30,000 infantry and only 1,000 cavalry. Knowing that Pompey would exploit his superiority in horsemen, Caesar created a special force of six cohorts (some 2,000 men), placing them in the rear of his right flank.

The struggle began as the legions of Caesar advanced against the Pompeians stretched out along the base of the hill. As the footsoldiers came to grips, Pompey launched his cavalry, driving hard into Caesar's right wing. Hopelessly overmatched, Caesar's cavalry broke as the enemy pushed on. Suddenly the six cohorts appeared, surprising the cavalry. The Pompeian horse was scattered as the cohorts moved forward, striking against Pompey's left. At this moment, Caesar unleashed his last reserves. With the fabled X Legion leading the way, the forces of Pompey were smashed utterly. Caesar led his victorious troops in pursuit, crashing into the enemy's camp and making any recovery impossible.

Pompey fled the field, removed his insignia and made for the coast with only 30 riders as escort. Caesar had lost only a few hundred men, while inflicting more than 10,000 casualties and capturing another 24,000. Although he still had followers ready to fight on his behalf, Pompey sailed to Egypt, where he would meet his end. Sources include Caesar's *Civil War* and Lucan's *Civil War*, or *Pharsalia*.

Phasael (d. 40 B.C.E.) *Son of the minister Antipater of Idumaea and brother of Herod the Great*

Phasael, like his brother, was groomed for high office, holding command in Judaea with his father and eventually becoming governor of Jerusalem. After Antipater's death in 43 B.C., Phasael and Herod were the masters of Judaea, administering affairs in the name of the weak king Hyrcanus. In 40 B.C., when the Parthians invaded the kingdom, Phasael was either killed or, more likely, committed suicide.

Philae Island in the Nile River near Aswan; now submerged. Philae was heavily decorated by temples, built mainly by the last dynasties of Egypt and by the Ptolemies. Various Roman emperors took an interest in the site and repaired or improved its structures. These included Augustus, Hadrian, and Diocletian. The Temple of Isis there was visited by travelers from all over the Roman world. Philae served as one of the important boundary markers for the Roman province of Egypt, denoting the starting point of Ethiopia. Archaeologically, the island was very impressive. As a result of the modern Aswan Dam, Philae itself was submerged by the Nile, and the numerous structures that once graced the island were moved to a nearby island, Agilqiyyah, shaped to resemble the original in exact detail.

Philip I (d. 249 C.E.) *Emperor from 244 to 249*

Called "Philip the Arab" because he was the son of an Arabian chieftain who was also a member of the Equestrians (EQUITES), Philip served in the army, rising to the position of second in command of the Praetorian Guard, behind TIMESITHEUS, the prefect. Sometime in 243, Timesitheus died, with many assuming that he had been murdered by Philip. Emperor Gordian III then named Philip as the new prefect. Shortly after assuming his duties, he convinced the troops in the armies of Gordian in the East to remove the young emperor. Acclaimed by the legions, Philip immediately placated the Senate by having Gordian deified. He then terminated the campaign against Persia, signed a hastily arranged treaty with the Persians and journeyed to Rome to establish his claims. Once home, Philip elevated his son to the rank of Caesar and had his wife, Otacilia Severa, named Augusta. His brother, Gaius Priscus, became the governor of Mesopotamia.

With the imperial line apparently stabilized, Philip set out in 246 against the CARPI in DACIA. The operations along the Danube were extremely successful, as evidenced by his assuming the titles *Carpicus Maximus* and *Germanicus Maximus*. Philip's son was then promoted to Augustus or coemperor, and in Rome the Secular Games were held to celebrate the 1,000th birthday of the city. Problems soon erupted, however. The barbarian Goths, Germans, and Carpi once more created trouble. More important, usurpations, especially by Pacatianus and

Jotapianus, destroyed Philip's faith in himself. To aid in quelling the Danubian revolts, DECIUS was appointed general in Moesia and Pannonia. By 249, Decius had been so victorious that his troops proclaimed him emperor. Philip marched to give battle, but he was defeated near Verona and slain. His son joined him in death a short time later, putting an end to the first Arab line on the throne.

Philip II (d. 249 C.E.) *Son of Emperor Philip I (the Arab) and Otacilia Severa*

Following the elevation of his father to the throne in 244, Philip II was given the rank of Caesar, probably at age seven. Three years later (247) he was made Augustus, or coruler, with his father, sharing as well in two consulships. In 249, he was murdered, probably by the Praetorian Guard, following his father's defeat and death at the hands of DECIUS.

Philip the Tetrarch (d. 34 C.E.) *Son of Herod the Great*

By virtue of the will of Emperor Augustus, Philip was made the tetrarch of Gaulanitis, Trachonitis, and Batanaea. Although Herod despised Philip, an emotion that he visited upon all of his children, the son was able to survive the old king's reign, sharing in the inheritance of Herod when he died in 4 B.C.E. Augustus ensured that the extensive domain of Judaea was broken apart. Philip received control of his own districts, ruling them until his death. At that time, L. Vitellius, the governor of Syria, annexed the entire territory, but it was later given to Herod Agrippa I. Philip was married to the infamous Salome.

Philippi Founded in Macedonia by Philip of Macedon in the fourth century B.C.E., this town gained lasting fame as the site of the battle fought by Octavian (AUGUSTUS) and Antony against the Liberators, including Brutus and Cassius. Philippi was actually two battles, fought in early October and on October 23, 42 B.C.E.

Following the formation of the SECOND TRIUMVIRATE at Bononia (Bologna) in November of 43 B.C.E., by Octavian, Antony, and Lepidus, war was inevitable, for the cause of Julius Caesar had been assumed by his heir, Octavian. Marcus BRUTUS and Gaius CASSIUS LONGINUS, the ringleaders in Caesar's murder, had fled to the East, where they had taken control of Rome's provinces, brutally draining them and any Roman ally of all available wealth. By late summer of 42, they had collected an army of 19 legions, totaling some 80,000 infantry and 20,000 cavalry. In September they crossed the Hellespont and marched into Thrace.

Against them, Octavian and Antony gathered a host of 85,000 foot and around 12,000 or 13,000 horsemen. They sailed from Brundisium to Epirus, beginning immediately to maneuver around Macedonia for a suitable place to make a stand. With Antony in the lead, the forces of the triumvirate came upon the Republican legions near the town of Philippi. Brutus and Cassius had their forces positioned on both sides of the Via Egnatia, with a swamp protecting the lines of communication with their fleet at Neapolis.

Antony decided to attack through the swamp and thus gain a surprise. He made preparations with a causeway over the worst parts of the mire and then crashed into the camp of Cassius. The sorties was highly successful. Cassius, thinking the chances of victory were gone, had a servant kill him. Unbeknownst to him, Brutus's units had made a similar raid on the camp of Octavian, driving the young general from the field. Brutus and Antony returned to their respective camps, triumphant but faced with the same dire news.

Days passed as both sides waited for an opportunity. While Octavian could use the name of Caesar to motivate his cohorts, Brutus had to rely upon money. Sensing that this would keep his men loyal for just so long, he decided to give battle. Octavian recovered some of his honor as he and his troops stood firm against the enemy. Antony then routed the demoralized Republicans. Brutus escaped with only four legions, leaving thousands of prisoners behind. A short time later he committed suicide. So died the "noblest of the Romans" and, with him, the Republic.

Philippus, Flavius (d. 351 C.E.) *Praetorian prefect of Orientis from 344 to 351*

For many years a reliable agent of Emperor CONSTANTIUS II, Philippus was the son of a sausage maker but learned to read and write, mastered shorthand and entered imperial service as a *notarius* (*see* NOTARII). By 344, possibly through the influence of eunuchs at court, he was made praetorian prefect. In the name of Constantius he deposed the orthodox bishop of Constantinople, Paul, deporting him before putting him to death in Armenia. In place of Paul, Philippus placed the Arian prelate Macedonius. In 348 he toured Bithynia and held a consulship. To observe the disposition of forces by MAGNENTIUS, the usurper, Philippus was sent by Constantius to negotiate a peace settlement in 351. He spoke to Magnentius's troops, charging them with disloyalty to the House of Constantine. As retribution, Magnentius refused him permission to leave. Philippus died in custody. Constantius at first believed Philippus a traitor but, learning of his speech, restored his reputation and erected statues in his honor.

Philippus, Lucius Marcius (fl. first century B.C.E.) *Consul in 56 B.C.E. and stepfather of Emperor Augustus*

Philippus married the widow Atia and thus became the surrogate father of the young Octavian. Any influence he may have had with the lad was offset by Julius Caesar's interest in Octavian. Philippus was apparently opposed to Augustus's political rise but later sponsored the construction of the Temple to Hercules and the Muses at the prodding of his stepson.

Philo (Philo Judaeus [the Jew]) (c. 30 B.C.E.–50 C.E.) *A noted intellectual writer of the first century C.E.*

Little has survived of his life except that he was born in Alexandria to a wealthy Jewish family, was the uncle of Tiberius Alexander, learned Greek and emerged as the foremost spokesman of Hellenistic Judaism in the world. In 39–40 C.E. he was sent to Rome to act as envoy to Gaius Caligula. He presented accusations against the prefect of Egypt, Flaccus, and defended the cause of Jewish rights. These experiences were recorded in *Legatio ad Gaium* (Embassy to Gaius) and *Contra Flaccum* (Against Flaccus). As a philosopher, Philo was very influential, both in his own day and in the subsequent Christian theological school of Alexandria, especially with CLEMENT and ORIGEN. He pursued an allegorical interpretation of Jewish literature, especially the Old Testament, presenting Judaism to the Hellenic world in terms of mainly Platonic philosophy. Greek and Jewish philosophical ideas were thus combined. Many of his writings, complex and numerous, are extant.

Philopater I (first century B.C.E.) *King of Cilicia*

The son of Tarcondimotus I, Philopater was a minor ruler sponsored by Pompey and Julius Caesar. Philopater succeeded Tarcondimotus when he fell at ACTIUM in 31 B.C.E., fighting for Antony. Philopater tried to give his allegiance to Augustus but was deposed; Cilicia passed into Roman hands and in 20 B.C.E., Tarcondimotus II, Philopater's brother, was installed as the ruler.

Philopater II (d. 17 C.E.) *King of Cilicia*

Probably the son of Tarcondimotus II, Philopater II a minor client-ruler of Cilicia in the early first century C.E. Upon the demise of Philopater, most of the kingdom favored annexation by Rome, a wish that was granted.

philosophy

The history of Roman philosophy began in 155 B.C.E. with the arrival in the Eternal City of an Athenian embassy composed of three eminent Greek intellectuals: the Academic Carneades (214–129 B.C.E.), the Stoic Diogenes, and the Peripatetic Critolaus. Carneades astonished his Roman hosts with his feats of forensic prowess, including the skill of the Sophists to be able to represent either side of an argument with equal conviction. Of particular note were the many young Romans who flocked to hear his lectures, marking a decisive moment in the embrace by the Romans of Hellenic philosophy.

ROMAN PAGAN PHILOSOPHY

Traditionally, the Romans had a deep mistrust of the Hellenes and took to philosophy only slowly and reluctantly.

The influx of philosophers was opposed by elements in the more traditional and conservative Roman establishment. Cato the Censor, for example, made an effort in the early third century B.C.E. to have all of the Greek philosophers banned from the city and prohibited from ever returning. The campaign against the Greeks was not supported by the majority of Romans, and philosophy became a permanent aspect of Roman life in the centuries to follow. The backlash nevertheless helps to explain why the serious study and application of traditional Greek philosophy was undertaken only from the time of CICERO and VARRO in the first century B.C.E.

Cicero was the first truly notable Roman philosopher and remained arguably Rome's foremost practitioner. He was also the prime exemplar in the Roman world of the influence of Hellenism on the Romans and the flourishing of the so-called New Academy. The Old Academy had been founded by Plato and lasted until the fourth century B.C.E. The Middle Academy survived throughout the third and second centuries B.C.E., and the New Academy was established around 100 B.C.E. and survived until 529 C.E., when it was closed forever by Emperor Justinian.

The New Academy was characterized by its eclecticism in the way that it utilized Platonism, elements of Aristotle, Stoicism, and other schools. For Cicero, it was important to overcome the influence of Carneades and his application of skepticism. The solution to skepticism, which questions the reliability of knowledge, for Cicero was the formation of a *consensus gentium,* the common belief of the people, which would permit moral and ethical certainty.

The Eclectic School exemplified by Cicero was only one of several philosophical schools that flourished from the middle of the first century to 225 C.E., the founding date of NEOPLATONISM. The chief schools of this period were NEO-PYTHAGOREANISM, STOICISM, EPICUREANISM, and the CYNICS.

Neo-Pythagoreanism was most represented among the Romans by Nigidius Figulus. While never a formally organized school, it exercised considerable influence on the academy, on the Neoplatonists, and even on the later Christian mystics. The Pythagoreans evidenced a traditional fascination with numbers, but they also developed an intense interest in magic, mysticism, and the study of the transcendence of God.

The Stoics of the Late Stoa flourished during the first centuries of the Roman Empire and claimed three significant Roman adherents: SENECA (3 B.C.E.–65 C.E.), EPICTETUS (60–117 C.E.), and especially Emperor MARCUS AURELIUS (121–180 C.E.). Influenced by Heraclitus, the "Weeping Philosopher" (c. 544–484 B.C.E.), the Stoics placed much stress on morality. The writings of Seneca demonstrate this, with their focus on the moral depravity of Rome during the reigns of Emperors Claudius and Nero. Likewise, Epictetus authored a compendium on Stoic morality, the *Moral Enchiridion,* edited by his student, Flavius Arrianus. Marcus Aurelius was also intensely concerned with Stoic morality, although his own ethical system did not prevent him from continuing the persecution and execution of Christians, in large measure because he saw Christianity as baneful for society and the state. Stoicism's influence was felt, however, even among early Christian philosophers.

Established as a reaction to the strict moral and ethical system of the Stoics, the Epicureans placed pleasure as the essential requirement of happiness, although Epicurus (341–270 B.C.E.) argued that he was never a selfish hedonist. The Epicureans thus declared that while every pleasure was good on its own account, not every pleasure has to be pursued. Equally, they believed that humans do not have to avoid every pain, even if every pain is evil. Additionally, the Epicureans later developed theories pertaining both to physics and to logic and emphasized human freedom over the Stoic tendencies toward fate. For these reasons, Epicureanism found a wide following among the sensualist Romans and among those who saw the importance of the innate human pursuit of happiness.

Finally, the Cynics were never organized into anything approaching a formal school, such as the Stoics and Epicureans, but they nevertheless enjoyed wide public popularity in late first century C.E. Rome. The Cynics were founded upon the principles laid down by Diogenes of Sinope (including the attainment of happiness by meeting human needs in the easiest, most simple means possible), although many Cynics preferred giving credit to Antisthenes. They achieved considerable influence in the third century B.C.E. and then faded until a marked revival in the first century C.E. Dio Cassius noted the large numbers of Cynics in Rome during the reign of Vespasian. They troubled the Flavian establishment with their calls for austerity and rejection of all social conventions and were subsequently banished from the city by exasperated emperors. The chief representatives of the Cynics during this period were DEMETRIUS THE CYNIC, DEMONAX, and Oenomaus of Gadara. The movement declined steadily throughout the second century C.E. but remained in existence until at least the sixth century.

THE RISE OF
CHRISTIAN PHILOSOPHY

Christian philosophy emerged out of the desire of Christian writers and theologians to begin the process of expressing their faith in rational terms and so defend it against contemporary philosophies. In this sense, the works of early Christian philosophers must be distinguished clearly from their theological writings, as philosophy was not supported—as was religion—by claims of the facts of revelation. In its broad terms, the rise of Christian philosophy is divided into two main eras: the patristic (extending from the first to the eighth centuries) and the scholastic (from the ninth to the 14th centuries). The patristic era was itself divided into three main periods: the pre-Augustinian, the Augustinian, and the post-Augustinian.

The pre-Augustinian period encompassed the most formative years of Christian thought, from the Apostolic Age to the rise of ST. AUGUSTINE (354–430) in the late fourth century. It included the writings of the first apologists, JUSTIN MARTYR (105–165) and TERTULLIAN (160–230); the polemists, such as the Pastor of Hermas (second century); the Catechetical Schools of Alexandria and Antioch; and the first of the so-called church fathers, GREGORY OF NYSSA (d. c. 395).

Such was his towering intellect and influence, that St. Augustine not only established a rich and enduring theological system for Christianity but a detailed philosophical structure as well. His wide-ranging philosophical interests—put to use always to advance Christian thought—were encapsulated by his famous maxim, *Credo ut intelligam* (I believe that I may understand). He examined the questions of faith and reason, ontology, the senses and the intellect, freedom, and grace, the nature of evil, the origin of the soul, and the philosophy of history. He relied heavily upon Platonic philosophy for his own system, as seen in his reliance upon eternal truths (which are closely associated with Plato's subsistent ideas), but he deviated sharply from Plato in that eternal truths did not rest in themselves but in God. The way in which Augustine's philosophy was centered in God was clear in his proclamation in the *Confessiones (Confessions): Inquietum est cor nostrum, donec requiescat in te* (Our heart is restless until it rests in you). His philosophy was less rationalistic than those of his successors (most notably St. Thomas Aquinas in the 13th century), but he remained the most influential and widely read Christian philosopher for over a thousand years.

The post-Augustinian period of patristic philosophy included some of the last philosophers of the Roman Empire in the West. Perhaps the best known writer of this time was Anicius Manlius Boethius (d. 524), who was the chief source of information on Greek and Roman philosophy during the first centuries of the Middle Ages. His chief work, *De consolatione philosophiae (On the Consolation of Philosophy)*, examined the questions of God, evil, and personal freedom. It included his famous observation that God is "better than which nothing can be imagined," a phrase used subsequently by St. Anselm in the rise of Scholastic philosophy. Other Christian philosophers of the patristic period included Pseudo-Dionysius, Cassiodorus (d. c. 580), and Isidore of Seville (d. 636).

See also AMMONIUS SACCAS; AMBROSE; APOLLONIUS OF TYANA; APULEIUS; ARIUS; ARRIA; ARRIAN; ATHANASIUS; BASILIDES; CALCIDIUS; CELSUS; CHRISTIANITY; CHRYSANTHIUS; CLEMENT OF ALEXANDRIA; CLEMENT OF ROME; CORNUTUS, LUCIUS; EPICUREANISM; HYPATIA; IAMBLICHUS; JULIAN THE APOSTATE; KANUS, JULIUS; LONGINUS, CASSIUS; ORIGEN; PANTAENUS; PLOTINUS; PORPHYRY; PRISCUS; PRISCUS, HELVIDIUS; PROCLUS; RUFUS, MUSONIUS; SOPATER; THEMISTIUS; THRASEA PAETUS; and VICTORINUS, MARIUS.

Suggested Readings: Annas, Julia. *Ancient Philosophy: A Very Short Introduction.* Oxford: Oxford University Press, 2000; Clark, Stephen R. L. *From Athens to Jerusalem: The Love of Wisdom and the Love of God.* New York: Oxford University Press, 1984. Copleston, Frederick. *A History of Philosophy.* Vols. 1–2. New York: Image Books, 1985. Kaufmann, Walter, and Forrest E. Baird, eds. *Philosophic Classics.* Englewood Cliffs, N.J.: Prentice Hall, 1994; Kingsley, Peter. *Ancient Philosophy, Mystery, and Magic: Empedocles and Pythagorean Tradition.* Oxford: Clarendon Press, 1995; Walsh, Martin J. *A History of Philosophy.* London: G. Chapman, 1985; Wedberg, Anders. *A History of Philosophy.* Oxford: Clarendon Press, 1982.

Philostorgius (c. 368–439 C.E.) *Ecclesiastical historian and follower of Arius*
Philostorgius who came from Cappadocia. He became an ardent admirer of the Arian bishop of Cyzicus, Eunomius and this influence colored all of his subsequent writings while he lived in Constantinople. As a historian, Philostorgius continued the work of EUSEBIUS OF CAESAREA with a *History of the Church.* Covering the years from around 300 to 425, the history viewed Christianity from an Arian perspective and thus survived only in fragments and in an epitome by Photius, who was very disrespectful of Philostorgius and his views. Of value were the sources used by Philostorgius as well as his (biased) views of the leading figures of ARIANISM.

Philostratus, Flavius (fl. early third century C.E.) *Writer and rhetorician*
Philostratus was from a wealthy family of Sophists in Lemnos, an island off the coast of Mysia. Philostratus pursued the career of sophistry. After teaching at Athens he journeyed to Rome where his reputation brought him to the attention of JULIA DOMNA, wife of Septimius Severus. She was filling the imperial court with every intellectual that she could find, and Philostratus thus became a member of her inner circle. He was an author of numerous works, the two most important being *The Lives of the Sophists* and the *Life of Apollonius of Tyana.* The latter was written in eight books, sometime between 208 and 210, probably under the influence of Julia Domna. Philostratus created such a carefully drawn, sympathetic, and laudatory biography that over the next years Apollonius was held up by pagans and anti-Christians as a counterinfluence to the Gospels.

Phoebe (fl. late first century C.E.) *Freedwoman of Julia (3), daughter of Emperor Augustus*
Phoebe acted as a confidante and was thus privy to many of Julia's adulteries. When the scandal over Julia's behavior erupted in the court in 2 B.C.E., Phoebe killed herself to avoid punishment.

phoenix Legendary bird that had the capacity to be born again from its own ashes. Its appearance was considered an omen of impending death and the start of the new era, as in late 36 C.E. when bird's appearance was believed to prophesy Tiberius's death. The phoenix was adopted by Christians as a symbol of the resurrection. Lactantius, in *de Ave Phoenice* (On the phoenix), gave it a special significance to Christ.

Phraataces (d. 4 C.E.) *King of Parthia from 2 B.C.E. to 4 C.E.*

The son of King PHRAATES IV and an Italian slave girl who had been a gift to the monarch from Augustus, Phraataces was initially considered illegitimate, Phraataces became a genuine heir when Phraates married the slave, made her his queen and changed her name from Thesmusa to Thea Musa. Phraates replaced his sons with Phraataces, sending them to Rome as willing hostages of Augustus. As the designated successor to the Parthian throne, Phraataces no longer needed his father, murdering him in 2 B.C.E. He then began to meddle in the affairs of Armenia, demanding as his price for peace the return of his brothers. Augustus refused, sending Gaius Caesar to the East. Unable to rely upon his nobles, who viewed him as illegitimate and an upstart, Phraataces made a settlement with Rome that secured the recognition by the Roman Empire of Parthia as a prominent state in the world. Despite this tacit acceptance by Rome, Phraataces was never successful in gaining the support of his own aristocracy. In 4 C.E. he was ousted from power and probably murdered by Orodes III.

Phraates III (d. 57 B.C.E.) *King of Parthia from 70 to 57 B.C.E.*

Phraates succeeded Sinatruces as king and throughout the 60s had dealings with Pompey the Great, who was settling the question of the East for Rome. His view of Roman power in the region shifted from friendly to hostile and he was one of the monarchs of Parthia to interfere in the neighboring realm of Armenia. He was assassinated by his two sons, Orodes and Mithridates.

Phraates IV (d. 2 B.C.E.) *King of Parthia from 38 to 2 B.C.E.*

Phraates murdered his father, Orodes, and took the crown. Early troubles characterized his reign, for he could not bring all of the Parthian nobles into his political camp. Many he slaughtered, some fled the country. Only when he had purged the vast domain of unreliable aristocrats and massacred most of his own family did he sit with confidence upon the throne. Phraates staved off the invasion of Parthia by Marc Antony in 36, when his General Monaeses handled operations in the field and administered a humiliating defeat to Antony. Following the battle of Actium in 31, Augustus had taken immedi-

ate steps to improve relations. He refused to support a rival claimant, Tiridates, although the usurper tried repeatedly to overthrow Phraates. In the negotiations that followed with Rome, Phraates neglected to give back the legionary standards that had been captured over the years. To force matters, Augustus ordered Tiberius to organize an army and march it to Armenia. Not desiring a war, Phraates took the unpopular step of restoring the standards to the Romans in 20.

Relations with Augustus remained cordial. Around 10 or 9 B.C.E., Phraates even sent his four sons to Rome. His motivation was probably fear of assassination or usurpation. Phraates, however, was sent a gift by Augustus, a slave girl named Thesmusa, who bore him an illegitimate son, PHRAATACES. He loved her, eventually marrying her and changing her name to Thea Musa. Phraataces thus became heir apparent and in 2 B.C.E. murdered his father for the throne.

Phrygia A region of west-central ASIA MINOR. Phrygia was an ancient state, conquered repeatedly but never losing its intellectual vitality until quashed by the Persian Empire. Roman occupation placed the country in the province of Asia, later giving a portion of its eastern section to GALATIA. During the years of the Roman Empire, Phrygians were considered slow and stupid. In the second century C.E., Phrygia was the birthplace of the apocalyptic Christian movement of MONTANUS.

Piazza Armerina A site in Sicily known for its large, fourth-century C.E. imperial villa. It was originally believed that Piazza Armerina had been built for Emperor Maximian, but recent work has shown that it dates more likely to the reign of Constantine the Great (306–337 C.E.). Architecturally it is sprawling, with baths, audience chambers and numerous rooms. Most were positioned at different axes from the others, forming a less structured style both in terms of the interior and exterior. *See also* SPLIT; TIVOLI.

Picenum One of the regions of Italy, situated on the Adriatic coast, on the opposite side of the peninsula from Rome. Picenum spread along the Adriatic and was surrounded by Umbria, Samnium, and Apulia. The region was conquered by the Romans in 268 B.C.E. and was later one of the 11 districts of Italy.

Picts A wild people living in northern Britain (BRITANNIA), especially in CALEDONIA. Called "Picts" by the Romans, for their habit of painting their bodies, they were probably related to the Caledonians or MAEATAE by blood, sharing in their hatred of Rome. In the many wars with the Roman army, from 296 C.E. onward, the Picts were frequently allied with the Scots. Constantius I was planning an expedition against them when he died in

306. Constans defeated them in 343, and Lupicinus, the general of Julian, campaigned from circa 359 to 360 against them. Magnus Maximus was hailed by his troops in 383 after crushing them. When Constantius III left the islands in 407, however, all of Britain was subject to attack by the Picts, Scots, and Saxons.

Pincian Hills *See* HILLS OF ROME.

Pinus, Cornelius (fl. late first century C.E.) *Painter*
Pinus worked with Attius Priscus on Emperor Vespasian's Honos and Virtus Temple. The two were considered the finest painters in Rome during their age.

piracy Robbery at sea. The citizens of many nations ravaged the sea-lanes of the Mediterranean, and the Romans were no exception to the suffering caused by piratic attacks. Rome's problem was made more acute by the rise of the Republic and the acquisition of overseas possessions. The Roman NAVY had never been invulnerable, as the First Punic War demonstrated in the third century B.C.E. When fighting was necessary against the pirates of Illyria, the easiest solution was to wage a land war in Dalmatia. But as the naval arm of the Roman military developed, it became possible to take the struggle directly to the pirates. This policy proved only moderately successful in the second century B.C.E. and early in the first. From 79 to 68 B.C.E., numerous sorties were attempted throughout the Mediterranean, but a lack of organization in the Senate and the absence of gifted admirals made them ultimate failures.

All of this changed in 67, when pirate squadrons from CILICIA were virtually in possession of the Mediterranean. The Senate, realizing that drastic action was necessary, finally appointed POMPEY THE GREAT, giving him vast powers and the task of clearing the seas. Sectioning off the Mediterranean, he used every ship that he could find, strangling the freedom of movement for the Cilicians while battling them on the water and destroying their land bases. Within months his job was finished, and piracy had been dealt a severe blow.

The many years of relative peace on the seas were a testament to Pompey's success. In 40 B.C.E., however, Sextus POMPEY took up the life of a buccaneer in his effort to combat the Second Triumvirate. His ships and men soon dominated the western Mediterranean, pillaged the west of Italy and occupied Sicily, Sardinia, and Corsica. This eventually threatened the vital grain supplies of Rome. Sextus was not defeated until 36 at the battle of NAULOCHUS. His vanquisher was Marcus AGRIPPA, the lieutenant of Octavian (AUGUSTUS).

With the founding of the Roman Empire, the Imperial Navy stretched its control over the entire Roman world, from the North Sea to the Red Sea, including the Channel and the Mediterranean and Black seas, as well as the Adriatic and Ionian. Inventive solutions were found to stop local pirates, such as the Liburnians of Epirus, who were hired to build Roman ships. Although this strategy was effective for over two centuries, by the middle of the third century C.E., Roman military strength had declined to such a state that from around 253 to 268 the BLACK SEA was infested with the raiding vessels of the GOTHS, who roamed the coasts of Moesia, Thrace, and Asia Minor, burning and destroying everything in their wake. The Roman recovery begun by Emperor Claudius II Gothicus helped end the Black Sea instability, and a return to a more healthy empire was achieved by Diocletian.

A new bout of piracy, however, was felt in the north. The gifted admiral CARAUSIUS was named by Diocletian to clear the sea-lanes on the coasts of Gaul, Britain, and Germany. Germanic raiders were increasingly menacing the provinces there. He succeeded in his task, but by 287 he was declared a usurper by the imperial government. But Carausius remained in possession of Britain and northern Gaul, and only in 293 was his reign ended, as ALLECTUS, his own minister, murdered him.

Henceforth pirates from Germany and along the entire North Sea coast sailed with impunity. In the early fifth century larger invasions of Britain commenced, and the isle passed out of Roman control. It was a similar story in the Mediterranean. There the Imperial Navy, debilitated by years of disuse and unable to respond to the challenge of the new VANDAL nation in Africa, saw King Geiseric of the Vandals launch his fleets against Sicily in 440. The western Mediterranean was now his, as the Roman Empire in the West crumbled.

Pisidia Country of wild hill people stretching across the inland southern regions of ASIA MINOR. Pisidia was always trouble to any force of occupation, for its inhabitants were fiercely independent. Attached to the Roman province of GALATIA, Pisidia was subjected to a rigorous campaign of pacification and Romanization as colonists, veteran Italians, were planted in the territory, centering themselves around ANTIOCH (2), a colony founded by order of Augustus.

Piso, Gaius Calpurnius (d. 65 C.E.) *Focal figure in the Pisonian Conspiracy of 65 C.E., the most famous and wide-ranging plot against Emperor Nero*
Piso came from the ancient and noble house of the Calpurnii and thus enjoyed a reputation among the populace that far outweighed his achievements. According to Tacitus, Piso used his eloquence to defend his fellow citizens, was generous and gracious in speech but lacked earnestness and was overly ostentatious, while craving the sensual. But his public image convinced many in the various ranks of society in 65 C.E. to propose him as their candidate to replace Nero on the throne. When the entire

affair was exposed, Piso refused to make a desperate attempt at winning popular support. Returning to his home, he opened his veins and killed himself. In the hope of having his wife, Satria Galla, spared, Piso filled his will with flattery toward Nero, but his testament prompted only torture and death for those who had supported him.

Piso, Gnaeus Calpurnius (d. 19 C.E.) *Consul in 7 B.C.E.*

A successful imperial official whose career and life were destroyed by his running feud with GERMANICUS, Piso came from the nobility, enjoying the friendship of the emperors Augustus and Tiberius. He was by nature arrogant, unpleasant, and violent, a manner made worse by his marriage to the high-born and beautiful PLANCINA. In 18 C.E. he made himself very useful to Tiberius by accepting the post of governor of Syria. Succeeding Creticus Silanus, Piso understood that he was to act as a counterweight to Germanicus, who had been granted the IMPERIUM MAIUS, with total control of the East. Piso took Tiberius to mean that he should work against Germanicus, and thus, from the start, attempted to undermine both his authority and his command of the legions there. A bitter hatred developed in Agrippina the Elder, Germanicus's wife, even as Germanicus tried to keep the situation from erupting into a serious hostility.

It was unfortunate that Germanicus should die under suspicious circumstances in 19. Germanicus supposedly accused Piso and Plancina of his murder as he died, and Agrippina not only carried on a campaign of charges but also included Tiberius and Livia in her accusations. Piso did little to help his own cause by offering a sacrifice of thanks to the gods upon Germanicus's demise. A trial followed before the Senate, and Piso expected Tiberius to come to his aid. The emperor, however, proved moderate in his dealings with the proceedings. The important charge of poisoning broke down under scrutiny, but this inadequacy proved unimportant because it was obvious that the Senate and the Roman people viewed Piso as the agent of Germanicus's death anyway and were unforgiving of his treatment of their popular general.

When Plancina requested that she be allowed to conduct a separate defense, Piso had but one avenue of escape. After listening to the vicious comments of the Senate he went home, and was found dead the following morning, presumably by his own hand. The death left unanswered questions about Piso's guilt in Germanicus's passing and the degree of Tiberius's involvement in the actions of Piso while in Syria.

Piso, Lucius Calpurnius (1) (fl. mid-first century B.C.E.) *Consul in 58 B.C.E.*

A friend and partisan of Julius CAESAR, Piso used his ties to Caesar and the members of the newly formed TRI-

UMVIRATE to secure for himself the consulship. As a result of this position he became closer to Caesar and secured the triumvir's marriage to his daughter CALPURNIA, but earned the lasting enmity of CICERO by refusing to prevent his exile. From 57 to 55 B.C.E. he served as governor of Macedonia. In what was viewed as a very unsuccessful term, Macedonia was damaged by Thracian invasions; upon Piso's return to Rome he did not ask for a triumph. Cicero, who himself returned in 51, vented his fury against Piso in his *In Pisonem.* This speech was deliberately cruel, and Cicero made it worse by publishing it. Both in defense of Piso and to demonstrate that a client of Caesar could not be maligned, a pamphlet, probably written by Sallust, was circulated attacking Cicero. Piso held the post of censor in 50. During the Civil Wars (*See* CIVIL WAR, FIRST AND SECOND TRIUMVIRATE) he preferred to assume a neutral stance, while relying on his Caesarean associations to smooth his path with the victors.

Piso, Lucius Calpurnius (2) (d. 32 C.E.) *Consul in 15 B.C.E. and a successful general in the service of Emperor Augustus*

Piso had the rare distinction of a natural death. He served probably with P. Sulpicius Quirinius in Galatia, where both tried to establish Roman control over the region. In Thrace, however, he gained his greatest victory. Summoned to the territory around 13 (or 12) B.C.E., Piso found the tribes there in revolt. Three years of fighting were needed before the Thracians could be pacified. For his success Piso was given triumphal honors in Rome. The exact date of his assuming his duties as PREFECT OF THE CITY is unclear. He succeeded Statilius Taurus, possibly in 12 C.E., before the death of Augustus. During that time he earned the title *pontifex* and the reputation of being tactful and subtle in the execution of his broad powers. Piso died in 32 C.E., and Tiberius gave him a lavish funeral.

Piso Licinianus (d. 69 C.E.) *Adopted heir of Emperor Galba—briefly—in 69 C.E.*

Piso Licinianus was a young nobleman, descended from Crassus on his paternal side and from Pompey on the maternal. Although he possessed no experience in government, Galba admired his impressive lineage and what was said to be excellent character. Other candidates had been available, the most important being Otho, who had served as governor of Hispania Lusitania and was of the opinion that he alone deserved to be Galba's successor. Piso, however, had the support of Cornelius LACO, prefect of the Praetorian Guard, and on January 10, 69, was presented before an unenthusiastic Guard. Galba refused to see that the grumblings of the Guard were only a foreshadowing of brutal events that would come to pass on January 15. Under the guidance of Otho, the Praetorians assassinated every major figure in the imperial circle, including Galba and Piso, who met his end in the Temple of Vesta, where he had fled in the vain hope of escaping the blades of the assassins.

Pisonian Conspiracy   The most famous of many plots to remove Nero from the throne, involving every level of Roman society and crushed so pitilessly that a pall of gloom lingered over the remainder of Nero's reign. Already in 62 C.E., there had been talk among those of senatorial rank, in the nobility and among the Equestrians (EQUITES), that Nero was a disaster, both politically and morally. By 65, Rome had endured the terrible fire and the persecution of the Christians. The small groups of conspirators united, some favoring the Republic and others a new emperor, but all agreeing that Nero had to die. Seneca was suggested as a replacement, until it was decided that Gaius Calpurnius PISO was the best possible choice.

A list of members in the conspiracy reveals the extent of Nero's unpopularity. There were the consul Plautius Lateranus; the prefect of the Guard Faenius Rufus, joined by several tribunes and centurions of the Guard; senators Afranius Quintianus and Flavius Scaevinus; the knight Antonius Natalis, as well as Seneca and Lucan. There were certainly many others involved, a fact that helped to ensure the failure of the conspiracy. The date of the assassination was to be during the Circensian Games (see LUDI) in late April. This date was probably set too far in the future, for details of the coup leaked through a freedwoman, Epicharis, who tried to enroll Volusius Proculus, an officer of the fleet at Misenum. Proculus informed Nero, but Epicharis died before any names could be extracted.

On the night before the fateful day, the freedman Milichus, in the service of Scaevinus, informed on his master. One by one the plotters were arrested, and many, such as Lucan, Natalis, and Scaevinus, told of the others in the hope of staying alive. Nero responded to the plot by ordering the death of everyone involved. Some met their end heroically. Piso, Seneca, and Lucan committed suicide. In all, 19 were put to death and 13 exiled. Equally, membership in the plot was used as a charge against some of Nero's later victims, as a useful tool for execution or murder. Tigellinus, the perfect of the Guard, was also given a free hand in hunting down the emperor's potential enemies, a task that he fulfilled with enthusiasm.

Pituanius, Lucius   (early first century C.E.) *Astrologer in Rome during the reign of Tiberius (14–37 C.E.)*
In 16 C.E., as part of the emperor's campaign against astrologers in Italy, Pituanius was hurled to his death from the Tarpeian Rock as a warning to others.

See also ASTROLOGY.

Placentia   City in Gallia Cisalpina about 40 miles southeast of modern Milan; founded as a Roman colony circa 219 B.C.E. and located on the Via Aemilia, on the right bank of the Po River. In 69 C.E., it was the scene of intense fighting in the prelude to the first battle of BEDRIACUM; and much of the city was damaged.

The first bitter skirmish was fought in April between the converging forces of Emperor Otho and General CAECINA ALIENUS, a supporter of the claimant VITELLIUS. Knowing that his troops were too few to oppose successfully the larger columns of Vitellius, Otho dispatched Annius Gallus and Vestricius Spurinna to northern Italy to do what they could. With only three cohorts of the Praetorian Guard and some legionaries and cavalry, Spurinna barricaded himself into Placentia. Caecina arrived with his army, pushing his units into action. Amazingly, despite damage to the town, the Praetorians repulsed Caecina so successfully that his frontal assaults had to be abandoned. As the Othonians lacked enough troops to exploit their advantage, the battle of Placentia served only to attract the armies of both sides and thus ensure the first battle of Bedriacum.

In 270 C.E., Emperor Aurelian was severely defeated near Placentia by the JUTHUNGI, who had invaded Italy. Another engagement, fought in early 456 C.E., ended the reign of Emperor AVITUS. MAJORIAN, a claimant to the throne in the West, found a patron in RICIMER, the MAGISTER MILITUM, and in 456 moved with an army into Italy to depose Avitus. Gathering forces, the emperor accepted battle near Placentia. Unpopular with many elements of the government and army, he was unable to hold together his units, and the result was a crushing defeat. With his general killed, Avitus fled to Placentia, becoming a bishop, but was slain a short time later.

Placidia, Galla   (d. 450 C.E.) *Mother of Valentinian III and Augusta from 421 to 450*
Placidia was one of the most formidable figures of the fifth century C.E., the daughter of Emperor Theodosius and Empress Galla, born and educated in Constantinople before moving to the West with her half-brother Honorius around 395. Living in Rome, Galla Placidia was present in 410 for the sack of the city by Alaric and the Visigoths.

As a member of the imperial family she fascinated her barbarian captors, eventually being forced to marry Alaric's successor, ATHAULF, in 414. Galla gained considerable influence over her husband. Athaulf departed for Spain with Galla Placidia and their young son, Theodosius. The son died, followed by Athaulf himself. The princess returned to the status of bargaining tool, this time in the hands of Wallia, the new Visigothic ruler.

Her predicament would have continued had the Visigoths not faced difficulties in Spain and suffered military reverses at the hands of CONSTANTIUS III, Honorius's reliable lieutenant. Through negotiations Placidia was returned to her half-brother, who made her wed Constantius in early 417. This union must have been disagreeable to Galla Placidia, although it produced another son, Valentinian III. When Honorius accepted Constantius as his colleague in power, she became Augusta in 421. All seemed well, until Constantius suddenly died. A disagreement soon surfaced with Honorius, who apparently developed a passion for Placidia.

In 423, Galla Placidia departed for Constantinople, and Honorius died soon after. After the usurper John had been crushed, she and Valentinian III sailed for Rome in 425, where he was to sit upon the Western throne while she ruled in his name. Her influence was at first unquestioned and supreme. Around 433, however, the MAGISTER MILITUM AETIUS emerged as a potential rival. Galla Placidia tried to replace him with the *magister militum* BONIFACE but failed and lost her power. Defeated, she retired to private life as her son came under the influence of Aetius and his courtiers. She died on November 27, 450.

Plancina, Munatia (d. 33 C.E.) *Wife of Gnaeus Calpurnius Piso*

Munatia Plancina was probably the granddaughter of the famous Munatius Plancus. From a wealthy and prestigious family, she married Piso, a friend of AUGUSTUS and TIBERIUS, while she gained the status of client to LIVIA, an association of great importance later. In 18 C.E., Tiberius appointed Piso to be governor of Syria, no doubt with instructions to watch GERMANICUS, who had been appointed to the East. Livia perhaps ordered Plancina to vie with Germanicus's wife, AGRIPPINA THE ELDER. This she did, and a bitter hatred erupted between the two parties. Thus the death of Germanicus under suspicious circumstances was immediately attributed to Piso and Plancina.

Plancina certainly sensed that Piso was doomed, for a trial was set before the Senate. As his political future was ruined, she used her ties to Livia to secure for herself a secret pardon and then asked for a defense separate from his, this despite her friendship with the known poisoner Martina, who had died suddenly before she could testify at the proceedings. Piso killed himself, and Plancina was pardoned in 20. Thirteen years passed before Tiberius was willing to move against her. The hatred of Agrippina and the protection of Livia had shielded her from Tiberius's cruel nature, but by 33 both were gone. Condemned for the old crime, she killed herself.

Plancus, Lucius Munatius (fl. first century B.C.E.) *Consul in 42 B.C.E. and a supporter of Julius Caesar, Marc Antony and then Augustus*

Plancus began as a legate in the army of Caesar during the Gallic Wars, becoming Caesar's closest client and friend. Through the dictator's patronage he received the proconsulship of Gaul. As governor, sometime after Cae-

sar's assassination in 44, Plancus established colonies at Raurica (Augst) in 44 and Lugdunum (Lyon) in 43. As head of Gallia Transalpina, Plancus was initially on the side of the Republic in the war against Marc Antony, but deserted in 42 to Antony's cause. This transfer of allegiance dealt a cruel blow to Republicanism and caused, in large part, the death of Decimus BRUTUS ALBINUS. As a lieutenant of Antony, he pursued his master's interests, refusing to help Fulvia and Lucius Antony conduct the PERUSINE WAR against Octavian (AUGUSTUS) in 41 B.C.E., losing two legions anyway to Marcus Agrippa via defections.

As was the case with other followers of Antony, Plancus was unable to bear the influence of Cleopatra and, before Actium, offered his services to Octavian. Not only did Plancus bring with him great experience in politics and war, he also revealed details of Antony's will that were confirmed by Octavian's later seizure of the document. Used against Antony, the will was of help in swaying public opinion to Octavian's side. After Antony's defeat and death, Plancus was a firm adherent of the regime of Octavian, proposing that the month Sextilis be changed to Augustus (August). That Augustus trusted him was seen by his position of respect, his lavish spending on Roman buildings and his position as censor in 22. He was a friend and patron of literary figures, including Horace, who addressed one of his odes to him. Others viewed him harshly. Velleius Paterculus called him a vile traitor. The tomb of Plancus was a round structure at Gaeta, now part of a castle.

Plancus Bursa, Titus Munatius (fl. first century B.C.E.) *Tribune of the Plebs in 52 B.C.E. and the brother of Lucius Munatius Plancus*

Titus was involved in the politics of 52 and had a hand in the burning of the Curia following the death of CLODIUS PULCHER. Put on trial, he was condemned despite the help of POMPEY THE GREAT. Banished, he nevertheless returned in time to fight for Marc Antony at the battle of MUTINA in 43.

Platonism   *See* NEOPLATONISM; PHILOSOPHY.

Plautianus, Gaius Fulvius (d. 205 C.E.) *Prefect of the praetorian guard during the reign of Septimius Severus*

Coming from Africa, Plautianus possibly was related to Severus and thus gained a favorable position in the Praetorians. He was eventually named co-prefect, with Aemilius Saturninus, but murdered him sometime around 197 C.E. or earlier. Henceforth he ran the Guard by himself, jealously watching for any possible rivals. As with the prefects who preceded him, Plautianus made himself indispensable to the emperor and so acquired both influence over his master and control over every element of government. The historian Dio condemned his corruption by writing that he wanted everything, demanded everything and took everything, leaving no province or city unplundered. Severus surrendered sway over the empire to him, and the consular insignia as well, giving him a consulship in 203, with Geta, the emperor's younger son.

In 202, Plautianus became attached officially to the imperial family through the marriage of his daughter Plautilla to Geta's brother, CARACALLA. As a gift to his child he had 100 Romans, of all classes, castrated to act as her private eunuchs. Caracalla, however, resented the prefect, loathed the daughter and was probably responsible, in 205, for organizing the plot to destroy Plautianus. Accused of conspiring to murder the emperor, Plautianus was stripped of his offices and put to death.

Plautilla (d. 211 C.E.) *Wife of Caracalla, from 202 to 205* Daughter of the Praetorian Prefect G. Fulvius PLAUTIANUS, she was betrothed to Caracalla in 200, she wed him in 202, their union proving unhappy, for the imperial heir loathed her and resented Plautianus. The prefect fell from power in 205, and she learned of his death when bits of his beard were given to her. She and her brother Plautius were banished to Lipara, where they lived in constant dread. In 211, Caracalla came to the throne and they were slain. Although her father lavished many gifts upon her, the stories of her wanton habits and adulteries were probably untrue.

Plautius (d. 211 C.E.) *Son of Plautianus, prefect of the Praetorian Guard* When his father fell from power in 205 and was executed, Plautius and his sister Plautilla were exiled to Lipara. In 211, he and Plautilla were put to death by order of Caracalla, newly ascended to the throne.

Plautius, Aulus (fl. first century C.E.) *Consul in 29 C.E. and the conqueror of Britain for Emperor Claudius in 43* Aulus Plautius had served as the governor of Pannonia, when Claudius chose him in 43 to lead the Roman invasion of Britain. Using superior Roman legions, he defeated the British and Belgic tribes in southern Britain, capturing the capital of Camulodonum. Over the next four years he systematically pacified the old kingdom of Cunobellinus, returning to Rome to accept a deserved OVATIO. According to the historian Tacitus, in 57 he sat in judgment on his wife, Pomponia Graecina, to determine her guilt or innocence on charges of believing in foreign cults (*externa superstitio*); he found her innocent.

Plautius Lateranus (d. 65 C.E.) *Nephew of Aulus Plautius, the conqueror of Britain in 43 C.E.* In his time, became embroiled in two major scandals, with Empress MESSALLINA in 48 C.E. and in the PISONIAN CONSPIRACY in 65. Claudius's chief secretary was aware that Lateranus had become Messallina's lover but did

nothing until 48, when the empress married another paramour, Gaius Silius, in a mock ceremony, an act that brought her indiscretions to light. Because of his uncle, Lateranus was spared by Claudius but was ousted from the Senate. In 65, he became one of the ringleaders in a plot to assassinate Emperor Nero. He despised the tyrant, despite the emperor's restoration to him of his rights lost in the Messallina affair. When the plot was uncovered, the punishment of death was hurried in his case. Lateranus reportedly met his fate (at a site in the modern Porta Maggiore) with bravery and silence. Tacitus described him as a big man, firm and resolute in character. Juvenal wrote of his luxurious palace on the Caelian Hill as an example of fallen wealth.

Plautius Silvanus, Marcus (fl. early first century C.E.) *Consul in 2 B.C.E. and a successful general in the service of Augustus* Marcus Plautius Silvanus held the post of proconsul of Asia before becoming the legate of Galatia. There he possibly fought with the local tribesmen, perhaps the Isaurians. In 6 C.E. he marched to the aid of Tiberius in Pannonia with badly needed reinforcements, spending the next three years campaigning in Pannonia and Illyricum. For his victories he received the *ornamenta triumphalia* in 9. Plautius's two children achieved notoriety. His son, Plautius Silvanus, committed suicide in 24 rather than face condemnation for shoving his wife out of a window. A daughter, Plautia Urgulanilla, married Claudius. His mother, Urgulania, was a friend of Livia.

Plautius Silvanus Aelianus, Tiberius (d. 62 C.E.) *Consul suffectus in 45 and ordinarius in 74 C.E. and a successful general and governor* Plautius was a legate during the invasion of Britain in 43 C.E., where Claudius showed him favor, possibly because Plautia Urgulanilla, a relative, had once been married to the emperor. Appointed legate of MOESIA by Nero, Plautius achieved success along the lower Danube, despite the limited number of troops at his disposal. Much of the Danube was pacified under his administration, as more than 100,000 tribesmen were relocated to the south bank of the river. Treaties were made with local chieftains, and a massive corn supply was made available to Rome. Nero was typically unwilling to give him any honors, an oversight that Vespasian corrected. The new emperor gave him a second consulship in 74, the *ornamenta triumphalia* and the governorship of Hispania Tarraconensis. Upon his return to Rome after serving as governor in Spain (c. 74), Vespasian made him PREFECT OF THE CITY.

Plebeians Also called Plebs; the general populace of Rome, separate from the elite class of the PATRICIANS. Although tradition stated that Romulus divided the Roman people into two distinct classes, the differences between the Plebeians and the Patricians were not actually felt until the time of the early Republic. According to law and custom, the Plebs could not enter the priestly colleges, hold magistracies or marry into the class of the *patricii*. They did command certain rights, including positions in the army. The status of the Plebeians was greatly aided by increased organization, to the extent that they could challenge the Patricians as a legitimate order. The *plebeius ordo* soon had its own assemblies, magistrates, and officials, including TRIBUNES and AEDILES. As the Patricians dwindled in number by the end of the Republic, the Plebeians filled the vacuum. In the imperial epoch "Plebeian" actually referred to those of the lowest social strata.

See also SOCIAL CLASSES.

Pliny the Elder (Gaius Plinius Secundus) (c. 23–79 C.E.) *Writer, cavalry commander, and one of the greatest encyclopedists in Roman history*

Pliny was born at Comum, the son of an Equestrian, and received his education probably at Rome. Pursuing an Equestrian career, he helped create the harbor at Ostia for Claudius, drained the Fucine Lake and spent 12 years with the legions, mainly in Germany. Leader of a cavalry squadron, he later (54–68 C.E.) wrote on cavalry tactics.

On the accession of Vespasian in 69, he found an imperial patron, first in the new emperor and then in his son Titus, whom he had known from his days in Germania. He was given a procuratorship, and he also served as an adviser to Vespasian and Titus. Awarded the prefectship of the fleet at Misenum, he was there in the summer of 79 when Mount Vesuvius erupted. On August 24, he sailed from Misenum to Stabiae to observe the volcano. Poisonous gases killed him as he attempted to gather more information for his scientific works. His death was recorded by his nephew and adopted son, PLINY THE YOUNGER.

As a writer, Pliny used his vast energies and insatiable curiosity to author numerous histories and studies. Regrettably, only the *Natural History* survives. Other works included: *De iaculatione equestri*, the analysis of horse tactics; *De vita Pomponi Secundi*, a biography of Pomponius Secundus, a friend and patron; and *Bella Germaniae*, a 20-volume history of the wars between Rome and the German tribes down to 47 C.E., later used by Tacitus in both his *Annals* and *Germania*. Pliny also wrote *Studiosi*, a three-part guide on oratory; *Dubius Sernio*, an eight-volume treatise on suspect or doubtful language or linguistic forms; and *A fine Aufidi Bassi*, or *From Where Aufidius Bassus Left Off*, a continuation of the Roman history of Bassus in 30 books, covering possibly the reigns of Claudius and Nero with the civil war of 69, composed in the more liberal times of the Flavians, from 71 to 77.

While knowledge of these works comes only from descriptions by Pliny the Younger, Pliny's masterwork survived: the *Naturalis Historia*, 37 books with a preface, index and collections pertaining to the cosmos, geography, humanity, zoology, botany, medicine, mineralogy, art, and architecture. In his preface, Pliny wrote that he consulted 100 authors and 2,000 volumes, having amassed 20,000 individual facts. But as Pliny enlarged his work with each new discovery, the total number of books listed is over 4,000, and the facts were correspondingly higher. Although his approach was unscientific, he nevertheless succeeded in compiling a stunning array of data on the important, the trivial and even the absurd, and helped preserve many fragments of ancient works that would otherwise have been lost.

Pliny the Younger (Gaius Plinius Caecilius Secundus) (c. 61–122 C.E.) *Writer*

Born at Comum, Pliny was adopted by his uncle, PLINY THE ELDER, thus receiving an excellent education at Rome, including instruction by QUINTILIAN. After serving with a legion in Syria, he embarked upon a senatorial career. As an ADVOCATUS, he prosecuted several imperial provincial officials for extortion. He was a PRAETOR in 93, next serving as prefect of the *aerarium militare* and prefect of the *aerarium Saturni* from c. 94 to 100 and as consul in 100. Pliny enjoyed Trajan's favor and trust, sitting on the imperial board of advisers, the CONSILIUM PRINCIPIS. He was sent to Bithynia as a special legate in 110, where he died in office.

Pliny's historical notoriety lies in his extensive communication with friends and the Emperor Trajan. Two-hundred and forty-seven letters, written between 98 and 108, survive, including 121 dispatched to Trajan from before and during his period in Bithynia. His *epistulae* were filled with details of the social, political, historical, and domestic events of the time, each centered on a major theme or idea, especially on government, Christianity and the works of his uncle. Aside from the letters, he also attempted poetry and oratory, and in 100 delivered *Panegyricus* to Trajan in the Senate on reception of his consulship.

Plotina, Pompeia (d. 121/122 C.E.) *Empress from 98 to 117*

The wife of Trajan, Plotina was known for her humility, virtue, and dignity. Dio wrote that when she entered the imperial palace she exclaimed: "I would leave here the same woman as I now enter." In 100 she was offered the title Augusta but refused it and could not be convinced to accept the honor until five years later. She bore Trajan no children, but at his death in Cilicia in 117, she played an instrumental role in Hadrian's adoption as successor. Upon her death, he consecrated two temples in her honor, in the Forum of Trajan and in Nîmes.

Plotinus (205–270 C.E.) *Neoplatonic philosophers*

Plotinus was probably born in Egypt but spoke Greek. After deciding to pursue philosophy, c. 232–233, he spent

11 years studying with Ammonius Sarcas in Alexandria. In an attempt to learn Eastern or oriental thought, he joined the expedition of Emperor Gordian III against Persia (242–245). In 244–245, he moved to Rome, remaining there as a teacher until his death in Campania.

Of central importance to Plotinus was the idea of the One, the source of all things, from which all creation flowed. Individual unification with the One was possible through intense contemplation. It was the duty of all persons, he believed, to strive toward this goal. Most of Plotinus's doctrines were written only after 255. Fifty-four of his essays were assembled by his student PORPHYRY and published early in the fourth century under the title *Enneads*. Augustine is said to have quoted the pagan philosopher on his deathbed.

See also NEOPLATONISM.

Plutarch (Lucius [?] Mestrius Plutarchus) (before 50–after 120 C.E.) *Historian, writer, and one of the most popular and widely read authors of the ancient world*
Plutarch was from Chaeronea, born sometime during the reign of Claudius (41–54 C.E.) He studied at Athens and knew Egypt and Italy. Despite a successful tour as lecturer at Rome, Plutarch spent most of his years in Chaeronea, Boeotia, and perhaps as a procurator in Achaea, under Trajan and Hadrian. Noted for his devotion to the gods, he served for 30 years as a priest at Delphi. Among his friends were Sosius Senecio and FAVORINUS.

Plutarch was a prolific author. Most of his writings are collectively known as the *Moralia;* its 78 separate compositions include works of moral philosophy on Aristotle, Plato, Epicureanism, Stoicism, and atheism and dialogues concerning the intelligence of animals (*De sollertia animalium*), the genius of Socrates, and the nature of Platonism. Other titles included *Advice on Public Life, On the Fortune of the Romans,* and *Roman Questions (Quaestiones Romanae),* as well as treatises on the raising of children, marriage, divine fortune, and diatribes against Stoicism. But Plutarch's most famous work is his *Lives,* 23 paired biographies of Greek and Roman historical figures, notable for their vivid, anecdotal narrative style and historical detail. Written in the first century C.E., Plutarch's *Lives* prefigures the great second century C.E. movement to formalize the synthesis of Rome and Greece.

Pluton   Roman name for the god of DEATH, or the underworld. Confused with the older god of the dead, Orcus, Pluton, or Pluto, allowed the Romans to make reference to this feared deity without having to say his dreaded name: Hades. "Pluton" came from his association as the giver of wealth, for he controlled all that came from the earth. In this way he was similar to Dis Pater, the wealthy god of death. According to the Romanized Greek pantheon, Pluton was the son of Saturn and the brother of JUPITER and NEPTUNE. He was married to Proserpina, whom he abducted from the Upperworld. His cultic rites included the sacrifice of a black sheep, with his supplicants averting their eyes from the traditionally gloomy statue of the god, wielding his staff over his domain. Temples or altars to Pluton were very rare in the Roman world, for the Romans were reluctant to give prayers to such a fearsome deity.

See also GODS AND GODDESSES OF ROME.

poetry   One of the most popular and important forms of self-expression among the Romans. Few peoples produced the variety or the number of geniuses in poetical writing than the Romans did. From the time of Cicero, poets played an important role in describing and defining society, in verse ranging from the epic to the elegiac, bucolic, satiric, and erotic. Like the social system of the time, one could find a poet to satisfy one's tastes, be it grand as Virgil, raucous as Catullus or biting as Juvenal.

See LITERATURE for a discussion of poetry in literary history. *See also* the individual poets included in this volume.

first century B.C.E.   CATULLUS, Gaius Helvius CINNA, Cornelius GALLUS, HORACE, Aemilius Macer, Domitius Marsus, OVID, Sextus PROPERTIUS, Albius TIBULLUS, L. VARIUS RUFUS, VIRGIL.

first century C.E.   Caecius Bassus, Titus Calpurnius Siculus, Saleius Bassus, CORNELIUS SEVERUS, C. Valerius FLACCUS, Grattius, JULIUS CEREALIS, JUVENAL, LUCAN, Marcus MANILIUS, MARTIAL, Publius POMPONIUS SECUNDUS, STATIUS, SULPICIA.

second century C.E.   Lucius Arruntius Stella, HADRIAN, OPPIAN.

third century C.E.   COMMODIAN, M. Aurelius NEMESIANUS, Q. Seremus Sammonicus.

fourth century C.E.   AUSONIUS, Postumus Avienus, CLAUDIAN, Gaius Vettius JUVENCUS, PALLADAS, PAULINUS OF NOLA, Publilius Optatianus PORFYRIUS, PRUDENTIUS, QUINTUS OF SMYRNA, SYNESIUS OF CYRENE, TIBERIANUS.

fifth century C.E.   Flavius MEROBAUDES (2).

Polemo, Marcus Antonius (c. 88–145 C.E.) *Noted Greek rhetorician and Sophist*
Polemo came from Laodicea but spent most of his life at SMYRNA. As one of the leading orators of his generation, Polemo was an associate and friend of Emperor HADRIAN, accompanying him on the imperial tour of Greece. In a cause of improving the status of his adopted city of Smyrna, he spoke before the emperor, winning his favor at the expense of the rival city EPHESUS. This speechmaking was both a professional and a personal challenge, for Ephesus was represented by Polemo's archenemy, FAVORINUS. In 130, the Athenians asked Polemo to give an ora-

tion at the start of the Olympics in Athens. He claimed as his greatest pupil Aristides.

Polemo I (d. 8 B.C.E.) *King of Pontus*

Son of the great orator Zeno of Laodicea and a reliable client to Marc ANTONY, Polemo was appointed him ruler of Cilicia Tracheia around 39 B.C.E. As Antony later gave that domain to Cleopatra, he was forced to find a new kingdom for Polemo, settling on the vacant throne of Pontus. This was a more than suitable gift, for not only did Polemo now control Pontus, but Antony gave him as well parts of Bithynia, the Upper Euphrates and Armenia Minor. Polemo remained loyal to Antony, serving as a watcher on Parthia's northern flanks during Antony's war with the Parthians in 36. Just as the Romans fared poorly, so too did their allies and Polemo was captured by the Medes. Returned to his country, the king took an oath of allegiance to Antony before the campaign of ACTIUM and then watched the Armenian frontier while his master was away fighting Octavian (c. 32–31 B.C.E.).

When word arrived that Antony had been destroyed at the battle of Actium, Polemo took immediate steps to negotiate for peace with Octavian (AUGUSTUS). The new master of the Roman world perceived Polemo's value and allowed him to retain Pontus, removing Armenia Minor from his control. As part of his attempt at organizing the East, Augustus seized the kingdom of the BOSPORUS through his lieutenant, Marcus Agrippa. Polemo was then granted the region through a forced marriage to the widowed Queen Dynamis (c. 16 B.C.E.) The union proved unsuccessful, and Dynamis fled to the nearby Sarmatian tribes. The next years were spent trying to subdue the chieftain Aspurgus. Campaigning incessantly, Polemo fell in battle.

Polemo II (fl. first century C.E.) *King of Pontus*

The son of POLEMO I and his second wife, Pythodoris, Polemo ruler of the domains of Pontus and the BOSPORUS kingdom, given to him in 39 C.E. by Emperor Claudius. In 41, Claudius took away the territories of the Bosporus to bestow them upon Mithridates. As compensation, Polemo was given the Cilician districts of Alba, Cennatis, and Lalassis. After losing the Bosporus to Claudius, Polemo was forced to surrender the Pontic kingdom as well, to Emperor Nero in 64–65. Having had Pontus annexed by Rome, he retired to his Cilician holdings and there lived out his remaining years.

Pollentia

City about 20 miles inland from the Adriatic coast of central Italy; site of a military engagement fought on April 6, 402 C.E., between the armies of ALARIC and the VISIGOTHS and the MAGISTER MILITUM STILICHO. By the autumn of 401, Alaric felt confident enough to mount an invasion of Italy with the hope of inducing Emperor Honorius to surrender large sections of the Danubian frontier.

With his host of Visigoths, Alaric passed over the Italian Alps, probably captured Aquileia and moved toward Milan, where a terrified Honorius demanded that Stilicho come to his aid. Stilicho was busy that winter, defeating another barbarian ruler, Radagaisus, before moving to Italy in February of 402.

To prepare for Stilicho, Alaric maneuvered his forces to Hasta (Asti) and then took up a position at Pollentia (Polenza). Stilicho advanced, accepted the confrontation and a great slaughter ensued. Details of the battle are unclear, except that the losses on both sides were heavy. At day's end, Stilicho had the upper hand but refused to exploit it. Instead, he negotiated a Visigothic withdrawal from Italy. While he could claim that Rome was saved, Stilicho knew that Pollentia was only a temporary reprieve.

Pollio, Gaius Asinius (c. 76 B.C.E.–5 C.E.) *Consul in 40 B.C.E., governor and a literary figure*

A supporter of Julius Caesar, Pollio held the rank of PRAETOR in 45 and was governor of Hispania Ulterior around the time of Caesar's assassination in 44. In the subsequent division of the Roman world into armed camps, Pollio threw in with Marc ANTONY, marching two legions from Spain for his use. He backed Lucius Antony in the PERUSINE WAR (41) but was more enthusiastic as the representative of Antony in the negotiations with Gaius Maecenas leading to the TREATY OF BRUNDISIUM in 40. After serving as consul in 40, he was given 11 legions by Antony and sent to campaign against the Parthini tribes in the Balkans. As proconsul of Macedonia, Pollio crushed the Parthini in Illyricum in 39 and triumphed in that year, or perhaps 38. A falling out then took place with Antony, and Pollio, feeling that Octavian (AUGUSTUS) was too young to deserve his loyalties, retired from public life, refusing to help either side. During the reign of Augustus and following Antony's death, Pollio did not offer submission to the emperor, nor did he seek his downfall. This coolness remained a characteristic of Pollio until his death.

In matters of literature, Pollio was both a patron and a contributor. He began the first public library in 39 B.C.E., decorating it with portraits of famous authors. He gave exhibitions of his own art collections and initiated the system of recitations by invitation. Oratory was his area of expertise, and he spoke as a declaimer and often delivered orations of a legal or political nature. So effectively did he attack the Troy Games that Augustus cancelled them. A dislike of rhetoricians was evidenced in his criticism of Cicero and in the fragments of speeches preserved by Seneca the Elder.

Pollio was a poet who was overshadowed by some of his generation's greats: Catullus, Cinna, Horace, and Virgil. His tragedies were published and possibly performed. Another style that he pursued was erotic composition. Of greater note was Pollio's history of the Civil War, from around 60 to 42 B.C.E. Of a highly independent nature, the *historiae* covered the battles of Pharsalus and Thapsus, the death of Cato, the death of Cicero, and the battle of Philippi.

Pollio, Publius Vedius (d. 15 B.C.E.) *Equestrian of low birth and official under Augustus*

Pollio was renowned for his immense wealth and cruel nature. It was written that at his estate in Campania he kept a pool of man-eating lamprey. Any servant or slave with whom he was displeased was thrown into the pool. Augustus was visiting one day when a slave broke a crystal goblet. Pollio ordered him fed to the lampreys, but Augustus tried to dissuade him. When the imperial attempts failed, Augustus called for the remaining goblets and broke them himself, thus saving the unfortunate cup bearer. Pollio died in 15 B.C.E., leaving most of his property to Augustus, including his famous estate of Pausilypon ("grief-relieving" in Greek) situated at modern Posilipo, between Puteoli and Naples. Pollio declared in his will that some monument should be erected there. On the pretense that he was initiating the project, Augustus razed the estate to erase the memory of this unpleasant man.

Pollio, Rufrius (d.c. 47 C.E.) *Coprefect of the Praetorian Guard*

Pollio served with Catonius JUSTUS during part of the reign of Emperor Claudius. Pollio was probably the commander of the cohorts of the Praetorian Guard that accompanied Claudius on his British campaign of 43 C.E. As a reward for his services, he was granted a statue in 44 and given the right to sit in the Senate with the emperor. He was put to death later by Claudius, perhaps before 47.

Polybius (d. 47 or 48 C.E.) *Freedman in the service of Emperor Claudius*

Aside from his probable duties as A LIBELLUS, Polybius headed the recently created "literary office," the *a studiis,* concerned with all matters of literary importance. His power during the years 42–43 C.E. was made clear by SENECA's letter to him, *Consolatio ad Polybium,* a message of condolence on the death of his brother. Seneca used flattery and obvious exaggeration to implore Polybius to help in recalling him from exile. The freedman was also noted for his translation of Virgil into Greek and Homer into Latin. He was killed by Messallina, despite the fact that she was sleeping with him.

Polycarp (c. 69–115/6 or 167/8 C.E.) *Bishop of Smyrna and a leading Christian figure in Asia in the second century C.E.*

Polycarp was a staunch defender of orthodox CHRISTIANITY. Beyond that, and his martyrdom, few details of his life survived. He authored an extant *Epistle to the Philippians,* concerning their keeping the faith intact. At a very old age he visited Rome to discuss Easter traditions and upon his return to Smyrna faced arrest during a pagan festival. Refusing to give up his creed, Polycarp was burned alive. According to Eusebius's *Chronicle,* Polycarp was martyred in 167 or 168 during the time of Marcus Aurelius. Other sources probably more correctly put the date as 155 or 156, with the actual day traditionally listed as February 23. He died at the age of 86.

Polycleitus (fl. first century C.E.) *Freedman in the service of Nero (ruled 54–68 C.E.)*

Also called Polyclitus, he was sent in 61 C.E. to Britain to observe the actions of the legate SUETONIUS PAULINUS, while attempting to ease the rebellious spirit of the local tribes following the bitter war with BOUDICCA. Polycleitus infuriated the legions in Britain, representing as he did the class of former slaves (freedmen). Further, the Britons treated him with contempt. He reappeared in 67 as the assistant of the corrupt Helius in his administration of Rome during Nero's trip to Greece.

pomerium Also *pomoerium,* a space traditionally left within a city wall to denote the boundary of the original foundation. According to custom, a pair of oxen, one a bull, the other a heifer, drew a plough around the area of a desired city. This marking of upturned earth was the *pomerium.* No buildings could be constructed in a set distance from the *pomerium,* so as to clearly define the beginnings of a community. The *pomerium* of ROME was of considerable political importance for it symbolized the termination of power for any who held the IMPERIUM upon entrance into the city. The great exception to this rule was Augustus (ruled 27 B.C.E.–14 C.E.), who held the rank of proconsul given to him for life by the Senate. The *pomerium* was expanded several times, in the first century B.C.E. and in the first century C.E.; Julius Caesar did it in 44 B.C.E., Augustus in 8 B.C.E. and Claudius in 49 C.E.

Pomona
Roman goddess of the fruit trees. Pomona bore the title *pomorum patrona,* or patron of fruit, and was considered important as one of the divinites of nature. She had her own member of the FLAMENS, the Flamen Pomonalis, who presided over all of her ceremonies. According to Roman legend her beauty attracted other gods of nature, including Silvanus.

See also GODS AND GODDESSES OF ROME.

Pompeia (1) (fl. first century B.C.E.) *Second wife of Julius Caesar*

Daughter of Quintus Pompeius and granddaughter of Sulla, Pompeia wed Caesar in 67 B.C.E. but was divorced by him in 61, on suspicion of adultery with CLODIUS PULCHER, who reportedly dressed as a woman and violated the sacred BONA DEA rituals just to seduce her. Caesar refused to testify against her at the divorce. When asked why he had initiated such proceedings, he commented, according to Suetonius, "I cannot allow members of my house to be accused or under suspicion."

Pompeia (2) (fl. first century B.C.E.) *Daughter of Pompey the Great and sister of Sextus Pompey*
Pompeia was betrothed in 39 B.C.E. to MARCELLUS, son of Octavia, sister of Octavian (AUGUSTUS), but the marriage plans were later terminated.

Pompeianus, Ruricius (d. 312 C.E.) *Commander of Emperor Maxentius's cavalry and infantry in 312 C.E.*
In charge of VERONA and the surrounding area of Venetia during CONSTANTINE the Great's invasion of Italy, Pompeianus found himself besieged at Verona by Constantine and with an effective attack broke through the siege lines and rode for help. The nearest available reinforcements were gathered and marched back to Verona, where Pompeianus hoped to trap Constantine. He had Constantine's forces caught between himself and the city walls. Unfortunately, Constantine was too good a general to panic in the face of the charge. He gave battle while holding the lines of circumvallation secure. Pompeianus fell during the battle.
See also MILVIAN BRIDGE.

Pompeianus, Tiberius Claudius (fl. second century C.E.) *Consul in perhaps 167 and 173 C.E. and a one of the most reliable general in the army of Emperor Marcus Aurelius*
Despite only senatorial-level origins, he was the emperor's choice to marry Annia LUCILLA, the emperor's daughter, widowed after the death of Lucius Verus. Wed in 169, they were not happy together, but Pompeianus remained a fixture at court. When COMMODUS succeeded to the throne in 180, Pompeianus tried to convince him to continue the MARCOMANNIC WAR against the Germans, but the new ruler refused. Unable to bear the depths to which Commodus reduced the office of emperor, Pompeianus left the city of Rome. Following the successful murder of the emperor in 192, Pompeianus returned to Rome and was offered the throne. He refused in favor of Pertinax, who was killed in 193. Again Pompeianus's name surfaced, and again he declined.

Pompeii   History's most famous victim of a volcanic eruption and, aside from Rome itself, the best preserved archaeological site in the entire world. At the time of its burial by Mount Vesuvius at 10:00 A.M. on August 24, 79 C.E., Pompeii, southeast of Naples, was a thriving city and an ancient one. In existence since the eighth century B.C.E., it was built as a market community in Campania by the local Oscans, who were subsequently influenced by the Greeks, Etruscans, Samnites, Italians, and, finally, by the Romans. Actual inclusion in the Roman franchise did not come until after 89 B.C.E., so Pompeii was a latecomer to Romanization. Full Latinization and

A house from Pompeii *(Courtesy Fr. Felix Just, S.J.)*

Roman architecture were introduced only slowly, aided in large measure by an earthquake in 62 C.E., which was recorded by Tacitus and Seneca. The severe damage caused by this natural calamity allowed rebuilding in a completely Italian style. Thus, in 79, a perfect example of a first-century-C.E. Roman community was locked away, awaiting discovery by the modern world.

Begun simply as a market town, Pompeii became a major economic center and then an industrial city. Prosperous, it relied upon business and the continued expansion of its commerce for survival, unlike the quiet town of Herculaneum, which was situated nearby. Wealth allowed the most modern buildings, and production techniques to be employed in Pompeii—multistoried structures, workshops, villas—and fostered a vibrant, changing social system.

See also BATHS; CAMPANIA; HERCULANEUM; STABIAE; and especially VESUVIUS.

Suggested Readings: Andrews, Ian. *Pompeii.* New York: Cambridge University Press, 1978; Biel, Timothy L. *Pompeii.* San Diego, Calif.: Lucent Books, 1989; Caselli, Giovanni. *In Search of Pompeii: Uncovering a Buried Roman City.* New York: P. Bedrick Books, 1999; D'Avino, Michele. *The Women of Pompeii.* Naples: Loffredo, 1967; Mouritsen, Henrik. *Elections, Magistrates, and Municipal Élite: Studies in Pompeian Epigraphy.* Rome: L'Erma di Bretschneider, 1988.

Pompey, Gnaeus (d. 45 B.C.E.) *Eldest son of Pompey the Great, by his third wife, Mucia*
Gnaeus was a loyal officer to his father, joining him in the CIVIL WAR OF THE FIRST TRIUMVIRATE against Julius Caesar. During the DYRRHACHIUM campaign in 48 B.C.E., he burned part of Caesar's fleet and harassed the ships of Marc Antony. After Pompey's defeat and eventual death as a result of the battle of PHARSALUS, Gnaeus fled to Africa,

where he became one of the leaders of the declining Pompeian cause. When the Pompeians were dealt another blow at THAPSUS in 46, Gnaeus sailed away to the Balearic Islands, where he was joined by his brother, Sextus. Both then tried to gather support in Spain, where Caesar arrived in 45. The resulting battle of MUNDA, while fiercely contested, ended with Caesar's triumph. Gnaeus again escaped, but there were no more safe havens for him. In a few weeks he was hunted down and beheaded.

Pompey, Sextus (d. 36/5 B.C.E.) *Younger son of Pompey the Great by his third wife, Mucia, and a gifted pirate leader from circa 43 to 36 B.C.E.*

Sextus Pompey gained position among the Pompeians only after the death of his father in 48. Joining his brother, Gnaeus, in the Balearic Islands after the defeat at THAPSUS in 46, Sextus subsequently served in Spain as a general in the legions against Caesar. There, the battle of MUNDA was lost in 45, and Gnaeus was captured and executed. Titus Labienus and most of the Pompeians either were killed or surrendered. Sextus escaped to the remaining Pompeian fleet, where he acted as a rallying point for the remnants of Pompey's followers. After the assassination of Julius Caesar in 44, Sextus was won over to the cause of the Republic by Marcus Lepidus. The year after, the Senate gave Sextus command of the fleet with control over the Italian coast. This cooperation ended soon after, when the newly formed SECOND TRIUMVIRATE of Antony, Octavian, and Lepidus produced its list of proscribed names. Sextus was on it.

Taking Sicily, and with a vast fleet of ships at his disposal, Sextus began to menace the sea-lanes of Rome for profit. The Mediterranean became a dangerous place, as he threatened all seaborne traffic and launched raids on the entire Italian coast. Further, he provided a haven for all those condemned by the new triumvirs. An alliance was formed briefly with Marc Antony (c. 41–40) but was broken by the favorable terms given Antony at the Conference of BRUNDISIUM in 40. By 39, Sextus was endangering the vital corn supply of Rome. Octavian and Antony decided to meet with this pirate king. In the spring of 39, a conference was held at Misenum, resulting in the Treaty of MISENUM. By its terms Sextus agreed to respect Italy, to leave the corn shipments alone and to cease all hostilities. In return he was given a position of respect and the promise of an augurship and a consulship. Clearly, everyone knew that war would erupt again. In 38, Octavian reopened the struggle, needing to remove Sextus as a destabilizing force in the West. Campaigns were launched against Sicily, followed by two years of defeat. Finally, after careful preparations by Marcus Agrippa, another offensive was launched in 36, culminating in the battle of NAULOCHUS. Sextus was badly defeated and fled to Asia Minor, where, because of his continuing popularity in Rome, Antony allowed him to live in peace. When Sextus tried to regain his lost political fortune, M. Titius, Antony's lieutenant, put him to death. Years afterward, crowds drove Titius from the theater, having never forgiven him.

Pompey the Great (Gnaeus Pompeius Magnus) (106–48 B.C.E.) *Political and military leader*

Called Magnus (the Great), he played a major role in the terminal period of the Republic and was a legitimate claimant for absolute control of the Roman world. Aptly, Plutarch wrote of him, "More worship the rising than the setting sun."

Pompey was the son of Pompeius Strabo. Born on September 30, 106 B.C.E., he first appeared in 83 B.C.E. in the service of the dictator Sulla. Organizing an army in Picenum, he won battles for Sulla and was sent as a propraetor to Sicily and Africa, where he vanquished Cn. Domitius and King Iarbos. Despite his age and the cruel nature of his victories, Sulla reluctantly allowed him a triumph, giving him the name Magnus in 81. Anxious to maintain his political momentum, Pompey joined Catulus in defeating Lepidus in 77, before assuming proconsular powers to assist Metellus Pius in his Spanish war against Sertorius and his successor, M. Perperna. Returning to Italy, Pompey helped finish off the forces of Spartacus and compelled the Senate to grant him a consulship in 70, this despite his Equestrian (EQUITES) origins and his total lack of senatorial experience. VARRO, it was said, had to give him a guidebook on the procedures of the Senate. As consul, however, he proved characteristically gifted, working with his bitter rival, Crassus, to amend the Sullan constitution, restore the status of the censors and, pleasing the *optimates*, repair the power of the tribunes.

Having carefully nurtured his political connections, Pompey now vexed the Roman establishment by using his popularity to increase his influence. In 67, the *lex Gabinia* was passed, providing him with a rare IMPERIUM to hunt down and destroy the pirates marauding the Mediterranean Sea. Three months later he had annihilated their strongholds and had driven the buccaneers from the sea (*see* PIRACY). His imperium was extended to include the East, where he concluded brilliantly the Mithridatic War. Following the suicide of Mithridates VI of Pontus in 63, Pompey, on his own initiative and without relying upon the Senate's approval, made his own settlement of the East. He founded client states, reorganized Judaea, established colonies and claimed Syria for Rome. In large measure, subsequent Roman policy in the East was based upon this systematic adjustment.

Pompey triumphed once more in 62. Disbanding his army, he asked the Senate to find land on which to settle his troops and, more important, to accept his overhaul of the Eastern lands. Viewed as overly ambitious as well as too wealthy, Pompey found enemies in the Senate; Cato Uticensis and Lucullus led the opposition to his ACTA in the East. Sensing that he had no other means of securing senatorial approval, Pompey took the dramatic step in 59 of entering into a TRIUMVIRATE with CRASSUS (1) and the rising Julius CAESAR. Marrying Caesar's daughter JULIA (2) in 59, Pompey found Caesar a reliable ally as consul. Regret soon surfaced when Pompey, even as a member of the triumvirate, could not sustain his prestige in Rome. While Caesar was conquering Gaul (see GALLIC WARS), Pompey was beset in Rome by troubles from the unpredictable and dangerous CLODIUS PULCHER. Beginning in 58, Clodius refused to recognize Pompey's status. Defeats in the Senate followed, when he could not gain military authority to accompany his supervision of the grain supply. Another blow came when he was unable to bring the Republic to subsidize the return to Egypt of the fallen King Ptolemy XII Auletes.

A recovery was launched in 56 at the successful Conference of LUCA with his fellow triumvirs, and with another consulship (with Crassus) in 55. Julia died in 54, bringing irreparable damage to the relationship between Caesar and Pompey, a rift accentuated by the death of Crassus at the battle of CARRHAE in 53. Controlling Spain for five years, Pompey sent lieutenants to act as his representatives there, while he stayed at Rome to deal with the political crisis of Clodius. Summoning the unscrupulous tribune, Annius MILO, Pompey allowed a vicious struggle to erupt with Clodius, which ended only with Clodius's death in 52. Having wed CORNELIA (2), daughter of Metellus Scipio, Pompey found new alliances in the senatorial party against Caesar. They ensured that he held the consulship of 52 alone. Although he did fight corruption in the government, Pompey used the imperium given to him to seize the upper hand in the inevitable conflict with Caesar. Thus he demanded the recall of Caesar from Gaul before the consulship of 48, and in 50 he took over the command of the Republican forces being arrayed against his onetime father-in-law.

Civil war began. Officially, it was a confrontation of the Republic against Caesar. Realistically, Pompey was dueling with Caesar for the fate of Rome. Departing Italy for Greece, Pompey spent 49 B.C.E. preparing his many LEGIONS for battle. This strategy left Spain wide open for attack, and Caesar demolished the Pompeian cause there. Finally coming to grips with his enemy in Greece, Pompey defeated but did not annihilate Caesar at DYRRHACHIUM in 48. Controlling a much larger army, Pompey again collided with Caesar, this time at PHARSALUS on August 9, 48. The Pompeians were routed by Caesar's superior legions, and Pompey fled. Sailing to Egypt and its unpredictable Ptolemaic rulers was his final miscalculation. On September 28, 48 B.C.E., he was murdered when he landed in Alexandria. His head was offered to Caesar as a gift, with the words: "Dead men do not bite."

Pompey the Great was a genuine prodigy and a superb general. He applied these skills to his career and was propelled to the virtual dictatorship of Rome. Unfortunately, he was unable to match his martial prowess with political acumen, as did Caesar. He wavered between the *optimates* and the triumvirs, much as he did between his toleration of bloodshed and his attempts at government reform.

Pompey married five times. His first two wives were Antistia and Aemilia. His third wife, Mucia, bore him Gnaeus and Sextus, but in 59 B.C.E. he wed Julia, the daughter of Julius Caesar. She died in childbirth in 54. Two years later Pompey married Cornelia, the daughter of Metellus Scipio, who remained with him and witnessed his murder in 48 at the hands of the Egyptians.

Suggested Readings: Greenhalgh, Peter. *Pompey, the Republican Prince.* London: Weidenfeld and Nicolson, 1981. ———. *Pompey, the Roman Alexander.* Columbia: University of Missouri Press, 1981; Leach, John. *Pompey the Great.* Dover, N.H.: Croom Helm, 1986. Rawson, Beryl. *The Politics of Friendship: Pompey and Cicero.* Sydney: Sydney University Press, 1977; Seager, Robin. *Pompey: A Political Biography.* Berkeley: University of California Press, 1979.

Pomponius, Sextus (fl. second century C.E.) *Jurist and one of the most prolific of the Roman legal writers*
Born probably during the reign of Domitian (81–96 C.E.), Pomponius was instructed in law by such teachers as Pegasus and Octavenus and had as his contemporary the great Salvius Julianus. He thus wrote during the time of Hadrian, Antoninus Pius, and Marcus Aurelius (117–161 C.E.). Although Pomponius was greatly respected, he held no official post or title. Preferring to write and teach, he nevertheless received instructions from Hadrian to organize a commentary on the praetor's Edict that totaled perhaps more than 150 books. To this impressive study were added 300 other works on the IUS CIVILE, SENATUS CONSULTUM, various readings (*Varias lectiones*), and a large number of legal treatises. The influence of Sextus Pomponius was considerable, as he was often quoted as part of the legal reorganization under Justinian.
See also LAW.

Pomponius Proculus, Titus (d. after 176 C.E.) *Consul in 150 and 176 C.E. and a relative of the imperial family of Marcus Aurelius*
Pomponius was also one of the more reliable generals of the emperor. Of a noble line, he embarked upon a senatorial career, becoming governor of Spain during the reign of Antoninus Pius, then a legate in Moesia Inferior and a proconsul of Asia. Under Marcus Aurelius, Pomponius held the position of staff member, helping to organize the campaigns against the Germans in 168 and against the Sarmatians in 174.

Pomponius Secundus, Publius (fl. first century C.E.) *Consul suffectus in 44 C.E. and a notable poet and tragedian*

Pomponius Secundus possessed a reputation for being a fine individual of great intellect. Nevertheless, he was accused in 31 of aiding a friend (or perhaps the son) of SEJANUS during that prefect's fall from power. Through the defense of his brother Quintus, Pomponius was allowed to live with his brother. There he engaged in literary pursuits, surviving the reign of Tiberius. He was a consul in 44 and had his work booed by an audience in Rome in 47, for which they were rebuked by Claudius. Emperor Claudius appointed Pomponius governor of Germania Superior in 50. Remaining there from 50 to 51, he inflicted a serious defeat upon the CHATTI, receiving triumphal honors. Pliny the Elder was a friend of his, writing a biography in his honor.

Pontifex Maximus   Supreme head of Rome's state religion. According to Roman custom, the Pontifex Maximus was the leader of not only the PONTIFICES but also the entire religious establishment, including the colleges of priests and the VESTAL VIRGINS. This gave him vast powers. During the Republic, the office was considered one of the grandest posts available. Aside from the priesthoods and the Vestals, the pontifex fixed the calendar and festivals, had absolute authority in questions of doctrine and was, in large measure, above the jurisdiction of the Senate and the People of Rome. He required, however, political allies to attain the post, which was held for life, and the support of the pontifices for his own actions.

It was believed that the Pontifex Maximus was first appointed by the kings of Rome or possibly by the pontifices. Later, during the Republic, he was elected by the tribes. Julius Caesar combined his position as dictator with that of pontifex, making himself superior religiously, as he was politically and militarily. Henceforth the Roman emperors made certain that the title of Pontifex Maximus was included in their numerous titular powers. The last emperor to serve as pontifex was Gratian (reigned 367–383 C.E.), who instituted extreme anti-pagan activities, including the termination of the seat of the Pontiff.

See also PAGANISM; PRIESTHOODS.

Pontifices   Members of the one of the largest and most important of the priestly colleges in Rome. According to tradition, the pontifices (sing., *pontifex*) originated when King Numa appointed six Patricians to aid him in the sacred duties of his office. Their name came from the idea of building a bridge over water, or the divine stream. When the monarchy was abolished by the Romans, the religious aspect of the king was given to the *PONTIFEX MAXIMUS*. Increasing in number throughout the Republic, the pontifices eventually numbered 16, by order of Julius Caesar, and both Plebeians and Patricians were eligible for entry, as elections passed into the hands of the Senate. The duties of the pontifices extended into every facet of Roman RELIGION. They conducted the rites and sacrifices necessary to keep the gods and goddesses happy, rendered important decisions on the nature of worship, and ensured that every undertaking of the state was accompanied by the proper propitiating ceremonies. Finally, they organized the calendar to place all appropriate holidays and thus exercised considerable influence over Roman society.

See also PRIESTHOODS.

Pontius Pilate (d. after 37 C.E.) *Procurator of Judaea from 26 to 36 C.E.*
Few Roman officials of his rank gained the fame of Pontius Pilate, even though his time of administration was fraught with troubles and unrest. Appointed to the territory of Judaea as successor to Valerius Gratus, Pilate introduced himself in Jerusalem by carrying images of Emperor Tiberius on his standards, in violation of Jewish law. Only after severe complaints of the populace did he remove them.

This debacle was followed by his equally unfortunate attempt to improve the city's water supply. He ordered an aqueduct constructed but used money from the sacred treasury of the Jews to do it. Outbursts of violence followed, rioting that he suppressed with extreme measures. His subsequent condemnation of Jesus was probably a conciliatory gesture to the insulted Jewish establishment, although he showed a personal leaning toward Jesus. Around 36 C.E. an uprising of the Samaritans was crushed with such ferocity that they appealed to L. Vitellius, governor of Syria and Pilate's nominal superior. The complaint was passed on to Rome, and Emperor Tiberius summoned him home. He reached Rome just after Tiberius's death in 37, fading at that point from history. According to Eusebius, Pilate committed suicide. Historical sources varied as to their opinions of him. Josephus and Philo were extremely hostile to Pilate, while Christian chronicles took a more sympathetic view.

Pontus   A land situated along the southern shore of the Black Sea; its name derived from the Greek for the vast inland sea, the Pontus Euxinus. Pontus first appeared in the *Anabasis* of Xenophon but became an actual kingdom during the fourth century B.C.E. By far its greatest ruler was Mithridates VI, who extended the domain into ASIA MINOR, bringing Pontus into direct confrontation with Rome. He died in 63 B.C.E. at the hands of his own son, Pharnaces, whose ambitions were destroyed by Julius Caesar at the battle of ZELA in 47 B.C.E. Thenceforth Pontus was dependent upon the goodwill of Rome. Its most notable later monarchs were POLEMO I and his son, POLEMO II. Polemo I was an ally of Marc Antony but survived the political catastrophe of Actium in 31 B.C.E. to retain his throne under the auspices of Augustus. Gaius Caligula, in 39 C.E., made Polemo II the king of Pontus and the Bosporan kingdom, but Nero, in 64–65, forced him to retire to a small Cilician realm. Pontus was annexed and attached to Galatia, where it gave Rome not only strategic watch over Armenia but vast mineral wealth as well.

Poppaea, Sabina (d. 65 C.E.) *Empress from 62 to 65 C.E. and the second wife of Emperor Nero*

Poppaea was the daughter of Titus Ollius and granddaughter of the famed proconsul Poppaeus Sabinus. Her mother, of the same name, was hounded to death by Messallina in 47. According to the historian Tacitus, Poppaea was a stunning beauty whose charms, wealth, and apparent modesty hid a licentious nature, ambition, and an inability to love anyone.

Her first husband was the PREFECT OF THE PRAETORIAN GUARD, Rufrius Crispinus. Although she bore him a son, she became adulterously involved with Marcus OTHO. Accounts varied as to her affair, for the writer Suetonius reported that Otho acted merely as a screen for Nero, who had developed a passion for the woman, a story repeated by Tacitus in the *Histories* but corrected in the *Annals*. There, Tacitus had Poppaea engaged with Otho because of his youth and high position of favor with the emperor. As it was, she left Crispinus, married Otho and soon attracted Nero. Otho's position as a friend was sacrificed in favor of Poppaea's role as mistress. Nero appointed Otho the governor of Hispania Lusitania, a post that he retained until 69, when he supported Galba against Nero. Poppaea remained behind in Rome; in 62, Nero divorced Octavia, his first wife, and married Poppaea.

As empress she was ruthless. Even before the union with Nero she had pushed for the removal of his mother, AGRIPPINA THE YOUNGER, and now had the limitless resources of an empire at her disposal. She sat on Nero's council, exercising influence in equal parts with the Praetorian Prefect TIGELLINUS. Nero was totally devoted to her, granting her title of AUGUSTA, calling their newborn daughter by the same name after her birth in 63. In 65, Poppaea was expecting another child when Nero kicked her in the stomach during a fit of rage. She died from the injury, and Nero grieved over what he had done. He deified her and had her embalmed instead of cremated in the normal Roman manner. Public mourning masked private rejoicing, while Otho never forgot his wife, cherishing her even when he became emperor in 69.

Porcia (d. 43 B.C.E.) *Daughter of Cato Uticensis*

Porcia was twice married, first to Marcus BIBULUS, consul in 59 B.C.E., and then to Brutus, the assassin of Caesar, whom she wed in 45. It was said that she convinced her husband to reveal the plot to murder Caesar by stabbing herself in the thigh to prove her inner resolve. Porcia was present at the Conference of Antium in 44, journeying back to Rome while Brutus sailed to the East. Growing ill, she killed herself, perhaps through poisonous vapors, in 43, although some accounts put her death in 42, after the demise of Brutus.

Porcius Latro, Marcus (d. 4 C.E.) *One of the most famous rhetoricians in the time of Augustus*

Probably from Spain, Porcius displayed natural gifts for RHETORIC but preferred to teach. Porcius claimed as his students Ovid, Florus, and Fulvius Sparsus. So attached were they to their instructor that they reportedly drank *cuminum* (cumin) to acquire his paleness.

Porfyrius, Publilius Optatianus (fl. fourth century C.E.) *Poet and panagyricist*

Porfyrius was probably the governor of Achaea (Greece) in the early years of the fourth century, before being exiled by Emperor Constantine the Great. In an attempt to have his banishment lifted, he composed a skillful panegyric to Constantine, sometime before 325. Perhaps sent as part of the emperor's jubilee, the poems offered praise to Constantine, while mentioning both Apollo and Christ. Using ingenious wordplay, Porfyrius obtained his goal. Constantine recalled him, and he served twice as urban prefect, in 329 and 333.

Porphyry (233–c. 305 C.E.) *Neoplatonic philosopher and writer*

Also known as Porphyrius, he was born either in Tyre or, less likely, in Batanea in Palestine. Originally called Malchus, a Greek form of the Syrian-Phoenician name for king *(melech)*, he became "Porphyry" while studying under Cassius Longinus in Athens. From 262 to 263 he was a devoted pupil of Plotinus in Rome, who led him into full acceptance of NEOPLATONISM. Subsequently Porphyry taught at Rome, counting IAMBLICHUS as one of his students.

Around 300 he edited PLOTINUS's *Enneads* and wrote a biography of his deceased master. These writings, however, were only two books in a collection that eventually numbered 77 works. Philosophically, Porphyry focused on the nature of the soul in its need to find a way to the One so clearly shown by Plotinus. He penned studies on philosophy, biographies of great philosophers and treatises on Plato, Theophrastus, and Aristotle. There were also technical compositions, including those on music, astrology, logic (the *Isagoge*), embryology, the philology of Homer, and an analysis of Ptolemy's *Harmonica*.

Porphyry studied all of the religions of his time, especially those popular in Asia. While he viewed them all with a careful eye, he singled out CHRISTIANITY for special attack. Porphyry apparently respected Christ as a teacher but considered the ambitions of the Christian Church to be illogical, contradictory, and unpatriotic. In a 15-book treatise, *Against the Christians,* he expounded upon his ideas of anti-Christianity, earning the immediate response of Christian theologians, including EUSEBIUS OF CAESAREA. In 448, his writings on the subject were banned and, like much of his other literary achievements, survive only in fragments.

portorium   A kind of customs duty or tax placed upon incoming or outgoing goods at a harbor, at the gates of many cities, at tolls, or on the frontiers of the empire. The *portorium* (pl. *portoria*) was not a protective tariff but was seen as a useful source of revenue. Normally, as was seen in the Gallic provinces, it was levied at 2 to 2.5 percent of the value of the goods. This increased in some regions, especially on the imperial frontiers, where the levy might be as high as 25 percent. The primary target of revenue collection through the duty was the often lucrative trade with the East, notably along the Red Sea and through Palmyra, both of which had substantially higher levies. Most goods were subject to the *portorium,* with the few exceptions being animals and vehicles, as well as all military equipment used by the legions and the personal property of the emperor or materials owned by the government in general.

Collection of the *portorium* was originally the task of customs officials who worked in customs offices (*stationes*) attached to legionary posts or frontier stations. Eventually, the task was given to civil servants, such as the *publicani,* the traditional tax collectors. In the early empire *conductores* and in the later empire *procuratores* assumed the work of collecting revenue, largely in order to prevent the threat of fraud that was always present with the *publicani.* Under Emperor Tiberius, the entire empire was divided into five customs districts.

Portunus   God of communication, identified by the Romans with the Greek god Palaemon, and variously described as the patron of harbors (*portus*) and gates (*porta*); often confused with Janus, the god of doorways. The festival held in honor of Portunus was the Portunalia, each August 17. The date of the festival may have been associated with the dedication of his temple along the Tiber near the Aemilian bridge. The Tiber may have been associated with Portunus, given the proximity of the temple and the water as well as the similarity of date for the Portunalia and the Tibernalia.

See also GODS AND GODDESSES OF ROME.

Postumus, Marcus Cassianus Latinius (d. 268 C.E.) *Usurper and ruler of Gaul from 260 to 268*
Born to an obscure family in Gaul, Postumus rose through the ranks to be appointed by Emperor Valerian as commanding general of the Gallic and Germanic frontiers, with control over the legions of Germania Inferior and Superior. His main task was to protect the borders from the hostile Germans. This he did so well that in 259, when Valerian was defeated and captured in battle against the Persians, GALLIENUS, his successor, retained Postumus in his post.

However, one change in his assignment was made. Gallienus placed the entire Western theater under the authority of his son Saloninus. Postumus was to work in cooperation with young prince's preceptor, Silvanus. A disagreement with Silvanus escalated into violence in 260, as Postumus besieged Saloninus and his guardian at Cologne. Both were captured and put to death as Postumus extended his control over Gaul, Spain, and Britain.

Gallienus tried without success to destroy the usurper, most notably in 265, but neither claimant to the throne could devote their complete attention to the other. The Roman Empire was beset with internal usurpations and terrible barbarian invasions. Ironically, the inroads of the Germanic tribes gave Postumus a chance to solidify his hold over the West, for each victory brought further support from the populace. He thus issued coinage with the title *"RESTITVTOR GALLIARVM."* This claim of having restored Gaul was rendered inaccurate in 268, when LAELIANUS attempted his own revolt. Although put down, the uprising seemed to have weakened Postumus's position. He and his son were killed by the troops sometime in 268. A colleague, Victorinus, succeeded him in the West. The accounts in the *Historia Augusta* are generally unreliable.

Potamon of Alexandria (fl. late first century B.C.E.) *Philosopher*
Potamon was noted for founding his own school of philosophy based on Stoicism, Platonism, and certain elements of Peripatetic teachings. Called the Eclectic School, Potamon's institution was able to gain wide acceptance.

Pothinus (d. 48 B.C.E.) *Eunuch in the Egyptian royal palace of Ptolemy XIII and Cleopatra*
Pothinus was in charge of Ptolemy's funds and in 48 B.C.E. became a leader in the Alexandrian uprising against Julius CAESAR. His role was short-lived, however, for Caesar put him to death out of fear that he would kidnap Ptolemy and use him as a rallying point for the already aroused Egyptians.

praepositus sacri cubiculi   The title of the grand chamberlain in the imperial palace. According to custom, the *praepositus sacri cubiculi* was a eunuch who was in charge of the entire private palace staff of eunuchs in attendance upon the emperors. They were present in the years of the middle empire and became commonplace in the late empire. Because of the closeness to the imperial family that was inevitable in the office of chamberlain, the eunuchs came to amass considerable wealth and influence, much as the freedmen had in the first century C.E. By the fifth century, the *praepositus sacri cubiculi* could dominate his master and dictate not only palace affairs but also many facets of imperial policy.

Praetextatus, Vettius Agorius (c. 310–384 C.E.)

Praetorian prefect of Italy, Africa, and Illyricum in 384 and leading pagan intellectual

Praetextatus was born in Rome and embarked upon a highly successful career in government. From 362 to 364 he served as proconsul of Achaea, having received his post from fellow pagan, the Emperor Julian. Already a noted pagan, he convinced Emperor Valentinian I not to enforce the imperial ban on night sacrifices. Praetextatus was urban prefect for Rome in 367–368, where his administration was famous for its fairness. Although he was decidedly anti-Christian, he aided Pope Damasus, returning to him the Basilica of Sicininus. Once he said to Damasus that, if made pope, he would certainly become a Christian. His Praetorian prefecture was marked by his inquiry into the destruction of pagan temples in Italy by Christians. When he died in late 384, he was preparing to become consul.

Throughout his life Praetextatus had been a staunch pagan. Aconia Fabia, his wife of 40 years, was equally devoted to the tenets of PAGANISM. He held numerous priestly offices, including augur, *pontifex Solis* (to his beloved sun god), *quindecimvir, hierophanta,* and *pater patrum.* As a friend of SYMMACHUS he enjoyed immense popularity with the pagans of Rome. The Vestals proposed to erect a statue in his memory. Praetextatus brought an excellent literary mind to his duties and beliefs. He made a translation into Latin of Themistius' commentary on Aristotle's *Analytics.* MACROBIUS made him the central figure of the *Saturnalia,* and he was known by the later writer, Boethius.

praetor

At first, a title used to denote a CONSUL; later it came to signify the magistrates whose duties centered on the field of justice in Rome. In the Republic, the powers of the praetor were originally the province of the Patricians, but in 337 B.C.E. members of the Plebeians were elected to the praetorship by the *comitia centuriata.* Throughout the Republic, praetors increased both in number and in breadth of jurisdiction, but their position weakened in the days of the empire. From 242 B.C.E. there were at least two praetors elected each year, and more were added by Sulla, making eight. Julius CAESAR increased their number to 10, 14, and then 16. Their duties centered on the trying of cases, conducting legal business, and issuing edicts at the end of their term, which normally lasted one year. The two basic types of praetor were the *praetor urbanus* and the *praetor inter peregrinos,* later called the *praetor peregrinus.* The *praetor urbanus* was a legal expert for Rome, handling civil cases that fell within the jurisdiction of the IUS CIVILE (civil law). Any cases involving foreigners or any dispute arising from the IUS GENTIUM (international law) fell into the area of the PRAETOR PEREGRINUS. He was thus a reliable source for legal decisions regarding the place of the PEREGRINI in Roman law and the relations between Rome and other states.

From around 149 B.C.E., it was required that all praetors serve out their entire period of service within Rome. The principal reason for this was the adoption of the QUAESTIONES or *quaestiones perpatuae,* the standing criminal courts. This helped to ensure a smoother operation of the entire system. Praetors then had the right to make changes in the law, issued in the annual Edict of the Praetor. But such reforms were rare and never took place without the permission of the SENATE, meaning the emperor. The edicts were naturally important sources for the development of the law of Rome and were codified by the eminent jurist Salvius JULIANUS at the order of Emperor HADRIAN in the second century C.E. With the start of imperial ruler under AUGUSTUS (ruled 27 B.C.E.–14 C.E.), the praetors suffered a decline. Much of their burden was placed in the hands of the PREFECT OF THE CITY (*praefectus urbi*) and especially the PREFECT OF THE PRAETORIAN GUARD (*praefectus praetorio*). The collections of the edicts signalled the effective end of praetorian influence in law. Roman law now progressed through the JURISTS, the CONSILIUM PRINCIPIS, and the Praetorian prefect. Under Tiberius, election to the praetorship was transferred to the Senate. Each praetor was entitled to have six lictors; to bear the proper insignia of the *toga praetexta;* and, upon completion of their terms, to travel to the senatorial provinces to assume the role of PROCONSUL. Although virtually meaningless by the fourth century C.E., the praetors remained until the very end of the Roman Empire in the West.

Praetorian Guard

The imperial guard of the Roman Empire. Created by Augustus to act as a special, elite force for his protection, the Praetorians became a lasting influence upon Rome and its emperors.

HISTORY

The term *Praetorian* came from the tent of the legate of a legion in the field—the *praetorium.* It was the habit of many Roman generals to choose from the ranks a private force of soldiers to act as bodyguards of the tent or the person. In time, this cohort came to be known as the *cohors praetoria,* and various notable figures possessed one, including Julius CAESAR, Marc ANTONY, and Octavian (AUGUSTUS). As Caesar discovered with the X Legion, a powerful unit more dangerous than its fellow legions was desirable in the field. When Augustus became the first ruler of the empire in 27 B.C.E., he decided such a formation was useful not only in war but also in politics. Thus, from the ranks of legions throughout the provinces, Augustus recruited the Praetorian Guard.

The group that was formed initially differed greatly from the later Guard, which would murder emperors. While Augustus understood the need to have a protector in the maelstrom of Rome, he was careful to uphold the Republican veneer of his regime. Thus he allowed only nine cohorts to be formed, each of 500 to 1,000 men, and only three were kept on duty at any given time in the capital. While they patrolled inconspicuously, in the palace and major buildings, the others were stationed in the towns surrounding Rome; no threats were possible from these individual cohorts. This system was not radically changed with the arrival of two Praetorian prefects in 2 B.C.E., Q. Ostorius SCAPULA and Salvius Aper, although organization and command were improved.

Augustus's death in 14 C.E. marked the end of Praetorian calm. Through the machinations of their ambitious prefect, Lucius Aelius SEJANUS, the Guard was brought from the Italian barracks into Rome itself. In 23 C.E. Sejanus convinced Tiberius to have the CASTRA PRAETORIA (the Camp of the Praetorians) built just outside of Rome. Henceforth the entire Guard was at the disposal of the emperors, but the rulers were now equally at the mercy of the Praetorians. The reality of this was seen in 31 when Tiberius was forced to rely upon his own *cohors praetoria* against partisans of Sejanus. Though the Praetorian Guard proved faithful to the aging Tiberius, their potential political power had been made clear.

On campaign, the Praetorians were the equal of any formation in the Roman army. Seldom used in the early reigns, they were quite active by 69 C.E. They fought well at the first battle of BEDRIACUM for OTHO. Under DOMITIAN and TRAJAN, the Guard took part in wars from Dacia to Mesopotamia, while with MARCUS AURELIUS, years were spent on the Danubian frontier. Throughout the third century C.E., the Praetorians assisted the emperors in various crises.

From the death of Sejanus, who was sacrificed for the DONATIVUM (imperial gift) promised by Tiberius, the Guards began playing an increasingly ambitious and bloody game. At will, or for the right amount of money, they assassinated emperors, bullied their own prefects or turned on the people of Rome. In 41, GAIUS CALIGULA was killed by conspirators from the senatorial class and from the Guard. And the Praetorians placed CLAUDIUS on the throne, daring the Senate to oppose their decision.

It is important, however, not to overestimate the place of the Praetorians in the imperial government. They could slaughter emperors but played no role in administration, as did the personnel of the palace, Senate and bureaucracy. Further, it was often the case that, after outrageous acts of violence, revenge by the new ruler was forthcoming. For example, in 193 C.E. DIDIUS JULIANUS purchased the empire from the Guard for a vast sum. Later that year Septimius SEVERUS marched into Rome, disbanded the Praetorians and founded a new formation from his Pannonian legions. Even VESPASIAN in 69, who had relied upon the disgruntled cohorts dismissed by VITELLIUS, reduced their ranks in number when ascending the throne. Unruly mobs in Rome fought often with the Praetorians in MAXIMINUS's reign (c. 235–236) in vicious street battles.

DIOCLETIAN, in 284, reduced the status of the Praetorians; they were no longer to be a part of palace life, as Diocletian lived in Nicomedia. A new corps of guards, the Jovians and Herculians, replaced the Praetorians as the personal protectors of the emperors, a practice that remained intact with the tetrarchy. By the time Diocletian retired in 305, the Castra Praetoria seems to have housed only a minor garrison of Rome.

In 306, when MAXENTIUS, son of the retired emperor MAXIMIAN, was passed over as a successor, the troops took matters into their own hands and elevated him to the position of emperor in Italy on October 28. When CONSTANTINE the Great, launching an invasion of Italy in 312, forced a final collision at the MILVIAN BRIDGE, the Praetorian cohorts made up most of Maxentius's army. Later, in Rome, the victorious Constantine abolished the Guard. The soldiers were sent out to various corners of the empire, and the Castra Praetoria was pulled down. For over 300 years they had served, and the extirpation of the Praetorians was a grand gesture, inaugurating a new age of imperial history.

The following list indicates the relationships between various emperors and their Guard.

Augustus	27 B.C.E.–14 C.E. created the Praetorian Guard
Tiberius	14–37 C.E. allowed Sejanus to gain power as prefect
Caligula	37–41 C.E. murdered by the Guard
Claudius	41–54 C.E. proclaimed emperor by the Guard
Nero	54–68 C.E. deserted by the Guard
Galba	68–69 C.E. murdered by the Guard
Otho	69 C.E. elevated by the Guard
Vitellius	69 C.E. deposed by the Guard and then killed
Vespasian	69–79 C.E. reduced the size of Guard after victory in 69
Titus	79–81 C.E. served as Praetorian prefect, then as emperor
Domitian	81–96 C.E. murdered by his prefects
Nerva	96–98 C.E. humiliated by Guard and died
Hadrian	117–138 C.E. founded the FRUMENTARII
Commodus	180–192 C.E. murdered by his prefect in a plot
Pertinax	193 C.E. murdered by the Guard
Didius Julianus	193 C.E. purchased empire from the Guard
Septimius Severus	193–211 C.E. disbanded Guard and created a new one from the Pannonian Legions
Caracalla	211–217 C.E. murdered in a plot by his Prefect Macrinus

Macrinus	217–218 C.E. first prefect since Titus to become emperor
Elagabalus	218–222 C.E. murdered in the Castra Praetoria by the Guard
Balbinus	238 C.E. murdered by the Guard
Pupienus	238 C.E. murdered by the Guard
Gordian III	238–244 C.E. proclaimed emperor by the Guard but killed by his prefect, Philip the Arab
Philip	244–249 C.E. another prefect to become emperor
Aurelian	270–275 C.E. murdered by the Guard
Florian	276 C.E. prefect who became emperor
Probus	276–282 C.E. killed by Praetorian troops after a revolt
Carus	282–283 C.E. probably poisoned by Prefect Aper
Numerian	283–284 C.E. poisoned by Aper
Diocletian	284–305 C.E. effectively broke the power of the Praetorians
Maxentius	306–312 C.E. last emperor to command the Guard
Constantine	306–337 C.E. disbanded the Guard and destroyed the Castra Praetoria

ORGANIZATION AND CONDITIONS OF SERVICE

Although there were obvious similarities, the Praetorian Guard was unlike any of the other LEGIONS in the Roman army. Its cohorts were larger, the pay and benefits better, and its military abilities were reliable. As conceived by Augustus, the Praetorian cohorts totaled around 9,000 men, recruited from the legions in the regular army or drawn from the most deserving youths in Etruria, Umbria, and Latium. In time, the pool of recruits expanded to Macedonia, the Spanish provinces and Illyricum. Vitellius formed a new Guard out of the German legions, while Septimius Severus did the same with the Pannonian legions. He also chose replacements for the units' ranks from across the Roman Empire, undermining once more the primacy of Italy.

Around the time of Augustus (c. 5 C.E.) each cohort of the Praetorians numbered 1,000 men, increasing to 1,500 at the time of Severus—a highwater mark. As with the normal legions, the body of troops actually ready for service was much smaller. The ranks of the Praetorians were, in ascending order:

Miles   regular soldier
Immunes   After five years, these soldiers were allowed to serve in the *Equite singulares* (cavalry branch) or as SPECULATORES (special agents).
Principales   legionary administrators

Evocati   after 16 years of service, retirement was possible but most soldiers chose to stay in this honorary unit.
Centurions   soldiers transferred to the Guard after service in the legions, the VIGILES or the URBAN COHORT.
Tribunes   officers, also from the legions and usually of the Equestrian class, who commanded a cohort. Centurions could (rarely) be promoted to the tribuneship.
Procurators   a rank of the Equestrians
Prefects   available to Vigiles and urban cohorts; the highest rank of the Praetorian Guard.

The training of Guardsmen was more intense than in the legions because of the amount of free time available, when a cohort was not posted or traveling with the emperor. It followed the same lines as those elsewhere. Equipment and armor were also the same, with one notable exception—specially decorated breastplates, excellent for parades and state functions. Thus, each Guardsman probably possessed two suits of armor, one for Roman duty and one for the field.

For what was expected of them, the Praetorians were given substantially higher pay. They were paid by a system known as *sesquiplex stipendum,* or by pay-and-a-half. Thus, while the legionaries might receive 225 denarii, the Guards received 375. Domitian and Severus increased the *stipendum* (payment) to 1,500 denarii distributed three times a year, in January, May, and September. Upon retiring, a soldier of the Praetorians was granted 20,000 sesterces (5,000 denarii), a gift of land and a DIPLOMATA reading "to the warrior who bravely and faithfully completed his service." Many chose to enter the honorary EVOCATI, while others reenlisted in the hopes of gaining promotion and possible high positions in the Roman state.

Prasutagus (d. 61 C.E.) *King of the Iceni tribe in Britain for much of the first century* C.E., *and husband of the famous Boudicca*

For many years Prasutagus enjoyed a peaceful reign as a client of Rome. Seeking to ensure the continuation of his domain and the safety of his family after his death, he named as his heir "Caesar." Unfortunately, upon his death in 61, the land of the Iceni was plundered, his widow flogged and his daughters violated by the Romans. These crimes caused the terrible war that ended in the destruction of Iceni.

prefect of the city   Known as the *praefectus urbi,* or urban prefect; the administrator of Rome during most of the empire. The prefects had originally been appointed to act as deputies to the kings of Rome or the CONSULS. By custom they exercised their powers in the city only during the so-called Feriae Latinae, or Latin Festival, an event held each year in Mount Albanus that demanded the presence of the consul. In effect they ensured that Rome was not left without some sort of magistrate.

AUGUSTUS expanded the duties of this limited office. His *praefectus urbi*, as of 29 B.C.E., was to be a leading citizen who would govern Rome not just when the consuls were away but at all times. He would also decide all cases of law that fell within the jurisdiction of the city, up to the one-hundredth milestone from Rome. He was responsible for maintaining order in the burgeoning metropolis, with the Roman police, the URBAN COHORTS, at his disposal. Also wielded by these officials was the IMPERIUM; they were among the few holders of the title within the POMERIUM, the area denoting the original foundation of the city.

The first prefect of the city was MESSALLA CORVINUS, appointed in 25 B.C.E. He lasted only six days before stepping down, because of either dislike for the post or incompetence. In marked contrast to such a brief tenure was Lucius Calpurnius Piso (2), who succeeded STATILIUS TAURUS circa 12 C.E. and remained urban prefect until his death in 32. In its early history, the office was used by the emperor as a counterweight to the often ambitious PREFECT OF THE PRAETORIAN GUARD—as in 31 C.E., when Tiberius relied upon Urban Prefect Cornelius LACO to arrest and imprison Praetorian Prefect SEJANUS. Generally, however, just as the urban cohorts could not match the martial strength of the Praetorian Guard, neither could the prefect of the city compete with the prefect of the Guard in imperial influence. This was especially the case from the second century C.E. onward.

The role of prefect of the city did grow, however, in legal affairs. He began with his own court, but his area of jurisdiction expanded continually, so that eventually much of Italy appeared at his bench. With the founding of Constantinople, it was decided that another urban prefect should be created, and in 359 the *praefectus urbi* took up duties in the East that were almost identical to those of his Roman counterpart. The office continued until the end of the Roman Empire, and that of the Eastern capital until even later.

prefect of engineering

The *praefectus fabrum,* a post within each legion for the commander of all engineers. It eventually came to symbolize any appointed official sent out with the task of construction.

prefect of the grain   *See* ANNONA.

prefect of the Praetorian Guard

The commander of the PRAETORIAN GUARD; over time, the post evolved into one of the most powerful in the Roman Empire. Its political influence was such that, even when Diocletian disbanded the Praetorians in the late third century C.E., he could not completely eliminate the power of the prefect. In the later years of the empire, the office was still important enough to make the *praefectus praetorio* a key government administrator.

In 27 B.C.E., Augustus established the Praetorian Guard. For 25 years it functioned without the need of a supreme office, its tribunes answering directly to the emperor. In 2 B.C.E., however, Augustus appointed two prefects, Q. Ostorius SCAPULA and Salvius Aper, so that neither one would become overly ambitious. The pair directed the affairs of the Guard with moderation. Everything changed with the rise of Strabo's son, SEJANUS, to the prefectship in 14 C.E. This gifted, grasping prefect made himself so useful to TIBERIUS that vast ministerial authority was handed to him. Although destroyed in 31, he transformed the influence of the prefect. The prefectship became the highest attainable posting for members of the Equestrian Order, bearing with it both influence and prestige. At the same time, the emperors found it convenient to delegate certain perhaps unpleasant tasks to their prefects, knowing that they would not refuse. Because of this unique role, the prefects amassed more and more power.

In the first century C.E., BURRUS helped guide Nero's imperial policy, while the infamous TIGELLINUS destroyed it. TITUS became prefect for his father VESPASIAN. Throughout the second century there were further developments, beginning with the aggrandizement of the Equestrian class by HADRIAN. As the knights rose in prominence, so did the prefecture. Septimus SEVERUS, emperor at the start of the third century, did much to widen the scope of the prefectship, adding to it legal duties, to coincide with its martial and bureaucratic aspects. Great jurists such as ULPIAN and PAPINIAN became prefects.

Then, in 217, the prefect MACRINUS took the dramatic step of having Caracalla assassinated ensuring his own selection as emperor. The possibilities were obvious, and generals in the provinces spent much of the century not only fighting the barbarians pouring across the frontiers but also battling each other for the throne. The Praetorian Guard, led often by its prefects, did much to increase the chaos of the third century. DIOCLETIAN put to death by his own hand the Prefect Aper in 284, envisioning a total reform of the imperial system, and the Praetorian Guard was reduced in status. Stripped of his dangerous military role, the prefect was empowered with broader administrative tasks, overseeing the entire tax system, with control over most of the imperial finances.

When Constantine abolished the Praetorians in 312, he freed the prefects to play a new part in the Roman Empire. The provinces were divided into dioceses, in turn grouped into the four so-called Praetorian prefectures: Gaul, Illyricum, Italy, and the Orient. Each prefect had mastery over all of the dioceses and governors within his jurisdiction, the two most powerful being Italy and the East. In essence, there was no non-military government activity that did not involve the prefects. They had their own treasuries, paid and supplied the armies, named and removed governors, and made various decrees of a public nature. Prefects also exercised extensive legal privileges, hearing all appeals from the lower courts. From the prefect there was no appeal, not even to the emperor.

Because he possessed no military role, the prefect was adorned with the mighty symbols of his office. He rode in a golden chariot, wore an ornate purple robe (different from that of the emperor only in that it went to his knees and not to the floor), used a tripod silver bowl for holding petitions, carried a sword, and was honored by his audience with a required bent knee.

Following are the Praetorian prefects during the empire.

PREFECTS OF THE PRAETORIAN GUARD
2 B.C.E.–312 C.E.

Name	Emperor Served
Publius Aper	Augustus
Quintus Ostorius Scapula	Augustus
Valerius Ligur	Augustus
Lucius Strabo	Augustus, Tiberius
Lucius Sejanus	Tiberius
Macro	Tiberius, Caligula
M. Arrencinus Clemens	Caligula
Rufrius Pollio	Claudius
Catonius Justus	Claudius
Rufius Crispinus	Claudius
Lusius Geta	Claudius
Burrus	Claudius, Nero
Faenius Rufus	Nero
Ofonius Tigellinus	Nero
Nymphidius Sabinus	Nero
Cornelius Laco	Galba
Plotius Firmus	Otho
Licinius Proculus	Otho
Publius Sabinus	Vitellius
Junius Priscus	Vitellius
Tiberius Julius Alexander	Vespasian
Arrius Varus	Vespasian
Arrecinus Clemens	Vespasian
Titus	Vespasian
Cornelius Fuscus	Domitian
Casperius Aelianus	Domitian
Norbanus	Domitian
Petronius Secundus	Domitian
Casperius Aelianus	Nerva
Suburanus	Trajan
Claudius Livianus	Trajan
S. Sulpicius Similis	Trajan
C. Septicius Clarus	Hadrian
Marcius Turbo	Hadrian
Gaius Maximus	Hadrian, Antoninus Pius
Tattius Maximus	Antoninus Pius
Fabius Cornelius Repentinus	Antoninus Pius
Furius Victorinus	Antoninus Pius, Marcus Aurelius
Macrinus Vindex	Marcus Aurelius
Bassaeus Rufus	Marcus Aurelius
Tarutenius Paternus	Marcus Aurelius, Commodus
Tigidius Perennis	Commodus
Cleander	Commodus
Lucius Julianus	Commodus
Aemilius Laetus	Commodus, Pertinax, Didius Julianus
Flavius Genialis	Didius Julianus
Tullius Crispinus	Didius Julianus
Veturius Macrinus	Septimius Severus
G. Fulvius Plautianus	Septimius Severus
Papinian	Septimius Severus, Caracalla
Marcus Opellius Macrinus	Caracalla
Ulpius Julianus	Macrinus
Julianus Nestor	Macrinus
Valerius Comazon Eutychianus	Elagabalus
Antiochianus	Elagabalus
Ulpian	Severus Alexander
Iulius Paulus	Severus Alexander
P. Aelius Vitalianus	Maximinus
Philip the Arab	Gordian III
Gaius Julius Priscus	Philip
Aurelius Heraclianus	Gallienus
Florianus	Tacitus
Carus	Probus
Aper	Carus, Carinus, Numerian
Aristobulus	Numerian, Diocletian
Hannibalianus	Diocletian
Constantinus Chlorus	Diocletian
Asclepiodotus	Diocletian
Rufius Volusianus	Maxentius
Publius Cornelius Anullinus	Maxentius

prefect of the watch The head of Rome's fire brigades, the VIGILES. Called the *praefectus vigilum,* his duties included maintaining the readiness of the Vigiles both for fires and any other natural or paramilitary emergencies that might arise. Over the years the prefect of the watch also developed certain legal powers but was never a match for the PREFECT OF THE PRAETORIAN GUARD or for the PREFECT OF THE CITY.

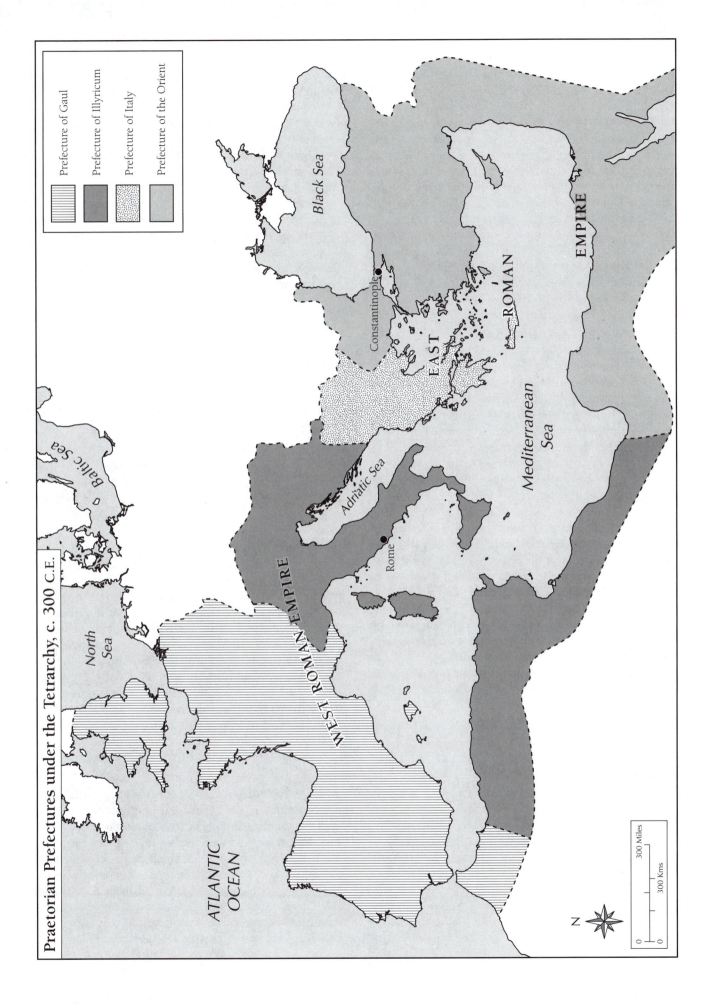

Praetorian Prefectures under the Tetrarchy, c. 300 C.E.

Prefecture of Gaul
Prefecture of Illyricum
Prefecture of Italy
Prefecture of the Orient

ATLANTIC OCEAN

North Sea

Baltic Sea

Black Sea

Mediterranean Sea

Adriatic Sea

WEST ROMAN EMPIRE

EAST ROMAN EMPIRE

Rome

Constantinople

N

300 Miles

300 Kms
0
0

Priapus   A male divinity of fertility, eventually considered the protector of gardens and orchards. According to legend, Priapus, the son of Dionysus (BACCHUS) and Aphrodite (VENUS), was born at Lampsacus on the Hellespont; hence he was also called Hellespontiacus. He was worshiped throughout Asia Minor as a major deity of nature, patron of gardens, flocks, vines, bees, and sometimes even fish. As the cult traveled into Greece and Italy, Priapus retained his obvious potency, but his power was restricted to that of guardian of gardens. Asses were traditionally sacrificed to him, while his statues and images were normally that of a dwarf with enormous genitalia. Such notables as CATULLUS, HORACE, and TIBULLUS wrote poems called *priapea*, dedicated to him.

See also GODS AND GODDESSES OF ROME.

priesthood   Collectively, the trained servants of the various cults and temples of Rome. According to the historian Dio, there were four major priesthoods in Rome at the start of the empire: the PONTIFICES, the augurs, the QUINDECIMVIRI and the SEPTEMVIRI. His statement was correct, but during the reign of Augustus (27 B.C.E.–14 C.E.) other priestly colleges were reinvigorated or resurrected as part of the emperor's campaign of promoting the Roman state religion. Thus, there were the ancient SALII of Mars, the Fratres Arvales or ARVAL BRETHREN, and, of course, the VESTAL VIRGINS.

As was traditional in Rome there was no sharp separation between the religious and the secular powers. Any priest could hold a magistracy, and the PONTIFEX MAXIMUS and Flamen Dialis sat in the Senate. Further, as the post was normally held for life, it was possible for one priest to serve in several different orders while fulfilling his duties to each. Specific regulations were enforced, depending upon the circumstances or the requirements of office. The importance of the various priesthoods was considerable in shaping Rome's religious life.

See also RELIGION; AUGURS AND AUGURY; FLAMENS; GODS AND GODDESSES OF ROME; PAGANISM.

Primus, Marcus Antonius (fl. mid-first century C.E.) *Adventurer, plotter and legate of the VII Galbiana Legion in Pannonia*

Primus was active in the year of the Four Emperors, 69 C.E. Tacitus wrote that Marcus Antonius Primus "possessed uncommon eloquence; an artful and insidious enemy, he had the art of involving others in danger." He was also to prove one of the most active of Vespasian's adherents during his drive for the throne of Rome. Nero disliked Primus and exiled him. Primus, however, attached himself to the next emperor, GALBA, who early in 69 C.E. succeeded the dethroned Nero. By his wits Primus managed to get command of the VII Galbiana Legion, joining the III and VIII legions on the Pannonia and Illyr-

ian frontiers. When Otho conspired to murder Galba and assumed the throne, he was accepted by the LEGIONS, Primus included. VITELLIUS, however, the master of the German Legions, started a second civil war, and despite an offer to assist in his campaigns, the Pannonian Legions were left out of the battles. Otho was defeated at the first battle of Bedriacum in Cisalpine Gaul, near Verona on April 14, and Vitellius assumed the throne.

Vitellius was despised, and the legions supported VESPASIAN in a bid for power. Primus, aided by Cornelius Fiscus, the procurator of Pannonia, used his considerable oratorical skills to gain the absolute devotion of his men Dalmatia and Illyricum soon joined the cause. Without waiting for Vespasian or any of his lieutenants, Primus ordered that the war should be taken to Italy. On October 27, the Vitellian forces were crushed at the second battle of Bedriacum. Together with Cerealis, Vespasian's brother-in-law, Primus captured Rome and, despite the Senate's acclamation of Vespasian as emperor, the city was sacked. The general now ruled the capital, appointing officials with the help of Arrius Varus, his cavalry commander. In December, 69 C.E., the arrival in Rome of Mucianus, Vespasian's true lieutenant, ended Antonius's power.

princeps   An unofficial but important title that meant "First Statesman." In the Republican era the *princeps* was used to give honor to special leaders or figures. POMPEY THE GREAT was called *princeps* out of recognition for his victories for the state and his position within Rome. Others received the name, including CICERO for the Catiline Affair in 63 B.C.E. Julius CAESAR won the title from Cicero in 49. As all of these great figures possessed the name *princeps* within the framework of the Republic, it was natural and astute of Augustus to choose the name for himself. In this regard, *princeps* allowed him to define his position—"first statesman" of the new Republic, who guided the ship of state with a firm but respectful hand.

While *princeps* carried with it no actual political power, such as IMPERATOR or the *TRIBUNICIA POTESTAS*, it was still a badge of prestige and status for the emperors. From the reign of GAIUS CALIGULA (37–41 C.E.) it was particularly meaningless, a mere titular possession.

See also PRINCEPS IUVENTUTIS; PRINCEPS SENATUS.

princeps iuventutis   Latin for "prince of youth." During the Republic the appellation *princeps iuventutis* was used to describe the chief of the Equestrian Order (EQUITES). Its use changed with the beginning of the empire, as it ceased to hold any political significance but came to be a designation of honor for certain princes of the imperial family who were obviously chosen as heirs. Thus, Gaius and Lucius, sons of Marcus AGRIPPA, received from the Equestrians silver shields and spears, as they were being raised to succeed AUGUSTUS. Henceforth, the *princeps iuventutis* was a common title, although it became traditional in some instances to grant the prince the rank of Caesar or junior emperor at the same time as the *princeps iuventutis*. It was also adopted as a title by several emperors, especially DOMITIAN.

princeps senatus   A term used during the late Republic to honor the leading senator, chosen by the CENSORS. It meant "first senator" and was considered very prestigious. Augustus (ruled 27 B.C.E.–14 C.E.), in his reorganization of the Senate, laid claim to the title; subsequently it was used by the emperors.

Prisca and Maximilla (fl. second century C.E.) *Christian leaders*
Leaders in the apocalyptic movement of Montanism. They assisted MONTANUS in spreading his prophecies that a heavenly Jerusalem would soon descend upon Pepuza in Phrygia.

Priscillian (fl. fourth century C.E.) *Christian heretic whose sect gained popularity in the West, most notably in Spain*
Priscillian was a Spanish layman, probably of a wealthy or noble family, who began to preach a severely ascetical, pseudo-Christian creed sometime in the early- to mid-370s. His exact aim and the tenets of his theology were not fully preserved. Clearly, however, he was influenced by GNOSTICISM, with his call for vegetarianism and adherence to strict living. Priscillian found support among many of the Spanish bishops but was opposed by Christian orthodoxy. In 380, at the Council of Saragossa, the prelates who were his antagonists managed only to have his sect condemned, and his patrons retaliated by ordaining him as the bishop of Avila. Drawn into the matter by appeals from the orthodox, Emperor Gratian sided with Priscillian.

Unfortunately, Gratian was murdered in 383, and Magnus Maximus, his successor, had to cultivate the goodwill of the orthodox Christians. At the Council of Bordeaux in 384, he allowed Priscillian to be condemned and, when the sect's followers appealed, listened to charges of sorcery. A tribunal of laymen, headed by Magnus Maximus's Praetorian prefect, found Priscillian guilty. St. MARTIN OF TOURS protested vehemently against the use of a secular court, to little avail. Priscillian was executed in 385. A controversy erupted over the death, the result of a lay committee, but the sect only increased in number throughout Spain. Steps were taken to reduce its impact, including the Council of Toledo in 400, aimed at bringing back into the church all less-stringent Priscillianists.

Priscus (1) (fl. late second century C.E.) *Designer of siege engines*

From Bithynia, Priscus came to the attention of Septimius Severus in 194 when that general was attempting to capture Byzantium, the city on the Hellespont, holding out in favor of the rival imperial claimant Pescennius Niger. The engines devised by Priscus were very strong and were positioned along the entire length of the city wall; they were helpful in preventing the capture of the site for almost three years. When Byzantium finally fell, Priscus was condemned to die, only to be spared by Severus. The new emperor wisely retained his services as a builder of siege engines. In Severus's campaign against the Parthians, Priscus created numerous siege devices for the assault on Hatra. His designs were so excellent that among the works destroyed by the Parthians only his were left standing.

Priscus (2) (fl. second century C.E.) *Officer of the legions in Britain*
Around 185–186, Priscus was chosen by the legionaries as emperor. He declined the nomination with the statement: "I am no more an emperor than you are soldiers."

Priscus (3) (c. 305–396 C.E.) *Neoplatonic philosopher*
Possibly born in Epirus, Priscus was a student of Aedesius at Pergamum. He taught at Athens before joining Maximus of Ephesus as one of the major influences in the intellectual development of Emperor JULIAN THE APOSTATE. He was invited to Julian's court in Gaul when the prince was Caesar and served as adviser during his reign as emperor from 361 to 363. Traveling with Julian, Priscus was at his side in Antioch in 362 and during the Persian Campaign in 363. He was also present at Julian's death. Returning to Antioch, Priscus enjoyed the favor of Jovian but was put on trial with Maximus of Ephesus by Emperor Valens. Acquitted in 370 or 371 on charges of conspiracy, Priscus was allowed to go home to Greece, where he taught for many years.
See also NEOPLATONISM.

Priscus (4) (fl. fifth century C.E.) *Greek historian from Panium in Thrace*
Priscus became a teacher of rhetoric before joining the embassy sent in 449 to ATTILA the Hun. He helped organize the meeting with Attila and presented the emperor's gifts to him. As a writer, Priscus composed a secular history in seven books of contemporary events and a history of Byzantium. Although extant only in fragments, it was used by such chroniclers as John Malalas and Procopius.

Priscus, Clutorius (C. Lutorius Priscus) (d. 21 C.E.) *Roman knight and poet*
Priscus received money from Tiberius for the beauty of *Ode to Germanicus,* upon the latter's death in 19 C.E. In

21, however, he supposedly composed another poem, in preparation for the demise of Drusus, Tiberius's son who had recently fallen ill. His hope, so the subsequent accusation claimed, had been to gain an even greater reward from the emperor. The Senate condemned him to death, angering Tiberius, not because they had killed someone but that they had shown such haste in doing so.

Priscus, Gaius Julius (fl. mid-second century C.E.) *Brother of Emperor Philip the Arab and a beneficiary of his sibling's rise to power*

In 244, when Philip had succeeded Gordian III and had concluded a peace treaty with the Persians, Priscus was named by him to be governor of Macedonia. Later he was made Praetorian prefect of the East, with full powers to administer the Eastern provinces. His style of rule, however, was extremely harsh, as he collected taxes aggressively. This caused civil unrest in the East, culminating in the rise of usurpers.

Priscus, Javolenus (Gaius Octavius Tidius Tassianus Lucius Javolenus Priscus) (fl. second century C.E.) *Leading jurist*

Aside from being the head of the Sabinian school of law, he was legate in Britannia, Germania Superior, and Africa, and proconsul of Africa. Among his writings were *Epistulae* and extensive analyses of previous legal experts.

Priscus, Junius (d. 39 C.E.) *A praetor and victim of Emperor Gaius Caligula*

Reputed to be very wealthy, Priscus was charged with various crimes and put to death. Discovering that Priscus, in fact, possessed little wealth, Gaius lamented: "He fooled me and thus needlessly died when he might as well have lived."

Priscus, Lucius Neratius (fl. early second century C.E.) *Influential jurist and one of the last heads of the Proculean School of Law*

Priscus's time of greatest power came during the reign of Trajan, when he sat on the CONSILIUM PRINCIPIS. It was widely reported that Trajan considered him an excellent choice as his successor, once saying that he entrusted the provinces to Priscus, should anything happen to him. Under Hadrian he retained his position as legal adviser with other notables, such as Juventius Celsus and Salvius Julianus. Priscus was mentioned frequently in the *Digest*.

Priscus, Statius (d. after 163 C.E.) *Consul in 159 C.E. and one of the most successful generals in the reigns of Marcus Aurelius and Lucius Verus*

Priscus was governor of numerous provinces, including Dacia, Moesia, Britannia, and Cappadocia. While serving in Cappadocia, in 163 he helped Lucius Verus conquer Armenia, destroying Artaxata, the Armenian capital. Ironically, Verus took the title Armeniacus. Priscus was replaced by Martius Verus.

Priscus Attius (fl. first century C.E.) *Artist in the time of the Flavians (69–96 C.E.)*

With Cornelius Pinus, Attius painted the Temple of Honor and Virtus for Emperor Vespasian. The writer Pliny the Elder noted that Priscus painted in a fashion very close to the old style.

Probus, Marcus Aurelius (c. 232–282 C.E.) *Emperor from 276 to 282 and one of the rulers of the late third century*

Born at Sirmium, Probus achieved great success as a general in the service of Emperor AURELIAN. Details of his early career, including his position as tribune under Valerian, are related by the *Historia Augusta* (see SCRIPTORES HISTORIAE AUGUSTAE) and thus present serious problems of reliability and accuracy.

After working for Aurelian along the German frontier, Probus held the post of commander in Syria and Egypt. This office apparently continued through the reign of TACITUS (2) and in 276, upon the emperor's death, Probus refused to recognize the claim of FLORIANUS. Proclaimed as emperor by his own troops, Probus avoided an actual battle with Florianus, causing instead mass defections in his opponent's army. Florianus was murdered by his own troops as Probus became master of the Roman world. Proceeding immediately to Rome he gained confirmation from the Senate, although his supposedly good relations with the senatorial elements in government had recently fallen under suspicion. Crises along the Rhine and Danubian frontiers called for immediate attention. The Franks were defeated, followed by the Vandals and Burgundians. Two years of fighting culminated in 278 with the final repulse of the Vandals and Probus's laying claim to the title of Restorer of Illyricum (Restitutor Illurici). Marching to the East, he crushed a number of local uprisings and a usurpation by one of his lieutenants, Julius Saturninus. After negotiating a truce with Persia, Probus returned to the West to put down two more rebels, Proculus and Bonosus. This accomplished, he made preparations in Rome for a long-awaited campaign against Persia. Unfortunately he announced that in the future the legions would be disbanded as there would be peace in the empire. Word soon arrived that the troops in Raetia and Noricum had elevated CARUS to the purple. Probus sent a detachment to murder him, but they defected, and the emperor himself was slain by his own mutinous legionaries in 282.

Probus, despite his fatal error with the army, had proven himself a gifted ruler. He was able to defeat the barbarians repeatedly, celebrated a rare triumph in Rome, had the political power necessary to retain the support of the Roman government and did much to restore the provinces economically. He thus had a major part in the revival of the Roman Empire that would be completed by Diocletian.

Probus, Marcus Valerius (fl. late first century C.E.)
Grammarian from Berytus
Probus wrote very little and took on a limited number of students. As an author, he specialized in commentaries on such writers as Horace, Virgil, Lucretius, and Persius, making critical and useful annotations. A large collection of works attributed to him were not genuine. When he did teach, it was orally. Suetonius called him the last of the grammarians.

Probus, Petronius (d. 388 C.E.) *Praetorian prefect in the latter half of the fourth century*
Probus was born around 328, perhaps at Verona. After serving as *quaestor* and *praetor,* he became proconsul of Africa in 358. Throughout much of the reign of Valentinian he held the post of Praetorian prefect; Illyricum in 364, Galliarum in 366 and Illyricum, Italy, and Africa from 368–375. He was also consul in 371. He married a daughter of Q. Clodius Olybrius. During his administration he faced several crises. In 371, Sirmium was under attack by the Sarmation tribes and the Quadi; years of fighting apparently followed, with much of Illyricum devastated. Ambitious rivals schemed to have him removed, using his ruthless financial policy as evidence of his unsuitability for office. He survived such assaults, remaining as prefect until the time of Valentinian II.

From 375 to 383 Probus held no post, but in 383 he received the prefectship of Illyricum, Italy, and Africa once more. A Christian, he authored poems dedicated to Emperor Theodosius. Considered one of the greatest statesmen of his era, Probus received praise from such intellectuals as Ausonius, Symmachus, and Ammianus Marcellinus. Ammianus wrote of his vast wealth, his fair disposition, and his charity. Probus was buried in a sarcophagus behind the altar in St. Peter's.

Proclus (c. 412–485 C.E.) *Neoplatonic philosopher of the fifth century*
From Lycia, Proclus studied in Rome and in Athens, and as a Neoplatonist he centered on pseudo-mysticism, theurgy and vague magical tenets. He developed a reputation for miraculous works and took over the leadership of the Athenian branch of the Neoplatonic movement. Proclus authored numerous treatises on philosophy, including commentaries on Plato. He is best known today for his *Elements of Theology (Stoicheiosis Theologike).*

See also NEOPLATONISM.

proconsul Title denoting the governor of a province (holding his *imperium,* or authority, in place of the *Consul*) during the Republic, the head of a senatorial province during the empire. According to custom, a proconsul held his post for one year, surrendering his authority to a successor and departing within 30 days of his expired term. He was, in official circumstances, accompanied by six lictors, 12 if he had once served as consul. An important difference between the proconsuls of the Republic and the empire was in power over troops. A proconsul in the Republic commanded any legions in his province, while an imperial proconsul had no units available to him.

See also IMPERIUM PROCONSULARIS for details of his power in terms of the imperial system.

Procopius (326–366 C.E.) *Usurper in the East from 365 to 366*
Probably related maternally to JULIAN. Procopius was born to a wealthy family in Cilicia, and under Emperor CONSTANTIUS II was an imperial secretary and tribune, reaching a position in the *schola notariorum.* When Julian became emperor in 361, he was promoted to the rank of COMES and held a command in the army during Julian's Persian campaign in 363. Apparently named by Julian to be his successor, Procopius was bypassed in favor of JOVIAN upon Julian's death in 363. He did not force the claim but returned instead to private life, discharging the duty of cremating Julian at Tarsus. Because of the doubts of Emperor Valens, Procopius went into hiding, but in 365 was back at Constantinople, where the local units, unhappy with Valens, proclaimed him emperor on September 28. Valens quickly recovered, and Procopius was put to death on May 27, 366.

Proculeans The Proculiani or Proculeiani, members of one of the leading schools of law in Rome. The name derived from the eminent jurist of the first century C.E., PROCULUS. The Proculeans, students of the law school of that name, were bitter opponents in Rome of the Sabinians. Differences between the two apparently originated in the Augustan period (27 B.C.E.–14 C.E.), between Ateius CAPITO and Antistius LABEO. The two disputed the nature of law; Capito held a more conservative view than Labeo's. Proculus adhered to Labeo and his less conservative outlook. They feuded with the Sabinians until the time of Hadrian, when the organizational centralization of Roman law merged the two. Lucius Priscus was probably the last head of the Proculean School.

Proculeius, Gaius (fl. late first century B.C.E.) *Member of the Equestrians (Equites)*
A friend and confident of Emperor Augustus, he was used in 30 B.C.E. with the freedman Epaphroditus, as ambassador to Cleopatra.

Proculus (fl. mid-first century C.E.) *One of Rome's most respected legal experts*

Little is known with certainty about Proculus. He centered himself in the tradition of M. Antistius Labeo, composing a *Notae* (a collection of notes) on him. Aside from his inclusion in numerous parts of the *Digest*, Proculus voiced his legal views in his *Epistulae* (Letters). The PROCULEANS of the Proculean School named themselves after him.

See also JURISTS; LAW.

Proculus, Licinius (fl. first century C.E.) *Prefect of the Praetorian Guard during the brief reign of Otho in 69 C.E.*

Proculus was one of two prefects, with Plotius Firmus, to be elected by the Praetorians themselves, following Otho's succession. He enjoyed a position of favor with the emperor, using it to convince Otho to give battle at BEDRIACUM. The Othonian cause was crushed, but Proculus was pardoned by VITELLIUS.

Proculus, Volusius (fl. first century C.E.) *An officer of the imperial fleet at Misenum*

Proculus was reportedly unhappy at being passed over for reward, despite his help in the murder of Agrippina the Younger in 59. In 65 C.E., hoping to win his support in the growing PISONIAN CONSPIRACY, the woman EPICHARIS invited Proculus to satisfy his desire for vengeance by joining the plot to murder Nero. He reported her words to Nero but, because there was no witnesses, could not prove the charge.

procurator   An agent of the emperor, with varying amounts of power throughout the years of the Roman Empire. Procurators fulfilled a number of tasks within the imperial civil administration, especially in the provinces. By far the most common duty for a procurator was to act as governor of a minor province or territory. His powers were those of any other governor of an imperial possession, with control over the law and local government, as well as the troops at hand. The most obvious examples were to be found in Mauretania and Judaea. Procurators assigned to senatorial provinces fulfilled different duties; there they cared for imperial estates and properties within the region. They had no other authority within that provincial jurisdiction. In 23 C.E., Tiberius had a procurator in Asia, Lucilius Capito, tried and condemned for overstepping his rights by laying claim to some prerogatives of the governor. Usurpations became a frequent occurrence in the late first century C.E., most notably in areas of financial concern.

Finances were the other major task of the procurator. When assigned to an imperial province with a legate (*legati pro praetore*), they acted as the financial overseer. Their equivalent in the senatorial domains was the QUAESTOR, but the procurator had to do more than collect taxes. All troops in the province had to be paid and accounts had to be maintained. Elsewhere, a procurator might be concerned more exclusively with tax collection or with the legal formalities connected with the taxes. Because of the trust and responsibilities given to them, the procurators were generally chosen from the ranks of the Equestrians (EQUITES). While freedmen were, from time to time, placed in a procuratorship, the office emerged as a bastion of Equestrian political expansion. Procurators thus survived the administrative changes of the second century C.E. In the fourth century C.E., with the termination of imperial and senatorial designations, they served as representatives of the central government in mints and mines.

See also PONTIUS PILATE; *RES PRIVATA*.

Prohaeresius (d. 367 C.E.) *Christian rhetorician*

Also known as Proaeresius, he studied RHETORIC at Athens and Antioch, becoming a teacher in the Athenian school. Famed for his eloquence, he received an honorary Praetorian prefecture from Constans and was given a statue by the Romans. When Emperor Julian the Apostate, in 362, forbade Christians from teaching, Prohaeresius was given a special dispensation; nevertheless he resigned his post in protest of the imperial policy. He claimed among his pupils Gregory of Nazianzus, Basil, and Eunapius.

Propertius, Sextus (d. 15 B.C.E.) *Elegiac poets*

Born between 54 and 49 or 47 B.C.E. at Assisi in Umbria, he was educated in Rome, showing early on a capacity for poetry. Propertius subsequently developed into a premier elegiac and erotic poet, surpassing Tibullus in his skills as an adherent of the Alexandrine style. Through the success of his book of elegies, devoted in the main to his love, Cynthia, Propertius acquired the patronage of Gaius MAECENAS. Although certainly a client and addressing works to him, the poet never seemed to enjoy familiarity with the circle of literary giants around Maecenas, which included Virgil and Horace. Ovid, however, repeatedly mentioned Propertius in a very favorable light. As a writer, Propertius underwent a fascinating transformation. Always original and imaginative, he nevertheless moved away from his characteristic nervousness into a forceful manner and perhaps even a didactic one in his last book (IV), where he treated various topics of Roman history. Beset throughout his life with poor health and catastrophe, he lost his father, home and the woman he loved—which possibly had an influence on his frequent mention of death. The date of his death is unclear and is placed sometime in the years between 16 and 2 B.C.E., but probably closer to 15.

proscription   From the Latin *proscriptio*, a list of individuals who, for various reasons and crimes, have been declared criminals. They were often those who lost in a major power struggle, such as the losers in the political and military conflicts following the death of Julius Caesar in 44 B.C.E. Among the proscribed at that time was Cicero. Victims of proscription lost their property and had a death sentence passed upon them. Anyone responsible for killing them received a reward. The sons and grandsons of the proscribed were banned from public office.

Prosper (Prosper of Aquitaine) (fl. fifth century C.E.) *Christian theologian and historian*

A follower of strict orthodoxy as symbolized by his patron, Augustine, Prosper composed polemics against the Pelagians and semi-Pelagians, and poems on various other subjects. The main work of Prosper was his *Chronicle*. A continuation of the effort of Jerome, the *Chronicle* included a brief epitome of Jerome's own history and then recorded events from around 379 to 455. Prosper wrote his book in Rome but subsequent revisions were made in Africa; final versions included the story of the Vandal Kingdom of Africa.

protectores

Precursor of the PROTECTORES DOMESTICI; they were organized probably during the reign of Gallienus (c. 260–268 C.E.) as part of his reform of the imperial armed forces. Membership among the *protectores* was based upon holding the rank of tribune in the PRAETORIAN GUARD and on other positions in the legions, including the centurionate. Based within the Castra Praetoria, the *protectores* were not divorced from the Praetorian Guard and thus did not offer a counterweight to the guardsmen. It was Diocletian and Constantine the Great who made an abrupt change in the structure of imperial palace politics.

provinces of the Roman Empire

While termed the Imperium Romani (the empire of Rome), the Roman Empire was, in fact, a conglomeration of far-flung territories, client-states, and regions that fell under Roman authority over the course of centuries. These acquired territories were divided for geographical and, especially, administrative purposes into provinces. The history of the Roman Empire—as distinct from the history of Rome or Italy—is one told by the events and the development of the provinces and the vast populations who lived under Roman imperial subjection.

As the city of Rome expanded its influence in Italy, the conquest of territory made it necessary to devise some structure for magistrates to administer justice and oversee public tranquillity. It was in this sense that the term *provincia* first came into use, to designate the task or specific jurisdiction granted to a magistrate by the Senate in the form of an IMPERIUM. Until the time of the First Punic War (264–241), all *provinciae* were situated in Italy. That changed throughout the long and bitter struggles with Carthage, when Rome seized control of extensive overseas territories. The Senate was reluctant to enter into direct administration of a new territory because of the cost in military personnel and administration, but the *provinciae* helped to establish important frontier buffers safeguarding the imperial interior and its swiftly developing trade and lines of communications. The loose system of assigned authority for a magistrate thus became understood to be an overseas territory administered by a magistrate supported by a staff. The number of provinces increased steadily during the first century through the campaigns of POMPEY THE GREAT and Julius CAESAR.

During the Republic, the governance and size of the provinces was never concretized in law. Rather, provinces were formed out of newly conquered territory, with the general establishing the specific terms for its foundation in consultation with members of the Senate. Actual administration was also loose in structure and subject to abuse and corruption. Customarily, cities and communities in the acquired province were permitted to retain local government and traditions. All, however, were subject to the edicts and even the whims of the governor. He governed through his provincial staff, which included quaestors and legates, as well as a variety of members from the civil service. As postings to often distant *provinciae* were considered undesirable, assorted incentives were given to governors and their friends (*cohors*). Lax oversight permitted severe abuses of the local population, so that many governors and their associates returned far wealthier than when they left Rome, although overly obvious corruption could be prosecuted by the Senate under the laws of *repetundae* (or retrieval of lost money by people in the provinces). The two most important functions of government were to maintain peace—either by watching the frontier or keeping the cities and town pacified—and to collect taxes. The latter task was left to quaestors or towns themselves, and surpluses were almost never reported to Rome as any excess taxes found their way into the coffers of the governor and his friends. Roman taxation, both direct and indirect, were often oppressive, becoming even more so in the later empire.

The long-standing system of provinces in the Republic was brought to an end by Emperor Augustus (r. 27 B.C.E.–14 C.E.). As part of his extensive political settlement with the Senate following the battle of Actium in 31 B.C.E., Augustus was granted control over his own *provincia,* which contained such extensive and important territories as Gaul, Syria, and Hispania. These he governed through *legati pro praetore* (or legates) who represented his interests. From this ad hoc structure emerged the recognition of the division of all provinces into one of two types, imperial and senatorial. The senatorial provinces (broadly the smaller and more established provinces) were governed by proconsuls, assisted by quaestors and legates. Even senatorial provinces were subject to imperial will, for Augustus and his successors possessed the IMPERIUM MAIUS, giving them the right to intervene in senatorial affairs. The most prestigious of the senatorial provinces were Asia and Africa, although it was traditionally accepted that appointment to the larger imperial provinces was a more certain way of guaranteeing advancement to higher office in Rome. All new provinces added after 14 C.E. were designated imperial provinces, a custom that did not change.

Egypt was a unique province in that it was held technically "subject to the Roman People." In reality, Augustus held Egypt as his own, which was logical given its strategic access to the Red Sea and, above all, its central role in supplying grain for the empire. Senators were forbidden to enter Egypt without direct imperial consent, and administration was in the hands of a prefect assigned from the ranks of the Equestrian class.

The system established by Augustus remained essentially unchanged until the late third century, when Diocletian inaugurated the system of the Tetrarchy in 293 C.E. and the redistribution of the provinces into 12 administrative units termed *dioceses*. The new system all but excluded senatorial participation and represented the climax of an imperial structure that had gradually ended the role of the Senate in the imperial machinery of state. The diocesan system became more complex throughout the fourth century C.E., keeping pace with the centralization of imperial government in the hands of the emperors and their bureaucracy.

The provinces in existence prior to the reforms of Diocletian were as follows:

Name	Year of Initial Creation
Achaea	27 B.C.E.
Aegyptus	30 B.C.E.
Africa	146 B.C.E.
Alpes Atrectianae et Poeninae	second century C.E.
Alpes Cottiae	c. 54 C.E.
Alpes Maritimae	14 B.C.E.
Armenia Major	114 C.E.
Armenia Minor	38 C.E.
Asia	129 B.C.E.
Assyria	116 C.E. (abandoned by Hadrian)
Bithynia et Pontus	65 B.C.E.
Britannia	c. 43 C.E.
Cappadocia	17 C.E.
Cilicia	72 C.E.
Cyprus	c. 27 B.C.E.
Cyrenaica	74 B.C.E.
Dacia	107 C.E.
Galatia	25 B.C.E.
Gallia Cisalpina	82 B.C.E.
Gallia Comata	27 B.C.E.*
Gallia Transalpina	121 B.C.E.
Germania Inferior	c. 90 C.E.
Germania Superior	c. 90 C.E.
Hispania Citerior	197 B.C.E.
Hispania Ulterior	197 B.C.E.
Illyricum	11 B.C.E.
Italia	c. 27 B.C.E.**
Lycia et Pamphylia	43 C.E.
Macedonia	c. 146 B.C.E.
Mesopotamia	c. 116 (abandoned by Hadrian; reconstituted in 197 and lost in the third century)
Moesia	c. 6 C.E.
Noricum	c. 15 B.C.E.
Raetia	after 15 B.C.E.
Sardinia et Corsica	227 B.C.E.
Sicilia	211 B.C.E.
Syria	64 B.C.E.
Thracia	46 C.E.

* Gallia Comata was reorganized by Augustus, c. 27 B.C.E., into three provinces: Gallia Aquitania, Gallia Lugdunensis, and Gallia Belgica. Together, they formed the so-called Tres Galliae.

** Italia came under the control of Rome over the course of several centuries, from the fifth century to the third century B.C.E. It was unified completely under Augustus around 27 B.C.E.

Suggested Readings: Balsdon, John P. *Romans and Aliens.* Chapel Hill: University of North Carolina Press, 1979; Barker, Graeme, John Lloyd, and Joyce Reynolds. *Cyrenaica in Antiquity.* Oxford, U.K.: B. A. R., 1985; Bowersock, Glen W. *Roman Arabia.* Cambridge, Mass.: Harvard University Press, 1983; Braund, David. *Rome and the Friendly King: the Character of the Client Kingship.* London: Croom Helm, 1984; Curchin, L. A. *Roman Spain. Conquest and Assimilation.* London: Routledge, 1991; De Alarcão, J. *Roman Portugal: Introduction and Gazetteer.* Warminster: Aris & Phillips, 1988; Dyson, Stephen L. *The Creation of the Roman Frontier.* Princeton, N.J.: Princeton University Press, 1985; Drinkwater, J. F. *Roman Gaul: The Three Provinces, 58 B.C.–A.D. 260.* Ithaca, N.Y.: Cornell University Press, 1983; ———. *The Creation of the Roman Frontier.* Princeton, N.J.: Princeton University Press, 1985; Julius Caesar. *The Conquest of Gaul.* New York: Penguin, 1982; Keay, S. J. *Roman Spain.* London: British Museum Publ., 1988; King, Anthony. *Roman Gaul and Germany.* Berkeley: University of California Press, 1990; Millar, Fergus. *The Roman Empire and Its Neighbours.* 2nd ed. London: Duckworth, 1981; Parker, S. Thomas. *Romans and Saracens: a History of the Arabian Frontier.* Philadelphia: American Schools of Oriental Research; Winona Lake, Ind.: Distributed by Eisenbrauns, 1986; Price, S. R. F. *Rituals and Power: the Roman Imperial Cult in Asia Minor.* Cambridge, U.K.: Cambridge University Press, 1984; Randsborg, Klavs. *The First Mil-*

lennium A.D. in Europe and the Mediterranean: an Archaeological Essay. Cambridge, U.K.: Cambridge University Press, 1991; Sullivan, Richard. *Near Eastern Royalty and Rome, 100–30 B.C.E.* Toronto: University of Toronto Press, 1990; Wacher, J., ed. *The Roman World* 2 vols. London: Routledge, 1987; Whittaker, C. R. *Frontiers of the Roman Empire.* Baltimore: Johns Hopkins University Press, 1994; Wightman, Edith M. *Gallia Belgica.* London: Batsford, 1985.

Prudentius (Aurelius Prudentius Clemens) (c. 348–410 C.E.) *Christian poet who specialized in apologetics and hymns*

Born in Spain, at the site of modern Saragossa, he studied law and was both a lawyer and government official. Despite a high position of respect in Rome, he spent his last years devoted to composition. Among the many works of Prudentius were *Apotheosis; Peristephanon,* in praise of martyrs; *Psychomachia,* a view of spiritual struggles between good and evil; *Cathemerinon,* hymns for each day; and the famous *contra Symmachum,* a polemic composed to refute the speech delivered by the pagan SYMMACHUS during the debates and struggles over the return of the pagan Altar of Victory to the Senate.

Ptolemais   Name given to numerous towns in Africa

and Egypt that were founded under Ptolemaic influence during that dynasty's three-century rule of the Egyptian kingdom. Two cities named Ptolemais were especially interesting, one in Africa and the other in Cyrenaica. Ptolemais in Egypt was situated along the Nile, south of the Faiyum and north of Thebes. As it was originally a Greek colony, its inhabitants steadfastly retained their Greek heritage and lifestyle. This was important to Emperor Hadrian, who, in 130 C.E., founded the city of ANTINOPOLIS just above Ptolemais. Many residents of the new community were drawn from Ptolemais, specifically because of their Hellenic cultural ties. Ptolemais in Cyrenaica was also a Greek colony, established probably in the third century B.C.E. It was positioned to the east of Cyrene along the coast and was probably very wealthy. The city possessed theaters, an odeon, an amphitheater and villas of exceptional beauty. Water was supplied through ingenious cisterns and decorated underground vaults.

Ptolemy (d. 40 C.E.) *King of Mauretania*

The son of King JUBA II and ruler of Mauretania from 23 to 40 C.E., Ptolemy was related to the imperial family though his mother, Cleopatra Selene, the daughter of Marc Antony. During the final years of Juba's reign, Ptolemy assumed greater importance to his kingdom and was thus well prepared to fulfill the duties of his office. His relations with Rome were always excellent. After aiding in the destruction of the brigand Tacfarinas he was

declared a "Friend of Rome," receiving from the Senate as well a scepter and a beautiful purple robe. In 40, however, he was summoned to Rome by Gaius Caligula and put to death. Various sources ascribed this murder to his wealth, his robe or to some imaginary offense. Mauretania was quickly seized by Rome.

Ptolemy, Claudius (f. second century C.E.) *Astronomer, mathematician, and geographer*

Claudius Ptolemy, or Ptolemaeus, lived in Alexandria when the city was still the heart of the Roman Empire's scientific life. Little survived to detail his life, except that he was Egyptian; only his monumental works stand as his personal legacy. Ptolemy's most famous treatise was his mammoth study on astronomy, the *Almagest.* Written in 13 books, it covered the entire extent of knowledge of the heavens, relying upon numerous ancient authorities, such as Menelaus and Hipparchus. Its mathematical computations were extensive. So impressive was the *Almagest* that it served as the accepted and definitive effort on the subject for the next millennium, even in the eras of Islam and the Byzantines. When combined with his many other astronomical studies, the *Almagest* provided a thorough presentation of the stars, geometrical systems, orbits, and constellations. Ptolemy thus knew something about virtually every science. One of his branches of expertise, geography, resulted in a detailed (but now inaccurate) geographical guide to the ancient world. All of his writings, however, were clear, methodical and important from a historical perspective in their preservation of sources from antiquity.

See also ASTROLOGY; MATHEMATICS.

Ptolemy XII Auletes (d. 51 B.C.E.) *King of Egypt from 80 to 51 B.C.E.*

Called officially Neos Dionysos, but popularly known as Auletes, he was the illegitimate son of Ptolemy IX Lathyrus, who died in 80 without any designated heir. With the support of the Alexandrian political parties, young Ptolemy was elevated to the throne, taking the name Ptolemy XII (because Ptolemies X and XI had reigned for brief periods when his father was off the throne, regaining it a few years before he died in 80). This accession took place without the blessings of the powerful Roman statesman Sulla, engendering the first thoughts of a possible Roman seizure of Egypt. This threat hung over Ptolemy's rule for many years and was partially resolved in 59 B.C.E. Through the help of Pompey and Julius Caesar, Ptolemy was given full status as the recognized head of Egypt by the Roman Senate in 59. This recognition came at the price of 6,000 talents of gold, and in order to pay vast bribes Ptolemy had to apply a ruthless taxation program to his own easily enflamed subjects. In 58, he fled Egypt, journeying to Rome to demand help in recovering the throne.

Pompey pressed the Senate to send troops to Egypt to win back the country, and had full approval for the consul Lentulus Spinther to march. Unfortunately, the SIBYLLINE BOOKS declared such a venture untimely. It was not until 55 that Ptolemy could find a means of returning home. The Roman official Aulus GABINIUS was offered 10,000 talents to forget the cause of Mithridates in Parthia. Gabinius accepted and reinstated Ptolemy but was then fined the money he received, a punishment for taking such a treasure. Ptolemy remained in Egypt until his death in 51. His children were CLEOPATRA, ARSINOE, PTOLEMY XIII, and PTOLEMY XIV.

Ptolemy XIII (d. 47 B.C.E.) *King of Egypt, brother of Cleopatra, and son of King Ptolemy XII Auletes*
Ptolemy XIII tried but failed to win the throne of his country from Cleopatra and Julius Caesar. In 51 B.C.E., Ptolemy XII died, leaving his heirs Cleopatra and Ptolemy, who was probably barely 10 years old. Although they were to rule Egypt together, a group of ambitious advisers surrounded both. The result was a tense political struggle for power within the palace. By 48, Cleopatra had been ousted from Alexandria through the maneuverings of Ptolemy's cunning counselors, such as POTHINUS and Theodotus. As she refused to give up so easily, the queen organized an army. Egypt stood on the verge of civil war when Pompey arrived on September 28, 48 B.C.E. Pompey the Great had just lost the battle of Pharsalus and had fled to Egypt with Caesar in hot pursuit. Ptolemy's adviser recommended murdering Pompey as an act of goodwill to Caesar. While the removal of such a foe was politically advantageous to Caesar, the shameful manner of his death virtually condemned Ptolemy. By the time Cleopatra became Caesar's lover, all of Alexandria was up in arms, and the Roman dictator was besieged. Sensing that it was to his advantage to send Ptolemy away from the palace, Caesar eventually allowed him to depart. Ptolemy joined his army, engaged at the time in trying to stop the advance of Mithridates of Pergamum. The young king showed flashes of real military talent, but he was no match for Caesar, who faced him in the battle of the NILE in February of 47. There the Egyptians were routed, and Ptolemy fell in the fray.

Ptolemy XIV (d. 43 B.C.E.) *King of Egypt*
The youngest son of King PTOLEMY XII AULETES of Egypt, and the brother of CLEOPATRA and PTOLEMY XIII, Ptolemy was placed on the throne with Cleopatra by Julius Caesar, in 47 B.C.E. Officially he was to be her consort, but as he was only 10 or 12 years old at the time, she was the true power in the land. He was presumably murdered by her sometime after Caesar's assassination, probably in 43 B.C.E.

Pulcheria, Aelia (399–453 C.E.) *Augusta from 414 to 453 and the sister of Emperor Theodosius II*
Pulcheria ran the Eastern Empire as regent for her brother, while earning a reputation for saintliness that resulted in her canonization. She was the daughter of Emperor Arcadius, growing up in Constantinople and living as the elder sister of the imperial heir. When Arcadius died in 408, Theodosius succeeded to the throne and both lived for the next six years under the fair administration of the Praetorian Prefect ANTHEMIUS. In 414, however, Anthemius was removed from his post. On July 4, 414, Pulcheria was proclaimed Augusta, taking control over virtually all aspects of her brother's education. She also introduced strict Christian practices into the court, eventually convincing her brother to condemn Nestorianism.

Theodosius married the formidable EUDOCIA in 421; with her elevation to the rank of Augusta in 423, she was on equal terms with Pulcheria. The next years were spent amidst intrigues as Eudocia quietly battled Pulcheria for control of the palace, and the ambitious eunuch and chamberlain, Chrysaphius ZSTOMMAS, sowed discontent between them. Pulcheria refused to take the bait of open war, retiring to a private life in the Palace of the Hebdomon in Constantinople. Eudocia was subsequently forced out of the Eastern capital, going to Jerusalem and leaving Zstommas to reign supreme during th 440s.

By the year 450, the officers of the army had risen up and defeated the eunuch. Pulcheria emerged once more as the main influence with Theodosius. He died in July of that year, leaving no appointed heir, although he was leaning toward the reliable soldier, MARCIAN. To ensure a smooth transition of power, Pulcheria married Marcian. She died a virgin in 453, having left a lasting mark on the East and on Christianity, with her support of orthodoxy and with her leadership at the Council of Chalcedon in 451.

Pulchra, Claudia (d. 26 C.E.) *A cousin of Agrippina the Elder*
Claudia's persecution in 26 C.E. marked the beginning of the end for Agrippina. Charged with adultery and the attempted assassination of Tiberius with poisons and incantations, she was condemned through the skillful oratory of Domitius AFER. Agrippina's angry response against Tiberius for allowing the trial to proceed only made Agrippina's position more dangerous.

Pupienus (d. 238 C.E.) *Senator and coemperor (with Balbinus) in 238 C.E.*
Marcus Clodius Pupienus Maximus was possibly of low birth, although the details of his life are rendered unclear by the wholly unreliable account in the *Historia Augusta* (*see* SCRIPTORES HISTORIAE AUGUSTAE). According to the

historian Herodian, Pupienus held numerous posts as governor, including that of Germania Inferior and Asia. When the Senate determined to be rid of Emperor Maximinus I Thrax, a committee of 20 was organized to prepare Italy for invasion. Both Gordians, whom the Senate had supported, were killed in 238, and Pupienus was raised with BALBINUS to the throne.

Even though the two colleagues were to be complete equals, Pupienus was the less popular of the two. To ensure their acceptance, the grandson of GORDIAN I, Gordian III, was made Caesar. This done, Pupienus set out to northern Italy, where he collected an army. It proved to be unnecessary, for Maximinus was slain by his own men. Returning to Rome with a German bodyguard, Pupienus infuriated both Balbinus and the PRAETORIAN GUARD with his ovation. As relations between the two rulers deteriorated, the Praetorians plotted their deaths, fearing that they were about to be replaced by the Germans. They thus stormed the palace, kidnapped the two emperors and murdered them in the CASTRA PRAETORIA.

Puteoli One of the major ports in Italy, on the Tyrrhenian Sea coast of CAMPANIA; a gateway for commerce from Alexandria and from Spain and much of the western Mediterranean. Puteoli (modern Pozzuoli) was founded by the Greeks, who were living in nearby Cumae at the time (c. 521 B.C.E.) and named their new community Dicaearchia. Popular usage turned it into Puteoli, probably from its many wells (*puteus,* well). Roman occupation came in 194 B.C.E. with colonists. Further efforts at colonization were made by Augustus, Nero, and Vespasian, each granting some new privileges. Under Nero, Puteoli was known officially as Colonia Claudia Augusta Neronensis. Such honors could not disguise the reality that from the reign of Claudius the port, despite its excellent harbor, was eclipsed as the commercial entry into Rome by OSTIA. As the residents of Puteoli watched their economic livelihood dry up in favor of Ostia and coupled with the growing independence of foreign markets, internal feuding between the populace and the magistrates erupted. In 58 C.E., riots and threats of arson brought the appointment of Gaius Cassius. He was replaced by the SCRIBONII BROTHERS who arrived with a cohort of the Praetorian Guard, striking suitable terror into the populace. Puteoli was sacked in 410 by Alaric and in 455 by Geiseric and again by the Huns in 545.

Pylades (fl. first century B.C.E.) *Actor*
Pylades was reportedly very old in 2 B.C.E. He quarreled with the other notable performer, Bathyllus, but was exiled from Rome and Italy for pointing out, with a middle finger, a spectator who had hissed at him. In 18 B.C.E. he was allowed to return to Rome. He commented to the emperor when rebuked for his feud with Bathyllus that: "It is fortunate for you, Caesar, that the people should devote their time to us." Pylades was also the name of two pantomime actors, one a favorite of Emperor Trajan (98–117 C.E.) and the other popular in the reign of Pertinax (193 C.E.).

Quadi A Germanic tribe of Suebi racial stock, situated in the area of the Main River late in the first century B.C.E. Moving into southeastern Germany, they came into contact with the MARCOMANNI, IAZYGES, and other minor peoples, such as the Osi. Subsequently, they developed close ties with both the Marcomanni and Iazyges while establishing themselves as a powerful tribal state. Under their chief, Vannius, the Quadi exercised considerable influence over the western Danubian frontier in the first half of the first century C.E. Around 50 C.E., however, Vannius and the Quadi were assailed by a barbarian confederation of the HERMUNDURI, Lugii and others. Vannius fell in battle while countering two usurpers, his nephews Vangis and Sido. They broke apart the Quadi, as large elements of Vannius's supporters fled to the Romans and were settled in PANNONIA. Henceforth the Quadi displayed hostility toward Rome. A war was fought with Emperor DOMITIAN, and the Quadi were a leading force in the MARCOMANNIC WARS in the second century. MARCUS AURELIUS inflicted a terrible defeat upon them in 174. By the end of the fourth century, the Quadi were part of the other Germanic states on the march into the Roman Empire. They probably traveled with the VANDALS into Spain.

Quadratus, Asinius (fl. early third century C.E.) *Senator and historian*
Probably proconsul of Achaea, Quadratus authored a *History of Rome* in 15 books and a work on the Parthians, both in Greek.

quaestiones The main criminal courts of the Republic, an institution that lasted until the third century C.E. According to early custom, crimes against the state were tried by a magistrate or, under certain circumstances, a special board summoned to handle the matter. This commission, called a *quaestio,* was not permanent. In 149 B.C.E., a major change was made as the term *quaestio perpetua* was now applied to the committee. At first presiding over civil cases, the *quaestio* assumed the bulk of criminal cases. Formed of senators, its jurors were non-senatorial, normally of the Equestrian class (EQUITES). Individual *quaestiones* were established to oversee various criminal jurisdictions, including *veneficia* (witchcraft and poisoning), MAIESTAS (treason), and *peculatus* (corruption). As part of the reorganization of the entire governmental system, AUGUSTUS retained the *quaestiones,* adding yet another court for crimes of adultery. While the *quaestiones* continued to operate as they had during the Republic, the trend from the first century C.E. was to take away some of the functions of law and place them elsewhere. The Senate itself assumed some of the duties of the *quaestiones* as did the central imperial administration. More important was the creation of widened jurisdictions in law for the PREFECT OF THE CITY and the PREFECT OF THE PRAETORIAN GUARD, especially with regard to the lower classes of Rome. The *quaestiones* lost much of their prestige.

See also LAW; PRAETOR.

quaestor The lowest ranking magistrate in the CURSUS IIONORUM and the first position taken by all candidates embarking upon a senatorial career. Quaestors were probably a creation of the Roman kings, becoming institutionalized during the Republic. Their numbers increased with the rise of Rome as an imperial power, until the dictator Sulla fixed their number at 20 with a minimum age of 30. From the earliest days of the quaestorships these officials were closely connected with finances in Rome and in the provinces. The *quaestores urbani* exercised their authority within the walls of Rome, attached to the AERARIUM until their position was usurped by new officers in the imperial system. *Quaestores provinciales* served the proconsuls in senatorial provinces. They managed the finances of the provincial treasury, acted as deputies to the proconsul and often assumed the proconsul's duties when he was away. Quaestors were synonymous with the procurators in imperial domains. Upon completion of a quaestorship, the newly declared ex-quaestor was promoted regularly to the SENATE and was eligible for other magistracies.

quaestor sacri palati Quaestor of the sacred palace, the chief legal minister. Appointed first during the reforms of CONSTANTINE THE GREAT in the fourth century, the *quaestor sacri palati* had the task of drafting laws and writing the replies of the imperial administration to legal petitions. He worked normally with the SCRINII for secretarial assistance.

Quietus, Lusius (d. 117 C.E.) *Chieftain of the Moors under Emperor Trajan*

A noted cavalry commander and one of the Roman Empire's most ruthless officials, Lusius Quietus was originally captain of a native cavalry detachment in the early second century C.E. Condemned for excessive behavior, he was pardoned by Trajan and put to use in the Dacian Wars; he also served the emperor in a series of operations in the Parthian Wars. The Moor captured NISIBIS before burning and sacking EDESSA in 116. Facing a massive Jewish uprising in Mesopotamia and elsewhere, Trajan charged the general with their suppression, which he accomplished mercilessly, assuming the governorship of Judaea. In 117 he held a consulship but the following year was put to death as part of the purge accompanying the accession of HADRIAN.

Quietus, Titus Fulvius Junius (d. 261 C.E.) *Son of General Fulvius Macrianus and younger brother of the usurper Junius Macrianus*

In 260 C.E., following the capture and death of Emperor VALERIAN at the hands of the Persians, Quietus was proclaimed emperor in the East with his brother. He remained in the Eastern provinces while his father and brother marched west to enforce their imperial claim. When both MACRIANUS and his father were killed by the usurper AUREOLUS in ILLYRICUM, Quietus was attacked at EMESA in 261 by ODAENATH, the ruler of PALMYRA, and was put to death.

quinarius A species of Roman silver coinage, in value roughly one-half of the DENARIUS. First coinage during the Republic, the quinarius was never issued in an organized fashion and mintings were not numerous.

See also COINAGE.

quindecimviri sacris faciundis Literally, the 15 men for performing the sacrifices, known also as the *quindecimviri*; one of the main priestly colleges of Rome. The 15 *quindecimviri* were in charge of the SIBYLLINE BOOKS and thus exercised great influence on the decisions of the government. Later they monitored all foreign religions or cults that were allowed to function in Rome after permission had been granted by the Sibylline Books. From the time of Julius Caesar they numbered 16.

See PRIESTHOODS.

Quintianus, Afranius (d. 65 C.E.) *Senator and a member of the Pisonian Conspiracy against Nero in 65 C.E.*

The historian TACITUS wrote that Quintianus desired revenge upon Nero for lampooning his effeminate nature. When the plot was uncovered, Quintianus hoped to have his life spared by implicating the other conspirators, including his closest friends. The betrayals did little good, for he was executed.

Quintilian (Marcus Fabius Quintilianus) (c. 34–100 C.E.) *Highly respected writer and teacher*

Born in Calagurris (Calahorra), Spain, possibly the son of a rhetorician, Quintilian was educated, at least in part, in Rome, perhaps under Remmius PALAEMON and certainly under Domitius AFER. After returning to Spain (c. 63), he was summoned by the Emperor GALBA back to Rome in 68, where he remained for many years. He prospered as a tutor, becoming the first recipient of a direct salary from the government, because of his rhetorical talents. In high favor with the Flavians, he also practiced as a lawyer and amassed vast wealth. He acted as instructor to Domitian's two great-nephews, the designated heirs to the throne, as well as to PLINY THE YOUNGER. Among his works were *De causis corruptae eloquentiae* (On the Causes of the Corruption of Eloquence), declamations, a discussion of rhetoric and the famed *Institutio Oratoria* (The Education of the Orator). Composed in 96, a few years before his death, this large treatise outlined the training of a rhetorician in all of its details: early education, proper schooling, subject matter, style, and the nature of speaking. Book 10 was particularly important for its information on Greek and Latin writers. A stout defender of Latin, Quintilian listed the greatest rhetoricians of his time, with his critical commentary.

Quintilii brothers *Dissenters during the reign of Emperor Commodus (177–192 C.E.)*

They earned a reputation for their learning, martial abilities, and wealth. Sextus Quintilius Condianus and Sextus

Quintilius Valerius Maximus were inseparable, agreeing in 182 C.E. that Commodus was an appallingly bad emperor. Their dissensions reached the ears of palace courtiers and both were killed together. The son of Maximus reportedly escaped, traveling for years to avoid imperial assassins.

Quintillus, Marcus Aurelius Claudius (d. 270 C.E.)
Brother of Emperor Claudius II Gothicus
Named by Claudius to serve as commander in Italy. When Claudius died in 270, Quintillus served briefly as emperor. His reign, perhaps only a few months, was cut short by his death, possibly at the hands of his troops.

Quintus of Smyrna (fl. fourth century C.E.) *Poet*
Quintus was known for his sequel to Homer's *Iliad*, composed in 14 books.

Quirinal hill   *See* HILLS OF ROME.

Quirinius, Publius Sulpicius (d. 21 C.E.) *Consul in 12 B.C.E. and imperial official under Emperor Tiberius (ruled 14–37 C.E.)*
Quirinius came from humble origins in Lanuvium and served in numerous provincial posts, including as proconsul of Crete and Cyrenaica, where he suppressed the Marmaridae, and perhaps as governor of Galatia and later of SYRIA, where he defeated the local Colician Homanadenses (a band of outlaws). Quirinius paid a flattering visit to Tiberius, in self-imposed exile on Rhodes, and became adviser to Gaius CAESAR in the East in 2 C.E. Appointed governor of Syria in 6 C.E., he was responsible for the census conducted in Judaea following the territory's annexation. Quirinius married Aemilia LEPIDA

(around 2 C.E.) but later divorced her in proceedings that were so vicious that his reputation was ruined. Tiberius gave him a lavish funeral while lauding his career and devotion.

Quirinus
Name given by the Romans to the deified Romulus. The title had a Sabine origin and was possibly derived from *quiris* or "spear." It had associations with Mars, the god of war and the father of Romulus. As a divinity, Quirinus ranked as one of Rome's most important patrons, along with Jupiter, Mars, and Juno. He had a temple and a festival, the Quirinalia, held on February 17 each year. A *Flamen Quirinalis* was in charge of all religious ceremonies pertaining to Quirinus.

See also GODS AND GODDESSES OF ROME; HILLS OF ROME.

quirites
General term meaning citizens of Rome. When applied to soldiers, as done by Caesar to his troops in 47 B.C.E., it assumed a derogatory sense, stripping them of their status as fighting men, calling them mere "civilians."

Quodvultdeus (d. 453 C.E.) *Bishop of Carthage during the mid-fifth century C.E.*
A Donatist, Bishop Quodvultdeus was captured in 439, during the invasion by GEISERIC, the king of the VANDALS. Strictly enforcing the Arian creed, Geiseric rounded up all the orthodox bishops and other clergy, put them on decrepit ships and sent them out to sea. They reached Naples, where the bishop died in exile. He was a friend of AUGUSTINE, with whom he corresponded, and the author of sermons and *On the Promises and Predictions of God*.

Rabirius (fl. late first century C.E.) *Architect*
Rabirius's masterpiece of design was produced at the order of Emperor Domitian, who hired him to create the DOMUS FLAVIA. He was a friend of MARTIAL.

Radagaisus (d. 406 C.E.) *Barbarian ruler of a loose confederation of tribes, mostly composed of Vandals*
Radagaisus led two invasions of imperial provinces in the West, in 401 and 405 C.E. The first onslaught by Radagaisus came at the same time that ALARIC and the Visigoths were threatening Italy and Rome. Advancing into Raetia and Noricum, Radagaisus was attached by the MAGISTER MILITUM. STILICHO and thoroughly defeated. The crushed tribes withdrew and even had to supply auxiliaries for use against Alaric. In 405, Radagaisus returned, with large elements of OSTROGOTHS. Ignoring the Danubian provinces, the host descended on Italy via Aquileia; they then split up into columns, the largest under Radagaisus. Stilicho once more devised a suitable strategy, massacring the barbarians. Throughout late 405 and 406 the forces of Radagaisus were ground down and destroyed until he was captured and executed in August 406.
See also POLLENTIA.

Radamistus of Iberia (d. 58 C.E.) *Son of King Pharasmanes of Iberia*
By 51 C.E., Radamistus was eager to have his own throne, and Pharasmanes, hoping to avoid losing his own kingdom, pointed his son toward MITHRIDATES (1) of Armenia, Pharasmanes's own brother. Feigning an argument with his father, Radamistus fled to Mithridates but returned, unable to bring down that king through conspiracies.

Gathering an army he invaded Armenia, besieging his uncle at Garneae. Through bribery of local Roman officials, Radamistus lured Mithridates out and had him killed. Assuming the throne, the new monarch of Armenia found himself under attack by his own subjects. Without support from his father, who had to balance himself politically with Rome and Parthia, Radamistus fled the country, abandoning his own wife. In 58, as an act of good faith to Nero, Pharasmanes put Radamistus to death.

Raetia One of Rome's smaller Danubian provinces, occupying the alpine territory between GERMANIA Superior and NORICUM, just north of Italy and just south of the DANUBE. The original inhabitants were called the Rhaeti (or Raeti). Believed to be of Illyrian or perhaps of Tuscan descent, they lived in northern Italy until the Celts pushed them out. Moving to the region of modern Tyrol, Bavaria and a part of Switzerland, the Rhaeti proved warlike and willing to cross the Alps to make raids into GALLIA CISALPINA.

Roman conquest of Raetia came in 16 B.C.E. when P. Silius Nerva defeated them in battle. This success was followed up by Drusus the Elder and Tiberius in 15, with a large-scale invasion that brought all of Raetia under imperial control. Initial policy put Raetia under the care of the governor of Gallia Belgica. After Germanicus departed Gaul and Germany in 16 C.E., the legate of Gallia Belgica appointed some kind of officer over the region. Opinions have varied among scholars as to the exact title of this officer, some favoring a prefect (*praefectus civitatum*), while others prefer an equestrian procurator. In any event, after the reign of Trajan (98–117 C.E.) a procurator was in charge. His seat was at Augustus Vindelicorum, with command over auxiliary units. There were four *alae* (auxiliary cavalry) and 11 cohorts at first, changing to three *alae* and 13 cohorts in the middle of the second century C.E.

Massive upheaval afflicted the province as a result of the MARCOMANNIC WARS, not only with bitter fighting, but also with changes in the administration. A legate (LEGATUS), in charge of the III Italica legion took over the duties of the procurator. The added troops allowed the frontiers to be watched, especially the area along the defensive perimeter of the LIMES, where the Rhine met the Danube, as well as the *agri decumates*. A procurator eventually returned, but under Diocletian, Raetia was divided into Raetia I and II, in the diocese of Italia. From the start of the fifth century pressures built up on the Danubian border, and by the fall of the Western Empire Raetia had ceased to be an imperial possession.

rationalis　Chief financial minister of the state, prior to the reforms of Emperor Diocletian and the late empire. Among the tasks of the *rationalis* were the collection of all normal taxes and duties, the control of currency, and the administration of mines and mints. After the reforms of Diocletian, the *rationalis* and the a RATIONIBUS were replaced by the *comes sacrarum largitionum*.

See also FINANCE.

rationibus, a　Secretary of finance, in charge of maintaining the accounts and expenditures of the FISCUS. His role in the finances of the early empire was considerable. Originally an office held by a freedman, from the second century C.E. and the reign of Hadrian, Equestrians (EQUITES) assumed total control. The *a rationibus* was rendered unnecessary by the *comes sacrarum largitionum* of the fourth century C.E.

See FINANCE.

Raurici　Tribe residing in Gaul between the SEQUANI and the HELVETII. Suffering from the inroads of Germanic peoples in Gaul, they joined the Helvetians in their attempted migration to better lands in southern Gaul, sharing in the defeat at the hands of Julius CAESAR in 58 B.C.E. In 52 B.C.E. some elements of the Raurici threw in with VERCINGETORIX but were again routed by Caesar at ALESIA. Subsequently, the tribe was under the influence and control of the Roman administration in Germania Superior, in such cantons as Basel and Augusta Rauricorum.

Ravenna　North Italian city; in Gallia Cisalpina, a few miles inland from the Adriatic coast in the middle of marshes. Ravenna may have been founded by the Thessalians, although the name was probably Etruscan in origin. It passed into the hands of the Umbrians and was insignificant in the affairs of Rome until the late first century B.C.E., when Emperor Augustus was looking for an ideal location for his Adriatic fleet. With its marshes, accessibility from only one direction by land, and its position far enough north to defend Aquileia, Ravenna was chosen.

Already a MUNICIPIUM in 49 B.C.E., the city underwent major reconstruction and improvement to accommodate its new status. Most important, a canal was dug from the Po River to the city and then to the coast to allow small-boat traffic along the route. The subsequent harbor, called Classis, came to dominate the economic and political life of the city, for it was its very heart. As one of the major ports in the Mediterranean, Ravenna flourished with exports, including wine, ships, and the goods produced throughout northern Italy, especially in MEDIOLANUM (Milan).

While the port held the fleet it remained strategically essential to imperial naval defenses; but by the fourth century C.E., the seagoing might of Rome had deteriorated. By the fifth century, Ravenna's fortunes improved as it became capital of the Western Empire. In 404 C.E., Emperor HONORIUS decided that Ravenna, with its defensively advantageous, mosquito-ridden environs and stout walls, was the safest place to conduct government. He thus moved there and subsequent emperors lived both there and in Rome. So easily defended was Ravenna that the barbarian king ODOACER adopted it as his chief city, as did the Ostrogoth Theodoric, the Byzantines and even the Lombards, centuries later.

Reburrus, T. Crispus　(fl. late first century C.E.) *Architect*
Reburrus was responsible for the design of two superb amphitheaters, in NEMAUSUS (Nîmes) and ARLES. Both were virtually identical in style and both have survived in amazingly fine condition.

rebus, agentes in　The imperial courier service that replaced the unpopular FRUMENTARII, sometime during the late third century C.E. under Emperor Diocletian, or perhaps around the year 319 C.E. As a result of the reforms of Diocletian, the *frumentarii* were disbanded; their sinister reputation had ended their usefulness. But the central imperial administration still needed couriers, and *agentes in rebus* filled this task perfectly. Originally they acted as the dispatch carriers for the Roman Empire. Eventually they assumed a variety of other duties. During the reign of Constantius II (337–361 C.E.), the *agentes* were sent out to the provinces and were expected to monitor the mail and communications and to send back reports on the events within their provincial jurisdictions. Their routine assignments brought them into contact with vast amounts of intelligence, and with the full approval of Constantius they ferreted out all possibly treasonous activities. Two were appointed to each province in 357, one in 395 and more again after 412. Each member of the *agentes in rebus* was normally promoted into other branches of government.

The corps, with its known activity of gathering secrets as the frumentarii had, acquired a name for terror. There has been debate as to the extent of their secret police work, for actual arrests and torture probably did not fall under their authority. However, in the hands of a ruthless emperor like Constantius II, they could be given considerable freedom in hunting down information or evidence of a crime. This facet of their activities overshadowed other, more mundane aspects, such as carrying letters or verifying that a traveler was carrying the right DIPLOMATA while using the CURSUS PUBLICUS (postal system).

Rebus Bellicis, De An anonymous fourth-century C.E. work, *On Matters of Wars*, that was addressed to Emperors Valentinian I and Valens. It is concerned chiefly with a series of proposed reforms touching upon the army, the law, administration in the provinces, and imperial finances.

Rectus (d. 40 C.E.) *A Stoic philosopher*
A friend of Julius KANUS, Rectus was put to death in 40 C.E., by Emperor Gaius Caligula as part of his purge of Stoics and other philosophers.

Rectus, Aemilius (early first century C.E.) *Prefect of Egypt early in the reign of Tiberius (14–37 C.E.)*
Rectus was overly zealous in the collection of taxes on the Nile. When he sent to Rome far more money than expected, Tiberius wrote him: "I expect my sheep to be shorn, not shaved."

Red Sea One of the main avenues of TRADE between the West and the Far East. Ships from INDIA sailed up the sea, passing the Troglodyte Coast on the left and ARABIA on the right. Important trading centers were Leuke Komo, belonging to the Nabataeans, and Arsinoe, opposite Pelusium, along the Sinai Peninsula. Roman vessels probably patrolled the region, at least as far as the borders of the province of EGYPT.

Regalianus (Regillianus) (fl. third century C.E.) *Roman general*
Regalianus served in the army of the emperors Valerian and Gallienus. In 260 C.E. was proclaimed emperor. He had supposedly been commander of the legions in ILLYRICUM when elevated; unable to hold the loyalty of his troops, he was murdered.

Regulus, Publius Memmius (fl. first century C.E.) *Consul in 31 C.E.*
Regulus held his office during the fall of the prefect SEJANUS. Loyal to Tiberius, it was Regulus who summoned Sejanus to face the charges read before the Senate, and he also led out the prefect to be arrested by Cornelius Laco, prefect of the city. As a reward for his services, he replaced Poppaeus Sabinus as governor of Macedonia and perhaps Achaea in 35. Married to LOLLIA PAULINA, he was forced to see her wed to Emperor GAIUS CALIGULA in 38, although the emperor later divorced her.

relegatio A form of banishment, less severe than EXSILIUM, during the Republic and early Roman Empire. It was similar to exile except that it did not include the loss of citizenship and possessions. The writer Ovid, for example, was ordered to live in Tomi, near the Black Sea.

religion One of the guiding forces of the life and sociopolitical systems of Rome. Although old and established, Roman religion was ever altered and influenced— and ultimately destroyed—by the foreign gods and cults brought into Rome by the conquering legions and by the emperors. The Italians, and later the Romans, sprang from the same agrarian background as the Greeks, and perceived that nature was controlled by powerful natural forces. However, the early gods and goddesses of Rome never developed the anthropomorphic tendencies so obvious in the Hellenic pantheon. Roman deities retained their identification with nature, being worshiped in this sense. As there were spirits at work in every corner of the cosmos, new gods sprang up and were worshiped, joining such established divinities as Jupiter, Juno, Mars, and Vesta. This accepted idea of adding gods to the cults of Rome had the most profound consequences on the development of Roman religion. It not only made Rome more tolerant of such foreign creeds as Judaism but also helped ensure the popularity of the gods of vanquished states.

The Greeks arrived in Rome probably before the end of the kingly era. Shrines by Tarquinius to Jupiter, Juno, and Minerva elevated these three to the level of supreme rulers of the Roman pantheon. Other Grecian imports included Apollo, Cybele, and Asclepius (Aesculapius). Total victory for the Greeks came only after the Punic Wars, when the Romans, now masters of the Mediterranean world, adopted wholesale Greek identities for their gods. Old, titanic forces of nature were replaced by new, more human deities, in an ironic replaying of Greece's own theological history. Zeus was Jupiter, Hera was Juno, Athena was Minerva, Poseidon was Neptune, and so on.

Early in Roman religious history a tendency developed to link political power with religion. The kings of Rome probably began this idea, acting as heads of the priesthoods of Rome while retaining their monarchical status. In the Republic this system was unchanged, placing, as it did, broad authority in the hands of the Patrician class. Magistrates formed the priestly colleges, performed the ceremonies of worship and responded to the decrees of the Senate, which decided most questions of a religious or doctrinal nature. But there was no centralization or institutionalization of the cult of state, a situation made worse by the rise of the *Plebeians*. Thus, while the sacred rites were performed right up until the end of the Republic, they had lost much of their meaning.

The fact that the fields of state and religion could be fused had been proven by the kings, to a lesser extent by the magistrates, and, in terms of literature, by Varro, with his *Antiquitates,* which combined his studies of human and divine antiquities. What was needed was the presence of one single figure at the center of the cult. Julius Caesar was certainly in a position to be that figure, but he died before most of his plan could be realized. The leader who did succeed was Augustus.

After becoming master of the Roman world by 27 B.C.E., the man named Octavian assumed the title of Augustus, an indication of his more than human stature. The title was taken presumably with the approval of the Roman gods, and he served as the Pontifex Maximus, or supreme head of all Roman worship, a position retained by his successors until the reign of Gratian in the late fourth century C.E. A revival accompanied his supremacy. The ARVAL BRETHREN were reinvigorated, and throughout the empire the divine station of the emperor and Rome was preached to the provinces (*see* IMPERIAL CULT for details).

It can be argued that the Augustan religious revival was neither long-lasting nor successful. The Romans willingly participated in the ceremonies necessary for keeping the favor of the gods or hailing the glory of their empire, but so politically entwined had the gods become that they had lost spiritual impact. For divine inspiration Rome looked elsewhere, finding its answers in the same place that the Roman soldier had looked: the Oriental cults. Unquestionably, foreign deities were popular at all levels of society, fitting into the Roman system because of its provisions for individual worship outside of the nationally revered pantheon.

Traditionally, the state of Rome took a dim view of strange cults, refusing at first to let them cross the sanctity of the POMERIUM, or the ancient line of the city. Cybele, with her bizarre priests, was not formally accepted until the time of Claudius, although a temple to her was allowed on the Palatine as early as 191 B.C.E. Augustus helped introduce his patron, Apollo. The most important early breakthrough came in the time of Gaius Caligula, who built a temple to Isis in Rome. Henceforth, as the Claudian favor to Cybele showed, strange gods were welcome.

Mithraism, with its connection to sun worship, arrived also in the first century C.E., from the East. It found followers in the ranks of the army and among the social elite. Oriental faiths soon spread throughout the Eastern Empire, with Serapis, Elagabalus and even Osiris offering choices to the soul-searching Romans. Two interesting trends evolved toward the end of the second century: syncretism and monotheism. Syncretism, the mixing together of one or more deities into a single form, was used in the Mithraic cult, as the god was sometimes equated with Sol Invictus. The effect of all this was to render Roman mythology into a debased and mystical mode of worship. Monotheism, born perhaps out of Mithraic-Solar belief and Christianity, was a partial return to the prime deity of the cult of state. Sol, sometimes known as Elagabalus in the early third century, was respected by the Flavians and placed at the heart of the Roman religion of state by Aurelian. All that Sol Invictus succeeded in doing, however, was to prepare the Roman Empire psychologically for the far more enduring god of Christianity.

This eastern cult, which came to conquer the entire empire, was one of the few creeds actively persecuted by Rome. After Judaism effectively separated itself from Christianity, Christians came under attack because of the realization that belief in Jesus Christ was exclusive. One could not attend Christian services as well as offer sacrifices to Jupiter. An eternal enmity erupted between Christianity and what came to be known as organized paganism.

In addition, a variety of creeds and cults were tolerated by Rome among its subject people, including:

Religion or Cult	Area of Influence
Apollo	Rome
Asclepius	Rome and Asia Minor
Bacchus	Rome
Ceres	Rome and Italy
Christianity	Roman Empire
Cybele	Rome, Italy, Africa, Greece, Spain, Gaul
Druidism	Celtic lands
Elagabalus (sun god)	Syria, the East, and, briefly, Rome
Hermes Trismegistos	Egypt and Roman intellectual circles
Imperial Cult	Roman Empire
Isis	Roman Empire
Judaism	Palestine and the lands of the Diaspora
Manichaeism	Parts of the Roman Empire and in the East
Mithraism	Social elite, the East, and military in the West
Osiris	Egypt, parts of the Roman Empire
Serapis	Egypt, Greece, and Rome

Suggested Readings: Beard, Mary, John North, and Simon Price. *Religions of Rome.* New York: Cambridge University Press, 1998; Benko, Stephen. *Pagan Rome and the Early Christians.* Bloomington: Indiana University Press, 1984; Burriss, Eli. *Taboo, Magic, Spirits; A Study of Primitive Elements in Roman Religion.* Westport, Conn.: Greenwood Press, 1972; Carter, Jesse Benedict. *The Religious Life of Ancient Rome: A Study in the Development of Religious Consciousness, from the Foundation of the City Until the Death of Gregory the Great.* New York: Cooper Square Publishers, 1972; Cumont, Franz. *After Life in Roman Paganism: Lectures Delivered at Yale University on the Silliman Foundation.* New York: Dover Publications, 1959; Dowden, Ken. *Religion and the Romans.* London: Bristol Classical Press, 1995; Dumézil, Georges. *Archaic Roman Religion.* Translated by Philip Krapp. Baltimore: Johns Hopkins University Press, 1996; ———. *Camillus: A Study of Indo-European Religion as Roman History.* Translated by Annette Aronowicz and Josette Bryson. Berkeley: University of California Press, 1980; Ferguson, John. *Greek and Roman Religion: A Source Book.* Park Ridge, N.J.: Noyes Press, 1980; ———. *The Religions of the Roman Empire.* Ithaca, N.Y.: Cornell University Press, 1982; Fishwick, Duncan. *The Imperial Cult in the Latin West: Studies in the Ruler Cult of the Western Provinces of the Roman Empire.* New York: E. J. Brill, 1987; Fox, Robin Lane. *Pagans and Christians.* San Francisco: Harper & Row, 1988; Glover, T. R. *The Conflict of Religions in the Early Roman Empire.* Boston: Beacon Press, 1960; Grant, Frederick. *Ancient Roman Religion.* New York: Liberal Arts Press, 1957; Grant, Michael. *Roman Myths.* London: Weidenfeld and Nicholson, 1971; Henig, Martin, and Anthony King, eds. *Pagan Gods and Shrines of the Roman Empire.* Oxford, U.K.: Oxford University Committee for Archaeology, Institute of Archaeology, 1986; Henig, Martin. *Religion in Roman Britain.* New York: St. Martin's Press, 1984; Liebeschuetz, J. H. W. G. *Continuity and Change in Roman Religion.* New York: Oxford University Press, 1979; Henig, Martin, and Anthony King, eds. *Pagan Gods and Shrines of the Roman Empire.* Oxford, U.K.: Oxford University Committee for Archaeology, Institute of Archaeology, 1986; Lyttelton, Margaret, and Werner Forman. *The Romans, Their Gods and Their Beliefs.* London: Orbis, 1984; MacMullen, Ramsay. *Paganism in the Roman Empire.* New Haven, Conn.: Yale University Press, 1981; Moeller, Walter O. *The Mithraic Origin and Meanings of the Rotas-Sator Square.* Leiden: Brill, 1973; North, J. A. *Roman Religion.* Oxford, U.K.: Oxford University Press, 2000; Ogilvie, R. M. *The Romans and Their Gods in the Age of Augustus.* New York, Norton, 1970; Rodwell, Warwick, ed. *Temples, Churches and Religion: Recent Research in Roman Britain; with a Gazetteer of Romano-Celtic Temples in Continental Europe.* Oxford, U.K.: B. A. R., 1980; Smith, John Holland. *The Death of Classical Paganism.* New York: Scribner, 1976; Szemler, G. J. *The Priests of the Roman Republic. A Study of Interactions between Priest-hoods and Magistracies.* Brussels: Latomus, 1972; Taylor, Lily Ross. *The Divinity of the Roman Emperor.* New York: Arno Press, 1975; Turcan, Robert. *The Cults of the Roman Empire,* transl. Antonia Nevill. Cambridge, Mass.: Blackwell, 1996; Warde Fowler, W. *The Religious Experience of the Roman People from the Earliest Times to the Age of Augustus.* London: Macmillan, 1922; Wardman, Alan. *Religion and Statecraft Among the Romans.* Baltimore: Johns Hopkins University Press, 1982; Watson, Alan. *The State, Law, and Religion: Pagan Rome.* Athens: University of Georgia Press, 1992.

See also ASTROLOGY; DEATH; FESTIVALS; GENIUS; GODS AND GODDESSES OF ROME; *LUDI;* MAGIC; NEOPLATONISM; NEO-PYTHAGOREANISM; PAGANISM; PRIESTHOOD.

Remigius (Remi) (c. 438–533) *So-called Apostle of the Franks*
Noted for his baptism of King Clovis I of the Franks and for converting the Frankish people, Remigius was the son of Emile, count of Laon (Laudunum). He studied at Reims and was so renowned for his intelligence and holiness that he was appointed archbishop of Reims at the age of 22. He thereafter devoted himself to the spread of Christianity in Gaul (Roman France), establishing sees at Tournai, Laon, Arras, Therouanne, and Cambrai. On excellent terms with Clovis, he brought the ruler into the faith, traditionally baptizing him in Reims on December 24, 498, in the presence of most of the Frankish army.

Remistus (fifth century C.E.) *Magister militum and Patrician*
Remistus was one of the most powerful figures in the Western Empire and a political shield for Emperor AVITUS in 455. The positions of *magister militum in praesentalis* and Patrician were coveted by his lieutenant, the *magister militum* RICIMER. To seize Remistus's post and to replace Avitus eventually with his own candidate, MAJORIAN, Ricimer plotted the assassination of his superior. This he accomplished in 456, while Remistus was at Ravenna.

Repentinus, Fabius Cornelius (fl. first century C.E.) *Prefect of the praetorian guard*
Repentinus served during the reigns of Antoninus Pius (138–161 C.E.), Marcus Aurelius (161–180 C.E.) and perhaps Commodus (177–192 C.E.). Repentinus succeeded to the prefecture with Furius Victorinus, following the death (date uncertain) of Tattius Maximus. He was forced to step down following a scandal that he had received his position through the influence of an imperial mistress.

Res Gestae Divi Augustus A set of inscriptions published in Rome following the death of Emperor Augustus in 14 C.E., detailing the political, social, religious, and architectural achievements of his reign. Written by Augustus before his death, the *Achievements of Divine*

Augustus was most certainly a propaganda device but characteristically was neither ostentatious nor pompous. In clear terms he listed the successes of his regime, its gifts to the Romans and the good services it had rendered to the world. The *Res Gestae* was a brilliant means of shaming any who might have questioned the efficacy of the Augustan principate, while preserving for posterity a record of considerable value. It is also known as the *Monumentum Ancyranum*, from a copy of a stone at Ankara.

res privata   Term used to describe the vast possessions of the emperors. Known officially as the *res privata principis*, it was the inevitable outgrowth of the *patrimonium* or private holdings of the imperial house, and came to be a rival to the FISCUS or state domains. Following the victory of Septimius Severus (ruled 193–211 C.E.) over his rivals, Pescennius Niger and Clodius Albinus, he was confronted with a major crisis in the finances of the Roman Empire. Among his solutions was the outright seizure of property belonging to his vanquished enemies. These new estates, coupled with the already extensive lands included in the *patrimonium* increased the personal wealth of the Severans to such a degree that an entirely new treasury had to be created, the *res privata* was under the care of procurators, with a parallel in the RATIONALIS of the fiscus. Under the later emperors, *res privata* passed into the hands of the *comes rerum privatarum*.

See also FINANCE.

Rheims   Originally the capital city of the Gallic tribe of the RHEMI, later made the capital of Gallia Belgica. Situated just south of the Aisne River and east of LUTETIA (Paris), in a position close enough to GERMANIA to make control of the Rhine frontier possible, the imperial governor had his residence there, while the Rhemi continued to occupy the *civitas* of Rheims.

See also GALLIA.

Rhemi   One of the largest and most powerful Gallic tribes of Gallia Belgica; located near their capital of RHEIMS. In 57 B.C.E., Julius CAESAR invaded Gallia Belgica, and the Rhemi (or Rheimi) wisely decided to make an alliance with Rome. Caesar received from them vast amounts of intelligence concerning the other peoples of the regions, and the Rhemi also provided him with scouts. Throughout the GALLIC WARS, the Rhemi remained steadfastly loyal to Caesar, emerging as the second leading state in Gaul (GALLIA). They continued to enjoy Roman favor, working against the uprising of CIVILIS in 69 C.E.

Rhescuporis of Thrace (Rhascyporis) (d. c. 19 C.E.)
King of Thrace
When his brother Rheometalces died sometime in the later years of Augustus's reign (27 B.C.E.–14 C.E.), Thrace

was divided between Rhescuporis and the old ruler's son, Cotys. By 19 C.E., Rhescuporis was plotting to take over the entire realm. Despite the intervention of Rome, Cotys was trapped and killed. Emperor Tiberius ordered L. Pomponius Flaccus to bring Rhescuporis to Rome, where he was accused by Coty's widow, Antonia Tryphaena. For his crime he was sentenced to exile in Alexandria and later put to death.

rhetoric   An art form brought to Rome from Greece, only to suffer a general decline in skill and originality with the advent of the Roman Empire. Rhetorical speaking, or persuasive speechmaking, that was aimed at achieving acclaim or some purpose saw considerable development during the Republic, nurturing such professional practitioners as Cicero. Training in rhetoric was available only in a rhetor's school, and it was considered essential for an educated individual aspiring to public office to be versed fully in rhetorical oration. This process changed with the rise of the emperors. No longer was speaking in the Senate or as an ADVOCATUS of the court the surest road to success. Favoritism and flattery of a ruler became more expedient tools.

Rhetoric did not die, however, for it found other avenues of acceptance. The most eminent and, arguably, the least redeeming was the *declamatio* or recitation in public of literary creations. Declamations had always been a useful method of teaching, but they were influenced by a pandering toward fashionable tastes. This corruption was made worse by Asinius Pollio, reportedly the first rhetorician to give his *declamatio* to an invited audience. Composed of the elite of Roman society, the private crowd could reward rhetors who pleased its members with influence and status. No longer was rhetoric aimed at influencing the public good; it was now focused on entertainment and public favor. Over time the *declamatio* came to be called *recitationes,* while the original term returned to its more formal legal meaning. Nevertheless, rhetoric had lost the vitality of its Republican roots and came to be used only by a dwindling number of experts.

Rhine   Called the Rhenus by the Romans, this river rises in the Swiss Alps and flows over 800 miles northward to the sea; one of the great dividing lines between the Roman Empire and the barbarian world. It first came to the attention of the Romans when the German leader ARIOVISTUS crossed westward over the river and menaced much of eastern Gaul. Although he was defeated, his vanquisher, Julius Caesar, perceived the threat coming from the Suebi and was determined to cross the river. This he did in 55 B.C.E., using a bridge of boats; he crossed again in 53.

Subsequently, the Roman legions passed over the Rhine frequently, especially during the reign of Augustus (27 B.C.E.–14 C.E.), when imperial policy was aimed at transforming inner Germany into a province. These hopes were destroyed with General Varus in 9 C.E. in the TEUTOBURG FOREST. Domitian's successful operations against the CHATTI in 83 gave Rome an extension into Germania Superior that carried beyond the Rhine, the so-called *agri decumates*. Using the LIMES along the entire border, Rome held this territory for centuries. Then instability on the frontiers brought the loss of the *agri*. Once more the Rhine was the natural termination point of civilization and Roman influence. Beyond lurked a barbaric and increasingly hostile collection of peoples.

Rhodes

Most easterly of the islands in the Aegean, situated off the coast of Caria in Asia Minor. From the time of Vespasian (ruled 69–79 C.E.), Rhodes, known as Rhodus, was attached to the province of ASIA. The island had a long history of excellent relations with Rome, helping in the Macedonian and Mithridatic Wars. Supporting the cause of Julius Caesar during the Civil War, Rhodes was plundered mercilessly by Gaius Cassius in 42 B.C.E. but was richly rewarded by Augustus for its loyalty. Starting in 6 B.C.E., Tiberius took up residence on the island in a self-imposed exile from the disappointments of Rome; he would depart to become adopted by Augustus in 4 C.E. Because of their act of crucifying several Roman citizens, the Rhodians were deprived of their independence in 44 C.E. by Claudius. Appealing to Nero in 53, they were given their own government again, although prosperity was never actually attained. An earthquake in 155 C.E. flattened most of the island, and henceforth it remained one of the least developed corners of the empire.

Rhoemetalces I (d. 12 C.E.) *King of Thrace*

Originally a dynastic ruler, Rhoemetalces was recognized as king as a result of siding with Octavian (AUGUSTUS) during his war with Marc ANTONY (c. 31 B.C.E.). With the help of Roman arms and influence, he was able to remain on the throne, serving as a reliable client to Augustus. Around 11 B.C.E., however, the tribe of the Bessi, under Vologaesus, burst upon Thrace, driving Rhoemetalces from the country and killing his son Rhescuporis. Only through direct imperial intervention and three years of fighting did he regain his crown. Rhoemetalces returned the favor of the Romans by defeating the rebelling Dalmatians in 6 C.E. Upon his death, Thrace was divided between his brother Rhescuporis and his son Cotys.

Ricimer, Flavius (d. 472 C.E.) *Magister militum from 456 to 472 and Patrician from 457*

Ricimer was the most pivotal imperial figure in the Western Empire during its final years. An Arian of mixed barbarian blood, he had a Suebian father and a Visigoth mother who was related to King Wallia of the Visigoths. His rise was typical of the gifted generals of the time, reflecting political power gained through his defeat of a

Vandal fleet in 456. For this triumph he was promoted to *magister militum* of the West. Once entrenched in this position he overthrew Emperor AVITUS in favor of his own candidate, MAJORIAN, crushing Avitus at Placentia in October of 456. By 457 he had the title of *patricius*, or patrician, presumably receiving it with the blessing of the Eastern court on February 28 of that year. Majorian became emperor with his help, but when the ruler outlived his usefulness, Ricimer deposed him in 461. After Majorian's execution, he was replaced by LIBIUS SEVERUS. Unacceptable to Constantinople, Severus nevertheless remained on the throne from 461 to 465, solely because Ricimer wanted him there.

The *magister militum* spent the next years scheming against a rival, MARCELLINUS OF DALMATIA, while defending against attacks by GEISERIC, king of the Vandals and Alans, who invaded Italy unsuccessfully. In 465 he removed Severus (perhaps by poison) and administered the empire for nearly two years, accepting a new emperor only in 467—ANTHEMIUS. To ensure his position in the new regime, Ricimer married Anthemius's daughter Alypia in 467 at Rome. Despite his supremacy in the empire he carefully avoided participation in the doomed expedition of 468 against the Vandals of Africa. This lack of concern for the expedition may have led to his rupture with Anthemius in 470. Temporarily reconciled in 472, another break took place. With the help of his nephew, Gundobad the Burgundian, Ricimer had the emperor put to death. Another weak successor was adorned with the purple in April of 472, but Ricimer died several weeks later, leaving the West in total chaos. Of all the *magistri militum*, Ricimer was one of the most destructive. He forced Libius Severus to surrender stretches of imperial territory to the barbarians and so routinely murdered his royal masters that no coherent policy or stability was ever possible while he lived.

Ricomer (d. 393 C.E.) *Magister militum from 388 to 393*

Ricomer, or Richomeres, was a Frank by descent, becoming an officer in the service of Emperor GRATIAN. By 377 he was a *comes domesticorum* and was sent to Thrace to help Emperor VALENS in fighting the Goths. He was one of the few survivors of the battle of ADRIANOPLE in 378. Appointed *magister militum* in 383, he took control of the East, meeting at Antioch the famed orator LIBANIUS, who subsequently became his friend. Consul in 384, he was made commanding general of the East (*comes et magister utriusque militiae*) four years later. Ricomer was employed against MAGNUS MAXIMUS and emerged as an important adviser to the emperor THEODOSIUS I. Ricomer introduced his nephew ARBOGAST to the later Western usurper, EUGENIUS, whom Arbogast would support. Like these two, Ricomer adhered to PAGANISM.

roads

The Romans had learned the value of superb roadmaking in their expansion in Italy, and later used a vast network of travel routes as one of the most important aspects of domination of the Mediterranean world and the Roman Empire. An oft quoted maxim that all roads led to Rome was, indeed, correct, save that to the Romans all roads led from Rome. According to the Roman system, a gilded pillar was placed by Emperor AUGUSTUS in the FORUM ROMANUM to mark the beginning point of a radiating transportation system clearly marked by milestones from the Eternal City. No journeyer could ever forget that he walked or rode upon an imperial domain.

The Roman imperial roads were a benefit for all residents of the empire and served a wide variety of purposes. The LEGIONS who most often created the roads used this efficient network to pass through provinces quickly to reach frontier posts or crisis spots. By marching through even mountainous terrain and along carefully designed ways (*viae*), there was no place they could not reach or defend. Campaigns very often centered on reducing an enemy country by destroying what was wild or natural. In Britain and Germany the local tribes were subdued and pacified by relentless roadmaking, cutting up the tribal boundaries, and isolating the tribes.

Once the legions had finished their tasks, administrators moved into a new province. Soldiers were used once more to refine the communications system, uniting all provincial areas to the main thoroughfare before linking them with the interprovincial *viae*. Progressively complex, this method allowed even the smallest province to stay directly in touch with the emperor, via the most advanced system in the world at the time for sending messages and reports—the CURSUS PUBLICUS (the Imperial Post).

One of the parallel developments with the *cursus* was the rise of roadside inns, taverns, and hotels. *Mutationes* were places where horses were changed, while *mansiones* offered a weary adventurer a bed for the night with food. Soon the roads were filled with traders and merchants bringing their wares to new markets. Economic expansion brought increased wealth to imperial coffers by means of taxes and duties, while fostering the ideals of internationalism so important to the Pax Romana.

Provinces varied as to how much roadwork was necessary to transform them into suitable imperial lands. Germany, Britain, Africa, parts of Spain and wilder sections of Asia Minor, such as Galatia, Cilicia, and Cappadocia, all needed extensive amounts of capital and effort. Regions with long histories needed only minor alterations. Among these were the provinces of Asia, Greece, Macedonia, and even Gaul. Outside of Italy, with its famous *viae*—the Appian, Flaminian, and others—the Roman Empire possessed several other important roads, including the impressive Via Egnatia, running from the Black Sea through Macedonia, all the way to the Adriatic port of Dyrrhachium. It was a lifeline for communications, not only for Achaea and Macedonia but also for the entire Danubian frontier. Trade passed from the western and eastern provinces, providing income for such cities as Nicopolis and Thessalonica.

Several books were published concerning the imperial roads, including the *Antonine Itinerary* and the *Jerusalem Itinerary*. The first is from the late third century C.E., detailing the main transportation routes through the empire, including the distances. The *Jerusalem Itinerary*, of the fourth century C.E., helped Christians find their way to Jerusalem.

See VIAE for major roads in Italy.

Robigus A Roman deity of nature whose main attributes were destructive powers through rust or blight. He could ruin crops if not appeased with the sacrifice of a sheep and a dog. Robigus (also called Robigo) was associated with Mars, hence all ceremonies in honor of him, especially the *Robigalia*, his festival on April 25, were under the direction of the Flamen Martialis.

See also FLAMENS.

Roles A tribal leader of the GETAE, who lived just north of the Danube River, near the Black Sea. He came to the aid of the Roman General Marcius Licinius CRASSUS (2), in his war against Deldo and the Bastarnae in 29 B.C.E. In turn, Crassus helped Roles to vanquish a Getae rival named Dapyx. Roles visited Augustus later and was honored. Subsequently, Roles and the Getae were stable clients of Rome on the eastern Danube.

Roma The divine personification of the city of Rome, a means of expressing in religious terms the greatness of the Eternal City, of the empire and the Republic. Through the use of coins bearing the likeness of a beautiful woman, and through temples erected in her honor, Roma impressed upon the world the status of the Eternal City. She had a temple in Rome, constructed during the reign of Hadrian, and was worshiped by the Greeks as well.

Romanus (fl. late fourth century C.E.) *Comes Africae from 364 to 373*
Romanus was in charge of Africa during the reign of VALENTINIAN I (364–375 C.E.). He defended LEPCIS MAGNA from barbarian attack but was accused by the inhabitants of failing in his duty. The resulting proceedings were suppressed through the use of influence at court. Later arrested, he relied upon the political leader MEROBAUDES to save him. The writers Ammianus Marcellinus and ZOSIMUS were extremely hostile to him.

See also GILDO.

Rome Capital of the Roman Empire from the reign of AUGUSTUS (27 B.C.E.–14 C.E.) until that of DIOCLETIAN (284–305 C.E.), and one of the most famous cities in history. Rome also came to symbolize the achievements of the empire in art, history, politics, culture, religion, and engineering. It was the first of the great urban centers, encountering, centuries before its time, the travails of crowded life, pollution, and social unrest.

GEOGRAPHY

According to the traditions, Rome was founded in 753 B.C.E. by Romulus and his twin brother, Remus. Under Romulus's guidance and that of the succeeding kings of Rome, what was once but a small village of shepherds grew strong and well organized. Rome was situated in the Italian region of Latium, approximately 16 miles from the sea. The two outstanding features of the Roman environment were the Tiber River and the hills. The Tiber flowed down from the Apennines in the northeast and made a cursive bend as it reached the Tiber Valley. Near the Capitoline Hill there was the important island, Insula Tiberina. Over the years additional territory was added until finally, in the time of King Servius Tullius (578–535 B.C.E.), Rome comprised the Seven Hills.

Primitive Rome was centered around the Esquiline and Quirinal hills. Later, the Capitoline Hill emerged as the very heart of the Roman establishment, with its magnificent temples; the Palatine contained residences and eventually the homes of the emperors. Between them lay the area of the Velabrum, leading to the Tiber. The river was on the entire western side, with the Pincian Hill to the east. To the south of the Pincian, the hills and valleys lead all the way to the Caelian Hill. Also in this group were the Quirinal, Viminal, and Esquiline hills. Upon these were gardens, baths, the CASTRA PRAETORIA and, at the foot of the Quirinal, the Subura. Between the Esquiline and Palantine was a valley, the Velia. To the west was another valley, in which the Fora of the Caesars were built. Toward the east, past the end of the Via Sacra, was an open area, surrounded by he Esquiline and Caelian hills and used by Nero for his Golden House. The Flavians filled in Nero's pond and erected the Colosseum on the site.

Beneath the Palatine were two areas of further interest. The Circus Maximus was in a depression between the Palatine and the Aventine. The Aventine Hill was an excellent place to see the separation of classes, for the poor lived at the base of the hill, and the wealthy had villas at the top, with a view of the city. Across the Tiber were the Vatican and Janiculus hills. The Vatican had its own Christian history, while the Janiculus played a minor role in Roman events with its early fortress.

Rome relied upon the mighty river Tiber for defense from the Etruscans but also for the divine patronage of the god TIBER, called Volturnus. At first all bridges across it were made of wood to allow the Romans to cut them down in time of attack. As the city grew in power, the bridges (*pons*) were built of stone. Numerous emperors sought to improve transportation out of the city with additional bridges. Most likely the earliest of bridges was the wooden structure of the Pons Sublicius, spanning the Tiber just below Insula Tiberina.

Interestingly the Pons Sublicius retained its wooden material even at a later time, when stone was the principal medium of construction. This was probably for religious reasons. Insula Tiberina was important to Rome, and thus two bridges connected it to the two banks—the Pons Fabricius on the east and the Pons Cestius on the west. The Pons Aemilius which connected the island to the Pons Sublicius was the first such bridge of stone. It was built around the middle of the second century B.C.E., marking a change in Roman engineering. Only one other span was notable from the days of the Republic, the Pons Milvius, or the Milvian Bridge, several miles to the north of Rome along the Via Flaminia.

GOVERNANCE

In 509 B.C.E., the Roman kings were ousted in favor of the CONSULS, the SENATE and the people of Rome. For the next 478 years the Eternal City was the very heart of the Republic, from which Rome launched its campaigns of expansion in Italy and throughout the Mediterranean. Here, too, the ambitious plotted schemes that came to fruition in the first century B.C.E. with CIVIL WARS OF THE FIRST AND SECOND TRIUMVIRATES raging off and on from 49 to 31 B.C.E. In that final year, at ACTIUM, Octavian defeated Marc ANTONY. Within four years he was called Augustus, and the Roman Empire was born. As PRINCEPS, or first man of the state, Augustus undertook the task of transforming Rome into the foremost city of the world.

The Augustan policy of imperial aggrandizement was the end result of careful thought and planning. Rome, with its many entertainments, glorious structures and tributes to Roman triumphs, was to be a model, the standard by which every provincial community would be measured. The IMPERIAL CULT was declared officially to be the cult of *Roma et Augustus;* as the emperors were to be worshiped, their abode was to be held in awe.

With the rise of the empire, the city was divided into 14 smaller *regiones,* replacing the four that were founded by Servius Tullius many centuries before; they were placed under the care of a magistrate, who, in turn, also looked after the so-called *vici* or districts within each of the *regiones.* They included all of Rome within the Servian Walls, but also went beyond them, even across the Tiber. The 14 *regiones* were I Porta Capena, II Caelimontium, III Isis et Serapis, IV Templum Pacis, V Esquiliae, VI Alta Semita, VII Via Lata, VIII Forum Romanum, IX Circus Flaminus, X Palatium, XI Circus Maximus, XII Piscina Publica, XIII Aventinus, XIV Trans Tiberim.

A new system of local division could do little to ease the growing congestion in the streets or the constant threat of fire. Therefore, over the entire city administration the emperor appointed the *praefectus urbi,* the PREFECT OF THE CITY, charged with trying cases within Rome and with maintaining the peace, aided by the URBAN COHORTS. In cases of emergency he could also use the VIGILES, the firefighters in the capital, formed to contain

A reconstruction of Rome in the early second century C.E. *(Hulton/Getty Archive)*

any serious conflagration before it could spread, or even the dreaded PRAETORIAN GUARD. The Praetorians were at first not kept in Rome, but from the time of TIBERIUS and his Praetorian prefect SEJANUS, the cohorts were stationed in the Castra Praetoria, east of the Viminal Hill on the Agger of Servius.

LIVING CONDITIONS

But these efforts fell short of alleviating the terrible conditions of life. According to the *Monumentum Ancyranum,* which contains Augustus's *Res Gestae,* the number of the Plebeian class at Rome in the time of Augustus was 320,000, not counting women and children. When added to the senatorial and Equestrian classes, the total free population would have been nearly 700,000. In addition, the slaves of the city probably equalled the general population, bloating the tally to well over a million. And Rome was also the destination of many foreign travelers. Some estimates have placed the combined population at 1.5 million.

Little wonder that all carts and wheeled traffic was forbidden in the city during the day. The only exception was the *carpentum* or small cart used by the VESTAL VIRGINS or the ladies of the court. Foot traffic was more than the streets could bear, as Rome acquired a lasting reputation for dirtiness and squalor, borne out by its housing. Two kinds of structure characterized Roman living. The wealthy occupied the *domus,* a large suite or inner-city villa. Frequently they were found on the more fashionable parts of the Hills of Rome. In marked contrast were the *insulae.* These tall apartment buildings housed the middle and lower classes, packing them into dirty little rooms as unsanitary as they were susceptible to fire.

Ironically, the fire of 64 C.E., in which nearly two-thirds of the city was burned, brought some relief. To Nero's credit, he ordered that in the future careful consideration be taken before any rebuilding could proceed. A proper code was instituted in construction: Stone was to be the preferred medium of building, with an eye toward fire resistance and a height limit. Streets were widened and the aqueducts leading into the city were refurbished and improved to provide enough water. Unfortunately, Nero's obsession with his Domus Aurea, or Golden House, overshadowed such genuinely progressive steps.

The value of Nero's brutally practical program was seen over the next few centuries, for there was no end to the ballooning population. If there had been over one million in the first century C.E., then the total number of inhabitants had no doubt surpassed two million by the second century. Inevitably the city grew beyond the old Servian Walls, especially into the Campus Martius, where Hadrianic apartment complexes have been excavated. In the late third century C.E. Emperor AURELIAN constructed a new wall, this time setting the boundaries of Rome beyond the Tiber.

BUILDING/EARLY HISTORY

Besides population, another major factor in the crowding was the incessant series of mammoth building programs. Rome, from the time of Augustus, was subjected to constant renovation and rebuilding. From the Capitoline to the Aventine hills to the Campus Martius and beyond, all the way to the Vatican Hill, emperors erected arches, columns, baths, circuses, palaces, temples (to themselves, gods or predecessors), theaters, basilicas, and forums. Everywhere there was a monument, so many in fact that free spaces were wholly consumed. And yet these architectural feats made Rome the envy of the world.

Augustus set the tone. He declared that he found Rome a city of bricks and left it a metropolis of marble. With the help of Marcus Vipsanius AGRIPPA this boast was true. The status of the Eternal City was celebrated while the broad policies of Julius Caesar were completed. With the TEMPLE OF CASTOR AND POLLUX and TEMPLE OF MARS ULTOR finished, the famed FORUM ROMANUM was altered significantly. Further, the CAMPUS MARTIUS to the north was discovered as a viable part of the city, largely due to Marcus Agrippa. There one could find theaters, the PANTHEON, the Baths of Agrippa and the Basilica of Neptune. A partial list of Augustus's other marvels in stone would include: the FORUM AUGUSTUM, the CURIA JULIA, the BASILICA JULIA, the TEMPLE OF DIVUS JULIUS, and the Theater of Marcellus.

Tiberius initiated little construction, in keeping with his own austere nature. He did finish the Augustan projects and ordered the creation of the TEMPLE OF DIVUS AUGUSTUS. Of note was the DOMUS TIBERIANA, the first great imperial palace on the Palatine, a plush home considered inadequate by GAIUS CALIGULA. That emperor not only upgraded the Domus but had the curious habit of raising temples to himself. He also allowed Isis to have a place of worship on the Campus Martius, and then desecrated the Temple of Divus Augustus by placing a bridge over it to connect the palace on the Palatine with the Temple of Jupiter Optimus Maximus on the Capitol. His successor CLAUDIUS focused on those imperial efforts that would most benefit the city. Aside from improving the harbor at Ostia to make the Tiber more accessible, he reformed the water system. The aqueducts at Rome had always been impressive, providing fresh water from the early days of the Republic. Their care was maintained by the censor and the AEDILES; later Claudius created the office of *curator aquarum*, or head of the water board.

Aside from the Golden House and the reconstruction of Rome, both springing from the fire of 64, Nero spent much time and money on buildings of a suitably grand scope, such as the CIRCUS Gai et Neronis and the Neronian Baths. His original DOMUS TRANSITORIA, linking the Palatine and the Esquiline hills, was a disappointment for it could not encompass Nero's vision of a proper home. The fire made the replacement, the Domus Aurea, possible, but that palace was appallingly expensive, as was his colossal statue of himself, a typically excessive gesture that lent his name to the FLAVIANS's gigantic amphitheater the COLOSSEUM.

Life in Rome began well under Nero, for he had able advisers and was stable and moderate under their guidance. With the death of Burrus in 62 and the retirement of SENECA, a reign of terror descended upon the city, made uglier even than that of Tiberius and Gaius Caligula because of Nero's obsession with art and music. The socio-political system was falling apart by 65, when elements of the Senate and the depleted nobility joined forces in the PISONIAN CONSPIRACY. Although crushed, the plot signalled the eventual downfall of Nero, who was ousted in 68 C.E. What followed was a bloody civil war in 69, which ended with the conquest of the city by legions supporting VESPASIAN. Damage to Rome was extensive, especially on the Capitoline, where a siege had taken place. The chaos in Rome mirrored the situation in the provinces, with rebellions in Germany and in Palestine.

Vespasian and the Flavian regime arrived in 70, and a reconstruction and return to prosperity were effected. The Forum Pacis, or Forum of Vespasian, and the Colosseum provided evidence of civic health, while pointing to the public spirit of administration. Care for the specific needs of the city continued under Titus and Domitian. The Baths of Titus gave the Romans yet another sumptuous watering place. Domitian built everywhere in the city, including the FORUM TRANSITORIUM, the Temple of Gens Flavia (the Flavian Temple), Temple of Minerva and the Odeum. He also erected a magnificent palace, the DOMUS FLAVIA, a building that would satisfy the needs of emperors for years to come.

Considered harsh and even autocratic, Domitian was assassinated in 96 C.E. Nerva ruled for only two years but adopted Trajan, thus beginning the glorius years of the second century C.E., when Rome would attain its fullest stature. In many ways the Golden Age of Rome was not so much an age of municipal opulence but of long-term bureaucratic and artistic stability. Trajan, Hadrian, Antoninus Pius, and, in part, Marcus Aurelius ran an empire that was at its peak. Rome reflected this.

Trajan was the founder of his Baths, the FORUM TRAIANI, and innovative market, designed by APOLLODORUS of

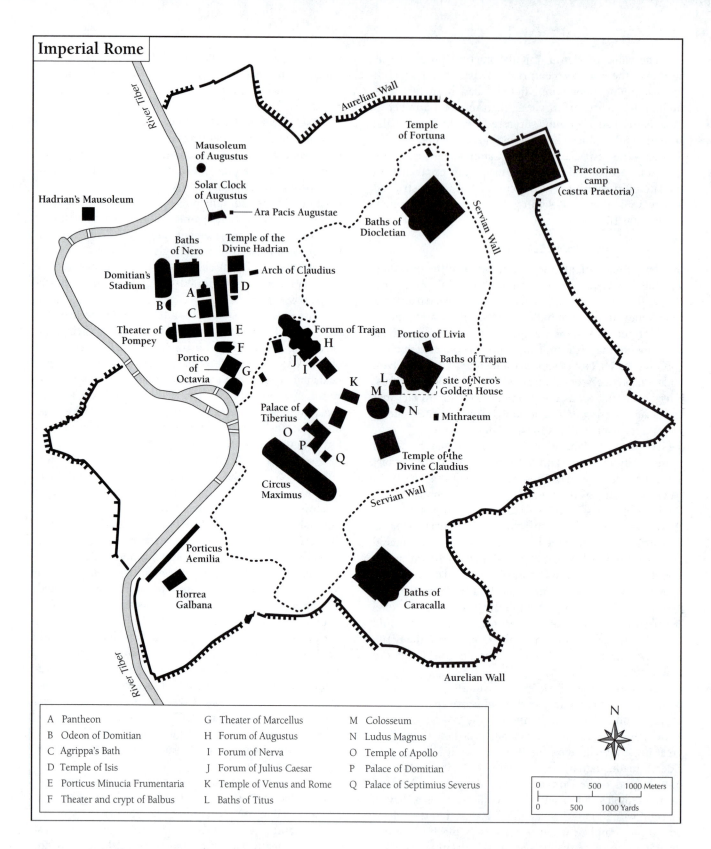

Imperial Rome

Map labels:

River Tiber
Aurelian Wall
Mausoleum of Augustus
Temple of Fortuna
Solar Clock of Augustus
Praetorian camp (castra Praetoria)
Hadrian's Mausoleum
Ara Pacis Augustae
Baths of Nero
Temple of the Divine Hadrian
Baths of Diocletian
Servian Wall
Domitian's Stadium
Arch of Claudius
A
D
B
C
Theater of Pompey
E
Forum of Trajan
Portico of Livia
F
Baths of Trajan
Portico of Octavia
H
J
site of Nero's Golden House
G
I
K
L
M
N
Palace of Tiberius
Mithraeum
O
P
Q
Temple of the Divine Claudius
Circus Maximus
Servian Wall
Porticus Aemilia
Horrea Galbana
Baths of Caracalla
Aurelian Wall
River Tiber

N

A Pantheon	G Theater of Marcellus	M Colosseum
B Odeon of Domitian	H Forum of Augustus	N Ludus Magnus
C Agrippa's Bath	I Forum of Nerva	O Temple of Apollo
D Temple of Isis	J Forum of Julius Caesar	P Palace of Domitian
E Porticus Minucia Frumentaria	K Temple of Venus and Rome	Q Palace of Septimius Severus
F Theater and crypt of Balbus	L Baths of Titus	

0   500   1000 Meters
0   500   1000 Yards

Damascus. HADRIAN brought both a Hellenism and an internationalism to the throne. Temples to his predecessor, his mother-in-law, his niece MATIDIA and Venus were sprinkled throughout the city. Loyal to tradition, he rebuilt Agrippa's Pantheon and gave no credit to himself but honored Agrippa. The reign of Hadrian, however, trumpeted an increasing universalism that was offset only briefly by ANTONINUS PIUS. Hadrian built his dream villa, TIVOLI, outside of Rome, in nearby Tibur. Antoninus Pius spent little money on the city, as did Marcus Aurelius. The former centered his energies on Italy and on the maintenance of self-government, while the latter faced plagues, political rebellion, and the terrible MARCOMAN-NIC WARS. Such concerns rendered a beautification program impractical.

One result of the era of sound imperial succession was a tendency toward centralization, especially from the time of Hadrian. Not surprisingly, the provinces now looked even more eagerly for the city to provide leadership and guidance. The reign of Commodus was a disaster, and his death touched off a bizarre episode in 193, when the Praetorian Guard auctioned off the throne to the highest bidder, DIDIUS JULIANUS, a sale that many felt epitomized the social decay of the times.

HISTORY FROM 193

Septimius SEVERUS then marched into Rome with his Pannonian legions and, after winning a protracted civil war, settled down to the business of running the state. Rome to him was a revered city, much as it had been for Augustus. The title *URBS SACRA*, or sacred city, was used to describe it. Romans paid no direct taxes and, unquestionably and for one of the last times, total power rested in Rome and in its institutions. Severus's son CARACALLA took the dramatic step of granting full citizenship to all of the inhabitants of the empire with the Constitutio Antoniniana, an act that would serve to dilute the special status of those who lived in Rome.

Throughout the early centuries of the Roman Empire, additional bridges were erected. The Augustan-era bridge was the Pons Agrippae, perhaps created by Marcus Agrippa and positioned in the north of the Campus Martius. To provide easy access to the Circus Gai et Neronis, Emperor Nero ordered the building of the Pons Neronis, or Pons Neronianus, at the eastern edge of the Campus Martius, pointing in the direction of the Vatican Hill, where the circus was located. Nearby, Hadrian put the *Pons Aelius*, the bridge that would lead right to his mausoleum, now known as the Castel San Angelo. Two more bridges were built in the third century: the Pons Aurelius Antoninus, or Pons Aurelius, established in all likelihood by Caracalla, and the Pons Probi, built by Probus.

The assassination of Caracalla in 217 brought the dawn of a new age for the city. For much of the third century, the empire was ravaged by barbarian invasions and usurping generals. Two vital developments contributed to the destruction of Rome's imperial preeminence. First, the emperors were frequently away from the city on military campaigns and getting themselves killed by other generals or in combat with the Goths or Persians. There would then be a vacuum in the political realm. Second, when an emperor did succeed in carving out a place of relative martial security it became necessary to keep the entire process of government traveling with him, as was done by GALLIENUS. Rome survived unchanged for a time, held in reverence because of its lingering prestige and because of the need for any new emperor to find allies in the old senatorial establishment.

Several developments in the city itself during this period should be observed. PHILIP THE ARAB celebrated the millennial anniversary of the founding of Rome with the *ludi Saeculares* in 247. In the early part of the reign of AURELIAN the JUTHUNGINE WAR made the city nervous for its safety from barbarian attack. Aurelian consequently built his wall. So it went, with soldier-emperors trying to stage a recovery. When it came, its very nature would be so momentous that Rome would be unable to withstand it.

In 284, DIOCLETIAN became emperor. He recognized the old system of governing as hopelessly inadequate, given the sheer size of the empire, and that one person was incapable of governing such a domain, especially from Rome. Diocletian imitated Tiberius and began to travel to the various provinces. A headquarters was established at Nicomedia, and the Praetorian Guard was downgraded to the rank of the garrison of Rome. New reforms were now instigated, not just for Rome but for the entire empire. Diocletian ended the division between imperial and senatorial provinces, placing all of them under his control. Italy lost all of its privileges, though Rome was allowed to keep many rights and was directed by the Senate. By the terms of the tetrarchy established by Diocletian, the two Augusti and two Caesars did not live in Rome but in widely separated parts of the East and the West. The closest capital to Rome in the tetrarchy was Mediolanum (Milan). Diocletian did not visit Rome, in fact, until 303. Two years later he and his colleague MAX-IMIAN retired, as GALERIUS and CONSTANTIUS I CHLORUS ascended to the rank of Augusti. Rome was again overshadowed.

Then in 306 the opportunity seemingly presented itself for the city to regain its honor. Maximian's son Maxentius resented being passed over as one of the Caesars, found support among the Romans and the Praetorian Guard, and was raised up as a rival emperor. For six years (306–312) Rome enjoyed a return to glory. At the battle of MILVIAN BRIDGE in 312, Maxentius was defeated by CONSTANTINE the Great, who would go on to conquer all of the empire.

Constantine built baths, smaller than those of Diocletian, and an ARCH in Rome, but his long-term policy neglected the city. The Praetorian Guard was disbanded ruthlessly and its camp, the Castra Praetoria, was destroyed, while CONSTANTINOPLE at the Bosporus between East and West was developed as the New Rome. All that remained to the Romans was the Senate and the city's marvelous art and architecture. The fifth century brought little promise of better things, for so weakened had the empire become in the West that in 410 ALARIC and the Visigoths captured and sacked Rome. Forty-five years later GEISERIC and the Vandals sailed from Africa and ravaged the city once more.

At the same time, a religious revolution was in process. Christianity had long been persecuted in the

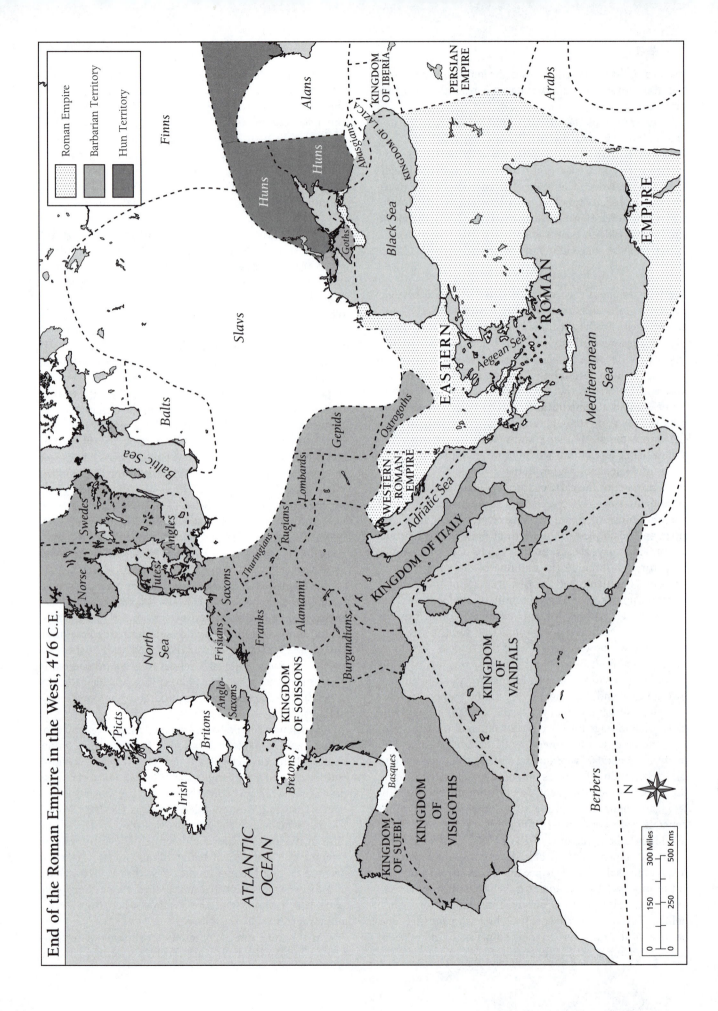

End of the Roman Empire in the West, 476 C.E.

Roman Empire
Barbarian Territory
Hun Territory

Finns

Huns

Alans

KINGDOM OF IBERIA

PERSIAN EMPIRE

Arabs

Huns

Slavs

Goths

Black Sea

Abasgians

KINGDOM OF LAZICA

EASTERN

Balts

Baltic Sea

Gepids

Ostrogoths

WESTERN ROMAN EMPIRE

Aegean Sea

ROMAN

Mediterranean Sea

Swedes

Norse

Angles

Jutes

Frisians

Saxons

Lombardi

Rugians

Thuringians

Franks

Alamanni

Burgundians

KINGDOM OF ITALY

Adriatic Sea

EMPIRE

Picts

Britons

Anglo-Saxons

Bretons

KINGDOM OF SOISSONS

Basques

KINGDOM OF VANDALS

Irish

North Sea

KINGDOM OF SUEBI

KINGDOM OF VISIGOTHS

ATLANTIC OCEAN

Berbers

N

0   150   300 Miles
0   250   500 Kms

empire, but Rome attracted Christian leaders and their disciples. Peter was executed, traditionally, on the Vatican Hill. That site was ever after considered the center of Christianity in Rome, and the bishop of Rome came to exercise ascendancy over the sees of the West when the office came to be known as the papacy. The EDICT OF MILAN, issued in 312 by Constantine the Great, granted Christianity a free hand. While Constantinople may have been the Christian city, Rome was eventually known as the city of churches, and numerous basilicas and shrines were built to honor martyrs. Domination by the Western bishops brought Rome's pope into direct conflict with the patriarchs of Constantinople and Alexandria, a disagreement that would last well into the Middle Ages and, in fact, continues today.

By the fifth century, the Senate was divided into Christians and pagans, the former holding the majority. But the pagans were ardent and formed an intellectual core that was not easily destroyed. With the brilliant oratory of SYMMACHUS, the final hopes of paganism fell before AMBROSE, the brutal bishop of Milan, and before THEODOSIUS I, who won the battle of FRIGIDUS in 394. Within 100 years of Constantine's edict, Christianity had brought an end to a cult of worship that had lasted for over 1,000 years.

Intellectualism was not dead, however. The absence of the emperors with their weighty administrations freed the still active Senate and allowed that body to function with a remarkable independence with respect to Rome's affairs. The Senate encouraged the pursuit of culture and the mind, even though many cultivated the patronage of the often strict Christian leaders. Symmachus, AVIENUS, MACROBIUS, and other writers and orators found a receptive and still sophisticated audience.

Founded by Romulus, Rome was, at least technically, last ruled by a Roman in 476—the appropriately named Romulus Augustulus. He fell in that year to the German Odoacer, who was himself overcome by the powerful Theodoric, king of the Ostrogoths, in 493. A succession of masters would follow. There remained, however, the incalculable legacy of Rome to the world and to history.

Suggested Readings: Anderson, James C. *The Historical Topography of the Imperial Fora.* Brussels: Latomus, 1984; Bandinelli, R. B. *Rome. The Centre of Power.* London: Thames and Hudson, 1969; Champlin, Edward. *Fronto and Antonine Rome.* Cambridge: Harvard University Press, 1980; Clayton, Peter *Treasures of Ancient Rome.* New York: Random House, 1986. Grimal, Pierre. *Roman Cities.* Translated and edited by G. Michael Woloch. Madison: University of Wisconsin Press, 1983; Hibbert, Christopher. *Rome: The Biography of a City.* New York: Penguin, 1985; Scullard, Howard H. *From the Gracchi to Nero: A History of Rome from 133 B.C. to A.D. 68.* 4th ed. London: Methuen, 1976; Storoni Mazzolani,

Lidia. *The Idea of the City in Roman Thought: From Walled City to Spiritual Commonwealth.* Translated by S. O'Donnell. Bloomington: Indiana University Press, 1982.

Romulus Augustulus (fl. late fifth century C.E.) *Last emperor of the Western Empire, ruling from October 475 to September 476 C.E.*
Romulus Augustulus (which means "little Augustus") was the son of the MAGISTER MILITUM ORESTES, who had been appointed to his post by Emperor Julius NEPOS. In August 475, Orestes used discontent among the Germanic troops in Italy to depose Nepos, forcing him to flee to Dalmatia. On October 31, he invested his son Romulus with the purple. Although the Eastern Empire, under Zeno, refused to recognize him, Romulus was de facto ruler of the West by virtue of the military and political power of his father. Orestes failed to hold his own troops, however, especially after refusing their demand to be settled on Italian soil. They found a new champion in Orestes's lieutenant, ODOACER, who besieged Orestes at Ticinum. Odoacer put the *magister militum* to death in August 476. Entering Ravenna, he deposed Romulus a month later. Surprisingly, the friendless monarch was not only allowed to live but was also given an estate in Campania (at Misenum) with a generous annual pension. Surviving until the sixth century, he was a living testimony to the defunct imperial system in the West.

Roxolani A people who originally occupied large stretches of land in the southern region of Russia, especially to the north of the related tribes of the IAZYGES. Starting in the second century B.C.E., they were pushed into the territory of the Iazyges by advancing SARMATIANS, driving the Iazyges toward the west, while the Roxolani occupied the lands of the Crimea and the Don. By the first century C.E. they had settled on the Danubian frontier, where they were viewed by the Romans as part of the broader Sarmatian menace. In 62–63 C.E. PLAUTIUS SILVANUS suppressed a widespread revolt along the BLACK SEA among the Sarmatian peoples, which probably were the Roxolani. They were the leading force in the Danubian troubles of 67–68, pushing across the river and necessitating stern military reprisals from Rome. Infrequent flareups marked their relations with Rome, although their ties with the Iazyges farther to the west were always a concern to the Romans. As part of his general operations against the Sarmatians, Marcus Aurelius made war upon the Roxolani from 179 to 180 C.E., claiming the title *Sarmaticus* in the process. With the rise of the GOTHS in the third century, the Roxolani were amalgamated into the ranks of the barbarian hosts that would ravage much of the Roman Empire.

Rubellius Plautus (d. 62 C.E.) *Son of Julia (5, daughter of Drusus the Younger)*
Plautus was, with NERO, one of the closest blood relatives to Augustus in the latter half of the first century C.E. Out of fear of Nero, and because of his own Stoic beliefs, Plautus led a secluded, blameless life, but in 55 his name was mentioned in connection with conspiracies against Nero and by 60 he was considered a successor to the emperor. This disquieted Nero, who ordered Plautus to retire to Asia, where Plautus moved with his wife Antistia and a few friends. Finally, in 62, Nero ordered his death, quipping when Plautus's head was brought before him, "Why did no one tell me Plautus had such a big nose?"

Rubicon Small river in the north of Italy south of Ravenna, in the region known as the Ager Gallicus; it rises in the Apennines and flows northeast to the Adriatic. The importance of the Rubicon was its role as boundary marker, during the Republic, for Italy and Gallia Cisalpina. It assumed a permanent place in history in 49 B.C.E., when Julius Caesar, at the head of his army, crossed over into Italy in direct violation of the Senate's orders.

Rubra Saxa Italian site in Etruria. Meaning "red rocks," Rubra Saxa was on the Via Flaminia and indicated the nearness of a traveler to Rome. In 312 C.E., it was the site of a skirmish between the armies of CONSTANTINE the Great and MAXENTIUS.

Rufina, Pomponia (d. 213 C.E.) *One of the four Vestal Virgins put to death in 213 for impurity*
Pomponia Rufina was buried alive for her indiscretions, according to custom.
> *See also* CRESCENTIA, CANNUTIA; LAETA, CLODIA; SEVERA, AURELIA; VESTAL VIRGINS.

Rufinus, Flavius (d. 395 C.E.) *Praetorian prefect of the East from 392 to 395 C.E.*
The most powerful figure in the early reign of Emperor Arcadius, Rufinus came from Gallia Aquitania and was known for his intelligence and his devout Christian ways. Rising through the ranks in Constantinople, he became increasingly important to THEODOSIUS I, serving as MAGISTER OFFICIORUM in 388. Consul in 392, he was then appointed Praetorian prefect. Systematically he destroyed all political opponents, maneuvering himself into an excellent position to bid for the throne. Upon the accession of Arcadius in 395, Rufinus encountered political opposition from EUTROPIUS (2), the chamberlain, and STILICHO, a MAGISTER MILITUM. First Eutropius blocked the marriage of Rufinus's daughter to Arcadius, securing a wedding with Eudoxia, a child of one of Rufinus's victims. Then Stilicho, presumably on the orders of a jealous Rufinus, sent back to Constantinople a large part of his army. Soldiers from this force then murdered the prefect in November of 395. Rufinus did build a monastery and shrine but was noted for his lobbying of anti-pagan legislation. Despite his obviously zealous Christianity, he was on good terms with the pagan LIBANIUS and had met with the orator SYMMACHUS.

Rufinus, Vulcacius (fl. fourth century C.E.) *Praetorian prefect of Italy, Illyricum, and Africa from 365 to 368*
A noble Roman pagan, Rufinus was consul in 347, and moved on to Illyricum and then Gaul in 354. His career was briefly endangered because of his being the uncle of Gallus Caesar, by his sister, Galla. In 365, he was named Praetorian prefect by Valentinian I, despite his old age, replacing Claudius Mamertinus.

Rufinus of Aquileia, Tyrannius (c. 345–410 C.E.) *Christian scholar and monk, a specialist in translating Greek theological texts into Latin*
Italian by birth, Rufinus was educated at Rome where he became a close friend of Jerome. Pursuing a monastic life he journeyed to the East around 371, visiting Egypt and studying in Alexandria. Arriving in Jerusalem, he established a monastery there before returning to Rome in 397. Living out his years in Aquileia, Rufinus made translations from the Greek of numerous important works, including the writings of such Christians as Basil, Gregory of Nazianzus, Eusebius of Caesarea, and especially Origen. His adherence to the teachings of Origen, even after Origen's condemnation as a heretic, caused a major rift between him and Jerome, who disagreed bitterly with the unorthodox nature of Origenism. This quarrel was never settled. Rufinus died after fleeing to southern Italy during Alaric's invasion.

Rufus, Bassaeus (fl. second century C.E.) *Prefect of the Praetorian Guard under Emperor Marcus Aurelius, from circa 169 to 172*
Rufus was singular as a prefect because of his humble origins and his apparent lack of education. Born into poverty, he nevertheless attained membership in the Equestrians (EQUITES) and held the order's highest post. By his own admission he did not know languages but was considered a good man in other respects.

Rufus, C. Valgius (fl. late first century B.C.E.) *Consul in 12 B.C.E.*
A writer during the Augustan Age (27 B.C.E.–14 C.E.), Rufus had a number of literary interests, including epigrams, a study of herbs, elegies, and a Latin translation of the rhetorical work of Apollodorus of Pergamum.

Rufus, Cluvius (fl. first century C.E.) *Consul in 66 C.E. and noted historian*
For many years a favorite of Emperor Nero, Rufus was used in 67 as the imperial herald, announcing the next songs that Nero would perform. Appointed one of the

governors of Spain, he supported the cause of Vitellius in 69, being acquitted of charges of planning to usurp the throne by virtue of his eloquence and reputation. As a writer, Rufus centered himself on a history of Nero and the civil war of 69 C.E. Written with accuracy, his work was used by the historian Tacitus in his *Histories* and probably served as a source for Plutarch and Suetonius.

Rufus, Quintus Curtius (fl. mid-first century C.E.?) *Historian*
Considerable questions exist with respect to Rufus. He has been dated to both the Augustan and the Flavian ages, but quite possibly lived and wrote in the middle of the first century C.E. Rufus's writings were highly imitative of Livy, and similar to the style of Seneca, which was in vogue in the time of Nero, and his affected rhetorical manner was typical of the Silver Age of Roman literature. His 10-volume *History of Alexander* relied heavily upon Greek sources. Books 1 and 2 as well as parts of the others were lost.

Rufus, Faenius (d. 65 C.E.) *Prefect of the Praetorian Guard from 62–65 C.E. and the successor of the great prefect Burrus*
Rufus had the misfortune of being appointed as coprefect of the Guard with Ofonius TIGELLINUS. He had made a reputation for himself as prefect of the grain (from 55–62), as an honest and decent leader. The post was given to him to hide the rise of Tigellinus, who completely dominated the prefecture, appealing to Nero's debauched lifestyle. Tigellinus spared no opportunity to attack his colleague as a lover of Agrippina the Younger, Nero's mother, or as a servant of her vengeance. Having lost all power, Rufus joined the PISONIAN CONSPIRACY in 65. When it was uncovered, he tried at first to play the role of inquisitor. He was discovered and put to death.

Rufus, Gaius Musonius (c. 30–101 C.E.) *A Stoic philosopher from Volsinii*

Acquiring a reputation as a Stoic, Rufus became the teacher of numerous philosophers, especially Epictetus and Dio Chrysostom. A friend of Rubellius Plautus, he followed him into exile in Asia Minor when Nero banished the courtier, c. 60. Returning to Rome after Plautus's death, Rufus again had to leave Rome as part of the PISONIAN CONSPIRACY of 65, living until 68 in Gyaros. The capital was safe when Galba became emperor, but under the Flavians he went into exile again by command of VESPASIAN. Through the liberal policies of Titus, Rufus was allowed to journey back to Rome, where he died sometime in 101.

Rufus, Verginius *See* VERGINIUS RUFUS, LUCIUS.

Rugila (d. 433 C.E.) *King of the Huns during the early fifth century C.E.*
With his brother MANDIUCH, Rugila controlled two of the three main clans of the Hunnic people. Rugila received tribute from Theodosius II in return for curbing his ambitions toward the Eastern Empire. He also probably supported Theodosius in his war against the GOTHS, receiving a slice of Pannonia for his reward.

Rusticus, Junius (fl. mid-second century C.E.) *Stoic philosopher*
One of the main instructors of the future emperor, MARCUS AURELIUS, Rusticus had much influence on the emperor. He earned both a second consulship in 162 (the first having been in 133) and a prefectship of the city. Upon his death Marcus asked the Senate to erect statues in his honor. He was, as well, an important adviser.

Rutilius Gallicus (Quintus Julius Cordinus Gaius) (fl. first century C.E.) *Consul circa 70 and 85 C.E. and governor of Germania Inferior under Vespasian*
During the period of 75–78 he launched an effective campaign against the BRUCTERI. He was honored by Domitian and died sometime around 92.

S

Sabellianism Also called Modalism, one of the two forms, with Adoptionism, of the theological movement of Monarchianism in the second and third centuries C.E. The Sabellians took their name from the theologian Sabellius (d. after 217), who argued that the Godhead (or the Creator) was essentially undifferentiated in its internal nature. This was in contrast to Christian teachings, which held that the Trinity was comprised of three distinct Persons and one substance. Sabellius was probably excommunicated in 217 and died most likely unreconciled to the church. Little else is known about him. The movement subsequently died out after Sabellius's death.

Sabina, Vibia (d. after 128 C.E.) *Empress from 117 to 136, the wife of Hadrian*
Sabina was the daughter of L. Vibius and Matidia, and granddaughter of MARCIANA, the sister of Emperor TRAJAN. Although Trajan apparently did not approve, Empress Plotina, in 100, organized Hadrian's marriage to Sabina. Hadrian was thus positioned perfectly to succeed Trajan as emperor and, in 117, Sabina became empress. Although she was made Augusta in 128, Sabina had a reputation for faithlessness. Hadrian reportedly ousted Septicius Clarus, Prefect of the PRAETORIAN GUARD, and Suetonius Tranquillus, an imperial secretary, because of their overly familiar attitude toward the empress. He supposedly once said that had he been a private citizen he would have sent her away. However, upon her death, sometime after 128, she was given full honors. There was a rumor that she had been poisoned.

Sabinians Members of one of the two important schools of LAW in Rome during the first and second centuries C.E. The Sabinians took their name from Masurius SABINUS but later were known as Cassians after Sabinus's student, CASSIUS LONGINUS. Sabinian views were based on the teachings of Gaius Ateius CAPITO, Sabinus's instructor and an adherent of conservatism in the reign of Augustus (27 B.C.E.–14 C.E.). Among the few characteristics discernable in the attitude of the Sabinians was a legal conservatism reflecting their founder. In opposition to the Sabinians were the PROCULEANS. A rivalry between the schools lasted well into the second century, when they were united. The most famous head of the Sabinians was Salvius Julianus.

Sabinus, Caelius (fl. late first century C.E.) *Leading jurist; consul in 69 with Flavius Sabinus*
Sabinus was a member of the Sabinian school of law and probably a contemporary of Pegasus. Both practiced with success under the Flavians.
See also PROCULEANS; SABINIANS.

Sabinus, Cornelius (d. c. 41 C.E.) *Tribune of the Praetorian Guard*
With Cassius CHAEREA, Sabinus was one of the ringleaders in the plot to assassinate Emperor GAIUS CALIGULA in 41 C.E. Among the conspirators Sabinus was least known and was overshadowed by the prefect of the Guard and his more bitter comrade. Nevertheless, he had a direct hand in the murder, later committing suicide when Chaerea was dead.

Sabinus, Flavius (d. 69 C.E.) *Brother of Emperor Vespasian*

Sabinus had a long career in government, serving as legate in MOESIA from around 49 to 56 C.E. and as PREFECT OF THE CITY (*praefectus urbi*) during the reign of NERO (c. 61). In 69, in an act of appeasement to Vespasian, Emperor OTHO appointed Sabinus once more as prefect of the city. Later that year, he was summoned by Emperor VITELLIUS to negotiate that ruler's hopeful abdication, but soldiers in ROME refused to accept Vitellius's resignation. Sabinus, with his friends, was besieged on the capitol and fought it out in the TEMPLE OF JUPITER. Captured, Sabinus was executed at the feet of Vitellius. His death was a rallying cry for the Flavians, who captured the city a short time later.

Sabinus, Julius (d. 79 C.E.) *Leader of the Germanic tribe of the Lingones*
In 70 C.E., Sabinus claimed descent from Julius CAESAR and began a revolt. Quickly defeated, he fled to his estates before disappearing for nine years with his wife Peponila. Captured in 79, he was executed with his family.

Sabinus, Masurius (fl. first century C.E.) *A student of Gaius Ateius Capito and an eminent jurist*
Sabinus possibly came from Verona, studying law in Rome. He achieved such notoriety that the school of law founded by Capito came to be known by his name (SABINIANS). Among the works of Sabinus was a study of the IUS CIVILE, used by subsequent jurists and thus influential in shaping the *Digest*. Written in three books, the treatise was called *Ad Sabinum*.

Sabinus, Nymphidius (d. 69 C.E.) *Prefect of the Praetorian Guard from 65 to 69 C.E.*
Sabinus was the son of a freedwoman of considerable beauty who had worked in the imperial court and claimed that he was born of Emperor GAIUS CALIGULA. Known for his height and forbidding looks, Sabinus entered the LEGIONS, eventually holding a command over auxiliaries in PANNONIA. Admitted to the Praetorian Guard as a TRIBUNE, he made himself useful to NERO and the corrupt Prefect TIGELLINUS, especially during the PISONIAN CONSPIRACY in 65. With the *consularia ornamenta*, Sabinus was made co-prefect of the Guard with Tigellinus. He proved a deft political manipulator, staying alive until 68, when Tigellinus became ill and Nero fell from power. Once Tigellinus was removed, Sabinus found the patronage of the new Emperor GALBA potentially profitable, promising in the claimant's name a hefty DONATIVUM in return for the support of the Guard. Disappointments soon confronted him as he realized that his position was not to be improved with the new administration. Overestimating his control of Praetorians, and probably with an eye on the throne, he marched into the Castra Praetoria, asking their help. The soldiers of the Guard not only rejected his offer but also killed him. This murder, unrewarded by Galba, was later an element in the unhappiness of the Guard with their new master.

Sabinus, Oppius (d. 85 C.E.) *Governor of Moesia in 85 C.E.*
The first of the Roman officials to confront the onslaught of the Dacians under DECEBALUS, he failed totally and was killed in battle as the Dacians ravaged much of the province.

Sabinus, Poppaeus (d. 35 C.E.) *Grandfather of Poppaea, the wife of Nero from 62 to 65 C.E.*
A highly successful imperial governor throughout the reign of TIBERIUS (14–37 C.E.) and CONSUL in 9 C.E., Sabinus was made legate in MOESIA by AUGUSTUS, probably in 11. Viewed by Tiberius as what TACITUS called competent and not more than competent, his services were retained by the new emperor, who added the governorships of MACEDONIA and Achaea as well. His tenure was extremely long, and he administered Moesia for 24 years. Only his death in 35 ended his term of office. In 26 he won a notable victory over the Thracians, receiving a triumphal insignia. Sabinus was typical of Tiberius's appointed officials, capable of fulfilling their duties but not in a manner that was overly skillful or remarkable.

Sabinus, Publius (fl. first century C.E.) *Prefect of the Praetorian Guard during the brief reign of Vitellius in 69 C.E.*
Sabinus was appointed prefect with Julius Priscus as part of the newly created Praetorians. He had been a mere prefect of an auxiliary cohort, probably in Germania, owing his promotion to the patronage of Fabius VALENS, one of Vitellius's important generals. However, he developed a friendship with CAECINA ALIENUS another legate, and when Caecina deserted the Vitellian camp, Sabinus was removed from his post and briefly imprisoned. He was succeeded by Alfenus VARUS.

Sabinus, Quintus Titurius (d. 54 B.C.E.) *Legate in the army of Julius Caesar during the Gallic Wars*
Sabinus was used against the Belgae in 57 B.C.E. before assuming command of three LEGIONS in 56 and defeating the Venelli in northwestern Gaul. Two years later, at ADUATUCA he was trapped and killed, with Cotta, by Ambiorix.

Sabinus, Titus Flavius (d. 84 C.E.) *Husband to his cousin, Flavia Julia (7), daughter of Emperor Titus*
Although Julia was known to be involved with her uncle, DOMITIAN, Sabinus married her anyway, sharing the consulship of 82 with Domitian, then emperor. Perhaps to remove him as an inconvenience or because of the banishment of DIO COCCEIANUS, Sabinus was put to death.

Sabis   The Sambre River of today's northern France and Belgium; site of a military engagement in July 57 B.C.E. between Julius CAESAR and the NERVII, the strong Gallic tribe of Gallia Belgica. Using surprise, the Nervii struck hard at Caesar's outnumbered legions; only by his sheer force of will was victory secured for the Romans. Haranguing his troops, especially the reliable X Legion, Caesar drove them on, eventually smashing the tribes so completely that the Nervii virtually disappeared as a nation. They had lost nearly 60,000 men, while the Roman losses proved relatively light. The battle of Sabis ensured the conquest of Gallia Belgica.

Sabratha   Coastal city in North Africa to the west of Lepcis Magna and Oea, in the region of TRIPOLITANIA. Smaller than Lepcis and less favored by the imperial government, Sabratha nevertheless was able to develop its resources. Archaeologically the site was important for its second-century-C.E. theater, designed along lines similar to the one in Lepcis, although this one was larger. There were also temples, a basilica, a CURIA, and a forum.

sacramentum   The oath of allegiance taken by members of the legions. The sacramentum began in the earliest of the Roman formations, when the troops swore to the standards to remain loyal for the length of a campaign. After the reforms of Marius, the pledge served for the entire period of service. Under the emperors, however, each legion took the *sacramentum* to the PRINCEPS, in recognition that he was the supreme ruler of Rome. Each January 1 and on the anniversary of the emperor's accession, the *sacramentum* was readministered. According to tradition, the *sacramentum* was taken by a legate and his tribunes, who then asked for it from the cohorts of the legion. One legionary was selected, reciting the oath, with his companions replying *"idem in me"* ("the same with me").

Sacred Way   *See* VIAE.

Sacrovir, Julius   (d. 21 C.E.) *King of the Gallic Aedui*
In 21 C.E. Sacrovir led an ineffective revolt against ROME, finding support only from within the Aedui and elements of the Treveri. Joined by Julius Florus, a Romanized Gaul, Sacrovir had around 40,000 followers when attacked by Gaius Silius and Visellius Varro, the legates of Germania Superior and Inferior. Defeated in battle, Sacrovir fled and later killed himself.

Sadducees   One of the leading Jewish religious movements, from the Hasmonaean Revolt until the fall of the Great TEMPLE OF JERUSALEM (c. 166 B.C.E.–70 C.E.). The Sadducees probably emerged as a legitimate element of JUDAISM after the Hasmonaean uprising. They believed in the sanctity of the Pentateuch, that only those laws actually written down were to be followed. Any others, espe-cially oral traditional laws, were not valid. Further, the Sadducees held that fate had no place in mortal affairs and that humanity decided its own course.

These views put them in direct opposition to the PHARISEES, who preached oral law and stressed the role of fate. Their fight with the Pharisees, bitter and violent at times, drew in as well the priest-kings of the Hasmonaeans, who derived their power from oral tradition. Consequently, the Sadducees enjoyed little political influence and even less popular appeal. Through an agreement with the Pharisees they were permitted to serve as priests in the Great Temple, eventually having several of their number named high priest, most notably Caiaphas, presider over the interview of Jesus. The Temple thus served as their main source of power. After its destruction in 70 C.E., the Sadducees could not survive the resulting collapse of structured Judaism, dying out over the next centuries.

Salacia   Minor and obscure Roman deity affiliated with NEPTUNE, perhaps as his wife or consort. Salacia was probably the goddess of springing water (*salire* means "jump").

Salarian Way   *See* VIAE.

Salii   The "leapers," a priestly college in Rome dedicated to MARS. Founded probably by King Numa but developed under King Tullus Hostilius, the Salii were actually two groups, the Salii Palatini and the Salii Agonenses or Collini. The former were connected to Mars, while the latter were once affiliated with Quirinus. Both, however, placed great importance in their ceremonies on the *ancilia* or holy shields. Although the Salii were to be found in towns throughout Italia, in Rome there were 12 members, all Patricians, whose parents were both living. Their head was a magister, with a *praesul* (dance leader) and *vates* (song leader). The normal costume was the war tunic, the *tunica picta,* a bronze breastplate, a peaked hat (*apex*), a military cloak (*trabea*), a sword at their side, a shield (the *ancile*) on the left arm and a spear in the right hand. The *ancile* was an eight-shaped replica of the gift of Jupiter to Numa. As their name would suggest (*salire,* dance or jump), the Salii performed rituals at certain times of the year. In October they danced at the *armilustrium* (October 19), closing the campaigning season. March was a busy time for them. On March 11 they presided over the *Equiria* or horse races in honor of Mars; on the 19 was the purifying of the shields, and on the 23 came the *tubilustrium* or cleansing of the trumpets. The song of the Salii was called the Carmen Saliare.

Salinator, Gnaeus Pedanius Fuscus   (d. 136 C.E.) *Grandson of Julius Servianus, great-nephew of Emperor Hadrian*

With his grandfather, Salinator was a leading candidate to succeed to the throne. The aging emperor seemingly groomed Salinator for the throne, granting him special status at the court. In 136, however, Hadrian changed his mind, choosing Lucius Ceionius COMMODUS (known as Lucius Aelius Caesar). When Servianus and his eighteen-year-old grandson became angry at this, Hadrian forced Servianus to kill himself and put to death Salinator.

Sallust (Gaius Sallustius Crispus) (c. 86–35/4 B.C.E.)
Historian
Sallust embarked on a political career through the patronage of the influential Clodius Pulcher, reaching the tribuneship in 52. As was the case with most of Clodius's followers, Sallust was outraged by his death at the hands of Annius MILO. A legate in Syria circa 50 B.C.E., he returned that year to Rome only to be ousted from the Senate by the CENSORS. Julius CAESAR reinstated him in 49, and Sallust became one of his supporters. After commanding a legion in Illyria, he served in 47 as a negotiator with the troublesome legions in Campania. Along with the rank of praetor in 46 came that of proconsul of AFRICA. His extortionist administration was so bad that in 45 charges were brought against him, only to be halted by Caesar. Nevertheless, the scandal rendered him useless. Sallust retired to his estates, which included the Horti Sallusti, or Gardens of Sallust.

Sallust turned to writing only in his later years and proved very influential. Instead of adhering to the models of the ANNALISTS, he tried to find new sources of ingenuity. Turning to the Greeks, especially Thucydides, he followed their style, using conciseness, speechmaking, and archaism, while chronicling recent events in the traditional Roman manner, with rhetoric and reflection. This unorthodox brand of writing was highly unique and left a marked impression upon his successors. Sallust authored several notable historical works. A monograph on Catiline relied upon literary sources to recreate the mood of the state at the time, rather than to document dryly the events. Another monograph, covering the Jugurthine War, was more carefully researched, and hence was smoother and objective. Of considerable ambition was his *History,* composed in five books, detailing the notable happenings from 78 B.C.E. until his own era. Unlike the first two, it has survived only in fragments.

Sallustius Crispus, Gaius (d. 20 C.E.) *Friend and adviser of Emperor Augustus and leading figure in the reign of Tiberius*
Sallustius was the grandnephew of the writer SALLUST; introduced into Roman society with his adoption by the historian, he subsequently pursued a career similar to that of Gaius MAECENAS. He gained great influence in the government without acquiring the routine senatorial position. Thus, while only an Equestrian (EQUITES) Sallustius Crispus far outweighed his friends in the Senate and came to be second only to Maecenas in imperial favor. When Maecenas died in 8 B.C.E., Sallustius Crispus was the most reliable bearer of secrets. This status was unchanged when Tiberius became emperor. He was not only responsible for the murder of the claimant AGRIPPA POSTUMUS in 14 C.E., but also helped arrest and execute Clemens, Agrippa's masquerading servant. His vast wealth and sumptuous lifestyle were mentioned by the historian TACITUS.

Sallustius Passienus Crispus, Gaius (fl. first century C.E.) *Consul in 27 and 44 C.E.*
The adoptive son of Sallustius Crispus, he earned a reputation as one of the foremost orators of Rome. He was famed for his comment on Gaius Caligula that "no man had ever been a better slave or a worse master." By marriage to NERO's aunt, Domitia Lepida, he became associated with the ruling family. Apparently seeking to improve his position even further, he abandoned Lepida and wed AGRIPPINA THE YOUNGER. Aside from starting a vicious enmity between the women, the union brought him little good. He was dead shortly thereafter, his wealth falling into his widow's hands. It was widely reported that Agrippina poisoned him.

Salluvii
Also called the Salyes, a large Gallic tribe living in GALLIA NARBONESIS. Of Ligurian stock, they presented difficulties to the early Roman occupiers of the region. Once subdued, their lands became part of the province of Gallia Narbonensis, and the colony of Aquae Sextiae was established to ensure continued cooperation.

Salona
City resting on the eastern shore of the Adriatic Sea; capital of the province of ILLYRICUM. Also called Salonae, the city was old but was vigorously developed in the hands of Roman traders (c. 47 B.C.E.), receiving a colony as well, Colonia Martia Julia Salona, through the patronage of Julius Caesar. From the time of AUGUSTUS, Salona served as the most important city in Illyricum. The legate of the province had his seat there and construction reflected its status. Salona was actually two cities in one, an old community known as *urbs vetus* and a new one, *urbs nova,* built just to the east. *Urbs vetus* had a temple and forum, and an amphitheater capable of holding more than 15,000 people. *Urbs nova* was even larger but was centered on housing and business, with many private homes and several basilicas. Both sectors were walled and connected by a large gate, the *Porta Caesarea,* erected by Augustus. One of the most successful metropolises in the Roman Empire, Salona was the birthplace of Emperor Diocletian (c. 240 C.E.). When he retired in 305, he took up residence in his palace at nearby SPLIT.

Salonina (Cornelia Salonina Chrysogone) (d. 268 C.E.) *Empress from 254 to 268*

Wife of Emperor GALLIENUS from around 249 to 268. Salonina was noted for intellectual and virtuous characteristics, both of which helped her survive the stress of being AUGUSTA at a time when the Roman Empire was facing severe crises and she was facing the pain of her husband's less faithful behavior. Unfortunately, she was murdered with Gallienus at the siege of Mediolanum (Milan).

Saloninus (Publius Licinius Cornelius Saloninus Valerianus) (d. 260 C.E.) *Son of Emperor Gallienus and Empress Salonina*

The youth was first appointed Caesar in 258. Two years later, under the guidance of his mentor Silvanus, and supposedly with the cooperation of the local general, POSTUMUS, Saloninus was elevated to Augustus, or co-emperor, and given command of the Rhine frontier. As Gallienus was away on campaign, the direction of imperial government in the West was ostensibly in the lad's hands, although real decisions were probably left to Silvanus. This proved unfortunate, for Silvanus and Postumus quarreled. A disagreement became violent, and the general gathered his troops, besieging Saloninus and Silvanus at Cologne in 260. The city was captured, and Saloninus was put to death.

Salutatio

The greeting given every morning from six to eight A.M. to the most powerful or high-ranking persons in the Rome of the imperial era. This form of flattery was typical of Roman society at the time, for those who desired advancement in the state sought the patronage of figures of influence. Although tiresome, the *salutatio* was deemed necessary, for favors could be asked and a small monetary gift, the *sportula*, was often given. The term also referred to the cheer given to a general by his troops, either in celebration of a victory or in recognition of his rank as IMPERATOR. On the basis of the *salutatio*, some generals assumed that their troops were saying that the general should aspire to the throne.

Salvianus (Salvianus of Massilia or Marseilles) (fl. fifth century C.E.) *Presbyter and writer*

Born probably near Cologne, Salvianus was a Christian by birth, later marrying and converting a pagan named Palladia. The couple broke up, in the mutual pursuit of religion, and Salvianus moved to a monastery on the island of Lerins, just off modern-day Cannes. From around 424 to 439 he taught there. Salvianus was the author of numerous books, the most important being *De Gubernatione Dei* (On the governing of God), a treatise in eight books arguing in favor of the divine retribution of the Almighty. An invaluable study of the prevailing social depravity within the Roman Empire, the work contrasted the social vices of the Romans with the cleansing vitality of the barbarian hordes. Morality clearly held the upper hand to society and declining sense of rectitude. Other efforts include *ad Ecclesiam* in four books, showing that Christians should donate their goods to the church, and letters.

Samaria

District in PALAESTINA situated to the north of JUDAEA and the south of GALILEE. Samaria was once one of the most important cities in the region, serving for a time as the capital of the kingdom of Israel. However, an intense dislike between the Samaritans and their Jewish neighbors dated as far back as the Babylonian Captivity. Thus, Samaria was considered a separate area of Palestine. Under POMPEY THE GREAT's reorganization of the East it was attached to SYRIA. AUGUSTUS presented it to HEROD THE GREAT, who spent large sums beautifying it. After Herod's death in 4 B.C.E., the Samaritans fell under the control of Archelaus, until he was removed, and then the legate of Syria assumed overall command via the procurator of Judaea. Around 36 C.E., a small local incident caused a major social upheaval, and PONTIUS PILATE called in troops to quell the unrest. Appalled at the bloodshed that resulted, the Samaritans protested to VITELLIUS, the governor of Syria. Their appeals eventually cost Pilate his career. By the fourth century C.E., Samaria was a place of no importance.

Samos

Island in the Aegean Sea, separated by a narrow channel from the coast of ASIA MINOR. Samos had a long and honorable history during the formation of the Mediterranean world, before passing into the hands of Rome in 84 B.C.E., when it was attached to the province of Asia. Through the work of Q. CICERO in 62 B.C.E., some of the island's wealth was returned to it, and further favor was shown during the time of its occupation by ANTONY and CLEOPATRA in 32. AUGUSTUS found Samos to be an excellent place to winter. He spent the cool months there in 21 and 20 B.C.E. For their hospitality, the residents were declared free by his decree. Subsequently the island had little to offer except as an abode for exiles.

Samosata

Capital city of the kingdom of COMMAGENE in northern SYRIA. It became a major site in the province of Syria after the annexation of the realm by VESPASIAN in 72 C.E. Subsequently the city was the birthplace of two notable philosophers, the pagan LUCIAN of Samosata and the Christian PAUL OF SAMOSATA.

Santones

Tribe in Gallia Aquitania that lived on the western coast of Gaul (Gallia); quickly subdued by the legions of Julius Caesar during the GALLIC WARS. By 56 B.C.E. and the successful conclusion of the operations of Crassus in Aquitania, the Santones were considered pacified. Although they took part in the widespread rebellion of VERCINGETORIX in 52 B.C.E., they eventually were declared a federated state of Rome. Their chief city, originally called Mediolanum, was later known as Santones (Saintes).

Saoterus (fl. second century C.E.) *Influential freedman during the reign of Emperor Commodus (177–192 C.E.)*
Saoterus was notable because of his origins. Coming from NICOMEDIA he used his position to reward his old city, receiving senatorial permission to hold games there and to build a temple to Commodus. He was murdered by the more ambitious CLEANDER.

Saracens A warlike and nomadic people who originated in northwestern Arabia but came to be known throughout a wide stretch of land, from Mesopotamia to the Nile. Although contact was made between the Saracens and ROME during the reign of MARCUS AURELIUS, actual dealings were uncommon until the third and fourth centuries C.E. Known as the Saraceni, one of their chiefs offered to be an ally to Julian but joined the Persians against the Roman Empire because of the terrible treatment given to him by Julian. The most famous leader of the Saracens was Queen Mavia, who carried on a war against the Romans in PALESTINE, from 373 to 378. When a treaty was finally arranged in 378, she sent a troop of her warriors to help defend CONSTANTINOPLE from Gothic attack, following the battle of ADRIANOPLE. Ammianus wrote of their sortie against the GOTHS, describing how one of the Saracens, dressed only in a loin cloth, killed a barbarian and then drank his blood. This so horrified the enemy that their normal bravado was severely shaken.

Sardanapalus The name of the last ruler of the Assyrian Empire; it was adopted by Emperor ELAGABALUS as part of his numerous Eastern titles.

Sardinia Large island in the Mediterranean, positioned strategically south of the island of CORSICA and about midway between Spain's Balearic Islands and the western shore of Italy. Fertile and rich in raw materials, Sardinia attracted the attention of the Phoenicians, Greeks, Carthaginians, and, ultimately, the Romans, who conquered it and neighboring Corsica in 227 B.C.E. Sardinia was originally placed under the provincial command of a PRAETOR, but with the founding of the Roman Empire a change was made. Under AUGUSTUS (ruled 27 B.C.E.–14 C.E.) the island, along with Corsica, was declared a senatorial province in the care of a proconsul. Just as local opposition to Roman occupation had surfaced in the third century B.C.E., civil unrest and bandit activity probably contributed to the transfer of Sardinia to the imperial provinces in 6 C.E. Procurators remained as governors until Nero's time, when he traded it back to the Senate in return for granting freedom to Achaea. Over the years Sardinia passed back and forth, depending upon various circumstances, until finally, in the reign of MARCUS AURE-

LIUS (r. 161–180 C.E.), senatorial rights were returned. Under the reforms of DIOCLETIAN, the isle belonged to the diocese of Italia.

When compared to its rocky and barren sister, Corsica, Sardinia was blessed with natural wealth. The plains in the western and southern sections offered great opportunities for agriculture. The full economic potential of the island was never developed, but crop production still yielded vast amounts of food for nearby Italy, especially ROME. With corn were to be found rich mines of iron and silver. Finally, beautiful springs provided salt, which was sold on the coast.

The seat of government for both Sardinia and Corsica was at Carales, the largest city. The Romans found the Sardinians to be quite uncivilized and fought for many years to subdue them. Most outbreaks of violence originated in the mountains dominating the east and parts of the north. Called the Insani Montes (the Mountains of Insanity), they were the hiding places of rebels and brigands. Operations were necessary against them, most notably in the reign of TIBERIUS (14–37 C.E.).

Sardis One of the great cities of ASIA MINOR and once the capital of Lydia. Known also as Sardes, it was situated in western Asia Minor, northeast of SMYRNA. Although still large and productive, it suffered a decline during the imperial era because of the continued development of Ephesus and Pergamum. In 17 C.E., Sardis was virtually destroyed in the earthquake that ruined numerous cities in the province of Asia. Although rebuilt through the help of Tiberius, the city was never able to recover its prestige. The clearest evidence of this was given in 26, when Sardis and Smyrna competed for the right to build a temple in honor of TIBERIUS. Smyrna won. Sardis was a very early place of Christian worship, mentioned by John in *Revelation* as one of the seven churches in Asia. He commented upon its state of ruin.

Sarmatians Called Sarmatae by the Romans, these large and powerful people of Indo-Iranian descent lived for centuries on the steppes of southern Russia, roughly east of the Don (ancient name, Tanais) River, near the Sea of Azov. They were closely connected racially to the Scythians, who possessed an extensive empire along the Black Sea. Contact between the two peoples was warlike but limited until the middle of the third century B.C.E., when migrations of Iranian-based tribes pushed the Sarmatians westward. This brought them into direct conflict with the Scythians, whom they eventually defeated for control of the entire region, except the Crimean Peninsula. The Scythians proved the more active of the two nations, and the Sarmatae broke into small tribal entities.

Sarmatian culture was surprisingly well developed and enlightened. Although nomadic, they had an organized aristocracy that ran a vast empire while accumulating wealth. The most interesting cultural feature was the probably-Iranian holdover of women possessing a major role in affairs, both domestic and military. Not only were women more free than their Hellenic or Roman counterparts, they also hunted and rode into battle with the men. Sarmatian possessions were always distinctive, with colors being used throughout their clothing. Pottery was often primitive, but they seemed to like imports from all over the East. As with the Scythians, the Sarmatians had an intense fondness for gold, using it in virtually every aspect of their life, especially in armor.

In battle, the Sarmatians adopted the same tactics and strategies as the Scythians, Parthians and most other Eastern states. This meant the use of massive units of cavalry, divided into heavy and light. Heavy cavalry usually meant the nobles, dressed in thick body armor varying in composition between iron and bone. They carried heavy lances and their charge was not easily broken. In support rode the light cavalry, less armored and bearing bows fired with a deadly accuracy.

Contact with the Roman Empire came in successive waves, ending in often bloody struggles. The first of the tribes was the IAZYGES, who settled in the Danube region. They were followed closely by the ROXOLANI and then the ALANS or Alani.

Sarmizegethusa

The capital of DACIA, both for the independent realm and the Roman province. Sarmizegethusa was the largest city in the kingdom and considered essential to the well-being of the Dacians. Throughout the wars of King DECEBALUS with Rome, Sarmizegethusa was kept safe from capture, but in the summer of 106 C.E. it fell to the legions of TRAJAN. The Romans chose to keep it as the center of the new province of Dacia. Trajan founded a colony there, renaming the city of Colonia Ulpia Traiana Augusta Dacica Sarmizegethusa Metropolis, more commonly known as Colonia Dacia.

Sassanid dynasty

Family ruling the so-called Persian Empire from 226 C.E. until the middle of the seventh century. Using a powerful combination of political domination, noble allies, and religious unity, the Sassanids forged a realm that came to be viewed as the equal of the Roman Empire. In 208 C.E., Papak King, a minor vassal lord of the Parthian Empire, was succeeded as ruler of the small realm of Persis by his son, SHAPUR. His youngest son, ARDASHIR, overthrew his brother and became king. With Shapur dead, Ardashir subdued the surrounding vassals of Parthia and, in 224, defeated and killed ARTABANUS V in battle. In 226 Ardashir took the title of "King of Kings," ascending the throne of a new empire, Persia.

From the start, the Romans had no idea that the Persians would be any different from the corrupt and deteriorated Parthians. Their blissful ignorance was shattered in

230, when Ardashir rolled into Mesopotamia. This war set off a long series of conflicts that raged over the next 133 years. Emperor SEVERUS ALEXANDER was able to respond effectively enough, but even when he departed in 233 for home no treaty was concluded. The Persians were back, under Shapur I, in 242. His reign was notable for one major victory, the annihilation of Emperor VALERIAN in 259–260, at Edessa. The Sassanids captured a Roman emperor, destroyed his entire army and justifiably laid claim to control of the East. Persian triumphs came at the darkest moment in imperial history, and total mastery of the Eastern provinces was prevented only by the rise of ODAENATH of PALMYRA. Shapur suffered crushing setbacks at the hands of the Palmyran, even enduring a siege of CTESIPHON in 267. There followed a period of decline, so that in 283, Emperor Carus felt confident enough to launch a major war upon Persia's King VARAHRAN II. Ctesiphon fell. Further inroads might have been made, but Carus died, probably murdered by his Praetorian Prefect Aper. With the accession of DIOCLETIAN, Varahran II was forced to surrender Mesopotamia and ARMENIA.

The era of weakness seemed ended in 293, when NARSES came to power. Narses invaded Syria in 296, thrashing the tetrarch GALERIUS in battle near Callinicus. Galerius, urged on by Diocletian, went back on the defensive in 298, not only routing Narses but seizing Ctesiphon as well. Roman terms of peace had to be accepted. Mesopotamia was lost, Armenia was a Roman client and other stretches of territory along the Tigris surrendered. It was a bleak moment for the Sassanids, but a brilliant recovery came in the person of SHAPUR II, who ruled from 309 to 379. Once of a mature age, he massacred all who might oppose him within the Persian nobility, firmly took hold of the army and declared war on the Roman Empire around 336. He fought with CONSTANTIUS II, losing an encounter in 344 or 348, and enduring a huge operation by Julian in 363. When that pagan emperor died in 363, his replacement, Jovian, accepted the Persian terms for peace, a humiliating and unnecessary treaty. Shapur was satisfied, and SHAPUR III (383–388) signed an important pact with THEODOSIUS I around 384–386.

This agreement ended the long, unbroken chain of hostilities between the Sassanids and the Romans. It was all the more remarkable because between 387 and 502 it remained in force, with only two minor violations. Thus, both states were able to focus on internal politics, while enjoying a warm if not uneasy relationship. For the Eastern Empire, the barbarians could be held in check, while for Persia the ever restless nomadic peoples on the frontiers could be repulsed or subjugated. Typical of the dealings between Constantinople and the Sassanids was the sending of emissaries to announce all successions or policy decisions; failure to do so was seen as a major breach of protocol.

The Sassanid dynasty came to power through the vigor of a young people, ready to explode, whose energy

Coins from the Sassanid Persian Empire. *(Courtesy Warren Esty)*

THE SASSANID KINGS

King	Dates
Papak	208–224 C.E.
Shapur	224
Ardashir	226–241
Shapur I	241–272
Hormazd Ardashir	272–273
Varahran I	273–276
Varahran II	293
Narses	293–302
Hormazd II	302–309
Shapur II	309–379
Ardashir II	379–383
Shapur III	383–388
Varahran IV	388–399
Yazdagird I	399–420
Varahran V	420–439
Yazdagird II	439–457
Hormazd III	457–459
Peroz	459–484
Valash	484–488
Kavad	488–531
Zamasp	496–498
Khusro I	531–579
Hormazd IV	579–590
Varahran Chobin	590–591
Khusro II	590–628
Kavad II	628
Ardashir III	628–629
Boran	629–630
Hormazd V	630–c. 632
Yazdagird III	632–651

was applied in the destruction of the Parthians and all who might oppose the Sassanid programs. But when actual governing was needed, the Persians chose to adopt much of the Parthian system. This was understandable, for the bureaucracy of the Parthians was, in Eastern terms, generally efficient. An essential difference was the strong centralization of the entire government. Unlike the Arsacids, the Sassanids kept the nobility in line while running the vast regions of the empire with governors or with reliable clients. No other Ardashir was to be allowed to rise up and declare himself king of kings. The monarchs of Persia were naturally more autocratic, leaning on the feudal nobility for support. The aristocracy supplied the army with its characteristic, mailed cavalry. With the state pillars of the Royal House and the Nobles stood the religion of the Sassanids, Zoroastrianism (or Mazdaism).

Coming from Iran, the Persians were firm adherents of Zoroastrian doctrines. The Sassanids converted their traditional faith into a leading political element. A priesthood, with influence over every social caste, jealously guarded its own place and watched for unacceptable heresies, such as MANICHAEISM. There were, however, many faiths in the Persian world, including Buddhism, Judaism, the original Zoroastrians as opposed to the Mazdean forms, and CHRISTIANITY.

Beneath the triad of throne, nobles, and priests there existed the bulk of the citizenry. There was probably a second class of nobles, answerable to the leading houses. Another class would have been the non-noble ministers and government officials, followed by the masses of common inhabitants. There was, no doubt, a complicated and ritualized social pattern that went with the various levels of life, a system in play until the fall of the Sassanids to the Muslims around 651.

satire   A form of versification with the object of ridiculing or mocking folly or social failings and thus correcting society on the whole while entertaining it. Quintilian once remarked that "Satire is wholly ours" ("*satura total nostra est*"). This was not inaccurate, for only in the spirited, spontaneous, biting, and practical hands of the Romans could satire so blossom.

Proto-Satire probably came to Rome in the early fourth century B.C.E., with itinerant minstrels who performed their improvised Fescennine verse on the public stage. In 364, Etruscan artists offered an actual ballet, beginning a tradition of combined humor with music and dance, to which were added influences from the Greeks. These included Stoic and Cynic speakers who addressed a multitude of sins in their *sermones,* using jokes and anecdotes to enliven their style.

In the second century B.C.E., Ennius penned poetry aimed specifically at satirizing life and death. He was followed by two influential writers of satire, Varro and Lucilius. Varro (d. 27 B.C.E.) came after Lucilius (d. 102/1 B.C.E.) but was unique in his Menippean satires by combining both prose and poetry. Serious subjects were treated in a humorous fashion. This mixed writing was adopted by other satirists. PETRONIUS found it useful, as did SENECA in his *Apocolocyntosis,* a vicious lampooning of the deification of Claudius. A much later application was made by Emperor Julian in his jocular *Caesares,* about the emperors before him.

However, Lucilius (second century B.C.E.) was credited by Horace with being the "Father of Satire." He observed many facets of life at the time, using humor, seriousness, or bitter attack. As his medium of expression was hexameter, he was quickly and easily mirrored by a host of imitators who, in the opinion of HORACE, could never match him. There were, however, several notable satirists.

Horace led the great revival of satire at the end of the first century B.C.E. Preferring to poke fun at less obscene parts of the human comedy, he was never particularly offensive. PERSIUS, in the early first century C.E., pursued the Lucilian form but did not attain the literary heights of JUVENAL, who was arguably the finest and the last of the satirists. With Juvenal, satire came to an end as a viable art form. It was too dangerous to apply rapier wit against a murderous imperial regime. Even Horace and Juvenal adopted the names of the dead or titles from other writers. Such restrictions made further growth quite impossible.

Saturnalia   The festival in honor of SATURNUS, held originally on December 17 of each year. Of the many holidays on the Roman calendar, Saturnalia was certainly the happiest. This was probably due to the adoption of so many Greek characteristics in the Roman pantheon. Just as Saturnus was heavily influenced by the Greek god Kronos, so was the Saturnalia transformed by the merry day of Kronia. When the Saturnalia originated is unclear, except that it was very old. Chief characteristics of the holiday were a temporary abolition of social standing so that slaves were given the day off, gambling was allowed, gifts were exchanged with family and friends, and a *Saturnalicus princeps* (a leading man of the Saturnalia or a "Lord of Misrule") was elected. Clearly, the Saturnalia had its own effect upon the celebration of the Christian Christmas and New Year.

Saturninus, Aemilius (d. c. 197 C.E.) *Prefect of the Praetorian Guard*
Saturninus was prefect with PLATIANUS during the reign of Septimius SEVERUS. He was murdered by his ambitious colleague.

Saturninus, Aponius (fl. first century C.E.) *Governor of Moesia in 69 C.E.*
Saturninus gained a victory for ROME against the SARMATIANS, the tribe that had hoped to use the chaos in the empire to its own advantage. Saturninus was given a triumph and retained in his office by both Emperors OTHO

and VITELLIUS. When the III Legion in ILLYRICUM revolted against Vitellius, Saturninus wrote the emperor of the events but later shrewdly deduced that the cause of Vespasian would eventually triumph. He thus joined Antonius Primus in marching on Italy. Suspected of being secretive and scheming, Saturninus had difficulty holding on to the loyalty of his troops. When he was charged with writing to Vitellius, the soldiers tried to murder him. He fled, retired to Patavium and surrendered total command to Primus.

Saturninus, Gnaeus Sentius (d. after 41 C.E.) *Consul*
Probably the son of a like named consul in 4 C.E. who attained the position in his own right in 41. Immediately after the assassination of Gaius Caligula he transferred the funds of the treasury to the capital, where they might be protected by the Senate. He then delivered a long address to the senators around him, proposing that the entire system of the principate be abolished. Although greeted with enthusiasm, his idea was not implemented because the Praetorian Guard had chosen Claudius the next emperor.

Saturninus, Julius (d. c. 278 C.E.) *Usurper in the East (c. 278)*
Probably a Moor, as reported by ZOSIMUS, instead of a Gaul, as listed in the *Historia Augusta.* One of the most reliable generals in the army of Aurelian, he was appointed overall commander of the East. Shortly after PROBUS succeeded AURELIAN, the LEGIONS of Saturninus elevated him to the purple. His period was brief. Although he minted coins at ANTIOCH, he own soldiers killed him at Apamea.

Saturninus, Lucius Antoninus (d. 89 C.E.) *Governor of Germania Superior during the reign of Emperor Domitian*
In January 89 Saturninus took control of his two legions at Moguntiacum (Mainz) and attempted a rebellion against the central government. When word reached ROME, Domitian set off at once, but his presence on the Rhine proved unnecessary. A. Lappius MAXIMUS, governor of Germania Inferior, had refused to join his colleague. He marched his troops to battle and destroyed Saturninus at a site near the Rhine. The German tribes who were supposed to help Saturninus could not cross the Rhine because of an early thaw. Maximus wisely burned Saturninus's papers to avoid unnecessary cruelties by Domitian.

Saturninus Secundus, Salutius (d. after 367 C.E.) *Praetorian prefect from 361 to 367*
Called the "Phoenix" by Libanius because of his ability to recover from political setbacks, Saturninus came from Gaul and was a pagan, earning the trust of Emperor JULIAN THE APOSTATE. Thus, in 361, Julian appointed him Praetorian prefect for the East. Remaining with Julian

throughout his short reign, he convinced his master that Christians should not be tortured in Antioch. As one of the leading generals of the time, he helped organize the Roman fleet to be used against the Persians. In the campaign of 363 he was very nearly killed in the same battle in which Julian was mortally wounded. After Julian died in 363, Saturninus was reportedly offered the throne, declining because of his age. He continued to serve Jovian and VALENTINIAN I, but was finally forced to retire in 367, because of his advanced years and the intrigues of other palace officials. Although a pagan, he was noted for his fair treatment of Christians and his incorruptible nature.

Saturninus Dogmatius, Gaius Caelius (fl. early fourth century C.E.) *Praetorian prefect of Gaul (Gallia) from 334 to 335*

A trusted servant of CONSTANTINE the Great, Saturninus was of non-senatorial descent, his career probably began during the reign of CONSTANTIUS I Chlorus (305–306 C.E.) and many of his early posts were held under that emperor. After serving as head of the RES PRIVATA, he held offices in Italia, including PREFECT OF GRAIN for Rome (*praefectus annone urbis*), and later came to the rank of VICARIUS for Moesia and PREFECT OF THE CITY of Rome. Around 324 Constantine elevated him to COMES and then appointed him to the Senate through ADLECTIO. Very reliable, Saturninus was made Praetorian prefect in his own right.

Saturnus God of time. One of the least known of the Roman gods, his origins and characteristics were mysterious. According to some legends he was a mythical king of Italia, but his origin was probably related to the Latin *satus* (sowing or planting). This made him a very old agricultural deity, identified by early Romans with the Greek god Kronos, and hence father of Jupiter, Neptune, Pluto, and Juno. Saturnus, like Kronos, was considered the oldest god in the Roman pantheon. Fleeing Jupiter, it was said, he appeared to King Janus and was given a temple on the Capitoline Hill, which later became the treasury (the *aerarium Saturni*). In return, he taught the Romans agriculture and headed Italia during a fabled age. The fact that he was a Greek import was demonstrated by the sacrifices made to him. The presiding priest had an uncovered head by tradition during ceremonies, as compared to a covered head for other ceremonies, although there is etymological argument for his origin in Etruria. The festival in honor of Saturnus, the SATURNALIA, was one of the most joyous holidays in ROME. Saturnus, however, did have a dark side, for he was associated with an unknown goddess, Lua (or Lua Mater), whose name implied *lues* (plague or disease).

See also GODS AND GODDESSES OF ROME.

Saxons One of the most powerful and active Germanic tribes in the late empire. The Saxons developed as a peo-

The Temple of Saturn *(Courtesy Fr. Felix Just, S.J.)*

ple in the region of the Cimbric Chersonesus, roughly between the Elbe and Trave rivers (modern Holstein). They made their presence felt by other Germans by overrunning the lands of the Chauci along the Elbe in the late second century C.E., before entering into conflict with others. The date of their contact with Rome has, by some, been put at 286 C.E. Henceforth they fought with the Franks for supremacy of both the Lower Rhine-Elbe territories and the confederations of tribes along the German frontier. Their attacks in Gaul caused considerable damage, while their savage piratic activity rendered the northern coast of Gaul virtually indefensible, hastening the demise of imperial control in Britain. From the middle of the fifth century, Saxons in large numbers took part in raids on Britain, with the Jutes and the Angles. Their raiders eventually settled permanently in the isles. Britain was soon conquered and occupied by this wave of invaders.

Scaevinus, Flavius (d. 65 C.E.) *Senator during the reign of Nero and a member of the Pisonian Conspiracy in 65 C.E.*

Scaevinus was one of the leading figures in the plot to murder the emperor, but he was unable to keep it a secret. Betrayed by his freedman Milichus, he at first denied any knowledge of the plan. But when his friend Antonius Natalis confessed everything, Scaevinus joined him, revealing the names of co-conspirators. He was then executed.

Scapula, Publius Ostorius (d. 52 C.E.) *Consul in 47 C.E. and general*

Of an Equestrian family, he was appointed by Emperor CLAUDIUS in 47 to succeed Aulus Plautius as governor of Britain, with orders to extend Rome's dominion over the isle and to certify its possessions. This operation, handled professionally and without mercy, was eminently successful. He designed the Fosse Way, the line of communications that stretched behind the frontier. Roman presence was made permanent with a colony at CAMULODUNUM (Colchester). These advances came at a terrible price, for Scapula made war on the rebellious ICENI, DECANGI, BRIGANTES, and Silures. This last tribe, led by CARATACUS, required severe methods of suppression. When Caratacus was taken to ROME in 51, Scapula was awarded a triumph. Much work remained, and subsequent campaigns were not as productive. The Silures refused to surrender, and Scapula died of exhaustion in the field.

Scapula, Q. Ostorius (fl. late first century B.C.E.) *First prefect of the Praetorian Guard, with Publius Salvius Aper*

A member of the Equestrians, Scapula was chosen by AUGUSTUS in 2 B.C.E. to assume joint command of the Praetorians. He was not to exercise any of the powers that would come to be a fixture of the prefectship and was removed (with Aper) in favor of Valerius Ligur, sometime before 14 C.E. He subsequently served as prefect of Egypt.

Scaurus, Mamercus Aemilius (d. 34 C.E.) *Great-grandson of the famous Republican figure, Marcus Amelius Scaurus*

A noted orator in his own right, wealthy, and a member of the SENATE, Scaurus earned the dislike and scorn of Emperor TIBERIUS, who called him a disgrace to his ancestors. Although no one could fault his oratory or skills as an ADVOCATUS, such imperial displeasure numbered his days. The prefect of the Praetorian Guard, MACRO, attacked his writing of a tragedy, *Atreus,* as treasonous. This and other supposed crimes brought his forced suicide in 34 C.E. He was the uncle and stepfather of Domitius CORBULO (2).

Scaurus, Q. Terentius (fl. second century C.E.) *Grammarian who specialized in Latin grammar*

His work, *De Orthographia,* was mentioned by such late writers as AUSONIUS and CHARISIUS and thus helped preserve important elements of the Latin language. Scaurus also authored commentaries on VIRGIL and HORACE.

Scholae Palatinae

One of the corps of bodyguards created by CONSTANTINE the Great to replace the defunct PRAETORIAN GUARD. Constantine desired his new force to be intensely loyal to the imperial household and thus gave the units on duty a special area of the palace in which they could await orders. Chosen, originally, from the German cavalry regiments, the Scholae was divided into so-called schools, seven in number and each 500 strong. Each school was under the command of a tribune, who was answerable to the MAGISTER OFFICIORUM. Most of their duties were in Constantinople with the new administration, but it is possible that some of the *Scholae* were posted in the West.

See also PALATINI; SCUTARII.

science and technology

See ART AND ARCHITECTURE, ASTRONOMY, ENGINEERING, FOOD AND DRINK, INDUSTRY, LEGIONS, MEDICINE, PLINY THE ELDER, SHIPS, TIME, TRANSPORTATION.

Scipio, Metellus (d. 46 B.C.E.) *Consul in 52 B.C.E. and a supporter of Pompey during the civil war with Julius Caesar*

A member of an ancient family, Scipio was a firm supporter of the aristocracy in the Republic and thus found POMPEY a useful counterbalance to CAESAR. A political alliance was cemented by the marriage of Scipio's daughter Cornelia to Pompey following the death of Julia, Caesar's daughter, who had been married to Pompey, in 54. A grateful Pompey then elevated Scipio to the consulship as his colleague; this despite his inability to win election as consul on his own. When the civil war began in 49, Scipio joined Pompey at Dyrrhachium and was assigned a proconsular command in the East. Following the defeat of Pompey at Pharsalus in 48, Scipio fled to Africa with the Pompeian remnant. There he was one of the leading generals with Cato Uticensis, Titus Labienus, and King Juba of Numidia. After taking part in the Pompeian defeat at the battle of Thapsus in February, 46, Scipio killed himself.

Scribonia (fl. first century B.C.E.) *Wife of Octavian (Augustus) before his marriage to Livia Drusilla*

Augustus wed Scribonia, sister of Lucius Scribonius Libo, out of political considerations, for Libo was the father-in-law of Sextus POMPEY. Scribonia was much older than Octavian and had already been married twice, to ex-consuls. Their union was not a happy one. On the day in 39 B.C.E. that she bore him a daughter, Julia (3), he divorced her in favor of Livia, claiming "I could not stand her nagging." When Julia was banished by Augustus in 2 B.C.E., Scribonia went into exile with her.

Scribonii brothers *Courtiers in the reign of Nero (r. 54–68 C.E.)*

In 58 C.E. Proculus and Rufus Sulpicii Scribonii were sent to PUTEOLI with a cohort of Praetorians to suppress the citizenry there, who were upset about the trade competition from Ostia. The Scribonii put down the revolt with total ruthlessness, restoring order very quickly. Later they were appointed governors of Germania Superior and Inferior, running the provinces together, for they did everything in unison and were very close. Hearing complaints about their habits, Nero summoned them to Greece and compelled them both to commit suicide.

scrinii Name given to the secretariat of the central imperial administration. Established during the early years of the empire, the *scrinii* had become a vast bureaucracy by the fourth century C.E., when they were placed under the *magistri scrinii*, who were answerable to the MAGISTER OFFICIORUM. There were originally three major sections of the *scrinii*—the *memoriae*, *libellorum*, and *epistularum*—followed later by the *dispositionum*. The *memoriae*, under the MAGISTER MEMORIAE, handled petitions to the emperor; the *libellorum* was concerned with legal cases; and the *epistularum*, which drafted correspondence, was split in two, one for Greek and the other for Latin. Finally, there was the *dispositionum* whose *comes dispositionum* worked out travel arrangements for the emperors.

See also COMES; EPISTULIS AB; LIBELLUS, A; NOTARII.

Scriptores Historiae Augustae Known also as the *Historia Augusta* and the Augustan History, a collection of biographies of the Roman emperors, caesars, and usurpers from the reign of Hadrian to that of Carinus and Numerian (roughly 117–284 C.E., with a gap c. 244–259). The *Historia Augusta* is one of the most debated and controversial ancient sources available to modern scholars. Originally called *Vitae Caesarum*, the collected biographies were first named the *Historia Augusta* by I. Casaubon in the early 17th century. It was claimed to have been written by six authors: Aelius Spartianus, Julis Capitolinus, Aelius Lampridius, Vulcacius Gallicanus, Trebellius Pollio, and Flavius Vopiscus. The influence of Suetonius's *Lives of the Caesars* is obvious, although these works were probably not a continuation of the *Lives*.

Such a question is only one of many concerning the *Historia Augusta*. Doubts as to the accuracy of the accounts, the number of actual authors, the reliability of the documents, changes made in the manuscripts, and the dating of their original composition have left authorities with little option but to form theories based on the most verifiable evidence. The amount of conjecture, coupled with the obvious falsification of sources and documents, rendered the entire *Historia Augusta* suspect. This is unfortunate, because the writings stand as the principle mine of information on the third century C.E. and its

many emperors. The biographies for this era are especially dubious with regards to the so-called Thirty Tyrants and a vicious treatment of Gallienus. Thus, when used, care must be exercised.

See THIRTY TYRANTS.

scutarii A part of the imperial bodyguard founded by Diocletian to act as a substitute to the PRAETORIAN GUARD. The *scutarii* were based on the *Equite scutarii* of the era of Gallienus, who used them as a special cavalry corps. Diocletian promoted them to the bodyguard, recruiting their numbers from the Illyrian legions, making them more reliable than the Praetorians. From the time of Constantine the Great, the *scutarii* were probably attached to the SCHOLAE PALATINAE.

Scythia A very ancient land that was, according to Roman thinking, a vast territory extending from the Volga and the north of the BLACK SEA to the borders of India. While the Scythians actually occupied a smaller area than this, their traditionally nomadic lifestyle and brilliant use of the endless steppes made them for several centuries the masters of the Ukraine and the Caucasus. Originally they were a very mobile nation, living and traveling in the skin-covered wagons so typical of the yurts of the Steppe people and the Mongols. They were superb horsemen, dangerous warriors, and self-sacrificing in war. Over time, they cultivated fields of grain in the south of the Ukraine, and groups of them became settled in the Crimea. Such agricultural endeavors made them responsive to economic ties with inhabitants of parts of the other Black Sea coast, especially through THRACE and ASIA MINOR. The Scythian Empire was thus wealthy and considerable, dealing especially with the Greeks.

Unfortunately, pressures from the East drove the related SARMATIANS into conflict with the Scythians in the middle of the third century B.C.E. After bitter fighting the Scythians were defeated but retained their holdings in the Crimean Peninsula. Here they remained, continuing to play a trading role in the region. A number of Scythian-based tribes did journey west to the Danube frontier. One of the largest was the tribe of the Bastarnae, responsible for ravaging parts of Thrace in 30–29 B.C.E. They were defeated and their King Deldo killed by Marcus CRASSUS (2) in 29 B.C.E. Other Scythians remained in the Danubian territory, some supplying troops to Rome; CARACALLA had Scythian bodyguards.

Sebastianus (d. 378 C.E.) *Magister peditum in the East in 378*
Described by the historian Ammianus Marcellinus as a quiet, peace-loving man who was very popular with the troops, Sebastianus was appointed to the post of leader in EGYPT in 356–358, giving support to Bishop George of ALEXANDRIA and the Arians, and removing all orthodox fol-

lowers of Athanasius, probably at the demand of the pro-Arian Emperor CONSTANTIUS II. Sebastianus next appeared in the service of JULIAN in 363, in the Persian Campaign before joining VALENTINIAN I on his trip to the West in 364. As one of the emperor's generals, he took part in operations against the Alamanni in 368, and, with MEROBAUDES, against the Quadi in 375. With the death of Valentinian in that year, the jealous Merobaudes sent Sebastianus, who was ignorant of the emperor's demise, to a post so far removed as to ensure no interference with the succession.

By 378 he held the rank of *magister peditum*, through the influence of Emperor VALENS, who requested his help in the battle against the GOTHS. While accounts differ as to the circumstances of his departure for the East (several mention the intrigues of the eunuchs in the West), his services were welcomed by the ruler of the East. Despite successes against the Goths in THRACE, he advised Valens not to wait for Gratian to arrive with reinforcements but to attack the barbarians immediately. His counsel was followed, with the result being the battle of ADRIANOPLE. Sebastianus was among the dead in the disaster.

Secundus, Pedanius (fl. first century C.E.) *Prefect of the city in 61 C.E.*

Secundus was murdered by his own slave. The case was of great public interest because of the old law that stipulated that in case of such a crime all of the slaves in the house should be put to death. When the soldiers arrived to carry out the punishment, a mob prevented them with stones. Emperor NERO then rebuked the people and ordered the executions to go forth.

See also SLAVERY.

Secundus, Petronius (d. 98 C.E.) *Prefect of the Praetorian Guard with Norbanus during the reign of Domitian*

In 96, he became a member of the plot to murder the emperor, joining his colleague and Domitia, the empress. Following Domitian's assassination, Secundus was replaced by Casperius AELIANUS, who incited the Praetorians to revolt and demand revenge for the dead emperor. Despite his friendship with Nerva, the new ruler, Secundus had to be handed over for execution by his own soldiers in 98.

Segovia

A town in Spain situated in the region of the Guadarrama Mountains in Hispania Lusitania. Segovia possessed one of the finest aqueducts in the Roman Empire. Built in the late first or second century C.E., the aqueduct carried water into the town from a nearby source at Rufrio and included an architecturally brilliant bridge over a steep valley.

Seine

River known as the Sequana to the local Celtic tribe of the SEQUANI; one of the main rivers in Gaul (GALLIA), it played a major role in trade and communications within the provinces of Tres Galliae. Cutting across Gallia Lugdunensis, the Seine, which rises near Dijon and flows northwestward to the English Channel, provided the Romans with a wide river and tributaries for waterborne traffic throughout the whole province and into Gallia Belgica. This system was one of the secrets to Gaul's success in trade and industry.

Sejanus, Lucius Aelius (c. 20 B.C.E.–31 C.E.) *Prefect of the Praetorian Guard from 14 to 31 C.E.*

One of the most ambitious yet enigmatic figures of the first century C.E., Sejanus, the son of the successful Equestrian Lucius STRABO, was born in Volsinii (modern Tuscany) and used family connections to have himself adopted by the Aelians, perhaps by Aelius Gallus, the prefect of Egypt. With his father and adoptive father, as well as his respected brothers, Sejanus was perfectly positioned to embark upon a glorious career.

One of his first posts was with Gaius CAESAR during the prince's posting to the East (1 B.C.E.–4 C.E.). After Gaius died Sejanus joined the staff of Tiberius before receiving the appointment as co-prefect of the Praetorian Guard with his father in 14 C.E. Soon, at the request of TIBERIUS (now emperor), Lucius Strabo took up the position of prefect of Egypt, and Sejanus became the sole master of the Praetorians. He made himself absolutely indispensable to Tiberius, acting as his workhorse and loyal supporter, while slowly amassing political influence. By having his own minions appointed to key positions he soon was the equal of virtually any other official of state. He was pleased by the death of GERMANICUS in 19, seeing it as the perfect chance to rid himself of the legitimate heirs to the throne, the children of Germanicus and DRUSUS (3), Tiberius's son.

Drusus was murdered in 23, probably by poison after Sejanus had seduced his wife Livilla. The party of Germanicus followed. AGRIPPINA THE ELDER and her sons, NERO and DRUSUS (2) were removed in 29, and their friends and allies faced condemnation, exile, or death. Tiberius secretly abetted Sejanus's annihilation of his enemies, receiving continued signs of the prefect's loyalty, first in 22, when Sejanus helped extinguish the fire in the Theater of Pompey, and then in 26, when the roof caved in at the grotto of SPELUNCA. There he leaped upon the emperor, shielding his body from the rocks.

Tiberius was ready to listen when the prefect had ideas for improving the principate. In 23, Sejanus received permission to centralize the cohorts of the Praetorian Guard in Rome, thereby creating the CASTRA PRAETORIA that brought so much unhappiness to the city. His statues appeared everywhere in the provinces, and Tiberius referred to him as *adjutor imperii,* or "imperial aide." Those seeking promotions or favors looked to him for help or patronage. A triumph came in 26, when he convinced Tiberius to depart from Rome to Capri. There he could keep close watch over the emperor while continuing to build his own strength in the capital.

Sejanus then asked for permission to marry Livilla, Drusus's widow; Tiberius denied him this reward, offering, instead, permission to marry Julia, Livilla's daughter. The betrothal was announced in 31. Sejanus was at the height of his power, serving as CONSUL and accepting the fearful respect of the Senate.

Perhaps through the warnings of Antonia, Claudius's mother, or because of his own sense of intrigue, Tiberius wakened to the threat of Sejanus. In a carefully laid plot he trapped the prefect in 31, having him arrested, taken to the dungeon of TULLIANUM and there executed. His three children, two sons and a daughter, were also slain. The daughter, being under age, was raped to make her eligible and then executed. They joined their father at the base of the GEMONIAN STAIRS. APICATA, Sejanus's divorced wife, was spared but committed suicide. A bloodbath ensued as the clients of Sejanus were hunted down without mercy.

There has been considerable debate as to the ultimate aim of Sejanus. He was destroyed before any plans could come to fruition, but through his work the principate was made absolute, the Praetorians awakened to their political potential and the prefectship of the Guard was made powerful.

Seleucia   A great and ancient city in Babylonia, on the Tigris River, near modern Baghdad. Seleucia was for many years the capital of the entire region until the rise of CTESIPHON. Despite its political decline at the hands of the Parthians, the city did not lose its prestige or importance in terms of trade. Seleucia retained its independence during the years of the Parthian Empire and was probably at the heart of numerous internal conspiracies and power struggles for the throne in the first century B.C.E. and C.E. Because of its location on the Tigris, Seleucia was one of the targets of Roman attack in any campaign against PARTHIA and later PERSIA. By the fourth century C.E. and the Persian War of Julian, the city was virtually deserted. The name Seleucia was used for other cities in the East, founded in the Greek style.

Senaculum   Name given to the Women's Senate established by Emperor ELAGABALUS around 218 or 219 C.E. Traditionally the Romans had what was called the *conventus matronalis,* a Republican board of matrons who concerned themselves with questions of social or political etiquette. A *senaculum* was originally the meeting place of the senators when the SENATE was not in session. Elagabalus thus took this title and applied it to the *conventus matronalis,* when he empowered it with certain privileges, mainly the formal recognition of their decisions. They met on the Quirinal Hill.

Senate   One of the oldest institutions in Rome, serving as a leading element in the emergence of the Republic from a minor political entity in Italy to the most powerful state in the world. This august body suffered degradations in the first century B.C.E. at the hands of Sulla and Julius CAESAR, and by the reign of AUGUSTUS (27 B.C.E.–14 C.E.) it was a mere instrument in the hands of the emperors. Although there would be moments of achievement during the imperial epoch, the Senate's era of glory had passed.

As the first emperor, Augustus was shrewd enough to retain to the furthest possible degree the trappings of the Republic, including the Senate. Once he had cleansed it and made it his own through ADLECTIO (enrollment) and censorial privilege, he returned to it extensive powers. The Senate was still in charge of the AERARIUM (state treasury), governed or administered all provinces outside the control of the emperor, including Italy, retained the privilege of minting all copper COINAGE, and eventually had legal and legislative rights. One by one, however, its original duties were curtailed or usurped by the rulers. The aerarium was one of the first to go as the Senate grew utterly dependent upon the goodwill of the PRINCEPS. The emperor heeded the advice of the senators selectively and even the election of magistrates, which passed to the Senate from the people, was merely a reflection of imperial wishes.

A serious blow to the Senate was the degree of supremacy exercised over the selection of its members by the emperors. As the PRINCEPS SENATUS, the ruler applied the gift of *adlectio* to appoint senators, while all candidates for the senatorial class were first approved by the palace. Nevertheless, the CURSUS HONORUM was intact, as senators were enrolled only after a long and possibly distinguished career in the military or government. High posts throughout the empire were often filled with them, a situation concretized by the transformation of the senatorial class into a hereditary one.

Clearly the Senate still had much to contribute to the Roman state. To be a senator was one of the greatest honors attainable in the empire, and even the *magistri militum* of the late empire wanted to be members. The emperors referred many legal cases to the body, as it began hearing those trials once brought before the *comitia.* All kinds of crimes were presented: capital, MAIESTAS (treason), financial improprieties, and appeals. In the second century C.E. any appeal decided by the Senate could not be taken to the emperor for further consideration.

Other legislative functions passed into its hands. Through the SENATUS CONSULTUM the enactments of the Senate were declared fully law after the rule of HADRIAN. Further, they could debate many aspects of imperial policy, expressing the opinions of the senatorial order, popular views, or the fears of the upper classes. Emperors always sought the Senate's official granting of the *princeps* with the IMPERIUM.

Ironically, all of these roles were fulfilled wholly in a manner pleasing to the imperial court. Thus, laws were promulgated as per the desires of the emperor, trials always ended with a condemnation or an acquittal as was expected, and a successor to the throne usually was accepted because he possessed the most legions. A fascinating exception to this came in 238 C.E., when the Senate condemned MAXIMINUS I THRAX, first elevating GORDIAN I in Africa but later naming two senators, PUPIENUS and BALBINUS. Through the activity of the senators, Maximinus was killed. Unfortunately, neither Balbinus nor Pupienus carried enough political power to prevent their own assassinations after a reign of barely 100 days. An emperor could run the empire quite effectively, either on good terms with the Senate (as in the case of TRAJAN) or on poor terms (as did HADRIAN). It mattered very little.

Increased centralization during the second century C.E., the full development of the CONSILIUM PRINCIPIS, and the transfer of legal jurisdiction in many areas to both the PREFECT OF THE CITY and the Praetorian prefect, debilitated the Senate even more. In time all that remained was the distinct privilege of being a senator. There were many social advantages. Members wore a tunic with a broad purple stripe (the *latus clavus*) in front, woven into the material. They were given a short boot with a letter "C" on the front, meaning *centum* for the first 100 members. Senators were also honored with a feast, and vast wealth could be accumulated but was necessary because of the expenditure made while in office. The taxes on properties were crushing.

Aside from its normal schedule, the Senate could be convened at the will of the emperor by virtue of his position as *princeps senatus*. Whereas the number necessary for a legal assembly was 400, this was ended by Augustus, who made the figure dependent upon the importance of a subject. Political impotence and apathy combined to drive down attendance so that in time a mere 70 senators constituted an assembly.

Membership was for centuries exclusively Roman, becoming diluted slightly in the Republic's last stages with Italians entering. During the empire, the fully Roman provinces made their contributions, especially HISPANIA and GALLIA NARBONENSIS. As with the family of Septimius SEVERUS, Africans took part by the late second century, as did deserving wealthy candidates from the East.

Much as Augustus had chosen the Senate to be a recipient of superficial aggrandizement, so too did CONSTANTINE the Great three centuries later. Through the interweaving of the Equestrian Order (EQUITES) with that of the senatorial, there was a caste of officials for many administrative positions in the vast bureaucracy of the later imperial government. With such a large pool of candidates, the Senate in Rome increased in size but continued to lack real power as a body, mainly because of the creation of the Senate of Constantinople. The new Senate was made the equal of Rome in 359 C.E. It too had no real sway in the working of either empire, East or West.

It was a strange twist of fate that the Senate of Rome should outlive the emperors. That happened when Odoacer ended the reign of Romulus Augustulus in 476 C.E., terminating the Western Empire. He kept alive the Senate, liking its capacity to legitimize his own regime. The barbarian successors to Odoacer felt the same, at least until 603, when the Senate was last mentioned. Senators in the West showed the final embers of independence in the fourth and fifth centuries by defending their ancient paganism, most notably the Altar of Victory in the Curia. The Senate of CONSTANTINOPLE remained until the ninth century.

senatus consultum   The power of the Senate to make a declaration of its opinion to the magistrates of the state and thus influence law. In the days of the Republic, the *senatus consultum* was enacted by the consent of the senatorial body; while officially it was not law, the pronouncement carried with it the AUCTORITAS (authority) of the Senate. Thus the *senatus consultum* could be viewed as binding upon the people of Rome. As an instrument of imperial rule, the *senatus consultum* was changed first under Augustus and later under Hadrian. From the Augustan principate, the decree was far more potent legally, and henceforth bore the names of the CONSULS or other high figures. During the reign of Hadrian, the *senatus consultum,* included in praetor's edicts, came to be considered direct law. Through it, the emperor could change administrative systems or decide religious questions or other laws. The letters "S.C.," for *senatus consultum,* appeared normally on Roman imperial coins of the brass or copper species as that was under the care of the Senate. The letters did not appear on the imperial coinage of gold or silver, displaying the differentiation between the Senate and emperors in terms of minting.

Seneca (Lucius Annaeus Seneca) (c. 5–65 C.E.)
Poet, writer, major literary figure, and Stoic philosopher
Seneca was the son of SENECA THE ELDER and was born at Cordova, Spain. Taken to Rome as a youth, he studied rhetoric and philosophy while using the reputation of his father and the connections of his aunt to begin a senatorial career. Made a quaestor in 32, Seneca quickly acquired his own name as an orator and master of the pen, earning the jealous attack from GAIUS CALIGULA of being a "textbook orator" and "sand without lime." Having survived the despotism of Gaius, he was suddenly exiled to Corsica in 41 by Emperor CLAUDIUS, most likely at the urging of Empress MESSALLINA. While the cause is unclear, Seneca took the banishment quite poorly, and in un-Stoic letters to Polybius, an influential freedman, he pleaded for an end to the exile. This came only in 49 when AGRIPPINA THE YOUNGER, now the most powerful figure in the palace, had him brought back to tutor her son, NERO. PRAETOR in 50, Seneca and the Praetorian pre-

fect Burrus were the two main ministers in Nero's government upon Claudius's death in 54. Through their influence the first years of the Neronian principate were stable, marked only by the graceless decline of Agrippina and Seneca's subtle reduction of her authority until her murder in 59, in which the minister was a passive participant.

Increasingly, Nero proved difficult to control, and both Seneca and Burrus lost political ground. With Burrus's death in 62 it was only a matter of time before the emperor decided that Seneca had outlived his usefulness. Of advancing age, Seneca retired, settling on his estates in Campania, as Nero sank into tyranny. In 65, Seneca, perhaps wrongly, was implicated in the PISONIAN CONSPIRACY and was allowed to choose the method of his death, settling finally, after a few failed attempts, on a lethal vapor bath. Twice married, his second wife was Pompeia Paulina.

Seneca had been attacked as a writer for being too eager a proponent of the gaudiness of the Silver Age of Roman literature. His was a conscious rejection of the past greatness of the Augustan Age, dressing his prose in an affected and overly decorated style. Nevertheless, the sheer volume of his work, stretching from prose to poetry, including satire, scientific studies, and letters, is astounding.

Dialogi The dialogues of Seneca, written between 37 and 41 C.E., can be divided into two categories, philosophical examinations and consolations. His philosophic dialogues were: *De Providentia* (On providence); *De constantia spientis* (On the constancy of the philosopher); *De Ira* (On anger); *De Vita Beata* (On the happy life), incomplete; *De Otio* (On leisure); *De Tranquillitate Animi* (On the tranquility of the spirit); *De Brevitae Vita* (On the brevity of life). Three *consolationes*, *Ad Polybium*, *Ad Marciam* and *Ad Helviam*, were addressed to POLYBIUS, MARCIA, and Helvia, his mother.

Other Prose Works Three treatises were composed that fell out of the scope of the *Dialogi*. They were: *de clementia* (On clemency), written in 55–56 and surviving only in part, stressing the need for mercy in a ruler; *de beneficiis* (On benefits), in seven books written after 56, covering benefits available to individuals; and *Naturales Quaestiones* (Natural questions), possibly 62–64, addressed to Lucilius and discussing many phenomena of nature.

Epistulae morales 124 moral letters, in 20 books, were also addressed to Lucilius, presenting various aspects of Stoic and philosophical doctrine (64–65). There were once more than those now extant.

Satire Seneca's adaptation of the Menippean Satire, combining verse and prose, was used in his *Apocolocyntosis*, the so-called Pumpkinification. Composed as a lampoon of Claudius's *apotheosis* (deification) in 54, the work was both bitter and deliberately cruel.

Tragedies As a poet, Seneca specialized in tragedies. He authored nine of them from the years 49 to 62. They were: *Hercules (Furens)*, *Troades*, *Phoenissae*, *Medea*, *Phaedra*, *Oedipus*, *Agamemnon*, *Thyestes*, and *Hercules Oetaeus*. A tenth, *Octavia*, was once ascribed to him but is generally considered the work of someone else. It is the only surviving *praetexta* (Roman tragic drama).

Suggested Readings: Seneca. *Apocolocyntosis*. Bryn Mawr, Pa.: Thomas Library, Bryn Mawr College, 1988; ———. *De Clementia*. Edited by F. Prechac. Paris: Les Belles Lettres, 1961; ———. *Epistulae*. Edited by L. D. Reynolds. Oxford: Clarendon Press, 1965; ———. *Hercules: The Madness of Hercules*. Translated by Ranjit Bolt. London: Oberon, 1999; ———. *17 Letters*. Translated by C. D. N. Costa. Warminster, U.K.: Aris & Phillips, 1988; ———. *Medea*. Translated by Frederick Ahl. Ithaca, N.Y.: Cornell University Press, 1986; ———. *Moral and Political Essays*. Translated by John M. Cooper and J. F. Procopé. Cambridge, U.K.: Cambridge University Press, 1995; ———. *Oedipus of Lucius Annaeus Seneca*. Translated by Michael Elliot Rutenberg. Wauconda, Ill.: Bolchazy-Carducci Publishers, 1998; ———. *Phaedra*. Edited by Michael Coffey and Roland Mayer. New York: Cambridge University Press, 1990; ———. *Seneca's Phoenissae: Introduction and Commentary*. Edited by Marica Frank. New York: E. J. Brill, 1995; ———. *The Tragedies*. Translated by David R. Slavitt. Baltimore: Johns Hopkins University Press, 1992–1995; Share, Don, ed. *Seneca in English*. New York: Penguin Books, 1998.

Seneca the Elder (Lucius Annaeus Seneca) (c. 55 B.C.E.–41 C.E.) *Rhetorician, writer, father of Seneca and Annaeus Mela and grandfather of Lucan*

Seneca was born in Cordova, Spain, to an Equestrian family, spending most of his life in Rome. The details of his life, beyond his marriage to Helvia, a Spanish woman, and his vast accumulated wealth, are unclear. He was, however, a prolific writer. He authored a (lost) history of the important events of his era but also penned from memory a vital collection on the declaimers. Dedicated to his sons, the compilation contained 10 books of *Controversiae* and seven books on *Suasoriae*. Each of the *Controversiae* had a preface, surveying various orations. Unfortunately, only a few excerpts survived. A fourth-century–C.E. Christian abridgement made a little more available, preserving the prefaces for Books 1, 2, 3, and 4. Even fewer of the *Suasoriae* are extant. Of the seven books but a few epigrams are known. As a writer, Seneca revealed himself as capable of humor and careful thought.

Senecio, Claudius (d. 65 C.E.) *Son of a freedman*
In the service of the emperors and a confidant of
Emperor NERO, Senecio joined OTHO in 55 C.E., another
friend of the ruler, in the conspiracy to hide Nero's affair
with the woman ACTE. He apparently fell out of favor (as
did Otho) and next appeared as a member of the PISO-
NIAN CONSPIRACY to murder Nero in 65. Discovered,
Senecio was promised a pardon by his former patron.
He thus revealed name after name but was put to death
anyway.

Senecio, Herennius (d. c. 93 C.E.) *An* advocatus *and
biographer from Hispania Baetica*
Senecio never pursued a public career beyond the office
of QUAESTOR but was highly successful in his legal pursuits. He also authored a work on HELVIDIUS PRISCUS and
was probably put to death by Emperor DOMITIAN for it.

Senecio, Sosius (fl. late first century C.E.) *Consul in 99
and 107 C.E.; a confidant of Trajan*
Senecio earned from Trajan a statue in his honor in 110.
He was also a friend of PLINY THE YOUNGER and was the
recipient of several dedications by Plutarch in his *Lives*.
Little else is known of him.

Sentius, Gnaeus (fl. early first century C.E.) *Successor
to Gnaeus Calpurnius Piso as governor of Syria in 19 C.E.*
Sentius was chosen by the legates and senators in Syria to
assume control of the province following the death of
GERMANICUS. He proved very firm, refusing to give Piso
any favors and even sent the alleged prisoner, Martina, to
Rome to take part in the inevitable trial against Piso and
his wife, PLANCINA. When the former governor attempted
to reclaim his office, Sentius defeated his plans, placing
him on a ship for Rome.

Septemviri   The so-called Board of the Seven, one of
the leading PRIESTHOODS of ROME. Originally known as
the Epulones, they were created in 196 C.E. to aid the
PONTIFICES in their duties. Specifically, they organized
the banquets (the *epulum*) on the Capitoline Hill in
honor of the Capitoline deities. Later the Collegium
Epulonum assumed the task of superintending the public amusements whenever the SENATE ceremoniously
dined on the Capitoline, normally as part of the *ludi
Romani*.

When founded, the priests were known as the *tresviri
epulones* as there were three of them. This number was
increased to seven, and the name Septemviri Epulones
was henceforth used, even after Julius Caesar had added
three more members. The Septemviri were still in existence in the fourth century but eventually faded in the
wake of Christianity.

See LUDI and PAGANISM.

Sequani   One of the large tribes inhabiting GALLIA Belgica in the first century B.C.E. They suffered very severe
deprivations at the hands of the chieftain ARIOVISTUS and
welcomed his defeat by Rome. Through a broad alliance
with the Germans, however, they succeeded in acquiring
supremacy over the federated tribes of the AEDUI. This
brief reign was ended by Caesar's conquests in Gallia Belgica. Subsequently their territory along the Seine was part
of the Roman province of Gaul. The district of the
Sequani was called Maxima Sequanorum.

Serapis   Deity who became a fixture in the pantheon of
Ptolemaic EGYPT and was later popular throughout the
Roman Empire. Serapis (also Sarapis) was created
through the patronage of Ptolemy 1 of Egypt, who combined the Memphite religious idea concerning the spirit
of the APIS Bull with Osiris, lending body to the new deity
with a huge statue. The worship of Serapis became connected with that of other, more Greek deities, especially
Zeus. Manifestations varied, depending upon the preference of the worshipers. He was Aesclepius, and hence
god of healing, or Jupiter, supreme god, or even Osiris-
Hades-Pluton as the god of death. The popularity of Serapis during the Republic and the early imperial age was
limited to Egypt and to parts of Greece. With the spread
of other cults, however, especially Serapis's superior rival,
ISIS, the cult found fertile ground in Mediterranean ports,
in the East and finally in the West. A temple to the divinity was constructed in York (*see* BRITANNIA) while the
famed Serapeum in ALEXANDRIA, with its host of cultic
altars, served as the center for the Roman world.

ROME did not grant permission for Serapis to enter
the city until the reign of GAIUS CALIGULA (c. 37 C.E.).
Henceforth the emperors of the first and second centuries
C.E. supported Serapis enthusiastically. By the third century Romans were ardent believers, most notably in the
so-called Zeus-Helios-Serapis or Serapis, the Sun god
Jupiter. This form lasted until the annihilation of the cult
by Christians in the fourth century. The destruction of
the Serapeum in Alexandria was one of the mortal blows
to organized PAGANISM in the Roman Empire.

Serena (d. 408 C.E.) *Niece of Emperor Theodosius I and
wife of the* magister militum *Stilicho*
Extremely unpopular in the courts of both ROME and
CONSTANTINOPLE, Serena wed Stilicho sometime before
385, bearing him children who were to be linked by marriage to the imperial household: Maria and Aemilia
Materna Thermantia both married HONORIUS, while a son
was mentioned as a possible husband to GALLA PLACIDIA.
Her general treatment of pagans and her ambitions for
her husband were enough to cause lasting dislike. When
Stilicho was murdered in 408, she was put to death,
mainly out of fear of her dealings with the VISIGOTHS'
King ALARIC.

Servianus, Julius (Lucius Julius Ursus Servianus)
(d. 136 C.E.) *Consul in 90, 120, and 134 C.E.*

Servianus was generally considered the heir apparent during the reign of HADRIAN (117–138). Like his great patron, Emperor TRAJAN, Servianus was a Spaniard, attaining the trust of both Trajan and his predecessor, NERVA. Appointed by Nerva in 98 to the governorship of Germania Inferior, he already possessed great political power as a senator. Trajan used Servianus extensively, naming him governor of PANNONIA and granting him important commands against the Dacians. He became a member of the imperial family by marrying Domitia Paulina, sister of Hadrian. By 136, Hadrian was increasingly ill and looking for a successor. Servianus was too old at 90 to be considered but not so feeble as to be viewed as no longer a threat to stability. To ensure a smooth transition of power, Hadrian ordered his death and that of his grandson, Gnaeus Fuscus. It was reported that Servianus exclaimed before his execution that "my only prayer is that Hadrian lingers for a long time, praying for death but unable to die."

Servius (fl. early fifth century C.E.) *Grammarian*
Servius was included by MACROBIUS in the *Saturnalia* and authored a major work on VIRGIL. The commentaries on Virgil are extant in two versions. The first, certainly by the hand of Servius, was a short treatise centering on the grammar, diction, and style of Virgil, while the second was longer, with additions and quotations of other writers. Called the *schola Danielis,* it was probably composed much later by a Christian. Servius himself was possibly a pagan.

sestertius (Also *sestertii* or *sesterces*)
One of the major species of Roman imperial COINAGE; the main coin of silver, worth approximately one-quarter the value of the DENARIUS. Originally issued during the Republic, its first minting was traditionally set in 296 B.C.E., when it bore a worth of two asses. With the monetary reforms of Emperor Augustus, the sestertius replaced the AS as a silver coin. Subsequently it was the most widely distributed money in the Roman Empire, earning the name *nummus* or the "coin." It suffered in the economic crisis of the third century C.E. and was dropped altogether as a form of currency after the usurper Postumus made a last issue during the years 259–267.

Severa, Aquilia *See* ELAGABALUS.

Severa, Aurelia (d. 213 C.E.) *One of the four Vestal Virgins put to death by Emperor Caracalla in 213 C.E.*
Along with Pomponia Rufina and Clodia Laeta, she was buried alive for crimes of unchastity.
See also CANNUTIA CRESCENTIA.

Samples of *sestertius (Courtesy Warren Esty)*

Severianus, P. Aleius (fl. late second century C.E.) *Roman legate in Armenia in 161 C.E.*
He was notable for his complete failure in preventing the invasion of the country by VOLOGASES III of PARTHIA and for leading virtually an entire legion to its destruction near Elegeia. His resounding defeat brought Lucius VERUS to the East, precipitating a major war with Parthia in 163.
See ARSACID DYNASTY.

Severus (1) *See* CELER AND SEVERUS.

Severus (2) (fl. first century C.E.) *Prefect of Egypt during the reign of Tiberius, in 32 C.E.*
Also called Hiberus, he did not come from the usual ranks of the Equestrians (EQUITES) but was a freedman. This was a singularly unusual appointment.

Severus I *See* SEVERUS, SEPTIMIUS.

Severus II (Flavius Valerius Severus) (d. 307 C.E.) *Joint emperor from 306 to 307*
Severus was an Illyrian soldier and a close friend of Emperor GALERIUS. When Galerius was promoted from Caesar to Augustus in 305 (*see* TETRARCHY) he nominated Severus as his replacement. This move gave Galerius a powerful hold over the Roman Empire, for the other Caesar, Maximinus II Daia, was also a supporter. The new Augustus, CONSTANTIUS I CHLORUS, was seemingly outnumbered. Severus's sphere of control was Italy, AFRICA and, later, PANNONIA. One year later, Constantius died in Britain, and Galerius used his authority to elevate Severus to the rank of Augustus in the West. Constantine, Constantius's son, was appointed as his Caesar. This infuriated MAXENTIUS, the son of the old Augustus, Maximian. In 307 Maxentius found allies in Rome and was proclaimed

emperor. Galerius sent instructions to Severus to march from Milan to Rome. His campaign was a disaster. Retreating to Milan, he surrendered to Maximian, who had come out of retirement. Galerius took to the field, and upon his entering Italy Severus was put to death by his captors.

Severus, Lucius Catilius (fl. second century C.E.)
Consul in 110 and 120 C.E.
An imperial officer and the greatgrandfather of MARCUS AURELIUS, Severus was of a distinguished senatorial family, embarking on a highly successful career as proconsul of Asia, *praefectus aerari militaris, praefectus aerari Saturni* and legate of CAPPADOCIA from 114 to 117, where he fought in TRAJAN's Parthian campaign. In favor with HADRIAN, he was put in charge of SYRIA in 117, holding the post until around 119. After serving as consul for a second time, he was made proconsul of AFRICA before being appointed PREFECT OF THE CITY in 138. Upon the adoption of Antoninus Pius as Hadrian's heir, Severus was reportedly so disappointed at not being named that Hadrian removed him from his post.

Severus, Septimius (Lucius Septimus Severus)
(145–211 C.E.) *Emperor from 193 to 211 and founder of a dynasty that influenced the Roman Empire from 193 to 235*
Severus was born at LEPCIS MAGNA in Tripolitania, to Publius Septimius Geta and Fulvia Pia, both members of successful families in the Equestrians (EQUITES) and the SENATE. After an unclear early career he became a QUAESTOR of Rome around 169, later returning to Lepcis Magna, where he married Paccia Marciana, who died childless after several years. The TRIBUNE of the Plebeians in 174, he was PRAETOR in 177 and a legate in SYRIA by 180. Emperor COMMODUS removed him after approximately two years.

The major turning point in his advancement came in 184 when he was reinstated as an imperial favorite, receiving the post of governor of Gallia Lugdunensis and several years later of Sicily; he was also married, to the formidable Julia Domna, the Syrian noblewoman who gave him two sons, CARACALLA in 188 and GETA in 189. Consul in 190, he was made governor of PANNONIA Superior in 191. Severus was still there in 192 when Commodus was assassinated and succeeded by Pertinax. The new emperor did not last long, and his death in 193 resulted in the auctioning off of the empire by the PRAETORIAN GUARD to DIDIUS JULIANUS, the highest bidder. Knowing that the sanctity of the throne had been violated, that omens and prophecies had predicted his rise to the purple and that he had the perfect solution militarily, Severus accepted the *SALUTATIO* from his troops. Hailed at Carnuntum, he and his legions marched to ROME, where Didius Julianus was sentenced to death and executed by the Senate. Once in the capital he entrenched himself politically by disbanding the Guard and forming a new,

A gold aureus of Septimius Severus, struck 201 C.E. in Rome *(Courtesy Historical Coins, Inc.)*

larger one with the select soldiery of the Danubian legions. The VIGILES and URBAN COHORTS were increased in size as well.

His position as emperor was not universally accepted, for PESCENNIUS NIGER, governor of Syria, claimed the empire, and CLODIUS ALBINUS, governor of Britain, was another obvious candidate. To gain time against the more dangerous Niger, Severus offered Albinus the rank of Caesar, with the obvious implication that he would be the heir. Albinus accepted this position, allowing Severus to launch his war with Niger. Crushing the Eastern claimant at the battle of ISSUS in 194, Severus turned on Albinus in 196, and at LUGDUNUM (Lyons) the governor of Britain was destroyed. Severus was now sole master of the Roman world, but the civil war had caused great ruin, both in terms of fighting and in the political executions necessary to bring the Senate and bureaucracy under heel. Once he had liquidated all possible enemies, Caracalla was designated as his heir, later joined by Geta.

There was little time to enjoy the comforts of Rome for war with Parthia was deemed essential. From 197 to 199, he waged a successful war of vengeance against Parthia for its support of Niger. CTESIPHON, the capital, fell, and MESOPOTAMIA was seized and became a Roman province. Visits to Syria and Africa ended in 203 with a triumphal return to Rome. In celebration of his tenth imperial year, two arches were erected, one in Lepcis Magna and the other in Rome. The gift to Lepcis was typical of his attentions to African cities, especially his hometown, which would know no brighter moment. From 203 until 207/8, Severus remained at Rome, falling under the influence of his own Prefect of the PRAETORIAN GUARD, PLAUTIANUS. Plautianus was allowed vast powers until 205, when Caracalla, who was forced to marry the prefect's daughter, led a coup that brought down the ambitious minister.

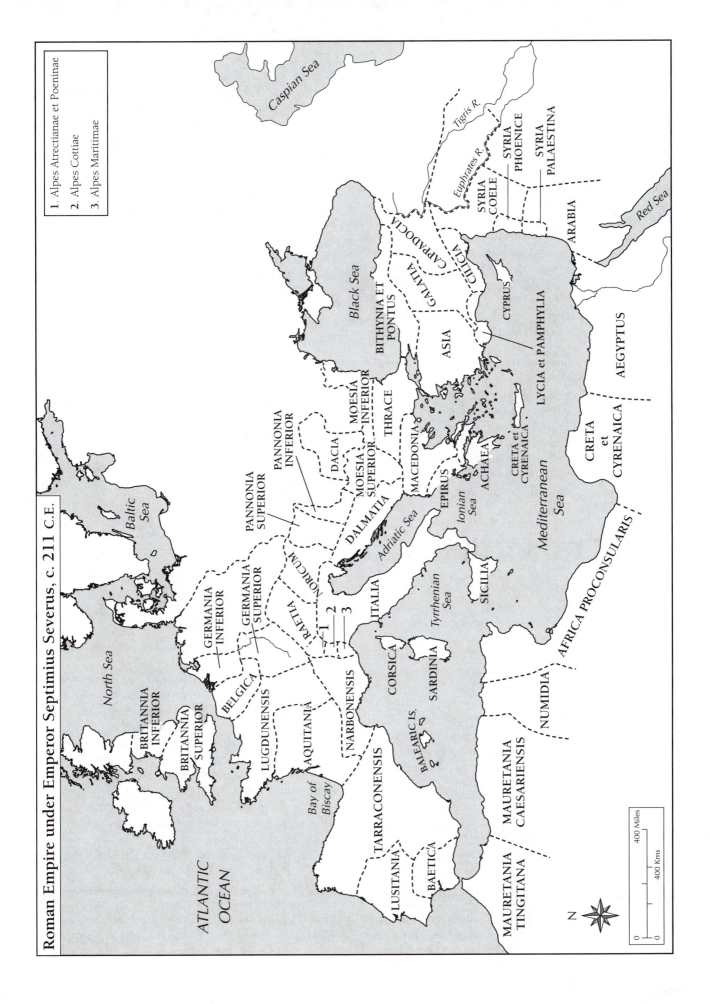

Roman Empire under Emperor Septimius Severus, c. 211 C.E.

1. Alpes Atrectianae et Poeninae
2. Alpes Cottiae
3. Alpes Maritimae

Caspian Sea

Baltic Sea

North Sea

ATLANTIC OCEAN

BRITANNIA INFERIOR

BRITANNIA SUPERIOR

BELGICA

GERMANIA INFERIOR

GERMANIA SUPERIOR

LUGDUNENSIS

AQUITANIA

Bay of Biscay

NARBONENSIS

RAETIA

NORICUM

1
2
3

ITALIA

PANNONIA SUPERIOR

PANNONIA INFERIOR

DACIA

DALMATIA

MOESIA SUPERIOR

MOESIA INFERIOR

Black Sea

THRACE

Adriatic Sea

MACEDONIA

EPIRUS

Ionian Sea

ACHAEA

CORSICA

SARDINIA

Tyrrhenian Sea

SICILIA

BITHYNIA ET PONTUS

GALATIA

CAPPADOCIA

CILICIA

ASIA

LYCIA et PAMPHYLIA

CYPRUS

Euphrates R.

Tigris R.

SYRIA COELE

SYRIA PHOENICE

SYRIA PALAESTINA

ARABIA

Red Sea

Mediterranean Sea

CRETA et CYRENAICA

CRETA et CYRENAICA

AEGYPTUS

AFRICA PROCONSULARIS

NUMIDIA

MAURETANIA CAESARIENSIS

MAURETANIA TINGITANA

BALEARIC IS.

TARRACONENSIS

LUSITANIA

BAETICA

N

400 Miles
400 Kms
0
0

Troubles appeared in Britain as the local tribes, especially the Caledonians, had pushed beyond the WALL OF ANTONINUS. In 208, Severus and Caracalla invaded Caledonia while Julia Domna and Geta remained behind at Eburacum (York). Fighting relieved the pressure on the frontier but did not make a long-lasting impression. Planning another attack, Severus fell ill at Eburacum in 211 and died. He had taken care to promote Geta as Caracalla's equal, reportedly telling them both on his deathbed: "Cooperate with each other, pay the soldiers and hate everyone else." His plea was well in keeping with the policies of the Severan regime. The legions now numbered 33, with vast units of NUMERI or irregular troops. The army, especially the centurions and officers, was deliberately cultivated to be loyal totally to the central government—namely, the emperor himself. He had won the throne because of them and never forgot where his true source of authority rested.

Further, the power of the imperial administration was widened throughout the empire, as was seen in the field of law. When Plautianus fell, his replacements would include the eminent jurists ULPIAN and PAPINIAN. Both did much to improve Roman legalism while Julia Domna kept alive intellectualism and artistry in the midst of a seemingly martial reign. Ultimately, Severus helped provide enough stability to the empire to ensure its survival, even in the hands of Caracalla and in the crises of the third century C.E.

Suggested Reading: Birley, Anthony R. *Septimius Severus: The African Emperor.* New Haven, Conn.: Yale University Press, 1989.

Severus, Sextus Julius *Consul in 127 C.E.; governor in numerous provinces under Emperor Hadrian and general*
Severus was a member of the Equestrians (EQUITES) from Dalmatia. After serving as legate in MOESIA and CAPPADOCIA, he was sent to Britain as its governor. Known by Hadrian to be reliable, he was ordered (c. 132) to JUDAEA to take command of the legions there in the campaign to suppress the rebellion of Simon BAR COCHBA. From 132 to 135 he waged a ruthless but successful campaign in PALAESTINA, crushing the uprising while devastating the prince. With pacification complete, he was made the first governor of Syria Palestine.

Severus, Sulpicius (c. 363–420 C.E.) *Christian historian*
Born in Aquitania, Severus came from a noble family, studying law before converting to CHRISTIANITY around 389. When his wife died in 392, he retired to the life of a monk, transforming his estates into an ascetic haven under the influence of St. MARTIN OF TOURS. After a brief involvement with Pelagianism, he died sometime around 420. He was the author of two important histories. One was a biography of St. Martin, composed during Martin's life but finished and published after the saint's death. The other, more important work, was a universal chronicle covering Christian events from creation to 400 C.E. In excellent Latin, it is a useful source on the events of the fourth century, especially Priscillianism (*see* PRISCILLIAN).

Severus Alexander, Marcus Aurelius (Marcus Julius Gessius Alexianus Bassianus) (208–235 C.E.)
Emperor from 222 to 235
Severus was born in a town in Phoenicia, the son of Gessius Marcianus and JULIA MAMAEA, the daughter of JULIA MAESA. As the cousin of Emperor ELAGABALUS, Severus Alexander received not only an education in being a priest of the sun god but also a stable and normal Roman upbringing. This was of importance as Elagabalus's eccentricities convinced Julia Maesa and Julia Mamaea that he had to be removed. Through Maesa's influence, Elagabalus adopted his younger cousin in 221, giving him the title Caesar and PRINCEPS JUVENTUTIS and the new name, Marcus Aurelius Severus Alexander. By 222 they were joint consuls, and Severus Alexander enjoyed greater popularity with the Senate and the PRAETORIAN GUARD. Elagabalus grew jealous, and his attempts at removing his cousin from power ended in his assassination by the Guard. Severus Alexander then assumed the throne.

It was the unfortunate image of the reign that Severus Alexander was dominated by the formidable women of the imperial palace, most notably the Julias. While they cultivated a series of sound policies, the apparent weakness of the emperor eventually cost him his life. Julia Maesa was at first the leading figure in the Roman Empire, until her death in 223. Shortly thereafter, the brilliant jurist and Praetorian Prefect ULPIAN was murdered by his own troops, and the imperial house lost an invaluable adviser.

Julia Mamaea stepped forward to direct policy. In 225 she arranged a marriage between her son and the noblewoman Barbia Orbiana. Within two years, however, the new empress had been driven out of Rome and her father put to death. Bearing the title AUGUSTA and Mother of the Emperor and the Camp and the Senate, Julia initiated in her son's name stern fiscal reforms to restore the financial strength of the Roman world. The SENATE was given a larger role in government and an enlarged CONSILIUM PRINCIPIS (council of advisers) provided advice.

All was not well on the frontiers, and the newly formed Persian Empire of the Sassanids required the emperor's attention. A campaign was waged in 232 with such success that upon his return to ROME Severus Alexander laid claim to the title of *bersicus maximus.* Word soon arrived from the DANUBE that the tribes in the region, especially the Alamanni, were threatening the provinces. The emperor and his mother set out in 234 with the legions but soon infuriated the troops by their insistence on negotiations. MAXIMINUS I THRAX was proposed as a rival for the throne, and the soldiers murdered both Severus Alexander and Julia Mamaea. His death signalled the age of the soldier emperors.

Sextus Caesar (d. 46 C.E.) *Cousin of Julius Caesar*
Sextus was appointed by the dictator to be the governor of SYRIA in 47 B.C.E. At his disposal was a legion to keep the peace, although the name of Caesar was far more valuable. Despite the support of the Jews, Quintus Caecilius BASSUS, an officer once in the service of POMPEY THE GREAT, arrived in 46. He stirred up the troops at Tyre, and in the resulting mutiny Sextus was killed.

Shapur I (d. 272 C.E.) *King of Persia; the second ruler of the Sassanid dynasty and the Persian Empire, from 241 to 272*
Assuming the throne at a time of great vitality in Persia and of instability in Rome, he was the son of the famous ARDASHIR, who died in 241. Although he was not crowned until 242, he immediately seized the initiative and campaigned against the numerous states within the Persian domain. With the title "king of kings," he then embarked upon a bitter war with the Roman Empire, from 241 to 244. Philip the Arab made peace with him. After subjugating the wild peoples of Media, he returned to the Roman provinces with an army. Armenia was invaded in 250 and SYRIA attacked two years later. With a combination of his power and the exploitation of Rome's weakness, Persian influence was spread over much of the East. Only Emperor VALERIAN, starting in 257, could march to oppose him. In 259–260, at the battle of EDESSA, the unlucky Valerian was captured, humiliated, and then put to death.

This major triumph was long remembered by the Persians. Shapur attempted to follow up this achievement with a direct assault upon ASIA MINOR, but in 262 a new opponent had emerged, ODAENATH of PALMYRA. The following years were filled with savage fighting, until (c. 267) ARMENIA had been lost and Shapur was in dire military straits. Defeats at the hands of Odaenath ended the king's ambitions for expansion.

Shapur was considered a cruel and grasping monarch. Nevertheless, he gave to his subjects a general freedom of worship, including the Christians and the Jews. The religious cult leader, Mani, found in Shapur an interested and sympathetic patron. Upon Shapur's death in 272, he left Hormazd ARDASHIR, his son, a stable government.

See also SASSANID DYNASTY.

Shapur II (d. 379 C.E.) *Ruler of the Persian Empire from 309 to 379*
Son of HORMAZD II, he came to the throne when still an infant. His mother acted as regent while relying upon the Persian nobility for political support. Growing up, Shapur kept in contact with Emperor CONSTANTINE the Great, sending embassies to him in 324 and 337. Upon reaching maturity, the King of Kings strove to gain total control of his empire, defeating the nobles who challenged his authority. Once possessing supremacy in the palace, he made war upon the Roman Empire, starting with an invasion of Mesopotamia around 336. Until 363, fighting continued, varying only in intensity or with brief rounds of peace. Battles raged over the East, in ARMENIA and MESOPOTAMIA, although a favorable treaty was secured from Jovian, following the death in the field of Emperor JULIAN in 363. He was succeeded by his brother, ARDASHIR II.

Shapur, III (d. 388 C.E.) *King of Persia from 383 to 388*
The son of SHAPUR II, he became ruler upon the overthrow of his uncle, ARDASHIR II, by the Persian nobility. His reign was notable for the peace that was made with Emperor THEODOSIUS I around 384–386.

See also PERSIA; SASSANID DYNASTY.

ships Seagoing vessels were improved and modernized during the imperial epoch as a result of Rome's expansion throughout the Mediterranean, the continued work of the Alexandrian shipbuilders and the large amounts of capital spent by Roman merchants. Although there were many differently rigged and designed vessels, most of them served either as merchant vessels or warships.

MERCHANT SHIPS

Traditionally, the vessels designed for commerce and trade were shorter, wider and of a heavier build than their military counterparts. Being stouter in design, such ships were more seaworthy in all weather, especially when filled with goods. As their purpose was purely economic, space was devoted to storage instead of weapons or implements of war. Oars were normally limited in number, as the crews were small. Merchantmen relied upon sails, using oars only for maneuvering in special situations or in an emergency. These limitations made merchant ships easy prey for a quick attack, even in convoys, although in a good wind and with enough warning sails made them faster. For defense they required assistance from the navy of Rome.

WARSHIPS

The Roman fleets that were created for the Punic Wars were, for the most part, based on Carthaginian design. CARTHAGE boasted the powerful ship called by Rome the quinquereme, or "Five," so named because of the five banks of oars used to propel it. By the end of the wars with Carthage, this was the principal design used by Roman builders. Afterward and up to the battle of ACTIUM, warships tended to be bigger and even heavier.

Octavian (AUGUSTUS) and his gifted admiral, Marcus AGRIPPA, chose to counter the heavy warships of Marc

A mosaic of a warship (right) and a trading vessel, from Ostia
(Courtesy Fr. Felix Just, S.J.)

ANTONY and Cleopatra off the coast of Actium in 31 B.C.E. with a new naval strategy. Agrippa's fleet was composed of faster, lighter triremes and the so-called *liburnicae,* vessels constructed by the builders of LIBURNIA in ILLYRICUM. Agrippa's brilliant tactics, the *HARPAX* (a special weapon for attacking and damaging enemy vessels) and the internal disorder of the Egyptian fleet contributed to Octavian's decisive victory. The battle of Actium ushered in a new era for the Roman world and signalled the supremacy of the trireme and *liburnicae* in the Roman imperial navy. These ships became the mainstay of the naval arm, although there were also smaller transports, privateers, and cutters, all of Greek design.

No longer concerned with massive warfare, Rome was now preoccupied with safeguarding the seas against infrequent but dangerous piratic activity and the defense of the merchants. This policy was successful only so long as the navy was capable of mounting operations. With the eventual deterioration of the navy, the Mediterranean and the north coast of Gallia and Germania became susceptible to aggressive piracy by the VANDALS of AFRICA and the SAXONS in GERMANIA, both in the fifth century C.E.

Typically, all warships were decorated with eyes painted on their bows just above the beak, the ram (*rostrum*) of three spikes used to smash an opponent or to destroy enemy oars. The *corvus* was attached to the bow during the Punic Wars; it was a boarding plank with another spike that connected the quinquereme to the enemy vessel. Agrippa's *harpax* replaced the *corvus,* proving more effective in combat, especially when used by the lighter ships in Octavian's fleet.

The trireme and the *liburnicae* were based on the older Greek *pentekontos,* which had reigned for centuries as the supreme weapon of naval warfare. On average, the trireme was some 110 feet long and 12 feet wide, with a crew of 200, not including detachments of marines. The quinquereme (also spelled quinquireme) was around 120 feet long and 20 feet wide, with a crew of 300, not including marines. If the quinquereme was big, the *deceres* was huge. This dreadnought was the fashion toward the end of the first century B.C.E. and could be considered the apex of massive ship building. It stretched 145 feet and was 20 feet wide, with a crew of nearly 600. Its value was limited tactically, as Antony, who had several at Actium, discovered. The triremes of Octavian and Agrippa proved victorious and set the naval standard for the next age.

Suggested Readings: D'Arms, John H., and Kopff, E. C., eds. *The Seaborne Commerce of Ancient Rome.* Rome: American Academy in Rome, 1980; Hodge, Peter. *Roman Trade and Travel.* London: Longman, 1978; Rodgers, William L. *Greek and Roman Naval Warfare; a Study of Strategy, Tactics, and Ship Design from Salamis (480 B.C.E.) to Actium (31 B.C.E.).* London: B. F. Stevens & Brown, Ltd, 1937; Starr, Chester G. *The Influence of Sea Power an Ancient History.* New York: Oxford University Press, 1989;———. *The Roman Imperial Navy, 31 B.C.–A.D. 324.* Ithaca, N.Y.: Cornell University Press, 1941; Warry, John. *Warfare in the Classical World.* Norman: University of Oklahoma Press, 1995.

Sibyl   Name given by the Romans to a famous group of prophetesses. By tradition, the first Sibyl (plural, Sibyllae) was the daughter of Dardanus and Neso. Subsequently, the number of her namesakes were placed at three, four, 10, and even 14. None of these other Sibyls could match in importance the one at Cumae in Italy. The Sibyl of Cumae offered to King Tarquinius Superbus nine books of prophecies for 300 gold pieces. This price was reached after she burned six of them. The remaining volumes became the SIBYLLINE BOOKS.

Sibylline Books   The legendary books of prophecy sold to King Tarquinius Superbus by the SIBYL of Cumae. Precisely when or how the Sybilline Books were written was never clear to the Romans, but the three volumes of prophetic verse became extremely important to the welfare of the Roman state. Entrusted to the quindecemviri, the Sibylline books were consulted at various times by the Senate. Whenever calamity, pestilence, unrest, or defeats took place, they were opened to determine the meaning of such events. Decisions of war or peace might be affected greatly by the poems inside, and the words of the Sibyl were taken seriously.

The Sibyllini Libri continued as a part of the life of the imperial era. In the care of the *quindecemviri,* the volumes were recopied in 18 B.C.E. at the order of Augustus as the original libri had been destroyed by fire in 83 B.C.E. Increasingly, however, the verses were not taken seriously, and by the end of the fourth century C.E., CHRISTIANITY attacked them as being obvious symbols of PAGANISM. Finally, during the reign of Emperor HONORIUS (395–423) the MAGISTER MILITUM STILICHO burned them. Interestingly, in the days of the empire a group of Jews and Christians produced their own version of the Sibylline Books, called the Sibylline Oracles.

Sicilia (Sicily) Province of the empire; the large island at the southern tip of Italia's boot. Sicilia was called Thrinacia or Trinacria, but was known to the Romans as Triquetra because of its shape; according to tradition, the first resident was the Cyclops. The beautiful, fertile island was contested by virtually every major Mediterranean culture, but the name Sicilia was derived from the tribe of the Siceli or Sicani. They were joined by Cretans, Phoenicians, Greeks, and Carthaginian colonists. The later seafaring states of Greek origin fought bitterly with CARTHAGE for years. Sicilia's western regions fell into Roman hands with the end of the First Punic War in 241 B.C.E., and the eastern part in 211 B.C.E. Sicilia, ROME's first imperial possession, was placed under the care of a PRAETOR and eventually a proconsul. Roman occupation was made somewhat easier by the granting of Latin rights (IUS LATII) by Caesar. AUGUSTUS placed limits on these but augmented the Latinization with full promotion to colonial status and the creation of numerous colonies of veterans.

The natural wealth and economic potential of the island were legendary. So rich in wheat and corn were its fields that it was known to be an abode of the goddess Ceres. There grains were produced in abundance, while other exports included fruits, almonds, honey, and wine. In purpose the province fulfilled a role similar to that of Sardinia, as a breadbasket for Italy and Rome. After the war of 36 B.C.E. and the defeat of Sextus POMPEY by Octavian (AUGUSTUS) and Marcus AGRIPPA, the island settled into a general tranquility for many years. SYRACUSE, an ancient city, was made the provincial capital. By the fifth century C.E., Roman protection had deteriorated. The VANDALS of GEISERIC attacked the province, and, after the fall of the Western Empire in 476, the OSTROGOTHS laid claim to it.

Sidonius Apollinaris (Gaius Sollius Apollinaris Sidonius) (c. 430–479 C.E.) *One of the last great orators and poets of the Roman Empire*
An associate of the final emperors of the West, and a superb panegyricist, Sidonius was born to a noble senatorial family at Lugdunum (Lyons), proving an excellent student. By marriage to Papianilla, daughter of Emperor AVITUS, he became connected to the imperial family when his father-in-law was crowned in July 455. In his honor, Sidonius delivered a panegyric on New Year's day, this latter receiving as a reward a statue in the Forum of Trajan. After the fall of Avitus, Sidonius eventually accepted the successor, MAJORIAN, composing another panegyric at Lugdunum in 458. He held some office in Rome until 461, when he returned to Gallia Lugdunensis. This semi-retirement was ended in 467 when he headed a delegation to the court of Anthemius. In early 468 he delivered a third panegyric and was made PREFECT OF THE CITY before going home. Offered the post of bishop of Auvergne in 469, he accepted, working to counter the influence of the advancing GOTHS. This opposition led to his brief imprisonment in 475, when the Gothic King

Euric was ceded Auvergne. Euric released him and even allowed him to return to his ecclesiastical duties. Tired and ill, Sidonius died around 479.

Sidonius Apollinaris was the author of more than these three panegyrics. In the *Carmina* these addresses were preserved (in reverse chronological order) along with a large number of poems. He also communicated with friends and associates, through *Letters*. In style he was neither original nor flawless, but he provided an important glimpse of life at the time of the dying Western Empire.

See also SYMMACHUS.

Silana, Junia (d. after 59 C.E.) *Wife of Gaius Silius (2)*
Silana was divorced her husband by the order of Empress MESSALLINA in 47 C.E.. She was, according to the historian Tacitus, a high-born, lovely woman, wealthy but abandoned. After the divorce she became a dear friend of AGRIPPINA THE YOUNGER. Their relationship soured in 55, when Agrippina, jealous of Silana's qualities, frightened away Sextius Africanus, a prospective husband. Vowing revenge, Silana used two clients, Iturius and Calvisius, to accuse Agrippina of planning to raise up Rubellius Plautus to the throne. Through a spirited defense Agrippina secured her acquittal and the punishment of the plotters. Silana was banished. After the death of Agrippina in 59, she was allowed to return to Italy, dying at her estates in Tarentum.

Silanus, D. Junius Torquatus (d. 64 C.E.) *Descendant of Augustus during the reign of Nero*
Silanus was put to death by the emperor. Nero killed him because he refused to allow members of the family of AUGUSTUS to survive in his reign.

See also RUBELLIUS PLAUTUS.

Silanus, Lucius Junius (d. 49 C.E.) *Praetor in 48 C.E.*
Silanus was the son of Aemilia Lepida and hence a descendant of AUGUSTUS. Although young, he was allowed to hold a magistracy five years before his time and was betrothed to OCTAVIA, daughter of CLAUDIUS. This proposed union was immediately attacked as dishonorable because of accusations that he had committed incest with his sister, Junia Calvina. A further threat came in the person of AGRIPPINA THE YOUNGER, who was conspiring to have her son Nero wed Octavia. Always impressionable, Claudius listened to the charges and terminated the betrothal. Silanus was then expelled from the SENATE and forced to resign from the praetorship. On the day of Claudius's wedding to Agrippina (in 49) he killed himself.

See also PRAETOR.

Silanus, M. Junius (d. 54 C.E.) *Brother of Lucius Junius Silanus, the Proconsul of Asia in 54*
He held the distinction of being the first victim of NERO's reign. The historian TACITUS reported that he died

because AGRIPPINA feared his reputation as being more capable as emperor than Nero. Nonetheless, Silanus was so sluggish that he had the nickname of "the golden Sheep." He had also been CONSUL in 46.

siliqua   A silver coin (plural, *siliquae*) issued from the time of CONSTANTINE the Great (c. 312 C.E.). It served as one of the foundations of the reorganized currency of the late empire, being worth approximately one–twenty-fourth the value of the gold SOLIDUS. *Siliquae* were minted for centuries after the fall of the Western Empire.

See also COINAGE.

Silius, Gaius (1) (d. 24 C.E.) *Consul in 13 C.E. and a legate of Germania Superior, from 14 to 21 C.E.*
One of the most competent generals in the service of Emperor TIBERIUS, in 15–16 he aided GERMANICUS in his German campaign, conducting operations against the CHATTI. In 21 he destroyed the rebel SACROVIR. For his victory over the Chatti he was awarded the triumphal insignia. Tiberius apparently resented his achievements, the loyalty of his troops to him personally and his friendship with GERMANICUS. Silius was charged with various offenses and committed suicide in 24.

Silius, Gaius (2) (d. 48 C.E.) *Son of Gaius Silius (1)*
Silius suffered an unhappy youth but was considered the most handsome man in Rome during the reign of CLAUDIUS. His good looks attracted the attention of Empress Valeria MESSALLINA, who, in 47, developed such a passion for him that he was forced to divorce his wife, Junia SILANA. Consul-designate, he seemingly joined their affair with ardor, and in 48, he and Messallina were married in a mock ceremony. The inevitable uproar brought down Messallina, and Silius went to his death without delay, asking only that it be swift.

Silius Italicus, Tiberius Catius Asconius (c. 26–101 C.E.) *Epic poet and author of the longest Latin work, the Punica*
Silius Italicus was probably from Spain but the place of his birth remains unclear. An accomplished orator, he was an associate of both PLINY THE YOUNGER and MARTIAL, attaining notoriety as a lawyer but also as an informer during the reign of Nero. CONSUL in 68, he was a supporter of VITELLIUS. Under the Flavians (69–96 C.E.) he held the post of proconsul of Asia (in 77), gaining praise for his stable regime. Retiring to Campania and ROME, Silius purchased an old estate of CICERO's, repaired VIRGIL's tomb and amassed a great collection of books. He died in a state of self-induced starvation because of a terminal illness. Silius Italicus probably began writing after his retirement, bringing a Stoic-influenced outlook to his work. In style he imitated very closely his contemporary, LUCAN, while relying on a disciplined technical method of versification. The *Punica* was a vast epic in 12,200 lines and 17 books, covering the Second Punic War. His main source was LIVY.

Silk Route   Traditionally, the great trade route between the West and the sources of silk, spices, and unique products in China. During the Roman Empire, an early version of the Silk Route ran through the Parthian Empire and such cities as PETRA, ANTIOCH, DOURA, and EDESSA. Full economic links were in place from the first and third centuries C.E. Decline in the financial health of the Roman world and hostility from the Persians terminated the system, not to be revived for several centuries.

Silva, Flavius (fl. first century C.E.) *Governor of Judaea in 73 C.E.*
The successor of Lucilius Bassus as general in charge of suppressing the remnants of the Jewish Rebellion, he was thus faced with the difficult task of besieging the fortress of MASADA, capturing it on May 2, 73. He served as CONSUL in 81.

Silvanus (fl. mid-fourth century C.E.) *Magister Peditum in Gaul from around 352 to 355 and a brief usurper in 355*
Of Frankish descent, Silvanus was originally a supporter of MAGNENTIUS, but deserted him in 351 for CONSTANTIUS II, before the battle of MURSA MAJOR. Rewarded with the rank of *magister peditum* in 352/3, he served in Gaul but found himself under attack by enemies in the court. Faced with a forged letter claiming his ambitions for the throne, he had little choice but to rebel against the injustice. His troops at Colonia Agrippina (Cologne) proclaimed him emperor. Constantius sent Ursucinus to crush him but learned of Silvanus's loyalty too late. The emperor spared Silvanus's son.

Silvanus, Gaius (d. c. 65 C.E.) *Tribune of the Praetorian Guard during the reign of Nero*
In 65, he became a member of the PISONIAN CONSPIRACY but was not revealed as a plotter for he was sent to question SENECA (the Younger) about his possible role. Silvanus later returned to inform Seneca that he would die. Although acquitted, the officer eventually killed himself.

Similis, S. Sulpicius (d. c. 124 C.E.) *Prefect of the Praetorian Guard during the last years of Trajan's reign*
He began his career as a soldier in the Guard, becoming a centurion before moving up the Equestrian ladder. He was PREFECT OF THE GRAIN, prefect of Egypt, and finally Praetorian prefect. When HADRIAN came to the throne in 117, Similis requested permission to retire because of his advanced age. The emperor agreed reluctantly, and Similis retreated to his estate in the country, where he died after seven peaceful years.

Sinope Important and old city situated on the northern Black Sea coast of ASIA MINOR, in the region of PAPHLAGONIA. Once the largest of the Greek colonies in the area, the city retained its status and wealth even after occupation by ROME. At the time of Julius CAESAR, a colony of veterans was founded there, known as Colonia Julia Caesarea Felix Sinope. The city relied primarily on the bountiful trade in the Black Sea for its survival. By the fourth century C.E., its position had declined considerably.

Siraci The name given to a SARMATIAN tribe that took part in the power struggles for the BOSPORAN KINGDOM. The Siraci joined the cause of MITHRIDATES (2) against Rome and were defeated in 49 C.E. by a Roman backed army.

Sirmium City on the Save River just south of the DANUBE and near modern Belgrade, in the region of Pannonia Inferior. Sirmium assumed a great strategic importance to the Romans because of its central location relative to the Danubian frontier. With communication possible with MOESIA, PANNONIA, ILLYRICUM, and MACEDONIA, it was ideal as a center for naval operations. For that reason the emperors DOMITIAN and TRAJAN took up quarters at Sirmium in their wars against the Dacians, and MARCUS AURELIUS found it convenient in his MARCOMANNIC WARS. The city boasted notable brick structures, including baths, granaries, and palaces.

Sitas (fl. late first century B.C.E.) *Blind ruler of the Thracian tribe of the Dentheleti*
An ally of ROME, Sitas and his people in 29 B.C.E. were menaced by the Bastarnae, who overran their lands in Thrace. Marcus Licinius CRASSUS (2) was sent into the region and rescued Sitas.

69 C.E. One of the bloodiest and most turbulent years in the history of the Roman Empire. In this terrible period the Roman world, especially ROME, endured assassinations, executions, coups, battles, invasions, and bitter rivalries, all reflecting the other name given to 69 C.E.—the Year of the Four Emperors.

On June 9, 68, Emperor NERO, uttering the words, "What an artist dies with me!" committed suicide. The SENATE recognized Servius Sulpicius GALBA (2), governor of Hispania Tarraconensis, as Nero's successor. He did not reach Rome until the fall of 68, but soon disappointed everyone in the city with a harsh, overly austere nature and a tendency to allow his advisers, Titus VINIUS, Cornelius LACO and ICELUS, a free hand in the tyrannical acquisition of monies. Consequently, on January 1, 69, the legions on the Rhine refused to take the oath of allegiance (the SACRAMENTUM) and demanded that a replacement be found.

To please the establishment, GALBA announced on January 10 that PISO LICINIANUS was his heir. Instead of satisfying his enemies, he merely infuriated the governor of Lusitania, Marcus Salvius OTHO, who felt more deserving of the throne than Piso. He found allies in the PRAETORIAN GUARD, for they were ready to commit murder after Galba refused to pay them their promised DONATIVUM, saying "I am used to levying soldiers, not paying them." Otho and his fellow conspirators struck on January 15, killing Galba and his heir.

Otho received the support of the Senate and the fealty of the legions in Syria (under VESPASIAN), the East and on the Danube. In Rome he took steps to placate those who suffered under Galba but then discovered that the troops in Germania had risen in revolt. The Rhine legions, urged on by their ambitious legates, CAECINA ALIENUS and Fabius VALENS, declared for VITELLIUS, the governor of Germania Inferior, even before Galba was dead. So, with an army of 100,000 men, Vitellius and his generals set out for Italy.

Inexplicably wasting time for weeks, Otho finally sprang into action to defend Rome and his throne. He had at his disposal only 25,000 men but positioned them well along the line of the Po River in northern Italy. The Vitellians, meanwhile, passed through Gaul and Helvetia, ravaging much of the countryside. Battle finally was joined at PLACENTIA and then at BEDRIACUM, on April 15. Othonian hopes were crushed in a confrontation that should not have taken place, and on April 17 Otho killed himself. Vitellius proceeded to Rome, where he indulged himself in a brief period of dissipation. His administration was worse than Galba's, far more corrupt and even more spiteful. The old Praetorian Guard was disbanded, replaced by a new one formed from the Germanic legions. Gladiatorial shows, endless feasts, and lavish spending were brought to a stunned end by the news that the Danubian armies had given their *SALUTATIO* (salute) to Vespasian in the East and were marching on Italy under the command of the legate Antonius PRIMUS.

Vespasian, governor of JUDAEA, had been directing the Jewish War before the outbreak of the hostilities in Rome. He was an excellent choice for emperor, well-respected and backed by the prefect of Egypt, TIBERIUS JULIUS ALEXANDER, and the governor of Syria, MUCIANUS. The legions in that part of the empire took their oath to him in July. Word reached the disaffected Danubian commands quickly. Vespasian soon had even more soldiers ready to die for him and his cause. Primus, using his gift for eloquence, convinced the Danube legions not to wait for Vespasian's eastern units, on their way under Mucianus. They marched west toward Italy, placing Vitellius in an ironically similar position to the one faced by Otho. The Vitellians tried to protect the line of advance into Italy but failed because of their stagnated military skills and the attempted treason of Caecina Alienus.

The climactic engagement between the Flavians (Vespasian's troops) and the Vitellians came at Bedriacum on October 27. Led by Primus, the Danubian cohorts won the day. The road to Rome lay ahead, while Vitellius made a few preparations for a siege and negotiated with Flavius SABINUS, PREFECT OF THE CITY and Vespasian's brother, for a surrender. Feelings ran high among the Vitellians, and Sabinus was soon besieged on the Capitol, perishing supposedly at the feet of Vitellius. Such treachery infuriated the Flavians. Primus was forced by his legionaries to attack Rome at once, pushing into the Eternal City in three great columns. A bitter fight ensued at the Castra Praetoria, while Vitellius was captured and executed on the Gemonian Stairs on December 20. Soon the entire city was pacified. Primus settled into the role of master of Rome, awaiting the arrival of Mucianus. The year ended as the Eastern legions approached, bringing to a close a truly grim time. Mercifully, there followed many years of stability.

slavery An ancient institution in ROME, and a major part of Roman society and economics for many centuries. Because of the pervasiveness of the practice of enslaving human beings, the Romans drew up strict laws and regulations to ensure that slaves were treated in a fair manner. Throughout the Republic, slaves were available, but it was only after the second century B.C.E. that they began appearing in massive numbers. The reason for this expansion in the slave trade was Rome's rise as the most powerful state in the Mediterranean. With territorial acquisitions in ASIA MINOR, many of the slaves came from the East and were Syrian, Jew, Greek, and even Egyptian. Further conquests along the Rhine, the DANUBE and in Gaul opened up even more sources for strong barbarians who made good fieldhands.

The wide variety of slaves in Rome, and throughout the Roman Empire, was broken down into precise classes. All slaves were either public or private. Public enslavement was usually preferable to private, as the *servi publici* had greater personal freedom, were rarely sold and could, to a small degree, own property—a condition unique in the history of slavery. Duties involved caretaking public buildings, serving officials, and performing as lictors and executioners.

Private slavery could be pleasant or hellish. Those slaves belonging to one person were called a *familia,* with three being necessary to constitute this body. All private slaves belonged either to the *familia urbana* or *familia rustica.* The *familia urbana* worked in the houses of their owners. This entailed traveling with the master to any country villa; the *familia urbana* did not lose their status by departing from the city because the villa was considered an extension of the main house. The slaves of the house were appointed to smaller groups, called *decuriae,* depending upon their specialities or appointed jobs. *Ordinarii* ran the housekeeping, with slaves under their command; they could be chief chambermaids or butlers. *Vulgares* constituted the bulk of house slaves. All household chores were handed to them, including cooks (*coqui*) and bakers (*pistores*). Some were janitors or doormen. The *literati* acted as readers or secretaries for the household and were highly prized because of their literacy.

All slaves outside of the house were called members of the *familia rustica.* They were herdsmen, farmhands or gatherers in the fields. The *familia rustica* were seen more often in the days of the Republic, for the maintenance of large numbers of slaves on farmlands was staggeringly expensive. More importantly, the government in Rome did not relish the idea of a landowner amassing a virtual army of slaves on a rural estate. Tenant farming thus replaced slavery in crop production and farming.

According to Roman law, the slave was utterly the property of his or her owner. Thus, the master could treat the slave as he pleased. Punishments, rewards, manumission, and even death were at the whim of the owner. While social norms and belief in the humane treatment of all human beings helped to improve the general lot of slaves, there were still many shocking acts of cruelty. Laws were passed to help regulate treatment, in particular, the *lex Petronia* (circa 61 C.E.) and the *lex Junia Petronia* (19 C.E.). Even with such laws, persons of influence committed acts of outright murder. Witness Publius Vedius POLLIO, who threw his slaves to man-eating eels.

Aside from the *lex Petronia* and the *lex Junia Petronia,* other steps were taken. The Roman constitution supposedly ensured fair living conditions for slaves. If a master was obscenely harsh, the slaves could protest, and Claudius decreed that any slave who was infirm and was left exposed could be considered free. Further, in the event of a slave's sale, any family, including wife and children, went with him, this despite the official refusal of the law to recognize any children at all or to accept a slave's marriage as legitimate.

Manumissio was the act of terminating enslavement. It was generally up to the owner to decide if a slave should go free. The custom developed to allow many slaves their independence, and by the time of Augustus this had become a distinct social problem. In 2 B.C.E., the *lex Fufia Caninia* was passed, restricting the mass manumissions that occurred upon the death of a master. Another law, the *lex Aelia Sentia* (in 4 C.E.), completed the intent of the *Fufia Caninia* by creating certain conditions for manumission. A board of magistrates determined the suitability of a slave, based on his or her moral or social character. As punishment for harsh treatment a slaveholder might lose the slave in question. During the Christian era, it was possible for a slave to leave his servitude to enter a monastery or to become an ascetic. Naturally, all such would-be clerics had to remain forever in their religious environment. Any departure from the monastic way or any grounds of corrupt living meant an immediate return to slavery.

CHRISTIANITY, long concerned with its own survival, did not have the opportunity to condemn slavery as contrary to the proper way of life. Once the Roman Empire was fully Christianized, steps were taken to eradicate the entire institution. Led by Christian leaders and writers, the slaveowners were openly discouraged from continuing the practice. The institution died hard, finding new strength in the barbarian invasions, bringing the so-called *silavi* or slaves.

Suggested Readings: Buckland, William W. *The Roman Law of Slavery; The Condition of the Slave in Classical Slavery.* Edited by M. I. Finley. London: F. Cass, 1987; Finley, M. I. *Ancient Slavery and Modern Ideology.* London: Chatto and Windus, 1980; Yavetz, Zvi. *Slaves and Slavery in Ancient Rome.* New Brunswick, N.J.: Transaction Books, 1988.

Smyrna   Venerable, wealthy, and naturally beautiful city on the western coast of ASIA MINOR. From the earliest days of Greek expansion in the Aegean, Smyrna attracted colonists. With fertile hills and a superb harbor it emerged as a major center for trade, both by sea and land, a reputation carefully and shrewdly cultivated by its leaders. They chose to aid ROME in its wars against Mithridates, earning the eternal gratitude of the Romans. As one of the foremost metropolises of the senatorial province of ASIA, Smyrna was a recipient of the intense development initiated by the emperors. An earthquake devastated it in 178 C.E., but MARCUS AURELIUS sent a senator of Praetorian rank to rebuild it, putting vast resources at his disposal. Unfortunately, Smyrna was not blessed with the presence of any imperial officials beyond the *conventus iuridicus.* This placed it at a disadvantage to EPHESUS and PERGAMUM. Christianity made the birthplace of HOMER a success, as Smyrna was included in the seven churches of Asia and as the site of martyrdom of POLYCARP.

social classes   A strict social order developed in the early days of Rome, when the kings called together the oldest families (*patres*) for advice and counsel. The heads of the families formed the SENATE (from the Latin for *senes,* old men) and thus constituted, with their families, the first class of Roman society, the *populus Romanus.* With the expulsion of the kings, the Republic was founded, with political power resting in the hands of PATRICIANS, who controlled not only the Senate but also the high positions of government. Their exalted position was in marked contrast to the status of increasingly numerous freeborn men. These came not from noble families but from the ranks of the commoners and could neither serve in the government nor hold any kind of office. In time, however, they constituted the majority of Roman citizens, winning entry into politics and recognition as a legitimate class, the Plebeians.

These two social orders were joined in time by the Equestrians (*see* EQUITES), who belonged both to the Patricians and the Plebeians. Importantly, the Equestrians fulfilled the needed task of acting as bankers and economic leaders. They received into their ranks numerous noblemen who opted for membership and commoners who could afford the large fees necessary for admission.

The entire Republican social system was not swept away by AUGUSTUS, but it was certainly reformed and changed. Imperial Roman society reflected both the rise of the emperors and their families and the acquisition and Romanization of vast stretches of once barbarian or enemy land. At the top of the imperial social classes was the palace, with the PRINCEPS. Augustus did not rely upon Oriental court ceremonies as a way of governing, but inevitably such a grandiose lifestyle took firm hold. GAIUS CALIGULA and NERO were the first practitioners, but the more cunning DIOCLETIAN used it to elevate the royal family and hence the entire central administration into a supreme position in the empire. Diocletian's precedent was followed by the house of the Constantines and became fully developed by the emperors of the fifth century C.E. and by the Byzantines. The notion of an emperor being a god (*apotheosis*) was an instrument of perpetuating the privileges of the ruler while indoctrinating the provinces into the IMPERIAL CULT.

The Patricians suffered severely under the emperors because of their social proximity to the imperial household and their ancient assembly of the Senate. Despite Augustus's complex attempts at retaining the Republican facade of government, it was a reality of life that his own position as princeps had come at the expense of the Senate. Further, the Patricians as a class were diluted by the appointment of Equestrians and even Plebeians to their ranks. Nevertheless, they survived the purges of the more tyrannical emperors and existed as best they could. From the third century C.E., members of the wealthy upper class of the empire came to be known as *honestiores* and were given special rights, especially in terms of law, with the aim of preserving their dwindling numbers.

Of the major classes in Roman Imperial society, the Equestrians were clearly the most successful. As they had access to all classes, were historically the most flexible and had long-standing ties to business and finance, the Knights were perfectly positioned to receive the patronage of the emperors. By the second century C.E., they began to take over vital roles in affairs of the empire.

Because of the infusion of new blood, the Equestrians were constantly drawing off members of the next class, the Plebeians. The departure of members of this group to the Equestrians was probably always welcomed, especially by the new knight's family. Political influence for the Plebeians was gone after 14 C.E., when Tiberius transferred the election of magistrates from the *comitia* to the Senate. Other problems surfaced as well. Slaves were being released by their masters (*manumissio*) in vast numbers, and it was necessary to pass the *lex Fufia Caninia* (2 B.C.E.) and *lex Aelia Sentia* (4 C.E.) to restrict such manumissions.

The plight of the Plebeians in the years of the empire was very often severe. Social advancement was difficult, and there was little incentive to work toward improving one's lot because of the public subsidies of food (*frumentationes*) given out by the emperor. When combined with the distracting games and shows that were held all years, many in Rome were content. Plebs found life even worse in the late empire, when they became known as the *humiliores*, or lower class. They were the most affected by the decay of central authority, for the food stopped coming and protection from brigands and invasions ceased.

For those Plebeians who were desirous of stepping up into a better existence, there were ways. Success in business made the Equestrian ranks attainable, while even a military career opened up avenues that in the Republic were utterly closed. Another method of self aggrandizement was the finding of a patron. Being a client to a wealthy or powerful Roman official could lead to appointments in the government or at least a small amount of gift money, the *sportula*. In the patronage relationship between a patron and a client, a client would flatter and scrape before his protector, giving early morning attendance (SALUTATIO), and in turn the patron would, if convenient, offer dinner, a few extra coins, some clothes, or even a kindly word. This parasitic existence has been seen as a major example of the degeneration of Roman society.

See also CURIALIS; DECURIONES; FARMING; INDUSTRY; SLAVERY; TRADE; TRIBUNE; *TRIBUNICIA POTESTAS*.

Suggested Readings: Boren, Henry C. *Roman Society: A Social, Economic, and Cultural History.* Lexington, Mass.: D. C. Heath, c1977; Bradley, K. R. *Discovering the Roman Family. Studies in Roman Social History.* Oxford, U.K.: Oxford University Press, 1991; Brown, Peter R. L. *Society and the Holy in Late Antiquity.* Berkeley: University of California Press, 1982; Carcopino, Jerome. *Daily Life in Ancient Rome.* New Haven, Conn.: Yale University Press, 1968; Garnsey, Peter. *The Roman Empire: Economy, Society, and Culture.* Berkeley: University of California Press, 1987; Goodman, Martin. *State and Society in Roman Galilee,* A.D. *132–212.* Totowa, N.J.: Rowman & Allanheld, 1983; Hallett, Judith P. *Fathers and Daughters in Roman Society: Women and the Elite Family.* Princeton, N.J.: Princeton University Press, 1984; Raaflaub, Kurt A., ed., *Social Struggles in Archaic Rome: New Perspectives on the Conflict of the Orders.* Berkeley: University of California Press, 1986; Syme, Ronald. *The Augustan Aristocracy.* New York: Oxford University Press, 1986; Yavetz, Zvi. *Plebs and Princeps.* London: Oxford University Press, 1969.

Socrates (c. 380–450 C.E.) *Lawyer and Christian historian*
A native of CONSTANTINOPLE, Socrates knew little of the West. This deficiency was apparent in his continuation of the *Ecclesiastical History of* EUSEBIUS. Composed in seven books, Socrates's work carried the chronicle from 305 to 439. He relied at first on Rufinus, but after the writings of Athanasius became available he corrected numerous historical errors, issuing a revised edition. In style, Socrates strove for straightforward and objective narrative. This being an ecclesiastical account, he displayed little interest in secular matters but conveyed his layman's aversion to the theological debates of the time. He used, however, numerous documents from the Eastern Church, in turn being the main source for SOZOMEN.

solidus Main gold coin of issue during the late empire. Whereas the AUREUS had served for centuries as the central species of gold currency, by the fourth century C.E. it had become too heavy and hence too expensive to mint. By the reforms of CONSTANTINE the Great (c. 312) the aureus was replaced by the solidus, a lighter coin but still of gold. The solidus received vast distribution and lingered as a form of currency in the Dark Ages.

See also COINAGE.

Solinus, Gaius Julius (fl. early third century C.E.) *Grammarian and author of the* Collectanea Rerum Memorabilium
Solinus borrowed extensively from PLINY THE ELDER'S *Natural History* and the writings of Pomponius MELA, without acknowledgement, presenting curiosities in geographical history from all over the empire. Considered inferior as a writer, Solinus has been attacked as a plunderer, whose own original contributions, notably on the British Isles, could not compensate for a lack of independent scholarship elsewhere.

Sol Invictus Roman god of the sun, called by the Greeks Helios. Sol to the early Romans was a Sabine god who possessed a temple on the Quirinal Hill and received public worship on August 8 of every year. When the Greek deity Helios was introduced into ROME, Sol assumed most of his attributes, including his identification with Apollo. The Greek city of Rhodes, with its Colossus, was dedicated to the deity.

Despite the connection to Apollo and the attempts of AUGUSTUS to give Apollo a high place of honor, worship of Sol was not widespread in Rome or in Italy. That changed with the introduction of the Eastern cults, especially that of Mithras. From the time of VESPASIAN and the Flavians (69–96 C.E.), Mithras and solar cults were officially sanctioned by the imperial government. Henceforth the rise of Mithraism was inexorably tied to the idea of Sol Invictus or the Invincible Sun.

Sol Invictus was part of the twofold process in Roman religion of increasing influence and the need to find a universal deity for the entire empire. As the sun was the most wondrous sight in the universe, held sacred by virtually every civilized culture in the Roman world, it was natural to make Sol the heart of imperial religious grandeur. A foreshadowing of this came in the reign of ELAGABALUS when the sun god of Emesa was brought to Rome. It found final fruition under AURELIAN, the soldier-emperor, who helped the Roman Empire recover from the catastrophes of the third century C.E. Celebrating his triumphs, he thanked Sol Invictus of the East for coming to his aid. Solar belief was ordered throughout the provinces, a decree upheld by DIOCLETIAN in his attempts to expunge Christianity. Even CONSTANTINE used the solar motif on his COINAGE. This first Christian ruler employed the idea of Sol Invictus on most of his species of coins, often with the motto, "SOL INVICTI COMITI," all the while acting as patron to the Christians. Sol Invictus, with Mithras, was revered by only one more emperor, Julian, from 361 to 363.

soothsayers Known to the Romans as HARUSPICES; important diviners used by both the state and private persons in a number of ways. According to tradition, soothsayers first developed in Etruria, mastering their craft before appearing in Rome during the reign of Tarquinius Superbus. They were subsequently summoned back to the city by senatorial decree to interpret any prodigies or omens left unexplained by the SIBYLLINE BOOKS. The soothsayers were requested with such frequency that by the time of the Punic Wars they had settled in Rome. Generals often consulted them, and their pronouncements were followed carefully by the priests of the city. They thus achieved popularity at the expense of the AUGURS, many going so far as to accept money for their services, an act that earned general condemnation. Although they possessed their own order, the *haruspices* lacked an actual *collegium*. This was changed by CLAUDIUS in 47 C.E. when he asked that a college of soothsayers be established with the object of preventing the old science from dying out.

Soothsayers could do three things: read entrails (*extispicium*); decide the meaning of an event; and name a way in which to appease the gods after some event of an ominous nature. The first form of divination, the reading of the *exta* or vital organs, was the most commonly used skill, for control could be exercised over the entire ceremony. The other two had to be in response to an event or happening. *Haruspices* remained under a leader, the *haruspex maximus*, until the early fifth century C.E., when their institutions were closed.

Sopater (early fourth century C.E.) *Neoplatonic philosopher following the death of his tutor, Iamblichus*

Sopater came from Apamea in SYRIA and was a noted pagan writer. Visiting Nicomedia and CONSTANTINOPLE, he became a close friend of CONSTANTINE the Great. It was to the emperor that he explained that no expiation was possible for the murder of CRISPUS. Sopater soon fell under attack by jealous courtiers, led by the Praetorian Prefect ABLABIUS. Accused of propagating PAGANISM and using magic to ruin crops, the philosopher was executed. His son, also a philosopher, was an associate of the emperors CONSTANTIUS II and JULIAN THE APOSTATE.

Sophistry A school of learning and artistic skill that was popular in ancient Greece and then died out as the Sophists lost their finesse and lore and degenerated into pomposity. A rebirth in sophistry came in the second century C.E., with an increased Roman appreciation of Hellenism under Emperor HADRIAN. Resurgent sophistry was a result of the success of the rhetorical speakers so much a part of the first century C.E., especially the declamations. Once more, orators roamed the world, attracting large, cheering audiences that included, at times, even Roman emperors. The greatest of these new Sophists were DIO COCCEIANUS, HERODES ATTICUS, and PHILOSTRATUS. The movement declined in the chaos of the third century, only to reappear in the fourth. Sophistry at this time became the weapon of leading pagans fighting Christianity's attacks on paganism. In their ranks were JULIAN THE APOSTATE, THEMISTIUS, LIBANIUS, and Himerius. SYNESIUS OF CYRENE was the last notable Sophist.

Soranus (fl. second century C.E.) *Physician and medical writer*

Soranus came from EPHESUS, studying at ALEXANDRIA before finally opening up a practice in Rome, where he remained during the reigns of TRAJAN and HADRIAN (98–138). Soranus authored some 20 volumes on medicine, specializing in specific diseases instead of generalities or symptoms. He wrote in Greek but Latin translations were common and popular.

Soranus, Barea (fl. mid-first century C.E.) *Noted Stoic philosopher and political figure*

Soranus was consul in 52 C.E. and proconsul of Asia from around 61–62. He fulfilled his duties with both integrity and energy, aiding EPHESUS in developing its harbor and refusing to punish PERGAMUM for preventing the city's plunder by Acratus, one of Nero's freedmen. For this and for his virtue, Soranus was singled out for destruction. NERO charged him with friendship with RUBELLIUS PLAUTUS and treasonable activities. Condemned, Soranus stoically took his own life.

Sororia Name given to JUNO as the goddess of puberty.

Sosigenes (fl. first century B.C.E.) *Peripatetic philosopher and astronomer*
He was hired by Julius CAESAR in 46 to reorganize the Roman calendar.

Sosius, Gaius (fl. first century C.E.) *Lieutenant of Marc Antony and governor of Syria in 38 B.C.E.*
The following year he marched with two legions in Palestine to aid HEROD THE GREAT in reclaiming his lost kingdom from the Parthians and from rival claimant Antigonus. In 37, Sosius besieged and captured JERUSALEM for Herod, commemorating the event by striking coins bearing the likenesses of Antigonus and JUDAEA (epitomized by a captive woman). Henceforth he was a follower of Antony against Octavian (AUGUSTUS), once delivering a stinging attack against Octavian in the SENATE. Consul in 32, when open warfare erupted between the triumvirs (see TRIUMVIRATE, SECOND), Sosius fled to the East to join ANTONY. He was at the battle of Actium in 31, where he fell into Octavian's hands but was spared. Sosius rebuilt the aged TEMPLE OF APOLLO in ROME.

Sozomen, Salmaninius Hermias (fl. early fifth century C.E.) *Christian historian*
Sozomen probably came from Gaza but lived in CONSTANTINOPLE as a lawyer. His main achievement was to write a continuation of EUSEBIUS's *Ecclesiastical History*. In nine books the chronicle extended the history from 323 to either 425 or 439, although the sections from approximately 421 are not extant. Sozomen relied heavily upon the writer SOCRATES, his older contemporary, but his own sources were more sound, especially in terms of Western development and the spread of CHRISTIANITY among the non-Romans.

Spain *See* HISPANIA.

Sparta Sparta fell under Roman domination with the rest of Greece, and from 146 B.C.E. it was included in the province of MACEDONIA until it became part of Emperor AUGUSTUS's creation of ACHAEA. Sparta was considered a federated state.

Speculatores. A department of the PRAETORIAN GUARD, originally created to act as the source of couriers, scouts, or special agents. Over time, the Speculatores and their sub-department, the Quaestionarii, acquired a sinister reputation as the private assassins and torturers of the Roman emperors. The need for special service soldiers was a natural one, as in Rome there were many non-military duties that accompanied enlistment in the Praetorians. The Speculatores thus became familiar with internal palace intrigues by carrying dispatches or running errands for the powerful. Lucius Aelius SEJANUS, the notorious Prefect in the reign of TIBERIUS, first used them as spies, assassins, or as experts in cruel torture (this was the purpose of the Quaestionarii, the Questioners).

Once the Speculatores had made themselves useful their existence was guaranteed. Membership was restricted to veterans of more than five years service. NERO, through his Prefect Ofonius TIGELLINUS, used the Speculatores to hunt down his enemies, especially those in the PISONIAN CONSPIRACY. And TITUS, it was said, sent them out as his own murderers, removing all political rivals while serving as prefect for his father, VESPASIAN. Because of their limited number and the necessity of keeping some of them involved in mundane tasks, the Speculatores never evolved into an empire-wide intelligence organization, such as the one created by HADRIAN, the FRUMENTARII.

Spelunca Now called Sperlonga; a country estate in Campania, built in the first century C.E. and used by Emperor TIBERIUS as a private retreat. Meaning "cave" or "grotto," Spelunca was a beautiful cavern on the coast, decorated and supported by masonry, Rhodian sculptures (a remembrance of his time on Rhodes), rooms, dining areas, show stages, and even a fish pond, or *vivarium*. According to TACITUS, Tiberius left Rome in 26 C.E. to live in Campania. On his way to the VILLA JOVIS, he stayed at Spelunca with an entourage, including Praetorian Prefect Lucius Aelius SEJANUS. While dining, the mouth of the cave collapsed. The courtiers ran for their lives, and only Sejanus remained, covering Tiberius's body with his own. This event prompted the emperor's explicit trust in his lieutenant.

Split A small village approximately three miles west of Salona on the Illyrian coast. Its significance dates from 305 C.E., when the retired Emperor DIOCLETIAN took up residence there, living out his life in a sumptuous palace. The villa at Split was constructed by Diocletian from around 300 to 305/6, and its architecture was both ingenious and practical, combining styles that were imperial, martial, and sound. Its military qualities could be seen in the stout rectangular walls surrounding the entire complex, with towers and easily defended gates. Two colonnaded avenues cut the palace into quarters, with the business sections and the barracks in the two northern portions. Here business could be conducted in preparation for seeing the emperor, who resided with his extensive entourage in the southern half.

Diocletian's suites, rooms, and audience chambers were very impressive. None more so than his Hall of Audiences, the Aula Palatina. There, dressed in his formal robes and sitting on a lavish throne, he would greet his guests. Pointed toward the sea, the throne rested beneath a hugh vaulted arch, designed to strike awe in any supplicant. Ironically, although Diocletian was an expert at creating imperial atmosphere, his happiest moments at Split were spent in his gardens, especially in his cabbage beds.

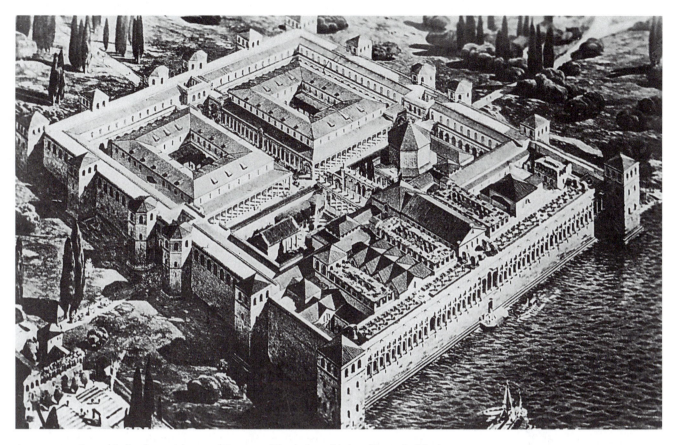

A reconstruction of Split, the residence of Emperor Diocletian *(Hulton/Getty Archive)*

Sporus (d. 69 C.E.) *Beautiful youth in Rome who was "married" to Emperor Nero around 65 C.E.*
The marriage was complete with a dowry and the title of mistress. Sporus had the nickname Sabina because of his similarity in appearance to POPPAEA, the dead empress and former wife of Nero. One of the more notorious lovers of the ruler, Sporus fled from Rome with Nero in 68, killing himself during the short reign of VITELLIUS in 69.

S.P.Q.R.   The four letters used by the Romans on their coins, standards, and monuments. They stood for *Senatus Populusque Romanus* (Senate and People of Rome). S.P.Q.R. was retained by AUGUSTUS and placed, in a variety of forms, on the Roman imperial COINAGE from his reign until the time of CONSTANTINE the Great. Other variations included "S.p.q.r.a.n.f.f., OPTIMI PRIN-CIPI," (the Senate and People of Rome [hope for] a prosperous and joyous New Year [*annum novum faustum felice*] to the foremost prince); or "S.P.Q.R. IMP. CAES. QUOD V.M.S.EX.EA.P.Q.IS.AD.A.DE" (*Senatus Populusque Romanus Imperatori Caesari quod viae munitae sint ex ea pecunia quam is aerarium detulit*), in gratitude to Augustus for his monetary contribution to the treasury and his gifts of the roads and improvement of public safety.

Spurinna (fl. first century B.C.E.) *Augur of Rome in 44 B.C.E. who uttered the warning to Julius Caesar: "Beware the Ides of March!"*
He also answered Caesar's retort that the Ides had come, saying: "Yes, they have come, but they have not passed."

Spurinna, Titus Vestricius (fl. first century C.E.) *Minor official in the cause of Emperor Otho against Vitellius in 69 C.E.*
Spurinna and Annius Gallus were appointed by Otho to be the forward commanders of the troops marching north to defend Italy from the invasion by the Vitellians. Spurinna proved his worth by protecting the town of PLA-CENTIA from attack by CAECINA ALIENUS. He then joined his fellow Othonians in the battle of BEDRIACUM.

Stabiae   Small town in Campania, to the southwest of POMPEII and north of Surrentum. Stabiae was very old when it was destroyed by Sulla during the Social War (90–89 B.C.E.), but it is noted for two happenings in 79 C.E. The first was its near total destruction by Mount VESUVIUS, along with that of Pompeii and HERCULANEUM. The second was the death of PLINY THE ELDER, witnessing the eruption from Misenum, when he sailed to Stabiae to get a better look and inhaled the toxic fumes pouring over the town.

Statius, Publius Papinius (c. 40 or 45–95 or 96 C.E.) *One of the great poets of the Flavian era (69–96 C.E.)*

Statius was born in Naples, the son of a school teacher. Competing at an early age in contests in Naples and Alba, he made a name for himself and his work. Upon his father's death he traveled to ROME, where he composed pantomimes and became a declaimer of high repute (*see* RHETORIC). Social connections, a marriage to a Roman woman named Claudia, and the successful reception of his work, especially the *Thebaid*, allowed him to live in some comfort in Alba for the remaining years of his life. His three main works are the *Thebaid*, *Silvae*, and *Achilleid*. Derived from Antimachos, the *Thebaid* was his earliest and longest composition. Published around 91, its 12 books of hexameter detail the struggle between Polynices and Eteocles. Very superficial, Statius seemed to thrive on rhetorical effect, willingly mixing pathos with the outrageous. *Silvae*, a collection of 32 poems on diverse topics, was published sometime before his death. It stands as the most popular of the poet's works because of its insights into the times and its more traditional style. *Achilleid* was never finished, as its second book was incomplete. On a massive scale, this epic was to augment the *Iliad*. Statius certainly possessed the talent and the eccentric vision to achieve its completion.

Statius Annaeus (fl. mid-first century C.E.) *Friend and physician of Seneca*

Statius helped his long-time associate to kill himself in 65 C.E. When SENECA did not die from the usual method of cutting his veins, Statius tried the traditional Greek way—hemlock. Seneca had lost too much blood, however, so a lethal vapor bath was prepared, the *Laconicum*.

Statius Priscus (fl. second century C.E.) *Consul in 159 and generals in the reign of Marcus Aurelius (161–180 C.E.) and Lucius Verus (161–169 C.E.)*

He was governor of numerous provinces, including Dacia, MOESIA, Britain, and CAPPADOCIA. While serving in Cappadocia in 163, he helped Lucius VERUS conquer ARMENIA, sweeping into the country and destroying Artaxata, the Armenian capital. Verus took the title Armeniacus. Statius Priscus was replaced by Martius VERUS.

Stephanus (d. 96 C.E.) *Murderer of Domitian in 96 C.E.*

Stephanus was a strong freedman in the palace, chosen as the main assassin. He struck Domitian, knocking him unconscious while his fellow conspirators completed the deed. In the fray that followed, Stephanus was slain.

Stephanus (Pope Stephen I) (d. 258 C.E.) *Pope from 245 to 257*

His years as the leader of the Roman Church were spent in bitter conflict with his colleagues, differing with them on such questions as lapsed Christians and baptisms by heretics. A disagreement occurred with CYPRIAN, the bishop of CARTHAGE, over the latter. Little else is known about Stephanus and doubts remain concerning his supposed martyrdom in 258.

Stilicho, Flavius (d. 408 C.E.) *Magister militum in the West from 394 to 408 and one of the major political figures in the later years of the Roman Empire*

Stilicho was the son of a VANDAL cavalry officer and a Roman lady. Probably through the influence of his father he was chosen in 383 to serve as part of a diplomatic mission to PERSIA. Upon his return (c. 394) he was married to Serena, Emperor THEODOSIUS I's niece, and given the rank of COMES, or count. From 385 to 392 he was *comes domesticorum*, accompanying the emperor on his campaign against Magnus Maximus while amassing influence and power in the court. Made MAGISTER MILITUM in THRACE (c. 392), he was a general during the war against Eugenius. After the battle of FRIGIDUS (394), Theodosius declared him *magister militum* in the West.

Stilicho now possessed virtually unlimited power, increasing his control by centralizing the bureaucracy of the Western provinces, making them answerable to him alone. Thus, when Theodosius named Stilicho as guardian of the young Honorius, he was ready to go beyond the letter of the emperor's aims, especially after Theodosius died in 395. De facto ruler of the West and master of the Eastern armies, Stilicho pronounced himself guardian of both emperors HONORIUS and ARCADIUS. Marching into Greece he was ready to annihilate ALARIC and the VISIGOTHS but received orders to desist from Praetorian Prefect RUFINUS, whom Stilicho subsequently had murdered.

The removal of Rufinus did nothing to end the hatred of Stilicho in both the Eastern and Western courts. In 397, Arcadius declared him a public enemy, and the *magister militum* in AFRICA, Gildo, revolted. Neither event could loosen his hold on the Western Empire, for he was CONSUL in 400. The following year Alaric invaded Italy, only to be beaten by Stilicho at the battle of POLLENTIA. Consul again in 405, the general took to the field once more, this time against Radagaisus, routing the barbarian king in 406. Deciding to use Alaric as an ally, he elevated the Visigoth to the rank of *magister militum* as part of a plan to take ILLYRICUM. His strategy was ruined by the emergence of the usurper CONSTANTIUS III in Gaul. Not only did he have to face a dangerous usurper, but also Alaric suddenly demanded compensation of 4,000 pounds of gold. Stilicho convinced the SENATE to oblige.

Fortune turned against Stilicho even more in 408. Arcadius died, and Stilicho convinced Honorius to allow him to settle affairs at Constantinople. Already weakened by Alaric's extortion, Stilicho was accused by members of the court of plotting to put his son on the throne. When the troops in Gaul mutinied, murdering their own officers, Stilicho was arrested by Honorius. After hiding briefly in a church, he was executed on August 22, 408.

Many accounts were very hostile to Stilicho, most notably that of the historian EUNAPIUS. He was, nevertheless, an accomplished general who proved skillful in defeating the hordes then threatening the empire and in dealing with them by negotiation and diplomacy. A vehement Christian, he helped destroy PAGANISM both through laws and with the burning of the SIBYLLINE BOOKS.

stipendium Translated most often as "payment," generally the pay given to the Roman soldier. Other meanings given to it were the length of service expected by the troops before their retirement, and even a tax. More specifically, the *emeritis stipendis* denoted the end of a man's military duty.

See also LEGIONS; DONATIVUM.

Stoicism Important philosophical movement founded in the third century B.C.E. by ZENO of Citium. Named after the Greek stoa or public meeting place, as in Athens where Zeno taught, the idea of Stoicism was to make the lives of humans as orderly as the cosmos. By adhering to the guiding principle of nature it was believed possible for someone to bring a sense of logic and order into existence. The history of Stoicism, like the ideas of its adherents, followed varied paths of development. Some Stoics stressed the ideal of virtue, while others used physics and reasoning. Nevertheless it had a profound effect upon the Romans, most notably in its last two eras, the Middle and Late Stoas.

The Middle Stoa lasted from the second to the first century B.C.E. and was brought to Rome by Diogenes of Seleucia. Although attacked by Cato, Stoicism found a home in the Roman intellectual environment. Its greatest proponents of the era were Panaetius, Posidonius, and Scipio Aemilianus, while other Stoics included Scaevola and Aelius Tubero. They allowed the philosophy to flourish, and thus it survived the upheaval that led to the foundation of the Roman Empire.

Roman fascination with the Stoic virtues and ethical pondering characterized the Late Stoa, roughly the first and second centuries C.E. The fact that ethics were important and pursued actively was seen in the list of practitioners of Stoicism: Rubellius Plautus, Thrasea Paetus, Helvidius Priscus, Junius Rusticus, C. Musonius Rufus, and Q. Junius Arulenus Rusticus.

Stoicism of this age found expression through three masters: L. Annaeus SENECA, EPICTETUS and MARCUS AURELIUS. Seneca the Younger accepted the more scientific outlook of Posidonius, while stressing, sometimes unsuccessfully, the idea of duty to society. Epictetus was most renowned as a teacher; his views on Stoicism helped shape later philosophers, especially Marcus Aurelius. That emperor came the closest of virtually any historical monarch to the idea of the philosopher king. Considered the last of the Stoics, he put his faith in the interior growth of himself, while bowing to the place of all creatures within the universe. From the time of Marcus Aurelius, Stoicism proved unable to retain its vitality, becoming partly absorbed by Neoplatonism and Christianity. It died out when the Athenian school was closed in 529 C.E. by Justinian.

Strabo (fl. late first century B.C.E.) *Famed geographer*
Strabo came from Ameseia in Pontus and was born sometime around 64 or 54 B.C.E. One of the foremost travelers in the Roman world, Strabo visited numerous countries and provinces and was a friend of Aelius Gallus, the prefect of Egypt. Educated in Rome, he returned sometime after 30 B.C.E. and spent a long time in the city. Strabo wrote his vast historical work in 43 books, continuing the history of Polybius probably down to the fall of Egypt in 30 B.C.E. None of these volumes survive, unlike his 17 books on geography that are in their entirety (minus book seven, in existence only as an epitome). Strabo's *Geography* was designed for use by educated readers or officials.

See also MELA, POMPONIUS; PLINY THE ELDER; PTOLEMY, CLAUDIUS.

Strabo, Lucius Seius (fl. early first century C.E.) *Third prefect of the Praetorian Guard and the father of the famous Praetorian Prefect Sejanus*
Strabo came from a good Equestrian (EQUITES) family and was appointed by AUGUSTUS in 14 C.E. to succeed Valerius Ligur as sole commander of the Praetorian Guard. Upon Augustus's death in 14, only the consuls preceded him in giving TIBERIUS the oath of allegiance. A short time later, his son Sejanus was promoted as his colleague, eventually replacing him. As a reward for his loyalty, Strabo was made prefect of Egypt.

Styx The chief river of the Roman underworld received its name from the daughter of Oceanus and Tethys, who watched the entrance of Hades from her beautiful grotto. The river supposedly flowed around the land of the dead seven times.

See also CHARON; DEATH.

Subura (or **Suburra**) A valley in Rome created by the Esquiline, Quirinal, and Viminal Hills; the area was heavily populated and described by the writer *martial* as filled with prostitutes, barbers, stores, and vendors. Arruntius Stella owned an estate there, with gardens and fountains. In the Subura, along the entrance to the FORUM ROMANUM, could be found as well the punishers of slaves in Rome, their blood-stained instruments hanging on hooks and awaiting use on the Via Turbina, the traditional site of death for slaves.

Suburanus (Saburanus) (fl. late first century C.E.) *Prefect of the Praetorian Guard during the reign of Trajan (98–117 C.E.)*
According to Dio, he was given his official sword by the emperor, with the words: "Take this sword and if I rule well use it for me, but if I rule poorly, use it against me."

Suburbicaria Name used in the later years of the Roman Empire for the diocese of southern Italy, comprised of Italy's south, Sicily, Corsica, and Sardinia.

Suebi Also called the Suevi; a collection of Germanic tribes occupying large stretches of territory in Germania Barbara, or "barbaric" Germany. Their domain stretched from the Vistula to the Elbe and along parts of the Rhine, to the Danube. The Suebi were rarely considered by the Romans as a single entity. Rather, it was never forgotten that they were a confederation of tribes, united for self defense. The historian TACITUS wrote of them in this manner, adding that they differed from other Germans in the practice of knotting their hair, tying it sideways, or allowing it to grow stiffly backward.

Rome first encountered the Suebi during Caesar's GALLIC WARS. He defeated ARIOVISTUS, king of the Suebi, in 58 B.C.E. but admitted that they were the strongest, fiercest people in the region, wearing only skins in the winter and refusing to purchase items of luxury from traders. Among the tribes that belonged to the Suebi, the three most powerful were the Hermunduri, Langobardi, and the Semnones. All of the chiefdoms convened once a year in the sacred groves of the Semnones to declare their continued cohesion. This did not always hold true, for many Suebi joined Marobodus, and others, with the Marcomanni, were settled on the lands of the Roman Empire.

Fighting between Rome and the Suebi occurred frequently. A bitter struggle raged in 97–98 C.E. along the Danube, and Marcus Arelius (c. 178) included them in his vast Germanic campaign north of the Danubian frontier. The tribes were still in existence in the early fifth century C.E., when they crashed across the Rhine, invading Gaul and pushing all the way to Spain with the other barbarian nations of the era.

Suessiones A large tribe living in GALLIA Belgica during the first century B.C.E.; under their King GALBA (1) they were forced to defend their lands from Roman invasion by Julius CAESAR in 57 B.C.E. Despite a heroic stand at the battle of AXONA, they were defeated utterly and forced to submit to Rome. Once second only to the

Bellovaci in strength, by their defeat they were forced to become clients for a time to the smaller Remi. Under Roman occupation of Gallia Belgica, the Suessiones were allowed to retain their lands. Romanization was pronounced within their territory; their capital, Noviodonum, was renamed Augusta Suessonum and later became known as Suessones (Soissons). The Suessiones were noted farmer, holding fertile soil just north of the Seine River and Lutetia (Paris).

Suetonius (Gaius Suetonius Tranquillus) (69 or 70–after 103 C.E.) *Important Roman historian and influential writer*
Born in Hippo, AFRICA, Suetonius was educated in law, probably teaching literature in Rome before serving as a lawyer and a member of the staff of PLINY THE YOUNGER, then governor of Bithynia (c. 110–112 C.E.). As a member of the Equestrians (EQUITES), Suetonius returned to Rome where a position at the imperial court awaited him. He was a minor secretary and then director of the imperial libraries, both positions most likely under TRAJAN (ruled 98–117 C.E.).

When HADRIAN became emperor in 117, Suetonius was promoted to AB EPISTULIS, or secretary of correspondence. This post remained his until around 122, when, with Praetorian Prefect Septicius Clarus, he was dismissed by Hadrian for being overly familiar with Empress SABINA. It is possible that he was able to return to Hadrian's favor some years later. He was alive in 130 after which date there is no record of him.

Suetonius first focused on his writing in the reign of Trajan, never stopping from that time on. As the first known Latin biographer, he seemed to deviate consciously from TACITUS's chronological style, preferring to arrange his material and sources in an anecdotal, even episodic manner. Rhetoric overshadowed exactitude. Aside from his works on grammar and history, two collections of biographies most displayed Suetonius's literary talent: *De Viris Illustribus (Lives of the Great Men)* and *De Vita Caesarum (Lives of the Caesars)*. *Lives of the Great Men* was a Greek-influenced group of biographies on the major figures of Roman literature. He included grammarians and rhetors (*De Grammaticus et Rhetoribus*); 33 poets (*De Poetis*), including VIRGIL, HORACE, LUCAN, and Terence; and historians, starting with SALLUST. Unfortunately, only fragments of these biographies have survived.

Preserved virtually in its entirety, with only a few early chapters of Julius CAESAR's life missing, the so-called *Twelve Caesars* covered the first Roman rulers from Caesar to DOMITIAN. It was dedicated to Septicius Clarus and relied heavily upon state archives, at least until Suetonius was dismissed and lost access to them. This happened perhaps after the Augustan account. For sources Suetonius certainly used the *Acts* of Augustus, as well as Cremutius Cordus and Gaius Asinius Pollio. Other sources are unclear, as he failed to mention them. Suetonius had a lasting effect on historical composition. Einhard's ninth-century *Charlemagne* and Petrarch's 14th-century *Lives* both looked to Suetonius as their model.

Suggested Readings: Hurley, Donna W. *An Historical and Historiographical Commentary on Suetonius' Life of C. Caligula.* Atlanta, Ga.: Scholars Press, 1993; Suetonius. *The Twelve Caesars.* Translated by Robert Graves. New York: Penguin, 1979; Wallace-Hadrill, Andrew. *Suetonius: The Scholar and His Caesars.* New Haven, Conn.: Yale University Press, 1984.

Suetonius Paulinus, Gaius (fl. first century C.E.) *Consul in 66 C.E. and general in Africa and Britain*
Suetonius first gained notoriety around 41 C.E., when he was sent as a legate to Mauretania to put down a violent local revolt. Although eventually replaced by Hosidius Geta, his reputation was so firmly in place that he was the obvious choice as governor of Britain in 58. According to the historian TACITUS, by 61 he was jealous of the great General CORBULO in Armenia and thus launched his own campaign against the Druid stronghold of Mona (now the island of Anglesey). While his troops conquered the isle, hacking down the sacred groves of the Druids, word arrived that in his absence, Queen BOUDICCA of the Iceni had launched her legendary uprising. Severe fighting was needed before the Britons could be pacified. Ordered to do nothing more by NERO, he was superceded by Petronius Turpilianus. A consulship followed in 66, and in 69, OTHO, looking for generals to bolster his political and military position, brought the aging Suetonius out of retirement. Having lost none of his sense of strategy, the old officer strongly recommended that the Othonians decline battle with VITELLIUS's legions at BEDRIACUM in April of that year. His advice was not heeded, and Otho was defeated. Vitellius, however, allowed Suetonius to return to his quiet life.
See also DRUIDS AND DRUIDISM; 69 C.E.

Suillius Rufus, Publius (fl. first century C.E.) *Consul in 46 C.E., governor of Asia, and a hated orator in Rome*
Suillius was once a QUAESTOR under GERMANICUS, and for this he was banished by TIBERIUS in 24 on a charge of judicial bribery, but was allowed to return by Claudius. He involved himself in accusations, acting as a *delator* (*see* DELATORES) with his excellent skills in speaking. Acquiring many enemies, he was finally tried for corruption by NERO in 58. Found guilty, Suillius Rufus was exiled to the Balearic Islands. Refusing to act like a criminal, he made certain that his life there was pleasant.

Sulla, Publius Cornelius (d. 46 B.C.E.) *Son of the famous Roman dictator and a minor political figure of the late Republic*

A lieutenant in the army of POMPEY THE GREAT. Sulla was with Pompey in 63 B.C.E. when Jerusalem was captured, distinguishing himself as one of the first soldiers to enter the city. Three years later he amazed ROME with a magnificent gladiatorial show in memory of his father. An AUGUR in 57, he was chosen by the SENATE to build a new meeting place, following the destruction of the Senate's CURIA HOSTILIA in 52. His work on the CURIA CORNELIA was aborted by Julius CAESAR, who wanted no interference with his CURIA JULIA. Not surprisingly, Sulla joined the Pompeian cause at the start of the CIVIL WAR. Present at the battle of PHARSALUS, he fled to Africa and was captured and put to death after the battle of THAPSUS in 46.

Sulpicia (fl. late first century C.E.) *Poetess*
She addressed her poems to her husband Calenas and was considered one of the few women writers of the era.

Sulpicianus, Titus Flavius (d. 197 C.E.) *Prefect of the city in 193*
Sulpicianus was a participant in the auctioning of the Roman Empire by the PRAETORIAN GUARD. Sulpicianus was appointed Pertinax's successor as urban prefect shortly after the new emperor's accession. He was sent to the CASTRA PRAETORIA on March 28, 193, to bring the mutinous Praetorians back to order, learning while there that Pertinax had been assassinated. Intriguing with the Guard to have himself elevated to the throne, he found a rival in the person of DIDIUS JULIANUS. The two of them bid for the throne, and Sulpicianus lost. He was allowed to live, but in 197, Emperor Septimius SEVERUS put him to death for being a supporter of Clodius Albinus.

Sulpicius Asper (d. 65 C.E.) *Centurion of the Praetorian Guard*
In 65 C.E., Sulpicius Asper joined the Pisonian Conspiracy bent on murdering Nero. When asked later by the emperor why he had entered into the plot, he replied, "I saw no other way to reform you."

Sura, Lucius Licinius (d. c. 110 C.E.) *Consul in 97, 102, and 107 C.E.*
One of the closest friends of Emperor TRAJAN, he was sent in 100 as an envoy to the Dacian King DECEBALUS; and he commanded a body of troops in Trajan's Dacian Wars. He was awarded a triumphal insignia but enjoyed greater fame for the absolute trust placed in him by Trajan. The ruler frequently spent days in Sura's home, without attendants, despite the jealous attacks of fellow courtiers. Sura was also partly responsible for introducing the future Emperor HADRIAN to Trajan, encouraging the two men to be on excellent terms. It was Sura who announced to Hadrian that he had been adopted as the royal heir. Sura died around 110 and was honored with a statue and a public funeral.

Surenas (d. 55 B.C.E.) *Parthian general*
Surenas was responsible for the destruction of the Roman general Marcus Licinius CRASSUS (1), at the battle of CARRHAE in 55 B.C.E. A powerful officer in the Parthian army, Surenas came to the aid of King ORODES II against his brother MITHRIDATES (c. 57–56), driving Mithridates out of the country and ensuring that Orodes became king. Thus, when Triumvir Crassus attempted his invasion of Mesopotamia, Orodes once more turned to his lieutenant. While the king made war upon Rome's Armenian allies, Surenas was given freedom to conduct operations against Crassus. Concerned that he might use this triumph to seize the throne, Orodes put Surenas to death a short time later.

Symmachus, Quintus Aurelius (d. c. 402 C.E.) *Consul in 391, prefect of the city of Rome, and one of the greatest orators in Roman history*
Symmachus was the SENATE's spokesman in the fourth century and served organized PAGANISM in the same fashion, while enjoying a reputation for poetry. He was a member of the old aristocratic family of the Symmachi, which owned estates on the Caelian Hill and in AFRICA. His education was entrusted to a Gallic teacher of RHETORIC. Embarking on a senatorial career, Symmachus served as a member of a priesthood (c. 365) and in 369 was sent to Gaul as a representative of the Senate to Emperor VALENTINIAN I, meeting and befriending the writer Ausonius. Presumably for his skills in speaking he was rewarded in 373 with the proconsulship of Africa. Back in Rome in 376, he spent several years delivering speeches on various subjects. In 382, an important cause presented itself, the defense of paganism.

Symmachus was an ardent pagan who had already complained during his priesthood that being a pagan was very difficult with a Christian imperial government. Under Emperor Gratian life became even worse. The emperor ordered the Altar of VICTORY removed from the Senate. When Symmachus attempted to have the policy changed, the ruler refused to see him. As Gratian increased the official persecution of paganism, Symmachus emerged as the leading figure in its defense. His powers were increased with the prefectship of the city, but each attempt at reinstating pagan rights, especially the Altar of Victory, was rebuffed, largely through the machinations of AMBROSE, bishop of Milan.

Despite a consulship in 391 and the honorific title of *PRINCEPS SENATUS*, Symmachus was intermittently ill and even had to leave Rome in 398, chased out by a mob for some unknown reason. He was allowed to return home a short time later, but fell ill again in 400 and died sometime around 402. Many of his speeches were preserved, mainly in fragments, but his greatest contribution came in the form of his 900 letters. Organized into 10 books, Symmachus's letters were very similar to those of PLINY THE YOUNGER, and were addressed to the most notable personages of the times. Thus they served as valuable documents of the social climate of the fourth century, although they were often superficial, decorated, and written with an eye to posterity.

Synesius of Cyrene (c. 370–413/414 C.E.) *Bishop of Ptolemais and poet*
Synesius was born in Cyrene and was raised as a pagan, studying in ALEXANDRIA under the Neoplatonist HYPATIA. Despite his PAGANISM, Synesius was chosen to be ambassador to CONSTANTINOPLE in 399. Before Emperor Arcadius he delivered a speech on the supreme ideal of a Roman emperor, *De Regno*. Returning to Cyrenaica, Synesius married a Christian woman in 403, had three children and faced a major decision in 410. Elected bishop of Ptolemais, he pondered for a long time and then gave up his family, was consecrated by Theophilus of Alexandria and became a prelate. It is possible that he was not yet a Christian at the time. A spiritual figure, Synesius proved a strong leader. He died in 413 or 414, spared the tragic news of Hypatia's murder in 415. Synesius authored numerous books. Aside from his letters and hymns he wrote *De Providentia* on Constantinople; *Calvitii Encomium*, a satire on baldness; *Dion*, a defense of learning and Greek culture; and *De Dono Astrolabii*, a study of astrolabes.

See also SIDONIUS APOLLINARIS, for a similar career.

Syracuse One of the oldest cities on the Italian peninsula and, during its Roman occupation, the chief seat of government for Sicily (SICILIA). Known as Syracusa, this famous site in southern Sicily was founded in the eighth century B.C.E. near the mouth of the Anapus River, close to the Syraco Marsh. Established by Corinthians and Dorians, Syracuse developed into a major port in the Mediterranean. It boasted two harbors, the Great, called *Porto Maggiore,* and the Small, *Laccius.* Athenian and later Carthaginian fleets were stationed there, at least until around 213/12 B.C.E., when Rome captured the island. It was natural for Syracuse to serve as the capital of the province of Sicily, and considerable effort was spent in the first century C.E. to restore its economic health. This was accomplished through colonists, sent in by AUGUSTUS, and with numerous building programs. Syracuse was thus an interesting blend of Greek and Roman designs. There was a temple of Apollo (sixth century B.C.E.), a temple of Jupiter, and one of the largest amphitheaters (third century B.C.E.) in the Roman Empire.

Syria One of the largest and most important provinces of the Roman Empire, the linchpin of imperial concerns in the East. Syria was the protector of the vital provinces of ASIA MINOR, the key TRADE routes from the Far East, and the Roman defense against the Parthian and later Persian Empires. A truly ancient country even before its conquest by Alexander the Great in the fourth century B.C.E., Syria's name was derived from the Aramaic *Surja*. It came to be applied to a vast portion of the Middle East, including the area west of the TIGRIS, east of Asia Minor, and north of the Arabians and Palestinians, who were themselves at times under its jurisdiction. The original inhabitants were Aramaeans, or Syro-Arabians, but throughout ancient history successive invasions brought Assyrians, Babylonians, Persians, Macedonians, and, after the battle of Ipsus in 301 B.C.E., the Seleucids of Seleucus Nicator, Alexander's general.

From 301 to 79 B.C.E., the Seleucids were players in the political game of the East. Suffering repeated setbacks they were reduced by the Romans and the Parthians to just the region of Syria by the first century B.C.E. and were conquered entirely by King Tigranes of ARMENIA in 79. Syria soon fell prey to chaos and bloody sorties from the surrounding nations. Nabataeans, Ituraeans, Arabs, and Parthians all had designs on the cities or the rich caravan routes. Such was the situation encountered by POMPEY THE GREAT when he arrived there in 64 B.C.E. He quickly declared Syria a Roman possession, transforming it into a province for the Republic. But instead of annihilating the host of petty kingdoms throughout Syria, he compelled them to become clients of Rome with the task of defending the frontiers. The numerous Greek towns he allowed to retain their independence, appreciating their influence in Syria as instruments of Hellenization and hence civilization.

With the founding of the Roman Empire, the vision of Pompey was proven correct. The client states were still in existence and still loyal to Rome: CHALCIS, JUDAEA, ARABIA, and NABATAEA. As part of his imperial policy of manning hostile frontiers with vassals, AUGUSTUS chose to keep Pompey's organization while encouraging the Hellenistic cities. The imperial province of Syria at this time, and throughout the first century C.E., stretched from Cappadocia to Arabia (including Judaea, from 6 to 66 C.E.), administered by a procurator. After the fall of Jerusalem in 70 C.E., Judaea was made a separate province under a Praetorian legate, with its own garrisons taken from a large four-legion command of the legate of Syria. The presence of such a sizeable force left little doubt as to where Rome felt it faced enemies. The post of governor of Syria was considered the most powerful imperial office in the East. The career opportunities open to a successful legate were endless, and authority as governor was such that even the IMPERIUM MAIUS could be questioned, as by Piso of Germanicus in 19 C.E.

These strengths increased throughout the final years of the first and second centuries C.E. Starting with VESPASIAN in 72 C.E., the clients were absorbed and put under the administration of the legate at ANTIOCH (1), the provincial capital. COMMAGENE was one of the first to be incorporated. There followed Ituraea, the Jordan-based realm, in 93, and other weak domains. Syria did lose two notable sections, aside from Judaea; CILICIA was made independent by Vespasian in 73, and NABATAEA was annexed separately by Trajan in 106; and subsequently became the province of Arabia.

A more serious blow to the status of the legate came around 194, when Emperor Septimius SEVERUS divided Syria into two provinces, Syria Coele in the north and Syria Phoenice in the south. His action was merely a continuation of the provincial reform seen in Britain, born out of concern that too many legions were available to one general. He had just endured a civil war with Pescennius Niger, governor of Syria, and did not want to repeat the experience or face another crisis, such as Avidius Cassius presented in Marcus Aurelius's time.

The changes in provincial government did little to curtail the vibrant life of the province. Throughout the imperial epoch, Syria was the most enduring example of generally positive Roman rule to be found anywhere. In marked contrast to Egypt, where the Romans pillaged all available financial and natural resources, Syria enjoyed three centuries of stable rule, careful imperial development of culture, and the long-term ideal of economic health. If Syria was remarkably different from Egypt, it was a stern rival in matters of industry and commerce. Linen weaving, agriculture (plums, nuts, and other fruits), purple-dying, and glass-blowing were the province's major source of locally produced income. Of immense value was the trade system that crossed the Syrian deserts to Antioch, TYRE, PALMYRA, PETRA, and DAMASCUS. While Egypt had Alexandria, Syria had many other cities, especially Antioch and Palmyra, that were directly connected to PARTHIA, INDIA, and the entire East. Syrian traders and merchants organized caravans, and Roman soldiers were given the task of protecting them from local insurrections or desert nomads.

Despite the risk of being ordered to war, as happened throughout the third century, service in Syria was a happy one for the legions. In the reign of TIBERIUS there were four legions: III Gallica, VI Ferrata, X Fretensis, and XII Fulminata. By 74 C.E. the JEWISH WAR had been fought, and there remained the III Gallica and the IV Scythica. The mid-second century saw three legions there: III Gallica, IV Scythica, and XVI Flavia. The Roman troops became acclimatized to the friendly environment of Syria. In fact, in 69 C.E. Governor Mucianus convinced the legions that they should support Vespasian, with the story that VITELLIUS in Rome planned to replace them with the Rhine legions, sending the Syrian units to the dangerous forts of Germania—that was enough to have them march off to war.

Because of the Seleucid tradition, Greek was both the language of domestic government and the culture imposed upon Syria. The Greek cities were given the right to have their own constitutions and had a certain autonomy. These privileges were kept by the emperors as a tool for introducing civilization to the millions of Syrians in the villages. The sheer number of villages, however, made the task virtually impossible. Aramaic persisted in the countryside, as did the native tongue in Egypt. Greek thus became the language of the educated, the upper classes, and business. In cities and with the help of Rome, Greek did find fertile ground among the workers of the lower classes.

Unfortunately, details of the Roman administration and sociopolitical life in Syria are limited. Clearly the presence of the legions had an impact, and Latin would have been spoken in those towns founded by Roman patronage. Most recruits from Syria, a very large group, would pick up some vulgar Latin through their years in the army.

The calm of Syria was shattered in the third century C.E. In 255–256, SHAPUR I, king of Persia, stormed into Syria, marching to the gates of Antioch. After the defeat and capture of VALERIAN (259–260 C.E.), Shapur was back, this time netting Antioch itself. Although rescued by ODAENATH of Palmyra, Syria would never again feel safe. With the reforms of DIOCLETIAN the province became part of the diocese of Oriens, but never lost its place as a first-class possession of a weakening empire.

See also ARSACID DYNASTY; BAALBEK; BERYTUS; EMESA; GALERIUS; IAMBLICHUS; LUCIAN; MANICHAEISM; MAXIMUS OF TYRE; MESOPOTAMIA; NEOPLATONISM; NICOLAUS OF DAMASCUS; PALAESTINA; PAPINIAN; SASSINID DYNASTY; SOL INVICTUS; STOICISM; TATIAN; ULPIAN; VERUS, LUCIUS; ZENOBIA.

Syrus, Publilius (fl. first century B.C.E.) *Syrian-born actor*
Syrus came to ROME during the middle of the first century B.C.E. Originally a slave, he acquired his freedom mainly through sheer talent, subsequently becoming the leading performer of his age. Known to Julius CAESAR, Syrus defeated the venerable Roman Laberius in a theatrical competition sponsored by the dictator in 45. Specializing in mime, Syrus authored several notable mimes, including *Murmurithon*. Praised by such writers as SENECA the Elder and Petronius, his verses were used in education. Some of his sayings became quite famous, especially "the end justifies the means" and "honor among thieves."

T

Tacfarinas (d. 24 C.E.) *Rebel chief in Africa from 17 to 24 C.E.*

A Numidian by birth, Tacfarinas became an auxiliary in the Roman army. In 17, he deserted, gathered together a group of followers, ravaged the provinces and became the leader of the local Musulamii. Four Roman generals campaigned against the rebel. Camillus defeated the Musulamii and their Moorish allies in 17, winning triumphal honors, while the new proconsul of Africa, APRONIUS, helped to thwart a Tacfarinas attack in 20 C.E. Blaesus used guerrilla tactics against him in 22, and in 24 P. Cornelius DOLABELLA arrived to finish the war. Marching through the country with four flying columns, Tacfarinas was trapped by the Romans and killed in battle.

Tacitus (1), Publius Cornelius (c. 55–120? C.E.) *Last of the great Roman classical historians*

Little has survived of his own life except for the barest details of a public career. He was probably of Gallic descent, attaining senatorial rank during the reign of VESPASIAN. Further advancement came after 77, when he married the daughter of AGRICOLA. He was made a QUAESTOR in 81 and a PRAETOR in 88, and received an appointment to the quindecemviri. With a consulship in 97, Tacitus had survived the harsh time of DOMITIAN, a period that saw the death of his father-in-law and a regime whose cultivated despotism left a major mark on his writings. Viewed as one of the foremost orators of the age, Tacitus delivered the funeral oration for L. VERGINIUS RUFUS in 97. Three years later he prosecuted Marius Priscus for extortion, receiving help from PLINY the Younger. In 112–113, Tacitus became proconsul of Asia, dying a few years later.

By 100, Tacitus had already turned to writing. Clearly an admirer of the Republic, Tacitus was willing (or driven) to describe the despotic rule of the emperors. His policy of reporting only verifiable accounts rather than rumor or gossip, made his narratives all the more vivid. His style was fluid and direct, his text a mixture of poetical color and classical methodology. Ultimately, the writer's own independence and vision transcend the often bitter, melancholy, and outrageous tales. His extant works are:

Annals The longest, and perhaps finest, of Tacitus's writings. His last project, he was possibly working on it at his death. It covers the entire Julian dynasty from after the death of AUGUSTUS in 14 C.E. to perhaps the death of NERO in 68. All or part of 11 books (of 16) are extant; there may have been more. Called also *Ob Excessus Divi Augusti* (After the death of the deified Augustus), the *Annals* was written chronologically, highlighting the events of each year, often with a list of the consuls, and including events both in Rome and in the provinces. Tacitus wrote that he hoped to finish with accounts of the reigns of Augustus, NERVA, and TRAJAN, the former for the *Annals* and the latter for the *Histories,* but he never attained his goal.

Dialogue on the Orators (Dialogus de Oratoribus) This treatise was once considered his first book, though new dating places it perhaps around 100 and not in the late 70s, as was theorized. There has always been debate about Tacitus's authorship, a view now held in scholarly disrepute because of the inability to find a contemporary capable of writing it. In the *Dialogue*, Tacitus pleads the decay of oratory, using Ciceronian RHETORIC, argument, and observation.

Germania (De Origine et Situ Germanorum) Germania was a monograph on the peoples inhabiting the barbarian lands behind the Rhine. While Tacitus was aware of the great threat posed to the empire by the Germans, his book displayed remarkable interest, detail, and even sympathy toward the tribes and their cultures. While much of his information was inaccurate, Tacitus compared the Germans to the Romans; although the Romans naturally fared well, the historian admitted to the vitality of the barbarians and to the deteriorated ways of his own people.

Historia With the *Annals*, Tacitus's most important work. Composed sometime around 106–107, the *Histories* covered the events of the Roman Empire from 69 to 96, under the rule of GALBA, OTHO, VITELLIUS, VESPASIAN, TITUS, and Domitian. Unfortunately, the latter sections did not survive; all that remains of perhaps 14 books are books one to four and part of book five, roughly the entire civil war and some of the events that followed. It is fascinating because of the emphasis placed on the major and minor players alike, each with their own, often three-dimensional character.

On the Life of Julius Agricola (De Vita Iulii Agricolae) This biography was published probably in 98. Centering on his father-in-law's campaigns in Britain (BRITANNIA), it is the primary source for the events of Agricola's life and career. *Agricola* was more of a *laudatio* than a mere biography. There was, as well, a reminder of the tyranny of Domitian, contrasted with the loyalty of Agricola.

Suggested Readings: Chilver, Guy E. F. *A Historical Commentary on Tacitus' Histories IV and V.* New York: Oxford University Press, 1985; Dudley, Donald R. *The World of Tacitus.* Boston: Little, Brown, 1969; Kraus, C. S., and A. J. Woodman. *Latin Historians.* Oxford, U.K.: Oxford University Press, 1997; Mellor, Ronald. *Tacitus.* New York: Routledge, 1993; Syme, Ronald. *Tacitus.* Oxford, U.K.: Clarendon Press, 1958; Tacitus, Cornelius. *Empire and Emperors: Selections from Tacitus' Annals.* Translated by Graham Tingay. New York: Cambridge University Press, 1983; ———. *The Annals of Imperial Rome.* Translated with an introduction by Michael Grant. New York: Penguin, 1964; ———. *Annales.* Edited by Henry Furneaux. Oxford, U.K.: Clarendon Press, 1965; ———. *De Vita Agricolae.* Edited by R. M. Ogilvie. Oxford, U.K.: Clarendon Press, 1967; ———. *Historiae.* Edited by H. Heubner. Stuttgart, Ger.: B. G. Teubner, 1978; ———. *The Histories.* New York: Penguin, 1989.

Tacitus (2), Marcus Claudius (d. 276 C.E.) *Emperor from November 275 to around June 276*
Tacitus is one of the least known emperors because of the large amount of wholly unreliable information about him. His reign was detailed in the writings of the SCRIPTORES HISTORIAE AUGUSTAE, EUTROPIUS (1) and others, who describe him as an old senator, chosen by the SENATE to succeed AURELIAN and to recreate the constitutional government of former days, but such accounts were probably inaccurate. Tacitus was most likely a senator elected by the army in 275 to follow Aurelian. The Senate naturally agreed, while Tacitus humbly accepted power. The new emperor asked that Aurelian be deified and then declared his half brother Florian his Prefect of the PRAETORIAN GUARD. The pair then set out against the GOTHS, who threatened to ravage ASIA MINOR once more. Tacitus won a major victory, taking the title Gothicus Maximus, but he died soon after, in June 276, either at the hands of the army or of natural causes.

Tamesis (Thames) The most important river in Britain, giving direct access to the sea to the provincial city and port of LONDINIUM (London). The river had potential in terms of economic growth that was not overlooked by the traders there, even before the Roman conquest. After the rise of Londinium, the river became even more valuable.

Tapae Dacian site of two battles fought between the Romans and the Dacians, in 88 and 101 C.E. The first battle was part of Emperor DOMITIAN's campaign against the Dacian King DECEBALUS, with the Roman legions under the command of Tettius Julianus. Taking place near the Iron Gates, a deep gorge cut by the DANUBE River about 100 miles east of modern Belgrade, the conflict was an absolute success for Rome. Not only were the Dacians soundly defeated, but also Decebalus's lieutenant Vezinas, died on the field. While the first battle ended the war, it did not prevent later struggles. Another war broke out between Decebalus and Emperor TRAJAN, at the head of his own LEGIONS. During his advance on Dacia, Trajan fought at the same site. Decebalus was unvanquished. The conflict continued.

Tarentum, Treaty of Agreement signed in the spring of 37 B.C.E. between Octavian (AUGUSTUS) and Marc ANTONY. The year 38 had proven an unhappy one for Octavian and Antony, for the pirate Sextus POMPEY had shown himself to be a fearsome opponent to Caesar's heir, and Antony was in desperate need of troops. Octavian had missed a meeting at BRUNDISIUM, blaming Antony for not waiting. By the spring of 37, a new place and date was set at Tarentum, and Antony arrived with 300 ships for use by Octavian against Pompey, expecting in return help for his war against PARTHIA. The meeting was fraught with mistrust and tension. A disaster might have occurred had not OCTAVIA intervened, bringing the two stubborn men to the table. In the end, the triumvirate was reaffirmed; the two men promised mutual support and stripped Sextus Pompey of all rights and privileges given at MISENUM. The two departed, but suspicions remained between them.

Tarsus Also spelled Tarsos; the capital of the province of Cilicia. Situated in Cilicia Campestris, on the river Cydnus, it was probably founded by the Syrians and later used as a focal colony for the Greeks. The city suffered from attacks in the first century B.C.E. by Tigranes of Armenia and the famed Cilician pirates. When POMPEY THE GREAT defeated the pirates in 67 B.C.E., he created the Cilician province, declaring Tarsus its capital. Tarsus was highly favored in the imperial administration of AUGUSTUS, due in part to the emperor's tutor, ATHENADORUS who came from that city, which hosted the imperial legate and provincial assembly. The first metropolis in Cilicia, Tarsus enjoyed considerable autonomy, including freedom from taxes. Her prized status was eventually challenged by the citizens of Anazarbus to the northeast. Two events made Tarsus memorable. In 41 B.C.E., Marc ANTONY greeted CLEOPATRA there after she had sailed up the Cydnus in her famous gold barge. And in the first century C.E., Tarsus produced its most famous son, the Christian Saint Paul of Tarsus.

Tatian (second century C.E.) *Christian writer and theologian, of Assyrian descent*
Tatian was educated in Greek RHETORIC and philosophy. Between 150 and 165, he converted to CHRISTIANITY, becoming a pupil of JUSTIN MARTYR. Tatian displayed tendencies toward GNOSTICISM, finding full expression for his heretical views during a trip to the East (c. 172), when he founded the sect of the Encratites, a Gnostic group of ascetics. He wrote two important works, the *Oratio ad Graecos* (Address to the Greeks), a vicious condemnation of Hellenic civilization, and the *Diatessaron,* a history of the life of Christ that remained a doctrinal source for the Syrian Church until the fifth century.

Tatianus, Flavius Eutolmius (fl. late fourth century C.E.) *Praetorian prefect of the Orient from 388 to 392*
From LYCIA, Tatianus served as an ADVOCATUS to various government officials and was appointed *praefectus augustalis* of Egypt in 367. In 370, he became head of Syria and the Orient (until 374), earning, according to LIBANIUS, the reputation of flogging criminals to death. In 381, Emperor THEODOSIUS I summoned him back to court, and in 388 made him Praetorian prefect. He acted as the main agent of government while Theodosius was in the West. He was made a consul in 391, while his son Proculus became prefect of the city of CONSTANTINOPLE.

Through the intrigues of RUFINUS, the *MAGISTER OFFICIORUM*, Tatianus's political position was slowly destroyed. He was forced to watch the execution of his son and was himself condemned. Reprieved, Tatianus was exiled to Lycia, where he remained until Rufinus suffered his own demise. Tatianus was rehabilitated but reportedly died a blind beggar. A pagan, Tatianus used legislation to further his own anticlerical views, refusing to allow criminals to find sanctuary among the clergy or for monks to enter towns.

Taurus, Titus Statilius (fl. late first century B.C.E.) *Highly respected general and consul during the later Republic*
Taurus became one of the leading supporters of Octavian (AUGUSTUS) against Marc ANTONY. Considered by the writer Velleius Paterculus to be second only to Marcus AGRIPPA in military importance, Taurus was used in a large number of operations by Octavian. In 36 B.C.E. he won over virtually all of Africa and, in 34 took over the campaign against the Dalmatians when Octavian departed for Rome to assume a consulship. When the Civil War erupted against Antony, Taurus made a successful charge against enemy cavalry near Actium that convinced Philadelphus, king of Paphlagonia, to desert Antony's cause. In 29 he was in Spain, suppressing local tribes, including the Cantabri and Astures. Consul in 26, he was given command of the city of Rome of Augustus, when the emperor set out on his tour of the provinces. Taurus also erected a stone amphitheater in the Campus Martius, the first of its kind in Rome. His heirs included four later consuls and NERO's third wife, Statilia MESSALLINA.

taxation For centuries, the imperial tax system was a demonstration of the favored status of Rome and Italy, and mirrored Rome's policy toward its provinces and subject peoples. The government of the Republic followed the Greek model in its program of taxation, in that it had no direct taxes, with the exception of emergencies or extraordinary situations. There were, however, forms of indirect revenue enhancement. The most important of these were the 5% charge on the manumission of slaves (*vicesima manumissionis*) and the harbor tax. Allies or clients of Rome did not pay any taxes either, but fulfilled their oaths with troops and with ships.

All of this changed as the Republic acquired provinces. Each territory had to yield a fixed sum in direct and indirect taxes, but there was no set method for collection. Whatever local system was in place at the time could be retained so long as it fulfilled the purpose and was reasonably efficient. A more uniform formula for taxation was put in place by the imperial regime of AUGUSTUS. The key to taxation was the census used in every province to determine populations. From those figures came new quotas. Rome and Italy were, of course, spared every kind of direct tax but continued to pay indirectly.

Thus the census was increasingly important to the entire imperial financial system.

All Roman citizens were immune to direct taxation until the year 217 C.E., when CARACALLA issued the monumental Constitutio Antoniniana, by which all residents of the empire were given full citizenship. All were now subject to payment, except for Italy, which retained its historic privilege until at least the time of DIOCLETIAN in the late third century. That emperor ended Italian supremacy and instituted direct taxation, the same found in every other province.

The direct tax, collected from the provinces, was called TRIBUTUM. During the Republican era the *tributum* consisted of a fixed amount (STIPENDIUM) or a tithe (*decumae*). With the dawning of the empire and the application of the census, more accurate means of judging population were available. Based upon the census figures, a number of taxable regions per province (areas eligible for taxation) was found (the *iuga* or *capita*), a group of taxable units that would vary from census to census. From the *capita* was calculated how much was owed in the main direct tax, the *tributum solis* or land tax. Anyone who owned land paid, but provinces also had to make payments in other items or services. These included arms, food, and or other supplies for the legions that defended them or the bureaucrats who administered the cities. For those who did not own land there was a different tax, the *tributum capitis*, or poll tax. All members of this group who were over the age of 20 or 25, male or female, were liable, but females paid only half. Two forms of the *tributum capitis* existed, one for the country and another for the city. Taxes in the city were based on whatever property was owned and on wages from a field of work.

Collection was in the hands of the provincial government, trickling down to the local community and the *exactores*, the loathed tax collectors. The treatment given to Matthew in the New Testament accounts was very typical, while in some regions any protest against the empire was often started with the wholesale slaughter the tax collectors, the most prominent image of imperial tyranny. In the later years of the empire all means were used to ensure the acquisition of revenues, the main burden falling on DECURIONES, or local magistrates. Any arrears in taxes had to be paid by them, an arduous and expensive obligation that could lead to imprisonment, torture, and even death if not fulfilled.

The indirect system of taxation was considerably adjusted by the fiscal policy of Augustus. Citizens had to pay the harbor tax but new taxes were added as well. A 4% tax on the price of slaves formed the *quinta et vicesima manicipiorum*, while the tax on manumission continued. The *centesima rerum venalium* levied a 1% charge on all goods sold at auction, and the *vicesima hereditatum et legatorum* imposed a 5% tax on inheritance of estates over 100,000 sesterces by persons other than the next of kin, or on all willed legacies.

Temple of Apollo

Large temple erected by AUGUSTUS (Octavian) on the Palatine Hill in Rome in 28 B.C.E., in honor of his Greek divine patron, APOLLO. Octavian had pledged to construct a suitable place of worship to the god as part of his vows to avenge the death of Julius CAESAR. Seemingly, Apollo blessed Octavian in this endeavor, for there was a small temple to the god at ACTIUM, overlooking the battle that sealed Octavian's final victory, in 31 B.C.E. As a clear indication of his devotion to Apollo, Augustus had the temple placed next to his own humble residence on the Palatine. Dedicated in 28 B.C.E., the sanctuary housed both an image of the god and two libraries, one in Greek and the other in Latin.

Temple of Castor and Pollux

A shrine dedicated to the gods Castor and Pollux (the DIOSCURI), situated prominently in the FORUM ROMANUM to honor the deities who, according to legend, came to the aid of the Romans in 496 B.C.E. at the battle of Lake Regillus against the Latins. For their help, Aulus Postumus Albinus, the commanding general, promised to build them a place of worship in the city. The site was well chosen, and the temple was completed in 484. In design the sanctuary was of average size, typically rectangular. It required renovation in 117 B.C.E., by Lucius Dalmaticus, by which time it had probably accumulated around it many *tabernae veteres*, or shops and vendors. The presence of these stalls no doubt contributed to the destruction of the temple in 14 B.C.E., when a fire struck the Forum. TIBERIUS, in Augustus's name, dedicated the rebuilt temple, the last structure finished in the Augustan principate, in 6 C.E. GAIUS CALIGULA, in 40, turned the temple into a vestibule, cutting the temple in two between the statues so that they might act as gatekeepers to his own divine person. CLAUDIUS returned them to their rightful place in 41. As typical of the decline in Rome, the temple was destroyed in the fourth century C.E. and never rebuilt. Of interest was the 1985 discovery by archaeologists of 86 teeth near the ancient entrance to the temple; the teeth belonged to the patients of a dentist who operated out of a nearby *taberna*. Popular usage changed the name of the temple to Aedes Castoris, or Temple of Castor.

Temple of Concord

One of the numerous temples within Rome's FORUM ROMANUM; dedicated to the goddess Concordia, a minor deity of unity. The first temple was founded by Marcus Furius Camillus in 367 B.C.E.; the site chosen was the *comitium*, or meetingplace of the Patricians. A new Temple of Concord was ordered to be built sometime after the death of Gaius Gracchus, by the unpopular consul Opimius (c. 121 B.C.E.), and yet another one was created by TIBERIUS in honor of himself and his brother DRUSUS in 10 C.E. In the Forum Romanum, the temple occupied the position just behind the later Arch of Severus, next to the Temple of Vespasian and the Dungeons of TULLIANUM. African marble was used in the construction of the lost temple, and the interior was apparently well decorated. The SENATE met there often, including the day in 31 C.E. when it condemned the Praetorian Prefect SEJANUS to death.

Temple of Divus Augustus The sanctuary constructed by Emperor TIBERIUS and his mother LIVIA in 14 C.E. as part of the ceremonies surrounding the deification of AUGUSTUS following his death. Where the temple was positioned has not been verified, but literary evidence places it between the Palatine and Capitoline hills. Quite possibly it was placed near the BASILICA JULIA, in the Velabrum. Augustus's temple was an example not only of the aggrandizement of the cult of the emperor, the IMPERIAL CULT, but also of the psychology of Tiberius and GAIUS CALIGULA. Tiberius ensured that the building was completed and then dedicated other edifices in his name. Gaius Caligula seemingly began his reign with a dedication to Augustus at the temple but then desecrated the sanctity of it with a bridge over the temple and connecting his palace to the Capitoline and the TEMPLE OF JUPITER. CLAUDIUS deified Livia in 41, and put a statue to her in the shrine.

The Temple of Castor *(Courtesy Fr. Felix Just, S.J.)*

Temple of Divus Claudius Temple constructed to the deified Emperor CLAUDIUS upon the Caelian Hill. Emperor NERO probably began construction of the sanctuary, setting it along the route of the Aqua Claudia, the aqueduct feeding that part of the city. The emperor apparently wished the outside of the temple to be decorated with fountains but focused so ardently upon this aspect of the construction that the temple itself was left incomplete. VESPASIAN, who came to power in 69 C.E., took upon himself the task of finishing the building. Despite its impressive arching, the shrine was never a major place of worship.

Temple of Divus Julius Small shrine devoted to the memory of Julius CAESAR that occupied one of the main axis points of the FORUM ROMANUM. It was positioned directly across the Forum from the TEMPLE OF CONCORD and was surrounded by some of the most beautiful edifices in Rome, the BASILICA AEMILIA, TEMPLE OF VESTA, TEMPLE OF CASTOR AND POLLUX, and the BASILICA JULIA. Caesar's temple was promised to him by Octavian (AUGUSTUS) as his avenger in 42 B.C.E. The site chosen was the very spot where Caesar was cremated after his assassination. Although work probably began and continued throughout the 30s, the temple was not dedicated until 29 B.C.E., by Octavian. It was part of his deliberate program to honor his family, while making Rome more grand.

Temple of Isis The sanctuary of the Egyptian goddess found in the CAMPUS MARTIUS. Worship of Isis was brought to Rome from the Nile, finding acceptance among the inhabitants but kept out of the POMERIUM (the sacred boundary) by the SENATE to preserve the inviolability of Roman social tradition. In 52 and 48 B.C.E., the Senate ordered her place of worship in Rome destroyed. Each time her devotees returned, and a new temple was decreed in 42 B.C.E. Official support for Isis came during the reign of GAIUS CALIGULA (37–41 C.E.), when this temple was ordered built to her in the Campus Martius. Although still outside the *pomerium*, Gaius ensured that Isis was surrounded by other beautiful structures, including the PANTHEON and the BATHS of Agrippa. In 80, a fire destroyed much of the area, but DOMITIAN saw to the repair of the temple, and a final renovation was made during the time of SEVERUS ALEXANDER (222–235).

Temple of Jerusalem, Great The center of worship in JERUSALEM that served for centuries as the heart of JUDAISM. Its destruction in 70 C.E. had a profound effect upon the Jewish religion and upon Jewish history. Biblical scholars consider that there were three such temples in Jerusalem: the first was Solomon's temple, built in the 10th century B.C.E; a second was named after Zerubabel, the local Persian governor at the time of reconstruction (c. 520 B.C.E.); and the third and most famous was

Herod's temple (c. 19 B.C.E.), an improvement completed to Herod's grand design. The last two temples figure prominently in Roman relations with the Jews.

In 63 B.C.E., POMPEY THE GREAT captured Jerusalem and desecrated the temple by entering the Holy of Holies, though he did not touch anything there. His fellow triumvir CRASSUS (1), however, plundered the temple treasury of 2,000 silver talents. HEROD THE GREAT became the king of JUDAEA in 37 B.C.E. and 18 years later began work on redesigning the entire structure. To convince the Jews of his plans, he had to finish all preparations for the new temple before touching a stone of the old edifice. In the end, the temple complex was very pleasing. Gold covered the temple, with a sanctuary along Solomonic dimensions, and the structure was placed on a large platform; the entire area was decorated with gates and columns. Further building made the temple a key part of Jerusalem.

During the Jewish Revolt, it was clear to the Romans not only that Jerusalem was the focus of the entire war, but also that the Great Temple had to be captured. Thus, when General TITUS laid siege to the city in 70, the entire operation was aimed at reaching the holy site. There has been debate as to whether or not Titus wanted the temple destroyed; JOSEPHUS the historian argued against this, but other sources pointed to Titus's acquiescence. In any event, the entire building was burned, except for two gates, its defenders dying rather than surrendering. The vessels of the temple that could be rescued were gathered up and carried by Titus's aides in his triumph in Rome.

Temple of Jupiter Capitolinus

The great structure devoted to Jupiter Optimus Maximus (Jupiter Greatest and Brightest) on Rome's Capitoline Hill. If the broad state RELIGION of Rome had an emotional or divine center, it was here, beneath the gilded roof of this vast shrine, where JUPITER, aided by MINERVA and JUNO, looked down upon the Eternal City.

The Temple of Jupiter Capitolinus was very old, dating to 509 B.C.E., when it was dedicated. It was built under the influence of the Etruscans; altars were erected not just to Jupiter but also to Juno and Minerva, the three major deities of the Roman religion: Jupiter as supreme god, Minerva as patroness of the arts and reason, and Juno in her incarnation as *Moneta,* goddess of finance. Here the consuls came upon entering office to sacrifice white bulls, and it was to Jupiter that a victorious general rode in a chariot as part of his triumph.

Because of its position on the Capitol, the temple figured in numerous historical events. It was burned in 83 B.C.E. and rebuilt. Emperor GAIUS CALIGULA connected it to his palace on the Palatine by building a bridge over the TEMPLE OF DIVUS AUGUSTUS. In 69 C.E., the brother of VESPASIAN, Flavius SABINUS, took refuge on the Capitoline from the aggression of Emperor VITELLIUS. He sealed up the entrance to the temple and was besieged. As a result of bitter fighting, virtually the entire structure was reduced to rubble. The Flavians then repaired the damage, only to have it burned again in 80. Completely restored, the temple served for centuries as one of the leading symbols of PAGANISM in Rome.

Temple of Mars Ultor

Shrine constructed by Emperor AUGUSTUS in honor of Mars Ultor, or Mars the Avenger, and placed in the most prominent position in the FORUM AUGUSTUM. In 42 B.C.E., before the battle of PHILIPPI, Octavian made a pledge to build a temple to Mars if he should prove victorious. As both BRUTUS and CASSIUS were killed in the battle, Octavian felt certain that Mars had been on his side. As Mars was also the supposed founder of the Julian *gens* (or clan), Augustus chose to situate the temple in his own Forum. The Forum was dedicated in 2 B.C.E., and the temple itself contained statues of Mars, Venus, and the deified Julius CAESAR—also the legionary standards lost at CARRHAE in 55 B.C.E. but restored to Rome in 20 B.C.E. As the Avenger, Mars Ultor received gifts from those who had achieved vengeance upon their enemies, such as GAIUS CALIGULA, who murdered Lepidus in 39 C.E. and, as though he had prevented his own assassination, sent three daggers in gratitude to the shrine.

Temple of Peace

Also called the Forum of Peace and the Forum of Vespasian; the so-called *Templum Pacis* was the creation of Emperor VESPASIAN, who began the work in 71 C.E., and dedicated the entire structure in 75. The Temple of Peace was one of numerous architectural projects started by Vespasian to celebrate both the triumph of Rome over the Jews and the return of tranquility to the Roman world. Desiring to find a prominent location for the sanctuary, Vespasian chose one of the last remaining sites available in the vast complex of the Roman forums, just to the north of the FORUM ROMANUM and to the east of the FORUM TRANSITORIUM. Within the temple were stored the many items removed from JERUSALEM and brought to Rome by TITUS. A fire destroyed the temple in 192, but Septimius SEVERUS repaired it, placing within it a marble model of Rome.

Temple of Saturn

One of the oldest temples in Rome, located in the FORUM ROMANUM and fulfilling both a religious and a political function. Dedicated in 498 or 497 B.C.E., the Temple of Saturn was near the TEMPLE OF CONCORD on the southwestern edge of the great Forum Romanum. Later, the BASILICA JULIA was constructed near it. Aside from the statue of SATURNUS, the government placed within the shrine the state treasury, or AERARIUM. Subsequently, the treasury was known as the Aerari Saturni.

Temple of Vesta

The home of the goddess of the Roman hearth. As VESTA was both an ancient deity and an important one in terms of the Roman state, her temple was situated in the FORUM ROMANUM, eventually located near the temples of Castor and Divus Julius, and the Arch of Augustus. King Numa (c. 700 B.C.E.) was the builder of the original temple of Vesta, choosing a round shape, probably imitating the original circular hut where she was worshiped. There was no statue of Vesta to be found, rather she was represented by an eternal flame. Anyone could enter during the day, but admission was restricted to the interior, where relics of Vesta were safeguarded, and at night all men were refused entry.

Temples of Minerva   Three notable sites of worship, particularly the shrine at the TEMPLE OF JUPITER CAPITOLINUS, that honored this goddess. As Moneta, or patroness of finance, Minerva had a chapel in the temple of Jupiter and two other temples, one in the FORUM TRANSITORIUM and one called Minerva Chalcidica, both constructed under the patronage of DOMITIAN, who revered the deity with fervor. Minerva's temple in the Forum Transitorium was the principle feature of the area. With columns supporting the entire forum, the temple itself was dominated by a statue of the goddess. Domitian died before he could complete his work, but NERVA finished the project, dedicating it in 97 C.E. The first temple of Minerva Chalcidica had been built in 29 B.C.E. by AUGUSTUS, but another temple of interest was erected in the Campus Martius by Domitian, near the PANTHEON and the BATHS of Agrippa.

Tenth Legion   One of the most famous legions in the Roman army. Julius CAESAR's Tenth Legion was involved in the GALLIC WARS and in the CIVIL WAR with POMPEY THE GREAT, as the "Old Guard" of Julius Caesar. The Legio X Fretensis, as it was known by its contemporaries, was the elite inspiration for Roman legions throughout the Republic. References to its battlefield achievements were considerable, as the cohorts assumed near-heroic proportions. Caesar first encountered the Tenth in Helvetia, when he arrived in Geneva to assume control of Gaul. He immediately marched the Tenth off to battle against migrating Helvetians. Henceforth, the soldiers of the legion were ever at his side. One of the earliest and most dramatic episodes of bravery came in 58 B.C.E. in the struggle with the German chieftain Ariovistus. Facing a shortage of cavalrymen, Caesar selected certain soldiers from the Tenth, and put them on mounts. The legion subsequently was known as the Legio X Equestris, or Legion of the Knights.

At the battle of PHARSALUS in 48 B.C.E., against Pompey, the cohorts served as the anchor of Caesar's line. Positioned on the right flank, where Caesar knew the main Pompeian blow would fall, the Tenth successfully withstood a furious assault, holding the flank long enough for Caesar to make his devastating counterattack and win the day. The legion no doubt would have partici-

pated in the Parthian War, had Caesar not been assassinated. His successor Octavian (AUGUSTUS) used the legionaries throughout the civil war with Marc ANTONY, but after the battle of Actium in 31 B.C.E. he disbanded the nucleus of the legion. The replacements had no sense of the original esprit de corps and the unit became once more the Legio X Fretensis. It had a long career during the imperial epoch, including participation in the Jewish War (c. 66–70 C.E.).

Terentia (fl. late first century B.C.E.)   *Wife of Maecenas*
Reportedly a very beautiful woman, Terentia was loved desperately by Emperor AUGUSTUS. She may have been one of the reasons for his leaving Rome in 16 B.C.E. to tour provinces and was possibly a cause for the deteriorating relationship between her husband and the emperor. That Augustus admired her was certain, despite the fact that her brother, Licinius MURENA, was executed in 22 B.C.E. for conspiracy against him.

Terentius, Marcus (fl. first century C.E.)   *Intimate associate of the Praetorian Prefect Sejanus spared by Emperor Tiberius, because of his honest (and ingenious) defense*
When placed on trial for his friendship with the fallen PRAETORIAN PREFECT, Terentius, a knight, refused to deny his status as a client but exclaimed loudly that, on the contrary, he had pursued the favor of Sejanus. After all, he argued, Sejanus had been honored by Tiberius, and "if the emperor did no wrong in having such a friend neither did I; if one such as he was deceived by the Prefect, what surprise is there that I was deceived? It is our duty to regard highly all whom the emperor trusts, regardless of what kind of men they might be—all that matters is that they please the emperor." He was immediately acquitted.

Tertullian (Quintus Septimius Florens Tertullian) (c. 160–c. 222)   *Apologist, Christian theologian, and controversialist*
Born in Carthage, North Africa, Tertullian was the son of a Roman soldier, probably a centurion. Raised as a pagan, he studied law and Latin and Greek literature. He became a lawyer and adherent to STOICISM before settling in Rome, where he acquired an excellent reputation as a jurist. Appalled by the state of social decay, he was drawn to Christianity and converted c. 195–196. He returned to Carthage and became a defender of the new faith, also devoting his time to teaching. According to St. Jerome, Tertullian was ordained a presbyter around 200. By 207, however, he had become disillusioned with the African Church, turning to the Montanist movement, which offered a strict morality and a rigorous lifestyle. He formally joined the Montanists in 211, but even they were not sufficiently rigorist for Tertullian; he left the heretical sect and established his own group, called the Tertullianists.

While he wrote against Catholic teaching during his Montanist period, Tertullian did retain many orthodox beliefs. His orthodox writings include the famous *Apologeticus* (c. 197), a popular treatise refuting the charges then being hurled against Christianity; *Ad nationes* (To the nations), an apology on which the *Apologeticus* was based; *Ad martyres* (To the martyrs), in praise of martyrs; *De praescriptione hereticorum* (c. 200; Prescription against the heretics), attacking heresies then facing the faith; *De spectaculis* (On shows), about pagan spectacles; *De oratione* (On prayer); *De baptismo* (On baptism); *De paenitentia* (On penance); *De Testimonio animae* (On the testimony of the soul), a declaration of the natural recognition of the existence of God; *De cultu feminarum* (On the apparel of women); and *Adversus Marcionem* (207; Against Marcion), a relentless criticism, in five books, of the heretic Marcion and his doctrine concerning the nature of Christ.

His works as a Montanist include *De idolatria* (On idolatry), a strict interpretation of Christian morality; *De carne Christi* (On the flesh of Christ); *De resurrectione carnis* (On the resurrection of the flesh); *De fuga in persecutione* (On flight in persecution); *De exhortatione castitatis* (On the exhortation to chastity); *De jejunio* (On fasting); *De monogamia* (On monogamy); *Ad Scapulam* (To Scapula), an open letter dated to 212 and sent to the proconsul of Africa Scapula condemning his persecution of Christianity. His last known treatise was *De pudicitia* (On modesty), questioning the measure of Pope Callistus I in making more lenient the penance required of Christians.

Considered the first true theologian of the West, he is distinguished as the first Christian author to compose chiefly in Latin. He utilized in his theology a legally exact mind, creating a comprehensive body of Latin terms that was ideally suited to the spread of the Christian faith throughout the West and the rapid development of theology. His contributions would earn him the eventual title of Father of Latin Theology and would influence the theological life of the Western Church for the next millennium. He mistrusted philosophy, holding it to be the source of all heresy, using it only as a tool rather than as a source of truth.

Suggested Readings: Barnes, Timothy David. *Tertullian: A Historical and Literary Study.* New York: Oxford University Press, 1985; Osborn, Eric. *Tertullian, First Theologian of the West.* Cambridge, U.K.: Cambridge University Press, 1997; Rankin, David. *Tertullian and the Church.* Cambridge, U.K.: Cambridge University Press, 1995; Tertullian. *Apology.* Translated by T. R. Glover. Cambridge, Mass.: Harvard University Press, 1998.

tessera Ticket or token. Tesserae were used as tickets of admission to game or circuses. Disk-shaped, the *tesserae* identified the seat number and section of a theater or amphitheater where the holder would be located (*see* COLOSSEUM). Bronze tokens, called *tesserae frumentariae* or *tesserae nummariae*, were part of the CONGIARIUM or gifts of food given out to the lower classes of Rome. Such coins were distributed to the crowds, either in an orderly fashion or by throwing large quantities right into the throng, thus giving the more cynical emperors amusement. Tesserae were normally minted for special occasions, such as anniversaries of imperial accession or for birthdays.

Tetrarchy The system of shared imperial rule established in 293 C.E. by Emperor DIOCLETIAN. It remained the accepted, albeit increasingly chaotic, form of government until around 308–309, when it broke apart completely. The idea of joint rule of the Roman Empire was not original. MARCUS AURELIUS (ruled 161–180 C.E.) had asked the SENATE to elevate Lucius VERUS to the post of coemperor, and other emperors had ensured a stable succession by appointing their sons as equals in imperial power. Diocletian, however, desired a process in which stability would be guaranteed beyond one or two reigns. He understood that the empire was now too vast and complex to be administered by only one man. Help was needed, and the tetrarchy would provide it.

In essence, the tetrarchy was a *concordia* between two senior emperors, each known as an Augustus and two *Caesares,* or lieutenant-emperors. They were to be masters of the Roman world, working in close cooperation and laboring for the good of all. Although they might be forced to reside or fight at opposite ends of the provinces, it was understood that they shared in the rank of Augustus and were heads of only one empire, not of an Eastern or Western territory. They would not necessarily be the son of the reigning Augustus but would be the most qualified officials available. A connection to the imperial family could be arranged through marriage to cement the political union. Theoretically sound, the system worked temporarily.

Diocletian laid the groundwork for his great experiment by promoting his friend MAXIMIAN to the rank of Augustus (or coemperor), this after Maximian had defeated the Bagaudae in Gaul, thus proving his worthiness for such a high office. By 286 there were two emperors (or Augusti); during the years of military campaigns that followed, struggles that would have exhausted one monarch were less taxing on two. In 293, having gained confidence in the arrangement, Diocletian named two Caesars (or subemperors), CONSTANTIUS I CHLORUS, and GALERIUS. The provinces were then handed out for each tetrarch to patrol and administer.

Aided by Galerius, Diocletian took the East, specifically Bithynia, Arabia, Africa, and Egypt, with Galerius in ILLYRICUM and Asia, as well as most of Asia Minor. Maximian, with Constantius as Caesar, possessed Rome, Italy, Sicily, Western Africa, and probably Hispania. Constantius was given the troubled regions of Britain and Gaul. Soon after the installations, frontier troubles and rebellions, most notably in Egypt, Africa, and Britain, put the tetrarchy to its first test. They all handled matters easily, justifying Diocletian's act of placing the twin dynasties under the protection of Jove (Jupiter) for himself, and Hercules for Maximian. From 293 to 305 the reign of the four emperors worked effectively. By 303, Diocletian was preparing to retire but found that Maximian did not share his desire to give up his exalted rank. Persuaded by Diocletian in 305, Maximian stepped down on May 1. Diocletian retired at Nicomedia in Bithynia, and Maximian did the same at Milan. Galerius immediately took up his duties in the East and Constantius in the West.

CONSTANTINE, the son of Constantius, and MAXENTIUS, son of Maximian, soon felt that they were entitled to a place in the new scheme of things; but they were ignored, as the rank of Caesar went to SEVERUS II and MAXIMINUS DAIA. Both Caesars were political clients of Galerius, who was now preeminent. The following year, Constantius died at Eburacum (York), and Constantine was hailed by the troops in Britain as his successor. To avoid civil war, Galerius named Severus the Augustus in the West and made Constantine his Caesar. Maxentius was angered by this act and, with the help of Rome's populace and the PRAETORIAN GUARD, declared himself emperor.

Galerius ordered Severus to march on Italy, only to have Maximian come out of retirement. Severus was defeated and later killed. Galerius took up the campaign, failing almost as badly. Meanwhile, Constantine married Fausta, daughter of Maximian, and the old emperor himself tried to overthrow his son Maxentius, who was forced to flee to Constantine when he failed. The entire fabric of government was thus rent. Galerius and his colleagues consequently summoned Diocletian from his gardens at Split and convened the Conference of Carnuntum in 308. With Diocletian's help the tetrarchy was supposedly restored. Galerius was to be the Augustus, alongside LICINIUS, with Maximinus Daia and Constantine as Caesars. Maxentius was outlawed, and Maximian ordered to return to retired life.

Events had taken such a turn that no such easy a solution was possible. Maximian tried to conspire against Constantine and had to be besieged at Massilia in 310, where he died, possibly a suicide. Maxentius refused to yield Italy, and Maximinus Daia, outraged at being passed over in favor of Licinius, claimed the title for himself. At one point there were as many as six Augusti: Galerius, Maximinus Daia, Maximian, Licinius, Maxentius, and Constantine. Maximian's death pointed the way to a lasting political answer, the eradication of the claimants, one by one.

Precisely what Diocletian had hoped to avoid was now inevitable. Galerius succumbed to illness in 311, and the following year Constantine crushed Maxentius and Licinius defeated Maximinus Daia. That left only two

rivals for supreme control, and in 323 Constantine won the battle of ADRIANOPLE. The tetrarchy became only a memory.

Tetricus, Gaius Pius Esuvius (fl. third century C.E.)
Last of the Gallic usurpers
Tetricus reigned in Gaul from 270 to 273. A senator from an old noble family, he was serving in Gallia Aquitania as governor in 270 when the army proclaimed him emperor. His decision to elevate his son to the rank of Caesar did nothing to help a regime that was soon troubled with barbarian inroads along the Rhine and a resurgent central government under AURELIAN. Tetricus very wisely submitted to Aurelian in 273 and was allowed to retire (his son eventually taking his place in the SENATE).

Teutoburg Forest Site of a massacre in 9 C.E. in Germania in which the Roman General Quinctilius VARUS was annihilated by the Cheruscan leader, ARMINIUS. Forever after, the Teutoburg Forest was seen as one of the worst defeats ever inflicted on a Roman army. After the successful campaigns of Drusus the Elder, TIBERIUS and other legates in Germania, Emperor AUGUSTUS decided to push for full provincial development of the wild German interior. To accomplish this the emperor appointed Varus to be governor. Varus had a reputation more for administration than martial skill and seemed the perfect choice for the intense Romanization of the Germanic tribes.

Unfortunately, Augustus was overly optimistic about the temperament of the Germans. When revolts erupted under the leadership of Arminius and his Cheruscans, Varus was ill-equipped to meet the challenge. He rashly departed from his summer camp, moving over impossible terrain and listening all the while to his German advisers. They led him through the Teutoburg Forest where, bogged down by his baggage train and unable to meet any attack, he was suddenly assaulted by the Cherusci and their few German allies.

As was the case at ADUATUCA many years before, the Romans put up the best resistance they could, but Varus lost heart and killed himself. His lieutenants fought bravely but were outnumbered and unable to move. A slaughter ensued as three legions were hacked to pieces, the few survivors being placed in wicker cages and burned alive. Rome's forts east of the Rhine fell to the triumphant Germans, and the empire received a terrible blow to its expansion policy for the region.

Teutons One of the largest Germanic tribes of antiquity. The Teutons, or Teutones, lived in the region of the Baltic Sea, near Jutland, with the equally extensive Cimbri. Sometime in the late second century B.C.E., both peoples moved from their northern homes, marching through the Celtic peoples of Gaul and hoping to settle in the area of GALLIA NARBONENSIS. Marius destroyed the Teutons in 102 B.C.E. at the battle of Aquae Sextiae, but some tribes in Gaul subsequently claimed descent from the remnant. Over time, the name Teuton was used generally to refer to any German tribe.

Thamugadi (Timgad) A Roman city in Africa, situated in NUMIDIA, just north of the Aurasius Mountains and to the east of Lambaesis. Thamugadi was founded in 100 C.E. by Emperor TRAJAN. As part of the intensive Romanization programs, only Roman army veterans were used to populate the colony. In turn, they helped to defend southern Numidia from the frequent incursions of local nomads. Built with the assistance of the III Augusta Legion, Thamugadi was remarkable because of its organization, with its streets laid out in perfect order. The city was, in fact, a nearly flawless square, with the usual Roman architectural necessities: baths, a basilica, a forum, the Arch of Trajan, and the Temple of Genius Coloniae. Thamugadi was also an example of too much growth in too confined an area. By the late second century C.E. any new monuments or buildings had to be placed outside of the city. Such was the case with the new baths, the temple, and the capitol.

Thapsus Ancient town on the east coast of modern Tunisia that was the site of a battle fought in February of 46 B.C.E. between Julius CAESAR and the combined remnants of the Pompeian forces. After defeating King Pharnaces at the battle of Zela in 47, Caesar understood that he had a great deal of fighting to do in Africa. In 49, his lieutenant there, G. Scribonius Curio, was defeated and slain by the Pompeians, supported by King JUBA of Numidia. Their position was strengthened in 48, when the survivors of the battle of PHARSALUS poured over the Mediterranean. By the time that Caesar was ready to deal with them, the Pompeians possessed 60,000 men under the command of such notables as METELLUS SCIPIO, King Juba, Sextus, and Gnaeus POMPEY, as well as Titus LABIENUS and CATO UTICENSIS. Against them came Caesar himself, with his veteran legions, 40,000 strong.

Caesar sailed from Lilybaeum in Sicily on October 8, 47. After arriving on the African coast, he set out for Ruspina but was nearly defeated by Labienus and Petreius. Caesar escaped brilliantly, taking up a strong enough position to allow his reinforcements to arrive. There followed a period of marches and counterattacks, as at the battle of Ilerda, in which Caesar compelled the Pompeians to give battle on the worst possible terms. Only a general of Caesar's caliber could be gifted or lucky enough to bring that about.

With the town of Thapsus nearby, the Pompeian-supported city that had served as bait, Caesar dressed his lines. The famed Tenth Legion was on the right flank, led the charge, and shattered Scipio's left; Scipio and his officers fled from the field. In a rare act of cruelty, Caesar's normally efficient and disciplined legions massacred the remaining enemy. Caesar was now a master of Africa, but he was also aware of the fact that others had escaped, including Gnaeus and Sextus Pompey and Labienus. The war was not yet over.

See also CIVIL WAR, FIRST TRIUMVIRATE.

theater There were several types of performance, in Rome, including comedy, drama, pantomime, and tragedy, although favorite types depended upon the social level of the audiences.

Theatrical performances owed their development to Greek culture and its foremost literary representative, Livius Andronicus, who came to Rome as a captive in 200 B.C.E. While there had been plays and productions prior to the time of Andronicus, it was this brilliant writer and translator who made available to the Romans the finest examples of original Greek tragedies and comedies. Eager successors either continued his tradition or initiated entirely new forms.

COMEDY AND MIME

Roman or Italian comedy actually began with the so-called *versus Fescennini* from Etruria, introduced around 390 B.C.E. as part of the general mime drama. The satire, a distinctly Roman creation, came from this early period and left an influence on later comedy by introducing such elements as music, dance, and verse. The Atellan Farce, or Atellana, was noteworthy, not only as comedy but also as a composition form with definite characters and traits.

Greek comedy or, more correctly, the New Greek comedy arrived with Livius Andronicus, who made translations of established Greek plays. The Roman imagination did the rest. Greek works were called *palliata*, after the Greek cloak, the *pallium*. In the second century B.C.E., the *togata* made its appearance. Again named after a cloak, or toga, this comedy was a departure from the Hellenic mold, for the stories, characters and atmosphere were Italian. Thus, two different styles of comedy coexisted, the Greek and the Italian, represented by the Atellan Farce and satire. Actual Latin Comedy was written by Plautus and Terence, many of whose plays survived. They were modeled after their Greek predecessors. Mimic comedy was equally produced, and by the end of the Republic was the favorite theatrical fare, remaining so throughout the imperial era. With easily understood plots, broad humor, and lightweight intellectual demands, the comedy had a wide appeal to the easily distracted mobs attending the festivals or games.

Famous writers of comedies, aside from Terence and Plautus, were Ennius, Naevius, Turpilius, Novius, Pomponius, Publilius, Syrus, and Laberius. Traditionally, the play consisted of a mixture of verse in iambic trimeter and straight dialogue. Music, called *cantica,* was used to score the action or as interludes usually played on the flute.

DRAMA AND TRAGEDY

Although Roman authors never matched the Greek models introduced by Livius Andronicus, there were some brilliant successes, most notably the purely Roman tragic form of the *fabulae praetextate* or *praetexta*. The *fabulae* were tragedies composed along the lines of a Roman character, with sources based on Italian or Roman history. The authors of the tragedies were some of the more notable literary figures in Rome: Naevius, Ennius, Pacuvius, Accius, during the Republic; and the imperial writers, Asinius POLLIO, OVID, POMPONIUS SECUNDUS, Curiatus Materna, and SENECA THE YOUNGER. Seneca wrote *Hercules Troades, Phoenissae, Medea, Phaedra, Oedipus, Agamemnon, Hercules Oetaeus*, and *Thyestes*. *Octavia*, the only extant *praetexta*, was not composed by Seneca, although attributed to him.

Drama (in the ancient sense both comedy and tragedy) took a more tenuous path to production. Considered a useful part of public or private spectacles, dramatic performances were staged by actor troupes called the *grex*. Their subject matter was chosen by the director (*dominus gregis*), who purchased the rights to a play from an often unknown playwright. The acquisition of a play was purely on speculation. If the production failed, no money was paid to the director. With dark themes, the drama was less popular with the mob but found an audience in the more educated upper classes, where plays might be given at parties or even at funerals.

ACTORS AND PERFORMANCES

The profession of acting presented some interesting contradictions. Acting was considered an *infamia* (disreputable), among the lowest of the Romans in social status, but some actors obtained reputations, adulation, and adoration from people of all walks of life, and others became the lovers of empresses or victims of emperors. Most actors began as slaves or as FREEDMEN who had been sent to work as members of a troupe. At first despised offstage, the influence of the Greeks was seen in the gradual acceptance of actors. By the late Republic, two actors, Roscius the comedian and Aesopus the tragedian, frequented the best social circles and were becoming wealthy.

With the founding of the Roman Empire, the acting profession took a major step forward. As all forms of performances became associated with either public recreation or private display, the lavishness of productions increased. Costumes were improved, decorations or sets made larger, and even the size of the cast grew from the traditional Greek three to many. In the Theater of Pompey, actual horses were used to show the sack of a city. Women were not a key part of the Roman theater. They were allowed some roles in mimes, and not until very late

did they appear in comedies. In drama or in tragedy their parts were played by men. It was Roscius who introduced the wearing of masks to heighten effect. Previously makeup and wigs served the same purpose.

The two most famous actors of the Augustan Age were Bathyllus and Pylades. While Pylades was eventually exiled, his rival was an excellent example of the rising station of the actor. Originally from Alexandria, he served as the freedman of Gaius Maecenas, who became his patron. With such help, Bathyllus received money and approval from AUGUSTUS. Later, in the reign of GAIUS CALIGULA, Mnester, the most famous and arrogant actor of the day, secured the favor of the emperor. Surviving Caligula's fall, he was honored at the court of CLAUDIUS. Unfortunately, he attracted MESSALLINA and spent much time unsuccessfully avoiding her unwanted attentions. When she was finally put to death in 48 C.E., Mnester joined her, mainly because of the plottings of Claudius's freedmen. A similar fate was suffered by two actors named Paris. The first tried to teach NERO how to mime, and when the emperor proved a dismal failure, Paris was put to death in 67. The other Paris, loved by DOMITIAN's wife, Domitia Longina, was hunted down by the emperor and murdered in the street.

theaters and amphitheaters Places of amusement for the Romans and an integral part of the government's commitment to entertaining the masses. In the provinces the structures were symbols of successful Romanization and the claim to civilization.

THEATERS

Theaters were virtually unknown in Rome throughout much of the Republic, owing to the absence of organized theatrical performances until the late third century B.C.E. Around 240 B.C.E., a drama was given in the circus, but the stage was torn down after each performance. Subsequently, senatorial opposition made construction of a permanent theater with seats very difficult. Even after the conquest of Greece and the importation of Hellenic culture, senators still opposed theaters, and such standing structures were not permitted.

Aemilius Scaurus, in 58 B.C.E., erected a wooden theater complete with nearly 80,000 seats and thousands of bronze statues. POMPEY THE GREAT took the decisive step in 55 B.C.E. of building a theater out of stone (the CURIA POMPEY). In 44 B.C.E., Julius CAESAR was stabbed to death in the Curia Pompey when the SENATE met there because of the unavailability of their normal curia. A fire broke out in 22 C.E. but was extinguished quickly by the Praetorian Prefect SEJANUS, who also saved the surrounding buildings, receiving a statue from Emperor TIBERIUS, who helped repair the damage. Cornelius Balbus funded a second stone theater in 13 B.C.E. but was overshadowed by Augustus, who dedicated in the same year the Theater of Marcellus, named after his nephew who died in 23 B.C.E.

These were the main examples of stone theaters in the empire; from then on, most would be constructed out of wood.

The Roman theater was usually in the shape of a semicircle, with seats sectioned off for the various levels of society. Two balconies over the *cavea* (where the musicians played) were for the emperors and their retinues, including the Vestal Virgins. Other rows were for senators, knights, ambassadors, and the rest of Roman society. As with other public spectacles, admission was free, entry being gained by the *tesserae,* or tickets, handed out to the public by the government.

AMPHITHEATERS

Roman amphitheaters were circular in design to afford everyone a view of the staged events, which were normally GLADIATOR displays or productions involving animals (the *venationes*).

The first amphitheater in Italy was built not in Rome but in nearby CAMPANIA, where Scribonius Curio erected a wooden stadium in 50 B.C.E., although his creation was actually the result of combining two theaters. Julius CAESAR funded one in 46 B.C.E., while Statilius TAURUS constructed the first stone amphitheater in 29 B.C.E. Destroyed by the great fire of 64 C.E., Taurus's structure was rebuilt by NERO, but this time out of wood.

Provincial and Italian amphitheaters actually displayed considerable beauty and imagination. The structures in ARLES and NEMAUSUS (Nîmes) were particularly impressive. Unfortunately, a Flavian project, the *Amphitheatrum Flavium,* dominated the attentions of the empire. This was, of course, the masterpiece of the COLOSSEUM, the zenith of amphitheater construction.

See also ART AND ARCHITECTURE; CIRCUS; FESTIVALS; LUDI; TESSERA; and individual entries for circuses.

Suggested Readings: Arnott, Peter D. *The Ancient Greek and Roman Theatre.* New York: Random House, 1971; Beacham, Richard C. *The Roman Theatre and Its Audience.* Cambridge, Mass.: Harvard University Press, 1992; Duckworth, George E. *The Nature of Roman Comedy: A Study in Popular Entertainment.* Norman: University of Oklahoma Press, 1994; *The History of the Greek and Roman Theater.* Princeton, N.J.: Princeton University Press, 1961; Simon Erika. *The Ancient Theatre.* Translated by C. E. Vafopoulou-Richardson. London: Methuen, 1982; Vince, Ronald W. *Ancient and Medieval Theatre: A Historiographical Handbook.* Westport, Conn.: Greenwood Press, 1984; Wiles, David. *The Masks of Menander: Sign and Meaning in Greek and Roman Performance.* Cambridge, U.K.: Cambridge University Press, 1991.

Themistius (c. 317–388 or 389 C.E.) *Philosopher of the late fourth century, writer, orator, educator, and political adviser*

Born at Byzantium, he came from a Paphlagonian family, his father the philosopher Eugenius. After studying under Hierocles at Sinope, near Pontus, he returned home in 337, to CONSTANTINOPLE. Taking up a career of teaching, Themistius centered on Aristotle and by 350 was considered a highly successful philosopher and orator. He earned wide acclaim by delivering a speech (extant) to Constantius II. A member of the SENATE in 355, henceforth he was a prominent member of the new senate of Constantinople, serving as one of its envoys to Constantius when he was at Rome in 357. As the last proconsul of Constantinople (before creation of the prefectship of the city), Themistius aided in the recruiting of senators for the Senate of Constantinople, now given equal power to that of its Roman counterpart.

Subsequently, Themistius was a confidant and favorite of three Christian emperors, despite his own PAGANISM, and was the author of a letter to JULIAN to remind him in 361 of the duties of a king. A speech to JOVIAN in 363 celebrated the brief-reigning monarch's first consulship, followed by numerous addresses and panegyrics to VALENS and later to THEODOSIUS I. All of his oratory reflected his own views in favor of fair rule and toleration in religious matters. Theodosius probably had a hand in the appointment of Themistius to the post of PREFECT OF THE CITY in 384. Although the philosopher was much criticized and left office after only a few months, he took care of the city and continued the education of Archadius during Theodosius's trip to the West. In 350 or 351, Themistius met the famed orator LIBANIUS, developing a friendship with him that lasted for many years. A quarrel erupted in 362, but by 364 the two were once more in touch, continuing to correspond until 388. Themistius was also married twice, the second time to a Phrygian woman.

Theodora (fl. late third century C.E.) *Stepdaughter of Maximian and wife of Constantius I Chlorus, whom she married around 293*
Theodora's union with Constantius was a purely political one, terminating his marriage to HELENA, mother of CONSTANTINE the Great. As the spouse first of a Caesar and then an Augustus, Theodora bore six children: Hannibalianus, Iulius Constantius, Flavius Delmatius, Constantia, Eutropia, and Anastasia. Constantine gave great honors to his mother, apparently neglecting Theodora; her children, however, were given a role in the court. Theodora's parents were Afranius Hannibalianus and EUTROPIA.

Theodore of Mopsuestia (c. 350–428) *Ecclesiastical writer, biblical exegete, theologian, and bishop of Mopsuestia*
Born in Antioch, he studied at the renowned school of rhetoric in the city under the pagan orator Libanius. While there, he met and became a friend of St. John Chrysostom and Maximus, the future bishop of Seleucia.

Around 369, influenced by the example of Chrysostom, Theodore entered the school run by Diodore (Diodorus), later bishop of Tarsus, and became an ascetic. Ordained sometime between 383 and 386, he left Antioch around 392 to join Diodore in Tarsus and was named bishop of Mopsuestia that same year, probably through Diodore's influence. He remained bishop until his death. During the controversy involving Chrysostom's dispute with Empress Eudoxia at Constantinople, he stood by his friend.

While friendly to the Pelagians and perhaps influenced by them, he accepted the condemnation of Pelagianism and was largely considered by his contemporaries to be an adherent of orthodoxy. Theodore was the author of a vast body of works, including exegetical commentaries (on the Old and New Testaments) and theological treatises such as *De Incarnatione* (15 books, written in Antioch c. 382–392), on the Incarnation; *De Sacramentis* (one book, now lost), on the sacraments; and *De Spiritu Sancto* (two books, now lost), on the Holy Spirit, against the Macedonians. His biblical commentaries are known for their high critical standard; he applied scientific, historical, and philological methods in marked contrast to the allegorical interpretations of Scripture used by members of the Catechetical School of Alexandria. Theologically, he proposed that Christ had two natures, divine and human, but his terminology was at times ambiguous, was common among Theologius in the era before the Council of Chalcedon (451). His views on the Incarnation were subsequently condemned at the Councils of Ephesus (431) and Constantinople (553). Theodore, however, had a major influence upon the Nestorians (*see* NESTORIUS), earning the title, with Diodore, *patres Nestorii blasphemiae* (fathers of the Nestorian blasphemy). He was revered by the Nestorians, who called him the Interpreter and looked upon him as one of their most important sources for doctrine. The rediscovery of many of Theodore's works in modern times has forced a careful reappraisal of the often harsh criticism of his views by historians and contemporary theologians.

Theodoret (c. 393–466 C.E.) *Bishop of Cyrrhus and an admirer and defender of Nestorius*

From Antioch, Theodoret entered a monastery sometime around 415 or 416 after giving away his possessions. Consecrated against his will as bishop of Cyrrhus in 423, he found himself embroiled in the bitter dispute between Nestorius, patriarch of CONSTANTINOPLE, and CYRIL, patriarch of Alexandria, over matters of doctrine. Despite the Council of Ephesus in 431, Theodoret continued to support Nestorius against Cyril and his successor Dioscorus. He was deposed and anathematized in 449 by the Council of Ephesus, which received the name *Latrocinium* or "Bandit Council." Exiled, he was summoned to Chalcedon in 451 and compelled to accept the condemnation of Nestorius.

Theodoret was an accomplished writer, although few of his works are extant. Notable among his compositions were a collection of heretical fables dealing with Arianism, Nestorianism, and Eutychianism; a church history from 323 to 428; a history of clerics, covering the lives of the monks; and the important apologetic, *Cure for the Pagan State of Mind*, a carefully composed defense of Christianity, with direct comparisons between Christian and pagan thinking.

Theodorus, Flavius Mallius (fl. late fourth century C.E.) *Government official*

His life and career were preserved by Claudian, the pagan panegyricist. Theodorus began as an advocate (ADVOCATUS) but was appointed a governor (377), MAGISTER MEMORIAE (379), probably *comes sacrarum largitionum* (380) and then Praetorian prefect of Galliarum under Gratian in 382. After retiring to his home in Mediolanum (Milan) he became an influential figure in literary and philosophical circles, including among the Neoplatonists. A writer, he authored several books on philosophy, earning the respect of St. Augustine, who dedicated to him the *De Beata Vita* (On the Happy Life), although he came to regret this action because of his return to politics. From 397 to 399 he held the rank of Praetorian prefect of Italy, Africa, and ILLYRICUM, through the influence of STILICHO. Through his initiative, Milan was favored over Rome. He was CONSUL in 399.

Theodosius I (d. 395 C.E.) *Emperor of the East from 379–392 and sole master of the Roman Empire from 394 to 395*

Theodosius was called "the Great" because of his ardent, although often cruel CHRISTIANITY. Like his father, the highly successful Count THEODOSIUS, the emperor was a Spaniard, born at Cauca. While his father emerged as one of the foremost generals of the time, Theodosius followed him into the army, eventually serving as a staff member for the count himself (c. 368). Around 373 or 374, he was made governor of Moesia Prima, also called Moesia Superior, defeating the SARMATIANS along the Danube. His career was seemingly terminated in 375, when his father was executed by the imperial government for treason.

Having retired to his estates in Hispania, Theodosius was suddenly called back to duty in 378 by Emperor GRATIAN, in the wake of the disaster at the battle of ADRIANOPLE, in which Emperor VALENS was killed. He was given the Danubian frontier as his theater of operations, launching such vengeful campaigns against the GOTHS that he was made Eastern emperor by Gratian at Sirmium on January 19, 379.

Years of war followed, but by 382 the emperor came to the conclusion that a total victory was impossible and negotiated an agreement with the Goths, which allowed the tribes to settle on land in Thrace and to receive imperial subsidies. In return, the barbarians promised to supply contingents for the armies and to maintain loyalty to the emperors. MARCUS AURELIUS had tried the same thing in the past, but Theodosius gave the barbarians vast territories, which proved in time to be dangerous to imperial stability, but it also enlisted the Visigoths.

In 383 Gratian was murdered by the usurper from BRITANNIA, the Spaniard, Magnus MAXIMUS. When Maximus occupied Gaul, he received recognition from Theodosius, who may have preferred a fellow countryman to Gratian. The usurper invaded Italy in 387 and spurned Theodosius's gesture. Theodosius organized an army of barbarian units and headed west, routing Maximus and beheading him at Aquileia. In his reorganization of the West, he transferred large parts of MACEDONIA and Moesia Superior to the Eastern Empire, placing them under the jurisdiction of the newly created prefecture of ILLYRICUM. This territory subsequently became a point of contention between the empires.

While in the West, Theodosius fell under the influence of AMBROSE, bishop of Milan. The emperor had always been devoutly Christian, persecuting eagerly all heretics and reversing the Arian favor shown by Valens. This policy of enforced Christianization culminated in 391 with the closure of pagan temples. In large measure his views were reinforced by Ambrose. Such was the position of Ambrose that in 390 he excommunicated Theodosius for massacring 7,000 people in Thessalonica for civil disorder—until the emperor did public penance.

Another episode in the West ended in complete triumph for Theodosius but at a terrible price. When he left the Western provinces in 391, he placed the MAGISTER MILITUM, ARBOGAST, as caretaker of the imperial administration of VALENTINIAN II. The following year Valentinian died, and Arbogast elevated a former school-teacher, Eugenius, to the throne. War began once more, ending in 394 with the battle of FRIGIDUS. Theodosius won the struggle, achieving unification of both imperial domains. Such unity was shortlived, for Theodosius died at Mediolanum (Milan) in January of 395. Theodosius was succeeded by his two sons, Arcadius and Honorius. Although his reign had been characterized by civil war and humiliating settlements with the Goths, his lasting achievement was the creation of a dynasty through his two empresses, Aelia Flavia Flaccilla and Galla. His children were Arcadius, Honorius, and Aelia Galla Placidia.

Theodosius II (401–450 C.E.) *Emperor of the East from 408 to 450 and the longest reigning ruler in the history of the Roman Empire*

Theodosius headed a government that epitomized the difference between the sound East and the increasingly chaotic and doomed West. Also, backed by the army and a fine administration he was proof of the degree to which Christianity had permeated the sociopolitical structure of imperial Rome.

Theodosius was the son of Emperor Arcadius and Aelia Eudoxia and was thus the grandson of THEODOSIUS I. Born at CONSTANTINOPLE, he was Arcadius's only male heir, succeeding to the throne in 408. He had already been raised to the rank of Augustus, and his claims were cemented by Arcadius's naming of YAZDAGIRD I, the king of Persia, as his guardian. The early years of his reign were remarkably smooth, mainly because of the efforts of the Praetorian Prefect ANTHEMIUS. This gifted and loyal regent improved the empire from 404–414. The grain supply of Constantinople was reorganized, the defenses of the city were strengthened, and the Walls of Anthemius, or the Walls of Theodosius, finished in 313. His services were terminated in 414 by Theodosius's sister, Aelia PULCHERIA, who, though only two years his senior, assumed the title of Augusta as well as near-total control of the state.

Pulcheria became the main influence in the life of the young emperor, supervising his education, indoctrination into Christianity, and even his marriage to Aelia Eudocia in 421. By 416, Theodosius was ready to take up the burdens of office, but the mark of Pulcheria was irrevocable. Theodosius preferred matters of the intellect, especially religion and literature. As a result, Constantinople blossomed with a university boasting departments in Greek, Latin, philosophy, and law. An interest in legal matters culminated with the monumental code of Theodosius (Codex Theodosianus), completed in 438 with the cooperation of VALENTINIAN III. In 16 books the decrees and enactments of the previous years were collected and codi-

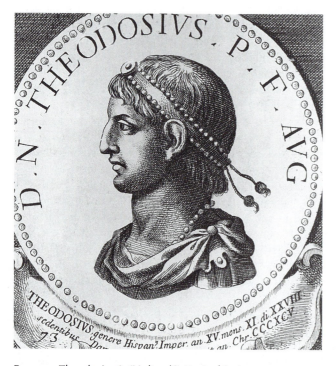

Emperor Theodosius I *(Hulton/Getty Archive)*

fied, preserving forever the nature of Roman law in the fifth century. The codes served as the basis for the equally important Code of Justinian.

Theodosius's preference for the less bloody aspects of rule, combined with an intensely devout nature and a pleasant demeanor, never changed. As he grew older, he paid even less attention to the murderous aspects of his office. Fortunately, he was surrounded by competent officials, allowing the administration to continue. Internal feuds did flourish, naturally. The eunuch Chrysaphius ZSTOMMAS replaced Pulcheria in the mid-440s as the most powerful adviser at court. Just before Theodosius died the eunuch fell, mainly through the efforts of Pulcheria and the Eastern generals. Relations between the capitals of East and West were repaired with the placing of Valentinian III on the throne of the Western Empire in 425. Not only did Theodosius travel to Ravenna to crown Valentinian, but in 437 he had his daughter, Licinia Eudoxia, marry Valentinian as well.

In foreign policy, Theodosius was highly successful in some areas and a failure in others. Around 422 he made a lasting peace with the Persian Empire that brought tranquility to the often war-ravaged Eastern provinces. The treaty remained in effect for over a century and was a contributing factor to the military and political vitality of Constantinople. While aid was sent to the West against ALARIC and the Visigoths, the East was faced with its own crisis, the Huns. Chrysaphius Zstommas nearly bankrupted the treasury by paying expensive subsidies to the Hunnic armies, a blackmail that ended with his fall. Despite the efforts of two MAGISTER MILITUMS, ARDABURIUS and ASPAR, much of the Danube was ravaged, and the question of what to do about the barbarians troubled the palace. A solution was not found in the time of Theodosius, for he died on July 28, 450, after falling from a horse just outside of the city. He was succeeded immediately by Marcian.

Theodosius, Flavius (Count Theodosius) (d. 375 C.E.) *Formidable general in the late part of the fourth century*

Theodosius was the founder of the House of Theodosius through his son, THEODOSIUS I, the Great. A Spaniard, he was serving as a *comes rei militari* in the West in 368–369, when Jovinus was recalled from Britain and he was sent to the isles as his replacement. In a campaign lauded by the historian Ammianus Marcellinus, the count restored Roman supremacy in Britain. For his victory, VALENTINIAN I promoted him to MAGISTER EQUITUM in 369, again replacing Jovinus. Years of war followed as Theodosius served as Valentinian's chief general. He defeated the Alani, the Alamanni, and the SARMATIANS. In 373 he was dispatched to Africa to quell a local uprising led by Firmus (*see* GILDO). Perhaps because of his political influence and potential for meddling in the succession, he was executed under mysterious circumstances at Carthage in

375. Survived by his wife Thermantia and his son, he made it possible for his family to lay claim to the throne in 379.

Theon of Smyrna (fl. second century C.E.) *Mathematician*

From Smyrna, authored an introduction an introduction to the field, in the tradition of the Peripatetic school. He was overshadowed by his great contemporary, Claudius PTOLEMY.

See also MATHEMATICS.

Theophanes of Mytilene (nicknamed Gnaeus Pompeius) (d. after 44 B.C.E.) *Historian*

Theophanes was one of the closest friends and advisers of POMPEY THE GREAT. From Mytilene on Lesbos, he stayed at the side of Pompey right up until the triumvir's departure for Egypt after Pharsalus. As a writer, Theophanes distinguished himself as the leading panegyrist in the cause of his patron, composing a history of Pompey's campaigns in the East.

Theophilus (1) (d. c. 412 C.E.) *Bishop of Alexandria from 385 to 412*

One of the most violent anti-pagans in the Church, Theophilus also worked tirelessly to improve his own religio-political position. As head of the Christians in Egypt, he suppressed ruthlessly the pagans, destroying the Serapeum in 391. Originally a supporter of Origenism, he turned against it, using his campaign against the sect to battle the see of CONSTANTINOPLE and St. JOHN CHRYSOSTOM for the supremacy of the Eastern Church. In 403 he manipulated the Council of Constantinople to condemn Chrysostom. His nephew was his successor, the equally severe CYRIL.

Theophilus (2) (fl. second century C.E.) *Bishop of Antioch and Christian apologist*

Theophilus was a distinguished theologian, writing numerous treatises on Christian doctrine. In these he expressed the superiority of the creed over paganism. He was important in his development of the nature of God and the Trinity. Little of his output has survived.

Thessalonica
Also called Therma, Saloniki, Thessalonika, and Salonica; an important city in MACEDONIA at the head of the Gulf of Therme, south of Pella and on the economically vital Via Egnatia. Known originally as Therma, the site was old but of little consequence, even during the glory years of Athens. Later, possessed by the Macedonians, the city was developed by King Cassander (c. 315 B.C.E.) and named after the sister of Alexander the Great. It grew in size until occupied by the Romans and made the capital of the province of Macedonia (c. 148 B.C.E.).

Thessalonica was administered by Cicero for a time and served throughout the CIVIL WAR between POMPEY THE GREAT and Julius CAESAR as the headquarters for the SENATE, as Rome was in Caesar's hands. Its loyalty to Pompey did not cause a loss of status upon the foundation of the empire. Not only did the governor have his residence there but also a high degree of independence was retained. A local government, headed by the so-called *politarchs*, was allowed from the time of Augustus (ruled 27 B.C.E.–14 C.E.).

The honor of being made a *colonia* was not given until the third century C.E., but Roman building was extensive from the second century until the early fourth, when Hellenic designs and fortifications were changed to meet Roman architectural needs. When Thessalonica was chosen as the capital for the territory given to Emperor GALERIUS as part of the TETRARCHY, Galerius constructed a large palace to the east of the city and a circus just to the south of the Via Egnatia. To the north was Galerius's mausoleum, finished sometime before 311. It was ironic that Thessalonica, the base for Galerius's personal campaign against Christianity, should in turn serve as an orthodox Christian center. St. Paul visited the city in 50 or 51, establishing the second Christian community in Europe. Thessalonica later was a bishopric and, by the late fourth or fifth century, was closely connected to the papacy.

Thessaly   In Latin, Thessalia; the largest territory in Greece, it encompassed the flatlands to the east of EPIRUS and just south of MACEDONIA. Thessaly was supposedly founded by descendants of Hercules, who became kings of the wild tribes in the region but were later deposed, their families emerging instead as the ruling nobility. In time, the Thessalians joined together to form separate confederations under individual councils, although oligarchical powers were retained by the nobles. They served Philip of Macedonia and Alexander the Great and fell under Roman domination after the battle of Cynoscephalae in 197 B.C.E.

For administrative purposes, the Romans decided to utilize the sense of independence that was a trademark of the Thessalians. Attached for practical and historical purposes to Macedonia, Thessaly was allowed its own local league and a *Koinon*, a version of the *concilium*. Under the reorganization of DIOCLETIAN, Thessaly was made an actual province, attached to the diocese of MOESIA.

See also ACHAEA.

Thirty Tyrants   Name given in the *Historia Augusta* (*see* SCRIPTORES HISTORIAE AUGUSTAE) to a group of usurpers in the middle of the third century C.E. Chosen to parallel the famous tyrants of Athens, the writings on the lists of 30 tyrants were supposedly composed by Trebellius Pollio. They were highly dubious and partly fictitious, designed to discredit the regime of Gallienus.

While 32 separate usurpers were actually mentioned, only nine were known to exist at the time of Gallienus; the others were either in different reigns or never existed at all. Thus, the entire *Thirty Tyrants* is more than questionable as a historical source.

Those usurpers verified either through coinage or sources, were, in the order of coverage in the *Historia*: Cyriades, Postumus, Lollianus (Laelianus), VICTORINUS, Mariius, Ingenuus, Regalianus, Aureolus, Macrianus, Macrianus the Younger, Quietus, Odaenath, Maeonius, Ballista, VALENS, Valens the Elder, Aemilianus, Tetricus the Elder, Tetricus the Younger, ZENOBIA, Victoria, and Titus. The suspect usurpers were: Postumus the Younger, Victorinus the Younger, Herodes, Piso, Saturninus, Trebellianus, Herennianus, Timolaus, Celsus, and Censorinus. Sulpicia Dryantilla, the wife of Regalianus, can be added to the list, for she appeared prominently on COINAGE.

Thrace   The large territory south of the DANUBE, north of the Aegean, west of the BLACK SEA and east of MACEDONIA. Thrace was one of Rome's important Danubian provinces, protecting the frontier and also securing the lines of communication from Macedonia, via Byzantium, to Bithynia and Asia Minor. Late in being annexed, the province was of even greater value to the empire after the fourth century C.E. because of the presence of CONSTANTINOPLE, the Eastern capital, on the Bosporus.

Thrace was an ancient land, still considered in the time of Herodotus to be a wild and cruel place. Its inhabitants, a conglomeration of tribes of mainly Indo-European stock, were savage, warlike, and brave. Although independent, they developed certain civilized habits and produced numerous Greek poets. Greek colonization brought Hellenic influence but the two cultures were never very compatible. A Thracian kingdom was founded in the fifth century B.C.E., remaining until the time of Philip of Macedon and Alexander the Great. Macedonia was henceforth the master of Thrace until 168 B.C.E. and the battle of Pydna, when the Romans defeated the Macedonians. Thrace, however, was left under the administrative control of Macedonia.

The importance of this pre-imperial history was in the ties between the Thracians and the Macedonians, a connection that had far-reaching consequences. In the revolt of Macedonia in 149 B.C.E., the Thracians were a major support to the rebels. It was not surprising that, after Rome seized Macedonia, it subjected Thrace to attack, often in response to raids and incursions. With the aim of stabilizing the region, a series of kings was established by the Romans, preferably loyal clients to Rome.

Rhescuporis was the first of the Thracian monarchs. He was not a friend to Caesar or his successor Octavian (AUGUSTUS), but aided POMPEY THE GREAT and Cassius and Brutus. Much of the country's future was shaped subsequently by the dynast RHOEMETALCES I, who wisely sided with Octavian against Antony at Actium. With the founding of the Roman Empire, Rhoemetalces was allowed to keep his throne, largely with the help of a Roman army, eventually receiving all of Thrace after being expelled briefly in 11 B.C.E. by the Bessi. Rhoemetalces lived until 12 C.E. when, upon his death, the realm was partitioned between his son COTYS of Thrace and his brother RHESCUPORIS.

Intrigues characterized the last years of the monarchy. In 19, Rhescuporis attacked and killed Cotys. TIBERIUS removed him, but again divided Thrace, this time between the sons of Rhescuporis—Rhoemetalces and Cotys. Rhescuporis was taken to Rome, accused by Cotys's widow, Antonia Tryphaena, condemned, exiled, and later put to death. One son of Cotys, Rhoemetalces III, was granted his father's domain in 39 by Emperor GAIUS CALIGULA. It is possible that he was granted all of Thrace, for in 46 a King Rhoemetalces was murdered by his wife. CLAUDIUS, having had enough of the Thracians, annexed the country and the province of Thrace was born.

Opposition to provincialization was acute, but the Roman administration was hampered more by the absence of urbanization. A procurator of the Equestrian (EQUITES) class was at first appointed but TRAJAN changed this to a Praetorian legate who was aided by procurators. The central government was based in Perinthus. Because of the lack of cities, a system was adopted similar to the one in Cappadocia. Thrace was divided into several *strategiai*, or local districts, headed by a *strategos* named by the governor. Tribes were answerable through their chief, called a *phylarch*, from *phyle*, the name of the tribal unit.

The Romans focused on the creation of cities and colonies. Under Claudius and VESPASIAN early colonization took place at Apri, Deultum, and Philippopolis, the latter by veterans. Through Trajan's imperial policy more colonies were founded, and the gradual flowering of Thrace's urban life commenced. Such cities as Plotinopolis, Marcianopolis, Traianopolis were very successful but also tended to inculcate the Thracians with Grecian lifestyles rather than Latin. Where the native tongue was not spoken, Greek was preferred; in the villages, even Greek was little known. Rome's greatest need was to create a province that was stable enough and urban enough to support the chain-link system of the Danubian frontier. In this Rome succeeded, but beyond this, hopes were limited.

Thrace was one of the provinces that paid for itself, largely through the flesh and blood of its inhabitants. Long accustomed to a martial lifestyle, the Thracians made excellent soldiers, especially in the *auxilia* of the legions. Economic life was a combination of mining, agriculture, and some trade along the Danube and the Black Sea. Growth and financial expansion were always hindered by the presence of the destabilizing barbarians just beyond the frontier. This was most true in the third century C.E., when the province suffered terrible privations at the hands of the GOTHS. King Kniva of the Goths earned lasting notoriety by campaigning in Thrace and then destroying Emperor Decius at Abrittus in 251. Over a century later, in 378, Emperor VALENS was annihilated at ADRIANOPLE in southern Thrace, again at the hands of the Goths.

With the reforms of Emperor DIOCLETIAN in the late third century and the subsequent Constantinian shift of imperial might to Constantinople, Thrace was not overlooked. Further cities were constructed and a diocese of Thrace was formed, comprising the province of Moesia Inferior, Scythia, Thracia, Rhodope, Haemimontus, and Europa. Such bureaucratic steps, while improving life to some degree, did nothing to prevent the continual ravaging of Thrace by the barbarians in the fourth and fifth centuries.

Thrasea Paetus, Publius Clodius (d. 66 C.E.) *Most famous Stoic dissenter during the reign of Nero (54–68 C.E.)* From Patavium (Padua), he studied philosophy before taking up his seat in the SENATE. Thrasea Paetus subsequently acted as the conscience of the state, opposing many of Nero's more abusive pieces of legislation but also receiving censure from his fellow Stoics for ignoring matters of supreme importance in favor of lesser ones. His reputation for stubborn moral opposition was such that TACITUS (1), his greatest admirer, called him "virtue itself." Thrasea married Arria the Younger, daughter of the noted Arria the Elder. His idol was the Republican orator Cato Uticensis, whom he honored with a biography, and he was a close friend of Persius, a relative of Arria. Associates also included the future Emperor VESPASIAN and Demetrius the Cynic.

Consul around 56 C.E., Thrasea was at first mentioned by the historian Tacitus as disliking a motion that would have given the Syracusans more facilities for gladiators. In 59, he walked out of the Curia when it was proposed to make AGRIPPINA's birthday a day full of evil omen, earning the dislike of Nero, who ensured that he was not among the delegates sent to offer senatorial condolences upon the death of the imperial daughter in 63. By 66, Thrasea had neglected to attend the Juvenalia and had been absent on purpose when divine honors were given to Empress Popaea. His fate was sealed. Capito Cossutianus charged him with treason. Condemned by Nero, Thrasea killed himself by opening his veins in a scene recorded with suitable emotion and drama.

Thrasyllus (d. 36 C.E.) *Private astrologer of Emperor Tiberius*
Thrasyllus became attached to the household of Tiberius c. 4 C.E., while that eventual emperor was on Rhodes. As Tiberius himself was fascinated by the stars, he allowed Thrasyllus to become an intimate, regretting this decision eventually. The astrologer would have been thrown to his death from a rocky cliff on the island had he not

supposedly predicted that he felt himself to be in danger and that the ship then sailing into the harbor of Rhodes brought good news. Right on both counts, Thrasyllus accompanied his patron to Rome on the same ship that had informed Tiberius of the deaths of Gaius and Lucius Caesar.

For the rest of his life he was a constant companion of Tiberius, even in 14, at the side of Augustus in his final days. After Tiberius became emperor, the ruler consulted him every day. Aside from his optimistic predictions, the astrologer used his influence to prevent executions by declaring that Tiberius need not be troubled with them as the emperor had many years to live and need not be concerned with killing them immediately. Thrasyllus died one year before Tiberius, in 36. His son was the equally successful astrologer, BALBILLUS.

Thugga (Dougga)

Old town at the center of the province of AFRICA, to the southeast of Bulla Regia and southwest of Utica and Carthage. Thugga, once a capital for a smaller Numidian kingdom, later developed into one of the more beautiful Roman communities in Africa. What made the site so interesting was its layout, a hill town with an impressive capital at the summit.

Thysdrus (El Djem)

Small town in Roman AFRICA, found to the south of Thapsus on the Roman roads leading away from the coastal line of communications and running from Carthage to Tripolitania. The amphitheater there, constructed during the governorship of the future Emperor GORDIAN I (c. 238 C.E.), was one of the largest in Africa.

Tiber

The chief river of Italy. Known by many other names, including Tibris, Tybris, Amnis Tiberinus, and Thyber, the river was, according to legend, originally called the Albula but its name was changed to Tiber after Tiberinus, king of Alba, was drowned in its swift current. Emerging from springs in the Apennines near Arretium, the Tiber flows south for over 100 miles to the Nar (Narnia); from then on it is a large, fast but navigable waterway. Continuing south for about 70 miles it connects with the Anio (Teverone), just above Rome, although there are many other tributaries along the entire route.

The Tiber was a dangerous river for navigational purposes and also noted for its flooding and the silt that passed down its length. After the rains, the Tiber overflowed, usually into the lower stretches of Rome. Most attempts to prevent such disasters, even by Augustus, were unsuccessful. Because of the silt that turned the water a muddy yellowish color, the river was nicknamed *flavus Tiberis* (yellow Tiber). This silt accumulated at the mouth of the river as it poured into the Tyrrhenian Sea just past OSTIA. Silt made the ports there increasingly dif-

A bridge across the Tiber *(Courtesy Fr. Felix Just, S.J.)*

ficult to maintain, and Claudius, needing a radical solution, built an artificial mouth.

Politically the Tiber divided two sections of Italia, Etruria to the east and Latium to the west. The Tiber was under the patronage of the divine personification of the river, and a Tiber festival was held every May 14. Normally, a bundle of rushes shaped to resemble a man, the *argii*, was thrown into the Tiber to appease the divine nature.

Tiberianus

(fl. fourth century C.E.) *Poet and probable government official in the latter part of the reign of Constantine the Great*

Possibly holding posts in AFRICA and in one of the Spanish provinces, Tiberianus was called by Jerome *vir disertus* (well-spoken man) in his *Chronicles*. He served as Praetorian prefect of Gallia in 335. Little of Tiberianus's writings has survived, beyond a few poems. He composed 28 hexameters on the evils of gold and a poem of praise to the Supreme Being, displaying Platonic and Orphic influences. Possibly to his pen can be ascribed a work on a bird and the famous *Pervigilium Veneris*.

Tiberias

City on the western shore of the Sea of GALILEE. It was built during the reign of TIBERIUS (14–37 C.E.) by HEROD ANTIPAS, in gratitude to the emperor for his help politically. In 43 C.E., the city was the scene of a brief meeting between Herod Agrippa I and the client kings of the nearby provinces, including Herod of Chalcis, Antiochus IV of Commagene, Cotys of Armenia Minor, Polemo of Pontus, and Sampsigeramus, king of Emesa. Viewed by the governor of Syria, Vibius Marsus, as potentially conspirational, the conference was terminated.

There was a strong anti-Roman movement in Tiberias. By 66 C.E. and the outbreak of the Jewish Rebellion, the city was one of the main supporters in Galilee of JOHN OF GISCHALA. Other factions included followers of

JUSTUS, the political and later literary rival of Galilee's Jewish head, JOSEPHUS, and a small but vocal pro-Roman party. Thus by the time VESPASIAN was launching his campaign in Palestine, Tiberias was divided, opening its gates in late 67 to the Romans.

Tiberius (Tiberius Claudius Nero) (42 B.C.E.–37 C.E.) *Emperor of Rome from 14–37 C.E.*

Thanks to the writings of TACITUS (1), SUETONIUS, and others, the reign of Tiberius was heavily documented. Tiberius suffered from the considerable burden of succeeding to the principate after AUGUSTUS. It would appear that whatever good qualities he possessed were blotted out eventually by the deterioration of his regime in its later years and by his desire to live away from the Rome that he hated.

Tiberius was a member of the family of the Claudians, the son of LIVIA Drusilla and TIBERIUS CLAUDIUS NERO, the ardent Republican. He was born on November 16, 42 B.C.E., probably on the Palatine Hill in Rome. Most of his early childhood was difficult because his family had to flee Italy as a result of his father's failed revolt against Octavian (AUGUSTUS) in 40. They returned in 39, per the terms of the treaty of Misenum, and Octavian fell in love with Livia. Tiberius's parents thus divorced, and the rest of his life was entwined in the fortunes of his stepfather. Tiberius did deliver the funeral oration for his natural father in 33.

He received a superb education as well as every opportunity to embrace the political lifestyle. A marriage was arranged with Vipsania AGRIPPINA, daughter of Marcus AGRIPPA, and Augustus began to entrust various military commands to him. In 20 B.C.E., he went to the East, where he restored Tigranes to the American throne and received back the standards of Crassus that had been captured at Carrhae in 53. By 12 B.C.E., he was a general of Rome in PANNONIA, proving himself extremely able in war. Pannonia was his posting from 12–9 B.C.E., and he served in Germania from 9–7 B.C.E. Then, various events brought him great loss and embarrassment. In 9 B.C.E, his beloved brother, DRUSUS (1) the Elder, died from an injury while on campaign in Germania. Tiberius walked in front of the body all the way back to Rome. Also, Augustus seemed to be choosing someone else as heir. Despite giving Tiberius the tribunician power, the emperor promoted his grandsons Gaius and Lucius. By 6 B.C.E. Tiberius found this so unbearable that he fled Rome for his private retreat at Rhodes. Another misfortune befell him in 12 B.C.E., when Augustus instructed him to divorce Agrippina and to marry his daughter JULIA. Tiberius loved Agrippina desperately, and his relationship with Julia deteriorated rapidly, contributing to his dark moods. Tragedies struck the imperial family in the next few years as Gaius and Lucius both died. Summoned back to Rome in 4 C.E., Tiberius was adopted by Augustus, granted tribunician power once more (for 10

years), and apparently chosen as the heir to the throne. That Augustus had qualms about him was obvious from the aging emperor's search for anyone else who might be suitable, and by the adoption of Agrippa Postumus, the surviving brother of Gaius and Lucius.

The revolt in Germania (4–6 C.E.) and the major uprising in Pannonia (6–9) demanded Tiberius's presence. When they had been suppressed, word arrived that the legate Quinctilius VARUS had been killed with his three legions, massacred in the TEUTOBURG FOREST. Tiberius stabilized the Rhine region and then went back to Rome, where the task of running the government fell to him. As Agrippa Postumus was exiled to Planasia, Tiberius was the only logical choice for emperor when Augustus died in 14, as he held the IMPERIUM PROCONSULARE.

With the knowledge that Augustus had cared little for him, Tiberius began his own imperial era with disastrous debates in the SENATE as to the extent and nature of his powers. The legions in Pannonia and Germania revolted for better pay and improved conditions of service. Drusus, Tiberius's son, was sent to Pannonia while GERMANICUS, son of Drusus the Elder and a respected figure in the empire, was dispatched to the Rhine. The unrest was eventually ended, and Germanicus launched a retributive campaign against the Germans. While these operations were more successful from the perspective of propaganda than actual military gain, Tiberius gave Germanicus, whom he had adopted, a triumph. This celebration made tensions in the palace more severe, as the mob in Rome preferred Germanicus to the somber emperor. The popularity of Germanicus probably had something to do with his being given the IMPERIUM MAIUS and sent to the East in 17.

The attempt to remove Germanicus from the public eye backfired badly, for in 19 he died suddenly in Antioch, after quarreling with the governor of Syria, Gnaeus Calpurnius PISO. A hot issue erupted as Piso and his wife Plancina were suspected of poisoning Germanicus. AGRIPPINA THE ELDER, the vocal widow, used the entire affair to hurl accusations at Tiberius and at his mother, Empress Livia. Ultimately Tiberius sacrificed his long-time supporter Piso but forever after hated the family of Germanicus, especially Agrippina the Elder.

As emperor, Tiberius proved faithful to his deified predecessor, declaring that the acts of Augustus were law. He certainly furthered the authority and the supremacy of the imperial house, but only after it became painfully clear that the Senate was incapable of wielding any true privileges or rights given to it. His mistrust of the senators, coupled with his search for a loyal aide, led him into the arms of SEJANUS, the PREFECT OF THE PRAETORIAN GUARD. Even during the rise and fall of this minister, Tiberius remained devoted to his imperial chores, running the provinces with a firm but surprisingly effective hand.

A silver denarius of Tiberius, struck between 16 and 37 C.E. at Lugdunum *(Courtesy Historical Coins, Inc.)*

Much of his trouble stemmed from his inability to communicate effectively. Almost an unwilling ruler and difficult to understand, it was little wonder that he had no patience with the flattering sycophants of Rome. His reign began well in terms of justice and power, for he treated the Senate with respect and refused to allow any case of treason (*maiestas*). When one man was charged with impiety against the gods, he replied that the gods must defend their own good name. Moderation declined as the years passed and as the weight of office increased. Informers (DELATORES) invaded the legal system, as accusations against persons high and low initiated a wave of treason trials and deaths. The main instigator of this policy was Sejanus. Having worked his way into the emperor's trust, he convinced Tiberius that there were plots everywhere, using the resulting fear to widen his own influence. The prefectship of the Guard became a key administrative office, and the Guard was moved into the CASTRA PRAETORIA, a barracks in Rome. Tiberius put absolute faith in Sejanus, calling him his friend and assistant; because of him, in 26, he could leave Rome once and for all, taking up residence on Capri at the Villa Jovis.

Tiberius was happy to leave Livia behind as well. She had guided his path to the throne, using every means, including murder to some, to secure his accession. He hated her for it, and her constant interference in his rule made his leaving all the more desirable. Upon her death in 29 he was intent that the Senate should give her as few honors as possible; promising to build her arch himself, he never did it. Capri also allowed Tiberius to indulge himself, away from the prying eyes of the Romans. A man with peculiar tastes, he has been portrayed as an old, dirty, perverted debaucher by many, a view perhaps exaggerated. Nevertheless, he shared some of his adventures in pornography with GAIUS CALIGULA, who was like in pursuits and appealed to Tiberius's own bitter sense of posterity. Know-

ing that history would judge him by comparison with his successor, Tiberius decided that Gaius Caligula, an obvious lunatic, would be perfect, inflicting at the same time lasting horrors upon the Romans. He thus enjoyed saying: "I am nursing a viper for the Roman people!"

As it turned out, Caligula was the only survivor of the entire reign who was available for the throne. One by one all other claimants died or were murdered. Germanicus died in 19, Drusus was probably poisoned by Sejanus in 23, and Germanicus's sons Drusus and Nero Caesar, the brothers of Caligula, were also arrested and done away with. Nero was exiled and died (like his mother) on a distant rock, and Drusus endured many years of misery in a Roman dungeon before succumbing. Sejanus tried to maneuver himself into the inheritance but was lured to his doom in 31 in a plot masterminded by Tiberius, who was probably awakened to the threat by the Lady Antonia. That left only Gaius and his own grandson, Tiberius Gemellus. In his will he named both as heirs. Tiberius Gemellus did not survive long.

The last years of Tiberius, from 31 until 37, were characterized by reigns of terror, as anyone associated with Sejanus or anyone guilty of often imaginary crimes was executed. He died on March 16, 37, at the Villa of Lucullus in Misenum. The cause of death was probably natural, although some reported that he was smothered to death under a pillow by the Prefect Macro, on the orders of Gaius Caligula. His tyrannies, especially at the close of his reign, were closely scrutinized by Tacitus, who viewed him with the jaundiced eye of the age of DOMITIAN, an emperor who studied Tiberius for clues on how to rule. The historian Dio summed him up by saying that he possessed many virtues and many vices.

Suggested Readings: Baker, G. P. *Tiberius Caesar.* New York: Barnes & Noble, 1967; Jonson, Ben. *Sejanus His Fall.* New York: Hill and Wang, 1969; Levick, Barbara. *Tiberius the Politician.* London: Thames and Hudson, 1976; Marañón, Gregorio. *Tiberius; a Study in Resentment.* London: Hollis & Carter, 1956; Marsh, Frank Burr. *The Reign of Tiberius.* Cambridge, U.K.: W. Heffer and Sons, 1959; Suetonius. *The Twelve Caesars.* Translated and with an introduction by Michael Grant. New York: Penguin, 1979; Tacitus, Cornelius. *Empire and Emperors: Selections from Tacitus' Annals.* Translated by Graham Tingay. New York: Cambridge University Press, 1983; Velleius Paterculus. *The Caesarian and Augustan Narrative.* Edited by A. J. Woodman. New York: Cambridge University Press, 1983; Velleius Paterculus. *The Tiberian Narrative.* Edited by A. J. Woodman. New York: Cambridge University Press, 1977.

Tiberius Claudius Nero (d. 33 B.C.E.) *Praetor in 42 B.C.E., the first husband of Livia and the father of Emperor Tiberius and Drusus (1) the Elder*

Tiberius Claudius Nero came from a good family, entering the service of Julius CAESAR at the siege of Alexandria. An ardent Republican, however, he proposed to the SENATE in 44 that Caesar's assassins be rewarded. In 43 or 42, he married Livia, daughter of the nobleman Marcus Livius Drusus CLAUDIUS, who bore him two sons, Tiberius in 42 and Drusus in 39. An opponent of Octavian (AUGUSTUS), Tiberius took part in the fighting in Italy in 40, raising an unsuccessful slave revolt in CAMPANIA to undermine Octavian's position. Forced to flee the country, he took his wife and son to Sicily and then to Marc ANTONY. According to the terms of the Treaty of Misenum in 39, he was able to return to Rome. This proved unfortunate, for Octavian fell in love with Livia. Tiberius soon divorced his wife and was so agreeable to the union that he gave the bride away three months before the birth of Drusus. The butt of many jokes in Rome, he nevertheless received from Octavian the right to raise his sons. He died in 33, his funeral oration delivered by the nine-year-old Tiberius, who was to become Augustus's heir to the throne.

Tiberius Julius Alexander (fl. first century C.E.) *One of the most successful Jews in Roman imperial history*

Born in Alexandria to wealthy Jewish parents, Tiberius was the nephew of PHILO. A fallen-away Jew, Tiberius rose far in the ranks of Roman government, becoming a member of the Equestrians (EQUITES). Procurator of JUDAEA from around 46–48 C.E., he helped to exterminate local dissidents, including the sons of Judas the Galilean. Promoted to the staff of General Corbulo in Armenia in 63, he was made prefect of Egypt in 66, Emperor NERO apparently relying upon his Jewish background and knowledge of the East. This experience was soon tested, for ALEXANDRIA was the scene of considerable unrest in 66. So violent did the rioting become that the prefect called in two legions, and over 50,000 people died. Of note was his (extant) edict discussing the provincial government, published under Galba. Tiberius Julius Alexander was a supporter of VESPASIAN and used his position as prefect of Egypt to convince the troops there and in the Eastern provinces to support the Flavian cause. On July 1, 69, he administered to his own troops the oath of allegiance for Vespasian. Subsequently he aided TITUS in his campaign against the Jews and was present in 70 at the siege of Jerusalem. Unsuccessfully, he tried to have the Great TEMPLE OF JERUSALEM saved from destruction. Despite this disagreement on policy, he was given command of the Praetorian Guard, the climax of his career.

Tibullus, Albius (c. 54–19 B.C.E.) *An Elegiac poet of the Augustan Age*

Tibullus was a follower of the Alexandrine School but expressed himself with (as Quintilian wrote) dry elegance. Of obscure but wealthy descent, he apparently suffered as a result of the civil wars, especially in the land seizures and the redistributions of 41. Tibullus became a client of the political figure Messalla Messallinus, a patronage that reversed his financial decline. Entering Messalla's literary circle he was soon a friend of HORACE and an associate of OVID. He probably accompanied Messalla on his trip to Asia, falling ill at Corcyra. He may have been part of the retinue of Messalla during his Gallic proconsulship in 27 as well, recording his patron's victory over the Aquitani. The output of Tibullus centered mainly on elegies and panegyrics. There are two elegies to his mistress Delia and to the homosexual Marathus, and six on Nemesis—all organized into two books. A third book contains earlier poems by Tibullus, as well as six elegies, supposedly by the pen of the virtually unknown poet Lygdamus, and six more to the woman writer Sulpicia. Thus the collection of poems from the circle of Messalla were added to the poet's authentic works. He also authored panegyrics to his patron, ending with an epigram and an elegy.

Tigellinus, Gaius Ofonius (d. 68 C.E.) *Prefect of the Praetorian Guard from 62 to 68 and the most infamous servant of Emperor Nero*

Although detailed information about him has not survived, Tigellinus was born to a poor family, working his way into the services of Gnaeus Domitius Ahenobarbus and Marcus Vinicius, probably by having affairs with their wives, AGRIPPINA THE YOUNGER and Livilla, GAIUS CALIGULA's sister. He was exiled to Achaea, where he sold fish for a time in order to survive. He eventually returned to claim an inheritance from a forged will, successful in the venture because of Agrippina. Living in Apulia, he then became a horse trainer, and in this capacity met Nero.

Ingratiating himself with the young emperor, Tigellinus was named commander of the VIGILES upon the death of Annaeus Serenus. Thus in 62, when the Praetorian Prefect Burrus died, Nero turned to Tigellinus to be his replacement. Knowing that such a choice would be opposed, given Tigellinus's lack of morality or qualifications, Nero appointed as well the respected Faenius RUFUS. True power in the Praetorians rested with Tigellinus, who shared in Nero's debaucheries. Through the use of informers and agents the prefect spun a web of terror around Rome, exposing treasonous activities and destroying the opponents of Nero. His value to the emperor increased by his ruthless extirpation of the PISONIAN CONSPIRACY in 65. This investigation and subsequent massacre netted as well the other prefect, Rufus, who had been a member of the plot. Tigellinus was now the second most important figure in the empire. But even his spies could not prevent wholesale discontent in the provinces and in Rome, and in 68 he fell ill. His co-prefect, the quiet but ambitious

Nymphidius SABINUS, assumed most of his duties, and Tigellinus distanced himself as much as possible from Nero and past events.

When Galba came to the throne late in 68, Tigellinus was relieved as prefect, while the mob cried for his death. But Titus VINIUS, an adviser to Galba, protected Tigellinus, repaying him for saving his daughter some years before. OTHO, Galba's swift successor, sought to appease the Romans and so ordered Tigellinus to die. Upon receiving the death sentence at the spas of Sinuessa in Latium-Campania, he enjoyed the favors of prostitutes and then slit his throat with a razor. The historian TACITUS accorded him particularly vicious treatment in both his *Annals* and the *Histories*.

Tigranes I (d. c. 56 B.C.E.) *"The Great," king of Armenia from c. 90 to 56 B.C.E.*

Tigranes secured improvements in his country through personal ambition and an alliance with Mithridates of Pontus. He helped finish off the Seleucids in SYRIA, assuming mastery over a vast region, from the Euphrates to Antioch. His expansionism brought him into conflict with Rome, first with Lucullus in 69 and then with POMPEY THE GREAT in 66, when he was defeated. Tigranes submitted to Pompey and was allowed to retain his domain as a client to Rome. He died sometime around 56. His importance in terms of imperial history was his act of bringing the Romans to Armenia and hence into conflict with PARTHIA. He was also the grandfather of Tigranes III.

Tigranes II (d. 6 B.C.E.) *King of Armenia*

The son of King ARTAVASDES I and ruler from around 20 to 6 B.C.E., he was captured in 34 when Marc ANTONY overran Armenia, he was taken to Rome, where he spent several years as a hostage while his brother Artaxes regained the throne and ran the country with a cruel and despotic hand. A pro-Roman element in the palace called for AUGUSTUS to send Tigranes back to Armenia as a replacement. In anticipation of the arrival of Tiberius with an army in 20 B.C.E., the courtiers murdered Artaxes. Tigranes was crowned with the royal diadem by TIBERIUS and remained as ruler until his death, leaving Armenia to a chaotic situation with ERATO and TIGRANES III.

Tigranes III *See ERATO.*

Tigranes IV (d. 36 C.E.) *King of Armenia*

Tigranes reigned c. 6–8; he was probably a grandson of HEROD THE GREAT through Alexander and his wife Glaphyra, daughter of Archelaus, king of CAPPADOCIA. One of Archelaus's wives was probably connected to the Armenian royal line, thus qualifying Tigranes, perhaps obliquely, for the succession. He was clearly not the first choice of Emperor Augustus (that had been Gaius Caesar's Mede, Ariobarzanus), but he had died, as had his

heir, Artavasdes. Tigranes was unable to hold the traditionally factious Armenian court in check and found himself deposed. Living in Rome, he was accused in 36 of some crime and put to death by Tiberius. The historian TACITUS recorded his demise, but did not include him in the list of Armenian kings.

Tigranes V (fl. first century C.E.) *King of Armenia from 60–62 C.E.*

Following the successful operations of General Corbulo (2) in Armenia against the deposed monarch TIRIDATES, NERO decided to return to the previously disastrous system of placing client kings on the Armenian throne. His choice was Tigranes, nephew of TIGRANES IV, greatgrandson of HEROD the Great and Archelaus of Cappadocia. Tigranes V was taken to his city and installed there by Corbulo, who left a legionary detachment of 1,000 men at TIGRANOCERTA, with auxiliaries and cavalry. The new king possessed little influence over his subjects. Perhaps driven by desperation to achieve some kind of success, he launched an attack on the Parthian client state of Adiabene. It is unclear whether Nero or Corbulo gave approval, but the campaign set off a wider conflict as Vologases, king of PARTHIA, invaded Armenia, besieging Tigranes at his capital. Through the threat of Roman countermeasures, the Parthians were convinced to withdraw from Armenia. Tigranes had suffered an irretrievable blow and fell from power in 62. Nero had to recognize the claims of Tiridates.

Tigranocerta One of the capitals of ARMENIA (with ARTAXATA); founded by King TIGRANES I to serve as the center for imperial expansion in the early first century B.C.E. It may have been situated just north of Nisibis and east of Edessa in a valley between the mountains of Masius and Niphates. Because of the position of Tigranocerta relative to PARTHIA and MESOPOTAMIA, it was susceptible to attack, and it fell to the Roman generals Lucullus in 69 B.C.E. and Corbulo in 60 C.E. That it was both large and powerful was seen in 61–62 C.E., when Vologases unsuccessfully besieged TIGRANES V there. The city was rebuilt in the late fourth or early fifth century C.E. as Martyropolis.

Tigris One of the major rivers of the ancient world and, with its companion to the west, the EUPHRATES, an important element in the development of MESOPOTAMIA. The Tigris, which formed Mesopotamia's eastern border, flowed out of ARMENIA into Assyria and then down through Babylonia until it reached the Persian Gulf. Like the Euphrates, with which it converges as it nears the Gulf, the Tigris was a political dividing line in the Parthian and Persian empires. Numerous cities were situated either on or near it, including Nisibis, Hatra, Apamea and one of the Parthian capitals, Ctesiphon. Roman campaigns into

Mesopotamia always took the Tigris into strategic account. Thus, when TRAJAN invaded Parthia in 115 C.E., he passed down the river, captured Ctesiphon and continued marching until he reached the Gulf. Such use of the Tigris was meant to define it as the easternmost region of the Roman Empire; such occupation was shortlived, as HADRIAN soon reestablished the traditional frontier. The Tigris was part of the economy of the East, as caravans stopped along its banks and shipping, to a small degree, could pass northward for some distance into Babylonia.

time The Roman day was divided into 12 hours of light and 12 hours of darkness. By the middle of the second century B.C.E., the Romans understood that the length of daylight varied throughout the year and also depended upon latitude. Midnight was counted as the sixth hour of the night, and noon the sixth hour of the day, with the first hour calculated at the start of sunrise and the 12th hour as the hour before sunset. As hours were not of a fixed length, varying with seasons, the key measurements were midnight and noon. The term *ante meridiem* designated the time "before the middle of the day," and *post meridiem* designated the time "after the middle of the day."

One of the chief methods used for telling time was the sundial, the *solarium* (pl., *solaria*), which first appeared in Rome around 263 B.C.E. as part of booty brought to Rome from Sicily during the Punic War. For nearly a century, the Romans remained ignorant of the fact that the sundials needed to be calibrated for a specific latitude and seasonal adjustments. Therefore, their sundial was telling Sicilian time rather than Roman. The *solarium* also had the disadvantage of needing sunlight to tell the time, so it was useless at night and on stormy days. The most famous of the *solaria* of Rome was the Solar Clock of Augustus, erected in 9 B.C.E. by Emperor Augustus in the Campus Martius. The solarium was designed with the help of the mathematician Manilius. Unfortunately, it was notoriously inaccurate, as was noted by PLINY THE ELDER.

In 159 B.C.E., the Romans began importing water clocks, *clepsydrae,* which told time by a regulated dripping of water. Variations of the *clepsydra* included very elaborate mechanisms that could tell time for an entire 24-hour period. The water clock was not especially accurate, but it did have the advantage of telling time at night. All Roman *horologia,* or clocks, sought to divide the day into equal parts, meaning that even if accurate, they ran counter to the accepted division of the day into two times, night and day, with unequal hours depending upon the time of year or the latitude.

See also CALENDAR.

Timesitheus, Gaius Furius Sabinus Aquila (d. 243 C.E.) *Prefect of the Praetorian Guard from 241 to 243*

The leading minister in the reign of Emperor GORDIAN III, Timesitheus was the foremost administrator in the Roman Empire, whose Equestrian (EQUITES) career had been a series of important provincial postings. He was especially adept at finances, with procuratorships in Gallia Belgica, Arabia, Syria, Palestine, Germania Inferior, Bithynia, Pontus, Paphlagonia, Gallia Aquitania, and Gallia Lugdunensis. Thus, in 241, when Gordian III was looking for a responsible imperial officer to serve as prefect of the Guard, the choice was obvious. From the start Timesitheus proved more than equal to the task, assuming the operation of the entire government with Gordian's support, demonstrated in the emperor's marriage to his daughter, TRANQUILLINA. Unlike other prefects in similar circumstances, Timesitheus was not ambitious for the throne. After working to improve the frontier defenses of AFRICA, including probably the construction of LIMES, the prefect began to organize a war with Persia. He served as general in 243, inflicting defeats in SHAPUR I in Syria and Mesopotamia, including the capture of Nisibis. Further campaigns were planned, but the prefect suddenly fell ill and died. Gordian named PHILIP I (the Arab) as the new Praetorian prefect, a man of much greater political ambition.

Tingis City in MAURETANIA just below the *fretum gaditanum,* or the Strait of Gibraltar. Tingis (Tangiers) was said to have been founded by Phoenician traders and was thus very old by the time its inhabitants chose to support Octavian (AUGUSTUS) in the civil wars of Rome. For their loyalty, they were given Roman franchise before being attached to Hispania Baetica for provincial administration. To aid in Romanization, however, veterans were sent there as colonists. Under Claudius, Tingis was transferred from Baetica to Mauretania where it became the capital of Mauretania Tingitana, with the full title of *colonia.* Little has survived of the original site, making it archaeologically limited in value.

Tiridates (fl. first century C.E.) *Unsuccessful claimant to the Parthian throne in 35–36 C.E.*
Certainly a member of the ARSACID DYNASTY and probably a grandson of PHRAATES IV, who had sent his sons to Rome during the reign of AUGUSTUS (27 B.C.E.–14 C.E.). Tiridates was chosen by TIBERIUS as a reliable Roman candidate for Parthian kingship and was sent as a rival to ARTABANUS III. When Artabanus was compelled to flee Parthia for Scythia, Tiridates was convinced that the moment was right for his own advance, and by 36 he was crowned at Ctesiphon. He listened to the counsel of the courtier ABDAGAESES, however, refusing to march to the various Parthian provinces and clients to win their fealty. Artabanus soon recovered, organized an army and expelled Tiridates, who had no stomach for war.

Tiridates of Armenia (fl. mid-first century C.E.) *King from around 51–60 and from 63*

The son of the Parthian King Vonones and brother of VOLOGASES I and PACORUS, Tiridates and Pacorus both agreed to the accession of Vologases in 51, presumably in return for their own kingdoms. Pacorus received Media Atropatene and Tiridates took Armenia. Following the murder of MITHRIDATES by RADAMISTUS in 51 and the latter's seizure of Armenia, Vologases decided that the country was ripe for retaking. Parthian troops swept into Armenia, capturing both ARTAXATA and TIGRANOCERTA. Radamistus departed hurriedly, only to return a year later, when disease and a vicious winter forced first the Parthians and then Tiridates himself to leave Armenia. Radamistus could not keep his throne, however, and Tiridates, backed by Vologases, was soon back and stayed until 60.

When NERO came to power, he was eager to establish policy with vigor wholly wanting in CLAUDIUS. Foreign (Parthian) occupation of Armenia was not to be tolerated in his view, and he dispatched General CORBULO (2) to the East in 55. Two years passed quietly as Corbulo made his preparations. In late 57, he entered Armenia and in 58, in conjunction with Roman clients in the region, he reduced Tiridates's position. The king opened negotiations but when these failed, Corbulo took and utterly destroyed Artaxata. The following year saw the fall of Tigranocerta, and in 60 Tiridates made a final, unsuccessful attack to reclaim his throne. From 60–62, TIGRANES V ran the Armenians with increasing impotence. An incursion of his into Adiabene allowed Vologases to return to Armenia. Tigranes fell, departing from the scene and allowing Tiridates to declare to Corbulo in 63 that he was willing to accept the diadem of rule from Nero, if need be. Thus, in 66 Tiridates journeyed to Rome, where he was treated with respect and honored with massive festivities. Relations were subsequently so calm that Nero gave him millions of sesterces and artisans to rebuild Artaxata, now renamed Neroneia (or Neronia).

Tiridates II (fl. first century B.C.E.) *Parthian usurper from c. 30–25 B.C.E.*

Tiridates tried unsuccessfully to unseat PHRAATES IV as king of Parthia. He may have been an officer in the army used to repulse Marc ANTONY's invasions in 36 and may then have tried to fulfill his own ambitions, ousting Phraates in 31 but proving unable to hold the throne. He was forced to flee to Octavian (AUGUSTUS) in 30, receiving sanctuary but no supplies or logistical support. In dealing with Parthia, Augustus came to look upon Tiridates as a useful tool in forcing Phraates to the bargaining table. Tiridates made another attempt at rule, but was beaten again in 26. Running to Augustus he brought with him Phraates, the king's son. Demands that both be surrendered to Parthian justice were made, and Augustus partially obliged, returning the prince to

his father. Tiridates remained in SYRIA, although his ambitions were ended when a peace treaty was signed in 20.

Tiridates III (d. 318 or 330 C.E.) *King of Armenia (c. 287–318 or 330 C.E.) and the first Christian king of that country*

Tiridates was taken as a child to the Roman provinces when Armenia was overrun by SHAPUR I around 252. Subsequently raised by the Romans, he took part in the campaigns against the GOTHS of Probus before being restored to the throne of Armenia in 287. Another Persian onslaught (c. 296), led by Narses, ousted him briefly until 298, when Emperor GALERIUS defeated the Persians. In 301, Gregory the Illuminator (GREGORY OF ARMENIA) appeared at his court performing miracles. Tiridates was immediately converted, transforming Armenia into a Christian domain. He was murdered either in 318 or 330.

Tiro, Marcus Tullius (fl. mid-first century B.C.E.) *Freedman and close friend of Cicero*

Tiro lived for many years after the death of Cicero, working hard in that time to preserve his friend's good name while developing his own literary reputation. Originally a slave in Cicero's household, Tiro was given his freedom in 54 B.C.E. and henceforth was indispensable to his former master, reading and preparing Cicero's multitudinous manuscripts. After the murder of Cicero in 43, Tiro was the editor of his collected orations and letters, as well as the author of a biography on him. The freedman authored his own poetry, a grammatical work and the *notae Tironianae*, an early version of shorthand, using abbreviations.

Titiana, Flavia (fl. late second century C.E.) *Wife of Emperor Pertinax*

Titiana was the daughter of Flavius SULPICIANUS, the PREFECT OF THE CITY during the auctioning of the Roman Empire in 193. Flavia Titiana was reportedly adulterous, carrying on, for example, with a lute player. The historian Dio called her an unchaste consort. This was probably why the newly elevated emperor refused in 193 to give her the title of AUGUSTA. Curiously, COINAGE and inscriptions show her with that rank.

Titius, Marcus (first century B.C.E.) *Son of the one of the victims of the triumviral proscriptions (see TRIUMVIRATE, SECOND)*

Titius was noted for trapping and executing Sextus POMPEY in 36 B.C.E. After the murder of his father (c. 40), Titius fled from Italy to GALLIA NARBONENSIS, where he organized a band of ships and followers. Captured by the Sextian officer, MENAS, Titius was spared because his men carried on their shields the name of Sextus. Eventually deserting Sextus for Marc ANTONY, Titius was charged with the task of hunting down the pirate in 36, after the battle of NAULOCHUS. Sextus was found and put to death. Titius became a legate in the service of Antony but, with Plancus, departed in 32 for the party of Octavian (AUGUSTUS). Prior to the battle of Actium (31 B.C.E.), Titius commanded cavalry with Statilius TAURUS, defeating Antony's horsemen and convincing Philadelphus, king of Paphlagonia, to join Octavian. Titius was later a trusted officer in the regime of Augustus, holding the post of governor of SYRIA (c. 10–9 B.C.E.). His action in the death of Sextus Pompey was never forgiven by the Romans, and a mob once chased him out of a theater.

Titus (41–81 C.E.) *Emperor from 79–81 and the brother of his successor, Domitian*
According to the historian SUETONIUS, Titus was feared and hated at the time of his accession but soon earned the loyalty and devotion of Rome through his goodness and sound rule. He was born on December 30, 41, in a slum section of Rome, the first son of VESPASIAN and Flavia Domitilla. Because of his father he was educated in the palace of Emperor CLAUDIUS and later in that of NERO, becoming the closest of friends with BRITANNICUS, Claudius's son. It was said that when Nero killed the prince with poison, Titus was reclining at the same table and actually drank some of the fatal brew, suffering severe illness as a result.

Having survived the court, Titus embarked upon a successful military career. A tribune in Britain and Germany, he was made a *quaestor* in 65 and two years later a legate in command of a legion in PALESTINE, under the supervision of his father. The young general proved quite able in the suppression of the Jewish uprising. Josephus recorded that he tried, when possible, to avoid destruction and bloodshed. Vespasian sent his son on a trip to Rome to congratulate Galba on his accession, but when Titus reached Corinth he heard of the new emperor's assassination in January 69 and returned to JUDAEA. Vespasian was soon persuaded by his son and fellow officers in the East to march on Rome and seize the throne. The completion of the Jewish War was left to Titus, who showed great strategic sense and energy over the next year, culminating in the capture and destruction of JERUSALEM and its great temple. Sources are at odds as to Titus's willingness to see the temple demolished, but, guilty or innocent, it was an act that earned him eternal condemnation and had a major influence on Jewish history.

With Judaea pacified and his father now emperor, Titus hurried home in 71, thus dispelling rumors that his excessive cultivation of praise following his triumph pointed to other ambitions. Vespasian heaped further honors upon him, making it clear whom he desired for his heir. Titus became his colleague, sharing his powers in every sense and even acting as the head of government in his father's name. As consul seven times and as PREFECT OF THE PRAETORIAN GUARD, he earned a reputation for ruthlessness, tyranny and political violence. Added to this was the habit of throwing lavish parties for his friends and an affair with BERENICE, a Jewish princess.

When Vespasian died in 79, the Romans were afraid that Titus's joke would come true. He claimed that to pay for the financial needs of the state he would have to be a second Nero. Roman anxiety was soon calmed and replaced by admiration, for Titus as emperor offered no faults for criticism. At every opportunity he gave public displays of his good nature. Gladiatorial games were held with other amusements to keep the Roman mobs happy in the face of stern but necessary economic policies. The highlight of his reign came with the opening of the COLOSSEUM, known then as the Amphitheatrum Flavium. With the shows held there and the pogrom launched against informers, Titus's time on the throne was remembered as stable, in spite of numerous, normally ominous natural disasters. Mount VESUVIUS erupted in 79, burying POMPEII, Stabiae, and HERCULANEUM. Titus hurried south to CAMPANIA, only to have a fire break out in Rome the next year. In the wake of the fire a plague descended upon Italy, one of the worst on record. Each calamity was met with concern and generous remedial action. After uttering that the fire "has ruined me," he sold or stripped imperial estates to hasten the recovery.

What would have happened in following years was never known, for Titus was dead on September 1, 81. He cried while at the games, for an unknown reason, took ill and succumbed in the same house where Vespasian died only two years before. Titus's last words were that he was bitter about dying because he had only one terrible sin on his conscience; the nature of that offense was never known. Mourning was widespread and sincere, increasing over the next few months as the Romans came to know their new Emperor DOMITIAN. Suetonius admired Titus, describing him as graceful and dignified but not tall and having a paunch. His memory was superb, he read Greek and Latin and could play music.

Tivoli Town about 15 miles from Rome, on one of the oldest inhabited sites in Italy (*see* LATIUM); also, the grandest villa ever constructed. Tivoli (also known as Tibur) is where Emperor HADRIAN constructed his huge villa complex of the same name in the second century C.E.

The town was situated on a hill to give it a commanding view of the nearby countryside. Flowing nearby was the Anio River, forming a waterfall. The city came under Roman rule in 338 B.C.E. and was subsequently developed as a retreat from Rome for the upper classes. It was the beauty of Tibur and its relative proximity to Rome that drew Hadrian there. Nobles and notables took up residence as well, and HORACE had a small house in Tibur. Emperor AURELIAN even decided that Queen

ZENOBIA, whom he defeated in 271 C.E., should reside there in relative comfort.

An emperor of considerable ambition and vision, Hadrian took one of the hills near Tibur and transformed it, between 118 and 134, into his own retreat. It may originally have been a villa owned by Empress Sabina, but by the time Hadrian was finished there was no similarity to the older, Republican-style villa. Indeed, Tivoli was the physical manifestation of Hadrian's great love for Hellenism. Throughout Tivoli could be found Greek references in statuary, mosaics, and design. Where Greek influence was not obvious, other nations contributed, such as Egypt (specifically, ALEXANDRIA) with an imitation of its Serapeum.

Arguably the most beautiful place in the villa was the isolated Island Villa, a moated series of rooms and suites, with bedrooms, a dining hall, and full facilities, including a bath. It was accessible by bridges but never lost its sense of quiet seclusion, with its white columns and continual breezes. Nearby was the so-called Poicile, or peristyle courtyard. It was designed most likely along the lines of the Greek *dromos* or exercise area so common in that country. There were columns along the entire perimeter and rooms at one end for the staff. Situated, no doubt, just below were the private imperial suites where Hadrian actually slept while visiting. Part of this section had a hippodrome, similar to the one found in Domitian's Domus Flavia, although this track was far more impressive.

Hadrian ordered that two baths be built, the small and the large. The smaller baths were perhaps for his own use, displaying niceties in design that seemed to reflect the personal imperial touches. Such were wholly absent in the larger baths, just to the south. These were more conventional. To the east could be found the Piazza d'Oro, another peristyle court topped with an unusual, eight-sided vault. Here again, with columns arranged in the fashion of a *stoa*, could be seen Hadrian's fascination with Hellenic style.

To the west of the piazza was a series of structures that were slightly removed from the main complex. The Serapeum, modeled on the Alexandrian shrine, was a half-dome, decorated with glass and built into the hillside. Stretching from it was the Canopus, a small canal-like pool surrounded by statues with Grecian motifs (Amazons, for example). Also belonging to Tivoli were an Academy and a temple to Venus. Hadrian, according to Spartianus, gave names to parts of the villa as he thought appropriate, with references to parts of the empire. He had an Academy, Canopus, Tempe, Poicile, and Lyceum. There was even a Hades, or an entrance to the land of the dead.

toga Allowed only to Romans, the toga became synonymous with the culture and society of Rome. It developed, as well, its own precise uses, official purposes, and popular nuances.

Togas were an ancient form of dress, dating far back into Roman history. Before the creation of the *sagum,* or military uniform, the toga was worn into battle. As Rome grew as a military power, the garment found expression as a symbol of peace. Essentially, a toga was a white woolen cloth, cut into a semicircular design of approximately five yards long, four yards wide, varying upon the size of the wearer. A part of it was pressed into plaits and doubled lengthwise so that one of the folds (called the *sinus*) would wrap comfortably around the hip and chest while allowing room enough to walk or move. The left shoulder was covered and the right shoulder remained free, although by design, the right shoulder and head could be covered for ceremonies, usually by pulling up the *sinus*.

There were special ways of wearing the toga, just as there were special togas. For sacrifices and certain religious ceremonies the *cinctus Gabinus* was arranged. Named after the town of Gabii, the Gabian toga had the *sinus* drawn over the head but the portion draped over the left shoulder was drawn around the body instead, to form a girdle by tucking it around the waist. In this way both arms were free. Over time, the *cinctus Gabinus* appeared only at religious observances, such as the opening of the Temple of Janus, sacrifices or the groundbreaking for a new town.

Men wore the so-called *toga virilis*, also known as the *toga pura* or common toga. Often the wool that was used was made whiter by applying chalk. Such treated togas were named *toga candida* and were found worn by candidates seeking office. Dark-colored togas, the toga *pulla* or toga *sordida*, were worn by the lower classes or by others in time of mourning or when under severe stress, as at a trial.

The *toga praetexta* was a toga with a distinctive purple stripe woven into the fabric, probably along the *sinus*. In the Republic it was the emblem of the curule magistrates, CENSORS, dictators, and priests (when performing their religious duties). Later it was adopted by the emperors. Children wore the *toga praetexta*: boys until they reached manhood and received the *toga virilis*; girls until marriage, when they took the *stola* or matron's dress. Prostitutes and disgraced wives always wore the toga.

Finally, there was the *toga picta* or ornate toga. This was a toga decorated with a red stripe and gold embroidery. Generals were adorned with it for triumphs, and CONSULS wore it upon entering office, as did magistrates when giving public games. The emperors, not surprisingly, took to wearing it themselves and with them it remained.

See also CLOTHING; DICTATOR; FESTIVALS; *LUDI*; PATRICIAN; PLEBEIANS; RELIGION; SENATE.

Tome of Leo Important letter (Epistola, XXVIII) composed by Pope (later St.) LEO I (r. 440–461) on June 13, 449, to Flavian, patriarch of Constantinople. While directed specifically against the heresy of Eutyches, the tome established the significant Christological doctrine concerning Christ's two natures in one Person. Leo made clear that Christ is one Person, but in him, permanently united, unconfused, and distinct, are two natures, the divine and the human. While each has its own faculties, they are performed entirely within the unity of the Person of Christ. When Emperor Theodosius II (r. 408–450) convened the Council of Ephesus in August 449, Leo expected that the tome would be read by his legates and given approval by the participants. The council failed to do this, restoring instead the monk Eutyches, thereby earning the name Latrocinium, or Robber Council, of Ephesus, from the displeased pope. At the Council of Chalcedon (451), however, the orthodox party triumphed. The tome was given full recognition and was declared the church's formal statement on the Incarnation, as the delegates at Chalcedon proclaimed that "the voice of Peter had spoken through Leo."

Trachalus, P. Galerius (fl. first century C.E.) *Consul in 68, with Silus Italicus, an advocatus and rhetor*
Quintilian wrote of him that he had the finest voice and delivery that he had ever heard. Trachalus was a minor player in the events of 69 C.E., when he acted as political adviser to OTHO, possibly writing some of his speeches. Although an obvious confidant of Otho, Trachalus was not attacked in the brief reign of VITELLIUS. His sister Galeria was married to Vitellius.

trade and commerce

WITHIN THE ROMAN EMPIRE

Province	Contribution to Commerce
Achaea	Major: olives
	Minor: wine
Africa	Major: olives; corn; cereal; fruits
	Minor: textiles
Arabia	Major: trade routes from East to West
Asia	Major: trade routes from East to West; cloth
	Minor: olives and corn
Bithynia	Major: trade routes from East to West
	Minor: agriculture; timber; iron
Britannia	Major: gold; iron; silver; tin
	Minor: agriculture and livestock
Cappadocia	Major: horses and livestock
	Minor: cereal and fruit
Cilicia	Major: timber
	Minor: wheat; olives; fruit; wine
Cyprus	Major: copper
Crete and Cyrenaica	Major: agriculture
Dacia	Major: gold and silver

Egypt	Major: corn and grain
	Minor: trade routes from East to West
Galatia	Major: none
	Minor: none
Gallia (Tres Galliae)	Major: pottery; glassmaking; metallurgy; woodcraft; textiles
	Minor: wheat; olives; fruits; corn; oil; wine; cheeses; ham
Germania (Germany)	Major: none
	Minor: none
Hispania (Spain)	Major: gold; silver; copper; tin; lead
	Minor: wheat; olives; oil; fruits; wine; livestock
Illyricum	Major: trade routes along the Danube
Italia (Italy)	Major: metallurgy, pottery; weapons
	Minor: olives
Lycia and Pamphylia	Major: timber
	Minor: corn
Macedonia	Major: mining and timber
	Minor: trade routes from East to West; agriculture; livestock
Mauretania	Major: olives and fruits
	Minor: marble; wine; livestock
Moesia	Major: trade along the Danube and Black Sea
	Minor: agriculture and mining
Noricum	Major: mining; iron
Numidia	Major: corn and grains
	Minor: wine and livestock
Pannonia	Major: mining; iron; silver
	Minor: wild bison and boars
Raetia	Minor: agriculture
Sardinia	Major: corn and salt
	Minor: iron and silver
Sicilia (Sicily)	Major: wheat; corn; fruits; almonds
	Minor: wine
Syria	Major: trade routes from East to West
	Minor: grain; fruits; cloth; glassmaking; dyes
Thrace	Major: trade along the Danube and Black Sea
	Minor: agriculture and mining

OUTSIDE THE EMPIRE

State	Contribution to Commerce
African kingdoms	slaves
Bosporus, Kingdom of	grain; fish; hides; hemp

Commerce in action, from Trajan's Column *(Courtesy Fr. Felix Just, S.J.)*

State	Contribution to Commerce
China	silk; incense; jewelry; perfumes; spices
India	spices; gems; ivory; perfumes; cotton; jewelry; incense; exotic animals
Parthian Empire	minor trade goods and caravan routes to the East and West
Persian Empire	minor trade goods and caravan routes to the East and West

See also COINAGE; ECONOMY; FARMING; PROVINCES; TRANSPORTATION; WEIGHTS AND MEASURES and under individual provinces for details on the industry and trade for each territory.

Suggested Readings: Casson, Lionel. *Ancient Trade and Society.* Detroit, Mich.: Wayne State University Press, 1984; Charlesworth, M. P. *Trade-Routes and Commerce in the Roman Empire.* New York: Square Publishers Inc., 1979; D'Arms, John H. *Commerce and Social Standing in Ancient Rome.* Cambridge, Mass.: Harvard University Press, 1981; D'Arms, John H. and Kopff, E. C., eds. *The Seaborne Commerce of Ancient Rome.* Rome: American Academy in Rome, 1980; Duncan-Jones, Richard. *Structure and Scale in the Roman Economy.* Cambridge, U.K.: Cambridge University Press, 1990; Duncan-Jones, Richard. *The Economy of the Roman Empire: Quantitative Studies.* Cambridge, U.K.: Cambridge University Press, 1982; Finley, M. I. *The Ancient Economy.* 2nd ed. London: Hogarth, 1985; Frank, Tenney, ed. *An Economic Survey of Ancient Rome.* New York: Octagon Books, 1975; Frayn, Joan M. *Sheep-rearing and the Wool Trade in Italy During the Roman Period.* Liverpool, U.K.: F. Cairns, 1984; Gar-

nsey, Peter, Keith Hopkins, and C. R. Whittaker, eds. *Trade in the Ancient Economy.* Berkeley: University of California Press, 1983; Glodariu, Ioan. *Dacian Trade with the Hellenistic and Roman World.* Translated by Nubar Hampartumian. Oxford, U.K.: British Archaeological Reports, 1976; Greene, Kevin. *The Archaeology of the Roman Economy.* Berkeley: University of California Press, 1986; Hodge, Peter. *Roman Trade and Travel.* London: Longman, 1978; Love, John R. *Antiquity and Capitalism: Max Weber and the Sociological Foundations of Roman Civilization.* London: Routledge, 1991; Rickman, Geoffrey. *The Corn Supply of Ancient Rome.* Oxford, U.K.: Clarendon Press, 1980; Whittaker, C. R., ed. *Pastoral Economies in Classical Antiquity.* Cambridge, U.K.: Cambridge Philological Society, 1988.

Trajan (Marcus Ulpius Traianus) (c. 53–117 C.E.)
Emperor from 98–117 and the most militarily ambitious ruler of the Roman Empire

The reign of Trajan was filled with some of the largest wars in Rome's history and characterized by the aggrandizement of Rome and its empire. Unfortunately, these events were recorded in scant detail, for literary sources on Trajan did not survive, except for the account of the historian Dio. Only through COINAGE of the era, correspondence with PLINY and Pliny's panegyric, and the grand arch of Trajan can evidence be found.

Trajan was born to a family originally from Umbria but settled in Hispania Baetica. His father, of the same name, was a successful senator, CONSUL and governor of Asia and SYRIA; his mother was Marcia, otherwise unknown. With the status of his father as a useful base, Trajan embarked upon his own career. A tribune with his parent while his father was governor of Syria, by the late 80s he was a legate in charge of a legion in Hispania Tarraconensis, the VII Gemina. In 89, in response to the summons of DOMITIAN, Trajan marched his cohorts toward Germania Superior, where Apronius SATURNINUS had rebelled. Although he arrived too late to participate in Saturninus's demise, the emperor was nevertheless grateful; in 91, Trajan held a consulship. Nerva apparently appointed him the governor of Germania Superior in 96, and then, after the PRAETORIAN GUARD humiliated the emperor, Trajan was suddenly adopted.

His adoption by the emperor probably stemmed from his military reputation, support from the SENATE and the real popularity that he enjoyed with the troops of the legions. Quite possibly Trajan and his allies in Rome applied enough pressure on the aged emperor to have him named as heir. Nerva died in 98, and Trajan was informed at Cologne by the young HADRIAN that he now ruled the Roman world. To demonstrate that the throne was his and to teach a lesson as to its rights, he summoned Casperius Aelianus, PREFECT OF THE PRAETORIAN GUARD, along with the leaders of the

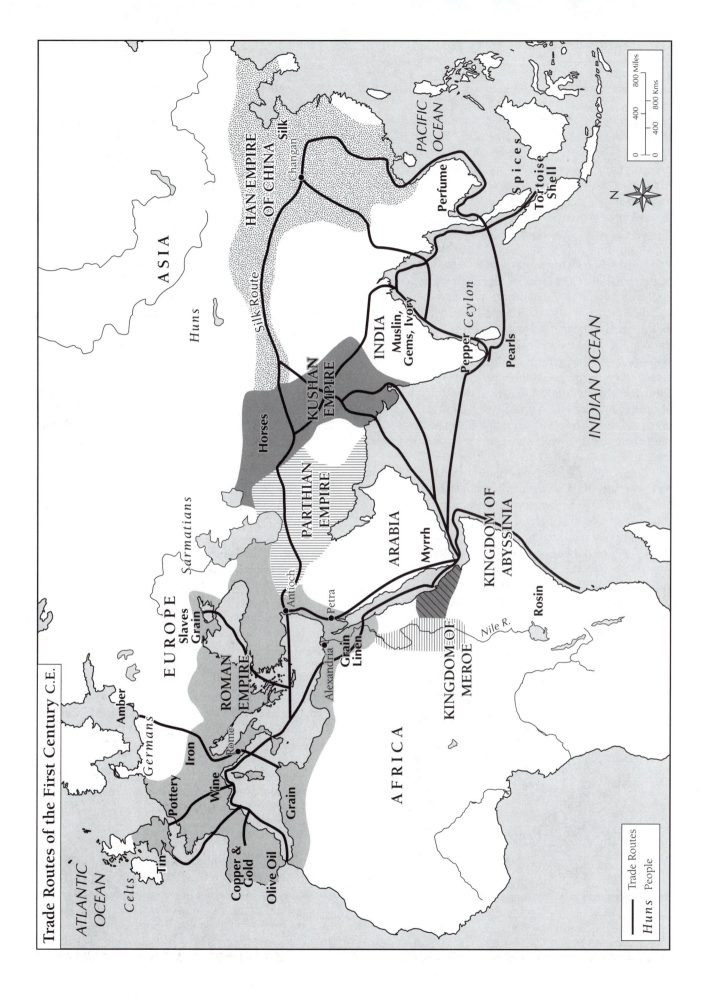

Trade Routes of the First Century C.E.

ATLANTIC
OCEAN

ASIA

HAN EMPIRE
OF CHINA

Huns

Silk Route

Changan

Silk

PACIFIC
OCEAN

Perfume

Spices

Tortoise
Shell

N

800 Miles
800 Kms
400
400
0
0

INDIA
Muslin,
Gems, Ivory

Ceylon

Pepper

Pearls

KUSHAN
EMPIRE

Horses

Sarmatians

EUROPE
Slaves
Grain

PARTHIAN
EMPIRE

Antioch

Petra

ARABIA

Myrrh

KINGDOM OF
ABYSSINIA

Rosin

INDIAN OCEAN

Amber

Germans

ROMAN
EMPIRE

Rome

Iron

Pottery

Wine

Celts

Tin

Copper &
Gold

Olive Oil

Grain

Alexandria

Grain
Linen

KINGDOM OF
MEROE

Nile R.

AFRICA

Trade Routes
Huns   People

group that had shamed Nerva. They were put to death, and Trajan entered Rome in pomp, with his austere wife PLOTINA.

What followed was virtually incessant warfare, as Trajan sought to extend the limits of the empire in every direction. He began by finishing what he considered a previous failure; the unsatisfactory war with DACIA and its King DECEBALUS. In two massive campaigns (101–102 and 105–106) Dacia was defeated and Decebalus driven to suicide. When Dacia was declared an imperial province, it represented a major Roman inroad into the region north of the DANUBE. At the same time, Cornelius Palma led a Roman army into Arabia Petra, subduing the Nabataeans of Petra and reducing the economically wealthy kingdom to the status of a province.

Back in Rome, Trajan celebrated his win over Dacia and devoted a number of years almost solely to running the empire. As emperor he displayed a remarkable restraint in dealing with the Senate. He showed the body great respect while presenting himself as the ideal ruler. Dio wrote of him in glowing terms, describing his sense of justice, bravery, and simplicity of habits. He envied no one, paid no attention to slander and was so beloved by the Senate and the people that he often went to homes without a guard.

This cultivated image of honesty and compassion was proven in more ways than by minor demonstrations or speeches. Trajan increased the CONGIARIUM or free distribution of food and took further steps to ensure that the grain supply was maintained. One of his finest creations in the field of public service was the *alimenta* or special subsidy paid to the poor of Italy. For the provinces he appointed governors who were reliable and could be trusted to deal honorably with the inhabitants. For those provinces or cities where finances were in a desperate

state, such as Achaea and Athens, he sent the CORRECTORES or administrators. One of his governors in Bithynia was PLINY THE YOUNGER. Military colonies were also established in those areas needing Romanization, especially in Germania and along the Danube, in MOESIA. Despite the reduction in taxes and his lengthy campaigns, Trajan found time and money to spend on public works in the empire and in Rome. With the help of APOLLODORUS of Damascus he built the Forum of Trajan (FORUM TRAIANI), the Market of Trajan (TRAJAN'S MARKET) and the Baths of Trajan. Roads were also repaired throughout the provinces.

Even as he made these popular gifts to the people, his thoughts were returning to war. Parthia was still a troubling enemy in the East and, much as he had done in Dacia, Trajan planned to do more than inflict a severe defeat upon them. Thus in 114, he invaded ARMENIA with a huge army. The country fell quickly, and in 115 he marched into Mesopotamia and captured the Parthian capitol of Ctesiphon. This acquisition made western Parthia Roman territory, and Trajan declared Mesopotamia part of the empire. He soon discovered that conquest was easier than holding a region filled with minor kingdoms and hostile populations. When Mesopotamia rose in revolt, Roman authority was reinstated, but tenuously. Trajan tried to reduce the city of Hatra and was so exhausted by the siege that he fell ill shortly thereafter. Other bad news reached him. The Jews in Cyrenaica, Cyprus, Egypt and even in parts of JUDAEA had risen in rebellion. Although suppressed, the uprising had left thousands of dead and entire parts of provinces in ruins.

Trajan departed the East in 117, tired and ill. In Cilicia he suffered some kind of stroke in early August and died. He had adopted Hadrian but may not have named him his successor. Whatever Trajan's view might have been is not known, for Plotina and the Praetorian Prefect ATTIANUS made certain that Hadrian followed him to the throne. Hadrian did not believe in wars of expansion, viewing them as too costly, thus undoing by policy and by inactivity Trajan's life's work. Nevertheless, Trajan had accomplished much to make Rome proud again, and Hadrian, despite his differing viewpoint, was a worthy successor.

Suggested Readings: Bennett, Julian. *Trajan: Optimus Princeps*. Bloomington, Indiana: University Press, 1997; Lepper, F. A. *Trajan's Parthian War*. London: Oxford University Press, 1948.

Trajan's Market Ingenious structure built by Emperor TRAJAN sometime between 100 and 112 C.E.; located just above the FORUM TRAIANI in Rome and designed by APOLLODORUS of Damascus, the great architect in the service of the emperor. The Market of Trajan, called the *mercatus Traiani* was a very large structure covering the side of the Quirinal Hill. There were five levels of shops (*tabernae*)

A gold aureus of Trajan and Plotina, struck posthumously under Antoninus Pius during the opening months of his reign, Summer 138 C.E., at Rome *(Courtesy Historical Coins, Inc.)*

and offices, including those for Trajan's *annona* and *alimenta*, or bureau of loans and subsidies. Architecturally, the market was startlingly different from virtually every other building in the city. Apollodorus used a simple design, abstaining from the opulent facades of the time in favor of concrete and plain brick. It was topped with a vaulted hall and a concrete half-dome.

Tranquillina, Furia Sabina (fl. third century C.E.)
Empress from 241 to 243

The wife of Emperor GORDIAN III, Tranquillina was the daughter of the Praetorian Prefect TIMESITHEUS. Her marriage to Gordian in 241 was an admission by the young emperor of both the political indispensability of her father and her own suitability as empress. In 243, she suffered the double loss of her husband and father. Her own fate is not recorded.

transportation

The Roman Empire has long been credited with creating and maintaining for centuries a highly developed, systematic, and relatively efficient transportation system throughout its provinces. The success of Roman ROADS, the MILESTONE system, and sea power made it possible for most of the citizens of the empire to travel, both for purposes of need and even for leisure during times of peace and stability. Travel remained a difficult—and often dangerous—undertaking, and most people journeyed during spring and summer when the roads were in better shape and the threats of the snow or storms did not pose insuperable obstacles to land and sea travel. From the third century C.E. on, the collapse of imperial dominance on the frontiers made leisure travel largely impractical, although the wealthy could still afford the carts, horses, and guards to make the journey from Rome or Italy to the provinces in some safety.

The most obvious element in Roman transportation was the network of roads that connected Italy with all of its provinces and the frontiers. First developed in the early republic, the road system expanded swiftly with the empire, becoming a specific and important facet in Roman strategic plans for conquest and pacification. Good roads ensured swift movement of the legions, easy communication between the cities and provinces, and ease of transport for merchants, travelers, and colonists. At the same time, great emphasis was placed by the Roman government on shipbuilding and the maintaining of a large imperial fleet and commercial shipping to supply Roman merchants with access by sea to Egypt, the Mediterranean coast, and the lands of the East.

LAND TRANSPORTATION

On land, travel was accomplished in several ways: the *cursus publicus,* on foot, on horseback, or in wheeled vehicles. The *cursus publicus* was the imperial postal system organized first by Emperor Augustus (r. 27 B.C.E.–14 C.E.) to ensure communications throughout the imperial world. A public transportation system, the *cursus publicus* used couriers (*tabellarii*) to carry messages along military roads. They made speedy progress thanks to the different stations (*mansiones, mutationes,* and *stationes*) posted along the routes. There they could find fresh horses, food, and rest before continuing on to the next station. The *cursus publicus* was also used by soldiers on missions, government officials, and anyone granted a formal diploma (or imperial authorization).

As the average citizen did not have access or use of the *cursus publicus,* they were forced to manage as best they could on their own. Most poor and typical citizens made their journeys on foot on the Roman roads. Given the rugged terrain and inevitable delays due to weather, the best one could hope to achieve on any given day was about 40 Roman miles.

For someone with a load to carry on the journey, options included hiring someone to carry it for you on the way, using a neck yoke (*iugum*), or using a pack animal. Wealthier travelers could also hire a litter (*lectica*), which would be carried by slaves or also by mules.

Pack animals were probably the most common form of transportation when there was also a load to be borne. Mules and donkeys were the most reliable pack animals; horses were generally used only for riding and racing, being too expensive for heavy labor. Pack saddles were attached by ropes to the mule's back, and trains of donkeys were a common sight throughout the empire. The legions also used mules in large numbers to transport equipment, food, and other supplies. Northern provinces, such as Britannia, Germania, and those along the Danube, necessitated hardier animals. Typical animals were draft horses and ponies. In desert climates, camels were an ideal pack animal. Mules, ponies, and also camels were adopted by travelers as a perfectly suitable means of transport.

It is known that Romans made extensive use of wheeled vehicles, although few details have been preserved. Literature provides few narrative explanations of the design or development of carts and wagons, and depictions, such as reliefs or paintings, offer few clues about how the harnesses worked, how the axles were configured, or how horses and other equines were shod. Typical horse shoes were designed to be fastened to the mule's foot by leather straps and were made of Sparta grass (*Solea sparta*) or iron (*Solea ferrae*). The shoes were naturally cumbersome, fell off easily, and made transport slow and inconvenient. A better solution to shoeing seems to have been the custom of guiding carts and wagons on a parallel dirt track to the road. Movement along the softer terrain would have extended the life of the animals.

Traveling along the dirt tracks also no doubt was preferred to riding along the roads for passengers. It is known that a typical cart was based on a Celtic design

Mosaic of trading ships, from Ostia *(Courtesy Fr. Felix Just, S.J.)*

and had no suspension. This would have made even a short trip physically demanding and extremely uncomfortable.

The noise and congestion that carts and wagons created in cities led to the promulgation of the *lex Julia municipalis*, part of the comprehensive set of laws under Julius Caesar in 59 B.C.E. The law made it illegal for wheeled traffic to be used in the daytime in Rome. The only exceptions to the law were those carts attached to public services, such as the rubbish sweepers and on holidays.

SEA TRANSPORTATION

Despite the dangers of storms, shipwreck, and even piracy, the Romans made extensive use of sea travel. Such was the competence and abundance of Roman sailors that by the first century C.E. it was a common boast that one could sail from Ostia (the chief port out of Rome) to Alexandria (the chief port of Egypt) in seven days. One of the most famous accounts of a journey at sea was provided by St. Paul in his Letter to the Ephesians. Arrested for being a Christian and taken under escort from Palestine to Rome for trial, Paul traveled by boat and was shipwrecked on the island of Malta.

Virtually all shipping was oriented toward commerce (or movement of troops by sea), and pure passenger SHIPS were unknown. Most ships were thus configured with a maximum of space oriented toward cargoes. Passengers were taken on as extra cargo at the discretion of the captain and remained on deck. Shelter was usually a makeshift tent, and the passengers themselves had to provide their own food, although they had permission to fix meals in the galley.

Trapezus   Also known as Trabezun or Trabzon; a Cappadocian city on the south coast of the BLACK SEA. Probably founded circa 8 B.C.E. as a trading colony, Trapezus was a possession of the kingdom of PONTUS before falling

into Roman hands. Subsequently, it had a major role in the development of the province of CAPPADOCIA. Trapezus was one of the connecting points between the Syrian frontier and the Black Sea, and was an important economic link for the seagoing commerce of the entire region. Trapezus replaced SINOPE as the leading port in the eastern Black Sea, was the homeport for the *classis Pontica* or Black Sea fleet of the Roman NAVY, and had a sizable garrison. HADRIAN constructed a new harbor by enclosing it between moles to provide protection from attack and the weather. Such measure could not prevent Trapezus from suffering terribly in the barbaric invasions of the mid-third century. During the reign of VALERIAN and Gallienus, the city fell to the GOTHS but was recaptured. After repairs were made, the dock reopened and Trapezus regained its wealth; the city still flourished in the reign of Eastern Emperor JUSTINIAN in the sixth century C.E.

treason   *See* MAIESTAS.

Trebellenus, Rufus (d. 21 C.E.) *Ex-praetor*
In 19 C.E., Trebellenus was appointed by Emperor TIBERIUS to act as a guardian to the children of COTYS, after that king of THRACE had been murdered by his uncle, RHESCUPORIS. His administration of Thrace brought severe complaints from the inhabitants, including the charge that any crimes committed by Romans went unpunished. In 21, he was condemned in Rome and killed himself.

Trebonianus Gallus, Gaius Vibius (c. 206–253 C.E.) *Emperor from 251 to 253 C.E.*
Born to a family from Persia, he held a consulship in 245 and the governorship of MOESIA in 250. He became one of the most important generals of Trajanus Decius, working with the emperor to repel the GOTHS under their king Kniva. In 251, however, Decius was defeated and slain at Abrittus by the Goths. Gallus received the blame for supposedly permitting the catastrophe but was proclaimed emperor by his troops anyway. He probably had nothing to do with Decius's defeat.

From the start the new emperor tried to placate the various political currents of the Roman Empire. A new treaty of peace was made with the Goths, designed to reward them for not violating the frontiers, a very unpopular admission of weakness. Freed from war, Gallus traveled to Rome, where the SENATE was honored and respect paid to Decius's remaining family members. The dead emperor's youngest son, Hostilianus, was made AUGUSTUS, and the widow, Etruscilla, retained her title of AUGUSTA.

Such attempts at unification failed because of the unremitting catastrophe that gripped the world during the brief years of Gallus's reign. The Goths returned in force, pouring over the borders and extending their marches all the way to Asia Minor, where they pillaged and burned its beautiful cities. In the East, the Persians under SHAPUR I seized ARMENIA and then devastated Antioch and SYRIA. To complicate things further, in 252, a horrible plague swept through the provinces, killing Hostilianus and debilitating the legions.

Gallus's response was to revive the persecutions of the Christians, pursued so actively by his predecessor. Begun in 253, the crises everywhere were too severe, and the legions put their trust in a new master, Marcus Aemilius AEMILIAN, a general on the DANUBE. He defeated the Goths and was hailed by his own troops as their savior. Aemilian marched on Italy, and Gallus's men, avoiding a massacre, murdered Gallus to pave the way for a new man on the throne.

Trebonius, Gaius (d. 43 B.C.E.) *Tribune of the Plebeians in 55 B.C.E.*
Trebonius began as a QUAESTOR in 60, when he was a supporter of the aristocratic party, but found greater opportunity for advancement with the members of the FIRST TRIUMVIRATE, Julius CAESAR, POMPEY THE GREAT, and CRASSUS. As TRIBUNE in 55, he authored the *lex Trebonia* and aided both Pompey and Crassus with commands in Spain and the East (for Crassus). Crassus was soon destroyed at the battle of Carrhae by Parthia, and the triumvirate broke apart only a few years later. From 55 to 50, he was a legate in the service of Julius Caesar in the GALLIC WARS. With the outbreak of the CIVIL WAR (of the First Triumvirate) in 49, Trebonius joined the cause of Caesar. He conducted with great success the siege of Massilia and served as *praetor urbanus* in 48. The following year he replaced Q. Cassius Longinus as the pro-praetor of Spain, where he proved unable to prevent the Pompeians from reuniting. Nevertheless, Caesar rewarded his loyalty in 45 with a consulship and the promise of the post of governor of Asia. Trebonius repaid this by joining the plot to murder Caesar in 44, actually taking part in the assassination. He then departed Rome and took up his duties in Asia. In 43, he was surprised by the infamous DOLABELLA, who killed him in his bed at Smyrna, later hurling his head at Caesar's statue. Trebonius was also noted for his collection of CICERO's witty sayings and puns, published for his friend in 47.

Treveri Also, Treviri; a large tribe in Gallia Belgica, living to the east of the SUESSIONES and close to the Rhine River. This proximity to the Germanic tribes made them, in the opinion of Julius CAESAR, the most German of the Gallic nations; they were also reported to be the bravest and most talented horsemen. Because of their fierce independence, the Treveri were difficult clients for Rome as they could be found in the thick of virtually every major revolt. But their factionalism was an aid to Rome, especially during the GALLIC WARS. In 54 B.C.E., Caesar was able to avert a rebellion by supporting the chief Vercingetorix over Indutiomarus. Unfortunately, a revolt did occur in 53 but was quickly suppressed.

Under the occupation of Rome, the Treveri supplied levies of auxiliaries to serve in the legions but continued to take part in movements against the Romans. In 21 C.E., they joined Julius SACROVIR but in 68 refused to back VINDEX in his attempt to begin a nationalistic Gallic revolution. As the rise of Vindex had helped Galba, the Treveri were punished for remaining loyal to NERO. As a consequence, they received warmly the pro-VITELLIUS march of the Rhine legions on Rome and then cheered Julius CLASSICUS in his creation of the Imperiim Galliarum in 69. Subsequently of reduced importance, their chief town, Trevi or Treves, was taken by the Romans to serve as a leading city in Gallia Belgica—Augusta Trevirorum (Trier).

tribune An important officer of the Roman state. Those tribunes who represented the PLEBEIANS were called the *tribuni plebis* or tribunes of the plebs, while in the legions there were the *tribuni militum* or military tribunes.

TRIBUNI PLEBIS

The tribunes of the Plebs were the elected, official representatives of the Plebeian class and acted as the champions and protectors of all Plebeians against any possible oppression by the PATRICIANS or the CONSULS. The tribunes were first organized in the early fifth century B.C.E., chosen by the *comitia curiata* and later by the COMITIA TRIBUTA, probably after 471 B.C.E. Originally two in number, they eventually became five and then (c. 457) 10. The position of the tribune relative to the Republic grew considerably as the Plebeians assumed greater power. While they were only magistrates in the fifth century B.C.E., so long as the oath taken to them by the Plebs remained intact, the aggrandizement of their office was both inevitable and desirable. By using their office, the tribunes kept in check competing officials of the Republic and came to a position where they could oppose anyone except the dictators.

By the first century B.C.E. it was widely recognized that the tribune of the Plebs was, within Rome, the most powerful position attainable. Although its rights and privileges, the TRIBUNICIA POTESTAS, extended only to the city and its environs, there was a desire to wield it for political advantage. SULLA (c. 80 B.C.E.) attempted to curtail the tribunes, but his limitations were revoked some 30 years later. With the civil war, the weight of the tribuneship passed into the hands of Julius CAESAR in 48 B.C.E., without any definite time limit and without any degree of restraint.

In Caesar was thus established the idea of a perpetual tribuneship. AUGUSTUS, beginning in 36 B.C.E., followed suit but for him the key was not so much the actual post but its real strength, the *tribunicia potestas*. The emperor took the *potestas* for himself, separate from the office, as part of his pledge to defend the people. His status in Rome was thus largely derived from the prerogatives of the *potestas*, which was marked each year by numerals. Actual tribunes continued to exist but shorn of their influences, elected by the SENATE. In order to make the weakened honor more appealing, Augustus made it a key step in the senatorial career of a Plebeian, mandatory before the praetorship. Tribunes continued to exist until the late fourth century C.E.

TRIBUNI MILITUM

Originally key military personnel in the legions of the Republic, the military tribunes had a reduced role in the imperial legions. They were elected at first by the people, later in conjunction with the CONSULS. Six were assigned each year to each legion but, as most field or combat duties were handled by the centurions, the tribunes held posts of an administrative nature. This reality of legionary life was probably a reflection of the pool from which the tribunes were taken. Only very rarely was a centurion appointed to the tribuneship. Rather, most candidates came from the senatorial or Equestrian (EQUITES) rank, were young and had already served as staff member or aide-de-camp to a general or a commander-in-chief. Eager to embark upon a political career, they viewed the tribuneship as a necessary first step in their advancement to higher office.

All tribunes wore a toga with a broad or narrow purple stripe, depending upon their membership in the senatorial or Equestrian class, but all bore an Equestrian ring. From the time of Julius Caesar the tribunes ceased to enjoy the senior positions in the legions because of the rise of the *legati* or legates (*see* LEGATUS), who ran the legions. During the imperial era this system was concretized; the tribunes did lead the legion on march, however, and still held commands of power in the auxilia.

See also EQUITES.

tribunicia potestas   The powers of the *tribuni plebis*, or TRIBUNES of the PLEBEIANS. Tribunes were originally considered mere magistrates, elected by the Plebeians to defend them against the cruelties of the PATRICIANS or the CONSULS. They lacked any insignia of office and were not honored by the lictors. They did not have attendants (*viatores*).

Very quickly, however, the tribunes amassed vast political powers, and the *tribunicia potestas* became the strongest protection from tyranny in the Roman Republic. According to the oath taken to them by the Plebeians, the *tribuni plebis* were made sacrosanct, free from persecution and prosecution in the fulfillment of their duties. They safeguarded all Plebeians (and later everybody) from excesses by the magistrates (excepting the dictators). The right to enact compulsory measures, including arrests, fines, imprisonment, and even death, was their to use. Troops could be levied, TRIBUTUM or taxes demanded, but appeals to these orders could also be made. Their privilege to veto certain enactments spread to allow them to curtail or even suspend activities of the SENATE.

Officially, any proposals made by the tribunes had to be approved by the Senate, but in time of crisis this legal technicality was ignored. The tribune was free to do this because of his immunity from prosecution. Changes in the law were also tolerated, and a place was provided for the tribunes in the Curia during proceedings of the Senate. From this bench, called the *subsellia*, the tribune used his *auxilium* to speak out in defense of his constituency, if he felt the need. This capacity to interfere in senatorial deliberations led to an actual seat in the body, a right to veto and, finally, the ability to summon the Senate.

It was not surprising that SULLA, in 80 B.C.E., took steps to curtail the *tribunicia potestas*. But the tribunes survived Sulla's machinations and were successful in restoring their status. In CAESAR and AUGUSTUS they encountered two more resilient manipulators. Augustus seized the *tribunicia potestas*, kept it forever as one of the keys to his omnipotence as PRINCEPS and then divorced it from the old tribuneship. Another important development was Augustus's granting to Marcus Vipsanius AGRIPPA full authority to wield the *potestas* (c. 19–18 B.C.E.) in his name. The years of its being held were numbered so that dating was characterized by the inscriptions "trib. pot. II" or "trib. pot. III." Elevating someone to hold the *tribunicia potestas* was, in the imperial age, considered a clear indication of the decision of the emperor that this individual would succeed to the throne.

Tribual Assembly   *See* COMITIA TRIBUTA.

tribute penny   Nickname used to describe the poll tax (*tributum capitis*) paid by residents of the provinces to Rome, but especially the form of TRIBUTUM collected from the inhabitants of JUDAEA after provincialization in 6 C.E. Their tax, for many years one DENARIUS, received the name tribute penny.

See also COINAGE; TAXATION.

tributum   The tax collected by the Roman imperial government from the inhabitants of the provinces. Under the Republic, taxes were normally paid as a fixed sum (STIPENDIUM) or a tithe (*decumae*). This system changed with the foundation of the empire, for the use of the CENSUS made possible accurate estimates of the size of the population and hence the amount of *tributum* to be paid. While there were exceptions, most notably in COLONIES, in cities with the IUS ITALICUM and in Egypt, the two basic forms of imperial TAXATION were the poll tax (*tributum capitis*) and the land tax (*tributum solis*).

Trier   (Augusta Treverorum)

Once the capital city of the Treveri but later developed into one of the leading cities of Gallia Belgica. Trier was situated on the Moselle River, just east of Germania Superior (modern Luxembourg). Also known as Treves, it came under direct Roman occupation probably in the reign of AUGUSTUS but most likely did not receive full status as a *colonia* (see COLONIES) until the time of CLAUDIUS. Strategically situated to serve as a gateway for the distribution of Gallic goods and services to the two provinces of Germania Inferior and Superior, Trier became noted in the first century C.E. for its cloth. Romanization was pronounced, and a school in the city taught Latin. Because of its wealth and Roman flavoring, Rome decided to move to Trier a part of the central administration from Gallia Belgica and the two Germanias. The finances of the provinces came under the control of a procurator who had his offices in Trier.

While the city eventually came to rival RHEIMS, the capital of Gallia Belgica, it was not until the third century C.E. and the reforms of DIOCLETIAN that it became one of the foremost metropolises of the West. Emperor CONSTANTIUS I CHLORUS, named a Caesar in the TETRARCHY, chose Trier as the center of operations for his portion of the empire (Gallia, Hispania, and Britannia).

Under Constantius and his son CONSTANTINE, Trier was improved architecturally. Although the city already had some interesting structures dating to the second century C.E. including the Baths of St. Barbara, a forum and an amphitheater, Constantius began work on the large basilica and imperial palace structure that occupied a good part of the eastern region of the city. Constantine completed these projects after 306, when he succeeded his father. He added his own touch with the sumptuous imperial baths, perhaps used only by the court. To this period also belongs the Porta Nigra, the famous gates of Trier.

Trio, Fulcinius   (d. 35 C.E.)

One of the most disliked Delatores (informers) during the reign of Tiberius (14–37 C.E.) Trio first gained prominence as an accuser of LIBO in 16 C.E. and then as a leading attacker on Gnaeus Calpurnius PISO in 19. After the suicide of Piso, Trio was promised public office but was not made CONSUL until 31, probably to allay the suspicions of the Praetorian Prefect SEJANUS, who was his political patron. Trio's colleague was the more reliable P. Memmius Regulus who subsequently helped to destroy the ambitious Sejanus. Despite being a known client of Sejanus, Trio evaded death in 31 by becoming a leading accuser of the fallen prefect's supporters. He complained about Regulus, claiming that he did not pursue the friends of Sejanus with enough vigor. In 35, Trio committed suicide, knowing that Tiberius would inevitably have him put to death.

Tripoli   *See* OEA.

Tripolitania

The eastern portion of the province of AFRICA; also called Tripolitana and Syrtica Regio, after the two branches of the Syrtes River that cut through the region. This was actually a very narrow strip of territory between the coast and the domain of the hostile Garamantes and the hot Sahara. Although fertile lands was hard to find, development in Tripolitania was considerable, with three main cities: Lepcis Magna, Oea (Tripoli), and Sabratha.

triumph

Ancient celebration in Rome that gave honor to a victorious general; the highest honor attainable for an officer in the legions of the Republic, it could be won on land or sea, so long as certain requirements were met by the victor. Throughout the Republic there were precise demands that had to be fulfilled. The battle celebrated had to be won under the auspices of the general, not his lieutenants; thus an underling who won would not be entitled to a triumph, but his superior would, even though the junior commander had clearly made the victory. Thousands of the enemy had to be killed in the battle, with only minor losses to the Romans, and the battle had to be a legitimate one, not the result of a civil struggle. Peace had to follow the battle, and only high magistrates were allowed to be so honored.

During the Late Republic these rules were broken. For example, POMPEY THE GREAT triumphed in 81 B.C.E. despite having held no major office and being only 24. Julius CAESAR's triumphs after the civil wars in the provinces (but not Pharsalus) were greeted with a sense of distaste. Caesar was typical, however, of the deteriorated Republic, for he celebrated his triumphs as a personal possession. From the founding of the empire by AUGUSTUS, only the emperors themselves received a triumph. The reason for this, officially, was that the legates (*legati Augusti pro praetore*) were viewed simply as the underlings of the emperor. They were not given triumphs, as the auspices were with their masters. Instead, the *legati* were recipients of the *ornamenta triumphalia*. The last known general to triumph, who was not a member of the imperial family, was Cornelius BALBUS (2) in 21 B.C.E.

According to custom, the general who laid claim to a triumph did not enter the city upon returning to Rome but gave his report to the SENATE in the Temple of Bellona. If it was satisfactory, a date was set for his jubilant entrance. The procession, strewn with flowers, began at the CAMPUS MARTIUS, went through the Porta Triumphalis into the Circus Flaminius and then to the CIRCUS MAXIMUS and up the Via Sacra to the Capitol, where two white bulls were sacrificed. The general was dressed in the robes of Jupiter Capitolinus, a purple tunic (the *toga picta*), with golden shoes and an ivory scepter with an eagle on the top. His hair was adorned with a laurel branch. Riding in an ornate chariot with him was a public slave, holding a golden crown of Jupiter and uttering in his ear: "Remember thou art only a mortal."

See IMPERATOR; IMPERIUM; LEGATUS; ORNAMENTA; OVATIO.

Triumvirate, First

Triumvirate, First   Political union formed in 60 B.C.E. by Julius CAESAR, POMPEY THE GREAT, and Marcus Licinius CRASSUS (1); its rise and subsequent success in the formation of government policy were mortal blows to the Roman Republic. By 60 B.C.E., all three were leading figures in the Roman Republic but had suffered defeats or humiliations at the hands of the SENATE and its suspicious spokesmen, such as CATO UTICENSIS and CICERO. Caesar had returned to Rome from his service in Spain in the hopes of celebrating a TRIUMPH and then serving his consulship. First, he encountered senatorial opposition to his plans and had to sacrifice his triumph in order to ensure his election as CONSUL, discovering then that his colleague was the strange M. Calpurnius BIBULUS. As a further act of cruelty, the Senate gave him the forests of Italy to manage, instead of the usual prominent provincial command.

Having been treated so poorly, Caesar determined to check the intrigues of the Senate by finding powerful allies who had likewise suffered. He quickly found Pompey. That famed and respected general had returned from the East and had been rebuffed in two of his projects, the ratification of his arrangements in the East and the granting pensions of land to his veterans. Crassus had failed to have his tax rebate for the farmers passed and thus was willing to listen to any reasonable offer.

Caesar first enlisted Pompey with a promise of mutual support. In return for Pompey's prestige, he guaranteed his own backing, including troops if needed. To seal the alliance, he wed his daughter JULIA (2) to Pompey in 59. Crassus had long disliked Pompey but decided to join in order to have a hand in guiding the state and to watch for his own interests. Thus was born the First Triumvirate, although its powers were only de facto and never received the full legal status enjoyed by the SECOND TRIUMVIRATE. Nevertheless, the triumvirs quickly became the foremost influence in the Republic. How effective the triumvirate could be was seen in 59, when Caesar entered into the consulship. The land bill introduced by Caesar was forced through the Senate, satisfying Pompey's veterans. Pompey's settlements in the East were ratified, and Crassus' farmers received their tax break. With his partners happy, Caesar asked for and got what he wanted most, a command of his own in the provinces. Through the *lex Vatinia de Caesaris Provincia* he became governor of Gallia Cisalpina and ILLYRICUM. A short time later, Gallia Transalpina was added (by Pompey's hand). He was now in a position to embark upon the famed GALLIC WARS, with the sanction of his colleagues. The senatorial opposition was, for a time, bullied into silence. Patience and skill would be needed if the triumvirate were to be broken by an outside source.

While at Rome the politician CLODIUS PULCHER became the workhorse of the triumvirate; both Cicero and Cato were removed from the scene by exile or by appointment to provincial positions (Cicero returned in 57). By 56 the old antagonism between Crassus and Pompey had arisen, as Caesar the mediator was absent in Gaul. Outbursts between them were aggravated by Cicero, who sought to break the triumvirate. He hoped to turn the members against one another, using Lucius DOMITIUS AHENOBARBUS (1), a candidate for the consulship in 55 who had promised to strip Caesar of his provinces. Caesar took immediate steps to solve the crisis by convening the Conference of LUCA in April of 56. The triumvirs reaffirmed their pact, and Cicero was so overcome that he later served as spokesman for the triumvirate. Domitius Ahenobarbus was defeated in the consular elections, and Caesar's position in Gaul was made secure by the *lex Pompeia Licinia*, guaranteeing him continued command until the year 50.

Crassus and Pompey both desired their own provincial possessions, clearly to counterbalance what they saw as Caesar's real success in Gaul. By the terms of the *lex Trebonia*, Pompey took Spain, with a vast army, and Crassus sought his fortune in the East. Two events, tragic and unforeseen, had the most profound effect upon the future of the triumvirate. First, Julia died in 54, ending the era of peaceful relations between Caesar and Pompey. Then, Crassus was crushed and killed at the battle of CARRHAE, by the Parthians. The death of Crassus left Rome with only two triumvirs. The following years were filled with Caesar's completion of his conquest of Gaul, while Pompey inched closer to the senatorial party. He avoided an open breach with Caesar for as long as possible, but the Senate's determination that Caesar should surrender his legions made war unavoidable. The triumvirate was over as Caesar rode over the RUBICON.

Triumvirate, Second

Triumvirate, Second   Political alliance formed in 43 B.C.E. among Octavian (AUGUSTUS), Marc ANTONY and Marcus Aemilius LEPIDUS (1). Following the battle of MUTINA in April of 43, Octavian understood that the cause of Republicanism was not the way for him to achieve power and thus arranged a meeting with the two leading figures of the Caesarean cause, Antony and Lepidus. They met at Bononia and, after several days of negotiations, agreed to start a new triumvirate.

This alliance differed from the original triumvirate of Crassus, Pompey, and Caesar in 60 B.C.E. in that by virtue of the *lex Titia* of November 27, 43, the official and legal status of *tresviri republicae constituende* was given to each, enabling them to make laws, issue decrees, appoint governors, make wars, and act with powers superior to that of any magistrate of Rome. Further, each member possessed a specific territory: Antony held Gallia Cisalpina and Transalpina; Lepidus had the remainder of the Gallic lands and Nearer and Further Spain, while Octavian received Africa, Sicily, and Sardinia. Lepidus was to govern Italy, while Antony and Octavian dealt with the immediate crisis of the LIBERATORS (Caesar's assassins) and the remnant of the Republican forces.

A war with BRUTUS and CASSIUS was accompanied by the terrible episode of the proscriptions. The triumvirs had their lists of enemies, and many died. One of the first was CICERO, Antony's hated enemy, cut down and his hands nailed to the Rostra. Others fled from Italy, many seeking safety with Sextus POMPEY, son of POMPEY THE GREAT. At the battle of PHILIPPI in 42, Antony and Octavian destroyed the Liberators and terminated the last hopes for the Republic in the Roman world. With the victory, Antony went to the forefront in the triumvirate, for an ill Octavian had not yet made his presence felt, and Lepidus was suspected of ulterior motives and secret negotiations with Sextus Pompey. According to the arrangements resulting from the victory, Antony commanded all of Gaul (including Gallia Cisalpina), Octavian had Spain, Africa and Sardinia, while Lepidus was to be granted Africa from Octavian, if he stayed loyal to the cause.

Italy became neutral territory as a result, but in truth it was in Rome that Octavian consolidated his power, as Antony abandoned the West and took up residence in the East. Strains developed quickly, not between Antony and Octavian but because Antony's wife FULVIA and his brother Lucius viewed Octavian as the enemy. The PERUSINE WAR in 41 was the result, and Octavian proved triumphant. Fulvia died in 40, making a reconciliation between the triumvirs possible. The Treaty of BRUNDISIUM was signed soon after. Lepidus retained Africa, but everything else was divided between Antony and Octavian. Antony chose the East, leaving Octavian the western regions, and the contract was sealed with Antony's marriage to Octavian's sister OCTAVIA (1). Sextus Pompey remained a threat, and a treaty signed at Misenum granted him Corsica, Sicily, and Sardinia. In return he ceased his piratic activities. Freed of this irritant, Antony launched operations against ARMENIA and PARTHIA, and Octavian returned to war with Sextus. By 37 both needed the other. Antony required troops, and Octavian needed ships. Through the intervention of Octavia the two met again, at TARENTUM, coming away barely satisfied with the extension of the *lex Titia.*

While Antony was being defeated by the Parthians and falling under Queen CLEOPATRA's spell, Octavian destroyed Sextus Pompey in 36 at NAULOCHUS. That victory brought about the destruction of Lepidus as well, for he tried to stage a coup and failed, spending his remaining years as the butt of Octavian's ill humor, becoming Pontifex Maximus until his death in 13/12 B.C.E. As had happened with the FIRST TRIUMVIRATE, two men now ruled Rome, a situation that could not last. With his title of *divus filius,* or son of the divine Caesar, Octavian had the upper hand. He won the ultimate victories and became Augustus.

Trogus, Pompeius (fl. late first century B.C.E.) *Historian of the early Augustan age (27 B.C.E.–14 C.E.)*
Trogus was a contemporary of LIVY; authored the *Historiae Philippicae,* or *Philippic Histories,* in 44 volumes. He came probably from GALLIA NARBONENSIS, and his father may have been used as an interpreter by Julius Caesar in 54 B.C.E. It has been argued that Trogus relied almost exclusively on Greek sources for his work, especially Timagenes, the evidence being his concentration on other states of the ancient world, such as MACEDONIA and PARTHIA. Ignored to a great degree was Rome, which could have been a result of using Greek sources. Other writers consulted by Trogus included Theopompus, Timaeus, Posidonius, and Polybius. Trogus's history survived only through its table of contents and the abridgement made by Justin (M. Junianus Justinius), who lived perhaps in the second or third century C.E.

Troyes City in northern GALLIA, on the Seine River about 90 miles southeast of Paris. Of little importance until the 10th century C.E., Troyes was converted to Christianity in the fourth century and figured in the legendary feats of St. Lupus. ATTILA the Hun was marching on Troyes in 453 but left the inhabitants unmolested when Lupus (or St. Loup), using the sheer power of his will, convinced the Scourge of God (as Attila was called) to move elsewhere.

Tubero, Lucius Aelius (fl. mid-first century B.C.E.) *Adherent of the New Academy*
Tubero was an intimate friend and brother-in-law to CICERO. He served as a lieutenant to Q. Cicero in Asia from around 61 to 58 B.C.E. and later joined the Pompeians in the war against Julius CAESAR. Pardoned by Caesar, he returned to Rome, where he pursued literary interests. His historical work may have been completed by his son Quintus Aelius TUBERO.

Tubero, Quintus Aelius (fl. late first century B.C.E.) *Minor literary figure*
Tubero was the son of Lucius Aelius TUBERO, and considered an excellent orator, historian, and writer on law. He was mentioned in the *Digest* but also authored a sizable history, dating from Rome's earliest days down to the CIVIL WAR between POMPEY THE GREAT and CAESAR. In that war he joined his father in aiding Pompey's cause but was granted a pardon by the victorious Caesar.

Tullianum, dungeons of   Dismal prison (*carcer*) at the base of the Capitoline Hill and just north of the FORUM ROMANUM. According to legend, the dungeons were built by Servius Tullius as an addition to the *carcer* of Rome and always had an unpleasant reputation; they achieved a special notoriety in the reign of TIBERIUS. Through the efficient work of SEJANUS, the Prefect of the PRAETORIAN GUARD, many died cruelly in the Tullianum until, in 31 C.E., Sejanus was himself taken there and executed.

Turbo, Quintus Marcius (fl. 117–138 C.E.) *Prefect of the Praetorian Guard*
Turbo was prefect throughout much of the reign of Emperor HADRIAN and one of the most trusted friends and political allies of the emperor. From Dalmatia originally, Turbo became Hadrian's friend early on and was no doubt accepted into the Equestrians (EQUITES) as a result of this relationship, which also probably aided his rise in the military. Upon the accession of Hadrian in 117, Turbo took command of the legions in the Eastern provinces, with orders to liquidate the Jewish rebels. This he accomplished ruthlessly, pacifying Egypt, Palestine, and Cyrenaica. Pleased, the emperor put him in charge of Mauretania where he crushed a Moorish uprising. There followed a rare honor. Turbo was named as legate for DACIA and PANNONIA, a highly unusual posting for a member of the Equestrian Order. He proved the perfect man for the job, reorganizing Dacia along Hadrian's personal lines of imperial policy. As a reward for his loyalty and success, Turbo was made prefect of the Praetorian Guard, succeeding the voluntarily retiring Attianus. According to the historian Dio, Turbo was an excellent prefect, humble and hardworking throughout his term of office. He spent virtually the entire day at the palace, laboring as well through the night. His response to Hadrian when told to remain in bed when sick: "The Prefect should die on his feet." As was the case with many friends of Hadrian, Turbo was persecuted as the ruler grew old. Hadrian probably put him to death or compelled him to take his own life.

Turin   City known originally as *Augusta Taurinorum;* a creation of the Augustan policy of colonization throughout the Roman world, it was located in the Po Valley of Gallia Cisalpina and in the shadow of the Alps. Turin was a city of little consequence until 69 C.E., when the inhabitants had to extinguish a blaze that burned down a large number of structures. The fire may have been caused by VITELLIUS's legions, who were on the point of murdering one another. Turin was rebuilt but figured only slightly in the events of succeeding centuries. As with other Roman colonies, its greatness lay in the future.

Turranius, Gaius (fl. first century C.E.) *Prefect of the Grain for Rome*
Turranius served from the time of AUGUSTUS until the reign of CLAUDIUS. This long-serving *praefectus annonae* was one of the first officials to take the oath of allegiance to Emperor TIBERIUS in 14 C.E.; he weathered the reigns of Tiberius and GAIUS CALIGULA and, incredibly, was still at his post in 48, aiding Claudius in the crisis caused by MESSALLINA.

Turrullius, Publius (fl. late first century B.C.E.) *Senator and one of the plotters against Julius Caesar*
He survived the proscriptions of the SECOND TRIUMVIRATE, probably through his friendship with Marc ANTONY. Subsequently, he lived with Antony as a client, escaping the vengeance of Octavian (AUGUSTUS). In 30 B.C.E., when Octavian was in a position of advantage after the battle of ACTIUM, Antony tried to appease him by sending to him Turrullius. Octavian then put him to death to avenge Caesar and to appease Asclepius, the god of medicine, whose groves on Kos had been desecrated by Turrullius when he chopped down the trees to build Antony's ships.

Tuscus, Caecina (fl. first century C.E.) *Prefect of Egypt during part of the reign of Nero*
Tuscus was removed from his post and banished for the sole reason that he had used the baths in ALEXANDRIA. The baths had been constructed for an intended visit of Nero in 67 C.E.

Twelve Tables   The oldest Roman legal code (dating from 451/450 B.C.E.) and the basis for all subsequent development in Rome's complex system of LAW. While the actual date of the Twelve Tables, among other questions, has not been verified, they were probably written as a LEX ordered by the Comitia Centuriata and published on bronze in the FORUM ROMANUM. Destroyed by Gallic invaders in 390 B.C.E., the Tables were subsequently known only in fragmented form. It can be deduced, however, that they centered on numerous aspects of law and were fundamental to Roman legalism, as evidenced by the continued adherence of subsequent law to the tenets supposedly laid down by the Tables. In time, Roman law surpassed the codes of the Twelve Tables, rendering them obsolete. Prior to the Twelve Tables, knowledge of the law had been the exclusive privilege of the PATRICIANS.

Tyre   Ancient metropolis built on the Mediterranean coast of Phoenicia (modern Lebanon) and considered one of the great ports of antiquity. Its period of grandeur ended in 322 B.C.E., when it was sacked by Alexander the Great. Henceforth it was overshadowed by ALEXANDRIA. As a city in the Roman province of SYRIA, Tyre was noted for its purple dye. From HEROD THE GREAT the city received financial aid, and CLAUDIUS gave it further assistance, after which it became known officially as Claudiopolis, although Tyre remained the common usage. STRABO wrote that it was not a pleasant place in which to live.

Tyrrhenian Sea Body of water roughly confined by the islands of Corsica, Sardinia, and Sicily and the western coast of Italy; known as the Tyrrhenum Mare. Colonists in Italy settled on the western side of the peninsula because the Tyrrhenian offered many advantages over the Adriatic on the east. First, it allowed for economic ties with southern Gaul (GALLIA), Spain (HISPANIA), and AFRICA. Second, its weather was normally superior, especially when compared to the dangerous Adriatic. The number of ports and landing sites was also greater, making navigation easier, and it offered accessible inland waterways, including the Arno and the TIBER. With the establishment of the Roman Empire, patrolling and defending the Tyrrhenian Sea became the responsibility of the imperial NAVY. At first the fleet for the Western Mediterranean was stationed at Forum Iulii, but later it was moved to MISENUM, on the western Italian coast near Naples.

U

Ubii Germanic tribe living on the east bank of the Rhine. The Ubii had had good relations with Julius CAESAR, but in 37 B.C.E., unable to withstand the incessant conflicts with the neighboring Germans, they asked Marcus AGRIPPA for permission to settle on Roman lands. Agrippa agreed, and the Ubii were transported over the Rhine to the area around what was later called Civitas Ubiorum. A colony founded there by Rome, Colonia Agrippinensis (COLOGNE), contributed to the Romanization of the tribesmen, who took to naming themselves the Agrippenses.

Uldin (d. c. 412 C.E.) *Chieftain of the Huns beyond the Danube during the reign of Arcadius (394–408) and into that of Theodosius II (c. 395–412)*
Uldin probably did not have total control of the Hunnic people. Uldin was first known to the imperial government in December 400, when he lopped off the head of a troublesome Roman minister, Gainas, and sent it to the emperor as a gift. Five years later, the Huns contributed troops, including their client Sciri, to the cause of the MAGISTER MILITUM, STILICHO, against the Visigoths' King ALARIC. An invasion of MOESIA around 408 was repulsed, with thousands of Uldin's Germanic allies falling into Roman hands. Uldin retreated. Upon his death around four years later, the Huns were divided into three great camps.

Ulfila (Ulphila; Ulphilas) (c. 311–383 C.E.) *Bishop of the Goths and one of the first Christian missionaries to preach to the barbarians*
Ulfila was descended from a Christian Cappadocian who had been captured by the Goths, and he was born sur-rounded by Goths and became adept at their language. Educated at CONSTANTINOPLE, around 341 he was consecrated a bishop by EUSEBIUS of Constantinople (formerly the bishop of NICOMEDIA.) He proselytized to the peoples beyond the Roman Empire, eventually returning to the Goths settled along the Danube. He translated the Bible into Gothic, and he led the tribes into ARIANISM, a heretical Christian doctrine pursued by his converts for centuries.

Ulpia Traiana Also called Vetera or Xanten; one of the colonies founded by TRAJAN within Germany. Ulpia Traiana was located on the Lower Rhine, approximately 66 miles north of Cologne. During the reign of AUGUSTUS (27 B.C.E.–14 C.E.) it was used as a legionary fortress, built first of wood and then of stone, in the mid-first century C.E. The entire station, its *canabae* or civilian settlements and much of the XV Primagenia Legion, was destroyed during the rebellion of CIVILIS in 69–70 C.E. Following the uprising, a new fortress was erected along with new *canabae,* and the city took on importance and increased in size, resulting in the foundation of a colony by Trajan c. 98–105. Ulpia Traiana had an amphitheater, baths, and various temples, which absorbed the original civilian settlement. For many years the site was the headquarters of the V and XXI legions.

Ulpian (Domitius Ulpianus) (d. 228 C.E.) *Prefect of the Praetorian Guard during the reign of Severus Alexander and a leading jurist*
Domitius Ulpianus was born in TYRE and received an education in LAW. He emerged as a brilliant legalist in

the time of the Severans, producing the bulk of his writings between the years 211 and 217, in the reign of CARACALLA. For some offense he was banished by ELAGABALUS but was recalled by Severus Alexander, who appointed him *magister libellorum*. He was later appointed prefect of the grain (*praefectus annonae*) and, in 222, the Praetorian prefect. He was assassinated by his own troops in 228. Ulpian's importance to Roman law rested in his mammoth output. He authored nearly 300 books which were the basis for a large part of the Code of Justinian. A compiler and commentator, Ulpian wrote *Ad Sabinum*, a 51-volume treatise on private law; *Ad dictum*, focusing on the edicts of the praetors, in 81 volumes; and the extant *Regularum liber singularum*, which survives in an abridged form composed in the fourth century.

ultor Latin for "avenger," applied to the god MARS by Octavian (AUGUSTUS) in 42 B.C.E., when he vowed to seek vengeance upon the LIBERATORS for the assassination of Julius CAESAR. Mars had a personal connection to the family of the Julians, who claimed the god as the legendary founder of their line. After fulfilling his vow, Octavian built the TEMPLE OF MARS ULTOR, or Mars the Avenger, placing it prominently in the FORUM AUGUSTUM. It was dedicated in 28 B.C.E.

Umbria Region of Italy to the south of Gallia Cisalpina and roughly between Etruria and Picenum. Called Ombrica by the Greeks, the region was the home of the powerful Umbri, who controlled most of central Italy. The Umbri were defeated and reduced by the Etruscans, the Gauls and finally by Rome, in 307 B.C.E. Throughout the Republic, Umbria was one of the northern borders of Italy with the Rubicon serving as the political demarcation point. Under AUGUSTUS it was made a district of Italia. The Via Flaminia ran through its rough, mountainous terrain.

Ummidius Quadratus (Gaius Ummidius Durmius Quadratus) (d. 60 C.E.) *Governor of Syria*
Ummidius served during the period of great tension between ROME and the Parthians (c. 54–60 C.E.). He held two consulships, the second probably during the reign of CLAUDIUS (41–54 C.E.) and was governor of Syria in 51, when a crisis in ARMENIA followed the murder of King MITHRIDATES (1). Radamistus, the usurper, had murdered Mithridates, and the ensuing involvement of Parthia's VOLOGASES I and TIRIDATES in Armenian affairs drew the Roman general CORBULO (2) to the scene. Ummidius and Corbulo disagreed over matters of policy in the East, but Ummidius retained his post until his death, when Corbulo succeeded him. Ummidius also was present in JUDAEA in 52, where he worked to repair the terrible records of previous procurators there.

urban cohorts (cohortes urbanes) The police force in the city of ROME, established by Emperor AUGUSTUS (ruled 27 B.C.E.–14 C.E.) as part of his extensive program of reorganization for the city. Within Rome, the cohorts were outmatched in strength and in political power by the PRAETORIAN GUARD, also stationed in the capital but infrequently used in the suppression of unrest. Throughout the imperial era the urban cohorts were, despite the presence of the Guards, responsible for maintaining order. The three *cohortes urbanae*, each 1,000 men strong, were under the command of tribunes answerable to the PREFECT OF THE CITY (the *praefectus urbi*). They were stationed in a barracks upon the Viminal Hill until the time of AURELIAN, who built them a new headquarters, the Castra Urbana, in the CAMPUS MARTIUS. Service for regular members of the three (later four) cohorts was normally for 20 years, although pay and service conditions were much better than in the legions. Tribunes often served in the urban cohorts before holding a similar post in the Praetorian Guard, while the prefect of the city emerged as a major figure politically, even in the late empire. Other urban cohorts were known outside of Rome, for example in LUGDUNUM (Lyons) and in CARTHAGE.

Urbicus, Lollius (d. after 139 C.E.) *Consul in 138 C.E. and a successful governor of Britannia from 139–142*
An African by birth, Urbicus attained imperial favor as an officer during the reign of Hadrian, especially during the Jewish rebellion, 132–135. Later, he served as governor of Germania Inferior and as consul. In 139, Antoninus Pius appointed him LEGATE in Britannia, where Urbicus faced an invasion of the province by the Brigantes from the north, who poured through the Wall of Hadrian. In a swift campaign, he defeated the barbarians, and to strengthen the borders of Roman Britain he constructed the Wall of Antoninus Pius (or Antonine Wall), which ran between the Firth of Forth to the Firth of Clyde in modern Scotland. After returning to Rome, he served as prefect of the city.

Urgulanilla, Plautia *See* CLAUDIUS.

Ursacinus *See* VALENS (BISHOP OF MURSA).

Ursicinus (fl. mid-fourth century C.E.) *Magister equitum from 349 to 359 and magister peditum from 359 to 360*
Ursicinus served during the reign of CONSTANTINE and was appointed master of the cavalry in 349 by CONSTANTIUS II, to help administer the East. He was summoned from the Persian frontier to Antioch by GALLUS CAESAR to assist in treason trials. After the fall of Gallus in 354, Ursicinus was recalled by Constantius II, who sent him to the West to crush the usurper SILVANUS; for a time he remained in Gaul as a *magister equitum* in the Western

provinces. He returned to the East in 357 to face the Persian invasion. Although promoted to master of the infantry in 359, he was unable to prevent the fall of Amida. The details of Ursicinus's life have survived mainly through the account of the historian AMMIANUS MARCELLINUS, who served on his staff.

Usipetes   Germanic tribe closely associated with the Tencteri and occupying the region of modern Metz (in eastern France) in the first century B.C.E. Along with the Tencteri, they felt increasing pressure from the SUEBI, and were eventually pushed to the Rhine. This migration came at the expense of the Gallic tribes, especially the Menapii and the TREVERI. The Usipetes battled with the Treveri in 55 B.C.E. until repulsed by Julius CAESAR. Again on the move, in 16 B.C.E. they resided for a time in the area north of the Lippe and east of the Rhine.

Utica   Large city on the African coast just west of CARTHAGE. Founded by Phoenician traders, Utica became a colony that predated nearby Carthage, with which Utica was a logical ally. When ROME emerged as the ultimate victor in the Punic Wars, Utica broke its alliance with Carthage and received from Rome extensive land grants in AFRICA. During the Roman CIVIL WAR the remnant of the Pompeians on the continent retreated to Utica following the battle of THAPSUS in 46 B.C.E.; and there CATO UTICENSIS killed himself. After Africa was taken by Julius CAESAR, Utica was made a provincial capital and a MUNICIPIUM, probably by Statilius TAURUS around 34 B.C.E. Although the provincial administration was moved by Emperor AUGUSTUS (ruled 27 B.C.E.–14 C.E.) to Carthage, Utica was still one of the leading centers of the province. A request was made during the reign of HADRIAN (117–138) for promotion to full status as a colony, but it was not until the time of Septimius SEVERUS (ruled 193–211), a native, that Utica enjoyed colonial privilege.

V

Vaballath (Lucius Julius Aurelius Septimius Vaballathus Athenodorus) (fl. mid-third century C.E.) *King of Palmyra*

The son of ODAENATH and Queen ZENOBIA, Vaballath was ruler of his land from 266 to 272. Vaballath assumed his father's title upon the latter's death in 266, and may also have taken the title of *corrector Orientis,* or leading official of the East for the Roman Empire. Realistically, Vaballath held little power, as his mother Zenobia was the driving force behind Palmyra's rise to leading state of the Eastern provinces. He finally did take the rank of Augustus in 272, but he was deposed when captured by Emperor AURELIAN a short time later.

Vadomar (mid-fourth century C.E.) *King of the Alamanni who shared power with his brother Gundomadus*

Together they launched attacks on Gaul but signed a peace treaty with Emperor CONSTANTIUS II in 356. When Gundomadus died shortly thereafter, elements of Vadomar's people took hostile actions in Gaul (c. 357); two years later Constantius put these incursions to use by encouraging Vadomar to make war upon Julian the Apostate, whom the emperor did not trust. Another peace was signed in 359, this time with Julian. In 361, Vadomar entered and pillaged a part of Raetia. Julian's solution was to kidnap the barbarian ruler. Ironically, Vadomar emerged as one of the first Germans to be hired by the emperors, for Emperor VALENS made him a general and sent him to recapture Nicaea from the usurper Procopius (356–366). He subsequently fought against the Persians but did not lose touch with his own people, his son Vithicab becoming king before being assassinated in 368.

valarshapat So-called "New City" in ARMENIA; founded in 163 C.E. by STATIUS PRISCUS as a replacement for the ancient Armenian capital of ARTAXATA. Priscus had earlier marched into Armenia and reclaimed the country from the Parthians, who had invaded a year before. To terminate the endless political bickering within Artaxata, he destroyed the city and founded Valarshapat some miles away.

Valens (d. 350 C.E.) *Bishop of Mursa and one of the most influential prelates of the Western Church*

With URSACINUS, bishop of Singidunum, he was an important leader of the Arian movement in the fourth century. Both prelates were pupils of ARIUS, joining together to fight the champion of Christian orthodoxy, ATHANASIUS. Through much of the reign of Emperor CONSTANTIUS II (337–361 C.E.), they acted as the emperor's spiritual advisers, opposing Athanasius at the councils of TYRE (335), Arles (353), Milan (355), and Sirmium (357). Nevertheless, Valens and his colleague swayed with the political winds and often changed their views to correspond to the fluctuating mind of Constantius or to make peace with Constans, his brother, ruler of the West until his death in 350. In Constantius, however, they found an ultimately reliable champion, working for him in the defense of ARIANISM.

Valens, Fabius (d. 69 C.E.) *Legate of the I Legion at Bonn, in Germania Inferior, in 69 C.E.*

Valens was a prime mover in the rise of VITELLIUS to the throne. An older general, he was described by the historian TACITUS (1) as both intelligent and enterprising. When Galba was raised to the throne in late 68, Fabius

Valens killed his own governor, Fonteius Capito, on suspicion of his plotting against the new emperor, and then kept an eye on L. VERGINIUS RUFUS, the governor in Germania Superior. For this loyalty, he was given no reward, and, feeling betrayed, he convinced his equally disillusioned colleague CAECINA ALIENUS, commander of the IV Legion in Germania Superior, to join him in the cause of Vitellius. Power and wealth could be gained if they were successful.

On January 2, 69, Valens marched to Cologne, where he draped Vitellius with the purple robes of emperor. Soon, both provinces of Germany followed enthusiastically as the march on Rome began. In the massive column that set out, Valens took the head of one, slashing his way violently through Gaul, extorting large sums of money from the towns and cities in return for not stationing his troops there. In April, he linked with Caecina and together they won the battle of BEDRIACUM, against OTHO. They informed Vitellius of their triumph and entered Rome.

CONSUL for 69, Valens continued to increase his wealth by plundering the property of returning exiles, turning what was left of popular opinion against his gluttonous patron. A short time later, word arrived that VESPASIAN had declared himself a claimant for the throne. Valens fell ill, and Caecina, already plotting the betrayal of Vitellius, was put in charge of Italy's defenses. When Caecina's attempted defection was reported. Valens left Rome with a camp of followers and eunuchs. Strangely inactive, he chose not to proceed to the front but journeyed to Gaul instead, to rally supporters of Vitellius. His hopes ended swiftly with his capture by a Flavian detachment. At Urbinum he was executed, his head used as a symbol of the demise of the Vitellians.

Valens, Flavius Julius (c. 328–378 C.E.) *Emperor of the East from 364 to 378*

Valens earned notoriety by suffering one of the worst defeats in Roman history at the battle of ADRIANOPLE, on August 9, 378, at the hands of the GOTHS. Valens was the second son of Gratianus the Elder, founder of the Valentinian house and brother of Emperor VALENTINIAN I. He was born around 328 and held various posts under Julian and Jovian but found greater advancement under Valentinian, who first made him a TRIBUNE and then promoted him to full status as co-emperor or Augustus.

Valens was given command of the East but lacked the drive and skill of his brother. These deficiencies, combined with the unpopularity of Petronius, father of his wife, Albia Domnica, caused internal dissension and a rebellion. In 365 the usurper PROCOPIUS was proclaimed at CONSTANTINOPLE but was defeated by Valens at NACOLEA the following year. After repulsing the Goths who had arrived to aid the usurper, Valens spent several years fighting conspiracies in Constantinople, the Persians in Mesopotamia and, once more, the Goths. This last enemy,

composed of the OSTROGOTHS and VISIGOTHS, had been pushed into the Danubian frontier by the advancing HUNS. Valens allowed the barbarians to settle, but Roman cruelty and manipulation caused war to erupt. The campaign of Adrianople began, a series of events culminating in the disaster of a battle. Valens was killed, and a state of panic descended upon Constantinople.

Valens was a failure as an emperor, never equaling his brother. He differed with Valentinian in his religious policy as well, having been baptized an Arian. He persecuted orthodox Christians, putting some of them to death or exiling them. AMMIANUS MARCELLINUS described him as cruel, greedy, unjust, and ever eager to listen to informers.

Valentinian I (321–375 C.E.) *Emperor in the West from 364 to 375*

Valentinian was the son of the Pannonian Gratianus the Elder, who emerged from peasantry to become a noted general. Valentinian traveled with his father to AFRICA, rising through the ranks while receiving a surprisingly extensive education. Although he could read and was a painter, his main talents were in war, serving under the emperors CONSTANTIUS II and JULIAN. Dismissed by the latter in 362, and banished to Egypt because of his CHRISTIANITY, he was recalled by Jovian in 363 and used to hold the allegiance of the troops in the Gallic provinces. He was also appointed commander of the SCUTARII.

He was stationed at Ancyra in Asia Minor when, on February 25, 364, Jovian died. The army generals, deliberating to find a successor, decided on Valentinian. Shortly after his elevation, he named as his colleague his brother VALENS, giving him total control of the East while he retained the rule of the West. This separation of the Roman Empire set a precedent for the subsequent splitting of the imperial realm and the inevitable estrangement between the two spheres. His decision was proven astute in the short term, however, for frontier troubles and barbarian crises dominated his entire reign. In 365, the Alamanni poured over the Rhine but were destroyed in battle by the MAGISTER MILITUM JOVINUS. Valentinian then launched brutal counterattacks across the river, and a campaign was carried across the Channel in 367 to help relieve Britain from the threat of the Picts and the Saxons—followed by more years of bloodshed and labor to improve the borders.

To aid in protecting the Western provinces, Valentinian rebuilt the fortifications along the entire Rhine, while placing greater emphasis on the armed forces. Soldiers were given the first places in imperial government, and taxes, when necessary, were often harshly exacted to pay for his wars and martial efforts. Petronius Probus was unfortunately given a free hand, reigning as Valentinian's agent in the West, with terror as his weapon. His excesses overshadowed the genuine concern the emperor had for his long-suffering subjects. Attempts were made to curtail governmental abuse and religious toleration was promoted to ease the social strains between Christianity and PAGANISM. Such decisions as increasing the powers of provincial heads and promoting coarse generals to the senatorial order, enraged the old members of the SENATE, who chafed at further reductions of their influence.

Hopes that the frontier would be stabilized were dashed in 374, when the SARMATIANS and Germans breached the walls of the forts on the DANUBE. Valentinian marched to the scene, repulsed the invasion and made a vengeful raid over the river. The following year he received a delegation of the Quadi, becoming so angry at their disrespectful attitude that he suffered a fit of apoplexy and died on November 17. The historian AMMIANUS MARCELLINUS thought little of him, reflecting the distaste of others. However, he left behind him a rejuvenated army, a sound bureaucracy and a competent son, GRATIAN.

Valentinian II (371–392 C.E.) *Emperor of the West from 375 to 392*

One of the characteristically weak rulers who came to occupy that throne, Flavius Valentinianus was the son of Emperor VALENTINIAN I and his second wife, Justina, and the half brother of GRATIAN. Born at TRIER, he was proclaimed coemperor with Gratian four years later upon the death of their father. The main instigator of his elevation was the MAGISTER MILITUM MEROBAUDES (1), ostensibly to prevent any political chaos, as Valentinian I died suddenly. Although Gratian accepted the demands of the Danubian troops that his brother be made co-emperor, from the start it was clear that Valentinian would possess little political power. In 378, when Valens was killed at the battle of ADRIANOPLE, Gratian nominated THEODOSIUS I to fill the vacant throne of the East, not Valentinian. This was a good choice, for Gratian was himself destroyed by the usurper Magnus MAXIMUS in 383.

By a treaty among Magnus, Theodosius and Valentinian, the young emperor was allowed to reside in Italy, with influence at court passing to his mother Justina. This arrangement was in force until 387, when Magnus invaded Italy, forcing Valentinian and his mother to flee to Theodosius. After the fall of Magnus, Theodosius sent Valentinian II back to his throne; but Theodosius, who chose to remain in the West until 391, and then the *magister militum* ARBOGAST, held true authority. Out of some strange belief that he could assume control of his own destiny, Valentinian tried to replace Arbogast but was found dead on May 15, 392, quite possibly from suicide. Valentinian had also been dominated by AMBROSE, the formidable bishop of Milan, who pressured the emperor into denying the petition of the SENATE to restore the Altar of Victory, a bitter blow to PAGANISM.

Valentinian III (c. 419–455 C.E.) *Emperor of the West (425–455)*

The last relatively stable ruler of the Western Empire and the final member of the House of Valentinian to occupy the imperial throne, he was the son of Galla PLACIDIA and Emperor CONSTANTIUS III. Galla was the half-sister of the childless Emperor HONORIUS, who named Valentinian to be his heir in 421. A bitter quarrel between Galla and Honorius in 423 forced Valentinian and his mother to flee to THEODOSIUS II in CONSTANTINOPLE, despite the lack of recognition that Theodosius had given to Valentinian's claims. In 423, Honorius died and Theodosius was forced to accept Valentinian as the only candidate for the Western throne in the face of JOHN THE USURPER. In 424, Valentinian was crowned, while the Eastern generals, Ardaburius and Aspar, captured Ravenna in 425 and executed John.

Valentinian arrived in Italy in 425, taking up his duties while the real power rested in the hands of his mother, who acted as regent. Her authority was at first challenged and then, in 433, broken by the ambitious MAGISTER MILITUM AETIUS, who defeated Galla's champion, the magister Boniface. With Aetius in control of the imperial administration, Valentinian had little impact upon policy but probably supported the failed attempt to subdue the VANDALS in AFRICA under their King GEISERIC. Twice an army was sent against the Vandals, but both were defeated, in part by Geiseric's outstanding leadership and in part by Aetius's jealousy of any rivals. By 442, the West admitted defeat just in time to learn of a new threat from the East, the HUNS. Angered by a planned marriage to a Roman whom she disliked, Honoria, Valentinian's sister, invited Attila the Hun to Italy to defend her honor in 450.

Attila's demands for her hand were rejected, precipitating the Huns' invasion of the empire's Gallic lands. Aetius won the great battle of CATALAUNIAN PLAIN in 452 but refused to annihilate the Huns, allowing them to again menace Italy. Rome was saved by Pope Leo, and Attila died a short time later. Such seemingly divine intervention could not prevent court conspiracies against Aetius. The conspiracy led by PETRONIUS MAXIMUS and HERACLEUS THE EUNUCH convinced Valentinian to remove his *magister militum*. This he did, personally murdering Aetius in September 454. Unfortunately, another struggle erupted in the palace between Petronius and Heracleus, with Valentinian favoring the latter. Angered, Petronius engineered another assassination on March 15, 455, just after Valentinian's third decade of rule. He was killed by two one-time lieutenants of Aetius. The West was doomed.

Valentinus (fl. second century C.E.) *Gnostic theologian and founder of the heretical sect of Valentinians*

According to Epiphanius, St. Irenaeus, and other sources, Valentinus was a native of Egypt, born probably on the coast. After studying in Alexandria, he journeyed to Rome, where he resided from about 136 to 165, arriving during the pontificate of Pope Hyginus (r. 136–140) and departing during that of Anicetus (r. 155–166). He was initially associated with the orthodox Christians of Rome and, as written by TERTULLIAN (*Adversus Valentinianos*), he had aspirations of being elected bishop of Rome, "quia et ingenio poterat et eloquio" ("because of his intellectual ability and eloquence"). Disappointed in this ambition, he shifted away from orthodoxy and established himself as a heretical theologian. Most likely excommunicated, he traveled to Cyprus, where he died. Few of his writings are extant, but he is the reputed author of *Evangelium Veritatis* (Gospel of Truth), a curious fusion of New Testament writings with Gnostic doctrines, a Coptic version of which was discovered in 1946 at Nag Hammadi. His original theology was highly influential in shaping subsequent Gnostic thought, especially as it was elaborated by his disciples, the Valentinians, including Bardesanes, Heracleon, and Theodatus.

Valentinus held that all things begin as emanations from the Bythos, or Primal Being. The first beings, called the aeons, numbered 30, made up of 15 pairs, the syzygies. As the result of the sin of Sophia, one of the youngest aeons, the visible (i.e., the lower) world came into being. Her child was Demiurge, at times considered the God of the Old Testament. Humankind was the highest being of the lower world, and redemption brought a freedom of the spiritual (higher) nature from servitude to the material world. The mission of Christ and the Holy Spirit was to bring that redemption. Christologically, Valentinus believed that the aeon Christ united himself with the man Jesus so that mankind might learn of its great destiny, that knowledge called gnosis. Such gnosis, however, was attainable only by the pneumatics, or men of the spirit, identified with the Valentinians. Christians and some pagans were classified as psychics and were able by good deeds to reach a middle kingdom ruled by Demiurge. All the others, deemed *hylics* (engrossed in matter) were doomed to eternal damnation. A complex theological system relying upon Christian, Pythagorean, and Platonic concepts, Valentinianism became divided into western and eastern (Oriental) branches. Its influence has been noted by scholars not only in broad Gnosticism but also in many heretical Christian movements such as Pelagianism.

Valeria, Galeria (d. 315 C.E.) *Empress from 293 to 311*

The daughter of Emperor DIOCLETIAN, she married when the system of the TETRARCHY (co-emperors) was established by her father, Galerius, the man appointed to be Caesar to Diocletian. This union cemented the ties between the emperor and his deputy. She eventually possessed the titles of AUGUSTA and Mater Castrorum, or Mother of the Camp. Galerius died in 311, and Valeria was entrusted to the care of Licinius Licinianus; not trusting him, she fled to MAXIMINUS DAIA, who wanted to marry her. When she refused, he sent her in exile to SYRIA. Upon the death of Maximinus in 313, her death sentence was passed by Licinius. For a time she eluded him, but finally she was caught and beheaded, perhaps in 315. According to the Christian writer Lactantius, Valeria was a Christian, a fact unverified in any other account.

Valerian (Publius Licinius Valerianus) (d. 260 C.E.) *Emperor from 253 to 260*

A persecutor of Christians, Valerian was captured and eventually killed by the Persians. Valerian was born late in the second century C.E., and his early career is unclear, although he was probably a CONSUL in the reign of SEVERUS ALEXANDER (222–235 C.E.). He played a part in the usurpation of Gordian I in AFRICA and was given a post in the administration of DECIUS (249–251), perhaps because of their mutual dislike of CHRISTIANITY. By 253 he was in command of the legions on the Rhine frontier, receiving a plea to march to the aid of Emperor Trebonianus Gallus against AEMILIAN. Gallus was killed before Valerian could arrive. He was proclaimed emperor by his troops in Raetia. Aemilian's army, not desiring a civil war, murdered their master and swore allegiance to Valerian. The new emperor then proceeded to Rome, where the SENATE accepted him and his son Gallienus as co-emperors.

One of Valerian's earliest policies was a purge of the Christians in the empire. His main problems, however, were to be found outside of the imperial borders. Barbarians poured over the DANUBE and across the Black Sea, bringing terror and devastation to the Balkans and parts of Asia Minor. Valerian had already chosen to attack these crises by appointing Gallienus to control the West, while he marched to the East to make war upon the GOTHS. A plague weakened his legions, however, and word suddenly arrived from SYRIA that the Persians under SHAPUR I had invaded ARMENIA, CAPPADOCIA, and the Syrian territories, capturing Hatra, Doura, and even Antioch. The danger posed by Shapur outweighed that of the Goths, and Valerian set out for Mesopotamia with a depleted and exhausted army in 259. In late spring of 260, he fought the battle of EDESSA but soon fell into the hands of the Persians. He was humiliated by Shapur, killed and reportedly stuffed to be put on display in a Persian temple as a trophy. The defeat and murder of a Roman emperor could not have come at a worse time for the empire.

Valerianus, Publius Licinius Cornelius (d. 258 C.E.) *Little known and short-lived older son of Emperor Gallienus*

Valerianus was, despite his young age, elevated around 256 to the rank of Caesar, owing to the crises besetting the empire. He was not a major participant in his father's campaigns. SALONINUS, his younger brother, replaced him.

Valerius Asiaticus, Decimus (d. 47 C.E.) *Courtier in the reigns of Gaius Caligula (37–41 C.E.) and Claudius (41–54 C.E.)*

CONSUL during the reign of Gaius and again in 46 C.E., Valerius was from Gallia Narbonensis. Valerius was a client of Lady ANTONIA (1), and probably met eventual emperor Gaius under her roof. He was a close adviser to Gaius, suffering severe insults at his hands but always managing to keep his head. In 41, he was jubilant at the assassination of Caligula, saying to a crowd afterward that he wished he had been the doer of the deed. Known to be wealthy and a superb athlete, Valerius purchased the old gardens of Lucullus and beautified them to such an extent that they were famed throughout Rome. Despite his friendship with Claudius, including journeying with him on the British campaign of 43, Valerius fell prey to the cruel greed of Empress MESSALLINA, who probably desired his gardens. Condemned, he killed himself, ordering that his body be burned on a pyre in the gardens.

See also GARDENS OF ASIATICUS.

Valerius Maximus (fl. early first century C.E.) *Writer*
Valerius's main work, *Factorum et dictorum memorabilium libri (The Book of Memorable Deeds and Words),* was dedicated to TIBERIUS and published after 31 C.E. Valerius was of unknown origin but probably of modest means. Through Sextus Pompeius (CONSUL in 14 C.E.) and by base flattery of Tiberius, he was able to survive the harsh reign. His *Factorum* was a compilation of historical events shallowly researched and written in an ostentatious style; nine books survived (there may have been more) although other works of Valerius may have been mistaken as part of this work by later compilers. In the work, Valerius lauded Tiberius and included an attack on the fallen prefect SEJANUS, thus dating the work to after 31.

Vandals One of the most powerful and successful of the Germanic tribes; not only ravaged the Western Empire but also established their own kingdom in AFRICA. Further, the Vandals produced GEISERIC, arguably the greatest barbarian king who ever battled ROME.

The Vandals (also called Vandilii) originally occupied a position along the Baltic coast of northern Germany but chose to migrate south, settling in the area of modern Hungary in the mid-second century C.E. This region, just to the north of the MARCOMANNI, became known as Vandalici Montes, and from there the Vandals launched punitive expeditions along much of the DANUBE, reaching as far east as DACIA and PANNONIA and as far south as RAETIA and Italy. The Rhine frontiers, normally impregnable to the barbarians, were ready to be breached at the start of the fifth century, and in 406 the Vandals joined with other Germanic peoples in crossing the river, passing through Germania and entering Gaul. After three years of fighting, they surrendered to pressures from others and moved into Spain, where they became somewhat divided, sharing the region with the SUEBI and the ALANS. In recognition of their supremacy, the imperial government invited the Vandals to live as a federation in Spain, a status accepted by the mobile clans.

This imperial policy ended in 416, after a treaty with the advancing VISIGOTHS. King WALLIA of the Visigoths then embarked upon a relentless war in Spain, smashing the Vandals, with the Suebi and Alans, in 416–418. At the conclusion of Wallia's campaigns, the Visigoths received parts of Gaul and the remnants of the states in Spain united under Gunderic, king of the Vandals and Alans.

Recognizing that they could not long survive in Europe, the Vandals and Alans constructed ships and went in search of a new home. (ALARIC, king of the Visigoths, had hoped to do the same thing but died before his plans could come to fruition.) Within a year the Vandal ships had taken the Balearic Islands and discovered Roman Africa on the horizon. In 428, Geiseric came to power, exerting a most profound effect upon his people and upon the entire empire. For nearly 50 years, until his death in 477, this half-brother of Gunderic made the Vandals a proud, organized power in the Mediterranean. In 429, he received an invitation from the MAGISTER MILITUM, BONIFACE, to enter Africa; he swept into the region, bringing the Alans and Suebi in his train. His initial goal was Mauretania, and his troops destroyed everything in their path, despite the efforts of the Romans to halt him. Africa fell and the Vandal kingdom there was established, By 439, Geiseric was in possession of CARTHAGE, where he made his capital. Old families in the region were liquidated or stripped of their privileges, and the Christians suffered terrible privations.

The Vandal kingdom of Africa prospered, and in 455 Geiseric even invaded Italy, sacking Rome while his fleets made war on much of the Mediterranean. Corsica, the Italian coast, Sardinia, and Sicily all felt the terror of his forces. Geiseric outlived the Western Empire by one year, while his kingdom was sustained until 535, when the famed Byzantine general, Belisarius, destroyed the Vandals and annexed their lands to the Byzantine Empire. The best source on the later Vandals is *De Bello Vandalico,* or *The Vandal War,* by PROCOPIUS.

Varahran I (d. 276 C.E.) *King of Persia, ruling from 273 to 276*
Also called Vahram I, he was the son of SHAPUR I and the brother of Hormazd I Ardashir (the successor to Shapur in 272), Varahran succeeded when the heir died. Little is known of his early years, except that he served as governor of Khorassan, one of the important steps for obtaining the Persian throne. He ruled briefly, noted only for reversing the policy of Shapur toward Mani and MANICHAEISM; Mani was put to death after having enjoyed imperial favor. Varahran II followed his father to the throne in 276.

Varahran II

Varahran II (d. 293 C.E.) *King of Persia, ruling from 276 to 293*

Also known as Vahram II, he was governor of Khorassan before succeeding to the throne. As a monarch, Varahran was involved in frequent struggles with both the Roman Empire and his own brother Hormazd (or Hormizd). When war broke out with the Roman Empire in 283, Emperor Carus proved victorious over Varahran, capturing Ctesiphon and Seleucia and subjugating Mesopotamia. The subsequent peace terms forced the Persian to surrender formally ARMENIA and Mesopotamia, and he may have lost more had Carus not dropped dead in the summer of 283. All thoughts of recovering the lost territory were put aside as Hormazd, then governor of Khorassan, began a revolt. Bitter fighting was necessary before order could be restored. To ensure stability, the king placed his own son, Varahran III, as ruler of the Sacae, who had aided Hormazd.

Varahran III (d. c. 293 C.E.) *King of Persia for only one year*

Varahran succeeded his father, Varahran II, in 293. He had earlier served as king of the Sacae after the revolt of his uncle Hormazd (c. 283–284) had been crushed. His powers were merely gubernatorial, but that training made him ostensibly ready for the Persian throne. Unfortunately, he was unprepared for the uprising of his great-uncle NARSES, who ousted him from power, probably after only four months.

Varahran V (fl. early fifth century C.E.) *King of Persia*

The son of YAZDAGIRD I, he ruled from 420 to 439, in a reign notable for persecution of Christians and for a temporary breakdown in relations with the Roman Empire. As an ardent Zoroastrian, Varahran allowed the Christians in his domain to be purged ruthlessly, combining this activity with hostility toward Roman merchants. A war broke out in 421, and General Ardaburius gained a Roman victory over the Persians. Negotiations followed but were broken by a sudden attack on the Romans that failed miserably. Peace was made in 422 and would last for nearly a century. The Christian persecution was eased as Varahran spent the rest of his life battling with barbarian peoples who were threatening the eastern regions of his realm.

Vardanes (d. 45 or 47 C.E.) *Ruler of the Parthian Empire*

Vardanes's authority was contested from 38 to 45/47. Sometime before 40 (probably in 38), Artabanus II died, and his successor was Vardanes, one of his sons. Another son, Gotarzes II, rose up with allies at court and ousted his brother. Gotarzes's cruel reign was brought to an end in 42, and Vardanes returned, only to face a second rebellion as his brother gathered an army from less loyal provinces. Bloodshed was averted by a reconciliation that made Vardanes the sole ruler, with Gotarzes serving as his chief ally and client king. Internal troubles continued, as Gotarzes, again supported by some of the Parthian nobles, made one last attempt at the throne. Vardanes gained a victory but was assassinated, in 45 or 47, and Gotarzes was triumphant.

Varius Rufus, Lucius (fl. first century B.C.E.) *Poet*

Varius supported first Julius CAESAR and then Octavian (AUGUSTUS), composing epic poems in their honor, and was also a friend of both HORACE and VIRGIL. Rufus joined Plotius Tucca in editing the *Aeneid* after Virgil's death. Rufus's two greatest works were *On Death*, an Epicurean-influenced poem reflecting the teachings of Philodemos, and the tragedy *Thyestes*, performed around 29 B.C.E.

Varro, Marcus Terentius (116–27 B.C.E.) *soldier, editor, and librarian*

Varro was born at Reate in the Sabine country, or possibly in ROME, receiving an excellent education from such instructors as L. Aelius Stilo and the noted scholar ANTIOCHUS OF ASCALON. Reaching the rank of PRAETOR, he saw service in ILLYRICUM before becoming a partisan of POMPEY THE GREAT. As one of Pompey's officers he fought in the Spanish region against the pirates, earning the *corona rostrata,* or crown of victory. In 49 B.C.E., he rejoined Pompey, this time against CAESAR. His field was once more Spain, but he failed miserably.

Varro was pardoned by Caesar, who returned him to public favor and appointed him chief librarian in 47. With the assassination of Caesar in 44, Varro suffered politically, as Marc ANTONY placed his name on the list of proscriptions in 43. He fled from ROME but lost his house and had his library plundered. Octavian's (AUGUSTUS) triumph permitted him to return to Rome, and his last years were spent writing and studying. His vast output on a great number of topics earned him the title "most learned of Romans."

Varro's works encompassed a depth of knowledge—science, history, literature, grammar, law, music, medicine, agriculture—although little has survived. He probably authored over 600 books, but only 55 are known today, either through fragments or titles. Of these, but two, *Res Rusticae* and *De Lingua Latina* (On the Latin language), are partially extant. The *Res Rusticae* (Agriculture) survived intact in three books containing his studies of agriculture, livestock breeding, and the animals that populated farms. While clever and imaginative, the study is intensely organized. *De Lingua Latina* was composed of 25 books; books 5 and 6 are complete, and 7 to 10 are incomplete. Dedicated at first to the Quaestor Septimius, it was, from book 5, written in honor of CICERO and was published before 43 B.C.E. Other efforts by Varro that were lost include a social history, portraits of famous Romans and Greeks, a compilation of all areas essential to study, and the 41 volumes of *Antiquitates* (Antiquities), dedicated to Caesar; books 1 to 25 centered on humanity, while the last 16 were concerned with divine affairs. The *Antiquitates* was dated to 47 B.C.E.

Varus, Alfenus (fl. mid-first century C.E.) *Prefect of the Praetorian Guard in the reign of Vitellius (69 C.E.)*
Varus was serving in the Rhine legion as prefect of the camp (a senior post as centurion) in 69, when the troops helped place Vitellius on the throne. He distinguished himself in the campaign by restoring discipline to the often unruly cohorts and fought well at the first battle of BEDRIACUM against OTHO. Thus, when Publilius Sabinus, the Praetorian prefect, fell from favor, Vitellius appointed Varus as his replacement, eventually naming Julius Priscus as his colleague. Later in that year the legions favoring VESPASIAN marched on ROME, and Vitellius sent his prefects to the north of Italy to organize defenses. At Narnia they allowed their troops to surrender, fleeing themselves to Rome as the Flavians advanced. Varus participated in the fight for the capitol but could not prevent its fall. He was spared by Vespasian.

Varus, Arrius (fl. mid-first century C.E.) *Prefect of the Praetorian Guard for a brief time in 69–70 C.E.*
A long-time soldier, Varus was noticed under CORBULO (2) in ARMENIA but gained a post as a senior centurion through Emperor NERO, reportedly for maligning the character of his superior. In 69, he was serving with the legions at the DANUBE and joined in the cause of VESPASIAN, with Antonius Primus. In the subsequent campaign, Varus was a leading, if not impetuous figure, heading an ill-advised cavalry charge in the early stages of the second battle of BEDRIACUM. After the fall of ROME, Varus was considered an important officer who could not be ignored by Mucianus, Vespasian's official representative in the city. A praetorship was given to him, as well as the prefectship of the reconstituted Praetorian Guard. Once Mucianus was in firm control, however, Varus was edged out and given the post of prefect of the grain. He may have been put to death during the reign of DOMITIAN, in vengeance for his betrayal of Corbulo. Domitian had married Corbulo's daughter, Domitia Longina.

Varus, Publius Quinctilius (d. 9 C.E.) *Consul in 13 B.C.E. and one of the most famous generals in Roman history*
Varus suffered a crushing defeat at the hands of the German chief ARMINIUS in the TEUTOBURG FOREST. Varus came form a noble family, improving his station by marrying Augustus's great-niece. In 6 C.E., he was appointed governor of SYRIA and sent two legions into JUDAEA to quell local unrest after the territory was converted to a province. By 9 C.E., it was the belief of AUGUSTUS that the vast region of Germania beyond the Rhine was ripe for Romanization and provincialization, and he hoped to use Varus to develop the region without war. The people of the territory were not prepared to accept his program, and Arminius and the CHERUSCI, joined by other allies, trapped Varus in the Teutoburg Forest of northwest Germany, annihilating the XVII, XVIII and XIX legions. In the battle, which lasted three days, the Romans fought bravely, but Varus, sensing doom, killed himself. When Augustus heard of the disaster, he tore his clothes and screamed: "Varus, bring back my legions!" Varus was thus blamed for the collapse of imperial policy in Germany, and no further attempts were made to subdue the Germanic peoples beyond the Rhine.

See GERMANIA.

Vasio Town (now Vaison-la-Romaine) in GALLIA NARBONENSIS near Avignon, situated east of the Rhone River and to the north of Massilia. Vasio was originally a small site, but around 20 B.C.E., in conjunction with the imperial policy of development, a new community was started nearby. Subsequently, Vasio mirrored Gallia Narbonensis in the adoption of Roman architecture and lifestyle, soon boasting a theater and a basilica, as well as numerous Roman houses. Archaeologically it has been of great value in offering examples of housing in the first century C.E., especially the state of the Gallic villa.

Vatican Hill The Mons Vaticanus and its surrounding area, the Campus Vaticanus. The most western of the HILLS OF ROME is located across the TIBER and was at first relatively unimportant. Under the emperors, however, a number of structures were founded upon or near it. HADRIAN's mausoleum, now called Castel Sant' Angelo, was constructed just to its east, and GAIUS CALIGULA began a private stadium there, called the Circus Gai, that was finished by NERO. It became known as the Circus Gai et Neronis or as the Circus Neronis. He also created the Horti Neroni, the Gardens of Nero. According to tradition, CHRISTIANITY endured one of its blackest hours in 64 C.E., when Nero used the Circus Gai to massacre Christians. With a reputation for martyrdom, Vatican Hill was sealed forever as a place of great importance by the upside-down crucifixion of St. PETER in that same year.

A shrine was established by the Roman Christians sometime in the second century C.E. to mark the tomb of St. Peter, thus designating the center of what would later become the papal Vatican, headquarters of Catholic Christianity. In 326, CONSTANTINE the Great made his patronage of the faith obvious by erecting a large, five-aisled basilica there, over the shrine of St. Peter. Around this original structure the Vatican grew, although the pontiffs of Rome actually resided in the Lateran Palace. Constantine's basilica did not survive the Renaissance, for Pope Julius II found the structural damage beyond repair and built a new one. For an idea of the original architecture, Constantine's other creation, St. Paul's Outside the

Walls, is a prime example. Archaeological work continues today, as the area below the Vatican is being excavated, at the site deemed the tomb of St. Peter.

Vatinius (fl. mid-first century C.E.) *Deformed courtier during the reign of Nero (54–68 C.E.)*
He came from Beneventum and was called a cobbler by the satirist Juvenal, possibly because of family connections to that profession. He was allowed to remain a fixture of palace life because of his dreadful appearance, while underneath he harbored ambition and cunning. Vatinius ingratiated himself with Nero and was soon accusing various people of crimes, emerging as one of the more hated DELATORES of Nero's reign. His nose provided the name for a kind of jug with a strangely shaped spout.

Vatinius, Publius (fl. first century B.C.E.) *Consul in 47 B.C.E. and a servant of the First Triumvirate in the last days of the Republic*
Vatinius was utterly detested by CICERO, who considered him corrupt and villainous. After serving as QUAESTOR in 63 B.C.E., he was a TRIBUNE of the Plebs in 59, more or less selling himself to Julius CAESAR (then a consul) and to his colleagues in the First Triumvirate, POMPEY THE GREAT and CRASSUS (1). He spearheaded any legislation they desired, most importantly the acceptance in the SENATE of Pompey's arrangements for the East and Caesar's command in Gallia Cisalpina and ILLYRICUM. The latter legislation, called the *lex Vatinia de Caesaris Provincia*, made possible Caesar's GALLIC WARS and subsequent supremacy over the Roman state. Despite appearing in court in 65 against two of Cicero's friends (for which he was attacked by the famed orator), Vatinius was defended by Cicero in 54 against a charge of having bribed his way into the praetorship of 55.

Vatinius was also loyal to Caesar in military ventures, serving as a legate in the closing stages of the Gallic Wars and then during the CIVIL WAR against Pompey and the Senate. As a general, Vatinius showed a certain imagination and energy in defending Brundisium from the Pompeians. He also won a naval engagement near Brundisium, even though his fleet was only an improvised gathering of ships. For this triumph and his devotion, he was made consul in 47. Caesar then appointed him governor of Illyricum, with three legions. His task was to defeat the Illyrians, which he accomplished, fighting and conducting wearying campaigns. He was still legate in Illyricum after the assassination of Caesar in 44. He opposed the LIBERATORS, but, being unpopular with his own troops, could not prevent their desertion to BRUTUS in 42.

Vegetius Renatus, Flavius (fl. later fourth century C.E.) *Military writer*
In his treatise *Epitoma de rei militaris,* Vegetius bemoaned the decline of Rome's capacity for war. Vegetius was probably a Christian, holding some post in government. His book called for a return to classical training in war while presenting the traditional methods of drilling, legionary organization, and tactics. While he wrote distinctly as an amateur, he did use numerous sources, including Celsus, SALLUST, and Frontinus. Vegetius may also have authored a veterinary work, MULOMEDICINA, attributed to a contemporary named P. Vegetius.

See LEGIONS.

Veiento, Fabricius (Aulus Didius Gallus Fabricius Veiento) (fl. first century C.E.) *Thrice Consul under the Flavians (in the 80s C.E.)*
In 62, he had been expelled from Italy by NERO for slandering the gods and their priests, but he apparently returned with VESPASIAN's accession. According to the satirist Juvenal, he had a reputation in DOMITIAN's time as one of the DELATORES (informers).

Veii One of the great Etruscan cities, possibly the capital of the so-called Etruscan Confederation that was contemporaneous with the early development of Rome. The inhabitants, called the Veientes, were bitter enemies of the Romans, with whom they struggled for centuries. Finally, in 396 B.C.E., the city was captured by the Roman dictator Camillus. Virtually destroyed after a siege, it was left unrepaired until the reign of AUGUSTUS (27 B.C.E.–14 C.E.), when the site, close to ROME, was declared a colony. Veii was never able to prosper, however, and was in a state of irretrievable decline by the middle of the second century C.E.

See also COLONIES; ETRURIA; ITALIA.

Velius Longus (fl. c. 100 C.E.) *Grammarian from the time of Trajan (98–117 C.E.)*
Velius was noted mainly for his precise and well organized treatise, *De Orthographia.* He was considered one of the major grammatical writers in the late first and early second centuries C.E.

Velleius Paterculus, Gaius (fl. early first century C.E.) *Minor writer of history*
Born in Campania around 19 B.C.E., he entered the legions and fought in PANNONIA and GERMANIA under TIBERIUS (c. 4–5 C.E.), he began to idolize Tiberius and his principate. In 7 C.E., he became a QUAESTOR and in 15 a PRAETOR, serving with his brother. His death, after 30 C.E., was most likely connected to the end of Lucius Aelius SEJANUS, who fell from power in 31, a man whom Paterculus had constantly lauded. Paterculus composed his *Historiae Romanae* over a relatively short period of time. Dedicated to his friend, M. VINICIUS, the history examined the development of Rome from the first Greek settlers to his own time. Book 1 was a mere outline, covering from Romulus to the fall of CARTHAGE in 146 B.C.E.

Book 2 went into more detail as the narrative reached Velleius's era. He followed the Annalists in general style but inserted his own reflections and interests. Literature, therefore, was covered extensively, focusing on Latin and Greek. Here he displayed considerable knowledge. He lacked, however, objectivity and perspective. Tiberius was presented as the ultimate monarch, the grand culmination of Roman political evolution.

Suggested Readings: Velleius Paterculus. *The Caesarian and Augustan Narrative.* Edited by A. J. Woodman. New York: Cambridge University Press, 1983; Velleius Paterculus. *The Tiberian Narrative.* Edited by A. J. Woodman. New York: Cambridge University Press, 1977.

Veneti A powerful seagoing people who inhabited the coastal areas of what was, in the first century B.C.E., Armorica (northwestern Gaul, modern Morbihan in Brittany). The Veneti were described by Julius CAESAR in his *Gallic Wars* as the foremost sailors in the region, conducting extensive trade with Britain. Their knowledge of the sea, combined with access to the few suitable harbors along the coast, gave them a virtual monopoly in trade, especially with the British tribes. The Veneti opposed Roman occupation of Armorica in 56 B.C.E., posing serious strategic and tactical problems for the legions of Caesar. After trying unsuccessfully to pin them down, Caesar allowed his captain, Decimus Brutus, to engage the Veneti offshore. With Caesar himself looking on, Brutus destroyed the proud seamen, and the tribe was soon subjugated. Deprived of their traditional means of life, the Veneti took up agriculture, surviving well into the fifth century C.E., when their land was suddenly flooded with British migrants who had fled the isles and the chaos there.

Venetia District of northern Italy; originally a part of GALLIA CISALPINA but later the tenth region of the Augustan division of Italy. Venetia was delineated by the Athesis River on the west, the Alps to the north, the Timarus River to the east and the Adriatic to the south. The major cities were AQUILEIA and PADUA (Patavium); later, Venetia (Venice) was founded there as well (see below). The original inhabitants of Venetia were a people called the Veneti (not the Veneti of Gaul), who were not Italian or Celtic but probably of Illyrian stock. Always peaceful, they detested the Celts, Etruscans, and Gauls, eventually allying themselves with ROME for protection, an alliance never broken. They profited from their inclusion among the Roman possessions in northern Italy and received full citizenship in 49 B.C.E. Considerable prosperity was enjoyed until the MARCOMANNIC WARS (c. 166–180 C.E.), when the region was overrun; in the fifth century, Aquileia was destroyed by ATTILA the Hun.

The city of Venetia (Venice), was founded in the fifth century C.E., but did not take shape until the reign of Jus-tinian in the sixth century. Following the destruction of Aquileia in 452, many survivors of the siege took refuge in the nearby islands and lagoons. Such a retreat had existed at least since the time of Alaric, early in the fifth century, and perhaps even earlier. After a time these settlements became united, and Venice was established.

Ventidius, Publius (d. c. 38 B.C.E.) *Consul in 43 B.C.E. and a general during Parthian War*
Ventidius came from a common lineage and was subjected to cruel jokes about his origins; he had to live down the reputation of having been a muleteer, probably as a supplier to the LEGIONS. In time, he became a supporter of Julius CAESAR, who was not afraid of using talented but undistinguished soldiers. Through Caesar, he entered the SENATE.

After Caesar's assassination in 44 B.C.E., Ventidius held a praetorship and a consulship in 43, replacing Octavian (AUGUSTUS) later that year in the second office. He levied three legions in preparation for the coming war, aiding Antony after the battle of MUTINA in 43 and later participating in the PERUSINE WAR. Promoted to proconsul, Ventidius was dispatched to the East in 39 to deal with the Parthian invasion of SYRIA and PALESTINE. In 39, the general defeat of Quintus LABIENUS (an ally of CASSIUS) and his Parthian army, along with the destruction of the Parthian Prince PACORUS, brought him fame. Ventidius killed Pacorus in battle and evicted the enemy from Roman territory. MARC ANTONY soon replaced him (perhaps out of jealousy or on the suspicion of corruption), and Ventidius returned to ROME to a TRIUMPH. He died soon after and was given a lavish public funeral.

Venus Roman goddess of love; an old deity to the Italians and quite unimportant in ROME until the influence of the Greeks was felt. From that point, Venus took on the characteristics of Aphrodite, her Greek counterpart, and in that form she came to Rome, via the Punic War with CARTHAGE. Romans were entranced by a temple in honor of Venus on Mount Eryx in Sicily, when it fell to them in 217 B.C.E. She was called Venus Eurcina and was brought into Rome after the SIBYLLINE BOOKS granted approval to the establishment of her cult. She assumed a number of incarnations in Rome. As Venus Verticordia, she changed the human heart. As Venus Genetrix, her most popular form, she was part of a legend that Aeneas was the son of Venus and Mars. Thus Julius CAESAR and Octavian (AUGUSTUS), who both claimed descent from Aeneas's line (via the *gens* Julia), held Venus Genetrix in great esteem and allowed the goddess to be a part of the IMPERIAL CULT and the Roman state religion. Temples to the goddess were common throughout Rome. Julius Caesar made the Temple of Venus Genetrix the focus of his FORUM CAESARIS, while HADRIAN (c. 135) dedicated the Temple of Venus in Rome near the COLOSSEUM.

See also GODS AND GODDESSES OF ROME; RELIGION; VINALIA.

Veranus, Quintus (fl. first century C.E.) *Consul in 49 C.E.*

A successful imperial officer, he was used as an effective founder of provinces. He first gained imperial attention in CAPPADOCIA in 18 C.E., when he was sent as a legate to organize the land under the administration of ROME. His steps for provincialization included a reduction of the royal tribute (TRIBUTUM) taxes, to make Rome more popular. Two years later he was back in Rome, spearheading the prosecution of Gnaeus Calpurnius PISO for the death of GERMANICUS; he served as a major figure in the popular condemnation of Piso, for which he was enrolled in a priesthood. In 41, after the murder of Gaius CALIGULA, Veranus was part of the senatorial deputation sent to CLAUDIUS. The emperor appointed him first legate of LYCIA in 43, where he spent five years pacifying the country and introducing Roman rule. Probably because of his previous provincial work, he was chosen by NERO as governor of Britain in 58, the replacement for Didius Gallus. After a bitter campaign there, he died and was succeeded by C. Suetonius Paulinus.

Vercingetorix (d. 46 B.C.E.) *Most famous of the Gallic chieftains and an opponent of Julius Caesar in the Gallic Wars*

Vercingetorix was the son of Celtillus, a leader of the major Gallic tribe of the AVERNI who was put to death by his own people for being overly ambitious. Vercingetorix declared in 52 B.C.E. his intent to rebel against Rome. Soon all the Averni and their confederates joined him, and he was elected commanding general. When other Gauls responded, Caesar found himself facing a major crisis.

Vercingetorix was aware of the dangers of fighting Caesar in the field, as the defeat inflicted upon him at Noviodonum proved. He adopted a more conservative military policy, which included laying waste everything that the Romans might need and making guerrilla attacks. The bulk of the Gauls retired to the large fortress of AVARICUM, where Rome's legions would have to struggle with both the enemy fire and stout walls. Although Avaricum was lost, this strategy proved valuable to the Gauls at GERGOVIA. Hoping to inflict a crushing blow, Vercingetorix accepted battle, and this time Caesar routed the tribes, driving them to ALESIA. Caesar opted for a siege, engulfing the city in Roman lines. His people starving, Vercingetorix watched helplessly as his allies were beaten in every attempt to penetrate the Roman siege and bring relief. With no other choice the Gallic chief surrendered. Taken to Rome, he lived another five years only to march in Caesar's triumph in 46. Then he was murdered in the Dungeons of TULLIANUM.

A statue in honor of Vercingetorix, at Alise-Sainte-Reine, France *(Hulton/Getty Archive)*

Verginius Rufus, Lucius (d. 97 C.E.) *Consul in 63, 69, and 97 C.E. and governor of Germania Superior*

As the head of a German province, Rufus was confronted with the uprising of the Gallic rebel VINDEX and marched immediately to suppress him. This he accomplished at Vesontio, reportedly mourning the suicide of the rebel. Although his victory and prime location could have made him a rival for the throne, he chose instead to support Galba. Rufus received little consideration from the new emperor, finding OTHO a more gracious patron. Throughout the remainder of his career he was hailed for his patriotic act of not seizing the crown in 68. NERVA had him serve as consul in 97, and on his tombstone was a laudatory epitaph. He was eulogized by the historian TACITUS (1). Rufus also had literary aspirations. A friend to PLINY THE YOUNGER, he wrote erotic poetry.

Verina, Aelia (d. 484 C.E.) *Augusta from 457 to 474 and the wife of Emperor Leo I*

Verina married Leo sometime before his accession in 457. Throughout his reign she supported her brother BASILISCUS, helping to have him appointed to the important command of the Eastern forces against GEISERIC in 468, a debacle that weakened the Eastern Empire and virtually sealed the doom of the West. Verina had three children by Leo; daughters Ariadne and Leontia, and a son, Leo, who died in 463 after only five months. Ariadne was wed to Leo I's heir, ZENO, and Verina thus became his mother-in-law. After Leo's death in 474,

Verina led a conspiracy to depose Zeno in favor of her lover Patricius, but was then superseded by her brother, who took the throne. He fell from power in 476, and Zeno returned. Verina remained adamant in her opposition to him, and aided General Illus in his rebellion in 483–484. She died during a siege in 484 and was buried in CONSTANTINOPLE.

Verona A leading city in northern Italy, at the base of the Alps on the Via Postuma, north of Mantua and west of PADUA (Patavium). Founded in antiquity, Verona became the leading city of the local Cenomani but inevitably passed into Roman hands. With the surname "Augusta," Verona was made a colony in the first century C.E., serving as an economic center whose success can be seen in surviving structures that include an amphitheater dating to the first century C.E. CATALLUS was from Verona.

The city figured in the strategies of the Flavians during the civil war of 69 C.E. Its capture was a blow to the Vitellian cause and netted the legions of Antonius Primus great booty. In military terms, Verona gave access to the Brenner Pass over the Alps and thus was a key site in the defense of Italy from attack from the north.

A conflict was fought there, probably in 402 or 403 C.E., between the VISIGOTH army of King ALARIC and the MAGISTER MILITUM of the West, STILICHO. Details of the actual battle are wanting, but what is clear is that Stilicho, reinforced by his barbarian auxiliaries, fought Alaric at Verona, inflicting yet another reverse upon the Visigoths. Alaric was nearly captured and might have been annihilated, but Stilicho once more stayed his hand, as he had after his victory at POLLENTIA in 402. The sources are not clear as to why the general allowed Alaric to withdraw again, although the writer Claudian blamed the unreliability of Stilicho's Alan levies. As it was, the Visigoths limped out of Italy, and Alaric was resourceful enough to recover once more.

Vertumnus A Roman god, probably of the changing seasons; his name was based on the Latin *verto*, or change. The deity was especially honored by the countryfolk of Italy as the patron of fruits. As a result, he was always depicted as holding fruits in one hand, or in his lap, with a pruning knife in the other hand. Despite being only a very minor deity, he was considered the consort of POMONA and had a chapel on the Aventine Hill.

Verulamium Town in the province of Britain (BRITANNIA), some miles north of LONDON (Londinium). Verulamium (St. Albans) served as the chief city of the Catuvellauni prior to the Roman conquest of the isles, and was built late in the first century B.C.E. by the tribal leader Tasciovanus near the Ver River. Following the fall of Britain in 43 C.E., the site underwent swift development as a military post for the advancing legions and then as a civilian town. This early prosperity was aborted in 61, with the revolt of BOUDICCA. According to the historian TACITUS (1), it was sacked and destroyed. In the rebuilding of the site, the original plan was probably duplicated, although improvements in the quality of the architecture bear witness to the success of the community, even though it did not possess the rank of colony. Archaeological excavations have revealed much, including the use of stone for houses after the mid-second century C.E. The city eventually possessed a theater, temples, centers of business, houses, and two gates, called the London and Chester. After the third century C.E., there was a long period of decline, interrupted by works begun in the later years of the Roman occupation.

Verus, Lucius (Lucius Aelius Aurelius Commodus) (130–169 C.E.) *Coemperor with Marcus Aurelius from 161 to 169*
Born Lucius Ceionius Commodus, he was the son of Lucius AELIUS CAESAR, the adopted heir of HADRIAN. His father died in 137, and ANTONINUS PIUS was adopted as heir. As part of Hadrian's attempt to ensure stability in the succession, Antoninus Pius took into his house both Marcus Aurelius and Lucius. Verus served as QUAESTOR in 153 and CONSUL in 154, and, in 161, with Marcus. Antoninus died in 161, and Marcus was proclaimed emperor and quickly declared that he wanted a colleague. With the new name of Lucius Aurelius Verus, or Lucius Verus, he became the political equal of Marcus Aurelius—but was never able to overcome the widely held view that he enjoyed a life of rest and recreation. He certainly was not the equal of Marcus Aurelius in terms of intellect, a fact particularly visible in his conduct of military operations.

Crises had been building for many years on the frontiers, and in 162 they erupted. Verus assumed command of the legions in the East, in response to an attack by VOLOGASES III of Parthia upon ARMENIA, the placement of a Parthian client on the throne, and the defeat of the Roman General SEVERIANUS at Elegeia. After months of delay, he finally arrived in SYRIA with badly needed reinforcements. Allowing his generals a free hand, most importantly Statius Priscus and Gaius Avidius CASSIUS, Verus laid claim to the title of *Armeniacus* in 163, with credit for the severe defeats inflicted upon the Parthians in 165–166. Verus returned in triumph to ROME in 166, where he and Marcus celebrated their positions of Fathers of the Country (*Pater Patriae*). The joy was short-lived, for barbarian incursions began in conjunction with a terrible plague brought back from the East by the legions. In winter 168, both emperors were at AQUILEIA. In the spring, Verus was at Altinum, where he suffered some kind of seizure and died. The body was entombed in the Mausoleum of Hadrian in Rome, as rumors began that he had been poisoned. Such stories were probably untrue. However, despite his marriage to Marcus's daughter LUCILLA, in 164, the passing of Verus was not entirely unwelcome, for in the future his presence could have become troublesome to imperial unity.

Verus, M. Annius (d. after 126 C.E.) *Consul under Domitian and in 121 and 126; grandfather of Marcus Aurelius*

A highly successful political figure, Marcus Annius Verus enrolled in the Patrician class with the sponsorship of Vespasian and Titus and was later prefect of the city. His son of the same name had embarked upon a similar career but died while still a praetor. Thus, Verus's grandson Marcus passed into his care and received the education that led to his remarkable character and intellect.

Verus, P. Martius (second century C.E.) *Governor of Cappadocia in the reign of Marcus Aurelius (161–180 C.E.)*

Verus was respected by the historian Dio, who stated that he not only could destroy an opponent but could also outwit enemies and anticipate their moves, preferring negotiations where he could rely upon his innate charm. In 164, he was sent to ARMENIA as a replacement for Statius Priscus and helped pacify the region, setting up a reliable client on the throne and serving Emperor Lucius VERUS loyally as a legate in the East. In 175, he was still at his post when word arrived of the revolt of Avidius CASSIUS, the governor of SYRIA. Verus immediately informed Marcus Aurelius and was instrumental in crushing all resistance to the imperial government following Cassius's death. Throughout Syria he made his presence felt, running the province until the emperor arrived in person. Appointed the governor of Syria by Marcus, Verus avoided all possible pogroms by burning most of Cassius's correspondence, as had Lappius MAXIMUS during the revolt of SATURNINUS in the reign of DOMITIAN (81–96 C.E.).

Vespasian (Titus Flavius Vespasianus) (9–79 C.E.) *Emperor from 69 to 79*

The restorer of Rome's stability after the reign of NERO and the chaos of the civil war of 69 C.E. Vespasian was a member of the old family of the Flavii, or Flavians, from the Sabine country. He was born at Reate to a knight, Flavius Sabinus, and the daughter of a knight, Vespasia Polla. Vespasian, however, was slow to apply for the advantages of membership in the Equestrians (EQUITES) and also slow in taking advantage of his uncle's membership in the SENATE.

His formal career began in 40 with a praetorship, followed by a position with the legions in Britain during the campaign of 43. There he won the *ornamenta triumphalia*; as the historian SUETONIUS recorded, he fought 30 battles, conquered two tribes and captured an island. His rise in imperial favor was furthered by the intercession of the

Emperor Vespasian *(Hulton/Getty Archive)*

imperial freedman NARCISSUS. After a consulship in 51, Vespasian entered a period of unhappiness, as AGRIPPINA THE YOUNGER hated anyone who had ever been a friend of the now-fallen Narcissus. The new Emperor Nero proved highly unpredictable as well. A reputation for competence probably brought Vespasian to the post of proconsul of AFRICA in 63, but his expenses were so severe that he went into virtual bankruptcy. Refusing to succumb to the larceny typical of provincial administrators, Vespasian had to mortgage his home to his brother and take up the profession of selling mules, earning him the nickname "the Mule Driver."

Back in Rome in 66, he was a member of Nero's court, where he committed the outrage of falling asleep during one of the emperor's recitals while on a tour of Achaea. He was dismissed for being boorish and fled to a small town to await the inevitable death sentence. Instead, he was given command of the legions in PALESTINE in February 67, the rank of governor of JUDAEA, and the task of suppressing the revolt of the Jews. Vespasian did not disappoint Rome. With his son TITUS at his side, he crushed the Jewish Rebellion and was preparing to lay siege to the TEMPLE OF JERUSALEM in 68 when word came that Nero had fallen and had been replaced by Galba. Vespasian sent Titus toward Rome to offer loyalty to the new emperor, but Titus stopped at Corinth when he heard that Galba had already been slain (in January 69). New Emperor OTHO was soon destroyed by VITELLIUS. Prompted by his son Titus, the governor of SYRIA (Licinius MUCIANUS) and the prefect of Egypt (Tiberius Alexander), Vespasian allowed himself to be proclaimed emperor. In the fall of 70, he arrived in Rome where Mucianus had held the reins of power in his absence. So began the actual reign of Vespasian, although he counted the days of his rule from July 1, 69, when the legions in the East saluted him as their imperial master.

From the start the Flavian regime celebrated the notion that, through Vespasian, peace and tranquillity had been restored to the Roman world. This claim was justified and paraded on imperial COINAGE and in the construction of the vast TEMPLE OF PEACE in the Forum of Vespasian. Equally, a stable succession was guaranteed because of Titus and DOMITIAN, his sons. Titus emerged as his most valuable assistant and later as his colleague, sharing in all of his imperial duties. While seemingly instituting a fair and even-handed style of government, Vespasian did much to reshape the very nature of the imperial system, assuming the powers of CENSOR in 73 (as had Emperor CLAUDIUS) to appoint new members to the long-depleted Senate and to give it a more international flavor. Senators arrived from all over Italy and from the provinces. Territories in the East were annexed, and the provinces, as needed, were reorganized; thus, Commagene and Armenia Minor were occupied in 72.

Neither the palace nor the Senate could forget where Vespasian's true power base rested, with the legions who put him on the throne. Rewards were given to the troops who had aided him, but steps were taken to prevent any bloody struggles as in 69. Legions were stationed farther away from each other, and their numbers kept constant at 28. Wherever possible, the soldiers were kept busy—not an easy task, given the overall quiet on the borders. Operations were launched, however, including entry into the Agri Decumates along the Rhine-Danube axis. In Britain, Wales was subjugated, and the governors continued to imprint Roman culture throughout the realm. The work of the General AGRICOLA was outstanding.

Perhaps more than any other emperor, Vespasian was practical and good-natured. In his fight with Roman philosophers, especially DEMETRIUS THE CYNIC and HELVIDIUS PRISCUS the Stoic, he was pushed to the fullest extent of his patience before taking retributive action. He laughed out loud at the flattering suggestion that Hercules was the founder of his family. Audiences were rarely held in the palace, as he preferred the GARDENS OF SALLUST, where anyone could speak with him. SUETONIUS noted that his early poverty made him greedy, but had to admit that he was generally very generous. He died on June 23, 79, after a bout with fever and dysentery. It was reported that his last words were: "Oh my! I think I am turning into a god!"

See also ART AND ARCHITECTURE; COLOSSEUM.

Vesta Important Roman goddess of the hearth; identified with the Greek deity Hestia. According to tradition, Vesta's cult was introduced to the Romans by King Numa, who brought it to Rome from Lavinium, the same site to which Aeneas had brought the sacred fire of Troy and the PENATES or household gods. As the goddess of the sacred fire, Vesta was honored in the homes of ROME and also by the state. Every house had its own hearth, where meals were eaten; thus she had a hand in the day-to-day existence of the Roman people. This idea was reinforced by the presence of an eternal flame in the TEMPLE OF VESTA, where the *praetors,* CONSULS and DICTATORS made sacrifices before embarking on their offices.

Worship of Vesta was detailed and highly ceremonial. On March 1, the flame at the temple in Rome was renewed along with the sacred laurel tree, which shaded the hearth. If the fire went out for some reason, there was great concern on the part of the VESTAL VIRGINS who attended it. They faced a charge of negligence and would be punished; the flame was rekindled by a burning-glass or by the ancient method of igniting a piece of bark from a fruit tree and using that to relight the temple flame. On June 9 was the Vestalia, when the women of Rome walked barefoot to Vesta's temple and asked for the continued blessings of the goddess with special sacrifices. A few days later, on the 15th, the temple was cleansed and purified. The dirt amassed by the cleaning was stored in a locked area so that no one could steal it. The first part of the day was considered *nefastus* or inauspicious. The priestess of Juno could not comb her hair to avoid bad

The Temple of Vesta *(Courtesy Fr. Felix Just, S.J.)*

luck. There were also daily purification rites. Vesta was a part of the Roman pantheon until 382 C.E., when Emperor GRATIAN abolished her and closed her temple.

Vestal Virgins Priestesses of Rome dedicated to the service of the goddess Vesta; important figures in Roman cultic worship, they bore many responsibilities but enjoyed numerous benefits, the greatest of which was a place of high honor. The Vestals dated probably to the earliest days of the worship of Vesta. There were originally two such Virgins, who served for five years. The number increased to four, then six, and the period of service extended to 30 years. Prospective members of the order were chosen by lot by the PONTIFEX MAXIMUS and had to be between six and ten years old; girls from free but not necessarily Patrician families. Immediately upon being named, the candidate left the authority of parents and became a child of Vesta. Entry into her new home, the Atrium of Vesta, near the goddess' temple, was followed by the shaving of her hair and the reception of the attire of the Vestals. The next 10 years were spent in training, then 10 in service and a final 10 in preparing successors.

The primary duty of a Vestal Virgin was to care for the eternal hearth of Vesta. The flame could not be allowed to die. If it did, punishments were meted out by

A Vestal Virgin (*Courtesy Fr. Felix Just, S.J.*)

the pontifex maximus. They also offered daily sacrifices, said prayers and participated in the festivals of the goddess and those of the deity BONA DEA. Vestals always wore white, with a headband called the *infula* that was decorated with ribbons (*vitae*) and covered with a veil at the time of sacrifice. Aside from the distinctive dress, there were many other privileges and powers. They had a lictor with them everywhere, had special seats at all public events and never took oaths, as their words were considered sacred. The Vestals could also save a criminal if they met the accused on the way to prison or execution, and they granted immunity from all attack to anyone with them. They also handled secret documents and wills. Equally, their code of behavior had to remain above reproach. Even the slightest offense warranted censure from the pontifex maximus or the chief vestal, the *Virgo Vestalis Maxima*. For violating chastity the punishment was death by live burial, and the lover involved was executed with rods. The most famous cases were in 83 C.E. and 213 C.E. In the first incident, Emperor DOMITIAN slaughtered the Vestals for breaking their vows, using some form of execution other than burial alive. Emperor CARACALLA had four Vestals die for being impure, although he had raped one of them himself. At the end of 30 years, any retired Vestal was allowed to marry. This was a rare occurrence, however, because it was deemed inauspicious to wed a former Vestal.

See also TEMPLE OF VESTA; CRESCENTIA, CANNUTIA; ELAGABALUS; LAETA; CLODIA; RUFINA, POMPONIA; SEVERA, AURELIA.

Vesuvius Also called Vesvus or Vesvius; the most famous volcano in the Roman world, located on the coast of CAMPANIA near the towns of POMPEII, HERCULANEUM, and Neapolis. Long considered dormant, the volcano served as a refuge for slaves during the revolt of Spartacus in the late 70s B.C.E. On February 5, 63 C.E., the first tremors of its reawakening were felt with earthquakes that caused extensive damage to Pompeii and Herculaneum and slight breakage at Naples. This small convulsion was only a preliminary to the disastrous eruption on August 24, 79 C.E. Spewing tufa, ash, stones, and mud, the volcano completely covered the surrounding cities, sealing them for centuries. PLINY THE ELDER lost his life trying to make scientific observations of the volcano. Although the blast in 79 was the most famous one, there were others in 202, 472, and 512.

Vetranio (d. 356 C.E.) *Magister peditum in Illyricum under Emperor Constantius II*
Constantius faced a severe crisis with the risk of losing both his Western and Eastern domains, his sister Constantia persuaded the veteran General Vetranio to proclaim himself emperor with the help of his troops. His sudden rebellion was certainly accomplished with the

consent of Constantius, for it disrupted MAGNENTIUS's political momentum while allowing the emperor to reorganize his own position. After artificial negotiations, Vetranio journeyed to Naissus and abdicated in favor of the Emperor of the East. Constantius then went on to defeat Magnentius while Vetranio, already old, retired to Prusa in Bithynia and lived for another six years.

Vetus, Lucius Antistius (fl. 55 C.E.) *Consul and one of the victims of the reign of Nero (54–68 C.E.)*

When Vetus was governor of Germania Inferior in 58, his plans for the connection of the Saone and Moselle rivers by a canal were destroyed by Aelius Gracilis, the legate of Gallia Belgica. Gracilis wanted to keep Vetus from gaining the favor of the Gallic people by claiming that the canal would endanger the safety of the empire. Vetus's personal life was marked with tragedy, for his son-in-law was RUBELLIUS PLAUTUS, who was forced to commit suicide in 62. The remaining family, including Vetus, his mother-in-law Sextia and daughter, Antistia Pollitta, were considered hated enemies of Nero. Vetus was charged with some crime by a freedman and, knowing his ultimate fate, took his own life, joined by his two relatives. They were condemned to death posthumously. Nero mockingly decreed that they could choose their manner of suicide.

vexillarii Special units in the imperial LEGIONS that were comprised of veterans who opted to remain in service after their full term. Under the conditions laid down, probably during the reign of AUGUSTUS (27 B.C.E.–14 C.E.), the *vexillarii* served for four more years, with lighter work and more privileges. In each legion the *vexillarii* were placed under the command of a *curator veteranorum* and belonged to a special force recognizable from its symbol, a standard or *vexillum*. In 14 C.E., following the death of Augustus, the mutinous soldiers of the Pannonian legions counted among their number many *vexillarii* who were unhappy about not receiving the promised rights and bonuses.

vexillationes *See* LEGIONS.

viae Highways constructed by the Romans to connect virtually every corner of the empire. While the transportation network throughout the provinces was extremely impressive, it was in Italy that the most famous *viae* were built. Through them ROME was able to extend its influence over the entire peninsula, ensuring rapid movement for the LEGIONS or CURSUS PUBLICUS (the Imperial Post), improved administration and commercial development. What follows is a list of those *viae* that were important throughout the imperial era for Italy. Virtually all were established during the early years of Roman history or in the Republican era.

Via Aemilia One of the most interesting roads in northern Italy. extending from Placentia, where it joined with the Via Postumia, to Ariminum, where it met the Via Flaminia. As it passed through much of Gallia Cisalpina, including Mutina and Forum Gallorum, it was a key element in the Romanization of the territory. With mountains to the southwest and the Adriatic in the east, any advance into the heart of Italy invariably used this highway. It was built in 187 B.C.E. by Marcus Aemilius Lepidus and was repaired by AUGUSTUS and later by TRAJAN. The Via Aemilia figured in several campaigns: Mutina in 43 B.C.E., the Civil War of 69 C.E. and the advance of CONSTANTINE the Great in 312 C.E. against Maxentius.

Via Annia Another *via* in northern Italy, constructed by T. Annius Luscus, probably in 153 B.C.E. Essential to Roman interests, it connected Bononia (on the Via Aemilia) to Aquileia and the provinces of the Danube River. Padua (Patavium) was on its route.

Via Appia Probably the most famous road in the Roman Empire, the main artery in southern Italy. It ran from Rome to Brundisium, through the districts of Latium, Campania, Samnium, and Calabria. Some of the more important cities on its route were Capua, Beneventum, Casilinum, and Venusia. Built originally in 312 B.C.E. by Appius Claudius Caecus, the censor, it went only from Rome to Capua. By the mid-third century B.C.E. it had been lengthened all the way to Brundisium and was paved by the end of the second century B.C.E.

Via Aurelia Actually two highways, the Via Aurelia was also called the Via Aurelia Vetus (Old Via Aurelia) and the Via Aurelia Nova (New Via Aurelia). The road stretched from Rome to Coas on the coast and was probably built in the third century B.C.E., many years before the Via Aurelia Nova of 109 B.C.E. This extension carried transportation.

Via Cassia A key road in central Italy that went from Rome to Arrentium, connecting the Eternal City to the Via Flaminia Minor and thence to Bononia over the Apennines. Its date of construction has been put to the middle of the second century B.C.E., perhaps 154 B.C.E. Over time the name Via Flaminia Minor was used for it, and the *via* stretched from Rome to Florentia (Florence) and even beyond.

Via Domitiana Road built by Emperor DOMITIAN in 95 C.E. with the object of improving the way through Campania. Essentially it was an off-branch of the Via Appia, traveling from the *via* to Volturnum and then to Cumae and Puteoli, two centers in Campania. The estates along the Campanian coast could thus be reached more easily.

The Appian Way *(Hulton/Getty Archive)*

Via Flaminia Indispensable highway cutting its way across the mountainous regions of central Italy, through the districts of Etruria and Umbria. It began in Rome and then went north to Interamna before turning northeast and ending at Ariminum on the Adriatic coast, where it linked up with the Via Aemilia. More so than the Via Cassia, the Via Flaminia was a lifeline from Rome to northern Italy, and its upkeep was a matter of great concern to the empire.

Via Flaminia Minor *See* Via Cassia.

Via Latina Road that traversed the area to the southeast of Rome and east of the Via Appia. It was apparently well traveled and used by those hoping to avoid the Via Appia for as long as possible or for anyone going into Samnium. The Via Latina was extremely old, its date of origin unclear. A new or repaired road went along the same route from Rome to Casinum (Cassino) just north of Capua and the Via Appia. This new version was built around 127 B.C.E. and was known as the Via Latina Nova.

Via Minucia An older road that has been the subject of considerable debate. It was mentioned by CICERO but details have been elusive. It may have been built in the late third century B.C.E. to connect Beneventum with Brundisium along a more northerly route than the Via Appia. What relation it might have had with the later Via Traiana is unclear.

Via Popillia Coastal route in northern Italy that connected Arminum to Aquileia by way of the Via Annia. Unlike the other roads, the founding date of the *via* is for certain, 132 B.C.E. by the CONSUL P. Popillius.

Via Postumia A highway at the far north of Italy, roughly along the Po River and the Alps, connecting the western and eastern ends of Gallia Cisalpina, from Genua (Genoa) to Aquileia. No entrance into Italy from the north was possible without passing over it. Along the road were Placentia, Cremona, Verona, and Opitergium. Advancing armies, hoping to march down the Via Aemilia, had to go across the Via Postumia. For that reason, in 69 C.E. two battles were fought near the junction to the west of Cremona, at BEDRIACUM. It was built in 142 B.C.E. by Sp. Postumius Albinus, with an eye on strengthening the Roman presence in Gallia Cisalpina.

Via Sacra Not so much a road as an institution and, one of the most important, roads in the Roman Empire. Along its path from the FORUM ROMANUM to the Palatine Hill, the Velia or outlying part of the Palatine, and the Via Appia, leading out of the city, were magnificent temples and grand structures. The Capitoline Hill looked down from above the Basilica Julia and the Forum. To the southwest was the Palatine and, over the years, other great forums to the northeast. In the time of the Flavians, the COLOSSEUM was built at the eastern edge of the *via* as it turned into the Via Appia.

The Sacred Way was so named for the obvious number of sacred buildings and for the rites celebrated with processions on its pavement. TRIUMPHS passed from the CAMPUS MARTIUS to the CIRCUS MAXIMUS, around the Palatine and up the Sacred Way to the capitol. The road was one of the few thoroughfares in Rome to be called a *via*.

Via Salaria One of the roads leading away from Rome, through the northeastern route to Reate and beyond. Its name suggests an ancient connection with the salt trade. Eventually two branches were made out of Reate, one to the north through Asculum to Castrum Turnetinum, and the other to the southeast, through Amiternum to Hadria. Both ended on the Adriatic. The small Via Caecilia extended from the south addition to Castrum Novum.

Via Aemilia Scauri Technically, an extension of the Via Aurelia Nova, journeying north from

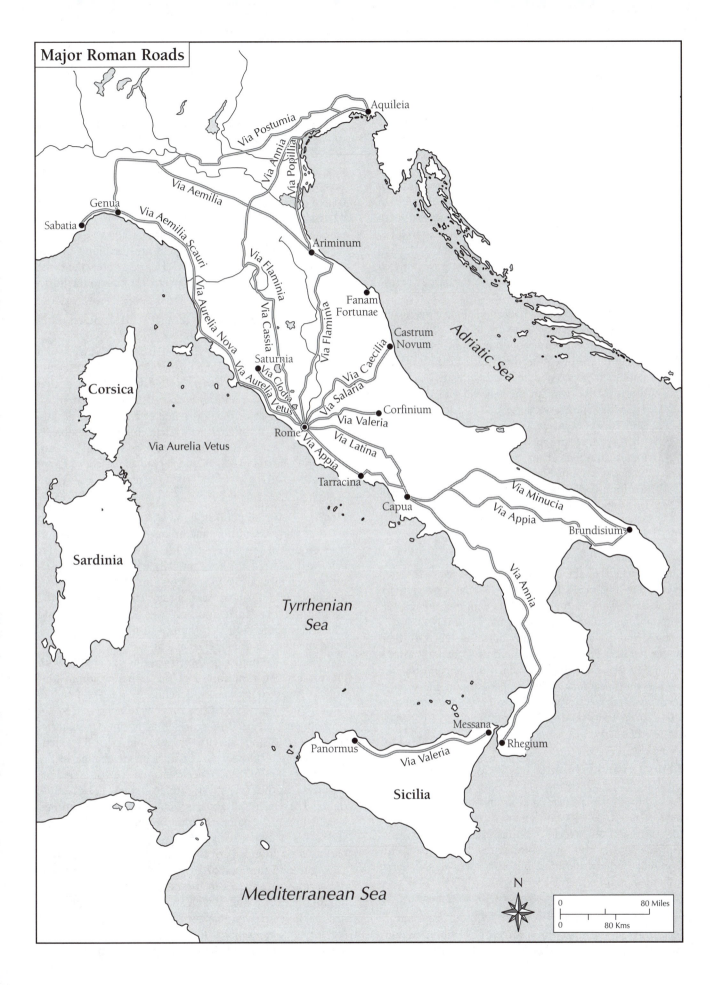

Major Roman Roads

Via Postumia

Via Annia

Via Popillia

Aquileia

Via Aemilia

Genua

Via Aemilia Scauri

Sabatia

Via Aurelia Nova

Ariminum

Via Flaminia

Via Cassia

Fanam
Fortunae

Via Flaminia

Castrum
Novum

Adriatic Sea

Corsica

Saturnia

Via Clodia

Via Aurelia Vetus

Via Caecilia

Via Salaria

Corfinium

Rome

Via Valeria

Via Latina

Via Appia

Sardinia

Via Aurelia Vetus

Tarracina

Capua

Via Minucia

Via Appia

Brundisium

Via Annia

**Tyrrhenian
Sea**

Messana

Panormus

Rhegium

Via Valeria

Sicilia

Mediterranean Sea

N

0   80 Miles

0   80 Kms

Populonia on the western coast to Sabatia beyond Genoa. Constructed in 109 B.C.E. or 107 B.C.E. by Marcus Aemilius Scaurus, it was of considerable value, for it connected Rome to the Via Postumia and Gallia Narbonensis.

Via Traiana The major road constructed by Emperor TRAJAN in 109 C.E. to improve the route from Beneventum to Brundisium (the southern portion of the Via Appia). It is possible that Trajan had the Via Traiana follow the approximate path of the ambiguous Via Minucia, but that is only speculation. Trajan's Way probably stretched across a more eastern line, bypassing the rugged Samnite terrain in favor of a coastal region through Apuleia.

Via Valeria A central Italian road, leaving Rome and winding its way eastward to the Adriatic. The Via Valeria was not begun and completed with the single intent of connecting Rome to the Adriatic. Rather, it proceeded forward at widely separate times. There was an ancient *via* called the Via Triburtina, but it was absorbed in initial construction by the Censor Valerius (309 B.C.E. or 307 B.C.E.). More progress was made in 154 B.C.E. under another censor, Marcus Valerius Messalla, who was responsible for advancing the highway to Corfinum. CLAUDIUS made the last improvement by adding more territory, all the way to the coast. Thus, on the Via Valeria were such towns as Tibur (with Tivoli), Alba Fucens, and Aternum.

viatores One of the classes of the *apparitores,* or civil servants to the magistrates in the Roman government. The *viatores* were the public bailiffs who had the duty of summoning senators to sessions, running assorted errands, and executing the many duties assigned to them by magistrates. They also had the duty of making arrests and confiscating goods. Like the other *apparitores,* the *viatores* were drawn from the freedmen and the sons of freedmen, and were organized into a corporation of several *decuriae* (panels) depending on the class of the magistrates they served.

Vibius Crispus, Quintus (c. 10–90 C.E.) *Orator from Vercellae*
He acquired the respect and friendship of Emperors NERO, VITELLIUS, VESPASIAN, and DOMITIAN, and served as CONSUL under all except Vitellius. He was never very popular, for he not only prosecuted many, using his formidable oratorical skills, but also survived the harsh years of war and tyranny.

Vibius Marsus, Gaius (fl. 17 C.E.) *Consul and legate*
According to the historian TACITUS (1), Vibius Marsus was descended from an illustrious family and was a man of great repute. He was on the staff of GERMANICUS in the East and in 19, after the death of the general, was considered as Cn. Calpurnius PISO's replacement as governor of SYRIA but lost to Gnaeus SENTIUS. Soon after he journeyed to ROME at the side of AGRIPPINA THE ELDER. Having supported one avowed enemy of Tiberius he was nevertheless made proconsul of AFRICA (from 27 to 29). In 36, he was charged with treason and adultery but was later spared. Appointment as governor of Syria came finally in 42, under CLAUDIUS. Until his departure in 45, Vibius maintained a suspicious eye on King AGRIPPA I, reporting on his strengthening of Jerusalem and breaking up the conference held by the ruler. He also prevented the designs of VARDANES, king of Parthia, on Roman territory.

Vibius Maximus, Gaius (fl. later first century C.E.) *Writer and government official*
Vibius was a friend of the literary figures STATIUS and MARTIAL, receiving from the former the dedication for the *Silvae.* From Statius's work it has been deduced that Vibius was a historian and authored a *Universal History.* While the history probably contained epitomes of SALLUST and Livy, it differed from them in terms of subjects treated. He was also the prefect of a cohort (III Alpinorum) in Dalmatia in 93–94 and served as prefect of Egypt from 103 to 107.

vicarii Powerful political figures of the late empire who acted as deputies to the Praetorian prefects, with control over groups of provinces. Traditionally, the term *vicarius* or *vicarii* referred to those officials who acted as substitutes or temporary replacements for a governor of a province who died or was away. They acted on the assumption that their position was extraordinary and would terminate either on the return of the governor or upon the naming of his replacement.

The special nature of the *vicarii* did not change with the increased centralization of the imperial administration in the second and third centuries C.E. Tied to the Equestrian Order (EQUITES), they were sent out by an emperor to act as his representative in a senatorial province or in some specific jurisdiction. With the extensive reforms of DIOCLETIAN came a major change in the nature of the office. Henceforth the *vicarii* acted as deputies to the Praetorian prefects with considerable rights. They heard all appeals from provincial governors, watched over the administration programs of individuals and oversaw the workings of groups of provinces, the DIOCESES, as founded by Diocletian. They were, in turn, answerable to the Praetorian prefects, who administered the various prefectures in the new system. There were a number of exceptions. AFRICA and Asia were private holdings of the emperors, managed exclusively by prefects of the imperial household. Further, Italy had two *vicarii,* one for Italy itself and the other for ROME, known as the *vicarius urbis Romae.* The *vicarii* remained part of the imperial government until disbanded by Justinian in the sixth century.

See GOVERNMENT and DIOCESE.

vicarius See VICARII.

Victor (fl. fourth century C.E.) *Magister equitum of the East from 363 to circa 379*
A SARMATIAN who married the daughter of the Saracen Queen MAVIA, he became an ardent Christian. Victor began his career in the service of CONSTANTIUS II and was later promoted by Julian to the rank of general; he commanded the rearguard of the imperial army during the Persian Campaign of 363. He was made MAGISTER PEDITUM by either Julian or Jovian but was appointed *magister equitum* by Jovian in 363. VALENS came to the throne in 364, and not only retained Victor but also used him extensively. In 366–367, he operated against the GOTHS but later negotiated with them (in 369) and with the Persians in 377. He held a consulship in 369. Prior to the battle of ADRIANOPLE in 378, Victor protested Valens's persecution of orthodox Christians and advised that the emperor await the reinforcements of Emperor Gratian before engaging the Goths in Thrace. He was able to extricate his own units from the disaster of Adrianople and informed Gratian. Victor retired at CONSTANTINOPLE after 382–383 and was in correspondence with GREGORY OF NAZIANZUS.

Victor, Claudius (fl. mid-first century C.E.) *Nephew of the Gallic rebel leader Civilis*
He was a commander of cavalry during the uprising of 69–70 C.E. He was sent, with Julius Maximus, to launch an attack upon the Roman General Dillius Vocula, but was unsuccessful.

Victorinus, Aufidius See AUFIDIUS VICTORIANUS, GAIUS.

Victorinus, Furius (d. 168 C.E.) *Prefect of the Praetorian Guard*
He served during the reign of ANTONINUS PIUS (138–161 C.E.) and into the reign of MARCUS AURELIUS (161–180 C.E.). He was appointed originally with Fabrius Repentinus, as a successor to Tattius Maximus. In 168, at the start of the MARCOMANNIC WARS, he was still at his post and was sent by Marcus Aurelius and Lucius VERUS to help defend Italy from barbarian invasions. While fighting near Aquileia he was killed, and a large part of his army was annihilated.

Victorinus, Gaius Marius (fl. fourth century C.E.) *Philosopher, rhetorician, and eventually a Christian theologian*
Born into a pagan African family, Victorinus became a noted and versatile intellectual of great reputation. Aside from his Neoplatonic books, translations of Aristotle, Porphyry, and Plato (now lost), he wrote commentaries on CICERO's *Topica* (lost) and *De inventione* (extant). There were, as well, an *Ars grammatica,* derived in the main from Aphthonius, in four books; texts; and writings on Christian thought. Converted circa 356 to CHRISTIANITY, he composed further commentaries on epistles by Paul and penned attacks on ARIANISM. Poems on the Bible and a number of texts attributed to him are now doubted.

Victorinus, Marcus Piavonius (fl. mid-third century C.E.) *Gallic usurper made coemperor to the major usurper, Postumus, in 267 or 268*
Victorinus took over virtual control of Gaul when both Posthumus and Laelianus died, but he was murdered, perhaps in 270. His mother Victoria was listed as one of the THIRTY TYRANTS, as was her son.

Victory Called Victoria by the Romans and Nice (Nike) by the Greeks, a goddess who was the personification of success or victory. According to legend she was the daughter of Pallas and Styx, becoming the patroness of heroes, guiding them along their appointed paths to greatness. Revered by the Roman people, she was given an altar in the SENATE. This sacred monument became one of the most important symbols of organized PAGANISM in the Roman Empire and a point of bitter confrontation between pagans and Christians in the fourth century C.E. Ordered removed several times by emperors, the altar was finally abolished in 394, after THEODOSIUS I defeated EUGENIUS and the *MAGISTER MILITUM,* ARBOGAST, in battle and decreed that the symbol of Victory be removed from the Curia, never to appear again.

Vienna Modern Vienne, not to be confused with modern Vienna (VINDOBONA), this was a leading town in GALLIA NARBONENSIS whose origins dated to the time of the Allobroges, when it served as the tribal capital of that generally peaceful people. A colony was founded sometime after the assassination of Julius CAESAR (c. 43 B.C.E.) but the title of *colonia* was not granted until the reign of GAIUS CALIGULA. By that time prosperity allowed an intense rivalry with nearby LUGDUNUM (Lyons). Thus, in 68 C.E., when VINDEX revolted against NERO, Lugdunum remained loyal but Vienne rejoiced at the rise of the usurper, serving as his headquarters. The following year the community was nearly destroyed by an advancing army of VITELLIUS, en route to Italy to defeat OTHO. Its extirpation was pressed by Lugdunum. Despite competition from the provincial capital, Vienne was able to thrive, building all of the usual Roman structures, including an odeon, a theater, and a Temple of Rome and Augustus.

vigiles Term used for the fire brigade of ROME during the imperial era. With its congestion and poorly constructed INSULAE (apartments), Rome was always susceptible to fires, but surprisingly the city possessed no official squad for fire-fighting. Prior to the reign of AUGUSTUS, prevention and extinguishing of blazes fell under the duties of various officials, including the AEDILES and the little known *triumviri nocturni*. They were in charge of a group of public slaves but received support from private contractors, normally wealthy slave owners who used their own workers. Such a system was inefficient.

Augustus reformed the entire administration of fire control, beginning around 23 B.C.E. The aediles were given a body of slaves numbering some 600. More fires brought several changes, culminating in 6 C.E. with the creation of the Vigiles, under the command of their own prefect (*praefectum vigilum*), a 7,000-man corps divided into seven cohorts, each under a TRIBUNE and composed of freedmen, not slaves. Seven cohorts were employed in order to provide the 14 regions of Rome with adequate protection; every two sections of the city were patrolled by one cohort. They not only put out fires but also probably aided in keeping order in the traditionally tempestuous streets of the capital. In 31 C.E., at the fall of the Praetorian Prefect SEJANUS, they proved indispensable under their Prefect Graecinus Laco. While they were at first quartered in numerous houses like the PRAETORIAN GUARD, they eventually had stations spread throughout the various districts of the city.

villa The Latin term for a country estate or rural dwelling, either a farmstead that was part of a larger property or a large country dwelling for the wealthy outside of a city. It should be noted, however, that the precise functions and nature of villas changed over time in the Roman world, and even the specific definition of a villa remains debatable.

The villa began as a rural dwelling that was built for agricultural purposes. Even the later models, luxurious residential estates in the country, depended on agriculture. Farming was the essential economic reality of the villa system, and virtually every villa was self-sufficient. Fields supplied the estate with its food and crops sold in nearby towns or cities provided income. Thus villas were commonly clustered around towns where the produce they raised could be sold easily at market. It is noted, of course, that not every farm with a central house was considered a villa. While the Romans themselves had differing definitions of a villa, it was differentiated from a farm by its degree of Roman culture (such as mosaics and wall paintings), its signs of wealth and status, and the presence of slave labor. It was long assumed that the owners of most provincial villas were wealthy Romans who had migrated from Rome. Recent indications are, however, that many villas were actually owned by prosperous citizens in the provinces who had adopted Roman customs.

The traditional Roman or Italian villa consisting of a farming estate with domestic buildings was described in great detail by such writers as Vitruvius and Varro. They were maintained for the owner—often an urban landholder—by slaves and other workers concentrated around a central house. There was also a simpler dwelling type, a *villa rustica* (house in the country), owned by poorer smallholders. Later, villas developed into large estates providing their wealthy owners a respite from stressful urban life. Naturally, a wide variety of architectural styles were employed, and the degree of obvious Roman characteristics might depend upon the wealth, taste, and personal tendencies of the owner.

Villas began appearing beyond the confines of Italia from about the first century B.C.E. They spread across much of the Roman world, but they were especially common in northern provinces, particularly the provinces of Gaul. They were also found in Hispania, Africa, Britannia, Germania, and along the Danube. They were less common in the eastern provinces, but knowledge is limited because of the fewer remaining models of eastern villas and the relatively limited archaeological work performed on surviving sites. Archaeology remains the chief source of knowledge, along with aerial photography and art history. Villas were represented in art, mostly in mosaics and wall paintings, and were mentioned by writers. Aside from the previously noted Varro and Vitruvius, another notable writer was Marcus Portius Cato, who wrote *De Agri Cultura* (On agriculture), including details of villas and their operations with slave labor, in the second century.

Early villas were of the *villa rustica* variety. They began as simple buildings and gradually assumed a peristyle structure in which the house was designed around a central atrium or courtyard or garden surrounded by a colonnaded portico. This basic design became increasingly more ornate and sophisticated in the hands of Roman architects and builders. One later form featured two courtyards, permitting the owner to have a more distinct separation between the farming activities of the villa and its residential quarters. From this emerged the trend for villas to become even larger and more grand, with the focus on the residence. The farming facilities were of secondary importance to the owners, who were concerned principally with the luxury and comfort of their surroundings when they visited.

A unique form of villa was the *villa maritima,* an immense estate owned by the most wealthy in Roman society or even emperors, situated on coasts or along the seaside. Several areas were famous for their seaside villas, including Baiae and Bauli, in Campania, where the most powerful figures in the capital owned estates. The best known *villa maritima* was the VILLA JOVIS, built by Emperor Tiberius on the island of Capri.

A villa in Herculaneum *(Courtesy Fr. Felix Just, S.J.)*

The typical villa owned by a smallholder was not ornately decorated and was a simple rectangular building divided into assorted rooms. Larger villas might have more extensive buildings, and decorations might include mosaics and paintings. In the villas of the very wealthy, there might be tiled roofs, mosaics, and plastered walls. Floor mosaics were made of fragments (or cubes termed *tessellae*) of stone, glass, tile, and pottery that were then arranged into often complex designs to form pictures. Typical designs were from Greek and Roman mythology. During winter months, heat was provided by charcoal braziers or by so-called hypocausts. The latter were a kind of underground heating based on the heating systems used in baths. A furnace produced hot air that was channeled throughout the house by stone-lined depressions beneath the flooring. Actual hot air was released into the rooms through flues cut into the floor or walls. Given the cost and the complexity needed for such heating, only several rooms were heated effectively. Second-story rooms were not heated.

Suggested Readings: Bowen, H. C. "The Celtic Background." In *The Roman Villa in Britain,* edited by A. L. F. Rivet. London: Routledge & Kegan Paul, 1969; Branigan, K., and Miles, D., ed. *The Economy of Romano-British Villas.* Sheffield, U.K.: University of Sheffield, 1989; D'Arms, John H. *Romans on the Bay of Naples; a Social and Cultural Study of the Villas and Their Owners from 150 B.C.E. to C.E. 400.* Cambridge, Mass.: Harvard University Press, 1970; Davies, Roy W. "Social and Economic Aspects." In *The Roman Villa in Britain,* edited by A. L. F. Rivet. London: Routledge, 1969, 173–216; Percival, John. *The Roman Villa: An Historical Introduction.* London: Batsford, 1976; Puppi, Lionello. *The Villa Badoer at Fratta Polesine.* Translated by Catherine Enggass. University Park: Pennsylvania State University Press, 1975.

Villa Jovis The Villa of Jove (Jupiter), constructed in CAPRI by Emperor TIBERIUS before 26 C.E. Always a private man who liked retreats such as his own on Rhodes, Tiberius desired a place in Campania where he could escape from the unpleasantness of ROME. A small seaside villa on Capri, built by AUGUSTUS, became his favorite place. From 14 C.E. he enlarged its dimensions and added to its beauty; by 26, when he abandoned Rome forever, he had a palace suitable as his home. The villa was situated on the top of a cliff, with a view of the eastern side of the island and a panorama of Campania's coast. There were baths, a main hall, private suites, and an observatory for the imperial astrologer, THRASYLLUS. A lighthouse helped the suspicious emperor to stay in touch with the fleet at Misenum and with Rome, via a relay system. In 31 C.E., when awaiting news concerning the fall of the Praetorian Prefect SEJANUS, Tiberius made plans to desert the villa for the nearby fleet. The lighthouse was destroyed by an earthquake just before his death in 37. Because of the terrible stories about his debaucheries on Capri, the Villa Jovis was not a favorite place of residence for subsequent emperors.

Vinalia The Roman festival of wine held every August 19 in honor of the new vintage for the year. It was widely but incorrectly believed that the Vinalia was associated with the goddess VENUS. In all probability, the fete was connected with Jupiter, for the Flamen Dialis sacrificed a ewe, cooked it and offered it on an altar of that deity. Once this had been done, the first of the grapes for the year were cut and the harvest began.

See also FLAMENS; JUPITER.

Vindex, Gaius Julius (d. 68 C.E.) *Governor in Tres Galliae (most likely, of Gallia Lugdunensis) in 68 C.E.*
Vindex's revolt against Emperor NERO was one of the major events leading to the fall of Nero that same year. Vindex was a Romanized Gaul, a member of the senatorial class and a figure of great importance with local Gallic tribes. He was also a member of a growing group of officials who had become tired of Nero's tyrannies. Thus he entered into communication with his fellow governors and, in the days before the summer of 68, openly declared himself in revolt from ROME.

He did not seek the throne for himself, but supported Servius Sulpicius GALBA (2), then head of Hispania Tarraconensis. His actual goals were never clear, except that he encouraged Galba to seek the purple and promised him the help of the Gallic provinces. Unfortunately, he failed in his task, as his command over the tribes other than the AEDUI and Arverni (Averni) was limited. Further, his headquarters had to be in Vienna (Vienne), not LUGDUNUM (Lyons), because that city refused to open its gates to him. Lugdunum proved fatal to his plans, for while he wasted precious time besieging it, VERGINIUS

RUFUS, legate of Germania Superior, gathered all available troops, marched to the scene and defeated Vindex near Vesontio (modern Besancon). It is possible that both commanders attempted to avoid bloodshed through negotiations, but a battle was eventually fought. After most of his troops died, Vindex killed himself.

Vindex, M. Macrinus (d. c. 169–170 C.E.) *Prefect of the Praetorian Guard*

Vindex served during the reign of MARCUS AURELIUS; possibly the successor to Furius VICTORINUS, who died in battle in 168 C.E. during the MARCOMANNIC WARS. He followed in Victorinus's footsteps, for in the continued fighting he too was slain (c. 169–170). The emperor erected three statues in his honor.

Vindobona

Modern Vienna, city on the DANUBE River, to the west of Carnumtum, in the province of PANNONIA Superior. Originally a Celtic community, the site was seen as ideal for Roman occupation, and by the end of the first century C.E., its status had been increased to *municipium*; it was headquarters of the X Gemina Legion and the main port of the *Classis Pannonica,* an imperial river fleet. While it did not possess the political power of the provincial capital, Vindobona was clearly important in a strategic sense.

Vingeanne

Minor engagement fought in 52 B.C.E. between the armies of Julius CAESAR and the chieftain VERCINGETORIX, leader of the rebelling Gallic tribes. The Gauls avoided an open-field confrontation with Caesar, remembering the other defeats suffered at his hands, but in July Vercingetorix allowed an attack to be made by the Gauls. Caesar put his cavalry to rout and captured three chieftains of the AEDUI. Vercingetorix ordered a retreat to the nearby site of ALESIA, setting the stage for a climactic siege and a Roman victory.

See also GALLIC WARS.

Vinicianus, Annius (fl. first century C.E.) *Conspirator*

He was a leading figure in the plots against the imperial house during the reigns of GAIUS CALIGULA (37–41 C.E.) and CLAUDIUS (41–54 C.E.). In 32 C.E., he was listed as a member of a treasonous group of politicians but escaped trial and condemnation when TIBERIUS set aside certain cases for personal review. Nine years later he became one of the organizers in a plot to kill Caligula. After the emperor's death, Vinicianus called for Valerius Asiaticus to withdraw from seeking the throne, hoping to avert a massacre of the SENATE by the PRAETORIAN GUARD, which had just proclaimed Claudius emperor. Immediately unhappy with Claudius, Vinicianus joined a conspiracy to elevate Scribonianus Camillus, governor of ILLYRICUM, to the throne in 42. When the attempt failed utterly, he was one of those who followed Scribonianus's example— and killed himself.

There was another Annius Vinicianus, said by the historian TACITUS (1) to be 26 years old in 63. He served with Domitius CORBULO (2) in ARMENIA and was married to Corbulo's daughter. In 66, he died as a result of a failed plot to replace NERO with his father-in-law. His exact relationship to the first Annius Vinicianus is curious, although he may have been his son.

Vinicius, Marcus (1) (fl. later first century B.C.E.) *Consul in 19 B.C.E. and general during the reign of Augustus (27 B.C.E.–14 C.E.)*

One of a new class of imperial favorites who owed their political careers to the new emperor, Marcus Vinicius repaid the faith placed in him with loyalty and competence. In 25 B.C.E. he was sent to the Alps to help quell the local tribes. Over the next few years he campaigned in PANNONIA, serving with Marcus AGRIPPA in 13 B.C.E. and later with TIBERIUS. He may also have been the legate of Illyricum mentioned in inscriptions as the conductor of operations over the DANUBE, sometime between 6 B.C.E. and 4 C.E.. His actions hemmed in the chieftain MAROBODUUS and extended Roman influence north of the Danubian frontier. Vinicius then replaced Lucius Domitius Ahenobarbus (c. 1 C.E.) as legate in Germany.

Vinicius, Marcus (2) (d. 45 C.E.) *Grandson of the Augustan general of the same name*

A successful Equestrian (EQUITES) and CONSUL in 30 C.E., Velleius Paterculus dedicated his history to him during his consulship and, in 33, Emperor TIBERIUS chose him to marry JULIA (6), daughter of GERMANICUS. Their marriage was not a happy one; she was banished by GAIUS CALIGULA in 39 but recalled by CLAUDIUS in 41, only to be put to death at the instigation of Empress MESSALLINA. Consul for a second time, in 45, Vinicius was an object of lust to Messallina. He was executed because he refused to have an affair with the empress. He was described as gentle, a graceful speaker, and one who minded his own business in the hope of staying alive.

Vinius, Titus (d. 69 C.E.) *Political ally of Emperor Otho*

A former officer of the Spanish provincial government and a greedy fortune hunter who journeyed to Rome in 68–69 C.E. with Emperor GALBA, becoming one of his leading advisers, along with Cornelius LACO and the freedman ICELUS. Described by the historian TACITUS (1) as the vilest of men, he became a stubborn supporter of OTHO for the position of Galba's heir and sought to wed his daughter to Otho, who was unmarried. He lost to Laco, who wanted Piso Licinianus. His backing of Otho was not enough to prevent his own murder in the assassination plot of Otho against Galba on January 15, 69. Vinius was cut down by the PRAETORIAN GUARDS outside of the TEMPLE OF DIVUS JULIUS.

Virgil (Publius Vergilius Maro) (70–19 B.C.E.) *Considered the greatest of all Roman poets*

Virgil was a master of the finest Roman poetical forms, including the pastoral, didactic, and epic. He was born in Andes, a small town near Mantua, on October 15, 70 B.C.E. to a family of moderate means that nevertheless provided him with the finest possible education, in Cremona (58), in Milan (55) and then in ROME (after 53). At first he probably studied oratory but moved on to philosophy, learning from the noted Epicurean Siro; also in his field of scholarship were mathematics and medicine. When he returned home is unclear, but in the years 41–40, he was included in the confiscations of land in Italy, begun at that time by the government. Virgil's family estate was seized, but, because of friends such as Asinius Pollio and Cornelius Gallus, Octavian (AUGUSTUS) was apparently convinced to intercede on his behalf. At the end of the PERUSINE WAR (40), however, Virgil was nearly killed when his home was again taken. With his father, he took up residence in an old house belonging to Siro. His friends recommended that he go to Rome, where, through the popularity of his *Bucolics,* he came under the patronage of the powerful MAECENAS. Not only were his possessions eventually returned, but he was also admitted to the literary circle of Maecenas (along with HORACE).

A friendship developed between these two writers that lasted some years, as Virgil rose in the ranks of the literary figures of the time. In 29, he read the *Georgics* to Octavian, and in 27 Augustus wrote to the poet, desiring some kind of monumental effort, the result being the *Aeneid.* When the imperial heir Marcellus died in 23, Virgil injected into the sixth book of his epic the tragic death of a youth. Octavia, Marcellus's mother, was overcome by the composition and rewarded Virgil with great praise. Possibly Virgil planned a trip to Greece, accompanying the emperor as far as Megara. Upon reaching Brundisium, his health, long in decline, gave out, and he died on September 22, 19. He was buried near the road from Naples to Puteoli.

Virgil was a gentle poet, popular and graceful in his style. Enemies, if he had any, could fault only his political views. Like Horace he was an ardent supporter of the Augustan regime, but lacked the ability to flatter the ruler or to seek his own interests. Eventually surrounded with luxuries, he maintained his gentle ways. As a poet Virgil was honored not only by his contemporaries but also by succeeding generations, who looked upon him as the epitome of the Golden Age of Roman Literature. Three brilliant works earned Virgil his eternal fame: the *Bucolics,* the *Georgics,* and the *Aeneid.*

The Bucolics Translated from the Greek, for poetry of oxherds; also called the *Eclogues.* These 10 poems were written between 41 and 39, based largely upon the Greek poet Theocritus. Originally, the *Bucolics* were probably published individually under their own titles. Each dealt with a particular subject but contained numerous historical allusions such as to the civil wars, the death of Caesar and promises of a new and better world. In this regard they were technically the least successful of all Virgilian creations, as there was always a certain tension between the original, rustic theme of the work and the nonbucolic insertions.

The Georgics Organized into four books, the *Georgics* were concerned about agriculture, nature, and animals, and were written sometime between 37 and 30 at the request of Maecenas, to whom the dedication was made. Here Virgil found a subject where his own enthusiasms and love could shine. While the information was not particularly accurate from a scientific view, or even from a practical viewpoint, it was presented with rare style. An atmosphere was created in which Virgil depicted the beauty of the countryside and the value of the simple life; it was an intense collection of his own experiences and research, using Greek and Roman sources. The *Georgics* were concerned with things that might be of value to the farmer. Book 1 was on agriculture, specially farming, while book 2 explored the field of cultivating trees. Book 3 covered domestic animals, and book 4 the raising of bees.

Aeneid Virgil's masterpiece was the *Aeneid,* written in 12 books between 29 and his death in 19, but never completed; ironically, published by L. Varius and Tucca, despite the poet's wishes to the contrary. For this task of compiling an epic on the scale of Homer's mighty works, Virgil studied carefully the structure and nuances of Homer, as well as earlier Roman masters of epic, Naevius and Ennius. All of these preceding works had an influence upon the *Aeneid,* but Virgil succeeded in retaining his own style and imagination, and the solemn tones so integral to the traditional Roman writings. With these elements at work, the poet forged an epic that did justice to the theme of Rome's foundation while embracing the future imperial era with enthusiasm.

The *Aeneid* was the story of Aeneas, a mighty hero of the Trojan War and the ancestral father of the Romans. Complex and sophisticated, the story was drawn from the accepted legends of Aeneas and included his flight to CARTHAGE, where he met Dido before sailing to Latium. The *Aeneid* was filled with powerful images, virtually flawless versification, and profound and compelling characterizations.

Suggested Readings: Horsfall, Nicholas. *A Companion to the Study of Virgil*. San Francisco: Brill Academic Publishers, 2000; Levi, Peter. *Virgil; His Life and Times*. New York: St. Martin's Press, 1998; Martindale, Charles. *The Cambridge Companion to Virgil*. Cambridge, U.K.: Cambridge University Press, 1997; Virgil. *The Aeneid*. Translated by Robert Fitzgerald. New York: Vintage Books, 1990; ———. *Eclogues and Georgics of Virgil*. Translated by David R. Slavitt. Baltimore: Johns Hopkins University Press, 1990; Virgil and G. P. Gould. *Eclogues, Georgics, Aeneid I–VI*. Translated by H. Rushton Fairclough. Cambridge, Mass.: Harvard University Press, 1999.

Virilis, Temple of   A shrine dedicated to the goddess FORTUNA but used only by men.

Virunum   One of the leading cities of the Roman province of NORICUM; situated in southern Noricum near the border of PANNONIA. From the start of ROME's occupation, the site was important because of its position on the road connecting the DANUBE frontier with the major areas of Italy (AQUILEIA) and Pannonia. When the traditional center of culture at Noreia (Magdalensberg) was destroyed to augment Romanization of the region, its replacement was Virunum. Here a MUNICIPIUM was founded and the procurator housed. The city enjoyed all of the usual architectural gifts of civilization, a bath, forum, basilica, and temples. So Italian did it become that *coloniae* were unnecessary, and it stood as a model both for the northern regions of the province and for Pannonia. Following the MARCOMANNIC WARS, in the mid-second century C.E., Ovilava replaced Virunum as the capital, but the procurator remained. Virunum was never fortified because of its location in southern Noricum, always a more peaceful territory.

Visigoths   Known as the Western Goths, one of the two major divisions of the GOTHS, the Visigoths developed separately from the OSTROGOTHS (Eastern Goths). By the close of the Western Empire they had become a powerful kingdom, occupying much of northern Spain and Aquitania. Splitting from their Ostrogothic kin in the early fourth century C.E., the Visigoths settled in DACIA in the area north of the DANUBE, remaining in that region throughout much of the century, pursuing a life based largely on agriculture. As with so many other tribes, by 376 the Visigoths were feeling the mounting pressure of the migrations of the HUNS from the East. Under their kings, FRITIGERN and ALAVIUS, the Visigoths moved to the Danube and sent representatives to CONSTANTINOPLE to ask Emperor VALENS for permission to enter imperial territory in THRACE. Fritigern, speaking to Valens on behalf of his people, was successful, although certain demands were made upon them in return, such as the surrendering of hostages and the handing over of all weapons.

Just at the Visigoths seemed ready to settle down, more refugees fleeing from the Huns arrived, renewing ties between the Visigoths and the Ostrogoths. The Roman administration of their domain was also harsh, bringing about war in Thrace. Alavius was slain in an ambush, but Fritigern, aided by the Ostrogoths under Alatheus and Saphrax, stunned and horrified the Roman world with his smashing victory over Valens on August 9, 378, at ADRIANOPLE. The Visigoths menaced Thrace and plundered the Balkans but were confronted with the lasting problem of finding a home. Fritigern was murdered in a power struggle, and the Visigoths remained, still unhappy, in MOESIA.

THEODOSIUS I, trying to end the threat of the barbarians and to create a buffer between the provincial cities and the more dangerous hordes of the Huns, made an offer to the Goths. In October 382, he allowed them to inhabit large stretches of Moesia, but as federates of the empire, with the duty of protecting the frontier. Whether or not this agreement could have lasted was rendered moot by the emergence of the influential King ALARIC around 395. Alaric, like his ambitious predecessors, desired a permanent domain for his people and moved out of the Danubian provinces and roamed through Greece before setting out for Italy. His ultimate goal was the granting of concessions by Emperor Honorius, but he had not counted on the presence of the MAGISTER MILITUM, STILICHO. Despite Stilicho's chronic reluctance to finish off any potentially useful barbarian host, he did repulse Alaric twice, at Pollentina (402) and at Verona (403). With plague, exhaustion, and starvation depleting his ranks, Alaric withdrew. Stilicho had a hand in his easy retreat, for the Visigoths no doubt figured in the magister's formula for annexing Illyricum from the Eastern Empire.

Alaric allowed himself to serve as a subject of the empire once more, holding Epirus for Honorius (c. 407). By 408, however, he was again strong enough to make his own demands. Sweeping into Noricum he called for payment for his services, and through Stilicho's influence received TRIBUTUM. Stilicho was put to death in that same year, and, with all restraints removed, the Visigoths marched on Italy. Rome was besieged three times during 409 and 410, and on August 24, 410, Alaric and his warriors entered the Eternal City. For two or three days Rome was pillaged and sacked. The Visigoths had thus not only annihilated a Roman emperor and his army but had desecrated the most venerable city in the empire.

Alaric was still seeking a home for his people and moved south to the edge of Italy, hoping to cross to AFRICA. A storm wrecked the ships and the king died soon afterward. His brother-in-law ATHAULF succeeded him, leading the Visigoths north, out of Italy and into southern Gaul (GALLIA NARBONENSIS). They had with them a prisoner, Galla PLACIDIA, as a bargaining tool and were soon encamped throughout Narbonensis and Gallia Aquitania. Athaulf then married Galla Placidia but was forced by the patrician CONSTANTIUS to evacuate into northern Spain.

Events took a dramatic turn in 415, when Athaulf was assassinated. A usurper named Singeric aborted the king's plans for better relations with Ravenna and the Western Empire, forcing Galla Placidia to endure humiliations. Singeric was replaced quickly by the far stronger WALLIA, who was king from 415 to 418 and was important in bringing his people into close relations with the Romans. He was elected ostensibly because of his anti-Roman sentiments but reinstated Galla Placidia; and, after his fleet bound for Africa was ruined by a storm, he entered into negotiations with Contantius (soon to be CONSTANTIUS III). According to the agreement, the Visigoths would make war on the VANDALS, Alans, and Suebi in Spain while surrendering Galla. In return, they received corn and large sections of Gaul—Narbonensis and Aquitania—to call their own. Wallia waged cruel war in Spain, virtually annihilating large elements of barbarian tribes, fulfilling his part of the bargain, as his people finally found a homeland in Gaul.

Wallia died in 418, followed on a throne by Theodoric I. Now settled, the Visigoths were able to consolidate and to expand. No opportunity was missed to add pieces of Roman land, although extensive acquisition was always difficult, given the constant movement of other peoples. As federates, the Visigoths had to aid the West, as it was in their own interest to do so. Such was the case in 451, as ATTILA the Hun threatened to wipe out every degree of order in Gaul. Theodoric joined the MAGISTER MILITUM AETIUS and his allies against Attila at the battle of CATALAUNIAN PLAIN. In the fierce fighting, Attila was halted but Theodoric fell in the fray. His son Thorismund screamed for revenge, only to

have Aetius fill his head with fears of losing his crown to scheming siblings. Thorismund rode home. Aetius may have been preserving the Huns to maintain a balance in the barbarian realms, but his warning came true. Thorismund was murdered by his brother, Theodoric II, in 453.

Theodoric helped AVITUS to occupy the Western throne and launched an assault upon the resurgent Suebi in Spain, destroying them at Astorga in 456. Angered by the fall of Avitus in 456, he rampaged through Gaul, besieging Arles. Avitus's successor, Marjorian, sent out his best general, Aegidius, against Theodoric, and the Visigoths were repulsed and forced into new negotiations. Barely 10 years later, in 466, Theodoric was himself assassinated by his brilliant, ambitious brother, EURIC. Eager to enhance the position of the Visigoths, Euric embarked upon a deliberate program of extending Gothic supremacy over all of Gaul. By 475 he was the master of most of Spain, southern Gaul and portions of Gaul's northern lands. The Visigoth kingdom extended from Spain to the Loire and the Rhine. He then took the dramatic step of declaring himself free of federate status to

Rome. Henceforth his possessions were his alone, a development that did much to sap the fleeting strength of the Western Empire. The Visigoths now owned a Gallic kingdom, a bastion of ARIANISM that would survive until 507, when Clovis the Frank would crush Euric's son, Alaric II, at the battle of Vouille. Spain would then be their home until the coming of the Moors early in the eighth century.

Vitalianus, P. Aelius (d. 238 C.E.) *Prefect of the Praetorian Guard in the reign of Maximinus I Thrax (235–238)*
A loyal supporter of the emperor, Vitalianus was left in charge of ROME during the emperor's campaigns. Feared and hated for what the historian Herodian called savage and merciless deeds, the prefect became the first target of removal for the African usurper, GORDIAN I. Assassins were sent to Rome with the task of carrying "important" documents to Vitalianus, pertaining to the emperor. Entering his study early in the morning they found him alone and stabbed him to death. The way was clear for the SENATE to elevate Gordian to the throne.

Vitellius, Aulus (15–69 C.E.) *Emperor from April until December 69 C.E.; one of the four emperors who came to power in the year of civil war*
Vitellius was the son of the powerful Claudian adviser, Lucius VITELLIUS (1), and used his father's position to advance his own career. CONSUL in 48, he had already acquired a loathsome reputation for vice and greed. GAIUS CALIGULA admired his chariot racing, CLAUDIUS his skill in dice and NERO his flattery. From the latter he won a procuratorship in AFRICA (c. 61–62) and then the post of CURATOR AQUARUM. The fame for gluttony and avarice that Vitellius possessed was probably the reason GALBA appointed him in 68 to the powerful office of governor of Germania Inferior. Galba claimed that he had little to fear from a glutton. From the start, however, Vitellius carefully cultivated the favor of the LEGIONS so that on January 2, 69, in conjunction with the plotting of Fabius VALENS and CAECINA ALIENUS, two legates of the Rhine legions, he was proclaimed emperor.

Thus began the march of the legions of Germania Superior and Inferior to ROME. They caused ruin as they advanced but won the first battle of BEDRIACUM in April, defeating the army of OTHO and winning Vitellius the throne. Their candidate, who lingered behind the advance, entered Rome in July. Enacting often thoughtless edicts, Vitellius proceeded to horrify much of the empire with an overly extravagant lifestyle and stupid appointments, such as the new PRAETORIAN GUARD. While the historians, especially TACITUS and SUETONIUS, were harsh and perhaps exaggerated in their coverage of his brief reign, Vitellius certainly did nothing to improve his political situation. He was a failure in terms of defending his throne.

The legions of the East declared for VESPASIAN on July 1, joined by their comrades on the DANUBE in August. Led by Antonius PRIMUS, the Danubian army set out for Italy. In October they won the second battle of Bedriacum. With the Flavians on their way to Rome, Vitellius considered abdication but was blocked by his own followers, who besieged SABINUS, Vespasian's brother, on the Capitol, eventually putting him to death. This act enraged the Flavians, and Rome fell on December 20 after a bitter fight. Vitellius was found in the palace and murdered. His reign would be condemned by Flavian propagandists, but he did initiate several good measures, including the freedom of all persons to express their opinion. These few acts of moderation were not enough to save him from his contemporaries or from the judgement of history.

Vitellius, Lucius (1) (fl. first century C.E.) *Consul in 34, 43, and 47, and a leading adviser to Emperor Claudius*
Lucius was also the father, as well, of Emperor VITELLIUS. Lucius Vitellius was the younger of four brothers, all of whom attained considerable success in the early first century C.E. He became a friend of Claudius but was appointed governor of SYRIA by TIBERIUS in 35 C.E. Although he had earned a bad reputation in ROME, as the legate of Syria he displayed skill in war and in diplomacy. Pontius Pilate was sent to him after massacring the Samaritans, and TIRIDATES was set up (briefly) on the Parthian throne, as a result of Vitellius's actions. After returning to the capital, his name was again dishonored because of his extreme flattery of GAIUS CALIGULA. Vitellius initiated the tradition of treating the deranged ruler as a god. When Claudius came to the throne, the flattery continued, this time directed at the freedmen and wives of the emperor. He kissed MESSALLINA's shoes and prodded the SENATE into approving Claudius's marriage to AGRIPPINA THE YOUNGER. For his services he was made consul, censor, and chief counselor and was left in charge of Rome during Claudius's campaign in Britain. Although aged, he was attacked in 51 as being treasonous, but Agrippina came to his rescue. He died after this affair injured the political future of his family. Sextilia was his wife. Vitellius was given a public funeral and a statue, inscribed with the epitaph: "Steadfastly Loyal to the Emperor."

Vitellius, Lucius (2) (fl. first century C.E.) *Brother of Emperor Vitellius*
He was the son of Lucius VITELLIUS (1), governor of SYRIA, and Sextilia. The historian TACITUS (1) wrote that he suffered from the same vices as his brother but was more active. After receiving the adulation of the SENATE upon his brother's elevation to the throne, he was appointed by Vitellius to command Rome during the civil war with the Flavians. As the enemy legions advanced on the capital, he moved against Tarracina in Latium, storm-ing the city and causing great loss of life. His wife Triaria supposedly put on a sword and helped slaughter the inhabitants. Captured by the Flavians, Lucius tried to negotiate for his life but was executed.

Vitellius, Publius (d. 31 C.E.) *Uncle of Emperor Vitellius and a leading political orator in the reign of Tiberius (14–37 C.E.)*
Vitellius served as an aide to GERMANICUS during the German Campaign (15 C.E.), taking command of two LEGIONS, the II and XIV, and withdrawing them by land from the theater of operations. A friend of Germanicus, he was horrified by the general's suspicious death in 19. Using all of his skills he helped secure the trial and downfall of Gnaeus Calpurnius PISO, the man believed to be Germanicus's murderer. He received a priesthood in 20 for his work but was implicated in the fall of the Prefect SEJANUS in 31 and imprisoned. According to TACITUS (1), he asked for a knife, slit his wrists, and died a short time later. SUETONIUS wrote that his wrists were bandaged, and he survived briefly, dying of illness and despair.

Vitruvius Pollio (fl. early first century C.E.) *Foremost architect of the Augustan Age (27 B.C.E.–14 C.E.)*
The author of the influential treatise *De Architectura* (*On Architecture*), Vitruvius apparently served in the CIVIL WARS, perhaps in the African campaign of 46 B.C.E., and wrote his book at an old age. Although clearly educated and experienced, he had an eccentric style and at times was unable to communicate clearly or managed to do so in a way that did little justice to Latin. *De Architectura*, however, was an important work in the field, in that he examined methods of construction, including private dwellings, aqueducts, and even sundials. He relied heavily upon Greek writers but did cover the training of architects. The entire 10-volume study was dedicated to AUGUSTUS, whom he called Imperator and Caesar. Its date was sometime around 14 B.C.E., for Vitruvius mentioned very few buildings in ROME and no great architectural achievements.

See also ART AND ARCHITECTURE.

Volcae The Volcae Tectosages and the Volcae Arecomici were Celtic tribes residing in GALLIA NARBONENSIS; largely peaceful, they were increasingly Romanized under the influence of the governor of the province. Some of the Volcae Tectosages migrated to GALATIA in Asia Minor.

Vologases I (d. 80 C.E.) *King of Parthia from around 51 to 80 C.E.*
Vologases was the greatest of the five kings who would bear his name, although Parthia was troubled throughout his reign on both its eastern and western borders. He was the son of VONONES II, a one-time monarch of Media-Atropatene. His mother was reportedly a Greek concu-

bine. Vonones was replaced by Vologases in 51, with the consent of his two brothers, TIRIDATES (of ARMENIA) and Pacorus, both of whom expected their own kingdoms. Pacorus was given the ancestral domain of Media, and Tiridates received the often contested realm of Armenia. Parthian armies then swept into Armenia and placed Tiridates in firm control, precipitating over a decade of hostilities with ROME. CORBULO (2) was sent by NERO to the East in 55, and in 58 Tiridates was ousted. Vologases could not exert his full strength during the crisis because of troubles in the East, but by 62, the Roman client TIGRANES V had fallen. Negotiations were favored over battle, despite the Parthian victory over PAETUS. Tiridates journeyed to Rome in 66 and was crowned by Nero. Relative peace followed between Parthia and Rome, especially in the reign of Nero. VESPASIAN had Vologases's backing in 69, and the emperor even pondered sending him troops to aid in the defeat of the barbarian ALANS. Better relations allowed domestic opportunities, as Vologases founded the city of Vologesia as a rival to SELEUCIA. He was followed on the throne by his SON PACORUS II.

Vologases II (d. 147 C.E.) *King of Parthia or possibly a vassal in the Parthian Empire from circa 105 to 147 C.E.*
Vologases was most likely the weaker co-ruler with OROSES for many years, perhaps administering the eastern affairs of Parthia while Oroses suffered humiliating defeats at the hands of TRAJAN. When Vologases finally came to the throne himself, he appointed MITHRIDATES IV to take over his duties in the east. He was succeeded by VOLOGASES III.

Vologases III (d. 192 C.E.) *King of Parthia; the successor to Vologases II and the ruler circa 149 to 192*
His reign was characterized by a renewed struggle with ROME. Around 161–162, Vologases declared war on Rome by placing a client king upon the throne of ARMENIA. Initial brilliant success was gained over the two Roman governors of CAPPADOCIA and SYRIA, but these triumphs proved only the deteriorated condition of the Eastern LEGIONS. Lucius VERUS launched a massive campaign in 163–164, recapturing Armenia and stretching Roman supremacy once more into MESOPOTAMIA, to CTESIPHON itself. Plague broke out in the Roman ranks, causing retreat in 165. Vologases remained in power until his death.

Vologases IV (d. 207 C.E.) *King of Parthia during the troubled period from 192 to 207*
Eager to avenge the Roman defeats inflicted upon his predecessors, but unable to do so, Vologases watched the numerous smaller kingdoms in MESOPOTAMIA, including Adiabene and OSROENE, rise against Roman supremacy. When Emperor Septimius SEVERUS marched into Mesopotamia (c. 197) to subdue the petty domains, cap-

turing CTESIPHON once again, Vologases could not respond, as a short time later the vassal states of his realm erupted. Vologases was succeeded by his son, VOLOGASES V.

Vologases V (d. after 224 C.E.) *King of Parthia and one of the last kings of the Parthian Empire*
He succeeded his father, VOLOGASES IV, around 207 and reigned until deposed by his brother, ARTABANUS V, sometime before 224. Parthia was on the verge of internal collapse. Recognizing his own political weakness, Vologases refused to be drawn into a war with ROME when Emperor CARACALLA made threatening gestures in 214–215. His caution, however, could not prevent a palace coup, for Artabanus desired the throne. Vologases was perhaps allowed to retain a minor post, although he had ceased to exert any influence on the affairs of his realm.

Volturnus One of the incarnations of the river god, TIBER, whose name implied a flowing stream. Volturnus, was held in high esteem, and a *Flamen Volturnalis*, or chief priest, conducted services dedicated to him. The Volturnalia was his festival, held every August 27.

Volusianus, Gaius Vibius Afinius Gallus Veldumnianus (d. 253 C.E.) *Son of Emperor Trebonianus Gallus; named Caesar by his father in 251.*
To cement Gallus's claim to the throne, Volusianus wed the daughter of the deceased Emperor DECIUS, and in 253 Volusianus became Augustus or co-emperor. When AEMILIAN, governor of MOESIA Inferior, revolted and marched on Italy, he convinced the outnumbered troops of Gallus to murder their master. Volusianus perished with his father.

Volusianus, Rufus (fl. early fourth century C.E.) *Probably Prefect of the Praetorian Guard during the reign of Maxentius (306–312)*
Volusianus was noted for his campaign in AFRICA to quell the revolt of DOMITIUS ALEXANDER, the prefect of CARTHAGE. Taking several cohorts of the Praetorian Guard with him, he crushed Alexander and destroyed most of Carthage in 311—for the support rendered by the city to the rebels.

Vonones I (d. 18 C.E.) *King of Parthia*
The Son of King PHRAATES IV and ruler of the Parthian Empire from circa 7 to 12 C.E. Vonones had been one of the children sent to ROME to serve as a hostage of good faith and to prevent his murder at the hands of his own family. As it was, Phraates was assassinated by Phraataces, his adopted son. There followed a period of instability as Phraataces and his successor, ORODES III, were killed. The Parthian nobility then requested that Vonones assume the throne, but from around 7 to 12 C.E. he ruled with such ineptness and foreign manner that a palace coup was

inevitable. Parthian nobles especially resented his Greek habits. With the connivance of the palace, Artabanus, an Arsacid from Media, launched a rebellion (c. 12) that ultimately ousted Vonones, who fled to SYRIA and took refuge in ANTIOCH (1). He lived royally there on the money that he had taken with him and in 16 asked Emperor TIBERIUS to sanction his seizing the vacant throne of ARMENIA as a springboard for regaining Parthia. Tiberius, however, detested him and with Artabanus promising war if Vonones was not restrained, Creticus Silanus, governor of Syria, was ordered to arrest the fallen king. In 18, GERMANICUS, then administering the Eastern provinces, agreed to a request from Artabanus and moved Vonones to Pompeiopolis in CILICIA. Knowing that he probably would not live to see another such move, Vonones bribed his guards and fled to Armenia, where the Roman cavalry caught up with him. An officer named Remmius, charged with his safety, ran him through, a death desired by Parthia and Rome.

See also ARSACID DYNASTY.

Vonones II (d. 51 C.E.) *King of Parthia for only a few months in 51*

Following the demise of King GOTARZES II, the throne of Parthia was vacant, largely because Gotarzes had killed virtually every possible claimant to ensure that no rivals could murder him. Vonones, the head of the vassal state of Media Atropatene, was given the throne by the Parthian nobility but died after a brief time and was succeeded by his son, VOLOGASES I. Two other sons, Pacorus and TIRIDATES, eventually became kings of Media Atropatene and ARMENIA, respectively.

See also ARSACID DYNASTY.

votive coins   Special coins minted to commemorate a vow taken by an emperor on some special occasion, such as a wedding or the Kalends of January, or a vow taken by a ruler who was eager to make a propaganda statement. AUGUSTUS, in 27 B.C.E., promised to bring peace to the entire Roman world within 10 years. In 18 B.C.E., he accepted government over ROME for two five-year periods; in 8 B.C.E. for 10 years more; in 4 C.E. for yet another 10, and in 13 C.E. for one more decade. Other emperors issued votive coins, including Antoninus Pius, MARCUS AURELIUS, COMMODUS, and other emperors in the fourth century C.E.

See also COINAGE.

Vulcan   Also Volcanus, and to the Greeks, Hephaestus; the great fire god of the Romans, whose power was always on display at the volcanos of Etna or VESUVIUS. Where he came from originally was never clear, except that he was ancient, perhaps arriving in Rome through the Etrurians and via the Mediterranean. He was not a Roman original. Later, when Greek influences were keenly felt in the Roman pantheon, Vulcan assumed all of the characteristics of Hephaestus. Thus he was viewed as the mighty smith of the gods, living and working beneath volcanos with his assistants, the Cyclops. According to legend, Romulus introduced Vulcan's worship to Rome. The deity received his own member of the FLAMENS, the *Flamen Volcanalis,* but was viewed as a counterpart to VESTA, the positive force of fire. Vulcan was the destructive side, the one that had to be appeased. His altar, the Volcanal, stood in the FORUM ROMANUM at the base of the Capitol, and a new temple, built around 214 B.C.E., was found in the CAMPUS MARTIUS.

Two festivals were held in his honor, the Festival of the Fishermen, and the Volcanalia. The former was staged in June, involving the offering of fish caught by fishermen as an act of appeasement. The Volcanalia, on August 23, was similar to the ceremony in June but was more state-oriented. Live fish were thrown into Vulcan's fire, again to avoid his wrath. The fish were always caught in the TIBER because the fires were extinguished with water from that river.

See also GODS AND GODDESSES OF ROME.

W

Wallia (d. 418 C.E.) *King of the Visigoths from 415 to 418* Wallia was responsible for their settlement in Roman territory. In September of 415, the Visigoth monarch ATHAULF was stabbed to death and replaced by Singeric, a cruel and brief-reigning usurper. Singeric was also slain, after only a week, and an election was held to find a legitimate successor. The Visigoths chose a little-known warrior, Wallia, who was selected because of his desire to have nothing to do with ROME, ironic given his subsequent actions.

Wallia first restored Galla PLACIDIA, Athaulf's Roman widow, to her rightful position of respect within the Visigoth community, making up for the harsh treatment meted out to her by Singeric. The most pressing problem, however, was securing the site of permanent Visigothic settlement. Spain, their current home, was overcrowded and blockaded by the Roman navy. When ships designed to carry the Visigoths to AFRICA were wrecked in a storm, Wallia looked northward to Gaul and began negotiations with the Roman government, resulting in a treaty in 416 between Wallia and CONSTANTIUS III. The Visigoths pledged to serve as clients or federates of Rome, which meant making war upon the VANDALS, Suebi, and ALANS in Spain. In return the Visigoths received massive amounts of badly needed corn and, ultimately, permission to take up residence in Gallia Aquitania and large sections of GALLIA NARBONENSIS as well. Over the next year, Wallia waged relentless war upon the barbarians in Spain and was so successful that by 418 the Visigoths were able to move into Gaul, according to their agreement with the Romans. This was Wallia's legacy, for he died in 418. He was succeeded by Theodoric I, a grandson of ALARIC.

Wall of Antoninus Also called the Antonine Wall; the second great barrier erected in the second century C.E. by the Romans in the province of Britain. Situated farther north than the Wall of HADRIAN, it stretched some 33 miles from the Firth of Forth to the Firth of Clyde in modern Scotland. The wall was made of turf, resting on a cobbled base, but lacked the sophistication or complexity of Hadrian's creation. The wall was only 14 feet wide, with a rampart and small wooden forts located at intervals along its length. A large ditch was dug in front of it, and a road to the interior of the province lay behind it. Only one road actually went through the wall, and was probably used by the LEGIONS for any advance into wild CALEDONIA beyond. The Antonine Wall was constructed by the II, VI and XX legions, under the supervision of Governor LOLLIUS URBICUS, in 142 C.E., some 20 years after work had begun on Hadrian's defenses. Occupation of the wall continued from 142 to 184–185. From the start, the wall was impractical because of the pressures from the peoples to the north. Any temporary evacuation to suppress provincial uprisings necessitated the virtual destruction of the turf to avoid capture. In 180 C.E., the wall was destroyed by the Caledonians, leading to the arrival of General Ulpius MARCELLUS in Britain. It was ultimately decided that the defense was a luxury the province could not afford. Roman troops were withdrawn, and the wall became a monument to Rome's declining strength.

Wall of Aurelian Large wall erected around Rome between 271 and 275 C.E. to defend the city from attack by barbarians; begun by AURELIAN but finished by PROBUS. The JUTHUNGINE WAR in Italy in 270 had demonstrated the vulnerability of the city, so construction was begun on the wall with the cooperation of the SENATE and the associations of workers and artisans in Rome. Because of the crises and internal threats of the time no LEGIONS were available, so virtually the entire wall was built by civilians. The Aurelian Wall was not strong enough to withstand a protracted siege, as inconceivable as that must have been to the Romans, but was built to repulse a sudden barbarian onslaught. It was 12 miles long, 12 feet wide and 20 feet high, intertwined with other, older structures. It had 18 gates and 381 rectangular towers, interspersed to provide adequate observation. Changes were made by Emperor MAXENTIUS (c. 306), who added to its height by installing galleries. A ditch was also initiated when the *MAGISTER MILITUM*, STILICHO (c. 401–403) made repairs, followed by similar activities by VALENTINIAN III (c. 442) and post-imperial rulers.

Wall of Hadrian   By far the most famous defensive barrier in the Roman Empire; served for nearly 300 years as one of the major dividing lines between Roman Britain and the barbarians of CALEDONIA. With the exception of the WALL OF ANTONINUS, built just to the north, the Wall of Hadrian was unique in all of the imperial provinces. Emperor HADRIAN ordered its construction in 122 C.E., and work was begun by Platorius NEPOS, governor of Britain, who completed it around 126. The wall extended some 73 miles (80 Roman miles) from Wallsend (Segedunum) to Bowness-on-Solway (or the Solway Firth). It was intended not as a formidable bastion but as a base from which Rome's presence could be maintained. Roman troops, mainly auxiliaries, manned its turrets and were to fight any large enemy force in the field while keeping watch on the frontier. In the event of a direct assault, the defenses were only adequate, perhaps explaining the collapse of Roman power in Britain from time to time.

The original plans were probably drawn by Hadrian. The barrier was to extend some 70 miles and be made mostly of stone, 10 feet thick, while the rest would be constructed of turf, 20 feet thick. The turf wall was completed, but the stone sections had only just begun when the plan was extended several miles to ensure that the barrier covered the area from sea to sea. Further, the stone portions were to be only 8 feet thick, instead of 10, and approximately 20 feet in height; the turf portions, 13 feet high. Forts were distanced some 5 miles from each other, with so-called milecastles spread out every Roman mile, connected by watchtowers. Two ditches were dug. The one in front was approximately 30 feet wide and 15 feet deep, designed for defense and V-shaped. The ditch behind the wall has caused considerable archaeological debate. Called the *Vallum* (trench), it was straight and flat-bottomed, 20 feet wide, 10 feet deep, and 10 feet across at the bottom, fortified on both sides by earthen walls (but then filled in). Scholars have speculated that it was once used for some other, nonmilitary purpose.

The Wall of Hadrian in Roman Britannia *(Hulton/ Getty Archive.)*

Until the construction of the Antonine Wall in 142, Hadrian's Wall was the only frontier marker in Britain. With the Antonine Wall in the north, its importance decreased briefly until 180, when the Antonine Wall was destroyed. In 196–197, CLODIUS ALBINUS took with him every available soldier in Britain for his bid for the throne, thus allowing the wall to be ruined. SEPTIMIUS SEVERUS repaired it from 205 to 207. Peace was maintained until the late third century C.E., when the chaotic situation in Roman Britain following the deaths of the usurpers CARAUSIUS and ALLECTUS brought the PICTS down from Caledonia. CONSTANTIUS I launched a restorative campaign but throughout the fourth century barbarian inroads put pressure upon the wall as Roman influence diminished. More invasions poured over the wall, only to be repulsed by Count Flavius THEODOSIUS in 369. The last garrison on the wall withdrew around 400 as the barrier became a monument to Rome's past.

weights and measures

ROMAN WEIGHTS

The Romans used a weight system that had as its basic measurement the *libra* (pound; literally "balance"), derived from the use of scales to calculate the exact weight of an item in question. This was reflected further by the word for weight, *pondus* (from *pendere*, to hang). One Roman pound was calculated at 11.849 ounces (or 335.9 grams). It was also termed an *as*, based in the custom of weighing bars of copper (*asses*) on balance scales.

Each of the bars was one Roman foot long and was divided into 12 inches (*unciae*), which in turn were termed ounces (likewise *unciae*). The lower weights were listed as follows:

libra (or as)	1 pound
deunx	11 ounces
dextans	10 ounces
dodrans	9 ounces
bes	8 ounces
septunx	7 ounces
semis	6 ounces
quincunx	5 ounces
triens	4 ounces
quadrans	3 ounces
sextans	2 ounces
sesuncia	$1^1/_2$ ounces
uncia	1 ounce
semuncia	$^1/_2$ ounce
sicilicus	$^1/_4$ ounce
sextula	$^1/_6$ ounce
semisextula	$^1/_{12}$ ounce
scriptulum	$^1/_{24}$ ounce
siliqua	$^1/_{144}$ ounce

Measurements of weight were made by use of a *libra*. It had a balance arm made of bronze or iron, and sometimes bone, with two bronze scale pans suspended from the balance at equal distances. The item being weighed was placed in one pan, and weights of stone, lead, bronze, or other metals were placed in the second. When the weights balanced on the scale, the weight was determined.

A second scale was the *statera*, a steelyard. The item weighed was suspended from the short end of a balance arm, and a steelyard, or counterbalance, was moved along the long arm until the balance was achieved. The balance arm was also suspended from hooks to permit different weights to be calculated.

ROMAN DISTANCES

The Romans made calculations of distance principally by using parts of the human body. Thus, the standard unit of measurement was the Roman foot (*pes*, pl. *pedes*). The *pes* had a standard length of around 11.65 inches in the early empire and 11.5 inches in the later empire. It was called the *pes monetalis*, from the official measure that was kept in the temple of Juno Moneta at Rome. Variations were found in some of the provinces, such as Gaul and Germania. The *pes* was subdivided into measurements of 12 Roman inches, although a Greek system was also used of 16 fingers (*digiti*). The divisions of the *pes* were:

as	12 unciae (inches)
deunx	11 unciae
dextans	10 unciae

dodrans	9 unciae
bes	8 unciae
septunx	7 unciae
semis	6 unciae
quincunx	5 unciae
triens	4 unciae
quadrans	3 unciae
sextans	2 unciae
uncia	1 uncia
semuncia	$^1/_2$ uncia
sicilicus	$^1/_4$ ounce
sesuncia	1.5 inches
dupondius	$1^1/_2$ feet

The Romans measured distances greater than a foot through the use of the *passus* (pace), which equaled five *pedes* and was roughly equal to the yard. The *passus* was approximately 4 feet 10 inches (1.48 meters). One thousand paces (5,000 *pedes*) were equal to a Roman mile; termed *milia passuum* or *mille passus,* they equaled 4,856 feet, 1,618 yards, or 1,480 meters. For measurements of distances at sea, the Romans used the *passus* again, with 125 paces equaling 1 *stadium.*

To measure distances of land, the Roman adopted an agricultural term, the *actus* (a driving), which reflected the distance that oxen would be driven in a field by a farmer before turning. It equaled 120 Roman feet (116 feet 6 inches; 35.48 meters). The square *actus* (*actus quadratus* or *acnua*) was the equivalent of 14,400 square Roman feet (0.312 acres), with two Roman square *acti* equaling 1 *iugerum,* or 28,800 Roman feet. Where the *actus* was the distance plowed by two oxen in a field before turning, the *iugerum* was the distance that could be plowed in one day. Two *iugera* equaled 1 *heredium* (1.246 acres), a term derived from the designation of inherited land used for one person. One hundred *heredia* equaled 1 *centuria* (approx. 124.6 acres).

women, status of   The status of women in the Roman Empire was characterized by a long period of legal subjugation and family dependence that improved gradually from the time of the late Republic. Throughout the imperial era, women gained for themselves a greater degree of personal, financial, and social freedom.

The subservient condition of women in early Roman society was maintained by the nearly all-encompassing right enjoyed by husbands and fathers within the paterfamilias. According to this dominating patriarchal system, women were excluded from all forms of public life and remained in a kind of legal servitude to their husbands, fathers or nearest male relative. In general terms, the Roman wife in the Republic existed *in manu*, meaning that she was subject to the authority (*manus*) wielded by her husband over her. *Manus* declined in practice toward the end of the Republic and women began to retain definite rights regarding property and status. However, women were still considered under the *patria potestas* of their fathers. The traditional separation of property ownership between husband and wife was altered considerably by the development of the *dos* (dowry), which made it possible for the wife to be returned the dowry at the end of a marriage.

Outside of MARRIAGE, women endured many social, legal, and political handicaps, beginning from birth. A girl born to a Roman was greeted with mourning, and it was not uncommon for a baby girl to be left to die from exposure, much as the Romans commonly put to death any infants with deformities, or severe mental illness. Growing up, a young girl was entirely under the power of her father, remaining so until he was able to find her a suitable husband. In some cases, a patriarch might even sell daughters into slavery. As noted, marriage *in manu* meant a form of legal subjugation to husbands, and the wife held no legal control or claim over her children.

For various reasons, the position of women improved gradually during the centuries of the empire. One cause was the established acceptance of the dowry system, which provided greater independence for women in marriage. Another was the tightening of the laws under Augustus concerning divorce and adultery that discouraged husbands from taking marriage vows too lightly. Finally, women, through determination and patience, created for themselves a better position in the Roman world.

Life for lower-class women was quite different from that of women of the upper classes and nobility. It was marked by a certain stultification, with the days of the peasant women cast in virtual stone from birth to death, in much the same way as that of her male counterpart. Few details are known about the work and habits of lower-class women, but it is acknowledged that they were engaged in various professions, such as textile production. Evidence for the involvement of women in industries is found in the remains of Pompeii. We also know little about the daily lives of middle-class women, although their days were certainly spent in more comfort than those of the poorer women of Rome.

The place of wealthy women in the empire was still handicapped by legal and social restrictions, including the inability to vote or participate openly in government, and by other traditional impediments in marriage and divorce. Nevertheless, women could exercise much independence and also political and cultural influence. Their position was assisted by the largely self-enclosed upper classes. The wealthy intermarried and knew each other, making it easier for women to play a role in political affairs by assisting husbands with their clients and the maintenance of the domus and villa.

Young girls of the upper classes were also frequently given an education equal to boys', and there are a number of examples of women becoming notable writers, poets, and artists. One of the best known was SULPICIA, wife of Calenus, who was praised by the poet MARTIAL.

Equally, Roman history is replete with women who came to wield great power and influence and who were of great importance in the administration of government. Among these remarkable women were EUDOXIA, GALLA PLACIDIA, and Theodora, wife of the sixth-century emperor Justinian.

Suggested Readings: Allason-Jones, Lindsay. *Women in Roman Britain.* London: British Museum Publications, 1989; Balsdon, J. P. V. D. *Roman Women: Their History and Habits.* London: Bodley Head, 1962; Clark, G. *Women in the Ancient World.* Oxford, U.K.: Oxford University Press, 1989; Gardner, Jane F. *Women in Roman Law & Society.* London: Croom Helm, 1986; Hallett, Judith P. *Fathers and Daughters in Roman Society: Women and the Elite Family.* Princeton, N.J.: Princeton University Press, 1984; Holum, Kenneth G. *Theodosian Empresses: Women and Imperial Dominion in Late Antiquity.* Berkeley: University of California Press, 1982; Lightman, Marjorie, and Benjamin Lightman. *Biographical Dictionary of Ancient Greek and Roman Women.* New York: Facts On File, 2000; Peradotto, John, and J. P. Sullivan, eds. *Women in the Ancient World: The Arethusa Papers.* Albany: State University of New York Press, 1984; Rowlandson, Jane, ed. *Women and Society in Greek and Roman Egypt: A Sourcebook.* New York: Cambridge University Press, 1998; Trager, James. *The Women's Chronology: A Year-By-Year Record from Prehistory to the Present.* New York: Henry Holt, 1994.

Worms   Domain ruled by the BURGUNDIANS in Gaul; centered around the city of Worms, on the Rhine between Mainz and Mannheim. The kingdom was founded in 413 C.E. when Emperor HONORIUS allowed Gundohar and his people to settle permanently in imperial territory, with the status of a federate state. Their task was to protect the Rhine frontier from invasion, and they remained faithful. Gundohar reigned until 436, when a Hunnic onslaught overran the Burgundian lands. He and thousands of his men were killed, and the remnants of the Burgundians departed for Savoy, to the south.

writing instruments and materials   As an exceptionally literate and literary people, the Romans relied on a wide variety of writing materials and instruments. There were two chief means of writing: pen and ink on parchment and papyrus or by a stylus on a waxed tablet.

The stylus (pl. styli) was made of bronze, bone, or iron, with a sharpened, pointed end for writing. The other end was flattened to serve as a counter weight, but it had the added practical value of serving to smooth out the excess wax that developed in the process of scratching the waxed tablet. Styli were often decorated. The pen for writing upon parchment of papyrus was a type of pen made of reed or bronze. The tip of the pen had a split nub. Ink was made of a mixture of carbon black, gum, and water. It was held in inkpots made of samian, bronze, and other pottery forms. They were crafted with a hidden lip to prevent easy spills and a small hole in the top where the pen could be dipped with ease.

The two main writing materials were papyrus and vellum. Papyrus was certainly the most common writing material in the ancient world, originating in Egypt and eventually adopted by the Romans around the third century B.C.E. Made from the pith of a water plant that grew along the banks of the Nile, papyrus was sold in rolls of 33 feet. Typical papyrus sheets were about 16 inches wide and 9 inches high.

Vellum (*vellus,* from skin or hide) was made from the skins of cattle, goats, and sheep that was scraped, rubbed with pumice, and then finished with alum. It was later termed *parchment,* from the city of Pergamum, which was the best-known center of vellum manufacturing. Over time, vellum, or parchment, replaced papyrus as the writing material of choice.

To use, the papyrus roll (*volumen*) was unrolled from the right and rolled up from the left. Once the scroll had been used, it was then rewound. Sometimes, the end of the scroll was attached to a wooden roller (*umbilicus*) with knobs. It was customary for the title of a book or document to be placed at the end of the scroll, as this was the part that was least exposed on a regular basis and was most likely to survive the passage of time. Scrolls housed in libraries were organized into pigeon holes and were identified by a hanging label, the *titulus* (pl. *tituli*). Additionally, important scrolls were rendered official by the attachment of imperial or other types of seals. One of the most common ways of protecting seals for perpetuity was to enclose them in seal boxes, normally made of bronze. The box had a hinged lid, and wax was poured into the depression of the box. The wax was then stamped by means of an official seal or by a seal ring.

Along with scrolls, papyrus and parchment were used in book form. Called a codex, it dates from around the first century C.E. and was made from eight folded sheets of papyrus or parchment, creating a "book" of 16 pages. The pages were then stitched together at the spine and bound between wooden boards. Slowly growing into popular usage, the codex replaced the scroll in the fourth century.

Important documents, such as business transactions, were written and preserved on waxed tablets. Normally, such a tablet was a recessed piece of wood filled with beeswax. Each tablet was then bound into a set by leather thongs or rings threaded through hinge holes in the outer edge. Two tablets bound together formed a diptych; three bound tablets formed a triptych, creating four or six pages of writing space. The first or outer page was left unwaxed; pages two and three were waxed; page four was either waxed or plain, and sometimes there was a groove down the middle of the page; page five was waxed and always contained a summary of the information on the other pages; page six was plain. Page four was used for the placement of signatures by witnesses, written either in ink or inscribed in wax. Seal impressions were then added into the groove running the length of the page. Writing was inscribed in the wax by use of a stylus.

Xanthus Ancient, chief city of the province of LYCIA, near the mouth of the XANTHUS RIVER; besieged in 42 B.C.E. by MARCUS BRUTUS, who wished to exact from the Lycians tribute for his war with ANTONY and Octavian (AUGUSTUS). The proud Lycians refused him, killed themselves and burned down the city. Marc Antony subsequently exempted the impoverished Lycians from TAXATION and invited them to rebuild Xanthus. They apparently refused.

Xanthus River The most important river in the province of LYCIA; rose in the Taurus Mountains and cut its way across the country to the south. Because of its size and location, the Xanthus was used as part of the water-borne trade system of ROME.

Xenophon (fl. first century C.E.) *Imperial physician* Xenophon served Emperor CLAUDIUS in the last years of his reign (c. 53–54 C.E.). Xenophon was originally from Cos (Kos), where his family was held in high esteem. As a gift to him in 53, Claudius granted a special IMMUNITAS (tax exemption) to the entire island. TACITUS (1) wrote that Xenophon had been bought by AGRIPPINA and was part of the murder of Claudius in 54. When the poisoned mushrooms failed to bring about the emperor's death, Xenophon was summoned to use a feather dipped in poison to ensure that Claudius died rapidly.

Yazdagird I (d. 420 C.E.) *King of Persia from 399 to 420*
Yazdagird's reign was noted for its improved relations with CONSTANTINOPLE and its easing of Christian persecutions begun under SHAPUR II. Considered powerful, Yazdagird was declared an honorary guardian to the young Emperor THEODOSIUS II in the will of ARCADIUS upon his death in 408. Yazdagird's willingness to protect the dynastic stability of the emperors was taken as a sign of improved relations between ROME and Persia, and in 409 an attempt was made to reestablish trading ties. CHRISTIANITY was allowed to flourish in Persian lands, especially ARMENIA, until the Christian clergy attempted widescale conversions and was suppressed harshly, ending the brief detente in 420. Yazdagird marched off to war but died on the way. His son VARAHRAN V succeeded him.

Yazdagird II (d. 457 C.E.) *King of Persia from 438 to 457*
Yazdagird succeeded VARAHRAN V to the throne. He soon made incursions into the Roman portions of ARMENIA until bought off probably by the *MAGISTER MILITUM*, ASPAR. Henceforth his reign was characterized by chronic troubles in Armenia, where the Christians refused to be converted to Persian Zoroastrianism and fought to the death. These pockets of resistance, however, could not entice CONSTANTINOPLE into widening hostilities, mainly because of the threats from the HUNS in the West. Yazdagird died, probably in the saddle, in 457 and was followed by HORMAZD III.

Z

Zabdas, Septimius (fl. mid-3rd century C.E.) *General in the service of Queen Zenobia of Palmyra; also called Saba or Zaba*

Zabdas led the armies of Palmyrene expansion in 270–271, sweeping into EGYPT and, with the aid of the pro-Palmyrene political faction, annexing the entire province in the name of his queen. Further advances were made throughout the entire East, including SYRIA and ASIA MINOR, until Emperor AURELIAN took to the field in 271. Zabdas focused on ANTIOCH as his strategic base and moved north to the banks of the Orontes where he had his first engagement with the Romans. Zabdas probably had a numerical advantage, especially in cavalry units, his horsemen being strongly armored on huge mounts, but this failed to serve him. Aurelian's infantry allowed the cavalry to charge and then simply rolled up the Palmyrene flank. Defeated but not destroyed, Zabdas retreated to Antioch but had to leave there because of the inhabitants' unrest. Aurelian entered the city and pushed on, following Zabdas's circuitous route to Emesa. Zabdas hoped for Persian aid, which did not materialize, and turned to give battle again. With some 70,000 men at his disposal and the cavalry still large and formidable, Zabdas repeated the tactics of his first encounter with Aurelian, with the same results. The Roman cavalry (mostly Moors and Dalmatians) was routed, but the LEGIONS weathered the charges and then advanced, demolishing the Palmyrene army. The survivors broke and fled to Emesa, while Zenobia retreated to her native city. What became of Zabdas is unknown.

Zanticus (d. after 175 C.E.) *Iazyges leader*
The chief of the IAZYGES tribe who, in 175 C.E., went before Marcus Aurelius and admitted defeat and submission to Rome. The terms of the subsequent treaty with the emperor demanded that all of the Iazyges abandon the Danube region.

See also MARCOMANNIC WARS.

Zealots Name given to a party of Jewish extremists in first century C.E. JUDAEA; they acted as the main organizers of resistance to Roman rule over the Jews. In 6 C.E., the Romans annexed Judaea and installed procurators to administer local government. Inevitably, small pockets of opposition emerged. From 6 to 66 C.E., the Zealots slowly organized themselves, their presence felt by sporadic incidents of unrest or violence. By 66, they were sufficiently manned to spearhead a major Jewish uprising, inducing the Judaean districts to rebel against ROME. JOSEPHUS, in his *Jewish War*, called them the Sicarii (Assassins), clearly depicting them as unrepresentative of the Jewish establishment. They pushed for war and then fought valiantly as the Roman LEGIONS under VESPASIAN and then TITUS reclaimed the country. In JERUSALEM, the Zealots caused dissension and bloodshed by terrorizing the moderates and murdering opponents, thereby inadvertently weakening morale and giving entrance to the unpopular and harsh Idumaeans. They shared in the destruction of Jerusalem in 70 but their cause was not so easily extinguished. At MASADA they fought bravely and survived total extirpation until 132–135, and the revolt of Simon BAR COCHBA.

Zela Town in north-central Turkey, about 75 miles inland from the Black Sea; site of a military engagement fought in May 47 B.C.E. between Julius CAESAR and PHARNACES II, king of the BOSPORUS, resulting in a complete triumph for Caesar. While the Roman world was engulfed by the CIVIL WAR of the FIRST TRIUMVIRATE, Pharnaces II, son of the famed MITHRIDATES the Great (of Pontus), attempted to emulate his father's achievements. He marched on Caesar's legate, Calvinus, in ASIA MINOR, and defeated him at the battle of NICOPOLIS in October 48. Caesar, embroiled in the siege of ALEXANDRIA, was unable to respond, and Pharnaces extended his conquests throughout Pontus and into CAPPADOCIA. By spring of 47, however, Caesar had finished his Egyptian campaign. The Asian monarch greeted the general's arrival on the Pontic borders with a delegation that sued for the retention of all lands taken. Two armies were camped near each other and close to Zela, the site of Mithridates' success in 67 B.C.E. Caesar had no intention of allowing Pharnaces to keep the lands but allowed the Asian to make new offers and counteroffers while he maneuvered the LEGIONS into a position of advantage. Made aware of Caesar's ploy, Pharnaces ordered his chariots and infantry to the attack, surprising the Romans, who did not expect such a foolhardy advance. Chariots armed with scythes tore through the confused Roman cohorts, but were soon rendered ineffective by massed archery and missiles. The legions, inspired by their tactical victory and by their position at the top of a steep hill, moved into action. The battle raged up and down the line, with the VI Legion, on the right, breaking through first. The rout was on, and Pharnaces fled from the field and was murdered a short time later. Caesar named MITHRIDATES OF PERGAMUM the new ruler of Pontus, now a reduced domain, and then headed for ROME. He summed up the defeat of Pharnaces with the famous words, "Veni, vidi, vici"—"I came, I saw, I conquered."

Zeno (d. 34 C.E.) *King of Armenia from 18 to 34 C.E.*

Zeno was the son of POLEMO I, king of PONTUS, and his second wife, Pythodoris, with the support and presence of the Armenian nobility, GERMANICUS crowned Zeno ruler of Armenia in 18 C.E., naming him Artaxias. His accession was greeted with approval, and the Parthians under ARTABANUS III were too distracted by internal strife to oppose anything in the client state. Zeno's reign was the most peaceful in Armenian history. When he died in 34, Artabanus was preparing to move against Roman supremacy in the region.

Zeno (Tarasicodissa) (d. 491 C.E.) *Emperor of the East from 474 to 475 and 476 to 491*

Born in ISAURIA, the wild region between Pisidia and CILICIA in ASIA MINOR, he bore the name Tarasicodissa and served as chieftain of the Isaurians. Emperor LEO I recruited him and his warriors as a military counterbalance to the Germans in the Eastern lands. Tarasicodissa changed his name to Zeno and was granted command of the newly formed (mostly Isaurian) imperial guard, the EXCUBITORS. A gifted and reliable officer, Zeno was given the hand of Leo's daughter, Aelia Ariadne, and the post of MAGISTER MILITUM in THRACE (c. 470). His official task was to repel an invasion of the HUNS, but Leo was developing him as a political weapon against the German *magister militum*, ASPAR.

Internal feuding followed as Aspar tried to have Zeno killed, but he fled to Serdica. Leo, in his absence, was forced to elevate Aspar's son PATRICIUS to the rank of Caesar, and Aspar moved to win the support of the Isaurian contingents. Zeno returned at once from Thrace, and in 471 Aspar and his son Ardaburius were murdered. What part Zeno played in this is unclear, although he profited handsomely from the deaths. By 473, he held a consulship (469) and the office of *magister militum* in the East, where he suppressed the banditry of the Isaurian tribes. Then he became the *magister militum* in CONSTANTINOPLE, where he advised the emperor on all important matters. In October 473, Leo's grandson (by Aelia Ariadne and Zeno) was elevated to Augustus, succeeding to the throne on February 3, 474. He lived only long enough to certify his father's already supreme authority, dying on November 17, 474.

Zeno was now sole master of the East, although considered a usurping outsider by the palace. VERINA, Leo I's widow, headed a conspiracy to remove him in favor of her lover, a secretary known as Patricius, and her accomplices included the Isaurian General Illus and Verina's brother BASILISCUS. Once more Zeno, forewarned, retired to safety, becoming chief of the tribe again in Isauria. Basiliscus betrayed his sister and took power for himself. The people of Constantinople rose up and rejected him, and Zeno returned in August of 476, remaining as emperor until his death in 491.

Meanwhile in the West, Emperor JULIUS NEPOS could not prevent the rise of ROMULUS AUGUSTULUS, son of Nepos's own magister, ORESTES, and fled to DALMATIA to plead his case. He found himself in competition with a delegation sent by the barbarian King ODOACER, who had deposed Romulus Augustulus and now sought recognition of his own control of Italy. Zeno chose a compromise, making Odoacer a patrician and reinstating Nepos. Odoacer agreed, having no intention of keeping his word. He called himself King of Italy until the invasion of the OSTROGOTHS in 489, and the West passed into history. The other major act of Zeno's reign was a peace treaty in 474 with King GEISERIC and the VANDALS that lasted half a century.

Zeno the Stoic (fl. third century B.C.E.) *Philosopher, found of Stoicism*

Zeno's views, crystallized by Chrysippus, had a most profound effect upon subsequent Greek and Roman thinking.

Zenobia (d. after 272 C.E.) *Queen of Palmyra from 266 to 272*

The daughter of Antiochus, she became the wife of ODAE-NATH and aided him in transforming Palmyra into a mighty ally of ROME. He campaigns against PERSIA secured Palmyran protection of PALESTINE, SYRIA, and parts of ASIA MINOR, with the blessing of Emperor GALLIENUS. When Odaenath was murdered sometime in 266 or 267, possibly by the Queen herself, she immediately assumed control of the government, ruling in the name of their son VABALLATH. She set about expanding her court, attracting the finest minds of the time, especially the Neoplatonists and CASSIUS LONGINUS, who urged her defiance of Rome.

When Emperor CLAUDIUS II GOTHICUS died in 270, Zenobia launched a campaign to increase her power. General ZABDAS took command of the Palmyrene army and invaded the provinces of Syria-Palestine, eastern Asia Minor and even into EGYPT. AURELIAN, new to the throne of Rome, was preoccupied with barbarian invasions until the summer of 271, when he marched against the Palmyrenes. Zabdas was defeated at ANTIOCH and Emesa, and the Palmyrene acquisitions in Asia Minor and Syria were lost. Zenobia fled to Palmyra, rejecting Aurelian's offer of peace. She then tried to escape to the Persians but was captured and forced to walk in Aurelian's TRIUMPH in Rome, where she was transported in a golden chair. She lived in Rome and on an estate at TIBUR for the rest of her life, on a state subsidy.

Zenonis (fl. fifth century C.E.) *Augusta in 475–476 and wife of Eastern emperor Basiliscus*

When Zenonis was proclaimed Augusta, she entered a torrid affair with a stunningly handsome courtier named Armatus, trying to conceal the relationship but working to have Armatus promoted to the highest positions in the city. When Basiliscus fell from power, Zenonis and her children were banished with him to Cucusus in CAPPADO-CIA, where they were starved to death.

Zeus   *See* JUPITER.

Zosimus (d. 418 C.E.) *Pope*

A brief reigning pope (417–418 C.E.), remembered for two stinging defeats of his policy. The first came in Gaul where he attempted to aggrandize the Bishopric of ARLES in 417, giving that prelate the right to co-consecrate the other bishops of GALLIA NARBONENSIS. A brief and bitter fight ensued, and other popes ended the special status of Arles. The second failure was in AFRICA, where Zosimus issued a decree in favor of the Pelagians, only to find himself facing St. Augustine, who forced him to recant his decree. He died in 418.

See PAPACY.

Zstommas, Chrysaphius (d. 450 C.E.) *Eunuch*

Highly influential during the reign of Emperor THEODO-SIUS II, Zstommas stirred up trouble between PULCHERIA, Theodosius's sister, and the emperor's wife EUDOCIA and then forced Pulcheria from the palace. Eudocia was exiled in 442 to JERUSALEM, where she lived until her death in 460. Zstommas filled the vacuum caused by the departure of those formidable women, using conciliatory policies and vast amounts of the treasury to buy off the HUNS, who were ravaging ILLYRICUM. His actions naturally brought him many enemies at court, and sometime in 450 Pulcheria returned to her former position, with the help of the army generals. Zstommas fell from power, and during the last months of Theodosius's reign Pulcheria gained complete control. After Theodosius died in July 450, MARCIAN, his successor, began his rule by executing Zstommas.

APPENDIX I

EMPERORS OF THE ROMAN EMPIRE 27 B.C.E.– 476 C.E.

Name	Period	Dynasty
Augustus	27 B.C.E. to 14 C.E.	
Tiberius	14–37 C.E.	
Gaius Caligula	37–41 C.E.	Julio-Claudian Dynasty
Claudius	41–54 C.E.	
Nero	54–68 C.E.	
Galba	69 C.E.	
Otho	69 C.E.	
Vitellius	69 C.E.	
Vespasian	69–79 C.E.	
Titus	79–81 C.E.	
Domitian	81–96 C.E.	Flavian Dynasty
Nerva	96–98 C.E.	
Trajan	98–117 C.E.	
Hadrian	117–138 C.E.	
Antoninus Pius	138–161 C.E.	
Marcus Aurelius	161–180 C.E.	Antonine Dynasty
Lucius Verus	161–169 C.E.	
Commodus	177–192 C.E.	
Pertinax	193 C.E.	
Didius Julianus	193 C.E.	
Septimius Severus	193–211 C.E.	
Clodius Albinus	193–194 C.E.	
Pescennius Niger	193–194 C.E.	
Caracalla	211–217 C.E.	
Geta	211–212 C.E.	Severan Dynasty
Macrinus	217–218 C.E.	
Diadumenianus	218 C.E.	
Elagabalus	218–222 C.E.	
Severus Alexander	222–235 C.E.	
Maximinus	235–238 C.E.	
Gordian I	238 C.E.	
Gordian II	238 C.E.	
Balbinus and Pupienus	238 C.E.	
Gordian III	238–244 C.E.	
Philip the Arab	244–249 C.E.	
Decius	249–251 C.E.	
Trebonianus Gallus	251–253 C.E.	
Aemilian	253 C.E.	
Valerian	253–260 C.E.	
Gallienus	253–268 C.E.	
Postumus	260–268 C.E.	
Claudius II Gothicus	268–270 C.E.	
Quintillus	270 C.E.	
Aurelian	270–275 C.E.	
Tacitus	275–276 C.E.	
Florian	276 C.E.	
Probus	276–282 C.E.	
Carus	282–283 C.E.	
Carinus and Numerian	283–284 C.E.	

Name	Period	Name	Period

Western Empire   *Eastern Empire*

DIOCLETIAN AND FIRST TETRARCHY
284–305 C.E.

Name	Period	Name	Period
Maximian (Augustus)	285–305	Diocletian (Augustus)	284–305
Constantius (Caesar)	293–305	Galerius (Caesar)	293–305

SECOND TETRARCHY

Name	Period	Name	Period
Constantius (Augustus)	305–306	Galerius (Augustus)	305–311
Severus (Caesar)	305–306	Maximin (Caesar)	305–309

COLLAPSE OF TETRARCHY

Name	Period	Name	Period
Severus (Augustus)	306–307	Galerius (Augustus)	305–311
Constantine I (Caesar)	306–308	Maximin (Caesar)	305–308
		Maximin (Augustus)	308–313

MAXENTIUS (USURPER) IN ITALY
306–312

Name	Period	Name	Period
Constantine I (Augustus)	307–337	Licinius (Augustus)	308–324

DOMITIUS ALEXANDER (USURPER) IN AFRICA
308–311

JOINT RULE OF CONSTANTINE I AND LICINIUS 313–324

CONSTANTINE I SOLE RULER
324–337

Name	Period	Name	Period
Constantine II	337–340	Constantius II	337–361
Constans	340–350		
Usurpation of Magnentius	350–353	Gallus Caesar	361–364
Julian Caesar	355–361		
Julian Augustus	360–363		

JULIAN SOLE RULE
361–363

JOVIAN SOLE RULE
363–364

Name	Period	Name	Period
Valentinian	364–375	Valens	364–378
Gratian	375–383	Theodosius I	379–395
Valentinian II	375–392		
Maximus (Usurper)	383–388		
Eugenius (Usurper)	392–394		

THEODOSIUS I SOLE RULER
394–395

Name	Period	Name	Period
Honorius	394–423	Arcadius	395–408
(Stilicho regent)	395–408		
		Theodosius II	408–450
Constantius III	421		
John (Usurper)	423–425		
Valentian III	425–455		
Petronius Maximus	455	Marcian	450–457
Avitus	455–456		
Majorian	457–461	Leo I	457–474
Libius Severus	461–465		
Anthemius	467–472		
Olybrius	472		
Glycerius	473		
		Zeno	474–491
Julius Nepos	473–475		
Romulus Augustulus	475–476		

Appendix II

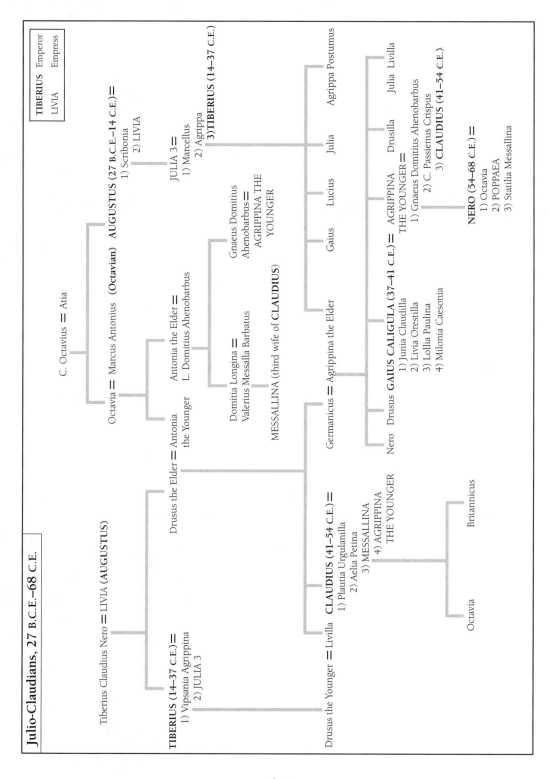

Julio-Claudians, 27 B.C.E.–68 C.E.

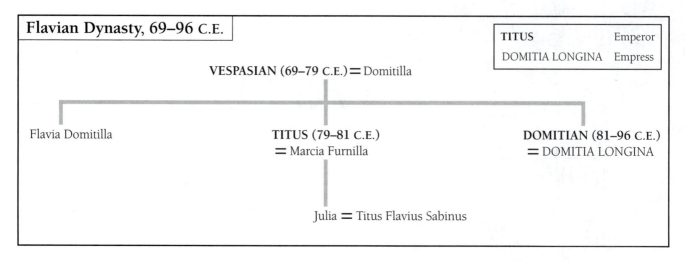

Flavian Dynasty, 69–96 C.E.

| TITUS | Emperor |
| DOMITIA LONGINA | Empress |

VESPASIAN (69–79 C.E.) = Domitilla

Flavia Domitilla

TITUS (79–81 C.E.)
= Marcia Furnilla

DOMITIAN (81–96 C.E.)
= DOMITIA LONGINA

Julia = Titus Flavius Sabinus

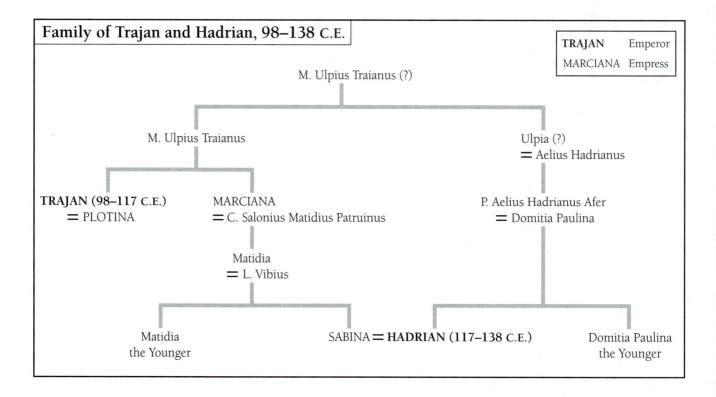

Family of Trajan and Hadrian, 98–138 C.E.

| TRAJAN | Emperor |
| MARCIANA | Empress |

M. Ulpius Traianus (?)

M. Ulpius Traianus

Ulpia (?)
= Aelius Hadrianus

TRAJAN (98–117 C.E.)
= PLOTINA

MARCIANA
= C. Salonius Matidius Patruinus

P. Aelius Hadrianus Afer
= Domitia Paulina

Matidia
= L. Vibius

Matidia
the Younger

SABINA = HADRIAN (117–138 C.E.)

Domitia Paulina
the Younger

Antonine Dynasty, 138–192 C.E.

ANTONINUS	Emperor
LUCILLA	Empress

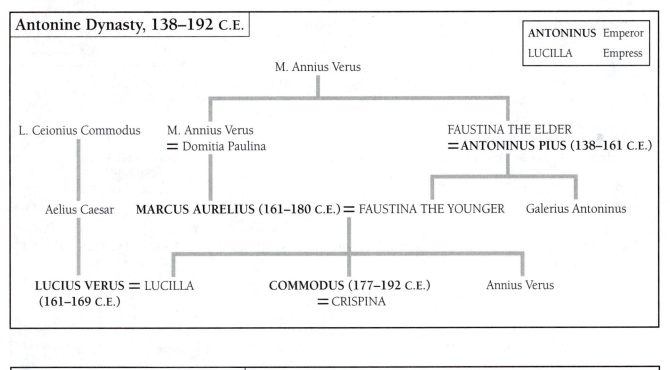

M. Annius Verus

L. Ceionius Commodus — M. Annius Verus = Domitia Paulina — FAUSTINA THE ELDER = **ANTONINUS PIUS (138–161 C.E.)**

Aelius Caesar — **MARCUS AURELIUS (161–180 C.E.)** = FAUSTINA THE YOUNGER — Galerius Antoninus

LUCIUS VERUS = LUCILLA (161–169 C.E.) — **COMMODUS (177–192 C.E.)** = CRISPINA — Annius Verus

Severan Dynasty, 193–235 C.E.

SEVERUS	Emperor
JULIA	Empress

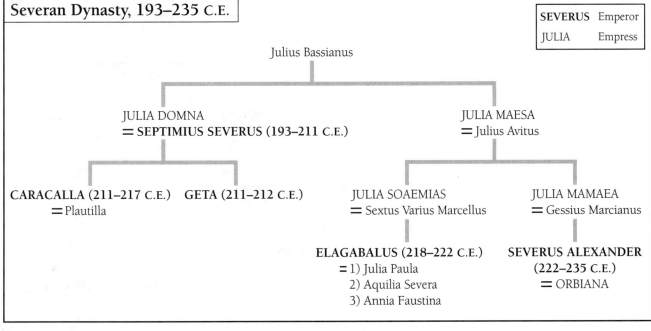

Julius Bassianus

JULIA DOMNA = **SEPTIMIUS SEVERUS (193–211 C.E.)** — JULIA MAESA = Julius Avitus

CARACALLA (211–217 C.E.) = Plautilla — **GETA (211–212 C.E.)** — JULIA SOAEMIAS = Sextus Varius Marcellus — JULIA MAMAEA = Gessius Marcianus

ELAGABALUS (218–222 C.E.) = 1) Julia Paula 2) Aquilia Severa 3) Annia Faustina

SEVERUS ALEXANDER (222–235 C.E.) = ORBIANA

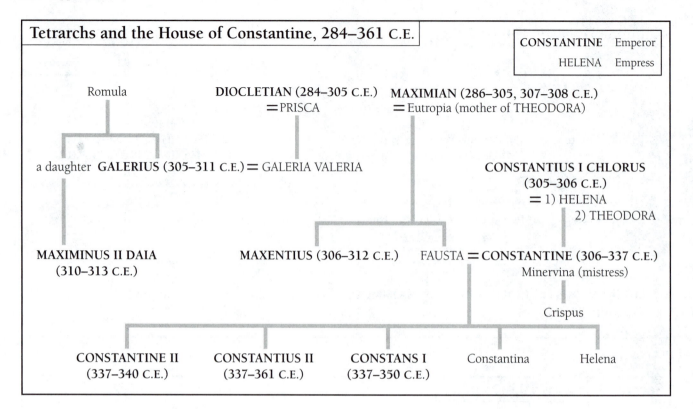

Tetrarchs and the House of Constantine, 284–361 C.E.

CONSTANTINE	Emperor
HELENA	Empress

Romula

DIOCLETIAN (284–305 C.E.)
= PRISCA

MAXIMIAN (286–305, 307–308 C.E.)
= Eutropia (mother of THEODORA)

a daughter   GALERIUS (305–311 C.E.) = GALERIA VALERIA

CONSTANTIUS I CHLORUS
(305–306 C.E.)
= 1) HELENA
2) THEODORA

MAXIMINUS II DAIA
(310–313 C.E.)

MAXENTIUS (306–312 C.E.)

FAUSTA = CONSTANTINE (306–337 C.E.)
Minervina (mistress)

Crispus

CONSTANTINE II
(337–340 C.E.)

CONSTANTIUS II
(337–361 C.E.)

CONSTANS I
(337–350 C.E.)

Constantina

Helena

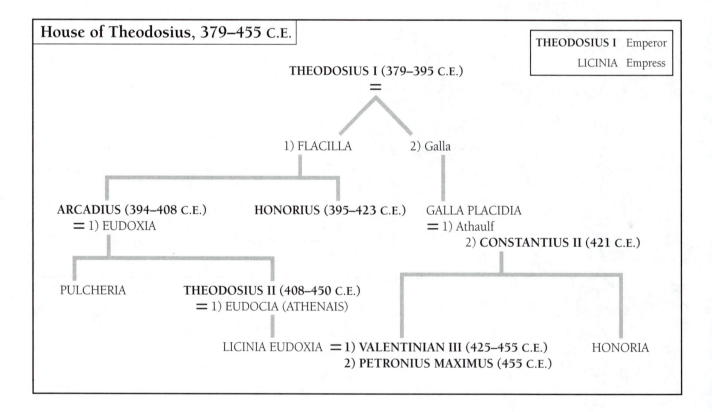

House of Theodosius, 379–455 C.E.

THEODOSIUS I	Emperor
LICINIA	Empress

THEODOSIUS I (379–395 C.E.)
=

1) FLACILLA   2) Galla

ARCADIUS (394–408 C.E.)
= 1) EUDOXIA

HONORIUS (395–423 C.E.)

GALLA PLACIDIA
= 1) Athaulf
2) CONSTANTIUS II (421 C.E.)

PULCHERIA

THEODOSIUS II (408–450 C.E.)
= 1) EUDOCIA (ATHENAIS)

LICINIA EUDOXIA = 1) VALENTINIAN III (425–455 C.E.)
2) PETRONIUS MAXIMUS (455 C.E.)

HONORIA

GLOSSARY

aedile   an administrator in Rome, below the PRAETOR, who was responsible for the care of temples, streets, and the corn supply, and the organization of public games.

annona   the tribute of grain paid by various provinces (in particular Egypt); it was used chiefly to feed the city of Rome and the legions.

as   (pl. asses) the smallest copper coin in use throughout the Roman Empire.

Augusta   the title of honor given to the empress or a woman of great influence in Roman imperial affairs.

Augustus   the title given to the emperor to signify his status above his subjects, used in some eras to signify as well a "senior" emperor.

Caesar   the name used to denote a "junior" emperor in some eras.

censor   an official with considerable power in the Republic, responsible for the citizen rolls and for the rolls of the Senate.

centurion   a Roman military officer; generally, each centurion commanded a century (100 men); each legion was composed of 60 centuries, when at full strength.

colonus   a tenant farmer in the empire who worked on an imperial estate; also the name given to someone operating a mine on a government contract.

comes   a title common in the Empire, meaning a count. Versions of the rank included *comes domesticorum* (count of the *domestici* or bodyguards) and *comes sacra largitionum* (a count in charge of the imperial finances).

consul   the supreme office during the Republic; remained honorific but of reduced power during the imperial era. Consuls wielded the executive authority in government that had been taken from the ancient kings.

cursus honorum   the process of bureaucratic promotions by which a magistrate of Rome rose in political power; the traditional sequence was quaestor, aedile, praetor, consul.

denarius   a Roman silver coin; it was worth approximately four sesterces.

dictator   a magistrate granted extraordinary supreme authority during a time of crisis or need, normally for a period of only six months.

drachma   the chief silver coin in the Greek monetary system; it remained in use in the Greek-speaking provinces of the empire and was approximately worth one denarius.

Equites   the Equestrian class of Rome. Originally referring to members of the cavalry, later the property-holding aristocracy, below the rank of senator.

fasces   a bundle of rods with an ax protruding from the upper end; it was carried by lictors before magistrates wielding the *imperium* as a symbol of their power.

imperator   an honorific title given to an emperor or to a victorious general.

imperium   the executive authority wielded by the emperors and by other magistrates, such as consuls or praetors.

legate   an officer who fulfilled a number of duties for the emperor or the Senate, either military or political in nature.

lictor   a minor official appointed to carry the fasces before a magistrate wielding the *imperium*.

magister militum   (master of the soldiers) the top-ranking commanders during the period of the late empire (fourth–fifth centuries C.E.); originating in the fourth-century creation of the titles *magister equitum* (master of the cavalry) and *magister peditum* (master of the infantry).

magister officiorum   the magistrate in charge of correspondence, petitions, and other areas for the imperial government of Rome.

notarii   the imperial service of notaries or secretaries, most active in the late empire.

Patricians   the hereditary nobility of Rome.

Plebeians   the general, nonaristocratic population of Rome, sometimes shortened to plebs.

Pontifex Maximus   the "supreme pontiff," the title of the head of the college of pontiffs and other priests in charge of the imperial cult of state; it was originally held by the emperor but was later granted to the pope.

praetor   a magistrate with legal and judicial powers, below a consul.

prefect of the Praetorian Guard   also Praetorian prefect; originally the commander of the Praetorian Guard and later a leading figure in the imperial government.

princeps   the term used to designate an emperor or politician as "First Statesman," an honorific title. *Princeps senatus* designated the most senior or honored member of the Roman Senate.

proconsul   the governor of a province during the Republic and the governor of a senatorial province during the imperial era.

publican   the term used for the tax collectors of the empire.

quaestor   the lowest-ranking magistracy in Rome, normally connected to finances.

Quirites   the broad term for Roman citizens.

sestertius   (pl. *sesterces*) a Roman coin with a value equal to one-quarter of a denarius and four asses.

tribune   a powerful magistracy in Rome and in the legions. A tribune of the plebs (*tribuni plebis*) protected the interests of the plebeians while the military tribune (*tribuni militum*) held administrative posts in the legions.

triumph   the procession made a general celebrating a major victory on behalf of the empire; the procession was made from the Campus Martius to the Capitol.

triumvirate   A tripartite leadership. Two triumvirates during the Late Republic wielded immense power and influence.

vir clarissimus   a title of honor meaning "most illustrious man" that was used for member of the Senate.

vir egregius   a title of honor meaning "distinguished man" that was used by members of the Equestrian class.

vir eminens   also *eminentissimus,* a title of honor meaning "prominent" or "most prominent"; it was granted as the highest title borne by public officials belonging to the Equestrian class.

vir perfectissimus   a title of honor meaning "most excellent man" that was used for official of high rank among the Equestrian class.

SUGGESTED READINGS

SELECTED PRIMARY SOURCES

The following are selected primary sources that may be of value to readers. The list is not comprehensive; rather, it seeks to offer a sampling of Roman writers readily available in translation for general readers.

Aili, Hans. *The Prose Rhythm of Sallust and Livy.* Stockholm: Almqvist & Wiksell International, 1979.

Anthologia Latina. Stuttgart, Ger.: Tuebner, 1982.

Barnes, Timothy David. *The Sources of the Historia Augusta.* Brussels: Latomus, 1978.

Benson, Thomas, W., and Michael H. Prosser, eds. *Readings in Classical Rhetoric.* Davis, Calif.: Hermagoras, 1988.

Cicero, Marcus Tullius. *Selected Political Speeches.* New York: Penguin, 1969.

Corpus Inscriptionum Latinarum. Edited by Theodor Mommsen. 16 vols. Berlin: Walter De Gruyter, 1873.

Courtney, E. *The Fragmentary Latin Poets.* Oxford, U.K.: Clarendon Press, 1993.

———. *Musa Lapidaria: A Selection of Latin Verse Inscriptions.* Atlanta, Ga.: Scholars Press, 1995.

Deeds of Famous Men (De viris illustribus). Translated and edited by Walter K. Sherwin, Jr. Norman, University of Oklahoma Press, 1973.

Deroux, Carl, ed. *Studies in Latin Literature and Roman History.* Brussels: Latomus, 1979.

Dio Cassius. *The Roman History: The Reign of Augustus.* London: Penguin, 1987.

———. *Roman History.* Books LXI–LXX. Cambridge: Harvard, 1985.

A Garden of Roman Verse. Los Angeles: J. Paul Getty Museum, c1998.

Grant, Michael, ed. *Readings in the Classical Historians.* New York: Scribner's, 1992.

Horace. *Carpe diem: Horace Odes I.* Translated by David West. Oxford, U.K.: Clarendon Press, 1995.

———. *The Complete Odes and Epodes.* Translated by David West. New York: Oxford University Press, 1997.

Julius Caesar. *The Civil War.* New York: Penguin, 1967.

———. *The Conquest of Gaul.* New York: Penguin, 1982.

Kennedy, Eberhard, ed. *Roman Poetry & Prose. Selections from Caesar, Virgil, Livy and Ovid.* Cambridge, U.K.: University Press, 1959.

Kraus, Christina Shuttleworth. *Latin Historians.* Oxford, U.K.: Oxford University Press, 1997.

Laistner, Max L. W. *The Greater Roman Historians.* Berkeley: University of California Press, 1977.

Latin Historians. Translated by C. S. Kraus and A. J. Woodman. Oxford, U.K.: Oxford University Press, 1997.

Lockwood, D. P. *A Survey of Classical Roman Literature.* Chicago: University of Chicago Press, 1982.

Lucan. *Pharsalia.* Translated by Jane Wilson Joyce. Ithaca, N.Y.: Cornell University Press, 1993.

———. *Civil War.* Translated by Susan H. Braund. Oxford, U.K.: Oxford University Press, 1992.

Martial. *The Epigrams.* Selected and translated by James Michie. Harmondsworth, U.K.: Penguin Books, 1978.

Murphy, James J., ed. *Quintilian on the Teaching of Speaking and Writing: Translations from Books One, Two, and Ten of the Institutio Oratoria.* Carbondale: Southern Illinois University Press, 1987.

Newman, John K. *Augustus and the New Poetry.* Brussels: Latomus, 1967.

Ovid. *Ovid in Love: Ovid's Amores.* Translated by Guy Lee. New York: St. Martin's Press, 2000.

———. *Fasti.* Book IV. Edited by Elaine Fantham. Cambridge, U.K.: Cambridge University Press, 1998.

———. *The Art of Love, and Other Poems.* Translated by J. H. Mozley. Cambridge, Mass.: Harvard University Press, 1979.

———. *Metamorphoses.* Book XIII. Translated by Neil Hopkinson. New York: Cambridge University Press, 2000.

———. *Ovid in English.* Edited by Christopher Martin. New York: Penguin Books, 1998.

———. *Ovid in Six Volumes.* Translated by Grant Showerman. Cambridge, Mass.: Harvard University Press, 1986–1988.

———. *The Love Poems.* Translated by A. D. Melville. Oxford, U.K.: Oxford University Press, 1998.

The Oxford Book of Latin Verse, From the Earliest Fragments to the End of the Fifth Century A.D. Oxford, U.K.: The Clarendon Press, 1968.

The Penguin Book of Latin Verse. Baltimore: Penguin Books, 1962.

Petronius Arbiter. *Petronius.* Translated by Michael Heseltine. Cambridge, Mass.: Harvard University Press, 1969.

Pliny the Elder. *Natural History: A Selection.* Translated by John F. Healy. London: Penguin, 1991.

Pliny the Younger. *Correspondence with Trajan from Bythinia.* (Epistles X). Translated by Wynne Williams. Warminster, U.K.: Aris & Phillips, 1990.

———. *The Letters of Pliny: a Historical and Social Commentary.* Edited by A. N. Sherwin-White. Oxford, U.K.: Clarendon Press, 1985.

Plutarch. *Life of Antony*. New York: Cambridge University Press, 1988.

Polybius. *The Histories*. Translated by W. R. Paton. Cambridge, Mass.: Harvard University Press, 1922–1927.

Ribaldry of Ancient Rome; An Intimate Portrait of Romans in Love. New York: F. Ungar Pub. Co., 1965.

Sacks, Kenneth. *Polybius on the Writing of History*. Berkeley: University of California Press, 1981.

Sallust. *The Histories*. Translated by Patrick McGushin. Oxford, U.K.: Oxford University Press, 1992.

———. *Catiline*. Edited by A. T. Davis. Bristol, U.K.: Bristol Classical Press, 1987.

Seneca. *De Clementia*. Edited by F. Prechac. Paris: Les Belles Lettres, 1961.

———. *Epistulae*. Edited by L. D. Reynolds. Oxford: Clarendon Press, 1965.

———. *17 Letters*. Translated by C. D. N. Costa. Warminster, U.K.: Aris & Phillips, 1988.

———. *Apocolocyntosis*. Bryn Mawr, Pa.: Thomas Library, Bryn Mawr College, 1988.

———. *Hercules: The Madness of Hercules*. Translated by Ranjit Bolt. London: Oberon, 1999.

———. *Medea*. Translated by Frederick Ahl. Ithaca, N.Y.: Cornell University Press, 1986.

———. *Moral and Political Essays*. Translated by John M. Cooper and J. F. Procopé. Cambridge, Mass.: Cambridge University Press, 1995.

———. *Phaedra*. Edited by Michael Coffey and Roland Mayer. New York: Cambridge University Press, 1990.

——— *The Tragedies*. Translated by David R. Slavitt. Baltimore: Johns Hopkins University Press, 1992–1995.

———. *Seneca's Phoenissae: Introduction and Commentary*. Edited by Marica Frank. New York: E. J. Brill, 1995.

Share, Don, ed. *Seneca in English*. New York: Penguin Books, 1998.

Silver Latin Epic: A Selection from Lucan, Valerius Flaccus, Silius Italicus & Statius. Bristol: Bristol Classical Press, 1985.

Suetonius *The Twelve Caesars*. Translated and with an introduction by Michael Grant. New York: Penguin, 1979.

Sussman, Lewis A. *The Major Declamations Ascribed to Quintilian: A Translation*. Frankfurt am Main: Verlag P. Lang, 1987.

Tacitus, Cornelius. *Empire and Emperors: Selections from Tacitus' Annals*. Translated by Graham Tingay. New York: Cambridge University Press, 1983.

———. *The Annals of Imperial Rome*. Translated and with an introduction by Michael Grant. New York: Penguin, 1964.

———. *The Histories*. Translated by Clifford H. Moore; *The Annals*. Translated by John Jackson. Cambridge, Mass.: Harvard University Press, 1925–1937.

———. *Annales*. Edited by Henry Furneaux. Oxford, U.K.: Clarendon Press, 1965.

———. *De Vita Agricolae*. Edited by R. M. Ogilvie. Oxford, U.K.: Clarendon Press, 1967.

———. *Germania*. Edited by D. R. Stuart. New York: Macmillan Co., 1916.

———. *Historiae*. Edited by H. Heubner. Stuttgart: B. G. Teubner, 1978.

———. *The Histories*. New York: Penguin, 1989.

Taylor, A. B., ed. *Shakespeare's Ovid: The Metamorphoses in the Plays and Poems*. Cambridge: Cambridge University Press, 2001.

Velleius Paterculus. *The Caesarian and Augustan Narrative*. Edited by A. J. Woodman. New York: Cambridge University Press, 1983.

———. *The Tiberian Narrative*. Edited by A. J. Woodman. New York: Cambridge University Press, 1977.

Virgil. *The Aeneid*. Translated by Robert Fitzgerald. New York: Vintage Books, 1990.

———. *Eclogues, Georgics, Aeneid I-VI*. Translated by G. P. Goold and Henry Fairclough. Cambridge, Mass.: Loeb Classical Library, 63, Harvard University Press, 1999.

Walbank, F. W. *Selected Papers: Studies in Greek and Roman History and Historiography*. New York: Cambridge University Press, 1985.

Woodman, A. J., ed. *Velleius Paterculus. The Tiberian Narrative*. New York: Cambridge University Press, 1977.

SELECTED SECONDARY SOURCES

The following is a suggested reading list of works in the English language for the general reader. The list is intended to provide the student or reader with readily available material for further reading or study. For suggested readings in specific topics beyond general histories and surveys, readers are encouraged to consult individual entries (e.g., ART AND ARCHITECTURE, LITERATURE, PAGANISM, and LEGIONS). The list is divided into general histories and references, the early Roman Empire, the late Roman Empire, and the Germanic invasions.

General Histories and References

Adkins, Lesley, and Roy Adkins. *Handbook to Life in Ancient Rome*. New York: Facts On File, 1994.

Boardman, J., Griffin, J., and Murray, O. *The Roman World*. Oxford, U.K.: Oxford University Press, 1986.

Brauer, George C. *The Age of the Soldier Emperors: Imperial Rome, A.D. 244–284*. Park Ridge, N.J.: Noyes Press, 1985.

The Cambridge Ancient History. Vols. 9, 10, 11, 12. New York: Cambridge University Press, 1929–1939.

The Cambridge Medieval History. Vol. 1. New York: Cambridge University Press, 1936–1949.

Christ, Karl. *The Romans*. Berkeley and Los Angeles: University of California Press, 1984.

Clare, John D., ed. *Classical Rome*. San Diego, Calif.: Gulliver Books, 1993.

Cornell, Tim, and John Matthews. *Atlas of the Roman World*. New York: Facts On File Publications, 1982.

Grant, Michael. *The Founders of the Western World: A History of Greece and Rome*. New York: Scribner, 1991.

————. *History of Rome.* London: Weidenfeld and Nicolson, c. 1978.

————. *The Roman Emperors: A Bbiographical Guide to the Rulers of Imperial Rome, 31 BC–AD 476.* New York: Scribner, 1985.

Hammond, Nicholas G. L., ed. *Atlas of the Greek and Roman World in Antiquity.* Park Ridge, N.J.: Noyes Press, 1981.

James, Simon. *Ancient Rome.* New York: Knopf, 1990.

Lewis, Naphtali, and Meyer Reinhold, eds. *Roman Civilization, Selected Readings,* Vol. 2, *The Empire.* New York: Columbia University Press, 1990.

Nicol, D. M. *A Biographical Dictionary of the Byzantine Empire.* London: Seaby, 1991.

Oxford Classical Dictionary. Edited by N. G. L. Hammond and H. H. Scullard. Oxford, U.K.: Oxford University Press, 1970.

Randsborg, Klavs. *The First Millennium A.D. in Europe and the Mediterranean.* Cambridge, U.K.: Cambridge University Press, 1990.

Ridley, Ronald T. *History of Rome: A Documented Analysis.* Rome: l'Erma di Bretschneider, 1987.

Schutz, Herbert. *The Romans in Central Europe.* New Haven, Conn.: Yale University Press, 1985.

Starr, Chester G. *The Beginnings of Imperial Rome: Rome in the Mid-Republic.* Ann Arbor: University of Michigan Press, 1980.

Starr, Chester G. *The Roman Empire, 27 B.C.–A.D. 476: A Study in Survival.* New York: Oxford University Press, 1982.

Wacher, J. S. *The Roman Empire.* London; Dent, 1987.

Wells, Colin M. *The Roman Empire.* Stanford: Stanford University Press, 1984.

The Early Roman Empire

Baker, G. P. *Augustus.* New York: Cooper Square Press, 2000.

Barrett, Anthony. *Caligula: The Corruption of Power.* London: Batsford, 1989.

Beard, Mary. *Rome in the Late Republic.* Ithaca, New York: Cornell University Press, 1985.

Bradford, Ernle. *Julius Caesar: The Pursuit of Power.* London: H. Hamilton, 1984.

Braund, David. *Augustus to Nero: A Sourcebook on Roman History 31 BC–AD 68.* London: Croom Helm, c. 1985.

Charles-Picard, Gilbert. *Augustus and Nero.* Translated by Len Ortzen. New York: Thomas Y. Crowell, 1968.

Dodge, Theodore. *Caesar: A History of the Art of War Among the Romans Down to the End of the Roman Empire, With a Detailed Account of the Campaigns of Gaius Julius Caesar.* New York: Da Capo Press, 1997.

The Early Principate: Augustus to Trajan. Oxford, U.K.: Clarendon Press, 1982.

Ferrill, Arthur. *Caligula: Emperor of Rome.* New York: Thames and Hudson, 1991.

Garnsey, Peter. *The Early Principate: Augustus to Trajan.* Oxford: Published for the Classical Association, at the Clarendon Press, 1982.

Gelzer, Matthias, Needham, Peter, trans. *Caesar: Politician and Statesman.* Cambridge, Mass.: Harvard University Press, 1985.

Griffin, Miriam T. *Nero: the End of a Dynasty.* New Haven, Conn. Yale University Press, 1985.

Gurval, Robert. *Actium and Augustus: The Politics and Emotions of Civil War.* Ann Arbor: University of Michigan Press, 1998.

Holland, Richard. *Nero: The Man Behind the Myth.* Stroud: Sutton, 2000.

Hurley, Donna W. *An Historical and Historiographical Commentary on Suetonius' Life of C. Caligula.* Atlanta, Ga.: Scholars Press, 1993.

Levick, Barbara. *Claudius.* New Haven, Conn.: Yale University Press, 1990.

Meier, Christian. *Caesar.* New York: HarperCollins, 1997.

Millar, Fergus, and Erich Segal, eds. *Caesar Augustus: Seven Aspects.* New York: Clarendon Press, 1984.

The Power of Images in the Age of Augustus. Translated by Alan Shapiro. Ann Arbor: University of Michigan Press, 1988.

Raaflaub, Kurt A., and Mark Toher, eds. *Between Republic and Empire: Interpretations of Augustus and His Principate.* Berkeley: University of California Press, 1990.

Shotter, David. *Nero.* London: Routledge, 1997.

Southern, Pat. *Augustus.* New York: Routledge, 1998.

Velleius Paterculus. *The Caesarian and Augustan Narrative.* Edited by A. J. Woodman. New York: Cambridge University Press, 1983.

The Later Roman Empire

Ammianus Marcellinus. *The Later Roman Empire (A.D. 354–378).* Translated by Walter Hamilton. New York: Penguin, 1986.

Athanassiadi-Fowden, Polymnia. *Julian and Hellenism: An Intellectual Biography.* Oxford, U.K.: Clarendon Press, 1981.

Baldwin, Barry. *Studies on Late Roman and Byzantine History, Literature, and Language.* Amsterdam: J. C. Gieben, 1984.

Barnes, Timothy D. *Constantine and Eusebius.* Cambridge, Mass.: Harvard University Press, 1981.

Carson, R. A. G., P. V. Hill, and J. P. C. Kent. *Late Roman Bronze Coinage.* New York: Sanford J. Durst, 1989.

Croke, Brian. *Religious Conflict in Fourth-Century Rome: a Documentary Study.* Sydney: Sydney University Press, 1982.

Drake, Harold A. *In Praise of Constantine: A Historical Study and New Translation of Eusebius' Tricennial Oration.* Berkeley: University of California Press, 1976.

Ferrill, Arther. *The Fall of the Roman Empire.* New York: Thames and Hudson, 1996.

Goffart, Walter A. *Rome's Fall and After.* London: Hambledon Press, 1989.

Gossman, Lionel. *The Empire Unpossess'd: an Essay on Gibbon's Decline and Fall.* New York: Cambridge University Press, 1981.

Johnson, Stephen. *Late Roman Fortifications.* London: B. T. Batsford, 1983.

Kaster, Robert A. *Guardians of Language: the Grammarian and Society in Late Antiquity.* Berkeley: University of California Press, 1988.

Macdowall, Simon, and Gerry Embleton. *Late Roman Infantryman 236–565 AD.* London: Osprey Publishing Ltd., 1994.

Nicolle, David and Angus McBride. *Romano–Byzantine Armies 4th–9th Centuries.* London: Osprey, 1992.

O'Flynn, John M. *Generalissimos of the Western Roman Empire.* Edmonton, Alta., Canada: University of Alberta Press, 1983.

Pelikan, Jaroslav J. *The Excellent Empire: The Fall of Rome and the Triumph of the Church.* San Francisco: Harper & Row, 1987.

Rollins, Alden M. *The Fall of Rome: A Reference Guide.* Jefferson, N.C.: McFarland, 1983.

Williams, Stephen. *Diocletian and the Roman Recovery.* London: B. T. Batsford, 1985.

Zosimus. *New History.* Translated by Ronald T. Ridley. Canberra; Australian Association for Byzantine Studies, 1982.

The Germanic Invasions

Cunliffe, Barry. *Greeks, Romans and Barbarians: Spheres of Interaction.* London; Batsford, 1988.

Goffart, Walter A. *Barbarians and Romans, A.D. 418–584: The Techniques of Accommodation.* Princeton, N.J.: Princeton University Press, 1980.

Grant, Michael. *Dawn of the Middle Ages.* New York: Bonanza Books, 1981.

Macdowall, Simon and Angus McBride *Germanic Warrior 236–568 AD.* London: Osprey, 1996.

Randers-Pehrson, Justine D. *Barbarians and Romans: The Birth Struggle of Europe, A.D. 400–700.* Norman: University of Oklahoma Press, 1983.

Thompson, E. A. *Romans and Barbarians: the Decline of the Western Empire.* Madison: University of Wisconsin Press, 1982.

Wolfram, Herwig. *The Roman Empire and Its Germanic Peoples.* Berkeley: University of California Press, 1990.

INDEX

Boldface page numbers indicate main headings. *Italic* page numbers indicate illustrations.

A

Abdagaeses **1**, 543
ab epistulis 199
Ablabius, Flavius **1**
ab ovo usque ad mala 216
Ab urbe conditi (Livy) 327
Acacius of Constantinople **1**
Academy **1–2**, 22, 428
accensi 28
Accius, Lucius **2**
acclamatio **2**
acetum 216
Achaea **2**, 53, 63
Achillas **2**, 15, 42
Achilleid (Statius) 514
Achilleus **2**
acnua 593
Acron, Helenius **3**
Acropolis 54
acta **3**
acta diurna **3**
acta Senatus **3**, 55
Acte, Claudia **3**, 11, 388, 397
Actium **3–4**, 10, 26, 27, 44, 58, 92, 127, 191, 252, 312, 313
actors 26, 331, 332, 373, 413, 461, 520, 531
Acts of the Pagan Martyrs **4**
actus 593
actus quadratus 593
adaeratio **4**
Ad dictum (Ulpian) 561
ad epistulis 198
Ad Eunapium (Oribasius) 400
Adiutrix (legion) 311
adlectio **4**, 495
Ad martyres (Tertullian) 528
Ad nationes (Tertullian) 528
adoptio **4**
adoptiominus plena **4**
adoption **4**
Ad Quirinam (Cyprian) 162
Adrianople **4–5**
   Constantine and Licinius at 4–5, 142, 143, 158, 321
   Valens and Goths at 5, 36, 168, 220, 247, 402, 471
Adriaticum Mare **5**
adrogatio **5**
Ad Sabinum (Sabinus) 483
Ad Sabinum (Ulpian) 561
Ad Scapulam (Tertullian) 528
Aduatuca **5**, 189, 232, 529
adultery 60, 318, 353

Adventus, Marcus Oclatinus **5–6**, 338
Adversus Marcionem (Tertullian) 528
Adversus Nationes (Arnobius) 325
Advice on Public Life (Plutarch) 437
advocatus **6**, 8, 91, 97
Aedesius **6**, 116, 259
aedile **6**, 7, 19, 475, 582
Aedui **6**, 37, 57, 63, 104, 228, 340, 484, 498
Aegidius **6**
Aelian (Claudius Aelianus) **7**
Aelianus, Casperius **7**, 388
Aelius Caesar, Lucius **7**, 24, 251, 349
Aemilian **7**, 51, 566
Aemilianus, Asellius 164, 422
Aeneid (Virgil) 323, 585–586
aerarium **7**, 211, 495
aerarium militare **7**, 60, 309
Aetius, Flavius **7–8**
   and Chlodius 219
   and Felix, Flavius Constantius 209
   and Heracleus 255
   and Huns 7–8, 54, 102, 342, 587
   and Majorian 343
   and Petronius Maximus 8
   and Placidia, Galla 434, 565
   and Valentinian III 8, 565
Afer, Gnaeus Domitius **8**, 231, 460
Afranius, Lucius **8**, 122, 269–270
Africa (province) **8–9**, 122, 159, 207, 224, 306
Africa Nova 8, **9**
African War (Caesar) 262
Africa Proconsularis 8, **9**, 97
Africa Vetus 8, **9**
Against the Christians (Porphyry) 444
agentes in rebus 466–467
Ager Helvetiorum See Helvetia
ager publicus 207, 301
Agricola (Tacitus) 259
Agricola, Gnaeus Julius **9**, 78, 79, 189
Agricultura, De (Cato) 207, 582
agriculture *See* farming
Agrippa I, Marcus Julius **9**, 75, 187, 228, 257, 281, 285, 288
Agrippa II, Marcus Julius **9**, 75, 211, 228, 235, 283
Agrippa, Marcus Vipsanius **9–10**
   at Actium 3, 10
   and architecture 10, 43, 71, 92, 410, 475
   and augurs 56
   and Augustus 3, 10, 58, 60

   and Baalbek 65
   and Chersonese 108
   and Cologne 134
   and Gallia 228
   harpax developed by 252, 382, 504
   and Hispania 262
   and literature 10, 323
   and Lucius 10
   and Pompey, Sextus 10, 58, 123
   sons of 10, 86, 88
   wife of 10, 289–290
Agrippa Postumus, Marcus Vipsanius **10**, 60–61, 326
Agrippina (Vipsania Agrippina) **10**, 50, 539
Agrippina the Elder **10–11**, *11*
   and Drusus 11
   and Gaius Caligula 11, 225
   and Germanicus 10–11, 241
   and Livia 10–11, 326
   and Piso, Gnaeus Calpurnius 432
   and Plancina, Munatia 434
   and Tiberius 10–11, 50, 460
Agrippina the Younger (Julia Agrippina) **11–12**
   and Anicetus 12, 19
   and Britannicus 11, 81
   and Burrus, Sextus Afranius 11, 84
   and Claudius 11, 56, 125, 328, 331, 381
   and Domitia 180
   and Domitius Ahenobarbus, Gnaeus 11, 183
   and Lollia Paulina 328, 381
   and Lucusta 331
   and Nero 3, 11–12, 56, 351, 386–387
   and Pallas, Marcus Antonius 408
   and Poppaea 11, 444
   and Sallustius Passienus Crispus 485
   and Silana, Junia 91, 505
Agrippinensis *See* Cologne
Alamanni (Alemanni) **12**, 35, 56, 62, 95, 240, 360, 564
Alans (Alani) **12**, 78, 229, 402, 567
Alaric **12**
   and Athaulf 12, 53
   and Attalus, Priscus 54
   and Constantius III 264
   and Honorius 12, 264, 438, 586
   and Pelagius 418
   and Stilicho 12, 264, 438, 465, 514–515, 560, 573, 586
Alaudae (legion) 311–312

Alavius 5, **220**, 586
Alesia **12–13**, 63, 228, 232
Alexander 32, 37–38
Alexander, Domitius 9, **13**, 97
Alexander Jannaeus 17, 267, 283
Alexander of Alexandria 35, 52
Alexander of Cotiaeon **13**, 37
Alexander of Seleucia **13**
Alexander the Great 13, 16, 95, 191, 253, 519
Alexandra Salom 37, 267
Alexandria **13–14**, *14*, 83, 87, 122, 191
Alexandria, battle of **15**
Alexandria, Library of **15–16**
Alexandria (*classis*) 383
Alexandria Troas **16**
Alexandrine War (Caesar) **16**, 88, 261
alimenta 550
Allectus **16**, 49, 80, 96, 329, 359, 431
Allobroges 6, **16**
Almagest (Ptolemy) 356, 459
Alps **16**
Altar of Peace 30, 42, 92
Altar of Victory 518, 581
Amandus and Aelianus **16**, 65
Amaseia (Amasia) **16–17**
Amathus **17**
Ambiorix 5, **17**, 189
Ambrose 5, **17**, 57, 63, 73, 406, 534
amici Caesaris 141
amici principis **17**, 122, 141
Ammianus Marcellinus **17–18**, 21, 325
   on Arabians 30
   on Armenia 48
   on Bassus Theotechnis 70
   on Constantina 142
   on Constantius II 149
   on Druids 186
   on Gallus Caesar 235
   on gluttony 244
   on Gratian 248
   on Sebastianus 493
   on silk 109
   on Valentinian I 565
Amminius 79, 95, 159
Ammonius Saccas **18**
Amores (Ovid) 404
Ampelius, Lucius **18**
amphitheaters 38, 211, **532** *See also* Colosseum
amphora **18**
Ampius, T. Balbus **18**
Amyntas 21, 226
Anabasis (Arrian) 40
Anabasis (Xenophon) 443

ancile 484
Andalusia 19
Andragathius 248, 361
Anicetus 12, **19**
Annalists **19**
Annals (Tacitus) xii, 50, 52, 171,
    324, 343, 521
Anna Perena 19, 245
Annius Verus, Marcus **19**
annona 19–20, 199
ante diem 90
ante meridiem 543
Anthemius (Emperor of West) **20**,
    48, 249, 342, 398, 471
Anthemius (prefect of Praetorian
    Guard) 20, 32, 146, 168, 460
Anti Cato (Caesar) 88, 102
anti-Gnosticism 67
Antigonus 16, 257
Antinopolis 20, 459
Antinous **20**, 43, 251
Antioch (capital of Seleucid Empire)
    20–21, 167, 519, 520
Antioch (colony) **21–22**
Antiochus I **22**, 26, 36, 139
Antiochus III **22**, 139
Antiochus IV **22**, 118, 139
Antiochus of Ascalon 1–2, **22**
Antipater of Idumaea **22–23**, 34, 37,
    257, 267, 269, 283, 287, 380
Antiquitates (Varro) 468, 569
Antistia 442, 480
Anti-Symmachus (Prudentius) 325
Antonia (daughter of Claudius) **23**
Antonia (mother of C. Domitius
    Ahenobarbus) **23**
Antonia (mother of Claudius) **23**,
    60, 187, 225, 327
Antonine Baths 72, 97
Antonine itinerary 279, 472
Antonines **23–24**, 43, 605 *See also*
    Antoninus Pius; Commodus;
    Marcus Aurelius; Verus, Lucius
Antonine Wall *See* Wall of
    Antoninus
Antoninianus 24, 95, 132, 133, 172
Antoninus, Arrius 24
Antoninus Pius 23, 24, **24**
    and adoptions 4
    and Alexander of Seleucia 13
    and architecture 92, 476–477
    and Christianity 111
    coinage of 24, *24*
    and Galatia 226
    and Gavius Maximus, Marcus
        236
    and Hadrian 24, 251, 349
    and literature 324
    ludi held by 332
    and Senate 24
    and Verus, Lucius 251, 573
    wife of 208
Antonius, Gaius 24
Antonius, Iullus **24–25**
Antonius, Lucius 25, 421
Antonius Musa 25, 61
Antony ("St. Antony") 25
Antony, Marc **25–26**
    at Actium 3, 10, 26, 27, 58, 92,
        127, 191, 252
    and Archelaus 32
    in Armenia 39

and Artavasdes 48
and Athens 53
and Augustus 25–26, 58, 82,
    123, 127, 217–218, 317, 522,
    556–557
and Bibulus, Lucius Calpurnius
    75
brothers of 24, 25
and Brutus, Marcus Junius 25,
    58, 75, 123, 217
and Brutus Albinus 83, 123, 379
and Caesar, Julius 87, 122
and Calenas, Q. Fufius 89
and Candidus Crassus, Publius
    92
and Cassius 58, 99, 123,
    426–427, 557
and Cleopatra 3, 16, 25–26, 58,
    107, 118, 123, 127, 523, 557
daughter of 23
and Domitius Ahenobarbus,
    Gnaeus 182
laws of 318
legions of 311, 313
and Lepidus, Marcus Aemilius
    25–26, 58, 317, 556–557
and Liberators 88, 320, 426–427
and Messalla Corvinus 366
and Parthia 22, 41, 47, 430
and Plancus, Lucius Munatius
    434
and Polemo I 438
and Pollio, Gaius Asinius 438
and Pompey, Sextus 370, 441
sons of 24–25, 26
and Sosius, Gaius 512
and Turrullius 558
wives of 221–222, 397
Antyllus 26
Anullinus, Publius Cornelius 26,
    422
Apamea Cibotus 26
Apamea Orontem 26
Apelles 26
Aper, Arrius 26–27, 37, 98, 175
Aper, P. Salvius 322, 447, 449, 492
apex 484
Apicata 23, 27, 327
Apicius 27, 215, 244
Apis 27
Apocolocyntosis (Seneca) 490, 497
Apocritica (Macarius Magnes) 336
apodyterium 71
Apollinaris (legion) 313
Apollinaris of Laodicea 27
Apollo 27, 60, 168, 245, 467, 468,
    510
Apollodorus 27, 45, 218, 475–476,
    550
Apollonius of Tyana 27–28, 385
Apologeticus (Tertullian) 528
Apologia (Apuleius) 28, 325, 340
Apology for Origen (Pamphylius)
    409
Apophoreta (Martial) 353
apotheosis 509
Apotheosis (Prudentius) 325, 459
apparitores 28, 580
appeal, rights of 304, 305
appearance 420–421
Appendix Vergiliana 28
Appian 32, 88

apprenticeship 190
Apronius, Lucius 28, 220, 521
Apuleius 8, **28**, 325, 340
Aqua Appia 29, 194
Aqua Ducto, De (Frontinus) 221
aquae **28–29**
aquae et ignis interdicto 205
aqueducts **29**, *29*, 43, 194–195, 221
Aquileia 5, 17, **30**, 42, 54, 266, 276,
    277
Aquitania **30**, 83, 202, 228, 232
Arabia **30**, 233
Arabia Petraea **30**, 422
Ara Pacis **30–31**, 42, 92
Ara Pacis Augustae 48
Arar, battle of **31**, 231
Arausio (Orange) **31**
Arbitio, Flavius **31**, 380
Arbogast **31**, 32, 201, 214, 220, 406,
    534
Arcadius, Flavius **31–32**, 56, 73,
    201, 204, 514
Archaic Latin 303
Archelaus **32**, 288
Archelaus of Cappadocia **32**, 39, 93,
    118
arches 29, **32–34**, 194
Architectura, De (Vitruvius) 588
architecture **43–46**, 475–477
    aqueducts 29, 194–195
    arches 32–34
    basilicas 68
    baths 70–72, *71*
    bridges 194–195
    Colosseum 135–137, *136*
    Pantheon 410, *411*
Arch of Augustus 33, 44
Arch of Beneventum 43
Arch of Caracalla 33
Arch of Constantine 33
Arch of Drusus 33
Arch of Germanicus 33
Arch of Septimius Severus 33
Arch of Tiberius 31, 33
Arch of Titus 32–33, *288*
Arch of Trajan 32–33, 316
Ardaburius 50, 100, 315
Ardashir I **34**, 39, 41, 47, 159, 252,
    488
Aretas III 22, **34**, 37, 267, 380
Aretas IV **34–35**, 258
Argentoratum '**35**
argentus 35, 133, 172
Argonautica (Flaccus) 213
Ariadne 276, 315, 572, 599
Arianism **35–36**, 115
    Ambrose and 17
    Antony and 25
    Arius and 38
    Athanasius and 52
    Basil the Great and 67
    Constantine and 144
    Constantius II and 142, 149
    Council of Nicaea and 389–390
    Cyril of Jerusalem and 164
    Eusebius and 202
    George of Cappadocia and 238
    Gregory of Nazianzus and 248
    Hilary and 260
    Hosius and 265
    Julius and 293
    Justina and 295

Liberius and 320
    Lucifer of Cagliari and 330–331
    Vandals and 98
    Visigoths and 587
Ariarathes X of Cappadocia 32, 36
Ariobarzanes III 36, 39
Ariobarzanes of Media 36, 47
Ariogaesus **36–37**
Ariovistus **37**, 239, 340, 470, 498,
    516
Aristides, Aelius 13, **37**, 49
Aristobulus II (king of Judaea) 22,
    34, 37, 267, 287, 380
Aristobulus (praetorian prefect) 37
Aristobulus (son of Herod the Great)
    37–38, 39
Aristophanes 38
Aristotle 385
Arius 35, **38**, 115, 203
Arles 38, 52, 119, 184, 186
armatura 307
Armenia and Armenia Minor **38–40**
    See also specific city
        Corbulo, Gnaeus Domitius and
            151–152
        kings of 47, 155, 371–372, 544,
            599
        Marcus Aurelius and 349
        Nero and 387
        patron saint of 248–249
        queen of 199–200
        rulers of 170, 413
armilustrium 484
Arminius 40, 60, 86, 109, 214, 239,
    241, 352, 529, 569
armor 307, *308*
army *See* legions
Arria 40
Arria the Elder 40
Arria the Younger 40
Arsacid dynasty 34, 39, **40–41**, 413,
    543
Ars Amatoria (Ovid) 403, 404
Ars grammatica (Charisius) 108
Ars grammatica (Diomedes) 178
Ars grammatica (Palaemon) 407
Arsinoe (daughter of King Ptolemy
    XII) 2, 15, **42**, 235
Arsinoe (Egyptian towns) 42
Ars major (Donatus) 185
Ars minor (Donatus) 185
Ars Poetica (Horace) 265, 323
art **42–43**
Artabanus III 41, **46–47**, 543
Artabanus V 34, 41, 47, 338, 488
Artagira 47, 86
Artavasdes (King of Armenia) 34,
    39, 47, 48, 92, 200
Artavasdes (King of Media
    Atropatene) 47
Artaxata **47–48**, 544
Artaxerxes 48 *See also* Ardashir I
Artaxes II 36, 39, 48
Artaxias *See* Zeno (king of Armenia)
Artemidorus Daldianus 48
Artes (Celsus) 104
Arulenus Rusticus, Q. Junius 48
Arval Brethren 48, 60, 168, 452,
    468
Arvandus 48
as **48–49**, 133, 172
Asclepiodotus 16, 17, **49**, 148, 329

Asclepius (Aesculapius) *49*, **49**, 50, 467, 468
Asconius Pedianus, Quintus **49**
Asia **49–50**, *50*
Asia Minor 49, **50**, 76, 93, 118, 335, 368, 379, 412, 430, 487
Asinius Gallus **50**
Aspar, Flavius Ardaburius **50**, 100, 200, 286, 315, 342, 415–416, 599
Aspurgus 77, 372, 438
assassinations **50–51**
astrology **51–52**, 340
Astronomica (Manilius) 345
astronomy **52**, 459
Athanasius (St. Athanasius) 25, 35, **52–53**, 68, 142, 149, 167, 238
Athaulf 12, **53**, 54, 149, 231, 264, 287, 433, 586–587
Athenadorus **53**, 523
Athenaeum **53**
Athens **53–54**
Atia 57, 427
Attalus, Priscus 53, **54**, 149
Attalus III 49, 335
"attendants" 112
Attianus, Publius Acilius **54**
attic 32
Attic Nights (Gellius) 237
Attila *54*, **54**, 266
  and Aetius 8, 54, 102, 342
  and Aquileia 30, 54
  and Avitus 63
  and Heruli 258–259
  and Honoria Augusta 54, 263
  and Leo I (pope) 316
  and Priscus 453
  and Theoderic I 587
  and Troyes 557
  and Valentinian III 565
auctoritas 55, 60, 496
Aufidius Bassus **55**
Aufidius Victorinus, Gaius **55**
Augsburg **56–57**
Augurium Canarium **55**
augurs and augury 52, **55–56**, 452
Augusta 11, 23, **56–57**
Augusta (legion) 311, 312
Augustan History *See Scriptores Historiae Augustae*
Augustans **56**
Augusta Taurinorum *See* Turin
Augusta Treverorum *See* Trier
Augusta Vindelicorum 56, 240
Augustine (St. Augustine) **57**, 429
  and Apollonius of Tyana 28
  as bishop of Hippo 261
  and Boniface 77
  and Donatus 115, 184
  and Orosius, Paulus 401
  and Pelagius 115, 418
  and Theodorus 533
Augustodonum 6, **57**, 104, 228
Augustus **57–61**, *58*, *59*
  acta of 3
  at Actium 3, 10, 26, 27, 58, 92, 127, 191, 252
  and Adriaticum Mare 5
  and Africa 8
  and Agrippa, Marcus Vipsanius 10, 56, 58, 60
  and Alexandria 13
  and *annona* 19

and Antioch 21
and Antonius, Lucius 25, 421
and Antony, Marc 25–26, 58, 82, 123, 127, 217–218, 317, 522
and Apollo 27, 60, 510, 524
and Aquae Sextiae 29
and Arabia 30
and Ara Pacis 30
and Archelaus 32, 118
and architecture 43, 68, 92, 217, 475, 524, 525, 526
and Ariobarzanes of Media 36
and Arles 38
and Armenia 39
and art 42
and Arval Brethren 48, 60
and Asia 49
and Asinius Gallus 50
on astrology 52
and Baalbek 65
and Balbus, Lucius Cornelius 66
and Bosporus kingdom 77
and Britannia 79
and Caesar, Gaius 86
and Caesar, Lucius 88
and Caesarea 89
and Calvinus, Gnaeus Domitius 91
and Cantabri 93
and Capito, Gaius Ateius 93
and Carthage 97
and Cassius 58, 99, 123, 426–427, 557
and Cassius Parmensis 100
and census 105
and Chalcis 107
and Chatti 108
and Cicero 118
and civil service 121
coinage of 131, 132, 133, 172
and *concilia* 140
and consulship 150
and Cordus, Aulus Cremutius 152
and Cornificius, Lucius 153–154
and Corsica 154
and Crassus, Marcus Licinius 156
and Crete 157
and *cursus publicus* 161, 551
and Cyprus 162
and Dacia 165
and Danube 168
daughter of 289–290
deification of 272
and *delatores* 171
and Druids 186
and Egypt 191
and Epaphroditus 196
and Epirus 198
and Equestrians 199
and Evocati 205
father of 397–398
fleets of 503–504
freedmen of 219
and Fulvia 222
and Gallia 228, 229, 239
and Gallus, Gaius Cornelius 234
games provided by 243
and Herod 38
and Herod the Great 257

and Hirtius, Aulus 261
and Hispania 262
and Horace 264, 323
and Illyricum 270
and imperium 272
and Juba II 287, 356
and Judaea 288
laws of 60, 304, 318, 319, 343, 352
legions of 307, 310, 311, 312, 313
and Lepcis Magna 316
and Lepidus, Marcus Aemilius 25–26, 58, 317, 556–557
and Liberators 88, 320, 426–427
and literature 323–324
and Macedonia 336–337
and Maecenas, Gaius Cilnius 339, 340
and Marcellus, Marcus Claudius 346
and Marcomanni 351–352
and Menas 364–365
and Messalla Corvinus 366
and Murena 377–378
and Nicopolis 391
and Noricum 392
and Ostia 402
and Ovid 403
and Pannonia 409
and Parthia 41, 430
physician of 25
and Plancus, Lucius Munatius 434
and Polemo I 438
and Pollio, Publius Vedius 439
and Pompey, Sextus 370, 441
and *praefectus urbi* 449
and Praetorian Guard 60, 185, 446, 447
and provinces 457–458
and *rationalis* 212
and Ravenna 466
Res Gestae Divi Augustus written by 469–470
and Rhodes 471
and Rhoemetalces I 471
and Salona 485
and Samaria 486
and Sardinia 487
and Senate 49, 58, 60, 228, 495, 509
sister of 397
and social classes 509
stepfather of 427
and Taurus 523
tax system of 523
and Terentia 527
and Tiridates II 544
and tribunes 554
and Turrullius 558
tutor of 53
and *vigiles* 582
wives of 58, 326, 492, 539
Aurelian 14, 16, **61–62**
  and architecture 46
  assassination of 51
  and Claudius II Gothicus 125
  coinage of 62, 132
  and Firmus 212
  and Goths 247

in Juthungine War 296, 433
  and Praetorian Guard 448
  and Probus, Marcus Aurelius 454
Aurelius Victor **62**, 186, 325
Aureolus, Manius Acilius **62**, 233
aureus **62**, 95, 132, 133, *500*, *550*
Ausonius, Decimus Magnus **62–63**, 83, 518
auspicia impetrativa 55
auspicia oblativa 55
Autun *See* Augustodonum
auxilia 229, 310, 554
auxilia palatina 310
Avaricum, Siege of **63**, 232, 238, 572
Aventine Hill 260–261, 473
Ave Phoenice, de (Lactantius) 430
Averni (Arverni) 6, 12, **63**, 104, 228, 232, 238, 340, 572
Avidius Heliodorus **63**
Avidius Nigrinus, Gaius **63**
Avidius Quietus, Titus **63**
Avitus **63–64**, 343, 433, 471, 505, 587
Axona **64**, 231, 516
Axum **64**

B

Baalbek **65**
Bacchus **65**, 245, 468
Bactria **65**
Baetica 19, **65**, 262
Bagaudae 16, **65**
Baiae **66**, 72, 277
Balbillus, Tiberius Claudius **66**
Balbinus 30, 51, **66**, 132, 246, 448, 496
Balbus, Lucius Cornelius (ally of Julius Caesar) **66**
Balbus, Lucius Cornelius (nephew of Lucius Cornelius Balbus) **66**
Balbus, T. Ampius **66**
Balearic Islands **66–67**
Ballista **67**, 337
baptismo, De (Tertullian) 528
barber shops 421
Barbia Orbiana **67**, 502
Bar Cochba, Simon **67**, 251, 258, 284, 289, 502
Bardasanes of Edessa **67**
Bargoia, Simon **67**, 286
Barnabas **67**
Basil the Great 36, **67–68**, 115, 203
Basilianus **68**
basilica **68**, 92, 114
Basilica Aemilia 44, **68**, *68*, 218
Basilica Julia 44, **68–69**, 218
Basilica Maxentia 46, **69**
Basilica Ulpia 45, **69**, 219
Basilides **69**
Basilina 149, 291
Basiliscus **69**, 200, 237, 315, 345
Bassianus **69**
Bassus, Aufidius **69**
Bassus, Betilinus **69–70**
Bassus, C. Julius Quadratus **70**
Bassus, Caesius **69**
Bassus, Junius **70**
Bassus, Quintus Caecilius **70**
Bassus, Saleius **70**
Bassus Theotechnis, Junius **70**

Batavi 70, 74, 82, 121, 239 *See also*
　　Civilis, Gaius Julius
baths 28, 70–72, 71, 226, 420, 475
Baths of Agrippa 43, 92, 475
Baths of Caracalla 46, 71–72, 95
Baths of Hadrian 72, 316
Baths of Titus 136
Bathyllus 72, 531
Bato (chief of Breucian tribes) 72,
　　85
Bato (chief of Dalmatians) 72, 85
Bato (gladiator) 72
Battarius 72
Bauli 72–73, 277
Bauto 31, 32, 73, 201
beards 420–421
Beata Vita, De (Augustine) 533
beauty aids 420
Bedriacum 73–74
　　Otho and Vitellius at 16, 70, 73,
　　　　85, 104, 212, 233, 311, 403,
　　　　452, 507, 569
　　Vitellius and Primus at 73–74,
　　　　376, 452
beds 222
Belgae 74, 79, 103, 139, 226, 228,
　　232
Bella Germaniae (Pliny) 436
Belle Civile (Lucan) 324, 330
Bello Africa, De (Caesar) 262
Bello Alexandrino, De (Caesar) 16,
　　88, 261
Bello Gallico, De (Caesar) 88, 261,
　　571
Bello Hispaniensi, De (Caesar) 262,
　　377
Bellona 74
Bello Vandalico, De (Procopius) 567
Bellum Africum (Caesar) 88
Bellum Germanicum (Bassus) 55, 69
beneficiarii 74, 383
beneficiarii legati legionis 74
beneficiarii procuratoris 74
beneficiarii tribuni 74
beneficium 74
Beneventum 74–75
Berenice 75, 162, 187, 545
Berytus 75
Betriacum *See* Bedriacum
Bibliotheca Alexandrina 16
Bibliotheca Historica (Diodorus) 178
Bibracte 6, 75, 231
Bibulus, Lucius Calpurnius 75
Bibulus, Marcus Calpurnius 75, 87,
　　173, 444, 556
bidentes 207
bipalium 207
birds 56
biscuits 215
bishops 112, 411–412, 415
Bithynia 50, 76, 164, 335, 389,
　　390–391
Black Sea 76
Black Sea (*classis*) 383
Blaesus, Quintus Junius 76–77, 396,
　　521
Bleda 54, 266
bodyguards 322, 492, 493 *See also*
　　domestici, protectores; Praetorian
　　Guard
Bolanus, Vettius 77
Bona Dea 77, 129, 439, 576

Boniface (magister militum) 8, 77,
　　100, 236, 266, 418, 567
Boniface (pope) 38, 103, 107
Book of the Laws of the Nations
　　(Bardasanes) 67
Bordeaux itinerary 279, 472
Bosporus kingdom 76, 77–78, 155,
　　372, 425
Boudicca 78, 79, 80, 103, 105, 269,
　　329, 387, 517
braca 130, 307
brazier 223, 583
bread 215
breakfast 215
Breucian tribes 72
Breviarum ab urbe condita
　　(Eutropius) 325
bridges 29, 194–195, 473, 477, 538
Brigantes 78, 79, 89, 98, 189
Britannia (British Isles) 79–81, 80
　　See also specific city
　　Augustus and 79
　　Caesar, Julius and 79, 87, 100,
　　　　103, 232
　　Catuvellauni in 95, 103, 124,
　　　　131, 159
　　Celts in 104–105, 228
　　Claudius and 95, 125, 269, 329,
　　　　435
　　Constantine and 80, 142, 189
　　Constantius I Chlorus and 80,
　　　　96, 329
　　culture in 9, 80–81
　　Decangi in 169
　　Diocletian and 80
　　Druids in 186
　　Gaius Caligula and 79
　　Hadrian and 251
　　Iceni in 269
　　Picts in 430–431
　　Severus, Septimius and 80, 329,
　　　　339, 502
Britannia (coin) 81
Britannica (*classis*) 383
Britannicus 11, 81–82, 84, 125, 331,
　　367, 387
bronze coinage 132
Bructeri 82, 239, 481
Brundisium 82, 188
Brundisium, Treaty of 58, 82, 123,
　　182, 557
Bruttidius Niger 82
Brutus, Marcus Junius 82–83, 320
　　and Antony, Marc 25, 58, 75,
　　　　123, 217
　　and Ariobarzanes III 36
　　and Caesar, Julius 88, 99
　　and Domitius Ahenobarbus,
　　　　Gnaeus 182
　　at Philippi 426–427, 557
　　suicide of 83
　　wife of 444
Brutus Albinus, Decimus Junius 83
　　and Antony, Marc 83, 123, 379
　　and Gallia Cisalpina 230
　　and Hispania 262
　　and Veneti 232
Bucolici 83, 99
Bucolics (Virgil) 207, 585
buildings 194, 475–477 *See also*
　　houses
Bulla Regia 83

Burdigala 83, 228
Burebista 83, 165, 169
Burgundians 8, 83–84, 229, 249,
　　594
burial 169
Burrus, Sextus Afranius 11, 81, 84,
　　91, 101, 387, 449
Byzantium 84, 145

C

Cabiri 85
Caecina, Paetus 40, 85
Caecina Alienus, Aulus 85
　　at Bedriacum 73, 74
　　and Chaerea 106
　　and Gallus, Appius Annius 233
　　and Helvetii 254–255
　　at Placentia 433
　　and Sabinus, Publius 483
　　and Valens, Fabius 564
　　and Vitellius, Aulus 85, 587
Caecina Severus, Aulus 40, 82,
　　85–86
Caelian Hill 260, 473
Caelius Rufus, Marcus 86, 128
Caenis 86
Caesar, Gaius 25, 30, 36, 47, 60–61,
　　86, 326
Caesar, Gallus *See* Constantius II
Caesar, Julius 86–88
　　and *acta diurna* 3
　　and Aedui 6
　　and Afranius 8
　　and Africa 9, 122
　　and Alexandria 13–14, 15, 122
　　and Ambiorix 5, 17
　　and Ampius, T. Balbus 18
　　and Antioch 21
　　and Antonius, Gaius 24
　　and Antonius, Lucius 25
　　and Antony, Marc 87, 122
　　and architecture 44, 68, 119,
　　　　160, 217
　　and Ariobarzanes III 36
　　and Ariovistus 37
　　and Aristobulus 23
　　and Arles 38
　　and Arsinoe 42
　　assassination of 82, 88, 98, 99,
　　　　119, 123, 160, 320, 553
　　and Augustodonum 57
　　and Augustus 57–58
　　and Balbus, Lucius Cornelius 66
　　and Balbus, T. Ampius 66
　　and battle of Arar 31
　　and Bibracte 75
　　in Britannia 79, 87, 100, 103,
　　　　232
　　and Burdigala 83
　　and Burebista 83
　　and Caelius Rufus, Marcus 86
　　and Calenas, Q. Fufius 89
　　calendar reform of 88, 89, 512
　　and Calvinus, Gnaeus Domitius
　　　　91
　　and Carthage 97
　　and Cato Uticensis 88, 102
　　and Chatti 108
　　and Cicero 117
　　and Cleopatra 87, 122, 127
　　and Clodius Pulcher 129
　　coinage of 132

　　and Commius 139
　　and Corinth 152
　　and Crassus 156
　　and Crassus, Marcus Licinius
　　　　87, 156, 231, 556
　　daughter of 289
　　and Deiotarus 171
　　as dictator 173, 174
　　and Domitius Ahenobarbus,
　　　　Gnaeus 182
　　and Domitius Ahenobarbus,
　　　　Lucius 183
　　and Druids 186
　　and Eburones 189
　　and Equestrians 199
　　and Evocati 205
　　and Gabinius, Aulus 224
　　and Galba 64, 226
　　Gallic Wars of *See* Gallic Wars
　　Gardens of 236
　　and Hirtius, Aulus 261
　　and Hispania 262
　　and Illyricum 270
　　and Juba I 287, 395
　　and Juba II 287
　　and Labienus, Titus 298
　　laws of 318, 319
　　legions of 307, 311, 312
　　ludi held by 333
　　and Mamurra 344
　　and Mithridates of Pergamum
　　　　372–373, 391
　　and Moors 375
　　and Oppius, Gaius 399
　　and Ostia 402
　　as Pater Patriae 414
　　and Pedius, Quintus 418
　　and Petreius, Marcus 423
　　and Piso, Lucius Calpurnius 432
　　and Plancus, Lucius Munatius
　　　　434
　　and Pompey the Great 87, 122,
　　　　188, 231, 269–270, 307, 330,
　　　　355, 356, 377, 425, 442, 530,
　　　　556
　　and Ptolemy XII Auletes
　　　　459–460
　　and Raurici 466
　　and Sallust 485
　　and Sinope 507
　　sister of 289
　　son of 26, 88
　　and Trebonius 553
　　and tribunes 553–554
　　and Varro 568
　　and Vatinius 570
　　Vercingetorix and 12
　　wives of 86, 88, 90–91, 153,
　　　　439–440
　　and Zela 598–599
Caesar, Lucius 60–61, 86, 88, 326
Caesar, Ptolemy 26, 88
Caesarea 89, 94, 257, 283, 284
Caesares (Julian) 490
Caesarion *See* Caesar, Ptolemy
Caesaropapism 115–116
Caesar (Plutarch) 88
Caesars (Aurelius) 62
The Caesars (Julian) 292
caldarium 71, 72
Caledonia 79, 89, 140, 430–431,
　　502

Calenas, Q. Fufius **89**
calendar 88, **89–90**, 512
caliga 130
Caligula *See* Gaius Caligula
Callistus 90, 261
Callistus, Gaius Julius **90**, 106
Calpurnia 88, **90–91**, 432
Calpurnius Siculus, Titus **91**
Calvinus, Gnaeus Domitius 29, 36, **91**, 425
Calvisius 91, 180
Calvus, Gaius Licinius Macer **91**
camels 551
Camillus, Furius Scribonianus 28, 40, **91**
Cammuni **91**
Campania **91–92**, 255, 370, 532
camps 240, 309, 447
Campus Agrippa **92**
Campus Martius 42, 71, 74, **92**, 119, 475, 525
Camulodonum 78, 79, **92**, 100, 103, 159, 329
canabae 240, 410
Candidus, Tiberius Claudius **92**
Candidus Crassus, Publius 4, **92–93**
candles 223
Cantabri **93**, 262
cantica 530–531
Cantii 328
Capella, Martianus **93**, 190
Capellianus **93**, 97, 246
Caper, Flavius **93**
capita 524
Capito, Cossutianus 69–70, **93**
Capito, Fonteius 121, 564
Capito, Gaius Ateius **93**, 99, 298, 455, 482
Capitoline Hill 260, 473
Cappadocia 32, 36, 50, 70, **93–94**, 137
Capri **94**, 540, 583
Capua **94**, 243, 277
Caracalla **94–95**, *95*, 290, 477, 502
  and Adventus, Marcus Oclatinus 6
  and Alamanni 12, 240
  and Antioch 21
  and Apollonius of Tyana 27–28
  and architecture 46
  assassination of 51, 55, 205, 338, 354
  and Bato 72
  and Castra Praetoria 101
  coinage of 24, 95, 132, 133, 172
  Constitutio Antoniniana of 119, 150, 277, 280, 377, 523–524
  and Geta, Lucius Septimius 241–242
  and gladiators 243
  and Macrinus, Marcus Opellius 338
  and Papinian 412
  and Pertinax, Publius Helvius 421
  and Praetorian Guard 447
  tax system of 523–524
  tutor of 119
  and Vestal Virgins 157, 299, 499, 576
  wife of 435

Caratacus 78, 79, **95–96**, 98, 103, 124, 159, 492
Carausius, Marcus Aurelius Mausaeus 80, **96**, 148, 329, 358, 431
carbatina 130
carcer 558
cardinal numbers 394
Caria **96**
Carinus, Marcus Aurelius **96**, 98, 175, 395
Carmen Apologetica (Commodian) 325
Carmen Saeculare (Horace) 265
Carmina (Horace) 264–265
Carmina (Sidonius) 505
Carna **96**, 245
Carneades 1, 427, 428
carne Christi, De (Tertullian) 528
carpentum **96**, 207, 474
Carpi **96**, 166
Carrhea 87, **96–97**, 99, 156, 414, 442, 518
Carthage 8, 72, **97–98**, 119, 567
Cartimandua 78, 79, 95, **98**
carts 551–552
Carus, Marcus Aurelius 26, 51, 96, **98**, 448, 454
Casca, Gaius **98**
Casca, Servilius **98**
Cassian, John **98–99**, 103
Cassian law 318
Cassius, Gaius Avidius 83, **99**, 159, 209, 349, 350
Cassius (Gaius Cassius Longinus) **99**, 320
  and Antipater of Idumaea 23
  and Ariobarzanes III 36
  and Augustus and Antony 58, 99, 123, 426–427, 557
  and Caesar, Julius 87, 88, 99
  at Carrhae 97, 99
  at Philippi 99, 123, 426–427, 557
  suicide of 83
Cassius Longinus, Gaius **99–100**, 295, 482
Cassius Longinus, Lucius **100**
Cassius Parmensis **100**
Cassius Severus **100**, 187
Cassivellaunus 79, 92, **100**, 103
Castinus 77, **100**, 286
Castor 179, 182, 245
castra 195
castra aestiva 309
Castra Peregrina 100, 419
Castra Praetoria **100–101**, 143, 447, 473, 494, 540
castra stativa 309
catacombs *101*, **101–102**
Catalaunian Plain **102**, 266, 342, 565, 587
Catalepton 28
Catecheses (Cyril) 164
Catechetical Orations (Gregory) 248
Catechetical School 126, 179
Catena *See* Paulus (Catena)
cathedra 222
Cathemerinon (Prudentius) 459

Catholicae Ecclesiae Unitate, De (Cyprian) 162
catholicos 275
Cato (Cicero) 102
Cato the Elder 253, 428
Cato Uticensis, Marcus Porcius 82, 88, **102**, 129, 162, 183, 423
Catullus **102**
Catullus, Gaius Valerius **102–103**, 119, 128, 161, 344
Catus Decianus 78, **103**
Catuvellauni 95, **103**, 124, 131, 159
causis corruptae eloquentiae, De (Quintilian) 463
cavalry 309, 310
cavea 532
Celer, Caninius **103**
Celer, Publius **103**
Celer (architect) **103**, 245
Celestine I 38, 98, **103**, 163, 196, 315, 389
Celsus **103–104**
Celsus, Aulus Cornelius **104**, 324, 362
Celsus, L. Publius **104**
Celsus, Library of 196
Celsus, Marius 73, **104**
Celsus, Publius Juventus **104**
Celts 78, 79, 80, **104–105**, 186, 228–229
cena 215, 216
Cena Trimalchionis (Petronius) 423
censor 105, 124, 150
censoria potestas 10, 105
Censorinus **105**
census **105**
centenionalis 132, 133
centesima rerum venalium 524
centum 393, 496
centumviri 69
centuria 593
centuriation **105**, 135
centuries 306, 310
centurions 307, 308, 310, 448
Cerealia 105, 332
Cerealis **105–106**
  and Batavi 70, 121, 234
  and Brigantes 79, 98
  and Bructeri 82
  and Civilis 375
  and Classicus, Julius 123
  and Iceni 78, 105
  and Treveri 105–106
Ceres 105, 106, 245, 468
Cerretani **106**
Cervidius, Scaevola Q. **106**
Cestius Gallus 89, **106**
Cestus, Gallius **106**
Chaerea, Cassius **106–107**, 225
chairs 222
Chalcedon **107**
Chalcedon, Council of **107**, 115, 204, 316, 375, 547
Chalcis **107**
Chaldaea **107**
Chaldaean Oracles 107
Châlons, battle of *See* Catalaunian Plain
Charisius, Aurelius Arcadius **108**
Charisius, Flavius Sosipater **108**
Charon **108**
Chatti **108**

  and Domitian 108, 181, 322, 471
  and Drusus 108, 187, 239
  and Galba 224
  and Germanicus 353
  and Hermunduri 256
  and Pomponius Secundus 108, 443
  and Saturninus 360
Chauci **108**, 151, 235, 240
Chersonese **108**
Cherusci **108–109** *See also* Arminius
  and Batavi 70
  and Drusus 108, 187, 239
  and Franks 219
  and Ingiuomerus 274
  and Italicus 279
  and Marsi 353
  prince of 214
  and Varus 109, 569
children, clothing for 130, 546
China **109**, 129
Christianity **109–116**, 468, 477–479
  in Africa 8
  in Alexandria 14
  in Antioch 21
  Antoninus Pius and 111
  Antony and 25
  in Arabia 30
  Arianism and 35, 38, 52, 67, 115
  in Armenia 39, 40
  and art 43
  in Asia 50
  and astrology 52
  Aurelian and 62
  in Bithynia 76
  in Cappadocia 94
  in Carthage 97–98
  and catacombs 101–102
  Celsus and 103–104
  in Cilicia 118
  conflicts in 114–116
  Constantine and 112, 114–115, 144, 367–368, 389–390, 406, 479, 569
  Constantius II and 406
  Council of Chalcedon and 107
  Council of Ephesus and 196
  Council of Nicaea and 389–390
  Decius and 112, 114, 170, 206, 320
  Demetrius and 172
  Diocletian and 112, 176, 299, 364
  Domitian and 111, 182
  in Doura 186
  and Druidism 186
  in Egypt 192
  Galerius and 227
  and gladiators 243
  Gnosticism and 244–245
  Hadrian and 111
  in Hibernia 416
  hierarchies in 112–114
  Hierocles, Sossianus and 259
  history of 110–112
  and Imperial Cult 111
  in Jerusalem 284
  Jovian and 287
  Julian and 291–292, 406

and literature 325
Marcionism and 347
Marcus Aurelius and 111
Maximinus Daia and 359–360
Neoplatonism and 385
Neo-Pythagoreanism and 385
Nero and 111, 433
and paganism 406
and philosophy 428
Prophyry and 444
and science 356
Severus and 111
and slavery 509
spread of *113*
in Thessalonica 536
Trajan and 111
Valerian and 112, 566
Chronica (Nepos) 386
Chronicle (Eusebius) 203
Chronicle (Hydatius) 267
Chronicles (Tiberianus) 538
Chrysanthius (philosopher) **116**
Chrysanthius (vicarius of Britain)
    116–117
Cicero, Marcus Tullius (orator)
    117–118, 171, 323, 428
    and Antiochus 2, 22
    and Antony, Marc 25, 58, 117
    and Asconius Pedianus 49
    and Augustine 57
    and Caelius Rufus 86
    and Caesar, Julius 88
    and Catullus, Gaius Valerius 102
    and Clodius Pulcher 117, 129
    on education system 190
    and Equites 199
    and Figulus, Nigidius 211
    and Labeo Marcus Antistius 298
    and Licinius Macer Calvus 322
    as Pater Patriae 414
    and Piso, Lucius Calpurnius 432
    and Tiro, Marcus Tullius 544
    and Vatinius 570
Cicero, Marcus Tullius (son of
    Cicero) 118
Cicero, Quintus Tullius 5, 17, **118**
Cilicia **118**, 398, 427, 519, 523
Cilo, Lucius Fabius **119**
cinctus Gabinus 546
Cinna, Gaius Helvius 98, 102, **119**
Cinna, Lucius Cornelius 98, **119**
circumcelliones 184
Circumnavigation of the Black Sea
    (Arrian) 76
circumvallation 195
circus **119**
Circus Maximus **119**, *120,* 473
Ciris 28
Cirta **119**
citizenship, Roman **119–121**
The City of God (Augustine) 57
Civilis, Gaius Julius **121**, 229, 239
    and Bructeri 82
    and Cerealis 70, 105
    and Classicus, Julius 123
    and Cologne 134
    and Gallus, Appius Annius 234
    and Moguntiacum 374–375
civil eervice **121–122**, 219, 393,
    445, 456
Civil War (Appian) 88
The Civil War (Caesar) 88, 425

Civil War, First Triumvirate 87,
    122–123, 188, 376–377, 442, 530
    Afranius, Lucius in 8
    Deiotarus in 171
    in Gallia Cisalpina 230
    in Illyricum 270
    Labienus in 299
    legions in 307
    in Mauretania 356
    Trebonius in 553
Civil War, Second Triumvirate 16,
    123, 230
civitas 228, 229
civitas sine suffragio 120
clabulae 161
claqueurs **123**
Clarus, C. Septicius **123**, 482
classiarii 351
Classical Latin 303
Classicus, Julius 106, 121, **123**
Claudian **123–124**
Claudius **124**, **124–125**
    acta of 3
    and Agrippa I 9, 285
    and *annona* 19
    and Antiochus IV 22
    and architecture 44, 475, 524,
        525
    and Armenia 39
    assassination of 51, 331, 567
    on astrology 52
    and Athens 53
    and Balbillus 66
    and Bosporus kingdom 77
    and Brigantes 78
    in Britannia 95, 125, 269, 329,
        435
    and Burrus, Sextus Afranius 84
    and Caecina, Paetus 85
    and Caligula 124, 151
    and Callistus, Gaius Julius 90
    and Camillus, Furius
        Scribonianus 91
    and Castra Praetoria 101
    and civil service 121
    coinage of *124,* 131
    and Commagene 139
    and *consilium* 141
    and Crispinus, Rufrius 158
    daughter of 397
    and *delatores* 171
    and Druids 186
    father of 187
    freedmen of 124, **125**, 219
    and Gallicus, Julius 231
    games provided by 243
    and Geta, Lusius 242
    and Julia Livilla 290
    ludi held by 332
    and Macedonia 337
    and Mauretania 356
    and Mithridates 371
    and Moesia 373
    mother of 23
    and Narcissus 381
    and Ostia 402
    physician of 301
    and Pomponius Secundus 443
    and Praetorian Guard 185, 447
    and Rhodes 471
    sons of 81, 188
    and Thrace 537

and Tiberius 124, 151
    and Veranus 572
    wives of 11, 56, 81, **125**, 317,
        367, 381, 387
Claudius II Gothicus 61, **125–126**,
    143, 431
clay pots 18
Cleander, Marcus Aurelius **126**, 140,
    178, 419, 487
Clemens, Arrecinus 106, **126**, 181
Clemens, Flavius 111, **126**, 182
Clemens, M. Arrecinus **126**
Clement of Alexandria **126**, 400
Clement I (Clement of Rome) 114,
    126–127
Cleopatra 127, **127–128**, 191
    at Actium 3
    and Antony, Marc 3, 16, 25–26,
        58, 107, 118, 123, 127, 523,
        557
    and Arsinoe 42
    and battle of Alexandria 15
    and Caesar, Julius 87, 122, 127
    and Epaphroditus 196
    and Nicolaus of Damascus 390
    and Ptolemy XIII 13, 460
    and Ptolemy XIV 460
    son of 26, 88
clepsydrae 543
client states **128**
clocks 543
Clodia 86, 102, **128**, 367
Clodius Albinus, Decimus 80,
    128–129, 300, 334, 395, 500
Clodius Pulcher, Publius 4, **129**,
    556
    and Bona Dea 77, 129
    and Calenas, Q. Fufius 89
    and Cato Uticensis 102, 129,
        162
    and Cicero 117
    and Deiotarus 171
    and Metellus Celer 367
    and Milo, Titus Annius 369
    and Pompeia 88, 439
    and Pompey the Great 442
    and Sallust 485
clothing 109, **129–130**, 546
codex 595
Codex Euricianus 202
Codex Justinianus 304
Codex Theodosianus 534
coemptio 352
Cogidubnus, Tiberius Claudius
    131
cognomina 310
cohors equitata 310
cohors miliaria 310
cohors praetoria 446, 447
cohors quingenaria 310
cohortes urbanes *See* urban cohorts
coinage *131,* **131–134**, *132, 133,*
    307 *See also specific coin*
    of Antoninus Pius 24, *24*
    of Augustus 132, 133, 172
    of Aurelian 62, 132
    of Caesar, Julius 132
    from Christian era *111*
    of Claudius *124,* 131
    of Commodus *140*

of Constantine 132, 134, 506,
        510
    of Constantius II 132, 133, 134
    of Diocletian 132, *133*
    of Domitian *181*
    of Gaius Caligula 131
    of Hadrian 81, *250*
    of Julian 132
    of Nero 131
    from Parthian Empire *414*
    from Sassanid Persian Empire
        489
    of Severus, Septimius 132
    of Severus Alexander 132
Collectanae Rerum Memorabilium
    (Solinus) 510
collectiones medicae (Oribasius) 400
collegia 273–274, 511
Cologne **134–135**, 239, 240, 277
Colonia Agrippina *See* Cologne
coloniae civium Romanorum 135, 377
colonies 135
Colosseum *44, 45,* **135–137**, *136,*
    181, 243, 245, 475, 545
Columella, Lucius Junius Moderatus
    137, 216
Column of Antoninus Pius 137
Column of Marcus Aurelius 137
Column of Trajan 43, 137, *138, 307*
columns 137, 307
Comana (town in Cappadocia) **137**
Comana (town in Pontus) **137**
Comazon 193, 204
come domesticorum 77
comedy 530
comes **138**
comes Aegypti 14
comes Africae 138
comes Avernorum 138
comes Britanniarum 138
comes dispositionum 138
comes domesticorum 138, 180
comes Hispaniarum 138
comes Orientis 138
comes privatae largitionis 138, 143
comes rei privatae 407
comes rerum privatarum 138, 141,
    207, 212
comes sacrae vestis 138
comes sacrarum largitionum 138,
    141, 143, 212
Comitatenses **138**, 143, 176, 310,
    341
Comitates **138**
comites 122, 138
comites largitionum 212, 407
comitia 150, 524
Comitia Centuriata 4, 150, 303, 446
comitia curiata 553
Comitia Tributa **139**, 553
Commagene 22, **139**, 486, 519
commendatio 392
commentarienses 74
Commentary (Macrobius) 339
commerce *See* trade and commerce
Committee of Twenty 66
Commius 79, 104, **139**
Commodian **139**, 325
Commodus 23, **139–140**
    assassination of 51, 151, 300,
        381
    and Aufidius Victorinus 55

and Callistus 90
and Candidus, Tiberius Aurelius
    92
and Capri 94
and Cleander, Marcus Aurelius
    126
coinage of 140
and Dionysius, Papirius 178
and Eclectus 189
and Marcia 346
and Marcomanni 348, 349, 350
and Mithras cult 371
and Paternus, Tarrutenius 414
and Perennis, Sextus Tigidius
    419
and Pertinax 421
and Pompeianus, Tiberius
    Claudius 440
and Praetorian Guard 447
and Quintilii brothers 463–464
and Saoterus 487
wife of 158
Compendiosa doctrina ad filium
    (Marcellus) 346
concilia **140–141**, 229, 272
conclamare 2
conclamatio 169
concordia 528
Condianus, Sextus Quintilius
    463–464
conductores 445
confarreatio 352
Conferences of the Egyptian Monks
    (Cassian) 99
Confessions (Augustine) 57, 429
Confessio (Patrick) 416
congiarium **141**, 181, 528, 550
Consilium Principis **141**, 143, 150,
    199, 251, 496, 502
Consistorium **141**, 143, 146, 393
consolatione philosophiae, De
    (Boethius) 429
Consolation (Julian) 292
Constans, Flavius Julius 35, 51,
    141–142, 144, 148, 342, 431
Constantia 35, **142**, 143, 149, 235,
    321
Constantina **142**, 149, 251
Constantine ("the Great") **142–144**,
    143, 477
    and Acacius of Constantinople 1
    and Adrianople 4–5
    and Africa 9
    and architecture 46, 69
    and Arianism 35, 38, 52
    and art 43
    and Bassus, Junius 70
    and Britannia 80, 142, 189
    and Castra Praetoria 101
    and Christianity 112, 114–115,
        144, 367–368, 389–390, 406,
        479, 569
    coinage of 132, 134, 506, 510
    and Consistorium 141
    and Constantinople 143,
        144–146
    daughter of 142
    and farming 207
    and Franks 219
    and Germania 240–241
    and gladiators 243
    and Hannibalianus 251

legal system of 304
legions of 310
and Licinius, Valerius Licinianus
    5, 143, 144, 321–322, 359
and literature 325
and *magister militum* 341
and Maxentius 142, 143, 227,
    358, 369, 477
and Maximian 142–143
mother of 252
and Musonianus, Strategius 378
and Pompeianus, Ruricius 440
and Praetorian Guard 143, 180,
    341, 447, 448, 449–450, 492
and Senate 496
sons of 141, 144, 148, 158, 321
and Sopater 511
and Trier 555
wife of 208, 358
Constantine II 141, **144**, 321
Constantine III 80, **144**, 229, 264
Constantinople 20, 114, 143,
    144–148, *145, 147*, 164, 240, 279
Constantinople, Council of 36, 115,
    148, 248, 364, 375, 415
Constantius I Chlorus *148,* **148**
    and Allectus 16, 49
    and Britannia 80, 96, 329
    and Carausius, Marcus Aurelius
        Mausaeus 96, 329
    daughter of 142
    and Eumenius 202
    and Galerius 227
    and Maximian 112, 176, 358,
        359
    son of 142
    and Trier 555
    wives of 252, 532
Constantius II 144, **148–149**
    and Ablabius 1
    and *agentes in rebus* 466
    and Arbitio 31
    and Arianism 35–36, 115
    and Athanasius 52
    and Christianity 406
    coinage of 132, 133, 134
    and Constans 141
    and Dalmatius 167
    and Datianus 168
    and Eusebius 202
    and Gallus, Caesar 235
    and Julian 291–292
    and Lucifer of Cagliari 330–331
    and Lupicinus, Flavius 334
    and *magister militum* 341
    and Magnentius, Flavius Magnus
        342–343, 378
    and Musonianus, Strategius 378
    and Paulus 417
    and Philippus, Flavius 427
    and Shapur II 488
    and Vadomar 563
    and Vetranio 576–577
    wife of 202
Constantius III 53, 77, 100, **149**,
    433–434
Constantius , Julius 149
Constitutio Antoniniana 95, 111,
    119, 121, 150, 277, 280, 377,
    523–524
constitutiones **149–150**, 304
Consualia 150

consul **150–151**, 160, 446, 448
consules ordinarii 150
consules suffecti 150
consul perpetuus 151
consultum 55
Consus 150, **151**
contagious magic 340
Contra Apionem (Josephus) 286
Contra Celsum (Origen) 400
Contra Flaccum (Philo) 427
contra Symmachum (Prudentius)
    459
controversia 170
conubium 119
conventus 49, **151**
conventus matronalis 495
cookbook 27, 215
cooking 215–216
coqui 508
Corbulo, Gnaeus Domitius (praetor)
    151
Corbulo, Gnaeus Domitius (Roman
    general) **151–152**
    and Armenia 41, 47, 151–152,
        387, 517, 542, 544, 561, 589
    and Bolanus 77
    and Chauci 151, 235
    and Frisii 151, 220
    and Paetus 406
    and Tiridates 41, 47, 152, 542,
        544, 561, 589
    and Vologases I 41, 152, 561,
        589
Cordius (Gordius) 152
Corduba 152
Cordus, Aulus Cremutius 152
Corinth 152–153
corn 8, 19–20, 50, 159
Cornelia (Vestal Virgin) 153
Cornelia (wife of Julius Caesar) 86,
    153
Cornelia (wife of Pompey the Great)
    153, 367, 442
Cornelius (legislative reformist) 318
Cornelius (pope) 153
cornicularis 74, 308
Cornificius, Lucius 153–154
Cornutus, Caecilius 154
Cornutus, Lucius Annaeus 154, 330
Corpus Hermeticum 256
Corpus Iuris Civilis 303, 304
correctores 2, 49, **154**, 274, 277
Corsica 154
corvus 504
cosmetics 420
Cotta Messalinus, M. Aurelius 154
Cottiaen Alps 16, **154**
Cottius 154–155
cotton 129
Cotys (king of Armenia Minor) 39,
    155
Cotys (king of Bosporus) 77–78,
    155, 372
Cotys of Thrace 155, 470, 537
couch 222
courier service 161, 221, 466–467,
    551
craftsmen 273–274
Crassus, Candidus 4, **155** *See* Can-
    didus Crassus, Publius
Crassus, Marcus Licinius (triumvir)
    155–156

and Artavasdes 47
and Balbus 66
and Bassus 70
and Caesar, Julius 87, 156, 231,
    556
and Cassius 99
and Orodes II 401
and Pompey the Great 87,
    155–156, 231, 556
and Surenas 41, 96–97
Crassus, Marcus Licinius (general)
    156, 171–172, 191, 336–337, 518
Crassus, Publius Licinius 83, 97,
    156, 228, 232
Credo ut intelligam 429
cremation 169
Cremutius Cordus, Aulus **156**
Crescentia, Cannutia **156**
Crete and Cyrenaica **156–157**, 163
criminal court *See quaestiones*
Crispina **157–158**
Crispinilla, Calvia **158**
Crispinus, Rufrius **158**, 242, 444
Crispinus, Tullius **158**
Crispus, Flavius Julius 144, **158**,
    321, 511
Crispus of Vercellae, Vibius
    158–159
Crocodilopolis 42
Ctesiphon 41, **158–159**, 189, 292,
    401, 495, 500, 543
cucullus 130
Cuicul **159**
Culex 28
cultu feminarum, De (Tertullian) 528
Cunobellinus 79, 92, 95, 103, **159**
cura annonae 6, 19, **159**
cura aquarum 93, **159**
curae palatiorum 159
curator aquarum 221, 475
curatores 151, **159–160**, 207, 277
curatores aquarum 105
curator veteranorum 577
curator viarum 151
curia 159, 218
Curia Cornelia **159–160**
Curia Hostilia **160**, 173
Curia Julia 68, **160**
curialis 160, 188
Curia Pompeia **160**
currency 133
curses 340
cursus honorum **160**, 190, 199, 306,
    308, 341, 462–463, 495
cursus publicus **160–161**, 179, 251,
    378, 472, 551
curule 173
customs duty 445
customs offices 445
Cybele **161–162**, 245, 332, 363,
    467, 468
Cynegetica (Grattius) 248, 324
Cynegetica (Nemesianus) 384
Cynegetica (Oppian) 399
Cynegius, Maternus **161**, 406
Cynics 162, 172, 266, 428
Cyprian of Carthage 97, 112, 115,
    162, 300, 325
Cyprus **162–163**
Cyrenaica 157–158
Cyrenaica (legion) 311
Cyrene **163**

Cyril of Alexandria **163**, 196–197, 204, 389
Cyril of Jerusalem **163**, 296
Cyrus, Flavius 146, **164**
Cyzicus **164**
Cyzicus, battle of **164**, 422

D

Dacia **165–167**, 522
   capital of 488
   and Domitian 166, 170, 181, 223, 522
   Goths in 247
   and Hadrian 250
   kings of 83 *See also* Decebalus
   and Trajan 70, 166, *166*, 168, 169, 488, 517, 522, 550
Dalmatia *See* Illyricum
dalmatic 130
Dalmatius, Flavius 167
Dalmatius, Flavius Julius 167
Damascus **167**
Damasus **167**, 282, 446
damnati 243
damnatio memoriae **167–168**, 168
Danube **168**
Daphne **168**, 245
Datianus **168**
deacons 112
Dea Dia 48, **168–169**, 245
death **169**
death penalty 305
Decangi **169**
Decebalus 165, 168, **169–170**, 181, 223, 522, 550
decemviri legibusscribundis 303
deceres 504
Decius, Gaius Messius Quintus (Trajanus) 168, **170**
   and Christianity 112, 114, 170, 206, 320
   and Goths 170, 247, 297
   and Philip I 170, 426
   wife of 256
declamatio **170**, 470
The Decline and Fall of the Roman Empire (Gibbon) 17
decreta 150, 304
decumae 524, 554
decuriae 199, 508
decuriones 170, 188, 377, 524
Deiotariana (legion) 313
Deiotarus **170–171**, 226
delatores **171**, 319, 343 *See also frumentarii*
   and Libo 171, 321
   Nero and 387
   Suillius Rufus as 517
   Tiberius and 154, 171, 540
   Titus and 171
   Trio as 555
Deldo 156, **171–172**
Demetrius **172**, 400
Demetrius the Cynic 162, **172**, 428
Demonstratio Evangelica (Eusebius) 203
denarius 24, 35, 132, 133, *172*, **172**, *181*, *540*
Densus, Sempronius **172–173**
Dentheleti **173**, 507
Deo Socratis, De (Apuleius) 28, 325
deportatio in insulam 205

deportatio in metalla 305
Desert Fathers 336
dessert 216
Dexippus, Publius Herennius **173**, 202, 325
Diadumenian 68, **173**
diakonoi 112
Dialogue on the Orators (Tacitus) 521
Dialogue (Tacitus) 324, 355, 399
Dialogues (Lucian) 330
Dialogue with Trypho the Jew (Justin) 295
Dialogus de Vita S. Joannis Chrysostomi (Palladius) 408
Diana **173**, 245
Diatessaron (Tatian) 523
dictator **173–174**
Didius Julianus **174**
   assassination of 51
   and Chauci 108
   and Genialis, T. Flavius 238
   and Juvenalis 296
   and Praetorian Guard 101, 158, 174, 447, 500, 517
diet **215–216**
Digest (Cervidius) 106
Digest (Eutropius) 204
Digest (Julianus) 293
digiti 593
dinner 215
Dio Cassius **174**, 325
   on Antioch 21
   on Antiochus IV 22
   on Antonia 23
   on Apicata 27
   on Apollodorus 27
   on Ariovistus 37
   on Armenians 40
   on Athenadorus 53
   on Bar Cochba, Simon 67
   on battle of Issus 276
   on Bibulus, Marcus Calpurnius 75
   on Boudicca 78
   on Britannia 79
   on Burrus, Sextus Afranius 84
   on Caesar, Julius 319
   on Caledonia 89
   on Caligula 73
   on Caracalla 55, 95
   on Cleopatra 4
   on Commodus 140
   on Crassus, Marcus Licinius 97, 156
   on Cynics 428
   on Decebalus 170
   on Densus, Sempronius 172–173
   on Domitia Longina 180
   on Domitian 181
   on Drusus the Younger 187
   on Hadrian 53, 256
   on Hatra 252
   on India 273
   on Livia 326
   on Livilla 327
   on Maeatae 339
   on Marcellus, Lucius Ulpius 345
   on Marcus Aurelius 243
   on Maternas, Curiatius 355
   on Numerianus 395

   on Pannonia 409
   on Perennis, Sextus Tigidius 419
   on Pescennius Niger 422
   on Plautianus, Gaius Fulvius 434–435
   on Plotina, Pompeia 436
   on Suburanus 516
   on Titiana 544
   on Trajan 548, 550
   on Turbo 558
   on Verus, P. Martius 574
   on Vespasian 236
diocese 143, **175**, 176
diocetes 192
Diocletian **175–176**, 477
   and Achaea 2
   and Alexandria 14
   and Amandus and Aelianus 16
   and Aper, Arrius 26–27
   and architecture 46, 69, 72, 160
   and Aristobulus 37
   and Armenia 39
   and Asia 49
   and Bagaudae 65
   and Britannia 80
   and Carinus, Marcus Aurelius 96, 175
   and Christianity 112, 176, 299, 364
   and civil service 122
   coinage of 132, 133
   coin of 35
   and Consistorium 141
   and Constantius I Chlorus 148
   and *curiales* 160
   dioceses of 175, 176
   and Egypt 192
   and Equites 199
   and farming 207
   financial reform of 212
   and *frumentarii* 221, 466
   and Galerius 227
   and Germania 240
   and Jovians and Herculians 287
   legions of 310
   and Manichaeism 344
   and Maximian 358–359
   and Mithras cult 371
   and Praetorian Guard 341, 342, 447, 448
   provinces of *177*, 458
   and Sardinia 487
   and Split 512, *513*
   and Syria 520
   tax system of 524
   and Thrace 537
   and Trier 555
   and *vicarii* 580
Dio Cocceianus 76, 162, **178**
Diodorus, Siculus **178**, 186
Diogenes, Laertius **178**, 186, 515
Diomedes **178**
Dionysius, Papirius **178**
Dionysius of Alexandria 14, **178**
Dionysius of Halicarnassus 19, **178**
Dionysius the Areopagite **179**
Dionysius the Great **179**
Dioscorides **179**
Dioscuri **179**, 182, 245
diplomata 161, **179**, 383
diplomata militaria 179
Dirae 28

Discourses Against the Arians (Athanasius) 53
Discourses (Arrian) 40
distances 593
distributives 395
Divinae Institutiones (Lactantius) 299
divorce 318, **352–353** *See also* marriage
doctors 361–362
Doctrina Christiana, De (Augustine) 57
Dolabella, Publius Cornelius 86, 99, **179–180**, 396, 521, 553
dolphin **180**
domestici, protectores 26, 138, 143, **180**, 287, 457
domestici et notarii 393
domi 223
domina 352
dominus gregis 531
Domitia **180**
Domitia Lepida *See* Lepida, Domitia
Domitia Longina 56, **180**, 181
Domitia Lucilla *See* Lucilla, Domitia
Domitian **180–181**, *181*
   and Aelianus, Casperius 7
   and Agricola, Gnaeus Julius 9
   and Annius Verus, Marcus 19
   and Apollonius of Tyana 27
   arch constructed by 33
   and architecture 45, 92, 119, 136, 137, 181, 219, 475, 525, 527
   assassination of 51, 413, 494, 514
   on astrology 52
   and Athens 53
   and Chatti 108, 181, 322
   and Christianity 111, 182
   and Clemens, Arrecinus 126
   coinage of *181*
   and Dacia 166, 170, 181, 223, 522
   and *delatores* 171
   and Fuscus, Cornelius 223
   and Gallia 229, 239
   and Illyricum 270
   and John 285
   and Julia Flavia 290
   legion of 311
   and literature 324
   ludi held by 332
   and Marcomanni 348
   and Moesia 374
   and Nerva 388
   palace of 183–184
   and Paris 413
   and Praetorian Guard 447
   and Saturninus 490
   and Sirmium 507
   and Titus 181, 545
   and Vestal Virgins 153, 181, 576
   wife of 56, 180, 181
Domitianus, Gaius 62, **182**
Domitilla, Flavia (daughter of Vespasian) 182
Domitilla, Flavia (granddaughter of Vespasian) 111, 126, **182**
Domitilla, Flavia (wife of Vespasian) 180, **182**
Domitius Ahenobarbus **182**

Domitius Ahenobarbus, Gnaeus (consul in 32 B.C.E.) **182**
Domitius Ahenobarbus, Gnaeus (consul in 32 C.E.) 11, 23, **182–183**, 386
Domitius Ahenobarbus, Lucius (praetor in 58 B.C.E.) 87, 102, **183**
Domitius Ahenobarbus, Lucius (consul in 16 B.C.E.) 23, 108, 168, **183**
Domitius Domitianus, Lucius 2, **183**
Domitius Ulpianus **183**, 295
domus 183, *184*, 474
Domus Augustana **183**
Domus Aurea *See* Golden House of Nero
Domus Flavia 181, **183–184**, 475
Domus Tiberiana **184**, 475
Domus Transitoria 44, **184**, 475
Donatism 57, 98, **184–185**, 275
donativum 51, 124, 125, 174, **185**, 226, 299, 421, 447, 507
Donatus, Aelius **185**
Donatus, Tiberius Claudius **185**
donkeys 551
Doryphorus **185–186**, 388
dos 352, 594
Doura **186**
drama 531
drink, Roman 215–216
dromos 546
Druids and Druidism 78, 79, 104, **186**, 228, 468
Drusilla, Julia 23, **186–187**, 317
Drusilla **187**, 209
Drusilla, Livia *See* Livia
Drusus (son of Claudius) 125, **188**
Drusus (son of Germanicus) **187**
Drusus, Julius Caesar ("Drusus the Younger") **187–188**
  and Asinius Gallus 50
  daughter of 290, 388
  father of 10, 11, 187
  and Germanicus 11, 187
  mother of 10
  and Pannonia 76, 187
  and Sejanus 23, 187, 494
  wife of 187, 327
Drusus, Nero Claudius ("Drusus the Elder") 23, 70, 108, **187**, 239, 326, 333, 539
Dubius Sernio (Pliny) 436
dungeons 558
duoviri 377
dupondius 133
duumviri **188**
duumviri honorarius **188**
duumviri municipales **188**
dyes 129
Dynamis 77, 372, 438
Dyrrhachium 8, 87, 117, 122, **188**, 425, 440, 442

E

Early Latin 303
eating 215–216, 244
Eburacum (York) 78, **189**
Eburones 5, 17, **189**, 232
Ecbatana **189**
Ecclesiastical History (Eusebius) 14, 67, 281, 282, 325, 510, 512

Eclectus 140, **189**, 300, 346
Eclogues (Virgil) *See* Bucolics (Virgil)
economy 50, 277, 508 *See also* farming
Edessa **190**, 503, 566
edicta 304
education **190**
Egypt 58, *127*, **190–192**, 207, 306, 458, 459
Egypt, prefect of **192**
Elagabalus **193**
  assassination of 51, 193, 259
  and Cordius 152
  courtier of 259
  and Diadumenian 173
  and Julia Maesa 193, 291
  and Macrinus 21, 193
  and Praetorian Guard 448
  Senaculum established by 495
  and Severus Alexander 193, 502
  tutor of 235
Elagabalus (sun god) 468, 511
"elders" 112
El Djem *See* Thysdrus
Elegira **193**
emancipatio 415
Embroidered Girdles (Julius Africanus) 293
Emerita *See* Merida
emeritis stipendis 515
Emesa **193**
Empiricus, Sextus **193**
enarratio 190
engineering **193–195**
Enneads (Plotinus) 385
Ennia Thrasylla **196**, 338
entertainment 242–244
Epagathus **196**
Epaphroditus (freedman of Nero) **196**, 387
Epaphroditus (freedman of Octavian) **196**
Ephemeris (Ausonius) 63
Ephesus 49, **196**, 419, 437
Ephesus, Council of 107, 163, **196–197**, 316, 547
Ephesus, Library of 196, *197*
Epicharis **197**, 433, 456
Epictetus 40, **197**, 428
Epicureanism **197–198**, 428
Epicurus 197, 428
Epigrams (Martial) 324, 353
Epiphanius **198**
Epiphanus (Augustus) 61
Epirus **198**
episkopoi 112
Epistles (Horace) 265
Epistle to the Philippians (Polycarp) 439
Epistola ad milites Corotici (Patrick) 416
Epistola Dogmatica (Leo) 107
epistrategus 192
Epistulae ex Ponto (Ovid) 404
Epistulae Heroidum (Ovid) 404
Epistulae morales (Seneca) 497
epistulis, ab **198**
epitaphion 409
Epitoma de rei militaris (Vegetius) 570
Epodes (Horace) 264

Eprius Marcellus, Titus Clodius **198**, 255
epulum 498
eques 244
Eques militia 199
Equester ordo *See* Equites
Equestrians *See* Equites
equipment of legions 307–308
Equites **198–199**, 509
  Augustans recruited from 57
  Augustus and 60, 121, 199
  chief of 452
  and freedmen 199, 219
  Hadrian and 212, 251
  tribunes from 199, 308, 554
  and *vicarii* 580
Equite scutarii 493
equites equo publico 199
equus publicus 199
Erato 36, **199–200**
Ermanaric **200**
errore profanarum religionum, De (Firmicus) 212
Erucius Clarus, Sextus **200**
Esquiline Hill 261, 473
essedarii 244
Essenes **200**, 425
ethnarch 192
etiarii 244
Etruria **200**, 242
Etruscan language 301
Etruscans 230, 378
Eubulus, Aurelius **200**
Eucherius **200**
Eudocia, Aelia 164, **201**, 266, 398, 460
Eudoxia, Aelia 32, 56, 73, 99, 116, **201**, 204, 285
Eudoxia, Licinia **201**, 237, 343, 424
Eugenius, Flavius 31, 38, 161, **201**, 214, 219–220, 406
Eulogy of Cato (Brutus) 61
Eumenius **202**
Eunapius 116, **202**, 515
Euphrates River **202**
Euric 20, 48, **202**, 386, 505, 587
Eusebia **202**
Eusebius **202**
Eusebius of Caesarea **202–203**, 325
  on Alexandria 14
  on Bar Cochba 67
  and Basil the Great 68
  on Constantine 144
  on James 281
  tutor of 6
Eusebius of Nicomedia 35, 38, **203**, 390
Eustathius of Antioch 35, **203**
Eustathius of Sebaste **203**
Eutherius **203–204**
Eutropia **204**
Eutropius (eunuch) **204**, 480
Eutropius (historian) **204**, 325
Eutyches 107, **204**, 316
Eutychianus, Valerius Comazon **204**
Evagrius Ponticus **204–205**
Evangelium Veritatis (Valentinus) 566
Evocati **205**, 354, 448
exactores 524
Excubitors **205**
executioners 322

Exegetica 69
Exempla (Nepos) 386
Exhortation to Martyrdom (Origen) 400
exile 205, 305, 467
Exploratores **205**
Exsilium **205**
extispicium 511
extremum vale 169

F

Fabatus, Rubrius **206**
Fabian 112, **206**
Fabianus, Papirius **206**
Fabiola **206**
fabulae preatextate 531
Factorum (Valerius) 567
Falco, Sosius **206**
falx messoria 207
falx putatoria 208
falx veruculata 207
falx vinitoria 208
familia 508
familia rustica 508
familia urbana 508
family life 60, 415
farming **206–208**, 582
  in Africa 8
  in Crete 157
  in Egypt 191
  in Gallia 229, 230–231
  in Hispania 263
  slaves working in 508
fasces 173, **208**, 322
fasciae 244
fashion 129–130, 546
Fasti (Ovid) 404
Faunus 208
Fausta, Flavia Maxima 141, 142, 144, **208**, 358
Faustina, Annia Galeria ("the Elder") **208–209**
Faustina, Annia Galeria ("the Younger") 99, 139, **209**, 349, 350
Favonius Eulogius 209
Favorinus **209**
Felicitas **209**, 245
Felix, Flavius Constantius **209**
Felix, M. Minucius **209**, 325
Felix, Marcus Antonius 187, **209**, 417
Fenestella **210**
Ferrata (legion) 312
festivals 210
Festus, Porcius 209, **210–211**, 417
Festus, Rufius **211**
Festus, Sextus Pompeius **211**, 213
fibulae 129
Fidenae, Amphitheater of **211**
Fides **211**, 245
Figulus, Nigidius 51, **211**, 385, 428
finance 131–134, **211–212**, 470
financial minister 466
fire brigade 582
fires 474, 582
Firmicus Maternus, Julius **212**
Firmus **212**, 242
Firmus, Plotius **212**
First Apology (Justin) 295
First Principles (Origen) 400
First Triumvirate *See* Triumvirate, First

fiscus 121, 200, 211, **212–213**, 466, 470
fiscus frumentarius 20
Flaccilla **213**
Flaccus, A. Persius **213**
Flaccus, C. Valerius **213**
Flaccus, Verrius 211, **213**
Flamen Dialis 213, 452, 583
Flamen Martialis 213, 214, 353
Flamen Quirinalis 213, 214, 464
flamens **213–214**
Flamen Volcanalis 590
Flamen Volturnalis 589
Flavia Felix (legion) 311
Flavia Firma (legion) 313
Flavian Amphitheater *See* Colosseum
Flavians 79, **214**, 604 *See also* Domitian; Titus; Vespasian
    and architecture 475
    and art 42
    coinage of 131
    and *delatores* 171
    and Gallia 239
    and Jerusalem 284
Flavianus, Virius Nicomachus 214
Flavius **214**
flavus Tiberus 538
flax 129
fleets 382–383, 503–504
floors 222
Flora **214**, 245
Florentia **214**
Florianus, Marcus Annius 51, **214–215**, 454
Florida (Apuleius) 28
Florus, Gessius 106, **215**, 283
Florus, Julius **215**, 484
Florus, Publius Annius **215**
flutes 378
food and drink, Roman **215–216**, 244
footwear 130
foricea **216–217**
Formulus 42, **217**
fornix 32
fortresses 309
forts 309
Fortuna **217**, 245, 376
forum 27, 60, 68, **217**
Forum Augustum 27, 44, **217**
Forum Caesaris **217**
Forum Gallorum 123, **217–218**
Forum Julium **218**
Forum Nervae 219
Forum of Constantine 146
Forum Pacis *See* Temple of Peace
Forum Romanum 44, 68, 217, **218**, *218*, 475, 524, 525, 527
Forum Tauri 146
Forum Traiani 137, **218–219**, 550
Forum Transitorium 219, 475
fossa regia 8
Fosse Way 492
Franks 6, 82, **219**, 469
fratres 6
freedmen 19, 60, 124, 125, 199, **219**
Fretensis (legion) 312
fretum gaditanum 543
frigidarium 71
Frigidus 31, **219–220**, 406, 534
Frisii **220**, 239

Fritigern 5, **220**, 402, 586
Frontinus, Sextus Julius 79, 194, **220–221**
Fronto, Marcus Cornelius 8, 37, 119, 209, **221**, 324, 349
fruits 235
frumentarii 5–6, 171, **221**, 251, 389
    See also delatores
frumentationes 510
fuga in persecutione, De (Tertullian) 528
fullers 129, 130
Fulminata (legion) 312–313
Fulvia 25, 82, 123, **221–222**, 421
funeral 169, 271
funestum 169
Furnilla, Marcia **222**
furnishings **222–223**
Furrina 223, 245
Furtius 36, **223**
Fuscus, Cornelius 74, 166, 169, 181, **223**

G

Gabinius, Aulus 34, 97, **224**, 287, 318, 372, 460
Gabinius, P. **224**
Gaetulia **224**
Gaius **224–225**, 294
Gaius Caligula **225**
    and Africa 8
    and Agrippa I 9
    and Antiochus IV 22, 118
    and Apelles 26
    and architecture 44, 524, 525, 526
    and Armenia 39
    assassination of 51, 90, 106, 447, 482
    and Bacchus 65
    and Bassus, Betilinus 69–70
    and Bauli 72–73
    and Bosporus kingdom 77
    and Britannia 79
    and Callistus, Gaius Julius 90
    and Carthage 97
    and Chaerea, Cassius 106
    and Claudius 124, 151
    coinage of 131
    and Commagene 139
    and Cotys 155
    courtiers of 317, 567
    and Domitius Ahenobarbus, Gnaeus 183
    and Drusilla 186
    and Ennia Thrasylla 196, 338
    freedmen of 219
    and Gemellus, Tiberius 237
    and gladiators 243
    grandmother of 23
    and Herod Antipas 257
    horse of 225, 273
    and Judaea 288
    and Julia Livilla 290
    and *legatus* 306
    and literature 324
    and Livia 326
    and Macro 338–339
    and Mithridates 371
    and Mnester 373
    mother of 11
    and Numidia 396

    and Ostia 402
    and Petronius Turpilianus 423
    and Praetorian Guard 447
    and Priscus, Junius 454
    and Thrace 537
    and Tiberius 225, 540
    wives of 328, 467
Galatia 16, 50, **226**
Galba 51, 64, **226**, 231, 516
Galba, Servicus Sulpicius **226–227**
    and Aedui 6
    assassination of 101, 172, 227
    and Caecina Alienus 85
    and Celsus, Marius 104
    freedman of 268–269
    and Helvidius Priscus 255
    and Laco, Cornelius 226, 299
    legion of 312
    and Lycia 335
    and Otho 227, 403, 507
    and Piso Licinianus 432–433, 507
    and Praetorian Guard 51, 226, 447
    and Primus, Marcus Antonius 452
    and Sabinus, Nymphidius 226, 483
    and Tigellinus 542
    and Vindex 226, 583
Galen (Claudius Galenus) **227**, 349, 362, 400
Galerius **227–228**
    and Christianity 112, 227
    and Constantine 142–143, 227
    and Diocletian 176, 227, 358, 359
    and Licinius 321
    and Maximinus Daia 227, 359
    and Mesopotamia 366
    and Narses 381, 488
    and Severus II 227, 499–500
    and Thessalonica 227, 536
    wife of 566
Galilee **228**
Galla, Satria **228**, 432
Galli 244
Gallia **228–229** *See also specific city*
Gallia Aquitania *See* Aquitania
Gallia Belgica 228 *See also* Belgae
Gallia Cisalpina 8, 87, 104, **230**
Gallia Narbonensis 16, 31, 38, 218, 228, **230–231**, 381, 384, 569
Gallia Transalpina *See* Gallia Narbonensis
Gallica (legion) 311, 313
Gallicus, Julius **231**
Gallic Wars 87, 228–229, **231–232**, 556
    Aduatuca in 5
    Ampius, T. Balbius in 18
    Averni 238, 572, 584
    Belgae in 74
    in Britannia 79
    Celts in 104
    in Gallia Cisalpina 230
    in Germania 239
    in Helvetia 254
    Rhemi in 470
    Siege of Avaricum in 63
    Suebi in 516
    Suessiones in 516

    Tenth Legion in 527
    Treveri in 553
    Veneti in 571
Gallic Wars (Caesar) 88, 261, 571
Gallienus, Publicus Licinius Egnatius **232–233**
    and Alamanni 12
    and art 43
    assassination of 51
    and Aurelian 61
    and Aureolus 62
    and Claudius II Gothicus 125
    and Franks 240
    and Heraclianus, Aurelius 255
    ludi held by 333
    and Odaenath 398
    and Postumus 445
    son of 486
    and Trapezus 552
    wife of 486
Gallio, Junius **233**
Gallio, Lucius Annaeanus Junius **233**
Gallus, Aelius 30, 34, 191, 200, **233**, 273
Gallus, Appius Annius 73, 105, 121, **233–234**, 403, 433
Gallus, Aulus Didius **234**
Gallus, Cestius 215, **234**, 283
Gallus, Gaius Asinius **234**
Gallus, Gaius Cornelius **234**, 323–324
Gallus Caesar 149, **234–235**
Gamala **235**, 242
games 242–244, 331–333
Gannascus **235**
Gannys **235**
Ganymedes **235**
gardens 92, **235–236**
Gardens of Antony **236**
Gardens of Asiaticus **236**
Gardens of Caesar **236**
Gardens of Sallust **236**
garum 216
Gaul *See* Gallia
Gavius Maximus, Marcus **236**, 361
Geiseric **236–237**, 567
    and Anthemius 20
    and Basiliscus 69
    and Boniface 77, 567
    and Carthage 98, 567
    and Eudoxia, Licinia 201, 424
    and Hippo 261
    and Leo I (emperor) 315
    and Leo I (pope) 316
    and Libius Severus 320
    and Majorian 344
    son of 266
    and Valentinian III 565
Gellius, Aulus 15, 209, **237**, 325
Gemellus, Tiberius 225, **237**
Gemina (legion) 312, 313
Gemonian Stairs **237–238**
Geneva **238**
Genialis, T. Flavius **238**
genius **238**, 301
geocentricism 52
geography 473, 515
Geography (Strabo) 515
George of Cappadocia **238**
Georgics (Virgil) 207, 585
Gepaepyris 77, 155, 372

Gergovia 232, **238**
Germania 181, 187, **238–241**
Germania (*classis*) 383
Germania Inferior 134–135, 239, 555
Germania Superior 239, 555
Germania (Tacitus) 324, 522
Germanica (legion) 311
Germanicus Julius Caesar **241**
  and Antioch 21
  and Apis 27
  and Batavi 70
  and Bructeri 82
  and Caecina Severus 86
  and Chatti 40, 108
  and Cherusci 109
  daughter of 290
  and Drusus the Younger 187
  and Egypt 191
  father of 187
  and Flavius 214
  and Gallia 229
  mother of 23
  and Piso, Gnaeus Calpurnius 432, 434
  and Silius, Gaius 506
  sons of 187, 225, 388
  and Tiberius 241, 539
  wife of 10–11
Geta, Lucius Septimius 51, 94, **241–242**, 290, 435, 502
Geta, Lusius 158, **242**
Getae **242**, 472
Gildo **242**, 514
Gischala **242**
gladiators 72, 140, **242–244**, 305, 532
gladius 307
gluttony **244**
Glycerius **244**, 386
gnosis **244**
Gnosticism 69, 114, **244–245**, 275, 385, 453, 523, 566
gods and goddesses of Rome **245**, 467–468
gold coinage 131, 132, 133 *See also specific coin*
Golden Ass (Apuleius) 28, 325
Golden House of Nero 42, 44, 71, 136, 217, **245**, 387, 474–475
Gordian I 8–9, 93, 97, **245–246**, 360, 587
Gordian II 93, **246**, 360
Gordian III **246**
  assassination of 51
  and Balbinus 66, 246, 461
  and Carthage 9
  and Philip I 426
  and Praetorian Guard 448
  and Pupienus 66, 246, 461
  and Shapur I 246
  and Timesitheus 246, 543
  wife of 551
Gotarzes II **246**, 363, 568
Goths **246–247** *See also* Kniva; Ostrogoths; Visigoths
  in Bithynia 76, 247
  Christianity and 36, 560
  and Claudius II Gothicus 125
  in Dacia 167, 247
  and Decius 170, 247, 297
  and Gallienus 233

and Herennia Etruscilla 256, 297
and Huns 383–384, 402–403
and Trebonianus Gallus 247, 552–553
and Valens 5, 168, 564
and Victor 581
gourmands **244**
Gradivus 353
Graecina, Pomponia **247**, 435
grammaticus 190
Gratian **247–248**
  and Arbogast 31
  assassination of 51
  and Ausonius 63, 247
  and Bauto 73
  and Danube 5
  and Maximus, Magnus 247, 361
  and paganism 406, 518
  and Symmachus 518
  and Theodosius I 36, 247, 533
  and Valentinian II 247, 565
gratiarum acto 409
Grattius **248**, 324
Great Collection (Ptolemy) 52
Great Forum 218
Great Harbor 14
Great Mother *See* Cybele
Greek culture xiii, 42–43, 253–254, 428, 467
Gregorian calendar 90
Gregory of Nazianzus (St. Gregory Nazienzen) 36, 67, 68, 115, 204, **248**
Gregory of Nyssa 36, 67, 115, **248**, 429
Gregory the Illuminator **248–249**
gremio matris 190
grex 531
groma 195
Gubernatione Dei, De (Salvianus) 486
guilds 273–274
Gunderic 567
Gundioc **249**
Gundobad 244, **249**, 471
Gundohar 83, 287, 594
Gundomadus 563
Gurio, Gaius 395
gustatio 216
gymnasiarch 192
gymnasium 27

H

Hadrian 23, *250*, **250–251**, 604
  and Achaea 2
  and Aelius Caesar 7, 251
  and Antinopolis 20
  and Antoninus Pius 24, 251, 349
  and Apollodorus 27
  and architecture 45–46, 92, 251, 410, 476
  and Arrian 40
  and art 42–43
  and Athenaeum 53
  and Athens 53
  and Attianus, Acilius 54
  and Avidius Heliodorus 63
  and Avidius Nigrinus 63
  and Baiae 66
  and Bar Cochba, Simon 67

beard of 421
and Britannia 251
and Celsus, L. Publius 104
and Christianity 111
and civil service 121
and Clarus, C. Septicius 123
coinage of 81, *250*
and consilium 141
and Dacia 166, 250
and Egypt 192
and *frumentarii* 221, 251
and Galatia 226
and Gavius Maximus, Marcus 236
and gladiators 243
and Heliodorus, C. Avidius 252
and Jerusalem 284
and literature 324
and Lycia 335
and Marcus Aurelius 349
and Pannonia 410
and Parthia 41
physician of 256
and Polemo, Marcus Antonius 437
and Praetorian Guard 447
and *rationalis* 212
and Salinator 485
and Servianus, Julius 499
and Severus, Sextus Julius 502
sister of 416
and Suetonius 516
and Tivoli 545–546
and Trajan 250, 548
and Trapezus 552
and Turbo 558
wife of 54, 250, 356, 482
hair dyes 420
hairstyles 420
Halieutica (Oppian) 399
Halieutica (Ovid) 404
"Hand-on-Hilt" 61
Hannibalianus 142, **251**
harbor tax 523
harpax 3–4, **251–252**, 382, 504
harpists 378
haruspices 361, 511
haruspicium 56
hastatus posterior 308
hastatus prior 308
Haterius, Quintus **252**
Hatra **252**
heating 223, 583
Hebe 296
Hegesippus **252**
Helena **252**, 532
heliocentricism 52
Heliodorus, C. Avidius **252**
Heliopolis 65
Helius **252–253**
Helix, Aurelius **253**
helladarch 2
Hellenism xiii, 42–43, **253–254**, 428, 467
helmets 307
Helvetia 238, **254–255**
Helvetians 31, 231, 254–255, 399
Helvidius Priscus 48, **255**
heptastadium 14, 15
Hera 293–294
Heracleus the Eunuch 255, 565
Heraclianus, Aurelius 233, **255**

Herculaneum *255*, **255–256**, 440
heredium 593
Herennia Etruscilla **256**
Herennius Etruscus 170, **256**, 297
heres 4
Hermes Trismegistos **256**, 365, 468
Hermogenes **256**
Hermopolis 20
Hermunduri **256**, 462
Herod Antipas 9, 32, 228, **256–257**, 258, 538
Herod the Great **257**, 288
  and Antony, Marc 257
  and Augustus 257
  brother of 23, 257, 426
  and Caesar, Julius 283
  and Caesarea 89, 257
  father of 23, 257
  and Jericho 282
  and Masada 257, 354
  and Nicolaus of Damascus 390
  and Parthians 257, 269
  and Samaria 486
  sons of 32, 37, 256, 257, 426
  and Sosius, Gaius 512
  and Temple of Jerusalem 257, 526
Herodes Atticus 13, 37, 53, **257–258**, 349
Herodian 6, 30, 80, 94, **258**, 325
Herodias 257, **258**
Herodion **258**
Heruli 233, **258–259**
Hesychius of Jerusalem **259**
Hexapla (Origen) 400
hiberna 309
Hibernia **259**, 416
Hierocles 6, **259**, 385
Hierocles, Sossianus **259**
Hieronymian Martyrology **259**
highways *See viae*
Hilarianus, Q. Iulius **259**
Hilary (Hilarius) **260**
Hilary (Hilary of Arles) **259–260**
Hilary (Hilary of Poitiers) **260**, 354
Hills of Rome **260–261**, 473
Hippicus Tower 285
Hippo 77, **261**
Hippolytus 90, **261**
Hirtius, Aulus 88, 123, 217, **261–262**
Hispana (legion) 312
Hispania **262–263**, 365
Hispania Citerior 262
Hispania Ulterior 262
Historia Augustae See Scriptores Historiae Augustae
Historia adversus Paganos (Orosius) 401
Historia Ecclesiastica (Eusebius) 203
Historiae Philippicae (Trogus) 557
Historiae Romanae (Velleius) 570
Historia (Tacitus) 522
Historical Library (Diodorus) 178
Histories (Sallust) 19
Histories (Tacitus) 215, 324
History (Ammianus) 17
History (Cordus) 152
History (Cremutius) 156–157
History (Eunapius) 202
History (Sallust) 485
History of Alexander (Rufus) 481

History of Parthia (Arrian) 40
A History of the World (Julius Africanus) 293
Histria 276
Holy Land *See* Judaea
homeopathic magic 340
homoiousios 36, 53
homoousios 35, 164, 265, 390
honestiores 509
honores 120
Honoria Augusta 54, 263
honorific arches 32–34
Honorius, Flavius 263–264
   and Alaric 12, 264, 438, 586
   and Athaulf 53, 264
   and Attalus 54
   and Burgundians 84
   and Castinus 100
   and Claudian 124
   and Constantine III 144
   ludi held by 333
   and Ravenna 466
   and Stilicho, Flavius 124, 200, 264, 514–515
   and trousers 130
   wives of 124, 200, 351
hoplomachi 244
Horace 216, 264–265, 300, 323, 339, 340
Hormasdas 265
Hormazd Ardashir (Hormazd I) 265
Hormazd II 265
Hormazd III 265
horologia 543
horses 551
Hortensius (Cicero) 57
hortis, De (Martialis) 354
Hosius 265, 390
Hostilian 256, 265–266
Hostilianus 266, 552–553
houses 183, 275, 474, 582
humiliores 243, 510
Huneric 237, 266, 398
Huns 266–267 *See also* Attila; Mandiuch; Rugila; Uldin
   and Aetius, Flavius 7–8, 54, 102, 342, 587
   and Alans 12
   and Anthemius 20
   and Constantinople 146
   and Goths 383–384, 402–403
   and Italia 279
   and Marcian 347
   and Theodosius II 535
   and Valentinian III 565
   and Visigoths 5
   and Worms 84
Hunting Baths 72
Hydatius 267
Hyginian legionary camp 309
Hyginus, Gaius Julius 267, 309
hylics 566
Hypatia 163, 267, 356
hypocausts 583
Hyrcanus 22–23, 34, 37, 257, 267, 287, 380, 426

I

iaculatione equestri, De (Pliny) 436
Iamblichus 6, 268, 385
Iazyges 36, 268, 479, 598
Iberia 268, 424–425

Ibis (Ovid) 404
Icelus 226, 268–269
Iceni 78, 79, 269
Ides 90, 269
idiologus 192
idolatria, De (Tertullian) 528
Idumaea 269
ientaculum 215
Ignatius (St. Ignatius) 269
Ilerda 8, 87, 122, 269–270
Illyricum (Dalmatia) 72, 270–271, 514
Illyricum Inferius 270
Illyricum Superius 270
imagines 271
immunes 308, 448
immunitas 271
imperator 58, 76, 271
Imperial Cult 271–272, 406, 468, 509
   in Achaea 2
   in Britannia 81
   in Camulodunum 92
   and Christianity 111
   and flamens 214
   in Gallia 229
   in Lepcis Magna 316
   in Lugdunum 333
   in Macedonia 337
   and Mithraism 371
   in Narbo 381
   in Nemausus 384
   in Nicomedia 390
   in Pergamum 419
   in Rome 473
Imperial Guard *See* Praetorian Guard
Imperial mints 131, 134
Imperial Post 161, 378, 472, 551
Imperial Secret Service 221
Imperiim Galliarum 553
imperium 150, 272
Imperium Galliarum 121, 123
imperium maius 60, 272, 272–273, 458
imperium proconsulares 61, 149, 272, 273
impetrativa 56
inauguration 151
Incarnatione, De (Theodore) 533
Incarnatione Domini, De (Cassian) 99
Incitatus 225, 273
India 273
Indike (Arrian) 40
industry 273–274, 277
infamia 531
Infancy Gospel 281
inflation 132
informers *See delatores; frumentarii*
infula 576
Ingenuus 62, 233, 274
Ingiuomerus 274
inheritance tax 524
ink 594–595
Innocent I 274–275
In Pisonem (Cicero) 432
Insani Montes 487
Institutes (Gaius) 225
Institutes of the Monastic Life (Cassian) 99
Institutio Oratoria (Quintilian) 324, 463

Instructiones (Commodian) 325
Insubres 230
insula 175, 474
Insula Batavorum 70
insulae 194
Insulae Britannicae See Britannia (British Isles)
Insula Tiberina 473
intelligence service 221, 466–467
intercalation 89
internship 190
The Interpretation of Dreams (Artemidorus) 48
io hymen 2
Ionia 275
io triumphe 2
Ireland *See* Hibernia
Irenaeus 275, 412
Isaac the Great (St. Sahak) 275
Isauria 205, 275–276, 342
Isis 276, 468
Issus 276, 500
Istria 276
Italia 135, 276–279, 278
Italica (legion) 311
Italicus 214, 279
itineraria 279, 420
Itinerarium Antoninianum 279, 472
Itinerarium Burdigalense sive Hierosolymitanum 279, 472
Itinerarium Egeriae 279, 303
Iturius 91, 180
iudices 199
iudicium 190
Iuga 279
iuga 524
iugerum 593
iugum 551
iurisprudentes 190
ius civile 279–280, 280, 304
ius emphyteuticum 280
ius gentium 280, 304, 446
ius honorum See praetor
ius Italicum 135, 277, 280, 316
ius Latii 120, 280, 377, 505
iusta facere 169

J

James 110, 281
James the Greater 281
James the Less 281–282
Janiculus Hill 473
Jannaeus 17, 267, 283
Janus 48, 245, 282, 445
Janus bifrons 282
javelin 307
Javolenus Priscus, Gaius Octavius Tidius Tassianus Lucius 282
Jericho 282
Jerome ("St. Jerome") 36, 185, 206, 282, 364, 400
Jerusalem 282–285, 283, 288
Jerusalem, Council of 67, 110, 281
Jerusalem itinerary 279, 472
Jewish Antiquities (Josephus) 9, 286
Jewish rebellion (66–70 C.E.)
   Apollinaris legion in 313
   in Galilee 228, 235
   Gallus, Cestius and 234
   and Herodion 258
   in Idumaea 269

   and John of Gischala 286
   Josephus, Flavius in 286
   Justus in 295
   Silva, Flavius and 506
   and Temple of Jerusalem 526
   Vespasian and 288, 574
Jewish revolt (132–135 C.E.) 67, 192, 251, 258, 284, 289, 502
Jewish War (Josephus) 9, 284, 286, 598
Jews, and Christianity 110–111
John 285
John Chrysostom 285
   and Cassian 99
   and Eudoxia, Aelia 32, 116, 201, 285
   and Innocent I 275
   and Isaurians 276, 285
   and Palladius 408
   and Theodore of Mopsuestia 532–533
   and Theophilus 285, 535
John of Gischala 242, 283–284, 286, 538
John the Usurper 50, 100, 286
Josephus, Flavius 9, 187, 228, 235, 284, 286, 286, 295
Jotapianus 286–287
Jovian (Flavius Jovinus) 168, 287, 292
Jovians and Herculians 287
Jovinus 53, 287
Juba I 88, 122, 224, 287, 395
Juba II 224, 287, 356
Judaea 287–289, 407 *See also* Jewish rebellion; Jewish revolt; *specific city*
   Agrippa I and 9
   Archelaus and 32
   Aretas III and 34
   Herod the Great and 257
   Hyrcanus and 22–23
   procurators of 209, 210–211, 289, 443
Judaism 289, 425, 468, 484
Judaizers 110
Jugurthine War 395
Julia (Caesar's aunt) 86
Julia (daughter of Augustus) 289–290
   and Agrippa, Marcus Vipsanius 10, 25
   and Antyllus 26
   and Marcellus 60, 346
   and Phoebe 429
   sons of 86, 88
   and Tiberius 50, 234, 539
Julia (daughter of Drusus Caesar) 290, 388, 495
Julia (daughter of Julius Caesar) 88, 289, 442, 556
Julia (daughter of Marcus Agrippa) 290
Julia (sister of Julius Caesar) 289
Julia Domna 94, 193, 290–291, 429, 500
Julia Flavia 180, 290, 483
Julia Livilla 290
Julia Maesa 193, 235, 291, 338, 502
Julia Mamaea 56, 67, 172, 291, 502
Julia Soaemias 193, 235, 291
Julian calendar 90

Julian the Apostate 149, **291–292**, 292
  and Aedesius 6
  and Alamanni 12, 292
  and Ammianus Marcellinus 17
  and Apollinaris of Laodicea 27
  and Arbitio, Flavius 31
  and Arianism 53
  and Aurelius Victor 62
  and battle of Argentoratum 35
  and Christianity 291–292, 406
  coinage of 132
  and Donatism 184
  and Eutherius 203–204
  and Franks 219, 292
  and Libanius 320
  and Lupicinus, Flavius 334
  and Maximus of Ephesus 361
  and Mesopotamia 366
  and Mithras cult 371
  and Neoplatonism 385
  physician of 400
  and Priscus 453
  and Procopius 455
  and Saturninus 490–491
  tutor of 116
  and Vadomar 563
Julianus, Salvius 96, **292–293**, 294–295, 338
Julianus, Tettius 170, 181, 522
Julio-Claudians 603 *See also* Augustus; Claudius; Gaius Caligula; Nero; Tiberius
Julius **293**
Julius, Clemens **293**
Julius Africanus, Sextus **293**
Julius Caesar (Suetonius) 88
Julius Gabinianus, Sextus **293**
Julius Nepos 51, 244
Julius Victor, Gaius **293**
Junia 99, **293**
Junius Otho 82, **293**
Juno 245, 279, **293–294**, 331, 355, 375, 467, 511, 526
Jupiter 48, 60, 179, 213, 245, **294**, 467
jurists 6, **294–295**, 303, 325, 446
Justina **295**
Justinian 2, 4, 36, 304
Justin Martyr **295**, 429
Justus **295**
Justus, Cantonius **295**, 439
Jutes **295–296**
Juthungi 433
Juthungine War 62, 296
Juvenal 213, 284, **296**, 490
Juvenalia **296**
Juvenalis, Flavius **296**
Juvenal of Jerusalem **296**
Juvencus, Gaius Vettius Aquilinus **296**
Juventas 245, **296**

K

Kalends 90, **297**, 590
Kanus, Julius **297**
katholikos 275
Knights *See* Equites
Kniva 7, 168, 170, 247, **297**
Koblenz **297**
koin 253–254
koinon 272

L

Labeo, Pompnius **298**
Labeo Marcus Antistius 93, 295, **298**, 455, 456
Labienus, Quintus **298**, 405
Labienus, Titus 12, 139, 232, **298–299**, 377, 530
lacerna 130
Laco, Cornelius 226, 269, **299**, 432, 449, 467
Laco, Graecinus **299**
laconicum 71, 514
Lactantius 112, 158, 227, **299**, 430
Laelianus, Upius Cornelius **299**, 445
Laeta, Clodia **299**
laeti 299
Laetus **299–300**, 334
Laetus, Quintus Aemilius 140, 189, **300**, 421
Lamia, Aelius Plautius **300**
lamps 223
land tax 524, 555
land transportation 551–552
Langobardi 279, 300, **300**, 348
languages 301, *302*, 303
lanista 243
Laodicea, Canons of **300**
lapis manalis 344
lapsi 153, 162, **300**, 393, 422
Lapsis, De (Cyprian) 162
Lara 245, **300**, 301
lararium 184, **300–301**
Lares 169, 245, 300, **301**, 418
Lares compitales 301
Lares praestites 301
Lares publici 301
Lar familiaris 301
Large Baths 72
Largus, Scribonius 301, 362
Lateranus, Plautius **301**, 433
Late Stoa 515
latifundia 207, **301**
Latin language **301–303**
Latium **303**
latrine 216–217
Latrocinium Council 107, 316
latus clavus 496
laudatio funebris 409
Laureolus (Catullus) 102
lavatory 216–217
law 3, 149–150, **303–305**, *304*, 318–319, 455, 482 *See also specific law*
Lawrence (Laurence) **305**
leagae 368
lectica 551
lectio 190
lectus 222
legal system *See* law
Legatio ad Gaium (Philo) 427
legati pro praetore 456
legatus **305–306**
legatus Augusti pro praetore 306, 555
legatus legionis 306
leges 303
legibus, De (Cicero) 117
legionary camps 240, 309, 447
legiones palatinae 310
legions **306–314**, *307*
  development of 306–307
  in late Empire 310
  list of 310–314

organization of 308–309
  training and equipment of 307–308
lemures 169, **314**
Lemuria 169, 344
Lentulus, Gnaeus Cornelius **314**
Lentulus, P. Cornelius 25
Lentulus Gaetulicus, Gnaeus Cornelius 225, **314–315**, 317
Leo I (emperor of the East) **315**
  and Aspar 50, 315
  and Basiliscus 69, 200, 315
  and Excubitors 205
  and Glycerius 244
  and Isauria 276, 315, 342
  legions of 310
  and Nepos, Julius 386
  and Olybrius 398
  and Vandals 237, 315
  wife of 572–573
  and Zeno 276, 315, 342, 599
Leo I (pope) 20, 38, 54, 107, 260, 263, **315–316**, 546, 565
Leo II **315**
Leontia 315, 416, 572
Lepcis Magna 46, 69, 72, **316**, 472, 500
Lepida, Aemilia 187, **316–317**, 464
Lepida, Domitia 317, 367, 386–387, 485
Lepidus, Marcus Aemilius (courtier) **317**
Lepidus, Marcus Aemilius (Triumvir) 25–26, 58, 82, 312, **317**, 556–557
Lepidus, Marcus Aemilius (would-be assassin) **317**
Lepidus, Paullus Aemilius **317–318**
"Lesbia" *See* Clodia
The Letter of Aristeas 15
Letters (Cicero) 118
Letters (Pliny) 123
Letters (Sidonius) 505
lex **318–319**
lex Aelia Sentia 318, 508, 510
lex Annales 318
lex Antonia de actis confirmandis 318
lex Appuleia 343
lex Calpurnia de ambitu 318
lex Cassia de plebeis in patricious adlegendis 318, 415
lex Clodiae 318
lex Cornelia 318
lex curiata 4
lex de adulteriis coercendis 318
lex de imperio Vespasian 318
lex de maritandis ordinibus 23
lex Fufia Caninia 318, 508, 510
lex Gabiniae 318, 441
lex Iulia de maiestate 171
lex Julia agraria 318
lex Julia de adulteriis 60, 352–353
lex Julia de ambitu 319
lex Julia de maiestate 319, 343
lex Julia de maritandis ordinibus 60, 319, 352
lex Julia et Papia Poppaea 4
lex Julia municipalis 552
lex Junia Petronia 319, 508
lex Licinia de provincia Caesaris 319
lex Malacitana 319
lex Manciana 319
lex Manilia 117

lex Munatia Aemilia 319
lex Papia Poppaea 171, 319, 352, 412
lex Petronia 319, 508
lex Pompeia Licinia 556
lex Rufrena 319
lex Saenia 415
lex Titia 319, 556, 557
lex Trebonia 553, 556
lex Vatinia de Caesaris Provincia 556, 570
lex Vatinius 319
Libanius 21, 285, **319–320**, 325, 378, 471
libellatici 300, **320**
libelli pacis 162, 320
libellis 199, **320**
libellis respondens 320
Liberators 88, **320** *See also* Brutus, Marcus Junius; Cassius (Gaius Cassius Longinus)
  and Antonius, Lucius 25
  at battle of Philippi 58, 75, 99, 426–427, 557
  and Cicero, Marcus Tullius 118
  and Labienus, Quintus 298
  and Messalla Corvinus 366
Liberatrix (legion) 311
Liberius 167, 203, 320
Liber memorialis (Ampelius) 18
Liber spectaculorum (Martial) 353
libertas 271
libertini 219
Libitina **320**
libitinarius 320
Libius Severus 6, 20, 51, **320–321**, 471
Libo, M. Drusus 171, 321, 340
libra 592, 593
Library of Alexandria **15–16**
Library of Celsus 196
Library of Ephesus 196, *197*
Liburnia **321**
liburnicae 321, 504
Licinius, Valerius Licinianus **321–322**
  and Constantine 5, 143, 144, 321–322
  and Edict of Milan 112, 321, 367–368
  and Maximinus Daia 321, 359
  wife of 142
Licinius Macer Calvus, Gaius 19, **322**
lictors 151, 208, **322**
Life of Apollonius of Tyana (Philostratus) 429
Life of Pompey (Plutarch) 370
lighting 223
Ligur, Valerius **322**
Liguria 29, **322**
Ligurians 154, 230
limes 240, 310, **322–323**
Limitanei 143, 176, 310, **323**
limites 322–323
Lincoln *See* Lindum
Lindum (Lincoln) 78, **323**
Lingua Latina, De (Varro) 568
liquamen 216
literati 508
literature xii, **323–325**, 437
litterator 190

Lives of Famous Men (Nepos) 386
Lives of the Caesars (Suetonius) 123, 493, 516
Lives of the Great Men (Suetonius) 516
Lives of the Sophists (Eunapius) 116, 202
The Lives of the Sophists (Philostratus) 429
Livia 56, **326**, 327
   and Agrippa Postumus 10, 326
   and Agrippina the Elder 10–11, 326, 434
   and Antonia 23
   and Augustus 58, 61, 326
   and Gaius Caligula 225
   and Plancina, Munatia 434
   sons of 187, 326, 539–540
Livianus, Claudius **326**–327
Livilla 23, 27, 86, 187, 290, **327**, 494–495
living conditions 474–475
living quarters 183, 275
Livius, Drusus Claudius 327
Livy (Titus Livius) 69, 282, 324, **327**–328
loincloth 130
Lollia Paulina **328**, 467
Lollius, Marcus **328**
Lollius Urbicus, Quintus 78, **328**
Londinium 78, 80, 189, **328**–329, 522
London *See* Londinium
Longinus 144, 145, **329**
Longinus, Cassius **329**
Longus, Velius **329**
lorica hamata 307
lorica segmentata 307
lorica squamata 307
Luca, Conference of 156, 183, **329**–330, 442
Lucan, Marcus Annaeus 186, 324, **330**, 363
Lucania **330**
Lucian 203, **330**
Lucian of Antioch 38, **330**
Lucifer of Cagliari (Lucifer of Sardinia) **330**–331
Lucilius, Gaius **331**, 489, 490
Lucilla, Annia Aurelia Galeria 140, 158, **331**, 440
Lucilla, Domitia 174, **331**, 349
Lucina **331**
Lucullus 39, 542
Lucusta the Poisoner 81, **331**
ludi 243, **331**–333, 378
ludi Actiaci 332, 391
ludi Apollinares 331
ludi Augustales 331–332
ludi Capitolini 253, 332
ludi Ceriales 332
ludi Circenses 331, 332
ludi Decennales 332
ludi Florales 332
ludi magister 190
ludi Megalenses 332
ludi Palatini 332
ludi Plebeii 332
ludi Pontificales 332
ludi Romani 332
ludi Saeculares 27, 331, 332–333, 477

ludi Scaenici 331
ludi Terentini 332
ludi Victoriae Caesaris 58, 333
ludi Volcanalici 333
ludi votivi 331
ludus 243
Lugdunum 119, 131, 228, 239, 300, 333–334
Lugdunum, battle of 334, 500
Luna 245, 334
lunch 215
Lupercalia 208
Lupicinus, Flavius 334, 431
Lusitania 262, 365
lusoria arma 243
Lutetia 119, 228, 232, **334**
Lycaonia **334**
Lycia 335
Lydia 49, 50, **335**
Lydia 28

M

Macarius Magnes 336
Macarius the Egyptian 336
Macedonia 2, 253, **336**–337
Macedonica (legion) 311, 312
macellum 337
Macer, Aemilius 337
Macriana (legion) 311
Macrianus, Titus Fulvius 62, 67, 233, 337
Macrianus, Titus Fulvius Junius 67, 337–338
Macrinus, Marcus Opellius 6, 21, 68, 95, 173, 193, **338**, 448
Macrinus, Veturius 338
Macro, Quintus Naevius Cordus Sutorius 126, 196, 225, 299, **338**–339
Macrobius, Ambrosius Theodosius 339, 499
Maeatae 339, 430
Maecenas, Gaius Cilnius 72, 264, 339, 378, 456, 585
Maecianus, Lucius Volusius 339–340
maeniana 136
Magetobriga 340
magic 340
magister equitum 31, 143, 310, **340**–341
magister equitum praesentalis 341
magister libellorum 320
magister memoriae **341**
magister militum 6, 100, 143, 201, 310, **341**–342, 383, 415
magister militum praesentalis 341
magister militum praesentis 341
magister officiorum 122, 138, 141, 143, 212, **342**
magister peditum 31, 50, 143, 310, 340, 341, **342**
magister populi 173
magister scriniorum **342**
magistrates 303, 304, 446
magistri scrinii 493
Magnentius, Flavius Magnus 31, 142, 148–149, **342**–343, 378, 386, 427
maiestas 167, 171, 224, 319, 343, 462, 540
maiores 213

Majorian 6, **343**–344, 433, 471, 505
Mamertinus, Claudius 344
Mamurra 344
manceps 161
mancipationes 4
Mandiuch 54, 266, **344**, 481
manes 169, 301, **344**
Mani 344–345
Manichaeism 57, **344**–345, 468, 567
Manilius 345
Manilius, Marcus 345
manipulus 306
mansiones 161, **345**, 472
Manu ad ferrum 61
manumissio 510
manumission of slaves 508, 523
manum viri 352
manus 352, 593
map 424
Marcella 10, 25
Marcellinus of Dalmatia 342, 345, 471
Marcellus, Lucius Ulpius 140, **345**–346
Marcellus, Marcus Claudius 10, 60, 289, 326, **346**
Marcellus, Nonius 346
Marcellus, Sextus Varius 193, **346**
Marcellus, Ulpius 346
Marcellus of Gaul 346
Marcia 189, **346**
Marcian 50, 64, 107, **346**–347
Marciana, Ulpia 347
Marcianus, Aelius 347
Marcionism 347
Marcius, Publius 347
Marcomanni 62, 256, 277, **347**–348, 351–352
Marcomannic Wars 13, 139, 240, 348–349, 350, 466
Marcus Aurelius 251, **349**–351, *350*
   adoption of 23, 24
   and Aelius Caesar 7
   and architecture 476–477
   and Ariogaesus 36
   assassination of 243
   and Athens 53
   and Aufidius Victorinus 55
   and Battarius 72
   and Candidus, Tiberius Aurelius 92
   and Cassius, Gaius Avidius 99
   and Castra Praetoria 101
   and Chatti 108
   and China 109
   and Christianity 111
   daughter of 331
   legions of 311
   and literature 324
   and Marcomanni 348–349, 350
   and Pertinax 421
   physician of 227
   and Pompeianus, Tiberius Claudius 440
   and Pomponius Proculus, Titus 442
   and Sardinia 487
   sons of 139
   and Stoicism 350–351, 428, 515
   and Suebi 516
   tutors of 13, 221, 257, 339, 349, 481

   and Verus, Lucius 349–350, 573
   and Verus, P. Martius 574
   wives of 209, 349, 350
Mare Internum 363
Maria 264, **351**
Mariamme Tower 285
Mariamne 37, 257
marines 252, **351**
Maritime Alps 351
Marius 351
Marius, Marcus Aurelius **351**
Marius (consul) 86, 306
Marius Maximus, Lucius 351
Maroboduus 274, 300, 348, 351–352, 366, 516
marriage 60, 319, **352**–353, 594 *See also* divorce
Mars 48, 60, 213, 245, 353, 484, 561
Marsi 353
Martial xi, 296, 324, **353**–354, 421
Martialis, Julius 205, 354
Martialis, Q. Gargilius 354
Martianus Capella 354
Martin of Tours 354, 453, 502
martyrology 259
martyrs 111–112, 281, 305, 330, 409, 439
Masada 269, **354**–355
Massilia 87, 122, 183, 230, **355**
Materia Medica (Dioscorides) 179
Mater Matuta 355
Maternas, Curiatius 355
Mater Regina 355
mathematics 355–356, 459
Matheseos (Firmicus) 212
Matidia 356
Mattiarii seniores 315
Mauretania 8, 287, **356**–357, 459
Mauretania Caesariensis 357
Mauretania Tingitana 357
Mauriac, battle of *See* Catalaunian Plain
Mavia 357, 487
Maxentius, Marcus Aurelius Valerius **357**–358
   and Alexander, Domitius 13
   Basilica Maxentia built by 69
   and Carthage 97
   and Constantine the Great 142, 143, 227, 358, 369, 477
   father of 208, 359
   and Fausta, Flavia Maxima 208
   and grain supply 20
   and Licinius 321
   and Praetorian Guard 358, 447, 448
   and Severus II 358, 499–500
Maximian **358**–359
   and Bagaudae 65
   baths built by 72
   and Carausius 96
   and Diocletian 175–176
   son of 208, 357–358, 359
   wife of 204
Maximinus 359
Maximinus Daia 5, 112, 142, 143, 321, **359**–360
Maximinus I Thrax 360
   and Alamanni 12, 360
   and Aquileia 30, 360
   assassination of 51, 360

and Capellianus 93
and Carthage 97
and Gordian I 246, 360
and Goths 247
and Senate 496
Maximus, A. Lappius 181, 360
Maximus, Gaius Julius Verius 360
Maximus, L. Marius 6, 360–361
Maximus, Magnus 73, 247, 341,
361, 431, 534
Maximus, Sextus Quintilius
463–464
Maximus, Tattius 361
Maximus of Ephesus 116, 361
Maximus of Tyre 361
meals 215–216
measures 592–593
meat market 337
Media Atropatene 361
medicamentis, De (Marcellus) 346
medici 362
medicine 49, 227, 301, 346,
361–362, 400, 511
Mediolanum 264, 277, 358, 359,
362–363, 466
Meditations (Marcus Aurelius) 13,
221, 351
Mediterranean Sea 363
Megalesia 161, 363
Meherdates 246, 363
Mela, Annaeus 93, 363–364
Mela, Pomponius 364
Melania the Elder 364
Melania the Younger 364
Melitian Schism 364, 390
Melitius and the Melitians 364, 422
Melitius of Antioch 364
memoria 341
men
clothing for 129, 546
footwear for 130
Menas (Menodorus) 364–365
mensores frumentarii cereris 106
merchant ships 503, 552, 552
Mercury 245, 300, 301, 365
Merida (Emerita) 262, 365
Merobaudes, Flavius (consul) 247,
340, 365, 565
Merobaudes, Flavius (poet) 365
Mesopotamia 252, 365–366, 392
Messalla Corvinus, Marcus Valerius
154, 366, 449
Messalla Messallinus, Marcus
Valerius 72, 366
Messallina, Statilia 366–367, 388
Messallina, Valeria 367
and Claudius 125
daughter of 397
and Julia Livilla 290
and Lateranus, Plautius 301,
435
and Mnester 373
mother of 317
and Narcissus 381
and Polybius 439
and Silana, Junia 505
and Silius, Gaius 505, 506
son of 81
Metamorphoses (Apuleius) 28, 325
Metamorphoses (Ovid) 404
Metellus Celer, Quintus Caecilius 8,
37, 128, 367

Metellus Scipio, Quintus Caecilius
367
methodo medendi, De (Galen) 227
Middle Academy 428
Middle Stoa 515
Milan *See* Mediolanum
Milan, Edict of 112, 114, 144, 321,
367–368, 406, 479
miles 307, 308
Milestones 368, 551
Miletus 368
milia 393
milia passuum 368, 593
miliarense 132, 133
Milichus 368, 433, 491
military engineering 195
military treasury 7
mille 393
mille passus 368, 593
Milo, Titus Annius 86, 117, 173,
368–369, 485
Milvian Bridge 4, 143, 208, 369, 473
mime 530
minerals 262–263
Minerva 48, 245, 369–370, 467, 526
Minervia (legion) 311
Minervina 144, 158
minimi 370
minores 213
mints 131, 134
mirrors 420
Misenum 72, 370
Misenum (*classis*) 383
Misenum, Conference of 370, 441
Mithraism 468
Mithras 30, 52, 370–371
Mithridates (king of Armenia)
371–372, 424, 465, 561
Mithridates (king of Bosporus) 77,
372
Mithridates (king of Iberians) 47,
372
Mithridates of Pergamum 15, 122,
372–373, 391, 599
Mithridates III (king of Parthia)
224, 372, 401, 518
Mithridates IV (coruler of Parthia)
372
Mnester 373, 531
Modalism 482
Modestus, Domitius 373
Moesia 156, 165, 181, 337,
373–374, 391
Moesia (*classis*) 383
Moesia Inferior 374
Moesia Superior 374
Moguntiacum (Mainz) 239, 240,
374–375
Monarchianism 417, 482
Moneta 375, 526, 527
monetary system 131–134
monogamia, De (Tertullian) 528
Monophysitism 375
monotheism 468
Mons Aurasius 375
Mons Aventinus 260–261
Mons Caelius 260
Mons Capitolinus 260
Mons Esquilinus 261
Mons Janiculus 261
Mons Palatinus 260
Mons Vaticanus *See* Vatican Hill

Montanism 114, 375
Montanus, Votienus 375, 453
Monumentum Ancyranum 470, 474
Moors 263, 356–357, 375–376, 463
Moral Enchiridion (Epictetus) 428
Moralia (Plutarch) 437
Moretum 28
Mortibus Persecutorum, De
(Lactantius) 299
mosaic floors 222, 223
Mosella (Ausonius) 63
"Mother of all Gauls" 38
Mucianus, Gaius Licinius 74, 121,
181, 234, 376
mules 551
Muliebris, Temple of Fortuna 376
mulsum 216
Munda 88, 123, 356, 376–377, 441
munera 120
munera municipalia 120
municipia civium Romanorum 377
municipium 120, 135, 254, 316, 377
Munitionibus Castrorum, De
(Hyginus) 309
munus publicum 120
Murena, Licinius Aulus Terentius
Varro 339, 377–378
Murmurithon (Syrus) 520
Mursa Major 31, 343, 378
music 378, 530–531
Musonianus, Strategius 378
must 216
mutationes 378, 472
Mutina 123, 317, 379
Mysia 49, 379, 419
mysticism 385

N

Nabataeans 30, 380, 422
Nacolea 380
Namatianus, Rutilius Claudius
380–381
Narbo 31, 230, 381
Narbonensis *See* Gallia Narbonensis
Narcissus (freedman) 367, 381
Narcissus (slayer of Emperor
Commodus) 140, 346, 381
Narses 39, 265, 381, 392, 488
Nasamones 381–382
Nasidius, Q. 382
Natalis, Antonius 382, 433
natatio 71
Natura Animalium (Aelian) 7
natura Deorum, De (Cicero) 117
Natural History (Pliny) 68, 109, 186,
324, 340, 362, 436
Naulochus 58, 382, 441
naumachia 137
navarch 383
navy 251–252, 382–383, 431,
503–504
Nedao 266, 383–384
nefastus 575
Nemausus 29, 29, 384, 384
Nemesianus 91, 325, 384
Nemesius 384
Neoplatonism 57, 244, 356,
384–385, 428 *See also specific
philosopher*
Neo-Pythagoreanism 385–386, 428
Nepos, Cornelius 386
Nepos, Julius 202, 386, 398, 479

Nepos, Platorius 386
Nepotianus, Julius 342, 386
Neptune 245, 386, 484
Nero 386–387 *See also* Pisonian
Conspiracy
and Achaea 2
on adoption 4
and Apollo 27
and architecture 44–45, 103,
387, 475, 525
and Armenia 39, 387
and art 42, 387
Augustans formed by 57
Augustiani established by 2
and Baiae 66
and Bosporus kingdom 78
and Boudicca 78, 387
bureaucratic system of 7
and Burrus, Sextus Afranius 84,
387, 449
and Capito, Cossutianus 93
and Cassius Longinus, Gaius
99–100
and Christianity 111, 433
coinage of 131
and Corbulo, Gnaeus Domitius
151–152, 387
and Doryphorus 185–186
and Drusus 187
and Epaphroditus 196
and Eprius Marcellus, Titus
Clodius 198
father of 182, 386
and Formulus 217
freedmen of 219, 424
and Galba, Servius Sulpicius 226
and Helius 252–253
legion of 311
and literature 324
lovers of 3, 158, 397, 513
and Lucan, Marcus Annaeus 330
and Messalina, Statilia 366–367
and Moesia 373
mother of 11–12, 56, 81, 386
and Nerva 388
and Otho 403
and Paetus, Lucius Caesennius
406
palace of 184, 245
and Pallas, Marcus Antonius
408
and Paris 413
and Petronius 423
and Praetorian Guard 447, 512
and Primus, Marcus Antonius
452
and Rhodes 471
and Rufus, Cluvius 480–481
and Scribonii brothers 492–493
and Seneca 3, 11, 19, 387, 416
and Silanus, M. Junius 505–506
and Soranus, Barea 103
suicide of 387, 507
and Thrasea Paetus 537
and Tigellinus 449, 541
and Tiridates 47–48
tutors of 387, 496–497
and Vespasian 574
and Vetus, Lucius Antistius 577
and Vindex 387, 583
wives of 125, 387, 388, 397,
444

Nero, Julius Caesar 288, **388**
Nerva, Marcus Cocceius **388**
  and Aelianus, Casperius 7
  and Beneventum 74
  and Dio Cocceianus 178
  and Domitian 52
  Forum Transitorium built by
    219
  and Frontinus, Sextus Julius 221
  and John 285
  and Praetorian Guard 338, 447
  and Raetia 465
  and Trajan 388, 548
Nervii 104, 231, **388–389**
Nestor, Julianus **389**
Nestorianism 375, 533
Nestorius 103, 163, 196, 204, **389**
Nevitta, Flavius **389**
New Academy 428
The New Testament 116
Nicaea **389**
Nicaea, battle of **389**
Nicaea, Council of 35, 38, 52, 76,
    112, 114, 115, 179, 203, 265,
    300, 364, **389–390**, 415
Nicator 20, 26
Nice **390**, 581
Nicene Creed 35, 36, 203, 248, **390**
Nicolaus of Damascus **390**
Nicomedia 46, 76, 176, 277,
    390–391
Nicopolis (city in Epirus) 198, **391**
Nicopolis (city in Moesia) **391**
Nigrinus, Gaius Avidius **391**
Nike 390, 581
Nile 87, 191, **391**
Nile, battle of **391**
Nîmes *See* Nemausus
Nisibis **392**
noble class 415
Noctes Atticae (Gellius) 237, 324
nominatio **392**
non conveniendo cum haereticis, De
    (Lucifer) 331
Nones 90, **392**
Norbanus 181, 388, **392**
Noricum **392–393**
notarii 141, **393**
Notitia Dignitatum **393**
Novatian 114, 115, 162, **393**
Novatianism 300, **393**
novendiale sacrificium 169
Nuceria **393**
Numa 378, 443, 484, 527, 575
numeral adverbs **394–395**
numerals, Roman **393–395**
numeri **395**
Numerian 26, 51, 96, 98, 175, **395**,
    448
Numerianus **395**
Numidia 8, 9, 93, 159, 261,
    395–396 *See also* Juba I; *specific*
    city
nummus 499
nummus castrensis **396**
nutrition 215–216
Nux (Ovid) 404
nymphaeum 316

O

oath of allegiance 484
oblativa 55

Obodas 34, **397**
Octavia 3, 23, 25, 58, 82, 123, **397**
Octavia, Claudia 11, 19, 84, 125,
    367, 387, 388, **397**, 505
Octavian *See* Augustus
Octavius, Gaius **397–398**
Octavius (Felix) 209
Odaenath 67, 233, **398**, 408, 488,
    503, 600
Odes (Horace) 264–265
Ode to Germanicus (Priscus) 453
Odoacer 386, **398**, 479, 496, 599
Oea (Tripoli) **398**
offenses 305
oil lamps 223
Olba **398**
Old Academy 428
olive press 274
olives 50
Ollius, T. **398**
Olybrius 20, 237, 244, 320, **398**
Olybrius, Quintus Clodius
    Hermogenianus **398–399**
Olympiodorus of Thebes **399**
On Alexander (Dexippus) 173
On Anatomical Procedure (Galen)
    227
On Faith (Ambrose) 17
On Fishing (Nemesianus) 384
On His Consulship (Cicero) 118
On His Own Times (Cicero) 118
On Hunting (Nemesianus) 384
On Man's Nature (Nemesius) 384
On Medical Experience (Galen) 227
On Perfection (Gregory) 248
On Seamanship (Nemesianus) 384
On the Christian Life (Gregory) 248
On the Fortune of the Romans
    (Plutarch) 437
On the Holy Spirit (Ambrose) 17
On the Holy Spirit (Basil) 68
On the Incarnation (Athanasius) 53
On the Life of Julius Agricola (Tacitus)
    522
On the Marriage of Mercury and
    Philosophy (Martianus) 354
On the Movement of the Muscles
    (Galen) 227
On the Natural Faculties (Galen) 227
On Virginity (Ambrose) 17
On Virginity (Gregory) 248
On Widows (Ambrose) 17
Opalia 399
operculum 18
Oppian **399**
oppidium 119
Oppius, Gaius **399**
Ops, goddess of the harvest 245,
    399
optimo genere oratorum, De (Cicero)
    117
optimo iure Quiritium 280
optio 308
optio equitum 309
Opus agriculturae (Palladius) 408
Orange *See* Arausio
Oratio ad Graecos (Tatian) 523
oratione, De (Tertullian) 528
Orator ad M. Brutus (Cicero) 117
oratore, De (Cicero) 117
oratory **399**
orbi 319

orchards 235
ordinal numbers 394
ordinarii 508
Ordo Nobilium Urbium (Ausonius)
    63
Orestes 386, 398, **399**, 479
Orgetorix **399**
Oribasius **399–400**
Oriens **400**
Origen 14, 18, 38, 103, 172, 179,
    198, **400**
Origenes **400**
The Origin of Sin (Prudentius) 325
Origo gentis romanae (Aurelius) 62
ornamenta **401**
ornamenta triumphalia 555
Orodes II 47, 97, 298, 372, **401**,
    518
Orodes III **401**
Oroses 41, **401**, 413
Orosius, Paulus 15, **401**
Orthographia, De (Scaurus) 492
Orthographia, De (Velius) 570
Osiris 276, **401**, 468
Osroene 190, 300, **401–402**
Ostia **402**
Ostrogoths 5, 220, 244, 402,
    402–403, 564
Otho, Lucius Salvius Titianus 104,
    403, 432–433
Otho, Marcus Salvius **403**
  and Caecina Alienus, Aulus 433
  and Castra Praetoria 101
  and Celsus, Marius 104
  and Firmus, Plotius 212
  and Galba 227, 403, 507
  and Gallus, Appius Annius 233
  legions of 311
  and Poppaea, Sabina 158, 444
  and Praetorian Guard 73, 447
  and Primus, Marcus Antonius
    452
  and Proculus, Licinius 456
  and Tigellinus 542
  and Vitellius, Aulus 16, 73, 233,
    403, 433, 507, 587
ovatio 403
oven *216*
"overseers" 112
Ovid 323, **403–404**, *404*, 456

P

Pacatianus, Titus Claudius Marinus
    405
Pacatus, Latinus Drepanius **405**
Pachomius **405**
pack animals 551
Pacorus 401, 405, 571
Pacorus II **405–406**
paenitentia, De (Tertullian) 528
paenula 130
Paetus, Lucius Caesennius 48, 152,
    406
paganism **406–407** *See also*
    Imperial Cult
  Cynegius, Maternus and 162
  Eugenius, Flavius and 201
  Flavianus and 214
  and gladiators 243
  Julian and 291–292, 320
  and philosophy 427–428
  Praetextatus and 446

  and science 356
  Symmachus and 518
Paidogogus (Clement) 126
Palace of Lausus 69
Palaemon 445
Palaemon, Quintus Remmius 37,
    407
Palaestina **407**
Palatine Hill 260, 473
Palatini 143, **407**
Pales 245, **407**
palestra 71
Palfurius Sura **407**
palla 129
Palladas **407**
Palladius 103, **407–408**
Palladius, Rutilius Taurus
    Aemilianus 408
Pallas, Marcus Antonius 23, **408**
palliata 530
Palma Frontonianus, Aulus
    Cornelius 30, 104, 408, 423,
    550
Palmyra 167, 186, 398, **408**, 600
paludamentum 130
Pammachius **409**
Pamphylia 50, **335**
Pamphylius of Caesarea **409**
Pandateria 290, **409**
panegyric 365, **409**
Pannonia 26, 72, 96, 187, 270,
    409–410
Pannonia (*classis*) 383
Pannonia Inferior 409, 410
Pannonia Superior 409, 410
Pansa Caetronianus, Gaius Vibius
    123, **410**
Pantaenus **410**
Pantheon 43, 46, 92, 251, 410, *411*,
    475
papacy **411–412** *See also specific*
    pope
Papak 34, **412**, 488
Paphlagonia **412**
Papinian 122, 295, **412**, 417
Papius Mutilus, Marcus **412**
papyrus 594, 595
Parcae **412**
parchment 595
Parentalia 169, 344
Parentalia (Ausonius) 63
Paris (actor) 180, **413**
Paris (city) *See* Lutetia
pars pro toto 340
Parthamasiris of Armenia 401, **413**
Parthamaspates of Parthia **413**
Parthenius **413**
Parthenon 54
Parthia **413–414** *See also specific*
    city
  Candidus Crassus and 92
  Cassius and 99
  Crassus, Marcus Licinius and
    97, 401
  Herod the Great and 257, 258
  Orodes II and 401
  Pacorus and 405
  Phraataces and 430
  Phraates III and 430
  Phraates IV and 430
  Tiridates and 1, 543
  Tiridates II and 544

Trajan and 550
Vologases I and 588–590
Parthian campaign 22, 25–26, 401
Parthian War 26
Parthica (legion) 311
Parthicus 159
partitione oratoria, De (Cicero) 117
passus 368, 593
Patavium 414
Paternus, Tarrutenius 140, 414, 419
Pater Patriae 60, 117, 414
patres 509
patres Nestorii blasphemiae 533
patria potestas 4, 414–415, 594
patriarch 415
Patricians 129, 130, 415, 509
Patricius 50, 69, 315, 415–416
Patrick 416
patrimonium 211, 470
patristic Christian philosophy 428,
   429
patrocinium 301
patromonium sacrae 212
Patruinus, Valerius 416
Paulina, Domitia 416, 499
Paulina, Pompeia 416
Paulinus of Nola 416–417
Paullus, Lucius Aemilius 290, 336,
   417
Paul of Samosata 417
Paul of Tarsus (St. Paul) 67, 110,
   111, 304, 305, 417
Paulus, Julius 121, 295, 417
Paulus (Catena) 417–418
Pausanias 418
Pax 418
Paxaea 298
Pax Romana 30, 418
Peace, Altar of 30, 42
Peasant Letters (Aelian) 7
peculatus 462
pecunia 132, 133
pecunia maiorina 133
Pedius, Quintus 418
Pelagia 418
Pelagianism 115, 275, 315, 416, 418
Pelagius 98, 115, 418
Peloplato 13
Penates 245, 418–419
pens 594
pentekontos 504
Peponila 419, 483
Peraea 419
Percennius 419
perduellio 343
Peregrinatio Aetheriae 279
peregrini 119, 280, 377, 419, 446
Perennis, Sextus Tigidius 140, 414,
   419
performances 531
Pergamum 49, 419
periploi 279, 419–420
Periplus Maris Erythraei 420
Periplus of the Euxine Sea 420
Periplus of the Outer Sea 420
Peristephanon (Prudentius) 325, 459
Peroz 420
Persia 26, 361, 420, 488, 503,
   567–568
Persians and Athenians 420
Persius Flaccus, Aulus 69, 420, 490
personal appearance 420–421

Pertinax, Publius Helvius (Emperor
   in 193) 421
   assassination of 51
   and Castra Praetoria 101
   and Didius Julianus 174
   and Eclectus 189
   and Laetus, Quintus Aemilius
      300
   and Praetorian Guard 421, 447
   wife of 544
Pertinax, Publius Helvius (son of
   Pertinax) 421
Perusine War 25, 123, 222, 421
Pervigilium Veneris (Tiberianus) 538
pes 593
Pescennius Niger 422
   coinage of 132
   and Severus, Septimius 21, 26,
      276, 334, 389, 391, 422, 500
pes monetalis 593
Peter of Alexandria 364, 422
Peter (St. Peter) 110, 112, 412, 422,
   569
Petra 380, 422–423
Petreius, Marcus 122, 269–270, 423
Petronius 303, 324, 423, 490
Petronius Maximus 8, 63, 201, 237,
   343, 423–424, 565
Petronius Turpilianus, Publius (con-
   sul in 19 C.E.) 423
Petronius Turpilianus, Publius (gov-
   ernor of Britain) 424
Peutinger Table 424
Phaedrus 424
phalanx 306
Phaon 424
Pharasmanes 371, 424–425, 465
Pharisees 425, 484
Pharnaces 36, 39, 87, 91, 425
Pharsalia (Lucan) *See Belle Civile*
   (Lucan)
Pharsalus 8, 70, 82, 87, 122, 191,
   307, 312, 425, 442, 527
Phasael 23, 257, 283, 288, 426
Phasma (Catullus) 102
Philae 426
Philip I 39, 170, 247, 426, 448, 454,
   477
Philip II 426
Philip the Tetrarch 426
Philippi 58, 75, 99, 426–427, 557
Philippic Histories (Trogus) 557
Philippics (Cicero) 117
Philippus, Flavius 427
Philippus, Lucius Marcius 60, 427
Philo (Philo Judaeus) 1, 22, 427
Philocalia (Gregory) 248
Philopater I 427
Philopater II 427
philosophy 1–2, 427–429 *See also*
   Cynics; Epicureanism;
   Neoplatonism; Neo-
   Pythagoreanism; Platonism;
   Stoicism; *specific philosopher*
Philostorgius 429
Philostratus, Flavius 13, 28, 429
Phoebe 429
phoenix 430
Phraaates 430
Phraates III 401, 430
Phraates IV 25, 39, 47, 48, 97, 401,
   430, 544

Phrygia 49, 85, 430
phylarch 537
Piazza Armerina 430
Picenum 430
Picts 80, 430–431
pilum 307
pilus posterior 308
pilus prior 308
Pinakes 15
Pincian Hills 261, 473
Pinus, Cornelius 42, 431
piracy 118, 157, 382, 431, 441
Pisidia 49, 431
Piso, Gaius Calpurnius 228, 387,
   431–432, 433
Piso, Gnaeus Calpurnius 241, 432,
   434, 572, 588
Piso, Lucius Calpurnius (consul in
   15 B.C.E.) 432, 449
Piso, Lucius Calpurnius (consul in
   58 B.C.E.) 432
Piso Licinianus 173, 227, 403,
   432–433, 507
Pisonian Conspiracy 387, 433, 475
   Lateranus, Plautius in 301, 435
   Lucan, Marcus Annaeus in 330
   Milichus and 368
   Natalis, Antonius in 382
   Petronius Turpilianus and 424
   Piso, Gaius Calpurnius in 66,
      431–432
   Proculus, Volusius and 456
   Quintianus, Afranius in 463
   Rufus, Gaius Musonius in 481
   Scaevinus, Flavius in 491
   Seneca in 497
   Senecio in 498
   Silvanus, Gaius in 506
   Sulpicius Asper in 517
   Tigellinus and 541
pistores 508
Pituanius, Lucius 433
Placentia 73, 433, 507
Placidia, Galla 433–434
   and Aetius, Flavius 8, 434
   and Aspar 50, 286
   and Athaulf 53, 149, 433
   and Boniface 77, 100, 434
   and Felix, Flavius Constantius
      209
   and Honorius 264, 434
   son of 565
   and Wallia 433, 591
Plancina, Munatia 432, 434
Plancus, Lucius Munatius 183, 333,
   421, 434
Plancus Bursa, Titus Munatius 434
Plato 1, 361, 428, 429
Platone et euis dogmate (Apuleius)
   325
Platonism 13 *See also*
   Neoplatonism
plaudite 2
Plautianus, Gaius Fulvius 94, 241,
   296, 338, 434–435, 500
Plautilla 94, 435, 435
Plautius 435
Plautius, Aulus 79, 92, 435
Plautius Lateranus 435
Plautius Silvanus, Marcus 435
Plautius Silvanus Aelianus, Tiberius
   435

Plebeians 129, 130, 435–436,
   509–510, 553–554, 554
plebeius ordo 436
plebiscitum 303–304
pledge of allegiance 484
Pliny the Elder 68, 109, 186, 324,
   340, 362, 436, 576
Pliny the Younger 24, 48, 76, 111,
   123, 181, 324, 436
plostellum 208
plostellum poenicum 208
Plotina, Pompeia 54, 436
Plotinus 18, 385, 436–437
Plutarch 4, 97, 370, 437
Pluton 245, 437
poena capitis 305
poetry 117–118, 437
Polemo, Marcus Antonius 437–438
Polemo I 438
Polemo II 77, 155, 438
police 60, 561
polis 253–254, 377
politarchs 536
Pollentia 438, 514
Pollio, Gaius Asinius 50, 82, 234,
   366, 438–439, 470
Pollio, Publius Vedius 439
Pollio, Rufrius 295, 322, 439
poll tax *See tributum capitis*
Pollux 179, 182, 245
Polybian legionary camp 309
Polybius 125, 309, 439
Polycarp 111, 439
Polycleitus 439
polytheism *See* paganism
Pomaxathres 97, 156
pomerium 272, 439, 468, 525
Pomona 245, 439
Pompeia (wife of Julius Caesar) 88,
   439–440
Pompeia (daughter of Pompey) 440
Pompeianus, Ruricius 369, 440
Pompeianus, Tiberius Claudius 331,
   440
Pompeii 42, 243, 277, 440, 440
Pompey, Gnaeus 37, 440–441, 530
Pompey, Sextus 431, 441
   and Agrippa, Marcus Vipsanius
      10, 382
   and Antony, Marc 370, 441, 522
   and Augustus 370, 382, 441,
      522
   and Caesar, Julius 123, 441, 530
   and Cornificius, Lucius 154
   and Domitius Ahenobarbus,
      Gnaeus 182
   and Lepidus, Marcus Aemilius
      317, 441
   and Menas 364–365
   and Titius, Marcus 544–545
Pompey the Great 441–442
   and Achillas 2
   and Afranius, Lucius 8
   and Alexandria 13
   and Amathus 17
   and Ampius, T. Balbus 18
   and Antioch 21
   and Aretas III 34
   and Ariobarzanes III 36
   and Armenia 39
   and Balbus, Lucius Cornelius 66
   and Balbus, T. Ampius 66

and battle of Alexandria 15
and Brutus, Marcus Junius 82
and Burebista 83
and Caesar, Julius 87, 122, 188, 231, 269–270, 307, 330, 355, 356, 377, 425, 442, 530, 556
and Cappadocia 93
and Cato Uticensis 102
and Cicero 117
and Cilicia 523
and Cleopatra 127
and Clodius Pulcher 129, 442
and Commagene 139
and Crassus 99, 155–156
and Crassus, Marcus Licinius 87, 155–156, 231, 556
and Figulus, Nigidius 211
and Gabinius, Aulus 224, 318
and Illyricum 270
and Jerusalem 283
and Juba I 287, 395
and Labienus, Titus 299
legions of 307
and Metellus Scipio 367
and Milo, Titus Annius 369
and Petreius, Marcus 423
and Pharnaces 425
and piracy 431
and Ptolemy XII Auletes 459–460
and Samaria 486
and Scipio, Metellus 492
sons of 440–441
and Sulla 441
and Syria 519
and Temple of Jerusalem 526
and Tigranes I 542
and Varro 568
wives of 153, 289, 367, 442
Pomponius, Sextus 442
Pomponius Proculus, Titus 442
Pomponius Secundus, Publius 442–443
pondus 592
Pons Aelius 477
Pons Aemilius 473
Pons Agrippae 477
Pons Aurelius Antoninus 477
Pons Cestius 473
Pons Fabricius 473
Pons Neronis 477
Pons Probi 477
Pons Sublicius 194, 473
Pont du Gard 29, 29, 384
Pontes longi 183
Pontifex Maximus 56, 169, 443, 452, 468, 576
pontiff 415
Pontifices 55, 443, 452
Pontius Pilate 288, 443, 486
Pontus 50, 77, 94, 137, 438, 443
Poppaea, Sabina 11, 56, 158, 388, 397, 403, 444
population growth 474–475
populi auctoritate 4
populus Romanus 509
Porcia 83, 183, 444
Porcius Latro, Marcus 444
Porfyrius, Publilius Optatianus 444
Porphyry 18, 385, 437, 444
portorium 445

ports 383
Portunus 245, 445
Portus Augusti 402
Portus Romanus 402
posca 216
post meridiem 543
Postumus, Marcus Cassianus Latinius 51, 125, 229, 233, 299, 445
Potamon of Alexandria 445
potestas 4
Pothinus 445
pozzolana 194
praecones 28
praefecti 7
praefecti aerarii 7, 134
praefectus annonae 14, 19, 159
praefectus castrorum 308
praefectus civitatum 392
praefectus fabrum 449
praefectus praetorio 446
praefectus praetorio praesens 141
praefectus urbi 446, 448–449, 473
praefectus vehiculorum 161
praefectus vigilum 450, 582
praelectio 199
praemia militiae 309
praenomen 168
Praeparatio Evangelica (Eusebius) 203
praepositus sacri cubiculi 141, 159, 445, 445
praescriptione hereticorum, De (Tertullian) 528
praesul 484
Praetextatus, Vettius Agorius 446
praetor 7, 211, 303, 304, 306, 446
Praetorian Guard 199, 446–448 See also prefect of the Praetorian Guard
    Augustus and 60, 185, 446, 447
    Claudius and 185, 447
    Constantine and 143, 180, 341, 447, 448, 449–450, 492
    Didius Julianus and 101, 158, 174, 447, 500, 517
    Diocletian and 341, 342, 447, 448
    donativum paid to 185
    Galba and 51, 226, 447
    history of 446–448
    Maxentius and 358, 447, 448
    military camp of 100–101
    Nero and 447, 512
    Nerva and 388, 447
    organization of 448
    Otho and 73, 447
    Pertinax and 421, 447
    Severus, Septimius and 447, 500
    Speculatores in 54, 171, 221, 512
    Tiberius and 185, 447
    Titus and 447, 512
    Vitellius, Aulus and 101, 447, 587
praetorium 195, 309
praetor peregrini 280, 419
praetor peregrinos 446
praetor urbanus 446
prandium 215, 216
Prasutagus 78, 79, 103, 448

prefect of the city 448–449, 473, 496
prefect of engineering 449
prefect of the Praetorian Guard 17, 122, 175, 199, 341, 447, 448, 449–450, 451
prefect of the watch 450
presbyteroi 112
Priapea 28
Priapus 245, 452
pridie 90
priesthood 452, 468, 498
priests 55–56, 112, 213–214, 303, 443, 468, 484
primicerius notariorum 286, 393
Primigenia (legion) 313–314
primi ordines 308
Primus, Marcus Antonius 73, 121, 181, 214, 223, 452, 507–508
primus pilus 308
princeps 55, 452
princeps iuventutis 61, 88, 452–453
princeps posterior 308
princeps prior 308
princeps senatus 60, 453, 495
principales 74, 179, 448
principia 309
Prisca and Maximilla 453
Priscillian 354, 361, 453
Priscus (designer of siege engines) 453
Priscus (historian) 453
Priscus (officer of legions in Britain) 453
Priscus (philosopher) 453
Priscus, Attius 42, 454
Priscus, Clutorius 453–454
Priscus, Gaius Julius 426, 454
Priscus, Javolenus 454
Priscus, Junius 454
Priscus, Lucius Neratius 454
Priscus, Statius 454, 563
private offense 305
private slaves 508
probatio 199
Probus, Marcus Aurelius 51, 98, 215, 448, 454–455
Probus, Marcus Valerius 455
Probus, Petronius 455, 564
Proclus 385, 455
proconsul 49, 76, 273, 446, 455
Procopius 31, 455, 567
Proculeans 455
Proculeius, Gaius 455
Proculus 456
Proculus, Licinius 73, 104, 212, 456
Proculus, Volusius 433, 456
procurator 49, 392, 445, 448, 456
Prohaeresius 456
promulsio 216
Propertius, Sextus 28, 323, 456
prophecy 504
Pro S. Athanasio (Lucifer) 331
proscription 456–457
Proserpina 245, 320, 437
Prosper 457
protectores 457
protectores et domestici See domestici, protectores
Protoevangelium (James) 281
Protrepticus (Clement) 126

provinces of the Roman Empire 457–458
Prudentius 70, 325, 459
psalterium vetus 282
Pseudo-Cynics 162
Psychomachia (Prudentius) 459
Ptoleimais 459
Ptolemy 459
Ptolemy, Claudius 52, 356, 459
Ptolemy XI Auletes 372
Ptolemy XII Auletes 23, 191, 224, 459–460
Ptolemy XIII 2, 13, 15, 87, 122, 127, 445, 460
Ptolemy XI Lathyrus 459
Ptolemy XIV 127, 460
publicani 445
public offense 305
public slaves 508
pudicitia, De (Tertullian) 528
Pulcheria, Aelia 20, 56, 107, 201, 346, 460, 534, 600
Pulchra, Claudia 8, 460
Punica (Silius Italicus) 506
Punic Wars 306, 402, 457, 503, 511
punishments 304, 305, 467
Pupienus 30, 51, 66, 132, 246, 448, 460–461, 496
Puteoli 402, 461
Pylades 461, 531
Pythagoras 211
Pythagorian philosophy 385

Q

Quadi 36, 98, 223, 277, 348, 462, 565
quadrans 133
Quadratus, Asinius 462
quadrivium 190
quaester sacri palati 143
quaestio 462
quaestiones 198, 304, 446, 462
Quaestiones (Papinian) 412
quaestio perpetua 462
quaestor 7, 211, 462–463
quaestor provinciales 463
quaestor sacri palati 141, 463
quaestor urbani 463
Quietus, Lusius 104, 289, 357, 375, 463
Quietus, Titus Fulvius Junius 67, 337, 463
quinarius 133, 463
quindecimviri sacris faciundis 55, 161, 452, 463, 504
quingenaria 310
quinquennales 377
quinquereme 504
quinta et vicesima manicipiorum 524
Quintianus, Afranius 140, 433, 463
Quintilian 55, 69, 70, 170, 190, 324, 463
Quintilii brothers 463–464
Quintillus, Marcus Aurelius Claudius 61, 464
Quintus of Smyrna 464
Quirinal Hill 260, 473
Quirinius, Publius Sulpicius 157, 335, 464
Quirinus 213, 245, 464, 484
quirites 464
Quodvultdeus 464

R

Rabirius 45, **465**
Radagaisus 438, **465**, 514
Radamistus of Iberia 372, 424, **465**, 544, 561
Raetia 187, **465–466**
Rapax (legion) 313
The Rape of Prosperpina (Claudian) 124
rastra 207
rationales summarum 212
rationalis 192, 212, **466**
rationibus 134, **466**
Raurici 56, **466**
Ravenna 176, 243, 264, **466**
Ravenna-Aquileia *(classis)* 383
Ravenna Cosmography 279
razors 421
Reburrus, T. Crispus 38, 384, **466**
rebus, agentes in **466–467**
Rebus Bellicis, De **467**
recitationes 470
recognitio 199
Re Coquinaria, De (Apicius) 27, 215
Rectus **467**
Rectus, Aemilius **467**
Reditu Suo, De (Namatianus) 381
Red Sea **467**
Refutations of All Heresies (Hippolytus) 90, 261
Regalianus 62, 233, **467**
regibus apostacis, De (Lucifer) 331
regiones 473
Regularum liber singularum (Ulpian) 561
Regulus, Publius Memmius 328, **467**, 555
relegatio 467
religion 60, 238, 344–345, 443, 452, **467–468** *See also* Christianity; Imperial Cult; *specific god*
Remedia amoris (Ovid) 404
Remigius **469**
re militari, De (Frontinus) 221
re militari, De (Paternus) 414
re militari, De (Vegetius) 307
Remistus **469**
Repentinus, Fabius Cornelius **469**
repetundae 457
repotia 352
republica, De (Cicero) 117
repudium 352
Rerum cotidianarum (Gaius) 225
re rustica, De (Columella) 137
rescripta 150, 304
Res Gestae Divi Augustus 42, 61, **469–470**
responsa 304
Responsa (Papinian) 412
res privata 138, 207, 212, **470**
Res Rusticae (Varro) 568
Restitutor Orbis 62
resurrectione carnis, De (Tertullian) 528
retiarii 244
Rheims 228, **470**
Rhemi 470
Rhescuporis of Thrace 78, **470**, 536
rhetoric **470**
Rhetorica (Cicero) 117
Rhine **470–471**
Rhodes 49, **471**

Rhoemetalces I 72, 155, 328, 470, **471**, 536–537
Ricimer, Flavius **471**
   and Aegidius 6
   and Anthemius 20, 471
   and Arvandus 48
   and Avitus 64, 471
   and Gundobad 249
   and Libius Severus 320, 471
   and Majorian 344, 433, 471
   and Marcellinus 342, 345, 471
   and Merobaudes, Flavius 365
   and Olybrius 398
Ricomer 471
roads 161, 195, 231, 322, 329, 337, **471–472**, 551, 577–580, *579*
Robigus 213, 245, **472**
Roles 472
Roma 245, **472**
Roman Antiquities (Dionysius) 178
Romanitas 121, 194, 195
Roman Questions (Plutarch) 437
Romanus **472**
Rome 277, **472–479**, *474, 476, 478*
   geography of 473
   governance of 473–474
   history of 475–479
   living conditions in 474–475
Romulus Augustulus 386, 398, **479**
rostra 44
Round Temple of Cybele *161*
Roxolani 165, 167, **479**
Rubellius Plautus 91, **480**
Rubicon **480**
Rubra Saxa **480**
ruderatio 195
rudus 195
Rufina, Pomponia **480**
Rufinus, Flavius 32, 204, **480**, 514, 523
Rufinus, Vulcacius **480**
Rufinus of Aquileia, Tyrannius **480**
Rufus, Bassaeus **480**
Rufus, C. Valgius **480**
Rufus, Cluvius **480–481**
Rufus, Faenius 387, 433, **481**, 541
Rufus, Gaius Musonius 103, 172, **481**
Rufus, Quintus Curtius **481**
Rufus, Verginius *See* Verginius Rufus, Lucius
Rugila 77, 266, 344, **481**
rugs 222
Rusticus, Junius **481**
Rutilius Gallicus 82, 239, **481**

S

Sabellianism 179, **482**
Sabina, Vibia 54, 250, 356, **482**, 516
Sabinians **482**
Sabinus, Caelius **482**
Sabinus, Cornelius 106, **482**
Sabinus, Flavius 105, 290, **482–483**, 588
Sabinus, Julius 121, 419, **483**
Sabinus, Masurius 295, 482, **483**
Sabinus, Nymphidius 226, **483**
Sabinus, Oppius 165, 169, **483**
Sabinus, Poppaeus 337, 373, 467, **483**
Sabinus, Publius **483**

Sabinus, Quintus Titurius 5, 17, 189, **483**
Sabinus, Titus Flavius 232, **483**
Sabis **484**
Sabratha **484**
sacellum 309
sacra 4
Sacramentis, De (Theodore) 533
sacramentum **484**
sacrarium 68
Sacred Teachings (Aristides) 37
Sacred Way 33
sacrificati 300
sacrifices 169, 170, 216, 332–333, 352, 406, 463
Sacrovir, Julius 6, 57, 215, 229, **484**, 506, 553
sacrum aerarium 212
sacrum consistorium 141
Sadducees 425, **484**
sagum 546
Salacia **484**
Salii **484**
Salinator, Gnaeus Pedanius Fuscus **484–485**
Sallust 19, 236, **485**
Sallustius Crispus, Gaius **485**
Sallustius Passienus Crispus, Gaius **485**
Salome Alexandra 37, 267
Salona 270, **485**
Salonina **486**
Saloninus 233, 445, **486**
Salutatio 271, **486**, 500, 510
Salvianus **486**
Samaria **486**
Samos **486**
Samosata **486**
sandals 130
Santones **486–487**
Saoterus **487**
Saphrax 5, 402
Saracens **487**
Saragossa, Council of 453
Sardanapalus **487**
Sardica, Council of 35, 265, 378
Sardinia 154, **487**
Sardis **487**
Sarmatians 12, 76, 77, 98, 268, 479, **487–488**, 507, 565
Sarmizegethusa 167, 170, **488**
Sassanid dynasty 34, 41, 265, 420, **488–489**, 503
satire 324, **489–490**
Satires (Horace) 264
Saturnalia 490, **491**
Saturnalia (Macrobius) 339, 499
Saturnalicus princeps 490
Saturninus, Aemilius 434, **490**
Saturninus, Aponius **490**
Saturninus, Gnaeus Sentius **490**
Saturninus, Julius 454, **490**
Saturninus, Lucius Antoninus 181, 360, 375, 490
Saturninus Dogmatius, Gaius Caelius **491**
Saturninus Secundus, Salutius **490–491**
Saturnus 245, 490, **491**
Satyricon (Petronius) 303, 324, 423
sauces 216

Saxons 80, **491**
Scaevinus, Flavius 382, 433, **491–492**
Scalae Gemoniae 237–238
scale 593
Scapula, Publius Ostorius 78, 79, 131, 269, **492**
Scapula, Q. Ostorius 322, 447, 449, **492**
Scaurus, Mamercus Aemilius 22, 34, 82, **492**, 531
Scaurus, Q. Terentius **492**
Scholae Palatinae 176, 180, **492**
schola labri 71
scholastic Christian philosophy 428, 429
School Master General 395
schools 190
Scipio, Metellus 88, 123, 395, **492**, 530
Scipio Aemilianus 97, 262
Scipio Africanus 9, 420
"Scourge of God" *See* Attila
scribae 28
Scribonia 58, 321, 326, **492**
Scribonianus, M. Furius 124
Scribonii brothers 152, **492–493**
scrinii 146, 341, **493**
Scriptores Historiae Augustae 2, 66, 125, 173, 186, 212, 233, 296, 325, **493**
scutarii 287, **493**
scutum 307–308
Scythia **493**
Scythians 77, 171, 173
Scythica (Dexippus) 173, 325
Scythica (legion) 311
sea transportation 551–552 *See also* ships
sea travel 382–383
Sebastian 5
Sebastianus **493–494**
Second Apology (Justin) 295
Second Triumvirate *See* Triumvirate, Second
secretaries 393, 493
secret service 221, 466–467
secunda mensa 216
Secundus, Pedanius **494**
Secundus, Petronius 181, 388, 392, **494**
securis 173, 208
secutor 244
Segestes 40, 109
Segovia **494**
Seine **494**
Sejanus, Lucius Aelius **494–495**
   and *acta Senatus* 3
   and Agrippina the Elder 11
   and Antonia 23
   and Asinius Gallus 50
   and Blaesus, Quintus Junius 76
   and Bruttidius Niger 82
   and Castra Praetoria 100–101, 447, 494, 540
   and Cordus, Aulus Cremutius 152
   and Drusus (son of Germanicus) 187
   and Drusus (son of Tiberius) 187, 494
   and Gallio, Junius 233

and Junius Otho 293
and Laco, Graecinus 299
and Lentulus Gaetulicus
 314–315
and Lepida, Aemilia 316–317
and Livilla 327
and Macro 338
and Nero, Julius Caesar 388
and Terentius, Marcus 527
and Tiberius 17, 44, 100, 338,
 449, 494–495, 540
and Trio, Fulcinius 555
wife of 27
Seleucia 20, 159, 335, **495**
Seleucia, Council of 35, 260
Seleucid dynasty 39, 413, 519
sella 222
sella curculis 151
Semi-Arians 36, 53
semis 133
Senaculum **495**
Senate **495–496**, 509
 and Achaea 2
 and *acta* 3
 adlectio and 4
 and *aerarium* 7
 Antoninus Pius and 24
 Augustus and 49, 58, 60, 228,
  495, 509
 Caesar, Julius and 122
 Caracalla and 94
 Claudius and 124
 against colonization 135
 and *constitutiones* 150
 Gaius Caligula and 225
 immunitas granted by 271
 imperium maius granted by 273
 and law 304
 meeting house of 160
 and monetary affairs 211–212
 in municipal towns 170
 Nero and 387
 Nerva and 388
 Severus Alexander and 502
 Tiberius and 3, 539
 Trajan and 548
 Women's 495
senatus consultum 4, 131, 304, 409,
 496
Senatus Populusque Romanus 513
Seneca **496–497**
 and Fabianus Papirius 206
 on Lentulus, Gnaeus Cornelius
  314
 on Library of Alexandria 15
 and Nero 3, 11, 19, 324, 387,
  416, **496–497**
 physician of 514
 wife of 416
Seneca the Elder 387, **497**
Senecio, Claudius **498**
Senecio, Herennius **498**
Senecio, Sosius **498**
Sentius, Gnaeus **498**
Septemviri 55, 452, **498**
Sequani 340, 494, **498**
Serapis 468, **498**
Serena **498**, 514
sermo cotidianus 303
Servianus, Julius 7, 104, 251,
 484–485, **499**
servi publici 508

Servius **499**
Servius Tullius 306, 473
sesquiplex stipendum 448
sestertius 62, 81, 133, **499**, *499*
Severa, Aurelia **499**
Severan Dynasty 605 *See also*
 Caracalla; Elagabalus; Severus,
 Septimius; Severus Alexander
Severianus, P. Aleius **499**
Severus (architect) **103**, 245
Severus (prefect of Egypt) **499**
Severus, Valerius 356
Severus II 359, **499–500**
Severus, Lucius Catilius **500**
Severus, Septimius 477, *500*,
 500–502, *501*
 and Africa 8
 and Alexandria 13
 and Antioch 21
 and Anullinus, Publius
  Cornelius 26
 and architecture 46
 and art 43
 and Bacchus 65
 in battle of Cyzicus 164
 and Britannia 80, 329, 339,
  502
 and Caledonians 89, 502
 and Candidus, Tiberius Aurelius
  92
 and Christianity 111
 and Cilo, Lucius Fabius 119
 and Clodius Albinus 128–129,
  300, 334, 500
 coinage of 132
 and Ctesiphon 159, 500
 and Didius Julianus 174
 and Egypt 192
 and Hatra 252
 and Juvenalis 296
 and Laetus 299–300
 legions of 311
 and Lepcis Magna 316
 ludi held by 333
 and Macrinus, Veturius 338
 and Nisibis 392
 and Numidia 396
 and Palmyra 408
 and Papinian 412
 and Pescennius Niger 21, 26,
  276, 334, 389, 391, 422, 500
 and Praetorian Guard 447, 500
 sons of 94, 241, 500
 and Syria 519
 wife of 290, 429, 500
Severus, Sextus Julius 67, **502**
Severus, Sulpicius **502**
Severus Alexander, Marcus Aurelius
 502–503
 and Alamanni 12
 and architecture 46
 and Ardashir I 34
 assassination of 51, 503
 and Baiae 66
 coinage of 132
 and consilium 141
 and Elagabalus 193, 502
 and Goths 247
 and Isauria 276
 and Maximinus I Thrax 360
 mother of 56
 and Persians 488

and Senate 502
 wife of 67
Sextus Caesar 118, **503**
Shapur I 488, **503**
 and Antioch 21
 and Armenia 94, 544
 and Bactria 65
 and Ballista 67, 337
 and Cappadocia 94
 father of 39, 503
 and Gordian III 246
 and Manichaeism 344
 and Odaenath 398, 503
 and Syria 94, 520
 and Valerian 65, 67, 190, 232,
  503, 566
Shapur II 287, 292, 488, **503**
Shapur III 488, **503**
shield 307–308
ships 168, 321, 382–383, **503–504**,
 504, 552
shoes 130
Sibyl **504**
Sibylline Books 27, 361, 369, 460,
 463, **504**, 511
Sicilia **505**
Sicily (Augustus) 61
Sidonius Apollinaris 48, **505**
siege engines 453
Silana, Junia 91, 180, **505**
Silanus, D. Junius Torquatus 252,
 505
Silanus, Lucius Junius 198, 397, **505**
Silanus, M. Junius **505–506**
silavi See slavery
silex 195
siliqua 133, **506**
Silius, Gaius (consul-designate)
 301, 367, 435, 505, **506**
Silius, Gaius (consul in 13 C.E.) 6,
 506
Silius, Publius 8, 91
Silius Italicus, Tiberius Catius
 Asconius **506**
silk 109, 129
Silk Route 109, **506**
Silva, Flavius 355, **506**
Silvae (Statius) 514
Silvanus **506**
Silvanus, Aelianus 373–374
Silvanus, Gaius **506**
silver coinage 131, 132, 133 *See
 also specific coin*
similia similibus 340
Similis, S. Sulpicius 123, **506**
Sinope **507**, 552
sinus 546
siphons 29
Siraci **507**
Sirmium 86, **507**
Sitas 173, **507**
situ orbis, De (Mela) 364
69 C.E. **507–508**
slavery 207, 273–274, 301, 318,
 319, **508–509**, 510
Small Baths 72
Smyrna 196, 437, 487, **509**
Snake Path 354
soccus 130
social classes **509–510** *See also*
 Patricians; Plebeians
Socrates **510**

solarium 543
soldiers 57 *See also* legions
 clothing for 130
 footwear for 130
 pay of 309
solea 130
Solea ferrae 551
Solea sparta 551
Solemnitate Paschali, De (Eusebius)
 203
solidus 132, 133, **510**
Solinus, Gaius Julius **510**
Sol Invictus 62, 371, 468, **510–511**
solium 222
soothsayers 361, **511**
Sopater 1, **511**
Sophistry **511**
Soranus **511**
Soranus, Barea 103, **511**
Sororia **511**
Sosigenes 52, **512**
Sosius, Gaius **512**
Sozomen, Salmaninius Hermias **512**
Spado 187
Spain *See* Hispania
Spanish War (Caesar) 262, 377
Sparta **512**
Spartacus 155, 243, 441
spas 28
Speculatores 54, 171, 221, **512**
speechmaking 470
Spelunca 494, **512**
spherical trigonometry 356
spies 221
Spiritu Sancto, De (Theodore) 533
Split 46, 176, **512**, *513*
spolia opima 156
sportula 486, 510
Sporus 388, **513**
S.P.Q.R. **513**
Spurinna **513**
Spurinna, Titus Vestricius 233, 239,
 403, 433, **513**
srategos 537
Stabiae **513–514**
Stabian Baths 70
Stadiasmus Maris Magni 420
stadium 593
Stairs of Sighs 237–238
statera 593
state treasury 7
stationes 445
Statius, Publius Papinius **514**
Statius Annaeus **514**
Statius Priscus 48, **514**
statumen 195
steelyard 593
stenographers 393
Stephanus 27, 181, 413, **514**
Stephanus (Pope Stephen I) **514**
Stilicho, Flavius **514–515**
 and Alaric 12, 264, 438, 465,
  514–515, 573, 586
 and Arcadius, Flavius 32, 514
 and Claudian 123, 124
 and Eutropius 204, 480
 and Gildo 242, 514
 and Honorius 124, 200, 264,
  514–515
 and Radagaisus 465
 and Rufinus, Flavius 480, 514
 son of 200

wife of 498
stipendium 515, 524, 554
stoa 68
Stoicism 1, 51–52, 428, **515** *See also specific philosopher*
stola 129
stola matronalis 352
stool 222
Strabo **515**
    on Archelaus of Cappadocia 32
    on Armenians 40
    on Druids 186
    on Hannibal 47
    on Library of Alexandria 15
Strabo, Lucius Seius **515**
strategiai 537
Stratonis Turri *See* Caesarea
Stromateis (Clement) 126
students 190
Studiosi (Pliny) 436
stuprum 353
stylus 594
Styx 108, **515**
suasoria 170
subsellia 554
Subura 473, **515–516**
Suburanus **516**
Suburbicaria **516**
Suebi 37, 108, 228, 232, 239, 340, 347, 462, **516**
Suessiones 64, **516**
Suetonius (Gaius Suetonius Tranquillus) xii, 324, **516–517**
    on Agrippina 10
    on Augustus 60, 61
    on Balbus, T. Ampius 66
    on Caesar, Gaius 86
    on Chaerea, Cassius 106
    and Clarus, C. Septicius 123
    on Colosseum 137
    on Domitian 181
    on Domitius Ahenobarbus, Gnaeus 182
    on Figulus, Nigidius 211
    on Gaius Caligula 225
    on Golden House of Nero 71, 245
    on Icelus 269
    on Laco, Cornelius 299
    on Rome 43
    on Titus 171, 545
    on Vespasian 574
    on Vitellius, Aulus 244, 587
    on Vitellius, Publius 588
Suetonius Paulinus, Gaius 73, 78, 79, 104, 186, 387, **517**
suffragium 119, 120
sui iuris 4
Suillius Rufus, Publius **517**
Sulla, Publius Cornelius 173, **517**
    and Athens 53
    and Caesar, Julius 86, 153
    and Crassus, Marcus Licinius 155
    and Equestrians 198
    and Mithridates II 41
    and Ostia 402
    and Pompey the Great 441
    and Ptolemy XII Auletes 459
    and Stabiae 513
    and tribunes 553
Sulpicia **517**

Sulpicianus, Titus Flavius 101, 174, **517**
Sulpicius Asper **517**
summa crusta 195
summer legionary camps 309
sundial 543
Sura, Lucius Licinius **517**
Surenas 41, 97, 156, 372, 401, **518**
sword 307
Symmachus, Quintus Aurelius 17, 57, 214, 325, 406, 446, 479, **518**
sympathetic magic 340
syncretism 468
Synesius of Cyrene 267, **518**
Synodis, De (Hilary) 260
Synopsis ad Eustathium (Oribasius) 400
Syracuse **518**
Syria 20–21, 70, 106, 107, **518–520**, 561
Syria (*classis*) 383
Syria Coele 519
Syria Phoenice 519
Syrus, Publilius **520**

T

tabellarii 551
tabernae veteres 524
tables 222
tabularium 7
Tacfarinas 28, 76, 396, **521**
Tacitus, Publius Cornelius xii, 324, **521–522**
    on Achaea 2
    on *acta diurna* 3
    on aedile 6
    on Anicetus 19
    on Archelaus 32
    on Ariobarzanes 36
    on Armenians 40
    on Artabanus III 47
    on Asinius Gallus 50
    on astrology 52
    on Augusta Vindelicorum 56
    on Bassus, Saleius 70
    on Batavi 70
    on Bedriacum 73, 74
    on Boudicca 78, 80
    on Capri 94
    on Celer, Publius 103
    on Cestus, Gallius 106
    on Chatti 108
    on Christians 111
    on Cotta Messalinius 154
    on *delatores* 171
    on Densus, Sempronius 172–173
    on Domitian 181
    on Drusilla 187
    on Flavius 214
    on Florus, Gessius 215
    on Florus, Julius 215
    on Fuscus, Cornelius 223
    on Galba 227
    on Gallus, Gaius Asinius 234
    on Germania 240
    on Golden House of Nero 245
    on Hermunduri 256
    on Hibernia 259
    on Iberia 268
    on Lateranus, Plautius 301, 435

    on *maiestas* 343
    on Maternas, Curiatius 355
    on Metellus Celer 367
    on Mucianus, Gaius Licinius 376
    on Petronius 423
    on Piso, Gaius Calpurnius 431
    on Poppaea, Sabina 444
    on Primus, Marcus Antonius 452
    on Quintianus, Afranius 463
    on Silana, Junia 505
    on Suebi 516
    on Suetonius Paulinus 517
    on Tiberius 10
    on Tigellinus 542
    on Valens 563
    on Verulamium 573
    on Vibius Marsus 580
    on Vinius, Titus 585
    on Vitellius, Aulus 587
    on Vitellius, Lucius 588
    wife of 9
Tacitus, Marcus Claudius 214–215, **522**
Tamesis **522**
Tapae 181, **522**
Tarasicodissa *See* Zeno (Tarasicodissa)
Tarentum, Treaty of 58, 82, 123, **522**
tariffs 445
Tarquinius Superbus 504, 511
Tarsus **523**
Tasciovanus 79, 92, 103
Tatian **523**
Tatianus, Flavius Eutolmius **523**
Taurini 83, 230
Taurus, Titus Statilius 449, **523**
taxation 457, **523–524** *See also specific tax*
    Caracalla and 95
    comes sacrarum largitionum and 212
    curialis and 160
    Diocletian and 176, 277
    Gaius Caligula and 225
    migration and 207
tax collectors 524
teachers 190
tempestiva convivia 244
Temple of Apollo 43, 333, **524**
Temple of Bacchus 65
Temple of Castor and Pollux 44, 68, 218, 475, **524**, 525
Temple of Concord 44, 218, **524**
Temple of Cybele 161
Temple of Divus Augustus 44, 475, **525**
Temple of Divus Claudius 525
Temple of Divus Julius 43, 218, **525**
Temple of Isis 426, **525**
Temple of Jerusalem, Great 423, **525–526**, 541, 574
Temple of Jupiter Capitolinus 294, 333, **526**
Temple of Mars Ultor 43, 353, *353*, 475, **526**
Temple of Peace 45, 475, **526**, 575
Temple of Saturn 68, 218, *491*, **526**
Temple of Solomon 283
Temple of Venus-Atargatis 65
Temple of Vesta **526–527**, 575

Temples of Minerva **527**
Tenth Legion **527**
tepidarium 71
Terentia 118, 339, **527**
Terentius, Marcus **527**
Tertullian 8, 90, 97, 114, 429, **527–528**, 566
tessellae 583
tessera **528**, 532
tesserae frumentariae 528
tesserae nummariae 528
Testimonio animae, De (Tertullian) 528
Tetrarchy 176, 359, **528–529**, 606
Tetricus, Gaius Pius Esuvius 61, 62, **529**
Teutoburg Forest 109, 241, 310, 313, 352, 353, 471, **529**, 539, 569
Teutons **529–530**
textile production 129
Thamugadi 396, **530**
Thapsus 8, 9, 88, 123, 441, **530**
theater **530–532**
Theater of Balbus 92
Theater of Marcellus 92, 119
Thebaid (Statius) 514
Themistius **532**
Theodora 252, **532**
Theodore of Mopsuestia **532–533**
Theodoret 196, **533**
Theodorus, Flavius Mallius 124, **533**
Theodosius I **533–534**, *534*
    and Christianity 36, 115
    and Cynegius 162
    and Eugenius, Flavius 201, 219–220
    and Gildo 242
    sons of 31–32, 263–264
    and Stilicho, Flavius 514
    and Tatianus 523
    and Themistius 532
    and Visigoths 12, 220, 586
Theodosius II **534–535**
    and Aelia Pulcheria 56
    and Anthemius 20, 32
    and *curialis* 160
    daughter of 201
    and Ephesus Council 196
    and Huns 266
    and Latrocinium Council 107
    legal system of 304
    and Nestorius 389
    sister of 460
    wife of 201
    and Zstommas 600
Theodosius, Flavius 31, **535**
Theological Orations (Gregory) 248
Theonas of Marmarica 390
Theon of Smyrna 52, **535**
Theophanes of Mytilene **535**
Theophany (Eusebius) 203
Theophilus (bishop of Alexandria) 99, 163, 201, 285, 406, 407, **535**
Theophilus (bishop of Antioch) **535**
Theotokos 163, 389
thermae See baths
Thessalonica 46, 85, 227, **535–536**
Thessaly **536**
Thirty Tyrants **536**
Thrace 173, 242, **536–537**
Thraeces 244

Thrasea Paetus, Publius Clodius 40, 48, 198, 255, **537**
Thrasyllus 52, 66, 72, **537–538**
"The Three Cappadocians" 67
throne 222
Thugga (Dougga) **538**
thurificati 300
Thysdrus (El Djem) **538**
Tiber **538**
Tiberianus **538**
Tiberias **538–539**
Tiberius **539–540**, *540*
 and Afer, Gnaeus Domitius 8
 and Agrippina the Elder 10–11
 and Antioch 21
 and Antiochus III 22
 and Apelles 26
 and Ara Pacis 31
 and Archelaus of Cappadocia 32
 and architecture 44, 475, 524, 525
 and Armenia 39
 and Artabanus III 47
 and Asinius Gallus 50
 assassination of 51
 on astrology 52
 and Blaesus, Quintus Junius 76
 and Bructeri 82
 and Bulla Regia 83
 and Capito, Gaius Ateius 93
 and Capri 94, 540, 583
 and Chaerea, Cassius 106
 and Chatti 108
 and Cherusci 108–109
 and Claudius 124, 151
 and Commagene 139
 and consilium 141
 and Cornutus, Caecilius 154
 and Cotta Messalinus 154
 and Dacia 165
 and *delatores* 171
 and Domitius Ahenobarbus, Gnaeus 183
 and Druids 186
 and Drusus the Elder 187, 539
 and Egypt 191
 father of 539, 541
 freedmen of 219
 and Gaius Caligula 225, 540
 and Gallus, Gaius Asinius 234
 and Germania 239, 539
 and Germanicus 241, 539
 and Herod Antipas 257
 and Lentulus, Gnaeus Cornelius 314
 and Lentulus Gaetulicus 314–315
 and literature 324
 and Macedonia 337
 and Macro 338
 and Marcomanni 348, 352
 and Messalla Messallinus, Marcus Valerius 72
 and Mithridates 371
 mother of 56, 326, 539
 palace of 184
 and Pannonia 270, 409–410, 539
 and Piso, Gnaeus Calpurnius 432
 and Plancina 434
 and *praefectus urbi* 449

 and Praetorian Guard 185, 447
 and Regulus, Publius Memmius 467
 and Rhodes 471
 and Sejanus, Lucius Aelius 17, 44, 100, 338, 449, 494–495, 540
 and Senate 3, 539
 and Silius, Gaius 506
 son of 187–188
 and Thrace 537
 and Thrasyllus 537–538
 treason law of 343
 wives of 234, 290, 539, 540
Tiberius Claudius Nero 326, 539, **540–541**
Tiberius Julius Alexander 14, 74, 75, 192, **541**
Tibullus, Albius 324, **541**
tickets 528
Tigellinus, Gaius Ofonius **541–542**
 and Capito, Cossutianus 93
 and Demetrius the Cynic 172
 and Nero 387, 449
 and Pisonian Conspiracy 433
 and Rufus, Faenius 481
 and Sabinus, Nymphidius 483
Tigranes I 39, 47, **542**
Tigranes II 199, **542**
Tigranes III 199–200
Tigranes IV **542**
Tigranes V 39, 152, **542**
Tigranocerta 152, 542, 544
Tigris **542–543**
time **543**
Timesitheus, Gaius Furius Sabinus Aquila 39, 246, 426, **543**
Tingis **543**
Tiridates 1, 430, **543**
Tiridates II **544**
Tiridates III 249, **544**
Tiridates of Armenia 39, **544**
Tiro, Marcus Tullius 118, **544**
tirocinium fori 190
tirocinium militiae 190
Titiana, Flavia **544**
Titius, Marcus 441, **544–545**
titulus 595
Titus **545**
 and Aquae Cutiliae 29
 and architecture 45, 71, 136, 245, 475
 and Berenice 75
 daughter of 290
 and *delatores* 171
 and Domitia Longina 180
 and Domitian 181, 545
 father of 545, 574–575
 games provided by 243
 and Gischala 242
 and Jerusalem 283–284
 and Judaea 288
 and Praetorian Guard 447, 512
 wife of 222
Tivoli 46, 251, 476, **545–546**
toga 130, **546**
toga candida 546
toga praetexta 130, 151, 446, 546
toga pura 546
toga sordida 546
togata 530
toga virilis 86, 130, 190, 546

Togodumnus 79, 95, 124, 159
toilet 216–217
toiletries 420
tokens 528
Toledo, Council of 453
Tome of Leo 107, 316, 347, **546–547**
Topica (Cicero) 117
To Sister Marcellina on Virginity (Ambrose) 17
trabea 484
Trachalus, P. Galerius 547
trade and commerce 273, **547–548**, *548, 549*
 with Britannia 81
 with China 109, 129
 with India 273
 with Nabataeans 380
 with Parthia 414
 Red Sea and 467
 roads and 472
 ships and 503
 Silk Route and 506
 with Syria 519
trading ships 503, 552, *552*
traditors 184
tragedy 531
Traiana *Fortis* (legion) 311
training of legions 307–308
Trajan **548–550**, *550*, 604
 and Aelianus, Casperius 7
 and *annona* 19–20
 and Antioch 21
 and Arabia 30
 and architecture 27, 45, 69, 218–219, 475–476, 550
 and Armenia 39, 413
 and art 42
 and Avidius Nigrinus 63
 and Bassus, C. Julius Quadratus 70
 and Beneventum 74
 and Bithynia 76
 and Cappadocia 94
 and Celsus, L. Publius 104
 and Christianity 111
 and *correctores* 154
 and Ctesiphon 159, 543
 and *curatores* 159
 and Dacia 70, 166, *166*, 168, 169, 488, 517, 522, 550
 and Doura 186
 and Galatia 226
 games provided by 243
 and Hadrian 250, 548
 and Hatra 252
 legions of 311, 314
 and literature 324
 and Livianus 327
 and Mesopotamia 366
 and Moors 375
 and Nerva 388, 548
 and Nisibis 392
 and Oroses 401
 and Ostia 402
 and Palma Frontonianus 408
 and Parthia 41, 543, 550
 and Quietus, Lusius 463
 and Raetia 466
 and Senate 548
 and Senecio, Sosius 498
 and Servianus, Julius 499

 and Sirmium 507
 sister of 482
 and Sura 517
 Thamugadi founded by 530
 and Thrace 537
 Ulpia Traiana founded by 560
 wife of 436
Trajan's Market 337, **550–551**
Trajanus *See* Decius, Gaius Messius Quintus (Trajanus)
Tranquillina, Furia Sabina 543, **551**
transitio ad plebem 415
transportation 229, 471–472, **551–552**, 577–580, *579*
Trapezus 94, **552**
travecto equitum 199
treason *See maiestas*
treasury 7, 121, 211–212, 212–213, 466, 470
Trebellenus, Rufus **552**
Trebonianus Gallus, Gaius Vibius 7, 51, 170, 247, 297, **552–553**
Trebonius, Gaius 122, **553**
tresviri epulones 498
tresviri republicae constituende 556
Treveri 105–106, 232, **553**, 562
tribulum 208
tribune 150, 180, 306, 448, **553–554**
tribunicia potestas 60, 61, 553, 554
tribuni et notarii 393
tribunii aerarii 7
tribuni militum 554
tribuni plebis 553–554
tribunus laticlavius 308
tribunus plebis 4
tribute penny **554**
tributum 524, **554–555**
tributum capitis 135, 280, 524, 554, 555
tributum solis 524, 555
Trier (Augusta Treverorum) 46, 228, 240, **555**
trigonometry 356
Trinitate, De (Hilary) 260
Trio, Fulcinius 171, 321, **555**
Tripoli *See* Oea
Tripolitania **555**
Tristia (Ovid) 404
tritheism 179
triumph **555–556**
triumphal arches 32–34
Triumvirate, First 87, 231, **556** *See also* Civil War, First Triumvirate
 and Bibulus, Marcus Calpurnius 75
 Conference of Luca and 329–330, 442
Triumvirate, Second 25, 58, 317, **556–557** *See also* Civil War, Second Triumvirate; Liberators
 and Antonius, Lucius 25
 and battle of Philippi 58, 75, 99, 426–427
 and Cicero 117
 and Munatia Aemilia 319
triumviri nocturni 582
trivium 190
Trogus, Pompeius **557**
trousers 130, 307
Troyes **557**

Troyes, battle of *See* Catalaunian Plain
True History (Lucian) 330
Tubero, Lucius Aelius 19, **557**
Tubero, Quintus Aelius 557
tubilustrium 484
Tullia 118, 179
Tullianum, dungeons of 238, 299, **558**
tunica 129
tunica picta 484
tunica recta 352
Tunisia 9, 83
tunnels 194
Turbo, Quintus Marcius 17, **558**
Turin 558
turmae 310
Turrantus, Gaius 558
Turrullius, Publius 558
Tuscus, Caecina 558
Tutor, Julius 121, 123
The Twelve Caesars (Suetonius) 324, 516
Twelve Tables 303, 304, **558**
Two Books Against the Pagans (Athanasius) 53
Tyre 52, **558–559**
Tyrrhenian sea 559

U

Ubii 348, **560**
Uldin 20, 266, **560**
Ulfila 36, **560**
Ulpia Traiana 240, **560**
Ulpian (Domitius Ulpianus) 122, 196, **560–561**
Ulpia Noviomagus 240
Ulpia Victrix (legion) 314
ultor **561**
umbilicus 595
umbo 195
Umbria **561**
Ummidius Quadratus 140, 152, 424, **561**
unciae 593
undergarments 130
Uni 293–294
uniforms 307, 546
United Nations Educational, Scientific and Cultural Organization 16
Universal History (Vibius Maximus) 580
urban cohorts 60, 369, 449, 500, **561**
Urbicus, Lollius **561**
urbs nova 485
urbs sacra 477
urbs vetus 485
Ursicinus 167, 202, **561–562**
Usipetes 232, **562**
usus 352
Utica 8, **562**

V

Vaballath 563
vacarii 175
Vadomar 563
valarshapat 563
Valens 563
Valens, Fabius 73, 85, 123, **563–564**

Valens, Flavius Julius **564**
and Arianism 36, 68, 564
and Goths 5, 168, 564
and Modestus, Domitius 373
and Ostrogoths 402, 564
and Ricomer 471
and Vadomar 563
and Victor 581
and Visigoths 5, 220, 564, 586
Valentinian I **564–565**
and Arianism 36
and Ausonius 63
and Maximinus 359
and Merobaudes, Flavius 365
son of 247
wife of 295
Valentinian II **565**
and Arbogast 31, 565
assassination of 51
and Bauto 73
and Gratian 247, 565
and Merobaudes, Flavius 365, 565
Valentinian III **565**
and Heracleus the Eunuch 255, 565
and Leo I 315, 565
and Majorian 343
mother of 149, 434, 565
sister of 263
and Vandals 565
wife of 201
Valentinus **565–566**
Valeria, Galeria 227, **566**
Valerian **566**
and Aemilian 7, 566
and Christianity 112, 566
and Shapur I 65, 67, 190, 232, 503, 566
son of 232
and Trapezus 552
Valerianus, Publius Licinius Cornelius 566
Valeria Victrix (legion) 313
Valerius Asiaticus, Decimus **566–567**
Valerius Maximus 567
Vallum 592
vallus 207–208
Vandals 567
and Alans 12, 567
and Anthemius 20
and Arianism 36
and Aurelian 62
and Basiliscus 69
and Boniface 77, 100, 567
and Carthage 98, 567
and Eudoxia, Licinia 201, 424
and Gallia 229
and Hippo 261
and Italia 279
kings of *See* Geiseric; Huneric
and Leo I (emperor) 315
and Leo I (pope) 316
and Libius Severus 320
and Majorian 344
in Marcomannii Wars 348
and Valentinian III 565
and Visigoths 567, 587
Varahran I 567
Varahran II 568
Varahran III 381, **568**

Varahran V 568
Vardanes 568
Varia Historia (Aelian) 7
Varius Rufus, Lucius **568**
Varonilla 153
Varro, Marcus Terentius 51, 52, 56, 207, 468, 489, **568–569**
Varus, Alfenus 569
Varus, Arrius **569**
Varus, Publius Quinctilius 539, **569**
and Arminius 40, 60, 239, 529, 569
and Chatti 108
and Cherusci 109, 569
and Marsi 353
Vasio 569
vates 484
Vatican Hill 473, 479, **569–570**
Vatinius 231, **570**
Vatinius, Publius 319, **570**
vegetables 216, 235
Vegetius Renatus, Flavius 307, **570**
vehicles 551
Veiento, Fabricius 570
Veii 570
velaria 136, 383
Velius Longus 570
Velleius Paterculus, Gaius xii, 324, 328, **570–571**
vellum 595
venationes 532
veneficia 462
Veneti 232, **571**
Venetia **571**
"veni, vidi, vici" 87, 123
Ventidius, Publius 405, **571**
Venus 245, **571**
Venutius 78, 98
Veranus, Quintus 241, **572**
verborum significatu, De (Flaccus) 213
Vercingetorix 12, 16, 17, 63, 195, 232, 238, 486, 572, **572**
Vergilius orator an poeta (Florus) 215
Verginius Rufus, Lucius 521, **572**
Verina, Aelia 69, 386, **572–573**
Verona 440, **573**
Versus Fescennini 352, 530
Vertumnus 573
Verulamium 78, 80, 103, **573**
Verus, Lucius 23, **573–574**
and Antoninus Pius 251, 573
and Eclectus 189
and Faustina the Younger 209
and Marcomanni 348
and Marcus Aurelius 349–350, 573
tutors of 221, 257
and Vologases III 41, 573
wife of 331
Verus, M. Annius 208, 349, **574**
Verus, P. Martius 99, **574**
Vespasian 574, **574–575**
and Achaea 2
and Agricola, Gnaeus Julius 9
and Annius Verus, Marcus 19
and *annona* 20
and Antoninus, Arrius 24
and Aquae Cutiliae 29
and architecture 45, 135–136, 245, 475, 525, 526, 575

and Armenia 39
and art 42
on astrology 52
auctoritas of 55
and Bassus, Saleius 70
and Bedriacum 73, 85
and Bolanus, Vettius 77
and Brigantes 78, 98
and Cappadocia 94
and Cassius Longinus, Gaius 100
and Cerealis 105
and Cilicia 118
and Civilis, Gaius Julius 121
and Clemens, Arrecinus 126
coinage of 131, 575
and Commagene 139
and *concilia* 141
concubine of 86
and Cynics 162, 172
daughter of 182
and Gischala 242
and Helvidius Priscus 255
and Jerusalem 283
and Judaea 288
laws of 318, 319
legions of 311, 312
and Lycia 335
and Mithras cult 371
and Mucianus, Gaius Licinius 376
and Nero 574
and Nerva 388
and Paetus, Lucius Caesennius 406
and Praetorian Guard 447
and Primus, Marcus Antoninus 452
and Rhodes 471
sons of 180, 545, 574–575
and Syria 519
and Thrace 537
and Tiberius Julius Alexander 541
and Vitellius 507–508, 588
vesperna 215, 216
Vesta 245, **575–576**
Vestal Virgins 452, 575, *576*, **576**
and Bona Dea 77
Caracalla and 157, 299, 499, 576
carpentum used by 96, 474
Domitian and 153, 181, 576
Vesuvius 256, 513, 545, **576**
veterans 306
Vetranio 142, 149, 342, **576–577**
Vetus, Lucius Antistius 70, **577**
vexaillarii 577
vexillarii 251
vexillationes 251
vexillationes palatinae 310
Via Aemilia 577
Via Aemilia Scauri 578–580
Via Annia 577
Via Appia 82, 577, 578
Via Aurelia 577
Via Aurelia Nova 577
Via Aurelia Vetus 577
Via Cassia 577
Via Domitiana 577
viae 195, 472, **577–580**, *579*
Via Egnatia 337
Via Flaminia 578

Via Flaminia Minor 577
Via Latina 578
Via Minucia 578
Via Popillia 578
Via Postumia 578
Via Sacra 418, 578
Via Salaria 578
viatores 28, 580
Via Traiana 580
Via Valeria 580
Vibius Crispus, Quintus 580
Vibius Marsus, Gaius 580
Vibius Maximus, Gaius 580
vicarii 138, 277, 580–581
vicarii praetectorum praetorio 175
vicesima hereditatum et legatorum 524
vicesima manumissionis 523
Victor 581
Victor, Claudius 581
Victorinus, Aufidius *See* Aufidius
    Victorianus, Gaius
Victorinus, Furius 581
Victorinus, Gaius Marius 581
Victorinus, Marcus Piavonius 125,
    581
Victory 581
Victrix (legion) 312
Vienna (Vienne) 42, 581–582
Vienna (Vindobona) 584
vigiles 199, 212, 500, 582
villa 223, 301, 582–583, 583
Villa Jovis 583
villa maritima 583
villa rustica 582
Viminal Hill 261, 473, 561
Vinalia 294, 583
Vindex, Gaius Julius 583–584
    failure of 229, 584
    and Galba 6, 226, 584
    and Nero 387, 583
    and Rufus, Verginius 481, 572
    and Treveri 553
Vindex, M. Macrinus 584
Vindobona 584
vineyards 235
Vingeanne 584
Vinicianus, Annius 106, 152, 584
Vinicius, Marcus (consul in 19
    B.C.E.) 584
Vinicius, Marcus (consul in 30 C.E.)
    290, 584

Vinius, Titus 226, 269, 584–585
Vipsania 234, 290
vir clarissimus 199
vir egregius 199
vir eminentissimus 199
Virgil 28, 207, 323, 339, 340, 499,
    585–586
Virgo Vestalis Maxima 576
Virilis, Temple of 586
Virinum 392–393
viris illustribus, De (Aurelius) 62
Viris Illustribus, De (Nepos) 386
Viris Illustribus, De (Suetonius) 516
vir perfectissimus 199
Virunum 586
Visigoths 586–587
    and Arianism 587
    and Huns 8, 587
    kings of 6, 63 *See also* Alaric;
        Alavius; Athaulf; Euric;
        Fritigern; Wallia
    and Namatianus 380
    and Theodosius I 220, 586
    and Theodosius II 535
    and Valens 5, 220, 564, 586
    and Vandals 567, 587
Vita Caesarum, De (Suetonius) 123,
    493, 516
Vitae Caesarum See Scriptores
    Historiae Augustae
Vitalianus, P. Aelius 587
vita Pomponi Secundi, De (Pliny) 436
Vita Pythagorae (Iamblichus) 268
Vitellius, Aulus 587–588
    and architecture 526
    assassination of 51
    and astrologers 52
    and Caecina Alienus 85, 587
    and civil service 121
    and Domitian 180
    and Fuscus, Cornelius 223
    as glutton 244
    and Helvetii 254–255
    and Otho 16, 73, 233, 403, 433,
        507, 587
    and Praetorian Guard 101, 447,
        587
    and Primus, Marcus Antoninus
        73, 121, 452, 588
    and Sabinus, Flavius 483, 588
    and Sabinus, Publius 483

and Samaritans 486
    and Valens 564
    and Varus, Alfenus 569
    and Vespasian 507–508, 588
Vitellius, Lucius (brother of Emperor
    Vitellius) 588
Vitellius, Lucius (consul) 125, 588
Vitellius, Publius 588
Vitruvius Pollio 44, 194, 588
vivarium 512
Volcae 588
Vologases I 39, 41, 561, 588–589
Vologases II 41, 589
Vologases III 41, 349, 573, 589
Vologases IV 589
Vologases V 47, 589
Volturnus 245, 473, 589
volumen 595
Volusianus, Gaius Vibius Afinius
    Gallus Veldumnianus 589
Volusianus, Rufus 9, 13, 97, 589
vomitoria 137, 244
Vonones I 46, 589–590
Vonones II 590
voting rights 119, 120
votive coins 590
Vulcan 245, 590
vulgares 508
Vulgar Latin 303

W
wagons 551–552
Wallia 149, 567, 587, 591
Wall of Antoninus 24, 78, 79, 140,
    591
Wall of Aurelian 62, 591–592
Wall of Hadrian 78, 79, 80, 89, 386,
    592, 592
walls 323
warehouse 216
warships 503–504, 504
water clocks 543
water supply 29, 159, 194, 475
waxed tablet 594, 595
wax masks 169
weapons 307, 308
wedding 352
weights and measures 592–593
wheeled vehicles 551
wigs 420
wine 216

winter legionary camps 309
women
    clothing for 129, 546
    footwear for 130
    status of 593–594
Women's Senate 495
wool 129
Worms 83, 594
writing instruments and materials
    594–595

X
Xanthus 596
Xanthus River 596
Xenia (Martial) 353
Xenophon 40, 276, 301, 443, 596

Y
Yazdagird I 534, 597
Yazdagird II 597
Year of the Four Emperors 507–508

Z
Zabdas, Septimius 62, 598, 600
Zanticus 598
Zealots 283, 286, 288, 354, 598
Zela 36, 77, 87, 123, 598–599
Zeno (king of Armenia) 47, 599
Zeno (Tarasicodissa) 599
    and Ermanaric 200
    and Leo I 276, 315, 342, 599
    and Nepos, Julius 386
    and Odoacer 398
    and Patricius 416
    and Verina, Aelia 69, 572–573
Zeno the Stoic 515, 599
Zenobia 408, 600
    and Aurelian 16
    and Firmus 212
    and Heraclianus, Aurelius 255
    and Longinus, Cassius 329
    and Odaenath 398
    son of 563
Zenodotus of Ephesus 15
Zenonis 69, 600
Zosimus 38, 73, 98, 212, 600
Zstommas, Chrysaphius 347, 460,
    535, 600